Cross on Evidence

Cross on Evidence

Seventh edition

by the late **SIR RUPERT CROSS**, FBA, DCL,
Solicitor, formerly Vinerian Professor of English Law
and Fellow of All Souls College, Oxford

and **COLIN TAPPER**, MA, BCL,
of Grays Inn, Barrister, All Souls Reader in Law
and Fellow of Magdalen College, Oxford,
Special Consultant to Masons (Solicitors)

Butterworths
London, Dublin, Edinburgh
1990

United Kingdom	Butterworth & Co (Publishers) Ltd, Halsbury House, 35 Chancery Lane, LONDON WC2A 1EL and 4 Hill Street, EDINBURGH EH2 3JZ
Australia	Butterworths, SYDNEY, MELBOURNE, BRISBANE, ADELAIDE, PERTH, CANBERRA and HOBART
Canada	Butterworths Canada Ltd, TORONTO and VANCOUVER
Ireland	Butterworth (Ireland) Ltd, DUBLIN
Malaysia	Malayan Law Journal Sdn Bhd, KUALA LUMPUR
New Zealand	Butterworths of New Zealand Ltd, WELLINGTON and AUCKLAND
Puerto Rico	Butterworth of Puerto Rico, Inc, SAN JUAN
Singapore	Butterworths Asia, SINGAPORE
South Africa	Butterworths Publishers (Pty) Ltd, DURBAN
USA	Butterworth Legal Publishers, CARLSBAD, California and SALEM, New Hampshire

A CIP Catalogue record for this book is available from the British Library.

First edition	1958
Second edition	1963
Third edition	1967
Reprinted	1969, 1970, 1972, 1973
Fourth edition	1974
Reprinted	1975, 1977
Fifth edition	1979
Reprinted	1982, 1983, 1984
Sixth edition	1985
Reprinted	1987
Seventh edition	1990
Reprinted	1994

ISBN Hardcover 0 406 51560 3
      Softcover 0 406 51561 1

Typeset in Great Britain by William Clowes Limited, Beccles and London.
Printed in Great Britain by Redwood Books, Trowbridge, Wiltshire.

∞ This text paper meets the requirements of ISO 9706/1994. Information and Documentation — paper for documents — requirements for permanence.

Preface to the seventh edition

This seventh edition of *Cross on Evidence* rests upon the foundations laid by Sir Rupert Cross. Much of the superstructure has changed, partly as a result of the restless tide of legislation, partly in response to changes in the social background. The fundamental principles have remained the same.

I have tried to maintain the balance between practical guidance and theoretical enquiry, between English and overseas authority, and between description and suggestion. It is a matter for concern, and for remedy in subsequent editions, that the book appears to have increased in length. In part this is due to the state of the law on the admissibility of confessional statements which has advanced beyond the bare statutory framework which could be no more than outlined in the previous edition, to a situation where a mass of detail has accumulated at an appellate level, but has yet to be condensed into succinct principle.

The major statutory innovation has been the advent of the Criminal Justice Act 1988 which has again changed the law relating to the admissibility of hearsay in criminal cases, though in a less revolutionary way than at one time seemed likely. The whole question of hearsay is nevertheless due to be re-examined again, this time by the Law Commission. The law of evidence has further declined in importance in civil litigation, though the area of privilege retains considerable vitality.

Fewer changes have been made to the form of this edition than were made to the last. The principal difference is that the whole of the law relating to the burden and standard of proof has been combined together into one chapter, and further simplification of the introductory sections has been attempted with the topic of identification expanded and moved to the last chapter among other particular matters of proof.

I am grateful to all of those who made suggestions for the improvement of the book, and who pointed out my mistakes. I have tried to correct them all, but will doubtless have introduced a new set. Their number has however been reduced by the kindness of friends and colleagues who have read and commented upon portions of the text, in particular Katharine Grevling and Peter Mirfield. I must also offer grateful thanks to my student David Kell who undertook to read the proofs, a task which proved to be unexpectedly demanding; so demanding, indeed, that a second proof-reading was required. Dr Grevling undertook, at great personal inconvenience, to help me. I owe much to her generous support at that time, and must express my heartfelt gratitude for it. May I finally offer my thanks to the editorial staff of Butterworths for their help and consideration, and to the Tables Department for saving me from the most egregious errors. I have attempted to state English law as at the end of January 1990, and overseas authority as available to me at that date.

Colin Tapper
Magdalen College
Oxford
June 1990

Extract from the preface to the first edition

In the preface to the first edition of his *Law of Evidence*, the late S L Phipson said that he had endeavoured to supply students and practitioners with a work which would take a middle place between 'the admirable but extremely condensed *Digest* [*of the Law of Evidence*] of Sir James Stephen, and that great repository of evidentiary law, *Taylor on Evidence*'. Those words were written as long ago as 1892, and Phipson's book now has claims to be regarded as *the* great English repository of evidentiary law. I realise therefore that I am flying high when I say that I hope to have supplied students and practitioners with a work which will take a middle place between those of Stephen and Phipson. The needs of students and practitioners are not, of course, identical; but I have catered for the students by including a good deal more theoretical discussion in the text than is customary in the case of a book designed solely for the practitioner, and I have catered for the latter by including many more cases in the footnotes than any student could conceivably wish to consult. Nearly all the decisions that are really important from the student's point of view are mentioned in the text. Though I have primarily borne in mind the requirements of those who are working for a law degree, I trust that the book may not prove too long for those working for the professional examinations. The long book may often be tedious, but it is sometimes more digestible than the shorter one.

I have adopted the growing practice of citing a number of decisions of the courts of the Commonwealth. My citations are not intended to be exhaustive. I have, in the main, chosen those Commonwealth decisions in which English cases have been discussed or which provide a neat illustration of what is pretty clearly English law.

I have laid myself open to the charge of having quoted at too great length from English judges and American writers. My answer is that I have endeavoured to meet the undoubted need of an up-to-date account of the theory of the subject—a need that is made plain by the fact that, in nine cases out of ten, any advocate can say whether evidence is admissible or inadmissible, but he is frequently at a loss to explain why this should be so. It is impossible to give a satisfactory account of the theory of our law of evidence without frequent reference to the ipsissima verba of the judges and the work of such great American exponents of the subject as Thayer, Wigmore, Morgan and Maguire.

Rupert Cross
January 1958

Contents

Table of statutes

References in this Table to *Statutes* are to Halsbury's Statutes of England (Fourth Edition) showing the volume and page at which the annotated text of the Act may be found. Page references in **bold** type indicate where the section of the Act is set out in part or in full.

Table of cases

Q

PAGE

PAGE

U

V

W

CHAPTER I

Introduction

The evidence of a fact is that which tends to prove it—something which may satisfy an inquirer of the fact's existence. Courts of law usually have to find that certain facts exist before pronouncing on the rights, duties and liabilities of the parties, and such evidence as they will receive in furtherance of this task is described as 'judicial evidence'. After mentioning the development of the law of evidence in section 1, the extent to which it applies to all of the different stages and matters considered by the courts, and to other tribunals, will be considered in section 2. The main purposes and categories of evidence will be considered and exemplified in section 3 together with the question whether any broad general rules can usefully be elaborated. The chief such rule is that of relevancy and is discussed in section 4.

SECTION 1. THE DEVELOPMENT OF THE LAW OF EVIDENCE

Although some of the modern rules of evidence can be traced to the middle ages, the story of their development really begins with the decisions of the common law judges in the seventeenth and eighteenth centuries. Those decisions were responsible for a complex and now almost defunct body of law concerning the competency of witnesses and the exclusion of all but the best evidence, together with other far from defunct rules such as the rule against hearsay with its numerous exceptions, the rule excluding evidence of opinion and the rudiments of the modern law of character evidence. The nineteenth and twentieth centuries have witnessed a number of statutory reforms, but it is the older decisions of the common law judges which dictate the form in which much of the law of evidence must be stated for this law still consists to a large extent of exclusionary rules, rules declaring that certain matters which might well be accepted as evidence of a fact by other responsible inquirers will not be accepted by the courts, rules declaring, in other words, what is not judicial evidence. There are however also signs of an increasing tendency, especially in civil cases, to develop guidelines relating to the weight of such evidence,[1] and to elaborate rules relating to the circumstances in which its disclosure can be compelled.[2] Three factors which have contributed to the largely exclusionary character of the law of evidence are the jury, the oath and the common law adversary system of

1 Eg Civil Evidence Act 1968, s 6(3), though the tendency was first discerned long ago, 'People were formerly frightened out of their wits about admitting evidence lest juries should go wrong. In modern times we admit the evidence and discuss its weight.' (Cockburn CJ in *R v Birmingham Overseers* (1861) 1 B & S 763 at 767).
2 See ch XI below.

procedure.[3] Allowance must also be made for a deep-seated fear that evidence will be manufactured by or on behalf of the parties:

> [T]he presumption ... is, that no man would declare anything against himself, unless it were true; but that every man, if he was in a difficulty, or in the view to any difficulty, would make declarations for himself.[4]

No doubt it was this fear which lay at the root of the extraordinary common law rule that the parties to litigation were unable to give evidence. It was abolished for civil cases by the Evidence Act 1851, but not until the Criminal Evidence Act 1898 came into force was the accused allowed to give evidence for himself in all criminal cases.

Changes such as those mentioned are climacteric, and have a bearing upon other rules of evidence. Thus it was the removal of many of the restrictions and disqualifications upon other witnesses by the Evidence Act 1843 which paved the way for the competence of parties under the Evidence Act 1851, and the anomalies thereby created between civil and criminal proceedings provided much of the impetus towards making the accused generally competent in 1898. A policy of piecemeal reform is liable to have particularly unfortunate results in relation to a subject so highly integrated as this department of the law.

The persistent application of the policy led one commentator to speak of the law of evidence in the following terms:

> Founded apparently on the propositions that all jurymen are deaf to reason, that all witnesses are presumptively liars and that all documents are presumptively forgeries, it has been added to, subtracted from and tinkered with for two centuries until it has become less of a structure than a pile of builders' debris.[5]

Yet it must not be supposed that all assessments of the modern law of evidence are equally critical. In *A-G v Horner (No 2)*[6] Hamilton LJ consoled himself with the following reflections when holding that a map was inadmissible evidence of the extent of Spitalfields market, in the eighteenth century:

> Generally I quite agree that I should desire to know the historical evidence about Spitalfields which, for every purpose except that of deciding the issue as to property as between private persons, nobody would think of excluding; but I yield to authority on the law of evidence without reluctance, because I am satisfied that in the main the English rules of evidence are just, and I am satisfied also that there is no portion of the English law which ought more rigidly to be upheld. My experience is that the public have in the result derived great benefit from their strict application.

Most lawyers would, however, probably have agreed that the time had come for a comprehensive survey of the whole field when, in September 1964, the Lord Chancellor and Home Secretary referred the law of evidence in civil and criminal cases respectively to the Law Reform Committee and the Criminal Law Revision Committee. The terms of reference were:

---

3 Modern scholarship suggests that judicial control of lawyers also played its part. Langbein 'The Criminal Trial before the Lawyers' (1978) 45 U Chi LR 263.
4 *R v Hardy* (1794) 24 State Tr 199 at 1093 per Eyre CB.
5 C P Harvey *The Advocate's Devil* (1958) 79.
6 [1913] 2 Ch 140 at 156.

To review the law of evidence in civil [criminal] cases and to consider whether any changes are desirable in the interests of the fair and efficient administration of justice, and in particular what provision should be made for modifying rules which have ceased to be appropriate in modern conditions.

The Law Reform Committee produced a series of reports which resulted in the Civil Evidence Acts of 1968 and 1972.[7] The Criminal Law Revision Committee made practically all its recommendations in one highly controversial report, the 11th Report, 'Evidence (General)' published in June 1972.[8] It is unlikely that some of its controversial recommendations will be adopted for a very long time, if at all; but a number of other recommendations, some of them extremely far-reaching,[9] were implemented by the Police and Criminal Evidence Act 1984.[10] The result of the references of 1964 has therefore been to increase the pre-existing differences between the rules of evidence in civil and criminal cases. Some disquiet was however expressed by the Roskill Fraud Trials Committee Report[11] about the current extent of such divergence, especially in view of the more radical approach adopted in civil cases as a result of the enactment of the Civil Evidence Act 1968. As a result some further relaxation of the rules applicable to criminal cases was implemented by the Criminal Justice Act 1988.[12] It remains the case that there are still many differences between the rules applying to criminal and to civil proceedings.[13] The common law rules of evidence were evolved for jury trial, a procedure which is obsolescent in civil cases although it is still the mode of trial for serious criminal charges and, even in the case of less serious ones, the fact that they are for the most part heard by lay magistrates may be thought to justify a greater restriction of the area of

7 Hearsay Evidence in Civil Proceedings, Cmnd 2964 (1966); The rule in *Hollington v Hewthorn & Co Ltd*, Cmnd 3391 (1967); Privilege in Civil Proceedings, Cmnd 3472 (1967); Evidence of Opinion and Expert Evidence, Cmnd 4489 (1970). The 19th report on the Interpretation of Wills, Cmnd 5301 (1973) contains recommendations which are relevant to the law of evidence, but has not yet been acted on. Part I of the Act of 1968 and the equivalent part of the Act of 1972 have not yet been extended to magistrates' courts. This produces a further complexity in the current law of evidence which cannot be made fully plain in this book as there is no space to deal adequately with the Evidence Act 1938, the predecessor of the Act of 1968.
8 Cmnd 4991. The 9th Report, Cmnd 3145 (1966) contained recommendations on evidence now embodied in ss 9–11 of the Criminal Justice Act 1967. For comment on the 11th Report see Tapper 35 MLR 621, 36 MLR 66 and 167; Zuckerman 36 MLR 609; MacKenna [1972] Crim LR 605; Williams [1973] Crim LR 76 and 139; Cross [1973] Crim LR 329 and 400; Muir [1973] Crim LR 341; Miller [1973] Crim LR 343. Memoranda on the Report submitted to the Home Office and separately published are also of great value, notably those of the Bar Council, Law Society, Magistrates' Association and Justice.
9 Among the most fundamental is the total reform of the law relating to the admissibility of documentary hearsay.
10 The Act also made very important changes to the law relating to the admissibility of confessions in evidence in criminal proceedings, inspired by the report of the Royal Commission on Criminal Procedure, Cmnd 8092 (1981), but adopting more the form of the recommendations on the topic made in the 11th Report.
11 (1986), paras 5.7 and 5.8.
12 Principally in relation to documentary hearsay, the presentation of evidence, expert reports, securing evidence from abroad, and the evidence of children.
13 The principal differences are that in criminal proceedings the standard of proof is higher; the accused is incompetent as a witness for the prosecution, unsworn evidence may be given by young children, special rules govern the competence and compellability of the accused's spouse, corroboration is necessary in more cases, there is no issue estoppel, and the reception of hearsay and opinion evidence is governed in part by the common law.

admissible evidence than is suitable in proceedings before a legally qualified judge sitting alone. Subject to the solution of the vexed problem of the right extent of the difference between the rules governing civil and criminal cases, the law of evidence is a fit subject for codification. If this task is ever undertaken in England, there will be some useful precedents which are mentioned from time to time in this book. There is the Indian Evidence Act 1872, drafted by Sir James Stephen, which still forms the basis of a number of Evidence Ordinances in the Commonwealth; then there is the Model Code of Evidence published by the American Law Institute in 1942, and the Uniform Rules of Evidence first published by the American Commissioners on Uniform Laws in 1953.[14] Unlike the Federal Rules of Evidence, approved by Congress in 1975, these are complete codes, but the Federal Rules contain some interesting novel provisions. The code of evidence published by the Law Reform Commission of Canada in 1976 is distinguished by its simplicity and clarity. It has now been followed in Canada by a draft set of Uniform Rules of Evidence,[15] and the Australian Law Reform Commission is currently engaged upon a mammoth enquiry into the Australian federal law with a view to comprehensive reform. In both Canada[16] and Australia[17] the respective Law Reform Commissions have undertaken extensive work in this field, but, as yet, it has not proved possible to enact comprehensive legislation to implement the various proposals.

SECTION 2. RANGE OF THE LAW OF EVIDENCE

The most cursory glance at the table of contents of this, or of any other, general work on the law of evidence reveals a wide diversity of topics and rules. Some rules deal with essentially procedural matters, such as those relating to the ability to secure the disclosure of relevant evidence, and the validity of reasons for not doing so, or rules about the form in which questions may be put to a witness; some deal with witnesses, such as the rules relating to their competency and the extent to which their evidence requires corroboration; some deal with the admissibility of particular sorts of evidence, such as rules relating to the use which might be made of evidence of the previous discreditable conduct of the accused or of potentially unreliable evidence such as hearsay or opinion; and some deal with questions of proof, such as rules about judicial notice or the amount of proof required. These various categories overlap and interlock. The interesting thing is that they can be fitted together into so many different patterns. There is no type of proceeding to which all of the rules of evidence apply. There are a number of ways of dividing the rules up, into those which apply to different types of proceedings, civil and criminal for example. Yet cutting across this is a division between the rules applying in the higher and in the lower courts. These two cross-cuts alone manage to yield three quite different versions of the rule against hearsay, applying variously to civil cases in the higher courts, to criminal cases in the higher courts and to civil cases in the lower courts.

14 See G D Nokes (1956) 5 ICQL 347.
15 Report of Federal/Provincial Task Force on the Uniform Rules of Evidence (1982).
16 See draft Code of Evidence published by Law Reform Commission of Canada in 1976 and the Report of the Federal/Provincial Task Force on the Uniform Rules of Evidence (1982).
17 See Law Reform Commission of Australia Report No 38 'Evidence' (1987).

It is worth a brief glance at some of the more important patterns. The most significant difference is probably that between the rules which apply to judicial proceedings in the courts, and those which apply to the determination of facts in other tribunals.

A. PROCEEDINGS IN COURTS

It is to be expected that the fullest range of the rules of evidence will apply to proceedings in courts, but there are still important variations in the precise mixture of rules which apply to different types of jurisdiction, to different types of court, and at different stages in the proceedings. Something will be said of each of these in turn.

1. DIFFERENT TYPES OF JURISDICTION

Notwithstanding many assertions of the common character of the law of evidence in civil and criminal proceedings, it is obvious, even to those making such assertions, that many of the rules are different, and that those that are the same are often applied differently. Thus in *R v Christie*[18] Lord Reading having stated the theoretical similarity went on to say that in practice 'it is desirable in certain circumstances to relax the strict application of the law of evidence.' He had in mind the need to temper the strictness of the law when it was applied to the accused in a criminal case, and in particular the need to preserve the accused from the effect of admitting evidence more prejudicial to the accused than probative of the prosecution case. This factor undoubtedly underlies many of the differences between the rules applied in the two types of proceeding. It has, in some areas, been implemented by statutory provisions. Thus the Criminal Evidence Act 1898 imports a special regime to apply to the accused as a witness, different from that applying to other witnesses, just because of his greater vulnerability. Even here the matter is not straightforward, for strictly such a consideration should lead not to discrimination between civil and criminal proceedings, but rather between rules applying to the accused in criminal proceedings, and those applying to others. This can lead to difficulty when the true adversary is not the prosecutor, but a co-defendant, for whom similar consideration must be shown, leading to further modification in the rules.[19] Another factor which contributes, perhaps even more strongly, to the differences between the rules applying in criminal and civil proceedings is the difference between the form of procedure and method of trial. In criminal cases pleading is generally oral, and there are commonly no interlocutory hearings. In civil cases there is hardly ever a jury. Here too the consequences of such differences find statutory expression, for example in the different methods of reforming the hearsay rule to be found in the Civil Evidence Act 1968 and the Criminal Justice Act 1988. It cannot be maintained that all of the differences stem from such considerations. For many it is hard to find any rational explanation, for example, why the admissibility of dying declarations by way of exception to the hearsay rule

18 [1914] AC 545 at 564.
19 See eg *Murdoch v Taylor* [1965] AC 574, [1965] 1 All ER 406.

should be limited not only to criminal cases, but to those involving the trial of the accused for the homicide of the declarant. Many statutory differences are equally puzzling. It is not at all obvious why the admissibility of the unsworn evidence of children should ever have been confined to criminal cases by s 38 of the Children and Young Persons Act 1933.[20]

In general the courts are concerned with a lis, a dispute between the parties before them, which is resolved by the adversarial process so typical of the common law. There are other aspects of their jurisdiction which are of a different character. Interlocutory applications often have to be heard urgently without recourse to the full panoply of evidential rules, often admitting hearsay, and even when such an application is treated as the trial of the action still the more relaxed rules to the admission of hearsay will be applied.[21] Though if proceedings of an interlocutory nature, such as an interim care order in respect of a child, involve making serious allegations against a party, and may lead to serious consequences for that party, it seems that he is entitled to have the matter determined by evidence tendered on oath. In *Scott v Scott*[1] Viscount Haldane singled out the paternal jurisdiction exercised in relation to wards of court and lunatics. In *Official Solicitor v K*[2] the House of Lords considered how far the ordinary principles of judicial inquiry were to apply to such proceedings. In particular the House considered whether it was open to the judge to find facts relevant to the exercise of his discretion upon a basis of hearsay. Lord Devlin distinguished between those rules which may vary and those which are so fundamental that they have to be observed by everyone who acts judicially, and which constitute the rules of natural justice. He was quite clear that many of the rules of evidence fell into the former category:[3]

> There are also rules of less importance designed to aid in the administration of justice and to regulate procedure. They are rules of convenience rather than of principle; and the rule against hearsay . . . is among them. No one would suggest that it is contrary to natural justice to act on hearsay.

The particular application to hearsay has been overtaken by statute, but the general principle remains, that the precise mixture of rules is not fixed, but determined by the nature of the jurisdiction. As Lord Evershed said[4] in the same case:[5]

> [I]t [is] not enough to say that the proceeding is a judicial proceeding. It is necessary to define or to have in mind what is the true character of this judicial proceeding and what is its end or purpose.

This consideration has also been allowed to determine a somewhat different

20 See now Children Act 1989, s 96(2).
21 See *Rose v Information Services Ltd* [1987] FSR 254.
 1 [1913] AC 417.
 2 [1965] AC 201, [1963] 3 All ER 191; see also *Re W* (1989) Times, 10 November.
 3 At 238, 208.
 4 With whom Lord Reid expressly agreed.
 5 At 217, 195. But see *Bradford City Magistrates' Court v K* [1990] 2 WLR 532 in relation to the care jurisdiction of magistrates, subsequently modified by Children Act 1989, s 96(3), and the Children (Admissibility of Hearsay Evidence) Order 1990 (SI 1990 No 143). See *Re Hogue and Haines Marriage* (1977) 29 FLR 186, for the approach in Australia.

approach to the question of the standard of proof of abuse of a child for the purposes of wardship proceedings from the normal judicial approach.[6]

Courts will be cautious to limit their departure from the rules which apply in ordinary cases.[7] Thus in *Re WLW*[8] the Court of Appeal distinguished between issues arising under the paternal jurisdiction, and the issue of whether the paternal jurisdiction should continue to be exercised, being more prepared to permit cross-examination of witnesses in the latter.[9] It has also been held that where allegations in wardship proceedings are both serious and central it would be better for the source of such allegations to depose the relevant affidavits so as to make himself available for cross-examination, if required.[10]

Many administrative functions involving the finding of facts used to be performed by the ordinary courts. Most of these have now been transferred to special administrative tribunals, but a few have been retained by the ordinary courts. In the performance of these the courts also apply a different set of rules of evidence, including at least one set permitting the admission of hearsay.[11] Similarly when magistrates act in committal proceedings the rules of evidence differ from those which apply when they are conducting a summary trial.[12] Even in extradition proceedings where the evidence must be such as would, according to the law of England, justify the accused's committal for trial,[13] the magistrate is justified in not applying rules of practice which would apply in an English trial.[14] It has been said that in conducting judicial proceedings which have a strong administrative element a judge is entitled to take into account material of the type which would be accepted by a responsible administrator.[15]

2. DIFFERENT TYPES OF COURT

It has already been noted that different courts often apply different mixtures of rules of evidence. This is sometimes accomplished by explicit legislation

6 *Re G* [1987] 1 WLR 1461.
7 Thus in *H v H and C, K v K* [1989] 3 All ER 740, [1989] 3 WLR 933 the Court of Appeal distinguished carefully between its wardship jurisdiction, where the ordinary rules of evidence do not apply and hearsay can be admitted, and its matrimonial jurisdiction where, although equally concerned with the welfare of children, those rules do apply and hearsay must be excluded.
8 [1972] Ch 456, [1972] 2 All ER 433. See also *Pallin v Department of Social Welfare* [1983] NZLR 266, where rules of statutory privilege were observed, although it was held that hearsay might be admitted in custody proceedings.
9 Though even there the court was prepared to contemplate the reception of evidence otherwise than on oath.
10 *Re N* [1987] 1 FLR 65.
11 *Kavanagh v Chief Constable of Devon and Cornwall* [1974] QB 624, [1974] 2 All ER 697. The position with regard to cross-examination was less certain, but in *R v Crown Court at Aylesbury, ex p Farrer* (1988) Times, 9 March it was held that the court had no power to order a licensing authority to call a witness to give oral evidence as opposed to the admission of hearsay.
12 Compare *R v Horsham Justices, ex p Bukhari* (1982) 74 Cr App Rep 291 (no discretion to exclude admissible evidence in committal proceedings) with *R v Sang* [1980] AC 402, [1979] 2 All ER 1222 (discretion at summary trial affirmed).
13 Extradition Act 1989, s 9.
14 *R v Governor of Pentonville Prison, ex p Schneider* (1981) 73 Cr App Rep 200 (rules of practice relating to competence of co-accused as witness for the prosecution); *R v Governor of Pentonville Prison, ex p Voets* [1986] 2 All ER 630 (rules of practice excluding identifying photographs of accused clearly indicating possession of a police record).
15 *R v Sanghera* [1983] 2 VR 130 at 131, per McGarvie J.

in the statute establishing the court. Thus the legislation establishing the new County Courts in 1846 for the first time made the parties competent witnesses, and not until 1851 was the position in the High Court brought into line. In other cases the result has been achieved by manipulation of commencement provisions. Thus the reason for the discrepancy in the hearsay rule in civil cases between cases heard before magistrates and in the High Court is simply that the Civil Evidence Act 1968 has never been commenced for the former.[16] Occasionally legislation establishes totally new courts, and sometimes explicitly abridges the rules of evidence to be applied in them. Thus when the Industrial Court was set up under the Industrial Relations Act 1971, it was provided that 'it should not be bound by any enactment or rule of law relating to the evidence which is admissible in proceedings in other courts.'[17] Such provisions are however to be construed narrowly, and it has been said in Australia that:[18]

> the rules of evidence should not be treated as excluded from the proceedings of a court unless the words are clear or the context compelling.

A similarly cautious approach has also been adopted in that jurisdiction to a more general authorisation of relaxation in Ord 33, r 3 of the rules governing the Federal Court of Australia, where the Court has said that it will be slow to apply the rule to admit hearsay in respect of a central issue.[19]

3. DIFFERENT STAGES OF PROCEEDINGS

Even if judicial proceedings in the ordinary higher courts alone are considered, deviations are still to be found between the rules which apply to the finding of facts at different stages within those proceedings. This may be illustrated by considering some of the variations which apply, before trial, to issues of fact which arise in relation to a plea in a criminal case or to those which arise in relation to the admissibility of evidence, and, after trial, to those which arise on questions of sentence or on appeal. At the pre-trial stage such scanty authority as exists suggests that the courts try to follow the rules, which apply at the trial stage as far as possible.[20] Thus in *R v Podola*[1] a full Court of Criminal Appeal overruled *R v Sharp*,[2] in favour of the view that

---

16 This is especially ironic in view of the deliberate decision to include such courts within the ambit of the Act contrary to the recommendation of the Law Reform Committee.
17 Industrial Relations Act 1971, Sch 3, para 18(5).
18 *Geschke v Del-Monte Home Furnishers Ltd* [1981] VR 856 at 863, construing Market Court Act 1978, s 13(2) providing that 'The Court may inform itself in such a manner as it thinks fit and is not required to conduct any proceedings in a formal manner.'
19 *Pearce v Button* (1986) 65 ALR 83 at 90, 97 and 102.
20 In *Savings and Investment Bank Ltd v Gasco Investments (Netherlands) BV* [1984] 1 All ER 296, Gibson J in interlocutory proceedings adhered to the rules for admissibility at trial as far as the nature of the issue allowed, and was against using in affidavits 'material which cannot be proved because it is mere opinion or is otherwise inadmissible'. Hearsay may however be admissible in interlocutory proceedings, see RSC Ord 41, r 5(2) as interpreted in *Savings and Investments Bank Ltd v Gasco Investments (Netherlands)BV (No 2)* [1988] Ch 422, [1988] 1 All ER 975.
1 [1960] 1 QB 325, [1959] 3 All ER 418. In this case expert witnesses were called on each side and cross-examined, and the accused also testified and was cross-examined. In the Scottish case of *Russell v HM Advocate* 1946 SC(J) 37, a similar issue of fact was determined by the judge, and not by the jury. See also *Jessup v Mahon* [1989] SCCR 600.
2 (1958) 41 Cr App Rep 197.

the burden of proving unfitness to plead was, like the substantive defence of insanity, on the accused who raised it rather than on the prosecution.[3] If raised by the prosecution it must be proved by them beyond reasonable doubt.[4] So far as issues of fact relevant to the admissibility of evidence are concerned the general rule is that such questions should be tried by the judge on the voir dire, at a trial within the trial.[5] It would however be unrealistic for such evidence to be considered in total isolation from that already adduced at the trial proper.[6] Most such trials have dealt with the admissibility of confessions, and it is well-established in such cases that the prosecution bears the burden of proving the issue of voluntariness beyond reasonable doubt,[7] and that witnesses, including the accused,[8] can be called, and cross-examined. The general question of the range of rules which does apply at this stage of judicial proceedings has been examined very thoroughly in the United States.[9] While it appears that in general the rules here relating to evidence are more similar to those governing the trial, there are some indications of a few differences. Thus in one case[10] the court took the view that the proponent of the evidence, there the prosecution, need make out only a prima facie case to show that a tape-recording satisfied the condition of originality. It must also often be the case just because the purpose of the preliminary issue is to determine the admissibility of a disputed piece of evidence, or the competency of a witness, that the rules at the preliminary stage must be different from those operating at the trial so as to allow the piece of evidence to be perused, or the witness examined.[11] How much further the rules are different is obscure in the modern English law.[12]

There are also significant differences in relation to the mixture of rules which apply to issues of fact which arise to be determined after the trial has concluded. In criminal cases issues of fact often arise in relation to the basis

3 This was regarded as a suitable analogy for other pre-trial issues such as autrefois convict or autrefois acquit in *R v Martin Coughlan* [1976] Crim LR 631, where an accelerated procedure for reading statements was also approved.
4 *R v Robertson* [1968] 3 All ER 557, 52 Cr App Rep 690. The Canadian task force on Uniform Rules of Evidence has recommended that the burden should be borne by the prosecution, Draft Act, s 13.
5 In the United States only the rules of privilege apply at this stage, see Federal Rules of Evidence, rr 104(a), 1101(d)(1); *Bourjaily v US* 107 S Ct 2775 (1987).
6 *R v Tyrer* (1989) Times, 26 July.
7 Now as a result of Police and Criminal Evidence Act 1984, s 76(2), in this respect re-enacting the common law, see *R v Sartori, Gavin and Phillips* [1961] Crim LR 397. The position is the same in Canada, (*Horvath v R* [1979] 2 SCR 376) and in New Zealand (*R v McCuin* [1982] 1 NZLR 13). In the United States (*Bourjaily v US* above) the standard is merely proof on the balance of probabilities, as it is generally believed to be in Australia (*Wendo v R* (1963) 100 CLR 559, HCA), though there is also some support for an intermediate standard, see *R v Askeland* (1983) 8 ACR 338.
8 *R v Cowell* [1940] 2 KB 49, [1940] 2 All ER 599.
9 See Maguire and Epstein 'Rules of Evidence in Preliminary Controversies as to Admissibility' (1927) 36 Yale LJ 1101. Rule 104(a) of the US Federal Rules provides that the judge is not bound by any of the rules of evidence except those relating to privileges in deciding such questions.
10 *R v Robson and Harris* [1972] 2 All ER 699, [1972] 1 WLR 651.
11 A procedure endorsed, though not implemented, in *R v Yacoob* (1981) 72 Cr App Rep 313 at 317, in relation to calling the witness on the preliminary question of her competency at the trial.
12 In *Duke of Beaufort v Crawshay* (1866) LR 1 CP 699 an affidavit which would have been inadmissible at the trial seems to have been admitted at this preliminary stage.

for sentencing the accused,[13] or making some other order.[14] Such factual issues are preferably to be determined by the judge after conducting a hearing,[15] at least when facts alleged by the prosecution as part of its case are disputed. At such a hearing it is established that the ordinary rules of burden and standard of proof apply.[16] In many cases it will be impracticable to secure a decision from a jury trying the issue of guilt or innocence, and if no evidence is called before the judge he must accept the defendant's version, unless it is manifestly false,[17] merely a matter of inference from undisputed primary facts,[18] or involves matters of mitigation unconnected with the case for the prosecution.[19] In cases tried on indictment where the accused has a criminal record, a statement of his previous convictions and antecedents is prepared by the police in the form of a proof of evidence.[20] This is intended to be used at the sentencing stage, though it is clear that many of the statements in it will amount to hearsay.[1] It seems that this is immaterial so long as the facts are not disputed,[2] but that if they are, it is necessary to prove them by evidence admissible under the rules for the trial.[3] The vestigial stage of development of an apparatus of rules of evidence for determining these matters is indicated by a recent clutch of cases considering whether or not evidence of the accused's involvement in other crimes may be admitted at this stage. Some cases can be reconciled on the basis of whether the evidence of the other crimes emanates from a third party, in which case it is,

13 See Thomas 'Establishing a Factual Basis for Sentencing' [1970] Crim LR 80 and *Principles of Sentencing* (2nd edn, 1978) ch 12. For an examination of the Australian situation see, Fox and O'Brian 'Fact Finding for Sentences' (1975) 10 MULR 163. In Canada the Supreme Court has pronounced it commonplace that the strict rules which govern at the trial do not apply at a sentencing hearing (*R v Gardiner* (1982) 140 DLR (3d) 612 at 648), an attitude in accord with that of the Task Force on the Uniform Rules.

14 Such as a compensation order to which similar principles apply, see *R v Horsham Justices, ex p Richards* [1985] 2 All ER 1114 construing Criminal Justice Act 1982, s 67; or the basis for a forfeiture order, see *R v Pemberton* (1982) 4 Cr App Rep (S) 328. See also Drug Trafficking Offences Act 1986 for a somewhat more stringent procedure in relation to proof of benefiting from the proceeds of drug trafficking so as to justify making a confiscation order.

15 *R v Newton* (1982) 77 Cr App Rep 13. This procedure applies equally to appeals to the Crown Court, *R v Williams* (1983) Times, 25 April.

16 *R v McGrath and Casey* (1983) 5 Cr App Rep (S) 460.

17 *R v Hawkins* (1985) 7 Cr App Rep (S) 351; *R v Walton* [1987] Crim LR 512.

18 *R v Lawrence and Carnegie* [1988] Crim LR 62; *R v Jackson* [1988] Crim LR 184.

19 *R v Connell* (1983) 5 Cr App Rep (S) 360; *R v Hopkins* [1987] Crim LR 204.

20 *Practice Direction* (Court of Criminal Appeal) [1966] 2 All ER 929, 50 Cr App Rep 271. In *R v Butterwasser* [1948] KB 4, [1947] 2 All ER 415, Lord Goddard CJ drew attention to a practice of substituting for the normal trial oath the special voir dire oath for such evidence given at the sentencing stage.

1 In the analogous case in domestic proceedings in the magistrates' courts of a report by a probation officer on the means of the parties, received to help in determining the amount of an order, after a decision on the merits, it is expressly provided by statute that the ordinary exclusionary rules of evidence do not apply. See Magistrates' Courts Act 1980, s 72(5). The position is the same in Canada, see *Albright v R* (1987) 45 DLR (4th) 11 explicitly approving this work, and permitting the proof of previous convictions by hearsay.

2 *R v Marquis* (1951) 35 Cr App Rep 33.

3 In the somewhat similar situation of a report by a court welfare officer to a court considering a family matter relating to children hearsay may be included, but any critical issue should be decided by original evidence, see *Thompson v Thompson* [1986] 1 FLR 212, approved by the Court of Appeal in *H v H and C, K v K* [1989] 3 All ER 740, [1989] 3 WLR 933. See also Children Act 1989, s 7.

as against the accused, hearsay;[4] or from the accused himself, in which case it would be admissible by way of exception to that rule.[5] More recently however this line of reasoning has become overlaid with another more generally concerned with the propriety of admitting evidence of other crimes beyond those of which the accused has been found guilty at his trial, or asked to have taken into consideration.[6] In evidential terms this seems more akin to the rule excluding evidence of discreditable extrinsic conduct, or similar fact evidence. At present the indetermination of definition of the issues which it is proper to raise at the sentencing stage precludes precise analysis. Nevertheless the result is exactly the same as would be achieved by the application of the ordinary rules of evidence, namely that evidence may be excluded because it is hearsay,[7] or even if it falls under an exception, if it infringes the general rule excluding evidence of discreditable extrinsic conduct.[8] It is perhaps superfluous to note that little consideration appears to have been given to questions such as the compellability of an accomplice of the accused at this stage, any need for the corroboration of such evidence,[9] the extension of rules relating to the protection of victims of sexual offences,[10] or the permissible range of cross-examination.[11] So too if an inference is to be drawn as to the facts of the offence either from the facts as stated by the prosecution on a plea of guilty, or from the evidence at the trial, any matters upon which it is proposed to rely for the purposes of sentencing should be indicated to the accused in advance,[12] and supported by evidence, including the calling of witnesses,[13] if the facts are disputed. It is immaterial that the evidence relied upon for sentencing was erroneously admitted at the trial, and this applies even though it favours the accused.[14] Another disputed question relates to the burden and standard of proof required to establish facts at this stage of the proceedings. In Canada the Supreme Court has rejected the American view,[15] that a lesser standard is appropriate, in favour

---

4 *R v Wishart* (1979) 1 Cr App Rep(S) 322. See also *R v Bryant* [1980] 1 NLZR 264.
5 *R v Russen* (1981) 3 Cr App Rep (S) 134.
6 *R v Connor* (1981) 3 Cr App Rep (S) 225, and *R v Ayensu and Ayensu* [1982] Crim LR 764. Nor should the sentence be based upon facts justifying a more serious count than any included in the indictment, *R v Solomon and Triumph* (1984) 6 Cr App Rep (S) 120.
7 *R v Wishart*, above.
8 *R v Connor and R v Ayensu and Ayensu*, above. Though it is clear that the exclusion rules are less strict at this stage, see *R v Butterwasser* [1948] 1 KB 4, [1947] 2 All ER 415.
9 But see *R v Huchison* [1972] 1 WLR 398, where this was raised in the context of corroboration of allegations made by the victim of a sexual offence. See also *R v Cooksley* [1982] Qd R 405.
10 But see *R v Ashmeil* [1988] Crim LR 474 where the court discouraged even the taking of a statement of the effect of a rape upon the victim, despite this being a consideration relevant to sentence.
11 It seems clear that the provisions as to cross-examination in the Criminal Evidence Act 1898, s 1(f) are inappropriate for proceedings after verdict, notwithstanding its terminology. It is generally inappropriate for the judge to cross-examine the accused on the matter, *R v McGrath and Casey* (1983) 5 Cr App Rep (S) 460.
12 *R v Lester* (1975) 63 Cr App Rep 144.
13 *R v Robinson* (1969) 53 Cr App Rep 314; *R v Hearne* [1976] Crim LR 753.
14 *Flewitt v Horvath* [1972] RTR 121, where the evidence admitted at the trial was hearsay, and wrongly taken into account by the magistrates in determining not to disqualify the accused driver; see also *James v Morgan* [1988] RTR 85 where hearsay evidence that the accused's drink had been 'laced' by his friends was rejected on the same issue. By contrast the Supreme Court of the United States has held it an unconstitutional denial of due process of law to exclude hearsay favouring the accused at the sentencing stage, *Green v Georgia* 442 US 95 (1979).
15 In *Williams v New York* 337 US 241 (1949). But see 81 HLR 821 (1968).

of adherence to the ordinary criminal standard of proof beyond reasonable doubt, resting upon the prosecution, on the basis that, in the words of Stephen, the question of sentence is the gist of criminal proceedings, being to them as the bullet is to the powder.[16] In England the authorities are less august, and less clear, but point in the same direction, both on the incidence,[17] and on the standard of proof.[18] It has been held in Australia that statistical material is more readily admissible at this stage than at the trial proper.[19]

The final situation to be mentioned here is that concerned with the rules to be applied to evidence adduced on an appeal.[20] There are provisions on both civil[1] and criminal appeals[2] for allowing fresh evidence to be heard. In each case the relevant provisions narrow, rather than broaden, the range of material which may be adduced compared with that admissible in the court below.[3] There are however some differences between the extent to which the courts are prepared to limit the ambit of the fresh evidence to be received in the two types of proceedings. The reason for this appears to be that in criminal proceedings the need to avoid inflicting injustice upon the accused may more readily override the need to achieve finality in litigation.[4] The rules of evidence are often relaxed in civil cases by agreement between the parties. Thus in one case no objection was taken, to the admission of a hearsay report in a local newspaper to show what had taken place at the trial, no proper note having been taken.[5] In civil cases the same rules apply whether or not the issue arises on an appeal from a summary judgment,[6] a hearing with, or without a jury, or in deciding whether or not to re-open a trial,[7] but not on an appeal by case stated on a question of law.[8] Order 59, r 10(2) requires special grounds before such fresh evidence is admitted, and the classic statement of the conditions to be applied in such cases was made by Denning LJ in *Ladd v Marshall*:[9]

16 *R v Gardiner* (1982) 140 DLR (3d) 612, quoting Sir James Fitzjames Stephen 'The Punishment of Convicts' (1863) Cornill Magazine 189.
17 *R v Pemberton* (1982) 4 Cr App Rep (S) 328.
18 See *R v Taggart* (1979) 1 Cr App Rep (S) 144 at 149. In Australia the situation is more confused, the standard of beyond reasonable doubt has been taken in South Australia (*Weaver v Samuels* [1971] SASR 116), New South Wales (*R v O'Neill* [1979] 2 NSWLR 582), ACT; (*Bierkowski v Pearson* (1971) 18 FLR 110), and Northern Territory (*Browne v Smith* (1974) 4 ALR 114); the standard of the balance of probabilities has been taken in Queensland (*R v Welsh* (1982) 7 ACR 249) though even there the accused cannot be sentenced on the basis of an offence in respect of which he has been acquitted, *R v Boney* (1986) 25 ACR 37.
19 *Morris v East* (1988) FLR 23.
20 Similar principles have been applied in Queensland to setting aside a judgment obtained by fraud, see *Brough v Abel* [1987] 1 Qd R 138.
1   RSC Ord 59, r 10(2).
2   Criminal Appeal Act 1968, s 23.
3   Although r 10(2) contains no such explicit limitation to evidence which would have been admissible at the trial as does s 23(2)(a), such limitation may be implied. As it may in relation to s 23(1), see *R v Lattimore* (1975) 62 Cr App Rep 53 at 56.
4   *Braddock v Tillotson's Newspapers Ltd* [1950] 1 KB 47 at 54, [1949] 2 All ER 306 at 311.
5   In *Re Cowburn, ex p Firth* (1882) 19 ChD 419 at 424.
6   *Langdale v Danby* [1982] 3 All ER 129 at 137, [1982] 1 WLR 1123 at 1132.
7   *Sincroflash Ltd v Trusthouse Forte PLC* (1983) Times, 7 January, but not when reviewing a discretionary decision taken on an interlocutory injunction, *Hadmor Productions Ltd v Hamilton* [1983] 1 AC 191 at 220, [1982] 1 All ER 1042 at 1046.
8   *Brady (Inspector of Taxes) v Group Lotus Car Companies plc* [1987] 2 All ER 674 at 688, as approved by the Court of Appeal, [1987] 3 All ER 1050.
9   [1954] 3 All ER 745 at 748, [1954] 1 WLR 1489 at 1491. Expressly approved by the House of Lords in *Skone v Skone* [1971] 2 All ER 582 at 586, [1971] 1 WLR 812 at 815, and in *Langdale v Danby* [1982] 3 All ER 129 at 137, [1982] 1 WLR 1123 at 1133.

[F]irst, it must be shown that the evidence could not have been obtained with reasonable diligence for use at the trial: second, the evidence must be such that, if given, it would probably have an important influence on the result of the case, although it need not be decisive: third, the evidence must be such as is presumably to be believed, or in other words, it must be apparently credible, though it need not be incontrovertible.

The first condition will normally not be satisfied if the evidence could have been secured before the trial by discovery,[10] though the court may permit fresh evidence to be taken to replace that contained in a note which has been lost by accident.[11] This condition also covers a case where a witness who can be found could not reasonably have been expected to testify to the desired effect, but a court will be slow to accept fresh evidence upon this basis.[12]

The second condition represents a compromise between two formulations suggested in *Brown v Dean*, the stronger expressed by Lord Loreburn LC, that 'if believed it would be conclusive',[13] the weaker by Lord Shaw, that it be 'so gravely material and so clearly relevant . . . that it should have been before the jury.'[14] The test is even more stringent when the fresh evidence relates solely to credit,[15] but it may nevertheless be admitted even then in an exceptional case if the court has been deceived and the evidence may reasonably have tipped the scales.[16]

The third condition relates to the cogency of the evidence and is really implicit in the second. In particular it seems that fresh evidence is unlikely to be admitted if it amounts to no more than a witness wishing to renege on the evidence he gave at the trial.[17]

The rule in *Ladd v Marshall* is designed to ensure that litigation is not unduly prolonged, but as such, it is subservient to the principle that a litigant should not succeed by fraud, and in such a case fresh evidence may be admitted notwithstanding the restrictions imposed by the rule.[18]

In criminal cases the situation is different, first because of the importance of securing justice for the accused,[19] and second, because of the width of the power to order a new trial.[20] Thus the relevant section of the Criminal Appeal Act 1968 contains two separate provisions for the adduction of fresh evidence on a criminal appeal, s 23(1) conferring a wide discretionary power,[1] and s 23(2) imposing a more circumscribed duty to do so. Even so

10 *Turnbull & Co v Duval* [1902] AC 429, though this will not necessarily bar admissibility in a case where a party has been misled into believing that discovery would be ineffective, *Skone v Skone* [1971] 2 All ER 582 at 587.
11 In *Re Cowburn, ex p Firth* (1882) 19 ChD 419 at 426.
12 See *Williams v Reason* [1988] 1 All ER 262.
13 [1910] AC 373 at 374.
14 At 376.
15 *Braddock v Tillotson's Newspaper Ltd* [1950] 1 KB 47 at 57, [1949] 2 All ER 306 at 313.
16 *Meek v Fleming* [1961] 2 QB 366 at 379, [1961] 3 All ER 148 at 154, per Holroyd Pearce LJ. Willmer LJ thought it enough that such evidence be of vital significance, and Pearson LJ that it merely be material.
17 *Pursell v Railway Executive* [1951] 1 All ER 536.
18 See *Meek v Fleming* above; endorsed by *Brady (Inspector of Taxes) v Group Lotus Car Companies plc* [1987] 3 All ER 1050.
19 Said in *Hughes v Singh* (1989) Times, 21 April to be the overriding consideration.
20 Criminal Appeal Act 1968, s 7.
 1 So wide as to justify its reception in exceptional cases even after a plea of guilty, *R v Foster* [1984] 2 All ER 679, or on the factual basis for a sentence, *R v Frankum* (1983) 5 Cr App Rep (S) 259.

the court will not, even under s 23 (1), admit evidence which could not have been adduced at the trial, such as hearsay,[2] nor will it admit fresh expert evidence in rebuttal, preferring to order a new trial.[3] It will also insist upon the observance of the procedural requirements which apply by statute to the admission of evidence at the trial.[4] Section 23(2) provides that if the fresh evidence is credible and would have been admissible at the trial, it should be received on appeal unless the court is satisfied that it would afford no ground for allowing the appeal[5] or that there was no reasonable ground for failing to adduce it at the trial. It seems probable that this provision will be accorded the same generous interpretation as that given to the predecessor of s 23(1), and will permit the reception of fresh evidence going to credit whether it relates directly to evidence adduced by the relevant witness at the trial,[6] or to the previous convictions or previous inconsistent statements of an important witness on an important matter.[7]

B. PROCEEDINGS IN OTHER TRIBUNALS[8]

There is a very wide variety of proceedings of a quasi-judicial, administrative and legislative nature in which issues of fact require authoritative determination. Many of them are susceptible of control by courts of law. It is sometimes a matter of dispute how far and how many of the rules of evidence apply, or should apply, in such proceedings.[9] It is largely because the concerns and purposes of these bodies vary so widely that few general principles can be discerned. Even when the formal rules of evidence apply to a non-judicial tribunal, to an arbitration for example, a more tolerant attitude to the enforcement of the rules is likely to be exhibited.[10]

Many of the bodies charged with these functions are set up by statute, and it is not uncommon in such cases for some express provision to relate to the procedure to be applied.[11] In some cases where the inquiry is of a formal nature the statute may expressly import rules of evidence as they apply in

2 *R v Dallas* [1971] Crim LR 90; *R v Lattimore* (1975) 62 Cr App Rep 53 at 56, though hearsay may be used to determine what fresh evidence should be produced, *R v Callaghan* [1988] 1 All ER 257.
3 *R v Merry* (1970) 54 Cr App Rep 274.
4 *R v Conway* (1979) 70 Cr App Rep 4, where the procedure of first putting an inconsistent statement to a witness before contradicting him, prescribed by the Criminal Procedure Act 1865, s 4, was insisted upon.
5 In Australia it must be such as would be *likely* to have affected the result, *Mickelberg v R* (1989) 86 ALR 321.
6 *R v Hamilton* (1917) 13 Cr App Rep 32.
7 *R v Parks* [1961] 3 All ER 633, 46 Cr App Rep 29. For full discussion of the cogency required of fresh evidence in criminal cases, see the High Court of Australia in *Gallagher v R* (1986) 65 ALR 207, and the Supreme Court of Canada in *Stolar v R* (1988) 62 CR(2d) 313.
8 See generally E. Campbell 'Principles of Evidence and Administrative Tribunals' in Waller and Campbell (eds) *Well and Truly Tried* (1982) p 36, and for the position in the United States see Davis 3 *Administrative Law Treatise* (2nd edn, 1980) ch 16.
9 Very occasionally a general revision of the rules of evidence will provide explicitly for its application outside the ordinary courts, for example the Civil Evidence (Scotland) Act 1988, s 9 so applies the abolition of the hearsay rule in civil proceedings in Scotland to a wide range of non-curial proceedings.
10 See *Re Enoch and Zaretzky, Beck & Co's Arbitration* [1910] 1 KB 327.
11 For example, the Building Societies Act 1986, ss 48(3), 52(8), 57(4) and 57(5).

the ordinary courts.[12] Thus the Race Relations Act 1976 regulates compulsory provision of information and disclosure of documents by reference to civil proceedings in the High Court.[13] It is however more common for the provision to exclude the strict application of the rules of evidence which apply in ordinary courts.[14] Sometimes the statute contents itself with bestowing a power to prescribe the rules of evidence which are to apply. In *R v Deputy Industrial Injuries Comr, ex p Moore*[15] where there was such a power, no regulations had been made under it. It was said that the existence of the power indicated that Parliament did not intend the strict rules of evidence to apply.[16] It would however be rash to construe the non-existence of such a power as indicating any intention in the matter at all. The precise pattern of rules depends upon a very wide range of factors defining the nature of the proceedings:[17]

> [T]here are degrees of judicial hearing, and those degrees run from the borders of pure administration to the borders of the full hearing of a criminal cause or matter in the Crown Court. It does not profit one to try to pigeon-hole the particular set of circumstances either into the administrative pigeon-hole or into the judicial pigeon-hole. Each case will inevitably differ, and one must ask oneself what is the basic nature of the proceeding.

Flexibility is the essence of the matter. The precise concatenation of rules of evidence and procedure should be adapted to the purposes of the proceedings, and to their circumstances. Where the procedure is in some sense judicial it is common to invoke the rules of natural justice, but this carries the matter little further:[18]

> Natural justice requires that the procedure before any tribunal which is acting judicially shall be fair in all the circumstances, and I would be sorry to see this fundamental general principle degenerate into a series of hard and fast rules. For a long time the courts have, without objection from Parliament, supplemented procedure laid down in legislation where they have found that to be necessary for this purpose.

Even if it were possible, it would not be appropriate to specify here all of the various mixtures of rules of evidence which apply in all of the different tribunals which have to decide issues of fact. It is however worth drawing attention to some of the main rules which have been controverted, and to give a few examples of the approaches adopted by the courts in order to resolve them. The rules involved have principally been those dealing with the calling of witnesses, the administration of an oath, the right to cross-examine, the admissibility of hearsay and the need to disclose.

It is clear that the nature of the issues of fact to be decided and the

---

12 In Canada a reference simply to 'all relevant evidence' has been held to exclude hearsay, *R v Zeolkowski* (1987) 39 DLR (4th) 45.

13 S 50(3)(a).

14 See e g CCR Ord 19, r 5(3) governing reference to arbitration, and Town and Country Planning (Enforcement) (Inquiries Procedure) Rules 1981, SI 1981 No 1743, r 11(4).

15 [1965] 1 QB 456, [1965] 1 All ER 81.

16 At 474, 85.

17 *R v Commission for Racial Equality* [1980] 3 All ER 265, [1980] 1 WLR 1580.

18 *Wiseman v Borneman* [1971] AC 297 at 308, [1969] 3 All ER 275 at 277, per Lord Reid. In Australia in *Hempel v A-G* (1987) 77 ALR 641 it was held to be consistent with natural justice in extradition proceedings to cast the onus of proof upon the party resisting extradition, and not allow him to cross-examine witnesses, or even an oral hearing.

consequences of a finding must have an important bearing on the nature of the rules which govern that finding.[19] Thus in *R v Board of Visitors of Hull Prison, ex p St Germain (No 2)*[20] where the board of visitors were adjudicating upon allegations of very serious offences, guilt of which would involve substantial loss of liberty, the requirements were very stringent. Nevertheless they differed quite substantially from those which would have operated in a court. Thus while the court thought it necessary to allow the accused to call witnesses and to cross-examine, it nevertheless permitted discretion to the chairman to limit the number of witnesses upon proper grounds, and to insist upon cross-examination being channelled through himself.[1] In view of the notorious difficulty of some of the issues involved, questions of identification at a distance for example, the court was reluctant to permit disposal simply on the basis of hearsay,[2] but here too its solution was not exclusion, as it might have been at common law, but rather to give the accused an adequate opportunity to deal with it. This decision may be compared with that in *R v Commission for Racial Equality*[3] where questions of the right to cross-examine and to rely upon hearsay were also raised. Here however the point arose in relation to the issue of a non-discrimination notice by the Commission for Racial Equality within the statutory framework of the Race Relations Act 1976. The allegations did not involve the commission of a criminal offence, nor did an adverse determination involve loss of liberty, or, at least in the absence of a series of further steps, interference with the discriminator's business. It was for these reasons that the court distinguished the prison visitors' case, and decided that the scheme of the Act neither required to be supplemented by an automatic right to cross-examine, nor excluded the admission of hearsay. Indeed since the statute made it proper for the commission to delegate its investigatory functions, the court thought it right for the commission to act upon the basis of the hearsay necessarily contained in reports by those carrying out such functions. Such statutory support is not however necessary. In cases where the statute provides little more than a requirement that a tribunal shall act upon the basis of evidence, the general view is that this entitles it, in the absence of special considerations, to act upon any material, including hearsay, which is logically probative:[4]

> [T]echnical rules of evidence form no part of the rules of natural justice. The requirement that a person exercising quasi-judicial functions must base his decision upon evidence means no more than that it must be based on material which tends

---

19 In *R v Milk Marketing Board, ex p Austin* (1983) Times, 21 March, QB, where a tribunal decision could deprive a man of his livelihood the full criminal standard of proof was required.

20 [1979] 3 All ER 545, [1979] 1 WLR 1401.

1 This course was also required by the Court of Appeal in *Chilton v Saga Holidays plc* [1986] 1 All ER 841, where although the rules for the arbitration of small claims authorised an informal and equal approach to be adopted they were nevertheless held not to permit the Registrar to disallow cross-examination by a legally represented party, the other party not being so represented.

2 The United States has now abandoned its old rule that such an issue could not be decided solely on the basis of hearsay, *Johnson v US* 628 F2d 187 (1980) at 190.

3 [1980] 3 All ER 265, [1980] 1 WLR 1580; see also *R v Haringey London Borough Leader's Investigative Panel, ex p Edwards*, (1983) Times, 22 March.

4 *R v Deputy Industrial Injuries, ex p Moore* [1965] 1 QB 456 at 488, [1965] 1 All ER 81 at 94, per Diplock LJ. See also *Minister for Immigration and Ethnic Affairs v Pochi* (1980) 31 ALR 666.

logically to show the existence or non-existence of facts relevant to the issue to be determined, or to show the likelihood or unlikelihood of the occurrence of some future event the occurrence of which would be logically probative. It means that he must not spin a coin or consult an astrologer; but he may take into account any material which as a matter of reason, has some probative value in the manner mentioned above. If it is capable of having any probative value, the weight to be attached to it is a matter for the person to whom Parliament has entrusted the responsibility of deciding the issue. The supervisory jurisdiction of the High Court does not entitle it to usurp this responsibility and to substitute its own view for his.

Disciplinary proceedings seem close to the model of a criminal trial, but nevertheless application of the civil standard of proof has been approved,[5] the use of confessions which would there be inadmissible has been allowed,[6] facts have been permitted to be proved by reference to criminal convictions otherwise inadmissible at law,[7] and there is even no absolute entitlement to cross-examine,[8] though in some cases the rule excluding evidence of similar facts seem to have been applied.[9] As the issue departs further and further from the model of a criminal prosecution so the likelihood of importing rules of evidence which apply there diminishes. Thus the wholly inquisitorial procedure before a coroner is inimical to the application of the rules of evidence, which accordingly do not apply to such proceedings.[10] Indeed in the case of local inquiries in planning matters Lord Diplock has refused even to adopt the terminology of natural justice as suggesting that 'the prototype is only to be found in procedures followed by English courts of law.'[11] Instead he referred simply to the need for the procedure to be fair. Indeed so far from finding that rights to cross-examine constitute one of the ingredients of a fair procedure he suggests that they might make it unfair:[12]

> To 'over-judicialise' the inquiry by insisting on observance of the procedures of a court of justice which professional lawyers alone are competent to operate effectively in the interests of their clients would not be fair.

He also drew attention to the totally different conditions of a planning inquiry in relation to the nature of the issues, the number of interested parties, and of their witnesses, and the length of the proceedings. He felt that in determining even so apparently straightforward a matter as the fairness of allowing cross-examination a multitude of factors needed to be considered, such as, in the case of an expert opinion witness, the nature of the topic on which the opinion was expressed, the qualifications of the witness and competence of the cross-examiner, and the inspector's view of whether his report would be more useful if cross-examination were allowed.

5 *R v Hampshire County Council, ex p Ellerton* [1985] 1 WLR 749, disapproving remarks in *R v Police Complaints Board, ex p Madden* [1983] 1 WLR 447. In Canada, Charter guaranties of non-compellability and the presumption of innocence do not apply automatically to them, *Starr v Houlden* (1990) 64 DLR (4th) 285.
6 *Dhaliwal v British Airways Board* [1985] ICR 513.
7 *Re Del Core and Ontario College of Pharmacists* (1985) 19 DLR (4th) 68; cp *Hill v Clifford* [1907] 2 Ch 236.
8 *Shakespeare v British Coal Corpn* (1988) Times, 5 April.
9 *Lanford v General Medical Council* [1990] AC 13, [1989] 2 All ER 921; *Re College of Physicians and Surgeons of Ontario and K* (1987) 36 DLR (4th) 707.
10 *R v West London Coroner, ex p Gray* [1987] 2 All ER 129, [1987] 2 WLR 1020; *McKerr v Armagh Coroner* [1990] 1 All ER 865, [1990] 1 WLR 649.
11 *Bushell v Secretary of State for the Environment* [1981] AC 75 at 95, [1980] 2 All ER 608 at 612.
12 At 97, 614.

In general, powers to compel attendance and to administer an oath require to be endowed by statute, though it is possible for a tribunal recognised by law, even though not set up by statute, to secure a subpoena to secure the attendance of a witness.[13] The power to administer an oath does not preclude the reception of unsworn testimony, if appropriate.[14] The application of spousal immunities may depend upon how close the issues are to an accusation of crime.[15] In those cases where a witness can be compelled to give evidence, the normal range of privileges will presumably apply in the absence of specific statutory provision,[16] since it would be odd for a court to be in a weaker position than a tribunal in securing relevant evidence. It may however be preferable to save any desired exclusionary privilege when the ordinary rules are relaxed. Thus under the rules for some planning inquiries it has been thought necessary to prevent the disclosure of material inimical to public policy by express provision.[17] It may finally be noted that the nature of the issue before a tribunal may dictate the application of different, and more restrictive, rules as to the admissibility of fresh evidence on appeal.[18]

It need hardly be added that the purposes and position of legislative committees are so far removed from those of a court, that quite different sets of rules apply,[19] including some abrogating protection so well-established in the ordinary courts as that of the privilege not to disclose communications between solicitor and client.

It may also be the case that where the inquiry is essentially governmental, for example, in England under the Tribunals of Inquiry (Evidence) Act 1921, there may be no need to claim immunity on the basis of public policy.[20]

SECTION 3. PURPOSES AND CATEGORIES OF JUDICIAL EVIDENCE

Judicial evidence is used to prove either facts in issue, or facts from which facts in issue may properly be inferred. It comprises the testimony of witnesses, documents and things. The first part of this section will consider the main categories of facts in issue, and will categorise and give examples of different sorts of circumstantial evidence. The second part will explain and give examples of the different types of judicial evidence.

13 *Currie v Chief Constable of Surrey* [1982] 1 All ER 89, [1982] 1 WLR 215, QB.
14 *General Medical Council v Spackman* [1943] AC 627.
15 See *Com of the Australian Federal Police v McMillan and Hordes* (1987) 24 ACR 278.
16 *AM & S Europe v EC Commission* [1983] QB 878 at 896, [1983] 1 All ER 705 at 720; but see *Parry-Jones v Law Society* [1969] 1 Ch 1 at 9, [1968] 1 All ER 177 at 180. See further p 434 below.
17 Town and Country Planning (Enforcement)(Inquiries Procedure) Rules 1981, SI 1981 No 1743, r 11(4).
18 *R v Immigration Appeal Tribunal, ex p Weerasuriya* [1983] 1 All ER 195, distinguishing *Hadmor Productions Ltd v Hamilton* [1983] 1 AC 191, [1982] 1 All ER 1042.
19 See May *Treatise on the Law, Privileges and Usages of Parliament* (20th edn, 1983), *First Report of Select Committee on Procedure* (1978); for Australia see *Parliamentary Committees; Powers Over and Protection Afforded to Witnesses* (Parl Pap No 168, 1972); and for Canada see *Witnesses Before Legislative Committees* (Ontario Law Reform Committee, 1981).
20 For a general discussion of the evidential rules relating to such bodies see Hallett *Royal Commissions and Boards of Enquiry* (1982). The evidential rules relating to inquiries by bodies like Royal Commissions have been much debated in the Commonwealth, see e g *Bisaillon v Keable* (1983) 2 DLR (4th) 193; *Bercove v Hermes* (No 3)(1983) 51 ALR 10.

A. OBJECTS OF PROOF

The objects of proof are either facts in issue or facts, relevant to facts in issue, of which circumstantial evidence is the clearest example.

1. FACTS IN ISSUE

There are two principal types of facts in issue, those which are in issue as a matter of substantive law, and those which are in issue as a matter of the law of evidence itself.[1]

The main facts in issue are all those facts which the plaintiff[2] in a civil action, or the prosecutor in criminal proceedings, must prove in order to succeed, together with any further facts that the defendant or accused must prove in order to establish a defence. A few examples will show that the main facts in issue in a particular case can only be ascertained by reference to the substantive law and the pleadings.

Suppose the plaintiff is claiming damages for personal injuries which he alleges were caused by the negligent driving of a motor car by the defendant. The question whether the defendant owed a duty of care to the plaintiff is the concern of the law of tort; the respects in which the plaintiff contends that the duty was broken are to be gathered from the particulars of negligence set out in his statement of claim; and, if negligence is denied in the defendant's defence,[3] the law of evidence indicates how the plaintiff may substantiate, or the defendant disprove, the allegations of negligence. If negligence is not denied in the defence, and there is no plea of contributory negligence, the only issue between the parties will most probably concern the amount of damages to which the plaintiff is entitled; thus the sphere of the law of evidence may be restricted to one issue by the pleadings in a given case.

Most cases involve more than one issue. Even the simplest claims for damages for assault or breach of contract normally give rise to disputes about the amount of damages to be awarded as well as to questions whether the defendant inflicted the blows, or made the agreement, as the plaintiff contends; while further issues may be raised by the defendant by means of such pleas as those of self defence and contractual incapacity. In criminal cases:

whenever there is a plea of not guilty, everything is in issue, and the prosecution has to prove the whole of their case, including the identity of the accused, the nature of the act and the existence of any necessary knowledge or intent.[4]

1 In *R v Robertson; R v Golder* [1987] QB 920 at 927, [1987] 3 All ER 231 at 236 the Lord Chief Justice characterised the former as the 'restricted meaning' and the latter as the 'extended meaning'.
2 This term must be taken to include the applicant or petitioner where appropriate, and the word 'defendant' must be taken to include the respondent.
3 Under RSC Ord 18, r 13(3), every allegation of fact made in a statement of claim or counterclaim which the party on whom it is served does not intend to admit, must be specifically traversed by him in his defence or defence to counterclaim, as the case may be; and a general denial of such allegations, or a general statement of non-admission of them, is not a sufficient traverse of them. Under r 13 (4) allegations as to damage are deemed to be traversed unless admitted.
4 Per Lord Goddard CJ, in *R v Sims* [1946] KB 531 at 539, [1946] 1 All ER 697 at 701.

Failure to discriminate clearly between different issues is one of the most potent, and least recognised, sources of confusion and difficulty in the law of evidence. It is especially acute in criminal proceedings just because no formal pleadings are made or required in advance.

As Thayer has shown,[5] failure to recognise the dependence of the law of evidence on the substantive law and rules of procedure has led to the inclusion in textbooks of much that is not comprised in the subject. For example, formal admissions, and some branches of estoppel belong to the heading of procedure, while other branches of estoppel and the rules governing the admissibility of evidence of character in civil cases are based on the substantive law. These matters are briefly discussed in this book for the sake of completeness and conformity with tradition, but every endeavour is made to avoid reference to decisions that turn exclusively on the substantive law or questions of pleading.

Subordinate or collateral facts which may be in issue are those affecting the competence or credibility of a witness and those affecting the admissibility or cogency of certain items of evidence; they may be in issue in a particular case on account of the law of evidence itself, and not on account of the substantive law or pleadings.

An illustration of such a fact in relation to competency occurred in *R v Yacoob*[6] where the competence of the witness depended upon whether or not she was married to the accused. Similarly it may be relevant to know of the existence of a relationship which would tend to make a witness biased in favour of a party calling him. He may thus be asked about the relationship in cross-examination and, if it is denied, the relationship may be proved by the opposite party.[7]

An example of a fact relating to the admissibility of an item of evidence is furnished by the normal requirement that a document be shown to be genuine before being produced to the jury.[8] The cogency of a piece of evidence may also become a subordinate fact, for example, when a challenge is mounted to the accuracy of a new device for measuring the speed of a motor car.[9]

2. FACTS AS EVIDENCE OF OTHER FACTS: CIRCUMSTANTIAL EVIDENCE

If the only evidence which could be adduced were that directly of facts in issue, or direct evidence, many claims would fail for lack of adequate proof. At some stage, resort almost always has to be had to 'circumstantial evidence' which may be defined as any fact (sometimes called an 'evidentiary fact', *'factum probans'* or 'fact relevant to the issue') from the existence of which the judge or jury may infer the existence of a fact in issue (sometimes called a 'principal fact' or *'factum probandum'*). A typical instance is afforded by the statement of a witness at a trial for murder that he saw the accused carrying a blood-stained knife at the door of the house in which the deceased was found mortally wounded. The prosecutor invites the jury first, to assume

---

5 *Preliminary Treatise on Evidence at the Common Law* passim.
6 (1981) 72 Cr App Rep 313.
7 *Thomas v David* (1836) 7 C & P 350.
8 See *R v Wayte* (1982) 76 Cr App Rep 110.
9 *Kent v Stamps* [1982] RTR 273.

that the witness is speaking the truth, and secondly, to infer that the accused inflicted the mortal wound with the knife.

Evidentiary facts may be proved by testimony, admissible hearsay, documents, things and other evidentiary facts. An example of the proof of one such fact by another is afforded by the statement of a witness at a trial for murder that he saw blood on the coat pocket in which the accused's knife was found. The jury is asked, first, to assume that the witness is telling the truth, secondly, to infer that the blood on the pocket came from the knife, and finally to infer that the blood was on the knife because the accused stabbed the deceased with that weapon. This process might be prolonged still further, but as the number of steps which have to be taken from the first evidentiary fact to the ultimate inference of a fact in issue increases, the weaker becomes the former as a means of proving the latter and the opportunities of adducing evidence in favour of a contrary conclusion are increased.[10]

The common fear of manufactured evidence applies, perhaps even more strongly, to circumstantial evidence: 'Circumstantial evidence may sometimes be evidence, but it must always be narrowly examined, if only because evidence of this kind may be manufactured to cast suspicion on another.'[11]

No useful purpose is served by a comparison of the merits of direct and circumstantial evidence. Although, in legal parlance, circumstantial evidence does not mean a detailed account of what happened (as it formerly did in popular speech), the phrase retains an important element of its original meaning when used by lawyers because circumstantial evidence derives its main force from the fact that it usually consists of a number of items pointing to the same conclusion. The blood on the accused's knife may not be of much significance, but additional facts, such as the accused's animosity towards the deceased, benefits to be derived by the accused from the death of the deceased, and the accused's efforts to conceal the knife may give it a very damning complexion.[12]

3. EXAMPLES OF CIRCUMSTANTIAL EVIDENCE

This section adopts one of the classifications of circumstantial evidence devised by Wigmore.[13] His division of the subject into 'prospectant', 'concomitant' and 'retrospectant' evidence involves the use of strange words,

10 'Arguments upon evidence are generally arguments from effects to causes; and in proportion as the number of possible causes of a given effect increases, the force of the argument is diminished. It is impossible to fix the precise point at which the argument becomes so weak as not to be worth noticing' (Stephen *General View of the Criminal Law* (1st edn) 307).

11 *Teper v R* [1952] AC 480 at 489.

12 'It has been said that circumstantial evidence is to be considered as a chain, and each piece of evidence as a link in the chain, but that is not so, for then, if any one link break, the chain would fall. It is more like the case of a rope comprised of several cords. One strand of the cord might be insufficient to sustain the weight, but three stranded together may be quite of sufficient strength. Thus it may be in circumstantial evidence—there may be a combination of circumstances, no one of which would raise a reasonable conviction or more than a mere suspicion; but the three taken together may create a conclusion of guilt with as much certainty as human affairs can require or admit of' (per Pollock CB in *R v Exall* (1866) 4 F & F 922 at 929). See also *Thomas v R* [1972] NZLR 34.

13 Wigmore *A Treatise on the Anglo-American System of Evidence* (Tillers revn, 1983) vol 1A para 43.

but it has the merit of stressing the main types of argument by which the relevance of one fact to another may be established.

When considering some of the illustrations given in the following paragraphs, the reader would do well to bear in mind that the number of witnesses allowed to give evidence at common law trials was greatly restricted down to the middle of the nineteenth century. Those who had any interest in the outcome of the proceedings were generally unable to testify before the Evidence Act 1843 came into force, parties in civil cases, and their spouses, were only made competent by the Evidence Acts of 1851 and 1853 respectively, and, as a general rule, the accused and his spouse were unable to give evidence at a criminal trial before the Criminal Evidence Act 1898 came into force.[14] The result was that circumstantial evidence was often all that was available on points upon which direct evidence would probably be given nowadays.

(i) Prospectant evidence

In its most general form, the argument for the reception of this kind of evidence is that the occurrence of an act, state of mind or state of affairs in the past justifies an inference that the act was done, or state of mind or affairs existed at the moment of time into which the court is inquiring.

(a) Continuance. If the speed at which someone was driving at a particular time is in issue, evidence of the rate at which he was travelling a few moments earlier is admissible;[15] in cases turning on the existence of a partnership, evidence of its existence at a time earlier than that with which the court is concerned is likewise admissible.[16] Evidence has been received of a person's theological opinions four years before the time at which their nature was in issue;[17] while the fact that someone was alive at an antecedent date may support an inference that he was alive at a subsequent date.[18] Evidence of this sort is given so frequently that it is sometimes said that continuance in general, and the continuance of life in particular, is the subject of a rebuttable presumption of law; but the question is simply one of relevance, depending on the common experience of mankind, and it would be best to avoid the use of the word 'presumption' altogether in this context, or, if that term must be

---

14 During the previous twenty-five years the total exclusion of this evidence had been relaxed by sundry statutes applying to specific offences.
15 *Beresford v St Albans Justices* (1905) 22 TLR 1. Compare *R v Horvath* [1972] VR 533; and see *R v Martin* (1981) 4 ACR 302.
16 *Brown v Wren Brothers* [1895] 1 QB 390.
17 *A-G v Bradlaugh* (1885) 14 QBD 667 at 711.
18 In *MacDarmaid v A-G* [1950] P 218, [1950] 1 All ER 497, Hodson J inferred the continuance of life of a healthy woman of 28 for a further three years; in *Re Peete, Peete v Crompton* [1952] 2 All ER 599, Roxburgh J inferred the continuance of life of a healthy man for three years; in *Chard v Chard* [1956] P 259, [1955] 3 All ER 721, Sachs J inferred the continuance of life of a woman of 26 for a further sixteen years. For a case in which death was inferred after a prolonged lapse of time see *Re Watkins, Watkins v Watkins* [1953] 2 All ER 1113, [1953] 1 WLR 1323. For other cases turning on the inference of continuance of life see *R v Harborne Inhabitants* (1835) 2 Ad & El 540, *R v Willshire* (1881) 6 QBD 366; *R v Jones* (1883) 11 QBD 118; and *R v Yacoob* (1981) 72 Cr App Rep 313.

employed, it should be qualified by the use of some such expression as a 'presumption of fact' or a 'provisional presumption'.[19]

It is important to remember that there are degrees of relevancy when this kind of evidence is being considered. Proof of the theological beliefs entertained by a man thirty years earlier, would not support a reasonable inference concerning his beliefs at the time which the court was examining,[20] and neither law nor logic can specify the stage at which such evidence ceases to be of any weight—everything depends upon the facts of the particular case. If it were proved that a husband was in good health the day before his wife married someone else:

> the inference would be strong, almost irresistible, that he was living on the latter day, and the jury would in all probability find that he was so. If, on the other hand, it were proved that he was then in a dying condition, and nothing else was proved, they would probably decline to draw the inference.[1]

(b) Course of business. To prove postage, evidence may be given that a letter was copied in an office letter book, and that, according to the practice of the office, all letters dealt with in this way were posted immediately.[2] Similarly, if delivery of a document to a particular individual must be proved, the jury may be invited to infer it was handed to him by his servant on proof that it was delivered to the latter although he was not authorised to receive the document on behalf of his master.[3] It seems however that these two steps cannot be combined and proof of a practice of postage accepted as evidence of receipt by the intended recipient.[4]

(c) Habit. The fact that someone was in the habit of acting in a given way is relevant to the question whether he acted in that way on the occasion into which the court is inquiring. Thus, in *Joy v Phillips, Mills & Co Ltd*[5] a claim was made for workmen's compensation in respect of the death of a stable boy caused by a kick from a horse. The deceased was found near the horse, holding a halter which there was no occasion for him to use at that time of

---

19 'Nothing can be more absurd than the notion that there is to be any rigid presumption of law on such questions of fact, without reference to accompanying circumstances, such, for instance, as the age or health of the party. There can be no such strict presumption of law. I think that the only questions in such cases are, what evidence is admissible? and what inference may fairly be drawn from it?' (per Denman CJ in *R v Harborne Inhabitants* (1835) 2 Ad & El 540 at 544–5).

20 *A-G v Bradlaugh* (1885) 14 QBD 667 at 711.

1 Per Lush J in *R v Lumley* (1869) LR 1 CCR 196 at 198.

2 *Trotter v McLean* (1879) 13 Ch D 574; cf *Hetherington v Kemp* (1815) 4 Camp 193 (proof letter put on office table where letters for posting usually put insufficient). Proof of postage is evidence of delivery to addressee (*Watts v Vickers* (1916) 86 LJKB 177). See Interpretation Act 1978, s 7 as to service by post.

3 *McGregor v Keily* (1849) 3 Exch 794. Cf *Tanham v Nicholson* (1872) LR 5 HL 561, which turned on substantive law.

4 *Bogdal v Hall* [1987] Crim LR 500 (though this decision may merely express scepticism of the efficiency of the computerised operation of public bureaucracy, at least to the prejudice of the accused).

5 [1916] 1 KB 849; *Lahrs v Eichsteadt* [1961] Qd R 457. It is not always easy to distinguish between the proof of isolated acts and of habit; the fact that the evidence amounted to no more than the former may have accounted for its exclusion in *Manenti v Melbourne Tramways* [1954] VLR 115.

day. It was held that the defendant might call evidence of the boy's practice of teasing the horse as tending to negative the applicant's claim that the accident arose out of and in the course of the deceased's employment. Phillimore LJ said:

> wherever an inquiry has to be made into the cause of the death of a person and, there being no direct evidence, recourse must be had to circumstantial evidence, any evidence as to the habits and ordinary doings of the deceased which may contribute to the circumstances by throwing light upon the probable cause of death is admissible, even in the case of a prosecution for murder.[6]

There is no rule against the reception of relevant evidence prejudicial to the character of the deceased when his death, its cause, or the state of mind of the person who brought it about is in issue,[7] but, when the evidence of habit refers to the practice of a party to the dispute, the prohibition on evidence which merely goes to show that his disposition is that of a man likely to do the wrongful act in question must always be borne in mind.

(d) Motive or plan. Facts which supply a motive for a particular act, such as the impending discovery by the deceased that the man accused of his murder had procured loans from him by means of forged documents,[8] or the impecuniosity of an alleged forger,[9] are among the items of circumstantial evidence which are most often admitted. Further examples are afforded by more or less any murder trial at which proof is given of facts supplying a motive for revenge, financial or amatory[10] gain, or the removal of someone who was in a position to disclose unpleasant information concerning the accused.[11] Conversely, facts which tend to show a total absence of motive may be adduced, as where the lack of pecuniary embarrassment on his part is proved by someone accused of arson with intent to defraud an insurance company.[12] It is, however, easy to attach too much weight to evidence of motive: 'Almost every child has something to gain by the death of his parents, but rarely on the death of a parent is parricide even suspected'.[13] So far as lack of motive is concerned, 'there is a great difference between absence of proved motive and proved absence of motive'.[14]

Facts, such as the purchase of poison by someone who is accused of murder,[15] which suggest the existence of a plan or design, or preparation for a given course of action may always be proved, and this evidence is of considerable weight because it calls for an explanation of his conduct from the person against whom it is given. When it consists of declarations of an intention to act in a particular way, the hearsay rule has to be borne in mind. If the declarations are made by a party, they may often be brought

6 [1916] 1 KB 849 at 854.
7 The prosecution unsuccessfully contended that such a principle existed in *R v Hector* [1953] VLR 543. Cf *R v Biggin* [1920] 1 KB 213.
8 *R v Palmer* (1856) 5 E & B 1024; Stephen *History of Criminal Law* ch III, 389.
9 *Roupell v Haws* (1863) 3 F & F 784.
10 *Plomp v R* (1963) 110 CLR 234, refuting the suggestion that evidence of motive is relevant only to mens rea.
11 *R v Clewes* (1830) 4 C & P 221.
12 *R v Grant* (1865) 4 F & F 322.
13 Best *Principles of the Law of Evidence* (12th edn) 384.
14 Per Channell J in *R v Ellwood* (1908) 1 Cr App Rep 181 at 182.
15 *R v Palmer*, above.

within the category of admissions and thus be received under a well-recognised exception embodied in s 76 of the Police and Criminal Evidence Act 1984 in criminal cases, and applicable to civil cases by virtue of s 9(1) of the Civil Evidence Act 1968. Even if the declarations are not those of a party they are certainly admissible in civil cases under the Act of 1968, and possibly in criminal cases under an ill-defined exception to the hearsay rule; but, assuming that such remarks are admissible, the judges seem to have taken different views about the relevance of the intention to the question whether an act said to have been intended was, in fact, performed. If the statement was that of the accused, and the conclusion that it was carried out would be favourable to his case, it may be excluded on account of the ease with which the evidence could have been manufactured.[16] When there is no such obvious risk, some cases suggest that the statement is admissible as tending to establish the performance of the act said to have been intended,[17] while others are against admitting it for this purpose.[18] The question whether evidence is sufficiently relevant to be admissible is pre-eminently one on which different views may be taken, and, assuming that a person's present declaration of his intention is admissible as evidence of that fact, it is probably best not to try to lay down any general principle on the subject of its relevance to the performance of a subsequent act by the declarant.[19]

(e) Knowledge or capacity. Facts which tend to prove or negative a person's capacity to do an act into which the court is inquiring may be highly relevant.

Thus, the accused's knowledge of the effects of certain drugs, his skill in their application, and his ability to procure them, would be admissible evidence at his trial for murder by means of their use, and the absence of

---

16 *R v Petcherini* (1855) 7 Cox CC 79.

17 *Johnson v Lyford* (1868) LR 1 P & D 546 (declaration of intention to execute copy will, evidence that will which was in fact executed was in terms of copy); *R v Buckley* (1873) 13 Cox CC 293 (declaration by police officer to superior that he would go in search of accused after dark admitted as evidence that he did so).

18 *R v Wainwright* (1875) 13 Cox CC 171 (declaration by deceased that she was going to accused's premises inadmissible because intention might not have been carried out); *R v Thomson* [1912] 3 KB 19 (declaration by deceased that she intended to perform illegal operation on herself inadmissible, but no attempt made by Court of Criminal Appeal to distinguish between these statements and statements that she had in fact operated on herself; both treated as inadmissible hearsay); see below, p 672.

19 A person's intention at a particular time may be in issue as when it is necessary to ascertain with what intention an act was done, and accompanying declarations are often tendered to establish this fact. It may also be relevant to the question of his intention at a later time on the principle of continuance.

There have been occasional suggestions that all declarations of intention which do not amount to admissions must be excluded as hearsay, but most difficulty has arisen on the score of relevancy when a declaration of intention has been tendered to prove the performance of the act said to have been intended. Similar problems have arisen in the United States, where the case of *Mutual Life Insurance v Hillmon* 145 US 284 (1892) in which a deceased's declarations of his intention to go on a journey were admitted as evidence that he went on it has attracted an extensive literature; see the citations in Morgan, Maguire & Weinstein *Cases and Materials on Evidence* (4th edn) 668. For the position in Canada see *R v Workman and Huculak* [1963] 1 CCC 297 affd on other grounds [1963] SCR 267 and criticized in 3 Alberta Law Review 299.

any of these factors would likewise be admissible on his behalf.[20] The most frequently cited case in which this type of evidence was discussed is, however, a civil suit. In *Dowling v Dowling*[1] the plaintiff claimed repayment of money lent, and evidence of his consistent impecuniosity extending over a period of seven years up to the date of the alleged loan was received in support of the defendant's denial that it was ever made.

(ii) Concomitant evidence

The general argument for the reception of evidence of this type is that circumstances existing contemporaneously with the transaction into which the court is inquiring render the facts alleged by one or other of the parties more or less probable. It is best illustrated by what is usually described as evidence of opportunity, but reference must also be made to the reception of evidence as part of the res gestae and the general question of the use of standards of comparison.

(a) Opportunity. The presence of the accused at the time and place of an alleged crime is something which must be proved by the prosecution on practically every criminal charge, and the establishment of an alibi is conclusive in favour of innocence.[2] Any evidence which tends to prove either of the above facts is therefore admissible, and, if the defence consists of an allegation that other named persons committed the crime, their alibis in turn become relevant and admissible as part of the case for the prosecution.[3] It is however regarded as too remotely relevant that such persons advance a false alibi.[4] The prosecution may be prejudiced by its inability to investigate an alibi of which it is made aware for the first time at the trial, and adjournments to enable an investigation to take place give rise to practical difficulties, especially at trials on indictment. Section 11 of the Criminal Justice Act 1967, accordingly provides that, at such trials the defendant shall not, without the leave of the court, adduce evidence in support of an alibi, unless he has given notice of particulars of the alibi (including the names and addresses of witnesses thereto if known) not later than 7 days after the end of the proceedings before the examining justices.[5]

Opportunity is an important feature in many cases in which adultery is alleged. In *Woolf v Woolf*[6] the Court of Appeal decided that the fact that a couple occupied the same bedroom must be treated as clear evidence of

---

20 In the United States such knowledge is often subsumed under a broadened category of opportunity, see *US v Green* 648 F2d 587 (1981) at 592.

1 (1860) 10 ICLR 236. For discussion, see H H Glass, QC (ed) *Seminars on Evidence* 83.

2 On the whole subject see R N Gooderson *Alibi*. The fact that the defence of alibi is raised does not mean that a judge should never leave some other defence such as self-defence to the jury (*R v Bonnick* (1977) 66 Cr App Rep 266).

3 *R v Dytche* (1890) 17 Cox CC 39.

4 *R v Steel* as reported in (1981) 73 Cr App Rep 173 at 186.

5 For cases on the construction of the section see *R v Hassan* [1970] 1 QB 423, [1970] 1 All ER 745; *R v Lewis* [1969] 2 QB 1, [1969] 1 All ER 79; *R v Sullivan* [1971] 1 QB 253, [1970] 2 All ER 68; *R v Cooper* (1979) 69 Cr App Rep 229. Whether or not the prosecution should be permitted to put in an alibi notice as part of its case will depend upon the circumstances, see *R v Rossborough* (1985) 81 Cr App Rep 139. See also Tosswill 'The Definition of an Alibi Defence', [1978] Crim LR 276.

6 [1931] P 134; but see *Ross v Ross* [1930] AC 1, as applied in *Webster v Webster* [1945] NZLR 537.

adultery in all but the most unusual circumstances. There is, however, no irrebuttable presumption of law to this effect, even if the evidence of opportunity is accompanied by evidence of inclination arising from the previous association of the parties.[7]

(b) Res gestae. A fact may be relevant to a fact in issue because it throws light on it by reason of proximity in time, place or circumstance. This is frequently expressed by the statement that the relevant fact is part of the res gestae, although it is difficult not to sympathise with Sir Frederick Pollock when he described this as an unmeaning term which 'merely fudges the truth that there is no universal formula for all the kinds of relevancy'.[8] The doctrine is mainly concerned with the admissibility of statements made contemporaneously with the occurrence of some act or event into which the court is inquiring, and it is best discussed later, but this seems to be the proper place to illustrate the part which contemporaneity may play in the relevance of one fact to another. In *R v Moore*[9] the accused were charged with obtaining two pounds by false pretences in consequence of a card trick practised on the prosecutor in a railway train. As he alighted, the prosecutor said he would fetch the police, and he caused the accused to be arrested almost immediately. His evidence was that a total stranger handed him two pounds forthwith, and the Court of Criminal Appeal held that this fact was rightly admitted because 'it related to part of the res gestae and an inference might fairly be drawn from it'.[10] The fact's relevance to the issue is obvious enough. If someone is handed the exact sum of which he says he has been defrauded shortly after making a complaint to this effect, the two events are probably connected with each other. It is likely that the person who handed the money over was acting on behalf of the person against whom the complaint was made, and the payment suggests that the complaint was justified. If the prosecutor had received two pounds from an anonymous donor two days after his railway journey, that fact might still be regarded as relevant to the question whether he was defrauded in the train, but the relevance of such a payment would become more and more remote with the passage of time until it lapsed into insignificance so far as the guilt of the accused was concerned. The relevant degree of contemporaneity may depend upon the particular issues raised by the parties. Thus in *Ratten v R*[11] it was the fifteen-minute period during which the deceased must have been shot, within which the accused denied that the telephone call in question had been made.[12] It is questionable whether anything is gained by using such phrases as 'pars rei

---

7 *England v England* [1953] P 16, [1952] 2 All ER 784.
8 Pollock-Holmes *Correspondence* vol 2, 285. Lord Tomlin suspected it of being 'A phrase adopted to provide a respectable legal cloak for a variety of cases to which no formula of precision can be applied' (*Homes v Newman* [1931] 2 Ch 112 at 120). 'If you wish to tender inadmissible evidence, say it is part of the res gestae' (Lord Blackburn). Professor Julius Stone speaks of the law as to res gestae as 'the lurking place of a motley crowd of conceptions in mutual conflict and reciprocating chaos' (55 LQR 66).
9 (1914) 10 Cr App Rep 54.
10 At 56.
11 [1972] AC 378.
12 Though in *Teper v R* [1952] AC 480, it might be thought that insufficient attention was paid to the fact that the accused's alibi was inconsistent not only with his presence on the scene at the time of setting the fire, but also with his presence there at the time at which the utterance in question was made.

gestae' to describe relevancy due to contemporaneity, but the terminology is in constant use in the courts.

(c) Standards of comparison. Whenever it is necessary to determine whether someone's conduct complies with some objective standard, as where negligence is alleged, evidence is admissible to show how others might be expected to behave in similar circumstances. This, in appropriate cases, may comprise evidence of moral standards or of professional practice. Thus in *Fraser v Thames Television Ltd*[13] witnesses were allowed to testify that they would never use ideas for programmes without the consent of their originators. Similarly in *Ladenbau (G & K) (UK) v Crawley & de Reya*[14] a number of solicitors testified to their individual practice in conducting searches of registers during the course of conveyancing transactions. In *Banque Keyser Ullmann SA v Skandia (UK) Insurance Co Ltd*[15] the evidence related to the practice in the London insurance market when an underwriter learned of deception practised by a broker upon his principal. Where the practice of a particular branch of a trade is in question, evidence may be tendered of the practice in closely related branches.[16]

No special rules apply to such cases beyond those which require the evidence tendered to be more than remotely relevant to the issue, and unlikely to raise a number of collateral questions. It is, however, essential that the point in dispute should concern some matter as to which the argument from analogous situations to the situation under inquiry is likely to be of real assistance to the court. For instance, if it becomes necessary to determine whether a book is obscene, i e whether it is likely to corrupt the morals of its readers, the court must answer this question by reading the book itself. It has been said that no useful purpose would be served by a perusal of other books in order to compare them with the one under consideration, and that if such other books are tendered in evidence, the evidence will be rejected because it is collateral, i e irrelevant, or insufficiently relevant to the issue.[17]

The courts are frequently asked to apply standards of comparison when the identity of handwriting is in issue, but this question is best considered in connection with documentary evidence.

(iii) Retrospectant evidence

(a) In general. In its most general form, the argument for the reception of this kind of evidence is the converse of that which demonstrates the relevance of prospectant evidence: the subsequent occurrence of an act, state of mind or state of affairs justifies an inference that the act was done, or the state of mind or affairs existed, in the past. Thus, a driver's excessive speed may be proved to support the conclusion that he was going too fast a short distance

13 [1984] QB 44, [1983] 2 All ER 101.
14 [1978] 1 All ER 682, [1978] 1 WLR 266.
15 [1987] 2 All ER 923, [1987] 2 WLR 1300 expressly approving the statement in Cross.
16 *Noble v Kennoway* (1780) 2 Dough KB 510 (practice in Labrador trade to prove practice in Newfoundland trade); *Fleet v Murton* (1871) LR 7 QB 126 (evidence of practice in colonial fruit trade to prove practice in London fruit trade).
17 *R v Reiter* [1954] 2 QB 16, [1954] 1 All ER 741; cf *Dalton v Higgins* (1964) 43 DLR (2d) 574 (evidence of other provinces' fire prevention regulations excluded in action concerning a fire).

further back.[18] A classic and simple example is provided by *Gumbley v Cunningham*[19] where the House of Lords permitted an inference to be drawn from the proportion of alcohol in the accused's blood some four hours after an accident to what it must have been at the time of the accident, given the normal rate of elimination. A person's anterior intention may also be proved by his subsequent acts, although this general principle of relevancy has often had to give way to precedent based on the dread of manufactured evidence as in advancement cases.[20]

Similarly, the court may be invited to infer that an event occurred from subsequent events which followed it in the ordinary course of business, as when an endorsed cheque is produced by the drawer to show that a payment was made.[1] Servants usually claim arrears of salary shortly after their employer has defaulted, so failure to make such a claim is some evidence that no salary was due.[2] Quite apart from any question of the course of business, delay in taking action may always have to be explained in order to prevent the conclusion that the circumstances of which complaint is ultimately made did not justify such action.

(b) Omnia praesumuntur rite esse acta. Proof that someone acted as holder of a public office is evidence of his title to do so.[3] On a charge of assaulting a police officer in the course of his duty, formal proof of his appointment is not essential as evidence that he acted as a police officer will suffice.[4] Similarly, if a solicitor claims damages for words spoken of him in the way of his profession, it is unnecessary for him to produce his practising certificate, or an extract from the roll of solicitors, provided there is evidence that he acted as a solicitor.[5]

The principle applies to corporations, so proof that a company has acted as such is evidence that it was duly incorporated.[6] In short, there is a rebuttable presumption of law establishing due appointment and capacity to act—'*omnia praesumuntur rite ac solemniter esse acta*'.[7]

So far as its application to the validity of appointments is concerned, the presumption is confined to those affecting the public at large. Although the fact that a man is a solicitor may be proved by his having acted in that capacity, retainer by a particular client cannot be proved in this way;[8] a letter in his handwriting relating to the client's affairs will not suffice,[9] any more than the appointment of other private agents can be proved by the

18 *R v Dalloz* (1908) 1 Cr App Rep 258. Cf *Beresford v St Albans Justices* (1905) 22 TLR 1.
19 [1989] AC 281, [1989] 1 All ER 5.
20 See *Warren v Gurney* [1944] 2 All ER 472 at 473.
1 *Egg v Barnett* (1800) 3 Esp 196.
2 *Sellen v Norman* (1829) 4 C & P 80. But see *Bogdal v Hall* [1987] Crim LR 500 where failure to complain of non-receipt of social security cheques was not accepted as proof of their receipt.
3 For a full citation of authorities see Phipson *Law of Evidence* (13th edn) 138.
4 *R v Gordon* (1789) 1 Leach 515.
5 *Berryman v Wise* (1791) 4 Term Rep 366. See now Solicitors Act 1974, s 18 and s 63, rendering authorised Law Society lists admissible evidence.
6 *R v Langton* (1876) 2 QBD 296. As to companies incorporated under the Companies Acts, see s 15 of the Companies Act 1948.
7 The judgment of Lord Ellenborough in *R v Verelst* (1813) 3 Camp 432 is strong authority for treating the presumption as a rebuttable presumption of law.
8 *Bright v Legerton* (1861) 2 De G F & J 606.
9 Such evidence might now be admissible to prove the relationship of solicitor and client under the Civil Evidence Act 1968 or under the Criminal Justice Act 1988.

fact that they purported to act on behalf of named principals. On the other hand, if a statute provides that trustees of public property shall take an oath before acting, proof of their having acted as trustees dispenses with the necessity of showing compliance with this provision.[10] The distinction can be justified on the ground that absence of a right to act in a certain capacity is more likely to be discovered if the capacity is public than if it is private, but the matter has never been fully considered by the courts, and there is no doubt that private authorisation may sometimes be inferred from retrospectant circumstantial evidence. For example, if A is injured by B's car, B's ownership of the car is some evidence that it was being driven by his servant or agent, and this is because those who drive other people's cars are, more often than not, authorised to do so.[11]

As has been truly said 'The wheels of business will not go round unless it is assumed that that is in order which appears to be in order'.[12] Much trouble and expense is saved when the courts act on this assumption, as when they hold that the fact that speed limit signs were erected is prima facie evidence that the local authority had carried out the duties imposed upon it by the Road Traffic Acts.[13] The maxim *omnia praesumuntur rite esse acta* must, however, be used with care in criminal cases. It cannot be relied upon to prove the existence of facts central to an offence.[14] Nor should it be relied upon to presume a fact contrary to the liberty of the subject, such as that a prisoner is being held in lawful custody.[15] The presumption cannot be invoked to support the conclusion that a breathalyser was approved by the Secretary of State in accordance with statutory requirements from the mere fact that an instrument of that type was issued to the police.[16]

Those who are concerned to establish that things were done in the right order in the absence of affirmative evidence to that effect may be able to rely on an extension of the principle *ut res magis valeat quam pereat* even when it is clear that the maxim *omnia praesumuntur rite esse acta* is inapplicable because the evidence shows that at least one act was performed prematurely. Thus, in *Eaglehill Ltd v J Needham (Builders) Ltd*[17] a notice of dishonour of a bill of exchange which plainly could not be met because it was drawn on a company which had since gone into liquidation was mistakenly posted on 30 December, the day before, instead of the day after, the bill was presented. The notice was received on 31 December and it was presumed that the bill had already been dishonoured on that day because, if two acts are done, one of which ought to be done after the other, it is presumed that they were done in the right order.[18]

(c) Mechanical instruments. A presumption which serves the same purpose of saving the time and expense of calling evidence as that served by the maxim

10 *Pritchard v Walker* (1827) 3 C & P 212.
11 *Barnard v Sully* (1931) 47 TLR 557; *Manawatu County v Rowe* [1956] NZLR 78.
12 Per Lord Simonds in *Morris v Kanssen* [1946] AC 459 at 475; [1946] 1 All ER 586 at 592.
13 *Gibbins v Skinner* [1951] 2 KB 379, [1951] 1 All ER 1049.
14 *R v Willis* (1872) 12 Cox CC 164; *Scott v Baker* [1969] 1 QB 659, [1968] 2 All ER 993; *Dillon v R* [1982] AC 484, [1982] 1 All ER 1017.
15 *Dillon v R*, above.
16 *Scott v Baker*, above, though there were then so many cases that formal proof of approval of that device was no longer required, *R v Jones* [1969] 3 All ER 1559, [1970] 1 WLR 16.
17 [1973] AC 992, [1972] 3 All ER 895.
18 In *Cooper v Chief Comr of Land Tax* (1988) 12 NSWLR 660 this was restricted to cases where the order of events was necessary to the efficacy of the acts.

omnia praesumuntur rite esse acta is the presumption that mechanical instruments were in order when they were used. In the absence of evidence to the contrary, the courts will presume that stopwatches and speedometers[19] and traffic lights[20] were in order at the material time. The court will be reluctant to limit the range of evidence admissible to challenge the reliability of such an instrument in the absence of clear statutory authority to do so.[1] Although in *Castle v Cross*[2] the court omitted the qualification that the instrument must be one of a kind as to which it is common knowledge that they are more often than not in working order, it is submitted that some such qualification is necessary. As Lord Griffiths observed in *Cracknell v Willis*[3] 'trial by machine' is an entirely novel concept and should be introduced with a degree of caution. Such caution is accorded by not applying this presumption to instruments in respect of which there is no common knowledge that they are more often than not in working order. If there is no such knowledge, expert evidence should be adduced.[4]

(d) Possession as evidence of ownership. A further rebuttable presumption of law is that of lawful origin. It lies at the root of the substantive law of acquisitive prescription:

> Modern possession and user, being prima facie evidence of property and right, the judges attached to them an artificial weight, and held that uninterrupted, uncontradicted, and unexplained, they constituted proof from which a jury ought to infer a prescriptive right, coeval with the time of legal memory.[5]

Quite apart from any question of prescriptive right, possession is always treated as prima facie evidence of ownership of real[6] or personal[7] property. As Wills put it in a well-known passage:

> The acts of enjoyment from which the ownership of real property may be inferred, are very various, as for instance, the cutting of timber, the repairing of fences or banks, the perambulation of boundaries of a manor or parish, the taking of a wreck on the foreshore, and the granting to others of licences or leases under which possession is taken and held; also the receipt of rents from tenants of the property; for all these acts are fractions of that sum total of enjoyment which characterises dominium.[8]

---

19 *Nicholas v Penny* [1950] 2 KB 466, [1950] 2 All ER 89; *Skalde v Evans* [1966] SASR 176; *Re Appeal of White* (1987) 9 NSWLR 427; *R v Amyot* [1968] 2 OR 626.
20 *Tingle Jacobs & Co v Kennedy* [1964] 1 All ER 888, [1964] 1 WLR 638. See also *S v Lund* 1987 (4) SA 548.
 1 *Cracknell v Willis* [1988] AC 450,[1987] 3 All ER 801, overruling *Hughes v McConnell* [1986] 1 All ER 268,[1985] RTR 244.
 2 [1985] 1 All ER 87, [1985] 1 WLR 1372.
 3 At 459, 806.
 4 As required by s 69 of the Police and Criminal Evidence Act 1984 in the case of computers; cp *R v Spiby* (1990) Times, 16 March. See also *Leonard v Newell* [1983] Tas R 78 (requirement of expert evidence of operation of local radar); *Chiou Yaou Fa v Morris* (1987) 46 NTR 1 (requirement of expert evidence of operation of satellite navigation system); *State Insurance Comr v Whyatt* (1984) 37 SASR 454 (breathalyser not sufficiently notoriously reliable).
 5 Best *Principles of the Law of Evidence* (12th edn) 322.
 6 *Doe d Graham v Penfold* (1838) 8 C & P 536.
 7 *Robertson v French* (1803) 4 East 130.
 8 *Law of Evidence* (3rd edn) 62.

Moreover, in disputes concerning the title to a small piece of land, the plaintiff's possession of other parts of the same property is admissible evidence of his right to possession of the strip in question, as in *Jones v Williams*[9] where the plaintiff claimed to be the owner of the entire bed of a river at a certain spot, and his possession of the bed lower down the river was admitted to rebut the presumption of law that the defendant, the owner of land on the bank opposite to the plaintiff's land, owned the bed up to the middle of the stream. In these cases there must be such a common characteristic of locality as would raise an inference that the place in dispute belonged to the plaintiff if the parts over which he is proved to have exercised possession belonged to him, and, in modern times, questions of the admissibility of such evidence will normally arise only where the title deeds are not clear. In most cases, the matter is, in the first instance, governed by some such rebuttable presumption of law as that riparian owners have the right to the bed of a river up to midstream, or that, where two properties are separated by a hedge and ditch, the ditch is the boundary.

(e) Absence of an explanation and failure to give evidence or call a witness.[10] The evidence against a man may be greatly strengthened by his failure to give an explanation of conduct proved or alleged against him or the inadequacy of the explanation which he does give; those negative facts can therefore be regarded as a species of retrospectant evidence. It is of particular importance in relation to the inferences that may be drawn from the accused's possession of recently stolen goods, and this will be discussed before some more general illustrations are given, after which an attempt will be made to place the absence of a prompt explanation and a party's failure to give evidence in their proper perspective.

People react to charges in very different ways and this means that all inferences from silence must be made with caution. The silent party may have been confused or taken by surprise, he may have considered the allegation to be unworthy of an answer, or he may have wished to conceal matters concerning himself or others which are irrelevant to the case before the court. Reflections of this nature suggest that before a person's silence is allowed to count against him the circumstances must have been such that an explanation was called for, and there must have been no apparent reason, apart from a consciousness of guilt, for its absence. The matter calls for special consideration only in relation to criminal cases. Failure to give evidence is specially mentioned because its effect has been the subject of a good deal of judicial observation in both civil and criminal proceedings. A court should take care to distinguish between the inference properly arising from failure to offer an explanation and any suggestion of consciousness of guilt drawn from failure to answer questions after caution, or from failure to testify.[11]

Possession of recently stolen goods. If someone is found in possession of goods soon after they have been missed, and he fails to give a credible explanation of the manner in which he came by them, the jury are justified in inferring that he was either the thief or else guilty of dishonestly handling the goods,

---

9   (1837) 2 M & W 326; *Doe d Barrett v Kemp* (1835) 2 Bing NC 102.
10 J D Heydon, 'Silence as Evidence', (1974) 1 Monash ULR 53.
11 *Bruce v R* (1987) 61 ALJR 603 where the High Court of Australia pointed out that an explanation could have been given before the accused was cautioned.

knowing or believing them to have been stolen, contrary to s 22 of the Theft Act 1968. The absence of an explanation is equally significant whether the case is being considered as one of theft or handling, but it has come into particular prominence in connection with the latter because persons found in possession of stolen goods are apt to say that they acquired them innocently from someone else. Where the only evidence is that the defendant on a charge of handling was in possession of stolen goods, a jury may infer guilty knowledge or belief (a) if he offers no explanation to account for his possession, or (b) if the jury are satisfied that the explanation he does offer is untrue. If, however, the explanation offered is one which leaves the jury in doubt as to whether he knew or believed the goods were stolen, they should be told that the case has not been proved, and therefore the verdict should be not guilty.[12] It goes without saying that what constitutes recent possession within the meaning of the above doctrine is a question of fact depending on the circumstances of the particular case,[13] but it must be emphasized that, even if no explanation is given by the handler, 'the jury are entitled, but not compelled to convict'.[14] In the absence of further incriminating circumstances, an inference is not warranted that someone in possession of goods obtained by means of blackmail or deception[15] knew of the unlawful obtaining, even if no explanation is forthcoming. On the other hand the mere fact that a reasonable explanation is forthcoming does not mean that the jury must be directed to acquit.[16] The inference of guilty knowledge is warranted in the case of recently stolen goods because theft is by far the most common means of unlawful acquisition.[17] Now that theft and handling, unlike the former larceny and receiving, are not mutually exclusive offences because most handlers by receiving become thieves through a later appropriation, it is probably safer to convict of theft, where both offences are charged and the evidence justifies the conclusion that one or other of them was committed.[18]

General illustrations. The importance of a party's failure to give a credible explanation of apparently damning circumstances can be illustrated by numerous isolated instances throughout the whole law of evidence. If someone who is charged with burglary was found in the hall of a house without having been asked to come there, it is incumbent on him as a matter

---

12 *R v Aves* [1950] 2 All ER 330, this is the effect of *R v Schama, R v Abramovitch* (1914) 84 LJKB 396 (the leading case); see also *R v Garth* [1949] 1 All ER 773; *R v Raviraj* (1986) 85 Cr App Rep 93.

13 *R v Marcus* (1923) 17 Cr App Rep 191. The circumstances of the receipt may be relied on as proof that the goods were stolen (*R v Sbarra* (1918) 87 LJKB 1003; *R v Fushillo* (1940) 27 Cr App Rep 193; *R v Guidice* [1964] WAR 128). The accused's demonstrably false testimony is evidence to the same effect (*R v Young* (1952) 36 Cr App Rep 200). The circumstance of statements by third parties that the goods were stolen, even though believed and acted upon by the accused, is inadmissible to show that the goods were in fact stolen, but it is admissible to show that the accused believed that they had been, *R v Hulbert* (1979) 69 Cr App Rep 243; *R v Korniak* (1983) 76 Cr App Rep 145. It might in some circumstances be very difficult to draw the inference against a particular one of two co-habiting spouses, see *R v Myall* (1986) 43 SASR 258.

14 Per Lord Goddard CJ in *R v Cohen* [1951] 1 KB 505 at 508, [1951] 1 All ER 203 at 206.

15 Theft Act 1968, s 24(4).

16 *R v Ately* (1985) 9 NSWLR 226.

17 *DPP v Nieser* [1959] 1 QB 254, [1958] 3 All ER 662, where it was said that one way of supporting an inference that the accused knew of the unlawful obtaining would be to prove an association with the obtainer showing that they were in each other's confidence.

18 *Stapylton v O'Callaghan* [1973] 2 All ER 782.

of common sense, though not as a matter of law, to give a satisfactory explanation of his presence, and, if this is not forthcoming, the jury will be justified in inferring the existence of the requisite guilty intent.[19] On a charge of theft, proof of the accused's possession of a cheque drawn by the receiver in respect of the goods in question, coupled with his failure to give evidence, will warrant a conviction.[20] In *R v Nash*,[1] the appellant was charged with the murder of her child whose body was found in a well. She had been seen near the well with the child for whom she could not find a home, and she also told lies concerning the child's whereabouts. When affirming the conviction Lord Coleridge CJ said 'the facts which are proved call for an explanation, and beyond the admittedly untrue statements, none was forthcoming'.[2] Where the law does impose a duty to provide an explanation, as in some statutory offences, the inference to be drawn from failure to reply may be stronger still.[3]

To turn to civil cases, if two cars are involved in a collision, and a passenger in one of them claims damages from both drivers, it has been said that 'proof of the collision is held to be sufficient to call on the two defendants for an answer'.[4] The principle underlying the cases in which reliance has been placed on the maxim *res ipsa loquitur* is based on the importance of the absence of an explanation. In *Ellor v Selfridge & Co* for instance, the plaintiffs were hit by a van which mounted the pavement, and Scrutton LJ said:

> The fact that in the present case the van appeared upon the pavement, where it had no business to be, and injured the plaintiffs on the pavement, and *the further fact that the defendants offered no explanation why their van was there* seem to be more consistent with negligence than with the exercise of reasonable care.[5]

In cases of racial discrimination it is rarely possible to prove more than discrimination and difference of race, if this is done, then in the absence of any credible explanation it is permissible to infer that the discrimination was made upon racial grounds.[6]

Failure to give a prompt explanation. There are at least two reasons why a belated explanation should be suspect. In the first place the delay in giving it may have been due to the fact that it had to be contrived, secondly it may have impeded investigation by the opposite party. We have seen that this possibility has led to special provisions concerning notice of alibi in the case

---

19 *R v Wood* (1911) 7 Cr App Rep 56.
20 *R v Kelson* (1909) 3 Cr App Rep 230.
 1 (1911) 6 Cr App Rep 225.
 2 At 228.
 3 *Elliot v Loake* [1983] Crim LR 36.
 4 *Baker v Market Harborough Industrial Co-operative Society* [1953] 1 WLR 1472, at 1476, per Denning LJ. See also *Bray v Palmer* [1953] 2 All ER 1449, [1953] 1 WLR 1455 and *France v Parkinson* [1954] 1 All ER 739, [1954] 1 WLR 581. The effect of these decisions is that if two cars are in collision on cross-roads of equal status, and there is no further evidence, the correct inference is that both parties were negligent. *Hummerstone v Leary* [1921] 2 KB 664 is a decision to the same effect; but it was pointed out in *Nesterczuk v Mortimore* (1965) 115 CLR 140 that all these decisions are explicable on narrower grounds and the High Court of Australia held that the trial judge had rightly dismissed both claim and counter-claim where one of the two cars involved in a collision must have swerved and there was no evidence which. An inference of joint negligence may not be justified where the collision was not head-on but between rear portions of two vehicles (*Wotta v Haliburton Oil Well Cementing Co Ltd* [1955] 2 DLR 785).
 5 (1930) 46 TLR 236, italics supplied.
 6 See *North West Thames Regional Health Authority v Noone* [1988] ICR 813.

of trials on indictment, and there can be little doubt that a deferred explanation must be treated as weaker than a prompt one in other situations. Someone found in another's house in suspicious circumstances has nothing to say at the time, but swears at his trial for burglary that he entered the house in order to have a sleep in the warmth. A man charged with an indecent assault upon a little girl had nothing to say when interviewed by the police but alleges at his trial that he took her into the bushes in order to show her a bird's nest. It is difficult to believe that a court or jury would not be minded to treat these belated defences with the contempt that they usually deserve, but there are undeniable difficulties in drawing inferences adverse to the accused from his failure to give an out of court explanation to a police officer inquiring into the questions whether and by whom an offence has been committed. Subject to a few statutory exceptions, no one commits an offence by refusing to answer police questions, and once a police officer has reasonable grounds for suspecting that person has committed an offence, he must caution him before asking further questions. The caution begins with a reminder of the suspect's common law right to silence by telling him that he is not obliged to say anything,[7] it would therefore be wrong to draw adverse inferences from his failure to speak. If the caution was administered he had been told that he need not say anything, if it was not administered his silence might have been due to his determination to rely on his common law right and not to the fact that he had nothing to say. The logical result of this line of reasoning would be a refusal on the part of the courts to pay any attention to the fact that the explanation ultimately advanced by the accused was belated, and this now seems to have been recognised by the Court of Appeal in *R v Gilbert*:

> In our view it may not be a misdirection to say simply 'this defence was first put forward at this trial' or words to that effect, but if more is said, it may give rise to the inference that a jury is being invited to disregard the defence put forward because the accused exercised his right of silence . . . .[8]

In earlier cases an attempt was sometimes made to distinguish between inviting a jury to draw an inference of guilt from the belated nature of the accused's explanation and commenting on the belatedness of the explanation as a factor to be taken into account when assessing its weight. An example is provided by the following observations of Melford Stevenson J in *R v Ryan*:[9]

> It is, we think, clear . . . that it is wrong to say to a jury 'Because the accused exercised what is undoubtedly his right, the privilege of remaining silent, you may draw an inference of guilt'; it is quite a different matter to say 'this accused, as he is entitled to do, has not advanced at an earlier stage the explanation that has been

---

7 See Code of Practice for the Detention, Treatment, Questioning and Identification of Persons by the Police, para C 10 replacing the Judges' Rules.

8 (1977) 66 Cr App Rep 237 at 244 per Lord Dilhorne, sitting in the Court of Appeal; see also *R v Lewis* (1973) 57 Cr App Rep 860, citing Humphreys J in *R v Tune* (1944) 29 Cr App Rep 162.

9 (1964) 50 Cr App Rep 144 at 148. This distinction continues to attract support in Australia, see *R v McNamara* [1987] VR 855; *R v Maiden and Petty* (1988) 35 ACR 346, though discretion may nevertheless come into play.

offered to you today; you, the jury, may take that into account when you are assessing the weight that you think it right to attribute to the explanation.'

The difference was imperceptible to the Court of Appeal in *R v Gilbert*:[10]

The second of the statements quoted seems to us an invitation to the jury to draw an inference adverse to the accused on account of his exercise of the right to silence, though in an oblique fashion . . .

The judgment went on to say that the court considered the present position to be unsatisfactory:

A right of silence is one thing. No accused can be compelled to speak before, or for that matter, at his trial. But it is another to say that if he chooses to exercise his right of silence, that must not be the subject of any comment adverse to the accused. A judge is entitled to comment on his failure to give evidence. As the law now stands, he must not comment adversely on the accused's failure to make a statement.

The right of silence has come under increasing attack from authority. In Northern Ireland inroads have already been made by Order in Council[11] which permit the judge to direct the jury to draw adverse inferences from the accused's failure to explain any incriminating fact, such as the presence of bloodstains on his shoes, or for his failure to account for his presence at a particular location. The law in England and Wales is currently under review by a working party, but the Home Secretary has indicated[12] his inclination to introduce similar proposals as soon as he receives its report.[13]

Failure to give evidence or call a witness: civil cases. In *McQueen v Great Western Ry Co*[14] the plaintiff claimed that his goods had been lost owing to the crime of one of the defendant's servants. All he could prove was that the goods were delivered to the company, and placed on a truck in a siding to which the public had access, after which they disappeared. It was held that the defendant's failure to explain the loss did not make the plaintiff's evidence sufficient to sustain his case. As Cockburn CJ said:

If a prima facie case is made out, capable of being displaced, and if the party against whom it is established might by calling particular witnesses and producing particular evidence displace that prima facie case, and he omits to adduce that evidence, then the inference fairly arises, as a matter of inference for the jury and not a matter of legal presumption, that the absence of that evidence is to be accounted for by the fact that even if it were adduced it would not displace the prima facie case. But that always presupposes that a prima facie case has been established; and unless we can see our way clearly to the conclusion that a prima facie case has been established, the omission to call witnesses who might have been called on the part of the defendant amounts to nothing.[15]

Very soon after the parties were enabled to testify in most civil cases by the Evidence Act 1851, Alderson B recognised that the failure of one of them to deny a fact which it is in his power to deny 'gives colour to the evidence

10 (1977) 66 Cr App Rep 237 at 244, 245.
11 Criminal Evidence (NI) Order 1988 (SI 1988 No 1987 (NI 20)).
12 138 Official Report H C 20 October 1988 col 944.
13 Until some such change is made the law remains as stated above, see *R v Raviraj* (1986) 85 Cr App Rep 93.
14 (1875) LR 10 QB 569.
15 At 574. See also *Hughes v Liverpool City Council* (1988) Times, 30 March.

against him'.[16] Almost a hundred years later the same point was made more forcefully by an Australian judge, Rich J, when he said:

> When circumstances are proved indicating a conclusion and the only party who can give direct evidence of the matter prefers the well of the court to the witness box, a court is entitled to be bold.[17]

Dixon J added a note of caution in a dissenting judgment in the same case:

> It is proper that a court should regard the failure of the plaintiff to give evidence as a matter calling for close scrutiny of the facts upon which he relies and as confirmatory of any inferences which may be drawn against him. But it does not authorise the court to substitute suspicion for inference or to reverse the burden of proof or to use intuition instead of ratiocination.[18]

But Lord Diplock may be thought to have gone further than Rich J in a case in which the defendants called no evidence:

> this is a legitimate tactical move under our adversarial system of litigation; but a defendant who adopts it cannot complain if the courts draw from the facts which have been disclosed all reasonable inferences as to what are the facts which the defendant has chosen to withhold.[19]

There does not appear to be much discussion in the English authorities of the effect of the failure of a party to a civil case to call a witness who might have been expected to give evidence favourable to him. A variety of explanations could be given for such a failure but, subject to these, it is difficult to believe that an English judge would dissent from the following observations in a joint judgment delivered in the Supreme Court of Victoria on an appeal in a civil case tried with a jury:

> [W]here a party without explanation fails to call as a witness a person whom he might reasonably be expected to call, if that person's evidence would be favourable to him, then, although the jury may not treat as evidence what they may as a matter of speculation think that that person would have said if he had been called as a witness, nevertheless it is open to the jury to infer that that person's evidence would not have helped the party's case; if the jury draw that inference, then they may properly take it into account *against the party in question* for two purposes, namely (a) in deciding whether to accept any particular evidence, which has in fact been given, either for or against that party, and which relates to a matter with respect to which the person not called as a witness could have spoken; and (b) in deciding whether to draw inferences of fact, which are open to them upon evidence which has been given, again with respect to matters to which the person not called as a witness could have spoken.[20]

Failure to give evidence, call a witness or provide an intimate sample: criminal cases. At one time it may have seemed that the failure of the accused to call

16 *Boyle v Wiseman* (1855) 10 Exch 647 at 651.
17 *Insurance Comr v Joyce* (1948) 77 CLR 39 at 49. See also *Black v Tung* [1953] VLR 629, and *Albus v Ryder* [1956] VLR 56. Much more attention has been paid to this question in Australia where it is referred to as the rule in *Jones v Dunkel*, see *Cross on Evidence* (3rd Australian edn, 1986) para 1.43.
18 77 CLR at 61.
19 *British Railways Board v Herrington* [1972] AC 877 at 930.
20 Newton and Norris JJ in *O'Donnell v Reichard* [1975] VR 916 at 929.

evidence in a criminal case would have been treated at least in the manner suggested by Rich J, if not in that proposed by Lord Diplock, but the need to stress the accused's right not to testify and the provisions of the Criminal Evidence Act 1898, have made a big difference, and the treatment of an accused who fails to call a witness who might have been favourable seems to be assimilated to the treatment of an accused who fails to give evidence himself.[21] As long ago as 1820 Abbot CJ said:

> No person is to be required to explain or contradict until enough has been proved to warrant a reasonable and just conclusion against him, in the absence of explanation or contradiction; but when such proof has been given, and the nature of the case is such as to admit of explanation or contradiction if the conclusion to which the prima facie case tends to be true, and the accused offers no explanation or contradiction, can human reason do otherwise than adopt the conclusion to which the proof tends?[1]

In those days the accused was incompetent to give evidence on his own behalf, but the explanation might have been given by other witnesses, or it might have been advanced out of court.[2]

Proviso (b) to s 1 of the Criminal Evidence Act 1898, prohibits comment by the prosecution on the accused's failure to give evidence, but, almost immediately after the Act came into force, it was decided that the judge may comment on this fact in his summing-up[3] and it has since been held that comment by or on behalf of a co-accused is permissible.[4] The nature and extent of the comment which is permissible varies from case to case and the matter is discussed in ch X. The justification of the need for caution in this matter is the undesirability of suggesting to the jury that the exercise by the accused of his privilege not to testify is equivalent to an admission of any part of the prosecution's case;[5] but the result has been another questionable distinction, viz that between judicial comment on the accused's failure to testify and a direction to the jury about inferences which may properly be drawn from that fact, a distinction which is applied to the accused's failure to call a witness.[6]

Most of the law of the pre-trial treatment of a suspect by the police has been revised and codified in the Police and Criminal Evidence Act 1984. One of the matters regulated by the Act is that of taking various types of samples. The Act makes explicit provision for appropriate inferences to be drawn from refusal to consent to the taking of an intimate sample[7] without good cause, and for such refusal to amount to corroboration of other evidence

21 *R v Wheeler* [1967] 3 All ER 829, 52 Cr App Rep 28, though the ban on comment is not quite so stringent in relation to a witness who is available *only* to the defence, *R v Wilmot* (1988) 89 Cr App Rep 341.
1 *R v Burdett* (1820) 4 B & Ald 95 at 120. See also *Purdie v Maxwell* [1960] NZLR 599, and *Sanders v Hill* [1964] SASR 327.
2 Though an English court would almost certainly agree with the decision of the Cape Provincial Court in *S v Kibido* 1988 (1) SA 802 that the failure of an unrepresented defendant to put his defence to particular witnesses in cross-examination should ground no adverse inference.
3 *R v Rhodes* [1899] 1 QB 77.
4 *R v Wickham* (1971) 55 Cr App Rep 199.
5 *Tumahole Bereng v R* [1949] AC 253 at 280.
6 *R v Gallagher* [1974] 3 All ER 118, [1974] 1 WLR 1204; *R v Staines* (1974) 60 Cr App Rep 160.
7 As defined in s 65.

against the accused.[8] The Act authorises non-intimate samples to be taken without consent, but before the Act came into force refusal to provide such a sample was considered to be evidence against the accused, and capable of amounting to the corroboration of other evidence against him.[9]

Here too the government is intent upon change, and already in Northern Ireland the jury may be instructed to draw adverse inferences from the failure of the accused to testify once the prosecution has made out a prima facie case against him, or from his introduction at his trial for the first time of something which he could have raised earlier in answer to questions. This may be taken as an augury of the government's intention to change the law in England and Wales in a similar way.

It has been held in Canada that no inference adverse to the accused can be drawn from the failure of an alleged co-conspirator to testify for the Crown.[10]

(f) Fingerprints, bodily samples and tracker dogs.

Fingerprints. An expert witness informs the court, often with the aid of photographs, that he took the fingerprints of the accused and found them to be identical with those on some object with which the case is concerned. This is very strong retrospectant circumstantial evidence, and convictions have been upheld when there was no other evidence of identity.[11] The expert must point out the resemblances which lead him to say that the fingerprints are identical but the jury has to decide whether his conclusion is correct. It has been held in Victoria that a statement by the expert to the effect that it is impossible for two people to have the same prints is inadmissible.[12]

Subject to this point it seems that no special rules apply to the admissibility of fingerprint evidence. In *Callis v Gunn*[13] such evidence was held to be admissible although the accused had not been cautioned when asked by a police officer for his prints. The ordinary principles governing the judge's discretion to exclude evidence at a criminal trial would of course apply to such a case. The procedure for taking fingerprints is now governed by the Police and Criminal Evidence Act 1984.[14]

Bodily samples. Scientific advance has supplemented the possibility of identification by comparison of fingerprints with newer methods. First, blood testing was employed to help determine paternity. Although it gradually became more refined, this technique suffered from defects. It involved what some regarded as a peculiarly objectionable intrusion upon their bodily integrity,[15] and in most cases it operated only negatively to rebut a purported identification. Its use in paternity cases was thus often controversial, since it might seem capable only of bastardising, but not of legitimising, a child. Nevertheless its usefulness was recognised, and its use regulated, by the Family Law Reform Act 1969.[16]

8 S 62(10).
9 *R v Smith* (1985) 81 Cr App Rep 286.
10 *Grabowski v R* (1987) 57 CR 3d 89.
11 *R v Castleton* (1909) 3 Cr App Rep 74; cf *R v Court* (1960) 44 Cr App Rep 242 (fingerprints on car wind-screen insufficient evidence of possession on receiving charge).
12 *R v O'Callaghan* [1976] VR 676.
13 [1964] 1 QB 495, [1963] 3 All ER 677.
14 S 61.
15 See *S v S* [1972] AC 24, [1970] 3 All ER 107.
16 Ss 20-25.

The situation has been transformed by the further development of DNA testing of bodily samples.[17] This technique has the advantage that it can use any tissue carrying the relevant genetic code, that the sample need be neither large nor recent, and, most significantly of all, that it furnishes effectively conclusive positive proof of identity, or of family relationship.

The Family Law Reform Act 1969 has now been amended[18] to allow for the use of this new technique. The new provisions permit tests to be ordered not only upon the application of the parties, but also by the court of its own motion. The amended s 20 now recognises the possibility of obtaining a positive result, and the establishment of maternity as well as paternity. While s 21 still prevents a blood test from being taken without the consent of the subject, and this will remain the normal case, it is less clear that consent is required for tests of other substances. Probably where any taking would involve an assault the common law would dictate a similar result, at least in the absence of explicit authorisation by the court. It is however possible, in some circumstances, to secure testable tissue without an assault, and in such a case there seems to be no obstacle to using it, even without the consent of the subject. If the court's direction to submit to such a test is refused, s 23 permits the court to draw any inference from such refusal as seems proper in the circumstances.

These provisions apply only to civil proceedings in which parentage is in issue, but there seems no reason why such tests should not be used with the consent of the parties in other civil, or in criminal, procedings. In Northern Ireland provision has been made for suitable samples to be taken without the consent of those suspected of any of a wide range of offences, by the technique of defining non-intimate samples to include swabs taken from the mouth.[19] Consultations are taking place with the police upon whether there is any necessity to introduce similar powers in England and Wales.[20]

Tracker dogs.[1] There does not appear to be any fully reported English case on the admissibility in evidence of the behaviour of tracker dogs. If, after being taken to the scene of a crime, a dog picks up a scent and leads those in charge of him to the accused, a useful piece of retrospectant circumstantial evidence may have been brought into existence. The South African Appellate Division regard it as too unreliable to be received on account of the danger of misunderstanding the dog's behaviour.[2] Such evidence has,

17 For descriptions of this technique see White and Greenwood 'DNA Fingerprinting and the Law' (1988) 51 MLR 145; Goelwitz 'DNA Fingerprinting: What's Bred in the Bone' (1988) 65 CR 3d 122; Burk 'DNA Fingerprinting: Possibilities and Pitfalls of a New Technique' (1988) 28 Jur J 455; Note 'DNA Identification Tests and the Courts' (1988) 63 Wash LR 903. For a cautionary note see Hall 'DNA Fingerprints—Black Box or Black Hole' (1990) NLJ 203.
18 By s 23 of the Family Law Reform Act 1987. See also Scottish Law Commission Discussion Paper No 80 'Blood Group Tests, DNA Tests and Related Matters' (1988) for comparable proposals to amend Scots Law.
19 Criminal Justice Act 1988, s 159 and Sch 14. See Gelowitz 'Yet he opened not his mouth': A Critique of Schedule 14 to the Criminal Justice Act 1988' [1989] Crim LR 198.
20 135 HC Official Report 16 June 1988, col 653.
1   See McCormick 'The Admissibility of Tracker Dog Evidence' [1985] Crim LR 202. In *Pierce v Minister of Community Welfare* (1987) 27 ACR 119 evidence derived from observation of the manipulation by a child of anatomically explicit dolls was analogised to that obtained from the observation of tracker dogs.
2   *R v Tupedo* [1960] AD 58.

however, since been received in Scotland,[3] Northern Ireland[4] and New Zealand.[5] It would in every case be necessary for evidence to be received about the training, skills and habits of the particular dog and its handler, and evidence or judicial notice of the fact that each human being has a different scent which is liable to be picked up by a well-trained dog would be necessary. The person giving such evidence must not express his opinion about what the dog was thinking at the material time.[6]

(g) Corpus delicti.[7] Every contested criminal case raises two questions, although there may often be no dispute about the first. The questions are was the crime charged committed? and was it committed by the accused? The first is often said to be concerned with the 'proof of the corpus delicti'.

On a trial for murder, for example, the courts will be loath to convict unless someone deposes to the death of the deceased, or this fact is admitted by the accused who either denies malice aforethought[8] or withdraws his confession[9] at the trial. It was once thought that there could not be a conviction of murder or manslaughter in the absence of some direct proof of death. Great caution is obviously required before there can be a conviction of homicide without a corpse but people have been convicted of murder in the absence of such evidence,[10] when the facts were such as to render it highly probable that the accused killed the deceased and disposed of his body. DNA fingerprinting has enhanced the chances of convicting in these circumstances by enabling such things as bloodstains to be attributed to the offspring of particular parents.[11]

In *R v Burton* the accused was seen to come out of a warehouse with a quantity of pepper. As there was a great deal of pepper inside the warehouse, none was proved to be missing, but the accused was nevertheless convicted of stealing pepper. In fact he made statements amounting to confessions of guilt, but Maule J said:

> If a man go into the London docks sober, without means of getting drunk and come out of one of the cellars very drunk wherein are a million gallons of wine, I think that would be reasonable evidence that he had stolen some of the wine in the cellar though you could not prove that any wine was stolen, or any wine was missed.[12]

---

3 *Paterson v Nixon* 1960 JC 42.
4 *R v Montgomery* [1966] NI 120.
5 *R v Lindsay* [1970] NZLR 1002; *R v McCartney* [1976] 1 NZLR 472.
6 *R v Te Whiu and Buckton* [1964] NZLR 748.
7 See Norval Morris in 68 LQR 391, and Delaney in 68 LQR 560 (Irish cases).
8 As in *R v Camb* (1947) Notable British Trials (admission corpse pushed through porthole, though death alleged to have been accidental).
9 As in *R v Davidson* (1934) 25 Cr App Rep 21.
10 *R v Onufrejczyk* [1955] 1 QB 388, [1955] 1 All ER 247. See also *R v Horry* [1952] NZLR 111, and case note by Northey, 15 MLR 348; *R v Chamberlain* (1984) 51 ALR 225.
11 A conviction of murder upon such a basis was reported in (1989) Times, 15 March.
12 (1854) Dears CC 282 at 284. See *R v Joiner* (1910) 4 Cr App Rep 64, on the need for caution where the accused is in possession of goods in suspicious circumstances, but there is no evidence that they were stolen.

B. MEANS OF PROOF

1. TESTIMONY

To revert to the principal items of judicial evidence, 'testimony' is the statement of a witness in court offered as evidence of the truth of that which is stated. Many of the rules of evidence, such as those concerned with the oath, the competency of witnesses and their cross-examination, are designed to ensure that testimony shall be as reliable as possible. There is a sense in which testimony is the only item of judicial evidence. A hearsay statement, if oral, has to be narrated to the court; if it is contained in a document, the document has usually, though not invariably, to be produced to the court and identified by a witness. The same is true of things.[13] In all the above cases, however, testimony is used for a widely different purpose from that of inducing the court to accept the witness's direct statement concerning a relevant fact, and that is why hearsay statements, documents, and things, though normally proved by a witness,[14] may properly be regarded as separate items of judicial evidence.

The general rule is that a witness can give evidence only of facts of which he has personal knowledge, something which he has perceived with one of his five senses. His statement must be accepted as prima facie evidence of his possession of such knowledge for there would be an infinite regress if this fact had to be proved by another witness. The only exception to the general rule is the expert witness testifying to matters calling for expertise. Parts of his testimony may be based on information derived from textbooks or on what he has learnt from other people. The party against whom testimony is given has a right to cross-examine the witness and this right, coupled with the personal knowledge rule, lies at the root of the ban on hearsay evidence. The probative value of a statement is diminished if it is not made by a witness when giving evidence in the proceedings.

2. HEARSAY

A litigant may endeavour to prove a fact in issue by direct testimony, that is by swearing to it himself, or calling a witness to swear to it, but it sometimes happens that the best he, or his witness, can do is to depose to what someone else was heard to say on the subject, and the rule against hearsay must then be borne in mind. In spite of the etymological ineptitude the rule applies to what people wrote as well as to what they were heard to say, and to what the witness himself said out of court as well as to what he proves to have been said by others whether they are or are not called as witnesses.

The following will suffice as a succinct statement of the rule: 'an assertion other than one made by a person while giving oral evidence in the proceedings is inadmissible *as evidence of any fact asserted.*'[15]

The rule against hearsay is not stated in any statute, and it has never been

---

13 See *R v Forrester* [1985] 2 NZLR 85 where the jury was not entitled to take into account real evidence which it discovered for itself in an exhibit handed to it in the course of a trial.
14 The only exception is a public document which proves itself, ie may simply be handed to the judge.
15 This formulation was explicitly approved by the House of Lords in *R v Sharp* [1988] 1 All ER 65 at 68, [1988] 1 WLR 7 at 11.

definitively formulated judicially; but the formulation in the last paragraph is in effect contained in s 1(1) of the Civil Evidence Act 1968. It fuses two closely connected common law rules which are also fused in a number of other formulations of the hearsay rule.[16] Under the first of these rules, the previous assertions of the witness who is testifying are inadmissible as evidence of the facts asserted. If the statement is consistent with the maker's testimony, it is generally inadmissible, and, even when it is admissible, it is never admissible as evidence of those facts;[17] if the assertion is inconsistent with the maker's testimony, he may be asked in cross-examination whether he made it, and, if he denies having done so, it may be proved by another witness,[18] but, at common law, it is admissible as evidence of the facts asserted only if the maker is a party to the proceedings; in all other cases it merely casts doubts on the credibility of the testimony. If a non-party witness swears in court that he saw A on 1 January, and it is proved that he previously asserted that he did not see A on that day, the previous assertion is inadmissible as evidence of the negative fact; it is merely something which would justify the conclusion that it would be unsafe to act on the positive assertion contained in the testimony.

The second common law rule embodied in the statement of the rule against hearsay adapted from the Civil Evidence Act 1968, is what may be described as 'the rule against hearsay in the strict sense'. The rule is that assertions by persons other than the witness who is testifying are inadmissible as evidence of the facts asserted. To this rule there are many exceptions at common law. For example, A is charged with the murder of X, where on his deathbed X said to Y 'I know there is no hope; A shot me; see that he is caught.' Y will be allowed to prove X's assertion at A's trial as evidence of the fact that A shot X. This is because dying declarations by the deceased are admissible in homicide cases as evidence of the cause of death under a well known common law exception to the hearsay rule in the strict sense.

The reasons for describing the second rule as the rule against hearsay in the strict sense are that the witness who proves the out of court assertion has no personal knowledge of the facts asserted, and the party against whom the assertion is tendered has no opportunity of cross-examining its maker. These are the principal reasons why the probative value of testimony is generally greater than that of hearsay. They are often inapplicable when the maker of the assertion gives evidence. In such cases the justification of the exclusion of such assertions as evidence of the facts asserted is that it is superfluous if consistent with the testimony of the person who made it and generally of little probative value if inconsistent with that testimony. The merits of conflating the two common law rules which have just been mentioned are perhaps debatable, although the conflation is the common practice of codifiers of the law of evidence as well as of many writers on the subject.

Having formulated the rule against hearsay as the fusion of the two rules which have just been mentioned, the Civil Evidence Act 1968 proceeds to provide (subject to conditions to be mentioned in ch XV) for the admissibility, as evidence of the facts asserted, of the previous assertions of witnesses and of those who are not called as witnesses because they are unavailable through,

---

16 Stephen *Digest of the Law of Evidence* art 15; Cowen and Carter *Essays on the Law of Evidence* 1; Uniform Rules, r 63.
17 Assertions admitted as part of the res gestae may be an exception.
18 Criminal Procedure Act 1865, ss 3–5. These sections apply to civil as well as criminal cases.

for example, death or illness. The common law exceptions to the rule are abolished in civil cases by the express terms of the Act. These common law exceptions continue to apply in criminal cases and there are quite a lot of statutory exceptions applicable to criminal proceedings.[19] There is thus a number of situations in which assertions which are not made by a person while giving oral evidence in the proceedings are admissible as evidence of the facts asserted. It seems proper to describe these assertions as 'admissible hearsay assertions' and a hearsay statement may be defined as 'an assertion other than one made by a person while giving oral evidence in the proceedings tendered as evidence of the facts asserted'.

When a witness is asked to narrate another's assertion for some purpose other than that of inducing the court to accept it as true his evidence is said to be 'original'. Original evidence may therefore be defined as evidence of the fact that an assertion was made, tendered without reference to the truth of anything alleged in the assertion. Examples are afforded by a witness's testimony concerning the terms of an alleged slander, or his account of the words used when one party to a contract was making an offer to the other. These examples are simple enough, but it is not always easy to distinguish original evidence from hearsay. To do so with precision has even been said to be 'the chief, if not the whole difficulty of the art of judicial evidence'.[20] As is the case with so many other problems relating to this subject, it is crucially important to have regard to the purpose for which the evidence is tendered to the court. It is also necessary to beware of the terminological difficulties which beset the exposition of the entire law of evidence,[1] for the word 'hearsay' is occasionally used in a broad non-technical sense to denote all assertions by a witness of that which he heard someone else say. From the etymological point of view, this usage is beyond criticism but it is confusing from the point of view of the lawyer because 'hearsay' has acquired a technical meaning on account of the rule which bears its name, and this prohibits its reception only as evidence of the truth of that which was heard or recorded.

3. DOCUMENTS

The contents of a document may be incorporated in the evidence of a witness who swears, for instance, that he entered into a written contract, and the court may be referred to them because they contain admissible hearsay statements, as when an entry made by a registrar of births, deaths and marriages is produced to prove one of these occurrences. Strictly speaking, the contents of a document need not be treated as a separate item of judicial evidence, although it is convenient to do so because they are governed by special rules.

A document may be put in evidence either as a chattel—a substance such as a paper or parchment bearing an inscription, or else as a statement—the inscription on the substance. This distinction was very clearly expressed by Hoffman J in *Huddleston v Control Risks Information Services Ltd*[2] in distinguishing

19 Many of them contained in the Criminal Justice Act 1988.
20 Gulson *Philosophy of Proof* (2nd edn) 279.
 1 'The law of evidence has suffered in its most vital parts from an ailment almost incurable,— that of confusion of nomenclature' (IV *Wigmore* 20 para 1058).
 2 [1987] 2 All ER 1035 at 1037, [1987] 1 WLR 701 at 703.

between the application of the Supreme Court Act 1981 to 'property' and to 'documents':

> a written instrument or any other object carrying information such as a photograph, tape recording or computer disk can be both 'property' for the purposes of s 33(1) and a 'document' for the purposes of s 33(2). Whether for the purposes of a particular case it is the one or the other depends on the nature of the question which it is said may arise.

When treated as a chattel, there is no doubt that it constitutes real evidence, as when a deed alleged to have been stolen is produced to the court in order to show that it bears the finger-prints of the accused. When treated as a statement, a document constitutes testimonial evidence in the vast majority of cases; but it may be used as circumstantial evidence, as when ancient leases are tendered to prove that the lessor, through whom the plaintiff claims a prescriptive title, was in possession of the locus in quo:

> Ancient documents coming out of proper custody, and purporting on the face of them to show exercise of ownership, such as a lease or licence, may be given in evidence . . . as being in themselves acts of ownership and proof of possession.[3]

Although it is produced and identified by a witness, the document is not incorporated in his testimony as having been written or read by him, neither are its contents tendered as proof of anything they may assert. It is offered to the court as the kind of document which would only have been executed by someone in possession. In other words, its existence is a relevant fact proved by real evidence—the production of a material object for examination by the court.

4. THINGS OR REAL EVIDENCE

Things are an independent species of evidence as their production calls upon the court to reach conclusions on the basis of its own perception, and not on that of witnesses directly or indirectly reported to it. If a witness swears that he saw a knife, and that it bore blood-stains, the court is asked to assume that both statements are true; but, if the witness swears that the bloodstained knife he produces is the one he saw on a particular occasion, only one assumption has to be made by the court in order to reach a conclusion as to the condition of the knife.

Although it was devised by Bentham and adopted by Best, 'real evidence' is not a term which has received the blessing of common judicial usage. There is general agreement that it covers the production of material objects for inspection by the judge or jury in court, but it is debatable how much further the term should be extended.

(i) Material objects

If the condition of a material object is among the facts in issue, as where it is alleged that a suit made by a tailor does not fit his customer,[4] or the

3 *Malcomson v O'Dea* (1863) 10 HL Cas 593 at 614, per Willes J.
4 Thayer 263 (n).

defendant's dog is vicious,[5] the object may be produced to the judge and jury to enable them to form their own opinion on the matter.[6] Indeed, failure to produce such an object may be the subject of observation by the judge,[7] and, if its value is in issue, a presumption adverse to his case operates against a party who fails to produce the thing.[8] In exceptional circumstances the court will accept secondary evidence of real objects rather than requiring their physical production, for example photographs of aircraft parts.[9]

Real evidence may be used as a means of proving facts in issue, it may also be used in an endeavour to establish relevant facts, as when a knife found in the hands of a person accused of murder is produced in order to show the jury that it bears the stains of blood. But, although the production of exhibits is a common enough occurrence, the above example shows that real evidence is of little value unless accompanied by testimony identifying it as the object the qualities of which are in issue, or relevant to the issue. It is of great value so far as it goes, but it rarely goes very far.

(ii) Appearance of persons

A person's physical characteristics are frequently included among the possible items of real evidence, and these may often serve as a valuable means of proof. For instance, the fact that the accused is left-handed, tall or short, strong or weak, may frequently render it more or less probable that he committed the crime charged; a physical deformity such as a rupture may lead almost inevitably to the conclusion that a man was not guilty of rape;[10] and the resemblance which a child produced to the court bears to its alleged father or mother may be some, though very weak, evidence of parentage.[11] If, at the hearing of a claim for damages for personal injuries, the court examines those injuries or their effects, it may be said to be receiving real evidence,[12] but great caution is exercised in allowing wounds to be exhibited owing, no doubt, to the prejudice which might be excited.[13]

5 *Line v Taylor* (1862) 3 F & F 731.
6 Though any experiment to be performed upon it must be conducted in the presence of the parties, so that they may make submissions, *R v Higgins* (1989) Times, 16 February.
7 *R v Francis* (1874) LR 2 CCR 128, at 133, per Lord Coleridge CJ.
8 *Armory v Delamirie* (1722) 1 Stra 505.
9 *R v Uxbridge Justices, ex p Sofaer* (1986) 85 Cr App Rep 367. See also *Tudhope v Stewart* 1986 SCCR 384.
10 1 Hale, PC, 635–6.
11 *Burnaby v Baillie* (1889) 42 Ch D 282; *Slingsby v A-G* (1916) 33 TLR 120 at 122, where Lord Loreburn regarded such evidence as of some weight, and Lord Shaw regarded it as worthless except where there was a difference in colour between the alleged parent and child (see *MacLeod v Hill* [1976] 2 WWR 593); *Russell v Russell and Mayer* (1923) 129 LT 151 at 153, where the evidence was admitted, but spoken of as unsafe and conjectural; *C v C and C* [1972] 3 All ER 577, [1972] 1 WLR 1335 (photographic evidence of resemblance of child to alleged father admissible).
12 And where the court proposes to rely upon such observations they should be drawn to the attention of counsel so as to permit representations to be made, see *Angaston and District Hospital v Thamm* (1987) 47 SASR 177.
13 See *Gray v La Fleche, Saskatchewan Power Corpn* (1962) 31 DLR (2d) 189, showing that the fact that liability is admitted makes a difference. In *Niznik v Johnson* (1961) 28 DLR (2d) 541 motion pictures were shown to the court in order to establish the fact that the plaintiff's manifestations of pain in court were faked. See also *Stevens v William Nash Ltd* [1966] 3 All ER 156, [1966] 1 WLR 1550 and *Draper v Jacklyn* (1969) 9 DLR (3d) 264.

Again, the court is acting on real evidence when it determines the age of a child by inspection.[14]

(iii) Demeanour of witnesses

Nokes included the demeanour of witnesses among the items of real evidence. If a witness gives his evidence in a forthright way, unperturbed by cross-examination, the court will no doubt be more disposed to believe him than would be the case with a halting and prevaricating witness. So far as its bearing on the facts in issue is concerned, this type of demeanour is analogous to the answers given by a witness who is being cross-examined as to credit, and may rightly be regarded as evidence in the case.[15]

When the court acts on the remarks or behaviour of a witness as constituting a contempt, it may be said to accept real evidence because it is not asked to do more than act on its powers of perception in determining the existence of a fact in issue—the contemptuous conduct.

(iv) View

A view is an observation undertaken out of court during the course of a trial. When that which is shown at the view is something that might have been produced as an exhibit had it been convenient to do so, as when omnibuses are examined in the yard of the court,[16] or the tribunal visits a place so that witnesses can show where they were standing at the relevant time,[17] the court is being asked to act on real evidence. Although in *Goold v Evans & Co*[18] Hodson LJ regarded a view of a factory to observe the reconstruction of an accident as no more than a means of interpreting evidence given in court,[19] Denning LJ regarded it as a species of real evidence, a view subsequently endorsed by the Court of Appeal. In *Buckingham v Daily News Ltd*[20] it held that the trial judge had rightly taken into account his opinion of the working of the machine formed at a view. Parker LJ said that the occurrences at the view were part of the evidence; it was as if the machine had been brought into the well of the court and the plaintiff had there demonstrated what had occurred on the occasion under inquiry. It is for this reason essential that such a demonstration should take place in the presence of judge,[1] parties,[2]

---

14 Children and Young Persons Act 1933, s 99. In *R v Colgan* [1959] SR NSW 96, it was held that, subject to the judge's discretion, it was proper to allow the jury to see a girl alleged to be mentally defective with whom the accused was charged with having had intercourse, although the girl was not called as a witness.

15 If the inference might be controversial there is something to be said for drawing the matter to the attention of the parties in case they wish to make submissions about it, see *Newell v Cronje* 1985 (4) SA 692.

16 *London General Omnibus Co Ltd v Lavell* [1901] 1 Ch 135 where, however, the Court of Appeal regarded the evidence as insufficient; too much importance has been attached to the dicta of Lord Alverstone CJ in this case, see *R v De Grey, ex p Fitzgerald* (1913) 109 LT 871. Where relevant, musical or dramatic performances may be given in or out of court.

17 *Karamat v R* [1956] AC 256, [1956] 1 All ER 415, where the view was treated as a substitute for, or supplementary to photographs and plans. See also Megarry J in *Tito v Waddell* [1975] 3 All ER 997 at 1002, [1975] 1 WLR 1303 at 1307.

18 [1951] 2 TLR 1189.

19 A view also held in Australia, see *Railways Comr v Murphy* (1967) 41 ALJR 77.

20 [1956] 2 QB 534, [1956] 2 All ER 904; see also *Webster v Burns* [1964] NZLR 749.

1 *Tameshwar v R* [1957] AC 476, [1957] 2 All ER 683; *R v Hunter* [1985] 2 All ER 173, [1985] 1 WLR 613.

2 *Salsbury v Woodland* [1970] 1 QB 324, [1969] 3 All ER 863.

and, where there is one, jury. Such a demonstration may be distinguished from a visit to a relevant public place to appreciate better the evidence adduced in court. Even in such a case however it has been said to be better for the judge to give prior warning to the parties of any such proposed visit.[3] The purpose of such a warning is to give the parties an opportunity to suggest possibly misleading features such as a change since the events in question, or allow the parties to answer points raised by the judge at such a view.[4] Such a visit by the jury in the absence of the judge is also undesirable since it is so highly likely that questions will be asked and things said transforming the character of the visit into something more akin to a demonstration.[5]

As with other types of real evidence, there is no intrinsic objection to the reception of photographs, or in the case of demonstrations, film or video recordings. Thus the recording of the route taken by a car was admitted in *R v Thomas*.[6] The main consideration is relevancy. In the case of inanimate objects it is important to film them as close to the relevant happening as possible, so as to minimise the possibility of material change. In the case of demonstrations involving animate bodies, such as an allegedly obscene dance, it is exceedingly unlikely that a sufficiently accurate or trustworthy reconstruction can be made, because,[7]

> it would be almost impossible to analyse motion by motion those slight differences which may in the totality result in a scene of quite a different character from that performed on the night in question.

No such objection would apply to a film of the very dance that was the subject of the charge.[8]

If considered, not as real evidence, but as a species of testimony by conduct, the evidence is equally objectionable as hearsay.[9] Such an objection can, however, be overcome if such a reconstruction can be brought within an exception to the hearsay rule, as in *Li Shu-ling v R*[10] where the accused's re-enactment of his crime could be considered to come within the exception for confessions.

(v) Automatic recordings

Most discussion has hitherto centred on the admissibility of tape-recordings,[11] but this has now been supplemented by a thin trickle of authority on the admissibility of other media such as film, video-tape and computer output.[12]

---

3 Lord Widgery in *Salsbury v Woodland* at 344, 874.
4 See *Parry v Boyle* (1986) 83 Cr App Rep 310.
5 *R v Hunter*, above.
6 [1986] Crim LR 682.
7 *R v Quinn and Bloom* [1962] 2 QB 245 at 259, [1961] 3 All ER 88 at 93.
8 As in *S v W* 1975 (3) SA 841.
9 This was the essence of the objection to the admission of a video recording of an interview between a child and a social worker in a sexual abuse case involving the use of anatomically accurate dolls, *Re E Re G* (1986) 136 NLJ Rep 843.
10 [1989] AC 270, [1988] 3 All ER 138. See also Children Act 1989, s 7.
11 See articles in [1954] Crim LR 96, [1961] Crim LR 598 and (1977) 51 ALJ 94. Many of the relevant authorities are cited in *R v Maqsud Ali*; *R v Ashiq Hussain* [1966] 1 QB 688, [1965] 2 All ER 464.
12 For commentary on visual media see Goldstein 'Photographic and Videotape Evidence in the Criminal Courts of England and Canada' [1987] Crim LR 384.

In all of these cases the evidence is real evidence when it is tendered to show what it was that was recorded. The relevance of what was recorded, and the operation of other exclusionary rules may determine ultimate admissibility. Thus if a recording were obtained illegally[13] or in breach of public policy[14] it might be rejected on these grounds, but not because it was a recording. If the matter recorded is itself in issue, then the recording is capable of constituting real evidence of it.

At a trial by jury the party relying on a recording or film must satisfy the judge that there is a prima facie case that it is authentic, and it must be sufficiently intelligible to be placed before the jury. The evidence must define and describe the provenance and history of the recording up to the moment of its production in court.[15] There is no need to account for the absence of the original if the copy is shown to be authentic.[16] If only part of the original recording has been retained, a court may treat that as a very material factor influencing the exercise of any discretion to exclude the part which is tendered.[17] Where it is helpful, a copy in the shape of a transcript of a sound recording may be adduced in evidence to help the jury.[18] If such a transcript is put in evidence the court will, of course, have to be satisfied of its accuracy. It should be noted that while a literal transcription of a tape in which a language understood by the jury was used may help it to understand the sound recorded on the tape, it is very common to permit the jury to receive written translation in cases where a foreign language was used. In such a case it cannot help the jury to understand the sounds, and experts must testify to the accuracy of their translation. Provided that this has been done there is no objection to the receipt of such translations by the jury.[19] It has been held in Scotland that a typist who prepares a transcript after familiarising herself with the contents of the recording by playing it over many times, may be treated as an expert for the particular occasion, her evidence verifying the transcript as truly representing the contents of the recording being evidence of expert opinion.[20] It is also acceptable for such a transcript to be authenticated not by the typist, but by a police officer who was present at the interview, and who has compared the transcript with the recording. In such a case the judge has a discretion to permit the jury to be supplied with the transcript but only so as to help them to understand the tape recording, which remains itself the only evidence of what was said.[1]

While the use of such transcripts is clearly a great convenience to the jury some doubt has been expressed as to how far the recording may be supplemented by evidence explaining it. In the case of video-tapes a number

---

13 See *R v Senat, R v Sin* (1968) 52 Cr App Rep 282.
14 *R v Migliorini* (1981) 38 ALR 356.
15 *R v Robson and Harris* [1972] 2 All ER 699, [1972] 1 WLR 651; *Butera v DPP* (1987) 76 ALR 45 at 47.
16 *Kajala v Noble* (1982) 75 Cr App Rep 149.
17 *R v Curran and Torney* [1983] 2 VR 133.
18 This applies equally to the sound-track of a video recording, see *Re G* [1987] 1 WLR 1461 at 1472.
19 *R v Maqsud Ali, R v Ashiq Hussain* [1966] 1 QB 688, [1965] 2 All ER 464. The same view has prevailed in Australasia, see *Butera v D P P* (1987) 76 ALR 45; *R v Menzies* [1982] 1 NLZR 40, and in Canada, see *Papalia v R* [1979] 2 SCR 256.
20 *Hopes and Lavery v HM Advocate* 1960 JC 104. See also *R v Menzies*, above.
 1 *R v Rampling* [1987] Crim LR 823; see also *R v Rowbotham* (1988) 41 CCC (3d) 1 at 48. There seems to be no objection to a witness using a tape to help refresh his memory in an appropriate case, see *R v Sitek* [1988] 2 Qd R 284.

of cases have accepted the principle of permitting a witness to testify to the identity of the accused and the person shown on the film.[2] This seems correct in principle since evidence is always admitted when required to supplement the production of an exhibit, and in these cases the testimony of a witness who knows the accused well and has observed his personal characteristics and body movements in everyday life is likely to be helpful to the jury who will only have seen the accused at the trial. In *Taylor v Chief Constable of Cheshire*[3] this was taken a step further in allowing evidence of the commission of an offence by the accused to be tendered by witnesses who had seen a video recording of an incident, even though the video recording had been accidentally erased before the trial. The court took the view that their evidence was just as much direct evidence of the commission of the offence as would have been that of someone observing an event through binoculars, in other words the recording was simply an extension of the human senses. It should perhaps be noted that in *Maqsud Ali* the actual recording was unintelligible to the jury, and it is perhaps not going too far to assimilate a situation in which the actual recording is unavailable. Although objection to the evidence in *Taylor* contended that it was hearsay, this cannot be sustained since the recording was automatic, and the only human mind through which the information passed was that of the witnesses, who were present and available for cross-examination.[4] The argument that such cross-examination might be less effective in the absence of the recording seems speculative, and to be, in principle, a consideration going more to weight than to admissibility.

Exactly the same principles apply to more complex automatic recordings, such as those of a radar trace of the movements of a ship.[5] The same principles were not at first applied to automatic recordings made by computers, because of confusion with the rules governing the exclusion of hearsay.[6] It then became settled that when the computer was operating as no more than an automatic recorder, or calculator, the usual rules relating to automatic recordings could apply.[7] These continue to apply outside the special area of statements contained in documents produced by computers which, when submitted in criminal cases, must comply with the special statutory conditions set out in s 69 of the Police and Criminal Evidence Act 1984.[8] It might be supposed that in the case of any new and unfamiliar form

---

2 *Kajala v Noble* (1982) 75 Cr App Rep 149; *R v Fowden and White* [1982] Crim LR 588; *R v Grimer* [1982] Crim LR 674. See also *R v Palmer* (1980) 1 ACR 458; *R v Goodall* [1982] VR 33; *R v Smith* (1983) 33 SASR 558; *R v Sitek*, above (where the issue was not the identity but the actions of the accused).

3 [1987] 1 All ER 225, [1987] 1 WLR 1479.

4 Evidence of what appeared on the visual display of a breath-testing device was accepted as being real evidence in *Owen v Chesters* [1985] RTR 191, and in *Gunn v Brown* 1986 SCCR 179 at 183.

5 *The Statue of Liberty* [1968] 2 All ER 195.

6 See *R v Pettigrew* (1980) 71 Cr App Rep 39, and discussion in Smith 'The Admissibility of Statements by Computer' [1981] Crim LR 387; and Tapper *Computer Law* (4th edn, 1990) p 374.

7 *R v Wood* (1982) 76 Cr App Rep 23; *Castle v Cross* [1984] Crim LR 682; *R v Spiby* (1990) Times, 16 March; and see *R v McHardie and Danielson* [1983] 2 NSWLR 733. An error similar to that made in *Pettigrew* seems to have been made in *R v Wiles* [1982] Crim LR 669, in relation to an automatic record made by a meter in an automatic petrol vending system, even though no computer was involved.

8 Though these will be little, if at all, more difficult to satisfy than the conditions for admissibility at common law (see further below p 635).

of automatic recording the court will require more in the way of foundation testimony to prove the ordinary working of the device.[9]

It has been held in Scotland in the case of tape-recorded interviews with suspects at police stations that the evidence of the recording and of the memory of those present are equally primary evidence of what was said.[10] As such recording becomes more common[11] some care may be necessary in evaluating the testimony authenticating the tape, which may well be tendered by one of the parties whose primary evidence of what was said is the subject of the dispute which the adduction of the tape is designed to resolve.

SECTION 4. RELEVANCE, ADMISSIBILITY AND WEIGHT OF EVIDENCE[12]

The main general rule governing the entire subject is that all evidence which is sufficiently relevant to an issue before the court is admissible and all that is irrelevant, or insufficiently relevant, should be excluded.[13]

The affirmative aspect of this rule (the exceptions to which constitute much of the law of evidence) and its negative aspect (to which there are no exceptions at common law)[14] must be considered separately. When this has been done the distinction between the relevancy, admissibility and weight of evidence will be examined.

A. THE ADMISSIBILITY OF RELEVANT EVIDENCE

1. DEFINITION OF 'RELEVANCE'

It is difficult to improve upon Stephen's definition of relevance when he said that the word 'relevant' means that:

> any two facts to which it is applied are so related to each other that according to the common course of events one either taken by itself or in connection with other facts proves or renders probable the past, present, or future existence or non-existence of the other.[15]

Elsewhere the same writer suggested as a test for determining whether

---

9 But see *Castle v Cross*, above, and compare *Mehesz v Redman* (1980) 21 SASR 569; *Holt v Auckland City Council* [1980] 2 NZLR 124.
10 *HMA v Swift* 1983 SCCR 204 at 207.
11 For plans to expand tape-recording of interviews see Home Office Research Study No 97 'The Tape-Recording of Police Interviews with Suspects: A Second Interim Report' (1988) pp 2–4.
12 See R Eggleston *Evidence, Proof and Probability* (2nd edn, 1983), especially ch 6, together with the same author's earlier papers in Glass (ed) *Seminars on Evidence* ch 3; and 4 Melb ULR 180; ALRC Res Paper No 7 'Relevance'; see also G F James in 29 Calif LR 689.
13 See per Goddard LJ in *Hollington v Hewthorn & Co Ltd* [1943] KB 587 at 594, [1943] 2 All ER 35 at 39.
14 Some statutory rules provide for the admission of evidence of dubious logical relevance, for example s 6 of the Criminal Procedure Act 1865 (permitting *any* criminal conviction to be put to a witness in cross-examination with a view to attacking credibility), see further below, p 315; Theft Act 1968, s 27(3) (inferring guilty knowledge from previous convictions), see further, below, pp 377–8.
15 *Digest of the Law of Evidence* (12th edn) art 1.

one fact should be regarded as evidence of, or relevant to another, that the matter under discussion should be cast into the form of a syllogism of which the alleged evidentiary fact constitutes the minor premise; it is then only necessary to consider whether the major premise is a proposition the truth of which is likely to be accepted by the person who has to draw the conclusion—in the case of a lawsuit, a reasonable man.[16] For example, suppose that goods were found in the possession of the accused shortly after they were missed, and he was unable or unwilling to give an adequate explanation of the manner in which he came by them. These would be relevant facts on a charge of stealing because, if the matter were cast into the form of a syllogism, it could be stated in the following way: men found in possession of goods which have recently been missed are frequently guilty of stealing them if they do not give an adequate explanation of their possession (major premise); the accused was found in possession of the goods in question shortly after they were missed, and he gave no adequate explanation of this fact (minor premise); therefore the accused may have been guilty of stealing the goods (conclusion). As the validity of the major premises on which courts are invited to act can usually be taken for granted, the deductive method outlined above is seldom used in practice, but the test of the syllogism may be found useful whenever there is any doubt about the relevance of evidence.

In applying the test care may have to be taken with regard to the selection of the appropriate major premise. For example no one knows whether a majority of those who plan to kill a particular person actually do so, but no one doubts the relevance in a murder case of the accused's plan to kill the deceased. The appropriate major premise is not 'those who plan to kill a particular person usually do so,' but 'those who plan to kill a particular person are more likely to do so than those who have no such plan.' The whole point of a lot of circumstantial evidence is to establish the accused's membership of a number of different classes of persons more likely than non-members to have done or omitted to do some act, purchasers of poison, those with a grudge against a certain person and those standing to gain by his death, for instance.[17]

2. EXCEPTIONS

The general rule that all relevant evidence is admissible is subject to numerous exceptions because:

> our law . . . undoubtedly excludes evidence of many matters which anyone in his own daily affairs of moment would regard as important in coming to a decision.[18]

The following four exceptions are frequently stressed, but there are many others.

(i) Hearsay

Hearsay which is highly relevant on account of the contents of the statement and because the circumstances in which it was made greatly enhance the

16 *General View of the Criminal Law* (1st edn) 236.
17 R Eggleston *Evidence, Proof and Probabilty* (2nd edn) 80.
18 Per Darling J in *R v Bond* [1906] 2 KB 389 at 410. See also the remarks of Hamilton LJ, p 2 above.

probability of its truth is often excluded, as when an attesting witness's death-bed confession of having altered a deed was rejected in an action on the document.[19]

(ii) Opinion

Witnesses are generally not allowed to inform the court of the inferences they draw from facts perceived by them, but must confine their statements to an account of such facts.

It frequently happens that a bystander has a complete and full view of an accident. It is beyond question that, while he may inform the court of everything which he saw, he may not express an opinion on whether either or both of the parties were negligent.[20]

Opinion is often said to be excluded because it is irrelevant, but something more will have to be said on this subject in ch XIII; expert witnesses may testify to their opinion on matters involving their expertise.

(iii) Character

An accused person's reputation among his neighbours as a man likely to have committed the offence charged is usually inadmissible evidence of his guilt, although it might be regarded as a relevant fact, and witnesses' opinions about a person's disposition to act in a particular way are generally excluded.

(iv) Conduct on other occasions

It might be thought that the fact that someone behaved in a particular way on one occasion is relevant to the question whether he behaved in a similar fashion on the occasion which is being considered by the court, merely by reason of the general tendency of human behaviour to repeat itself. Nevertheless, evidence may generally not be given of a party's misconduct on other occasions if its sole purpose is to show that he is a person likely to have conducted himself in the manner alleged by his adversary on the occasion which is under inquiry. 'You must not prove, for example, that a particular engine driver is a careless man in order to prove that a particular accident was caused by his negligence.'[1]

3. MULTIPLE RELEVANCE AND ADMISSIBILITY

An item of evidence may be relevant for more than one reason. In other words, the major premise of a syllogism may be altered, although the minor

---

19 *Stobart v Dryden* (1836) 1 M & W 615. The confession could now be proved under the Civil Evidence Act 1968, but it would still be inadmissible in a criminal case as evidence that the deed was forged.
20 Per Goddard LJ in *Hollington v Hewthorn & Co Ltd* [1943] KB 587 at 595, [1943] 2 All ER 35 at 40.
1 Per Stephen J in *Brown v Eastern and Midlands Rly Co* (1889) 22 QBD 391 at 393. The context makes it plain that Stephen J was concerned with conduct on other occasions as proof of disposition. See also *R v Westfield Freezing Co* [1951] NZLR 456.

premise and conclusion remain the same. To enlarge upon an example cited in an old case,[2] suppose that A is charged with stealing a shirt from B's house, that shortly before the alleged theft a shirt was stolen from C's house, and that C's shirt was found in B's house in circumstances suggesting that it had been inadvertently left there by the person who stole B's shirt. Evidence tending to show that A stole C's shirt might be regarded as relevant on either of the following grounds: (a) people who steal one thing frequently steal another, A stole C's shirt, therefore A probably stole B's shirt; (b) the man who stole B's shirt probably had C's shirt in his possession, A stole C's shirt, therefore A probably stole B's shirt. The first argument is of a general nature and is based on the tendency of thieves to repeat their conduct; the second is more specific and is based on the particular facts of the case. The evidence would be inadmissible on the first ground because it would merely show bad disposition, but it would be admissible on the second ground as tending to identify the thief of B's shirt. If evidence is admissible for one purpose, it cannot be rejected on the ground that it is inadmissible for some other purpose. It is desirable that in such circumstances the two purposes are kept clearly distinguished in the mind of the trier of fact. In criminal cases tried by a jury the judge should be particularly careful in his direction. Thus if evidence of the previous convictions of the accused should be admissible in the course of cross-examination for the purpose of impugning his credibility as a witness, it is necessary for the judge to instruct the jury that it must not take the evidence into account as showing the accused's guilt directly.[3] Some scepticism may reasonably be expressed as to how effectively such directions can prevent the evidence from being used for the wrong purpose.[4] Indeed in some cases the danger is recognised as being so great as to require the principle of multiple admissibility to be overridden, and the evidence excluded altogether, though only as a matter of discretion.[5] These remarks must also be understood to be subject to the operation of some rules, such as that excluding evidence the admission of which would be likely to damage the interests of the state, which override arguments for admission based on any type of relevancy.

Wigmore described the principle involved as one of 'multiple admissibility'.[6] The term is not particularly well chosen, because it suggests that evidence may be admissible for more than one purpose. This is undoubtedly true, but the point of the rule under consideration is that evidence may be admissible for one purpose although it is inadmissible for another. It is,

2 *R v Whiley* (1804) 2 Leach 983 at 985. Cf *R v O'Meally* (No 2) [1953] VLR 30 (proceeds of robberies left at scene of murder, accused's participation in the robberies could be proved); *R v Sims* [1967] Qd R 432 (prison boot found near house broken into by escaped prisoner).
3 The desirability of giving this sort of guidance was emphasised by Lord Pearce in *Selvey v DPP* [1970] AC 304, [1968] 2 All ER 497 at 528. For examples of such directions see p 410 below.
4 Some of the strongest expressions have been made by American judges. Justice Jackson described it as 'unmitigated fiction' in *Krulewitch v US* 336 US 440 (1949) at 453; Judge Learned Hand as 'a mental gymnastic' in *Nash v US* 54 F2d 1006 (1932) at 1007, Judge Jerome Frank as 'a judicial lie' in *US v Grunewald* 233 F2d 556 (1956) at 574, while Traynor CJ remarked that a jury 'cannot segregate evidence into separate intellectual boxes', in *People v Aranda* 407 P2d 265 (1965) at 272.
5 *R v Shepherd* (1980) 71 Cr App Rep 120; *R v Watts* [1983] 3 All ER 101 at 104, 77 Cr App Rep 126 at 129, where Lord Chief Justice Lane said that the jury was required 'to perform difficult feats of intellectual acrobatics' which were 'practically impossible'.
6 1 *Wigmore* para 13.

however, difficult to suggest anything better, and, although the term is not employed by English judges, the doctrine it embodies is mentioned in numerous dicta. The application of the doctrine is fraught with danger, but the total exclusion of the evidence could be productive of even greater injustice.[7]

B. THE INADMISSIBILITY OF IRRELEVANT AND INSUFFICIENTLY RELEVANT EVIDENCE

1. ILLUSTRATIONS

A few illustrations may be given of the exclusion of evidence which is irrelevant, or insufficiently relevant, to any issue before the court.

(i) Remoteness

In *Hart v Lancashire and Yorkshire Rail Co*[8] the fact that the defendant's method of changing the points was altered after an accident was held to be inadmissible as evidence that the accident was caused by the defendant's negligence. According to Bramwell B:

> People do not furnish evidence against themselves simply by adopting a new plan in order to prevent the recurrence of an accident. Because the world gets wiser as it gets older, it was not therefore foolish before.

In *Hollingham v Head*,[9] the defence to an action for the price of guano was that an express condition in the contract of sale provided that the goods should be equal to Peruvian guano. The defendant wished to call witnesses to swear that the plaintiff had entered into contracts with other customers containing a term similar to that for which he contended, but the Court of Common Pleas held that he was not entitled to do so:

---

7 'No doubt it renders the administration of justice more difficult when evidence which is offered for one purpose or person, may incidentally apply to another; but that is an infirmity to which all evidence is subject, and exclusion on such a ground would manifestly occasion greater mischief than the reception of the evidence' (Tindall CJ in *Willis v Bernard* (1832) 8 Bing 376 at 383). 'It often happens, both in civil and criminal cases, that evidence is tendered on several alternative grounds, and yet it is never objected that if on any ground it is admissible, that ground must not prevail, because on some other ground it would be inadmissible and prejudicial. In such cases it is usual for the judge (not always very successfully) to caution the jury against being biased by treating the evidence in the objectionable sense' (per Jelf J in *R v Bond* [1906] 2 KB 389 at 389). There is, however, no rule of practice requiring such a warning to be given, the matter is entirely one for the judge's discretion (see per Murray CJ in *R v Kennewell* [1927] SASR 287 at 302). For an application in the context of statutory rules, see *R v Wall* [1983] NZLR 238.
8 (1869) 21 LT 261 at 263. Cf *State Electricity Commission of Victoria v Gray* [1951] VLR 104, at 116 (change in lighting system after accident admissible to show warning could have been given before accident) and *Anderson v Morris Wools Pty Ltd* [1965] Qd R 65 (evidence of alteration of machine after accident admissible to show precaution which might have been taken). The US Federal Rules, r 407 reads: 'When, after an event, measures are taken which, if taken previously, would have made the event less likely to occur, evidence of the subsequent measures is not admissible to prove negligence or culpable conduct in connection with the event. This rule does not require the exclusion of evidence of subsequent measures when offered for another purpose, such as proving ownership, control, or feasibility of precautionary measures, if controverted, or impeachment.'
9 (1858) 27 LJCP 241.

It may be often difficult to decide upon the admissibility of evidence, where it is offered for the purpose of establishing probability, but to be admissible it must at least afford a reasonable inference as to the principal matter in dispute.[10]

In *Holcome v Hewson*,[11] a brewer claimed damages for breach of a publican's covenant to buy beer from him. The defence was that the plaintiff had supplied bad beer, and evidence to the effect that he had supplied other publicans with good beer was rejected. He 'might deal well with one and not with the others'.[12]

Relevancy is a matter of degree and it is as idle to enquire as it is impossible to say whether the evidence was rejected in the above two cases because it was altogether irrelevant, or merely because it was too remotely relevant; but there are decisions in which evidence has been held to be inadmissible on the score of insufficient relevancy when it would, by common consent, have been of considerable probative value if it had been easy to examine and adequately reliable, for two facts which may affect the relevance of evidence for the purpose of a legal inquiry are the danger that it will give rise to a multiplicity of issues, and the danger that it might have been manufactured. Each danger affects the probabilities because it raises doubts about the reliability of the premises by means of which it is sought to justify the reception of the item of evidence in question.

(ii) Multiplicity of issues[13]

The judgment of Willes J in *Hollingham v Head* contains a timely reminder that litigants are mortal, and Rolfe B once pertinently observed that:

> if we lived for a thousand years instead of about sixty or seventy, and every case was of sufficient importance, it might be possible, and perhaps proper . . . to raise every possible inquiry as to the truth of statements made . . . In fact mankind finds it to be impossible.[14]

Evidence which might even be highly relevant in a protracted academic investigation is treated as too remote from the issue in a forensic inquiry because the body which has to come to the conclusion is controlled by the time factor, not to mention considerations such as the danger of distracting the jury,[15] and the undesirability of pronouncing upon matters which are not being litigated. Thus, in *Agassiz v London Tramway Co*[16] the plaintiff, a passenger on a tram, claimed damages for personal injuries caused by a collision which she contended was due to the negligence of the driver. She

10 Per Willes J at p 242.
11 (1810) 2 Camp 391. Cf *R v Whitehead* (1848) 3 Car & Kir 202, where, on a charge of manslaughter against a doctor, evidence of his skilful treatment of other patients was excluded.
12 Per Lord Ellenborough CJ.
13 The extent to which the rules of relevance may be moulded to meet the exigencies of other facts has been examined quite independently in two modern essays: from a theoretical point of view by Dworkin 'Principle, Policy, Procedure' in Tapper (ed) *Crime, Proof and Punishment* (1981); and from a more practical point of view by Mr Justice Fox 'Expediency and Truth Finding in the Law of Evidence' in Waller and Campbell (eds) *Well and Truly Tried* (1982).
14 *A-G v Hitchcock* (1847) 1 Exch 91 at 105.
15 'The fewer and simpler the issues left to the jury, the less chance there is of a miscarriage of justice' (per Byrne J in *R v Patel* [1951] 2 All ER 29 at 30).
16 (1872) 21 WR 199.

said that she heard a fellow passenger tell the conductor that the driver ought to be reported, only to be met by the disconcertingly frank reply 'he has already been reported, for he has been off the line five or six times today—he is a new driver'. Kelly CB rejected the evidence, not because it infringed the rule against hearsay, but because it would have given rise to many collateral issues as to whether the driver had been reported, and whether he had been off the points five or six times or was a new driver.

The desire to avoid a multiplicity of issues accounts in whole or in part for several of the exclusionary rules of evidence,[17] and it explains the caution with which the courts approach arguments to the effect that A caused B because, whenever A occurred, B followed. Farwell J considered that 'the conclusion depends on the universality of the premise, and a negative instance unexplained breaks the chain'. He added that the reception of evidence in support of such an argument 'raises side issues upon which the court cannot decide without injustice to other parties'.[18] In *Folkes v Chadd*,[19] the question was whether an embankment erected by the plaintiff caused silting in the defendant's harbour. Mr Smeaton, the distinguished engineer, testified to his opinion as an expert that the silting was not caused by the embankment, and the plaintiff sought to reinforce this opinion by showing that silting had occurred in other harbours on the same coast. The additional evidence was held to be admissible in so far as it concerned harbours in which there were no embankments, because it tended to confirm Mr Smeaton's opinion that the silting arose from some other cause, but it was held to be inadmissible as to harbours in which there were embankments, since '*Litem lite resolvit*'.[20] Lord O'Hagan took this cryptic remark to mean that the existence of embankments 'made . . . the case in controversy and the case of illustration identical, proof as to the one could scarcely avail to explain, or vary, or confirm the proof as to the other'.

The last quotation is from the case of *Metropolitan Asylum District Managers v Hill*,[1] which was concerned with the effect of a smallpox hospital on the health of the inhabitants of the neighbourhood, and a majority of the House of Lords was disposed to hold that evidence of the effect of similar institutions on other localities was admissible, although the point was not finally decided. From time to time the courts have admitted evidence of particular instances to show that wherever A has occurred B has followed in support of an argument that A caused B, but generally only when a striking coincidence would have to be assumed if A did not cause B. In *Hales v Kerr*,[2] for instance, the plaintiff claimed that he had contracted barber's itch from the implements used by the defendant, a hairdresser, and he was allowed to prove that two other customers of the defendant contracted the same disease in the previous month after he had cut their hair. It certainly would have been a coincidence of some magnitude if three customers of the same barber had not contracted a disease connected with hairdressing from the same source.

---

17 It accounts in whole for the rule that a witness's answers in cross-examination to credit are generally final, in part for the hearsay rule and the rules governing evidence of disposition.
18 *A-G v Nottingham Corpn* [1904] 1 Ch 673 at 680 and 682–3.
19 (1782) 3 Doug KB 157.
20 Per Lord Mansfield CJ.
1 (1882) 47 LT 29 at 32.
2 [1908] 2 KB 601; see also *Akerele v R* [1943] AC 255, [1943] 1 All ER 367.

(iii) Danger of manufactured evidence

The courts rightly take the view that the degree to which an item of evidence is relevant to an issue diminishes in proportion to the likelihood of its having been manufactured, but it is open to question whether people are as prone to manufacture evidence as some judgments suggest,[3] and the bogey has led to certain exclusionary rules, the mechanical application of which may lead to the rejection of evidence of real probative value.

It has certainly played a large part in the development of the rule excluding hearsay, and especially the rule excluding evidence of previous consistent statements of a witness. The dread of manufacture has retarded and complicated reform of this branch of the law to no small extent. The major inroads made by common law were mainly confined to statements made by deceased persons;[4] the first major statutory reform, the Evidence Act 1938, excluded from its ambit statements made by a person with an interest of his own to serve,[5] and even the fresh and liberal approach adopted by the Civil Evidence Act 1968 adopts special rules in the case of previous statements made by witnesses whom it is proposed to call.[6]

This spectre still haunts attempts to reform the hearsay rule in criminal proceedings. The Criminal Law Revision Committee admitted that '[t]he need to provide for safeguards against the use of manufactured evidence caused ... more difficulty than did any of the other questions relating to hearsay evidence.'[7] In order to meet this danger the Committee proposed an even more elaborate provision relating to the admissibility of proofs of evidence than that made by the Civil Evidence Act 1968,[8] insisted on a strict notice procedure,[9] and wished to bar altogether any statement said[10] to have been made after the accused had been charged. This final provision reveals the absurd straits into which the cause of reform of the laws of evidence can be driven by the fear of manufacture. The reasoning appears to assume that there are some who are prepared to manufacture everything about a document except its date.

A slightly less timorous approach was adopted by the Roskill Committee[11] which felt that the exposure of fabrication was likely to be so devastating as to operate as an adequate deterrent. Even so it felt constrained to require documents prepared specifically for the purposes of legal proceedings to be admitted only with the leave of the court.[12]

2. APPARENT EXCEPTIONS

Three exceptions to the general prohibition on irrelevant evidence have been suggested, but it is submitted that all of them are unreal so far as English law is concerned.

3 See the remarks of Eyre CJ, p 2 above.
4 See further ch XVIII below.
5 S 1(3).
6 S 2(2).
7 11th Report on Evidence (General) Cmnd 4991 para 240, see also para 229.
8 Draft Bill cl 32(3).
9 Clause 32(3) and (4).
10 Para 237(iv). But see Police and Criminal Evidence Act 1984, Sch 3, para 2.
11 Fraud Trials Committee Report (1986) para 5.36.
12 This requirement effectively putting the burden of showing non-fabrication upon the party tendering the document was enacted as s 26 of the Criminal Justice Act 1988.

(i) Facts affecting the admissibility of evidence

Phipson said that Thayer was inaccurate when he asserted that 'without any exception, nothing that is not logically relevant is admissible', because numerous facts are legally admissible although they have no logical bearing on the issue the court has to decide.[13] He referred to such facts as that a witness was not sworn in a particular way, that a hearsay declarant was dead at the date of the trial, and that due search had been made for a lost document. It seems, however, that the criticism is a purely verbal one, because it assumes that by 'logically relevant' Thayer meant relevant to the main facts in issue. His statement might equally well be taken to mean that nothing is admissible which is not relevant, either to the main facts in issue, or else to such subordinate facts as those relating to the credibility and admissibility of evidence, in which case the relevance of the facts mentioned by Phipson is obvious enough.

(ii) Curative admissibility[14]

It is sometimes said that, if irrelevant evidence is adduced by one party, his opponent may seek to dispel its effect by calling irrelevant evidence himself. Whatever the position may be in certain American jurisdictions, this principle (which Wigmore described as one of 'curative admissibility') is not recognised by the English courts. Thus, in *R v Cargill*,[15] on a charge of unlawful intercourse with a girl between thirteen and sixteen, the prosecutrix swore that she had been chaste before the accused seduced her. This was irrelevant, because absence of consent and hence the girl's character, is immaterial in such a case, but it did not entitle the accused to call evidence concerning the girl's behaviour with other men because the court was not prepared to say that, if the prosecution introduced a matter irrelevant to the issue, the defence was entitled to call evidence with regard to that irrelevant issue.

(iii) Conditional admissibility[16]

One fact may only be relevant to another if it is taken together with some further matter, and it may well be the case that this can be proved only by a witness who will be called after the one who testifies to the fact the relevancy of which is being considered. In such circumstances, the court allows the evidence to be given conditionally on its turning out to be relevant. If it proves to be irrelevant, the judge will tell the jury to disregard it. An excellent example is provided by the rules governing the admissibility of statements made in the presence of a party. These only have probative value in the light of the conduct of the person to whom they were made. If A confronts B and alleges that he has committed a crime against him, and B is

---

13 *Manual of Law of Evidence* (7th edn) 28; Thayer *Preliminary Treatise on Evidence at the Common Law* 266. The view taken in the text is followed by the editor of Phipson's Manual (12th edn) p 25.

14 I *Wigmore* para 15.

15 [1913] 2 KB 271. See also *Ready v Brown* (1968) 118 CLR 165.

16 I *Wigmore* para 14; Phipson *Law of Evidence* (13th edn) para 6–05, citing *Haig v Belcher* (1836) 7 C & P 389. The same notion is involved in the statement that evidence will be received de bene esse for the origin of which see FDM in 62 LQR 38, and Plucknett in 68 LQR 130.

later tried for that offence, evidence of what A said will usually be relevant only if B's conduct is something other than a stalwart denial of the charge; but there is no doubt that A's statement may always be proved in the first instance, although the judge may subsequently be obliged to tell the jury to disregard it altogether.[17] Such a state of affairs is better regarded as a concession to the fact that the evidence in a case often emerges slowly, and from the mouths of many witnesses, rather than an exception to the rule prohibiting the reception of irrelevant, or insufficiently relevant, matter.

C. RELEVANCE AND ADMISSIBILITY

Although there are no real exceptions to this rule, the existence of important exceptions to the rule that all sufficiently relevant evidence is admissible renders it essential to draw a sharp distinction between the relevancy and admissibility of evidence. The former is a concept arrived at inductively from experience, and its applicability can be tested deductively by the construction of a syllogism. It is not primarily dependent on rules of law.[18] The admissibility of evidence, on the other hand, depends first on the concept of relevancy of a sufficiently high degree, and secondly, on the fact that the evidence tendered does not infringe any of the exclusionary rules that may be applicable to it. To quote Wigmore:[19] 'Admissibility signifies that the particular fact is relevant and something more,—that it has also satisfied all the auxiliary tests and extrinsic policies.'

Although the distinction between relevancy and admissibility is expressly recognised in many English judgments, an over-simplification of Stephen's has exercised a somewhat baneful influence, and, by way of reaction perhaps, demands are sometimes made for the recognition of further basic concepts in the law of evidence.

1. STEPHEN'S TERMINOLOGY

In his *Digest of the Law of Evidence* Stephen attempted to state the rules concerning the matters that may be proved in court wholly in terms of relevancy. The result was that he had to explain the rejection of hearsay on the ground that it was irrelevant or deemed to be irrelevant, while its reception under exceptions to the hearsay rule was based on the fact that it was relevant or deemed to be so. Other exclusionary rules were likewise said to involve the rejection of evidence which is irrelevant or deemed to be irrelevant. The objection to this mode of expression is that much of the evidence which English law rejects is highly relevant, and no one would now

17 *R v Christie* [1914] AC 545. Such a direction may be exceedingly difficult to phrase, see *Hoch v R* (1988) 81 ALR 225.
18 Thayer sometimes wrote as though the doctrine of precedent was wholly inapplicable to questions of relevance (see (1900) 14 HLR 139, answering Fox 14 HLR 39). Wigmore, on the other hand, said 'So long as courts continue to declare in judicial rulings what their notions of logic are, just so long will there be rules of law which must be observed' (I *Wigmore* (Tillers revn) 691). For once the truth really does lie between the two views and Thayer conceded as much when he said decisions concerning relevance may 'stand as a precedent to half settle other cases'.
19 I *Wigmore* (Tillers revn) 689.

wish wholeheartedly to adhere to the terminology of the *Digest*, although its influence has been considerable.

2. THE DEMAND FOR MORE BASIC CONCEPTS

It is sometimes said that, in addition to recognising the separate concepts of relevancy and admissibility, we should allow for the two further concepts of 'materiality' and 'receivability'.[20] If this were done, 'relevant' would imply that the evidence tendered tends to prove the fact it purports to establish, 'materiality' would mean direct relevance to a fact in issue, 'admissibility' would denote that the evidence did not infringe an exclusionary rule, while 'receivability' would mean that the evidence was relevant, material and admissible. All that need be said here is that the additional concepts are not employed in practice, and it is by no means certain that their adoption would render the exposition of the law any clearer.

D. ADMISSIBILITY AND WEIGHT OF EVIDENCE

Questions concerning the admissibility of evidence must be distinguished from those relating to its weight. The former is a matter of law for the judge (although it may sometimes depend upon a preliminary finding of fact by him); the weight of evidence, on the other hand, is a question of fact, although, in cases tried with a jury, the summing-up frequently contains observations on the cogency of certain matters, and the judge can always withdraw an issue from the jury because the proponent has not adduced sufficient evidence in support of his claim. The distinction between admissibility and weight does not require further elaboration, but it is not clear-cut. The weight of evidence may affect its admissibility as this is to some extent dependent on the degree of relevancy of the matter under consideration.[1] The tendency of the modern law is in favour of a broad basis of admissibility.[2]

---

20 Montrose (1954) 70 LQR 527. The concept of materiality is employed by Wigmore, that of receivability is canvassed by Professor Montrose.
1 *R v Quinn and Bloom* [1962] 2 QB 245, [1961] 3 All ER 88. This is a complicating factor in the modern law relating to the admissibility of 'similar fact' evidence in criminal cases, see further, below, p 361.
2 'People were formerly frightened out of their wits about admitting evidence lest juries should go wrong. In modern times we admit the evidence and discuss its weight' (Cockburn CJ in *R v Birmingham Overseers* (1861) 1 B & S 763 at 767).

CHAPTER II

Matters not requiring proof and judicial findings as evidence

The general rule is that all of the facts in issue or relevant to the issue in a given case must be proved by evidence—testimony, hearsay statements, documents or things. While the question of which facts are in issue in any given proceedings is really a matter of substantive law it should be noticed that such rules occasionally masquerade as rules of evidence. This is the case with so-called irrebuttable presumptions of law, whether at common law in the case of the presumption that a boy under fourteen years of age cannot commit rape, or by statute, as for example s 50 of the Children and Young Persons Act 1933[1] which says that it shall be conclusively presumed that no child under ten can be guilty of any offence.[2] Similarly it is not uncommon for a statute to dispense with proof of a matter which it might be expected would be in issue, for example s 79(1) of the Animal Health Act 1981 dispenses with proof of the appointment or handwriting of certain officials for the purposes of the Act.

If, in a moment of forgetfulness, the plaintiff or prosecutor fails to prove an essential fact, his opponent may well succeed on a submission that there is no case to answer although the evidence was readily available, for the court only rarely exercises its discretion to allow a witness to be recalled.[3] There are a number of exceptions to this general rule. In some cases the judge, or trier of fact, is entitled to find a fact of his own motion, he may take judicial notice of it. In others a party may make a formal admission of a relevant matter. Even if he does not go so far, a matter may still be determined against him as a result of certain circumstances which the law treats as preventing him from contesting it. In such circumstances he is said to be estopped. One example of such a circumstance is when the same matter has been determined against him and in favour of his opponent by a binding and conclusive judgment of a court. It is thus convenient to consider also in this chapter the whole question of the status of judicial findings in other proceedings. Each of these topics, judicial notice, formal admissions, estoppel and evidence of judicial findings will be considered in turn, the second of them very briefly indeed.

1 As amended by Children and Young Persons Act 1963, s 16.
2 See also Bankruptcy Act 1914, s 137(2) (now repealed by Insolvency Act 1986).
3 See *Middleton v Rowlett* [1954] 2 All ER 277, [1954] 1 WLR 831; *R v Pilcher* (1974) 60 Cr App Rep 1; *R v Gainsborough Justices, ex p Green* [1983] Crim LR 627.

SECTION 1. JUDICIAL NOTICE[4]

When a court takes judicial notice of a fact, as it may[5] in civil and criminal cases alike, it declares that it will find that the fact exists, or direct the jury to do so, although the existence of the fact has not been established by evidence. If, for instance, the date of Christmas should be in issue, or relevant to the issue, it will not be necessary for the party who desires to establish that fact to call a witness to swear that the birth of our Lord is celebrated on 25 December, because this is a matter of which judicial notice is taken. There are two classes of case in which the court will act in this way, for, to quote Lord Sumner:

> Judicial notice refers to facts which a judge can be called upon to receive and to act upon either from his general knowledge of them, or from inquiries to be made by himself for his own information from sources to which it is proper for him to refer.[6]

From time to time statute has provided that judicial notice shall be taken of certain facts. It will therefore be convenient to illustrate the application of the doctrine by reference to facts which are judicially noticed without inquiry, facts judicially noticed after inquiry, and those of which notice must be taken under various statutory provisions. Certain theoretical questions are raised at the end of the section.

A. FACTS JUDICIALLY NOTICED WITHOUT INQUIRY

It would be pointless to endeavour to make a list of cases in which the courts have taken judicial notice of facts without inquiry. The justification for their acting in this way is that the fact in question is too notorious to be the subject of serious dispute. Familiar examples are provided by the rulings that it is unnecessary to call evidence to show that a fortnight is too short a period for human gestation,[7] that the advancement of learning is among the purposes

---

4 For theoretical discussion see Thayer *Preliminary Treatise on Evidence at the Common Law* ch 7; Morgan *Some Problems of Proof Under the Anglo-American System of Litigation* 36; Nokes *The Limits of Judicial Notice* (1959) 74 LQR 59; Schiff 41 Can B R 335 at 344f; M McConville 'The Doctrine of Judicial Notice—its Relationship to Evidence' (1979) 1 Liverpool LR 62; Carter 'Judicial Notice: Related and Unrelated Matters' in Waller and Campbell (eds) *Well and Truly Tried* (1982).

5 The court has a discretion, and if the facts to be noticed would, for example, go a long way towards establishing a major part of the prosecution's case, may decline to take notice and instead require evidence to be called, see *R v Zundel* (1987) 35 DLR (4th) 338.

6 *Commonwealth Shipping Representative v P and O Branch Services* [1923] AC 191 at 212. Morgan (*Some Problems of Proof* p 61) says the party who asks that judicial notice be taken of a fact 'has the burden of convincing the judge (a) that the matter is so notorious as not to be the subject of dispute among reasonable men, or (b) the matter is capable of immediate accurate demonstration by resort to readily accessible sources of indisputable accuracy'. Davis (see for example 'Judicial Notice' (1955) 55 Columbia LR 945) has promoted a distinction between the judicial notice of adjudicative and legislative facts which was accepted by the Canadian Law Reform Committee in its draft code, though it is more common to restrict judicial notice to adjudicative facts. See US Federal Rule 201; Report of Canadian task force on Uniform Rules of Evidence s 4.4(c); Australian Law Reform Commission, Research Paper 10 'The Judge—Adducing Evidence and Judicial Notice' Part C proposal 5.

7 *R v Luffe* (1807) 8 East 193.

for which the University of Oxford exists,[8] that cats are kept for domestic purposes,[9] that the streets of London are full of traffic[10] and that a boy riding a bicycle in them runs a risk of injury,[11] that young boys have playful habits,[12] that criminals have unhappy lives,[13] that the reception of television is a common feature of English domestic life enjoyed mainly for domestic purposes,[14] and that the Riding of York is coterminous with the city of that name.[15] The court may be taken to know the meaning of any ordinary expression in the English language,[16] and that the value of money has declined since 1189.[17] Judicial notice will also be taken of the fact that a post card is the kind of document which might be read by anyone,[18] but not that husbands read their wives' letters.[19] These conclusions have been reached without reference to any extraneous sources of information, but there is a number of cases in which judicial notice has been taken only after such reference has been made.

B. FACTS JUDICIALLY NOTICED AFTER INQUIRY

Foremost among these are cases in which the court acts on information supplied by a Secretary of State with regard to what may loosely be described as political matters; but other illustrations are provided by cases concerning inquiries into historical facts, questions concerning the existence of various customs and matters of professional practice. It is sometimes said that the judges take judicial notice of the common law, but there is no need to deal separately with this aspect of the subject.

The sources consulted by the judge may include reports of previous cases, certificates from various officials, works of reference and oral statements of witnesses.

What was once a notorious fact to be noticed without further ado may become one of which notice will only be taken after the court's memory has been refreshed. In *Hoare v Silverlock*[20] for instance, the plaintiff had applied to a benevolent society for assistance, and she alleged that the defendant had defamed her by saying her friends would realise the truth of the fable about the frozen snake. Erle J said:

---

8 *Re Oxford Poor Rate Case* (1857) 8 E & B 184 (a decision that university premises came within special rating provisions).
9 *Nye v Niblett* [1918] 1 KB 23 (cats protected by Malicious Damage Act 1861).
10 *Dennis v A J White and Co* [1916] 2 KB 1 at 6.
11 Ibid. [1917] AC at p 492.
12 *Clayton v Hardwicke Colliery Co Ltd* (1915) 85 LJKB 292.
13 *Burns v Edman* [1970] 2 QB 541, [1970] 1 All ER 886.
14 *Bridlington Relay Ltd v Yorkshire Electricity Board* [1965] Ch 436, [1965] 1 All ER 264.
15 *R v St Maurice Inhabitants* (1851) 16 QB 908.
16 *Chapman v Kirke* [1948] 2 KB 450 at 454, [1948] 2 All ER 556 at 557.
17 *Bryant v Foot* (1868) LR 3 QB 497. A South Australian court has taken judicial notice of a general increase in the cost of living, but not of particular statistics (*Re Richardson* [1920] SASR 25); cf *National Trustees Executors and Agency Co of Australasia Ltd v A-G for State of Victoria* [1973] VR 610 (general inflationary trend in economy).
18 *Huth v Huth* [1915] 3 KB 32.
19 *Theaker v Richardson* [1962] 1 All ER 229, [1962] 1 WLR 151.
20 (1848) 12 QB 624.

I may take judicial notice that the words 'frozen snake' have an application very generally known indeed, which application is likely to bring into contempt a person against whom it is directed.[1]

If such a point were to come before a jury today, they would require a good deal of instruction in the mysteries of Aesop's fables.[2]

1. POLITICAL MATTERS

In *Duff Development Co v Government of Kelantan*[3] the government of Kelantan applied for an order against the enforcement of an arbitration award on the ground that Kelantan was an independent sovereign state. The Secretary of State for the Colonies in reply to an inquiry from the Master wrote that Kelantan was a sovereign state and the Sultan ruler thereof. The House of Lords held that this concluded the matter because:

> It has for some time been the practice of our courts, when such a question is raised, to take judicial notice of the sovereignty of a state, and for that purpose (in case of any uncertainty) to seek information from a Secretary of State; and when information is so obtained the court does not permit it to be questioned by the parties.[4]

The source of information to which the court resorts is treated as one of indisputable accuracy for reasons of public policy—the undesirability of a conflict between the courts and the executive. As in all cases in which the courts renounce their powers of determining facts on the basis of evidence, the practice may be represented as something like a submission to official dictatorship, but, in this instance, it is difficult to see how else a judge should act when confronted with such questions as the sovereignty of a foreign state, the membership of a diplomatic suite, the extent of our territorial waters or the existence of a state of war.[5] Moreover the courts form their own opinion of the effect of the Secretary of State's answer and they may differ inter se on this point.[6]

2. HISTORICAL FACTS

In *Read v The Bishop of Lincoln*[7] the question was whether the mixing of communion wine with water and various other practices were contrary to

---

1 At 633.
2 Nokes *Introduction to Evidence* (4th edn) 54.
3 [1924] AC 797. See also *Taylor v Barclay* (1828) 2 Sim 213 (judicial notice of non-recognition of South American republic after consultation with Secretary of State); *The Fagernes* [1927] P 311 (Admiralty's statement of extent of territorial waters conclusive); *Engelke v Musmann* [1928] AC 433 (Secretary of State's letter as to membership of diplomatic suite conclusive); *R v Bottrill, ex p Kuechenmeister* [1947] KB 41, [1947] 2 All ER 434 (judicial notice of continuance of war with Germany after consultation with Secretary of State).
4 Per Lord Cave [1924] AC at 805.
5 See cases cited in n 3 above and *Preston v Preston* [1963] P 141 at 149, [1962] 3 All ER 1057 at 1060 f. Judicial notice will not be taken of a particular event, such as the date of a military operation, in a modern war; *Commonwealth Shipping Representative v P and O Branch Services* [1923] AC 191.
6 *Carl-Zeiss-Stiftung v Rayner and Keeler Ltd* (No 2) [1967] 1 AC 853, [1966] 2 All ER 536.
7 [1892] AC 644.

the law of the church. It was held, against an objection to their doing so, that the courts might consider historical and ritualistic works on the subject. In the course of his speech in the House of Lords Lord Halsbury made it clear that the judge can rely on his own historical learning in such a case, although 'where it is important to ascertain ancient facts of a public nature the law does permit historical works to be referred to'.[8] If questions concerning the tenets of a political creed were to arise, the English courts would no doubt do what Australian courts are prepared to do and consult the appropriate literature.[9] A similar practice would no doubt be adopted with regard to general scientific or aesthetic questions. The courts will also take notice of what people must have believed at a given time about such contemporary matters as the likelihood of a war.[10]

3. CUSTOM

As a general rule a court cannot treat a fact as proved on the basis of the evidence in a previous case,[11] but this rule does not apply to the proof of custom, for it has been recognised that a time must come when the courts, having had the question of the existence of a custom before them in other cases, are entitled to say that they will take judicial notice of it and will not require proof in each case.[12] This recognition was made by Bray J in the Divisional Court when upholding a County Court judge's right to take judicial notice of the custom whereby a domestic servant might terminate her employment within the first month of her engagement by less than a full month's notice but the doctrine he enunciated lies at the root of the court's recognition of a vast number of mercantile customs.[13] It is not always easy to say when a custom has been recognised with sufficient frequency to become the subject of judicial notice. Whereas the courts were not prepared to recognise that it was the usual practice of a hotel-keeper to be in possession of furniture under hire purchase agreements in 1875, they were prepared to do so in 1881.[14]

4. PROFESSIONAL PRACTICE

In *Davey v Harrow Corporation*,[15] Lord Goddard CJ said:

---

8 At 653; *Evans v Getting* (1834) 6 C & P 586 (history of Breconshire not received on question of boundaries of Welsh parishes because of possible prejudice of author); *Darby v Ouseley* (1856) 1 H & N 1.
9 *Australian Communist Party v Commonwealth* (1951) 83 CLR 1.
10 *Monarch S S Co Ltd v Karlshamns Oljefabriker A/B* [1949] AC 196 at 234, [1949] 1 All ER 1 at 20, per Lord Du Parcq.
11 *Roper v Taylor's Central Garages (Exeter) Ltd* [1951] 2 TLR 284.
12 *George v Davies* [1911] 2 KB 445 at 448.
13 *Brandao v Barnett* (1846) 12 Cl & Fin 787.
14 *Re Matthews, ex p Powell* (1875) 1 Ch D 501; *Crawcour v Salter* (1881) 18 Ch D 30.
15 [1958] 1 QB 60 at 69.

Where a boundary hedge is delineated on an ordnance survey map by a line, that line indicated the centre of the existing hedge. That is in accordance with the practice of the ordnance survey and courts can take notice of that practice as at least prima facie evidence of what a line on the map indicates.

Judicial notice will likewise be taken of the practice of conveyancers.[16]

C. STATUTORY PROVISIONS[17]

The doctrine of judicial notice can be made to render assistance in connection with the proof of documents. We shall see in ch XIX that, subject to the presumption of due execution arising from the production of a document more than twenty years old from the proper custody, the due execution of a document, i e, the fact that it was signed or sealed by the person by whom it purports to be signed or sealed, must be proved before the court will receive it in evidence. This would lead to endless trouble in the case of various documents in constant use, and there are numerous statutes which provide that judicial notice shall be taken of the signatures of various persons attached to official documents.[18] Difficulties formerly experienced with regard to the proof of statutes, i e, showing that the document before the court corresponded with those of the Act duly passed by both Houses of Parliament, have been resolved by what is now s 3 of the Interpretation Act 1978. Its effect, when read together with the second schedule and s 9 of the repealed Interpretation Act 1889, is that every Act passed after 1850 shall be a public Act and judicially noticed as such in the absence of an express provision to the contrary. Judicial notice has always been taken of a public Act of Parliament, ie, no evidence has ever been required concerning its passage through Parliament and its contents, but, before 1850, such evidence was required in the case of private Acts unless, as was often the case, they contained some special provision about judicial notice. Even now, if reliance is placed upon a private Act passed before 1850, it may be necessary to produce a Queen's Printer's copy of the statute.[19]

It is unfortunate that there is no express provision for the taking of judicial notice of statutory instruments because, even in modern times, the courts have varied in their insistence on the production of a Stationery Office copy[20] and it is not even clear that proof by this method is authorised in the case of all statutory instruments.[1] It is however clear that proof of a statutory instrument is not required once constant reliance upon it has made it a matter of which judicial notice may be taken.[2]

---

16 *Re Rosher* (1884) 26 Ch D 801.
17 See European Communities Act 1972, s 4(2), for judicial notice by the English courts of community treaties and decisions of community courts, and Patents Act 1977, s 91, for judicial notice of the European Patent Convention.
18 E g, the Evidence Act 1845, s 2.
19 Evidence Act 1845, s 3. Before this statute it might have been necessary to call someone to prove that a private Act was duly passed. Now it is sufficient that a copy of any such statute passed before 1850 should purport to be that of the printer to the King or Queen. By the Documentary Evidence Act 1882, a Stationery Office copy is made equivalent to a Queen's Printer's copy.
20 [1962] Crim LR 334.
1 But see *R v Clarke* [1969] 2 QB 91, [1969] 1 All ER 924.
2 *R v Jones* [1969] 3 All ER 1559, 54 Cr App Rep 63; the same is true in Scotland, see *Valentine v McPhail* 1986 SCCR 321.

D. THEORETICAL QUESTIONS

The principal theoretical questions raised by the practice of taking judicial notice concern its relationship to the reception of evidence, the use which a judge can make of his personal knowledge, the rationale of the practice and its scope.

1. JUDICIAL NOTICE AND THE RECEPTION OF EVIDENCE

No problem arises with regard to the distinction between receiving evidence and taking judicial notice of a fact when the subject of judicial notice is a matter of common knowledge with regard to which no inquiry is made by the judge. In such a case the judge is acting on his own knowledge and that is a completely different procedure from the reception of evidence. The processes begin to approximate when the judge makes inquiries before deciding to take judicial notice. If learned treatises are consulted, it is not easy to say whether evidence is being received under an exception to the rule against hearsay or whether the judge is equipping himself to take judicial notice.[3] When the certificate of a Minister is sought on the question of the sovereignty of a foreign state, Law Lords have said both that evidence is not being taken and that the best evidence is being received.[4] Speaking of the class of case in which assessors may be consulted under statutory powers, Lord Denning said:

> The court must possess itself of necessary information. Some judges may have it already because of their previous experience. Others may have to acquire it for the first time, but in either case the information they glean is not evidence strictly so-called. When an assessor explains the technicalities, he does not do it on oath, nor can he be cross-examined, and no one ever called the author of a dictionary to give evidence. All that happens is that the court is equipping itself for its task by taking judicial notice of all such things as it ought to know in order to do its work properly.[5]

The approximation of taking judicial notice to the reception of evidence is even more marked when sworn testimony is heard before judicial notice is taken. In *McQuaker v Goddard*[6] the trial judge held that, in the absence of any evidence of scienter, those in control of a zoo had no case to answer when a claim for personal injuries was made in respect of a bite from a camel because camels are mansuetae naturae. He reached this conclusion after consulting books about camels and hearing witnesses, some of whom spoke of the wild habits of camels but the more expert of whom deposed to the tameness of these animals. The judge's decision was affirmed by the Court of Appeal, Clauson LJ being careful to point out that, when hearing the witnesses, the

---

3 The distinction can be of practical importance only in a case tried with a jury. If evidence is being taken, the judge must place it before the jury. If judicial notice is taken he can direct the jury to find the fact judicially noticed.

4 Contrast Lord Finlay and Lord Sumner in *Duff Development Co v Government of Kelantan* [1924] AC 797 at 813 and 824 respectively.

5 *Baldwin and Francis Ltd v Patent Appeal Tribunal* [1959] AC 663 at 691.

6 [1940] 1 KB 687, [1940] 1 All ER 471; cf *Turner v Coates* [1917] 1 KB 670. These cases were decided under the common law concerning liability for animals.

judge had not been taking evidence in the ordinary sense. The witnesses were simply assisting him in 'forming his view as to what the ordinary course of nature in this regard in fact is, a matter of which he is supposed to have complete knowledge'.[7] It seems that, even where the processes of taking judicial notice and receiving evidence approximate most closely, they remain essentially different, firstly, because, when the judge decides to take judicial notice of a fact after hearing witnesses, he may withdraw that fact from the jury although the witnesses do not speak with one voice. Secondly, the judge's decision constitutes a precedent.

If the processes of taking judicial notice and receiving evidence of a fact are essentially different, no evidence should be admissible in rebuttal of a fact which is judicially noticed. It appears that this is the case in spite of occasional remarks suggesting that taking judicial notice is merely the equivalent of prima facie proof of a fact. These remarks turn on the extreme generality of the facts of which judicial notice may be taken. Judicial notice that the seal or signature on a document is that of a particular court or official merely means that the seal or signature is recognised as similar to that of the court or official, and evidence of forgery in a particular case, though plainly admissible, does not rebut the fact of which judicial notice is taken.[8] Similarly, evidence that a particular practice was not followed on a particular occasion would not rebut the existence of the practice of which judicial notice is taken, nor, strictly speaking, would evidence of a change of practice for judicial notice is simply taken of the current practice at a particular time. There are of course many cases of judicial notice in which there can be no question of evidence in rebuttal, as when judicial notice is taken of the facts stated in the certificate of a government department.

There is something to be said for a practice under which a judge could state that he proposed to take notice of the existence of certain facts within his personal knowledge, subject to anything urged upon him to the contrary,[9] but this raises the whole question of the extent to which a judge can make use of his personal knowledge.

2. PERSONAL KNOWLEDGE[10]

The general rule is that neither a judge nor a juror may act on his personal knowledge of facts.[11] Nor may the court take steps to acquire such knowledge in private, for example, by applying a scientific instrument to an exhibit in

---

7 [1940] 1 KB 687 at 700. The ambiguity of this distinction between taking judicial notice and receiving evidence has been reflected in the need to give alternative bases for judgment in *Tutin v Mary Chipperfield Promotions Ltd* (1980) 130 NLJ 807.

8 *Holland v Johns* (1917) 23 CLR 149 at 154.

9 Cf *Thomas v Thomas* [1961] 1 All ER 19, [1961] 1 WLR 1, where the magistrates did not give the defendant an opportunity of urging them to take contrary action. Cf Federal Rules 201(e) reading in part as follows: 'A party is entitled upon timely request to an opportunity to be heard as to the propriety of taking judicial notice and the tenor of the matter noticed'. See also Australian Law Reform Commission Research Paper 10, 'The Judge—Adducing Evidence and Judicial Notice', Part C proposal 2(b) (iii).

10 See Colin Manchester 'Judicial Notice and Personal Knowledge' (1979) 42 MLR 22.

11 *R v Rosser* (1836) 7 C & P 648; *Manley v Shaw* (1840) Car & M 361; *R v Antrim County Justices* [1895] 2 IR 603; *Palmer v Crone* [1927] 1 KB 804.

the absence of a party.[12] This rule has reference to particular facts. When taking judicial notice a judge frequently makes use of his general knowledge, and justices can certainly make use of their knowledge of local conditions such as the extent of tidal waters,[13] or the topography of a road.[14] The distinction is not always easy to draw. In *R v Field JJ, ex p White*,[15] for instance, the issue was whether cocoa must necessarily contain a quantity of foreign ingredients. This is not a matter of general notoriety or even something which can be put beyond dispute by reference to the appropriate sources of information. Nevertheless, some of the justices had acquired knowledge of the subject in the navy, and the Divisional Court did not dispute the propriety of their making use of it. Wills J, a distinguished mountaineer, said:

> In the nature of things, no one in determining a case of this kind, can discard his own particular knowledge of a subject of this kind. I might as well be asked to decide a question as to the sufficiency of an alpine rope without bringing my personal knowledge into play.

In *Reynolds v Llanelly Associated Tinplate Co* in which the Court of Appeal held that the county court judge had gone too far in making use of his personal knowledge of the prospects of employment of a workman of a particular age and skill, Lord Greene said:

> The practice of county court judges of supplementing evidence by having recourse to their own local knowledge and experience has been criticised, praised as most beneficial, objected to and encouraged in different decisions.[16]

This case was cited in *Wetherhall v Harrison*[17] in which a Divisional Court held that a distinction should be drawn between the use of their private knowledge by judges and arbitrators on the one hand and by justices and jurors on the other hand. The latter are not trained to exclude certain matters from their consideration and, in any event, as a cross-section of the community they should pool their general knowledge. The issue had been whether a motorist whose roadside breath test had proved positive had simulated a fit in order to prevent a specimen of his blood being taken. One of the justices was a doctor and he communicated his views about the possible effects of the prospect of having his blood taken on the accused to the other members of the bench. They also made use of their wartime experience of the effect of innoculations on certain people. The accused was held to have had a reasonable excuse for not providing a specimen and the Divisional Court held that the conduct of the justices had been proper for there had been no question of one of their number giving evidence to the others.[18]

---

12 *R v Tiverton Justices, ex p Smith* [1981] RTR 280. See also *R v Stewart and Sappleton* (1989) 89 Cr App Rep 273 (scales disallowed); cp *R v Maggs* (1990) Times, 2 March (tape measure allowed).

13 *Ingram v Percival* [1969] 1 QB 548, [1968] 3 All ER 657. See also *Keane v Mount Vernon Colliery Co Ltd* [1933] AC 309.

14 *Chesson v Jordan* [1981] Crim LR 333; *Kent v Stamps* [1982] RTR 273.

15 (1895) 64 LJMC 158; cf *R v Tager* [1944] AD 339.

16 [1948] 1 All ER 140 at 142 where a number of the relevant authorities are cited. See also *R v Wood* [1982] 2 NZLR 233 (New Zealand court not entitled to take judicial notice that 'supertoms' grafted).

17 [1976] QB 773, [1976] 1 All ER 241.

18 Cf *Mangano v Farleigh Nettheim* (1965) 65 SR (NSW) 228 (juror with special knowledge should give evidence).

Similarly in *R v Blick*[19] the Court of Criminal Appeal upheld the conviction of the accused after the reception of evidence in rebuttal precipitated by a note passed to the judge by a juror, based upon the juror's personal knowledge of the locality in question.

Nor should it be forgotten that some judges, like those in the Patent Court, are selected just because they have some technical expertise, and they may probably take notice of a wider range of matters, though their not having such expertise does not mean that they can take notice that there is none.[20] All that can be said is that, within reasonable and proper limits, a judge, and, to a greater extent, a justice or juror, may make use of his special knowledge of general matters, but no formula has yet been evolved for describing those limits.[1]

3. RATIONALE

There are at least two reasons why we should have a doctrine of judicial notice. In the first place, it expedites the hearing of many cases. Much time would be wasted if every fact which was not admitted had to be the subject of evidence which would, in many instances, be costly and difficult to obtain. Secondly, the doctrine tends to produce uniformity of decision on matters of fact where a diversity of findings might sometimes be distinctly embarrassing. It was used to promote such consistency in the application to flick-knives of the definition of offensive weapons in *R v Simpson*.[2] It has been said that the basic essential is that the fact judicially noticed should be of a class that is so generally known as to give rise to the presumption that all persons are aware of it.[3] No doubt this is the justification for taking judicial notice in the vast majority of cases, but it is not always so. It would be idle to pretend that the particulars with regard to the behaviour of camels of which the court heard evidence in *McQuaker v Goddard* could be presumed to be generally known.[4]

4. SCOPE

Thayer spoke of judicial notice as 'an instrument of great capacity in the hands of a competent judge ... not nearly as much used in the region of practice and evidence as it should be'.[5] This is an exaggeration for there cannot be a much greater scope for the doctrine of judicial notice than there is at present, but perhaps the cases do indicate an excessive caution on the part of the courts, although the caution is often more apparent than real.

In *Brune v Thompson*[6] the question was whether an undertaking to call evidence from London (made under the old procedure) had been satisfied

19 (1966) 50 Cr App Rep 280.
20 *Hauni-Werke Korber & Co KG's Application* [1982] RPC 327.
1 They are however clearly exceeded when argument is supplemented not by expert evidence, but by handing up a technical article from a journal, *Dawson v Lunn* (1984) 149 JP 491 (justices). See also *R v Wood* [1982] 2 NZLR 233 (jurors).
2 [1983] 3 All ER 789, citing this passage.
3 *Holland v Jones* (1917) 23 CLR 149 at 153, per Isaacs CJ; *Auckland City Council v Hapimana* [1976] 1 NZLR 731.
4 That they require help in the act of copulation.
5 *Preliminary Treatise on Evidence at the Common Law* 309.
6 (1842) 2 QB 789.

by production of a document from the Tower, and the court refused to take judicial notice of the fact that the building is in London. Thayer pointed out that this was correct because part of the Tower was in Middlesex, as opposed to the County of London.[7] The courts may be thought to have been over cautious in refusing to take judicial notice of the time of sunset on a particular day as they had been referred to an almanac,[8] assuredly a source of indisputable accuracy. But allowance must be made for borderline cases in which the time of sunset in a place at some distance from any of those mentioned in the almanac is in issue. In such circumstances the safest course may be to require the evidence of an astronomer.[9]

An example of caution which can only described as excessive is provided by *Deybel's* case[10] where the question was whether an arrest had been effected between Beachy Head and the North Foreland in Kent. The arrest took place eight leagues from Orford Ness in the county of Suffolk, but the court would not take judicial notice of the fact that this spot was outside the specified area because parts of Suffolk might have been in Kent. Lest it should be thought that such caution merely represents the timid approach of a past period, a further reference must be made to *Preston-Jones v Preston-Jones*.[11] In that case the only fact of which the House of Lords would take judicial notice was that the duration of the normal period of gestation is about nine months. Only Lord Morton of Henryton was prepared to follow Denning LJ in inferring from that fact that a child born to a woman 360 days after she last had intercourse with her husband could not be his child. As is so frequently the case, the problem is where to draw the line between the realm of facts which will be judicially noticed and those which must be proved by evidence. But there does not appear to be more enthusiasm for a bold application of the doctrine of judicial notice in the twentieth century than there was in the nineteenth.

5. TACIT APPLICATIONS

The tacit applications of the doctrine of judicial notice are more numerous and more important than the express ones. A great deal is taken for granted

---

7 Thayer pp 310–311. Cf the same author's explanation of *Kearney v King* (1819) 2 B & Ald 301, sometimes erroneously cited for the proposition that judicial notice will not be taken of the fact that Dublin is in Ireland, when in fact it only decided that an allegation that a bill was drawn in Ireland was not proved by showing that it was drawn in Dublin for non constat that there was not a place called Dublin outside Ireland. See also *Thorne v Jackson* (1846) 3 CB 661.

8 It has been held in South Africa that times of sunrise and sunset cannot be proved satisfactorily from a diary, *S v Sibuyi* 1988 (4) SA 879.

9 *Collier v Nokes* (1849) 2 Car & Kir 1012; *R v Crush* [1978] Crim LR 357; *R v Trawick* (1972) 8 CCC (2d) 471; cf *Dugas v Leclair* (1962) 32 DLR (2d) 459.

10 (1821) 4 B & Ald 243. It has even been said that the courts cannot take judicial notice of the relative distance of places (per Wilde J arg. in *Kirby v Hickson* (1850) 14 Jur 625). The question was whether Russell Square was within 20 miles of Grosvenor Square in London. A South Australian court has taken judicial notice of the fact that a suburb of Adelaide is less than 100 miles away from that city (*Blatchford v Dempsey* [1956] SASR 285). But see *R v Dodd* [1985] 2 Qd R 277 where it was held, it is submitted correctly, that even though judicial notice might be taken of geographical locations, it would not necessarily extend to the time needed to drive from one to another, since this might require evidence of likely traffic conditions at different times.

11 [1951] AC 391, [1951] 1 All ER 124 (above). See M McConville 'The Doctrine of Judicial Notice—its Relationship to Evidence' (1979) 1 Liverpool LR 62 at 74.

when any question of relevance is considered or assumed. For example, evidence is constantly given that persons accused of burglary were found in possession of jemmies or skeleton keys, that powder puffs and pots of vaseline were found on the premises of those charged with homosexuality, and that the accused became confused when charged; these facts are relevant only provided there is a common practice to use such things in the commission of the crime, or provided that guilty people tend more than innocent ones to become confused when charged, but no one ever thinks of calling evidence on such a subject.

SECTION 2. FORMAL ADMISSIONS

A party may admit facts for the purposes of the trial, thus saving his adversary the trouble and expense of proving them. In a civil case he may be induced to do this by the possibility that he will be made to bear the cost of proving such facts if he does not admit them. These formal admissions which cannot be contradicted by the person who makes them, and which are binding only for the purposes of the particular case in which they are made, must be distinguished from the informal admissions that are received under an exception to the rule against hearsay discussed in ch XVI. Unlike formal admissions, informal admissions are an item of evidence. Their maker may endeavour to explain them away at the trial at which they are proved.

Under s 10 of the Criminal Justice Act 1967, a formal admission may be made by or on behalf of the prosecution or defendant before or at any criminal proceedings, and may, with the leave of the court, be withdrawn.

The procedural details, with regard to formal admissions in civil and criminal cases, are beyond the scope of this book.

SECTION 3. ESTOPPEL

When an estoppel binds a party to litigation he is prevented from placing reliance on or denying the existence of certain facts. This justifies the treatment of estoppel as an exclusionary rule of evidence. So regarded, it is less rigorous than the rules governing the exclusion of evidence on the ground of public policy because estoppels only operate if they are pleaded, but, like the exclusion of evidence on that ground, and unlike the exclusion of evidence under the rule relating to similar facts, estoppels operate without reference to the purpose for which reliance is placed on a particular fact. From the point of view of the party in whose favour they operate, estoppels could be regarded as something which renders proof of certain facts unnecessary; also it is possible to argue that estoppel is better regarded as a matter of pleading or substantive law, rather than a rule of evidence.

Estoppels are of three kinds—by record, by deed and by conduct. After each of them has been considered, reference will be made to the question of the right place for estoppel in a comprehensive exposition of the law. The whole notion is of primary, if not exclusive, importance in civil cases.

A. ESTOPPEL BY RECORD[12]

The principles underlying estoppel by record are '*Interest rei publicae ut sit finis litium*'—it is for the common good that there should be an end to litigation, and '*Nemo debet bis vexari pro eadem causa*'—no one should be sued twice on the same ground. The practical consequence is that, generally speaking, the order of a court of competent jurisdiction[13] is conclusive. An application may be made to have it set aside if it was obtained by fraud,[14] and fraud or collusion in the obtaining of a judgment may be proved by a stranger to the proceedings.[15] These matters belong to the law of procedure, but the conclusive effects of judgments on the whole world as well as the parties to civil litigation have some bearing on the law of evidence. After they have been considered, reference will be made to the somewhat specialised question of estoppel by record in matrimonial causes and the position in criminal cases.

It is important to stress the point that we are at present concerned with the extent to which judgments constitute an estoppel and thus prevent any evidence from being given to contradict them. There is a wholly different problem of the extent to which they can be regarded as prima facie evidence of the facts upon which they were founded (discussed in the next section of this chapter). This distinction, together with that between the effect of a judgment on parties and strangers respectively, may be illustrated by a hypothetical case in which A has obtained judgment for a thousand pounds, damages against B on account of the negligence of C, B's servant, acting in the course of his employment. If B seeks to recover this sum from C, C will be estopped from denying that a thousand pounds was the sum which B was ordered to pay A because the judgment is conclusive as to its terms, even against strangers to the proceedings in which it was pronounced, but at common law it was not even admissible as evidence that C was, in fact, negligent. If, as would hardly be likely to be the case, the question of C's negligence were to be raised again in litigation between A and B, B would be estopped from denying it because, as between parties to the proceedings in which they were obtained, judgments are conclusive so far as their grounds, as well as their terms, are concerned.

It should be noted that an estoppel can be raised on a foreign judgment.[16]

---

12 Spencer-Bower *Res Judicata* (2nd edn, 1969, by Sir Alexander Turner). Letters patent may constitute estoppel by record between the Crown and the Grantee (*Cropper v Smith* (1884) 26 Ch D 700), but the only estoppel of this nature which is worth any discussion in a work of this sort is estoppel by a judgment or res judicata. Estoppel by record is a misnomer because the doctrine applies to judgments which are not those of a court of record (see Lord Guest in *Carl-Zeiss Stiftung v Rayner and Keeler Ltd* (No 2) [1967] 1 AC 853 at 933, [1966] 2 All ER 536 at 564).

13 *R v Hutchings* (1881) 6 QBD 300 shows that there is not estoppel where the justices exceeded their jurisdiction by declaring that a road was a highway.

14 In *R v Calcedo* [1986] VR 499 an acquittal obtained by a plea bargain from which the accused subsequently resiled failed to ground an estoppel.

15 *R v Duchess of Kingston* (1776) 20 State Tr 355.

16 *DSV Silo—und Verwaltungsgesellschaft mbH v Owners of the Sennar* [1985] 2 All ER 104, [1985] 1 WLR 490.

However it may sometimes be more difficult to discern the precise issues in such cases.[17]

1. CONCLUSIVE EFFECT OF JUDGMENTS ON THE WHOLE WORLD—JUDGMENTS IN REM

A judgment is conclusive as against all persons of the existence of the state of things which it actually effects when the existence of that state is in issue or relevant to the issue.[18] Obvious examples are provided by an action for malicious prosecution in which the record of the Criminal Court would be conclusive of the acquittal of the plaintiff,[19] or an action by a surety against the principal debtor in which a judgment obtained against the surety by the creditor would be conclusive of the fact that it was obtained and the amount for which it was pronounced.[20] These examples may seem somewhat trivial, but the conclusiveness of a judgment with regard to the state of things which it actually effects is of great importance if it is in rem.

A judgment in rem is:

A judgment of a court of competent jurisdiction determining the status of a person or thing, or the disposition of a thing (as distinct from a particular interest in it of a party to the litigation).[1]

Allen v Dundas[2] is a simple illustration of the effect of such a judgment so far as the whole world is concerned. The defendant was indebted to P, and, on P's death, X obtained probate of what purported to be P's will. The defendant paid X the amount of P's debt, and, when the grant of representation was set aside in favour of the plaintiff because the will was a forgery, it was held that the defendant was not liable to pay the debt over again to the plaintiff. Everyone was bound to give credit to the probate (a judgment in rem) until it was vacated, which meant that the plaintiff was estopped from denying X's executorship at the material time. Other examples of judgments in rem are provided by the condemnation of a ship by a Prize Court which precludes everyone from denying the non-neutral nature of the cargo,[3] a determination that a street is a highway,[4] and a decree of nullity or divorce.[5] A decree of jactitation of marriage, on the other

---

17 The matter is fully treated in textbooks on the Conflict of Laws, see, for example, Dicey and Morris *Conflict of Laws* (11th edn, 1987).
18 Stephen *Digest of the Law of Evidence* (12th edn) art 41. This article was adopted by Lord Goddard CJ in *Hollington v Hewthorn & Co Ltd* [1943] 2 All ER 35 at 39.
19 *Purcell v Macnamara* (1807) 9 East 157.
20 *Re Kitchin, ex p Young* (1881) 17 Ch D 668 at 673.
1 *Halsbury's Laws of England* (Hailsham edn), vol 13, 405, adopted in *Lazarus-Barlow v Regent Estates Co Ltd* [1949] 2 KB 465 at 475, [1949] 2 All ER 118 at 122, by the Master of the Rolls who added 'such a judgment is conclusive evidence for and against all persons whether parties, privies or strangers, of the matters actually decided'. The courts have not developed the statement made in *Hill v Clifford* [1907] 2 Ch 236 at 244, that there are two kinds of judgment in rem, one of which is conclusive against all the world, and the other of which is not. An instance of the latter was said to be an inquisition in lunacy which has always been allowed to be read in a subsequent suit between third parties, as evidence of the lunacy, though it is not conclusive, and may be traversed.
2 (1789) 3 Term Rep 125.
3 *Geyer v Aguilar* (1798) 7 Term Rep 681.
4 *Wakefield Corporation v Cooke* [1904] AC 31.
5 *Salvesen v The Administrator of Austrian Property* [1927] AC 641.

hand, only establishes that the petitioner is not married to the respondent so far as it appears to the court which enjoins him to remain silent on the matter. Accordingly, the judges advised the House of Lords on the prosecution of the Duchess of Kingston in 1776 for bigamously marrying the Duke in the lifetime of her husband, the Earl of Bristol, that the Crown was not estopped from asserting the validity of her marriage to the Earl by a jactitation decree she had obtained in the Ecclesiastical Court before going through the impugned marriage ceremony.[6]

2. EFFECT OF JUDGMENTS ON PARTIES TO CIVIL CASES

Whether a judgment is in rem within the meaning of the above definition or in personam—a term which can be taken to comprise all judgments that are not in rem, its effect on the parties and those claiming through them is much wider than its effect in litigation between strangers. This is because the rule is that parties and their privies[7] are estopped from denying not merely the state of affairs established by the judgment, that A has been adjudged liable to B in the sum of a thousand pounds, for example, or that C is divorced, but also the grounds upon which that judgment was based, that A broke a contract with B, or that C committed adultery.

(i) Cause of action estopped

Estoppel by record inter partes, or *'estoppel per rem judicatam'* as it is usually called, is of two kinds. The first, now generally coming to be known as 'cause of action estoppel', is dependent on the merger of the cause of action in the judgment. Although its bearing on the substantive law is of great importance, this kind of estoppel does not call for detailed consideration here. Once it appears that the same cause of action was held to lie or not to lie in a final judgment between the same parties, or their privies, litigating in the same capacity, there is an end of the matter: 'If one party brings an action against another for a particular cause and judgment is given on it, there is a strict rule of law that he cannot bring another action against the same party for the same cause.'[8] The effect can be draconian. Thus, in *Conquer v Boot*,[9] judgment for the plaintiff for damages for breach of warranty to build a house in a workmanlike manner was held to bar a claim for damages subsequently occurring in consequence of the breach of warranty.[10] Of course, this applies only to litigation arising out of the same facts. If the facts change, then a judgment arising out of the earlier facts raises no estoppel.[11]

There has nonetheless been a tendency to extend the idea underlying

---

6 20 State Tr 537.
7 The expression is a rough equivalent for those claiming through the original party. Privies are said to be either 'in estate'—lessor and lessee or vendor and purchaser, for instance; 'in blood'—ancestor and heir; or 'in law' testator and executor or intestate and administrator, for instance.
8 Per Lord Denning MR in *Fidelitas Shipping Co Ltd v V/O Exportchleb* [1966] 1 QB 630 at 640, [1965] 2 All ER 4 at 8.
9 [1928] 2 KB 336.
10 This case was distinguished in *Purser & Co (Hillingdon) Ltd v Jackson* [1977] QB 166, [1976] 3 All ER 641 where there was a submission to arbitration and award was held to apply only to the matters covered by the submission.
11 *Thyssen-Bornemisza v Thyssen-Bornemisza* [1986] Fam 1, [1985] 1 All ER 328.

cause of action estoppel to claims which, though not the subject of formal adjudication, would have been brought forward as part of the cause of action in the proceedings which resulted in the judgment alleged to constitute an estoppel. In the frequently quoted words of Wigram VC:

> where a given matter becomes the subject of litigation in, and of adjudication by, a court of competent jurisdiction, the court requires the parties to that litigation to bring forward their whole case, and will not (except under special circumstances) permit the same parties to open the same subject of litigation in respect of matter which might have been brought forward as part of the subject in contest, but which was not brought forward, only because they have, from negligence, inadvertence, or even accident, omitted part of their case. The plea of res judicata applies, except in special cases, not only to points upon which the court was actually required by the parties to form an opinion and pronounce a judgment, but to every point which properly belonged to the subject of litigation, and which the parties, exercising reasonable diligence, might have brought forward at the time.[12]

Obviously it is desirable to protect defendants from plaintiffs who unnecessarily split up their claims against them;[13] but a rigid application of the words of Wigram VC could work great hardship on defendants who let judgment go against them by default, and the statement has been held to have no application to those judgments, the rules of cause of action estoppel being very narrowly applied in such cases.[14]

An illustration of the extension of cause of action estoppel mentioned by Wigram VC is provided by *Public Trustee v Kenward*.[15] The defendant and his deceased wife had carried on a farming business in partnership. He was one of the executors of his wife's will and an account was taken in administration proceedings of his indebtedness to his wife's estate. He made various counterclaims in respect of sums due to him, but he never raised the point that land forming part of the estate had been a partnership asset. It was held that he was estopped from doing so when the Public Trustee claimed payment of the amount certified to be due from the defendant to the estate. In such a case the failure to make the claim can reasonably be treated as an admission of its invalidity, but such an assumption will not always be justified and the explanation is inapplicable to cases in which the failure to make the claim was due to accident or inadvertence.

---

12 *Henderson v Henderson* (1843) 3 Hare 100 at 114; the dictum was applied in *L E Walwin & Partners Ltd v West Sussex County Council* [1975] 3 All ER 604, and in *Green v Hampshire County Council* [1979] ICR 861 at 865. The references to exceptions are as significant for the law of today as they were for that of 1843.

13 See *Chamberlain v Deputy Comr of Taxation* (1988) 62 ALJR 324 where the High Court of Australia applied the doctrine of res judicatae rigidly to prevent recovery of the balance of tax outstanding after a claim had been understated by a factor of ten as a result of omitting a last digit of zero. The question of mistake was not raised.

14 *New Brunswick Rail Co v British and French Trust Corporation Ltd* [1939] AC 1, [1938] 4 All ER 747; *Kok Hoong v Leong Cheong Kweng Mines Ltd* [1964] AC 993, [1964] 1 All ER 300; there is no estoppel by record where an action is dismissed for want of prosecution (*Pople v Evans* [1969] 2 Ch 255, [1968] 2 All ER 743) or where proceedings are withdrawn (*Owens v Minoprio* [1942] 1 KB 193, [1942] 1 All ER 30), but there could be an estoppel by conduct in such a case. For bastardy proceedings see *Robinson v Williams* [1965] 1 QB 89, [1964] 3 All ER 12. Lord Devlin was critical of Wigram VC in *Connelly v DPP* [1964] AC 1254 at 1356 f.

15 [1967] 2 All ER 870, [1967] 1 WLR 1062.

A further illustration is provided by *The Mekhanik Evgrafov (No 2)*[16] where the defendant failed to seek to limit his liability in a shipping case in respect of the only claim which could be made against him, and the court intimated[17] that where as a matter of practice such a defence should be raised, issue estoppel would apply to prevent a subsequent limitation action after final judgment on the original claim.[18]

(ii) Issue estoppel

The second kind of estoppel by record inter partes is often called 'issue estoppel'. It may be regarded as an extension of the first for, to quote Lord Denning MR: 'within one cause of action, there may be several issues raised which are necessary for the determination of the whole case. The rule then is that, once an issue has been raised and distinctly determined between the parties, then, as a general rule, neither party can be allowed to fight that issue all over again.'[19] Although Lord Denning went on to use words suggesting that the principle mentioned by Wigram VC in connection with cause of action estoppel might apply to issue estoppel, it may be better to regard the latter as restricted to issues actually determined in the former litigation for there may be many reasons why a litigant did not raise a particular issue, and it would be unjust to prevent him from raising it in later proceedings.[20] On the other hand when an issue has been determined, even by way of concession on an appeal, there is less reason to take a strict view, and every reason to uphold the estoppel.[1]

Issue estoppel is a branch of the law which has been developed recently and gradually. The basic principles were first clearly stated by Diplock LJ in *Mills v Cooper*,[2] and subsequently endorsed by the House of Lords in *Hunter v Chief Constable of West Midlands*.[3] The House of Lords rejected an attempt by Lord Denning MR in the Court of Appeal to eliminate the requirements of privity and mutuality on the basis that it is unjust that a party *against* whom an issue has been determined after a full opportunity to contest it, should be permitted to raise precisely the same issue again in subsequent proceedings involving another. The House of Lords preferred to decide the case upon an

---

16 [1988] 2 Lloyd's Rep 330.
17 Though it abstained from applying the doctrine in that case.
18 See also a thorough discussion of the rule by the High Court of Australia in *Port of Melbourne Authority v Anshun Pty Ltd (No 2)* (1981) 147 CLR 589 where the defendant in negligence proceedings claimed contribution from a co-defendant, but failed to claim an indemnity, and was held to be estopped. The analysis dwells on different types of defence, and in *Heid v Connell Investments Pty* (1987) 9 NSWLR 628 there is some suggestion that the rule applies more naturally to defendants than to plaintiffs, not least in respect of a different cause of action.
19 *Fidelitas Shipping Co Ltd v V/O Exportchleb* [1966] 1 QB 630 at 640, [1965] 2 All ER 4 at 8; see also the judgment of Diplock LJ in the same case and in *Thoday v Thoday* [1964] P 181, [1964] 1 All ER 341.
20 *Carl Zeiss Stiftung v Rayner and Keeler Ltd (No 2)* [1967] 1 AC 853 at 916 and 947, [1966] 2 All ER 536 at 555 and 573 per Lords Reid and Upjohn respectively. Lords Reid and Upjohn criticise the distinction taken by Diplock LJ in *Thoday v Thoday* [1964] P 181 at 198, [1964] 1 All ER 341 at 352, between issue estoppel and fact estoppel. Accordingly no reference is made to the latter in the text.
1 *Khan v Goleccha International Ltd* [1980] 2 All ER 259 at 267, [1980] 1 WLR 1482 at 1491, distinguishing *Jenkins v Robertson* (1867) LR 1 Sc & Div 117, and restricting it to cause of action estoppel proper.
2 [1967] 2 QB 459 at 468, [1967] 2 All ER 100 at 104.
3 [1982] AC 529 at 541, [1981] 3 All ER 727 at 733.

issue upon which the Court of Appeal had been unanimous; that it amounted to an abuse of the process of the court to launch a collateral attack upon a decision of a court of competent jurisdiction, by raising an issue for a second time.[4] The House noted that this involved recognising a difference between the operation of the doctrine in England and in North America.[5] The conditions were subsequently and concisely reformulated by Lord Brandon in *DSV Silo—und Verwaltungsgesellschaft mbH v Owners of The Sennar*:[6]

> In order to create an estoppel of that kind, [issue estoppel per rem judicatam] three requirements have to be satisfied. The first requirement is that the judgment in the earlier action relied on as creating an estoppel must be (a) of a court of competent jurisdiction, (b) final and conclusive and (c) on the merits. The second requirement is that the parties (or privies) in the earlier action relied on as creating an estoppel and those in the later action in which that estoppel is raised as a bar must be the same. The third requirement is that the issue in the later action in which the estoppel is raised as a bar must be the same issue as that decided by the judgment in the earlier action.

In addition to these requirements it should be noted that in relation to issue estoppel an earlier judgment may not raise an estoppel if fresh matter has become available showing that the earlier decision was wrong. It seems that for these purposes the fresh material showing the previous decision to have been wrong can consist either of new factual material conclusively showing it to be wrong,[7] or even of a subsequent change in the interpretation of the law giving at the least a very substantial chance that the earlier decision would be held to be wrong.[8]

Each of the requirements listed by Lord Brandon will be considered in turn.

(a) Previous judgment. This must first be one of a court of competent jurisdiction. This issue was analysed most clearly by Steyn J in *Speedlink Vanguard v European Gateway*.[9] In that case a collision at sea had been considered by a court of formal investigation, set up under the Merchant Shipping Act 1894. The court found negligence in the navigation of one of the ships, and it was argued that this finding estopped its being controverted in subsequent proceedings for damages in the Admiralty Court. It was held that as such a court of formal investigation acts primarily in an investigative role so far as the cause of the collision is concerned, and in an adjudicative capacity only so far as the certification of the relevant mariners is concerned, similarly it can be regarded as a court of competent jurisdiction only for its findings in the latter, and not in the former, respect. In similar vein it has

---

4 It is likely that a court will be slow to recognise such an abuse since it cuts right across the reasoning in this area of the law. Some indication that it will be confined to blatant cases is provided by *Bragg v Oceanus Mutual* [1982] 2 Lloyd's Rep 132 where there were good reasons why the issue would be presented differently on the second occasion.
5 See e g in the United States *Bernhard v Bank of American National Trust and Savings Association* 122 P 2d 892 (1942); *Bruszewski v US* 181 F 2d 419 (1950); *Blonder-Tonque Laboratories Inc v University of Illinois* 402 US 313 (1971); and in Canada *Royal Bank of Canada v McArthur* (1985) 19 DLR (4th) 762.
6 [1985] 2 All ER 104 at 110, [1985] 1 WLR 490 at 499.
7 *Phosphate Sewage Co Ltd v Molleson* (1879) 4 App Cas 801 at 814 approved unanimously by the House of Lords in *Hunter v Chief Constable of West Midlands* [1982] AC 529 at 545.
8 *Arnold v National Westminster Bank* [1990] 1 All ER 529, [1990] 2 WLR 304.
9 [1987] QB 206, [1986] 3 All ER 554.

been held that administrative decisions whether of magistrates[10] or of administrative tribunals[11] cannot raise an estoppel. If however an inferior tribunal has an adjudicative function its decisions may ground an estoppel, provided that it is acting within such jurisdiction.[12] It should be noted further that partly inquisitorial procedure adopted in any such proceedings will not by itself prevent a court from being one of competent jurisdiction.[13]

A second condition is that the previous judgment must have been final. Matrimonial decisions apart, a decision of an inferior court will operate as an estoppel in the High Court, but the decision must be one from which there could have been an appeal.[14] The mere fact that there was no appeal does not prevent a judgment from being final. A judgment can be final in this context even though made on an interlocutory application.[15] It seems also that a decision about the admissibility of evidence made by the judge on a voir dire may also amount to a final decision, at least when the jury returns its verdict after considering the evidence so admitted.[16] If, on the other hand, the jury disagrees, and a re-trial is ordered, no rulings made at the first trial can raise an issue estoppel at the re-trial,[17] even on substantial issues.[18]

The third condition relating to the prior judgment is that it should have been made 'on the merits', a phrase explained by Lord Diplock in *DSV Silo— und Verwaltungsgesellschaft mbH v Owners of The Sennar*:[19]

> What it means in the context of judgments delivered by courts of justice is that the court has held that it has jurisdiction to adjudicate on an issue raised in the course of action to which the particular set of facts give rise, and that its judgment on that cause of action is one that cannot be varied, re-opened or set aside by the court that delivered it or any other court of co-ordinate jurisdiction although it may be subject to appeal to a court of higher jurisdiction.

So expressed this condition seems to add little to the others, though it may be the most appropriate explanation for disregarding matters pronounced upon by way of obiter dicta.[20]

(b) Same parties acting in the same capacity. In *Townsend v Bishop*,[1] the plaintiff

10 *Wiest v DPP* (1988) 81 ALR 129.
11 *R v Secretary of State for the Environment, ex p Hackney London Borough Council* [1983] 3 All ER 358, [1983] 1 WLR 524; but see in Australia *Secretary of Department of Aviation v Ansett Transport Industries Ltd* (1987) 72 ALR 188.
12 *Crown Estate Coms v Dorset County Council* (1989) Times, 10 October.
13 In *DSV Silo—und Verwaltungsgesellschaft mbH v Owners of The Sennar*, above, the Dutch court's procedure in the decision creating the estoppel was partly inquisitorial.
14 *Concha v Concha* (1886) 11 App Cas 541.
15 *Midland Bank Trust Co Ltd v Green* [1978] 3 All ER 555, [1978] 3 WLR 149. Cp *Schlieske v Minister for Immigration and Ethnic Affairs* (1987) 79 ALR 554.
16 *Hunter v Chief Constable of West Midlands* [1982] AC 529 at 542, [1981] 3 All ER 727 at 734. But see in Canada *Duhamel v R* (1984) 14 DLR (4th) 92 where a ruling on the first voir dire in the accused's favour, crystallised by an acquittal, created no estoppel in respect of a second voir dire in respect of the same confession.
17 *Bobolas v Economist Newspaper Ltd* [1987] 3 All ER 121, [1987] 1 WLR 1101.
18 And certainly not rulings on the admissibility of evidence during a voir dire at the first aborted trial, *R v Blair* (1985) 1 NSWLR 584.
19 [1985] 2 All ER 104 at 106, [1985] 1 WLR 490 at 494.
20 See *Penn-Texas Corpn v Murat Anstalt* (No 2) [1964] 2 QB 647 at 660, [1964] 2 All ER 594 at 597; *Green v Martin* (1986) 63 ALR 627.
 1 [1939] 1 All ER 805. See also *Gleeson v J Wippel & Co Ltd* [1977] 3 All ER 54, [1977] 1 WLR 510; *Ramsay v Pigran* (1967) 118 CLR 271.

was injured in a collision with the defendant's lorry when he was driving his father's car. The plaintiff's father sued for damages to the car, when the defendant's plea that it was caused by the contributory negligence of the plaintiff who was acting as his father's agent succeeded. It was held that the plaintiff was not estopped from denying his contributory negligence in an action in which he claimed damages for personal injuries. This was simply because the parties to the two actions were different.

If allowance is made for the notion of privity under which one party may be estopped because the person through whom he derives his right would be estopped, the question of identity of parties is not usually likely to cause trouble; but the unusual case of *Carl Zeiss Stiftung v Rayner and Keeler Ltd (No 2)*,[2] shows that the requirements of identity and privity are narrowly construed by the English courts. In a previous action brought in the West German courts it had been held that the plaintiffs, a body known as the Council of Gera had no right to represent the Stiftung. The Stiftung then brought an action in the English courts by an English firm of solicitors, and it was held by a majority of the House of Lords that, although the solicitors were instructed by the Council of Gera, no estoppel precluded either the solicitors or the Stiftung from alleging that the action was duly authorised because the parties to the two proceedings were not identical and because there was no privity between the Council of Gera and the solicitors. Representation of a common principal does not lead of itself to privity.[3]

In *Marginson v Blackburn Borough Council*,[4] the defendant's omnibus was involved in a collision with the plaintiff's car which was being driven by his wife as his agent. She was killed, the plaintiff sustained personal injuries and some houses were damaged as well as the omnibus. The owners of the houses recovered damages in an action brought against Mr Marginson and the borough council on the footing that each of them was vicariously liable for negligent driving. Both drivers were held to have been equally to blame, and the council failed in a claim against Mr Marginson for damages to the omnibus because Mrs Marginson and the council's driver were equally to blame. Mr Marginson subsequently claimed damages for his own injuries and also sued as his wife's personal representative under the Law Reform (Miscellaneous Provisions) Act 1934 and the Fatal Accident Acts. The Court of Appeal held that Mr Marginson's personal claim failed because he was estopped from denying the contributory negligence of his wife by the finding that she and the council's driver were equally to blame for the damage to the omnibus and, under the substantive law as it then stood, contributory negligence was a complete bar to recovery. On the other hand, it was held that Mr Marginson was not estopped from denying his wife's contributory negligence in relation to his claims as her personal representative because he made those claims in a different capacity.

(c) Same issues. A strict construction of the requirement concerning identity of parties and their capacity can be justified on the ground that no one ought

2 [1967] 1 AC 853, [1966] 2 All ER 536.
3 Lord Wilberforce, unlike the other members of the House, tended to think that the only ground on which it could be held that there was no estoppel was that the West German judgment was not final. From a realistic point of view he thought the parties were the same (the Council of Gera) and the issues raised in the causes of action were the same (passing off). There is American authority in favour of this more flexible approach.
4 [1939] 2 KB 426, [1939] 1 All ER 273.

to be wholly precluded from arguing a point by a decision taken in proceedings at which he was not represented. It is open to question whether the requirement with regard to identity of issues should be applied so strictly for it is undesirable that there should be conflicting decisions on what is in substance the same issue of fact even though there is a technical ground for treating it as different from that which was the subject of earlier litigation.

Some cases favour a narrow and some a broad approach to this question. In *Hoystead v Taxation Comr*[5] the Privy Council held that a taxing authority was estopped from making an assessment for the year 1920–21 by a previous judgment relating to the assessment for the year 1918–19. In *Society of Medical Officers of Health v Hope (Valuation Officer)*,[6] on the other hand, the House of Lords held that a local valuation officer was not estopped from assessing the Society's premises for rates by a decision on a previous year's assessment that the Society was exempt. The question in these cases was basically whether one year's assessment raises a different issue from another year's assessment although the same legal point is involved, and special rules may be applicable to tax cases.

In *Re Manley's Will Trusts (No 2)*[7] a narrow view was taken in the matter of will construction for, although the point of construction involved was the same, it was held that the issues were different as the second concerned the devolution of a different share of the testator's estate. The decision was also based on the fact that the parties to the two proceedings were different.

There is an analogous conflict between broad and narrow views of issue estoppel in cases of negligence. *Marginson v Blackburn Borough Council*[8] favours a broad approach because Mr Marginson was held to have been estopped from denying that his wife's contributory negligence was, under the law as it then stood, the sole cause of his personal injuries as she had been held guilty of negligence on the claim by the council for damages to its omnibus; yet there is a technical difference between the issues of negligence and contributory negligence.[9]

A broad view was also taken in *Bell v Holmes*[10] and *Wood v Luscombe*.[11] In the first of these cases, there had been a collision between a taxi driven by Bell and a car driven by Holmes. A passenger in Holmes's car successfully sued both drivers for negligence and obtained judgment against each of them. As between the two defendants, Bell was held liable for five-sixths of the passenger's damages, Holmes for one-sixth. Bell then sued Holmes for damages for personal injuries negligently inflicted in the same collision. It was held that he was estopped from alleging that he was other than five-sixths to blame for the collision; yet Holmes's duty to Bell's passenger and the extent of his responsibility for its breach were in law different issues from his duty to Bell and the extent of his responsibility for its breach.

5 [1926] AC 155, not followed in *Mohamed Falil Abdul Carffoor (Trustees of the Abdul Caffoor Trust) v Commissioner of Income Tax Columbo* [1961] AC 584, [1961] 2 All ER 436.
6 [1960] AC 551, [1960] 1 All ER 317. Lord Keith of Avonholm also held (at 569) that an estoppel could not bind the rating officer as he was carrying out a statutory duty; this could hardly prevent a cause of action estoppel from arising. On the whole question of estoppel against statutes see an article by J A Andrews in (1966) 29 MLR 1.
7 [1976] 1 All ER 673.
8 Above. The cases down to 1957 are discussed in an article by Street, 73 LQR 358.
9 The argument was rejected by the High Court of Ireland in *Donohoe v Browne* [1986] IR 90 at 102.
10 [1956] 3 All ER 449, [1956] 1 WLR 1359.
11 [1966] 1 QB 169, [1964] 3 All ER 972.

The situation in *Wood v Luscombe* was the converse of that in *Bell v Holmes*. Motorcycles driven by Wood junior and Luscombe were in collision, and Wood senior, Wood junior's pillion passenger, sustained personal injuries. Luscombe sued Wood junior for personal injuries which he had sustained in the collision, and the parties were held equally to blame. Wood senior then sued Luscombe and recovered judgment against him. Luscombe had brought Wood junior in as a third party, and the question was to what extent Wood junior was liable to contribute to the sum which Luscombe had been adjudged liable to pay to Wood senior. It was held that he was estopped from denying that he was liable to contribute to the extent of fifty per cent; yet the duty owed by Wood junior to Luscombe and the extent, by which his responsibility for its breach was reduced by Luscombe's contributory negligence were in law different issues from their respective duties to Wood senior and the extent, as between themselves, of their responsibility for its breach.

A narrow view of issue estoppel was taken in *Randolph v Tuck*.[12] The plaintiff was a passenger in a car driven by Tuck, the first defendant, and that car collided with a car driven by Steale, the third defendant, in the course of his employment with the second defendant. In an action brought by Tuck against Steale, Tuck was held solely to blame for the collision. Randolph was, however, held entitled to judgment against all three defendants and, on the claim for contribution by the second and third defendants, it was held that Tuck was not estopped from denying his sole responsibility for the damages due to the plaintiff. The decision proceeded primarily on the basis that Steal's breach of duty to Tuck and Tuck's contributory negligence, which were in issue in the first action were, in law, different issues from that of the responsibility of the first and third defendants as between themselves for the damages sustained by the plaintiff.

Apart from *Marginson v Blackburn Borough Council*, a decision of the Court of Appeal the authority of which is impaired by the fact that it preceded both the Law Reform (Contributory Negligence) Act 1945, and the establishment of the principle that the basis of contributory negligence is the breach of the plaintiff's duty towards himself, all the English cases are decisions at first instance. As it is permissible to have regard to the pleadings, evidence and arguments in each action,[13] there is much to be said for the broad approach as it prevents the existence of conflicting judgments on what are substantially identical issues of fact. If the pleadings, evidence or points taken in argument in the second action are different from those of the first, the court hearing the second action would not, it seems, be bound to hold that there is an estoppel. The basis of the decisions in *Bell v Holmes* and *Wood v Luscombe* was that there was an estoppel because, though the issues were technically different, the issues of fact, and the evidence to support them, would be identical.

Both a broad and a narrow approach is also adopted in the Australasian cases on negligence.[14] Although it must be admitted that the narrow view

---

12 [1962] 1 QB 175, [1961] 1 All ER 814; *Johnson v Cartledge and Matthews* [1939] 3 All ER 654; *Association of Franciscan Order of Friars Minor v City of Kew* [1967] VR 732.
13 The county court judges' notes were consulted in *Marginson's* case and *Randolph v Tuck*. See also *Jenkins v Tileman (Overseas) Ltd* [1967] NZLR 484.
14 *Jackson v Goldsmith* (1950) 81 CLR 446; *Edwards v Joyce* [1954] VLR 216; *Clyne v Yardley* [1959] NZLR 617; *Hood v Commonwealth of Australia* [1968] VR 619; *Ramsay v Pigram* (1968) 42 ALJR 89; *Craddock's Transport Ltd v Stuart* [1970] NZLR 499.

greatly preponderates, the attractions of the broader view are made manifest by the South Australian case of *Black v Mount and Hancock*.[15] Black and Hunt were passengers in a car driven by Hancock. That car collided with a car driven by Mount, and both Mount and Hancock were held liable to Hunt for personal injuries sustained by him in consequence of the collision. As between Hancock and Mount, Hancock was held 85 per cent to blame for Hunt's injuries, Mount 15 per cent. Black then sued both drivers and was held entitled to judgment against each. It was also held that Hancock was estopped, as against Mount, from denying that he was 85 per cent to blame for the injuries sustained by Black. No doubt the duties owed by the drivers to each of the passengers were in law distinct, but the passengers were sitting in the same seat of Hancock's car, and it is difficult to dispute the force of the following remark of Chamberlain J in support of his view that there was an estoppel: 'The duties of care of each driver owed to the two passengers, the breach of those duties and the extent of their responsibility for the damage depended on precisely identical facts in each case'.[16]

Even when the issues are identical, differences in the onus of proof may sometimes prevent an estoppel from arising. For this, if for no other reason, it would probably be held that an acquittal on a criminal charge of assault would not estop the prosecutor, at common law, from suing in tort on the same facts.[17] A plaintiff might, however, be estopped from denying facts relied on by the defence as justification if he were to sue the Crown for damages for an assault by a police officer if those facts had been the subject of a criminal conviction for some such offence as drunkenness or using insulting words on the occasion in question.[18] In such a case the heavier burden borne by the prosecutor on a criminal charge could not possibly operate adversely to the plaintiff.

(iii) Pleading

In *Vooght v Winch*[19] it was held that the party alleging the existence of an estoppel by record must plead the former judgment and, if he fails to do so, it is merely an item of evidence in his favour which must be considered by the jury. If, notwithstanding the prior judgment or verdict, they are prepared to decide in favour of the opposite party, there is no reason why they should not do so, although they will no doubt be disposed to act as the tribunal did on the former occasion. The rules of pleading are, of course, less strict than they used to be, but it is still generally maintained that all estoppels must be specially pleaded.[20] The rule that, when a judgment is not pleaded, it may, nevertheless, be treated as evidence of the facts upon which it was based in later proceedings between the same parties is hard to reconcile on principle with the common law rule that the judgment is not admissible as evidence of

15 [1965] NZLR 499.
16 At 170.
17 *Kosanovic v Savapuu* [1962] VLR 321. There does not appear to be English authority directly in point. In practice the matter is liable to be affected by various provisions of the Offences Against the Person Act 1861, on which see an article by P M North in 20 MLR 16.
18 It would however be necessary for the normal conditions to be satisfied. *Hunter v Chief Constable of West Midlands* [1982] AC 529, [1981] 3 All ER 727.
19 (1819) 2 B & Ald 662. An estoppel may be pleaded in a second action although the writ was issued before judgment in the first (*Morrison Rose & Partners v Hillman* [1961] 2 QB 266, [1961] 2 All ER 891).
20 Odgers *Principles of Pleading and Practice* (22nd edn) 190.

these facts in proceedings between parties, or between one party to the earlier litigation and a stranger, but we shall see in the next section that there is good reason for regarding the latter rule as the questionable one.

3. MATRIMONIAL CAUSES[1]

There are numerous authorities on estoppel by record in matrimonial causes which are not easy to reconcile at first sight, but the apparent conflict can be largely, if not entirely, resolved if it is borne in mind that, whereas the ordinary principles of estoppel apply as between the parties, the divorce court is in a unique position on account of its special inquisitorial duty. It is true that several of the old cases must be read in the light of the Divorce Reform Act 1969, which abolished the bars to divorce and the concept of a matrimonial offence, but s 1(3) of the Matrimonial Causes Act 1973 (which now embodies the Act of 1969) provides, as did the corresponding section of the older statutes, that, on a petition for divorce, it shall be the duty of the court to inquire, so far as it reasonably can, into the facts alleged by the petitioner and into any facts alleged by the respondent. The facts alleged by the petitioner may include adultery and desertion, matters which seem expressly to render the old authorities relevant and conduct which makes it unreasonable to expect the petitioner to continue to live with the respondent, which may have the same effect by implication. It seems, therefore, still to be true to say that estoppels bind the parties to a matrimonial cause, but they frequently do not bind the court.

The statement that estoppels bind the parties means that:

> once an issue of a matrimonial offence has been litigated between the parties and decided by a competent court, neither party can claim as of right to re-open the issue and litigate it all over again if the other party objects ... But the divorce court has the right, and indeed the duty in a proper case, to re-open the issue or to allow either party to re-open it, despite the objection of the other party (that is what is meant by saying that estoppels do not bind the divorce court).[2]

Thus, in *Harriman v Harriman*,[3] where a wife who had obtained a separation order from the magistrates on the ground of the husband's desertion petitioned for divorce on the grounds of adultery and desertion at a time when it was necessary for her to establish both of these matrimonial offences, Cozens-Hardy and Fletcher-Moulton LJJ each stressed the point that, though the husband might be estopped from denying the desertion, the court was not bound by the findings of the magistrates.[4] Fletcher-Moulton LJ put the following case:

> The production of a decree for a judicial separation on the ground of cruelty is not as a matter of law sufficient to make it the judicial duty of the court to accept as a fact that the respondent has been guilty of such cruelty; and if the circumstances

1 The leading authorities on the subject include: *James v James* [1948] 1 All ER 214; *Winnan v Winnan* [1949] P 174, [1948] 2 All ER 862; *Thompson v Thompson* [1957] P 19, [1957] 1 All ER 161; *Bullock v Bullock* [1960] 2 All ER 307, [1960] 1 WLR 975; *Thoday v Thoday* [1964] P 181, [1964] 1 All ER 341; *Porter v Porter* [1971] P 282, [1971] 2 All ER 1037; *Rowe v Rowe* [1980] Fam 47, [1979] 2 All ER 1123.
2 Per Denning LJ in *Thompson v Thompson* [1957] P 19 at 29.
3 [1909] P 123.
4 At 132 and 142, respectively.

under which the decree was obtained are such as to raise a doubt in the mind of the court as to whether the cruelty was in fact committed, it would be entitled and bound to require such additional evidence as should be sufficient to convince it of the fact. But, although this is so, the respect paid to a judicial determination of a fact between parties (which in civil actions is evidenced by its creating a binding estoppel) would, I should presume, in ordinary cases lead the court to consider the fact of the cruelty to be adequately established by the production of the decree.

These views have, in effect, received statutory force, for s 4 of the Matrimonial Causes Act 1973[5] provides that the jurisdiction of the court in divorce is not excluded by the fact that the petitioner has been granted a judicial separation, or a magistrates' order, upon the same or substantially the same facts as are proved on a petition for divorce; and that the court may treat the decree or order as sufficient proof of the adultery, desertion or other ground upon which it was granted, but shall not pronounce a decree of divorce without receiving evidence from the petitioner. Even in cases to which the statute does not apply, it seems that, whereas a court of summary jurisdiction is bound by the previous findings of the divorce court[6] or another court of summary jurisdiction,[7] the divorce court is not bound by the previous findings of a court of summary jurisdiction,[8] although it seems that the divorce court is bound by findings of the same court,[9] subject to the provisions of the Act of 1973 which have just been mentioned.

One reason why the jurisdiction in divorce and nullity must be exercised with great circumspection is that it is concerned with status. In *Hayward v Hayward*,[10] a husband and wife both suspected that their marriage was bigamous when it was celebrated because the husband's first wife was still alive. The husband subsequently admitted liability in maintenance proceedings, and the consequential finding that he had neglected to maintain his wife would, in the ordinary case, have been sufficient to estop him from denying the validity of his marriage. It was nevertheless held that there was no estoppel affecting either party in nullity proceedings based on the bigamous nature of the marriage.

4. CRIMINAL CASES

In criminal cases the rule against double jeopardy[11] plays a role roughly equivalent to that played by cause of action estoppel in civil proceedings. It accounts for some extensions of the plea of autrefois acquit resembling, but

5 Re-enacting earlier provisions and amended by s 62 of the Domestic Proceedings and Magistrates' Courts Act 1978. On the evidential significance of an order of a court of summary jurisdiction, see *Fromhold v Fromhold* [1952] 1 TLR 1522; and *Turner v Turner* [1962] P 283, [1961] 3 All ER 944.
6 *James v James* [1948] 1 All ER 214.
7 *Stokes v Stokes* [1911] P 195.
8 *Winnan v Winnan* [1949] P 174, [1948] 2 All ER 862.
9 *Finney v Finney* (1868) LR 1 P & D 483.
10 [1961] P 152, [1961] 1 All ER 236, preferring *Miles v Chilton* (1849) 1 Rob Eccl 684 and *Andrews v Ross* (1888) 14 PD 15 to *Wilkins v Wilkins* [1896] P 108 (in so far as this case was based on estoppel) and *Woodland v Woodland* [1928] P 169. It was also held that there was no estoppel by conduct, *Bullock v Bullock* [1960] 2 All ER 307, [1960] 1 WLR 975, not being followed on this point. But on the point of estoppel by record, see Tolstoy 'Marriage by Estoppel' 84 LQR 245.
11 M L Friedland *Double Jeopardy* (1969) Clarendon Press.

distinct from, issue estoppel which has been held by the House of Lords to be inapplicable in English criminal law.[12]

(i) Autrefois acquit and autrefois convict

The most usual tests for determining the validity of the pleas in bar of autrefois acquit and autrefois convict are whether the accused had previously been acquitted or convicted of the same, or a substantially similar, offence; and whether he could have been convicted at the first trial of the offence with which he is charged at the second. The formulation and application of these tests has produced a great deal of case-law which need not be considered here.[13]

Earlier editions of this work canvassed the questions of whether convictions adduced either to the credit of the accused under s 1(f) of the Criminal Evidence Act 1898, or on a handling charge under the provisions of s 27(3) of the Theft Act 1968, could be denied by the accused. The latter seems now to have been resolved by s 74(3) of the Police and Criminal Evidence Act 1984.[14] Under that section it is clear that no estoppel operates against the accused. He does however bear the burden of proving his innocence.

Doubt still persists as to the former question which is unaffected by s 74(3) since such a conviction might do no more than impugn the accused's credit as a witness,[15] and thus would not be relevant to 'an issue in the proceedings' as the section requires.[16] It is thus possible that the Act has created a situation in which the accused is estopped as against the Crown from asserting that his previous convictions are wrong if they are put to him on the question of his credibility, but not if they are relevant to the issue. It can be argued in favour of this result that it is consistent with the general rule excluding rebuttal of collateral issues.[17] On the other hand it may be doubted whether in the case of the accused the distinction between credit and issue is readily separable by a jury, and if the accused can demonstrate his innocence of the crime for which he has been convicted it seems unjust to deny him the opportunity of doing so.

(ii) Extensions of autrefois acquit

In *Sambasivam v Malaya Federation Public Prosecutor*[18] the appellant had been charged with two offences, carrying a firearm and being in possession of

12 *DPP v Humphreys* [1977] AC 1, [1976] 2 All ER 497. It is however conceivable that issue estoppel could apply in criminal proceedings in respect of attacks upon a witness's credit, for example based upon a suggestion of guilt of a crime in respect of which the accused had been acquitted, see *R v Neville* [1985] 2 Qd R 398.
13 See the speech of Lord Morris of Borth-y-Gest in *Connelly v DPP* [1964] AC 1254, [1964] 2 All ER 401; and the judgments of Bray CJ and Wells J in *R v O'Loughlin, ex p Ralphs* [1971] 1 SASR 219.
14 Cmnd 4991 proposed the same result, but by different means.
15 *R v France* [1979] Crim LR 48; *R v Shepherd* (1980) 71 Cr App Rep 120; but see *R v Duncalf* [1979] 2 All ER 1116 and compare [1979] 1 WLR 918; for analysis see Pattenden, 'Purpose of Cross-Examination Under Section 1(f) of The Criminal Evidence Act 1898' [1982] Crim LR 707, and see below p 409.
16 That this phrase is designed to exclude questions going to credibility can be discerned from comparison of the terminology of cl 24 of the draft Bill annexed to the 11th Committee's Report from which this section derives and the terminology of cl 10 of that Bill which is not used in this Act.
17 Below p 309.
18 [1950] AC 458.

ammunition. He was acquitted of the second, but a new trial was ordered with regard to the first. At the second trial the prosecution relied upon a statement in which the appellant said that he was both carrying a firearm and in possession of ammunition. He was convicted of carrying a firearm but the Judicial Committee advised that his conviction should be quashed because the assessors had not been told that the prosecution had to accept that the part of the statement dealing with the ammunition must be regarded as untrue. Lord Macdermott said:[19]

> The effect of a verdict of acquittal pronounced by a competent court on a lawful charge and after a lawful trial is not completely stated by saying that the person acquitted cannot be tried again for the same offence. To that it must be added that the verdict is binding and conclusive in all subsequent proceedings between the parties to the adjudication, the maxim *'res judicata pro veritate accipitur'* is no less applicable to criminal than to civil proceedings. Here, the appellant having been acquitted at the first trial on the charge of having ammunition in his possession, the prosecution was bound to accept the correctness of that verdict and was precluded from taking any step to challenge it at the second trial. And the appellant was no less entitled to rely on his acquittal so far as it might be relevant in his defence.

The case fell outside the plea of autrefois acquit and there could have been no question of issue estoppel, but the knowledge that part of the accused's statement must be regarded as untrue might well have affected the assessors' attitude to the other parts. Any question that *Sambasivam* might not represent the current position in England has been resolved by the decision of the Court of Appeal in *R v Hay*.[20] There too the accused had confessed to two different crimes which were tried separately. It was held that after he had been acquitted of one of the crimes, having attacked the credibility of the confession, he was entitled to the benefit of that acquittal in his attack upon the same confession when he was subsequently tried for the other crime. It does not follow that because the accused was acquitted of earlier charges of a similar nature to that which he now faces, on the basis of evidence adduced by the same witness, that he may necessarily adduce evidence of his acquittal.[1] If the acquittal can be explained on some basis other than disbelief of the witness's evidence it is irrelevant.[2] In Canada the Supreme Court has applied[3] this view to a single confession to two crimes which was held inadmissible at the trial of the first which then resulted in an acquittal. The prosecution was nevertheless permitted to lead the same confession at the trial of the second, and the accused could rely on no issue estoppel, nor extension of autrefois acquit, to exclude it at the second, with the result that it was admitted, and his conviction was upheld. The only way of reconciling this result with that in *Hay*, must be that in *Duhamel* the question of the credibility of the confession was never reached at the first trial.

19 At 479.
20 (1983) 77 Cr App Rep 70. It has been repeatedly endorsed in New Zealand, see *R v Olsen* [1982] 1 NZLR 578; *R v Davies* [1982] 1 NZLR 584; and *R v Pene* [1982] 2 NZLR 652.
 1 See *R v Doosti* (1985) 82 Cr App Rep 181 where the evidence was of the finding of drugs in the same room by the same policeman.
 2 *R v Henri* [1990] Crim LR 51 where the question arose in relation to earlier proceedings for the same series of offences on some of which the accused had been acquitted and on some of which the jury had failed to agree.
 3 *Duhamel v R* (1984) 14 DLR (4th) 92.

In *G (an Infant) v Coltart*,[4] G, a domestic servant, was convicted of stealing goods from Mrs T, her mistress. Her defence was that she intended to return the goods to Mrs T. In order to rebut this the prosecution had adduced evidence that G had taken goods from Mrs Doig, a guest of Mrs T, and not returned them although told that she was going to South Africa. G had, however, been acquitted of stealing these goods at the instance of the prosecution on the mistaken assumption that the absence of Mrs Doig in South Africa was fatal to their case. It was held that the conviction of stealing from Mrs T must be quashed because it was not open to the prosecution to invite the court to make an inference that G was guilty of an offence of which she had been acquitted. Like *Sambasivam v Malaya Federation Public Prosecutor*, *Coltart's* case simply decided that the prosecution may not, in case B, rely on evidence which is only relevant on the assumption that the accused was guilty of the offence of which he was acquitted in case A.[5] What is alleged to have been wrongly challenged in the second case is the innocence of the accused in the first.

G (an Infant) v Coltart is to be contrasted with *R v Ollis*.[6] The accused had been charged and acquitted of obtaining a cheque by false pretences on 5 July, the alleged false pretence being that a cheque drawn by the accused and given to Ramsey would be honoured. Ollis was then charged with obtaining money by means of worthless cheques on 24 June, 26 June and 6 July respectively. He was convicted of these offences after Ramsey had given evidence concerning the incident of 5 July to the same effect as that given at the hearing which had resulted in an acquittal. The conviction was affirmed by a majority of the Court for Crown Cases Reserved. The court was unanimously of the opinion that the fact that he had been acquitted on the charge to which Ramsey deposed was immaterial, the judges differed over the question of the admissibility of the evidence under the similar fact rule. In *G v Coltart* Salmon LJ said:

> But it seems to me that the distinction between that case and the present one is that in the present case the only relevance of the evidence tendered was to prove guilt in the Doig case, whereas in *R v Ollis* the prosecution were able to say; we are not alleging let alone relying on the defendant's guilt in respect of the first cheque; we are relying on the fact that the first cheque was not met only to show what the defendant's knowledge or state of mind was when he gave the other three cheques.[7]

On the basis of the facts and judgments it is difficult to escape the conclusion that Ramsey's evidence was tendered in order to show that Ollis was acting dishonestly on 5 July in which case it went to show that he was at least guilty of an attempt to obtain by false pretences, an offence of which he was in danger of being convicted at his previous trial, but, whether or not it was applicable to the facts, the principle underlying the distinction drawn by Salmon LJ is clear enough. Evidence is no less admissible in the second case because it tends to show that the accused was guilty in the first provided that, in tendering it, the prosecution is not in effect denying the validity of the acquittal.

4 [1967] 1 QB 432, [1967] 1 All ER 271.
5 See also *Re Mulligan, ex p Isidoro* [1979] WAR 198, where the acquittal occurred after a licence had been refused in respect of the facts constituting the offence, and the appeal against the refusal was bound to give credit for the acquittal.
6 [1900] 2 QB 758; cf *R v Norton* (1910) 5 Cr App Rep 197.
7 [1967] 1 QB 432 at 440.

There could of course have been no question of a plea of autrefois acquit in *R v Ollis* because the accused was not in danger of a conviction on the Ramsey cheque. There was also no question of issue estoppel because it was impossible to say which particular issue, as distinct from the general one of his innocence had been decided in the accused's favour in the first case. Pleas of autrefois acquit and issue estoppel were likewise unavailable in *Connelly v DPP*[8] where the accused and others had previously been tried together and convicted of murder in the course of an armed robbery. Connelly had relied primarily on an alibi, but it was also submitted on his behalf that, even if he did participate in the robbery, he was not guilty of murder because he did not know that one of his co-accused was carrying a loaded gun. Connelly's conviction was quashed by the Court of Criminal Appeal on the ground of misdirection with regard to his alibi. Proceedings were then taken against him on the indictment concerning the robbery. He was convicted and his ultimate appeal to the House of Lords was unsuccessful.[9] Even if the quashing of the conviction of murder were treated as the equivalent of a verdict of acquittal, there could have been no question of an extension of autrefois acquit to cover the robbery charge because there never was a question of double jeopardy. Issue estoppel was unavailable because there was no way of establishing that any separate issue had been decided in favour of Connelly either by analysing the verdict of the jury or by examining the judgment of the Court of Criminal Appeal by which that verdict was quashed.

(iii) The rejection of issue estoppel in criminal cases[10]

Three of the Law Lords who heard *Connelly v DPP*[11] expressed the opinion that issue estoppel would be applicable on appropriate facts in an English criminal case. Lord Devlin thought that this would be undesirable if only because of the difficulty of ascertaining what precise issues are determined in criminal proceedings in which there are no pleadings, nothing but a general verdict of a jury and no reasoned judgments. There was the further problem of mutuality. If issue estoppel binds the Crown, it is hard to see why it should not also bind the accused. It was held that it did have this effect by Lawson J in *R v Hogan*,[12] a case in which it was possible to ascertain what

8 [1964] AC 1254, [1964] 2 All ER 401.
9 On the conviction for murder the robbery indictment had been marked 'not to be proceeded with without the leave of the court.' At the time there was a rule of practice against joining murder with other offences in one indictment. That rule was abolished by the House of Lords in *Connelly's* case. Today he would probably have been charged with both offences in the same indictment. Assuming that he was convicted of both, the quashing of the murder conviction for misdirection as to alibi would have entailed the quashing of the robbery conviction.
10 See Morris and Howard, *Studies in Criminal Law*, ch VII, a version of which was cited in *Connelly v DPP*. It deals with the Australian authorities up to the date of that decision. For an Australian case decided after *DPP v Humphreys*, but turning more on *Sambasivam's* case, see *Garrett v R* (1978) 52 ALJR 206; *R v Storey* (1978) 52 ALJR 737 contains divergent views as to whether issue estoppel applies in Australian criminal law. Issue estoppel remains part of the criminal law in Canada, *Gushue v R* [1980] 1 SCR 798. See also David Lanham 'Issue Estoppel in the English Criminal Law' [1970] Crim LR 428, containing some criticisms of *Sambasivam v Malaya Federation Public Prosecutor* and *G (an Infant) v Coltart*; and compare Mirfield 'Shedding a Tear for Issue Estoppel' [1980] Crim LR 336 presenting a powerful case for the retention of issue estoppel in criminal proceedings.
11 [1964] AC 1254, [1964] 2 All ER 401.
12 [1974] QB 398, [1974] 2 All ER 142.

issues had been determined by the jury at the first trial. Hogan had unsuccessfully relied on self-defence in answer to a charge of causing grievous bodily harm with intent to produce that result. He was then charged with murder after his victim had died. It was held that he was estopped from denying that he caused grievous bodily harm to the deceased without lawful excuse and with intent to do so. The result was that only such questions as whether the grievous bodily harm committed by Hogan had caused the deceased's death and the availability of a plea of provocation (inapplicable at the first trial) could be treated as live issues. Hogan was nonetheless acquitted.

This case was overruled by the House of Lords in *DPP v Humphreys*[13] when the House unanimously declared that issue estoppel does not apply in English criminal proceedings. Humphreys was acquitted on a charge of driving a motor vehicle on 18 July 1972 while disqualified from doing so. The only issue at the trial was whether a constable was correct in identifying him as the man he had stopped after seeing him drive a motorcycle on the day in question. Humphreys had given evidence in the course of which he denied having driven a motor vehicle at any time during 1972, and he was charged with perjury in having made this statement. Evidence tending to show that he had driven his motorcycle at various times during 1972 was tendered at the trial for perjury and, after the judge had overruled a submission that there was an issue estoppel, the same constable gave the same evidence as that which he had given on the former occasion, identifying Humphreys as the driver stopped by him on 18 July. Humphreys was convicted, his appeal to the Court of Appeal was allowed on the ground that the constable's evidence was precluded by issue estoppel, but the House of Lords restored the conviction. Differing views were expressed on the question whether a judge had power to stop proceedings for perjury based exclusively on evidence that had not been accepted at an earlier trial for another offence of which the accused was acquitted. It was also held that, even if issue estoppel does apply in English criminal law, it would have been inapplicable in Humphrey's case because no estoppel is created by a judgment obtained by fraud (including wilfully false evidence).[14]

In view of the unanimous rejection of issue estoppel it is unlikely that much will be heard about it in relation to English criminal proceedings,[15] but the same cannot be said of the extensions of autrefois acquit which have been mentioned. They give rise to a number of problems which have, as yet, not been considered, let alone solved.

B. ESTOPPEL BY DEED

'A party who executes a deed is estopped in a court of law from saying that the facts stated in the deed are not truly stated.'[16] Accordingly, if a deed contained a receipt for the purchase of property, the vendor was estopped in a common law action on the deed, from alleging that part of the money had

---

13 [1977] AC 1, [1976] 2 All ER 497.
14 In Canada where issue estoppel is part of the law it can be raised even in respect of a perjury charge unless the Crown produces new evidence that could not by reasonable diligence have been adduced at the first trial, *Grdic v R* (1985) 19 DLR (4th) 385.
15 But see *R v Pervez and Khan* [1983] Crim LR 108 and the commentary thereon.
16 *Baker v Dewey* (1823) 1 B & C 704 at 707 per Bayley J.

not been paid, provided the estoppel was duly pleaded.[17] Further examples of the operation of the same doctrine of common law are provided by decisions on priorities according to which someone who executed a conveyance on the footing that he was seised of the legal estate was estopped from denying this fact,[18] and by a case put by Lord Kenyon in *Hayne v Maltby*:[19]

> Where an heir apparent, having only the hope of succession, conveys during the life of his ancestor an estate, which afterwards descends upon him, he is estopped to say that he had no interest at the time of the grant.

In *Bowman v Taylor*,[20] the principle was applied to recitals in a deed so that the defendant, a licensee of patent rights, was estopped from denying that the plaintiff was the inventor as he had executed a deed of licence which recited that this was the case. The governing principle was said to be the same as that which underlies estoppel by statements contained in the body of the deed: 'If a party has by his deed directly asserted a specific fact, it is impossible to say that he shall not be precluded from disputing that fact.[1] It seems, however, that the basis of estoppel by recitals, if not of the entire doctrine of estoppel by deed, was formulated in a more satisfactory way in the later case of *Stroughill v Buck*.[2] It was said that:

> When a recital is intended to be a statement which all the parties to the deed have mutually agreed to admit as true, it is an estoppel upon all. But, when it is intended to be the statement of one party only, the estoppel is confined to that party, and the intention is to be gathered from construing the instrument.[3]

This was treated as the ground upon which *Bowman v Taylor* ought to have been decided in *Greer v Kettle*[4] where Lord Maugham said:

> Estoppel by deed is a rule of evidence founded on the principle that a solemn and unambiguous statement or engagement in a deed must be taken as binding between the parties and privies and therefore as not admitting any contradictory proof.[5]

Whatever may be the true modern basis of the doctrine of estoppel by deed, its scope is extremely limited under the present law.[6] In the first place, it applies only between parties to the deed and those claiming through them.[7] Secondly, it applies only in actions on the deed. In *Carpenter v Buller*,[8] for

---

17 *Potts v Nixon* (1870) IR 5 CL 45.
18 *Doe d Levy v Horne* (1842) 3 QB 757.
19 (1789) 3 Tem Rep 438 at 441; *Church of England Building Society v Piskor* [1954] Ch 553, [1954] 2 All ER 85.
20 (1834) 4 LJKB 58.
1 Lord Denman CJ.
2 (1980) 14 QB 781.
3 Patteson J.
4 [1938] AC 156, [1937] 4 All ER 396.
5 At 171 and 404, respectively.
6 Formerly the deed might have been an instrument of proof. There can be no estoppel by deed against a party claiming rectification (*Wilson v Wilson* [1969] 3 All ER 945, [1969] 1 WLR 1470).
7 It is uncertain whether there can be an estoppel by deed poll, see *Cropper v Smith* (1884) 26 Ch D 700.
8 (1841) 8 M & W 209. See also *Offshore Oil NL v Southern Cross Exploration NL* (1985) 3 NSWLR 337.

instance, the defence to an action of trespass was that the defendant was seised of the land in question and he produced a deed, made between himself, the plaintiff and a third party, in which this was stated to be the case; but it was held that the plaintiff was not estopped from denying the defendant's seisin because the action was not brought on the deed which did not directly concern the land. Thirdly, the doctrine applies only to clear and unambiguous statements,[9] and finally it does not prevent a party from setting up a plea of illegality or fraud or from availing himself of any fact which would have given rise to a right to rescind the deed in equity. This last limitation is of great importance, for it means that matters, such as the receipt for the purchase price of property in the body of the deed, which would formerly have supported a plea of estoppel at common law will now, generally speaking, be of little avail.

If the modern basis of the doctrine is agreement, there is not much point in preserving a separate head of estoppel by deed, for estoppel by agreement can easily be brought under the rubric of estoppel by conduct.

C. ESTOPPEL BY CONDUCT[10]

1. HISTORICAL

Although ideas of the sort had previously existed in equity, it was not until *Pickard v Sears*[11] that the doctrine of estoppel by conduct was clearly stated in a common law court. Then it was said that:

> Where one by his words or conduct wilfully causes another to believe in the existence of a certain state of things, and induces him to act on that belief, or to alter his own previous position, the former is concluded from averring against the latter a different state of things as existing at that time.

In *Freeman v Cooke*,[12] the word 'wilfully' in the above passage was treated as equivalent to 'with the intention that the belief which is induced should be acted upon', and it was accordingly held that the assignee of a bankrupt was not estopped from proving the latter's ownership of goods sold by the sheriff, although the bankrupt had said that the goods belonged to his brother under the mistaken impression that the sheriff was about to levy execution against his property and not that of his brother. There was clearly no intention to induce the sheriff to seize the goods as the brother's property, and the bankrupt had prevaricated to such an extent that no reasonable man would have given credence to any of his statements. When delivering judgment in *Freeman v Cooke*, Parke B nonetheless added that:

> If, whatever a man's real intention may be, he so conducts himself that a reasonable man would take the representation to be true, and believe that it was meant that he should act upon it, and did act upon it as true, the party making the representation would be equally precluded from contesting its truth; and conduct,

9 *Onward Building Society v Smithson* [1893] 1 Ch 1; *District Bank Ltd v Webb* [1958] 1 All ER 126, [1958] 1 WLR 148.
10 Ewart *Estoppel*; Pickering 'Estoppel by Conduct' (1939) 55 LQR 400; Spencer-Bower *Estoppel by Representation* (3rd edn, 1977, by Sir Alexander Turner).
11 (1837) 6 Ad & El 469.
12 (1848) 2 Exch 654.

by negligence or omission, when there is a duty cast upon a person, by usage of trade or otherwise, to disclose the truth, may often have the same effect. As, for instance, a retiring partner omitting to inform the customers of the fact, in the usual mode, that the continuing partners were no longer authorised to act as his agents, is bound by all contracts made by them with third persons on the faith of their being so authorised.[13]

These observations embody the main principles underlying estoppel by conduct,[14] and the subject may be considered in outline under the heads of estoppel by agreement, estoppel by representation and estoppel by negligence (an expression which has not escaped criticism)[15] although it must not be supposed that these divisions of the subject are mutually exclusive. When this has been done, some reference will be made to the limitations of estoppel by conduct.

2. ESTOPPEL BY AGREEMENT

It not infrequently happens that two people agree, expressly, or by necessary implication, that their legal relations shall be based on the assumption that a certain state of facts exists, and, when this has been done, the original parties to the agreement, as well as those claiming through them,[16] are sometimes said to be estopped from denying the existence of the assumed state of facts. The agreement may take the form of a contract supported by consideration, as where a party to an arbitration agreement who nominates an arbitrator is estopped from disputing the qualifications of his nominee by an implied term in the agreement,[17] and as we have seen an agreement may be inferred from the terms of a deed, but neither consideration nor a seal is essential to its efficacy as an estoppel. Acquiescence in a particular construction of a document may likewise lead to an estoppel by agreement,[18] and this is the

13 See now Partnership Act 1890, s 14(1). Further statutory provisions stating the common law of estoppel by conduct are ss 54–55 of the Bills of Exchange Act 1882.
14 A good modern statement of the principles underlying this branch of the law is that of Dixon J, as he then was, in *Grundt v Great Boulder Proprietary Gold Mine Ltd* (1937) 59 CLR 641 at 674: 'The principle on which estoppel in pais is founded is that the law should not permit an unjust departure by a party from an assumption of fact which he has caused another party to adopt or accept for the purpose of their legal relations.' See *Ishmael v Polish Ocean Lines* [1976] 1 All ER 902 at 907. 'He may be required to abide by the assumption because it formed the conventional basis upon which the parties entered into contractual or mutual relations such as bailment, or because he has exercised against the other party rights which would only exist if the assumption were correct, as in *Yorkshire Insurance Co v Craine* [1922] 2 AC 541, or because knowing the mistake the other laboured under, he refrained from correcting him when it was his duty to do so; or because his imprudence where care was required of him was the proximate cause of the other party's adopting and acting upon the faith of the assumption. But, in each case, he is not bound to adhere to the assumption unless, as the result of adopting it as the basis of action or inaction, the other party will have placed himself in a position of material disadvantage if departure from the presumption be permitted' (per Dixon J in *Thompson v Palmer* (1933) 49 CLR 500 at 547). Estoppel by conduct used to be called estoppel in pais because it depended on facts to be found by a jury (the country) and not on matter of record or deed.
15 Spencer-Bower *Estoppel by Representation* (3rd edn) 69, and, in the context of non est factum, Lord Pearson in *Saunders v Anglia Building Society* (on appeal from *Gallie v Lee* [1971] AC 1004 at 1038), but see the article by Professor Julius Stone 88 LQR 190.
16 *Taylor v Needham* (1810) 2 Taunt 278.
17 *Oakland Metal Co Ltd v D Benaim & Co Ltd* [1953] 2 QB 261, [1953] 2 All ER 650.
18 *Amalgamated Investment and Property Co Ltd v Texas Commerce International Bank Ltd* [1982] QB 84, [1981] 1 All ER 923.

basis of the rules that, generally speaking, a tenant is estopped from denying his landlord's title[19] (but only during the currency of the lease[20]), a bailee that of his bailor,[1] and a licensee that of his licensor.[2]

3. ESTOPPEL BY REPRESENTATION

The classic statement of the principle governing estoppel by representation is that of Spencer-Bower :[3]

> Where one person (the representor) has made a representation to another person (the representee) in words or by acts or conduct, or (being under a duty to the representee to speak or act) by silence or inaction, with the intention (actual or presumptive), and with the result,[4] of inducing the representee on the faith of such representation to alter his position to his detriment, the representor, in any litigation which may afterwards take place between him and the representee is estopped, as against the representee, from making, or attempting to establish by evidence, any averment substantially at variance with his former representation, if the representee, at the proper time, and in the proper manner, objects thereto.

The reference to presumptive intention is necessary because :

> If a man, whatever his real meaning may be, so conducts himself that a reasonable man would take this conduct to mean a certain representation of facts, and that it was a true representation, and that the latter was intended to act upon it in a particular way, and he with such belief does act in that way to his damage, the first is estopped from denying that the facts were as represented.[5]

There can, for instance, be little doubt that, if, on facts such as those of *Freeman v Cooke*, the debtor had contented himself with one positive assertion to the effect that the goods were his brother's, his assignee would have been estopped from claiming them.[6] On the other hand, in *Carr v London and North Western Rly Co*,[7] the defendant's agent told the plaintiff that the company held three consignments of goods to his order when only two had been received. The plaintiff purported to sell three consignments, and had to pay damages to the purchaser of one of them; but it was held that he could not recover these from the defendant. If an estoppel did operate against the company, it would have been liable in conversion through its servant's refusal to deliver the plaintiff's goods to his order but there was no estoppel because there was no evidence that the defendant's agent realised that the goods would be sold by the plaintiff. It was also held that there was no negligence, and that, if there was, it was not the immediate cause of the subsale; but it is not clear whether the court was using the word 'negligence'

19 *Terunnanse v Terunnanse* [1968] AC 1086, [1968] 1 All ER 651.
20 *Harrison v Wells* [1967] 1 QB 263, [1966] 3 All ER 524.
1 *Gosling v Birnie* (1831) 7 Bing 399. This type of estoppel may have been qualified to the point of extinction by the Torts (Interference with Goods) Act 1977, s 8.
2 *Crossley v Dixon* (1863) 10 HL Cas 293.
3 *Estoppel by Representation* (2nd edn), 4–5, adopted by Sir Raymond Evershed MR in *Hopgood v Brown* [1955] 1 All ER 550 at 559.
4 *The Skarp* [1935] P 134; *Cremer v General Carriers S A* [1974] 1 All ER 1, [1974] 1 WLR 341.
5 *Carr v London and North Western Rly Co* (1875) LR 10 CP 307 at 317 per Brett J.
6 See *Western v Fairbridge* [1923] 1 KB 667.
7 (1875) LR 10 CP 307.

in the sense of carelessness in the abstract, or that of a careless breach of duty towards a specific person.

A case in which the representation was by acts or conduct rather than words was one in which an employee was held to be estopped from denying his employment by the fact that he had given notice terminating it.[8]

A case in which there was a duty to speak or act within the meaning of Spencer-Bower's statement was *Greenwood v Martins Bank*[9] in which a husband's failure to disclose the fact that his wife had been forging his cheques was held to estop him from alleging this to be the case in an action to recover the amounts paid to his wife and debited to his account by his bank. Similarly, in *Oades v Spafford*,[10] a landlord agreed to sell property on the footing that the tenant would be liable for dilapidations, and it was held that his failure to disclose a release from this liability estopped him from denying its existence. Cases of the same species are those in which a person acquiesces in the erection of buildings on his land with the knowledge that the builder supposes that the land is his, for, in such circumstances, the landowner will be estopped from denying this fact,[11] or where a corporate body permits and encourages another to use a very similar name, and is estopped in a passing off action from denying entitlement to do so.[12] This whole area is experiencing rapid expansion, largely inspired by judicial reluctance to be constrained by excessive technicality, but rather inclined to adopt:

> a very much broader approach which is directed rather at ascertaining whether, in particular individual circumstances, it would be unconscionable for a party to be permitted to deny that which, knowingly or unknowingly, he has allowed or encouraged another to assume to his detriment rather than to inquiring whether the circumstances can be fitted within the confines of some preconceived formula serving as a universal yardstick for every form of unconscionable behaviour.[13]

D. ESTOPPEL BY NEGLIGENCE

In all the examples of estoppel by conduct that have been given so far, the party in whose favour the estoppel operated was either the person with whom an agreement was concluded or someone claiming through him, or else he was the person to whom a representation was made by the party estopped, or someone claiming through such person. There is, however, a type of estoppel, often called estoppel by negligence, in which the party in whose favour it operates is the victim of the fraud of some third person facilitated by the careless breach of duty of the other party. An example is provided by *Coventry Shepherd & Co v Great Eastern Rly Co*.[14] In that case the defendants carelessly issued two delivery orders relating to the same

---

8 *Smith v Blandford Gee Cementation Co Ltd* [1970] 3 All ER 154. Conversely, payment of a particular sum as wages may amount to a representation of entitlement to that amount, *Avon County Council v Howlett* [1983] 1 All ER 1073.

9 [1933] AC 51, distinguished in *West Country Cleaners (Falmouth) Ltd v Saly* [1966] 3 All ER 210, [1966] 1 WLR 1485.

10 [1948] 2 KB 74, [1948] 1 All ER 607.

11 *Ramsden v Dyson* (1866) LR 1 HL 129; *A-G to Prince of Wales v Collom* [1916] 2 KB 193.

12 *Habib Bank Ltd v Habib Bank A G Zurich* [1981] 2 All ER 650 at 668, [1981] 1 WLR 1265 at 1287.

13 *Taylors Fashions Ltd v Liverpool Victoria Trustees Co Ltd* [1982] QB 133 at 151, [1981] 1 All ER 897 at 915, 916.

14 (1883) 11 QBD 776.

consignment of goods, thus enabling the person to whom they were issued to obtain an advance from the plaintiff, and the defendants were held to be estopped as against him from denying the fact that the goods mentioned in the order were held on behalf of the assignor. Someone who puts documents of this nature into circulation owes a duty to those into whose hands they may come, and it is the fact that the documents were the creation of the defendants which distinguishes this case in the letter, if not in the spirit, from *Mercantile Bank of India Ltd v Central Bank of India Ltd.*[15] Railway receipts relating to a quantity of goods were pledged with the Central Bank as security for an advance when they were returned to their owners to enable them to get possession of the goods. The receipts were then delivered to the Mercantile Bank as security for a further advance, and it was held that the Central Bank was not estopped from asserting the priority of its claim to the goods. One ground of the decision was that the conduct of the first bank was not the legal cause of the detriment sustained by the second, for there was a well-known local practice under which receipts were returned by pledgees to their owners to enable them to get possession of their goods, but the decision was also based on the ground that the first bank owed no duty to the second when returning the receipts to their owners. The first bank did not bring the documents into existence, but it is open to question whether this warrants an opposite conclusion from that which was reached in the *Coventry Shepherd* case. Where there is no contractual duty of care, breach of which gives rise to an estoppel,[16] it is difficult to extract a safe guiding principle from the authorities on estoppel by negligence.[17]

It is possible that when the cases and underlying principles come to be authoritatively reviewed it will be found that the requirements of duty of care and proof of carelessness can be dispensed with. All that is necessary, it may be urged, is proof of intentional words, acts or conduct, which can reasonably be construed as a representation by the representor to the representee who need not be in direct relationship. To take a hypothetical case mentioned by Lord Pearson,[18] a busy managing director signs 'blind' a pile of documents handed to him by his secretary, disregarding the chance that an extraneous document may have been inserted. For such a man, such conduct may not amount to carelessness, yet he intends to sign whatever documents happen to be in the pile. It is difficult to escape the conclusion that he would be estopped from denying his liability on the fraudulently inserted document to anyone who reasonably took it to be his and acted

15 [1938] AC 287, [1938] 1 All ER 52.
16 *London Joint Stock Bank v Macmillan and Arthur* [1918] AC 777; contrast *Scholfield v Lord Londesborough* [1896] AC 514.
17 Compare the protection given to the innocent purchaser of shares by *Colonial Bank v Cady and Williams* (1890) 15 App Cas 267 and *Fuller v Glyn, Mills, Currie & Co* [1914] 2 KB 168, with the lack of protection accorded by the common law doctrine of estoppel to the innocent purchaser of goods in cases which are not covered by the Factors Act 1889 (see, for example, *Farquharson Bros & Co v King & Co* [1902] AC 325; *Central Newbury Car Auctions v Unity Finance Ltd* [1957] 1 QB 371, [1956] 3 All ER 905 and *Newtons of Wembley Ltd v Williams* [1965] 1 QB 560, [1964] 3 All ER 532). Note also the difficulty of reconciling *Mercantile Bank of India Ltd v Central Bank of India Ltd* [1938] AC 287, [1938] 1 All ER 52 with *Lloyds Bank v Bank of America, National Trust and Savings Association* [1938] 2 KB 147, [1938] 2 All ER 63. See further *Eastern Distributors Ltd v Goldring* [1957] 2 QB 600, [1957] 2 All ER 525; *Campbell Discount Co Ltd v Gall* [1961] 1 QB 431, [1961] 2 All ER 104; *Muskham Finance Ltd v Howard* [1963] 1 QB 904, [1963] 1 All ER 81; *Mercantile Credit Co Ltd v Hamblin* [1965] 2 QB 242, [1964] 3 All ER 592.
18 *Saunders v Anglia Building Society* [1971] AC 1004 at 1038.

upon it with detrimental consequences. Yet, ex hypothesi, he would not have been careless, and he could only be said to owe a duty to the person acting on his signature on the basis that anyone who intentionally signs documents, taking a chance on what they are, owes a duty to anyone into whose hands the documents may come. Lord Pearson's example was, however, mentioned in a case concerned with the very special plea of non est factum which, very exceptionally, enables signatories of documents to escape liability, and it cannot be denied that quite a number of the older decisions on estoppel by conduct turn on the requirement of a specific duty of care.[19]

E. LIMITS ON ESTOPPEL BY CONDUCT

There are a few well-defined rules which limit the operation of the doctrine of estoppel by conduct and it is convenient to collect them together at the end of our treatment of the entire topic.

1. MUST RELATE TO EXISTING FACT

The first universal requirement is that the estoppel must concern an existing state of facts. This is fundamental to all the common law cases, and *Jorden v Money*[20] conclusively established that there could be no common law estoppel founded on a statement of future intention.

2. MUST BE UNAMBIGUOUS

The second requirement of an estoppel by conduct is that it should be unambiguous. One reason why there was no estoppel in *Freeman v Cooke* was that the allegations of the debtor lacked this characteristic, and a more modern illustration is provided by *Canadian and Dominion Sugar Co Ltd v Canadian National (West Indies) Steamships Ltd*,[1] in which a receipt stating that cargo was in good order was held not to estop a purchaser from denying this fact because it referred to an ambiguous bill of lading.

3. RESULT MUST BE LEGAL

Finally, an estoppel cannot be relied on if the result of giving effect to it would be something that is prohibited by law. Accordingly, when a statutory undertaking mistakenly charged less for electricity than the amount specified in the relevant enactment, it was held that no estoppel covered the case although the recipients of the electricity had acted to their detriment.[2] Lord

---

19 For a recent example, see *Moorgate Mercantile Co Ltd v Twitchings* [1977] AC 890, [1976] 2 All ER 641.
20 (1854) 5 HL Cas 185. Although, to raise an estoppel, the statement must concern existing fact, the distinction between law and fact is no easier to draw in this context than others (see *De Tchihatchef v Salerni Coupling Ltd* [1932] 1 Ch 330). Promissory estoppel is outside the scope of this book.
 1 [1947] AC 46; *Woodhouse A C Israel Cocoa Ltd S A v Nigerian Produce Marketing Co Ltd* [1972] AC 741, [1972] 2 All ER 271.
 2 *Maritime Electric Co Ltd v General Dairies Ltd* [1937] AC 610, [1937] 1 All ER 748; *Roma Electric Light and Power Co Ltd v Hair* [1955] SRQd 311.

Maugham's opinion was that: 'this conclusion must follow from the circumstances that an estoppel is only a rule of evidence which, in certain special circumstances, can be invoked by a party to an action'.[3]

F. THE PLACE OF ESTOPPEL IN THE LAW

These words raise the general question of the rubric under which estoppel should be treated in an exposition of the whole of the law. The majority of the judges appear to have shared Lord Maugham's view that it is a rule of evidence, and the classic statement to this effect is that of Bowen LJ who said:

Estoppel is only a rule of evidence; you cannot found an action upon estoppel. Estoppel is only important as being one step in the progress towards relief on the hypothesis that the defendant is estopped from denying the truth of something which he has said.[4]

On the other hand, Lord Wright said: 'Estoppel is often described as a rule of evidence as indeed it may be so described. But the whole concept is more accurately viewed as a substantive rule of law'.[5]

If promissory estoppel associated with the decision in *Central London Property Trust Ltd v High Trees House Ltd*[6] is rightly so-called, estoppel must be treated as a rule of substantive law in at least one of its aspects. Provided the court comes to the conclusion that a promise was made with the requisite intention and acted upon, it will be treated as binding for certain purposes notwithstanding the absence of consideration. There is no question of the law preventing certain facts from being proved, and the rules of evidence do not enter into the matter at all.

For the rest it seems that the resolution of the apparent conflict of opinion between Bowen LJ and Lord Wright is a matter of words. Estoppel may have the effect of a rule of substantive law or a rule of evidence according to the type of estoppel which is under consideration. In either event the governing principle is one of public policy. The appropriate description of it within the dichotomy of substantive law and the law of evidence, is a mere matter of semantics which seems to be of no practical significance.

When speaking of estoppel by conduct Lord Wright once said that it 'may have the effect of creating substantive rights against the person estopped.'[7] This type of estoppel frequently has that effect, as when a wharfinger is estopped in an action for conversion from denying the plaintiff's title to goods on account of a statement that they were held on his behalf.[8]

---

3 At 620 and 753 respectively. See also *Re Companies' Acts, ex p Watson* (1888) 21 QBD 301; *Southend-on-Sea Corpn v Hodgson (Wickford) Ltd* [1962] 1 QB 416, [1961] 2 All ER 46; *Hayward v Hayward* [1961] P 152, [1961] 1 All ER 236; not following *Bullock v Bullock* [1960] 2 All ER 307, [1960] 1 WLR 975; *Western Fish Product Ltd v Penwith District Council* [1981] 2 All ER 204, extending the bar to inhibition of a statutory function. On the whole subject, see J A Andrews 29 MLR 1.

4 *Low v Bouverie* [1891] 3 Ch 82 at 105.

5 *Canadian and Dominion Sugar Co Ltd v Canadian National (West Indies) Steamships Ltd* [1947] AC 46 at 56.

6 [1947] KB 130, [1956] 1 All ER 256 n.

7 *Mercantile Bank of India Ltd v Central Bank of India Ltd* [1938] AC 287 at 297, [1938] 1 All ER 52 at 57.

8 *Gosling v Birnie* (1831) 7 Bing 399.

Nevertheless the principle of public policy according to which considerations of justice sometimes require that, even at the expense of truth, a person should be precluded, as against another, from denying or asserting a particular fact, can appropriately be described as one of the principles of the law of evidence.

Conversely, cause of action estoppel and issue estoppel have the effect of rules of evidence, but they do not belong to that branch of the law which, by definition, cannot tell us what are the issues in a given case. In the words of Lord Diplock:

> Whatever may be said about other rules of law to which the label of 'estoppel' is attached, 'estoppel' is not a rule of evidence. True, subject to the qualifications I have stated, it has the effect of preventing the party 'estopped' from calling evidence to show that the assertion which is the subject of the 'issue estoppel' is incorrect, but that is because the existence of the 'issue estoppel' results in there being no issue in the subsequent civil proceedings to which such evidence would be relevant. Issue estoppel is a particular application of the general rule of public policy that there should be finality in litigation.[9]

The general rule of public policy to which reference is made is at least better described as a rule of substantive law than as a rule of evidence, but why describe it as either?

SECTION 4. JUDICIAL FINDINGS AS EVIDENCE OF THE FACTS UPON WHICH THEY WERE BASED[10]

In order to appreciate the problem with which the section is mainly concerned, it is necessary to refer to two distinctions mentioned in the previous section—the distinction between a judgment and the facts upon which it was founded and the distinction between evidence and estoppel. Every judgment is conclusive as to the state of things it actually effects. If the question whether A is a convicted criminal should be in issue, A's conviction for crime is conclusive, even if he is a stranger to the proceedings in which the issue arises. No judgment is conclusive against all the world as to the facts which must have been proved before it could be pronounced. If A has been convicted of stealing a motor car, he is not precluded from denying his guilt in an action for conversion brought against him by the owner of the car, and the insurer of the car would not be precluded from denying it was stolen should this fact be relevant in proceedings brought against him by the assured. Parties and their privies are, however, estopped from denying the facts on which a judgment was founded when the same question is raised in subsequent proceedings between them. The problem with which this section is primarily concerned is whether and to what extent a judgment can be treated as evidence of the facts upon which it was founded when the proceedings in which this question is raised are between a party and a stranger, or two strangers. If A is convicted of murder or robbery and he

---

9 *Mills v Cooper* [1967] 2 QB 459 and 468. The qualifications related to the availability of new material.

10 The common law is fully discussed in Cowen and Carter *Essays on the Law of Evidence* Essay 6. There are valuable notes on *Hollington v Hewthorn & Co Ltd* in 59 LQR 299 and 21 Can B R 653. Reference may also be made to Coutts 'The Effect of a Criminal Judgment on a Civil Action' (1955) 18 MLR 331, and V *Wigmore* para 1671(a).

sues B for libel in describing him as a murderer or robber, would the conviction be admissible evidence in support of pleas of justification on B's part? If H obtains a divorce from W, involving a finding of her adultery with C, can Mrs C rely on this as evidence at the hearing of her petition for divorce alleging C's adultery with W? Before *Hollington v Hewthorn & Co Ltd*[11] was decided there was authority for an affirmative answer to each of these questions, but the bulk of the earlier case law favoured a negative response.[12]

In *Hollington v Hewthorn & Co Ltd*[13] the conviction of one of the defendants for careless driving was held to be inadmissible as evidence of his negligence in proceedings for damages on that ground against him and his employer. The main reason for the decision was that the conviction merely proved that another court, acting on evidence which was unknown to the tribunal trying the civil proceedings, was of opinion that the defendant was guilty of careless driving. The reception of the conviction as evidence of negligence would have infringed the hearsay as well as the opinion rule because it would have been treated as the equivalent of an assertion of negligence by a non-witness; but these points are indefensible technicalities.[14]

Rationalise it how one will, the decision in this case offends one's sense of justice. The defendant driver had been found guilty of careless driving by a court of competent jurisdiction. The onus of proof of culpability in criminal cases is higher than in civil; the degree of carelessness required to sustain a conviction of careless driving is, if anything, greater than that required to sustain a civil action for negligence. Yet the fact that the defendant driver had been convicted of careless driving at the same time and place of the accident was held not to amount to even prima facie evidence of his negligent driving at that time and place.

It is not easy to escape the implication in the rule in *Hollington v Hewthorn* that, in the estimation of lawyers, a conviction by a criminal court is as likely to be wrong as right.[15]

The rule in *Hollington v Hewthorn & Co Ltd* has now been overruled so far as it governs proof of convictions and findings of adultery and paternity in civil proceedings, by the Civil Evidence Act 1968,[16] and so far as it governs proof of convictions in criminal proceedings, by the Police and Criminal Evidence Act 1984.[17] Some statutes also make specific provision for the use of convictions, or other judicial findings, as evidence of their underlying facts.[18] These provisions will be discussed in the first two parts of this section.

11 [1943] KB 587, [1943] 2 All ER 35.
12 For an affirmative answer in the murder case see the judgment of Sir Samuel Evans P in *Re Crippen's Estate* [1911] P 108 at 115; for an affirmative answer in the divorce case see *Partington v Partington and Atkinson* [1925] P 34. The following were the principle authorities: *R v Warden of the Fleet* (1698) 12 Mod Rep 337 at 339; *Gibson v McCarty* (1736) Cas temp Hard 311; *Smith v Rummens* (1807) 1 Camp 9; *Blakemore v Glamorganshire Canal Co* (1835) 2 Cr M & R 133; *March v March* (1858) 2 Sw & Tr 49; *Leyman v Latimer* (1878) 3 ExD 352; *Yates v Kyffin-Taylor and Warl* [1899] WN 141.
13 [1943] KB 587, [1943] 2 All ER 35.
14 The *Hollington v Hewthorn & Co Ltd* rule originated in the days when interested witnesses, parties and their spouses were incompetent in civil proceedings and may have been based on the possibility that the conviction would have been obtained by evidence which was inadmissible in the subsequent civil proceedings.
15 15th Report of the Law Reform Committee, para 3.
16 Ss 11, 13 (as amended).
17 S 74.
18 See, for example, Company Directors Disqualification Act 1986, s 3.

The remaining parts will consider the status of evidence of acquittals, and of other findings.

A. THE CIVIL EVIDENCE ACT 1968, ss 11–13[19]

1. PREVIOUS CONVICTIONS IN SUBSEQUENT CIVIL PROCEEDINGS

Section 11 (1) of the Civil Evidence Act 1968, provides that:

> In any civil proceedings the fact that a person has been convicted of an offence by or before any court in the United Kingdom or by a court martial there or elsewhere shall . . . be admissible in evidence for the purpose of proving, where to do so is relevant to any issue in those proceedings, that he committed that offence . . . but no conviction other than a subsisting one[20] shall be admissible in evidence by virtue of this section.

Section 11(2) provides that:

> In any civil proceedings in which by virtue of this section a person is proved to have been convicted of an offence by or before any court in the United Kingdom or by a court martial there or elsewhere (a) he shall be taken to have committed that offence unless the contrary is proved; and (b) without prejudice to the reception of any other admissible evidence for the purpose of identifying the facts upon which the conviction was based, the contents of any document which is admissible as evidence of the conviction and the contents of the information, complaint, indictment or charge sheet on which the person in question was convicted shall be admissible in evidence for that purpose.

RSC Ord 18, r 7A requires a party to an action tried with pleadings who intends to rely on s 11 to state that intention in his pleading, to give particulars of the conviction and to indicate the issue to which it is relevant. On facts such as those of *Hollington v Hewthorn & Co Ltd* once the conviction has been proved, and the negligence in respect of which the driver was convicted identified, the court will be bound to find in favour of the plaintiff unless the driver or his employer disproves negligence on the balance of probabilities.[1]

Various observations have been made about the weight to be attached to the conviction in the subsequent civil proceedings in which it is proved. In *Wauchope v Mordecai*[2] the Court of Appeal did not suggest that the burden cast on the convicted defendant was a specially heavy one. In *Taylor v Taylor*,[3] on the other hand, it was said that the verdict of the jury finding the respondent to divorce proceedings guilty of incest was entitled to great weight, while Lord Denning MR and Buckley LJ took different views on this subject in *Stupple v Royal Insurance Co Ltd*.[4] In that case the plaintiff had

---

19 The provisions with regard to previous convictions must be read subject to the Rehabilitation of Offenders Act 1974 (p 315 below).
20 See *Re Raphael, Raphael v D'Antin* [1973] 3 All ER 19, [1973] 1 WLR 998. A conviction subject to appeal is subsisting but the civil court has power to adjourn the case pending the appeal.
1 *Stupple v Royal Insurance Co Ltd* [1971] 1 QB 50, [1970] 3 All ER 230.
2 [1970] 1 All ER 417, [1970] 1 WLR 317.
3 [1970] 2 All ER 609, [1970] 1 WLR 1148.
4 [1971] 1 QB 50, [1970] 3 All ER 230. See the note by Zuckerman (1971) 87 LQR 21.

been convicted of robbery from a bank which had been indemnified by the defendants. A sum of money found in the plaintiff's possession was paid over to the defendants under the Police (Property) Act 1897. The plaintiff claimed this sum and the defendants counterclaimed for the balance of their indemnity. The Court of Appeal upheld the judgment for the defendants. Lord Denning said:

> I think that the conviction does not merely shift the burden of proof. It is a weighty piece of evidence of itself. For instance, if a man is convicted of careless driving on the evidence of a witness, but that witness dies before the civil action is heard (as in *Hollington v Hewthorn & Co Ltd*) then the conviction itself tells in the scale in the civil action. It speaks as clearly as the witness would have done, had he lived. It does not merely reverse the burden of proof. If that was all it did, the defendant might well give his own evidence, negativing want of care and say: 'I have discharged the burden. I have given my evidence and it has not been contradicted.' In answer to the defendant's evidence the plaintiff can say: 'But your evidence is contradicted by the convictions.[5]

Buckley LJ said:

> In my judgment, proof of conviction under this section gives rise to the statutory presumption laid down in s 11(2)(a) which, like any other presumption, will give way to evidence establishing the contrary on the balance of probability without itself affording any evidential weight to be taken into account in determining whether that onus has been discharged.[6]

It is submitted that the approach of Buckley LJ is to be preferred. The assessment of the weight of the conviction would be an impossibly difficult task. As Buckley LJ pointed out, the propriety of the conviction is irrelevant in the civil action, the plaintiff would not discharge the onus cast upon him by s 11(2)(a) by proving that every witness who had given evidence against him at the criminal trial was guilty of perjury. He has to adduce sufficient evidence to satisfy the civil court that he was not negligent and, in spite of Lord Denning's suggestion to the contrary, his own testimony without more will generally not suffice.[7] The House of Lords has affirmed that the burden is the ordinary civil one, but nonetheless characterised as 'uphill' the task of a defendant[8] to persuade the court of the contrary of a verdict beyond reasonable doubt.[9]

As the conviction constitutes the basic fact of a presumption, it should be capable of corroborating other evidence where corroboration is required; it is stated by s 11(1) to be 'admissible in evidence for the purpose of proving that [the accused] committed the offence'. In *Mash v Darley*[10] a Divisional

---

5 At 72. If available, the transcript or proof of evidence of the deceased witness in the criminal case would be admissible under the Civil Evidence Act 1968.

6 At 76. This view was followed in *Wright v Wright* (1971) 115 Sol Jo 173. For an argument in support of Lord Denning based on the statutory wording see Phipson *Law of Evidence* (13th edn) para 28–95.

7 *Ludgate v Lovett* [1969] 2 All ER 1275, [1969] 1 WLR 1016 (negligent bailee); see also 15th Report of the Law Reform Committee, para 25.

8 The House regarded it as difficult to conceive of a plaintiff seeking to rely upon his own conviction. It is not however impossible, for example, if a salesman is dismissed for not visiting his sales area, he might want to put in evidence his conviction for a motoring offence in the area at the relevant time in a claim for unfair dismissal.

9 *Hunter v Chief Constable of West Midlands* [1982] AC 529 at 544, [1981] 3 All ER 727 at 735, 736.

10 [1914] 1 KB 1 affirmed on other grounds [1914] 3 KB 1226.

Court treated the respondent's conviction of unlawful intercourse with the applicant as corroboration of her evidence in affiliation proceedings. The decision could hardly have stood with *Hollington v Hewthorn & Co Ltd* but it may well have been resuscitated by the 1968 Act.

As long as convictions are not conclusive evidence of the guilt of the person convicted, it is possible for him to obtain a retrial of the issues raised in the criminal proceedings in a subsequent civil action by suing anyone implying that he was guilty of the offence for defamation. Even if the civil action were decided in his favour, the validity of the conviction would of course be unaffected. The Law Reform Committee took the view that, as a matter of substantive law, no-one ought to be at risk of incurring civil liability for stating that another was guilty of an offence of which he had been convicted; and conversely, no-one ought to be entitled, without incurring civil liability, to state that another person was guilty of an offence of which he had been acquitted.[11] The Committee therefore recommended that, in defamation actions, where the statement complained of alleges that the plaintiff has been guilty of a criminal offence, proof that he has been convicted of that offence should be conclusive evidence of his guilt, and proof that he was acquitted should be conclusive evidence of his innocence. The first, but not the second, of these recommendations was accepted. Section 13(1) of the Civil Evidence Act 1968 provides that:

> In an action for libel or slander in which the question whether a person did or did not commit a criminal offence is relevant to an issue arising in the action, proof that, at the time when the issue falls to be determined, that person stands convicted of that offence shall be conclusive evidence that he committed that offence.[12]

2. FINDINGS OF ADULTERY AND PATERNITY

Section 12(1) of the Civil Evidence Act 1968, as amended by s 29 of the Family Law Reform Act 1987, now provides that:

> In any civil proceedings—(a) the fact that a person has been found guilty of adultery in any matrimonial proceedings; and (b) the fact that a person has been found to be the father of a child in relevant proceedings before any court in England and Wales or has been adjudged to be the father of a child in affiliation proceedings before any court in the United Kingdom; shall ... be admissible in evidence for the purpose of proving, where to do so is relevant to any issue in those civil proceedings, that he committed the adultery to which the finding relates or, as the case may be, is (or was) the father of that child ....

Section 12(2), as also so amended, now provides that:

> In any civil proceeding in which by virtue of this section a person is proved to have been found of adultery as mentioned in subsection (1)(a) above, or to have been found or adjudged to be the father of a child as mentioned in subsection 1(b) above—(a) he shall be taken to have committed the adultery to which the finding

11 15th Report of the Law Reform Committee, paras 26–33.
12 On facts such as those of *Goody v Odhams Press Ltd* [1967] 1 QB 333, [1966] 3 All ER 369 in which one of those convicted of the great train robbery of 1963 claimed damages for a libel stating that he was guilty of the offence, the statement of claim, if it said no more, would be struck out.

relates, or, as the case may be, to be (or have been) the father of that child, unless the contrary is proved[13] . . . .

'Matrimonial proceedings' means, for the purposes of s 12(5)(a), 'Any matrimonial cause in the High Court or a county court in England or Wales, or in the High Court in Northern Ireland, any consistorial action in Scotland, or any appeal arising out of such cause or action', while 'relevant proceedings' for the purposes of s 12(2)(b) has been defined in an expanded form by s 29(4) of the Family Law Reform Act 1987 to include any public proceedings involving an adjudication of paternity.[14]

B. PREVIOUS CONVICTIONS IN CRIMINAL CASES[15]

Although there was very little authority on the point, it seems that the principle of *Hollington v Hewthorn & Co Ltd* applied to criminal cases.[16] For example, the conviction of a principal was inadmissible as evidence of the commission of the main crime at the trial of an accessory,[17] and the conviction of the thief was inadmissible as evidence that the goods received were stolen at the trial of the handler.[18] One of the oldest justifications of the principle we have been considering applied in such cases for it would have been possible for the principal or thief to have been convicted on evidence which was inadmissible against the accessory or handler, such as evidence of their spouses. The matter was put beyond doubt by the enactment of s 74 of the Police and Criminal Evidence Act 1984 which largely followed the recommendation of the 11th report of the Criminal Law Revision Committee.[19] It provides that:

> (1) In any proceedings the fact that a person other than the accused has been convicted of an offence by or before any court in the United Kingdom or by a Service court outside the United Kingdom shall be admissible in evidence for the purpose of proving, where to do so is relevant to any issue in those proceedings, that that person committed that offence, whether or not any other evidence of his having committed that offence is given.
> (2) In any proceedings in which by virtue of this section a person other than the accused is proved to have been convicted of an offence by or before any court in the United Kingdom or by a Service court outside the United Kingdom, he shall be taken to have committed that offence unless the contrary is proved.
> (3) In any proceedings where evidence is admissible of the fact that the accused has committed an offence, in so far as that evidence is relevant to any matter in issue in the proceedings for a reason other than a tendency to show in the accused a disposition to commit the kind of offence with which he is charged, if the accused is proved to have been convicted of the offence:
> (a) by or before any court in the United Kingdom; or
> (b) by a Service court outside the United Kingdom,
> he shall be taken to have committed that offence unless the contrary is proved.

13 On the balance of probabilities, *Sutton v Sutton* [1969] 3 All ER 1348 at 1352.
14 S 12(5).
15 See Munday 'Proof of Guilt by Association under Section 74 of the Police and Criminal Evidence Act 1984' [1990] Crim LR 236.
16 *R v Shepherd* (1980) 71 Cr App Rep 120.
17 *R v Xaki* 1950(4) SA 332.
18 *R v Turner* (1832) 1 Mood CC 347; *R v Lee* 1952(2) SA 67; see also *Taylor v Wilson* (1911) 76 JP 69 and *R v Hassan* [1970] 1 QB 423 at 426.
19 Cmnd 4991.

The proceedings referred to are defined as criminal proceedings.[20] It was necessary to depart slightly from the form of the draft bill in the 11th Committee's report because their recommendation of statutory reform of the similar facts rule was not implemented. It was perhaps somewhat surprising to find this section enacted in its current form in view of the failure to implement the Criminal Law Revision Committee's proposals for a radical revision of the hearsay rule in criminal cases, and especially in view of the withdrawal from the section dealing with confessions[21] of a provision making the out-of-court statements of one co-accused evidence against the other, and the disavowal of any intention to change the law in that respect.[1] The result has been to create some judicial disquiet. It first surfaced in *R v O'Connor*[2] where the conviction of another for the very conspiracy charged against the accused was adduced in evidence. The other conspirator had first admitted conspiring with the accused, and had then pleaded guilty to that charge. No other person was alleged to have been involved. Since the other conspirator was not called to give evidence for either prosecution or defence the accused was put in the difficult position of having damning evidence against him, based upon the statements of a third party, without being able to cross-examine that third party. These are the very dangers which the hearsay rule is designed to avert. So uneasy was the court that it invoked its discretionary powers under s 78 of the Police and Criminal Evidence Act 1984 to exclude on the basis of the adverse effect of the evidence upon the fairness of the proceedings.[3] Exactly the same approach has been taken to a co-defendant's plea of guilty to a charge of gross indecency with the accused, in respect of a charge, not of conspiracy, but of gross indecency with the co-defendant.[4] If the conviction relates to a conspiracy to which there were alleged to have been other parties, the court has felt more ready to admit the evidence of the conviction.[5] There has however remained a residue of unease, and in *Robertson* itself the court urged that s 74 should be used sparingly.[6] This has led in part to the development of a rather restricted view of what a conviction admitted under s 74 can be used to prove,[7] a view which finds little support in the terminology of s 75. It has further been held that the trial judge must be meticulous in his direction to the jury of precisely what use it is permitted to make of a conviction proved under s 74.[8] Some technicality also seems to be creeping in so as to permit the use of convictions in cases other than conspiracy, provided only that the guilt of the accused does not follow as a logical necessity from the establishment of the facts underlying the admitted conviction,[9] and that there is some other evidence supporting any inference of guilt which might be drawn.[10]

---

20 S 82(1).
21 S 76 of the Act as passed; the relevant provision was cl 69(5) of the Bill as introduced.
1 See the Lord Chancellor in 1262 H of L Official Report (5th series) col 705.
2 (1986) 85 Cr Ap Rep 298.
3 Though on the facts the court was then able to apply the proviso so as to uphold the conviction.
4 *R v Mattison* [1989] NLJ Rep 1417. In this case the court felt unable to apply the proviso.
5 *R v Robertson R v Golder* [1987] QB 920, [1987] 3 All ER 231; *R v Lunnon* (1988) 88 Cr App Rep 71.
6 At 928, 237.
7 See *R v Lunnon* above, and *R v Curry* [1988] Crim LR 527.
8 *R v Kempster* [1989] Crim LR 747.
9 See *R v Bennett* [1988] Crim LR 686.
10 *R v Kempster*, above.

Two more technical questions which have been resolved in these cases are that the 'matters in issue' to which reference is made extend beyond essential ingredients of the crime charged to more evidential issues,[11] and are by no means restricted to cases where the conviction relates to offences in which the accused played no part at all; and that reference to a 'conviction' applies to situations in which the third party has been found guilty, but has yet to be sentenced.[12]

It is unsatisfactory to have a situation in which the instincts of the judiciary so conflict with the clear terminology of the relevant provision, that resort is made to restriction by way of technicality, and to amelioration by way of discretion. It is to be hoped that an opportunity may be taken to reconsider the anomaly between the generally restricted ambit of hearsay in criminal proceedings against the interests of the accused, and its implicit admission by way of proof of the convictions of third parties.

C. ACQUITTALS

So far as the previous acquittal of a party is concerned, it may, of course, be proved when it is a fact in issue as would be the case in an action for malicious prosecution, but there is a variety of reasons why it should not be admitted as evidence of innocence in subsequent civil proceedings. Chief amongst these is the fact that the standard of proof is different, so that an acquittal means only that the case against the accused has not been proved beyond reasonable doubt. In *Packer v Clayton*[13] there are some observations of Avory J in a Divisional Court to the effect that, in affiliation proceedings, the acquittal of the respondent on a charge of a sexual offence against the complainant was something that could have been taken into account by the justices as showing that the girl's evidence did not convince the jury,[14] but it is doubtful whether this could be said to be so after *Hollington v Hewthorn & Co Ltd*.[15]

D. OTHER FINDINGS

1. JUDICIAL FINDINGS

Hollington v Hewthorn & Co Ltd could probably be cited as authority for the proposition that all judicial findings are inadmissible as evidence of the facts found in subsequent proceedings which are not between the same parties or their privies. From this it follows that judicial findings in cases falling outside ss 11–13 of the Civil Evidence Act 1968, are still, subject to other statutory

11 *R v Robertson*, above, at 927, 236; *R v Grey* (1988) 88 Cr App Rep 375; *R v Castle* [1989] Crim LR 567.
12 *R v Golder*, above, at 931, 240.
13 (1932) 97 JP 14; the opposite view was taken in *O'Donnell v Hegarty* [1941] IR 538. See further *Helsham v Blackwood* (1851) 11 CB 111; *Helton v Allen* (1940) 63 CLR 691; *Re Emele* [1941] 4 DLR 197; *Lingor v Lingor* [1955] 1 DLR 719.
14 This reasoning has been rejected as of general application in criminal cases, see *R v Doosti* (1985) 82 Cr App Rep 181; *R v Henri* [1990] Crim LR 51, and above p 88.
15 See *S & Y Investments (No 2) Pty Ltd v Commercial Union Assurance Co of Australia Ltd* (1986) 82 FLR 130 for refusal to apply *Hollington v Hewthorn & Co Ltd* to an acquittal in Australia.

provisions,[16] no evidence of the facts found. For example in an action for damages for negligence brought by a passenger injured in a bus accident, a finding of negligence in an earlier action brought by another passenger in respect of the same accident would be inadmissible. It was also argued in *McIlkenny v Chief Constable of West Midlands*[17] that an issue determined on the voir dire remains governed by the rule in *Hollington v Hewthorn & Co*, since the relaxation in s 11 of the Civil Evidence Act 1968 is restricted to the use of convictions as evidence of the commission of the offences charged. A number of answers to this problem were propounded. Lord Denning MR was prepared to disregard *Hollington v Hewthorn & Co* as having been wrongly decided.[18] Goff LJ and the House of Lords were able to avoid a direct decision on this point. Goff LJ clearly thought the voir dire outside the provisions of the statute.[19] The view of the House of Lords is less clear. It seems to have regarded the decision on the voir dire as so vital on the facts to the ultimate decision of guilt[20] that evidence of the conviction amounted to evidence of the factual basis of that holding under the terms of s 11.[1] Sir George Baker, the only judge to have addressed the question in any detail, held that the rule in *Hollington v Hewthorn & Co* did not apply to such holdings because they were never expressly considered, and fell outside the policy of the rule, being readily identifiable issues, the subject of public reasoning by the judge, and determined according to the criminal standard of proof.[2] In a case where a confession is not the only basis upon which the accused could have been convicted, a court may have to choose between these views, and that choice will indirectly determine the question of whether findings in civil proceedings are admissible as evidence of the factual basis of the finding in subsequent civil proceedings between different parties, unless that question has by then been decided directly. Evidence of findings in other jurisdictions remains subject to the rule in *Hollington v Hewthorn Ltd*, and is, as such, inadmissible as evidence of the underlying facts.[3]

2. INQUISITIONS

As a result of Part 1 of the Civil Evidence Act 1968 hearsay can be admitted in civil proceedings only by virtue of that Act, by statute or by agreement of the parties. It has been stated that the rule in *Hollington v Hewthorn & Co* still

16 See Phipson *Law of Evidence* (13th edn) para 28–93 n 27. S 33(2) of the Medical Act 1956 is repealed by the Medical Act 1978.
17 [1980] QB 283, [1980] 2 All ER 227, and on appeal as *Hunter v Chief Constable of West Midlands* [1982] AC 529, [1981] 3 All ER 727.
18 At 319, 237. A view shared in Western Australia, see *Mickelberg v Director of Perth Mint* [1986] WAR 365.
19 At 325, 241.
20 Cp *R v Vuckov and Romeo* (1986) 40 SASR 498 where an evidential issue arising on the voir dire was held to be sufficiently close to the issue of guilt to justify cross-examination under the local equivalent to s 1(f)(i) of the Criminal Evidence Act 1898.
1   At 542, 731, though it is also said at 543, 734 that *Hollington v Hewthorn & Co* is generally considered to have been wrongly decided which seems more consonant with Lord Denning's view.
2   At 342, 255.
3   *Union Carbide Corpn v Naturin Ltd* [1987] FSR 538.

applies to exclude from evidence the contents of reports of inspectors,[4] though in appropriate cases s 9(2)(d) could be relied upon to support the evidence mentioned by Phipson's *Law of Evidence*:[5]

> Inquisitions, surveys, assessments, reports and returns are admissible, but not generally conclusive, in proof of their contents when made under public authority, and in relation to matters of public interest or concern.

This common law exception to the combined operation of the hearsay and opinion rules covers a heterogeneous mass of cases ranging from extracts from Domesday book to a return by a bishop to a writ from the Exchequer directing him to ascertain the vacancies and advowsons in his diocese.[6] It was once thought that the verdict of a coroner's jury could be received under this head as evidence of the cause of a death, but it is now settled that that is not the case owing partly to the essentially preliminary nature of the enquiry, and partly to the unlikelihood of the coroner's attention being drawn to some points that might be of interest in the proceedings in which it was sought to adduce his return.[7] It is, however, settled that the old inquisitions and former master's orders in lunacy are admissible, though not conclusive, evidence of the unsoundness of mind of the person to whom they refer.[8] In *Hill v Clifford*[9] the Court of Appeal adopted this analogy with regard to a finding of the General Medical Council that a dentist had been guilty of professional misconduct. The majority of the Court was prepared to treat it as evidence in subsequent proceedings for the dissolution of the dentist's partnership. *Hill v Clifford* was not cited in *Hollington v Hewthorn & Co Ltd* but the cases can perhaps be distinguished because, being charged with the duty of inquiry, the General Medical Council fulfils a different function from that of a judge.

The combined operation of the hearsay and opinion rules would appear to exclude the fact that someone got a first in law on the issue whether he was a competent academic lawyer in for example, a libel action. The absurdity of this result may lead some to doubt the soundness of the principles enunciated by Parke B in *Wright v Doe d Tatham*,[10] a subject to which it will be necessary to refer again in ch XIV.

---

4 Peter Gibson J in *Savings and Investment Bank Ltd v Gasco Investments (Netherlands) BV* [1984] 1 All ER 296 at 303. And in New Zealand the report of a departmental inquiry, *R v Stephens* [1987] 1 NZLR 476.
5 Phipson (13th edn) p 528.
6 *Irish Society v Bishop of Derry* (1846) 12 Cl & Fin 641.
7 *Bird v Keep* [1918] 2 KB 692; *Calmenson v Merchants Warehousing Co Ltd* (1921) 90 LJPC 134; *Barnett v Cohen* [1921] 2 KB 461.
8 *Faulder v Silk* (1811) 3 Camp 126; *Harvey v R* [1901] AC 601.
9 [1907] 2 Ch 236.
10 See p 531 below.

CHAPTER III

Burden of proof

When an issue of fact has to be proved in a court of law it is first necessary to consider the burden of proof. The allocation of the burden helps to determine which party should begin calling evidence, a procedural matter to be discussed further in ch VII, and by extension how to decide upon a submission that there is no case to answer.

The nature of the burden of proof is obscured by the use of the term in a number of different senses which are distinguished and discussed in the first section of this chapter. The two principal senses are the burden of adducing evidence and the burden of proving facts. In relation to both, questions arise as to the incidence of the burden, and the discharge of the burden. The second section considers the allocation of the burden in these two senses, at common law and under statutory provisions, and how it is affected by presumptions of the law or by agreement of the parties. The third section of the chapter, dealing with the discharge of the two burdens, is principally concerned with the extent of those burdens, and with the way in which the burden of proof has to be explained to the jury.

The key to clarity in this whole area lies in the precise definition and discrimination of the issues to be tried, and of the facts upon the determination of which they depend. Unfortunately this is hindered by the absence of formal pleadings or pre-trial proceedings in criminal cases, and more generally by the lack of an agreed terminology. These factors have led to some confusion in the authorities, for example on such issues of whether burdens of proof can shift, and as to the precise effect of presumptions.

SECTION 1. NATURE OF THE BURDEN OF PROOF

Writing at the end of the nineteenth century, the American scholar J B Thayer claimed that the phrase 'burden of proof' is used in more than one sense. It is only necessary to discuss two of the three senses he mentioned because the third was said to be 'an indiscriminated use of the phrase, perhaps more common than either of the other two, in which it may mean either or both of the others.'[1]

Thayer's first sense of the term was:

> The peculiar duty of him who has the risk of any given proposition on which parties are at issue—who will lose the case if he does not make this proposition out, when all has been said and done.

This nearly corresponds to the legal burden, or burden of proof in the strict sense, which is discussed below. The correspondence is not complete

---

1 *Preliminary Treatise on Evidence at the Common Law* 355.

because no allowance is made in the passage quoted for the fact that the burden in question is confined to particular issues.[2] Most cases involve more than one issue, and the burden of proof upon the different issues may be variously distributed between the parties—a fact which can be readily appreciated by considering a claim in contract in which the terms of the agreement are in dispute and infancy is pleaded as a defence, a claim for damages for negligence in which the defendant raises the issue of contributory negligence, or a criminal charge on which insanity is pleaded. Owing to the possible multiplicity of issues, a party may have 'the risk' of a given proposition and yet not lose the case if he fails to make the proposition out; an example would be a claim in contract in which the defendant pleads both infancy and duress; the defendant bears the burden of proof on each of these issues, but failure on one of them does not entail the loss of the case.

Thayer's second sense of the phrase 'burden of proof' was:

The duty of going forward in argument or in producing evidence, whether at the beginning of a case, or at any later moment throughout the trial or discussion.[3]

This corresponds in part to the evidential burden discussed below, but it is a much broader concept because, in addition to embracing argument as well as the adduction of evidence, it covers not merely the obligation placed on a party by the law to be able to point to the existence of sufficient evidence to raise an issue before the tribunal of fact, but also the tactical obligation to lead counter-evidence placed upon a party against whom evidence has been adduced. To anticipate, Thayer's second sense of the term 'burden of proof' conflates the evidential burden with what is sometimes called a 'provisional' or 'tactical' burden.

Just because Thayer failed to distinguish between the strict senses of the legal and evidential burden as described below, and the burdens which arise as between different issues, or as a matter of tactics in the course of a trial, his successors, both in extra-judicial writings,[4] and in judicial opinions,[5] have had to refine his terminology. These refinements have not been uniform, and

2 Though surprisingly little attention is bestowed upon the critical matter of the precise discrimination of issues.
3 *Preliminary Treatise on Evidence at the Common Law* 355.
4 In addition to Thayer ch 9, reference should be made to IX *Wigmore* paras 2485–9; Stone (1944) 60 LQR 262, a commentary on *Joseph Constantine SS Line Ltd v Imperial Smelting Corpn Ltd* [1942] AC 154, [1941] 2 All ER 165 HL; Lord Denning 'Presumptions and Burdens' (1945) 61 LQR 379; Lord Bridge 'Presumptions and Burdens' (1949) 12 MLR 273, a reply to Lord Denning; Glanville Williams *Criminal Law, The General Part* (2nd edn 1961) ch 23; Sir Francis Adams 'Onus of Proof in Criminal Cases' in Clark (ed) *Essays on Criminal Law in New Zealand* (1971); Williams 'Placing the Burden of Proof' in Waller and Campbell (eds) *Well and Truly Tried* (1982).
5 Lord Denning has frequently used his own terminology, e g *Bratty v A-G for Northern Ireland* [1963] AC 386 at 413, [1961] 3 All ER 523 at 535. Professor Glanville Williams's distinction between the persuasive and evidential burdens was adopted in the judgment of the Court of Criminal Appeal delivered by Edmund Davies J in *R v Gill* [1963] 2 All ER 688, [1963] 1 WLR 841, and in *Henderson v Jenkins & Sons and Evans* [1970] AC 282 at 301, [1969] 3 All ER 756 at 766, Lord Pearson distinguished the 'evidential burden of proof' from the 'formal, or legal or technical burden of proof'; but he spoke of the evidential burden in terms of Lord Denning's provisional burden and doubted the propriety of calling it a burden of proof. The terminology of probative and evidential burden, having been used in the Court of Appeal by Bridge J, was repeated without question by the House of Lords in *DPP v Morgan* [1976] AC 182, [1975] 2 All ER 347. The distinction between the two principal burdens is frequently mentioned by Australian, Canadian and American judges.

have contributed substantially to the confusion over the question of whether burdens can shift, exacerbated by parallel problems over the role and terminology of presumptions. This section will first consider burdens in the strict sense, the other candidates for that terminology will then be considered in connection with the whole question of the shifting of burdens in the third part of this section.

A. THE TWO PRINCIPAL SENSES OF BURDEN

1. LEGAL BURDEN

The legal burden of proof is the obligation of a party to meet the requirement of a rule of law that a fact in issue be proved (or disproved) either by a preponderance of the evidence or beyond reasonable doubt as the case may be. The words in brackets are intended to cover the case in which a party has to negative a particular fact as the prosecutrix has to negative consent on a charge of rape. The words are also apt to cover a case in which a party has to negative a particular fact if his opponent adduces sufficient evidence of its existence. An example would be provided by a murder trial at which self-defence is pleaded; if there is sufficient evidence to raise a reasonable doubt in the minds of a reasonable jury, it is incumbent on the prosecution to prove beyond reasonable doubt that the accused was not acting in self-defence.

The phrase 'legal burden' is that of Lord Denning and it is justified by the fact that its incidence is determined by the substantive law. Other English writers refer to it as 'the burden of proof on the pleadings'[6] or 'the fixed burden of proof';[7] but the pleadings do not always indicate which party bears the burden, and the second principal burden, 'the evidential burden', also has claims to be described as 'fixed'. Wigmore spoke of the 'risk of non-persuasion' but this, like Professor Glanville Williams's 'persuasive burden', is open to the objection that both parties may bear such a risk on the same issue; for instance, when self-defence is pleaded on a charge of murder, the accused runs the risk of failing to induce a reasonable doubt in the minds of the jury although, provided the accused adduces sufficient evidence of self-defence, it is ultimately incumbent on the prosecution to negative the plea. Some recent judgments in which the distinction between the principal burdens is mentioned simply refer to this one as the 'burden of proof'[8] or the 'probative burden',[9] and such a course may be justified by the fact that the discharge of the other principal burden, the evidential burden, proves nothing.[10]

In a civil case where at the end of the day the evidence upon an issue is found to be too evenly balanced to determine the matter one way or the

---

6 Phipson *Law of Evidence* (13th edn).
7 Bridge 12 MLR 274.
8 Devlin J in *Hill v Baxter* [1958] 1 QB 277 at 284; *Bratty v A-G for Northern Ireland* [1963] AC 386 at 407, 414, [1961] 3 All ER 523 at 530.
9 *D P P v Morgan* [1976] AC 182, [1975] 2 All ER 347; *R v Bennett* (1978) 68 Cr App Rep 168.
10 *Jayasena v R* [1970] 1 All ER 219.

other, then the issue must be determined by the incidence of the legal burden of proof, as the House of Lords has recognised:[11]

No judge likes to decide cases on burden of proof if he can legitimately avoid having to do so. There are cases, however, on which owing to the unsatisfactory state of the evidence, or otherwise, deciding on the burden of proof is the only just cause for him to take.

2. EVIDENTIAL BURDEN

The evidential burden is the obligation to show, if called upon to do so, that there is sufficient evidence to raise an issue as to the existence or non-existence of a fact in issue, due regard being had to the standard of proof demanded of the party under such obligation. The concluding clause is designed to meet the point that the amount of evidence required to induce a judge to leave an issue to the jury varies according to whether the case is civil or criminal, and whether the party bearing the burden is plaintiff, prosecutor, defendant or accused.

The phrase 'evidential burden' is employed by Mr (now Lord) Bridge and Professor Glanville Williams (while Phipson spoke with equal accuracy of the 'burden of adducing evidence'[12]) a phrase which is coming to be increasingly used by the English judges.[13] Wigmore described it as the duty 'of passing the judge', and there is no doubt that the difference between the two principal burdens is best approached by considering the position of a plaintiff or prosecutor with regard to such issues which are about to be tried with a jury as defamation, or the doing of a criminal act by the accused. He has two hurdles to surmount. First, he must produce a sufficient quantity of evidence to prevent the judge from withdrawing the issue from the jury, and secondly he must convince that body. If he surmounts the first, he may yet fail at the second. This may be because the jury do not believe his witnesses, or will not draw the necessary inferences, or else because of the doubt raised by the counter-evidence. To quote Wigmore:[14]

The important practical distinction between these two senses of 'burden of proof' is this: the risk of non-persuasion operates when the case has come into the hands of the jury, while the duty of producing evidence implies a liability to a ruling by the judge disposing of the issue without leaving the issue open to the jury's deliberations.

Two further points must be stressed in connection with the definition of the evidential burden. In the first place, it caters for the abnormal situation where the party who starts with the legal burden of proof does not also bear the evidential burden, as well as for the normal situation where they are each borne by the same person in the first instance. To vary an illustration which has already been given with reference to self-defence, on a prosecution

---

11 *Rhesa Shipping Co SA v Edmunds* [1985] 2 All ER 712 at 718, [1985] 1 WLR 948 at 955, 956; see also *Morris v London Iron and Steel Co Ltd* [1987] QB 493 at 504, [1987] 2 All ER 496 at 503.
12 Phipson *Law of Evidence* (13th edn).
13 LEXIS reveals that the phrase has been used in more than one hundred and twenty-five cases since 1945.
14 IX *Wigmore* 284.

for murder, for example, the Crown has the legal burden of negativing provocation, but questions of provocation do not have to be considered by the jury unless there is evidence on the subject, and it is up to the accused to produce this evidence, although he has to raise only a reasonable doubt in the minds of the jury as to whether his conduct was provoked or unprovoked.[15] Secondly, it must not be supposed that the production of evidence always involves the giving of testimony. This will be necessary in the vast majority of cases in which an evidential burden has to be discharged, but there are rare instances in which the evidence called on the other side is sufficiently equivocal to have this effect.[16] On a prosecution for murder, the Crown witnesses might say enough in-chief about the provocation to make the judge feel obliged to raise the question in his summing up, although the matter will usually be brought before the court in consequence of the cross-examination of the Crown witnesses, reinforced by the accused's evidence-in-chief. It is also possible that evidence may be sufficient to raise a defence which the accused does not wish to advance. In such a case it should not be left to the jury.[17]

3. ILLUSTRATIONS OF CONFUSION

Two major sources of confusion in this part of the law are: first, failure to agree upon the discrimination of separate issues to which the rules are to apply; and second, failure to distinguish explicitly between the legal and evidential burden. One example will be given of each.

In *D P P v Morgan*[18] the accused were charged with rape. Their defence was that the victim consented, or at least that they believed her to be consenting. The trial judge directed the jury that it was for the prosecution to show that the act took place and to negative consent, but, in effect, that it was then for the accused to adduce some evidence to show that his belief in the victim's consent was reasonable. This view was upheld by the Court of Appeal where Bridge J distinguished between cases where the definition of the offence specified a particular mental state in which case the prosecution bore both legal and evidential burdens of showing it, and cases where there was no such definition in which case the issue of reasonable belief arose as a separate issue, the evidential burden of establishing which was on the accused. The House of Lords accepted Bridge J's analysis, but allowed the appeal because, by a majority, it took the view that in rape there was only one issue as to the accused's mental state, and as to that the prosecution bore both burdens. The whole difficulty arose simply because it was uncertain whether in relation to the accused's mens rea there was one issue, or two.

In *Woolmington v D P P*[19] the accused was charged with murdering his wife from whom he was separated, and he gave evidence to the effect that he had shot and killed her accidentally while endeavouring to induce her to return

---

15 *Mancini v D P P* [1942] AC 1, [1941] 3 All ER 272. See also *R v Lobell* [1957] 1 QB 547, [1957] 1 All ER 734 applying the same doctrine to self-defence; *Bullard v R* [1957] AC 635 at 642; *Rolle v R* [1965] 3 All ER 582, [1965] 1 WLR 1341.
16 See *Palmer v R* [1971] AC 814 at 823, [1971] 1 All ER 1077 at 1088.
17 *R v Campbell* (1986) 84 Cr App Rep 255.
18 [1976] AC 182, [1975] 2 All ER 347.
19 [1935] AC 462.

to live with him by threatening to shoot himself. Swift J's summing up to the jury contained the following passage:

> If the Crown satisfy you that this woman died at the prisoner's hands, then he has to show that there are circumstances to be found in the evidence which has been given from the witness box in this case which alleviate the crime, so that it is only manslaughter, or which excuse the homicide altogether by showing that it was a pure accident.

Woolmington was convicted, but his appeal was allowed when it reached the House of Lords because the jury had been misdirected.

The actual decision turned on the point that Swift J's direction suggested that, the killing having been admitted, the legal burden of disproving malice aforethought shifted to the accused, but Lord Sankey's speech in the House of Lords also shows that, even in cases in which the defence consists of something other than a denial of an essential element of the prosecution's case, a plea of provocation or self-defence for instance, the accused does not, as was formerly believed, bear a legal as well as an evidential burden. The speech can be regarded either as marking a change in the law[20] or as an insistence on the distinction, ignored by the old authorities, between the legal and evidential burdens.[1] Whichever be the correct view, there is no doubt that a number of appeals have been decided on the point that the judge wrongly instructed the jury that the accused bore the burden of proof on a particular issue whereas all that was borne by him was an evidential burden, a matter with which the jury has no concern.[2]

B. OTHER SENSES AND SHIFTING OF BURDEN

The definitions of the two principal senses of burden adopted above in this book render it difficult to speak meaningfully of the shifting of either of them. The evidential burden has been defined as the obligation to show, if called upon to do so, that there is sufficient evidence to raise an issue as to the existence or non-existence of a fact in issue. The legal burden, 'burden of proof', 'probative' or 'persuasive' burden has been defined as the obligation of a party to meet the requirement of a rule of law that a fact in issue must be proved or disproved. The question whether there is sufficient evidence to raise the issue of the existence of a particular fact can be answered only after both parties have called their evidence and, when there is a jury, the answer must be given by them after they have been instructed by the judge. Writing with reference to a criminal trial with a jury Professor Glanville Williams has said:

> [T]he evidential burden governs what the judge *does* in leaving the question to the jury or withdrawing it from them, the persuasive burden governs what he *says* in directing the jury how to reach their verdict.[3]

20 *Jayasena v R* [1970] AC 618 at 625.
1 Sir Francis Adams in Clark (ed) *Essays in New Zealand Criminal Law* 70–1.
2 *Chan Kau v R* [1955] AC 206, [1955] 1 All ER 266; *R v Lobell* [1957] 1 QB 547, [1957] 1 All ER 734; *R v Gill* [1963] 2 All ER 688; *R v Wheeler* [1967] 3 All ER 829; *R v Bone* [1968] 2 All ER 644; *R v Moon* [1969] 3 All ER 803; *R v Abraham* [1973] 3 All ER 694, [1973] 1 WLR 1270.
3 127 NLJ 156.

The concept of the evidential burden is the product of trial by jury and the possibility of withdrawing an issue from that body. Unlike the concept of the legal burden it is not a logical necessity of litigation about questions of fact; 'If it were to be said of any issue, that it was not covered by an evidential burden, the only effect would be to remove the judge's filtering power in respect of that issue.'[4] It is accordingly difficult not to sympathise with Browne-Wilkinson V-C who preferred the expression not to be used in civil proceedings since it was so apt to be applied to the provisional burden as defined and described below.[5]

It is true that, when dissenting in *D P P v Morgan*,[6] Lord Simon of Glaisdale spoke of the shifting of the evidential burden 'backwards and forwards in the course of a trial', but he was attempting to justify the view of the Court of Appeal that, as a matter of law, someone charged with rape bears the evidential burden on the issue of his mistaken belief that the woman was consenting to intercourse.[7] The decision turned on the substantive law, but, so far as the evidential burden was concerned, the majority of the House of Lords appears to have accepted the argument of counsel for the appellant summarised as follows by Lord Cross of Chelsea:

> If [the Crown] adduces evidence to show that intercourse took place and that the woman did not consent to it then in the absence of any evidence from the defendant the jury will certainly draw the inference that he was aware that she was not consenting. So as a practical matter he is bound—if he wishes to raise the point—to give evidence to the effect that he believed that she was consenting and as to his reason for that belief; and the weaker those reasons are the more likely the jury is to conclude that he had no such belief. But the issue as to the accused's belief in the woman's consent is before the jury from the beginning,[8] and is an issue in respect of which the evidential burden is on the Crown from the first to last. There is never any question of any evidential burden with regard to it being on the accused or of the judge withdrawing it from the jury.[9]

It remains to be seen what judges, and others, really have in mind when they refer to the shifting of a burden.[10] Three possibilities are worthy of consideration. The first is that the concept of a burden has been attenuated to refer only to the provisional or tactical desirability of adducing evidence in order to avoid an adverse decision of the issue by the trier of fact. The second is that the concept of a burden has been expanded to apply outside

4 127 NLJ 156 at 158.
5 *Brady v Group Lotus Car Companies plc* [1987] 2 All ER 674 at 686, 687, approved by the Court of Appeal [1987] 3 All ER 1050 at 1056.
6 [1976] AC 182 at 217. See also *Dunlop Holding Ltd's Application* [1979] RPC 523, where Buckley and Bridge LJJ take a similar view, though Waller LJ analyses the situation entirely in terms of the distribution of legal and evidential burdens.
7 Even if that were law it would not have justified the trial judge's action in leaving to the jury the question whether the accused had reasonable grounds for their belief, although it might have justified the withdrawal of the issue of the accused's belief from the jury on the ground of insufficiency of supporting evidence.
8 The definition of rape being unlawful sexual intercourse with a non-consenting woman knowing that she does not consent or being reckless as to whether she does so.
9 [1976] AC 182 at 200. S 1(2) of the Sexual Offences (Amendment) Act 1976 declares that the presence or absence of reasonable grounds for an alleged belief in the woman's consent is a factor to be taken into account by the jury in conjunction with any other relevant evidence when considering whether the accused had such a belief.
10 For a judge's own explanation see Mustill LJ in *Brady v Group Lotus Car Companies plc* [1987] 3 All ER 1050 at 1058.

the confines of a single issue, and to refer instead to the fluctuation of fortunes in a multiple issue case, considering the cumulative effect of the sequential resolution of each successive issue. The third uses burden in the sense so far discussed, but directs attention to cases where the allocation of one of the burdens is made conditional upon the proof of some other fact. The first two of these are considered in turn here, and the third in the next section in relation to the allocation of the burden of proof.

1. THE PROVISIONAL BURDEN

A provisional burden is one which is borne by the opponent of an issue after the proponent has discharged his evidential burden. The opponent must, in the words of Lord Denning, 'call evidence or take the consequences which may not necessarily be fatal'.[11] An example is provided by any criminal case in which the prosecution relies on the actus reus as evidence of mens rea. By not calling evidence on the subject the accused runs the risk of an adverse finding with regard to his mental state if the jury accepts the Crown's version of his external conduct. The degree of risk run by an opponent who does not adduce evidence on a particular issue varies from case to case. In civil proceedings the proponent's evidence may be so weighty that a verdict or decision in his favour will be demanded by common sense and a judge would be justified in directing a jury or himself accordingly.[12] In criminal cases tried with a jury[13] the situation is complicated by the rule that there cannot be a directed verdict of guilty, but judges sometimes allude to a shifting of the burden of proof on account of the strength of the evidence adduced by the accused on issues as to which he bears the evidential and legal burdens.[14]

Lord Denning even speaks of the provisional burden shifting to and fro in the course of a case.[15] No doubt judges often have something of this sort in mind when they refer to a shifting of the burden of proof, but the concept of a provisional burden (sometimes called a 'tactical burden') is devoid of legal significance because there is no means of telling when it has been brought into existence or when it has been discharged. It is evidential in the sense that it entails the calling of evidence but, by definition, it is non-existent at the beginning of a case when judicial ruling with regard to burdens may be obtained. Such a ruling may likewise be obtained at the end of a proponent's case if the judge is required to decide whether enough evidence to raise a particular issue has been adduced, but, in the first instance at any rate, a provisional burden is borne by the opponent. There can be no further ruling on burdens until the end of the case when the legal burden is the all important matter.

If a fact in issue may be inferred from the proof of another particular fact in a commonly recurring situation, the language of presumption is often

---

11 61 LQR 380.
12 *Ajum Goolam Hosen & Co v Union Marine Insurance Co* [1901] AC 362; cf *Pickup Thames and Mersey Marine Insurance Co Ltd* (1878) 3 QBD 594.
13 The Queen's Bench Divisional Court frequently remits a case to magistrates on an appeal by the prosecutor on the ground that the weight of the evidence adduced by him was such that there was a case to answer.
14 *R v Matheson* [1958] 2 All ER 87, [1958] 1 WLR 474.
15 In *Amoco Oil Co v Parpada Shipping Co Ltd* [1989] 1 Lloyd's Rep 369 Lord Donaldson MR seems to have had such a burden in mind though he confusingly refers to it as an evidential burden.

employed. The fact which is proved can be referred to as the basic fact, and the fact inferred as the presumed fact. Thus Lord Denning refers to such a presumption as casting a provisional burden upon the opponent of the presumed fact. In other words the party proving the basic fact is likely to win on the issue to which the presumed fact relates in the absence of evidence to the contrary adduced by the other. According to older classifications, presumptions having this limited effect are described as 'presumptions of fact', and instances which need to be mentioned are the presumption of continuance,[16] the presumption of guilty knowledge arising from the possession of recently stolen goods[17] and the presumption of unseaworthiness in the case of a vessel which founders shortly after leaving port.[18] These are all inferences which may be drawn by the tribunal of fact. It is not obliged to draw them as a matter of law even if there is no further evidence, although there may be occasions on which a civil jury should be directed that they ought to draw the inference as reasonable men, and, in civil cases, a verdict, or even the decision of a judge sitting alone, might be set aside if the inference was not drawn.

A further example is the presumption of intention in its modern form. *D P P v Smith*[19] decided that, in certain circumstances, there was a conclusive presumption that normal people intend the natural consequences of their acts, and it is possible to point to many statements made before *Woolmington v D P P*[20] to the effect that the presumption applies until the contrary is proved. But s 8 of the Criminal Justice Act 1967 provides that:

> A court or jury, in determining whether a person has committed an offence,—
> (a) shall not be bound in law to infer that he intended or foresaw a result of his actions by reason only of its being a natural and probable consequence of those actions;
> (b) shall decide whether he did intend or foresee that result by reference to all the evidence, drawing such inferences from the evidence as appear proper in the circumstances.

What used to be a presumption of law in criminal cases has thus become a presumption of fact. In the words of Lord Sankey in *Woolmington*'s case: '[I]f it is proved that the conscious act of the prisoner killed a man and nothing else appears in the case, there is evidence upon which the jury *may* not *must* find him guilty of murder.'[1] Although there are many statements in civil proceedings suggesting that the presumption of intention is one of law, it is best regarded as one of fact. As in the case of the presumption of seaworthiness, the tribunal of fact may be virtually obliged to find in favour of the presumption when there is nothing to suggest a contrary conclusion.

2. THE ULTIMATE BURDEN

The 'ultimate burden' as used by Lord Denning is a phrase appropriate only to a case involving more than one issue, but it is often used by other judges as a synonym for the legal or persuasive burden. To quote Lord Denning:

16 See p 22, above.
17 See p 32, above.
18 *Ajum Goolam Hossen & Co v Union Marine Insurance Co* [1901] AC 362.
19 [1961] AC 290, [1960] 3 All ER 161.
20 [1935] AC 462.
 1 [1935] AC 462 at 481, emphasis supplied.

Where the ultimate decision of a case depends on the determination of a number of separate issues, the burden on the ultimate issue needs to be distinguished from the burden on the separate issues.[2]

The ultimate burden is thus the burden borne by the party against whom the legal burden on a particular issue has been discharged. Lord Denning illustrates his meaning by reference to an action brought by the holder against the acceptor of a bill of exchange. The ultimate decision depends on whether the plaintiff is a holder in due course. He might begin by proving that he was the holder of a bill signed by the defendant as acceptor. He will succeed on his claim unless the defendant makes good some such defence as fraud in the negotiation of the bill. In his turn the defendant will succeed unless the plaintiff makes good a reply such as value in good faith subsequent to the fraud: 'this shifting to and fro is often described as shifting of the burden of proof and so it is, but it is a shifting of the ultimate burden'.[3] No doubt such progression towards Lord Denning's ultimate burden (sometimes spoken of as 'the burden of proof on the whole case' or the 'general burden of proof') is what judges sometimes have in mind when they say that burdens have 'shifted',[4] but the concept is subject to the same objections as those which have been advanced against the provisional burden, and to the further objection that, in the context of the law of evidence, the expression 'burden of proof' is meaningless unless it is used with reference to a particular issue.

The interaction of legal, evidential, provisional and ultimate burdens was conveniently illustrated in *Ratford v Northavon District Council*.[5] The authority levied a rate upon the receivers of a company occupying rateable property in their area. It was held that, provided there was some reasonable basis for supposing a person to be in occupation of such property, the authority was entitled to levy a rate upon them. In proceedings for non-payment the authority bore both evidential and legal burdens of showing that the rate had been duly made, demanded and not paid. The non-payer would then lose unless he satisfied the evidential and legal burden upon the next issue, that of showing a valid reason why he had not paid. In this case the receivers adduced evidence showing that, although empowered to do so, they had not in fact taken possession of the relevant premises. Once this had been done, and the evidential burden upon that issue satisfied, the only sense in which a burden could further shift was in the provisional sense, but its ultimate determination would decide the whole case. On this point the court endorsed the remarks of Donaldson LJ in *Forsythe v Rawlinson*[6] that it was like all burdens of proof in litigation a swinging burden in the sense that:[7]

As the evidence of varying weight develops before the magistrates, the eventual burden of proof will, in accordance with ordinary principles of evidence, remain with or shift to the person who will fail without further evidence.

2 61 LQR 380.
3 For a case in which the burden of proof was said to shift in this way see *Medawar v Grand Hotel Co* [1891] 2 QB 11; for a case of this type disposed of without any reference to the shifting of the burden of proof, see *Neal v Fior* [1968] 3 All ER 865, [1968] 1 WLR 1875.
4 See Mustill LJ in *Brady v Group Lotus Cars Companies Ltd* [1987] 3 All ER 1050 at 1058.
5 [1987] QB 357, [1986] 3 All ER 193.
6 [1981] RVR 97.
7 At 202.

SECTION 2. ALLOCATION OF THE BURDEN[8]

The burden of proof is, as noted above, capable of having a decisive effect upon the outcome of a case. It is generally allocated as a matter of common law, sometimes unconditionally, and sometimes conditionally upon the proof of certain facts, as in the case of true presumptions, though occasionally unconditional allocation borrows the language of presumption. The allocation may also be a matter of explicit provision, either by way of statutory allocation, itself either general or specific, or by agreement of the parties. These different modes of allocation will be considered in turn, and although all are capable of applying to burdens in either of the two principal senses of legal or evidential burden, it will be found that by far the greater attention has been paid to the allocation of the legal burden.

A. UNCONDITIONAL ALLOCATION AT COMMON LAW

1. EVIDENTIAL BURDEN

According to Taylor,[9] the right test for determining the incidence of the burden of proof is to consider first, which party would succeed if no evidence were given on either side, and secondly, what would be the effect of striking the allegation to be proved out of the record. The onus lies on whichever party would fail if either of these steps were taken. A moment's reflection should suffice to show that these tests are applicable only to the evidential burden; they cannot apply to the legal burden in all cases. Suppose, for example, that want of testamentary capacity is pleaded as a defence to a probate action. The defendant would fail on the issue if no evidence was given on either side, and the plaintiff would likewise succeed if the allegation was struck out of the record. Therefore, Taylor would have had to say that the burden of proof is on the defendant but the fact remains that the legal burden of establishing testamentary capacity is borne by the plaintiff.[10] Taylor's test is undoubtedly sound so far as the incidence of the evidential burden is concerned, although it has been said to be the statement of the effect of a rule, rather than the formulation of the principle underlying it.[11]

In other words resort must be had to the precedents. This is particularly true of criminal cases where the absence of pleadings makes it unreal to speak of striking allegations out of the record. Even so general statements are attempted from time to time.[12] The general rule is that the party bearing the legal burden on an issue also bears the evidential burden. This means that, in a criminal case, the prosecution must normally adduce evidence fit to be left to a jury of the essential ingredients of the offence charged. It is not

---

8 See generally Williams 'Placing the Burden of Proof' in Waller and Campbell (eds) *Well and Truly Tried* (1982).

9 *A Treatise on the Law of Evidence* (12th edn) para 365.

10 *Sutton v Sadler* (1857) 3 CBNS 87. Taylor's test was applied by Farwell LJ in *Talbot v Von Boris* [1911] 1 KB 854 at 863, but the court was there concerned with the evidential burden (see per Kennedy LJ at 866). The test is based on *Amos v Hughes* (1835) 1 Mood & R 464, and is supported by Bowen LJ in *Abrath v North Eastern Rly Co* (1883) 11 QBD 440 at 457, where, however, the different burdens are not distinguished.

11 Wills *Law of Evidence* (3rd edn) 29.

12 See Glanville Williams 'Evidential Burdens on the Defence' 128 NLJ 182.

enough to adduce evidence which would be sufficient on one of two mutually exclusive hypotheses, and leave the jury to choose between them.[13] The general rule also means that the defence bears an evidential burden on the issue of insanity, by virtue of the common law, and on sundry other issues by virtue of statutory provisions, on which the legal burden is placed upon the accused by way of exception to the rule in *Woolmington v Director of Public Prosecutions*.[14] In these cases he has to adduce evidence sufficient, if believed, to satisfy the jury of the existence of the defence on the balance of probabilities.[15] It seems that on issues arising out of special pleas the accused will bear an evidential burden, for example in relation to unfitness to plead[16] or autrefois convict[17] or acquit where the legal burden is on the accused; and perhaps even in cases where the legal burden is borne by the prosecution.[18]

With regard to a number of general common law defences it is settled that, although the prosecution bears the legal burden of disproving them, the accused bears the burden of adducing sufficient evidence to raise the issue of their existence.[19] Even when there are no words dealing expressly with the burden of proof, a statute will frequently be construed so as to place an evidential, if not a legal, burden on a particular issue on the accused.[20] Although there is little direct English authority on the point, it seems that where the accused bears an evidential, but not a legal burden, he may discharge it by adducing evidence of a reasonable possibility of the existence of the defence.[1]

It is hardly surprising that there should be no direct authority because judicial generosity or, as the cynics would have it, the possibility of an appeal, leads to a disinclination to withdraw issues of which there is some defence evidence from the jury. This disinclination may also account for the dearth of authority on the question whether the accused bears an evidential burden in respect of all defences which are more than mere denials of an allegation necessary to the prosecution's case. Sir Francis Adams, a retired judge of the Supreme Court of New Zealand, answers the question in the affirmative[2] but Professor Glanville Williams takes the contrary view.[3] His contention is that it is logically impossible that both sides should carry an

---

13 *Tsang Ping-Nam v R* [1981] 1 WLR 1462.
14 [1935] AC 462.
15 *R v Dix* (1982) 74 Cr App Rep 306, holding that some medical evidence must be adduced before the defence of diminished responsibility can be left to the jury.
16 *R v Podola* [1960] 1 QB 325. But see *R v Bradley* (No 2) (1986) 85 FLR 111 for some doubt in Australia.
17 *R v Coughlan and Young* (1976) 63 Cr App Rep 33.
18 See *R v Graham* (1983) 11 ACR 21 where this is true of a plea to the jurisdiction of the court.
19 *Mancini v DPP* [1942] AC 1, [1941] 3 All ER 272 (provocation); *Chan Kau v R* [1955] AC 206, [1955] 1 All ER 266 (provocation and self-defence); *R v Lobell* [1957] 1 QB 547, [1957] 1 All ER 734 (self-defence); *D P P v Walker* [1974] 1 WLR 1090 (no need to leave self-defence to the jury where no evidence that it was necessary); *R v Gill* [1963] 2 All ER 688, [1963] 1 WLR 841 (duress); *R v Bone* [1968] 2 All ER 644, [1968] 1 WLR 983 (duress).
20 See for example *R v John* [1974] 2 All ER 561, [1974] 1 WLR 624.
1 See per Lord Devlin in *Jayasena v R* [1970] AC 618 at 624, see *R v Newcastle-upon-Tyne Justices, ex p Hindle* [1984] 1 All ER 770 (drink imbibed after accident but before breath-test), and also *R v Thornton* (1967) unreported, a Northern Irish case discussed by E Comerton 'Automatism and the Criminal Justice Act 1966' (1968) 19 NILQ 60.
2 *Criminal Onus and Exculpations* para 3.
3 127 NLJ at 157–8.

evidential burden on the same issue. This leads him to conclude that the accused cannot bear an evidential burden with regard to alibi because his presence at or absence from the scene of the crime is put in issue by the prosecution. The prosecution also puts the accused's mens rea in issue at the outset of a criminal trial with the result, it is said, that he cannot bear an evidential burden with regard to the defence of accident. However weak the evidence on these matters may be, it must be left to the jury. The judge, Professor Williams maintains, has no power to censor it as he has in the case of such general defences as self-defence and duress. There is much force in these arguments, but there are counter-arguments. It could be said that, when the accused raises the defence of alibi,[4] or even accident, he is raising a fresh specific issue within the general issue. Such authority as there is leaves the point fairly open.[5] So far as principle is concerned, there is surely something to be said for preventing the jury from considering the possibility of defences which lack any reasonable foundation: '[i]t is not every facile mouthing of some easy phrase of excuse that can amount to an explanation. It is for a judge to decide whether there is evidence fit to be left to a jury which could be the basis of some suggested verdict'.[6]

In civil cases the nature of the defence will usually be raised on the pleadings from which the allocation of the respective burdens can be deduced. Where this does not occur the principles which apply are similar to those in criminal cases. Even though the proponent of a proposition may bear the persuasive burden of proving an issue to the satisfaction of the court, he is not necessarily bound to anticipate every possible defeasing defence, especially when it could easily have been pleaded. Thus in *Dunlop Holdings Limited's Application*[7] the opponents of a claim to patent a wheel had the burden of proving that the wheel had been in prior use. They were not however bound to anticipate a contention that such prior use had been secret. It was for the applicant to raise the issue by adducing some evidence, or at least by cross-examining the opponents' witnesses so as to show that the use had been in secret. Until this had been done proof of prior use without more was sufficient to entitle the opponents to succeed, though if the issue had been so raised they would have had to prove that the use was not secret upon the balance of probabilities.

4 *R v Johnson* [1961] 3 All ER 969, [1961] 1 WLR 1478 cited by Sir Francis Adams and by R N Gooderson *Alibi* 23, does not turn on the evidential burden because the judge was held to have misdirected the jury by suggesting that the accused bore the legal burden, but the judgment of the Court of Criminal Appeal contains the suggestion that alibi should be treated in the same way as self-defence and provocation. (See Sir Rupert Cross's Rede lecture *The Golden Thread of the English Criminal Law* (1976) CUP pp 12–13).

5 What appears to have been the view of the majority in *D P P v Morgan* [1976] AC 182, that the prosecution bears the evidential burden with regard to the accused's belief in consent might be cited in support of Professor Williams, but the Court of Appeal had trailed a red herring by referring to the evidential burden when the point at issue was one of substantive law. The incidence of the evidential burden was irrelevant to the decision of the majority of the House of Lords. *Bratty v A-G for Northern Ireland* [1963] AC 386, [1961] 3 All ER 523 decides that the accused bears the evidential burden on the issue of non-insane automatism although the plea could be said to be no more than a means of contradicting the prosecution's allegations, already before the jury, of actus reus and mens rea. Moreover Lord Kilmuir LC said (at 405) that the accused bears the evidential burden with regard to accident. See also *R v Bennett* (1978) 68 Cr App Rep 168, placing an evidential burden on the accused with regard to impossibility in a conspiracy case.

6 Lord Morris of Borth-y-Gest in *Bratty v A-G for Northern Ireland* [1963] AC 386 at 417.

7 [1979] RPC 523.

2. LEGAL BURDEN

So far as the legal burden is concerned, Wigmore has truly said 'There are merely specific rules for specific classes of case resting for their ultimate basis upon broad reasons of expedience and fairness',[8] but this does not often lead to difficulty in ascertaining the party upon whom the burden rests, for a fundamental requirement of any judicial system is that the person who desires the court to take action must prove his case to its satisfaction.[9] This means that, as a matter of common sense, the legal burden of proving all facts essential to their claims normally rests upon the plaintiff in a civil suit or the prosecutor in criminal proceedings.

The rule is sometimes expressed in terms of such maxims as '*omnia praesumuntur pro negante*', and '*ei incumbit probatio qui dicit, non qui negat*' but this must not be taken to mean that the onus of proof cannot lie upon a party who makes a negative allegation. If this were so, the application of the rule could be made to depend upon the language in which a case happened to be pleaded. For instance, a claim for damages for breach of covenant to keep a house in repair may be stated by saying, either that the defendant did not repair the house, or else that he allowed it to become dilapidated, but the legal burden is borne by the plaintiff, however the claim is expressed.[10] It is probably true to say that a positive averment can always be converted into a negative statement by appropriate linguistic manipulation. However this may be, there are numerous instances in which a plaintiff or prosecutor assumes the legal burden of proving a negative.[11] Absence of consent must be established by the Crown on a charge of rape or assault,[12] and where lack of consent[13] or want of due notice of a particular fact[14] is alleged in a civil action, these matters must be proved by the plaintiff. As Bowen LJ said in the leading case of *Abrath v North Eastern Rly Co*,[15] which decided that the legal burden of proving absence of reasonable and probable cause rests on the plaintiff in an action for malicious prosecution, 'If the assertion of a negative is an essential part of the plaintiff's case, the proof of the assertion still rests upon the plaintiff.'

Difficulty may sometimes arise with regard to the question whether an assertion is essential to a party's case or that of his adversary. This is strikingly illustrated by *Joseph Constantine Steamship Line Ltd v Imperial Smelting Corporation*

---

8 IX *Wigmore* 278.
9 *Dickinson v Minister of Pensions* [1953] 1 QB 228 at 232, [1952] 2 All ER 1031 at 1033.
10 *Soward v Leggatt* (1836) 7 C & P 613.
11 On the difficulties of proving a negative see Gulson *Philosophy of Proof* (2nd edn) 72–3, and Gulson Part 1, ch 18. Generally speaking, negative facts are not observed to the same extent as positive ones—it is easier to find a witness to swear there was a clock in the room than to say that no clock was there. 'Negative evidence, therefore, is always in some sort circumstantial or indirect, and the difficulty of proving the negative lies in discovering a fact or series of facts inconsistent with the fact which we are seeking to disprove, from which it may be possible to infer its absence with anything like an approach to certainty' (Gulson 153). Though true of some of the instances in which the law requires a negative to be proved, e g absence of fault, this is not true of all of them, e g absence of consent, nor is the difficulty so acute in cases where it is possible to use a computer to establish a negative averment, see e g *U S v Greenlee* 517 F2d 889 (1975).
12 *R v Horn* (1912) 7 Cr App Rep 200; *R v Donovan* [1934] 2 KB 498.
13 *Toleman v Portbury* (1870) LR 5 QB 288.
14 *Williams v East India Co* (1802) 3 East 192.
15 (1883) 11 QBD 440 at 457. This decision was affirmed by the House of Lords (1886) 11 App Cas 247.

Ltd[16] where the charterers of a ship claimed damages from the owners for failure to load. The owners pleaded that the contract had been frustrated by the destruction of the ship owing to an explosion, and the only question of fact was whether this had been caused by their fault. As the evidence was scanty, it became necessary to determine which of the parties bore the legal burden with regard to this matter. If the rule were that charter parties cease to be binding when the vessel, without default of either party, is disabled by an overpowering disaster, the negation of fault would be an essential of the defendant's case; on the other hand, proof of fault would be an essential of the plaintiff's case, if the rule were that charter parties cease to be binding when the vessel is disabled by an overpowering disaster, provided that disaster is not brought about by the fault of either party. The House of Lords decided that the latter was the correct formulation, and accordingly held that the plaintiff has the legal burden of proving fault when frustration is pleaded as a defence to an action on a contract. Their Lordships' speeches referred to principles, such as the difficulty of proving a negative and the presumption of innocence, but, as Professor Julius Stone has shown, general considerations of public policy probably constituted the decisive factor.[17] If such considerations are the guide where there is no governing precedent, it is obviously vain to seek for any set formula determining what facts are essential to a party's case and hence the incidence of the legal burden of proof can only be ascertained by consulting the precedents concerned with the various branches of the substantive law. In the case of bailment, for example, it is settled that the bailee has the onus of proving that the goods were lost without his fault,[18] and, at a criminal trial, the accused has the legal burden on a plea of insanity.[19] No a priori tests could have produced these results; it is pointless to collect numerous isolated precedents.

3. USE OF TERMINOLOGY OF PRESUMPTION

As noted earlier, the burden of proof is sometimes allocated by way of the terminology of presumption. The terminology is properly applied to a situation in which the proof of one fact affects the burden relating to another, and consideration of this is postponed to the next part of this section. In some cases however there is no basic fact at all, and the presumption does no more than express the incidence of the relevant burden. Typical examples are

16 [1942] AC 154, [1941] 2 All ER 165.
17 It seems to be the case that frustration occurs more often than not without fault on anyone's part, and absence of fault is undoubtedly difficult to prove. Hence 'a rule requiring the defendant pleading frustration to negative fault will then ex hypothesi do injustice to the great majority of defendants. While, on the other hand, a rule requiring the plaintiff to prove fault will ex hypothesi do injustice to only a small minority of plaintiffs' (60 LQR 278).
18 *Coldman v Hill* [1919] 1 KB 443; *Brook's Wharf and Bull Wharf Ltd v Goodman Bros* [1937] 1 KB 534, [1936] 3 All ER 696, and cases there cited; *Hunt and Winterbotham (West of England) Ltd v B R S (Parcels) Ltd* [1962] 1 QB 617, [1962] 1 All ER 111; *Houghland v R R Low (Luxury Coaches) Ltd* [1962] 1 QB 694, [1962] 2 All ER 159.
19 *McNaughten's Case* (1843) 10 Cl & Fin 200; *R v Smith* (1910) 6 Cr App Rep 19. For criticism, see Glanville Williams *Criminal Law (The General Part)* (2nd edn) 516. Under s 2(2) of the Homicide Act 1957, it is for the accused to prove diminished responsibility, see *R v Dunbar* [1958] 1 QB 1. Though in Canada it has been held contrary to the Charter for a legal burden of disproving sanity to be placed upon the accused, and it has been reduced to an evidential burden, *R v Leblanc* (1989) 68 CR (3d) 155.

provided by the presumption of innocence, and the presumption of sanity in criminal cases.

(i) Presumption of innocence[20]

When it is said that an accused person is presumed to be innocent, all that is meant is that the prosecution is obliged to prove the case against him beyond reasonable doubt. This is the fundamental rule of our criminal procedure, and it is expressed in terms of a presumption of innocence so frequently as to render criticism somewhat pointless; but this practice can lead to serious confusion of thought, as is shown by the much discussed decision of the American Supreme Court in *Coffin v The United States*.[1] The accused had been convicted of misappropriating the funds of a bank after the jury had been told that they should acquit him unless satisfied of his guilt beyond reasonable doubt, and a new trial was ordered because the judge did not enumerate the presumption of innocence among the items of evidence favourable to the accused. In other words, the Supreme Court considered that the presumption was something different from the rule concerning the onus of proof on a criminal charge, for they regarded it as an instrument of proof—an item of evidence which had been withheld from the jury. This decision has been universally condemned, it could hardly have been pronounced if the court had not been misled by the verbal dissimilarity between the rule that the prosecution bears the legal burden of proof, and the presumption of innocence.

This should be contrasted with the presumption that a child between the ages of ten and fourteen is unable to distinguish right from wrong. Although in such a case the prosecution also bears the burden of adducing evidence to show that such a child can so distinguish,[2] the additional burden arises only after proof of the age of the child which may be regarded as the basic fact of the presumption, so in such a case the language is properly applied.

(ii) Presumption of sanity

In criminal cases, the presumption of sanity is no more than a conclusion which must be drawn until the contrary is proved[3] for the McNaughten Rules have decreed:

> that the jurors ought to be told in all cases that every man is presumed to be sane and to possess a sufficient degree of reason to be responsible for his crimes until the contrary be proved to their satisfaction.

The McNaughten Rules apply to criminal charges, and the presumption of sanity which they entail must be distinguished from the same presumption in some other branches of the law. If a rational will is produced, and shown to have been duly executed, the jury ought to be told to find in favour of the

---

20 Allen *Legal Duties* 253. For a broader approach to this concept see Healy 'Proof and Policy: No Golden Threads' [1987] Crim LR 355 at 364, 365.

1 (1895) 156 US 432 discussed by Thayer *Preliminary Treatise on Evidence at the Common Law* App B.

2 *J M v Runeckles* (1984) 79 Cr App Rep 255; *IPH v Chief Constable of South Wales* [1987] Crim LR 42.

3 In Canada it is regarded as contrary to the Charter for the presumption to place a persuasive burden on the accused, *R v Leblanc* (1989) 68 CR (3d) 155.

testator's competence.[4] The legal burden rests on the party who propounds the will, but the rule that he does not have to adduce evidence of capacity in the first instance is sometimes said to raise a presumption of sanity in testamentary cases. This presumption is dependent on the proof of a basic fact—the execution of a rational will, therefore it is an illustration of the proper use of the term.

(iii) Other examples

Allowance must be made for a number of presumptions without basic facts, for example Lord Kilmuir and Lord Denning spoke of 'the presumption of mental capacity' in *Bratty v A-G for Northern Ireland*[5] simply as a compendious way of expressing the fact that the accused bears the evidential burden on the issue of non-insane automatism. Although it is common enough to speak of a presumption that mechanical instruments were in working order as a means of indicating the fact that an evidential burden is borne by the party denying that this was the case,[6] it can hardly be said that any basic fact is involved.

Statutes occasionally employ exactly the same technique, thus s 79(2) of the Animal Health Act 1981 presumes that the owner of an animal knows of the existence of diseases from which it suffers unless and until he proves to the satisfaction of the court that he did not and could not with reasonable diligence have known of it.[7] Thus the effect of this section as against the accused is a precise counterpart of the operation of the presumption of sanity in criminal cases.

B. CONDITIONAL ALLOCATION AT COMMON LAW: PRESUMPTIONS

The structure of all true presumptions requires first the proof of a basic fact or facts. Once this has been done different consequences follow so far as the establishment of the presumed fact is concerned. In the weakest form of presumption the only effect of proving the basic fact is that the presumed fact may be found by the trier of fact. In other words the logical inference of the presumed fact from proof of the basic fact attracts a measure of formal endorsement.[8] Such presumptions have no effect upon the burden of proof in either of its two principal senses and need here be considered no further.[9] Two possibilities remain, one relating to the evidential, and one to the legal, burden.[10] If, after proof of the basic fact, the presumed fact must be taken to be established in the absence of evidence to the contrary, then an evidential burden has been cast upon the opponent of the presumed fact and the presumption can reasonably be described as an evidential presumption.[11] On the other hand, if, after proof of the basic fact, the presumed fact must

---

4 See *Sutton v Sadler* (1857) 3 CBNS 87.
5 [1963] AC 386 at 407 and 413 respectively.
6 See p 50 above.
7 See also s 79(3).
8 A number of examples were given above, see p 118.
9 In traditional terminology these would be described as presumptions of fact.
10 In traditional terminology these would be described as rebuttable presumptions of law.
11 See Glanville Williams *Criminal Law (The General Part)* (2nd edn, 1961) 877ff.

be taken to be established unless the trier of fact is persuaded to the appropriate standard of the contrary, then a legal burden has been cast upon the opponent of the presumed fact, and the presumption can reasonably be described as a legal presumption. It is more accurate to speak of a shift in the burden of proof in the case of these stronger presumptions because they affect what the judge does in leaving an issue to the jury or withdrawing it from them, and they may determine the manner in which he must direct the jury at the end of the case.[12]

It would be unreasonable to expect anything approaching neat precision in this area of the law. Indeed it has been the subject of an extraordinary catalogue of complaints such as that,

> Every writer of sufficient intelligence to appreciate the difficulties of the subject-matter has approached the topic of presumptions with a sense of hopelessness, and has left it with a feeling of despair.[13]

There are a number of reasons for this. The precise delimitation and distinction of basic fact and presumed fact is assumed by the approach indicated above, but often not realised in practice.[14] This can mean that the same evidence rebuts both basic fact and presumed fact; for example, in the case of the presumption of death, evidence that the subject has been seen alive by one of his family may rebut both one of the basic facts of the presumption, that he has not been seen alive, and the presumed fact, that he is dead.[15] This could cause serious problems where the legal burden of proving the basic fact of the presumption is on the proponent of death, and the legal burden of rebutting the presumed fact of death upon his opponent.

Another example of overlapping between basic fact and presumed fact is provided by the presumption of legitimacy. The basic fact of that presumption is either the birth of a child to a married woman during wedlock, or its conception during wedlock. In one case however the child was born slightly more than the normal period after the termination of a marriage by divorce.[16] In order to establish the basic fact of the presumption of legitimacy it was accordingly necessary to rely upon a different, and hitherto, unrecognised presumption the basic fact of which appeared to be the birth of a child within a possible period of gestation after the termination of a marriage, and the presumed fact that conception took place during the marriage.

Nowadays presumptions have much less importance than they did when the exclusionary rules were very much more restrictive. It is much less common for them to operate so as to determine the outcome in the absence of directly relevant evidence. Many of them reflect the evidential value of their basic facts. In the absence of further evidence, it would be highly unreasonable not to infer legitimacy from a child's birth in wedlock. On the other hand, a presumption may have the effect of increasing the probative

12 When a statute speaks of a shifting of the burden of proof it is usually in relation to a rebuttable presumption of law created by the statute (see Bills of Exchange Act 1882, s 30 (2) below).

13 E Morgan 'Presumptions' (1937) 12 Wash LR 255.

14 For a convincing demonstration of this, see Treitel (1954) 'The Presumption of Death' 17 MLR 530. See also Stone 'The Presumption of Death: A Redundant Concept?'(1981) 44 MLR 516 for the view that this presumption no longer has any practical effect.

15 See *Prudential Assurance Co v Edmonds* (1877) 2 App Cas 487.

16 *Knowles v Knowles* [1962] P 161, [1962] 1 All ER 659.

value of the basic fact where there is no evidence contradicting such inferences as might be drawn from it. In the case of the presumption of death, for example, there is no special magic in seven years' absence so far as the ordinary tests of probative value are concerned. Someone who has been absent unheard of by those who would be likely to have heard from him for six and a half years is, for all practical purposes, just as likely to be dead as someone who has been absent in similar circumstances for seven years; but seven years' absence brings into play a rebuttable presumption of law, while absence for a shorter period merely gives rise to a more or less cogent presumption of fact that the person in question is dead. Reflections of this nature have led to the remark that: 'presumptions of law are nothing else than natural inferences or presumptions of fact which the law invests with an artificial or preternatural weight'.[17] While this may often be the case, it is by no means always the case. Some presumptions are clearly designed merely to resolve an impasse either of proof or procedure. Thus the statutory presumption contained in s 184(1) of the Law of Property Act 1925 provides that where two or more persons have died in circumstances rendering it uncertain which of them survived the other, such deaths shall (subject to any order of the court), for all purposes affecting the title to property, be presumed to have occurred in order of seniority, and accordingly the younger shall be deemed to have survived the elder. In such a case the evidential value of the basic fact is non-existent, and the whole effect of the presumption is expended on the allocation of the burden of proof.

It is however sometimes suggested that presumptions have an evidential effect in excess of the true probative worth of their basic fact, and quite independent of their effect in allocating the burden of proof.[18] It is submitted however that Lord Reid's words in *S v S* of the effect of the presumption of legitimacy are of more general application:

> Once evidence has been led it must be weighed without using the presumption as a makeweight in the scale of legitimacy. So even weak evidence against legitimacy must prevail if there is no other evidence to counter-balance it. The presumption will only come in at that stage in the very rare case of the evidence being so evenly balanced that the court is unable to reach a decision on it.[19]

If this is correct, and if the artificial force of presumptions is achieved by allocation of burden, it is hardly surprising to find that it is affected by other policies also directed to that end.[20] This is most obvious in criminal cases, especially in view of the decision of the House of Lords in *Woolmington v D P P*.[1] Although there is some older authority to the contrary[2] it is hard to

17 Gulson *Philosophy of Proof* (2nd edn) 371.
18 See per Lord Denning in *Stupple v Royal Insurance Co Ltd* [1971] 1 QB 50 at 72, [1970] 3 All ER 230 at 235–6, discussed in more detail above. It is however possible that the difference between Lord Denning and Buckley LJ in that case related only to the probative worth of the basic fact.
19 [1972] AC 24 at 41, [1970] 3 All ER 107 at 109.
20 For an interesting suggestion that presumptions should be classified on the basis of the policies they are designed to promote, see L Cohen 'Presumptions According to Purpose: A Functional Approach' (1981) 45 Albany LR 1079.
 1 [1935] AC 462.
 2 See *R v Curgerwen* (1865) LR 1 CCR 1; *R v Audley* [1907] 1 KB 383.

believe, since the decision in *Woolmington*, that an English court[3] would be prepared to apply a common law presumption so as to cast a legal burden upon the accused in a criminal case.[4] It is rare for an evidential burden to operate against the accused, but an example is provided by *R v Willshire*.[5] The accused had been convicted of bigamously marrying Miss D during the life of his wife C. He had married A in 1864 and, in 1868, he was convicted of bigamously marrying B in A's lifetime. The prosecution proved a formally valid marriage ceremony between the accused and C in 1879, together with a further marriage ceremony with D in 1880. The accused was therefore guilty of the offence charged in the indictment if he was validly married to C. His defence was that this was not the case because A, who was alive in 1868, was still alive when he married C in 1879. The conviction was quashed because the jury had not been properly directed with regard to the burden of proof. To quote from the judgment of Lord Coleridge CJ:[6]

> It is said, and I think rightly, that there is a presumption in favour of the validity of this latter marriage [the marriage to C] but the prisoner showed that there was a valid marriage in 1864, and that the woman he then married was alive in 1868 ... The Common Serjeant did not leave the question to the jury ... but held that the burden of proof was on the prisoner, who was bound to adduce other or further evidence of the existence of his wife in 1879; ... I am clearly of opinion that in this the learned Common Serjeant went beyond the rules of law. The prisoner was only bound to set up the life; it was for the prosecution to prove his guilt.

At one stage Lord Coleridge spoke of a conflict between the presumption of the validity of the 1879 ceremony and the presumption of continuance of A's life, but this is a presumption of fact, a recurrent item of circumstantial evidence. The prosecution bore the legal burden of proving the validity of the 1879 ceremony, but the presumption of the validity of that marriage placed an evidential burden of raising the issue of its invalidity on the accused. He discharged his burden by 'setting up' the life of A, and the jury should have been told that they could only decide the issue in favour of the Crown if they were sure that A was dead when Willshire married C.

The stringent modern approach is illustrated in relation to the presumption of the lawfulness of official action, *praesumuntur rite esse acta* in *Dillon v R*.[7] The accused, a policeman, was charged with negligently permitting the escape of two prisoners who were lawfully within his custody. The prosecution failed to offer formal evidence of the lawfulness of the custody. The accused submitted that there was no case to answer, but both trial judge and appellate court held that the prosecution could rely upon the presumption. The Privy Council rejected this view, holding that the courts will not presume the existence of facts which are central to an offence, and that when the liberty

---

3 Though it has been done in Australia, see *R v Bonnor* [1957] VLR 227. In the United States this issue gives rise to constitutional problems, see *Re Winship* 397 US 358 (1970) at 364, for comment see Jeffries and Stephan 'Defenses, Presumptions and Burden of Proof in the Criminal Law' (1979) 88 Yale LJ 1325. Canada has been plagued with a flood of cases on this problem since the enactment of its Charter, see, for example, *R v Oakes* (1986) 26 DLR (4th) 200; *R v Whyte* (1988) 51 DLR (4th) 481.

4 See, for example, *R v Yacoob* (1981) 72 Cr App Rep 313 at 364, a strong case since the issue was merely collateral.

5 (1881) 6 QBD 366.

6 At 369.

7 [1982] AC 484, [1982] 1 All ER 1017.

of the subject is involved there is no room for presumptions in favour of the Crown. It also expressed the view that:

> it would be contrary to fundamental principles of law that the onus should be on a prisoner to rebut a presumption that he was being lawfully detained, which he could only do by the (notoriously difficult) process of proving a negative.[8]

It should be noted that when the issue is a central one, the prosecution will bear both an evidential and legal burden in relation to it, and the effect of the ruling is to deny even the provisional force of the presumption in such cases, that is to say, the presumption is insufficient to discharge the burden of adducing evidence to show the custody to have been lawful, and the accused is entitled to a directed verdict in his favour, in the absence of any other evidence on this issue.

Proof of the basic facts of a common law presumption can cast nothing more than an evidential burden on to the accused and nothing less than a legal burden on to the prosecution. If someone charged with incest with his daughter contends that, though conceived and born in wedlock, she is the child of another man, it is difficult to believe that any court would hold it incumbent upon him to do more than adduce such evidence as would suggest a reasonable possibility of illegitimacy. If, on the other hand, the prosecution were to contend that, though born during his wife's marriage to another man, the girl was in reality the accused's daughter, the judge should withdraw the case from the jury if the prosecution can do no more by way of rebuttal of the presumption of legitimacy than prove statements by the accused to the effect that the girl was his child.[9]

C. ALLOCATION BY STATUTORY PROVISION

It is not uncommon for statutes to provide explicitly for the allocation of the burden of proof, though none seems so far ever to have distinguished explicitly between evidential and legal burdens. It has also been determined that it is possible for a statute to allocate the burden of proof implicitly.[10] Such an implicit allocation can be divined only by a process of statutory interpretation, and the common law developed certain principles which were subsequently encapsulated in a series of more general statutory provisions relating to summary proceedings.[11] It was at one time thought that these general statutory provisions for summary trials diverged in their effects from their counterparts at common law, perhaps because the accused could not before 1898 generally testify in his own defence, and perhaps because trial on indictment led to more serious consequences, thus justifying the imposition of a more onerous burden upon the prosecution. It is now clear that the rules are the same for both types of proceedings.[12] The accused

---

8 At 487, 1020.
9 *R v Hemmings* [1939] 1 All ER 417.
10 *R v Hunt* [1987] AC 352, [1987] 1 All ER 1.
11 Culminating in the Magistrates' Courts Act 1980, s 101. In Scotland the comparable provisions apply both to summary trials and to trials on indictment, see Criminal Procedure (Scotland) Act 1975, ss 66 and 312(v). Similar provisions abound in Commonwealth jurisdictions.
12 Such assimilation may be thought inherent in the classic statement of Lord Sankey in *Woolmington v D P P* [1935] AC 462 at 482 that the rules are the same 'No matter what the charge or where the trial', see below, p 133.

has been a competent witness in his own defence since 1898, and it can be argued that since so many statutory offences are triable either upon indictment or summarily,[13] that it would be confusing, impractical, and undesirable to apply different burdens in respect of the same offence depending upon how it came to be tried, especially if this were to involve offering advantages in the more expensive and time-consuming proceedings upon indictment. The principal distinction is now between those statutes which make explicit and those which make implicit allocation of the burden of proof, and they will be addressed in turn.

1. EXPLICIT ALLOCATION BY STATUTORY PROVISION

It is not uncommon for statutes to provide that certain facts shall be deemed to exist until the contrary is proved. The precise words that are employed vary from statute to statute, and they could have a decisive effect. It is possible to do no more here than provide a few representative examples. Examples are furnished by s 30(2) of the Bills of Exchange Act 1882, s 2 of the Prevention of Corruption Act 1916, and s 57(3) of the Employment Protection (Consolidation) Act 1978 (as amended).[14]

(i) Bills of Exchange Act 1882, s 30(2)

Section 30(2) of the Bills of Exchange Act 1882 provides that every holder of a bill is prima facie deemed to be a holder in due course; but if in an action on a bill it is admitted or proved that the acceptance, issue, or subsequent negotiation of the bill is affected by fraud, duress, or force and fear, or illegality, the burden of proof is shifted, unless and until the holder proves that, subsequent to the alleged fraud or illegality, value has in good faith been given for the bill. In the light of cases decided before and after the Act came into force, when the subsection speaks of 'proof' it is clear that all that is meant is 'evidence upon which a jury would be entitled to base a verdict'.[15] The result is that the holder has the legal burden of proving that he gave value for the bill in good faith, but he does not bear the evidential burden on the point until the defendant has made out a prima facie case that the bill was tainted with fraud, duress or illegality. No doubt this is commercially fair even if, from the point of view of literal interpretation, there is something to be said for a construction less favourable to the defendant.[16]

(ii) Prevention of Corruption Act 1916, s 2

By s 2 of the Prevention of Corruption Act 1916, on a charge under the Prevention of Corruption Act 1906, a consideration is to be deemed to be given corruptly unless the contrary is proved. In *R v Evans-Jones and Jenkins*,[17]

13 With various permutations of options and consents by prosecution and defence.
14 By Employment Act 1980, s 6.
15 *Talbot v Von Boris* [1911] 1 KB 854 at 866 per Kennedy LJ; *Hall v Featherstone* (1858) 3 H & N 284.
16 For the commercial justification of the law on this subject see Alderson B in *Elkin v Janson* (1845) 13 M & W 655 at 664.
17 (1923) 87 JP 115.

this was held to mean that, if the jury are in doubt as to whether they should accept the accused's explanation of a gift to a public officer, it is their duty to convict, and this construction was also adopted by the Court of Criminal Appeal in *R v Carr-Briant*,[18] where however, the conviction was quashed because the jury had been misdirected with regard to the standard of proof. Humphreys J stated the judgment of the court in the following terms:

> In any case where, either by statute or at common law, some matter is presumed 'unless the contrary is proved' the jury should be directed that it is for them to decide whether the contrary is proved, that the burden of proof required is less than that required at the hands of the prosecution in proving a case beyond reasonable doubt, and that the burden may be discharged by evidence satisfying the jury of the probability of that which the accused is called upon to establish.[19]

These observations were plainly intended to apply to all cases in which a criminal statute casts the burden of proof on the accused, and it seems that they will be applied to all such cases by the courts.[20]

(iii) Employment Protection (Consolidation) Act 1978, s 57(3) (as amended by Employment Act 1980, s 6)

The provision is concerned with the determination of the question whether or not the dismissal of an employee was unfair. In the 1978 version the employer must first show a proper reason,[1] and then the question of fairness shall:

> depend on whether the employer can satisfy the tribunal that in the circumstances (having regard to equity and the substantial merits of the case) he acted reasonably in treating it as a sufficient reason for dismissing the employee.

This was rightly regarded as placing the persuasive burden on this issue upon the employer. Such a burden was however regarded as being unduly onerous, and the provision was accordingly amended so as to make the question of fairness:

> depend on whether in the circumstances (including the size and administrative resources of the employer's undertaking) the employer acted reasonably or unreasonably in treating it as a sufficient reason for dismissing the employee; and that question shall be determined in accordance with equity and the substantial merits of the case.

It seems that this form of words is intended to leave the persuasive burden neutral between the parties,[2] the evidential burden presumably being satisfied by adduction of a reason sufficient to satisfy s 57(1). An interesting, and perhaps unintended, result of this technique is to effect a change in the standard of proof. As will be seen in the next section of this chapter, the normal standard of proof in civil proceedings is proof on the balance of probabilities. It is fundamental to that standard that it involves weighing

18 [1943] KB 607, [1943] 2 All ER 156; followed in *Public Prosecutor v Yuvaraj* [1970] AC 913.
19 [1943] KB 607 at 612, [1943] 2 All ER 156 at 158.
20 *Jayasena v R* [1970] AC 618, [1970] 1 All ER 219; *Mizel v Warren* [1973] 2 All ER 1140, [1973] 1 WLR 899.
1 As defined by s 57(1) and (2).
2 983 H of C Official Report (5th series) col 512.

the evidence to see if the required standard has been achieved. If it has not, the party bearing the legal burden loses, *however little evidence his opponent has adduced*. The effect of this change is that the only standard against which evidence can be weighed is that adduced by the opponent, in other words, if neither party bears the legal burden, then, if the case is to be decided at all, the party who adduces the greater amount wins, *however little evidence he has adduced*. In future in this area a party will win if he has adduced more evidence than his opponent, even though it may not, seen objectively, make his contention more probable than not. This is highly unsatisfactory, and the result may be that in an effort to avoid it cases will be fought out whenever possible on the question of the reason for dismissal, where the legal burden remains on the employer,[3] though the nature of the issue often makes that very difficult.[4]

2. IMPLICIT ALLOCATION BY STATUTORY PROVISION

A statute may allocate the burden of proof without explicit reference, and such statutes may concern civil,[5] or criminal liability. The most contentious issue relates to the imposition of a burden upon the accused in criminal proceedings. As noted above the general rule is that the prosecution bears both the evidential and legal burden in relation to issues necessary for the imposition of criminal liability. This general position was graphically expressed by the House of Lords in *Woolmington v D P P*:[6]

> throughout the web of the English Criminal Law one golden thread is always to be seen, that it is the duty of the prosecution to prove the prisoner's guilt subject to what I have already said as to the defence of insanity and subject also to any statutory exception . . . No matter what the charge or where the trial, the principle that the prosecution must prove the guilt of the prisoner is part of the common law of England and no attempt to whittle it down can be entertained.

It should be noted that Lord Sankey allowed for the defence of insanity, and for statutory exception. The question has arisen of how to construe the reference to statutory exception. It is quite clear that it applies to explicit statutory exceptions of the type exemplified above. Many statutes create offences without making any such explicit reference. The question is whether they too are capable of being construed as casting a burden upon the accused, and if so, in what circumstances, and how it should be decided. Some guidance was provided at common law, these common law guides were encapsulated into general statutory provisions, and recent case law has clarified the situation. Various suggestions have been made for reform. Each of these matters will be considered in turn.

(i) Common law

The common law used to attach importance to the distinction between exceptions and provisos and the effect of the defendant's peculiar knowledge

---

3 As in *Maund v Penwith District Council* [1982] ICR 732.
4 See Freedland 'The Burden of Proof in Claims of Unfair Dismissal' (1972) 1 ILJ 20.
5 For example the Factories Act 1961, s 29(1) construed in *Nimmo v Alexander Cowan & Sons Ltd* [1968] AC 107, [1967] 3 All ER 187.
6 [1935] AC 462 at 481, 482.

of material facts. Something must be said about each of these matters before
the effect of *R v Edwards*[7] is set out.

(a) Exceptions and provisos. There was an old rule of pleading dating back to
the seventeenth century according to which an indictment had to negative
exceptions, but not provisos. In the words of Lord Mansfield: '[I]t is a known
distinction that what comes by way of proviso in a statute must be insisted
upon by way of defence by the party accused; but, where exceptions are in
the enacting part of a law, it must appear in the charge that the defendant
does not fall within any of them.'[8] But it did not follow from the fact that the
prosecutor had to negative exceptions in the indictment that he bore any
kind of burden with regard to them at the trial. This was the main point at
issue in the leading case of *R v Turner*[9] in which the validity of an information
under the game-laws was challenged on certiorari before the King's Bench.
The accused was prosecuted for having pheasants and hares in his possession
without the necessary qualifications or authorisation. Ten possible qualifications were mentioned in the relevant statute and the court held that,
although the existence of any one of them was an exception, a fact which
necessitated the reference to want of qualification in the information, it was
unnecessary for the prosecution to adduce evidence on the subject. Lord
Ellenborough made the point that proof of qualification was 'easy on the one
side' whereas proof of total disqualification was 'almost impossible on the
other'. It is arguable that *Turner*'s case decided no more than that, where a
statute provides a plurality of excuses, the accused must raise the issue of the
existence of those on which he relies.[10] The decision did not put an end to
the distinction between exceptions and provisos if only because reliance was
occasionally placed on the fact that an exempting clause was a proviso as a
justification of the absence of any reference to it in the indictment and the
imposition of some burden with regard to it on the accused.[11] There is
however little doubt that *R v Turner* had a great influence on the law
concerning the incidence of the burden of proof because it showed that the
mere fact that an allegation negativing an exception occurs in an indictment
does not impose any burden on the Crown. Bayley J's justification of this
result was treated as specially significant in a number of later cases.

(b) Facts peculiarly within the knowledge of the accused. Bayley J said that he had
always regarded it as a general rule that:

> If a negative averment be made by one party, which is peculiarly within the
> knowledge of the other, the party within whose knowledge it lies, and who asserts
> the affirmative, is to prove it and not he who asserts the negative.[12]

It is important to grasp the limited extent of Bayley J's general rule. It is a
rule of statutory interpretation confined to cases in which the affirmative of

---

7 [1975] QB 27, [1974] 2 All ER 1085.
8 *R v Jarvis* (1756) 1 East 643n.
9 (1816) 5 M & S 206.
10 See per Bowen LJ in *Abrath v North Eastern Rly Co* (1883) 11 QBD 440 at 457; and per
    Palles CB in *Graham v Belfast and Northern Counties Rly Co* [1901] 2 IR 13 at 26.
11 *R v James* [1902] 1 KB 540; *R v Audley* [1907] 1 KB 383.
12 5 M & S 211. For a civil case in which the doctrine was applied see *General Accident, Fire and
    Life Assurance Corpn v Robertson* [1909] AC 404 at 413.

negative averments is peculiarly within the knowledge of the accused. There is nothing in the nature of a general rule that the burden of establishing any defence based on facts peculiarly within his knowledge is borne by him. Were there such a rule, someone charged with murder would bear the burden of proving many facts connected with provocation or self-defence, or even the burden of disproving an intention to kill, for few things can be more especially within a person's peculiar knowledge than his state of mind. The existence of such a rule was emphatically repudiated by the Court of Criminal Appeal in *R v Spurge*, a case in which a mechanical defect was the accused's answer to a charge of dangerous driving.[13] The most that can be said by way of generalisation is that a party's knowledge of essential facts may lessen the amount of evidence required to discharge an evidential burden borne by his adversary.[14] To quote Lord Mansfield:

> It is certainly a maxim that all evidence is to be weighed according to the proof which it was in the power of one side to produce, and in the power of the other to have contradicted.[15]

In consequence of Bayley J's rule of statutory interpretation the prosecution has been relieved of the necessity of showing that an apothecary charged with practising without a certificate did not possess one,[16] that a person charged with selling cocaine without a licence did not have a licence,[17] that a driver charged with infringing insurance regulations did not have a certificate,[18] that a sugar dealer charged with an offence against the Defence Regulations 1939 had not been granted a licence,[19] that a motorist had not got a licence when he was charged with driving without one,[20] and that the accused was in the possession of drugs without a prescription.[1]

Some of these holdings have been criticised as unjustifiable extensions of the decision in *R v Turner* from statutes containing a number of qualifications under which the acts charged would be lawful to issues concerning a single negative which would be as easy to prove by prima facie evidence as the affirmative. Suppose, for example, that a motorist is charged with driving without a licence. It would be as easy for the prosecution to provide prima facie evidence of guilt by calling a witness to swear that the accused was asked to produce his licence and failed to do so,[2] as it would be for the

---

13 [1961] 2 QB 205, [1961] 2 All ER 688, (the appeal was dismissed because the accused was negligent); *R v Mandry, R v Wooster* [1973] 3 All ER 996 at 1000. See also the striking decisions on ordinances based on s 106 of the Indian Evidence Act 1872: 'When any fact is essentially within the knowledge of any person the burden of proving that fact is upon him': *Attygalle v R* [1936] AC 338, [1936] 2 All ER 116; *Seneviratne v R* [1936] 3 All ER 36; *Ng v R* [1958] AC 173.

14 See *Dunlop Holding Ltd Application* [1979] RPC 523 at 544 per Buckley LJ.

15 *Blatch v Archer* (1774) 1 Cowp 53 at 65. See also *R v Burdett* (1820) 4 B & Ald 95 at 140, cited in *Joyce v D P P* [1946] AC 347 at 380; Stephen *Digest of the Law of Evidence* (12th edn) art 104 applied in *R v Kakelo* [1923] 2 KB 793 at 795 and cited in *R v Cohen* [1951] 1 KB 505, [1951] 1 All ER 203.

16 *Apothecaries Co v Bentley* (1824) 1 C & P 538.

17 *R v Scott* (1921) 86 JP 69.

18 Per Talbot J in *Williams v Russell* (1933) 149 LT 190 at 191.

19 *R v Oliver* [1944] KB 68, [1943] 2 All ER 800.

20 *John v Humphreys* [1955] 1 All ER 793, [1955] 1 WLR 325, not followed in *McGowan v Carville* [1960] IR 330 where the authorities are reviewed. See also *A-G (Comer) v Shorten* [1961] IR 304; cf *R v O'Brian* (1965) 50 DLR (2d) 92.

1 *R v Ewens* [1967] 1 QB 322, [1966] 2 All ER 470.

2 As in *Buchanan v Moore* [1963] NI 194.

defendant to attend court and produce his licence or explain its non-production, but *John v Humphreys* decides that this latter course must be adopted.[3]

There is, however, a further difficulty about the application of the doctrine of Bayley J. Precisely when can the negative of a positive averment be said to be 'peculiarly within the knowledge' of the defendant? This question is particularly pertinent in a case in which there is a single readily accessible register of licencees, and the charge is one of carrying on a certain activity without a licence.

(ii) General statutory provision

Statutory guidance for the construction of statutes creating summary offences was first enacted as s 14 of the Summary Jurisdiction Act 1848. This was periodically re-enacted and amended until it achieved its present form in s 101 of the Magistrates' Courts Act 1980 which provides:

> Where the defendant to an information or complaint relies for his defence on any exception, exemption, proviso, excuse or qualification, whether or not it accompanies the description of the offence or matter of complaint in the enactment creating the offence or on which the complaint is founded, the burden of proving the exception, exemption, proviso, excuse or qualification shall be on him; and this notwithstanding that the information or complaint contains an allegation negativing the exception, exemption, proviso, excuse or qualification.

There is comparatively little authority on the construction of this section or of its predecessors, s 39(2) of the Summary Jurisdiction Act 1879,[4] and s 81 of the Magistrates' Courts Act 1952. This is partly due to the fact that decisions which could have been reached by means of a direct application of s 39(2) or s 81 were based on the common law principles which govern trials on indictment,[5] but the matter has ceased to be of any importance since the Court of Appeal concluded in *R v Edwards*[6] that s 101 reproduces the common law. Before that decision it could be argued that there was a difference with regard to the burdens borne by the accused. The wording makes it difficult to escape the conclusion that s 101 is concerned with the legal burden and the authorities support this view,[7] but it was thought that the common law rules might cast nothing more than an evidential burden on an accused relying on an exception, exemption etc. Even in cases where as a matter of statutory construction the legal burden does not shift, it may nevertheless as a matter of tactics be desirable for the accused to adduce some

---

3 [1955] 1 All ER 793. In *Buchanan v Moore* (above) Lord Macdermott would express no opinion about the correctness of *John v Humphreys*. In *Everard v Opperman* [1958] VLR 389 Sholl J said that it was irreconcilable with the Australian cases.

4 The proviso to s 14 of the Summary Jurisdiction Act 1848, the predecessor to s 39(2), was restrictively interpreted (see the remarks of Blackburn J in *Roberts v Humphreys* (1873) LR 8 QB 483 at 489).

5 The much discussed case of *John v Humphreys* [1955] 1 All ER 793, [1955] 1 WLR 325 is one such decision.

6 [1975] QB 27, [1974] 2 All ER 1085.

7 *Gatland v Metropolitan Police Comr* [1968] 2 QB 279, [1968] 2 All ER 100; *Taylor v Ellis* [1956] VLR 457 at 461–2; *Everard v Opperman* [1958] VLR 389 at 391; *Akehurst v Inspector of Quarries* [1964] NZLR 621.

evidence, for example, on a charge of supplying liquor to non-members of a club, that the persons in question were members.[8]

Various tests have been suggested for determining when s 101 or one of its equivalents is applicable. One of the best known is the following:

> Does the section [under which the accused is prosecuted] make the act described an offence subject to particular exceptions, qualifications, etc, which, where applicable, make a prima facie offence an innocent act, or does the statute make an act prima facie innocent an offence when done under certain conditions? In the former case the exception need not be negatived; in the latter words of exception may constitute the offence.[9]

But this, like the other proposed tests, assumes that there is a logical distinction between the definition of an offence and an exception to it. In all cases turning on the applicability of s 101 the question is whether the words alleged to constitute an exception etc are an integral part of the definition of the offence or the equivalent of a defence which would operate by way of confession and avoidance. This is not a question which can be answered on principle. The form of the statute under consideration will often provide the answer. Words like 'unless',[10] 'other than'[11] or 'provided always' being fairly safe indications of the applicability of s 101, but there can be borderline cases.

Nimmo v Alexander Cowan & Sons Ltd,[12] a Scottish appeal to the House of Lords in civil proceedings, was concerned with the construction of s 29(1) of the Factories Act 1961, under which a place at which any person has to work 'shall, so far as is reasonably practicable, be made and kept safe for any person working therein'. Contraventions of the Act are made summary offences by s 155(1) and this accounts for the references which were made to the Scottish equivalent of s 101 of the Magistrates' Courts Act 1980. The issue was whether it was necessary for the plaintiff, a workman who had sustained injuries at his place of work, to plead and prove that it was reasonably practicable to keep the premises safe or whether it lay upon the defendant, his employer, to prove the contrary. By a majority of three to two the House held that the defendant had to plead and prove impracticability. The minority, Lords Reid and Wilberforce, took the view that the words 'so far as is reasonably practicable' are an integral part of the definition of the offence, but two members of the majority, Lords Guest and Pearson, considered that they were a qualification or excuse.[13] The status of the decision as a binding authority on the construction of s 101 of the Magistrates' Courts Act 1980, is debatable, but the importance of some observations of Lord Pearson is beyond dispute. He said that, while exceptions, exemptions and provisos would be easily recognisable from the use of such words as 'except' or 'provided always', the words 'excuse or qualification' showed an

8 *Oxford v Lincoln* (25 February 1982, unreported) QBD, (LEXIS), applying s 101 to construction of Licensing Act 1964, s 161.
9 Gibson J in *Shehan v Cork Justices* [1908] 2 IR 1 at 11.
10 *Buckman v Button* [1943] KB 405, [1943] 2 All ER 82.
11 *Baker v Sweet* [1966] Crim LR 51.
12 [1968] AC 107, [1967] 3 All ER 187.
13 The third member of the majority, Lord Upjohn, did not base his opinion on the construction of the equivalent to s 101, but he was generally in agreement with Lord Pearson's speech. The assumption that the incidence of the burden of proof should be the same in civil proceedings and at a summary trial is questioned by the Hon Sir Francis Adams *Criminal Onus and Exculpations* (New Zealand 1968) para 125.

intention to direct attention to the substance rather than the form of the enactment. It therefore seemed that, at any rate when the form of words did 'not speak for itself', the courts could have regard to the object of the statute creating the offence charged when considering the applicability of s 101.[14]

(iii) Recent developments

The aspect of this area of the law has changed dramatically as a result of two recent cases, one in the Court of Appeal[15] and the other in the House of Lords.[16]

The accused in *Edwards*[17] had been convicted of selling intoxicating liquor by retail without holding a Justices' licence authorising him to do so. He had not given evidence, the prosecution had adduced ample evidence from which sales might be inferred, but none with regard to the absence of a licence. The judgment of the Court of Appeal was delivered by Lawton LJ. He recognised the force, on the particular facts, of the point taken with regard to peculiar knowledge and raised some questions by way of general criticism of doctrines such as that enunciated by Bayley J in *R v Turner*. Who is to decide whether a fact is within the peculiar knowledge of the defendant? Is it a matter on which evidence is receivable? A very learned review of the authorities culminating in the following statement ensued:[18]

> In our judgment this line of authority establishes that over the centuries the common law, as a result of experience and the need to ensure that justice is done both to the community and to defendants, has evolved an exception to the fundamental rule of our criminal law that the prosecution must prove every element of the offence charged. This exception, like so much else in the common law, was hammered out on the anvil of pleading. It is limited to offences arising under enactments which prohibit the doing of an act save in specified circumstances or by persons of specified classes or with specified qualifications or with the licence or permission of specified authorities. Whenever the prosecution seeks to rely on this exception, the court must construe the enactment under which the charge is laid. If the true construction is that the enactment prohibits the doing of acts, subject to provisos, exceptions and the like, then the prosecution can rely upon the exception.

This part of the judgment concludes with the clearly expressed opinion that the burden borne by the accused in cases covered by the statement was persuasive.

Lawton LJ's reformulation of the common law rules with regard to exceptions had the two great merits of avoiding problems with regard to the meaning of 'peculiar knowledge' and of equiparating the law governing trials on indictment with that applicable to summary trials. Moreover the reference to the court's duty to construe the statute under which the charge is laid left room for a consideration of the object of the legislation before

---

14 See 92 LQR at 418.
15 *R v Edwards* [1975] QB 27, [1974] 2 All ER 1085.
16 *R v Hunt* [1987] AC 352, [1987] 1 All ER 1. The speech of Lord Griffiths, in whose reasoning Lords Keith and Mackay explicitly concurred, is taken to express the decision of the House.
17 [1975] QB 27, [1974] 2 All ER 1085. For a criticism of some of the historical statements in the judgment and of the utility of the general principle stated in it see Adrian Zuckerman 'The Third Exception to the Woolmington Rule' 92 LQR 401.
18 [1975] QB 27 at 39–40.

concluding that it prohibits the doing of acts subject to provisos, exceptions and the like.[19] Some guidance to the application of the principle was provided by *Guyll v Bright*[20] where the Divisional Court held the burden to be cast upon the defendant pursuant to these rules, despite the presence in the same statute of a provision explicitly casting upon the defendant the burden in relation to offences created by some other sections of the Act, but not by the one actually charged.

The whole matter was reviewed by the House of Lords in *R v Hunt*.[1] The accused was charged with unlawful possession of a controlled drug. The prosecution proved that the substance in question contained the relevant drug, but did not specify in what proportion it existed. Regulations made under the Act defined exempted substances to include those with a specified very small proportion of the otherwise illicit drug. It was argued that since the prosecution had not shown the proportion to exceed the low threshold, there was no case to answer. This view was rejected[2] both by the Crown Court and by the Court of Appeal. The House of Lords was invited to review the whole area, and to overrule *R v Edwards* on the basis that it was inconsistent with the decision of the House in *Woolmington*. The Misuse of Drugs Act 1971, s 5(2) under which the accused was charged does not in terms contain a proviso or exception, but is made subject to the relevant regulations. The regulations[3] did not themselves individually refer to exceptions or provisos, but were generally headed 'Exemptions from Certain Provisions for the Misuse of Drugs Act 1971', and were made pursuant to a power[4] granted to 'except' from the provisions of the Act by regulation. It should also be noted that the Act provides a number of defences capable of applying to an offence under s 5(2) whereby a persuasive burden is explicitly cast upon the accused.

The House of Lords took the opportunity to endorse the decision and reasoning in *R v Edwards*, subject only to widening its scope so that it applied not only to provisions which could be brought within the linguistic boundaries of exceptions and provisos,[5] but to provisions the import of which was to create exemptions from otherwise generally applicable provisions.[6] Its approach endorsed that taken in *Nimmo v Alexander Cowan & Sons Ltd*,[7] in suggesting that:[8]

> if the linguistic construction of the statute did not clearly indicate on whom the burden should lie the court should look to other considerations to determine the intention of Parliament, such as the mischief at which the Act was aimed and practical considerations affecting the burden of proof and, in particular, the ease or difficulty that the respective parties would encounter in discharging the burden.

19 In accordance with the views of Lords Pearson and Guest in *Nimmo v Alexander Cowan & Sons Ltd* [1968] AC 107, [1967] 3 All ER 187.
20 (1986) 84 Cr App Rep 260.
1 [1987] AC 352, [1987] 1 All ER 1.
2 Though for different reasons.
3 Misuse of Drugs Regulations 1973, SI 1973/797.
4 Misuse of Drugs Act 1971, s 7.
5 No attention was paid to r 6(C) of the Indictment Rules 1971 excusing reference to exceptions etc in the statement of the offence in the indictment, presumably because of r 8 which provides that nothing in the rules affect the law of evidence.
6 This also seems to be the position in Australia, see *Dowling v Bowie* (1952) 86 CLR 136; *Bannister v Bowen* (1985) 65 ACTR 3; *Macarone v McKone, ex p Macarone* [1986] 1 Qd R 284.
7 [1968] AC 107, [1967] 3 All ER 187.
8 At 374, 11.

Especial stress was laid upon the final consideration which was regarded as making it generally unlikely that Parliament would be taken to have imposed an onerous burden upon a defendant. It was by reference to this point that the House distinguished between the earlier decisions in *R v Oliver*[9] and *R v Putland and Sorrell*.[10] In the former the Court of Criminal Appeal upheld a conviction for selling sugar without a licence although the prosecution had offered no evidence of the absence of a licence, while in the latter it quashed a conviction for buying clothing without surrendering coupons because no evidence had been offered by the prosecution that no coupons had been surrendered. In the House's view a licensed trader could easily prove that he had a licence, but it would have been much more difficult for a purchaser of clothing to prove that he had surrendered coupons. It should also be noted that this was no mere incantation of high sounding theory, but was expressed in practical terms by reversing the Court of Appeal, and quashing the conviction upon the basis of a very strict construction of the relevant provision, which could be taken to reduce to a minimum the number of cases in which a persuasive burden would be cast upon the defence.

Despite the result of its application in *Hunt* the reasoning of the House of Lords has been widely attacked by commentators.[11] The main burden of this criticism is that the argument gives insufficient weight to the principle of *Woolmington* by breaking down the strict limitation upon the exceptions to the general rule that the prosecution always bears the burden of proof in criminal cases, and substituting for it considerations of policy to be determined by the judges upon only the very vaguest of criteria. It has to be conceded that there has been inconsistency of interpretation of the position in summary proceedings.[12] It can further be argued that this may encourage much looser drafting of statutory offences by releasing the draftsman from the need to consider carefully each element of each new statutory offence with a view to deciding whether by explicit provision, or formulation as an exception or proviso, so as to cast a burden upon the accused.[13] On the other hand it can also be argued that by departing from the tyranny of verbal formulation the decision in *Hunt* permits reconsideration, even of those provisions which do contain the appropriate verbal formulae if policy argues against the imposition of a burden upon the defence.[14]

It is submitted that the effects of *Hunt* are unlikely to prove so deleterious as its critics assert, nor so beneficial as its supporters may hope. Statutory provisions are likely to go on being drafted in the same careful way, and draftsmen will not willingly run the risk of an unwelcome construction if it can be pre-empted by use of an appropriate formula. It is doubtful whether judges will regard the reasoning in *Hunt* as a licence to re-write Acts of

9   [1944] KB 68, [1943] 2 All ER 800.
10   [1946] 1 All ER 85.
11   See Healy 'Proof and Policy: No Golden Threads' [1987] Crim LR 355; Smith 'The Presumption of Innocence' (1987) 38 NILQ 223; and Mirfield 'The Legacy of *Hunt*' [1988] Crim LR 19 and 'An Ungrateful Reply' [1988] Crim LR 233. It has also attracted some support, see Zuckerman 'No third exception to the *Woolmington* Rule' (1987) 103 LQR 170; Birch 'Hunting the Snark: The Elusive Statutory Exception' [1988] Crim LR 221.
12   See Smith 'The Presumption of Innocence' (1987) 38 NILQ 285 at 231–236.
13   For a more sceptical view of the draftsman's approach, see Bennion 'Statutory Exceptions: A Third Knot in the Golden Thread' [1988] Crim LR 31.
14   This probably accounts for its acceptance by the High Court of Australia, see *DPP v United Telecasters Ltd* (1990) 91 ALR 1.

Parliament, or to subvert existing canons of construction. Its boundaries should also be noted. It was dealing only with statutory offences, and leaves unaffected the major common law defences where the prosecution will continue to bear the legal, though often not the evidential, burden. It also seems that the court will be unlikely to extend its effects to those statutory offences which explicitly require mens rea by including some such term as 'knowingly',[15] or 'willfully'.[16]

It was regarded as virtually axiomatic in *Hunt* that if a burden were to be cast upon the accused by a statutory provision it must be a persuasive burden, to be satisfied by proof upon the balance of probabilities. This was regarded as mandated by the need to provide congruence with the position in cases governed by s 101 of the Magistrates' Courts Act 1980 which, as noted above,[17] is worded so as to connote a persuasive burden by using the verb 'prove'. It is not obvious that this will always be the appropriate analogy. If there is nothing in the language of the statutory provision to be construed to indicate more than the need to distinguish the case from the general rule imposing both evidential and legal burdens upon the Crown, then general policy should be allowed to dictate whether the imposition should be of the one or of the other.

It remains to be seen how far these developments will impinge upon previously unsettled and unsatisfactory areas, such as the rules relating to the construction of s 57 of the Offences Against the Person Act 1861. The first proviso excludes foreigners from the definition of bigamy if the second marriage ceremony was celebrated elsewhere than in England or Ireland. It was held in *R v Audley*[18] that, in such a case, the accused must allege and prove that he was not a British subject at the material time. The decision is consistent with the rule laid down in *R v Edwards* provided the word 'prove' is taken to refer to the legal burden, but *R v Curgerwen*[19] is inconsistent with the rule. In that case the Court for Crown Cases Reserved held that the prosecution bears what must certainly be regarded as the legal burden of negativing part of the second proviso exempting persons marrying a second time whose husbands or wives shall have been continually absent for seven years 'and shall not have been known by such persons to be living within that time.' The decision was that the Crown bears the burden of proving the requisite knowledge. *R v Jones*[20] does no more than place an evidential burden on the accused on the issue of continuous absence; it is very difficult to see why, so long as *R v Curgerwen* stands, he should also bear a legal burden.[21]

(iv) Reform

We have seen that is is difficult to believe that what may be called the '*Carr-Briant*' construction will not be applied by the courts to all criminal statutes

15 See *Westminster City Council v Croyalgrange Ltd* [1986] 2 All ER 353, [1986] 1 WLR 674.
16 *Hirst and Agu v Chief Constable of West Yorkshire* (1987) 85 Cr App Rep 143.
17 At p 136.
18 [1907] 1 KB 383.
19 (1865) LR 1 CCR 1.
20 (1883) 11 QBD 118.
21 *R v Broughton* [1953] VLR 572 decides that he does not, but the case was criticised in *R v Bonnor* [1957] VLR 226. See the discussions by Norval Morris in 18 MLR 482 and by D J MacDougall 21 MLR 510.

which expressly place the burden of proof on the accused, state that 'proof' lies upon him or require him to 'prove' something. It is in accordance with the ordinary principles of literal statutory construction that the burden imposed on the accused should be the legal burden. The discharge of an evidential burden does not prove anything, and the construction of s 30 of the Bills of Exchange Act 1882, according to which 'proved' means 'sufficient evidence has been adduced', can be explained on the footing that the section is a statement of the pre-existing common law.

Up to a point, the policy underlying statutes which place a burden upon the accused is justifiable because, in the absence of such a provision, a number of unmeritorious submissions of no case to answer, on account, for example, of the prosecutor's failure to give evidence of the lack of a lawful excuse, would have to be accepted. There is, however, an overwhelming objection to placing the legal burden on the accused in these cases, even after allowance has been made for the fact that the standard of proof would be that appropriate to civil proceedings; it means that the tribunal of fact may be obliged to convict a person of whose guilt they are so far from being sure as to regard the probabilities of the existence of a lawful excuse as equally balanced. The danger of unmeritorious submissions of no case can be met by placing an evidential burden with regard to lawful excuse etc on the accused. This was the recommendation of the 11th Report of the Criminal Law Revision Committee,[1] and it would have applied to the common law burden of proving insanity placed upon the accused as well as to existing statutory burdens. The recommended clause[2] could of course have been expressly excluded by subsequent legislation, and there was a necessary exception covering cases in which the accused could bring in a third party and was entitled to an acquittal on proof that his default was due to that of a third party; an example is provided by proceedings against a retailer under the food and drugs legislation who alleges that he was blameless and that the fault lay with the manufacturer.[3]

Clause 8(1) read in part as follows:

Where by virtue of any rule of law or existing enactment there falls on the accused in any procedings any burden of proof with respect to a matter relevant to his guilt or innocence, then, ... (a) unless there is sufficient evidence to raise an issue with respect to that matter, that matter shall be taken as proved against him.

It was a little less favourable to the accused than s 25(3) of the Theft Act 1968, under which, on a charge of going equipped for stealing, proof that the accused had with him any article made or adapted for use in committing a burglary, theft or cheat 'shall be evidence' that he had it with him for such use. This subsection merely provided for the discharge of the prosecution's evidential burden on the issue of unlawful purpose. It did not place an evidential burden upon the accused. Clause 8(1) would have had this effect and the generality of its application rendered it desirable that it should have done so for it applied to such matters as the common law burden of proving insanity or raising the issue of self defence, as well as statutory provisions such as s 101 of the Magistrates' Courts Act 1980, in relation to which the phraseology of s 25(3) of the Theft Act would be inept. Casual observation

1 Paras 137–142.
2 Cl 8.
3 See Wasik 'Shifting the Burden of Strict Liability' [1982] Crim LR 567.

of the multitude of statutory provisions passed since the publication of the 11th Committee's Report and imposing a legal burden on the accused might lead one to suppose that its recommendations in this area had passed unheeded. Such an impression is misleading. In most such cases the clauses simply dilute what would otherwise be offences of strict liability, by making it a defence to prove absence of negligence.[4] That the general principle espoused in the 11th Report carries weight can be seen in the government response to the proposal of the Whitford Committee on the Reform of Copyright and Design Law to impose upon the accused the legal burden of proving lack of knowledge, in a criminal prosecution for infringement of copyright.[5] The significant difference between these situations is that in the former the government is prepared to impose a burden of proof on the accused by way of alleviation of otherwise strict liability, but it is not so prepared where to do so would be to deprive the accused of the benefit of the general rule which he currently enjoys.

These matters were reconsidered in a report to the Law Commission on the question of the codification of English criminal law.[6] It was felt that the Criminal Law Revision Committee had been too radical in proposing, first, that the legal burden should immediately and automatically be assumed by the prosecution in relation to all existing statutory offences,[7] and, second, in proposing that the common form of casting a burden upon the defence by the use of the term 'prove' in one of its forms in relation to a matter of defence should be construed as casting only an evidential burden.[8] Instead the report favoured the more limited measure of abandonment of the exceptions rule for future statutory provisions by requiring express drafting to cast a burden upon the defence, though by appropriate drafting, such as by using the term 'prove' in one of its forms, it would still be possible to cast a legal burden upon the accused. It has however been suggested that even this proposal is likely to be impractical,[9] and one of its authors has, in the light of *Hunt*, reverted to advocating the more radial proposals of the Criminal Law Revision Committee.[10] The truth of the matter is that most lawyers find it distasteful that a jury should ever have to be directed to convict when it thinks, after considering all of the evidence, that it as likely as not that the accused is innocent.

D. THE INTERPRETATION OF AGREEMENTS AFFECTING THE BURDEN OF PROOF

The incidence of the burden of proof may be determined by the agreement of the parties in civil cases,[11] and, where there is such an agreement, there

---

4 Examples are legion; Companies Act 1985, s 343(8), illustrates a common form of provision. See generally Glanville Williams *Textbook of Criminal Law* (1983) para 2.5.
5 Compare 'Copyright and Designs Law' (Cmnd 6732) para 711 and the subsequent Consultative Document (Cmnd 8302) ch 14 para 12. No such presumption is made in the Copyright, Designs and Patents Act 1988.
6 Law Com 143 (1985).
7 Because there should be an opportunity to re-examine each such provision in detail.
8 Because this would fly in the face of ordinary English usage.
9 By Bennion 'Statutory Exceptions: A Third Knot in the Golden Thread' [1988] Crim LR 31 at 32.
10 See Smith 'The Presumption of Innocence' (1987) 38 NILQ 223 at 243.
11 *Levy v Assicurazioni Generali* [1940] AC 791, [1940] 3 All ER 427.

can be little doubt that the burden in question would generally be taken to be the legal one. This is also the burden which has been the subject of discussion in cases concerned with the construction of contracts for the carriage of goods by sea, and insurance against various types of loss.

1. PERILS OF THE SEA—*THE GLENDARROCH*

If a plaintiff claims damages from shipowners for breach of contract to carry goods safely, and the defendants rely on a clause exempting them from loss or damage occasioned to the goods by a peril of the sea, they must prove that the latter occurred, and alone[12] caused the damage in question; but, if the plaintiff relies upon a proviso to the exemption clause relating to negligence on the part of the defendants, the legal burden of proving negligence rests on him. These points were established in the leading case of *The Glendarroch*[13] where the ship on which the goods had been placed struck a rock, and Lord Esher said:

> The plaintiffs would have to prove the contract and the non-delivery. If they leave that in doubt, of course they fail. The defendants' answer is 'Yes; but the case was brought within the exception—within its ordinary meaning'. That lies upon them. Then the plaintiffs have a right to say there are exceptional circumstances, viz that the damage was brought about by the negligence of the defendants' servants, and it seems to me that it is for the plaintiffs to make out the second exception.[14]

2. INSURANCE EXCEPTIONS

This case was among those followed by Bailhache J in *Munro, Brice & Co v War Risks Association*,[15] which was concerned with an insurance policy covering the loss of a ship through the perils of the sea, subject to an exception in respect of enemy action. He held that the defendants bore the legal burden of proving that the ship was lost in consequence of the latter with the result that the plaintiffs succeeded on their claim as the ship had not been heard of after she set sail, and there was no evidence of the cause of her disappearance. The law on this point cannot, however, be regarded as completely settled for, in the earlier case of *Hurst v Evans*,[16] Lush J had decided that, where an insurance policy against loss of jewellery contained an exception in respect of theft by the plaintiff's servants, it was incumbent on the plaintiff to negative loss from this cause. This is not the kind of problem that can be solved by logical argument, for there is no difference between a clause which is construed to read 'The insurers shall be liable for loss except that which occurs in specified circumstances' and a rule which says 'the insurers shall be liable for loss arising from all causes other than those specified',[17] but it is

---

12 Such provisions are sometimes expressly controlled by statute, see Merchant Shipping Act 1979, Sch 3 art 18.
13 [1894] P 226.
14 At 231; contrast *Slattery v Mance* [1962] 1 QB 676, [1962] 1 All ER 525. In the case of insurance of a ship against fire the insurer must establish scuttling on the balance of probabilities. See also *Doats v Weekes* (1986) 82 FLR 334.
15 [1918] 2 KB 78.
16 [1917] 1 KB 352.
17 Cf the arguments of Professor Stone in 60 LQR 278.

submitted that practical considerations as well as previous authority[18] are in favour of the view of Bailhache J. He said that if he had been asked to advise on evidence in *Hurst v Evans*, it would not have occurred to him to suggest that the plaintiff should call all his servants, one after the other to swear that they had not stolen the jewels, 'The procession would be a long one if Messrs Whiteley were the plaintiffs.'[19]

SECTION 3. DISCHARGE OF THE BURDEN

Once the party who bears the evidential burden has discharged it by adducing evidence sufficient to justify consideration of a particular issue, it becomes necessary for the party bearing the legal burden on that issue, the proponent, to persuade the trier of fact that it should be decided in his favour. If his evidence is less persuasive than that of his opponent he must inevitably fail. If it is more persuasive, the question is whether he must equally inevitably succeed. The answer to that question demands consideration of the requisite standard of proof and how it should be explained to the jury. It is generally accepted that English law applies two main standards, though their precise connotation, formulation and application, the possibility of a third standard and their relationship to precisely quantifiable evidence, raise debatable issues which will be discussed in this section of the chapter. It is first necessary to consider the standard which must be achieved to discharge an evidential burden.

A. DISCHARGE OF EVIDENTIAL BURDEN[20]

No precise formulae have been laid down with regard to the standard of proof required for the discharge of an evidential burden and, as this is not a matter upon which it can ever be necessary for a judge to direct a jury, there is no reason why it should ever become the subject of formulae. It is, however, possible to distinguish between criminal cases in which the evidential, but not the legal, burden on a particular issue such as provocation or automatism, is borne by the accused, and criminal cases in which the evidential burden is borne by the Crown.

When the accused bears the evidential burden alone, it is necessary for there to be only such evidence as would, if believed and uncontradicted, induce a reasonable doubt in the mind of a reasonable jury as to whether his version might be true, for example as to whether he was provoked or in a state of automatism. To quote from the speech of Lord Morris of Borth-y-Gest in *Bratty v A-G for Northern Ireland*:

> There was no sufficient evidence, fit to be left to a jury, on which a jury might conclude that the appellant had acted unconsciously and involuntarily or which *might leave a jury in reasonable doubt whether this might be so*.[1]

18 *Gorman v Hand-in-Hand Insurance Co* (1877) IR 11 CL 224; his dictum was approved by Donaldson J in *Golodetz & Co v Czarnikow-Rionda Co* [1979] 2 All ER 726 at 743.
19 [1918] 2 KB at 86.
20 See Wood 'The Quantum of Proof in Criminal Trials, The Submission of No Case to Answer' (1961) 77 LQR 491, and Glass 'Insufficiency of Evidence to Raise a Case to Answer' (1981) 55 ALJ 842.
1 [1963] AC 386 at 419 (italics supplied). See also *USA v Shephard* [1977] SCR 1067.

In the words of Lord Devlin in the same case, the evidence must be enough to 'suggest a reasonable possibility'. There must be some *evidence*, derived either from the prosecution or adduced by the defence; it is not enough to rely upon an out of court self-serving statement,[2] and probably not enough to give equivocal evidence from which the jury is invited to draw a medical inference, itself contradicted by the evidence of a doctor.[3] Where the accused bears both the legal and evidential burdens, for example in relation to insanity and related defences such as diminished responsibility, it is necessary for him to go further and to adduce evidence such as might satisfy a jury on the balance of probabilities. Thus in *R v Dix*[4] it was held incumbent upon the accused to adduce some medical evidence before the defence of diminished responsibility could be left to the jury. When the evidential burden is borne by the Crown, it must be discharged, to quote Lord Devlin once more, by 'such evidence as, if believed, and if left uncontradicted and unexplained, could be accepted by the jury as proof'.[5] It is not enough that the accused fails to deny an allegation made by the prosecution, if no evidence is finally called by the prosecution to prove the allegation.[6] 'Proof' in this context must mean proof beyond reasonable doubt, and, in spite of occasional suggestions to the contrary,[7] the standard must, at least from the theoretical point of view, be higher than that required to discharge an evidential burden borne by a party to civil proceedings.

For the sake of theoretical completeness it may be added that when, in a civil case, the party with the legal burden on a particular issue also bears the evidential burden, it is discharged by the adduction of sufficient evidence to satisfy a reasonable trier of fact on the balance of probabilities.[8] If the party bearing the evidential burden does not bear the legal burden, the former is discharged by the adduction of sufficient evidence to leave the mind of a reasonable trier of fact in a state of equilibrium.

B. DISCHARGE OF LEGAL BURDEN[9]

1. DEGREE OF THE BURDEN

The cases show that there is a difference between the standards of proof in criminal and civil proceedings. The distinction was stated as clearly as it can be stated by Denning J in *Miller v Minister of Pensions*.[10] Speaking of the degree of cogency which the evidence on a criminal charge must reach before the accused can be convicted he said:

2 *R v Newcastle Justices, ex p Hindle* [1984] 1 All ER 770.
3 *R v Bailey* (1983) 77 Cr App Rep 76.
4 (1982) 74 Cr App Rep 306.
5 *Jayasena v R* [1970] AC 618 at 624.
6 *Chappell v DPP* (1988) 89 Cr App Rep 82.
7 *R v Smith* (1865) 34 LJMC 153: *Wilson v Buttery* [1926] SASR 150 at 154.
8 It is not discharged by the exhibition of an anonymous letter from a third party to an affidavit sworn by the defendant, *Barclays Bank plc v Anderson* (1987) Times, 10 March.
9 See further Cowen and Carter *Essays on the Law of Evidence* 242–249, and Glanville Williams 'The Direction to the Jury on the Burden of Proof' [1954] Crim LR 464. For the standard of proof at a trial within a trial, see p 171 below.
10 [1947] 2 All ER 372 at 373–374. For an earlier statement see *Cooper v Slade* (1858) 6 HL Cas 746 at 772.

That degree is well settled. It need not reach certainty, but it must carry a high degree of probability. Proof beyond a reasonable doubt does not mean proof beyond the shadow of a doubt. The law would fail to protect the community if it admitted fanciful possibilities to deflect the course of justice. If the evidence is so strong against a man as to leave only a remote possibility in his favour, which can be dismissed with the sentence 'of course it is possible but not in the least probable' the case is proved beyond reasonable doubt, but nothing short of that will suffice.[11]

When speaking of the degree of cogency which evidence must reach in order that it may discharge the legal burden in a civil case, his Lordship said:

That degree is well settled. It must carry a reasonable degree of probability, but not so high as is required in a criminal case. If the evidence is such that the tribunal can say: 'we think it more probable than not', the burden is discharged, but if the probabilities are equal it is not.

The validity of the distinction has not gone unquestioned. Lord Goddard once confessed that he had some difficulty in understanding how there are or can be two standards,[12] and Hilbery J is reported to have said: 'I personally have never seen the difference between the onus of proof in a civil and criminal case. If a thing is proved, it is proved, but I am not entitled to that view.'[13] Yet it can hardly be doubted that there are degrees of probability. If this much is conceded, the law can intelligibly require that a very high degree must be established by the prosecution at a criminal trial. So long as the proportions do not become excessive, it is better that people who are probably guilty should go free than that those whose innocence is reasonably possible should be convicted. The importance of the liberty of the subject contributes to the applicability of the criminal standard to cases of contempt of court in civil proceedings.[14] It is not the complete explanation however since the application of the civil standard to a contempt by a corporate defendant[15] was subsequently disapproved by the Court of Appeal.[16] The criminal standard is also required before summary judgment will be granted in civil proceedings, and in such cases is different from even the high standard required by the application of the flexible *Bater v Bater* standard before an interim payment order will be ordered.[17] That standard may also be explicitly required by statute or statutory instrument for other good reasons of policy.[18]

It will be submitted that there are no more than two standards of proof recognised by the law, though allowance must be made for the fact that some occurrences are antecedently more probable than others, and the conse-

---

11 The propriety of summing up in terms of probability and possibility was questioned in *R v McKenna* (1964) 81 (Pt 1) WN NSW 330; but the reference to probabilities can be regarded as a direction to use commonsense (*R v Coe* [1967] VR 712).

12 *R v Hepworth and Fearnley* [1955] 2 QB 600 at 603.

13 In the course of argument in *R v Murtagh and Kennedy* (1955) 39 Cr App Rep 72.

14 *Re Bramblevale* [1970] Ch 128, [1969] 3 All ER 1062; *Nelson v Nelson* [1988] SCLR 663; *Dean v Dean* [1987] 1 FLR 517. Conversely its absence contributes to the application of the civil standard to prove breaches of conditions upon which recognisances may have been entered into criminal proceedings, *R v Marlow Justices, ex p O'Sullivan* [1984] Crim LR 106.

15 In *West Oxfordshire District Council v Beratec Ltd* (1986) Times, 30 October (sequestration of company assets for breach of undertaking in action for nuisance).

16 In *Dean v Dean*, above.

17 See *Ricci Burns Ltd v Toole* [1988] NLJR 312.

18 *Judd v Minister of Pensions and National Insurance* [1966] 2 QB 580, [1965] 3 All ER 642.

quences of some decisions are more serious than others. People are less likely to commit murder than to drive recklessly, and less likely to be fraudulent than to be negligent. It is more serious to be imprisoned for life for murder than to be conditionally discharged by a magistrate for assault, and it is more serious to determine the legitimacy of a child than whether or not a civil trespass has occurred. For these reasons prosecutors on the more serious criminal charges or those carrying graver consequences, and plaintiffs in some civil cases, have higher hurdles to surmount than when they are making less serious allegations or those with more trivial consequences. This led Denning LJ to speak of degrees of proof within the same standard:

> It is of course true that by our law a higher standard of proof is required in criminal cases than in civil cases. But this is subject to the qualification that there is no absolute standard in either case. In criminal cases the charge must be proved beyond reasonable doubt, but there may be degrees of proof within that standard ... So also in civil cases the case must be proved by a preponderance of probability, but there may be degrees of probability within that standard. The degree depends on the subject-matter. A civil court, when considering a charge of fraud, will naturally require for itself a higher degree of probability than that which it would require when asking if negligence is established. It does not adopt so high a degree as a criminal court, even when it is considering a charge of a criminal nature; but still it does require a degree of probability which is commensurate with the occasion.[19]

The point was put more succinctly by Morris LJ when he said:

> Though no court and no jury would give less careful attention to issues lacking gravity than to those marked by it, the very elements of gravity become a part of the whole range of circumstances which have to be weighed in the scale when deciding as to the balance of probabilities.[20]

This view cannot, of course, be taken to suggest the imposition of a *stricter* standard than that of proof beyond reasonable doubt in relation to the most serious criminal cases.[1] The application of a flexible standard has been endorsed and applied by the House of Lords to the judicial review of the decisions of immigration officers in illegal entry cases:

> The reviewing court will therefore require to be satisfied that the facts which are required for the justification of the restraint put on liberty do exist. The flexibility of the civil standard of proof suffices to ensure that the court will require the high degree of probability which is appropriate to what is at stake.[2]

It was generally agreed that the civil standard was more appropriate than

19 *Bater v Bater* [1951] P 35 at 36–7. The passage has met with frequent judicial approval, for example that of Lord Pearce in *Blyth v Blyth* [1966] AC 643 at 673. See also *Thomas Bates & Son v Wyndhams (Lingerie) Ltd* [1981] 1 All ER 1077, [1981] 1 WLR 505.
20 *Hornal v Neuberger Products Ltd* [1957] 1 QB 247 at 266. This answers the observation of Sir Carleton Allen (*Legal Duties* 288) that it would startle the legal world and the public if, when trying an action for damages, the judge were to say to the jury, 'You need not be as careful in arriving at your conclusion as if you were trying a criminal case.'
1 See *R v RLR* (1988) 65 CR (3d) 235.
2 *Khawaja v Secretary of State* [1984] AC 74 at 113–14, [1963] 1 All ER 765 at 784.

the criminal,[3] but Lord Scarman himself, echoing Lord Denning in *Bater v Bater* described this as largely a matter of words.[4] Even the difference in words is eroded however when the House speaks of requiring to be satisfied with nothing less than 'probability of a high degree' or 'convincing proof'.[5]

2. DESCRIPTION OF THE BURDEN

It is possible that the law governing the different standards of proof is more settled and better understood than the preceding passages might suggest. Some of the difficulty is created by the words in which the standard is formulated. In ordinary civil cases it is usually expressed as involving the 'preponderance of probability', the 'balance of probabilities', or the 'preponderance of evidence'. It might be argued that the last of these seems to involve no more than the preponderance of the evidence adduced by the proponent of an issue over that adduced by its opponent.[6] It is more common however to regard all of these terms as synonymous, and as connoting not merely relative preponderance over the evidence of the opponent but satisfaction of a prescribed level of probability.[7] The House of Lords has pronounced any other view as being contrary to common sense since a judge should not be forced to find proved an occurrence which he regards on the evidence as extremely improbable.[8]

[The trial judge] adopted an erroneous approach to this case by regarding himself as compelled to choose between two theories, both of which he regarded as extremely improbable, or one of which he regarded as extremely improbable and the other of which he regarded as virtually impossible. He should have borne in mind, and considered carefully in his judgment, the third alternative which was open to him, namely that the evidence left him in doubt . . ., and that, in these circumstances, the shipowners had failed to discharge the burden of proof which was upon them.

It has however been proposed that to avoid confusion a new formulation should be adopted which recognises the variability of amount required to satisfy the standard in different situations:

---

3 Lord Bridge described his conversion from one view to the other at 124, 792. See *R v Milk Marketing Board, ex p Austin* (1983) Times, 21 March, QBD, for a case where the issue was regarded as so serious as to demand the traditional formulation of the full criminal standard.
4 At 112, 783.
5 At 124, 792.
6 Some support for this view can be gleaned from the speech of Viscount Simon in *Hickman v Peacey* [1945] AC 304 at 318, [1945] 2 All ER 215 at 220; and from that of Lord Reid in *S v S* [1972] AC 24 at 41, [1970] 3 All ER 107 at 109.
7 See *Ong Ah Chuan v Public Prosecutor* [1981] AC 648 at 669; *Larby v Armement L Hermans SA* [1956] 2 Lloyd's Rep 43 at 45. See also *Briginshaw v Briginshaw* (1938) 60 CLR 336. The same view prevails in the United States, see Devitt and Blackman *Federal Jury Practice and Instructions* (3rd edn, 1977) para 71.14. 'To establish by a preponderance of evidence means to prove that something is more likely so than not so.'
8 *Rhesa Shipping Co SA v Edmunds* [1985] 2 All ER 712 at 718, [1985] 1 WLR 948 at 956. Lord Brandon attributed the contrary view to an unjudicial dictum of Mr Sherlock Holmes.

the plaintiff (or the party on whom the burden rests) must satisfy the court that it is reasonably safe in all the circumstances of the case to act on the evidence before the court, bearing in mind the consequences which will follow.[9]

It is extremely rare to find a jury in a civil case, but even when one is present it is not necessary for the judge in every case to which it is relevant to give a direction about the flexibility of civil standards under the doctrine of *Bater v Bater* since this will often be no more than a matter of common sense.[10]

The problem of formulation is still more acute in criminal cases where a direction has to be given to the jury.

In 1949 Lord Goddard CJ said:

> Once a judge begins to use the words 'reasonable doubt' and to try to explain what is a reasonable doubt and what is not, he is much more likely to confuse the jury than if he tells them in plain language, 'It is the duty of the prosecution to satisfy you of the prisoner's guilt'.[11]

He returned to this theme in *R v Summers*,[12] but his words were much stronger as they amount to a prohibition on the use of the phrase 'reasonable doubt' by trial judges when summing up in criminal cases. He said:

> If the jury is told that it is their duty to regard the evidence and see that it satisfies them so that they can feel sure when they return a verdict of guilty, that is much better than using the expression 'reasonable doubt' and I hope in future that that will be done.

Lord Goddard subsequently indicated that his objection to the old formula was the difficulty of following explanations of what does, and does not, constitute a reasonable doubt. He thought that no real guidance is afforded by saying it must not be a fanciful doubt, and to say it must be such a doubt as would make jurymen hesitate in their own affairs does not suggest any particular standard because one juryman might hesitate where another would not do so.[13] In another case Lord Goddard said:

> Let us leave out of account, if we can, any expression such as 'giving the prisoner the benefit of the doubt'. It is not a question of giving the benefit of a doubt; if the jury are left with any degree of doubt whether the prisoner is guilty, then the case has not been proved.[14]

An appeal founded on the ground that the trial judge had not told the

9 *Re J S (a minor)* [1981] Fam 22 at 29, [1980] 1 All ER 1061 at 1066.
10 See *Lawrence v Chester Chronicle* (1986) Times, 8 February.
11 *R v Kritz* [1950] 1 KB 82 at 90, [1949] 2 All ER 406 at 410.
12 [1952] 1 All ER 1059.
13 *R v Hepworth and Fearnley* [1955] 2 QB 600 at 603, [1955] 2 All ER 918 at 919. For similar criticisms see *Brown v R* (1913) 17 CLR 570. The idea of a doubt which would cause jurymen to hesitate in their own affairs is traceable to the summing-up of Pollock CB in *R v Manning* (1849) 30 CCC Sess Pap 654: 'If the conclusion to which you are conducted be that there is that degree of certainty in the case which you would act upon in your own grave and important concerns, that is the degree of certainty which the law requires and which will justify you in returning a verdict of guilty.'
14 *R v Onufrejczyk* [1955] 1 QB 388 at 391, [1955] 1 All ER 247 at 249. The reference to giving the prisoner the benefit of the doubt has been traced back to the eighteenth century and appears to have the blessing of the House of Lords: *Woolmington v D P P* [1935] AC 462 at 481; *Mancini v D P P* [1942] AC 1 at 11, [1941] 3 All ER 272 at 279.

jury to give the accused the benefit of the doubt was dismissed in *R v Blackburn*[15] where a direction which did no more than stress the point that the jury must be satisfied of the accused's guilt was approved. In *R v Murtagh and Kennedy*,[16] on the other hand, an appeal was allowed because the summing up had not made it sufficiently clear that the jury must acquit if they were left in doubt concerning the accused's explanation of the facts. In *R v Hepworth and Fearnley*[17] an appeal was allowed on the ground that a direction to the effect that the jury must be satisfied of the accused's guilt was inadequate when the charge was one of receiving. The judgment of the Court of Criminal Appeal was delivered by Lord Goddard CJ:

> One would be on safe ground if one said in a criminal case to a jury: 'you must be satisfied beyond reasonable doubt', and one could also say, 'you the jury, must be completely satisfied', or better still, 'you must feel sure of the prisoner's guilt'.[18]

In spite of this approval of three different ways of saying the same thing, including the reference to the time-honoured standard of proof beyond reasonable doubt, the Court of Criminal Appeal and the Court of Appeal have had to express their disapproval of the trial judge's summing up concerning the standard of proof in a number of subsequent cases,[19] and similar difficulties have been experienced in other common law jurisdictions.[20]

It is hardly surprising that the English courts[1] and the Judicial Committee of the Privy Council[2] are against any set form of words:

> If the jury are made to understand that they have to be satisfied and must not return a verdict against the defendant unless they feel sure, and that the onus is all the time on the prosecution and not on the defence, then whether the judge uses one form of language or another is neither here nor there.[3]

It is the effect upon the jury of whichever words are used that matters, although the Court of Appeal has endorsed the specimen direction contained in guidance published by the Judicial Studies Board, and approved by the Lord Chief Justice, which recommends 'The burden of proof is upon the prosecution. It is for the prosecution to establish the defendant's guilt.' It is

---

15 (1955) 39 Cr App Rep 84 n. The Attorney-General refused his fiat for an appeal to the House of Lords in this case, but it is difficult to say what is left of the decision after *R v Murtagh and Kennedy* and *R v Hepworth and Fearnley* (above).
16 (1955) 39 Cr App Rep 72.
17 [1955] 2 QB 600, [1955] 2 All ER 918.
18 At pp 603, 920, respectively.
19 *R v Jones* [1961] Crim LR 322; *R v Johnson* [1962] Crim LR 52; *R v Head and Warrener* (1961) 45 Cr App Rep 225; *R v Attfield* [1961] 3 All ER 243, [1961] 1 WLR 1135; *R v Stafford* and *R v Luvaglio* [1968] 3 All ER 752 n; *R v Gray* (1973) 58 Cr App Rep 177; *R v Sweeney* (1983) Times, 22 October.
20 *People (A-G) v Byrne* [1974] IR 1; *Thomas v R* (1960) 102 CLR 584; *Dawson v R* (1961) 106 CLR 1; *Green v R* (1971) 126 CLR 28.
1 *R v Allan* [1969] 1 All ER 91, [1969] 1 WLR 33.
2 *Walter v R* [1969] 2 AC 26; the direction upheld in this case is criticised in 32 MLR 217; but it was also upheld, with a preference for the time-honoured formula of 'beyond reasonable doubt' in *Ferguson v R* [1979] 1 All ER 877, [1979] 1 WLR 94.
3 Lord Diplock [1969] 2 AC at 30.

unwise[4] to go further. The Court of Appeal has recommended that judges stop trying to define that which it is impossible to define.[5]

It is vitally important for the judge to direct the jury both as to the allocation and standard of the burden of proof,[6] but in very exceptional cases the Court of Appeal may nevertheless apply the proviso despite failure to direct the jury on either the allocation,[7] or standard,[8] of proof. In both of these cases however the decision was assisted by the fact that the failure to direct on the one question was compensated by a full and proper direction on the other. It is hard to conceive of circumstances in which the proviso would be applied if there were no proper direction on either.

From time to time it has been suggested that further precautionary instructions are required in criminal cases but the House of Lords has refused to lay down a rule that, in addition to directing the jury that the prosecution bears the burden of proving the accused's guilt beyond reasonable doubt, the judge must, where the evidence is purely circumstantial, direct them to acquit unless the facts are not only consistent with the accused's guilt, but also inconsistent with any other rational conclusion.[9] Such a requirement was at one time assumed to exist by the Canadian courts on the authority of *Hodge's Case*.[10] In that case great stress was properly placed on the destructive effect on the cumulative force of circumstantial evidence pointing to guilt, of one rational hypothesis of innocence; but the direction to the jury was, rightly it is submitted, treated by the House of Lords as no more than a formula suitable in some cases, for instructing the jury that they must be satisfied of the accused's guilt beyond reasonable doubt.

The Court of Appeal has held that it is unnecessary for the judge to direct the jury that it need be unanimous as to any single piece of evidence when various pieces, all capable of leading to the conclusion that a given ingredient of an offence exists, have been adduced.[11] On the other hand if a necessary ingredient of the offence can correspond to only one item of evidence, the jury must be directed that it cannot convict unless it is sufficiently agreed upon one of those pieces of evidence.[12] If there are alternative ingredients satisfaction of either of which would lead to a conclusion of guilt and each corresponds to one of different pieces of evidence, the court has reserved its opinion, though intimating, it is submitted rightly, that it more resembles the former than the latter situation.[13] An even more esoteric question has been raised: can there be satisfaction beyond reasonable doubt of the guilt

---

4   Though not quite necessarily a misdirection, see *R v Pahuja* (1987) 30 ACR 118 (judge did misdirect); *R v Finlay and Grellette* (1985) 23 DLR (4th) 532 (judge did not misdirect).

5   *R v Ching* (1976) 63 Cr App Rep 7. See also further Commonwealth cases, *R v Flesch* (1986) 7 NSWLR 554; *R v Wilson* (1986) 42 SASR 203.

6   In *R v Gibson* (1983) 77 Cr App Rep 151 an appeal was allowed because the direction as to allocation and standard had been given only once.

7   *R v Donoghue* (1987) 86 Cr App Rep 267.

8   *R v Edwards* (1983) 77 Cr App Rep 5.

9   *McGreevy v D P P* [1973] 1 All ER 503, [1973] 1 WLR 276.

10 (1838) 2 Lew CC 227; for Australia see *Plomp v R* (1963) 110 CLR 234; *Barca v R* (1974) 133 CLR 82; *Stanton v R* [1981] WAR 185; for New Zealand see *Police v Pereira* [1977] 1 NZLR 547; for the current Canadian view see *Monteleone v R* (1987) 41 DLR (4th) 746.

11 *R v Agbim* [1979] Crim LR 171. See also *Thomas v R* [1972] NZLR 34.

12 *R v Brown* (1983) 79 Cr App Rep 115. Still less can a finding be based upon the absence of reasonable doubt in one or other of two offences, see *A-G for Hong Kong v Yip Kui Foon* [1988] HKLR 544; or upon the responsibility of one or other of two defendants, *Ricci Burns Ltd v Toole* [1988] NLJR 312.

13 *R v Flynn* (1985) 82 Cr App Rep 319.

of the accused when there is no such satisfaction with regard to any of the evidentiary facts? On this the full court of South Australia has expressed itself as follows:[14]

> There is a clear distinction between drawing an inference of guilt from a combination of several proved facts, none of which by itself would support the inference, and drawing an inference of guilt from several facts whose existence is in doubt. In the first place {sic} the combination does what each fact taken in isolation could not do; in the second case the combination counts for nothing.

In the second case much would depend upon the degree of doubt entertained about the existence of the several facts whose existence was doubtful. An accumulation of evidentiary facts each of which is proved on a balance of probabilities may suffice to dispel all doubt about the existence of the fact to be proved. The South Australian court concluded that facts from which inferences are to be drawn must be 'clearly proved'.

These remarks have been subsequently considered by the High Court of Australia in *R v Chamberlain*[15] and by the Supreme Court of Canada in *R v Morin.*[16] The majority of the High Court in *Chamberlain* seems to have taken the view that no inferences can be drawn from facts which are not themselves proved beyond reasonable doubt,[17] and that the jury should be so directed. Deane J adopted a more discriminating approach.[18] The Supreme Court of Canada was divided on this question in *Morin*, but it was the minority[19] which took the view of the majority in the High Court of Australia, and even they qualified it by stressing that no fact was to be considered in isolation, but only in the light of all of the surrounding facts. Deane J and the majority[20] in *Morin* felt that this was to intrude too far into the jury's fact-finding process. They accepted that if guilt depends upon a chain of elements, each corresponding to a different piece of evidence, then the jury must be, and must be instructed to be, satisfied beyond reasonable doubt that the required elements have been established. This does not however imply that no inferences can be drawn from facts less well established, if they are not synonymous with essential elements of the offence.[1] Egglestone rightly points out that any other view would make nonsense of the rules relating to corroboration. As Deane J put it:[2]

> There is certainly no requirement of the law that the members of the jury must examine separately each item of evidence adduced by the prosecution and reject it unless they are satisfied beyond reasonable doubt that it is correct. Nor is it the law that a jury is in all circumstances precluded from drawing an inference from a primary fact unless that fact is proved beyond reasonable doubt.

The Supreme Court of Canada indeed requires the jury to be directed that

---

14 *R v Van Beelan* [1972] 4 SASR 353 at 374; criticised by Egglestone *Evidence, Proof and Probability* (2nd edn) p 122.
15 (1984) 51 ALR 225.
16 (1988) 66 CR (3d) 1.
17 See Gibbs CJ and Mason J at 239, 240; Murphy J at 266; and Brennan J at 291.
18 At 313.
19 Wilson and Lamer JJ.
20 Sopinka J with whom Dickson CJC, McIntyre and La Forest JJ concurred.
 1 Or at any stage constitute single links in a chain of reasoning to the inference of such an essential element.
 2 At 313. See also *Thomas v R* [1972] NZLR 34.

the facts are not to be examined 'separately and in isolation with reference to the criminal standard'. These decisions fortify the view that whatever may be the proper direction in the circumstances of a particular case, it is to be hoped that questions such as those which have just been raised will never be allowed to become the basis of prescribed rules.[3]

A rule is very properly prescribed for the direction which must be given on issues on which the accused bears the legal burden. To repeat the words of Humphreys J:

> In any case where, either by statute or at common law, some matter is presumed against an accused person 'unless the contrary is proved', the jury should be directed that it is for them to decide whether the contrary is proved, that the burden of proof required is less than that required at the hands of the prosecution in proving the case beyond a reasonable doubt, and that the burden may be discharged by evidence satisfying the jury of that which the accused is called upon to establish.[4]

In this context the word 'satisfy' connotes satisfaction on the balance of probabilities. It is sometimes questioned whether, in a comparatively brief summing up, it is possible to make clear to a jury the distinction between the standard to be applied on issues on which the prosecution bears the legal burden and that to be applied when this burden is borne by the accused. If there is any difficulty in this regard, it is a further argument against placing the legal burden on the accused on any issue in a criminal case.

Special considerations apply when the question of whether a crime has been committed arises in other proceedings. The difficulty is that the court in those proceedings is placed in a dilemma in which it must abandon either consistency of standard of proof as between two different proceedings relating to the same issue, or abandon it as between two different issues arising in the same proceedings. Such a dilemma can arise in administrative proceedings for the recovery of compensation for criminal injuries,[5] or in an ordinary civil case. A claims damages for a libel in which B referred to him as a bigamist,[6] the insurer's defence to an action on a policy of fire insurance is that the assured is guilty of arson[7] or the plaintiff simply claims damages for a conspiracy to defraud. This is precisely what happened in *New York State v The Heirs of Phillips*[8] where the advice of the Judicial Committee of the Privy Council delivered to Lord Atkin stated that the standard appropriate to criminal proceedings was the right one as 'the proposition has been laid

3 A sentiment explicitly endorsed by the majority of the Supreme Court of Canada at 17. It has also been endorsed in Australia, see *R v Shepherd* (1988) 85 ALR 387.

4 *R v Carr-Briant* [1943] KB 607 at 612, p 117 above; see also *Public Prosecutor v Yuvaroj* [1970] AC 913; *Sodeman v R* [1936] 2 All ER 1138 (insanity); *R v Dunbar* [1958] 1 QB 1, [1957] 2 All ER 737 (diminished responsibility); *R v Podola* [1960] 1 QB 325, [1959] 3 All ER 418 (fitness to plead); *R v Milnes and Green* (1983) 33 SASR 211 (pardon).

5 *R v Criminal Injuries Compensation Board, ex p Crangle* (1981) Times, 14 November.

6 *Willmett v Harmer* (1839) 8 C & P 695 where the same strictness of proof was required in support of B's plea of justification as on a trial for bigamy. See also *Chalmers v Shackell* (1834) 6 C & P 475.

7 *Thurtell v Beaumont* (1823) 1 Bing 339 (jury should be as satisfied as in a criminal case); *Issaias v Marine Insurance Co Ltd* (1923) 15 Ll LRep 186, where the same view is taken by Atkin LJ at 192. In *Slattery v Mance* [1962] 1 QB 676, [1962] 1 All ER 525 it was decided that the insurer has the burden of proving that the assured set fire to the insured ship on balance of probability only.

8 [1939] 3 All ER 952.

down time and again by the courts of this country and appears to be just'.[9] If this remark was intended to apply to all civil cases in which criminal conduct is alleged, it must be admitted that observations which were capable of bearing a contrary meaning had previously been made in the House of Lords,[10] and in *Doe d Devine v Wilson*,[11] the Judicial Committee had favoured the contrary view when holding that a party relying on a deed could discharge the legal burden of negativing its forgery on a preponderance of probability. *Doe v Wilson* was preferred by the High Court of Australia in *Helton v Allen*,[12] and again in *Rejfek v McElroy*.[13] Similar views in favour of the civil standard have prevailed in Scotland,[14] New Zealand[15] and Canada.[16]

In *Hornal v Neuberger Products Ltd*[17] the Court of Appeal recognised that the earlier English cases conflicted, and concluded, in apparently general terms, that proof on a preponderance of probability will suffice when the commission of a crime is alleged in a civil action. The plaintiff claimed damages for breach of warranty and fraud on the ground that the defendant had falsely stated that a machine sold by him to the plaintiff had been reconditioned. So far as the alleged breach of warranty was concerned, the trial judge held that the words were spoken by the defendant, but the claim failed because he considered that the parties did not intend them to have contractual effect. The judge proceeded to award damages for fraud, although he said that he was merely satisfied on the balance of probability, and not beyond reasonable doubt, that the statement was made. If the statement had in fact been made, the defendant would have been guilty of obtaining money by false pretences, for it was beyond dispute that he knew that the machine had not been reconditioned. The Court of Appeal dismissed the appeal mainly because:

> it would bring the law into contempt if a judge were to say that on the issue of warranty he finds that the statement was made, and on the issue of fraud he finds it was not made.[18]

Yet this would have been the result of holding that the claim for damages for fraud had to be established beyond reasonable doubt.

Although there were several previous decisions which were not discussed

9 At 954.
10 *Lek v Mathews* (1927) 29 Ll LRep 141 at 164 per Lord Sumner.
11 (1855) 10 Moo PCC 502.
12 (1940) 63 CLR 691.
13 (1964–5) 112 CLR 517. There seems to be no point in referring to other Australian authorities.
14 *Fisher and Donaldson Ltd v Steven* 1988 SCLR 337.
15 *Ellis v Frape* [1954] NZLR 341; *Cheape v New Zealand Law Society* [1955] NZLR 63; *W V Middleditch & Cons v Hinds* [1962] NZLR 570.
16 *Mutual Life Assurance Co of Canada v Aubin* [1979] 2 SCR 298.
17 [1957] 1 QB 247, [1956] 3 All ER 970.
18 At 258, 973, respectively, per Denning LJ. See also remarks of Sholl J in *McClelland v Symons* [1951] VLR 157 at 166. Lord Denning's remarks may be thought to conflict with his earlier observations in *Bater v Bater* (p 148 above) where he said the court will require a higher degree of probability for fraud than for negligence; but the ingredient of fraud which requires a high standard of probability is the defendant's knowledge of the falsity of his statement rather than the fact that he made it, and, if the statement was made, the defendant's knowledge of its falsity was beyond dispute in *Hornal's* case. On the question whether the statement was made there is no reason why the degree of probability for fraud and warranty should differ.

by the Court of Appeal, *Hornal's* case may be taken to have settled the English law for the time being. An allegation of criminal conduct, even of murder,[19] need be established only on a preponderance of probability in a civil action. When the commission of a crime is alleged in civil proceedings, the stigma attaching to an affirmative finding might be thought to justify the imposition of a strict standard of proof; but the person against whom criminal conduct is alleged is adequately protected by the consideration that the antecedent improbability of his guilt is 'a part of the whole range of circumstances which have to be weighed in the scale when deciding as to the balance of probabilities'.[20] By applying the flexible civil standard the civil court may thus discriminate between the standard required to prove the commission of the same crime by different individuals.[1]

C. THE QUESTION OF A THIRD STANDARD AND THE POSSIBILITY OF ANOMALIES

Three standards of proof appear to be recognised in the United States, proof by 'clear, strong and cogent' evidence lying midway between proof on a preponderance of probability and proof beyond reasonable doubt.[2] It is certainly not difficult to find support for the view that English law recognises standards other than those of proof beyond reasonable doubt and on a balance of probabilities. A claim for rectification must, it has been said, be established by 'strong, irrefragable evidence',[3] and the Law Reform Committee, whilst conceding that the meaning, like the pronunciation of this expression is not beyond argument, considered it to be clear that a mere balance of probability is not enough.[4] A high standard has been called for in cases of alleged professional misconduct as the Judicial Committee could not envisage professional men condemning each other on a mere balance of probabilities.[5] The evidence in rebuttal of the presumption of the formal validity of a marriage must, it has been said, be 'strong, distinct and satisfactory';[6] while an intention to change domicile must be 'clearly and unequivocally proved'.[7] Observations of this sort will no doubt continue to

19 *Re Dellow's Will Trusts, Lloyds Bank Ltd v Institute of Cancer Research* [1964] 1 All ER 771; *Nishina Trading Co Ltd v Chiyoda Fire and Marine Insurance Co Ltd* [1969] 2 QB 449, [1969] 2 All ER 776 (theft proved on balance).
20 Per Morris LJ (see p 148 above).
 1 *Re G* [1987] 1 WLR 1461 (more required to show father guilty of sexual abuse of child than would have been required for another).
 2 Morgan *Problems of Proof in the Anglo-American System of Trials* 82; Uniform Rules 1.04, see *Addington v Texas* 441 US 418 (1979). When the issue is what might happen in the future, e g whether an alleged offender might be prejudiced at his trial if returned to a designated country, something less than a preponderance of probability will suffice, *Fernandes v Government of Singapore* [1971] 2 All ER 691, [1971] 1 WLR 987. See also *R v Askeland* [1983] Tas NC 224 for an unequivocal view that the standard of proof of the voluntariness of a confession is in Australia intermediate between the usual two.
 3 *Countess of Shelburne v Earl of Inchiquin* (1784) 1 Bro CC 338 at 341; *Roberts & Co Ltd v Leicestershire County Council* [1961] Ch 555, [1961] 2 All ER 545; cf *Earl v Hector Whaling Ltd* [1961] 1 Lloyd's Rep 459. See also *Re Snowden, Smith v Spowage* [1979] 2 All ER 172.
 4 19th report para 26.
 5 *Bhandari v Advocates Committee* [1956] 3 All ER 742, [1956] 1 WLR 1442. See also *Willcox v Sing* [1985] 2 Qd R 66.
 6 *Piers v Piers* (1849) 2 HL Cas 331 at 389; *Mahadervan v Mahadervan* [1964] P 233 at 236.
 7 *Moorhouse v Lord* (1863) 10 HL Cas 272 at 286.

be cited by the courts,[8] but they do not support the importation of a third standard, for as Nourse J remarked in connection with the proof of mutual wills:

> that does not mean that there has to be a departure from the ordinary standard of proof required in civil proceedings. I have to be satisfied on the balance of probabilities that the alleged agreement was made, but before I can be satisfied of that I must find clear and satisfactory evidence to that effect.[9]

In the same vein Lord Tucker was, it is believed, expressing the commonly held opinion when he said: 'I am quite unable to accede to the proposition that there is some intermediate onus between that which is required in criminal cases and the balance of probability which is sufficient in civil actions.'[10]

D. MATHEMATICS AND THE STANDARD OF PROOF

Since the standard of proof is concerned with the question of the amount of evidence which is required to persuade the trier of fact, there is an understandable tendency to attempt to apply the techniques of mathematics to its assessment. The temptation to count is an old one,[11] which still persists in some corroboration requirements as will be seen in ch V. It has appealed most to those of a theoretical disposition. Bentham was attracted to it, influenced by the observation that wagering and insurance both attach numerical values to probabilities.[12] As the number of ways in which modern technology can assist judicial enquiry grows, it has become increasingly necessary for courts to adopt methods of combining evidence of mathematical precision with less exact sources of information. It is also common knowledge that many important decisions in fields such as business, national defence, and the formation of economic policy are increasingly taken upon the basis of the mathematical modelling of probabilities and decision theory. Whatever the reason, there has been a burgeoning of attention on the question of the possibility of applying mathematical techniques to law.[13] Much of this debate is, to say the least, remote from the practical concerns of trial lawyers. There has been a recent judicial reminder of this:

8 See eg per Lord Simon of Glaisdale in *Steadman v Steadman* [1976] AC 536 at 563–4.
9 *Re Cleaver, Cleaver v Insley* [1981] 2 All ER 1018 at 1024, [1981] 1 WLR 939 at 947.
10 *Dingwall v J Wharton (Shipping) Ltd* [1961] 2 Lloyds Rep 213 at 216. See also the remarks of Dixon J in *Murray v Murray* (1960) 33 ALJR 521 at 524.
11 It appears in late Roman Law, Corpus Juris 4.20.9 (AD 334).
12 *Treatise on Judicial Evidence* (1825) ch 17.
13 Such techniques are canvassed in Cohen *The Probable and The Provable* (1977); Eggleston *Evidence, Proof and Probability* (2nd edn, 1983); Finkelstein and Fairley 'A Bayesian Approach to Identification Evidence' (1970) 83 Harv LR 489; Tribe 'Trial by Mathematics: Precision and Ritual in the Legal Process' (1971) 84 Harv LR 1329, see also pp 1801 and 1810 for continuation of debate; Glanville Williams 'The Mathematics of Proof' [1979] Crim LR 297, 340; Cohen 'The Logic of Proof' [1980] Crim LR 91, and see p 103 for a rejoinder by Glanville Williams; and Jackson 'Probability and Mathematics in Court' (1980) 31 NILQ 223. The subject has generated massive theoretical attention in the United States, see the report of a symposium in (1986) 66 Boston ULR 377 running to more than 500 pages.

The concept of 'probability' in the legal sense is certainly different from the mathematical concept; indeed, it is rare to find a situation in which the two usages co-exist although, when they do, the mathematical probability has to be taken into the assessment of probability in the legal sense and given its appropriate weight.[14]

In that case the Court of Appeal refused to 'transmute a mathematical probability into a forensic certainty' by determining the paternity of a child upon the basis of statistical blood grouping evidence, at least in the absence of a full investigation of all the surrounding circumstances. One of the problems is that the proper foundation for the application of the mathematical techniques is rarely present. A striking example of this, and one which sparked off much of the modern American interest, is provided by *People v Collins*.[15] In that case the trial judge admitted statistical evidence in an attempt to identify the accused with the perpetrators of the robbery in question. There was evidence that the guilty couple possessed six characteristics. A statistician was allowed to testify that the likelihood of their all being present in any couple was, upon certain assumptions, 12 million to one against. The accused couple possessed these six characteristics, and were found guilty. As was pointed out on appeal this procedure was quite inappropriate. There was no basis for the assumptions of the likelihood of each of the characteristics occurring independently, and there was no ground for supposing that they were independent, indeed there was every ground for supposing that they were not. It will be extremely rare for the information required to make such estimates of probability to be available to a court. Nor should the court attempt to manufacture its own statistics where there is no evidence at all. A cautionary example here is provided by the opinion of Murphy J in *T N T Management Pty Ltd v Brooks*.[16] The plaintiff sought damages in respect of a road accident in which both drivers had been killed, and there was little evidence which was to blame. Murphy J took the view that it was too little. He was however prepared to uphold the claim on the basis that there were three possibilities, both to blame, plaintiff to blame or defendant to blame. Since two of these favoured the plaintiff's claim and only one opposed it, the balance of probabilities was satisfied. It is not clear why he excluded the possibility of neither to blame. Quite apart from that the procedure is obviously prone to cause injustice, for example in a case where only one of three injured employees caused the damage by his negligence in the course of his employment, but it is unknown which of them it was. In such a case the odds of any one being an innocent victim are also two to one on, with the startling consequence that all three can succeed although the whole calculation presupposes that one of them is not in fact entitled to do so.

If part of the difficulty is that there is usually an insufficient evidential basis for the mathematical exegesis, another is that the mathematical techniques are themselves controversial. Thus the statistical appendix to the judgment in *Collins* which purported to substitute an accurate statistical

---

14 *Re J S (a minor)* [1981] Fam 22 at 29, [1980] 1 All ER 1061 at 1066. See also *R v Shepherd* (1988) 85 ALR 387 at 392 by Roden J: 'Degrees of probability and degrees of proof with which juries are concerned are rarely capable of expression in mathematical terms.'
15 438 P2d 33 (1968).
16 (1979) 53 ALJR 267, the rest of the court decided the case upon the quite different basis that the evidence adduced was just sufficient to prove negligence.

analysis for the faulty methods proposed by the trial judge has itself been attacked as being mathematically unsound,[17] and the inapplicability of classical Pascalian probability to law is the whole theme of Cohen's book.

There will, of course, be some statistical evidence which does have a satisfactory foundation, and some issues to which that evidence is relevant. Such evidence will not automatically be excluded on the basis that it falls short of absolute scientific certainty.[18] Blood group evidence may be of that character. If a question arises as to the paternity of a child it may be possible to establish that if the husband of the mother is not the father then it could be one in ten of the population. In such a case the court must be wary of the alluring precision of the figures, and must not be seduced from the path of weighing together all of the circumstances, for example the terms of the relationship between husband and wife, the opportunities and inclinations of the wife for extra-marital intercourse, and the motives of the parties in making any allegations.[19] It will be a rare case where mathematical techniques will make a decisive contribution to the resolution of forensic uncertainty.[20]

17 Fairley and Mosteller 'A Conversation about Collins' (1974) 41 U Chi LR 242.
18 *S v S* [1972] AC 24, [1970] 3 All ER 107; *R v Bracewell* (1978) 68 Cr App Rep 44.
19 In *R v Chedzey* (1987) 30 ACR 451 where there was little other evidence to show that the accused was the maker of a malicious telephone call the court refused to uphold a conviction based on evidence that the automatic trading procedure was 99.96% accurate.
20 But not unknown; fingerprint or other forensic matching is often decisive.

CHAPTER IV

The functions of the judge and jury

Historically, the separation of the functions of the judge and jury has left so deep a mark upon English jurisprudence that the rules and habits of juristic thought, which it has engendered, are scarcely touched by the present day decline of jury trial in civil matters. If jury trial is ever abolished, many of these rules and conceptions will yet remain as long as the common law system is in being. The judge sitting alone must constantly be aware of the line which divides his two quite distinct functions. And the proper observation of the distinction is by no means a mere academic matter, but of the highest practical importance in its bearing on the exercise of appellate jurisdiction.[1]

A due appreciation of the respective functions of the judge and jury is therefore essential to a proper understanding of the law of evidence, and that is why a separate chapter has been allotted to them. The general rule is discussed in the first section, and some of the more direct methods of judicial control are considered in section 2.

Empirical research is beyond the scope of this book. It must be admitted, however, that no discussion of the law of evidence in criminal cases will ever be completely satisfactory until we have some idea of the extent to which the average jury understands the directions which the law requires the judge to give, and whether jurors are as comprehending, uncomprehending or prejudiced as some of the rules of evidence suppose. Does the jury understand the direction that it is to use the victim's out of court complaint of rape, not as evidence of it, but only as confirming the victim's evidence in court? Does the jury assume that the accused who elects not to testify has previous convictions? And if he does testify, and has previous convictions put to him in cross-examination, does the jury understand that these do not prove his guilt directly, but only impair his credibility? These, and a number of similar questions could be answered satisfactorily only by controlled, and secret, monitoring of the deliberations of real juries in real cases. Unfortunately such monitoring would amount to contempt of court.[2] Recourse must be had to simulations and generally less reliable methods of obtaining the information needed to provide a basis for understanding and improving the law of evidence.[3]

---

1 Nigel Bridge (now Lord Bridge) 12 MLR 275. Many of the matters considered in this chapter are discussed by Sir Patrick Devlin (now Lord Devlin) in *Trial by Jury* (The Hamlyn Lectures for 1965, revd 1966). See also W R Cornish *The Jury*; and G D Nokes 'The English Jury and Law of Evidence' 31 Tul LR 153.
2 Contempt of Court Act 1981, s 8.
3 For examples, see Kalven and Zeisel *The American Jury*; McCabe and Purves *Bypassing the Jury*; and *The Jury at Work* (occasional pamphlets published by Basil Blackwell and Co for the Oxford Penal Research unit); W F Cornish and others 'Juries and the Rules of Evidence' [1973] Crim LR 208; A P Sealey and W R Cornish 'Jurors and Their Verdicts' (1973) 36 MLR 496.

SECTION 1. THE GENERAL RULE

The general rule is that questions of law must be determined by the judge and questions of fact must be determined by the jury, but there are some special cases as well as exceptions to the general rule.

A. SOME SPECIAL CASES

1. CONSTRUCTION

'The meaning of an ordinary word of the English language is not a question of law. The proper construction of a statute is a question of law'.[4] Lord Reid said this on the hearing of an appeal in a criminal case from a Divisional Court, but his remarks have since been held to apply to a criminal trial by jury.[5] The appeal was concerned with the meaning of the words 'insulting behaviour' in s 5 of the Public Order Act 1936. Lord Reid continued:

> If the context shows that a word is used in an unusual sense the court will determine in other words what that unusual sense is. But here there is in my opinion no question of the word 'insulting' being used in an unusual sense. It is for the tribunal which decides the case to consider, not as law but as fact, whether in the whole circumstances the words of the statute do or do not as a matter of ordinary usage of the English language cover or apply to the facts which have been proved.

Concern has been expressed lest this gives the jury too free a hand, but account must be taken of a number of limiting factors. The proper construction of a statute may require a judge to do more than decide whether words are used in an unusual sense and if so, what that sense is. He may have to choose between a variety of possible meanings, including ordinary meanings of which there is sometimes more than one, and this will result in a direction on the law. Even when the sole question is the ordinary meaning of a word, the fact that it is a matter for the jury does not mean that they have an unfettered choice for Lord Reid recognised the possibility of an appeal on the ground that 'no tribunal acquainted with the ordinary use of the language could reasonably reach that decision'. The judge may therefore direct the jury that it is not open to them to give a particular meaning to ordinary words because that would be unreasonable, and, provided he makes it plain that the decision must be theirs, he can illustrate the application of a word or phrase to various factual situations including that of the instant case.

Even so there is a danger of uncertainty when a jury is left to pronounce on such general matters as the question whether property was 'dishonestly' appropriated or obtained by the accused without anything more than a direction on what 'dishonestly' cannot reasonably mean and some illustrations of what it can mean. There could well be contradictory verdicts in different cases concerned with substantially the same facts. If this is undesirable it is the price we pay for the rule that, although a judge may

---

4 *Brutus v Cozens* [1973] AC 854 at 861.
5 *R v Feeley* [1973] QB 530, [1973] 1 All ER 341.

direct an acquittal on appropriate facts, he has no power to direct a verdict of guilty even though he is satisfied that an acquittal would be perverse.[6]

The extent to which Lord Reid's words with which this section began can be generalised is an open question. It is tempting to say that the meaning of an ordinary word of the English language is always a matter of fact to be determined by the jury while construction is always a matter of law. There can be no doubt about the second of these propositions, but there is a good deal of eighteenth and nineteenth-century authority in support of the view that in a civil case tried with a jury the meaning of ordinary words comes within the sphere of construction.[7] The jury's role tended to be confined to the determination of specific facts such as the surrounding circumstances with reference to which a private document was executed and the intention of the parties. The rarity at the present time of jury trial in civil cases renders it impossible to predict, and pointless to speculate on, the extent to which the old authorities would be followed today.

2. DEFAMATION

Endeavours to restrict the role of the jury in accordance with those authorities in cases of criminal libel were the precipitating cause of Fox's Libel Act 1792. It provides that, in criminal prosecutions for libel, the jury shall, after direction by the judge on the law, give a general verdict upon the whole matter. In consequence of this statute, it has come to be the practice for the judge to determine whether the document in question is capable of bearing the meaning alleged by the prosecution, while the jury decides whether it does in fact amount to a criminal libel. This has been said to be because the intention of the parties is always a question for the jury, and the meaning of the document is part of that intention;[8] but the same procedure is adopted in civil cases where the intention of the parties is, to say the least, not so important as on a criminal charge.[9] It is therefore best to regard the established practice as a compromise. A literal adherence to the rule that the construction of documents and the ordinary meaning of words is a matter of law for the judge would mean that the jury simply determines whether the alleged libel was published and whether the circumstances from which any suggested innuendo could be inferred existed. This was the usual practice before Fox's Libel Act, but it proved to be objectionable on political grounds, and because it contravened the jury's right to return a general verdict in criminal cases.[10]

3. PERJURY

Under s 11(6) of the Perjury Act 1911, the question whether a statement on which perjury is assigned is material is one of law to be determined by the court of trial. In most cases the materiality of a statement would naturally

6 See articles by Glanville Williams in [1976] Crim LR 472 and 532, and by D W Elliott in [1976] Crim LR 707.
7 See for example *Neilson v Harford* (1841) 8 M & W 806 at 823.
8 Per Lord Abinger CJ in *Morrell v Firth* (1838) 3 M & W 402 at 404–5.
9 *Nevill v Fine Arts and General Insurance Co* [1897] AC 68.
10 Holdsworth *History of English Law* (vol 10) 688.

be treated as a question of fact, and there are some express statutory provisions to this effect,[11] but, in the case of perjury, it is probably convenient that the matter should be treated as one of law in the interests of certainty and uniformity.[12]

B. EXCEPTIONS

1. FOREIGN LAW

So far as the courts of England and Wales are concerned, the law of other countries, including Scotland, Eire[13] since 1921, and the British dominions and colonies, is a matter of fact to be determined on the evidence adduced in a particular case.[14] Thus, if the validity of a ceremony of marriage is among the facts in issue, proof of the ceremony will not be sufficient, for it must usually be shown to have constituted a formally valid marriage according to the law of the place of celebration.

Down to 1920, the evidence relating to the foreign law was submitted to the jury, but s 15 of the Administration of Justice Act of that year provided that, where for the purpose of disposing of any action or any other matter which is being tried by a judge with a jury in any court in England or Wales it is necessary to ascertain the law of any other country which is applicable to the facts of the case, any question as to the effect of the evidence with respect to that law shall, instead of being submitted to the jury, be decided by the judge alone.[15] The difficulty of the points which may be involved is no doubt an ample justification for this provision which has been held to be wide enough to cover criminal proceedings.[16] A similar procedure applies to the determination of questions as to the meaning or effect of community treaties, or the validity, meaning or effect of community instruments.[17] They too are questions for the judge to decide, if necessary after hearing evidence, which in a criminal case would not be heard by the jury.[18]

11 Eg Marine Insurance Act 1906, s 20(7).
12 See *R v Traino* (1987) 27 ACR 271.
13 See G D Nokes 'Irish Law in English Courts' (1960) 9 ICLQ 564. The Ireland Act 1949 under which Eire is for many purposes not a foreign country, has not affected the position (*Todd v Todd* [1961] 2 All ER 881). So far as Northern Ireland is concerned the English courts would probably take judicial notice of the common law of Northern Ireland and of English statutes applying to Northern Ireland but not of statutes of the Northern Ireland Parliament. Under the Maintenance Orders Act 1950, s 22(2), judicial notice may be taken of the laws of all parts of the United Kingdom in maintenance proceedings.
14 Except that the House of Lords takes cognisance of the law of Scotland, and the Privy Council takes cognisance of the law of the British Commonwealth (*Elliot v Lord Joicey* [1935] AC 209 at 213 and 236). See also European Communities Act 1972, s 4(2), providing for the taking of judicial notice by the English courts of the community treaties and decisions of the European court.
15 S 15 of the Administration of Justice Act 1920, has been repealed so far as the High Court is concerned by the Judicature Act 1925, but a similar provision is contained in s 69(5) of the Supreme Court Act 1981. See also s 68 of the County Courts Act 1984 as to county courts.
16 *R v Hammer* [1923] 2 KB 786. For proof of foreign law see ch XX.
17 European Communities Act 1972, s 3(1), judicial notice may be taken of the primary sources of community law, s 3(2).
18 *R v Goldstein* [1983] 1 All ER 434, [1983] 1 WLR 151.

2. REASONABLENESS

The reasonableness of a particular belief or course of conduct is essentially a question of fact, and, as such, it normally has to be determined by the jury, but, in certain civil cases, it must be decided by the judge, although he may leave subsidiary issues upon which the question of reasonableness ultimately depends to the jury. In an action for malicious prosecution, the question whether the defendant had a reasonable and probable cause for initiating the criminal proceedings must be answered by the judge.[19] It is also the duty of the judge to determine whether the terms of a covenant in restraint of trade are reasonably necessary for the protection of the covenantee;[20] but he may require the jury to find relevant facts concerning the information on which the defendant acted in the first case, and the nature of the covenantee's business in the second.

3. FACTS AFFECTING THE ADMISSIBILITY OF EVIDENCE[1]

There are conditions precedent which are required to be fulfilled before evidence is admissible for the jury. Thus, an oath, or its equivalent, and competency, are conditions precedent to admitting viva voce evidence; and the apprehension of immediate death to admitting evidence of dying declarations;[2] a search to secondary evidence of lost writings; and stamps to certain written instruments;[3] and so is consanguinity or affinity in the declarant to declarations of deceased relatives.[4] The judge alone has to decide whether the condition has been fulfilled. If the proof is by witnesses, he must decide on their credibility. If counter-evidence is offered, he must receive it before he decides; and he has no right to ask the opinion of the jury on the fact of a condition precedent.[5]

Other examples of the application of the rule are afforded by cases in which the accused objects to the reception of a confession on the ground that it does not satisfy the conditions of s 76 of the Police and Criminal Evidence Act 1984, or a witness claims to be privileged from answering a particular question.[6] In all such instances, the judge, and not the jury, must determine disputed facts, and the entirely separate nature of these preliminary or incidental issues was emphasised by the old practice under which witnesses who deposed to them were required to take a different oath, known as the 'voir dire' from that sworn by those giving evidence which was to be

19 *Herniman v Smith* [1983] AC 305, [1983] 1 All ER 1. A similar rule applies in the case of false imprisonment.
20 *Dowden and Pook Ltd v Pook* [1904] 1 KB 45.
 1 See also ch I, section 2, part A (iii) above. For thorough, if, from the English point of view, rather elaborate, discussions of this subject see Maguire and Epstein 'Preliminary Questions of Fact in Determining the Admissibility of Evidence' (1926) 40 Harv LR 392, and Morgan 'Functions of Judge and Jury in Determining Preliminary Questions of Fact' (1929) 43 Harv LR 165. See also Morgan *Some Problems of Proof* ch 3.
 2 Under an exception to the rule against hearsay as to the cause of death in prosecutions of homicide. For an early example of the exclusive control of the judge in such a case, see *R v Hucks* (1816) 1 Stark 521.
 3 For an example see *Bartlett v Smith* (1843) 11 M & W 483.
 4 Admissible under a common law exception to the rule against hearsay on genealogical issues (now only applicable in criminal cases).
 5 *Doe d Jenkins v Davies* (1847) 10 QB 314 at 323 per Lord Denman CJ.
 6 *Stace v Griffith* (1869) LR 2 PC 420 at 427–8.

submitted to the jury. The trial of the incidental issues is often called 'a trial within a trial'.

It is often impossible to decide the question of admissibility without disclosing the evidence on which the dispute turns. If it is alleged that a confession was made under pressure, the question can often only be settled by considering the terms of the accused's statements, and the jury could scarcely help being influenced by them even if they were to conclude that the surrounding circumstances rendered the confession inadmissible.[7]

Although the validity of the reasons for the rule under consideration seems to be beyond dispute, its application has given rise to three practical difficulties—the question whether the evidence of facts constituting a condition precedent to admissibility should invariably be heard in the absence of the jury, the course which should be adopted when the facts are identical with the facts in issue and the distribution of the functions of judge and jury with regard to the admissibility of confessions.

(i) Absence of the jury

Two settled rules in criminal cases are first, that the accused must be present throughout the entire trial of an indictable offence,[8] and secondly, that all the evidence should generally be given in the presence of the jury. Some qualifications are obviously necessary so far as the second of these rules is concerned, otherwise the accused might be prejudiced, and there is no doubt that the judge has power to dismiss the jury while hearing arguments on the admissibility of evidence or while holding a trial within a trial.

In *R v Dunne*,[9] however, the judge withdrew to his private room of his own motion in order to question a witness of tender years so as to ascertain whether she was competent to testify. In *R v Reynolds*,[10] the judge dismissed the jury while a similar question was considered. The ensuing convictions were quashed in both cases. The decision in *R v Dunne* is generally accepted as correct because the conduct of the trial infringed the first of the rules mentioned in the previous paragraph; but *R v Reynolds*, in which dicta in *R v Dunne* were applied, has been criticised on the ground that the question of a witness's competence ought to be disposed of in the absence of the jury. Against this it may be urged that the jury has to consider the weight of all the evidence concerning the facts in issue, and, although a schoolmaster testified concerning the competence of the witness in *R v Reynolds*, the judge usually deals with the matter by questioning the proposed witness himself. The answers to his questions may affect the weight of the witness's evidence when it comes to be given, and it is unlikely that the judge would put them to the witness again in the presence of the jury. Moreover, there is always the danger that the jury will think they are asked to withdraw because statements prejudicial to the accused are about to be made.[11] It is probably

---

7 See per Lord Goddard CJ in *R v Reynolds* [1950] 1 KB 606 at 608, [1950] 1 All ER 335 at 336.
8 *Lawrence v R* [1933] AC 699 at 708. There are exceptions; for example in cases in which the accused renders his continued presence in court impossible by his violence. See *R v Browne* (1906) 70 JP 472.
9 (1929) 99 LJKB 117. Dicta in this case are criticised in 46 LQR 130.
10 [1950] 1 KB 606, [1950] 1 All ER 335 (criticised 66 LQR 157). The rule is different in Australia, *Demirok v R* (1977) 137 CLR 20.
11 See per Lord Hewart CJ in *R v Anderson* (1929) 21 Cr App Rep 178 at 183.

better that they should remain in court while evidence concerning facts constituting a condition precedent to admissibility is given, unless it is impossible to take such evidence without disclosing matters which the judge might ultimately hold to be inadmissible.[12]

(ii) Identity of preliminary fact with fact in issue

In *Doe d Jenkins v Davies*,[13] the issue in an action of ejectment was whether one Elizabeth Stevens was legitimate. She was dead, and the defendant sought to call evidence of a declaration made by her to a solicitor when she handed him a certificate which apparently related to her parents' marriage. Statements by deceased persons as to pedigree are admissible at common law by way of exception to the rule against hearsay if they were made by legitimate members of the family in question. The plaintiff argued that the judge ought not to have received evidence on behalf of the defendant, tending to show that Elizabeth Stevens was legitimate, offered with a view to inducing him to admit her declaration. The answer given by Lord Denman CJ[14] was that:

> neither the admissibility nor the effect of the evidence is altered by the accident that the fact which is for the judge as a condition precedent is the same fact which is for the jury in the issue

The Court of Exchequer accordingly held that, after deciding that Elizabeth Stevens was legitimate (presumably without relying on her declaration), the judge had rightly allowed this declaration to form part of the evidence to go to the jury on the issue of legitimacy.

The judge had heard evidence on the voir dire from both sides before deciding the preliminary question of legitimacy. This course has two disadvantages when the preliminary question of fact to be determined by the judge as a condition precedent to the admissibility of an item of evidence is identical with the issue which has ultimately to be decided by the jury. In the first place it means that the judge has to sum up to the jury on an issue which he has already decided; secondly, it may mean that all the evidence given on the voir dire will have to be given over again, and this will certainly be so when the trial within a trial is held in the absence of the jury. Considerations of this nature led Lord Penzance, in *Hitchins v Eardley*,[15] a later case raising the same point as *Doe d Jenkins v Davies*, to reject evidence tendered on the voir dire by those denying legitimacy. He held that he ought to admit the declaration on being satisfied that those alleging legitimacy had adduced sufficient evidence of the fact to be left to the jury.

On practical grounds, the course taken by Lord Penzance may be preferable to that followed by *Doe d Jenkins v Davies*. However that may be there are certainly cases involving the reception of documentary evidence in which all that the judge can require, as a condition precedent to the admissibility of a copy, is prima facie evidence of the existence of a genuine

12 R 104(c) of the United States Federal Rules reads: 'Hearings on the admissibility of confessions shall in all cases be conducted out of the hearing of the jury. Hearings on other preliminary matters shall be so conducted when the interests of justice require.'
13 (1847) 10 QB 314.
14 At 323–4.
15 (1871) LR 2 P & D 248.

original. In *Stowe v Querner*,[16] the plaintiff succeeded in a claim on an insurance policy which the defendant alleged had never been executed. The judge had allowed the plaintiff to give secondary evidence of the contents of the policy on the basis that the original had been lost and left the jury to decide the validity of the defendant's contention that the policy had never existed. It was held that the course followed by the judge was the right one for:

> Where the objection to the reading of a copy concedes that there was primary evidence of some sort in existence . . . the judge must, before he admits the copy, hear and determine whether the objection is well founded. But where the objection goes to show that the very substratum and foundation of the cause of action is wanting, the judge must not decide upon the matter, but receive the copy and leave the main question to the jury.[17]

A similar situation would arise in a case in which the defendant contends that the document on which the plaintiff is relying as giving him a cause of action is forged.

Cases such as *Stowe v Querner* must be carefully distinguished from those in which the preliminary issue is whether a document has been lost, or which of two originals is the proper one to place before the jury;[18] in such cases the question of fact to be decided by the judge is not the same as that which has to be decided by the jury. There is then no doubt that the judge must hear evidence on both sides on the voir dire and come to a definite decision on the preliminary issue instead of being content with prima facie evidence from the party arguing for admissibility.

The question whether the maker of a dying declaration was under a settled hopeless expectation of death, a condition precedent to its admissibility at a trial for homicide, should on principle be decided by the judge.[19] By way of contrast, the question whether a tape-recording was the original, being one which must ultimately be determined by the jury, the judge need do no more than decide whether there is sufficient evidence to leave the issue to it.[20]

(iii) Confessions

If there is a dispute about it, it is for the judge to decide whether there is prima facie evidence that a confession was made, leaving the jury to determine whether it was in fact made.[1] In respect of many other issues relating to the admissibility of confessions the common law has been superseded by the provisions of s 76 of the Police and Criminal Evidence Act 1984, as will be explained in more detail in ch XVII below. Its effect on the division of responsibilities between judge and jury will alone be considered here. It is for the prosecution to prove beyond reasonable doubt that the confession has not been obtained by oppression,[2] or in consequence of

16 (1870) LR 5 Exch 155.
17 At 158.
18 *Boyle v Wiseman* (1855) 11 Exch 360.
19 But see *R v Christensen* [1923] 2 DLR 379; cf *R v Donohoe* [1963] SR NSW 38, where the question was decided by the judge in accordance with English authorities.
20 *R v Robson* and *R v Harris* [1972] 2 All ER 699, [1972] 1 WLR 651.
 1 *R v Roberts* [1954] 2 QB 329, [1953] 2 All ER 340; *Ajodha v The State* [1982] AC 204, [1981] 2 All ER 193; *R v Mulligan* [1955] OR 240; *R v Gleeson* [1975] Qd R 399.
 2 S 76(2)(a).

anything likely to make it unreliable.[3] These issues must, as a result of the wording of the relevant provision[4] of the Police and Criminal Evidence Act 1984, be resolved by a trial within a trial before a confession can be admitted into evidence.[5] This represents a change in English[6] law,[7] and can lead to a 'pantomime',[8] if the accused prefers to withhold his attack upon the confession until the trial. It is nevertheless still possible for a judge to achieve much the same result as under the old law by exercising his discretion at common law[9] to direct the jury to disregard the confession, or to discharge them.[10] In most cases the accused will seek determination of the admissibility of a confession at a trial on the voir dire. If he does not do so there is now a statutory power for the court to initiate such a trial of its own motion.[11] In *R v Brophy*[12] the House of Lords decided that if the accused should, on the voir dire, adduce evidence of the truth of a charge against him, such a confession would, nevertheless, be inadmissible at his trial if he should plead not guilty at that stage. Where such evidence is led by the prosecution there is an unedifying conflict between the decision of the Court of Criminal Appeal in *R v Hammond*[13] that such evidence could be elicited on the voir dire, and the decision of the majority of the Privy Council in *Wong Kam-ming v R* that it could not. Now that one of the conditions for excluding a confession is the existence of circumstances likely to render a confession unreliable the case for excluding the evidence has, if anything, become even stronger. The statute does not however deal with any of the other matters which exercised the courts in these cases. One of these is the extent to which statements made by the accused on the voir dire could be used against him, either as an admission or as a previous inconsistent statement. The view which prevailed before the Act was that, if the confession were held to be inadmissible, then no later use could be made of admissions relevant to the issue of admissibility which had been made by the accused on the voir dire. In *R v Brophy* the House of Lords regarded this as fundamental:

> If such evidence, being relevant, were admissible at the substantive trial, an accused person would not enjoy the complete freedom that he ought to have at the voire dire to contest the admissibility of his previous statements. It is of the first

3 S 76(2)(b).
4 S 76. The same applies to s 78 in relation to exclusion by discretion.
5 *R v Sat-Bhambra* (1989) 88 Cr App Rep 55 at 62. The same applies to summary trial before magistrates, *R v Liverpool Juvenile Court, ex p R* [1988] QB 1, [1987] 2 All ER 668; but not to a preliminary examination, *R v Oxford City Justices, ex p Berry* [1988] QB 507, [1987] 1 All ER 1244.
6 It was already the case at common law in South Africa, see *S v Nieuwoudt* (No 3) 1985 (4) SA 510.
7 For the previous position see *Ajodha v The State* [1982] AC 204 at 223, [1981] 2 All ER 193 at 202.
8 As it was judicially described in *R v Millard* [1987] Crim LR 196.
9 Expressly preserved by the Police and Criminal Evidence Act 1984, s 82(3).
10 *R v Sat-Bhambra*, above.
11 Police and Criminal Evidence Act 1984, s 76(3), following the recommendation of the Criminal Law Revision Committee, Cmnd 4991 para 54, and following the old rule, see *Ajodha v The State* [1982] AC 204 at 222, [1981] 2 All ER 193 at 202. It is the same in Australia, see *McPherson v R* (1981) 55 ALJR 594.
12 [1982] AC 476, [1981] 2 All ER 705, although it is not clear that in *Brophy* there was an extra-judicial confession confirmed on the voir dire, this ought, in principle, to be immaterial.
13 [1941] 3 All ER 318, 28 Cr App Rep 84, supported in this view by the Supreme Court of Canada in *De Clercq v R* [1968] SCR 902, and by Lord Hailsham in *Wong Kam-ming v R* [1980] AC 247, [1979] 1 All ER 939.

importance for the administration of justice that an accused person should feel completely free to give evidence at the voire dire of any improper methods by which a confession or admission has been extracted from him, for he can almost never make an effective challenge of its admissibility without giving evidence himself. He is thus virtually compelled to give evidence at the voire dire, and if his evidence were admissible at the substantive trial, the result might be a significant impairment of his so-called right to silence at the trial.[14]

This ban on the use of a statement made on the voir dire applied both to use in chief by the prosecution as an admission, or use in cross-examination as a previous inconsistent statement to impeach the accused's credit, whether the trial was by judge alone or by judge and jury in the normal way.[15] The force of this reasoning seems undiminished by the passage of the Act. It is not quite so clear that it is equally unaffected by the statutory language. It should be noted that most of s 76 follows the recommendations and draft provisions proposed by the Criminal Law Revision Committee in its 11th Report.[16] The question of the use of admissions made by the accused on the voir dire had not by 1972 come into much prominence,[17] and was not considered by the Committee, so their draft Bill contained no explicit provision on the matter. The problem is created by the impact of the new subsection. Subsection 76(1) in effect provides that a confession may not be given in evidence unless the prosecution is able to negate the circumstances mentioned in sub-s 76(2). An admission made by the accused on the voir dire would not appear either to have been obtained by oppression or in circumstances likely to render it unreliable. It would thus seem to be admissible under sub-s 76(1) as a matter of ordinary statutory interpretation. It is however submitted that there is nothing in the policy of the new Act which justifies such a departure from the existing position, and that a court will be tempted to exclude any such admissions in most ordinary cases as a matter of its discretionary control of a criminal trial.[18] It must however be accepted that this is an unsatisfactory solution, and one explicitly rejected by the House of Lords in *Brophy*.[19]

The resolution of this question must also determine the case where the admission is used as a previous inconsistent statement in order to discredit the accused's testimony. In *Brophy* the House of Lords felt that there was no difference between this situation and that where the evidence was led by the prosecution. It was settled in the old law that the terms of the excluded confession could not be used for this purpose,[20] and in *Wong Kam-ming*[21] the same reasoning was applied to admissions made on the voir dire. The Bill appended to the Criminal Law Revision Committee's 11th Report explicitly prevented such use being made of a confession inadmissible under that Bill.[1]

14 [1982] AC 476 at 481, [1981] 2 All ER 705 at 709.
15 At 482, 710. For criticism of this result see Pattenden 'Informal Judicial Admissions of Criminal Activity' (1983) 32 ICLQ 812.
16 Cmnd 4991 paras 53–69, and draft Bill cl 2.
17 The question had been aired in Australia in an article by Neasey 'Cross-examination of the Accused on the Voir Dire' (1960) 34 ALJ 110 and see *R v Monks* (1955) an unreported Tasmanian case referred to in the article; *R v Gray* [1965] Qd R 373; *R v Wright* [1969] SASR 256; and *R v Banner* [1970] VR 240.
18 Expressly preserved by Police and Criminal Evidence Act 1984, s 82(3). It might alternatively choose to exercise the new statutory discretion provided by s 78.
19 At 483, 710. But see *Burns v R* (1975) 132 CLR 258 at 263.
20 *R v Treacy* [1944] 2 All ER 229, 30 Cr App Rep 93.
21 [1980] AC 247 at 259, [1979] 1 All ER 939 at 945.
 1 See note to cl 2 of draft Bill.

No such words appear in the Act, no doubt because there is no such far-reaching acceptance of hearsay as proposed by the committee. If those words had remained it would have been easier to argue against the use of the accused's statements on the voir dire for this purpose also.

It had also become quite settled in the old law that when the admissibility of the confession has been challenged unsuccessfully on the voir dire, counsel retained the right to cross-examine at the trial proper the witnesses who had previously given evidence at the voir dire.[2] It should be noted that the judge retains his control over the evidence ultimately to be submitted to the jury throughout the trial. Accordingly, if having admitted a confession on evidence given in the absence of the jury, the judge concludes, in the light of subsequent evidence, that the confession ought not to have been admitted, he may either direct the jury to disregard it, or, where there is no other sufficient evidence against the accused, direct an acquittal, or, presumably, direct a new trial,[3] though the circumstances in which he will decide to take any of these courses are likely to be rare, especially now that this is no more than a matter of the judge's residual discretion.[4] After some uncertainty[5] it became accepted that the primary purpose of such re-examination at the trial was simply to ascertain the weight to be attached to the confession, and not to try again the issue of its admissibility.[6] This position was accepted by the Criminal Law Revision Committee in the 11th Report,[7] and the terminology of ss 76 and 78, by referring to the position only before the admission of the confession, strengthens this view, so it may be taken as representing the current law. When this issue has been ventilated again in this way the court will often be well-advised to direct the jury specifically on the credibility of the confession.[8]

It was also established in *Wong Kam-ming v R* that even when a confession was admitted after a voir dire, other admissions made at it by the accused could not be led against him. The problem is similar to that discussed above in relation to cases where the confession was *excluded* after a voir dire, except that even under the old law the argument for exclusion was recognised to be weaker when the confession was admitted.[9] The statutory interpretation argument also applies more strongly in favour of admissibility. If, as submitted above, exclusion can now, after the statute, only be by way of discretion, then that discretion may be more rarely exercised in favour of the accused when the confession has been admitted after a voir dire. If so, this will be consistent with the general admission of such statements to impeach the credit of the accused by putting them to him in cross-examination. This use of statements made by the accused at the voir dire,

---

2 *R v Murray* [1951]1 KB 391, [1950] 2 All ER 925. See also *Jackson v R* (1962) 108 CLR 591; *People (A-G) v Ainscough* [1960] IR 136 (unrepresented accused, having cross-examined on the voir dire, must be told of his right to cross-examine again at the trial).
3 Only the first two possibilities were mentioned by Lord MacDermott in *R v Murphy* [1965] NI 138 at 144. See also *Cornelius v R* (1936) 55 CLR 235.
4 See above p 168.
5 Engendered by dicta in *R v Bass* [1953] 1 QB 680 at 684, [1953] 1 All ER 1064 at 1066.
6 *Chan Wei-Keung v R* [1967] 2 AC 160, [1967] 1 All ER 948; *Hunter v Chief Constable of West Midlands* [1982] AC 529, [1981] 3 All ER 727. See also *Basto v R* (1954) 91 CLR 628; *R v McAloon* [1959] OR 441.
7 Cmnd 4991 para 67.
8 *R v McCarthy* [1980] 70 Cr App Rep 270, as explained in *Prasad v R* [1981] 1 All ER 319, [1981] 1 WLR 469.
9 [1980] AC 247 at 258, [1979] 1 All ER 939 at 944.

and inconsistent with his testimony at the trial, was allowed by the Privy Council in *Wong Kam-ming* in cases where the confession was admitted.[10] Under the new provisions this reasoning will be stronger still.

It will have been noted that a distinction has been drawn between cases where the accused denies that any confession was made, and those where he asserts that it was made only as a result of improper pressure. In the latter case alone is there an issue to be tried on the voir dire. In real life the situation will be less clear-cut. The accused may both deny some material parts of the confession, and assert that the whole was obtained by improper pressure, or he may admit having signed a statement but complain that he was induced to do so by threats, or misrepresentation of the contents. These more complicated situations were considered in *Ajodha v The State*.[11] The Privy Council held that there was no difference between a case where the accused claimed that the confession had been obtained by improper means, and those in which he claimed that he had been induced to sign or acknowledge one obtained by such means. In both cases it was appropriate to hold a trial on the voir dire. The only situation where there is no issue to be tried on the voir dire is that in which the accused simply denies having made or acknowledged the statement.[12]

(iv) The burden and standard of proof at a trial within a trial

We have seen in ch III that decisions on the question of which party bears the burden of establishing a particular issue are generally decisions on the substantive law. Decisions as to which party bears the burden of establishing a fact constituting a condition precedent to the admissibility of an item of evidence belong to the law of evidence. However, there is very little authority on the subject, no doubt because, as a matter of common sense, the conditions of admissibility have to be established by those alleging that they exist.

It is settled that the burden of proving the facts constituting the condition precedent to the admissibility of confessions[13] and dying declarations[14] is borne by the person seeking to tender them in evidence. These items of evidence are admissible as exceptions to the rule against hearsay, and it is reasonable to suppose that the burden of establishing the facts rendering hearsay admissible is always borne by the party tendering the evidence.

It was held in *R v Yacoob*[15] that the persuasive burden of establishing the competence of its witnesses beyond reasonable doubt is borne by the prosecution, though the evidential burden of raising the issue is naturally upon the accused. In the case of a claim to privilege by a witness, the burden of establishing the privilege would presumably be borne by the witness. It is much less clear who bears the burden on disputed issues of fact when the question of the exclusion of evidence by discretion is being tried on a voir dire.[16]

10 At 260, 946, subject only to the provisions of the Criminal Procedure Act 1865, s 4, discussed in ch VII below.
11 [1982] AC 204, [1981] 2 All ER 193.
12 See also *MacPherson v R* (1981) 55 ALJR 594.
13 Police and Criminal Evidence Act 1984, s 76(2).
14 *R v Jenkins* (1869) LR 1 CCR 187 at 192.
15 (1981) 72 Cr App Rep 313.
16 Cp *Vel v Owen* [1987] Crim LR 496 apparently putting it upon the defence and *R v Keenan* [1989] 3 All ER 598 at 605 apparently asserting this not necessarily to be the case.

We have seen in ch III that there are two standards of proof according to which facts may have to be established, proof on a balance of probabilities, the standard appropriate to civil cases, and proof beyond reasonable doubt, the standard demanded of the prosecution in criminal cases. Where the issue is one which must be decided once and for all by the judge, it would seem proper to hold that, in civil cases, the preliminary fact must be proved to the satisfaction of the judge on a preponderance of probability and that, in criminal cases, when the evidence is tendered by the prosecution, such fact must be proved beyond reasonable doubt.[17] The English rules on confessions[18] and the authorities on dying declarations[19] and proof of handwriting tendered for comparative purposes[20] bear out the above views, at least so far as the standard of proof demanded of the prosecution on the voir dire is concerned.

It has, however, been held in Australia with regard to both confessions[1] and dying declarations,[2] that the prosecution need only establish facts justifying admissibility on the balance of probabilities. The English rule at least has the merit of ensuring that the utmost care is taken before a confession is placed before the jury, and this is particularly important because, in many cases, to admit a confession is virtually to ensure the conviction of the accused.

Where the judge merely has to be satisfied that there is prima facie evidence, for example, that a confession was made, that a previous consistent statement amounted to a complaint, or that a tape-recording was the original, he need only hear evidence from the party tendering the confession, previous consistent statement or tape-recording. In *R v Robson*[3] the Court of Appeal regarded this as equivalent to a requirement that such evidence need reach only the standard of the balance of probabilities for fear of usurping the function of the jury. It is submitted that the better view is that the requirement is no different from that applying to the satisfaction of an evidential burden, namely whether the evidence, if believed by the jury, would be sufficient to prove the matter asserted to the standard required to satisfy the legal burden, namely beyond reasonable doubt, when borne by the prosecution in a criminal case. This involves no usurpation of the function of the jury since the jury is free not to believe the evidence, and may well not do so after taking into account its contravention by the other side. Such a view is in complete harmony with the ordinary rules on the discharge of an evidential burden, the determination of whether or not there is a case to answer, and the proper distribution of functions between judge and jury.[4]

17 If the evidence is tendered by the defence, the civil standard would seem appropriate, but there is no authority.
18 Police and Criminal Evidence Act 1984, s 76. See also *R v Pickett* (1975) 31 CRNS 239.
19 *R v Jenkins* (1869) LR 1 CCR 192; in *R v Booker* (1924) 88 JP 75 the words used were 'If it appears to the satisfaction of the judge.'
20 *R v Ewing* [1983] QB 1039, [1983] 2 All ER 645, overruling *R v Angeli* [1978] 3 All ER 950, [1979] 1 WLR 26. See also *R v Mazzone* (1985) 43 SASR 330; *R v Sim* [1987] 1 NZLR 356.
 1 *Wendo v R* (1963) 100 CLR 559; *R v Clark* (1984) 11 ACR 257. The Federal position in the United States is the same for all preliminary matters, *Bourjaily v US* 107 SCt 2775 at 2779 (1987).
 2 *R v Donohoe* [1963] SR NSW 38.
 3 [1972] 2 All ER 699, [1972] 1 WLR 651.
 4 See *Timm v R* [1981] 2 SCR 315, applying this principle to the question of whether a complaint was made by the victim of a rape (but distinguishing the questions of whether it was spontaneous or recent).

SECTION 2. JUDICIAL CONTROL OF THE JURY

The exceptions to the general rule that questions of fact must be determined by the jury are one facet of the subject of judicial control of that body. Another facet of the same subject is illustrated by the rules governing rebuttable presumptions of law which restrict to some extent the jury's power of finding facts but this section is concerned with more direct methods of control by means of withdrawing an issue from the consideration of the jury, by exercising discretion to exclude otherwise admissible evidence, by summing up and by setting aside verdicts on appeal.

A. WITHDRAWAL OF AN ISSUE FROM THE JURY

Before an issue can be submitted to the jury the judge must be satisfied that there is sufficient evidence in support of the proponent's contention for their consideration, and, if he is of opinion that the evidence is insufficient, he must decide the issue in favour of the opponent.[5]

> It has always been considered a question of law to be determined by the judge, subject, of course, to review, whether there is evidence which, if it is believed, and the counter-evidence if any, not believed, would establish the facts in controversy. It is for the jury to say whether and how far the evidence is to be believed. And if the facts, as to which evidence is given, are such that from them a further inference of fact may legitimately be drawn, it is for the jury to say whether that inference is to be drawn or not. But it is for the judge to determine, subject to review, as a matter of law, whether from those facts that further inference may legitimately be drawn.

These remarks were made in the case of *Metropolitan Rly Co v Jackson*,[6] in which a passenger's thumb had been crushed by the slamming of the door of a railway carriage. There was evidence that the defendants had been guilty of negligence in allowing the carriage to become overcrowded, but there was no evidence that the overcrowding had caused the plaintiff's thumb to be where it was when the door was slammed, and the House of Lords held that the judge should have withdrawn the case from the jury for this reason.

When a judge comes to the conclusion that evidence in support of the contention of the proponent of an issue is insufficient, the course which he should adopt will vary from case to case. Sometimes he should discharge the jury and enter judgment for the opponent of the issue, as in a civil suit in which there is insufficient evidence in support of the plaintiff's allegation of negligence,[7] on other occasions, he will direct the jury to return a verdict in favour of the opponent, as in a criminal case where the prosecution's evidence is insufficient; while there may be other issues to be left to the jury,

---

5 The proponent is the party by whom the issue must be raised in the first instance. He is usually the plaintiff in a civil case, and the prosecutor on a criminal charge, but this is not necessarily so. The proponent bears the evidential burden in the first instance. He usually bears the legal burden also, but this is not always the case. Wigmore uses the term to describe the party bearing the legal burden of proof.

6 (1877) 3 App Cas 193 at 207 per Lord Blackburn. If substantially similar facts were to occur today, it is possible that the Law Reform (Contributory Negligence) Act 1945 would be applied. This is also true of *Wakelin v London and South Western Rly Co* (1886) 12 App Cas 41, another leading case on the subject under discussion.

7 Even in this kind of case it may be desirable to have the damages assessed by the jury.

as on a criminal charge when the judge rules that there is insufficient evidence of insanity (an issue of which the accused is the proponent), and it is none the less necessary for the jury to decide whether the prosecution has established the accused's guilt in other respects. Whichever of these courses is adopted, the judge is obviously exercising considerable control over the jury, for he is either totally withdrawing facts from their consideration, or else directing them to come to a certain conclusion, whatever their own views may be.

The extent of this method of control increased during the nineteenth century, for as Willes J said in *Ryder v Wombwell*:[8]

> It was formerly considered necessary in all cases to leave the question to the jury if there was any evidence, even a scintilla, in support of the case; but it is now settled that the question for the judge (subject of course to review) is, ... not whether there is literally no evidence but whether there is none that ought reasonably to satisfy the jury that the fact sought to be proved is established.

The test to be applied by the judge in order to determine whether there is sufficient evidence in favour of the proponent of an issue, is for him to inquire whether there is evidence which, if uncontradicted, would justify men of ordinary reason and fairness in affirming the proposition which the proponent is bound to maintain, having regard to the degree of proof demanded by the law with regard to the particular issue.[9] This test is easy to apply when the evidence is direct, for, unless their cross-examination was utterly shattering, the question whether witnesses are to be believed must be left to the jury, but it is necessarily somewhat vague when circumstantial evidence has to be considered. In that case, little more can be done than inquire whether the proponent's evidence warrants an inference of the facts in issue, or whether it merely leads to conjecture concerning them.[10] At this stage the submission should succeed only if the circumstantial evidence raises no hypothesis consistent with guilt.[11]

Although it is sometimes the judge's duty to withdraw an issue from the jury of his own motion, questions of the sufficiency of evidence are usually raised on a submission that there is no case to answer made by the opponent of the issue.[12] The judge must rule in favour of the submission if there is insufficient evidence to prove an essential element in the proponent's case, or if the evidence which has been adduced is so tenuous that no jury properly directed could convict upon it. It is not enough when any weakness in the proponent's case depends upon matters within the exclusive jurisdiction of

---

8 (1868) LR 4 Exch 32 at 39. In *Jones v Great Western Rly Co* (1930) 144 LT 194, the trial judge referred to the scintilla rule in deciding to leave the case to the jury.

9 *Bridges v North London Rly Co* (1874) LR 7 HL 213 at 233 per Brett J. The last seventeen words which appeared in the first edition have been reinstated out of deference to a paper by Professor Eric Edwards in (1970) 9 Western Australian Law Review 169.

10 Mere improbability is not enough, *Rafidain Bank v Agom Universal Sugar Trading Co Ltd* [1987] 3 All ER 859, [1987] 1 WLR 1606. See also *Kerr v Ayr Steam Shipping Co* [1915] AC 217 at 233; *Jones v Great Western Railway Co* (1930) above at 202; *Caswell v Powell Duffryn Associated Collieries Ltd* [1940] AC 152 at 169, [1939] 3 All ER 722 at 733.

11 See *Torrance v Cornish* (1985) 79 FLR 87; *R v Haas* (1986) 22 ACR 299.

12 On the whole subject see articles by Glanville Williams in [1965] Crim LR 343 and 410, and Pattenden 'The Submission of No Case—Some Recent Developments' [1982] Crim LR 558.

the jury, such as the reliability of witnesses.[13] If he rules against the submission, the issue must be determined by the jury, but, even when the opponent calls no evidence, their decision will not necessarily be in favour of the proponent. The jury may disbelieve the testimony given on his behalf, or, if they do accept it, they may not be prepared to draw the requisite inference.

There are certain practical differences in the procedure which ought to be followed by the judge according to the class of case which he is trying.

1. CIVIL CASES TRIED BY A JUDGE ALONE

A submission that there is no case to answer may be made by one of the parties to proceedings before a judge alone, but, if this is done in a civil case, the judge must decline to rule on the submission unless the party making it elects not to call evidence.[14] At least two considerations justify this requirement. In the first place, the judge has to determine the facts as well as the law, and he ought not to be asked to express an opinion on the evidence until it is complete. No one would ask a jury at the end of a plaintiff's case to say what verdict they would be prepared to give if the defendant called no evidence.[15] Secondly, the parties might be put to extra expense if the judge ruled in favour of the submission before the evidence was complete, for, if the Court of Appeal were to decide against his ruling, a new trial would be necessary so that the party who made the submission could call his evidence.

2. CIVIL CASES TRIED WITH A JURY

Neither of these considerations apply to civil cases tried with a jury. Accordingly, it has been held that the judge has a discretion in such cases, and he may rule on the submission without putting the party who makes it to his election whether to call evidence.[16] If the judge decides in favour of the submission, there would have to be a new trial if his ruling is reversed on appeal, but this would also be the case if he deferred his ruling until the

---

13 *R v Galbraith* [1981] 2 All ER 1060, [1981] 1 WLR 1039. *Haw Tua Tau v Public Prosecutor* [1982] AC 136 at 151, [1981] 3 All ER 14 at 19. Similar principles apply to committal for extradition. *R v Governor of Pentonville Prison ex p Osman* [1989] 3 All ER 701 at 721. For discussion of the possible impact of s 2(1)(a) of the Criminal Appeal Act 1968, see p 197 below. See also *Mezzo v R* (1986) 30 DLR (4th) 161 illustrating special problems with evidence of identification in this area.

14 *Alexander v Rayson* [1936] 1 KB 169. In matrimonial causes, the cases establish that the judge has a discretion whether to put a party to his election on a submission of no case although the party making the submission will normally be put to his or her election (*Yuill v Yuill* [1945] P 15, [1945] 1 All ER 183; *Beal v Beal* [1953] 2 All ER 1228 n, [1953] 1 WLR 1365; *Gilbert v Gilbert* [1958] P 131, [1957] 3 All ER 604; *Wilson v Wilson* [1958] 3 All ER 195, [1958] 1 WLR 1090; *Meyer v Meyer* [1959] 2 All ER 633 n, [1959] 1 WLR 957; *Storey v Storey* [1961] P 63, [1960] 3 All ER 279; *Holzer v Holzer (Morley intervening)* [1964] 3 All ER 989, [1964] 1 WLR 1478; *Inglis v Inglis and Baxter* [1968] P 639, [1967] 2 All ER 71). It is only in the most exceptional circumstances that a new trial will be ordered by the Court of Appeal after an election (*Portland Manufacturers Ltd v Harte* [1977] QB 306, [1976] 1 All ER 225).

15 Per Romer LJ [1936] 1 KB 169 at 178.

16 *Young v Rank* [1950] 2 KB 510, [1950] 2 All ER 166 where the authorities are reviewed by Devlin J.

evidence was completed, for the verdict of the jury would have to be obtained in either event.

Whether a civil case is tried with a jury or not, it seems that, if a judge rules that there is a case to answer and the defendant gives evidence, the defendant's liability must be judged on the whole of the evidence and an appeal may be dismissed although the Court of Appeal is of opinion that the judge should have ruled in favour of the submission when it was made.[17]

3. CRIMINAL CASES TRIED WITH A JURY

In criminal cases tried with a jury, the accused is never put to his election whether to call evidence or not before a ruling is made on his submission that there is no case to answer. Even where the accused bears the evidential burden in respect of a special defence he may rely upon its having been raised by evidence adduced by the prosecution as part of its case.[18] If the ruling is in favour of the submission the jury are directed to acquit. If the submission fails, the accused calls his evidence in the ordinary way. Contrary to what was once decided by the Court of Criminal Appeal,[19] it has been said that on an appeal against conviction, the Court of Criminal Appeal considers the evidence as a whole, and they can therefore dismiss the appeal although they may be of opinion that the judge ought to have ruled that there was no case to answer at the close of the prosecution's evidence if, as sometimes happens, the accused is incriminated by his own evidence.[20] But this does not apply to a case in which the Court of Appeal is of opinion that there was no case to answer and the trial judge only allowed the case to go to the jury in fairness to a co-accused, who incriminates the accused.[1]

4. MAGISTRATES

A submission of no case may be made in proceedings before magistrates. If the proceedings are criminal, there is no question of the accused being put to his election.[2] If the proceedings are civil, the party making the submission may be put to his election. If the magistrates rule against the submission, they should give the party making it a further opportunity to address them on the facts.[3] This is because a finding that there is a case to answer is not a decision of the whole case against the party making the submission. It is perfectly proper for magistrates to hold that there is a case to answer and decide the issue in favour of the party making the submission. They may

---

17 *Payne v Harrison* [1961] 2 QB 403, [1961] 2 All ER 873.
18 Even when only by the exculpatory part of a mixed statement, *R v Duncan* (1981) 73 Cr App Rep 359; *R v Hamand* (1985) 82 Cr App Rep 65.
19 *R v Joiner* (1910) 4 Cr App Rep 64.
20 *R v Power* [1919] 1 KB 572.
 1 *R v Abbot* [1955] 2 QB 497, [1955] 2 All ER 899. See the discussion of the authorities by J C Wood 77 LQR 491.
 2 An unsuccessful submission that there was no sufficient case to answer does not deprive the accused of his right to give evidence at committal proceedings (*R v Horseferry Road Stipendiary Magistrate ex p Adams* [1978] 1 All ER 373, [1977] 1 WLR 1197).
 3 *Disher v Disher* [1965] P 31, [1963] 3 All ER 933; *Mayes v Mayes* [1971] 2 All ER 397, [1971] 1 WLR 679.

come to the conclusion that the evidence of the opposite party is not to be believed.[4]

B. DISCRETION TO EXCLUDE EVIDENCE[5]

If the judge has not altogether dictated the decision on an issue by withdrawing it from the trial or by directing a verdict, the next most powerful way in which he can affect its decision is by overriding the rules governing the admission of evidence relevant to that issue. The general question is how far the judge has a discretion to do so. In 1790, Grose J dreaded 'that rules of evidence should ever depend upon the discretion of the judges', he wished to find the rule laid down and to abide by it.[6] Channell J also believed it to be 'better to apply the rules strictly than to allow it to be supposed that a judge has a discretion to relax them if he thinks they will work an injustice.'[7] Lord Halsbury expressed himself in similar vein in 1914,[8] but he was in a minority and since then there have been many dicta concerning the judge's power to exclude admissible evidence because its reception would create undue prejudice or be unfair in some other respect. In *R v Sang*[9] the House of Lords affirmed the existence of a discretion to control the use of evidence so as to ensure a fair trial, and the matter has been put upon a new statutory footing by s 78 of the Police and Criminal Evidence Act 1984. The implications of that affirmation and the impact of the new statutory provision must both be explored. It will also be necessary to distinguish between the different situation in criminal and civil cases, but first the very nature of discretionary control must be examined.

1. NATURE OF THE DISCRETION

Not for the first, or last, time in the exposition of the law of evidence, it is necessary to beware of the danger inherent in the loose use of terminology, in this case the use of the word 'discretion' in a number of different senses.[10] It is particularly important to distinguish between the idea that the judge has the responsibility of deciding upon the application to the facts before him of an inherently vague term, and the idea that he is free to act in any way he chooses upon the facts which he finds to exist.[11] The difference is that

4 *De Filippo v De Filippo* (1963) 108 Sol Jo 56.
5 This has become a much more prominent issue in recent times and reflects a fundamental shift away from rigid exclusionary rules. For fuller examination see Pattenden *Judicial Discretion and Criminal Litigation* (1990); Livesey 'Judicial Discretion to Exclude Prejudicial Evidence' [1968] CLJ 291; Weinberg 'The Judicial Discretion to Exclude Relevant Evidence' (1975) 21 McGill LJ 1; Cross 'Discretion and the Law of Evidence: When it Comes to the "Forensic Crunch"' (1979) 30 NILQ 289.
6 *R v Inhabitants of Eriswell* (1790) 3 Term Rep 707 at 711. Exactly the same sentiments prevented the adoption of the United States Model Code. See Wigmore 'The American Law Institute Code of Evidence Rules: A Dissent' (1942) 28 ABA Jo 23.
7 *R v Cargill* (1913) 8 Cr App Rep 224 at 229.
8 *R v Christie* (1914) 10 Cr App Rep 141 at 149.
9 [1980] AC 402, [1979] 2 All ER 1222.
10 Dr Pattenden (n 5 above) distinguishes a number of senses. Three different exclusionary discretions were urged upon an Australian court in *R v Rowley* (1986) 23 ACR 371, see also *R v Duke* (1989) 38 ACR 305.
11 Dworkin in *Taking Rights Seriously* (1977) pp 31–33 describes these as weak and strong senses of discretion.

in the former case the judge must act in a particular way once he has found the facts, and in the latter he is still free to choose which action to take after finding them. In many practical situations the dichotomy may not appear so clear, the distinction has not always been present in the mind of judges, and the terminology of discretion has been used indiscriminatingly to apply to both. Nevertheless there are signs that the distinction is now being taken. Thus in considering Lord Edmund Davies' speech in *D v National Society for the Prevention of Cruelty to Children*[12] Professor Cross deplored 'the use of the word "discretion" to describe the judge's duty to perform the contemplated balancing act.'[13] Nor is such criticism limited to academic commentators. In *R v Viola* the Court of Appeal said of the court's earlier judgment in *R v Mills*[14] on the issue of allowing questions to be asked in cross-examination about the complainant's sexual history that:

> it is wrong to speak of a judge's 'discretion' in this context. The judge has to make a judgment whether he is satisfied or not in the terms of s 2 [of the Sexual Offences (Amendment) Act 1976]. But once having reached that judgment on the particular facts, he has no discretion. If he comes to the conclusion that he is satisfied it would be unfair to exclude the evidence, then the evidence has to be admitted and the questions have to be allowed.[15]

It is also significant that s 78(2) of the Police and Criminal Evidence Act 1984 explicitly provides that the stated exclusionary discretion is to operate without prejudice to any exclusionary rule.[16]

One practical consequence of making this distinction is simply that the grounds upon which an appellate court will review a discretion, although now much more extensive than was once the case,[17] are still not so extensive as those in which it will reverse the incorrect application of a rule.[18] Nor will it even consider exercising an exclusionary discretion for the first time on appeal when the matter has not been put to the trial judge.[19] In general terms the exercise of a discretion will stand so long as the judge 'does not err in law, takes into account all relevant matters and excludes consideration of irrelevant matters',[20] though there may be less reluctance to intervene when the trial judge's view was clearly obiter, and designed merely to bolster

12 [1978] AC 171 at 246, [1977] 1 All ER 589 at 618.
13 (1979) 30 NILQ 289 at 294.
14 (1978) 68 Cr App Rep 327.
15 [1982] 3 All ER 73 at 77, [1982] 1 WLR 1138 at 1142. See also *R v Murukami* [1951] SCR 801 at 803.
16 In *R v Gill and Ranuana* [1989] Crim LR 358 the Court of Appeal expressed the view that the operation of s 78 also involved the exercise more of judgment than discretion.
17 *Evans v Bartlam* [1937] AC 473, [1937] 2 All ER 646, is often seen as the turning point. See also *House v R* (1936) 55 CLR 499.
18 *Charles Osenton & Co v Johnston* [1942] AC 130, [1941] 2 All ER 245, where it was said that there is a presumption that the discretion has been exercised correctly. In *Cookson v Knowles* [1979] AC 556 at 566, [1978] 2 All ER 604 at 607, Lord Diplock explicitly distinguished between the role of an appellate court in relation to rule and discretion.
19 *R v Goldenberg* (1988) 88 Cr App Rep 285 at 289, though it seems immaterial that the first reference to the discretion at the trial was too late for its valid exercise, *R v Kempster* [1989] Crim LR 747.
20 *R v Scarrott* [1978] QB 1016 at 1028, [1978] 1 All ER 672 at 681. Thus in New Zealand where the old categorisation criticised in *Viola* still prevailed, the court refused to reverse the trial court's decision to disallow cross-examination of the victim of rape as to sexual history because it was an exercise of discretion, *R v Bills* [1981] 1 NZLR 760.

exclusion by rule.[1] A further consequence is that it becomes much more difficult for even consistent practice to mature into a rule. Thus in *Selvey v D P P*[2] the House of Lords rejected an attempt to claim that this had happened, and been recognised to have happened,[3] in relation to disallowance of cross-examination of the accused as to his bad character under the provisions of s 1(f)(ii) of the Criminal Evidence Act 1898. Thus Lord Pearce said:[4]

> The courts have been right, however, in thinking that the question is whether *this* attack on the prosecution, ought to let in *these* convictions on the particular facts of the case, and on such a point rules are no substitute for a discretion in producing a fair trial. I appreciate that in the result an accused cannot be certain exactly how far he can go without letting in his convictions.

In some situations the nature of the rule of evidence which is in question is defined in such terms that it is difficult to discern any possible role for the application of an exclusionary discretion.[5] Sometimes the rule is drafted in much more rigid terms, and in such cases it is feasible to construct guidelines for the exercise of a discretion designed to avoid injustice.[6]

If the distinction mentioned above is accepted it is tolerably clear that the only exercise of a discretion can be to exclude otherwise admissible evidence. It cannot be used to admit otherwise inadmissible evidence as remarked by Lord Reid in *Myers v D P P*:

> It is true that a judge has discretion to exclude legally admissible evidence if justice so requires, but it is a very different thing to say that he has a discretion to admit legally inadmissible evidence.[7]

It is true that some exclusionary rules are phrased in such vague terms that some judges occasionally appear to suppose that they are exercising an inclusionary discretion, but such cases are best explained as ones in which the vague question is resolved in such a way that the exclusionary rule does not apply.[8]

A true inclusionary discretion is sometimes conferred by statute, as where s 8 of the Civil Evidence Act 1968 empowers the court to admit hearsay statements even though the conditions for their admissibility prescribed by the Act have not been fulfilled,[9] and where s 26 of the Criminal Justice Act

1 As in *R v Samuel* [1988] QB 615 at 630, [1988] 2 All ER 135 at 147.
2 [1970] AC 304, [1968] 2 All ER 497.
3 In *R v Flynn* [1963] 1 QB 729, [1961] 3 All ER 58.
4 At 360, 528, emphasis in original.
5 It is arguable that this is the situation with regard to the admissibility of similar fact evidence, see p 372, below. The High Court of Australia has expressed a similar view in relation to the exclusion in that jurisdiction by discretion of confessions which have passed the local test for exclusion by rule, see Brennan J in *Collins v R* (1980) 31 ALR 257 at 315.
6 *R v Britzman* [1983] 1 All ER 369 at 373, [1983] 1 WLR 350 at 355. This course is favoured by Dr Pattenden.
7 [1965] AC 1001 at 1024, [1964] 2 All ER 881 at 887. But see *R v Greasby* [1984] Crim LR 488.
8 Eg *R v Dodd* (1982) 74 Cr App Rep 50. See also *R v Wilson* (1987) 32 ACR 286 at 293.
9 On the court's discretion with regard to affidavits see *Rossage v Rossage* [1960] 1 All ER 600, [1960] 1 WLR 249, and *Re J (an infant)* [1960] 1 All ER 603, [1960] 1 WLR 253; *Savings and Investment Bank Ltd v Gasco Investments (Netherlands) BV (No 2)* [1988] Ch 422, [1988] 1 All ER 975.

1988 permits the discretionary acceptance of documentary hearsay even though made in contemplation of criminal proceedings.

It is interesting to note that in proceedings where the general exclusionary rules of evidence do not apply, for example in some tribunals,[10] there is no room for an exclusionary discretion. Where statute has sought to extend the range of material available to the tribunal, it is not for the tribunal to cut it down as it chooses by the exercise of any such discretion.[11] It has also been held that in cases where the function of the tribunal is merely to establish the existence of a case to answer, as in the case of magistrates on committal proceedings, there is no room for an exclusionary discretion. That discretion comes into play only at the trial.[12]

2. DISCRETION TO EXCLUDE RELEVANT EVIDENCE IN CRIMINAL PROCEEDINGS

The existence of some such discretion at common law[13] has been recognised in criminal cases in the highest appellate tribunals since *R v Christie*.[14] In *Selvey v D P P* when the prosecution mounted a general attack on the existence of such a discretion in the context of the Criminal Evidence Act 1898, 1(f)(ii), Viscount Dilhorne said:

it is far too late in the day even to consider the argument that a judge has no such discretion. Let it suffice for me to say that in my opinion the existence of such a discretion is now clearly established.[15]

Lord Hodson made it clear that in his opinion the discretion applied in all criminal cases.[16] The general question was certified once again in *R v Sang*:

Does a trial judge have a discretion to refuse to allow evidence, being evidence other than evidence of admission, to be given in any circumstances in which such evidence is relevant and of more than minimal probative value.[17]

Their Lordships were unanimous in agreeing to an answer which distinguished two situations:

(1) A trial judge in a criminal trial has always a discretion to refuse to admit evidence if in his opinion its prejudicial effect outweighs its probative value.
(2) Save with regard to admissions and confessions and generally with regard to evidence obtained from the accused after commission of the offence, he has no discretion to refuse to admit relevant admissible evidence on the ground that it was obtained by improper or unfair means. The court is not concerned with how

10 See ch 1 section 2 above.
11 *Rosedale Mouldings Ltd v Sibley* [1980] ICR 816 at 822.
12 *R v Horsham Justices, ex p Bukhari* (1982) 74 Cr App Rep 291; *R v Governor of Pentonville Prison, ex p Voets* [1986] 2 All ER 630, [1986] 1 WLR 470. For criticism of the former see commentary in [1982] Crim LR 180, and for a different approach in Australia see *Seymour v A-G for Commonwealth* (1984) 53 ALR 513 at 540.
13 A new statutory discretion has been superimposed as s 78 of the Police and Criminal Evidence Act 1984, but discussion of this provision is deferred until the end of this section.
14 [1914] AC 545, [1914–15] All ER Rep 63.
15 [1970] AC 304 at 341, [1968] 2 All ER 497 at 510.
16 At 346, 515.
17 [1980] AC 402 at 431, [1979] 2 All ER 1222 at 1225.

it was obtained. It is no ground for the exercise of discretion to conclude that the evidence was obtained as the result of the activities of an agent provocateur.[18]

Strictly speaking, the ratio decidendi is expressed by the last sentence of this answer.[19] Nevertheless the rest of it might have been expected to have a very powerfully persuasive effect. In a subsequent case Lord Roskill asserted not only that *Sang* settled existing doubts, but that it would be a retrograde step to 'enlarge the now narrow limits of that discretion or to engraft an exception'.[20] It is useful first to examine these limits.

Two situations seem to be distinguished, those in which the court is concerned to afford the accused a fair trial, and those in which it is concerned to afford him fair treatment. In the former case the accused is to be protected by the exclusion from his trial of evidence which might have an unreliable effect upon the result; in the latter case he is to be protected by the exclusion from his trial of evidence which has been obtained by improper methods, however reliable the effect might be. There is a wide variety of discretions operating in relation to evidence in a criminal trial.[1] Of those which have mainly occupied the courts, any discretion relating to the exclusion of evidence of extrinsic discreditable conduct upon the basis that it is more prejudicial than probative,[2] and the exclusion of cross-examination about broadly similar matters under s 1(f) of the Criminal Evidence Act 1898, comes into the former category. Conversely any discretion to exclude real evidence obtained from the accused by improper means, or in breach of the principle underlying the privilege against self-incrimination, comes into the latter category. Confessional material straddles the two categories, especially in view of s 76(2) of the Police and Criminal Evidence Act 1984 which excludes confessions obtained:

in consequence of anything said or done which was likely, in the circumstances existing at the time, to render unreliable any confession which might be made by him [the accused] in consequence thereof.

The section itself recognises that a confession obtained in such circumstances might in fact be reliable, or even true. It is also obvious that a confession can be unreliable for many other reasons, for example that the person who confesses is mentally defective,[3] or confesses to something of which he has no knowledge.[4]

It will be convenient to consider the application of the discretion to exclude separately in relation to each such category, and then in relation to confessional statements.

Two major sub-categories in relation to which the discretion operates, if

18 At 437, 1231.
19 See Lord Diplock at 431, 1226 and Lord Scarman at 456, 1246.
20 *Morris v Beardmore* [1981] AC 446 at 469, [1980] 2 All ER 753 at 767.
1 For a very comprehensive list, see Pattenden *Judicial Discretion and Criminal Litigation* (1990).
2 For Australian analysis of these terms in this content, see *R v Hasler, ex p A-G* [1987] 1 Qd R 239.
3 See *R v Isequilla* [1975] 1 All ER 77 at 84, [1975] 1 WLR 716 at 723; *R v Miller* [1986] 3 All ER 119, [1986] 1 WLR 1191; and the statutory recognition of such a possibility by the prescription of a special direction in s 77 of the Police and Criminal Evidence Act 1984.
4 See *Comptroller of Customs v Western Electric Co* [1966] AC 367 at 371, [1965] 3 All ER 599 at 601.

at all, in pursuance of a fair trial, are evidence of the accused's[5] discreditable extrinsic conduct, and cross-examination of the accused as to the otherwise excluded matters under s 1(f) of the Criminal Evidence Act 1898. As will be seen in ch IX below, evidence of discreditable extrinsic conduct is generally inadmissible in chief at common law. It will be argued that this results from a rule that such evidence is inadmissible when its prejudicial effect exceeds its probative value. If this is the rule it is clear that evidence which is admitted after applying it cannot be excluded by the exercise of a discretion cast in the same terms.[6] It must be conceded however that the language of discretion is still used in this context.[7] This can be explained as no more than the wider use of the word 'discretion' to apply to a situation in which the operation of the exclusionary rule depends upon the comparative weight of indeterminate concepts such as probative force and prejudicial effect which can be accomplished only by the most delicate exercise of judgement. Even if this is the case there is still scope for discretion in the true sense in cases where the admissibility of such evidence is governed not by the common law, but by statute. Clear instances are provided by prosecutions for receiving stolen goods in which reliance is placed on s 27(3) of the Theft Act 1968.[8] Evidence of the accused's previous convictions of offences involving fraud or dishonesty is admissible in chief on the issue of guilty knowledge, but it has been held that the judge has an exclusionary discretion when there is a danger that the jury may consider such evidence also on the question of possession.[9] The convictions that may be proved on a handling charge are restricted to those of handling and theft. The reason for applying a discretion in these cases is simply that the statute gives a blanket power to the judge to admit the evidence for the stated purpose without expressing any restriction at all. In some circumstances this can lead to prejudice, and so the court exercises a discretion to prevent it. Exactly the same rationale applies to cross-examination about convictions, commission of offences, charges and bad character under s 1(f) of the Criminal Evidence Act 1898, the substance of which will be discussed fully in ch X below. There too the statute gives a blanket permission without any explicit qualification once the conditions have been satisfied. The whole question was ventilated in the House of Lords in *Selvey v D P P*[10] where the prosecution launched a full-scale argument against the existence of any discretion to prevent cross-examination once the conditions prescribed by s 1(f)(ii) of the statute had been satisfied. The question of the existence of any discretion is intimately connected with the construction of the conditions permitting cross-examination. It was just because the conditions were unqualified[11] in s 1(f)(ii) that the discretion was

---

5 There is no discretion to exclude relevant evidence of discreditable disposition or conduct adduced by the defence, for example in relation to the conduct of a victim to support a claim of self-defence, see *R v Masters* [1987] 2 Qd R 272.

6 See Tapper 'Proof and Prejudice' in Campbell and Waller (eds) *Well and Truly Tried* (1982).

7 Even in *D P P v Boardman* [1975] AC 421, [1974] 3 All ER 887; and such reference persists, see *R v Lunt* (1987) 85 Cr App Rep 241 proposition 5 at 244, and repeated in *R v Shore* (1988) 89 Cr App Rep 32 at 41. See further at p 370 below.

8 Repealing, and re-enacting with some modifications, Larceny Act 1916, s 43(1).

9 *R v Perry* [1984] Crim LR 680, *R v Wilkins* [1975] 2 All ER 734, 60 Cr App Rep 300. Under the old provisions, *R v List* [1965] 3 All ER 710, [1966] 1 WLR 9; *R v Herron* [1967] 1 QB 107, [1966] 2 All ER 26.

10 [1970] AC 304, [1968] 2 All ER 497.

11 *R v Hudson* [1912] 2 KB 464 at 470.

developed.[12] The subsequent history of the interpretation of the section confirmed this with each fresh re-affirmation of the rigour of the statutory wording closely followed by a new re-avowal of the existence of the discretion to soften its effect. Thus in *Selvey* itself Lord Guest said:[13]

> If I had thought that there was no discretion in English Law for a judge to disallow admissible evidence, as counsel for the Crown argued, I should have striven hard and long to give a benevolent construction to s 1, proviso (f)(ii).

The problem here is one common to all attempts to replace, or even to supplement, rules with discretion, namely the unpredictability of its exercise. This is vitally important in this context since it is necessary to make important decisions as to whether or not to call the accused to give evidence, and whether or not to run a particular line of defence, the validity of which are likely to depend entirely upon the accuracy of such a prediction. Awareness of such problems has fostered attempts to improve predictability by the creation of guidelines for the exercise of the discretion. It has been settled since *R v Turner*[14] that a defence of consent to a charge of rape does not justify cross-examination under the section, though it is less clear that such a result reflects consistent exercise of this discretion.[15] A more general guideline was promoted in *R v Flynn*[16] that where the very nature of the defence necessarily involves an imputation upon the prosecution then the discretion should, as a general rule, be exercised in favour of the accused. The court then acted upon this view by holding that the trial judge had there exercised his discretion wrongly in principle. The notion of any such general rule was emphatically rejected in *Selvey*. Lord Guest went so far as to assert that:

> If it is suggested that the exercise of this discretion may be whimsical and depend on the individual idiosyncracies of the judge, this is inevitable where it is a question of discretion, but I am satisfied that this is a lesser risk than attempting to shackle the judge's power within a straight jacket.[17]

Other members of the House saw the contrast in less vivid hues. Lord Pearce was prepared to accept that the conditions mentioned in *Flynn* were valid factors to be weighed in exercising the discretion, but not that they could constitute even presumptive rules subject to exceptions in individual cases.[18] It is hard to reconcile these dicta with the apparent accession of the whole House to the view expressed in *R v Cook*[19] that an appellate court could interfere with the exercise of a discretion by a trial judge on the basis that he had erred in principle. Such a view clearly demands the existence of some principle upon which the discretion should be exercised. It was explicitly

12 *R v Watson* (1913) 8 Cr App Rep 249 at 254.
13 [1970] AC 304 at 351, [1968] 2 All ER 497 at 519.
14 [1944] KB 463, [1944] 1 All ER 599.
15 Although the question was left open in *Selvey* it must militate against any such view that the same result was reached in *R v Sheean* (1908) 21 Cox CC 561, without reference to any discretion and some years before any was recognised in the context of the Criminal Evidence Act.
16 [1963] 1 QB 729, [1961] 3 All ER 58.
17 [1970] AC 304 at 352, [1968] 2 All ER 497 at 520.
18 At 360, 527.
19 [1959] 2 QB 340 at 348, [1959] 2 All ER 97 at 101.

recognised by the House in *Selvey*[20] that the decision provided no guidance to the accused. It is hard to understand how the guiding star of a fair trial avowed in *Selvey* could be regarded as leading to a situation in which the accused was left completely in the dark as to the best way in which to conduct his defence. Practice has continued to diverge,[1] and once again the Court of Appeal has attempted to propound guidelines for the exercise of the discretion.[2] It is noteworthy that a number of the considerations mentioned in those guidelines cannot easily be subsumed under the need to balance probative force and prejudicial effect. It will be interesting to discover whether or not the court's abstinence from the terminology of rules will protect the decision. Similar abstinence is to be found in *R v Nye*[3] where the court first referred to a *principle* of exercising the discretion so as to prevent cross-examination upon the basis of convictions 'spent' under the Rehabilitation of Offenders Act 1974, and then acted upon it by allowing an appeal against the trial judge's failure to do so.

It has subsequently become clear that *Selvey* still represents English law in this area. Its guidance has, in a series of decisions,[4] been re-affirmed by the Court of Appeal. In *Burke* the relevant convictions were for drug-related offences; in *Powell* for controlling prostitutes; and in *Owen* for theft from the person. These decisions have resulted in the endorsement of a number of points[5] for the judge to bear in mind in exercising this discretion: first, that the judge's duty is to ensure a fair trial, alike for both defence *and* prosecution, by weighing the prejudice to the accused of the cross-examination against the damage done to the prosecution by the attack upon its witnesses; second, that cases will occur where such prejudice unreasonably[6] outweighs that damage; third, that in the ordinary and normal case it is only fair that the jury should know of the credit-worthiness of both attacker and attacked; and fourth that it is not enough to justify quashing a conviction that the court would itself have exercised the discretion differently.

It is significant that attention was drawn to the similarity of the convictions put to the witness in *Selvey* with the offences with which he was charged, for sexual offences, while those which were withheld related to offences of dishonesty. It is particularly disturbing that some emphasis has been placed upon the possibility of putting convictions showing such similarity, especially in *Powell*,[7] though this was still recognised to be a factor to be taken into account militating against permitting cross-examination, and in *Owen*[8] it seems that prejudicial detail of similarity was omitted. Even after allowing for this, the result still seems to be that evidence which would not have been admissible in chief as similar fact evidence may be put in cross-examination,

---

20 [1970] AC 304 at 361, [1968] 2 All ER 497 at 528; see above p 179.
1 See *R v Britzman* [1983] 1 All ER 369 at 372, [1983] 1 WLR 350 at 353.
2 At 355, 373.
3 (1982) 75 Cr App Rep 247.
4 *R v Burke* (1985) 82 Cr App Rep 156; *R v Powell* [1986] 1 All ER 193, [1985] 1 WLR 1364; *R v Owen* (1985) 83 Cr App Rep 100.
5 Described in *Burke* at 161 as 'cardinal principles'.
6 This is the adverb used in *Owen*, the most recent of the series; in the earlier case of *Burke*, and repeated in *Powell*, the adverb was 'immeasurably'.
7 At 198, 1370 and in the criticism of the earlier decisions of the court in *R v Watts* [1983] 3 All ER 101, 77 Cr App Rep 126, and in *R v John and Braithwaite* (24 November 1983), (unreported) where this had been regarded as a particularly important factor in the decision to allow the appeals.
8 At 107.

ostensibly to credit. This tendency is exacerbated by the formulation noted above in terms of disallowance only in the case of 'unreasonable' prejudice to the accused. The formulation of the similar fact rule adopted here regards any preponderance of prejudice as justification for exclusion.

It should be noted that a similar direction has been approved by majorities in the High Court of Australia,[9] the Supreme Court of Canada,[10] and the Court of Session in Scotland.[11] In *Phillips v R* the majority[12] was concerned that the discretion should be unfettered by rules,[13] and attached weight to the fact that since in the case before them the convictions were for offences of dishonesty they would not be particularly prejudicial on a charge of rape.[14] In his dissenting judgment Deane J raised the interesting point that the nature of the imputation, namely that the victim and the accused had been associated in the misuse of drugs, reflected equally badly on both of them, so there was no upset balance to redress.[15] In Canada, as in the United States, once the accused chooses to testify he enjoys no such special regime of protection as that conferred by the Criminal Evidence Act 1898, s 1(f). In such circumstances a majority[16] of the Supreme Court of Canada regarded such discretionary protection as nevertheless available. In Scotland the legislation is in the English form, but used to be interpreted differently,[17] and the situation is complicated by statutory restriction on the use of previous convictions in court.[18] In *Leggate* however the rule, and apparently[19] its discretionary gloss, was assimilated to that applied in England.

It must be emphasised that this discretion is based upon the need for a fair trial to be conducted. That this may differ from the rationale of fair treatment of the individual concerned is illustrated by cases in which there is more than one accused. In such a case the court has no discretion to intervene so as to prevent one of several co-accused from adducing evidence which is more prejudicial than probative, nor to prevent cross-examination by the co-accused under the provisions of the Criminal Evidence Act.[20]

If, as suggested earlier, the former question really turns on judgment about the application of a vague rule rather than discretion, authority for that view in this context is to be found in the judgment of Devlin J in *R v Miller*:

> In the case of the prosecution, a question of this sort may be relevant and at the same time prejudicial, and, if the court is of the opinion that the prejudicial effect outweighs its relevance, then it has the power, and, indeed, the duty, to exclude

9 *Phillips v R* (1985) 62 ALR 479 at 488.
10 *Corbett v R* (1988) 41 CCC (3d) 385.
11 *Leggate v HM Advocate* 1988 SLT 665 at 672.
12 Mason CJ, Wilson, Brennan and Dawson JJ.
13 Deane J also agreed on this point.
14 Even though it had been accomplished by breaking into a dwelling house.
15 For an analysis stressing this factor see Seabrooke 'Closing the Credibility Gap: A New Approach to section 1(f)(ii) of the Criminal Evidence Act 1898' [1987] Crim LR 231.
16 Dickson CJC, Beetz, Lamer and La Forest JJ (agreeing on this point).
17 *O'Hara v HM Advocate* 1948 JC 90.
18 Criminal Procedure (Scotland) Act 1975, s 161.
19 Though no reference was made to the most recent English authority, and the tenor of the decision, which applied the discretion to exclude such cross-examination, might suggest that practice will continue to diverge.
20 Though evidence adduced by the prosecution and probative of the case against one co-accused may be excluded because it is unduly prejudicial against the other, *R v Rogers, R v Tarran* [1971] Crim LR 413. I am grateful to Dr Pattenden for bringing this situation to my attention.

the question . . . No such limitation applies to a question asked by counsel for the defence. His duty is to adduce any evidence which is relevant to his own case, and assists his client, whether or not it prejudices anyone else.[1]

The same point is nevertheless sometimes expressed more loosely in the terminology of discretion as in *R v Neale* where Scarman LJ speaking for a particularly strong court[2] said:

> The discretionary control the judge has in a joint trial or indeed in any trial, that is to say the discretion to refuse to allow the Crown to adduce, or elicit, evidence which though probative is so prejudicial that it should not be accepted, does not exist or arise when application is being made by a co-defendant.[3]

The existence of a discretion to disallow cross-examination by one co-accused as to the other co-accused's record when the conditions specified under sub-s 1(f)(ii) of the Criminal Evidence Act 1898 apply, although recognised in the earlier practice, divided the House of Lords in *Murdoch v Taylor*.[4] The majority took the view that there was no discretion in such a case, it is not explicit in the statute, and the co-accused is entitled to insist on his strict rights. Lord Pearce dissented on the ground that such an unrestricted right could lead to unfairness to the co-accused, either because one co-accused had been trapped into giving evidence against the other, or where the conflict between the stories was trivial and far out-weighed by the prejudice created by the revelation of the record. It is interesting to note that the Criminal Law Revision Committee in endorsing the majority view opined that since there was a conflict of evils, to grant a discretion would lead to inconsistency of application.[5] In some cases the injustice of not disallowing cross-examination in these circumstances can be alleviated by the operation of a different discretion, to permit separate trials; but not in all.[6]

The existence of such residual discretion at common law to exclude any otherwise admissible evidence, if its admission would be prejudicial to a fair trial, was reaffirmed by the Privy Council in *Scott v R; Barnes v R*[7] in relation to depositions of deceased persons identifying the accused.[8] It should also be noted that the new statutory discretion to preserve the fairness of the proceedings in s 78 has, perhaps surprisingly, been held, even to permit the exclusion of evidence of convictions in other proceedings, despite their clearly satisfying the relevant statutory conditions.[9]

Two apparent examples of a discretion to exclude evidence pursuant to a desire to achieve the fair treatment of the accused seemed to be those designed to protect him from compulsory self-incrimination, and from the

1 [1952] 2 All ER 667 at 669, 36 Cr App Rep 169 at 171, emphasis supplied.
2 The other members were Lane LJ and Donaldson J.
3 (1977) 65 Cr App Rep 304 at 306.
4 [1965] AC 574, [1965] 1 All ER 406.
5 Cmnd 4991 (1972) para 132.
6 *R v Varley* [1982] 2 All ER 519 at 522, (1982) 75 Cr App Rep 242 at 246.
7 [1989] AC 1242, [1989] 2 All ER 305.
8 In England such matters would now be governed by the statutory discretion embodied in s 78 of the Police and Criminal Evidence Act 1984, see *R v O'Loughlin and McLoughlin* [1988] 3 All ER 431, 85 Cr App Rep 157 (depositions, see also Criminal Justice Act 1988, s 26, below, pp 632–3), for the position in Australia see *R v Collins* [1986] VR 37; and *R v O'Leary* (1988) 87 Cr App Rep 387 (identification).
9 Police and Criminal Evidence Act 1984, s 74, see further, above, p 105.

use of improper methods to procure evidence against him. This whole area was reviewed by the House of Lords in *R v Sang*.[10] The accused was charged with conspiracy to utter forged banknotes. He argued that he had been entrapped by the activities of an agent provocateur, and that evidence obtained as the result of such activities could be excluded by the trial judge at his discretion on the basis that it had been obtained by unfair methods. If this argument were correct it would in effect have endowed the judge with the discretion to allow a defence of entrapment in the circumstances of that case, since there was too little other evidence to secure a conviction. The House of Lords had no doubt that whatever the extent of this discretion it did not go so far as that.

There was less unanimity on the precise ambit of the discretion, though all of their Lordships subscribed to the answer to the certified question quoted above.[11] The difficulty resides in the precise delineation between the general denial of a discretion to exclude evidence obtained by improper means, and the exclusion from that denial of evidence obtained from the accused after the commission of the offence. It seems that Lord Fraser understood the exclusion to extend to evidence obtained from the premises of the accused.[12] He also expressed the view that the decision left judges with a discretion to exclude in accordance with their individual views of what is unfair, oppressive or morally reprehensible. It is hard to reconcile that view of the discretion with Lord Diplock's view that there is no discretion to exclude evidence discovered as a result of an illegal search.[13] It is also difficult to be sure exactly what relation there is between the discretion as applied to confessions and that applying to improperly obtained evidence. Lord Diplock explains the cases of *R v Barker*[14] and *R v Payne*[15] on the basis of an analogy between the two situations.[16] In the former, incriminating books of account of impeccable reliability were obtained by deception; while in the latter, the accused was persuaded by similar means to submit to a medical examination, once again yielding perfectly reliable evidence. It seems then that the analogy is achieved by explaining the confession rule not on considerations of unreliability, but on those restricting self-incrimination.[17] In this way it is possible to by-pass the argument that evidence obtained by these means may be quite reliable. That is secured however only at the cost of blurring the line between the role of the discretion in ensuring a fair trial which is legitimate, and that of ensuring fair treatment of the accused independent of his trial which is not. It is thus not at all surprising to find that Viscount Dilhorne who draws this distinction most strongly of all their Lordships refuses to extend the exclusionary discretion to improperly obtained evidence outside the special case of confessions, and pointedly makes no reference to self-incrimination.[18] It is however baffling to find

10 [1980] AC 402, [1979] 2 All ER 1222.
11 See above, p 180.
12 At 450, 1241.
13 At 436, 1230.
14 [1941] 2 KB 381, [1941] 3 All ER 33.
15 [1963] 1 All ER 848, [1963] 1 WLR 637.
16 At 436, 1229.
17 Lord Diplock at 436, 1230, Lord Fraser at 449, 1241, and Lord Scarman at 456, 1247.
18 Though he is apparently prepared to equate a case like *Barker* with the confession cases.

Lord Fraser and Lord Scarman still insisting that the discretion is exercisable solely as a by-product of a fair trial.[19]

Inconsistencies in the reasoning immediately attracted the attention of academic commentators.[20] The lack of guidance was also recognised by the Court of Appeal which remarked that the limited exception to the general denial of exclusionary discretion in respect of improperly obtained evidence had not been fully considered, though it was clear that where it existed one of its purposes was to control the police:

> As there was no deliberate misconduct by the officer, this hardly seems to be a case in which the Court should seek to discipline the police, even though there may be cases where the exclusion of the evidence for disciplinary purposes may be justified.[1]

Subsequent English case law failed to take matters very much further before the advent of the new statutory discretion in s 78 of the Police and Criminal Evidence Act 1984.[2] In other jurisdictions very different approaches are adopted.[3] They will be discussed more fully in ch XII. It is sufficient to note here that the Canadian approach was, before the enactment of the new Charter, arguably more restrictive than that illustrated in *Sang*,[4] and the Irish,[5] Scottish[6] and Australian more expansive. In the leading Australian case it was denied that the discretion:

> takes as its central point the question of unfairness to the accused. It is, on the contrary, concerned with broader question of high public policy, unfairness to the accused being only one factor which, if present, will play its part in the whole process of consideration.[7]

The High Court also explained that the reason for this was that:

> it is not fair play that is called in question in such cases but rather society's right to insist that those who enforce the law themselves respect it, so that a citizen's precious right to immunity from arbitrary and unlawful intrusion into the daily affairs of private life may remain unimpaired.[8]

This position has now been affected by the passage of s 78 of the Police and Criminal Evidence Act 1984 which provides:

19 Lord Diplock at 436, 1230, Lord Fraser at 450, 1241, Lord Scarman at 456, 1247.
20 See commentary in [1979] Crim LR 656; Cross 'Discretion and the Law of Evidence: When it Comes to the Forensic "Crunch"' [1979] 30 NILQ 289; Polyviou 'Illegally Obtained Evidence and *R v Sang*' in Tapper (ed) *Crime, Proof and Punishment* (1981), and Pattenden *Judicial Discretion and Criminal Litigation* (1990).
 1 *R v Trump* (1979) 70 Cr App Rep 300 at 303. A similarly disciplinary discretion was mentioned in *R v Heston-Francois* [1984] QB 278, [1984] 1 All ER 785.
 2 Many of the cases have concerned breath-testing, compare *Trump* where there was discretion to exclude the evidence (although it was held right not to exercise it) and *Winter v Barlow* [1980] RTR 209, where there was held to be no discretion.
 3 See Pattenden 'The Exclusion of Illegally Obtained Evidence in England, Canada and Australia' (1980) 29 ICLQ 664; Yeo 'The Discretion to Exclude Illegally Obtained Evidence: A Choice of Approaches' (1981) 13 MULR 31.
 4 *R v Wray* [1971] SCR 272.
 5 *People v O'Brien* [1965] IR 142.
 6 *Lawrie v Muir* 1950 JC 19.
 7 *Bunning v Cross* (1978) 141 CLR 54 at 74; affirmed as being of quite general application in *Cleland v R* (1983) 43 ALR 619. See also *R v Ireland* (1970) 126 CLR 321.
 8 (1978) 141 CLR 54 at 75.

(1) In any proceedings the court may refuse to allow evidence on which the prosecution proposes to rely to be given if it appears to the court that, having regard to all the circumstances in which the evidence was obtained, the admission of the evidence would have such an adverse effect on the fairness of the proceedings that the court ought not to admit it.

(2) Nothing in this section shall prejudice any rule of law requiring a court to exclude evidence.

This section was introduced at a very late stage, and replaced a clause introduced in the House of Lords on the motion of Lord Scarman which would have spelled out a reverse onus exclusionary rule, linked explicitly to the codes of practice issued under the Act. An important difference between that approach and this, is that under s 78 exclusion is by discretion, and, unlike Lord Scarman's clause, not by rule. It is interesting that the section uses the phrase 'evidence on which the prosecution proposes to rely'. This may be construed more widely than Lord Scarman's phrase which was 'evidence (other than a confession) proposed to be given by the prosecution'. The new section is wider in abstaining from any explicit exclusion of confessions, and in perhaps extending to evidence assisting the prosecution, but tendered by, say, a co-accused. The section appears to follow the reasoning of those of their Lordships in *Sang* who sought to blur the distinction between fair trial and fair treatment in its explicit linkage of the circumstances of obtaining the evidence with the fairness of the proceedings. It is by no means obvious what sorts of impropriety will be regarded as having such an effect. The provenance of the section made it doubtful whether mere breach of one of the codes of practice would necessarily suffice, since this was explicitly and separately mentioned in Lord Scarman's provision, but was omitted here. It is noteworthy also that while Lord Scarman's version referred to 'the fair administration of the criminal law', the section as enacted refers to 'the fairness of the proceedings'. The former phrase would more easily have been capable of being construed in the spirit of *Bunning v Cross*.

Since its enactment s 78 has become the focus of attempts to secure the exclusion by discretion of evidence, both real and confessional, which has been unfairly obtained. It is used exclusively in the former case, and as a discretionary backstop to the exclusionary rules in the latter. Some general points have become clear. First, the discretion is at least as broad as the discretion at common law,[9] second, as part of a codifying provision, it will not be construed as subject to any common law restrictions expressed in *Sang*,[10] and third, impropriety is not a necessary pre-condition to its exercise.[11] It should be noted that there is some doubt how far s 78 has affected the principle expressed in *Sang* that the substantive rule that entrapment is no defence cannot be undermined by the use of an evidential discretion.[12] The very terms of s 78 do however indicate that some forms of unfair treatment

9 Though this is immaterial since the common law discretion is preserved by s 82(3) of the Police and Criminal Evidence Act 1984.
10 *R v Fulling* [1987] QB 426 at 432, [1987] 2 All ER 65 at 69.
11 *Fulling*, above; *R v O'Leary* (1988) 87 Cr App Rep 387.
12 Compare *D P P v Marshall* [1988] 3 All ER 683 and *R v Harwood* [1989] Crim LR 285 with *R v Gill and Ranuana* [1989] Crim LR 358. In Australia it seems that while the discretion in *Bunning v Cross* is capable of applying to evidence of entrapment, the conditions for its satisfaction will rarely be held to be satisfied, see *R v Papoulias* [1988] VR 858; *R v Romeo* (1987) 45 SASR 212. For the position in New Zealand see Orchard 'Unfairly Obtained Evidence and Entrapment' [1980] NZLJ 203.

will be capable[13] of leading to the discretionary exclusion of real evidence. Thus in *Matto v Wolverhampton Crown Court*[14] the adoption of an illegal and oppressive procedure to secure a breath test from a motorist was regarded as capable of triggering the discretion, and in *R v Fennelley*[15] it was held to be enough to exclude evidence of drugs found on the accused after a body search that he had not been informed of the reason for his arrest or the grounds for searching him.

The final area in which the discretion must be considered is that relating to confessional statements which was at first carefully excluded from all of the cases mentioned above which were concerned with real evidence, but to which it was explicitly applied by the High Court of Australia in *Cleland v R*,[16] and to which the operation of the statutory discretion in s 78 of the Police and Criminal Evidence Act 1984 has been held to apply.[17] As noted earlier it has hitherto been possible to explain the exclusion of some confessional statements either on the basis of the need for a fair trial, in which case the unreliability of such statements, and perhaps the question of self-incrimination, will be emphasised, or on the basis of the need for fair treatment, in which case the protection of the accused, and perhaps of the community's self-respect, will become more prominent.

The Police and Criminal Evidence Act 1984, s 76 has changed the basis of rules relating to the admissibility of confessions. Quite apart from the application to confessions of the discretion in s 78, it has also retained the court's general discretion to exclude in s 82(3):

> Nothing in this Part of this Act shall prejudice any power of a court to exclude evidence (whether by preventing questions from being put or otherwise) at its discretion.

It is thus necessary to see what discretion existed before 1984. It was recognised when the rule excluding involuntary statements was put into its traditional form in *Ibrahim v R*.[18] In *R v Voisin*[19] the exclusionary discretion was considered in relation to the Judges' Rules which had been devised to govern questioning by the police. The court was unwilling to concede the force of law to the Rules, but recognised the discretion of the judge to exclude statements 'obtained from prisoners, contrary to the spirit' of the Rules. Some stress was laid upon the use of the discretion to exclude statements which had not been made voluntarily, or which were unreliable, but a residual category of unfairness was also mentioned. By 1964 when a new set of Judges' Rules were produced,[20] oppression had been added as a second ground of mandatory exclusion. Perhaps the most common argument advanced for the exercise of the exclusionary discretion in relation to confessions was that they had been obtained after breaches of the Judges'

---

13 Though not all will in fact do so, see *R v Alladice* (1988) 87 Cr App Rep 380 where the accused himself denied that the conduct complained of had induced the relevant confession.
14 [1987] RTR 337.
15 [1989] Crim LR 142.
16 (1983) 43 ALR 619, subject only to the unlikelihood of being able to make out a case for the application of the discretion if the rules for admissibility had been satisfied. See also *Seymour v AG for Commonwealth* (1984) 53 ALR 513, for a full discussion.
17 *R v Mason* [1987] 3 All ER 481, [1988] 1 WLR 139 at 144.
18 [1914] AC 599 at 609.
19 [1918] 1 KB 531.
20 *Practice Note* [1964] 1 All ER 237, [1964] 1 WLR 152.

Rules. After a few early successes such arguments began to fall on stonier ground. The nadir of this aspect of the exclusionary discretion was reached in *R v Prager*. In that case the Court of Appeal seemed to submerge any breach of the Judges' Rules within the ordinary voluntariness test for exclusion by rule:[1]

> Their non-observance may, and at times does, lead to the exclusion of an alleged confession; but ultimately all turns on the judge's decision whether, breach or no breach, it has been shown to have been made voluntarily.

This proved to be an ephemeral stage in the development of this discretion which was re-affirmed by the Court of Appeal.[2] It should be noted that it was immaterial whether a breach of the Judges' Rules themselves was alleged, or breach of the principles accompanying the Rules,[3] or of the administrative guidelines published by the Home Office for the use of the police.[4] The essence of this discretion was concern for the fair treatment of the accused,[5] and governed by the principles which inspired the exclusionary rule itself as Lord Hailsham expressed them in *Wong Kam-ming v R*:[6]

> This is not only because of the potential unreliability of such statements, but also, and perhaps mainly, because in a civilised society it is vital that persons in custody or charged with offences should not be subjected to ill-treatment or improper pressure in order to extract confessions.

The exercise of the discretion before 1984 was not accordingly limited to breaches of the rules and their direct accompaniments, but was equally inspired by other similar factors such as the detention of the accused in excess of the period permitted by statute,[7] or in breach of other statutory requirements.[8] It was also unsurprising to find that discretion remained a second string for the exclusion of statements obtained after oppressive behaviour. Before 1984 voluntariness had often been treated as a rather rigid and technical concept thus permitting some scope for the exercise of an exclusionary discretion in cases falling outside its confines. In *R v Hudson* the existence of such a discretion was accepted quite unequivocally.[9]

The new discretion in s 78 has been exercised in relation to confessional statements in two main areas, first in respect of conduct clearly falling outside the exclusionary provisions of s 76 of the Police and Criminal Evidence Act 1984,[10] and second as a buttress to those provisions.[11]

Statutory exclusion of confessions on the basis of potential unreliability is

---

1 [1972] 1 All ER 1114 at 1118, [1972] 1 WLR 260 at 266.
2 *R v MacIntosh* (1983) 76 Cr App Rep 177.
3 *R v Gowan* [1982] Crim LR 821.
4 *R v Westlake* [1979] Crim LR 652; but see *R v King* [1980] Crim LR 40.
5 Though it was implausibly ascribed to the balance of probative force and prejudicial effect in *R v Ovenell* [1969] 1 QB 17 at 26, [1968] 1 All ER 933 at 939.
6 [1980] AC 247 at 261, [1979] 1 All ER 939 at 946.
7 *R v Hudson* (1980) 72 Cr App Rep 163.
8 *R v Platt* [1981] Crim LR 622 (breach of s 62 of Criminal Law Act 1977 in not informing parent of accused child's arrest).
9 At 170. See also *R v Wilson* [1981] 1 NZLR 316.
10 See further ch XVII, section 1, part D, below.
11 Both in New Zealand and in the state of Victoria, where broadly similar provisions have been in force for many years, it has been held that there is still scope for an exclusionary discretion alongside, see *R v Phillips* [1949] NZLR 316 at 345; *R v Lee* (1950) 82 CLR 133 at 150.

limited to those made 'in consequence of anything said or done' by an interlocutor.[12] It is clear that this cannot apply to one who spontaneously blurts out a confession, and has been held not to apply where the effective cause of confessing is some defect inherent in the speaker,[13] rather than proper questioning by the police. Even in cases where the police act improperly, for example by interviewing a juvenile in the absence of an appropriate adult,[14] it seem that a confession will be excluded under the s 78 discretion only when deliberate advantage has been taken of the juvenile.[15] In the case of a deranged person,[16] or one suffering from some other disability,[17] a court may also consider excluding a confession under s 78.[18] It should be noted that a direction warning of a special need for caution in cases substantially relying upon confessions by the mentally handicapped made otherwise than in the presence of independent persons, has now been prescribed for such cases by s 77 of the Police and Criminal Evidence Act 1984. Such a provision clearly contemplates that some such confessions will be admitted. A different aspect of unfairness may arise if the accused is induced to confess by being led to believe that what he says will be 'off the record', but is then confronted with his statement at the last minute.[19]

The second area of application of s 78 to confessional statements is when it is used as a secondary argument in favour of discretionary exclusion if a principal argument based upon exclusion by rule should fail.[20] In many cases such a claim is linked to a breach of the Codes of Practice issued pursuant to s 66 of the Police and Criminal Evidence Act 1984. It is now clear that breach of the Code is neither a necessary, nor a sufficient,[1] condition for discretionary exclusion of a confession under this provision. It has indeed been held that the wording of s 78 itself indicates that some breaches may not lead to exclusion.[2] On the other hand although police impropriety is not a necessary condition for the application of s 78 it seems that it is a powerful factor inclining the court to infer from such unfair treatment that the fairness of the proceedings has also been sufficiently adversely affected.[3]

It must be stressed that the discretion to exclude operates only in respect of confessional statements. It is not available to exclude statements made by

12 In most Commonwealth jurisdictions a 'voluntariness' test applies, but it tends to be interpreted less technically than was the case in England, so, eg in Australia, in extreme cases of impairment a confession may be excluded by rule, while in some cases it is a matter for discretion, see *Sinclair v R* (1946) 73 CLR 316; *McDermott v R* (1948) 76 CLR 501 at 507; *R v Bradshaw* (1978) 18 SASR 83 at 87.

13 *R v Goldenberg* (1989) 88 Cr App Rep 285.

14 Contrary to Code of Practice, C.13.1.

15 Compare *R v Fogah* [1989] Crim LR 141 with *R v Maguire* [1989] Crim LR 815.

16 *R v Miller* [1986] 3 All ER 119, [1986] 1 WLR 1191.

17 *R v Clarke* [1989] Crim LR 892 (deafness).

18 Since a plea of guilty was disregarded in *R v Swain* [1986] Crim LR 480 and the conviction quashed, it would be odd if the court had no power to exclude evidence of the overturned plea as a confession at a retrial, should one have been ordered.

19 As in *R v Woodall* [1989] Crim LR 288.

20 See eg *R v Alladice* (1988) 87 Cr App Rep 380; *R v Delaney* (1988) 88 Cr App Rep 338; *R v Doolan* [1988] Crim LR 747; *R v Maguire* [1989] Crim LR 815.

 1 *R v Parris* (1989) 89 Cr App Rep 68 at 72 where the trial judge seems to have regarded it as the former, and the Court of Appeal negated, in addition, the latter.

 2 *R v Walsh* [1989] Crim LR 822.

 3 *R v Alladice* (1988) 87 Cr App Rep 380 at 386. For the converse view that punctilious observation of the Code of Practice militates against a finding of unfairness, see *Re Walters* [1987] Crim LR 577.

witnesses, however oppressively they may have been induced by the police. That is a matter going only to weight.[4]

3. DISCRETION TO EXCLUDE RELEVANT EVIDENCE IN CIVIL PROCEEDINGS[5]

It remains to be seen whether the fair trial or fair treatment rationales for the exercise of an exclusionary discretion apply in civil proceedings. In England consideration has been given to the existence of such a discretion in cases where evidence has been unlawfully obtained, and in cases where information is being withheld from the court. There seem to be no English cases asserting a discretion to exclude, pursuant to the fair trial categorisation, on the basis that the evidence will be more prejudicial than probative in revealing evidence of extrinsic discreditable acts.[6] It was explicitly rejected in *Bradford City Metropolitan Council v K*.[7]

It was denied in *Ibrahim v R*[8] that there was any discretion to exclude improperly obtained statements in civil proceedings. In *Helliwell v Piggott-Sims* where the Court of Appeal assumed the evidence to have been obtained by improper means the same view was repeated:

> in criminal cases the judge may have a discretion. That is shown by *Kuruma v R*.[9] But so far as civil cases are concerned, it seems to me that the judge has no discretion. The evidence is relevant and admissible. The judge cannot refuse it on the ground that it may have been unlawfully obtained in the beginning.[10]

The other context in which the question has been raised is in relation to claims of privilege which will be dealt with in detail in chs XI and XII below. If an established privilege already exists no question of discretion arises because in the words of Lord Wilberforce: 'to substitute for the privilege a dependence on the courts' discretion would substantially be to the defendant's detriment'.[11] It arises only when a witness makes an unsuccessful claim to be privileged from answering a question. Does the judge then have a residual discretion not to allow the question to be put? In *D v National Society for the Prevention of Cruelty to Children* Lord Simon was quite

---

4 *R v Austin* (1982) Lexis Transcript, 18 June.
5 See Forbes 'Extent of the Judicial Discretion to Reject Prejudicial Evidence in Civil Cases' (1988) 62 ALJ 211.
6 Such a discretion has been denied in Australia, *Manenti v Melbourne Tramways* [1954] VLR 115 at 118; but see *Taylor v Harvey* [1986] 2 Qd R 137 at 142. It may be noted that the corresponding r 403 of the US Federal Rules does apply to civil proceedings. Although the terminology of discretion was employed in this context in *Berger v Raymond & Son Ltd* [1984] 1 WLR 625, it seems likely that it was used no more than loosely to characterise those elements of the exclusionary rule of an essentially indeterminate nature or perhaps to prevent prejudice in the case of surprise or unduly lengthening the proceedings by adducing evidence of dubious relevance. See further below at p 380.
7 [1990] 2 WLR 532. Although in terms applying only to the civil jurisdiction of magistrates the language is general, and contains no hint of restriction to lower courts.
8 [1914] AC 599 at 610, [1914–15] All ER Rep 874 at 878.
9 [1955] AC 197.
10 [1980] FSR 356 at 357, echoing similar sentiments expressed in *R v Christie* [1914] AC 545, [1914–15] All ER Rep 63, by Lord Moulton at 559, 69 and by Lord Reading at 564, 71. See also *ITC Film Distributors v Video Exchange Ltd* [1982] Ch 431, [1982] 2 All ER 241.
11 *Rank Film Distributors Ltd v Video Information Centre* [1982] AC 380 at 442, [1981] 2 All ER 76 at 81.

clear that in such a case 'it must be law, not discretion, which is in command'.[12] Unfortunately Lord Hailsham took the opposite view, accepting the views expressed in the sixteenth report of the Law Reform Committee on privilege in civil proceedings:

> Privilege in the main is the creation of the common law whose policy, pragmatic as ever, has been to limit to a minimum the categories of privileges which a person has an absolute right to claim, but to accord to the judge a wide discretion to permit the witness, whether a party to the proceedings or not, to refuse to disclose information where disclosure would be a breach of some ethical or social value and non-disclosure would be unlikely to result in serious injustice in the particular case in which it is claimed.[13]

The position has been reconsidered in subsequent authority though the issue has, at best, arisen on the periphery of a claim based on a resistance to discovery. Since discovery is an equitable remedy it always has a discretionary element.[14] It is far from clear that the same principles apply to prevent evidence from being adduced. Thus in *McGuiness v A-G of Victoria* Sir Owen Dixon in refuting a claim that the rules limiting discovery applied to evidence said: 'The answer is that it is not a rule of evidence but a practice of refusing in an action for libel . . . to compel discovery of the name of . . . informants.'[15] It might be argued that this passage relates only to the question of total immunity as a matter of law, and does not touch the question of discretionary exclusion. When the issue arises during a trial a judge has control over the propriety of the proceedings before him, and can certainly disallow vexatious or irrelevant questions. It is possible that the dicta in the authorities cited to justify the Law Reform Committee's view in its report, relied upon that power.[16] At first instance in *Granada* Megarry VC urged separate consideration of the position first in interlocutory proceedings, second at the trial, and third in deciding upon a remedy.[17] In the Court of Appeal Lord Denning rejected this view and asserted that the same principles applied at each stage.[18] In the House of Lords it is less clear how far the decision that the court has a discretion extends beyond the precise question of pre-trial disclosure. The better view is that it does extend to evidence at the trial. Lord Wilberforce refers to the duty as one to disclose *to a court*,[19] not as one to disclose to an opponent. Then in his final summary of his reasons, after asserting that the court undoubtedly has a discretion, he goes on to consider those parts of Megarry VC's reasons which explicitly related to a

---

12 [1978] AC 171 at 239, [1977] 1 All ER 589 at 613. The House was numerically equally divided on this point. Lord Edmund Davies delivered a speech to the same effect as Lord Simon, Lord Diplock did not mention the matter, and Lord Kilbrandon contented himself with agreeing with Lord Hailsham. In *British Steel Corpn v Granada Television Ltd* [1981] AC 1096 at 1113, [1981] 1 All ER 417 at 431, Megarry VC thought the balance favoured Lord Hailsham's view.

13 Para 1, citing *A-G v Clough* [1963] 1 QB 773, [1963] 1 All ER 420 and *A-G v Mulholland* [1963] 2 QB 477, [1963] 1 All ER 767, which, however do not entirely justify the statement. See also para 51.

14 In *British Steel Corpn v Granada Television Ltd* [1981] AC 1096 at 1174, [1981] 1 All ER 417 at 459, Lord Wilberforce said 'the remedy *(being equitable)* is discretionary' (emphasis supplied).

15 (1940) 63 CLR 73 at 104, a passage quoted with approval by Viscount Dilhorne in *Granada*.

16 As decided in *Re Buchanan* (1964) SR NSW 9.

17 [1981] AC 1096 at 1111, [1981] 1 All ER 417 at 427.

18 At 1129, 441.

19 At 1168, 455.

discretion in relation to evidence, and not to the discretion in relation to a remedy which he had carefully segregated.[20] It seems that the principle upon which the discretion is to be exercised is that stated by the House of Lords in *Science Research Council v Nasse*, namely:[1]

> to consider fairly the strength and value of the interest in preserving confidentiality and the damage which may be caused by breaking it; then to consider whether the objective, to dispose fairly of the case, can be achieved without doing so.

It is probably now too late to argue that this process relates only to the determination of the initial obligation to answer, rather than to that of determining whether the obligation should be overridden in the circumstances of a particular case at the discretion of the judge.[2] In the particular case of the disclosure of the source of information contained in a publication, the matter is now regulated, not by judicial discretion, but by a statutory rule that disclosure may be compelled only in the interests of justice or national security or for the prevention of disorder or crime.[3] It has been faintly suggested that an inclusionary discretion might exist in some cases, but this has been rejected in relation to the discretionary admission of hearsay in proceedings involving children, both in the higher,[4] and lower,[5] courts. It is also significant that in *Savings & Investment Bank Ltd v Gasco Investments (Netherlands) BV (No 2)*[6] where the Court of Appeal held contempt proceedings to be civil for the purposes of the admission of hearsay, it asserted, not that such hearsay could be excluded at the court's discretion, but rather that it would be unlikely to be accorded sufficient weight to satisfy the heavy burden of proof.

C. THE SUMMING UP

It is difficult to estimate the amount of control which a judge exercises over a jury by means of his summing up, for, quite apart from the legal rules that govern the matter, juries expect and receive considerable guidance with regard to the evidence submitted to them, and this guidance may be expressed in emphatic terms.[7] The legal rules on the subject have never been precisely formulated, but it seems that a judge must always put defences raised by the evidence to the jury[8] and he can never be justified in directing a jury that they must accept his view of disputed facts,[9] although he may, in a civil case, and sometimes should, tell them they ought to do so as reasonable

---

20 At 1175, 460.
1 [1980] AC 1028 at 1067, [1979] 3 All ER 673 at 681. Although in terms limited to questions arising in relation to discovery, it should be noted that this passage is justified by reference to cases like *Mulholland* and *Clough* where no question of discovery arose.
2 As argued by Professor Cross in 'Discretion and the Law of Evidence: When it Comes to the "Forensic Crunch"' (1979) 30 NILQ 289.
3 Contempt of Court Act 1981, s 10.
4 *K v K* [1989] 3 All ER 740 at 754, [1989] 3 WLR 933 at 956.
5 *Bradford City Metropolitan Council v K* [1990] 2 WLR 532.
6 [1988] Ch 422, [1988] 1 All ER 975.
7 For general statements see *Clouston & Co Ltd v Corry* [1906] AC 122 at 130 per Lord James of Hereford and *R v O'Donnell* (1917) 12 Cr App Rep 219 at 221 per Lord Reading CJ.
8 *R v Keith Keba Badjan* (1966) 50 Cr App Rep 141.
9 *Dublin Wicklow and Wexford Rly Co v Slattery* (1878) 3 App Cas 1155 at 1186.

men.[10] If a party tenders no evidence on a contested issue the judge may instruct the jury to draw the most favourable inference possible from the evidence tendered by the other.[11]

In *D P P v Stonehouse*[12] Lord Salmon referred to the judge's duty to direct an acquittal in a criminal case if satisfied that there is no evidence before the jury to justify them in convicting and said:

> This rule which has long been established, is to protect the accused against being wrongly convicted. But there is no converse rule—although there may be some who think that there should be.[13] If the judge is satisfied that, on the evidence, the jury would not be justified in acquitting the accused and indeed that it would be perverse of them to do so, he has no power to pre-empt the jury's verdict by directing them to convict. The jury alone have the right to decide that the accused is guilty.

The trial judge had directed the jury to find the accused guilty of an attempt to obtain money for his wife by deception if they were satisfied that he staged his death with the dishonest intention of causing an insurance company to pay over the amount due on his life policies. The question whether the accused's conduct was sufficiently proximate to the crime attempted, a question of fact for the jury,[14] was thus withdrawn from that body. By a majority of three to two the House of Lords held that the direction was wrong, although the House was unanimous in applying the proviso to s 2 of the Criminal Appeal Act 1968 and affirming the conviction.

In cases decided before *D P P v Stonehouse* in which the facts were undisputed the Court of Appeal had held it proper for the judge to direct a verdict of guilty,[15] but it is very doubtful whether they are any longer authoritative. The ultimate independence of the jury over all issues of fact raised by the evidence is not a thing to be trifled with and Lord Salmon went on to suggest in *Stonehouse's* case that, when a judge has, as he is fully entitled to do in an appropriate case, expressed himself forcefully on the facts, he should reiterate the point which he will no doubt have made previously that all questions of fact are for the jury to decide. Even in the case of medical evidence the judge ought not to direct them to accept it although there is no apparent reason for not doing so.[16]

It is clearly the duty of the judge to instruct the jury on all matters of law, including the effect of any relevant presumption of law and the incidence of the onus of proof.[17] This may oblige him to direct the jury that they must find one of the facts in issue to be proved if they are satisfied as to the existence of some other fact, for, when a rebuttable presumption of law

10 See for example *Pickup v Thames and Mersey Marine Insurance Co* (1878) 3 QBD 594 at 600.
11 *Ross v Associated Portland Cement Manufacturers Ltd* [1964] 2 All ER 452, [1964] 1 WLR 768.
12 [1978] AC 55 at 80.
13 See Lord Diplock at 69 and Lord Dilhorne at 72. They both dissented on this point although they concurred in affirming the conviction.
14 See Criminal Attempts Act 1981, s 4(3).
15 *R v Kelly* [1970] 2 All ER 198, [1970] 1 WLR 1050; *R v Morris* [1972] 1 All ER 384, [1972] 1 WLR 228; *R v Herd* (1973) 57 Cr App Rep 560; but see *R v Bates* [1973] 2 All ER 509, [1973] 1 WLR 718 and *R v Martin* (1972) 57 Cr App Rep 279. See also Lord Devlin's *Trial by Jury* (1966 edn) App 2, p 188; and articles by Griew [1972] Crim LR 204, McConville [1973] Crim LR 164, and Glanville Williams [1976] Crim LR 472 and 532.
16 *R v Lanfear* [1968] 2 QB 77, [1968] 1 All ER 683.
17 *R v Zarrabi* (1985) Times, 23 February where a conviction was quashed because the judge directed only upon the standard, and not upon the incidence of the burden, of proof.

applies to a case, proof of one fact is legally equivalent to proof of some other fact in the absence of further evidence. Thus, if the legitimacy of a child is among the facts in issue in civil proceedings, and the proponent adduces evidence to show that the child was born in wedlock, the judge must direct the jury to find in favour of the proponent if they accept this evidence, unless the opponent satisfies them on a balance of probabilities that there was no intercourse between the child's mother and her husband by which it could have been begotten. Similarly, if it becomes necessary to establish that a particular person is dead, the judge may have to tell a civil jury that they must find in favour of the proponent on being satisfied that the person in question had been absent for more than seven years, without having been heard of by those with whom he would most probably have communicated if he were alive. In criminal cases, where the accused is the opponent, it is probably necessary for him only to adduce or elicit or point to evidence adduced or elicited by his adversary which is sufficient to raise a reasonable doubt.

When the judge directs the jury on the effect of a presumption of law, he is not telling them that they must accept his view of the facts. As a matter of ordinary reasoning, many people, including the judge, might not be prepared to infer legitimacy from birth in wedlock if there was evidence of prolonged intimacy between the child's mother and her lover, any more than they would be prepared to infer her death from seven years' absence if the person in question was young and healthy when she was last heard of. For a number of different reasons, the law attaches what may be an artificial probative value to certain facts, and the judge's direction in such a case informs the jury of the legal consequences which follow upon their finding these facts to exist.

D. APPEALS

1. CRIMINAL CASES TRIED WITH A JURY

Under s 2(1)(a) of the Criminal Appeal Act 1968, the Court of Appeal (Criminal Division) must allow an appeal if they think that the conviction[18] should be set aside on the ground that under all the circumstances of the case it is unsafe or unsatisfactory. The corresponding provision in the Criminal Appeal Act 1907 required the court to think that the verdict of the jury was unreasonable or could not be supported by the evidence. The change was recommended in the Report of the Donovan Committee on the Court of Criminal Appeal published in 1965.[19] Some members thought that a verdict could be set aside on the ground that it was unsafe or unreasonable under the 1907 provision, but others thought that such a construction would have conflicted with the court's own pronouncements concerning its powers under the Act. Speaking of the change Lord Widgery CJ has said that it requires the court to set aside a verdict if there is a 'lurking doubt' in the minds of its members which makes them wonder whether an injustice has been done.[20]

18 Substituted for 'verdict' by the Criminal Law Act 1977, s 44.
19 Cmnd 2755.
20 *R v Cooper* [1969] 1 QB 267 at 271.

The Devlin Committee on Evidence of Identification[1] considered the impact of the change to be revolutionary. The new words were said to mean that an appellate judge 'and as an inevitable consequences a trial judge also—has to ask himself whether he thinks that a verdict is or would be safe and satisfactory'.[2] Although this interpretation attracted some support,[3] it was decisively rejected in *R v Galbraith*.[4] It was argued that the fact that the Court of Appeal had power to quash a conviction on those grounds was insufficient to justify granting similar powers to trial judges at the close of the case for the prosecution. This can be justified on the basis that the Court of Appeal must decide upon the evidence as a whole, not merely on how it appeared at the end of the case for the prosecution. It is however undeniable that in many cases the weakness of the prosecution case will reside in the unreliability of its witnesses which the trial judge who has heard them is in a better position to assess than the judges on appeal who have not.

The Court of Appeal has power to hear fresh evidence[5] and, having done so, to order a new trial.[6] When considering how the court should act on fresh evidence each member should ask himself whether he thinks the conviction to be unsafe or unsatisfactory. The court's views about what a jury would have decided in the light of the fresh evidence are not conclusive.[7]

For the sake of completeness, it may be added that the court may allow an appeal on account of a wrong decision of any point of law, or because there was a material irregularity,[8] and these provisions are, of course, wide enough to cover any wrongful admission or rejection of evidence by the judge as well as an irregularity in his summing up. Its entire jurisdiction is subject to the important proviso contained in s 2(1) of the Criminal Appeal Act 1968 under which an appeal may be dismissed if the court considers that no miscarriage of justice has actually occurred, notwithstanding its opinion that the point raised in the appeal might be decided in favour of the appellant. This proviso, like the corresponding rule in civil cases,[9] is of considerable significance in relation to the practical operation of the law of evidence, for it deters counsel on either side from taking frivolous technical objections at the original hearing with the result that an English trial bears little resemblance to that which occurs in many American films with constant interjections by the barristers on each side. The mere fact that an objection was overruled when an appellate court thinks it should have been sustained,

---

1 See p 718 below.
2 Para 4.67 of the Committee's Report.
3 *R v Mansfield* [1978] 1 All ER 134, [1977] 1 WLR 1102, but see *R v Barker* (1977) 65 Cr App Rep 287. Academic support was afforded by Glanville Williams 'Evidence of Identification: The Devlin Report' [1976] Crim LR 407 at 409.
4 [1981] 2 All ER 1060, [1981] 1 WLR 1039. This decision appears to depart from the practice in magistrates' courts which had previously been thought to apply to jury trial also, *Practice Note* [1962] 1 All ER 448, [1962] 1 WLR 227. See also *Haw Tua Tau v Public Prosecutor* [1982] AC 136 at 151, [1981] 3 All ER 14 at 19. For criticism see Pattenden 'The Submission of No Case—Some Recent Developments' [1982] Crim LR 558.
5 Criminal Appeal Act 1968, s 23; *R v Parker* (1960) 45 Cr App Rep 1.
6 Criminal Appeal Act 1968, s 7, as extended by s 43 of the Criminal Justice Act 1988.
7 *Stafford v D P P* [1974] AC 878, [1973] 3 All ER 762. See also *R v McMahon* (1978) 68 Cr App Rep 18.
8 Criminal Appeal Act 1968, s 2(1)(b) and (c).
9 RSC Ord 59, r 11(2).

or vice versa, does not mean that an appeal must succeed as it does in some American jurisdictions.[10]

2. CIVIL CASES TRIED WITH A JURY

After a civil case has been tried with a jury, the party against whom their verdict has been given may apply to the Court of Appeal for an order for a new trial and, if such an order is made, the verdict of the jury is set aside. A new trial may be sought on the ground that there was no evidence which ought properly to have been left to the jury in favour of the proponent of the issue in question, or because the verdict of the jury was against the weight of the evidence.[11] In order that a new trial should be granted on the latter ground:

> it is not enough that the judge who tried the case might have come to a different conclusion on the evidence than the jury, or that the judges in the Court where the new trial is moved for might have come to a different conclusion, but there must be such a preponderance of evidence, assuming there is evidence on both sides to go to the jury, as to make it unreasonable, and almost perverse, that the jury when instructed and assisted properly by the judge should return such a verdict.[12]

If the Court of Appeal concludes that the judge ought not to have left an issue to the jury because there was insufficient evidence in support of the proponent's case, it will enter judgment for the opponent forthwith. It may also adopt this course where the evidence in support of the opponent's case was very strong, although there was some evidence favourable to the proponent, provided it is clear that no further material would be available at a second trial.[13] This is the result of the construction which has been placed on Ord 59, r 10(3) of the Rules of the Supreme Court under which the Court of Appeal has power to draw inferences of fact and make any order which ought to have been made, but serious doubts have been expressed on the question whether it entitles the Court of Appeal to enter judgment for the proponent of an issue after setting aside a verdict for the opponent.[14]

---

10 I *Wigmore* 271. On the proviso to the Act of 1907 see *Stirland v D P P* [1944] AC 315, [1944] 2 All ER 13, confirming *R v Haddy* [1944] KB 442, [1944] 1 All ER 319 and rendering earlier authorities obsolete. See also *R v Farid* (1945) 30 Cr App Rep 168; *R v Oster-Ritter* (1948) 32 Cr App Rep 191; *R v Collins* (1950) 34 Cr App Rep 146; *R v Whybrow* (1951) 35 Cr App Rep 141 and *R v McVitie* [1960] 2 QB 483, [1960] 2 All ER 498. Although the beneficial character of the provisions mentioned can hardly be disputed they may have had a bad effect on the development of the law of evidence as they account, to some extent, for its being a body of rules which is nearly as much honoured in the breach as the observance.

11 A new trial may be ordered on a number of other grounds conveniently discussed in Odgers *Pleading and Practice* (22nd edn) 343–347.

12 Per Lord Selborne in *Metropolitan Rly Co v Wright* (1886) 11 App Cas 152 at 155.

13 See the judgment of Lord Aitkin in *Mechanical and General Inventions Co and Lehwess v Austin and the Austin Motor Co* [1935] AC 346.

14 [1935] AC 346 at 369 and 379 per Lord Wright reiterating doubts of Lord Halsbury in *Toulmin v Millar* (1887) 12 App Cas 746; but see *Croker v Croker* [1932] P 173 and *Winterbotham Gurney & Co v Sibthorp and Cox* [1918] 1 KB 625 at 634.

3. CIVIL CASES TRIED BY A JUDGE ALONE

The appeal is a rehearing when a civil case has been tried by a judge alone, so the result is usually judgment for one of the parties rather than an order for a new trial. The Court of Appeal may hear fresh evidence, but only on special grounds, except on matters which have occurred after the decision from which the appeal is brought, and the case is usually dealt with on the basis of a transcript or note of the proceedings in the court below.[15] Appeals on matters of law may involve questions of the wrongful admission or rejection of evidence, and these are disposed of in the same way as appeals involving any other legal issue. The Court of Appeal will naturally be loath to disturb a finding of fact by the trial judge who has had the advantage of observing the demeanour of the witnesses, 'their candour or their partisanship, and all the incidental elements so difficult to describe which make up the atmosphere of an actual trial'.[16] Although the court occasionally takes the view that the judge was wrong to give credence to a particular witness,[17] it will be far more ready to reverse his decision in a case which depends on inferences from admitted or undisputed facts.[18]

Appeals lie from decisions of judges who have sat without a jury in civil cases tried in the county court, and there may be appeals in matrimonial causes as well as criminal cases tried by the magistrates, but they do not call for separate discussion in a work of this nature.

15 RSC Ord 59, r 10(2). There is no distinction between cases tried with and without a jury so far as the hearing of fresh evidence is concerned (*Leeder v Ellis* [1953] AC 52, [1952] 2 All ER 814). On the refusal to hear fresh evidence see *Ladd v Marshall* [1954] 3 All ER 745, [1954] 1 WLR 1489 and *House v Houghton Bros (Worcester) Ltd* [1967] 1 All ER 39, [1967] 1 WLR 148, contrast *Skone v Skone* [1971] 2 All ER 582, [1971] 1 WLR 812.

16 Per Lord Macmillan in *Watt v Thomas* [1947] AC 484 at 490–1, [1947] 1 All ER 582 at 590.

17 Eg *Coghlan v Cumberland* [1898] 1 Ch 704; *Yuill v Yuill* [1945] P 15, [1945] 1 All ER 183; and *M v M (Custody Application)* [1988] 1 FLR 225 at 233.

18 Cf *Powell v Streatham Manor Nursing Home* [1935] AC 243 with *Flower v Ebbw Vale Steel Co* [1936] AC 206, and see *Benmax v Austin Motor Co Ltd* [1955] AC 370 together with an article by Goodhart in (1955) 71 LQR 402. See also the propositions of Lord Thankerton in *Watt v Thomas* [1947] AC 484 at 487–8, [1947] 1 All ER 582 at 586–7.

CHAPTER V

The competence and compellability of witnesses

It is necessary to distinguish between several separate, though closely related concepts—the competence, compellability, privileges and duties of a witness. A witness is competent if he may lawfully be called to give evidence. Nowadays, most people are competent witnesses, but, under the law which applied to civil cases down to the middle of the nineteenth century, and to criminal trials until the end of that century, many of those who could give relevant evidence were not allowed to do so. The older books on evidence are largely concerned with the competence of witnesses, and it was not until Bentham had scathingly ridiculed the old law, that it was cast into a rational shape by statute.

A witness is compellable if he can lawfully be obliged to give evidence. The general rule is that all competent witnesses are compellable, but there are a few exceptions which will have to be mentioned in due course. If a compellable witness refuses to testify he may be sent to prison, and this is the sanction by which someone who has entered the witness box and been sworn is generally obliged to answer the questions that are put to him.

While competence and compellability regulate the circumstances in which a witness may or must give testimony as a whole, different rules regulate evidence which he may not, or must not, answer. In some circumstances a witness who is both competent and compellable may refuse to give relevant, material and otherwise admissible evidence relying upon a privilege conferred by the law, while in others he may be under a public duty to withhold such evidence. The different privileges of witnesses will be discussed in ch XI, and the range of public interest immunity in ch XII. The modern law of competence and compellability is the subject of section 2 of this chapter, while section 1 is purely historical.

Generally speaking, the term 'witness' must be taken to include parties to the proceedings. The latter expression comprises the parties to a civil action and the accused, but not the prosecutor, on a criminal charge. There are several respects in which the position of a party differs from that of an ordinary witness, and attention is drawn to them where it is necessary to do so, but subject to these points of difference, everything that is said in this book about witnesses applies to parties.

SECTION 1. HISTORICAL INTRODUCTION

Incompetence due to youth or defective intellect is perforce recognised under the modern law, but there were formerly five further classes of persons who were wholly or partially prohibited from testifying, namely, non-Christians, convicts, persons interested in the outcome of the proceedings, parties and their spouses. Something must be said about the way in which these people were rendered competent, by case-law and various Oaths Acts so far as the first class was concerned, and, with regard to the remaining four classes, by the Evidence Acts of 1843 and 1851, the Evidence Amendment Act 1853, the Evidence Further Amendments Act 1869, and the Criminal Evidence Act 1898. These five statutes together with the Police and Criminal Evidence Act 1984 govern the modern law of competence and compellability. They could be consolidated with advantage.

A. NON-CHRISTIANS

Until the end of the seventeenth century the law was that evidence had to be given on oath and that oath had to be taken on the Gospel. If it could be shown that the proposed witness did not accept the authority of the Gospel, he would be held to be incompetent to give evidence. Coke included Jews as well as heathens in this class, and, although his views were not entirely shared by Hale,[1] it was only when Lord Hardwicke sought the advice of the common law judges in *Omychund v Barker*[2] in 1744 that the law on this subject was decisively modified. In that case, described by Wigmore as a great landmark of enlightened legal opinion,[3] it was held that the depositions of Gentoos should be received as they believed in a governor of the universe in whose name the depositions were sworn. Parker CB disposed of the old authorities by saying that they proved no more than that oaths are adapted to the natives of the kingdom,[4] while Willes CJ founded his judgment on the fact that our Saviour and St Peter have said God is no respecter of persons: 'Lord Coke is a very great lawyer, but our Saviour and St Peter are in this respect much better authorities than a person possessed with such narrow notions.'[5]

Willes CJ was, however, clearly of opinion that those who either did not believe in God, or did not think that he would punish them in this world or the next, could not be witnesses in any case because 'an oath cannot possibly be any tie or obligation upon them'.[6] The law has been put on its modern basis by statute in the nineteenth century, although Quakers had previously been permitted to make a solemn affirmation. The present position is discussed in section 3 of this chapter.

B. CONVICTS

Until the nineteenth century, a person who had once been convicted and sentenced for an infamous crime was incompetent as a witness for the rest of his life. A great deal of technicality was involved concerning the definition of an infamous crime which certainly included treason, felony and perjury, while an almost equal amount of learning was devoted to the effect of a pardon; but it is unnecessary to go into these matters any further because

1 2 PC 279.
2 (1745) 1 Atk 21. A previous decision pointing in the same direction was *Robeley v Langston* (1668) 2 Keb 314.
3 II *Wigmore* p 603 n 1.
4 1 Atk 40.
5 1 Atk 44.
6 As reported in Willes at p 545.

the incompetence of convicts to act as witnesses, incompetence through 'infamy' as it used to be called, has been totally abolished. In 1828 the Civil Rights of Convicts Act rendered convicts capable of acting as witnesses after they had served sentence, unless they had been found guilty of perjury. The Evidence Act 1843 provided that no person should thereafter be excluded by reason of incapacity on account of a conviction from giving evidence in any proceedings. Under the present law, therefore, the fact that a witness has been convicted is a matter which concerns the credibility and not the competency of his testimony.

C. INTERESTED PARTIES

Until the nineteenth century, those who had a pecuniary or proprietary interest in the outcome of the proceedings were incompetent to act as witnesses in them. This is also a subject which attracted a considerable amount of learning, but, once again, it is unnecessary to go into detail because the Evidence Act 1843 abolished incompetence through interest except in the case of the parties and their spouses. Interest is now something which affects only the weight of a person's evidence.

D. PARTIES

1. CIVIL CASES

The parties to most civil proceedings at common law were made competent and compellable witnesses by the Evidence Act 1851.[7] Section 4 contained an exception in respect of proceedings instituted in consequence of adultery and actions for breach of promise of marriage; it was repealed by the Evidence Further Amendments Act 1869, and there is no doubt concerning the competence and compellability of parties at the present day; this means that, should he be minded to do so, a plaintiff can compel a defendant to testify.[8]

2. CRIMINAL CASES

A party's incompetence in a civil case was due to his interest in the proceedings and the Act of 1851 was merely the corollary of that of 1843. The accused's interest in the outcome of the proceedings was one reason for his inability to give evidence at the hearing of a criminal charge against him, but there was a further reason based on what was largely an illogical application of the maxim '*Nemo tenetur prodere seipsum*'—no one should be obliged to give himself away. This lies at the root of the witness's privilege against self-incrimination discussed in ch XI. At first sight it may seem odd that a privilege against self-inculpation should be allowed to militate against self-exculpation by prohibiting all accused persons from giving sworn

7 The parties were already competent in Chancery proceedings, and the County Courts Act 1846 made the parties in county court actions competent and compellable.
8 Except perhaps in a penal action, see *Amway Corpn v R* (1986) 34 DLR (4th) 190.

evidence on their own behalf; but there was an historical reason for this attitude. It had been the practice of the Star Chamber to oblige those who were brought before it to answer questions on oath, and the practice came to share the unpopularity of the tribunal by which it was instituted. To quote Professor Glanville Williams:[9]

> The strong insistence, after the abolition of the Star Chamber, that the administration of an oath to a defendant was contrary to the law of God and the law of nature, was a race-memory from those evil days.

During the nineteenth century the accused came to be allowed to make an unsworn statement from the dock, a right preserved by the Act of 1898, but now abolished by s 72 of the Criminal Justice Act 1982.[10]

The prohibition against the accused giving sworn evidence on his own behalf may have had its advantages if he was guilty, for the jury could be left with the impression that he had a complete defence to the charge but was unfortunately prevented from deposing to its exact nature,[11] but the situation could not be viewed with equanimity owing to the extreme hardship that might be caused to an innocent accused. Accordingly, a number of statutes were passed between 1872 and 1898 under which the prisoner was made a competent witness in the case of specified charges such as those under the Criminal Law Amendment Act 1885. It is unnecessary to refer to them in detail because they have been superseded by the Criminal Evidence Act 1898, which provides in s 1 that every person charged with an offence shall be a competent witness for the defence at every stage of the proceedings, whether he is charged solely or jointly with any other person.[12]

E. SPOUSES OF THE PARTIES

1. EXTENT OF THE COMMON LAW DISABILITY

Subject to comparatively unimportant exceptions which were confined to criminal cases, a party's spouse was incompetent as a witness for or against him at common law.[13] The incompetence extended to spouses of either sex and to testimony concerning events occurring before as well as during the marriage.[14] It was immaterial that the marriage was contracted after the occurrence of the relevant events,[15] or even after the commencement of proceedings,[16] and whatever the motive for marrying. In *Monroe v Twisleton*[17] it was decided that the incompetence endured after the marriage had been dissolved by private Act of Parliament so far as transactions which occurred

---

9 *The Proof of Guilt* (3rd edn) 41.

10 The right is still retained in many Commonwealth jurisdictions.

11 It became so common for counsel for the defence to adopt this approach that judges used to remind them of the prisoner's right to make an unsworn statement.

12 The accused was allowed to give evidence on his own behalf a little earlier in parts of the Commonwealth and of the United States.

13 *Bentley v Cooke* (1784) 3 Doug KB 422; *Davis v Dinwoody* (1792) 4 Term Rep 678.

14 *Pedley v Wellesley* (1829) 3 C & P 558.

15 *Hoskyns v Metropolitan Police Comr* [1979] AC 474, [1978] 2 All ER 136.

16 See *S v Leepile (No 3)* 1986 (2) SA 352.

17 (1802) Peake Add Cas 219, though where the marriage no longer subsisted ex-spouses could testify to matters which occurred before it, *R v Algar* [1954] 1 QB 279, [1953] 2 All ER 1381; *R v Ash* (1985) 81 Cr App Rep 294.

during its subsistence were concerned. Accordingly, the plaintiff in assumpsit could not call the divorced wife of the defendant to prove the contract as it was concluded during her marriage. This case was followed in *O'Connor v Marjoribanks*[18] where personal representatives claimed damages for conversion of part of an estate from a bank, and it was held that the deceased's widow's evidence with regard to instructions received by her from her late husband concerning the disposal of his goods during his lifetime could not be received. It has however been determined that where an ex-spouse was competent to testify on matters occurring before or since the marriage, cross-examination as to matters occurring during the marriage was permissible for the purpose of attacking the credit of the witness.[19]

From time to time it has been suggested that, in addition to rendering the spouse of the parties incompetent, the common law prohibited the disclosure of marital communications by any witness, whether they passed between him and his spouse or were other people's marital communications overheard by him; but it has been authoritatively decided that the only relevant common law rule is that of incompetency.[20]

There was one clear exception to the common law rule and two further ones concerning which there is a high degree of uncertainty. The one clear exception was constituted by criminal charges involving personal violence by the accused against his or her spouse. This was established in *Lord Audley's Case*[1] in which a wife was held competent to testify against her husband who was charged as accessory to her rape. The decision was based on necessity. Were the law otherwise the injured spouse would frequently have no remedy.

The first of the uncertain exceptions is treason. If it exists it can be justified on the ground that the public interest in the safety of the state outweighs whatever public interests are promoted by preventing one spouse from testifying against the other.[2] The second uncertain exception relates to cases in which it has been held that on prosecutions under old statutes for abducting and marrying a girl against her will, she was a competent witness even if the marriage happened to be legally valid.[3] These may be accounted for on the ground that something in the nature of personal violence was involved.[4]

In *R v Sergeant*[5] it was said that a wife is in all cases a competent witness for her husband when admissible against him, and there is no reason to doubt that this doctrine applies to all the exceptions to the common law rule of the incompetency of spouses, and to husbands as well as wives. In the absence of some compelling reason to the contrary, what is sauce for the goose is sauce for the gander in the administration of justice no less than in other spheres of life.

---

18 (1842) 4 Man & G 435. *Monroe v Twistleton* was preferred to the contradictory decision in *Beveridge v Minter* (1824) 1 C & P 364. See also *Doker v Hasler* (1824) Ry & M 198.
19 *R v Ash* (1985) 81 Cr App Rep 294.
20 *Rumping v D P P* [1964] AC 814, [1962] 3 All ER 256; *Shenton v Tyler* [1939] Ch 620, [1939] All ER 827 criticised on historical grounds by Holdsworth in 56 LQR 137.
1 (1631) 3 State Tr 401 followed in *R v Azire* (1725) 1 Stra 633.
2 See per Lush J in *DPP v Blady* [1912] 2 KB 89 at 92. The other dicta for and against the competency of the accused's spouse in treason are collected in Cohen *Spouse Witnesses* 23.
3 *R v Wakefield* (1827) 2 Lew CC 279.
4 See the judgment of Blackburn J in *Reeve v Wood* (1864) 5 B & S 364.
5 (1826) Ry & M 352.

2. STATUTES AFFECTING CIVIL CASES

The spouses of parties to litigation are now competent and compellable in all civil cases. This is the effect of s 1 of the Evidence Amendment Act 1853, the exception of proceedings instituted in consequence of adultery having been repealed.

3. STATUTES AFFECTING CRIMINAL CASES

The modern law is contained in s 80 of the Police and Criminal Evidence Act 1984, which repeals earlier provisions in the Criminal Evidence Act 1898 and Theft Act 1968. In broad terms it makes the accused's spouse a competent and compellable witness for the accused, a competent witness for a co-accused, and a generally competent, but sometimes compellable, witness for the prosecution. It is discussed in detail in the next section.

SECTION 2. COMPETENCE AND COMPELLABILITY UNDER THE MODERN LAW[6]

The general rule is that anyone is a competent and compellable witness in any case; but there are exceptions relating to children, persons of defective intellect, the accused and the accused's spouse.

A. CHILDREN[7]

Attention has been increasingly focused upon the competence of children, partly as a result of heightened concern about the sexual abuse of children,[8] and partly in consequence of the passage of s 34 of the Criminal Justice Act 1988, which removed many of the existing corroboration requirements in relation to the evidence of children. One focus of concern has been the possibility of harm being caused to a child witness. The evidence is however inconclusive,[9] and it has been decided in England that competent children are also compellable,[10] and, in the case of wards of court, even without any need to seek leave to call them.[11] This requirement has however been mitigated by statute in relation to committal proceedings, at least where the defence raises no objection.[12] In both civil and criminal proceedings children can give sworn testimony at common law and unsworn by statutory

---

6 See generally Australian Law Reform Commission Research Paper No 5, 'Competence and Compellability of Witnesses'.
7 For reference to recent research on this topic see Spencer and Flin 'Child Witnesses—Are They Liars?' (1989) 139 NLJ 1601 part of an intended monograph by the joint authors on the general topic of the evidence of children.
8 See Butler-Sloss 'Report of the Inquiry into Child Abuse in Cleveland 1987' Cmnd 412 (1988).
9 See 'Report on Criminal Procedure in Scotland, (1975).
10 Certainly in public prosecutions.
11 *Re K* (1988) 1 All ER 214. Though leave is required to interview the ward prior to proceedings being commenced, see *Practice Direction* [1988] 1 All ER 223.
12 Magistrates' Courts Act 1980, s 103, as amended by Criminal Justice Act 1988, s 33, and subject to some other qualifications.

provision.[13] It should also be remembered that the situation is to some extent alleviated by the greater admissibility of hearsay in civil proceedings relating to children.[14]

1. SWORN EVIDENCE

It was decided in *R v Brasier*[15] that at common law no evidence could be given otherwise than on oath.[16] The judges to whom this question had been referred in the case of a child tendered to give evidence of an assault nevertheless took a flexible approach:[17]

[t]here is no precise or fixed rule as to the time within which infants are excluded from giving evidence, but their admissibility depends upon the sense and reason they entertain of the danger and impiety of falsehood, which is to be collected from their answers to questions propounded by the court.

It seems that the judge should first conduct an enquiry to determine whether the child is competent to give sworn testimony,[18] and that such an enquiry should take place in the presence of the jury.[19] Now that affirmation is available as an alternative to swearing on oath as an outward pledge of reliability in the case of mentally competent adults, a more secular approach is taken to the determination of the competency of a child. In *R v Hayes*[20] the Court of Appeal held the relevant decision to be whether:

the child has a sufficient appreciation of the solemnity of the occasion, and the added responsibility to tell the truth which is involved in taking an oath, over and above the duty to tell the truth which is an ordinary duty of normal social conduct.

If the judge is satisfied of this he should allow the child to be sworn, and, irrespective of theological ignorance, not merely to affirm.[1] At the end of the day the decision is likely to be taken more upon the basis of the judge's general impression of the child's demeanour than upon that of the answer to any particular questions.[2] In civil cases, before there was any statutory power to admit unsworn testimony, it seemed that the proceedings could be adjourned to permit the child to be instructed.[3]

---

13 In criminal proceedings by virtue of the Children and Young Persons Act 1933, s 38, and in civil by virtue of the Children Act 1989, s 96(2).
14 See *Official Solicitor v K* [1965] AC 201, [1963] 3 All ER 191 and *Re W* [1990] 1 FLR 203 in relation to wardship, and the more general extension in the Children Act 1989, s 96(3).
15 (1779) 1 Leach 199.
16 Despite the contrary suggestion of Hale in relation to the evidence of young children, 1 Pleas of the Crown 634.
17 At 238.
18 *R v Khan* [1981] Crim LR 330.
19 *R v Bird* (1988) Times, 22 June.
20 [1977] 2 All ER 288 at 291, [1977] 1 WLR 234 at 237. See also *R v Campbell* [1983] Crim LR 174.
1 *R v Bellamy* (1985) 82 Cr App Rep 222. But see *R v TCD* (1987) 61 CR (3d) 168.
2 *Re X, Y and Z* (1989) Times, 3 November.
3 *Baker v Rabetts* (1954) 118 JPN 303.

2. UNSWORN EVIDENCE[4]

Section 38(1) of the Children and Young Persons Act 1933 provides that:

> Where, in any proceedings against any person for any offence, any child of tender years called as a witness does not in the opinion of the court understand the nature of an oath, his evidence may be received, though not given upon oath, if, in the opinion of the court, he is possessed of sufficient intelligence to justify the reception of the evidence, and understands the duty of speaking the truth; . . .

It will be noted that this provision applies only to criminal proceedings,[5] and to witnesses of 'tender years', a phrase which is not further defined. It is best to regard it as a matter for the good sense of the court.[6] In *R v Lee*[7] the trial judge seemed to think that it could not extend to a child of fifteen-and-a-half, while in *R v Khan* it was thought that enquiry should have been made in respect of a child of twelve. In *R v Hayes* the Court of Appeal seems to have accepted the view that the dividing line between sworn and unsworn testimony generally runs between the ages of eight and ten. Although the substantive test is cast in terms of intelligence and moral integrity it seems that an English[8] court will be unlikely to accept the evidence of a very young child, since in *R v Wallwork*[9] Lord Goddard CJ remarked that:

> The court deprecates the calling of a child of this age as a witness, . . . A jury could not attach any value to the evidence of a child of five; it is ridiculous to suppose that they could.

It is arguable that the substantive test is too abstract in referring to understanding of a duty to tell the truth,[10] but it is submitted that courts are unlikely to take too pedantic an approach, and will be content to accept any indication of a commitment to tell the truth, given sufficient intelligence to recognise it. Although there seems little difference in the terminology of the conditions required for the sworn and unsworn testimony of children, it has been held in Canada[11] that a less onerous standard of understanding is required for the tender of unsworn testimony, and in one case[12] an appeal has been allowed because the child was permitted to testify unsworn although the enquiry required to determine whether she could tender sworn testimony had not been conducted.

---

4 Such unsworn testimony, if wilfully false, is punishable as perjury just as if it had been sworn.
5 Though civil proceedings have now been assimilated as a result of the passage of the Children Act 1989, s 96, and this was already the case in some Commonwealth jurisdictions such as Canada.
6 *R v Campbell* [1956] 2 QB 432 at 436, [1956] 2 All ER 272 at 274.
7 [1988] Crim LR 525.
8 Though in Scotland the evidence of a child of three has been accepted, *R v Miller* (1870) 1 Coup 430; and in some jurisdictions in the United States, see Jones 'The evidence of a Three Year Old Child' [1987] Crim LR 677 (where the evidence was videotaped).
9 (1958) 42 Cr App Rep 153. See also now *R v Wright* (1987) 90 Cr App Rep 91; cp *R v B* (1990) Times, 1 March.
10 See Spencer 'Reforming the Competency Requirement' (1988) 138 NLJ 147.
11 *R v Khan* (1988) 64 CR (3d) 281.
12 *R v D (RR)* (1989) 69 CR (3d) 267.

3. REFORM OF THE LAW[13]

In England, now that the mandatory corroboration requirement for unsworn testimony has been abolished, there seems still more to be said in favour of the proposal of the Criminal Law Revision Committee[14] that all children under the age of fourteen should, if sufficiently competent, give evidence unsworn, and those over that age, sworn. The same rule might well be extended to evidence in civil proceedings. One significant advantage of such a proposal is that in avoiding any overlapping, and hence any choice between different forms, it will overcome the difficulty currently experienced if a judge wishes to resile from his initial decision as to whether the child should give evidence sworn or unsworn.[15] The Committee also recommended that the second part of the test be changed from understanding the duty to understanding the importance of telling the truth. It is suggested that a court is likely to take a flexible and sensible view whatever form of words is chosen.

B. PERSONS OF DEFECTIVE INTELLECT

At one time it appears to have been thought that lunatics so found were absolutely excluded from testifying, but *R v Hill*[16] decides that, in all cases where it is contended that the witness is of too weak an intellect to admit of his giving evidence, it is for the judge to decide whether he understands the nature of an oath and, if the judge answers this question in the affirmative, it is for the jury to say what degree of credit is to be given to the testimony. The inmate of an asylum whose only delusion was that spirits talked to him was accordingly allowed to give evidence at a prosecution for manslaughter. In *R v Bellamy*[17] where the mental ages of the adult witnesses were equivalent to those of children, the common law rules for children were regarded as appropriate to determine competence. If it appears that, though duly sworn before the jury, the witness was in fact too weak-minded to testify or that, for some other reason, such as deafness or dumbness, the evidence cannot be taken, the judge may declare the witness to be incompetent.[18] Temporary incapacity occasioned by illness or intoxication would presumably lead to an adjournment in an appropriate case.

---

13 See Scottish Law Commission Discussion Paper No 75 'The Evidence of Children and other Potentially Vulnerable Witnesses' (1988); Flin 'Child Witnesses: The Psychological Evidence' (1988) 138 NLJ 608; Spencer 'Evidence: Reforming the Competency Requirement' (1988) 138 NLJ 147; McEwan 'Child Evidence: More Proposals for Reform' [1988] Crim LR 813.

14 11th Report 'Evidence Cmnd 4991, paras 204–8 (1972).

15 See, for example, *R v Lee* [1988] Crim LR 525; *R v Chapman* [1980] Crim LR 42.

16 (1851) 2 Den 254. See also *R v Dunning* [1965] Crim LR 372.

17 (1985) 82 Cr App Rep 222. See also *R v TCD* (1987) 61 CR (3d) 168. In *R v Hall* (1987) 86 Cr App Rep 159 it appears that a woman with an IQ in the bottom 1% of the population, and held to be severely mentally impaired, was allowed to testify, though without conspicuous success.

18 *R v Whitehead* (1866) LR 1 CCR 33; cf *Jacobs v Layborn* (1843) 11 M & W 685. It was held in *The People (A-G) v Keating* [1953] IR 200 that the judge must examine the witness although he has examined the same witness in a previous case; cf as to children *R v Surgenor* [1940] 2 All ER 249.

C. THE ACCUSED[19]

1. AS A WITNESS FOR THE PROSECUTION

The general rule is that the accused is not a competent witness for the prosecution in any criminal case. The rule is the result of the common law which, so far as this point is concerned, has not been modified by the Criminal Evidence Act 1898, because that statute confers competence on the accused only as a witness for the defence. In *R v Grant*[20] and *R v Sharrock*[1] committals were quashed because one co-prisoner had been called on behalf of the prosecution at the preliminary examination. In so far as these cases decided that an indictment based on inadmissible evidence is necessarily bad, they have been overruled,[2] but they still serve as a warning to over-zealous prosecutors.

Where several people are charged in the same indictment there are various devices by which the prosecution can render one of them competent and compellable against the others. A nolle prosequi may be filed with reference to his case; it may be stated that no evidence will be offered against him when he will be acquitted; an order for separate trials may be obtained or he may plead guilty. In this last event it is desirable that the witness should be sentenced before being called on behalf of the prosecution.[3] If the former co-accused was an accomplice, a warning against the danger of acting on his uncorroborated testimony will have to be given to the jury; this is discussed in the next chapter.

It was said in *R v Pipe*[4] that an accomplice[5] against whom proceedings are pending must not, as a matter of practice, be called on behalf of the prosecution unless it is made plain that the proceedings will be discontinued. No doubt the ban would apply to a case in which proceedings, though not actually pending, were likely, but the judgment of Lawton LJ in *R v Turner*[6] suggests that the matter is basically one of judicial discretion. An accomplice who had turned 'King's evidence' was, together with his family, accorded police protection, an advantage which he might have lost if he had not testified in accordance with statements previously made by him. Lawton LJ said that it could not always be irregular to call an interested witness on behalf of the prosecution. He instanced a case in which a reward would be due to an informant on the conviction of the person against whom he testified.

---

19 Likely to be construed strictly so as to permit even a policy-making director to be compelled to testify for the prosecution against the firm whose policy he makes, see *Penn-Texas Corpn v Murat Anstalt* [1964] 1 QB 40, [1963] 1 All ER 258, distinguishing between officer and corporation in the context of compulsory process. See also *R v N M Peterson & Sons* [1980] 2 SCR 679, to the same effect in Canada.

20 [1944] 2 All ER 311.

1 [1948] 1 All ER 145.

2 *R v Norfolk Quarter Sessions, ex p Brunson* [1953] 1 QB 503, [1953] 1 All ER 346.

3 *R v Payne* [1950] 1 All ER 102. The devices were mentioned in *R v Pipe* (1966) 51 Cr App Rep 17. See also R N Gooderson 'The Evidence of Co-prisoners' (1953) 11 CLJ 279, an article to which the text is much indebted.

4 (1966) 51 Cr App Rep 17.

5 Presumably including an accessory after the fact, see *R v Bleich* (1983) 150 DLR (3d) 600.

6 (1975) 61 Cr App Rep 67, applied *R v Governor of Pentonville Prison, ex p Schneider* (1981) 73 Cr App Rep 200. See also *R v Weightman* [1978] 1 NZLR 79; *R v Brown* (1983) 74 FLR 97.

2. AS A WITNESS FOR HIMSELF

The effect of s 1 of the Criminal Evidence Act 1898 is that the accused is a competent witness on his own behalf at every stage of a criminal trial.[7] The section contains important provisos concerning comment on his failure to testify, marital communications and the cross-examination of the accused; they are discussed elsewhere in this book.[8]

Doubts have been raised whether that which an accused person says when testifying on his own behalf may be used against a co-accused whether the statement was made in-chief or in cross-examination.

(i) Evidence in-chief

In *R v Rudd*,[9] the most recent case on the availability of the testimony of one of several accused given on his own behalf as evidence for the prosecution, the Court of Criminal Appeal held that the trial judge had rightly refrained from telling the jury to disregard the evidence implicating the appellant given by his co-accused. Humphreys J said:

> While a statement made in the absence of the accused person by one of his co-defendants cannot be evidence against him,[10] if the co-defendant goes into the witness box and gives evidence in the course of a joint trial, then what he says becomes evidence for all the purposes of the case including the purpose of being evidence against his co-defendant.

These remarks are well supported by authority, if not entirely to the extent suggested by Humphreys J,[11] and it is submitted that they are sound on principle because it is the common lot of a party to litigation to have adverse as well as favourable testimony given by his own witnesses and, not infrequently, by himself. But, even in modern times language is sometimes used which suggests that nothing said by one or two accused in the witness box is evidence against the other.[12] There was some authority in support of this view before the Act of 1898 when doubts were expressed whether the evidence of a prisoner who had been acquitted and testified for one of the two remaining co-accused was admissible against the other,[13] but it is submitted that this, and similar hesitancy, sprang from a failure to distinguish between one co-accused's out-of-court testimonial assertions or unsworn

---

7 Even after a plea of guilty he may give evidence in mitigation of sentence (*R v Wheeler* [1917] 1 KB 283). The accused may also give evidence on the voir dire (*R v Cowell* [1940] 2 KB 49, [1940] 2 All ER 599).

8 See ch X as to comment and cross-examination, and ch XI as to marital communications.

9 (1948) 32 Cr App Rep 138. To the same effect are *R v Hunting and Ward* (1908) 1 Cr App Rep 177; *R v Paul* [1920] 2 KB 183; and *R v Garland* (1941) 29 Cr App Rep 46n. See also *Young v H M Advocate* 1932 JC 63 where the earlier English and Scottish authorities are reviewed.

10 Because of the hearsay rule, but see *Mawaz Khan v R* [1967] 1 AC 454, [1967] 1 All ER 80 where such a statement was regarded as original evidence.

11 His Lordship said it had been the invariable rule to state the law in the same way (32 Cr App Rep 138 at 140).

12 For a ruling that comes near to telling the jury to disregard the evidence of one accused when considering the case against the other see *R v Meredith* (1943) 29 Cr App Rep 40. It was assumed that one accused's testimony was evidence against the other in *Rigby v Woodward* [1957] 1 All ER 391, [1957] 1 WLR 250.

13 *R v Burdett* (1855) Dears CC 431.

statements in court which were certainly not evidence against the other,[14] and his sworn evidence in court which is analogous to that of any other witness.

(ii) Evidence elicited in cross-examination

On principle there can be no doubt that what a witness says in cross-examination may be relied on by the person responsible for the cross-examination as evidence in his favour. This would mean that anything that one accused says when he is being cross-examined by the prosecution may be treated as evidence against the other; but principle sometimes has to give way to considerations of policy, and, if it is sound policy to prohibit the prosecution from calling accused persons to testify against each other, it is pertinent to remember that the policy is liable to be circumvented whenever the prosecution is allowed to rely on the statements of an accused elicited in cross-examination as evidence against his co-accused. To some extent it is only proper that this permission should be accorded, but it is arguable that the court went too far in *R v Paul*.[15] Paul, Goldberg and others were jointly charged with an offence. Goldberg was told that he need not give evidence, but nonetheless went into the witness-box, and declared that he was guilty. This was all he said in-chief, but the Court of Criminal Appeal held that the judge had rightly allowed the prosecution to cross-examine him on Paul's alibi—a subject on which his evidence assisted the Crown. This case was criticised by Lord Justice General Clyde in *Young v H M Advocate*.[16] The court has a discretion with regard to the cross-examination it will permit, and Lord Clyde considered that this discretion should have been exercised in favour of Paul. It is, however, possible to exaggerate the criticisms of *R v Paul* because, had the accused pleaded guilty in the first instance, he would have been compellable for the prosecution, although it is true that his evidence could not then have been obtained by means of leading questions and other forms of pressure permissible in cross-examination.

3. AS A WITNESS FOR A CO-ACCUSED

The general rule is that the accused is a competent but not a compellable witness for anyone being tried jointly with him. This is the effect of s 1 of the Criminal Evidence Act 1898.[17] It means that, if A and B are being tried together, B may call upon A to testify for him provided A is willing to do so. Within the meaning of the Criminal Evidence Act 1898, a prisoner who has pleaded guilty is not a 'person charged' because he is not concerned in any issue before the jury; he is therefore both competent and compellable for a co-accused.[18] For the same reason someone who was originally jointly

---

14 The right to make such an unsworn statement has now been abolished.
15 [1920] 2 KB 183.
16 1932 JC 63, though some of the views there expressed were regarded as out-moded in *Todd v HM Advocate* 1984 JC 13.
17 See *R v Payne* (1872) LR 1 CCCR 349 as to incompetence before the Act. The rule is expressly left unaffected in its application to a co-accused spouse, Police and Criminal Evidence Act 1984, s 80(4).
18 *R v Boal* [1965] 1 QB 402 at 414, [1964] All ER 269 at 275.

indicted with the accused but has been acquitted or directed to be tried separately is both competent and compellable for the accused.[19]

An accused who gives evidence is liable to be cross-examined by his co-accused as well as by the prosecution even if his evidence was in no way adverse to the accused,[20] although he will enjoy the protection of s 1(f) of the Criminal Evidence Act 1898 against certain types of cross-examination if he does not give evidence against someone charged in the same proceedings.

D. SPOUSES[1]

After a long, complicated and thoroughly unsatisfactory process of development, the modern law on this topic has been greatly simplified by the Police and Criminal Evidence Act 1984, s 80.[2] Most difficulties have been experienced in criminal proceedings, and the provisions of the new Act will be examined below. It will then be necessary to mention the situation in which ex-spouses testify to matters which occurred during the marriage.

1. CRIMINAL PROCEEDINGS

Section 80 of the Police and Criminal Evidence Act 1984 states the new law in its principal provisions as follows:

(1) In any proceedings[3] the wife or husband of the accused shall be competent to give evidence—
(a) subject to subsection (4) below, for the prosecution; and
(b) on behalf of the accused or any person jointly charged with the accused.

(2) In any proceedings the wife or husband of the accused shall, subject to subsection (4) below, be compellable to give evidence on behalf of the accused.

(3) In any proceedings the wife or husband of the accused shall, subject to subsection (4) below, be compellable to give evidence for the prosecution or on behalf of any person jointly charged with the accused if and only if—
(a) the offence charged involves an assault on, or injury or a threat of injury to, the wife or husband of the accused or a person who was at the material time under the age of sixteen; or
(b) the offence charged is a sexual offence[4] alleged to have been committed in respect of the person who was at the material time under that age; or
(c) the offence charged consists of attempting or conspiring to commit, or of aiding, abetting, counselling, procuring or inciting the commission of, an offence falling within paragraph (a) or (b) above.

19 *R v Conti* (1973) 58 Cr App Rep 387 (directed acquittal); *R v Richardson* (1967) 51 Cr App Rep 381 (separate trials).
20 *R v Hilton* [1972] 1 QB 421, [1971] 3 All ER 541.
1 See Creighton 'Spouse Competence and Compellability' [1990] Crim LR 34.
2 Similar reform has been undertaken in other jurisdictions, see e g Criminal Procedure (Scotland) Act 1975, s 143; Evidence Act (South Australia), s 21 (as amended); Evidence Act 1910 (Tasmania), s 55 (as amended); Crimes Act 1958 (Victoria), s 400 (as amended); and Crimes Act (New South Wales) 1900, s 407 (as amended).
3 Defined as criminal proceedings by s 82(1). In Australia proceedings for a penalty have not been regarded as criminal for these purposes, *Australian Federal Police Comr v McMillan* (1987) 70 ALR 203.
4 Defined by s 80(7) as an offence under the Sexual Offences Act 1956, the Indecency with Children Act 1960, the Sexual Offences Act 1967, s 54 of the Criminal Law Act 1977 or the Protection of Children Act 1978.

(4) Where an information or indictment charges a husband and his wife jointly with an offence neither spouse shall at the trial of the information or indictment be competent or compellable by virtue of subsection (1)(a), (2) or (3) above to give evidence in respect of that offence unless that spouse is not, or is no longer, liable to be convicted of that offence at the trial as a result of pleading guilty or for any other reason.

These provisions are modelled upon those proposed by the Criminal Law Revision Committee in its 11th Report, and set out in the draft bill annexed to the report.[5]

A major change from the position at common law is that the spouse becomes a competent witness for the prosecution in all cases subject only to the minor exception of proceedings in which the spouses are being tried jointly. The iniquity of the old rule was well illustrated in *R v Deacon*[6] in which the accused was charged with murdering his brother-in-law and attempting to murder his wife. She gave evidence that she saw her husband shoot and kill the deceased after which he shot at her. Deacon was convicted of murder, no verdict being taken on the charge of attempt. The conviction was quashed by the Court of Appeal because Mrs Deacon was an incompetent witness on the murder count. Her evidence was not wholly unhelpful to the accused for the killing was admitted and he relied inter alia on the defence of accident, but no application to have her called as a witness had been made on his behalf, and such an application could not be implied from his failure to object to his wife's being called as a witness by the prosecution. It seems also to have been the case that one spouse was incompetent to give evidence for the prosecution against the other's co-accused.[7] Incompetence extended to matters occurring before, as well as during, the marriage,[8] and to those occurring after a judicial separation.[9] The Criminal Law Revision Committee felt that the preservation of marital harmony could not justify the retention of such incompetence,[10] and that the only argument of any substance at all was the dilemma that would be created for spouses in cases where there was no compellability. Since the Act does not make the spouse compellable for the prosecution in all cases this dilemma still exists, but the committee's recommendation that it should not stand in the way of change has been accepted. The law of spouse competency is now clear and straightforward. Most of the old statutory provisions have been repealed.[11]

Since it was not thought desirable to apply to spouse witnesses the general rule of the common law that competence implies compellability,[12] many of the old problems which formerly related to spouse competence reappear in relation to spouse compellability for the prosecution. The Act deals with three situations, offences involving assault or injury to the spouse, offences of

---

5 Evidence (General) Cmnd 4991, paras 143–57 and Annex 1, draft Bill, para 9.
6 [1973] 2 All ER 1145, [1973] 1 WLR 696. See also *R v Mount* (1934) 24 Cr App Rep 135; *R v Boucher* (1952) 36 Cr App Rep 152.
7 *R v Mount* at 136, but see Cohen 'Are Wives Really So Incompetent?' [1980] Crim LR 222.
8 *Hoskyn v Metropolitan Police Comr* [1979] AC 474, [1978] 2 All ER 136.
9 *Moss v Moss* [1963] 2 QB 799, [1963] 2 All ER 829.
10 But see Lempert 'A Right to Every Woman's Evidence' (1981) 66 Iowa LR 725 criticising the similar situation recently arrived at by judicial interpretation in the United States in *Trammel v US* 405 US 40 (1980).
11 Although the Theft Act 1968, s 30(2) has, unlike s 30(3), not been repealed its continued existence should cause no difficulty in the light of the generality of the new provisions.
12 *Ex p Fernandez* (1861) 10 CBNS 3.

a similar character against children, and sexual offences against children. Each requires separate consideration.

At the time of the Criminal Law Revision Committee's report it was thought that in cases of violence against them, spouses were compellable at common law.[13] The policy underlying such a rule was accepted by the Criminal Law Revision Committee.[14] This position was overturned by the decision of the House of Lords in *Hoskyn v Metropolitan Police Comr.*[15] In that case the accused was charged with wounding a woman. They were married two days before the trial, and the wife was compelled to testify over her objection. Her evidence was unhelpful to the prosecution, but they secured leave to treat her as a hostile witness and the accused was convicted. His appeal to the Court of Appeal was rejected on the authority of *Lapworth.* The House of Lords allowed the appeal overruling *Lapworth* on the ground that it was inconsistent both with the common law,[16] and also with the analogy of the position in statutory offences scheduled to the Criminal Evidence Act 1898.[17] Neither ground was very plausible. As Lord Edmund Davies pointed out in his dissent[18] *R v Inhabitants of All Saints, Worcester* was decided on the basis not of non-compellability, but of privilege. *Leach v R* can be criticised on many grounds.[19] The House of Lords also doubted the policy underlying the law as understood in *Lapworth* and as accepted by the Criminal Law Revision Committee. That policy was simply that to allow the spouse a choice would often, in effect, be to subvert the rule of criminal law that the consent of a spouse is no defence to a charge of assault upon that spouse. It may also be argued that where one spouse has used such violence against the other as to be charged with it there can be little confidence that the victim's choice not to testify has been inspired by marital affection rather than by fear. The argument on the other side is that it is generally unsatisfactory to compel witnesses to testify against their will, and repugnant to compel a wife to testify unwillingly against her husband. The new Act reflects the policy applied in *Lapworth* and recommended by the Criminal Law Revision Committee. There are however differences in the drafting. The Bill annexed to the committee's report referred to cases where 'the act or any of the acts constituting the offence charged consists of an assault, etc'. The Act refers to cases 'where the offence charged involves an assault etc'. The effect of this change is obscure. Its construction is not assisted by the use of the verb 'consists' in sub-s 80(3)(c). It is arguable that the difference in wording suggests that 'involves' must be given a different meaning from 'consists' and a possible interpretation would be that it makes it sufficient for s 80(3)(a) that an assault or injury to the spouse occurs even though it is not reflected in the formal charge. The use of the present tense for 'involves' and the contrast with the past 'was' in relation to age makes this a somewhat forced interpretation however. Another possibility is that the new wording is simply an attempt to achieve the same result a little more elegantly. Such a view is

---

13 As decided in *R v Lapworth* [1931] 1 KB 117.
14 Cmnd 4991 para 149.
15 [1979] AC 474, [1978] 2 All ER 136.
16 As expounded in *R v Inhabitants of All Saints, Worcester* (1817) 6 M & S 194 at 200 by Bayley J, and as interpreted by Taylor *On Evidence* (9th edn, 1895) p 892.
17 As decided in *Leach v R* [1912] AC 305.
18 It may be noted that Lord Edmund Davies had been chairman of the Criminal Law Revision Committee at the time of the 11th report.
19 For some of them, see Zuckerman (1979) 94 LQR 321.

however weakened by observation that the Bill's original terminology for the substance of the matter covered by s 80(3)(a), although now abandoned for that purpose, has been taken over in s 80(3)(c), which did not appear at all in the Criminal Law Revision Committee's draft Bill. A further difference between the draft Bill and the new section is that the former referred only to assault or threat of violence, while the new section refers to assault, injury or threat of injury. It is perhaps clearer from the terminology of the new section that a case like *R v Verolla*,[20] where the accused was charged with attempting to murder his wife by poisoning her, would still be covered, though in view of the inclusion of s 80(3)(c) which covers that situation exactly there would be no need to rely upon 80(3)(a). The explicit reference to threat of violence also removes the difficulty found at common law in relation to competence in *R v Yeo*[1] where a wife was held not competent to testify against her husband who was charged with sending a letter threatening to murder her. On the other hand it seems clear that a wife would still not be compellable if her husband should be prosecuted for living on her immoral earnings.[2] It remains unclear whether a spouse would be compellable upon a charge like arson which had in the circumstances put the other in fear.[3] On balance the wording seems not apt to go quite so far. 'Injury' is less redolent of intent than 'violence', so it is possible that a spouse will be compellable for the prosecution in respect of offences where injury is caused recklessly or negligently. Retention of the concept of assault means that a wife is compellable in the prosecution of her husband for buggering her, presumably irrespective of her consent at the time, though it is hard to imagine any circumstances in which such a charge would be brought to trial if the wife were unwilling to testify.[4]

The next category, offences involving assault, injury or threat of injury to children under sixteen, had no predecessor at common law. It too was foreshadowed in the Criminal Law Revision Committee's Report. There is however one important difference. The committee's recommendation was that the scope of the offences should be limited to those against children who were also members of the same household as the accused.[5] It was felt that the basic reason for enacting compellability in such cases was to try to secure the availability of some evidence where otherwise there might be none, and some cases, for example of cruelty to children too young to testify, might otherwise have to go unpunished. This would be most likely to occur in cases where the child was a member of the same household as the accused. The Act has, it is submitted rightly, adopted a more expansive policy of protecting children generally. The Act also implements the committee's recommendation[6] that no distinction be drawn between offences involving injury to children and those of sexual offences. Here too consent is irrelevant. This means that the accused's wife will be compellable against him if he kisses a fifteen year old, however much encouragement she offers, but not if he rapes

20 [1963] 1 QB 285, [1962] 2 All ER 426.
 1 [1951] 1 All ER 864n.
 2 Assuming the absence of assault, injury or threat of injury. Under the old law she was not even competent, *D P P v Blady* [1912] 2 KB 89, though in the United States compellability has been achieved at common law, *Wyatt v US* 362 US 525 (1960).
 3 See *R v Sillars* [1979] 1 WWR 743; *R v Czipps* (1979) 101 DLR (3d) 323.
 4 *R v Blanchard* [1952] 1 All ER 114, 35 Cr App Rep 183.
 5 Para 151, draft Bill cl 9(3)(a).
 6 Para 150, draft Bill cl 9(3)(b).

and murders a sixteen year old. If the potential availability of evidence is an important consideration, cases of homicide might seem eligible for addition to the category where the spouse is compellable.

It is interesting to note that a totally different policy has been adopted in some Australian states and is recommended by the Australian Law Reform Commission, according to which the spouse is prima facie compellable for the prosecution in all cases, but the court is given a discretion to excuse the spouse from testifying according to certain guidelines set out in the statute.[7]

It should be noted that both the general provision as to competence, and these exceptional cases of compellability, apply to the spouse of a co-accused exactly as they do the spouse of a sole accused.

The Act also simplifies the law in relation to the competence and compellability of a spouse witness for the defence. The position before the Act appeared to be that a spouse was a competent,[8] but not a compellable, witness for the accused.[9] The new Act provides explicitly that one spouse is a competent,[10] and a compellable,[11] witness for the other subject only to the minor exception that in cases where both spouses are being tried jointly they are still not compellable.[12]

The old law provided that the accused's spouse was sometimes competent for a co-accused only with the consent of the accused,[13] and sometimes without the necessity for any such consent.[14] The Act provides that a spouse is always a competent witness for the other's co-accused,[15] but compellable for such a person only in the circumstances in which the spouse would have been compellable for the prosecution against the other spouse.[16] The result of these provisions upon spouse compellability can be expressed in the form of a table, first supposing A and B to be jointly tried for a non-sexual offence against neither a spouse nor a child, and then supposing them to be jointly tried for an assault on Mrs A.

	FOR PROSECUTION		FOR DEFENCE	
	Against A	Against B	For A	For B
GENERAL CASE				
Mrs A	No	No	Yes	No
	80(3)	80(3)	80(2)	80(3)
Mrs B	No	No	No	Yes
	80(3)	80(3)	80(3)	80(2)
ASSAULT on MRS A				
Mrs A	Yes	Yes	Yes	Yes
	80(3)(a)	80(3)(a)	80(2)	80(3)(a)

7 For example, South Australia and Victoria; Australian Law Reform Commission, Report No 38 'Evidence' para 82. A similar approach inspired s 57 of the Evidence Code recommended in 1975 by the Law Reform Commission of Canada, though it was not endorsed by the Task Force on the Uniform Laws.
8 Criminal Evidence Act 1898, s 1.
9 *R v Boal* [1965] 1 QB 402 at 416, [1964] 3 All ER 269 at 275.
10 S 80(1)(b).
11 S 80(2).
12 S 80(4).
13 Criminal Evidence Act 1898, s 1(c).
14 Eg Theft Act 1968, s 30(3).
15 S 80(1)(b).
16 S 80(3).

	FOR PROSECUTION		FOR DEFENCE	
	Against A	Against B	For A	For B
Mrs B	No	No	No	Yes
	80(3)	80(3)	80(3)	80(2)

These provisions are in line with the recommendations of the Criminal Law Revision Committee.[17]

2. EX SPOUSES

In the case of criminal proceedings the Act follows the recommendation of the Criminal Law Revision Committee[18] in providing that:

> In any proceedings a person who has been but is no longer married to the accused shall be competent and compellable to give evidence as if that person and the accused had never been married.[19]

This changes the position at common law as exemplified in *R v Algar*,[20] whereby the position of an ex-spouse, whether as a result of divorce or the annulment of a voidable marriage, was assimilated to that of a current spouse, following *Monroe v Twisleton*.[1] Parties to a void marriage are regarded as strangers to each other for these purposes.[2] As a result of this provision, competence and compellability is bestowed upon all of these categories of ex-spouses. The existing law whereby a marriage is treated as subsisting for these purposes notwithstanding that the parties are living apart, even pursuant to a judicial order for separation or non-cohabitation,[3] has been retained. Nor does there seem likely to be much basis for excluding the evidence of such a witness upon the basis of its making the proceedings unfair, though an unsuccessful attempt to do so has been made.[4]

It is generally assumed that *Monroe v Twisleton* is no longer law so far as civil cases are concerned. It is certainly difficult to believe that a modern court would hold the divorced wife of a party incompetent to testify concerning a contract made by her former husband during or before his marriage to her; but how is such a result to be avoided? One view would be that it cannot be avoided because *Monroe v Twisleton*, vested with the authority of the Court of Criminal Appeal, if not the House of Lords,[5] still governs the case; but the absurdity of a law of evidence according to which the present spouse of a party to civil proceedings is both competent and compellable while a divorced spouse is not even competent is sufficient to raise the gravest doubts concerning the soundness of this view. Assuming that the Evidence Act 1843 did not overrule *Monroe v Twisleton*,[6] the only alternative is to hold

---

17 Cmnd 4991 para 155, draft Bill cll 9(2) and 9(3).
18 Cmnd 4991 para 156, draft Bill cl 9(4).
19 S 80(5).
20 [1954] 1 QB 279, [1953] 2 All ER 1381.
 1 (1802) Peake Add Cas 219.
 2 So a party to a polygamous marriage, bigamous in England, is competent and compellable,
    R v Khan (1986) 84 Cr App Rep 44.
 3 *Moss v Moss* [1963] 2 QB 799, [1963] 2 All ER 829.
 4 *R v Mathias* [1989] Crim LR 64.
 5 The case was mentioned, although its present status was not considered, in *Rumping v D P P*
    [1964] AC 814, [1962] 3 All ER 256.
 6 To hold that it did would entail the conclusion that *R v Algar* [1954] 1 QB 279, [1953] 2
    All ER 1381 was wrongly decided.

that, so far as civil cases are concerned, the decision has been overruled by the Evidence Amendment Act 1853, s 1. This rendered the 'husbands' and 'wives' of parties competent and compellable, and it is submitted that the words 'husband' and 'wife' must be given an extended meaning to cover a divorced spouse testifying to matters occurring during the marriage.[7]

Lest the construction of s 1 of the Evidence Amendment Act 1853 suggested above should prove to be unacceptable, a statutory provision placing the matter beyond doubt may be thought to be desirable. Subject to this relatively minor point, there is no case for any reform in the law relating to the competence and compellability of the parties' spouses in civil cases.

E. OTHER RELATIONSHIPS

Little consideration seems to have been given in this country to claims in respect of other relationships. In Victoria[8] and in Israel[9] the rules relating to compellability have been relaxed as between parents and children. The Australian Law Reform Commission has also recommended some relaxation as between heterosexual cohabitants.[10]

F. THE SOVEREIGN AND DIPLOMATS

It goes without saying that the sovereign is not a compellable witness. The same applies to heads of other sovereign states, because they are not subject to legal process. Under various statutes diplomatic and consular officials, and officials of, and other persons connected with, certain international organisations, enjoy total or partial immunity from compellability to give evidence.[11]

G. BANKERS

Reference must finally be made to the limited immunity enjoyed by bankers under the Bankers' Books Evidence Act 1879. Section 6 provides that a banker or officer of a bank shall not, in any legal proceeding to which the bank is not a party, be compellable to produce any banker's book the contents of which can be proved under this Act, or to appear as a witness to prove the matters, transactions and accounts therein recorded, unless by

7 To obviate the effect of *O'Connor v Marjoribanks* (1842) 4 Man & G 435, the words must also be taken to include a widow or widower testifying to matters occurring during the marriage when proceedings are brought against his or her deceased spouse's estate.
8 Crimes Act 1958, s 400 (as amended).
9 Evidence Ordinance 1971, cl 4.
10 Research paper No 5 ch 7. The Law Reform Commission of Canada recommended extension of discretionary protection to those bound by 'family or similar ties', draft Code, s 57.
11 See in particular Diplomatic Privileges Act 1964 (c 81), s 2(1), Sch 1, arts 1, 31(2), 37(1), (2); Consular Relations Act 1968 (c 18), s 1(1), Sch 1, arts 1(1), 44, 58(2); International Organisations Act 1968 (c 48); Diplomatic and Other Privileges Act 1971 (c 64), s 4; International Organisations Act 1981; Arms Control and Disarmament (Privileges and Conventions) Act 1988. The assistance of G V Hart, late secretary of the Criminal Law Revision Committee, on this subject is acknowledged.

order of a judge made for special cause.[12] The object of this statute is to save the time of bankers and protect them and their customers from the inconvenience of producing the originals of their books. We shall see in ch XIX that, although it is sufficient to produce a copy of a public document to the court, the original of a private document has to be produced as a general rule. Bankers' books, apart from those of the Bank of England, rank as private documents, but the Act of 1879 provides for their proof by means of a copy. There are various safeguards which it is not necessary to mention, beyond saying that the authenticity of the copy can usually be established by affidavit, thus sparing any bank official the necessity of attending court.

SECTION 3. OATH, AFFIRMATION AND UNSWORN EVIDENCE[13]

A. OATH AND AFFIRMATION

We saw in section 1 that the law with regard to the swearing of witnesses developed from the notion that only those who were prepared to testify on oath on the Gospel were competent witnesses, but that other forms of oath and affirmation were gradually permitted. The present law is contained in the Oaths Act 1978, which consolidates earlier enactments.

Section 1 of the Act prescribes the form in which an oath shall be administered to Christians and Jews. It also allows for the administration of an oath to those with other religious beliefs in other forms. The fact that a person taking an oath has no religious belief does not prevent it from being binding on him.[14] Under s 5 anyone objecting to being sworn is permitted to make a solemn affirmation, and such an affirmation may be required of any person in relation to whom it is not reasonably practicable to administer an oath in the manner appropriate to his religious belief. An affirmation has the same force and effect as an oath which means that a false affirmer may be punished as a perjurer.

Although a majority of the Criminal Law Revision Committee advocated the abolition of the oath in favour of a declaration (subject to the same sanction in the event of falsity as that for perjury), no recommendation was made on account of the undesirability of a difference in this respect between civil and criminal proceedings. The Law Reform Committee was unwilling to report on the question of abolishing the oath in civil cases because they regarded the problem as a social one. There is the further point that oaths are used in many contexts other than that of litigation. The arguments for and against their employment in the latter are set out in paras 279–81 of the 11th Report of the Criminal Law Revision Committee.

B. UNSWORN EVIDENCE

It is necessary to distinguish between the different classes of case in which unsworn evidence may be given.

12 See also Companies Act 1985, s 452(3).
13 See generally Australian Law Reform Commission Research Paper No 6 'Sworn and Unsworn Evidence'.
14 S 4(2).

1. THE ACCUSED'S UNSWORN STATEMENT AT A CRIMINAL TRIAL[15]

The right of the accused to make an unsworn statement at his trial existed at common law and was expressly preserved by s 1 (h) of the Criminal Evidence Act 1898 which also made the accused generally competent to give sworn evidence in criminal cases. It was abolished by s 72 of the Criminal Justice Act 1982, in accordance with the recommendations of the Criminal Law Revision Committee.[16]

2. UNSWORN EVIDENCE OF CHILDREN

The unsworn evidence which children of tender years are allowed to give in criminal cases differs from the unsworn statement which the accused used to be able to give, in two respects. In the first place the witness is liable to be prosecuted for giving wilfully false testimony, and secondly he is liable to be cross-examined. Furthermore there never has been any doubt that the child's testimony does constitute evidence in the case in which it is given. It would be wrong to give the jury the direction as to weight formerly given in relation to an unsworn statement made by the accused.[17]

3. MISCELLANEOUS

The other cases in which a witness need not be sworn depend on the common law. Someone who simply produces a document pursuant to a subpoena duces tecum does not have to be sworn if there is another witness who can identify the document.[18] This means that the person producing it cannot be cross-examined. Another person who need not be sworn is the advocate giving evidence of the terms of a compromise reached between the parties to litigation in which he acted for one of them. It is customary for his statement to be made from the well of the court[19] but the matter is dependent on convention and there is really no authority on the question whether he can insist on his right not to take the oath.[20] Finally, it is said that if the sovereign were to give evidence she need not be sworn, but, in the absence of authority, there does not appear to be much point in making conjectures concerning the appropriate procedure in such a case.

---

15 Cowen and Carter *Essays in the Law of Evidence* essay 7; see also previous editions of *Cross on Evidence*.
16 Cmnd 4991 paras 102–6.
17 See *R v Wills* (1985) 16 ACR 247.
18 *Perry v Gibson* (1834) 1 Ad & El 48.
19 *Hickman v Berens* [1895] 2 Ch 638. But see *Pioneer Concrete Gold Coast Pty Ltd v Cassidy (No 2)* [1969] Qd R 290.
20 There are obvious objections to an advocate acting as a witness in a case in which he is professionally engaged (*R v Secretary of State for India, ex p Ezekiel* [1941] 2 KB 169, [1941] 2 All ER 546); but it would probably be going too far to say that he is not a competent witness in such circumstances.

SECTION 4. PROCEDURE

The procedure for determining whether or not a witness is competent, and if so whether or not the evidence should be sworn or unsworn, may occasion certain problems. Questions may also arise as to the role of the court in advising the witness upon matters of competence and compellability, and in commenting upon the decision not to call a witness.

In *R v Yacoob*,[1] where a question arose whether or not a witness in criminal proceedings was married to the accused, it was decided that the proper procedure was for the judge to resolve the matter on the voir dire in the absence of the jury. The witness could be heard on that issue, even though it related to the witness's own competency. Similarly in the case of a young child, when a question arises as to his being sworn, the judge will normally conduct a voir dire in which the child will be examined.[2] Indeed if the child is of tender years such an inquiry becomes mandatory.[3] It seems that the party suggesting incompetence bears an evidential burden on that issue, but that the legal burden resides upon the party calling the witness. If the witness is called by the prosecution, the standard is proof beyond reasonable doubt;[4] if called by the defence it is presumably proof on the balance of probabilities.

Judges have a wide general power over the procedure to be adopted before them, and may alter the arrangement of their court in the interests of doing justice. To this end they may permit vulnerable witnesses and especially children, to be screened from sight of the accused.[5] If such a course be adopted the jury should be directed not to allow the adoption of such an arrangement to create prejudice against the accused.[6]

The court takes an active part in matters affecting the competence and compellability of witnesses. In the case of children it must not only conduct an examination[7] to determine competence, but also has the power to instruct the child.[8] In the case of spouses it has been said to be desirable that the court should take the initiative and explain to a competent, but non-compellable, spouse the precise nature of that situation, so as to inform the witness's choice whether or not to testify.[9] The choice is particularly important because it is exhausted once a witness has decided to testify. There is then no further chance of refusing, and if a witness attempts to resile from his proof he is liable to be treated as hostile, and to be cross-examined on any previous statement he may have made, a procedure explained more fully in ch VII. In two recent reported cases the accused has been found guilty despite, or perhaps because, a spouse witness for the prosecution has attempted to shield him, and then been treated as hostile.[10]

The Criminal Evidence Act 1898 provided that the prosecution should not comment upon the failure of the accused, or the spouse of the accused, to

---

1 (1981) 72 Cr App Rep 313.
2 *R v Hayes* [1977] 2 All ER 288, [1977] 1 WLR 234.
3 *R v Khan* (1981) 73 Cr App Rep 190.
4 *Yacoob* at 317.
5 *R v Smellie* (1919) 14 Cr App Rep 128.
6 *R v X, Y and ʒ* (1989) Times, 3 November.
7 Though leading questions might be frowned upon, see *R v Ogden* [1985] 1 NZLR 344.
8 *Baker v Rabetts* (1954) 118 JPN 303.
9 *R v Acaster* (1912) 7 Cr App Rep 187; *R v Pitt* [1983] QB 25, [1982] 3 All ER 63. See also *Bates v HM Advocate* 1989 SCCR 338.
10 *Hoskyn v Metropolitan Police Comr* [1979] AC 474, [1978] 2 All ER 136; *R v Pitt* above.

give evidence.[11] The Criminal Law Revision Committee recommended that the prohibition should be lifted in both cases.[12] The recommendations of the Criminal Law Revision Committee relating to the position of the accused as a witness have not so far been accepted, and it is understandable in that case that the prohibition also remains unamended. As has been seen, the committee's recommendations on spouse witnesses have generally been accepted. This one however has not. The existing prohibition upon comment by the prosecution on failure to call the spouse has been expressly re-enacted.[13]

11 See ch X for comment on failure of accused to testify.
12 Cmnd 4991 paras 110 and 154, draft Bill cll 5(4) (by inference) and 9(6).
13 Police and Criminal Evidence Act 1984, s 80(8).

CHAPTER VI
Corroboration

The general rule of modern English law is that the court may act upon the uncorroborated testimony of one witness, and such requirements as there are concerning a plurality of witnesses, or some other confirmation of individual testimony are exceptional. This does not mean that the court must act upon the evidence of one witness, even if it is unshaken in cross-examination, and in no way discredited by the witness's demeanour. To quote Sir James Stephen:[1]

> The circumstances may be such that there is no check on the witness and no power to obtain any further evidence on the subject. Under these circumstances juries may, and often do, acquit. They may very reasonably say we do not attach such credit to the oath of a single person of whom we know nothing, as to be willing to destroy another person on the strength of it. This case arises where the fact deposed to is a passing occurrence—such as a verbal confession or a sexual crime—leaving no trace behind it, except in the memory of an eye or ear-witness ... The justification of this is, that the power of lying is unlimited, the causes of lying and delusion are numerous, and many of them are unknown, and the means of detection are limited.

It was to meet situations such as those which have just been mentioned that the judges developed rules of practice under which juries must be warned of the dangers of convicting on uncorroborated evidence. These rules are discussed in section 1 together with the statutory provisions under which corroboration in some form or other is required as a matter of law. When corroboration is required as a matter of law, a conviction or finding of fact in its absence will necessarily be set aside by an appellate tribunal. On the other hand, when corroboration is required as a matter of practice, the greatest caution must be exercised in coming to a conclusion in its absence, but, provided due precautions have been taken, the conclusion cannot be assailed on legal grounds. Section 2 is concerned with the nature of corroboration—what does and does not constitute corroboration in the legal sense of the term.

The history of this subject is not without interest, for one of the great differences between the modern English law of evidence and that prescribed by the canon or civil law, which usually applied the maxim *testis unus testis nullus*, consists in the absence of any general requirement of a plurality of witnesses.[2] More than one oath helper was required when compurgation was among the standard methods of trial, so English law started with

1 *General View of the Criminal Law* (1st edn) 249.
2 There is a similar distinction between English and Scots criminal law today; but any general requirement of corroboration in Scottish civil proceedings was abolished by s 1 of the Civil Evidence (Scotland) Act 1988, enacting recommendations made by the Scottish Law Commission in its paper on 'Evidence' SLC 100 (1986).

something like the requirements of a number of witnesses such as were demanded by the canon law under the influence of Roman law, although the compurgators were of course quite unlike the modern witness. The two systems diverged more or less completely when English jury trial began to assume its present form in the seventeenth century. Before that period, the jurors were themselves witnesses, rather than triers, of fact, so there was a sense in which it could be said that more than one witness was always necessary at a common law trial. It is of some significance that Coke maintained that more than one witness was necessary in proceedings without a jury as where the validity of challenges fell to be determined. When the jurors ceased to resemble the modern witness, some efforts to impose rules requiring two or more witnesses were made by statute; but provisions of this nature were never generalised, and they are now of no importance.

The agreement of witnesses on matters of detail is often of the greatest significance, but, if it were invariably required, the testimony of one honourable man could not, as Napoleon observed, prove a single rascal guilty.[3] Rigid rules concerning the number of witnesses can hardly be justified as a matter of policy, although it is generally assumed there is a limited class of case in which some form of corroboration is desirable in the interests of justice. In all the situations which are about to be discussed, except the first, the required corroboration will not necessarily consist in the testimony of a second witness. It will often take this form, but an admission, letter or piece of real evidence will also suffice.

SECTION 1. WHEN CORROBORATION IS REQUIRED

Most statutory provisions have been cast in terms of requiring some corroboration, but now there is also a provision requiring not corroboration but merely a warning that the jury be cautious about convicting solely upon the basis of the type of evidence in question.

A. STATUTORY PROVISIONS

1. STATUTES REQUIRING TWO OR MORE WITNESSES[4]

A few surviving criminal statutes provide that the accused can only be convicted on the oath of two or more credible witnesses. These include s 1 of the Treason Act 1795, penalising the compassing of the death or restraint of the Queen, and s 168(5) of the Representation of the People Act 1983 (replacing earlier legislation) dealing with impersonation at elections. These provisions are of no practical importance from the point of view of the general law of evidence, and their repeal was recommended in the 11th Report of the Criminal Law Revision Committee.

---

3 Cited IX *Wigmore* p 256, n 3. The foregoing historical account is based on IX *Wigmore* para 2031.
4 The same rule applies to an attempt to commit such an offence, Criminal Attempts Act 1981, s 2(1)(g).

2. SECTION 89 OF THE ROAD TRAFFIC REGULATION ACT 1984

Under s 89 of the Road Traffic Regulation Act 1984,[5] a person charged with the offence of driving a motor vehicle at a speed greater than the maximum allowed shall not be liable to be convicted solely on the evidence of one witness to the effect that in the opinion of the witness the person charged was driving the vehicle at such greater speed. The effect of this provision is that where the evidence is that of the opinion of witnesses concerning the speed at which the accused was travelling, there must be two or more of them, and it has been held that their opinion must concern the accused's speed over the same stretch of road at the same time. A's opinion that the accused was travelling at a particular speed in one place, and B's opinion that he was travelling at that speed a little further on will not suffice.[6] There may, however, be a conviction on the evidence of one witness if it amounts to something more than his opinion. In *Nicholas v Penny*,[7] a police officer's evidence that he followed the accused in a police car and consulted its speedometer which showed an excessive speed was held to be sufficient. The speedometer reading is prima facie evidence of the speed recorded, although it is of course always open to the accused to raise a doubt whether the instrument was working properly.[8] The reading is evidence of a fact, and not a statement of opinion. As a general rule the opinion of witnesses who are not experts is excluded, but we shall see in ch XIII that it is admissible in a number of cases in which its exclusion would be absurd. Estimates of the speed at which a vehicle was travelling are among these cases, but the fact that such estimates are more liable to be inaccurate than testimony concerning direct perception amply justifies the provisions of s 89 of the Road Traffic Regulation Act 1984. Where the opinion is not based upon an estimation from observation of the vehicle in motion, but upon calculation from real evidence, such as skid marks and the effects of impact, there is not the same danger, and a generous view has been taken allowing such evidence to supplement the testimony of the expert deriving the appropriate inference from it.[9]

3. PERJURY

Under s 13 of the Perjury Act 1911, a person shall not be liable to be convicted of any offence against this Act, or of any offence declared by any other Act to be perjury or subornation of perjury, or to be punishable as perjury or subornation of perjury solely upon the evidence of one witness as to the falsity of any statement alleged to be false. This confirmed the common law as settled in *R v Muscot*,[10] but the reason for the rule given in that case— 'else there is only oath against oath'—is open to question because it would

---

5 Re-enacting earlier legislation.
6 *Brighty v Pearson* [1938] 4 All ER 127.
7 [1950] 2 KB 466, [1950] 2 All ER 89, where earlier decisions are reviewed.
8 If no reason is adduced for doubting such a reading the trier of fact must accept it as corroboration, *Burton v Gilbert* (1983) 147 JP 441.
9 *Crossland v DPP* [1988] 3 All ER 712.
10 (1713) 10 Mod Rep 192, and extended it to a wider range of offences, see *R v Barker* [1986] 1 NZLR 252.

justify a requirement of corroboration in any number of situations in which it is not necessary as matter of law or practice. There is an historical basis for the rule in the fact that perjury was originally punished in the Star Chamber—a court whose procedure was to some extent influenced by the civil law which, as we have seen, usually applied the principle that the testimony of one witness is insufficient. The requirement of corroboration in the case of perjury and kindred offences may also be justified on the ground that nothing must be allowed to discourage witnesses from testifying, and the fact that a conviction for perjury might be secured on the oath of one witness could have this effect. A second witness to the falsity of the impugned statement is, however, not essential. A letter, the authenticity of which is duly proved or admitted, and which might be construed as a subornation to someone else to commit perjury in relation to the same matter will suffice.[11] If all that is proved is that the accused contradicted the impugned statement, there is not enough evidence to support a conviction for nothing more is established than that one of two allegations made by the accused is untrue. Additional evidence, such as the repetition of the contradiction of the impugned statement on a number of occasions to different people, will, however, be sufficient.[12]

Although it is necessary for the judge to give an appropriate direction to the jury,[13] it is noted that only the falsity of the statement need be corroborated.[14]

According to para 192 of the 11th Report of the Criminal Law Revision Committee, the provision in s 13 of the Act of 1911 that a person is not liable to conviction 'solely upon the evidence of one witness as to the falsity of any statement alleged to be false' is treated, 'rightly or wrongly', as requiring that a second witness should give evidence from his own knowledge of the falsity of the statement in question, at any rate where the falsity is not proved by the production of letters or repeated contradictions. Accordingly it is said not to be enough that a second witness should simply prove that the accused admitted the falsity of the statement. The committee accordingly recommended an amendment of s 13 according to which the accused shall not be liable to be convicted on the evidence of one witness only as to the falsity of the statement in question 'unless the evidence is corroborated in some material particular by other evidence'. The committee also recommended, as did the Law Commission, that the requirement of corroboration should be confined to perjury in judicial proceedings and should not, like the present law, apply to such other offences under the Act of 1911 as the making of false statutory declarations.[15] This is because the encouragement of people to testify without fear of too easy a prosecution is regarded as the justification of the requirement of corroboration.

11 *R v Threlfall* (1914) 10 Cr App Rep 112.
12 *R v Hook* (1858) Dears & B 606. See also *R v Atkinson* (1934) 24 Cr App Rep 123 and *R v Stokes* [1988] Crim LR 110.
13 *R v Hamid* (1979) 69 Cr App Rep 324.
14 *R v O'Connor* [1980] Crim LR 43. If the falsity of the statement is not an issue, or is formally admitted by the accused, no reference need be made to s 13, see *R v Rider* (1986) 83 Cr App Rep 207. See also *R v Willmot* [1987] 1 Qd R 53 where the falsity of the statement was admitted under oath in the earlier proceedings.
15 11th Report of the Criminal Law Revision Committee, para 191.

4. PROCURATION[16]

Sections 2–4 and 22 and 23 of the Sexual Offences Act 1956,[17] which punish such offences as the procuration of women for the purpose of prostitution, provide that no person shall be convicted of any offence under them upon the evidence of one witness, unless the witness be corroborated in some material particular by evidence implicating the accused. The requirement that the corroborating evidence must implicate the accused in a material particular is characteristic of several statutory provisions as well as the common law rules of practice on the subject. As will be explained more fully in the discussion of the evidence of accomplices, it is not enough that that which is relied on should confirm some part of the testimony of the witness to be corroborated, it must do so in relation to that part of the testimony which implicates the accused.[18] Procuration belongs to the class of charges which are easy to make and difficult to rebut. Moreover the chief witness for the prosecution is usually the procured who cannot be numbered among the most reliable accusers, so the requirement of corroboration in this instance may be thought to be justified on the score of public policy.

5. UNSWORN EVIDENCE OF CHILDREN

As explained in the last chapter a child may be allowed to give evidence unsworn in criminal cases, provided that it is of sufficient intelligence and understands the duty to speak the truth, as provided for by s 38 of the Children and Young Persons Act 1933. As originally enacted, and understood, such evidence required corroboration,[19] and could not itself corroborate other unsworn evidence.[20] Section 34 of the Criminal Justice Act 1988 has changed the law in both respects. Subsection 1 repeals the proviso to s 38, and sub-s 3 provides that:

> Unsworn evidence admitted by virtue of section 38 of the Children and Young Persons Act 1933 may corroborate evidence (sworn or unsworn) given by any other person.

This salutary provision has remedied the situation in which a sexual attacker could minimise his chances of conviction by confining his attacks to very young children. It should also be noted that as a result of sub-s 2 of the new provision any attempt to diminish the effect of the change by the mandatory requirement of a warning in such cases has also been pre-empted, though it may be expected that such a warning will often be given as an exercise of discretion by the judge in the course of his duty to secure a fair trial for the accused. Warnings may also be required in relation to such evidence when it is required by some other rule, such as that for the evidence of accomplices, or rather more likely for that of the victims of sexual offences.

---

16 It has been doubted whether attempts to commit such offences are subject to the same rules, *R v Chauhan* (1981) 73 Cr App Rep 232.
17 Re-enacting the Criminal Law Amendment Act 1885, as subsequently amended.
18 *R v Goldstein* (1914) 11 Cr App Rep 27. Other cases on these sections are *R v Staub* (1909) 2 Cr App Rep 6, and *R v Cohen* (1909) 3 Cr App Rep 234.
19 Proviso to s 38.
20 *DPP v Hester* [1973] AC 296, [1972] 3 All ER 1056.

6. CONFESSIONS BY MENTALLY HANDICAPPED PERSONS

Section 77 of the Police and Criminal Evidence Act 1984 imposes a special obligation upon the court to warn the jury of special need for care in convicting upon the confession of a mentally handicapped person, obtained by the police otherwise than in the presence of an independent person.[21] The section further provides that the reason for such need should also be explained.

B. RULES OF PRACTICE

The dangers of a jury acting upon the basis of uncorroborated testimony have in certain situations seemed so great as to have generated rules of practice requiring a warning of such danger in formal terms, and the elaborate dissection of evidence so as to instruct the jury whether it was, or was not, capable of amounting to corroboration. There is a strong current tendency to move to a more discretionary and flexible system, both by way of the formal elimination of rules of practice where they previously existed,[1] and by resolute refusal on the part of the judiciary to extend the categories in which mandatory rules of practice are enforced.[2] Indeed further erosion may be indicated by Lord Hailsham's rejection of the very terminology of categories.[3] At present however there remain two such clear categories, accomplices and victims in sexual cases,[4] where a full and formal direction is still mandatory.[5] These will be considered first, and then some other situations where a more diluted form of warning may well be desirable.

1. ACCOMPLICES

The desirability of some form of corroboration of the evidence of an accomplice of the accused has been stressed at criminal trials for a hundred years and more, but, down to 1954, the cases showed that two schools of thought existed on the subject. According to one school, it lay in the judge's discretion whether the jury were warned of the desirability of corroboration, while the other school insisted that the warning must be given. In *Davies v D P P*[6] the House of Lords settled this point in favour of what may be described as the 'peremptory' school:

21 The Code of Practice for Police Questioning provides that a mentally handicapped person shall be interviewed in the absence of an independent person only in cases of urgency under Annex C to the Code.
1 For example by the elimination of the obligation to give a warning where it was required only because the witness was a child, Criminal Justice Act 1988, s 34(2).
2 See, for example, *R v Spencer* [1987] AC 128, [1986] 2 All ER 928.
3 Ibid at 135, 932.
4 Corroboration requirements in sexual cases have been abolished in a number of Australian jurisdictions, see in New South Wales, Crimes Act 1900, s 405c construed in *R v Murray* (1987) 30 ACR 315; in Victoria, Crimes Act 1958, s 62(3) construed in *R v B* [1987] VR 276; in South Australia, Evidence Act 1929, s 341(5) construed in *R v G* (1987) 45 SASR 102.
5 See *R v Stewart* (1986) 83 Cr App Rep 327.
6 [1954] AC 378, [1954] 1 All ER 507, discussed by Edwards 'Accomplices in Crime' [1954] Crim LR 324.

In a criminal trial where a person who is an accomplice gives evidence on behalf of the prosecution, it is the duty of the judge to warn the jury that, although they may convict upon his evidence, it is dangerous to do so unless it is corroborated. This rule, although a rule of practice, now has the force of a rule of law. Where the judge fails to warn the jury in accordance with this rule, the conviction will be quashed, even if, in fact, there be ample corroboration of the evidence of the accomplice, unless the appellate court can apply the proviso to s 4(1) of the Criminal Appeal Act 1907.[7]

The danger that the accomplice will minimise his role in the crime and exaggerate that of the accused is the usual justification for the requirement of caution in such a case, although some authorities consider that it has become a mystique in the administration of justice and that the question whether the warning is given should depend on the facts of each case.[8] It will be observed that the passage that has just been quoted refers to an accomplice giving evidence on behalf of the prosecution. One of two co-accused may incriminate the other when giving evidence on his own behalf. On principle there does not appear to be any good reason for distinguishing the case in which an accomplice gives evidence on his own behalf from that in which he testifies on behalf of the prosecution. If there should, as a matter of law, be a warning of the dangers of acting on the uncorroborated evidence of the accomplice in the one case, it should be equally necessary in the other. It seemed at one time as if the substance of this result could be achieved by the practice of delivering a warning to the jury against his uncorroborated evidence whenever a witness had a purpose of his own to serve, whether or not an accomplice as defined by *Davies*, and whether called by the prosecution or by the defence.[9] This rather vague doctrine came under critical scrutiny as the implications of the standard corroboration warning became increasingly onerous.[10] It has now been re-examined. *R v Beck*[11] was a case of conspiracy to defraud a finance company by securing payment against bogus satisfaction notes. The directors of the allegedly defrauded finance company testified for the prosecution. They had themselves claimed substantial sums from their insurers in respect of the alleged frauds. It was suggested by the defence that the directors of the finance company had known all along that the notes were not genuine, and that this exposed them to risk of prosecution for attempting to defraud their insurers, so that they had a purpose of their own to serve which imposed upon the trial judge a duty to give a corroboration warning in respect of their evidence. They were not accomplices within the definition of *Davies*, not least because if the allegations were true there would have been no fraud on the finance company. The Court of Appeal, after reviewing all of the authorities, rejected the view ascribed to in *Prater*. It distinguished between 'the obligation on a judge to advise a jury to proceed with caution', and an 'obligation to

---

7   At 309, 513 respectively, per Lord Simons LC.
8   See *Vetrovec v R* (1982) 136 DLR (3d) 89 where the Supreme Court rejected such a formal requirement for Canada though appeals may still be allowed where the facts require a direction which is not given, see *R v Hayes* (1989) 68 CR (3d) 245. No similar requirement exists in the United States. The Criminal Law Revision Committee recommended its abolition in England, Cmnd 4991 para 185, draft Bill cl 20(1). See further section 3 below.
9   *R v Prater* [1960] 2 QB 464 at 466, [1960] 1 All ER 298 at 300.
10 *R v Stannard* [1965] 2 QB 1 at 14, [1964] 1 All ER 34 at 40; *R v Whitaker* (1976) 63 Cr App Rep 193. See also *R v Gibb and McKenzie* [1983] 2 VR 155.
11 [1982] 1 All ER 807, [1982] 1 WLR 461; see also *R v Stainton* [1983] Crim LR 171.

give the corroboration warning with all that entails'.[12] In particular it suggested that *R v Prater* had in no way extended the law as laid down in *Davies*. It is however interesting to note that in its detailed analysis of *Prater* the court in *Beck* concentrated entirely on the imprecision of the test propounded to trigger off the corroboration warning. The discussion of *Prater* may even have appeared to support the application of the mandatory rule to accomplices called by the defence. In *R v Loveridge*[13] that question became the central point of the case. The accused, who were charged in respect of a number of burglaries, raised inconsistent defences. It was held following a series of earlier cases, none of them by then fully reported in the regular series,[14] that there is no obligation to give the full corroboration warning in these circumstances, though it may nevertheless be desirable to do so. It seems that between them *Beck and Loveridge* have re-established the strict limits of *Davies* free from any extension by the decision in *Prater*.

When a prosecution witness who might have been an accomplice gives evidence which is partly favourable to the accused, the question whether the warning should be given is a matter of discretion.[15]

It is now necessary to consider who is an accomplice for the purposes of the rule requiring a warning when the witness is called on behalf of the prosecution, the respective functions of the judge and jury in determining this question, and what constitutes corroboration of an accomplice's evidence.

(i) Who is an accomplice[16]

In *Davies v D P P* it was recognised that the accomplice warning must be given with regard to the evidence of the following classes of witness when called by the Crown: (a) *participes criminis*, whether as principals or accessories before or after the fact in the case of felonies, or as persons committing, procuring, aiding or abetting a misdemeanour;[17] (b) receivers giving evidence at the trial of those alleged to have stolen the goods received by them;[18] the crimes are intimately allied and the relationship is that of 'one-sided dependence'—there could not be a receiver unless the goods had first been stolen; (c) the parties to other crimes alleged to have been committed by the accused, when evidence of such crimes is received on the ground that it is of particular relevance or that it tends to prove something more than mere criminal propensity.[19] Presumably, in spite of the abolition of the distinction between felonies and misdemeanours by s 1 of the Criminal Law Act 1967, and the provision that the old law and practice with regard to misdemeanours should prevail, a corroboration warning is still necessary in the case of prosecution witnesses who have impeded the apprehension or trial of someone charged with an arrestable offence. This would seem to be

---

12 At 468, 813.
13 (1983) 76 Cr App Rep 125.
14 *R v Bagley* [1980] Crim LR 572; *R v Knowlden and Knowlden* (1983) 77 Cr App Rep 94 (decided in 1981); *R v Blackman* (5 February 1982 unreported) (LEXIS).
15 *R v Royce-Bentley* [1974] 2 All ER 347, [1974] 1 WLR 535. Though the judge should explain his reasons, *R v Wilson* (1988) Times, 23 April.
16 The Anglo-American and Commonwealth authorities were helpfully reviewed in an article by Professor Heyden [1973] Crim LR 264.
17 Application to accessories after the fact was confirmed by the Supreme Court of Canada in *Sillars v R* [1980] 1 SCR 527.
18 *R v Jennings* (1912) 7 Cr App Rep 242; *R v Dixon* (1925) 19 Cr App Rep 36.
19 *R v Farid* (1945) 30 Cr App Rep 168.

required by Lord Simonds' speech, although the case for treating these witnesses, like that for treating the old accessory after the fact, as an accomplice, may be thought to be a weak one because it would so often be in their interest to give evidence tending to show that the principal offence had not been committed.[20]

Davies's case was treated as one in which there was no evidence that the witness was an accomplice, so an appeal which was primarily based on the absence of a warning against the danger of acting on his testimony without corroboration was dismissed. Davies was charged with murder by knifing the deceased. He and the witness were members of a gang who had assaulted the deceased—an offence for which the witness had been convicted, but the witness had desisted from the attack by the time the knife was used, and there was no evidence that he had previously been aware of Davies's possession of such a weapon. Although the judgment embodies the previous case-law on the question of who is an accomplice, it is arguable that the principle which underlies the rule that the warning should be given covers all parties to the transaction in the course of which the crime is committed. In the words of an Australian judge, Sholl J:

> the temptation to exaggerate or make false accusations would appear to be much more related to the nature and possible punishment of the offence than to its technical identity with that alleged against the accused.

If Sholl J had been free to do so, he would have held the true principle to be that:

> that person is an accomplice within the common law rule who is charged in relation to the same events as those founding the charge against the accused with an offence (whether the same offence or not) of such a character, that he would be, if convicted thereof, liable to such punishment, as might possibly tempt that person to exaggerate or fabricate evidence as to the guilt of the accused.[1]

The mere fact that the witness has already been acquitted or convicted ought not to relieve the judge from the necessity of giving the warning because the witness's evidence at his trial may have been affected by the consideration mentioned by Sholl J and it is likely that he would adhere to it on a subsequent occasion. *Davies v D P P* at least lends no countenance to the view that the fact that the witness has already been acquitted or convicted of the offence for which the prisoner is being tried can have any bearing on the question whether the warning should be given.

An agent provocateur or spy is not an accomplice,[2] however much his activities may be deplored. In some cases where an offence has been created to protect a consenting party the law takes the view that such a victim is not an accomplice, and hence no warning is required as a matter of law. Thus

---

20 This point is stressed in *Khan v R* [1971] WAR 44 where it is suggested that Lord Simonds's definition of an accomplice may be too narrow because it does not cover the case of a witness liable to be convicted of a crime of which the accused could have been convicted on the particular indictment. See also *R v Meston* (1976) 28 CCC (2d) 497.
1 *McNee v Kay* [1953] VLR 520 at 530.
2 *R v Mullins* (1848) 3 Cox CC 526; *R v Bickley* (1909) 2 Cr App Rep 53; *Sneddon v Stevenson* [1967] 2 All ER 1277; *Dental Board v O'Callaghan* [1969] IR 181; *R v Phillips* [1963] NZLR 855; *R v Turnbull and Davidson* [1988] 1 Qd R 266.

the youthful victims of sexual offences,[3] or those induced to participate in offences,[4] are sometimes not regarded as accomplices. Similar principles have also been applied to adult women in cases involving their buggery[5] or living upon their immoral earnings.[6] Much depends upon the particular facts, however, and there are cases involving youthful participants[7] and adult women[8] where the whole question has been made to depend upon the enthusiasm of their involvement. Occasionally mere consent has been regarded as enough to make such a witness an accomplice of the accused.[9] Such variation of approach supports a more general switch to flexibility and discretion.[10]

Although no accomplice warning is necessary on a charge of affray at which participants are called for the prosecution, the judge should point out that they are interested witnesses who might have been doing what the accused were charged with having done.[11] Subject to the considerations mentioned above it is arguable that in all bilateral illegal transactions a party without whose participation in it the crime could not be committed should be regarded as an accessory, and thus as an accomplice. In such a case it might be relevant to consider whether the legislature has made both parties criminally liable.[12]

The terms of Lord Simonds's speech in *Davies*'s case do not favour an extension of the meaning of 'accomplice' in this context. It does not suggest that thieves are to be regarded as the accomplices of receivers to whom stolen goods are passed on, and there are undoubtedly cases in which it would be wrong to treat the thief as an accomplice. For example, if A and B steal something and C is charged with receiving it from B, there may be good reasons for treating B as C's accomplice at C's trial, but there would be no reason for treating A as C's accomplice.[13] But there seems to be every reason for treating the thief from whom the accused receives goods as an accomplice in all cases, and some recent judgments support this approach.[14]

---

3 *R v Pitts* (1912) 8 Cr App Rep 126; *R v Tatam* (1921) 15 Cr App Rep 132; *R v Ross* (1924) 18 Cr App Rep 141.
4 *R v Cratchley* (1913) 9 Cr App Rep 232; *R v Bone* [1968] 2 All ER 644, [1968] 1 WLR 983.
5 *R v Jellyman* (1838) 8 C & P 604.
6 *R v King* (1914) 10 Cr App Rep 117.
7 *R v Dimes* (1911) 7 Cr App Rep 43; *R v Bramhill* (1933) 24 Cr App Rep 79; *Horsburgh v R* [1967] SCR 743.
8 *R v Pickford* (1914) 10 Cr App Rep 269; *R v Pollock* [1973] 2 NZLR 491.
9 *R v Tate* [1908] 2 KB 680 (victim of buggery); *R v Stone* (1910) 6 Cr App Rep 89 (sister in charge of incest); *A-G v Levison* [1932] IR 158 (client of abortionist).
10 As explicitly suggested by Lord Reading LC in *King*.
11 *R v Sidhu* [1976] Crim LR 379.
12 In South Australia in *Scott v Killian* (1985) 19 ACR 187 the Full Court divided on this question in a case where a woman was charged with receiving money for the purpose of prostitution, though under local legislation it was no crime for a man to pay money for such a purpose. Prior J thought that this must indicate that the man should not be regarded as an accomplice of the woman, but Matheson J took the contrary view, while the Chief Justice reserved his view and decided upon a different point.
13 Kenny *Outlines of Criminal Law* (17th Edn) p 483, n 9. The position might be different if A knew that the goods would probably be passed on to C by B.
14 *R v Jenkins* (1981) 72 Cr App Rep 354; *R v Hodgett* [1957] NI 1; *R v McDonald* (1955) 74 NZLR 699. For earlier authority see *R v Crane* (1912) 7 Cr App Rep 113 and *R v Reynolds* (1927) 20 Cr App Rep 125. See also *Mulcraft v R* [1982] WAR 33.

(ii) Functions of judge and jury and direction of judge to jury

It is at least arguable that it would be best if the question whether a witness is an accomplice were always to be decided by the judge, but such a view is untenable in the light of Lord Simonds's speech. It was said in *Davies*'s case that the question whether a witness is an accomplice is often answered by his own confession or plea of guilty, or by the fact that he has been convicted of the crime under consideration, otherwise it is for the judge to rule whether there is evidence that the witness is an accomplice, while the jury must decide whether this is so in fact, the judge having warned them against the danger of convicting on the witness's uncorroborated evidence if they come to the conclusion that he was an accomplice.

It seems that there are three possible situations. In the first place there may be no sufficient evidence that the witness was an accomplice in which case the judge is not required to say anything to the jury with regard to corroboration, and this was held to be the position in *Davies*'s case itself. In the second place, the question whether the witness was an accomplice may have to be left to the jury with a clear warning that, if they think he was, they should be cautious before convicting in the absence of corroboration.[15] In such cases the jury faces a prior question of fact, perhaps dependent upon the resolution of a conflict of evidence. There is little indication in the English authorities of how such a question should be decided, and in particular who bears the onus of proof. In general it is for the party tendering a witness to prove his competence to testify, and by analogy the prosecution should here have to disprove beyond reasonable doubt that the witness is an accomplice if a mandatory warning is to be avoided. On the other hand it might be argued that the side alleging the witness to be an accomplice should bear the burden of proving it, at least on the balance of probabilities. Sometimes however the defence wants both to deny all involvement, and to require a warning to be given in respect of prosecution witnesses.[16] The best solution seems to be to require some evidence adduced either by prosecution or defence of the witness being an accomplice, and where it exists to require the prosecution to show beyond reasonable doubt that the witness was not an accomplice.[17] In a close case the judge would in any event be prudent to give some warning to the jury of the danger of convicting solely on the evidence of one so involved, and probably with an interest of his own to serve. Finally, it may occasionally be the duty of the judge to direct the jury that a particular witness is an accomplice, and, according to an Irish decision, this may be so in cases other than those mentioned above in which the question whether he is an accomplice has been answered by the witness himself.[18] There is a possible difficulty with regard to joint trials which has not yet been faced by the courts, for anything in the nature of a direction that a co-accused is an accomplice may be taken by the jury to be an indication of the judge's views concerning the guilt of the co-accused.

15 *R v Riley* (1979) 70 Cr App Rep 1.
16 As in *R v Merritt and Roso* (1985) 19 ACR 360.
17 Cp *R v Kay* [1950] OR 235; *R v Turnbull and Davidson* [1988] 1 Qd R 266; *R v Cox* [1986] 2 Qd R 55.
18 *People v Carney* [1955] IR 324, discussed by Professor Coutts in (1958) J Cr L 61. In *R v Chrimes* (1959) 43 Cr App Rep 149, the trial judge directed the jury that a witness who had not confessed or been convicted was an accomplice, although the Court of Criminal Appeal said that he need not have done so.

A mandatory warning, coupled with the danger of provoking unmeritorious but successful appeals, tends to promote the adoption of standard forms of direction. Such an approach has generally been resisted, and such resistance was re-affirmed[19] by the House of Lords in *R v Spencer*:[20]

> It has been said both in the Court of Appeal and in your Lordships' House, that the obligation to warn a jury does not involve some legalistic ritual to be automatically recited by the judge, or that some particular form of words or incantation has to be used and, if not used, the summing up is faulty and the conviction must be quashed. There is no magic formula which has to be used with regard to any warning which is given to juries. As this is no mere idle process it follows that there are no set words which must be adopted to express the warning. Rather must the good sense of the matter be expounded with clarity and in the setting of a particular case. The summing up should be tailored to suit the circumstances of the particular case.

It may well be claimed that the use of the word 'corroboration' is actually unhelpful as not being a word in popular usage.[1] It is nevertheless necessary to convey to the jury in clear and simple language and without doubt that there is a serious danger of risk of convicting an innocent man by relying upon the evidence of the impugned witness alone.[2] It may not be enough to refer to the need to take care, despite being qualified by an adjective like 'great',[3] 'particular'[4] or 'utmost',[5] even if the reasons for requiring such care are also elaborated.

(iii) Corroboration of an accomplice's evidence

It was said in *R v Mullins*[6] that corroboration does not mean that there should be independent evidence of that which the accomplice relates, otherwise his testimony would be unnecessary, as it would merely be confirmatory of other independent testimony. In the leading case of *R v Baskerville*[7] Lord Reading LCJ said that what is required is some additional evidence rendering it probable that the story of the accomplice is true, and that it is reasonably safe to act upon his statement. This view of the law has recently been re-affirmed in *R v Beck*,[8] stilling any doubts which might otherwise have been engendered by a dictum of Lord Hailsham LC in *D P P v Kilbourne*.[9] The judgment of Lord Reading LCJ is of the greatest importance because it settled a conflict between two views concerning the nature and extent of corroboration.

According to the first view, independent evidence tending to verify any part of the testimony of the accomplice would suffice, while the second required that the evidence should not only show that part of the accomplice's

---

19 The context and citations indicate that these sentiments were not intended to be confined to cases requiring less than the 'full' warning.
20 [1987] AC 128 at 141, [1986] 2 All ER 928 at 937 (references omitted).
1 See Lord Diplock in *DPP v Hester* [1973] AC 296 at 327, [1972] 3 All ER 1056 at 1075.
2 *R v Stewart* (1986) 83 Cr App Rep 327 at 335.
3 *R v Holland* [1983] Crim LR 545.
4 *R v Price* [1969] 1 QB 541, [1968] 2 All ER 282.
5 *R v Riley* (1979) 70 Cr App Rep 1.
6 (1848) 3 Cox CC 526 at 531.
7 [1916] 2 KB 658.
8 [1982] 1 All ER 807 at 815, [1982] 1 WLR 461 at 471.
9 [1973] AC 729 at 741, [1973] 1 All ER 440 at 448.

testimony is true, but it should also implicate the accused. The distinction may be illustrated by the facts of *R v Birkett*.[10] The accused was charged with sheep-stealing and, after evidence of the theft, the accomplice repeated statements made by him to the police concerning the whereabouts of some of the sheep's skins. Another witness proved (a) that the skins were found where the accomplice said they would be discovered and (b) that mutton corresponding to the carcases of the stolen sheep was found in the accused's house. On the first view of the nature of the required corroboration, item (a) would have been sufficient, but this would not have been so on the second view, although item (b) sufficed according to either view. The second view was favoured by the Court of Criminal Appeal in *R v Baskerville* and it is unnecessary to go into the previous authorities. To quote Lord Reading LCJ:

> We hold that evidence in corroboration must be independent testimony which affects the accused by connecting or tending to connect him with the crime. In other words, it must be evidence which implicates him, that is, which confirms in some material particular not only the evidence that the crime has been committed but also that the prisoner committed it. The test applicable to determine the nature and extent of the corroboration is thus the same, whether the case falls within the rule of practice at common law or within that class of offence for which corroboration is required by statute. The language of the statute, 'implicates the accused', compendiously incorporates the test applicable at common law in the rule of practice.[11]

In *R v Beck*[12] the Court of Appeal recommended adherence to this form of words with as little embellishment as possible. It has however been rejected in Canada as over-cautious on the ground that the important thing is to restore trust in the witness, and it does not matter much how that trust is restored.[13] While this generally accords with the less technical approach advocated by the House of Lords in cases such as *D P P v Hester*,[14] it would be wrong to weaken the protection afforded to the accused by the *Baskerville* test, so long at least as some such protection is still regarded as being necessary. Such an approach also maintains consistency between the position at common law and under statutes which have adopted the same formula.[15]

Various decisions provide instances of corroboration similar to those which have been discussed in connection with the relevant statutory provisions. Compromising letters written by the accused to the accomplice will suffice,[16] as will any item of damning circumstantial evidence such as the discovery of the mutton in the accused's house in *R v Birkett*. The accused's silence when a reply was to be expected will also corroborate the testimony of an accomplice as in *R v Cramp*[17] where the evidence of a girl whose miscarriage the accused was alleged to have attempted was corroborated by his silence when her father came to him and said, 'I have here those things which you gave my daughter to produce abortion'.

10 (1839) 8 C & P 732; *James v R* (1970) 55 Cr App Rep 299 (sexual offence).
11 [1916] 2 KB 658 at 667.
12 At 815, 471.
13 *Vetrovec v R* (1982) 136 DLR (3d) 89 at 103.
14 [1973] AC 296 at 325, [1972] 3 All ER 1056 at 1073.
15 Eg Children and Young Persons Act 1933, s 38(1).
16 As in *R v Baskerville* [1916] 2 KB 658, [1916–17] All ER Rep 38.
17 (1880) 14 Cox CC 390.

There are some special points which should be noted with regard to the corroboration of an accomplice's evidence. An accomplice of the first class mentioned by Lord Simonds in *Davies v D P P*[18] (a party to the crime including, it may be, someone who has impeded the apprehension or trial of a person charged with an arrestable offence) cannot corroborate another member of that class so that, if A, B and C are accomplices, B's evidence against C is not corroborated by anything to which A deposes.[19] Although it has been recognised by the House of Lords,[20] the merits of this rule have never been fully considered by an English court. It has been rejected after due consideration in South Africa,[1] and it is certainly difficult to justify on principle. If A's evidence standing alone is, subject to a warning against the danger of acting on it in the absence of corroboration, sufficient to support a conviction, why should it not be sufficient to corroborate the evidence of A's accomplice B? Assuming that the evidence of each witness implicates the accused in a material particular, and assuming that there is no question of a conspiracy between the witnesses, A's evidence adds considerably to the probability of the truth of B's and vice versa.[2]

In *Director of Public Prosecutions v Kilbourne*[3] the House of Lords held that the sworn evidence of young boys against whom the accused was alleged to have committed buggery or indecent assaults in 1971 could corroborate the sworn evidence of young boys against whom similar offences by the accused were alleged in 1970 and vice versa, the evidence being of particular relevance on account of the similarity of the conduct alleged against the accused on every occasion. A warning of the danger of acting on the uncorroborated sworn evidence of children is necessary, as it is on any sexual charge, and the boys may have been accomplices of the accused. However that may be, the importance of *Kilbourne's* case is that it lays to rest the extraordinary notion, produced by earlier decisions, that evidence of the type in question is admissible because it may help the jury to decide whether the other evidence is true, although it cannot corroborate such evidence. This particular *bêtise* was the outcome of an undiscriminating adherence to the rule that the testimony of one accomplice cannot corroborate that of another accomplice. *Kilbourne's* case decides that this is not so when the accomplice belongs to the third class mentioned by Lord Simonds in *Davies v Director of Public Prosecutions*[4] (parties to other crimes alleged to have been committed by the accused when such evidence is admissible). Clearly there is far less danger of collaboration between accomplices called by the prosecution when they belong to different classes (one being a party to the crime charged and the other a party to a different crime) than when they are both alleged to be parties to the crime charged; but it is open to question whether this is something which ought to justify a rule of law that accomplices who are parties to the crime charged cannot corroborate each other. We have already seen that such a rule cannot

---

18 [1954] AC 378, [1954] 1 All ER 507, and see p 231 above.

19 *R v Gay* (1909) 2 Cr App Rep 327; *R v Prater* [1960] 2 QB 464, [1960] 1 All ER 298.

20 *DPP v Kilbourne* [1973] AC 729, per Lord Hailsham LC at 747, per Lord Reid at 751, and per Lord Simon of Glaisdale at 759. See also *DPP v Hester* [1973] AC 296, per Lord Diplock at 326 and per Lord Cross of Chelsea at 330.

1 *State v Avon Bottle Store Pty Ltd* 1963 (2) SA 389 (A); *Nkambule v R* [1950] AC 379 (construing the Swaziland Criminal Procedure Proclamation, s 231).

2 As recognised in the Judge's direction in *R v Turner* [1980] Crim LR 305.

3 [1973] AC 729, [1973] 1 All ER 440.

4 [1954] AC 378, [1954] 1 All ER 507.

be based upon the requirements of logic and the danger of collaboration between witnesses is something which naturally goes to the weight rather than the admissibility of their evidence.

The wife of an accomplice who is not called can corroborate one who does give evidence[5] and, after some uncertainty in the authorities, the Court of Criminal Appeal has decided that the wife of an accomplice who is called can corroborate his evidence, although her evidence naturally requires to be treated with caution.[6]

Finally, where an accomplice gives evidence against two prisoners, the fact that there is corroboration so far as one of them is concerned does not corroborate his testimony against the other.[7]

The Criminal Law Revision Committee[8] recommended the abolition of the requirement of the accomplice warning as a matter of law in the case of witnesses called by the prosecution. This is partly on account of the difficulty of stating who is an 'accomplice' and partly on account of the fact that it is as safe to act on the uncorroborated evidence of some accomplices as it is dangerous to act on the uncorroborated evidence of many other witnesses of questionable character with regard to whom no warning is required as a matter of law. The committee would also have abolished the rule that one accomplice cannot corroborate another.

2. SEXUAL OFFENCES

It is also the practice of the court to warn the jury of the danger of convicting the accused upon the uncorroborated evidence of the victim of a sexual offence.[9] This is best regarded as a peremptory requirement as appeals have been allowed because no such direction was given although there was abundant corroborative evidence.[10] The requirement operates whenever the commission of a sexual offence is an issue. It seems however that where the commission of such an offence is not being contested, for example where the accused simply denies all involvement, then unless the sexual nature of the offence has in some way affected the quality of the identification of the accused, all that is necessary is the direction customarily given in relation to contested evidence of eye-witness identification.[11] If the commission of the

5   R v Willis [1916] 1 KB 933.
6   R v Evans [1965] 2 QB 295, [1964] 3 All ER 401. For earlier authorities see R v Neal and Taylor (1835) 7 C & P 168; R v Payne (1913) 8 Cr App Rep 171; R v Willis [1916] 1 KB 933; A-G v Durnan [1934] IR 308; R v Ehberts (1912) 7 DLR 398; R v Munevich [1942] 3 DLR 482; Tripodi v R [1961] ALR 780.
7   R v Jenkins (1845) 1 Cox CC 177, approved in R v Baskerville [1916] 2 KB 658 at 670, and R v Donat (1985) 82 Cr App Rep 173 at 178. This seems not to apply to the corroboration of the evidence of the victims of sexual offences, see further below p 240.
8   11th Report, paras 183–5 and para 194.
9   R v Jones (1925) 19 Cr App Rep 40; R v Freebody (1935) 25 Cr App Rep 69; R v Winfield [1939] 4 All ER 164; R v Burgess (1956) 40 Cr App Rep 144; R v O'Reilly [1967] 2 QB 722, [1967] 2 All ER 766; R v Henry, R v Manning (1968) 53 Cr App Rep 150. The corroboration warning is not required as a matter of law in Australia, Kelleher v R (1974) 131 CLR 534. It seems that the need for caution applies in civil actions arising out of a sexual offence, M v Cain (1989) Times, 15 December.
10 Though it is not necessary to stick to any particular form of words as long as the substance of the problem is made clear to the jury, R v Dowley [1983] Crim LR 168.
11 As specified in R v Turnbull [1977] QB 224, [1976] 3 All ER 549. See further, below p 718. This is, in principle, sufficient even if the victim is also a young child, see R v McInnes [1989] Crim LR 889, considering R v Willoughby (1988) 88 Cr App Rep 91.

offence is formally admitted, or effectively left uncontested, then no additional warning is required.[12] This view has been justified, in part, upon the basis that if a fuller direction were to be required, then in a case where the primarily intended crime were burglary, the burglar would improve his evidential position in any subsequent proceedings by going on to commit a sexual offence against an occupant. It should also be noted that the offence must contain a sexual element. It is not enough that there is some sexual undertone in the circumstances in which an ordinary offence, with which the accused is charged, was committed.[13] This may be the best explanation of the decision in *R v Olaleye*[14] where it was held that no warning was required in respect of the accused, charged with aiding and abetting an attempted rape, and tried in the same proceedings[15] as the principal offender, in relation to whom a full corroboration warning was given. It may be thought that in such a case since no further sexual element is urged against the accessory beyond that made against the principal, so there is no need for any warning. In relation to the accessory the sexual element is not effectively in issue. If the commission of a sexual offence is in issue, however, it is immaterial whether the victim,[16] or the accused,[17] is male or female, and whether consent is, or is not, an ingredient of the offence.[18] The desirability of retaining this rule has been considered by a number of law reform committees,[19] and academic commentators.[20] It has been abolished in many jurisdictions. The most convincing ground for its retention is that sexual offences can be feigned more plausibly than other crimes, and that the psychological motives for doing so are not so much a part of common knowledge that the jury can be expected to possess it without special instruction, which the requirement of a corroboration warning ensures. On the other hand the wide variety of offences, victims, alleged perpetrators, and circumstances tells against any universal rule. This seems to cause some uneasiness, and courts have said that it is safer to act upon uncorroborated evidence in sexual cases than in those of accomplices,[1] and that allowance may have to be made for special facts, such as the age of the victim.[2]

12 *R v Atkinson* (1987) 86 Cr App Rep 359; *R v Chance* [1988] QB 932, [1988] 3 All ER 225.
13 *R v Simmons* [1987] Crim LR 630 (false imprisonment, probably for a sexual motive). Cp *R v Caswell* [1984] Crim LR 111 (common assault, but involving sexual intercourse without consent which could not be charged as rape since the parties were married).
14 (1986) 82 Cr App Rep 337.
15 If tried separately a warning would presumably still be required in each aspect of proceedings in respect of the victim's evidence.
16 Eg *R v Gammon* (1959) 43 Cr App Rep 155.
17 Few women are prosecuted for sexual offences against victims, but since some of the same statutory offences which attract a warning when committed by males can also be committed by females, there is every reason to suppose that the same requirement applies. Some indication that it does, can be gleaned from *R v Hare* (1933) 24 Cr App Rep 108 at 110, but the dictum is equivocal since the victim there, as in all the reported cases, was a child.
18 Eg *R v Marks* [1963] Crim LR 370.
19 Criminal Law Revision Committee, Cmnd 4991 paras 186–8; and in the context of rape, 'Rape Prosecutions' Working Paper No 4 Law Reform Commission of Victoria, section 13; Rape and Other Sexual Offences' Special report of Criminal Law and Penal Methods Reform Committee of South Australia, para 15.6; Report of the Criminal Law Review Division of Department of Attorney-General of New South Wales, part 10.
20 Williams 'Corroboration—Sexual Cases' [1962] Crim LR 662; *Wigmore* para 924a; and for a thorough rehearsal of all the arguments either way, Heydon *Cases and Materials on Evidence* pp 79–83.
1 *R v Crocker* (1922) 92 LJKB 428.
2 *R v Zielinski* [1950] 2 All ER 1114n, 34 Cr App Rep 193.

According to a majority of the Court of Criminal Appeal, if evidence of an earlier indecent assault is admitted against the accused in order to negative his defence of accident in relation to the indecent assault with which he is charged, there need be no warning against accepting the earlier evidence if it is uncorroborated.[3]

The alleged corroborative evidence must implicate the accused in a material particular. In a case of rape it must confirm that intercourse has taken place with the accused, and that it took place without the consent of the victim.[4] Where it is alleged that the crime was committed by more than one man, each is implicated by evidence that an act took place without the consent of the victim.[5] The strength of such corroboration against each of the accused might however be diminished, but that would be a matter for the jury. On the other hand evidence merely that a young girl was not a virgin when her step-father was charged with an offence against her would not be enough to implicate him,[6] nor where separate offences are charged against the same accused does corroboration of one amount to corroboration of the other.[7]

A majority of the Criminal Law Revision Committee was in favour of retaining a requirement of corroboration as a matter of law in the case of a sexual charge on which the complainant was under 14 (the age at which according to recommendations of the committee already mentioned[8] sworn evidence was to be given), and of providing that the jury must be directed that there was a special need for caution before convicting on the uncorroborated evidence of the complainant in every sexual case when he or she were 14 or over.[9]

Under the present law there could be several reasons why the same evidence should be received with caution if it is not corroborated for, in addition to coming under the present head, the evidence might be that of an accomplice, or it might be given by a person of tender years. In such a case each ground for the warning should be mentioned.[10]

3. SWORN EVIDENCE OF CHILDREN

It was formerly the case that a rule of practice required a mandatory warning in respect of the sworn evidence of children.[11] The Criminal Justice Act 1988, s 34(2) has removed it:

> Any requirements whereby at a trial on indictment it is obligatory for the court to give the jury a warning about convicting the accused on the uncorroborated evidence of a child is abrogated in relation to cases where such a warning is required by reason only that the evidence is the evidence of a child.

3 *R v Sanders* (1961) 46 Cr App Rep 60.
4 *James v R* (1970) 55 Cr App Rep 299 at 302. If both elements are in issue then the evidence requires corroboration as to both, *R v West* (1983) 79 Cr App Rep 45.
5 *R v Pountney* [1989] Crim LR 216. The same view has been taken in Canada, see *Murphy and Butt v R* [1977] 2 SCR 603.
6 *R v Kerim* [1988] 1 Qd R 426.
7 *R v West* (1984) 79 Cr App Rep 45.
8 See p 209 above.
9 Ibid.
10 *R v Gammon* (1959) 43 Cr App Rep 155.
11 See *R v Cleal* [1942] 1 All ER 203.

It should be noted that the reasons for the rule advanced in *R v Dossi*,[12] namely that children are more susceptible to the influence of third persons, and may allow their imagination to run away with them, may still persuade the judge to exercise his discretion so as to give an appropriate warning, and that a warning may still be mandatory as a matter of practice, if the child can be considered an accomplice, or is the victim of a sexual offence.

4. CLAIMS AGAINST THE ESTATES OF DECEASED PERSONS

A claim against the estate of a deceased person will not generally be allowed on the uncorroborated evidence of the claimant, but there is no rule of law against allowing it[13] in England. The absence through death of one of the parties to the transaction calls for caution in such a case, but claims have been allowed where there was no corroboration.[14]

5. OTHER POSSIBLE CAUSES

In *People (A-G) v Casey (No 2)*,[15] Kingsmill-Moore J speaking for the Supreme Court of Eire said:

> The category of circumstances and special types of case which call for special directions and warnings from the trial judge cannot be considered as closed. Increased judicial experience and, indeed, further psychological research, may extend it.

The case before the court concerned the reliability of evidence of visual identification and it was said that, in all such cases, whether or not there was a plurality of witnesses, the jury's attention should be drawn to the necessity of caution because there have been cases in the past in which responsible witnesses to identification have been subsequently proved to have been mistaken. The words of Kingsmill-Moore J were repeated with approval by the Lord Chancellor in *D P P v Kilbourne* ;[16] but, as we shall see,[17] the problem of identification has been dealt with by the English courts in a different way. The precautions mentioned in *R v Turnbull*[18] must be observed, but they do not prescribe an invariable requirement of corroborative evidence or a warning to the jury of the danger of convicting in its absence. Indeed the Report of the Devlin Committee on Evidence of Identification in Criminal Cases which preceded the decision in *R v Turnbull* speaks of the declining

---

12 (1918) 13 Cr App Rep 158 at 161.
13 *Re Hodgson, Beckett v Ramsdale* (1885) 31 Ch D 177; *Rawlinson v Scholes* (1898) 15 TLR 8; *Vavasseur v Vavasseur* (1909) 25 TLR 250; *Re Cummins, Cummins v Thompson* [1972] Ch 62, [1971] 3 All ER 782; see note in 87 LQR 268.
14 It is required by statute in some Canadian jurisdictions, see *Ken Ertel Ltd v Johnson* (1986) 25 DLR (4th) 233.
15 [1963] IR 33 at 38.
16 [1973] AC 729 at 740.
17 See p 718 below.
18 [1977] QB 224, [1976] 3 All ER 549.

belief in the value of a requirement of corroboration and says that the law on the subject has become too technical.[19]

The tide of judicial feeling seems to be running strongly against the ritualistic observation of rigid rules in this area, and for this reason new categories of witnesses[20] or further areas for the application of rules or practices of requiring a mandatory and full corroboration warning are very unlikely to open up.[21] The most that will be required is a direction tailored to the facts of the particular case so as to ensure that the accused enjoys a fair trial. Sometimes a warning equivalent to the full mandatory warning may be required to bring concealed dangers to the attention of the jury, in other cases where any danger would be obvious to the jury it may even be sufficient for the judge to say nothing.[22]

SECTION 2. THE NATURE OF CORROBORATION

Although it has been said that 'corroboration' is not a technical term, but simply means 'confirmation' or 'support',[1] it remains the case that in order to amount to 'corroboration' evidence must emanate from a source independent of the witness to be corroborated, and must implicate the accused in a material particular. It follows that not all evidence which might as a matter of common sense be thought to confirm or support the testimony of a witness will necessarily satisfy such a requirement. As a result of this divergence the exegesis of the requirements of corroboration has undeniably attracted a degeee of technicality, which, while it may have been reduced by recent decisions, including the decision of the House of Lords in *Hester* itself, has not yet been totally eliminated, at least in England. As noted above,[2] these requirements were laid down very deliberately by the Court of Appeal in *R v Baskerville*,[3] were intended to be of general application to all formal requirements of corroboration, and have generally been accepted as such.[4] The formulation is to be found in statutory provisions also, such as those now contained in the Sexual Offences Act 1956[5] requiring corroboration 'in some material particular by evidence implicating the accused', and its specific nature may have an important bearing on the kind of corroboration required by English law when the evidence is circumstantial.

In order to be corroborative, evidence must be admissible on the relevant count,[6] and admissible against the relevant person.[7] Examples of what does, and does not, amount to corroboration are scattered throughout the preceding paragraphs but, after some general observations, something

---

19 Paras 4.36 and 4.53. See ch XX, section 2, below for an account of the report and evidence of identification generally.
20 The House of Lords has refused to erect patients in a secure mental hospital into such a category, *R v Spencer* [1987] AC 128, [1986] 2 All ER 928.
21 In *Nembhard v R* [1982] 1 All ER 183, 74 Cr App Rep 144, extension to dying declaration cases was denied.
22 See *R v Simmons* [1987] Crim LR 630. The same view has been expressed in the High Court of Australia, see *Bromley v R* (1986) 67 ALR 12 especially Brennan J.
1 *DPP v Hester* [1973] AC 296 at 325, [1972] 3 All ER 1056 at 1073.
2 At p 236.
3 [1916] 2 KB 658 at 667.
4 *Thomas v Jones* [1921] 1 KB 22.
5 Ss 2, 3, 4, 22 and 23.
6 *R v Hickmet* (1988) 33 ACR 75.
7 *R v Jolen, R v Katz* (1989) Times, 5 October.

further will be said on the subject under the headings of the conduct or condition of the witness whose testimony requires corroboration, the conduct of the party against whom corroboration is required, and the functions of judge and jury.

A. GENERAL OBSERVATIONS

Three matters calling for general comment are the requirement that corroboration come from an independent source, the specific nature of the requirements for corroboration to which reference was made above, and some remarks of Lord Morris of Borth-y-Gest and Hailsham of St Marylebone stressing the point that the essence of corroboration is that one creditworthy witness confirm what another creditworthy witness has said.

1. EVIDENCE FROM AN INDEPENDENT SOURCE

It was stressed in *Baskerville*, and is clearly a matter of common sense that if the testimony of a witness requires confirmation it is desirable that it be provided by an independent source. It is clearly less convincing if one person says the same thing twice, than it is if two independent persons both say the same thing, or if it is confirmed by a fact. If a woman is raped, and testifies that X was her assailant and that he ran off through a muddy field, it adds little to the credibility of either the woman or her story that she told it to a number of different people. It adds greatly to her credibility if a close acquaintance of X saw him running out of the very field at about the right time, or if shoe prints corresponding exactly in terms of need for repair, size and all other characteristics are found in the field. Yet this seemingly simple requirement conceals considerable difficulty as demonstrated in two recent English cases.

In *R v Willoughby*[8] the only contested issue was whether the accused was the man who had committed an indecent assault upon a child. Soon after the crime the child described her assailant as having a spot, or spots, upon his face. She subsequently identified him upon an identification parade, and finally identified him in court as her assailant. Certainly at the time of the trial he had a spot upon his face.[9] The trial judge directed the jury that they could find corroboration in the correspondence of the witness's evidence of her assailant's appearance[10] with the real evidence of the spot upon the accused's face. The Court of Appeal however held this not to be sufficiently independent:[11]

the evidence constituted by the physical appearance of the appellant, however singular that may have been and however closely it may have corresponded to the description given by the victim, cannot amount without more to corroboration of

8 (1988) 88 Cr App Rep 91.
9 Though he alleged that he had not had such a spot at the time of the offence, and it is not made clear whether or not he had such a spot when attending the identification parade.
10 It seems that the judge was referring to her evidence of her immediate description of her assailant. Such evidence is customarily admitted though it arguably amounts to no more than evidence of a prior statement consistent with her testimony in court, and ought, as such, not to be received, see further below p 281.
11 At 94.

her evidence. The child described her assailant and gave evidence that he had a certain physical feature. She also identified the appellant as her assailant at an identity parade. The independent evidence is not that the assailant had that feature, but (at best) that the appellant has the same feature. There is nothing therefore in the latter evidence which tends to establish the reliability of the child's testimony that her assailant had that feature.

The argument seems to be that there is nothing to connect the accused, who happens to be a man with spots, with the crime, except the testimony of the victim both that her assailant had spots, and that the accused was her assailant. Proof, however independent, of the presence of the spots on the accused's face cannot connect him with the commission of the crime until the victim's testimony in one or other of the respects set out above is accepted, but it is her testimony that requires corroboration, and it cannot corroborate itself because of the independence requirement.

This problem reappeared in the subsequent decision of the Court of Appeal in *R v McInnes*,[12] also a case involving a sexual assault on a child. In this case the victim was assaulted in a car, and was able to give a vivid description not only of her assailant but of his car.[13] She subsequently identified the accused and his car on a 'video identity parade',[14] and gave unsworn testimony at the trial that the accused was her assailant. The *Willoughby* point was raised, but was met by the Court of Appeal by reference to the esoteric circumstantial knowledge of the victim which was regarded as independent of her testimony:[15]

> the circumstantial evidence consisted of the girl's knowledge and, in particular, her knowledge of the inside of the appellant's car. She could not possibly have had this knowledge unless her evidence was truthful. Putting it another way, the evidence which required to be corroborated was her identification of the defendant on the video identification parade. Her knowledge of the inside of the accused's car was a fact, independent of her evidence, which confirmed or supported her identification.

The Court felt that *Willoughby* could be distinguished because there was nothing there to confirm the girl's evidence that her assailant had a spot. This is hard to follow since there was equally nothing here to confirm that the assault took place in this car, independent of the victim's assertion to that effect. It may be true that the victim's evidence of circumstantial detail was more convincing in *McInnes*, it is far less clear that it was any more independently confirmed.[16] In both cases the victim's evidence of the identity of her assailant was supported by the consistency of detail. It remained the case however that the evidence of the identity of the assailant, and of the detail relating to the assailant equally emanated from the witness's statements. Either the description of detail should be regarded as independent of the act of identification, irrespective of the fact that both emanate from the same witness, or the independence requirement should be abandoned as an over-technical refinement.

12 (1989) 90 Cr App rep 99.
13 Including some quite unique features, among them the presence in it of a particular brand of sweet paper.
14 In this case another child was also able to identify the accused and his car.
15 At 104.
16 Apart from evidence of the other child which is here ignored, as it was, for this purpose, by the Court of Appeal.

2. THE SPECIFIC NATURE OF THE CORROBORATION REQUIREMENT[17]

Circumstantial evidence owes its strength to its cumulative effect: 'it is . . . like the case of a rope comprised of several cords. One strand of the cord might be insufficient to sustain the weight, but three stranded together might be quite of sufficient strength'.[18] The requirement that corroborative evidence must implicate the person against whom it is directed necessitates some elucidation of the doctrine in this context. If the evidence tendered as corroborative does not, taken piece by piece, implicate the accused in a material particular it should then be considered as a whole. If there is sufficient connection between the individual pieces of evidence for them to hang together circumstantially then they may together suffice, but such connection is crucial. This seems to be the best explanation of remarks of Atkin LJ in the old bastardy case of *Thomas v Jones*.[19]

> [I]t appears to me impossible, when dealing with the question of corroboration, that the accumulation of pieces of evidence, each of which by itself is not admissible as corroborative evidence, can amount in the whole to corroboration. *Ex nihilo nihil fit.* That appears to me to be different from circumstantial evidence, where evidence of independent facts, each in itself, insufficient to prove the main fact, may yet, either by their cumulative weight, or still more by their connection one with the other as links in a chain, prove the principal fact to be established.

In *R v Hills*[20] the Lord Chief Justice illustrated the application of this view to a hypothetical case of rape in which there was independent medical evidence of recent sexual intercourse; independent evidence of the accused's being alone with the victim during the relevant period; and independent evidence of the victim's torn clothing and injuries. The first of these does not implicate the accused or show absence of consent; the second does not show that intercourse took place or the absence of consent; and the third does not implicate the accused or show that intercourse took place. Together they show both of the required elements, that intercourse took place and that it took place without the victim's consent; and they implicate the accused in that act of intercourse. It is irrelevant that no one item shows all of these features, nor that they emanate from different sources.[21] It is however necessary that they emanate from sources independent of the witness required to be corroborated, and it was because this had not been made sufficiently clear that the appeal was allowed in *Hills*.

It seems that this way of illustrating the point is quite consistent with the view expressed by the Privy Council in *James v R*:[22]

---

17 See Thorp 'Cumulative Corroboration' [1984] Crim LR 142.
18 Pollock CB in *R v Exall* (1866) 4 F & F 922 at 929, cited more fully at p 21 n 12 above.
19 [1921] 1 KB 22 at 48.
20 (1987) 86 Cr App Rep 26 at 31. See also *R v McInnes* [1989] Crim LR 889.
21 The same view is taken in Australia, see *R v Galluzo* (1986) 23 ACR 211 at 216 'Taken individually they are . . . little more than straws in the wind. But taken together . . . they do present a pattern in which some degree of corroboration could be found'. See also *R v Lindsay* (1977) 18 SASR 103; *R v Freeman* [1980] VR 1; *R v Berrill* [1982] Qd R 508.
22 (1970) 55 Cr App Rep 299 at 302.

Where the charge is of rape, the corroborative evidence must confirm in some material particular that intercourse has taken place and that it has taken place without the woman's consent and also that the accused was the man who committed the crime.

Each individual element must, in England, be considered separately.[23] In Canada however rape[24] provided the catalyst for more wholesale jettisoning of the *Baskerville* requirements in the important case of *Vetrovec v R*.[25] Although reliance was placed upon dicta in cases decided by the House of Lords[26] to justify this decision further remarks explicitly endorsing the principles of *Baskerville* in those very decisions seem to have been ignored.[27] While there is much to be said for a general reappraisal of the position, it seems that in England if it is to come at all, it is now most likely to come from the legislature.[28]

3. CORROBORATION AND CREDITWORTHINESS

Some remarks of Lord Morris in *Director of Public Prosecutions v Hester*:[1]

The purpose of corroboration is not to give validity or credence to evidence which is deficient or suspect or incredible but only to confirm and support that which as evidence is sufficient and satisfactory and credible: and corroborative evidence will only fill its role if it is completely credible.

and of Lord Hailsham LC in *Director of Public Prosecutions v Kilbourne*:[2]

Corroboration is only required or afforded if the witness requiring corroboration or giving it is otherwise credible. If his evidence is not credible, a witness's testimony should be rejected and the accused acquitted even if there could be found evidence capable of being corroboration in other testimony. Corroboration can only be afforded to or by a witness who is otherwise to be believed. If a witness's testimony falls of its own inanition the question of its needing, or being capable of giving corroboration does not arise.

gave rise to the impression in some quarters that there was a two-stage test, first by the judge to determine whether evidence were capable of being creditworthy, and, only if it were, then by the jury to determine whether or not to believe it. Such a view then naturally gave rise to the question of whether the judge should at his stage take into account only the intrinsic quality of the evidence, rather as in determining whether or not there is a

23 *R v West* (1984) 79 Cr App Rep 45; *R v Willoughby* (1988) Cr App Rep 91.
24 *Warkentin v R* [1977] 2 SCR 355.
25 (1982) 136 DLR (3d) 89.
26 Especially in *DPP v Hester* [1973] AC 296, [1972] 3 All ER 1056 and *DPP v Kilbourne* [1973] AC 729, [1973] 1 All ER 440.
27 See in *Hester* by Lord Morris at 315, 1065; by Lord Pearson at 322, 1070; by Lord Diplock at 325, 1073; and in *Kilbourne* by Lord Hailsham at 746, 448; and by Lord Reid at 750, 459.
28 In *R v Spencer* [1987] AC 128, [1986] 2 All ER 928 the House of Lords notably failed to include the established categories of accomplices and victims of sexual cases from its relaxation of strict requirements, explicitly endorsing *R v Beck* [1982] 1 All ER 807, [1982] 1 WLR 461 without any reservation, and in *Beck* there is ringing reaffirmation of *Baskerville*.
1 At 315, 1065.
2 At 746, 452.

case to answer,[3] or whether he could take into account any personal deficiencies of the witness. The matter has subsequently been elucidated by the Privy Council in *A-G of Hong Kong v Wong Muk-ping*,[4] by drawing attention to the remarks of Lord Hailsham immediately following the passage quoted above in which he alluded to such estimation being made by the jury at the end of the case.[5]

The true position appears to be as follows. In a very few cases, after taking all the circumstances into account, the evidence of some witnesses will be wholly incredible, for example if the witness himself admits it to be false under cross-examination. In such a case the jury should be directed to acquit if the evidence is necessary for the prosecution to make out its case, or to disregard it entirely and to rely exclusively upon the rest of the evidence in the case, if that is by itself capable of sustaining the case for the prosecution. If, as will normally be the case, the evidence is capable of belief on some view or another, then the normal corroboration warning should be given if it is appropriate, and it will be for the jury to decide whether or not to believe it, taking all the circumstances, including any corroboration warnings and direction as to what evidence is, or is not, capable of amounting to corroboration, into account. Only if at the end of the day it does believe it, or finds that there is sufficient evidence to convict without reliance upon it, should it convict.

B. CONDUCT OR CONDITION OF THE PERSON WHOSE TESTIMONY REQUIRES CORROBORATION

'In order that evidence may amount to corroboration it must be extraneous to the witness who is to be corroborated.' This remark was made by Lord Hewart CJ in *R v Whitehead*[6] where the accused was charged with unlawful intercourse with a girl under sixteen. It was suggested that her testimony might have been corroborated by the fact that she spoke to her mother about her condition some time after the alleged intercourse, whereupon her mother laid an information against the accused. Lord Hewart demonstrated the absurdity of this contention when he said: 'the girl cannot corroborate herself, otherwise it is only necessary for her to repeat her story some twenty-five times in order to get twenty-five corroborations of it.' Another leading case which turned in part on the impossibility of self-corroboration is *R v Christie*.[7] The accused was charged with indecently assaulting a little boy who gave unsworn evidence. The boy's mother and a policeman testified to the terms in which the boy had described the assault shortly after it occurred when he also identified the accused; but the House of Lords held that these witnesses did not corroborate the boy's testimony and the conviction was quashed because the trial judge had suggested that the evidence of the mother and the policeman did have this effect.

We shall see in the next chapter that complaints by the victim of a sexual offence are admissible, provided certain conditions are fulfilled but, even

---

3 See above p 173.
4 [1987] AC 501, [1987] 2 All ER 488.
5 To the extent that Lord Morris's remarks diverged from this view they were to be disregarded. See also *R v McCormick* [1984] NI 50.
6 [1929] 1 KB 99 at 102.
7 [1914] AC 545.

when they may be proved, either by the complainant or by the person to whom they were made, they do not corroborate the complainant's testimony.[8] Even where such a complaint becomes admissible in evidence as proof of the facts which it relates under the provisions of the Civil Evidence Act 1968 or of the Criminal Justice Act 1988 its use to corroborate the complainant's testimony is explicitly prohibited.[9]

Even if the statement is rendered admissible by virtue of a common law rule of evidence such as that relating to cross-examination on a diary or address book used to refresh memory as discussed in the next chapter, it does not corroborate the evidence of the maker.[10]

The distressed condition of the complainant on a sexual charge can amount to corroboration only in exceptional circumstances, as when a bystander swears that the accused approached a child and that, shortly afterwards, he saw the child in a distressed condition.[11] If proved by the person to whom a complaint was made or by someone present on the occasion of the complaint, the distressed condition adds little, if anything, to the complainant's testimony and ought not to be left to the jury as corroboration.[12] It should not be forgotten that the circumstances should be such as to minimise the possibility of fabrication, and to maximise the implication of the accused.[13] The question whether the existence of physical injuries can amount to corroboration of the complainant's testimony concerning them implicating the person against whom the evidence is given is a question of fact varying from case to case.[14] It may become especially complicated when different rapes committed by different defendants, and accompanied by different amounts of force affording different reasons for distress, are tried together.[15]

C. CONDUCT OF THE PARTY AGAINST WHOM CORROBORATION IS REQUIRED

Sometimes the conduct of the defendant or accused will be held to constitute corroboration of the evidence against him, and sometimes it will not have this effect. The matter is best considered under the heads of the admission of

8 *R v Evans* (1924) 18 Cr App Rep 123; *R v Coulthread* (1933) 24 Cr App Rep 44; *R v Coyle* [1926] NI 208. The conversation between the girl and her mother in *R v Whitehead* would have been inadmissible as a complaint because it took place some months after the event of which complaint was made. The admissibility of the boy's statements as complaints was not argued in *R v Christie*. See also *Thomas v R* [1952] 4 DLR 306; *Eade v R* (1924) 34 CLR 154.

9 Civil Evidence Act 1968, s 6(4); Criminal Justice Act 1988, Sch 2, para 2. These provisions seem superogatory.

10 *Senat v Senat (K, H and B intervening)* [1965] P 172, [1965] 2 All ER 505.

11 *R v Redpath* (1962) 46 Cr App Rep 319; *R v Wilson* (1973) 58 Cr App Rep 304; *Forgie v Police* [1969] NZLR 101; *R v Murphy* (1976) 9 NR 329.

12 *R v Knight* [1966] 1 All ER 647, [1966] 1 WLR 230; *R v Richards* [1965] Qd R 354; *R v Pitman* (1985) 38 SASR 566.

13 *R v Moana* [1979] 1 NZLR 181; *R v Freeman* [1980] VR 1. Some recent English and Canadian decisions seem to show a laxer approach, see *R v Chauhan* (1981) 73 Cr App Rep 232; *R v Dowley* [1983] Crim LR 168; *Gracey v HM Advocate* 1987 SCCR 260; *The People v Mulvey* [1987] IR 502; *Murphy and Butt v R* [1977] 2 SCR 603.

14 *Fromhold v Fromhold* (1952) 1 TLR 1522; *R v Aubichon* (1964) 48 WWR 529; *R v Etherington* (1982) 32 SASR 230.

15 *R v Franklin* [1989] Crim LR 499.

the party against whom corroboration is required, lies told by him, his failure to give evidence, his silence when charged out of court, his failure to provide a sample of real evidence and his conduct on an occasion previous to that with which the trial is concerned.

1. ADMISSION OF DEFENDANT OR ACCUSED

A person's statement in court may well be held to corroborate the case against him. In *R v Dossi*[16] for instance, it was held that the accused's admission in evidence that he had platonically fondled the child who gave sworn testimony to the effect that he had indecently assaulted her could be treated as some corroboration of her statement. As Atkin LJ said: 'The question of corroboration often assumes an entirely different aspect after the accused person has gone into the witness box and has been cross-examined.'[17] Whether anything that emerges in the course of the evidence of the defendant or accused does corroborate his opponent's witnesses in a material particular is of course a question of fact dependent on the circumstances of the particular case. Much may depend upon the issues which remain contested, and the extent of any admission.[18]

2. LIES OF DEFENDANT OR ACCUSED[19]

As a matter of commonsense, to tell a lie may indicate consciousness of guilt and so corroborate suspect testimony. In *Tumahole Bereng v R*[20] Lord MacDermott said that a prisoner does not corroborate an accomplice merely by giving evidence which is not accepted and must therefore be regarded as false:

> Corroboration may well be found in the evidence of an accused person, but that is a different matter, for there confirmation comes, if at all, from what is said, and not from the falsity of what is said.

There is nothing in the context which suggests that this dictum is applicable only to the testimony of an accomplice, and there can be no doubt that it is generally true of all cases in which corroboration must be sought. To quote from a South Australian judgment in affiliation proceedings:

> The court cannot, as is sometimes suggested, prefer the evidence of the mother to that of the defendant and then use its disbelief of his evidence as the basis of an inference to be used in corroboration of the mother's testimony.[1]

This is the type of error into which the trial judge seems to have fallen in *R v*

16 (1918) 13 Cr App Rep 158. *Goguen and Goguen v Bourgeois and Bourgeois* (1957) 6 DLR (2d) 19.
17 At 162.
18 See Munday 'Corroboration and the Partial Admission' [1955] Crim LR 190, pointing out that in *R v Tragen* [1956] Crim LR 332 Lord Goddard CJ seems to have taken a different view of facts superficially similar to those in *Dossi*.
19 See J D Heydon 'Can Lies Corroborate?' (1973) 89 LQR 552.
20 [1949] AC 253 at 280.
1 Napier J in *Pitman v Byrne* [1926] SASR 207 at 211.

Chapman and *R v Baldwin*,[2] a case in which the judgment of the Court of Appeal could be construed as meaning that the accused's lies in court can never corroborate evidence given against him. This view has been rejected both in the Commonwealth,[3] and in England, where it has been said that:

> To be capable of amounting to corroboration the lie told out of court must first of all be deliberate. Secondly, it must relate to a material issue. Thirdly the motive for the lie must be a realisation of guilt and a fear of the truth. The jury should in appropriate cases be reminded that people sometimes lie, for example, in an attempt to bolster up a just cause, or out of shame or out of a wish to conceal disgraceful behaviour from their family. Fourthly the statement must be clearly shown to be a lie by evidence other than that of the accomplice who is to be corroborated, that is to say by admission or by evidence from an independent witness.[4]

It was regarded as sensible to apply exactly the same principles to lies told in court, and provided that the conditions can be satisfied there seems no reason to suppose that they cannot also be applied to the adoption of lies told by others.[5] Corroboration is provided by a lie only in respect of that part of the evidence to be corroborated which is contradicted by the lie.[6] Although it will sometimes be incumbent upon the judge to explain to the jury that there may be some other explanation for the lie than the truth of the evidence to be corroborated,[7] this is probably not an invariable requirement.[8] Nor, where the evidence is directly relevant to an issue, as well as being indirectly relevant as a lie, is it necessary to rehearse all of the matters considered in *Lucas*.[9] These principles are not limited to criminal cases, but will also apply to other situations in which corroboration is required such as affiliation proceedings.[10]

3. FAILURE TO GIVE EVIDENCE

In *R v Jackson*[11] Lord Goddard CJ, speaking for the Court of Criminal Appeal, said:

> One cannot say that the fact that the prisoner had not gone into the witness box is of itself corroboration of accomplices' evidence. It is a matter which the jury very properly could, and very probably would, take into account, but it should be clearly understood that the direction [that failure to testify can amount to corroboration] is wrong in law.

The distinction between a matter which the jury can take into account and

---

2 [1973] QB 774, [1973] 2 All ER 624.
3 *R v Collings* [1976] 2 NZLR 104, *R v Perera* [1982] VR 901.
4 *R v Lucas* [1981] QB 720, [1981] 2 All ER 1008, rejecting the construction of *Chapman* mentioned above.
5 See *R v Perera*, above.
6 *R v West* (1984) 79 Cr App Rep 45; *R v Barber* (1988) Times, 29 July.
7 See *R v Dowley* [1983] Crim LR 168 (where there was no other cooroboration).
8 Cp *R v Penman* (1985) 82 Cr App Rep 44 although no strict question of corroboration was there involved.
9 *R v Ensor* (1989) 89 Cr App Rep 139.
10 *Corfield v Hodgson* [1966] 2 All ER 205, [1966] 1 WLR 590. For a very full discussion see *Popovic v Derks* [1961] VLR 413.
11 [1953] 1 All ER 872, [1953] 1 WLR 591.

one which can amount to corroboration is perhaps, in this context, not as clear as it might be, and the Criminal Law Revision Committee recommended that the accused's failure to give evidence should, if the fact were such that an inference of guilt might properly be drawn therefrom, be treated as capable of amounting to corroboration of any evidence given by the prosecution;[12] but consideration of the merits of this proposal is best deferred until the proposal that such inferences as appear proper may be drawn from the accused's failure to give evidence are discussed in ch X.

The rule that a party's failure to testify does not constitute corroboration of the evidence against him applies to affiliation proceedings. Thus in *Cracknell v Smith*[13] the applicant admitted to intercourse with the respondent's brother as well as the respondent on various occasions, but alleged that she had had intercourse only with the respondent during the month in which her child was conceived. The applicant's mother gave evidence of meetings between her daughter and the respondent, but the Divisional Court held that mere evidence of opportunity could not amount to corroboration. The court came to a similar conclusion with regard to the fact that the respondent's brother gave what the magistrates considered to be false evidence concerning the periods at which he had had intercourse with the respondent, there being no evidence that he had been incited to do so by the respondent. The latter did not give evidence and, when allowing his appeal on the ground that this too did not corroborate the applicant's evidence, Lord Parker CJ said:

> If there is evidence and some corroborative evidence, it may be that the Justices are entitled to take into consideration the fact that he gave no evidence in considering the weight to be attached to the corroboration.

The distinction between corroboration and a fact which, though not itself corroboration, adds weight to corroborative evidence is another one which is not altogether easy to grasp. In affiliation proceedings the respondent is a compellable witness for the applicant, but there would normally be no point in her calling him because a party cannot cross-examine his own witness. If the law were to be changed so as to allow the respondent's failure to give evidence to be capable of amounting to corroboration, it would in effect be placed on a par with that of some Commonwealth jurisdictions according to which corroboration is required in affiliation proceedings only if the respondent gives evidence.

It is scarcely necessary to add that failure to cross-examine is never in itself corroboration of the witness's evidence.[14]

4. SILENCE WHEN CHARGED

There is a broad principle of common sense which was stated by Cave J in the course of his judgment in *R v Mitchell*:[15]

12 11th Report, para 111. The same reasoning would apply a fortiori to failure to call a spouse.
13 [1960] 3 All ER 569, [1960] 1 WLR 1239.
14 *Dingwall v J Wharton (Shipping) Ltd* [1961] 2 Lloyd's Rep 213 at 219.
15 (1892) 17 Cox CC 503.

Undoubtedly, when persons are speaking on even terms, and a charge is made, and the person charged says nothing, and expresses no indignation, and does nothing to repel the charge, that is some evidence to show that he admits the charge to be true.

This principle was acted on in *R v Cramp*[16] in which the accused's failure to answer the observation of the girl's father about some pills was held to be capable of corroborating her evidence that the accused had attempted to procure her miscarriage. But what if the persons in question are not speaking on even terms?

In *R v Tate*[17] it was held that the accused's silence when arrested did not corroborate the evidence of an accomplice, and *R v Cramp* was distinguished on the ground that the statement might reasonably have been expected to call for a reply from an innocent person. In *R v Feigenbaum*,[18] however, the accused's failure to reply to a police officer who told him he was about to be arrested and charged as an accessory on account of statements made by the youthful principals was held to have been rightly treated as corroborative of their evidence; but this decision of the Court of Criminal Appeal was not followed in *R v Whitehead*[19] where the same court held that the appellant's statement that he did not wish to say anything when served with a summons charging him with unlawful intercourse with a girl under 16 did not corroborate her testimony. When delivering the judgment of the Court of Criminal Appeal in *R v Keeling*,[20] Hallett J expressed a preference for *R v Whitehead* and the cases applying that decision. A similar preference was expressed by the Judicial Committee of the Privy Council in *Hall v R*,[1] when, in answer to a suggestion that *R v Feigenbaum* was distinguishable from the other cases because, in them, the accused had been expressly told that he need say nothing, Lord Diplock said 'the caution merely serves to remind the accused of a right which he already possesses at common law'. But, when he is being questioned in the presence of his solicitor by a police officer, the parties may be on equal terms.[2] Subject to this possibility it may be assumed with a good deal of confidence that silence when charged by a police officer can never amount to corroboration of evidence against someone charged with a crime.

One of the most controversial of the proposals of the 11th Report of the Criminal Law Revision Committee was that the silence of the accused when questioned by the police could in some circumstances amount to corroboration of the evidence against him.[3] This recommendation was not adopted in the Police and Criminal Evidence Act 1984, and the Code of Practice on

16 (1880) 14 Cox CC 390. See also *Bessela v Stern* (1877) 2 CPD 265, and contrast the position where the charge is made by letter when it would often, though not invariably, be wrong to draw an adverse inference from failure to reply (*Wiedmann v Walpole* [1891] 2 QB 534).
17 [1908] 2 KB 680.
18 [1919] 1 KB 431.
19 [1929] 1 KB 99, followed in *R v Charavanmuttu* (1930) 22 Cr App Rep 1 and *R v Naylor* [1933] 1 KB 685. See also *R v Littleboy* [1934] 2 KB 408 and *People (A-G) v Quinn* [1955] IR 57.
20 [1942] 1 All ER 507.
 1 [1971] 1 All ER 322. Cf *Parkes v R* [1976] 3 All ER 380, [1976] 1 WLR 1251 (accused's reaction to question by deceased's mother about stabbing her daughter admissible). No question of corroboration was involved in these cases.
 2 *R v Chandler* [1976] 3 All ER 105, [1976] 1 WLR 585. No question of corroboration was involved.
 3 Cmnd 4991 paras 40–42.

questioning retains the traditional caution. The one exception in the Act to this general attitude is the provision in s 62(10) that appropriate inferences may be drawn from refusal without cause to consent to the taking of an 'intimate sample,'[4] and that such a refusal may amount to corroboration of other evidence against the accused in the relevant particular.[5]

5. FAILURE TO PROVIDE A SAMPLE OF REAL EVIDENCE

Since no one is obliged to provide a sample of real evidence any more than to answer questions it might be thought that refusal to do so should no more be regarded as corroborative of other evidence. This seems not to be the case. It was held in *R v Smith*[6] that the accused's arbitrary refusal to provide a sample of his hair, after being told that the hair to which it was to be matched had been found at the scene of a robbery, could corroborate the testimony of a witness treated as an accomplice. In affiliation proceedings similar reasoning was applied in *McVeigh v Beattie*[7] to the refusal by a putative father to take a blood test at the direction of the court. It should perhaps be noted that in both of these cases the person who refused to provide the sample was at the time in receipt of legal advice. The matter has also been addressed in statutory provision. Section 62(10) of the Police and Criminal Evidence Act 1984 expressly permits inferences drawn from failure to provide an intimate[8] sample to be used to corroborate relevant evidence. In the case of fingerprints and non-intimate samples no such provision is made, but there is power to require the provision of such evidence in the absence of consent, upon satisfaction of the relevant conditions.[9]

If, as seems to be the case, a different approach is being taken to refusal to provide a sample of real evidence from that relating to refusal to speak some explanation must be advanced. In *Smith* the Court took refuge in common sense and denial of any analogy to refusal to speak. In *McVeigh v Beattie* it was said that anything else would prevent the provisions of the Family Law Reform Act 1969[10] from being effective. The Court there also pointed out that the sample of hair refused in *Smith* would not, under the provisions of the Police and Criminal Evidence Act 1984 have been regarded as intimate, and so would have fallen outside the class of refusal explicitly made corroborative. It is submitted that the best explanation is that now that real evidence may be so weighty its production will be sought by all acceptable means. In cases where it is possible, without shocking the conscience, to secure the samples without consent, that is the preferable course;[11] but where, as in the cases of a bodily invasion, it is thought not to be, then a provision permitting inferences to be drawn and to corroborate other evidence is the best alternative. Its availability may have the effect of securing such production once those required to produce such samples realise that they have little or nothing to gain by refusal.

4 As defined in s 65.
5 For further discussion of the right to silence, see below pp 384 and 626.
6 (1985) 81 Cr App Rep 286.
7 [1988] 2 All ER 500.
8 As defined in s 65. It is slightly differently defined in relation to Northern Ireland by the Criminal Justice Act 1988, Sch 14, para 6.
9 Police and Criminal Evidence Act 1984, ss 61 (fingerprints) and 63 (non-intimate samples).
10 As amended.
11 As in the case of fingerprints and non-intimate samples.

6. CONDUCT ON OTHER OCCASIONS

We shall see in ch IX that facts tending to show that someone committed a crime or civil wrong, or conducted himself improperly on other[12] occasions, may not be proved in order to establish his commission of the crime or civil wrong into which the court is inquiring, if they are relevant only as showing a disposition to commit crimes or civil wrongs generally, or the kind of crime or civil wrong with which the court is concerned. This will often exclude the previous conduct of the party against whom corroboration is required, but such conduct is admissible if of particular relevance to a matter in issue. In two instances of this nature, such conduct may clearly corroborate the evidence against the accused. In the first place it may show a propensity which is more specific than that of committing a certain crime because it involves doing so with a particular person or in a particular way, and secondly it may corroborate a witness's story about statements made by the defendant or accused.

(i) Previous conduct to show specific propensity

An example of corroboration by previous conduct showing a propensity to commit a crime with a particular person is provided by *R v Hartley*.[13] The accused was convicted of buggery with H on a named day. H gave evidence of the commission of the offence on the day in question, and also deposed to the fact that the accused had done the same thing to him on a previous occasion. There was no corroboration of H's evidence so far as the offence mentioned in the indictment was concerned, but his evidence with regard to the previous occasion was corroborated by another witness who saw the accused take H to his office, lock the door and draw the blinds. It was held that H's evidence with regard to the previous occasion was admissible because, where a person alleges that an offence such as that with which the court was concerned has been committed against him, he is entitled to show that the offence was indulged in habitually. It was also held that the corroboration of H's testimony concerning the former crime constituted corroboration of his evidence with regard to the crime charged, and in this respect the case may be compared with those in which a man's conduct before the intercourse alleged has been held to corroborate the testimony of the claimant in proceedings for affiliation.[14]

An example of corroborative evidence supplied by the accused's modus operandi is provided by *D P P v Boardman*.[15] The head of a language school was convicted of attempted buggery with S and incitement of H to commit buggery with him, S and H being his pupils. The House of Lords held that the trial judge had rightly treated the case as one of mutual corroboration. There were, it was said, striking similarities. Each boy was awakened in the dormitory and addressed in a low voice, in each case the alleged conduct occurred in the accused's sitting-room and in each instance he sought to play

12 It may be subsequent conduct, see *Masolini v Siebel* [1979] 1 WAR 115 (continued association after knowledge of pregnancy to corroborate on issue of paternity).
13 [1941] 1 KB 5; *R v Deen* [1964] Qd R 569.
14 *Cole v Manning* (1877) 2 QBD 611; cf *Wilcox v Gotfrey* (1872) 26 LT 481.
15 [1975] AC 421, [1974] 3 All ER 887. See also *D P P v Kilbourne* (1973) AC 729, [1973] 1 All ER 440, and see p 364 above.

the passive role. Factually the case was somewhat borderline, but the principle, derived from *R v Sims*[16] is clear enough:

> The probative force of all the acts together is much greater than one alone; for, whereas the jury might think one man might be telling an untruth, three or four are hardly likely to tell the same untruth unless they were conspiring together.

Striking similarities in the accused's manner of committing the offence charged and other offences (whether or not they are charged in the same indictment) certainly implicate him in a material particular within the definition of corroborative evidence laid down in *R v Baskerville*.[17] As Lord Cross said in *D P P v Kilbourne*:

> Once the 'similar fact' evidence is admitted—and it was common ground that it was properly admitted in this case—then of necessity it 'corroborates'—i e strengthens or supports—the evidence given by the boy an alleged offence against whom is the subject of the count under consideration.[18]

(ii) Previous conduct to corroborate statement to witness

Evidence which tends to show that the accused incited a course of conduct resulting in the commission of the crime charged certainly implicates him in a material particular. Accordingly anything which confirms a witness's story with regard to such incitement will be held to constitute corroboration when this is required, and it sometimes happens that the alleged incitement takes the form of a reference to previous misconduct. In *R v Mitchell*,[19] for instance, a clergyman was charged with indecently assaulting a girl named Sheila, who gave sworn evidence against him. In addition to deposing to the assault upon her, Sheila said that he told her about his behaviour with a girl named Judy and it was held that this girl's testimony with regard to the accused's conduct corroborated the evidence of Sheila who could hardly have heard of Judy from any other source as the two girls lived in different parts of the country.

D. FUNCTIONS OF JUDGE AND JURY

The technicality and rigidity of this branch of the law of evidence has been authoritatively, and repeatedly, deplored by the House of Lords.[20] It has been stressed that it is not appropriate or intelligible to treat a jury to a 'general disquisition on the law of corroboration, couched in lawyers' language.'[1] It has nevertheless been recognised that, given the rules, and given the unfamiliarity of the dangers which justify the rules, some direction is necessary. It is however recommended that it be cast in non-technical

16 [1946] KB 531 at 540.
17 [1916] 2 KB 658. See the discussion of this point in an article by Fallon and Bursell in [1978] Crim LR 188.
18 [1973] AC 729 at 760, [1973] 1 All ER 440 at 464.
19 (1952) 36 Cr App Rep 79.
20 *D P P v Hester* [1973] AC 296, [1972] 3 All ER 1056; *D P P v Kilbourne* [1973] AC 729, [1973] 1 All ER 440; *D P P v Boardman* [1975] AC 421, [1974] 3 All ER 887; and *R v Spencer* [1987] AC 128, [1986] 2 All ER 928 concur in their stigmatisation. See also *Vetrovec v R* (1982) 136 DLR (3d) 89.
1 Per Lord Diplock in *Hester* at 328, 1076.

language, that it eschew rigid formulae[2] and that it be tailored to suit the particular circumstances of the case.[3] It may often be desirable for the judge to discuss his intended direction with counsel in the absence of the jury.[4]

Some things have to be done. In a case where corroboration is required as a matter of law, the judge must direct an acquittal if there is none. If the case is one in which corroboration is required as a matter of practice, and there is no corroboration, the judge may often have to warn the jury of this fact, in addition to warning them of the danger of acting on uncorroborated evidence. If the dangers which justify the practice of giving a warning are less prominent in the circumstances of a particular case, this may be pointed out,[5] though the judge must be careful not to go too far in devaluing the warning.[6]

Although there is no model direction relating the evidence in a case to the warning which has been given, some general points emerge by which judges should be guided. It is usually necessary to warn the jury if there is no evidence at all capable of amounting to corroboration, although this is not an absolute rule, even in cases where a corroboration warning is mandatory.[7] If there is no such evidence, it is clearly pointless, and confusing, to define or describe it any further.[8] On the other hand, if in the opinion of the judge there is evidence capable of amounting to corroboration, then, as stated above, the jury should, at least in England, be told in general terms that it is material only from a source independent of the witness, and implicating the accused in a material particular, which is capable of amounting to corroboration of the witness's testimony.[9] This should, at least in general terms, be related to the evidence in the case.[10] It is now[11] in England[12] the judge's duty to point out to the jury which particular items of evidence are capable of amounting to corroboration, if necessary after considering relevant submissions from counsel in the absence of the jury.[13] It is also prudent for him to do so, since a comprehensive review of such material may be regarded as curing a direction technically defective for some other reason.[14] A conviction may be quashed if the judge directs the jury that items of evidence are corroborative when they lack that quality.[15] On the other

2 Though in *R v Stewart* (1986) 83 Cr App Rep 327 it was emphasised that it must convey to the jury the danger of convicting an innocent person.
3 Lord Hailsham in *Kilbourne* at 741, 447, repeating the substance of the remark of Lord Diplock quoted above.
4 *R v Nagy* (1989) Times, 31 October.
5 *R v Zielinski* [1950] 2 All ER 1114n, 34 Cr App Rep 193 (advanced age of victim of sexual offence); *R v Price* [1969] 1 QB 541, [1968] 2 All ER 282; *R v Turner* [1980] Crim LR 305 (absence of opportunity for accomplices to collaborate in story).
6 *R v Timmins* [1981] Crim LR 774.
7 *R v Allen, R v Evans* [1965] 2 QB 295 at 302, [1964] 3 All ER 401 at 404. Still less necessary where the corroboration warning is not itself mandatory, *R v Loveridge* (1983) 76 Cr App Rep 125.
8 *R v Fisher* [1965] 1 All ER 677, [1965] 1 WLR 464; *Hester*, above at 328, 1076.
9 *R v Clynes* (1960) 44 Cr App Rep 158. See also *Hester*, above at 325, 1073.
10 *R v Goddard* [1962] 3 All ER 582, [1962] 1 WLR 1282.
11 For the older view see *R v Zielinski*, above.
12 For a less stringent approach in Australia see, for example, *R v Sorby* [1986] VR 753.
13 *R v Lucas* [1981] QB 720, [1981] 2 All ER 1008; *R v Beck* [1982] 1 All ER 807, [1982] 1 WLR 461; *R v Cullinane* [1984] Crim LR 420; *R v Webber* [1987] Crim LR 412.
14 As in *R v Donat* (1985) 82 Cr App Rep 173.
15 *R v Thomas* (1959) 43 Cr App Rep 210 (immaterial matters); *Goddard*, above, (complaints in sexual cases); *R v Manning* (1968) 53 Cr App Rep 150 (corroboration of evidence against co-accused); *R v Lucas*, above, (simple disbelief of accused).

hand it is permissible for the judge to tell the jury that such evidence, although not amounting to corroboration, may make the evidence of the witness more credible.[16] It is hard to believe that such fine distinctions reflect much credit upon this branch of the law. It would be more helpful if there were a clearer correlative obligation to direct the jury what items are not capable of amounting to corroboration, particularly if it might otherwise think that they were. It has however been held that there is no need to direct the jury that one accomplice cannot corroborate another,[17] nor that mere determination that the accused is lying does not necessarily corroborate a witness he so contradicts.[18] It is nevertheless a misdirection to tell the jury that it can use a consistent statement by a victim of a sexual offence for any purpose it likes, after a warning has been given, and without any indication whether it is, or is not, capable of corroborating the victim's evidence.[19] Even if not strictly obligatory, it is clearly preferable to give such guidance whenever the jury might otherwise be confused. Where there is corroboration so far as some counts are concerned, but not with regard to others, this fact should be made plain to the jury.[20] While it is for the judge to direct the jury what evidence is capable of being corroborative, it is for the jury determine whether it is in fact corroborative, and whether they believe it. The judge's direction should not go so far as to collapse the first question for the jury into the second.[1]

SECTION 3. THE QUESTION OF REFORM IN CRIMINAL CASES

Most of the recommendations of the Criminal Law Revision Committee with regard to corroboration have already been mentioned, but it will be convenient to restate the major proposals as the starting point of a brief discussion of other possibilities. The committee's most important recommendations were: (i) corroboration of the victim's evidence should be required as a matter of law in the case of sexual offences against children under 14; (ii) the jury should be warned of the special need for caution before convicting on the uncorroborated evidence of the victim in the case of sexual offences against persons of and above the age of 14; (iii) any rule or practice whereby in criminal proceedings the evidence of one witness is incapable of corroborating that of another witness should be abrogated; (iv) the court should warn the jury of the special need for caution when the evidence of identification is disputed.

One of several other plausible views is that no change is necessary. The rule of law requiring a warning of the danger of acting on the uncorroborated evidence of accomplices can never increase, and may decrease, the chances of a conviction of an innocent person; the same is true of the rule that

---

16 This is the whole purpose of permitting evidence of complaints to be adduced, and the same reasoning has been applied to evidence corroborating testimony against a co-accused, *R v Webber* [1977] Crim LR 413.
17 *R v Rance and Herron* (1975) 62 Cr App Rep 118 at 122.
18 *R v Penman* (1985) 82 Cr App Rep 44.
19 *R v Askew* [1981] Crim LR 398.
20 *R v West* (1984) 79 Cr App Rep 45; *R v Franklin* [1989] Crim LR 499. See also *The People (A-G) v Shaw* [1960] IR 168.
1 *R v Willoughby* (1988) 88 Cr App Rep 91.

accomplices who are parties to the crime charged cannot corroborate each other; and it is open to the courts to recognise new situations in which something like the corroboration warning is necessary.

On the other hand, it can be argued with equal plausibility that the proposals of the Criminal Law Revision Committee do not go far enough. At last, it may be said, notice has been taken of the observations of Chief Baron Joy concerning accomplices made as long ago as 1836:

> Why the case of an accomplice should require a particular rule for itself; why it should not, like that of every other witness of whose credit there is an impeachment, be left to the unfettered discretion of the judge, to deal with as the circumstances of each particular case may require, it seems difficult to explain.[2]

But why not apply the observations to sexual offences? Is the following statement in para 186 of the 11th Report really convincing?

> In sexual cases [the reason for a requirement of a warning about the danger of acting on uncorroborated evidence] is the danger that the complainant may have made a false accusation owing to sexual neurosis, jealousy, fantasy, spite or a girl's refusal to admit that she consented to an act of which she is now ashamed. In the case of an accomplice any special danger that there may be in relying on the witness's evidence is apparent from the fact that he is an accomplice or it can easily be made apparent by the defence. In the case of a sexual offence the danger may be hidden.

Those who take the view that the proposals of the committee do not go far enough would applaud something like the following amended version of cl 20(1) of the draft Bill attached to the 11th Report:

> At a trial on indictment it shall be for the court to decide in its discretion, having regard to the evidence given, whether the jury should be given a direction about convicting the accused on uncorroborated evidence; and, accordingly, any rule of law or practice whereby at such a trial it is in certain circumstances obligatory for the court to give the jury such a direction is hereby abrogated.

References rendering the clause subject to the recommendations about sexual offences and the Perjury Act 1911, have been omitted, and the word 'direction' has been substituted for 'warning' because it is assumed that proponents of the view under consideration would approve of the abolition of requirements of corroboration as a matter of law such as that which the committee contemplated retaining in the case of sexual offences against children under 14.

The mention of trials on indictment in cl 20(1) serves as a reminder that the requirement of warnings about the dangers of acting on uncorroborated evidence is unrealistic in the case of the vastly more numerous summary trials. The Criminal Law Revision Committee did about all that can be done by recommending the following clause:

> At the summary trial of a person for an offence the court shall have regard to all such enactments as would or might in comparable circumstances at a trial on indictment require the court to warn the jury of a special need for caution before convicting the accused.[3]

2 See para 184 of the 11th Report.
3 Cl 28.

But is it not somewhat odd to require a magistrate to reason as follows on a charge of indecent assault brought by a respectable middle-aged female: 'I believe her evidence, but I must think twice before acting upon it because sex is a mysterious thing', whereas, on a charge of assault brought by a man with numerous convictions for violence, the magistrate can simply say to himself 'I believe his evidence and I need not think twice about acting upon it because there is no particular danger that charges of violence will be made on account of neurosis, jealousy, fantasy or spite'?

Those who, in general, favour what may be described as the 'unfettered discretion' approach, can, with perfect consistency, approve of a requirement of some kind of cautionary direction, whether it is to be administered by a judge to a jury or a magistrate to himself, in cases of disputed identification because there is a consensus of opinion that it is in such cases that there is a specially grave risk of convicting an innocent man. The weakness of the present law and the recommendations of the Criminal Law Revision Committee is that they are based on assumptions which do not appear to be supported on a consensus of opinion,[4] still less on anything that can be called 'empirical evidence'.[5]

It is therefore submitted that, subject to the precautions required by *R v Turnbull*[6] in cases of disputed identification, the unfettered discretion approach is the best answer that English law can give to the questions whether, when and to what extent corroboration should be required. The discretion would have to be subject to appellate control, and a possible argument against the commended approach is that it would lead to too many appeals; but this is exactly the same objection as that which is levelled against the present law. Such technical questions as 'who is an accomplice?', 'what is corroboration?' and 'was the jury warned in the right terms?' are currently quite a fertile source of appeals. At least it would be an improvement to speak to juries in terms of a 'special need for caution' rather than telling them that it is 'dangerous' to act on 'uncorroborated evidence' (whatever 'corroboration' may mean) although they may do so if they believe the evidence, but something which enhances the credibility of the evidence is not necessarily corroborative of it. Such a change would be in complete accord with the spirit of the speeches in recent cases in the House of Lords, and with the decisions of the Canadian courts.

---

4 In *D P P v Hester* [1973] AC 296 at 328, [1972] 3 All ER 1056 at 1075, Lord Diplock expressed the view that the current law may achieve the opposite of the results it intends, and in *Vetrovec v R* (1982) 136 DLR (3d) 89 at 95, the Supreme Court of Canada suggested that this occurred because cogent prejudicial testimony was repeated and highlighted.
5 Such as there is suggests that Lord Diplock and the Supreme Court of Canada are correct, see LSE Jury Project 'Juries and the Rules of Evidence' [1973] Crim LR 208 at 220.
6 [1977] QB 224, [1976] 3 All ER 549.

CHAPTER VII

The course of evidence[1]

In this chapter an account is given of the principal rules governing the examination-in-chief, cross-examination and re-examination of witnesses. Such an account can hardly hope to be entirely satisfactory because it is concerned with regulations that are either matters of common knowledge or else can be thoroughly mastered by experience, but the rules with which it deals are among the most characteristic of the English law of evidence. The elucidation of facts by means of questions put by parties or their representatives to witnesses summoned, for the most part, by them, called mainly in the order of their choice, before a judge, acting as umpire rather than inquisitor, is the essential feature of the English 'adversary' or 'accusatorial' system of justice. Not only is an appreciation of this procedure desirable for its own sake, but it is necessary for a proper understanding of such matters as the law concerning the admissibility of the convictions, character and credibility of parties and witnesses, or the structure of s 1(f) of the Criminal Evidence Act 1898, considered in the three following chapters.

Section 1, below, deals with some procedural matters which appear to be essential to the exposition of the subject covered in this and subsequent chapters.

SECTION 1. MISCELLANEOUS PROCEDURAL MATTERS

A. EVIDENCE BEFORE TRIAL

1. CIVIL CASES

In civil cases, all the evidence is normally given viva voce at the hearing,[2] but it may be taken before trial and read at the trial when it is given by affidavit, on commission, under letters of request, in answer to interrogatories or by way of perpetuation of testimony.

(i) Affidavits

In a number of cases, specially provided for by Rules of Court, evidence may be by affidavit. This is allowed in matters coming before the Chancery

---

1 See generally Australian Law Reform Commission Research Paper No 8 'Manner of Giving Evidence'.
2 Though the normal practice is to order an exchange of written proofs of such evidence in advance of the trial, except in cases where such an exchange would be oppressive, see *Richard Saunders & Partners v Eastglen Ltd* (1989) Times, 28 July, criticising RSC Ord 38, r 2A as amended by Rules of the Supreme Court (Amendment No 2) S1 1988 No 1340 (L16).

Division on originating summons or motion, and orders may be made for the proof of particular facts by affidavit on an interlocutory summons in any division of the High Court. The statements in the affidavit are, of course, not subject to cross-examination, and they may sometimes be based on the knowledge, information or belief of the deponent, but, in appropriate cases, he can be obliged to attend for cross-examination.

(ii) Commissions

Under Ord 39, r 1, of the Rules of the Supreme Court, the court or a judge may, in any cause or matter where it shall appear necessary for the purposes of justice, make any order for the examination upon oath before the court or judge or any officer of the court, or any other person, and at any place, of any witness or person, and may empower any party to any such cause or matter to give such deposition in evidence therein, on such terms, if any, as the court or a judge may direct. The order is usually made when the witness is ill or abroad or is likely to be abroad at the time of the hearing. A practising lawyer, rather than an officer of the court, is usually named as examiner. The witnesses, parties and advocates attend before him, the witnesses are examined, cross-examined and re-examined. The examiner takes a note of any objection to the admissibility of evidence that may be raised. The judge will allow the deposition to be read only at the hearing, without the consent of the party against whom it is given if the maker is still unable to attend court.[3]

(iii) Letters of request

Letters of request may be issued to a foreign, dominion or colonial court asking one of their judges to take the evidence of a specific person within the jurisdiction of the court. The depositions are remitted to the High Court, and may be read at the trial.[4]

(iv) Interrogatories

If an order for interrogatories is made, they are answered on affidavit, and the affidavit may be read at the trial. An order for interrogatories directs a party to answer written questions addressed to him by his adversary on oath. The procedure is designed to facilitate proof of the adversary's case and to save expense; but the court will not allow interrogatories of an oppressive nature.

---

3 Ord 39, r 9. The governing statute is now Supreme Court Act 1981, s 36, which applies both to securing evidence for civil and criminal cases, and for securing it both from within the United Kingdom and from abroad. The taking of evidence in England for the use of a foreign court is governed by the Evidence (Proceedings in Other Jurisdictions) Act 1975, see *State of Norway's Application* [1989] 1 All ER 745, [1989] 2 WLR 458; and is also subject to the Protection of Trading Interests Act 1980. See also Ord 70. Such evidence may be ordered to be supplied on videotape, *J Barber & Sons v Lloyd's Underwriters* [1987] QB 103, [1986] 2 All ER 845.
4 Ord 39, r 2.

(v) Perpetuation of testimony

Under Order 39, r 15, any person who would under the cirucmstances alleged by him to exist become entitled, upon the happening of any future event, to any honour, title, dignity, or office, or to any estate or interest in any property, real or personal, the right or claim to which cannot be brought to trial by him before the happening of such event, may commence an action to perpetuate any testimony, which may be material for establishing such right or claim. This procedure is rarely used, but it might have to be employed by someone who is contingently entitled to property if certain facts can be proved in the future when there is a danger that the evidence of these facts will not be available, and the court is unlikely to make a present declaration concerning future rights.

2. CRIMINAL CASES

Written statements may be made for the purpose of committal proceedings against a person charged with an indictable offence in accordance with the provisions of s 102 of Magistrates' Courts Act 1980, and depositions may be taken at such proceedings. When the makers of the statements or depositions attend the trial, their testimony, and not the statements or depositions, constitutes the evidence in the case; but a limited provision is made for the use of the depositions and statements as evidence of the facts stated therein in the absence of the deponents. Similar use may also be made of depositions taken before a coroner, or under s 105 of the Magistrates' Courts Act 1980, and s 6 of the Criminal Law Amendment Act 1867, or under various other statutory provisions.

(i) Committal proceedings

Some of the witnesses or makers of statements at the committal proceedings may be conditionally ordered to attend the trial, in which case their depositions or statements may be read as evidence if they have not been required to attend. This is the effect of s 13(3) of the Criminal Justice Act 1925, as amended by the Criminal Procedure (Attendance of Witnesses) Act 1965, as applied to committals without consideration of the evidence by s 102(7) of the Magistrates' Courts Act 1980. The subsection also enables the deposition to be read if the maker is proved to be dead or insane, or so ill as not to be able to travel, or to be kept out of the way by means of procurement of the accused.[5] The existence of these preliminary conditions must be proved beyond doubt by evidence which would be admissible at the trial, and if it is alleged that the witness is being kept away by the accused it is not enough that others may have been acting on his behalf.[6] These provisions were construed so as to prevent depositions which did not comply with their conditions from being adduced under s 68 of the Police and Criminal Evidence Act 1984.[7] These decisions depended in part upon the observation

---

5 Though this will not be allowed where prejudice to the defence might occur, for example because of the inability to cross-examine, *R v Blithing* (1983) 77 Cr App Rep 86.

6 *R v O'Loughlin and McLaughlin* [1988] 3 All ER 431.

7 *R v O'Loughlin* (above); *R v Martin* [1988] 3 All ER 440, [1988] WLR 655, despite an apparently clear indication in the wording of Sch 3 that the provision was intended to apply to statements prepared for the purposes of criminal proceedings.

that the relevant section had been enacted without repeal of or amendment to s 13(3) of the 1925 Act. It may be remarked that the supersession of s 68 by the provisions of the Criminal Justice Act 1988 has equally made no such alteration to s 13(3). Section 26 of the new Act does however deal so explicitly with statements in documents prepared for the purposes of criminal proceedings that it seems most likely to be construed as supplementing s 13(3), though it may well be the case that the absence of the ability to cross-examine will still influence the exercise of the court's discretion to give leave for the admission of any such deposition.[8]

(ii) Coroners

When depositions are taken by a coroner, there does not appear to be any similar statutory provision for their being read at any trial that takes place on the coroners inquisition; but in *R v Cowle*[9] it was held that the deposition of a dead deponent might be read if it was signed by him and the coroner, and the accused had an opportunity of cross-examination.

(iii) Section 105 of the Magistrates' Courts Act 1980, and s 6 of the Criminal Law Amendment Act 1867

Under s 105 of the Magistrates' Courts Act 1980, a deposition may be taken out of court by a magistrate from anyone who can give information with regard to a indictable offence if he is dangerously ill and it is impracticable to take the deposition in the ordinary way. The deposition may be read as evidence at the committal proceedings, but the provisions of s 6 of the Criminal Law Amendment Act 1867, apply. This enables a justice of the peace to take a deposition from someone who is dangerously ill for use at the trial. Reasonable notice must have been given to the person against whom the deposition is to be read in evidence, and he must have had an opportunity of cross-examining the deponent.[10]

(iv) Letters of request

Although there was, and still is, a limited power to secure depositions made abroad under the provisions of s 691 of the Merchant Shipping Act 1894, the power was stymied by the requirement of the presence of the accused when the deposition was made.[11] Now that hearsay has been made more widely admissible in criminal cases under the provisions of the Criminal Justice Act 1988, and following the recommendations of the Roskill Committee,[12] provision has been made for evidence to be secured for the purposes of criminal proceedings by the issue of letters of request.[13] Such

---

8 See the second of the considerations listed in the Criminal Justice Act 1988, s 26. For the discretion under the old law see *Scott v R* [1989] AC 1242, [1989] 2 All ER 305; *R v Neshet* (1990) Times, 27 February.
9 (1907) 71 JP 152, contra *R v Butcher* (1900) 64 JP 808; see also *R v Black* (1909) 74 JP 71 and *R v Marriott* (1911) 75 JP 288. In Australia there is discretion to reject such a deposition, *R v Collins* [1986] VR 37.
10 The sections should be consulted for further procedural requirements.
11 A similar restriction still applies even more generally in Canada, see *R v Branco* (1988) 62 CR (3d) 317.
12 Report of the Departmental Inquiry on Fraud Trials 1986 para 5.43.
13 Criminal Justice Act 1988, s 29.

evidence may be secured even before proceedings have been instituted, if they are likely to be so instituted if the evidence is obtained, and the procedure may also be invoked by the accused, though in his case only if proceedings have been instituted. Such evidence must satisfy the provisions of ss 23 or 24,[14] and is further subject to the discretionary control of s 25, though it is excluded from the requirements of s 26.

(v) Miscellaneous statutory provisions

Under s 42 and s 43 of the Children and Young Persons Act 1933, the deposition of a child or young person may be taken out of court, and used at the preliminary examination or trial of a person for an offence under the Act.[15] The conditions are that the child's attendance in court would cause serious danger to his life or health, and that the accused should have had an opportunity of cross-examining him.[16]

These provisions were not regarded as affording sufficient protection for young children, and have now been supplemented by permitting young children[17] to testify by live television link in certain proceedings by leave of the court.[18] The aim of providing for a live link was to preserve the possibility of cross-examination, but a strong body of opinion feels that this may still not provide sufficient protection, and that video recordings of interviews before the trial might be preferable.[19] The matter is highly controversial, and there is a clear danger of prejudice to the accused if he is unable to make an effective challenge to any possible leading of perhaps suggestible witnesses.[20] Further debate, and development, is to be expected.

B. THE RIGHT TO BEGIN

The plaintiff, prosecutor or their respective advocates open every case in the sense that they explain the issues to the court, but questions sometimes arise concerning the right to begin calling evidence.

The Crown will almost always have the right to begin in criminal cases where there is a plea of not guilty,[1] because there will be some issue upon which the evidential, if not the legal, burden will be borne by the prosecution; but, now that there can be formal admissions and agreed statements of fact

---

14 S 23(2)(b) will probably be invoked most often.
15 See Spencer and Tucker 'The Evidence of Absent Children' (1987) NLJ 816.
16 See also Children and Young Persons Act 1963, as to committal proceedings in the case of sexual offences.
17 And witnesses who are outside the United Kingdom, in their case without limitation as to the class of proceeding.
18 Criminal Justice Act 1988, s 32.
19 See Spencer 'Child Witnesses and the Law of Evidence' [1987] Crim LR 76.
20 Such fears find some justification in judicial criticism of commonly used interviewing techniques in cases of alleged sexual abuse of children where such recordings have been tendered in civil proceedings, see, eg *C v C* [1987] 1 FLR 321. In the United States it has been held contrary to the confrontation clause in the constitution even to screen a child witness from the accused, *Coy v Iowa* 108 S Ct 2798 (1988).
1 Where a special plea is raised, such as autrefois convict, and there is a dispute of fact, the accused would begin. A plea of guilty does not admit everything on the depositions (*R v Riley* [1896] 1 QB 309 at 318; *R v Maitland* [1964] SASR 332 according to which an accused pleading guilty should call evidence as to disputed facts).

under s 10 and s 9 of the Criminal Justice Act 1967, respectively, there can be exceptional cases in which the accused has the right to begin.

In civil cases, subject to the judge's discretion to direct the contrary,[2] the plaintiff has the right to begin unless the defendant has the burden of proof on every issue[3] and, in this context, 'burden of proof' may be taken to mean 'evidential burden'.[4] This was established in *Mercer v Whall*,[5] an action for wrongful dismissal in which the defendant admitted that he determined the plaintiff's contract of service prematurely, but alleged that he was justified in doing so. It was held that the plaintiff ought to begin calling evidence because the damages claimed by him were not agreed. If damages had not been in issue, the defendant would have had the right to begin, because there would have been no fact with regard to which the plaintiff bore the evidential burden.[6]

C. THE ADVOCATES' SPEECHES

The incidence of the right to begin may affect the order in which the advocates' speeches are made to the court. In civil cases, assuming that he has this right, the plaintiff opens the case to the court,[7] calls his witnesses and sums up if the defendant does not call witnesses. The defendant then replies and thus secures the last word. If the defendant calls witnesses, the plaintiff does not sum up at the conclusion of his case, but the defendant opens his case, calls his witnesses and sums up, leaving the plaintiff with the right of reply. The foregoing procedure is reversed if the defendant has the right to begin calling evidence.[8]

In criminal cases tried on indictment, the prosecutor opens and calls his evidence. If the accused does not call evidence, the prosecutor sums up leaving the accused with the right of reply. If the accused calls evidence, the prosecutor's closing speech is made after the close of the evidence for the defence with the result that the accused has the right of reply.[9]

In both civil and criminal cases, the above procedure may be interspersed with a submission that there is no case to answer, arguments about the admissibility of evidence,[10] or arguments on points of law.

2 Ord 35, r 7(1).
3 Ord 35, r 7(6).
4 *Re Parry's Estate, Parry v Fraser* [1977] 1 All ER 309, [1977] 1 WLR 93n; *Pontifex v Jolly* (1839) 9 C & P 202, showing that an amendment will not be allowed for the sole purpose of altering the right to begin. See *W Lusty & Sons Ltd v Morris Wilkinson & Co (Nottingham) Ltd* [1954] 2 All ER 347, [1954] 1 WLR 911 showing that, where a claim is admitted in court, the defendant may begin calling evidence on his counterclaim. See also *Seldon v Davidson* [1968] 2 All ER 755, [1968] 1 WLR 1083.
5 (1845) 5 QB 447.
6 For the right to begin in matrimonial causes see *Arding v Arding* [1954] 2 All ER 671n, [1954] 1 WLR 944 and *Hewitt v Hewitt* [1948] P 150, [1948] 1 All ER 242.
7 He must not allude to facts with regard to which he cannot call evidence (*Faith v M'Intyre* (1835) 7 C & P 44; *R v O'Neill* (1950) 34 Cr App Rep 108).
8 For details see RSC Ord 35, r 7.
9 Criminal Procedure (Right of Reply) Act 1964. For further details see Archbold (42nd edn) para 4–390. For summary trial see Magistrates' Courts Rules 1981, rr 13 and 14.
10 If, as will usually be the case, counsel knows that objection will be taken to an item of evidence, he should not refer to it in opening, and the objection should be raised when the evidence is about to be given (*R v Cole* (1941) 28 Cr App Rep 43; *R v Zielinski* (1950) 34 Cr App Rep 193). This procedure can be applied to civil cases tried with a jury. The point is not so important when there is no jury.

D. THE CALLING OF WITNESSES AND THE ROLE OF THE JUDGE

It was said in the first paragraph of this chapter that the essential feature of the English adversary or accusatorial system of justice is the questioning of witnesses by the parties or their representatives, summoned for the most part by them, and called mainly in the order of their choice before a judge acting as umpire rather than as inquisitor. A few words may now be added by way of enlargement on and qualification of these remarks. All the matters discussed belong rather to the realm of procedure than to that of evidence.

Most of the qualifications relate to criminal proceedings. In civil cases the parties may call as many or as few witnesses able to give admissible evidence as they choose, in the order which commends itself to them,[11] and the judge can call a witness only with their consent.[12] In criminal cases the prosecution is obliged to call certain witnesses and to have others available to be called by the defence, there is a restriction on the order in which defence witnesses may be called and the judge may call a witness without the consent of the parties.

It used to be a general practice for the names of the witnesses called by the prosecution at the committal proceedings to be written on the back of the indictment and the prosecution had to ensure that these witnesses were in court although it had a discretion whether to call them or leave them to be called, if they thought fit, by the defence.[13] A similar obligation now exists with regard to the makers of the statements served upon the accused committed without consideration of the evidence under s 6 of the Magistrates' Courts Act 1980. The discretion is not unlimited for the prosecution must call all the witnesses or makers of statements, favourable or unfavourable, whose testimony is essential to the narrative of its case. This rule was recognised in *R v Nugent*[14] where the prosecution had taken statements from eight alibi witnesses named by the defence before the committal. These statements were served with the other committal papers on the accused and their makers' names were mentioned in the formal notice of alibi defence served upon the prosecution. As their testimony was not essential to the prosecution's narrative, it was held to be under no obligation to call them as its witnesses.

The restriction upon the order in which defence witnesses may be called relates to the accused himself. In *R v Morrison*[15] Lord Alverstone CJ said:

> In all cases I consider it most important for the prisoner to be called before any of his witnesses. He ought to give his evidence before he has heard the evidence and cross-examination of any witnesses he is going to call.

11 *Briscoe v Briscoe* [1968] P 501, [1966] All ER 465. There is of course the sanction of liability for costs in any event if superfluous witnesses are called.
12 *Re Enoch and Zaretsky, Bock & Co's Arbitration* [1910] 1 KB 327: but such consent is unnecessary on motions to commit for contempt (*Yianni v Yianni* [1966] 1 All ER 231n, [1966] 1 WLR 120). Opinions differ as to whether the limitation still applies in Australia, cp *Obacelo Pty Ltd v Taveraft Pty Ltd* (1986) 66 ALR 371 and *Clark Equipment Credit Pty Ltd v Como Factors Pty Ltd* (1988) 14 NSWLR 552.
13 *R v Oliva* [1965] 3 All ER 116, [1965] 1 WLR 1028. This is still the position in Australia, see *Whitehorn v R* (1983) 49 ALR 448.
14 [1977] 3 All ER 662, [1977] 1 WLR 789. See also *R v Kizon* (1985) 18 ACR 59.
15 (1911) 6 Cr App Rep 159 at 165.

It has since been said that there are rare exceptions to this rule under which a formal witness, or one about whose evidence there is no controversy, might, with the leave of the court, give evidence before the accused.[16] A majority of the Criminal Law Revision Committee thought the rule a good one, but the committee unanimously recommended that the discretion to allow for exceptions should be unlimited.[17] This general rule, and the unfettered discretion to depart from it, has achieved statutory form in the Police and Criminal Evidence Act 1984, s 79.

In civil and criminal proceedings the parties must, as a general rule, call all their evidence before the close of their cases.[18] The authorities are mainly concerned with the question when the Crown may call evidence in rebuttal in criminal proceedings. It was once said that leave to call such evidence should only be given: 'if any matter arises ex improviso which no human ingenuity can foresee',[19] but this formulation of what is universally considered to be a rule of practice rather than law has since been said to be too wide.[20] In *R v Day*[1] a conviction of forgery was quashed because the judge allowed the prosecution to call a handwriting expert after the close of its case, and the Court of Criminal Appeal considered that the necessity of such evidence should have been foreseen at the outset. The prosecution is not, however, required to react to any suggestion emanating from the accused, especially if it comes outside the evidence given at the trial and appears insubstantial and unlikely to be repeated.[2] It seems that the rule has now become relaxed to the extent of investing the judge with a discretion to permit prosecution evidence in rebuttal of any line of defence which could not reasonably have been anticipated.[3] This seems more practicable and more just. The court will normally allow evidence in rebuttal to be called in order to make good a purely formal omission such as the prosecutor's failure to prove that the leave of the Director of Public Prosecutions to bring proceedings had been obtained.[4] It would, however, be wrong to allow the Crown to split its case as it wished, especially if in so doing the accused might be compelled to testify in reply, and be exposed to cross-examination.[5] Clause 23(1) of the Bill attached to the eleventh report of the Criminal Law Revision Committee would have given the court a complete discretion to allow evidence to be given by the prosecution or defence after the close of their respective cases.

Clause 23(2) would, if enacted, have made an even more drastic change in the law. It reads:

16 *R v Smith* [1968] 2 All ER 115, [1968] 1 WLR 636.
17 11th Report, para 107.
18 Though in civil cases the court has a general discretion in the interests of justice to allow evidence to be led at a later stage, *Neigut v Hanania* (1983) Times, 6 January; compare *R v Gainsborough Justices, ex p Green* [1983] Crim LR 627, illustrating the much more constrained situation in criminal cases, especially after a submission of no case to answer.
19 Per Tindal CJ in *R v Frost* (1839) 4 State Tr NS 85 at 376.
20 *R v Crippen* [1911] 1 KB 149 at 156 per Darling J; *R v Owen* [1952] 2 QB 362 at 366 per Lord Goddard CJ. See also *R v Francis* (1990) Times, 19 January.
1 [1940] 1 All ER 402. See also *R v McCarthy* (1984) 14 ACR 73.
2 *R v Hutchinson* (1985) 82 Cr App Rep 51.
3 *R v Scott* (1984) 79 Cr App Rep 49. See also *R v Harrington* [1984] Crim LR 487.
4 *Price v Humphries* [1958] 2 QB 353, [1958] 2 All ER 725.
5 See *John v R* (1985) 24 DLR (4th) 713; *R v Chin* (1985) 59 ALR 1 where the principle was extended to matters introduced for the first time in cross-examination.

In the exercise of its discretion under this section the court may allow evidence to be given at any time before delivery of the verdict or, at a summary trial, the decision of the court, and accordingly at a trial on indictment may do so *after the conclusion of the summing-up or after the jury have retired* and at a summary trial may do so *after the court has retired to consider its decision.*

The italicised words would have changed what is at present a sacrosanct rule, supported by numerous authorities,[6] that a witness cannot be called or recalled after the jury or justices have retired to consider their decision. The rule applies even though the jury has requested the action and the defence is agreeable. The Supreme Court of Eire has held that the judge has a discretion to allow a witness to be called up to the time when the jury returns its verdict.[7]

The English rule makes for tidiness because the witness who was called would have to be cross-examined and the process might lead to suggestions that further witnesses should be called, but the Criminal Law Revision Committee took the view that it was too rigid.

At a trial on indictment the rule prevents the judge from calling a witness after the jury has retired. Up to that point he has a discretion to do so, although it has been stressed that there must be good reason for such an interference with the adversarial process and reference has even been made to the ex improviso rule in this context.[8] The Court of Appeal will be extremely reluctant to interfere with the discretion of the trial judge, and in *R v Roberts*[9] remarked that it knew of no case where an appeal had been allowed because the trial judge had refused to exercise it to call a witness. Clause 23(4) of the Bill attached to the eleventh report of the Criminal Law Revision Committee empowered the court to call a witness at any time before the delivery of the verdict or, at a summary trial, the decision of the court.

The power to recall a witness in criminal cases serves as a reminder that the English judge is more than an umpire in the strict sense of the word. It is true that he must not descend into the dust of the arena,[10] but we have seen that he may exert a very considerable influence over the jury,[11] he has a discretion to exclude certain types of evidence[12] and he can question witnesses in the cause of clarification. His position was well summed up in the following passage from a judgment of Denning LJ:

6 *R v Owen* [1952] 2 QB 362, [1952] 1 All ER 1040; *R v Wilson* (1957) 41 Cr App Rep 226; *R v Gearing* (1965) 50 Cr App Rep 18; *R v Lawrence* [1968] 1 All ER 579, [1968] 1 WLR 341; *R v Nixon* [1968] 2 All ER 33, [1968] 1 WLR 577. As to proceedings before justices, see *Webb v Leadbetter* [1966] 2 All ER 114, [1966] 1 WLR 245, and *Pheland v Back* [1972] 1 All ER 901, [1972] 1 WLR 273.
7 *People (A-G) v O'Brien* [1963] IR 65.
8 *R v Cleghorn* [1967] 2 QB 584, [1967] 1 All ER 996 where the conviction was quashed and stress was placed on the fact that, in *R v Tregear* [1967] 2 QB 574, [1967] 1 All ER 989, the judge was in effect requested by the defence to call the witness in question. An examining magistrate probably has no such power in committal proceedings where the only issue is whether the prosecution has presented a prima facie case, *R v Epping and Harlow Justices, ex p Massaro* [1973] QB 433, [1973] 1 All ER 1011. For the position in Australia see *R v Apostilides* (1984) 53 ALR 445.
9 (1984) 80 Cr App Rep 89 at 96.
10 *Yuill v Yuill* [1945] P 15, [1945] 1 All ER 183; *R v Clewer* (1953) 37 Cr App Rep 37.
11 Ch IV above.
12 Ch IV, section 2 above.

In the system of trial which we have evolved in this country, the judge sits to hear and determine the issues raised by the parties, not to conduct an investigation or examination on behalf of society at large as happens, we believe, in some foreign countries. Even in England, however, a judge is not a mere umpire to answer the question 'How's that?' His object, above all, is to find out the truth, and to do justice according to law . . .[13]

SECTION 2. EXAMINATION-IN-CHIEF

The object of examination-in-chief is to obtain testimony in support of the version of the facts in issue or relevant to the issue for which the party calling the witness contends. The facts in issue and the concept of relevancy have already been discussed, while the various exclusionary rules which prohibit the proof of certain facts are considered elsewhere in this book. At present we are primarily concerned with the manner in which witnesses who can, ex hypothesi, give relevant and admissible evidence must be treated. Generally speaking they may not be asked leading questions, and, although a witness may refresh his memory by referring to documents previously prepared by him, he cannot usually be asked about his former statements with a view to their becoming evidence of the facts stated or in order to demonstrate his consistency. A party may call someone else to contradict his witness who has given unfavourable evidence with regard to a fact in issue or relevant to the issue, but he may discredit his witness only if the judge considers that witness to be hostile. We shall therefore be concerned with leading questions, refreshing memory, previous statements of witnesses consistent with their present testimony and unfavourable or hostile witnesses.

A. LEADING QUESTIONS

1. DEFINITION AND ILLUSTRATION[14]

A leading question is one which either (a) suggests the answer desired, or (b) assumes the existence of disputed facts as to which the witness is to testify.[15] An example of the first type would be the following question put to one of the plaintiff's witnesses in a running-down case—'Did you see another car coming very fast from the opposite direction?'[16] It should be split up into something like the following—'Did you notice any other traffic? Which direction was it coming from? Was it going fast or slow?' A typical example of the second type of leading question would be, 'What did you do after Smith hit you?' put to the plaintiff in an action for assault before he had deposed to being hit by Smith.

Lord Ellenborough once said that if questions are asked to which the answer 'yes' or 'no' would be conclusive, they would certainly be objectionable;[17] but this is untenable as a test for determining whether a question is leading. The answer 'yes' or 'no' would be conclusive to such a

13 *Jones v National Coal Board* [1957] 2 QB 55 at 63.
14 This discussion was approved in *R v Saunders* (1985) 15 ACR 115.
15 This is in effect the definition in Stephen *Digest of the Law of Evidence* (12th edn) art 140. The alternative is to describe questions of type (b) as improper rather than leading.
16 Munkman *Technique of Advocacy* 42–43.
17 *Nicholls v Dowding and Kemp* (1815) 1 Stark 81.

question as 'Did you notice any traffic?' but it would not be leading if put to a witness who had just said that he was standing on the side of the road. Again, such a question as 'Did you hear what A said?' would be a leading question of the second type if the presence of A in the witness's company, or the fact that A said anything were in dispute, and as yet unproved by the witness, otherwise it would fall outside the definition of a leading question. As Best said, 'It should never be forgotten that "leading" is a relative, not an absolute term';[18] everything depends on the context.

The answers to leading questions are not inadmissible in evidence although the method by which they were obtained may rob them of all or most of their significance.[19] Leading questions are objectionable because of the danger of collusion between the person asking them and the witness, or the impropriety of suggesting the existence of facts which are not in evidence. Account must also be taken of human laziness—it is easy to say 'yes' or 'no' on demand, and most leading questions can be answered in this way, even if the same is true of some questions that are not leading. There is, however, no doubt that leading questions save time, they are often an indispensable prelude to further interrogation and a travesty could be made of any examination-in-chief by an over-emphatic insistence on the prohibition. There are, therefore, numerous recurring situations to which it does not apply. If no objection is taken to a leading question any answer amounts to evidence in the case, but may be regarded as being of diminished weight.[20]

2. EXCEPTIONS TO THE PROHIBITION

A witness may always be led on the formal introductory part of his testimony. The following is the beginning of almost any examination-in-chief—'Is your name John Smith?' 'Are you a baker?' 'Do you live at 1 Any Street, Anywhere?' Undisputed matters belong to the same category. In a divorce case in which the marriage was not denied by the respondent, the examination might well continue 'Were you married at St John's Church, Tooting?' 'Did you live happily with the respondent until last June?'

It would often be impossible to persuade a witness to identify a person or thing in court without the aid of leading questions. Accordingly such questions as 'Was he the man you saw?' or 'Was that the book he lent you?' have to be allowed every day.[1]

Questions with regard to the identification of persons or things are, in fact, an example of a broader class of question rendered necessary in order to focus the witness's mind on a particular point. Someone is called to prove a partnership; in order to stimulate his memory, he may be asked whether named persons did, or did not, participate in the business.[2]

Lists are sometimes drawn up of the matters with regard to which leading questions are permissible. Introductory or undisputed matters, questions of identity and questions designed to bring the witness's mind to the point are among the items that commonly appear on such lists, but the subject does

---

18 *Law of Evidence* (12th edn) 562.
19 *Moor v Moor* [1954] 2 All ER 458, [1954] 1 WLR 927.
20 *Moor v Moor* [1954] 2 All ER 458, [1954] 1 WLR 927; *Gabrielsen v Farmer* [1960] NZLR 832 at 834.
1 *R v Watson* (1817) 2 Stark 116 at 128.
2 *Acerro v Petroni* (1815) 1 Stark 100; *Nicholls v Dowding and Kemp* [1815] 1 Stark 81.

not lend itself to exhaustive treatment of this nature. There are bound to be cases which do not fall within any list. A witness is in court while a previous witness is giving evidence about the contents of a letter; when the time comes for the second witness to give his evidence-in-chief, he says that he read the letter; he can be asked whether it contained a particular passage.[3] A magistrate dies in the course of a case in which many witnesses have given evidence; provided there is an opportunity of cross-examination, each witness can be recalled before a new magistrate. After the witness has considered his disposition, he can be asked whether the document represents his evidence because long leading questions may be allowed, even in-chief, at the discretion of the judge.[4] No one would have dreamed of including these cases in any list before they were decided.

It is said on good authority[5] that leading questions may always be put in cross-examination. No doubt this is true so far as questions suggesting the desired answer are concerned; but those which suggest the existence of unproved facts might well be disallowed, even in cross-examination, and in *R v MacDonnell*,[6] it was said that questions put to a prisoner in cross-examination ought to be put in an interrogative form; they should commence 'did you?' and not 'you did'. The judge has a wide discretion in these matters, and it is difficult to say more than that leading questions will usually be disallowed in-chief, or in re-examination, although they will generally be permitted in cross-examination.[7]

B. REFRESHING MEMORY[8]

Perhaps the most important feature of an English trial, civil or criminal, is its 'orality'. Much greater weight is attached to the answers given by witnesses in court on oath or affirmation than to written statements previously made by them. We shall see that all previous statements of witnesses, whether made orally or in writing, are now admissible, with the leave of the court, as evidence of the facts stated in civil cases under the Civil Evidence Act 1968;[9] but the persistence of our faith in orality is shown by the fact that the Act renders the admissibility of a witness's previous written statement far less a matter of course than was the case under the Evidence Act 1938. Under that statute, it was necessary only to call the maker of the statement, ask him whether the signature on it was his, and put the document in as of right without any examination-in-chief.[10] Such a course was frowned on and no doubt it was seldom adopted in practice, but it was undesirable as a possibility in any case in which the facts were seriously disputed because, contrary to

---

3 *Courteen v Touse* (1807) 1 Camp 43.
4 *Ex p Bottomley* [1909] 2 KB 14 at 21.
5 *Parkin v Moon* (1836) 7 C & P 408.
6 (1909) 2 Cr App Rep 322.
7 In a case where there are multiple parties, the effective role of witnesses may vary according to the function their evidence is serving as between the parties, and the right to ask leading questions will vary accordingly; see for example *Peabody Donation Fund (Governors) v Sir Lindsay Parkinson* [1983] CLY 1660 (unaffected on this point by subsequent proceedings).
8 Michael Newark and Alec Samuels 'Refreshing Memory' [1978] Crim LR 408.
9 Until Part I of the 1968 Act is applied to magistrates' courts, the Evidence Act 1938 will continue to apply to civil proceedings in those courts.
10 *Hilton v Lancashire Dynamo Nevelin Ltd* [1964] 2 All ER 769, [1964] 1 WLR 952.

what is commonly supposed by the layman, the way in which a witness responds to examination-in-chief is often more informative with regard to his reliability than his reaction to cross-examination. Accordingly, in addition to requiring the leave of the court for the reception of the previous statement of a witness at the behest of the party calling him, s 2(2) of the Act of 1968 stipulates that, in general, the statement shall not be admitted before the conclusion of the maker's examination-in-chief. Preference for orality is even stronger in criminal cases,[11] and was invoked to water down the originally radical proposals to admit documentary hearsay proposed by the Roskill Committee.[12] As a result the Criminal Justice Act 1988 requires oral evidence whenever it is available rather than documentary hearsay except in the case of expert reports, and accepts it there only with the leave of the court.[13]

1. OUT OF COURT

Yet, for all its apparent orality, an examination-in-chief is rarely conducted 'out of the blue'. The witness has usually given a statement (commonly called his 'proof of evidence') to the solicitor for the party calling him or, if he is a prosecution witness in a criminal case, he will have made a signed statement to the police. It is on the basis of these documents that the questions put to the witness in-chief will be framed. The statement will frequently have been made a considerable time before the trial, and the witness may or may not have retained a copy of it. In these circumstances, it is inevitable and desirable that the witness should read his proof shortly before the hearing or even be taken through it by the person to whom it was made. If it were to transpire that there had been anything in the nature of 'coaching' by such person, or some kind of pre-trial confabulation between the witnesses, the judge would no doubt treat the evidence with the contempt it deserved. It was, however, once suggested that it is objectionable for prosecution witnesses to be provided with copies of their statements to the police to be read or gone through shortly before the trial;[14] but it would have been difficult to justify or enforce a special rule for this particular case, and, if the statement were an elaborate one, as even statements to the police sometimes are, the rule would have been absurd. The practice has since been held to be perfectly proper,[15] although it is desirable, but not essential as a matter of law, for the defence to be notified of what has taken place.[16] The defence is free to cross-examine on a document used in this way, just as if refreshment had taken

---

11 The reasons for this were eloquently elaborated by the High Court of Australia in *Butera v D P P* (1987) 76 ALR 45 at 50.
12 Report of the Departmental Inquiry on Fraud Trials (1986).
13 Criminal Justice Act 1988, s 30(2).
14 *R v Yellow and Thay* (1932) 96 JP 826.
15 *R v Richardson* [1971] 2 QB 484, [1971] 2 All ER 773. Nor need the judge give any special direction to the jury, *Rooke v Auckland City Council* [1980] 1 NZLR 680. For criticism see M N Howard 'Refreshment of Memory Out of Court' [1972] Crim LR 351.
16 *Worley v Bentley* [1976] 2 All ER 449; *R v Westwell* [1976] 2 All ER 812. It is even more desirable for such refreshment to take place in court wherever feasible, *R v Tyagi* (1986) Times, 21 July.

place in court.[17] No other conditions concerning the documents which may be used to refresh memory out of court have been laid down.

2. IN COURT

Judging by the reported cases, the English courts have not had to deal with the problem of the amnesiac or near amnesiac witness, and it is anybody's guess whether they would follow the practice adopted by a British Columbian court in *R v Pitt*.[18] On a charge of attempting to murder her husband, the accused, who was suffering from functional amnesia, said in court that she could remember little of what happened. Her counsel then applied for leave to have her hypnotised in court, a hypnotist having given evidence that her memory might be refreshed by an hypnotic trance. The application was granted, the wife giving her evidence after she had emerged from the trance. The decision was partly based on the analogy of refreshment of memory, but reference was also made to the unfairness of not allowing the accused the benefit of the latest medical techniques.

It will be convenient to enumerate the conditions on which a witness is allowed to refer to a document in order to refresh his memory while giving evidence, before distinguishing between the two types of case in which memory is said to be 'refreshed' in court. The document must have been made substantially at the same time as the occurrence of the events to which the witness is required to depose, it must have been made or read over and accepted as accurate by the witness while the facts were still fresh in his memory.[19] It must be produced to the court or opposite party on demand, and, in one class of case, the document must be the original.

(i) Contemporaneity

Contemporaneity is, as always, a question of fact and much may depend upon the subject matter of the document. Although the requirement is usually treated as an independent condition, it can hardly amount to more than strong evidence of compliance with the further requirement that the writing must have been brought into existence while the facts were still fresh in the witness's memory. The matter is not one on which precedents are likely to be much help. In *R v Woodcock*[20] a prosecution witness was not allowed to refresh his memory from a deposition made by him three months after the events with which it dealt and, in *R v Graham*,[1] the Court of Appeal was doubtful about the propriety of allowing an accomplice to refresh his memory from his statement made a month after the relevant event. On the

17 *Owen v Edwards* (1983) 77 Cr App Rep 191. See also *R v Pachonick* [1973] 2 NSWLR 86; *R v Kingston* [1986] 2 Qd R 114.
18 (1968) 68 DLR (2d) 513. Distinguish *R v Eades* [1972] Crim LR 99 (below) where the accused claimed that his memory had been fortuitously refreshed out of court. The problem with which *R v Podola* [1960] 1 QB 325, [1959] 3 All ER 418 was concerned was of course quite different, the issue being whether amnesia affected fitness to plead not whether an amnesiac's memory can be refreshed.
19 It is sufficient if the documents are read to and accepted by the witness, *R v Kelsey* (1982) 74 Cr App Rep 213, but it is doubtful whether the English courts would follow *R v O'Linn* 1960 (1) SA 545, and allow refreshment of memory from a document dictated by the witness but not checked by him.
20 [1963] Crim LR 273.
1 [1973] Crim LR 628.

other hand a gap of twenty-two days was disregarded in *R v Fotheringham*.[2] In *Burrough v Martin*[3] a captain who had inspected his ship's logbook throughout a voyage and found the entries in it to be accurate was allowed to refresh his memory from it although the entries were made by the mate. In *R v Simmonds*[4] notes made by customs officers at the first convenient opportunity after returning to their office from lengthy interviews were held to comply with the condition of contemporaneity and the officers were permitted to read them to the court. It was said to be a course constantly adopted by police officers giving evidence of a long interview or series of interviews with suspects.[5]

In *R v Da Silva*[6] it was held that memory could be refreshed even from a strictly non-contemporaneous document if:

> (1)... the witness indicates that he cannot now recall the details of events because of the lapse of time since they took place, (2) that he made a statement much nearer the time of the events and that the contents of the statement represented his recollection at the time he made it, (3) that he had not read the statement before he continued to give evidence.

It is also made clear in that case that the degree of contemporaneity required will depend upon the nature of the matter, and that there is no rigid rule that a witness who has begun to give evidence cannot subsequently refer to such a statement for this purpose.

(ii) Document read over or accepted as accurate by the witness

Burrough v Martin[7] shows that it is unnecessary for the document to have been made by the witness. A more striking example is provided by *Dyer v Best*[8] where a witness was allowed to refresh his memory concerning the day on which certain proceedings were brought by referring to an article in a newspaper which he had read at the time and then believed to be true. Pollock CB said:

> If a man at the time he has a recollection of certain facts reads a document containing a statement, which he knows to be true, of the facts, he may again refer to it to refresh his memory although, at the time when he first read it, he made no memorandum.[9]

A witness may refresh his memory from a copy of a document provided the accuracy of the transcription is properly verified. In *Burton v Plummer*[10] a

---

2 [1975] Crim LR 710.
3 (1809) 2 Camp 112. See also *R v Langton* (1876) 2 QBD 296.
4 (1967) 51 Cr App Rep 316.
5 At 329. See also *R v Bryant* (1946) 31 Cr App Rep 146. There is no objection to police officers refreshing their memories from notes over which they have collaborated (*R v Bass* [1953] 1 QB 680, [1953] 1 All ER 1064), or from a fair copy made from jotted notes, *A-G's Reference No 3 of 1979* (1979) 69 Cr App Rep 411.
6 [1990] 1 All ER 29 at 33.
7 Above.
8 (1866) 4 H & C 189. See also Indian Evidence Act 1872, s 159.
9 At 192.
10 (1834) 2 Ad & El 341. In *Jones v Stroud* (1825) 2 C & P 196, a witness was not allowed to refresh his memory from a copy made six months after the date of the original, but the original was covered in figures when the copy was made and the judge's suspicions appear to have been justifiably aroused concerning the accuracy of the copy.

clerk was allowed to refresh his memory from a ledger which contained copies, made under his supervision, from a waste-book kept by him. In *Topham v McGregor*[11] the state of the weather at a particular period fourteen years earlier was a relevant fact. The author of an article which appeared at the time was allowed to refresh his memory from a copy of the newspaper containing it, the editor having deposed to the destruction of the manuscript and the accuracy of the copy. After reading the article the author swore that he had no doubt that the facts were as therein stated.

The courts are not over-insistent on the exactitude of the copy provided they are satisfied that the document by which memory is to be refreshed substantially reproduces what was said in the original. It has been held proper for a surveyor to refresh his memory from a printed report based on his original notes[12] and for a police officer to do likewise from the statement prepared by him for use in committal proceedings from his notebook which was not available at the trial.[13] In *R v Mills*[14] it was held that a police officer might refresh his memory by referring to a note which he had checked from a tape recording of a conversation between the two appellants. The officer had overheard the conversation but had used the recording, which was not put in evidence, to confirm and improve his note.

(iii) Production of the document

The document must be handed to the opposite party or his advocate to enable him to inspect it and, if he so desires, to cross-examine the witness with regard to its contents.[15] The jury may also see the document as it could assist them in estimating the witness's credibility.[16]

(iv) The original

It was held in *Doe d Church and Phillips v Perkins*[17] that a witness may refresh his memory by any book or paper if he can afterwards swear to the fact from his own recollection, but, if he cannot swear to the fact from recollection any farther than saying that he will do so because he finds it in some book or paper, the original must be produced.[18] Allowance must of course be made for cases in which the original is lost or destroyed in which event a witness will, if he is prepared to do so, be allowed to swear to a fact that he does not recollect, because he finds it in a copy.[19]

---

11 (1844) 1 Car & Kir 320.
12 *Horne v Mackenzie* (1839) 6 Cl & Fin 628.
13 *R v Cheng* (1976) 63 Cr App Rep 20; *A-G's Reference (No 3 of 1979)* (1979) 69 Cr App Rep 411.
14 [1962] 3 All 298, [1962] 1 WLR 1152.
15 *Beech v Jones* (1848) 5 CB 696. See below as to the effect of cross-examination.
16 *R v Bass* [1953] 1 QB 680, [1953] 1 All ER 1064; *R v Fenlon* (1980) 71 Cr App Rep 307 at 312.
17 (1790) 3 Term Rep 749; *Howard v Canfield* (1836) 1 Jur 71; *R v Harvey* (1869) 11 Cox CC 546; *Ames v Nicholson* [1921] SASR 224; *Collaton v Correl* [1926] SASR 87; *King v Bryant (No 2)* [1956] SRQd 570.
18 Some latitude in this respect appears to have been allowed in *McLeod v Fraser* [1986] SCR 271.
19 As in *Topham v McGregor* (above).

3. DISTINCTION BETWEEN CASES IN WHICH MEMORY IS REFRESHED AND THOSE IN WHICH IT IS NOT REFRESHED

The distinction between cases in which a witness's memory is refreshed by the sight of a document and those in which it is not, although he is prepared to swear to the accuracy of his former statement, appears to be of importance in English law solely in connection with the question whether the original should be produced. Wigmore systematised the distinction under the headings of 'present recollection revived' and 'past recollection recorded'. His main contentions were that there should be no conditions concerning the document by which the former might be achieved while in the latter case the document should be received in evidence under what is probably best regarded as an exception to the rule against hearsay.[20] These contentions have been influential in the United States and, although neither of them represents English law, a few words about each may not be out of place here.

(i) Present recollection revived

As long ago as 1835 Lewin made the suggestion that a witness should be allowed to refresh his memory by any means because:

> Common experience tells every man that a very slight circumstance, and one not in point to the existing inquiry, will sometimes revive the history of a transaction made up of many circumstances.[1]

The desirability of carrying out the suggestion has been enhanced by the acceptance of the practice, recognised by Lewin, of allowing a witness to refresh his memory out of court. If that is not subject to restrictions concerning the type of document which may be used, it is difficult to justify the retention of such restrictions when it is sought to refresh memory in court.[2] The document which 'triggered off' the train of memory is available for inspection should any question of credibility arise, but the witness's oral testimony is the evidence on which the tribunal of fact is invited to act.

(ii) Past recollection recorded

According to English law this is also the case when present recollection is not in the least revived by the sight of the document, although there are theoretical difficulties which do not appear to have been considered by our courts. The ineptitude of the term 'refreshing memory' in such circumstances has been the subject of judicial comment:

> That is a very inaccurate expression; because in nine cases out of ten the witness's memory is not at all refreshed: he looks at it [the document] again and again; and he recollects nothing of the transaction; but, seeing that it is in his own handwriting, he gives credit to the truth and accuracy of his habits and, though

20 III Wigmore ch 28. See in particular Chadbourn revision, paras 754 and 754A.
1 Note on *Lawes v Reed* (1835) 2 Lew CC 152 at 153. There is no English case-law on the refreshment of memory by the production of an object, but see *Smith v British Aerospace* [1982] ICR 98, where memory was refreshed from a photograph.
2 See per Lawton LJ in *R v Cheng* (1976) 63 Cr App Rep 20 at 23–4.

his memory is a perfect blank, he nevertheless undertakes to swear to the accuracy of his notes.[3]

The number of cases in which the witness's memory remains a 'perfect blank' may not be as high as that suggested, but allowance must be made for numerous situations in which memory is only partly revived. When police officers are allowed to read their notes of interviews in the course of their testimony, it is unlikely that their minds are in a state of complete oblivion with regard to the subject matter, but it is even more unlikely that they could give a coherent account of what was said by any means other than that of reciting their notes. Whether the case be one of total or partial oblivion, English legal theory maintains that the matters mentioned in the document are not proved by the statements contained in it under an exception to the hearsay rule but by the witness's oral testimony.[4] In many of the cases the document to the accuracy of which the witness deposes, though remembering nothing about the matters to which it refers, would have been inadmissible in evidence and the courts have been at pains to emphasise the fact that the evidence is oral, not documentary. Thus, in *Maugham v Hubbard*,[5] a witness was called to prove the receipt of money. Being unable to remember that the payment was made to him, he was shown an unstamped acknowledgement signed by himself whereupon he said that he had no doubt that he had received the sum specified in it, although he did not recall having done so. It was held that this was sufficient evidence of the payment in spite of the prohibition on the use of unstamped receipts in litigation:

> The paper was not used as evidence of the receipt of the money, but only to enable the witness to refresh his memory; and when he said that he had no doubt that he had received the money there was sufficient parole evidence to prove the payment.[6]

Exactly the same reasoning applies in cases of the refreshment of memory of the number of a motor car by reference to a contemporaneous note. If the number has been dictated to a third party who has not himself seen it, his note is inadmissible as evidence of the number since it is hearsay,[7] but it can be used by the dictator, who cannot remember the number, to 'refresh' his memory.[8] It is not surprising that this result has been judicially castigated as being absurd.[9]

Are these instances, of which others are mentioned in ch XIV, of the unwitting reception of evidence infringing the rule against hearsay? According to that rule as formulated in this book an assertion other than one made by a person while giving oral evidence in the proceedings is inadmissible as evidence of any fact asserted. The question can best be approached by distinguishing between the different circumstances in which someone who does not recollect an event might yet have no doubt that it

---

3 Hayes J in *Lord Talbot de Malahide v Cussack* (1864) 17 CLR 213 at 220. See also *R v Bryant* (1946) 31 Cr App Rep 146 at 150.
4 *Jacob v Lindsay* (1801) 1 East 460; *Kensington v Inglis* (1807) 8 East 273; *Maugham v Hubbard* (1828) 8 B & C 14; *R v St Martin's, Leicester* (1834) 2 Ad & El 210; *Birchall v Bullough* [1896] 1 QB 325; the rule against hearsay was not mentioned in any of these cases.
5 Above.
6 Lord Tenterden CJ at 16.
7 *Jones v Metcalfe* [1967] 3 All ER 205, [1967] 1 WLR 1286.
8 *R v Kelsey* (1982) 74 Cr App Rep 213.
9 By Diplock LJ in *Jones v Metcalfe*, above, at 208, 1291.

occurred. A man who regularly shaves every morning might well have no doubt that he did so on a named day a little while back, and accordingly be prepared to testify to that effect, although he does not remember shaving on the day in question. He vouches for the regularity of his habits and the absence of anything to lead him to suppose that they might have been broken on the day in question. The further back in time the question goes the less likely is he to be prepared to swear to having shaved on account of the greater chance of some forgotten reason for not having done so. The case may be described as one of 'reconstruction' and it is of a kind which counts as personal knowledge for the purpose of the rule that witnesses must have such knowledge of the facts to which they testify. Now let us suppose that someone who recollects having dined in his college hall on a particular day is asked what he was offered for dinner. His mind may well be a complete blank on the subject and his memory may be in no way refreshed by the sight of the menu prepared by the chef and used on the occasion in question; yet he might well be prepared to swear that he was offered the items of food mentioned on the menu. His reasoning might be: 'I have never known a college menu to err; therefore I have no doubt that I was offered the dishes mentioned on the menu for that day.' He is thus prepared to vouch for the accuracy of the chef. This too is a case of reconstruction, but the witness lacks personal knowledge of the matters to which he is testifying, for the knowledge is derived from the menu, not from the regularity of his habits. *Maugham v Hubbard* resembles this last example more than that of the regular shaver. The witness was vouching for the accuracy of what he had said in a document concerning a long forgotten event.[10]

As long as the rule against hearsay is formulated in such a way as to embrace previous statements of the witness who is testifying, it is difficult to escape the conclusion that it was infringed in such cases. A hearsay statement[11] is none the less a hearsay statement because someone who has no recollection of the matters to which it refers swears that it is accurate. To meet this point r 803(5) of the Federal Rules of Evidence of the United States provides for an exception to the rule against hearsay in the following terms:

> A memorandum or record concerning a matter about which a witness once had knowledge but now has insufficient recollection to enable him to testify fully and accurately, shown to have been made or adopted by the witness when the matter was fresh in his memory and to reflect that knowledge correctly.

In civil cases the previous statement of a witness, whether or not used to refresh memory, is admissible evidence of its contents under the Civil Evidence Act 1968, but in criminal cases this is so only if the person making or taking down the statement were acting in the course of a business at the time.[12] It may be thought little less absurd that under the new law the note of a car number will be admissible evidence of its number when taken down by a policeman,[13] but inadmissible as evidence of it when taken down by the

---

10 In some circumstances the fact that a statement was made may be in issue rather than whether or not it is true, and in such cases no question of hearsay arises and the recorder of that statement may refresh his memory from his record of what was said, see *Wentworth v Rogers (No 9)* (1987) 8 NSWLR 388 at 406.

11 For definition, see p 42 above.

12 Criminal Justice Act 1988, s 24.

13 As in *R v Kelsey* (1982) 74 Cr App Rep 213.

witness's wife.[14] While such anomalies remain there may be something to be said for preserving the requirement that certain conditions should be fulfilled before a witness is permitted to refresh his memory by referring to such a note.[15]

The practical effect of the present English law is that a judge must never treat, or allow the jury to treat, a document used to refresh memory as evidence merely because it has been so used. The point may be illustrated by the Canadian case of *Young v Denton*.[16] The date of a journey made on the defendant's behalf by a driver involved in an accident was relevant to the issue of the defendant's vicarious liability. The defendant swore that the journey was made some days before the accident, having refreshed his memory from a book kept by him. The judge treated the book as a contemporaneous record assisting him to decide in favour of the defendant. It was held that he was not entitled to do this because nothing occurred to make the entry in the book evidence in the case.

4. CROSS-EXAMINATION ON DOCUMENTS USED TO REFRESH MEMORY

There is an old general rule,[17] inadequately explored in the modern authorities, that, if a party calls for and inspects a document held by the other party, he is bound to put it in evidence if required to do so.[18] But:

> Where a document is used to refresh a witness's memory, cross-examining counsel may inspect that document in order to check it without making it evidence. Moreover he may cross-examine upon it without making it evidence provided that his cross-examination does not go further than the parts which are used for refreshing the memory of the witness.[19]

If, therefore, a witness refreshes his memory concerning a date or an address by referring to a diary, he may be cross-examined about the terms or form of the entries used to refresh his memory without there being any question of the right of the party calling him to insist that the diary should become evidence in the case.[20] On the other hand, if the witness is cross-examined

---

14 As in *Grew v Cubitt* [1951] 2 TLR 305.
15 Wigmore's views were acted upon by a majority of the New Zealand Court of Appeal in *R v Caesar Naidanovici* [1962] NZLR 334.
16 [1927] 1 DLR 426.
17 It has been held to apply just as much to documents used to refresh memory out of court, *Owen v Edwards* (1984) 77 Cr App Rep 191. See also *R v Kingston* [1986] 2 Qd R 114.
18 *Wharam v Routledge* (1805) 5 Esp 235; *Calvert v Flower* (1836) 7 C & P 386; *Palmer v Maclear and M'Grath* (1858) 1 Sw & Tr 149; *Stroud v Stroud* [1963] 3 All ER 539, [1963] 1 WLR 1080.
19 *Senat v Senat* [1965] P 172 at 177. This case probably does not, as the headnote suggests, conflict with *Stroud v Stroud* (above) where the documents called for and inspected were not used to refresh memory. See also *Gregory v Tavernor* (1833) 6 C & P 280; *Payne v Ibbotson* (1858) 27 LJ Ex 341; *R v Newall* (1983) 5 DLR (4th) 352.
20 *Lloyd v Freshfield* (1826) 2 C & P 325 (cross-examination on other half of entry used to refresh memory did not make entry evidence); *R v Ramsden* (1827) 2 C & P 603 (witness could be asked whether entry written on a particular day without making it evidence); *R v Fenlon* (1980) 71 Cr App Rep 307 at 312 (prosecution could not insist on notes used by policemen to refresh memory of interview, upon which they had been cross-examined, being put before the jury). See also *R v McGregor* [1984] 1 Qd R 256 (where two people wrote different things on the same piece of paper and only one was cross-examined about his entry, only that part could strictly become evidence).

about other parts of the diary, the party calling him may insist on its being treated as evidence in the case.[1]

The major difficulty about the formulation of the general rule and the exception to it concerns the implication of such expressions as 'making a document evidence'. It might be thought that the contents become admissible as evidence of their truth by way of exception to the rule against hearsay, but the decision of the Court of Appeal in *R v Virgo*[2] shows that, in a criminal case, they are only admissible by way of exception to the rule, about to be discussed, that a witness's previous statements are inadmissible to bolster up his credibility by proving his consistency. The principal prosecution witness against Wally Virgo, a police officer charged with conspiracy to accept bribes from dealers in obscene literature, and with the corrupt reception of specific payments was Humphries, one of the pornographers, an accomplice and a man of bad character. He was allowed to refresh his memory about dates of payments to Wally from his diaries. He was cross-examined extensively on these documents with a view to showing that they referred to another Wally. They thus became evidence in the case. Virgo's convictions were quashed because the judge should have directed the jury on the limited probative value of the diaries in addition to stating, as he did, that they could not corroborate Humphries' testimony. He had spoken of them as the most important documents in the case whereas they only went some way towards establishing Humphries' creditworthiness. They had an effect similar to a complaint in a sexual case and were not evidence of the facts stated.

Subject to one possible exception[3] previous statements of witnesses are never admissible at common law as evidence of the facts stated, but s 3(2) of the Civil Evidence Act 1968 provides that:

> Nothing in this Act shall affect any of the rules of law relating to the circumstances in which, where a person called as a witness in any civil proceedings is cross-examined on a document used by him to refresh his memory, that document may be made evidence in those proceedings; and where a document or any part of a document is received in evidence in any such proceedings by virtue of any such rule of law, any statement made in that document or part by the person using the document to refresh his memory shall by virtue of this subsection be admissible as evidence of any fact stated therein of which direct oral evidence by him would be admissible.

Clause 33(2) of the draft Bill annexed to the eleventh report of the Criminal Law Revision Committee is to the same effect. In each instance there is an express provision that the statement cannot corroborate the testimony of the maker where corroboration is required as a matter of law or practice.[4] Such provisions are declaratory of the common law under which corroboration must come from a source independent of the witness whose testimony requires corroboration.

---

1 *R v Britton* [1987] 2 All ER 412, [1987] 1 WLR 539, expressly approving the statement of law in this paragraph.
2 (1978) 67 Cr App Rep 323.
3 Statements received as part of the res gestae.
4 Civil Evidence Act 1968, s 6(4); draft Bill cl 36(5); this draft clause did not appear in the Police and Criminal Evidence Act 1984 nor in the Criminal Justice Act 1988, despite a powerful plea for such a measure, see Murphy 'Previous Consistent and Inconsistent Statements' [1985] Crim LR 270.

C. PREVIOUS CONSISTENT STATEMENTS

The general rule at common law is that a witness may not be asked in-chief whether he has formerly made a statement consistent with his present testimony. He cannot narrate such statement if it was oral or refer to it if it was in writing (save for the purpose of refreshing his memory), and other witnesses may not be called to prove it. The rule against hearsay as defined in this book[5] prohibits the reception of the statement as evidence of the facts stated, but there is an independent common law ban on proof of the previous oral or written statements of the witness as evidence of his consistency.[6] Thus, in *R v Roberts*,[7] the accused was charged with murdering a girl by shooting her as she was letting him into her house. His defence, supported by his evidence at the trial was that the gun went off accidentally while he was trying to make up a quarrel with the girl. Two days after the event he told his father that the defence would be accident. The trial judge would not allow this conversation to be proved, and the Court of Criminal Appeal held that he had been right.

In this case, the reason given for the ban (sometimes loosely described as 'the rule against narrative' or 'the rule against self-corroboration') was the ease with which evidence of this nature can be manufactured.[8] But, generally speaking, this can only be apposite when the witness is a party and, in any event, the ease with which evidence can be fabricated is a matter which should affect its weight rather than its admissibility. A more convincing reason was given by Sir W D Evans in his notes to Pothier[9] when he said that in an ordinary case, the evidence would be at least superfluous, for the assertions of a witness are to be regarded in general as true, until there is some particular reason for impeaching them as false. The necessity of saving time by avoiding superfluous testimony and sparing the court a protracted inquiry into a multitude of collateral issues which might be raised about such matters as the precise terms of the previous statement is undoubtedly a sound basis for the general rule.[10]

The distinction between receiving a witness's previous statement as evidence of the facts stated and as evidence of consistency is often of no practical importance because the statement is no more than an earlier version of the testimony. In some situations[11] the time at which, or circumstances in which, the statement was made may sometimes be an additional guarantee of the trustworthiness of the testimony.

In the case of the common law exceptions to the ban on the reception of

5 See p 42 above.
6 For this reason the Civil Evidence (Scotland) Act 1988 not only abolishes the hearsay rule in s 2, but also makes separate provision for the admission of previous statements in s 3.
7 [1942] 1 All ER 187.
8 At 191 per Humphreys J. See too per Swinfen-Eady LJ in *Jones v South Eastern and Chatham Rly Co's Managing Committee* (1918) 87 LJKB 775 at 778.
9 *Pothier on Obligations* (1806 edn) vol 2, p 289.
10 'Generally speaking, as is well known, such confirmatory evidence is not admissible, the reason presumably being that all trials, civil and criminal, must be conducted with an effort to concentrate evidence on what is capable of being cogent' per Lord Radcliffe in *Fox v General Medical Council* [1960] 3 All ER 225 at 230.
11 See e g the facts of *Gillie v Posho Ltd* [1939] 2 All ER 196 (timing of previous letter to same effect as testimony significant); and *Corke v Corke and Cooke* [1958] P 93, [1958] 1 All ER 224 (circumstantial inference of making telephone call to same effect as testimony significant) though the legal results would no longer be the same.

previous statements as evidence of consistency there is some reason, other than the mere fact that it preceded the testimony, why the statement should have enhanced the witness's credibility. When a witness's previous statement is admissible as evidence of the facts stated by way of exception to the hearsay rule, it is also received as evidence of consistency on the principle that the greater includes the lesser. If all previous consistent statements are not to be admissible as evidence of the facts stated in criminal cases, it is submitted that they should always be admissible as evidence of consistency when they are relevant for some reason other than the fact that they preceded the testimony.

Previous consistent statements of witnesses are now, with the leave of the court, admissible in civil cases as evidence of the facts stated in them, as a result of the Civil Evidence Act 1968, but they are not so admissible in criminal proceedings, because there is no comparable provision in the Criminal Justice Act 1988.[12] The reception of statements under the Act of 1968 is considered in ch XV, and under the Act of 1984 in ch XVII. At this stage it is proposed to consider three well recognised exceptions to the general common law prohibition of the proof of a witness's prior statements as evidence of consistency—complaints in sexual cases, statements forming part of the same transaction as that to which they refer (admitted as part of the res gestae) and previous statements admitted to rebut the suggestion that the witness's testimony was an afterthought. The first may almost certainly be taken to be confined to criminal cases, but the second and third are still relevant to civil as well as criminal proceedings because the leave of the court is not required for the reception of statements to which they apply. There are in addition some further ill-defined exceptions to the common law rule which probably only apply to criminal cases, and a word must be said in conclusion about the possiblity of the reception of the statements made by a witness out of court under the influence of a truth drug.

1. COMPLAINTS IN SEXUAL CASES

In the Middle Ages it was essential that the victim should have raised the hue and cry if an appeal of rape were to succeed. By the beginning of the eighteenth century, when the modern law of evidence was beginning to take shape, the absence of complaint was no longer an absolute bar to success, but Hawkins still referred to the strong presumption against a prosecutrix in a case of rape if she made no complaint within a reasonable time of the alleged offence.[13] If the absence of such complaint could tell against a prosecutrix it seemed to follow that the fact of having made a complaint ought to tell in her favour, and if failure to complain could be proved by the defence then the fact of making a complaint should be capable of proof by the prosecution. Such proof does however raise problems since it grates against the rule excluding previous consistent statements, the hearsay rule and the rule against self-corroboration. It is necessary to consider, first, the range of cases in which such a complaint is admissible, second, the definition of such a complaint and the conditions to which its admissibility is subject, third, the

---

12 Though such a change was recommended by the Criminal Law Revision Committee, Cmnd 4991 para 239, draft Bill, cll 31 and 32.
13 1 PC ch 41, s 9.

use which may be made of it, fourth, other rules which permit evidence of complaints to be led, and in conclusion whether it is worth retaining the rule.

(i) Range of application

As noted above the original point of admitting evidence of a complaint was to rebut the adverse inference that might otherwise be drawn from the victim's failure to complain of the attack upon her. It is sufficient to rebut any such inference to prove merely that a complaint was made. To have admitted the terms of the complaint would have courted the risk of the jury's using them as evidence of the facts which they asserted, contrary to the hearsay rule. Originally therefore no more than the fact of a complaint having been made was admitted, though this limitation was neither fully understood,[14] nor fully accepted,[15] by the judges. Nor was it clear how far the rule extended.[16] These matters were subsequently clarified.

In *R v Lillyman*[17] the Court for Crown Cases Reserved, without conspicuous understanding of the reason for the limitation to the admission of evidence of the complaint having been made, extended admissibility to its terms, influenced in part by the effect of persistent attempts to undermine it, like those countenanced in *Wink*. A further consideration was that the exclusion of evidence of the terms effectively left the decision of whether a statement amounted to a complaint to the complainant or her auditor. The problem of hearsay was proposed to be resolved by specific instruction to the jury that the complaint was to be used only as 'evidence of the consistency of the conduct of the prosecutrix with the story told by her in the witness box, and as being inconsistent with her consent to that of which she complains'.[18] In *Lillyman* consent was not formally in issue on the relevant count, but had, in fact, been denied.[19] In *R v Osborne*[20] the court took the matter a step further by holding that consent need be in issue, neither in form nor in fact, in order to admit evidence of the terms of a complaint. The ambit of the rule was, however, restricted to 'cases of this kind'. It seems that this ambiguous phrase was intended, somewhat unhistorically[1] and illogically,[2] merely to exclude non-sexual charges. Any further ambiguity as to whether or not it extended to complaints by young male victims was resolved in favour of such a view by the decision of the Court of Criminal Appeal in *R v Camelleri* to extend it to a complaint made by a young boy.[3] Lord Hewart CJ intimated that in the

14 See Parke B in *R v Walker* (1839) 2 Mood & R 212.
15 See *R v Wink* (1834) 6 C & P 397 where Patteson J was perfectly prepared to permit the limitation to be undermined.
16 In *Wink* it was applied to a complaint of robbery.
17 [1896] 2 QB 167.
18 At 170.
19 It seems that Hawkins J, who had delivered the judgment in *Lillyman*, himself regarded this as a necessary condition, see *R v Rowland* (1898) 62 JP 459.
20 [1905] 1 KB 551.
1 The original requirement of 'hue and cry' applied to all appeals of felony, and, as noted above, as late as 1834 the rule was being applied to non-sexual offences.
2 If consent is not in issue the only recognised purpose is to demonstrate credibility by reference to consistency of complaint and testimony, and the credibility of witnesses is relevant whatever the issue to which they testify.
3 [1922] 2 KB 122. This step had already been taken by the Court of Appeal in New Zealand, see *R v McNamara* [1917] NZLR 382, and by a lower court in England, see *Chesney v Newsholme* [1908] P 301.

case of adult males little weight might be ascribed to such a complaint, but the reason for this is obscure. The point is, however, virtually moot in the United Kingdom since the absence of consent is[4] now required in relation to offences against adult males, and the question of consistency seems not to be dependent upon age.[5] From time to time attempts have been made to extend the exception beyond sexual criminal offences, now that the principal purpose is to support the consistency of the witness's story. This view was espoused by Chapman J in *R v McNamara*[6] very soon after *Osborne* had made such rationale explicit. In Canada it was also applied to cases involving illegal confinement, even in the absence of any overt sexual purpose.[7] In England there are dicta in *Jones v South Eastern and Chatham Rly Co's Management Committee*[8] suggesting extension to any complaint of violence whether in criminal or civil proceedings. There are also isolated examples of complaints not being unreservedly rejected,[9] and even admitted,[10] in other cases. It is, however, submitted that the rule does not in England extend beyond sexual offences, whatever the sex of the victim. The best justification for singling out such offences is that more hinges on questions of the credibility of the participants than in most other areas, just because sexual activity tends to take place in private and is usually kept secret, thus restricting the amount of other evidence which is likely to be available. It is upon that basis that the rule of practice requiring corroboration warnings, again in relation to both sexes, is still maintained, and it might seem right to admit any other evidence which can perhaps help the jury to resolve the customary direct conflict of testimony.

(ii) Conditions of admissibility

In *R v Osborne*[11] Ridley J summarised the conditions governing this exception to the rule otherwise prohibiting proof of previous consistent statements:

> It applies only when there is a complaint not elicited by questions of a leading and inducing or intimidating character and only when it is made at the first opportunity after the offence which reasonably offers itself.

There are thus three conditions, although each is interpreted liberally: that the statement be spontaneous; that it be contemporaneous; and that it amount to a complaint. All are matters for the judge, though it has been suggested that the third may be further reconsidered by the jury.[12] These will be considered in turn.

---

4 In the vast majority of cases.
5 See, for example, *R v Hurst and Miller* (1966) 55 WWR 358 at 365.
6 Above, at 402.
7 *R v Frame* (1976) 31 CCC (2d) 332 (a girl): *R v MacHay* (1979) 48 CCC (2d) 468 (boys).
8 (1918) 87 LJKB 775 at 778. See Gooderson 'Previous Consistent Statements' (1968) CLJ 64.
9 *Fromhold v Fromhold* [1952] 1 TLR 1522 (complaint of cruelty rejected only because not sufficiently contemporaneous).
10 *O'H v O'H* (1916) 33 TLR 51 (complaint of marital difficulty); *McIlkenny v Chief Constable of West Midlands* [1980] QB 283 at 313, [1980] 2 All ER 227 at 232 where Lord Denning MR considers evidence of complaints of ill-treatment at the hands of the police made by prisoners.
11 [1905] 1 KB 551 at 561.
12 See *Lillyman* at 178.

(a) Spontaneous. In *R v Merry*[13] it had been held that a statement elicited by the questioning of the victim's mother could not be adduced because it was a conversation rather than a complaint. No details were given of the form of questioning, so in *Osborne*, where the complaint was made only after the girl had been asked by a friend why she had not waited in the chip shop as arranged, Ridley J attempted to discriminate between different forms of questioning:

> the mere fact that the statement is made in answer to a question in such cases is not of itself sufficient to make it admissible as a complaint. Questions of a suggestive or leading character will, indeed, have that effect, and will render it inadmissible; but a question such as this, put by the mother or other person, 'What is the matter?' or 'Why are you crying?' will not do so.

Even this was thought to be too dogmatic in relation to leading questions, and in *R v Norcott*, where the auditor refused to let the complainant go until she had spoken, the Court of Criminal Appeal explained *Osborne*:[14]

> The court is concerned to see that in the present case the statement made by the girl was spontaneous in the sense that it was her unassisted and unvarnished statement of what happened. That she may have been persuaded to tell her unassisted and unvarnished story is no reason why the evidence of her having made the statement should be rejected.

The whole matter was said in *Osborne* to be a matter for the discretion of the trial judge, and to depend upon all of the relevant circumstances. Thus in one case[15] a complaint elicited by the question 'have you been raped or something?' was admitted because the victim had already indicated sufficient distress for this to be regarded as merely accelerating, rather than suggesting, the complaint. On the other hand complaints elicited by threat of force,[16] or by cross-examination after disbelief of a different statement,[17] have been rejected on this basis. The ultimate consideration should be simply whether the purpose of enhancing the witness's credibility by showing consistency between complaint and testimony will be achieved by admitting the earlier statement.

(b) Contemporaneous. The general principle underlying this exception is that the nature of the offence is such that some complaint might be expected.[18] It might well be expected to be made soon after the event, but not necessarily to the first person to be encountered. It seems quite reasonable for the victim to choose to wait until she can complain to a congenial person.[19] On the other hand if a person is obviously appropriate, and a complaint is eventually made to her, a court will be less prepared to excuse the spurning of an earlier

13 (1900) 19 Cox CC 442.
14 [1917] 1 KB 347 at 350.
15 *R v Freeman* [1980] VR 1. See also *R v Gallagher* (1986) 41 SASR 73.
16 *S v T* 1963 (1) SA 484 (A).
17 *R v Adams and Ross* [1965] Qd R 255.
18 Though modern research suggests that very often complaint is not made, see Temkin *Rape and the Legal Process* (1987) pp 145, 146.
19 Thus in *R v Cummings* [1948] 1 All ER 551 it was held that a young woman in a strange camp need not complain to the male supervisor whom she hardly knew but could wait until morning and complain to an older lady friend.

opportunity.[20] In general the condition will be interpreted generously in view of the subjective condition of the victim who might easily be too upset to talk about the offence at all for some time.[1] If the victim testifies to having made a complaint, but the auditor either denies that it was made,[2] or it cannot be used because it is regarded as not having been sufficiently spontaneous,[3] then a subsequent complaint may be proved if made reasonably soon afterwards. In *Breen v R*[4] the High Court of Australia was prepared to admit several complaints made soon after the event, despite the victim not having referred to many of them in her testimony. This seems questionable, and there is force in the view[5] that if the only point is to demonstrate consistency then one is enough, and that more may be prejudicial, making it even more likely that the jury will be inclined to regard them as evidence of the truth of what they assert.

(c) Complaint. The third requirement is that the statement should amount to a complaint. This will rarely cause difficulty though some statements have been rejected as 'conversation'[6] or 'narrative'.[7] It has been held in Australia that the complaint must relate to the sexual element of the offence.[8] Here too a generally relaxed view is taken, perhaps because this condition is regarded as being capable of being reconsidered by the jury,[9] though it is hard to believe that any jury would really engage in so arcane an exercise.

(iii) Permissible use

Both in *Lillyman*[10] and in *Osborne*[11] reference was made to the complaint being used to show consistency with the victim's testimony, and being inconsistent with consent. In *Kilby v R*,[12] it is submitted rightly, the High Court of Australia emphasised that this could not be taken to mean that it amounted to evidence of the absence of consent, nor its absence to evidence of consent. That would be to make the very hearsay use of the complaint warned against by Hawkins J, in *Lillyman*. The correct view is that the victim's testimony is evidence of lack of consent, and the complaint does no more than support the credibility of the victim in so testifying.

It sometimes happens that the testimony of the victim is inconsistent with the complaint. In such a case there is no reason why it should not be used as such by the opponent in cross-examination, and there is some authority for permitting its use for this purpose as a complaint, apparently on the basis

---

20 Dicta in *R v Peake* (1974) 9 SASR 458 (though on the facts such a complaint was admitted).
 1 See *R v Freeman* [1980] VR 1.
 2 As in *R v Lee* (1911) 7 Cr App Rep 31 (where the complaint admitted was actually the third alleged to have been made, the first being denied in crucial details by the accused's mother to whom it had been made, and the second, to the victim's father, relating only to a physical injury). See also *R v McDonald* (1985) 17 ACR 297.
 3 As seems to have been the case in *R v Wilbourne* (1917) 12 Cr App Rep 280.
 4 (1974) 50 ALJR 536. See also *R v Roisetter* [1984] 1 Qd R 477.
 5 *R v Wilson* (1986) 42 SASR 203 at 226; *R v Tanda* (1986) 43 SASR 161.
 6 *R v Merry* (1900) 19 Cox CC 442.
 7 *De B v De B* [1950] VLR 242.
 8 *R v Saunders* [1965] Qd R 409 (where the victim was believed by her auditors to be male).
 9 *R v Manwaring* [1983] 2 NSWLR 82 at 91, so interpreting dicta in *Lillyman*.
10 [1896] 2 QB 167 at 170.
11 [1905] 1 KB 551 at 557, 558.
12 (1973) 129 CLR 460.

that if consonance of complaint and testimony enhances credibility, dissonance should be allowed to diminish it.[13]

Since the purpose of admitting evidence of the complaint is simply to enhance the credibility of the victim's testimony it follows that evidence of the complaint is inadmissible if the victim is unable to testify.[14] It seems, however, that if the victim can testify, it is immaterial that such testimony differs in some details from the terms of the original complaint.[15] When the victim does testify a complaint cannot amount to corroboration of her testimony, whether it is exceptionally proved by the victim herself,[16] or, as is more usual, by the auditor.[17]

If evidence of the absence of a recent complaint is to be used to weaken the credibility of the victim it seems only fair that evidence explaining why such a complaint was not forthcoming should be admissible. It clearly is admissible before the judge when he is deciding whether the conditions for admitting the statement as a complaint have been established. As a matter of fairness judges will normally direct juries not only as to the use they are permitted to make of the terms of an admissible complaint but also what inference they may draw from a failure to make such a complaint. While *Kilby v R*[18] proscribes any direction that this is evidence of consent, it approves a direction that it weakens the credibility of the victim, though in New South Wales, even before it became mandatory by statutory amendment,[19] it was customary for juries to be warned of the reasons which might inhibit such complaint.[20] Since this second direction sanctioned by *Kilby* has survived the statutory reform,[1] it is submitted[2] that it is only fair that evidence relevant to the reasons for not complaining sooner, or at all, should be admissible at the trial.

(iv) Other rules

As indicated above a complaint inconsistent with the eventual testimony of the victim may be put in cross-examination as a previous inconsistent statement, in which case also it will affect only credibility, and will not amount to evidence of the facts it states. It is, however, possible to imagine situations in which a recent complaint might become evidence of its assertions by way of exception to the hearsay rule. It is possible that the complaint might be made in the presence of the accused, and accepted by him.[3] If a complaint is made as a dying declaration it will be admissible as evidence of its truth in the limited circumstances in which such declarations are admissible.[4] Attempts have also been made to secure the admission of

13 *R v Askew* [1981] Crim LR 398.
14 *Sparks v R* [1964] AC 964, [1964] 1 All ER 727.
15 *R v Braye-Jones* [1966] Qd R 295; *R v Askew* [1981] Crim LR 398.
16 As in *R v Lee* (1911) 7 Cr App Rep 31 where the auditor refused to testify to the complaint, and in *R v Duell* [1964] Qd R 451 where she was unable to remember it.
17 *R v Lovell* (1923) 17 Cr App Rep 163. See also *Eade v R* (1924) 34 CLR 154; *Thomas v R* [1952] 4 DLR 306.
18 (1973) 129 CLR 460 at 465.
19 Crimes Act 1900, new s 405B.
20 *R v Zorad* [1979] 2 NSWLR 764 at 772.
 1 See *R v Davies* (1985) 3 NSWLR 276.
 2 This has been disputed in Canada, cp *R v Kistendey* (1975) 29 CCC (2d) 382; *R v Walters* (1980) 53 CCC (2d) 119 at 130.
 3 As it was argued had occurred in *R v Christie* [1914] AC 545.
 4 See further, below, ch XVI.

such complaints as part of the res gestae,[5] but this is usually unsuccessful, because the complaint is made only after the stress of the crime has somewhat subsided.[6] It is, however, possible to conceive of cases where the line is not so clear, and the protest is made, and heard, while the offence is taking place or in its immediate aftermath.[7]

(v) Reform

The Criminal Law Revision Committee recommended, as part of its general reform of the hearsay rule in criminal cases, that this rule be abrogated,[8] but this part of its proposals has not been, and now seems unlikely to be, enacted. The rule has been heavily criticised in the United States,[9] and abrogated in Canada.[10] It has also been abolished or severely restricted in a number of other Commonwealth jurisdictions,[11] though in South Australia after being abolished it was subsequently restored. The argument for abolition is its inconsistency with other rules, its illogicality, its capacity to prejudice the accused, its arbitrary scope, and the resentment created by allowing the credibility of one of the parties to the dispute to be bolstered, but not that of the other.[12] The argument for retention is that in a contest of credibility technical rules should not stand in the way of anything which assists the jury to resolve it satisfactorily, and that the legal rules still operate in sexual cases to the disadvantage of complainants to such an extent that it would be unfair to remove a rule which does a little to redress the balance. Technicality creates its own injustice however, not least in unmeritorious acquittals, and it is submitted that it is better to reform what is still shown to be wrong in the law of procedure as it applies to sexual offences directly, rather than to seek to counterbalance one injustice by a different anomaly. Most of the legitimate work to be done by the recent complaints rule could be better accomplished by use of the rule permitting the use of previous consistent statements to rebut any suggestion of afterthought.[13] There seems no reason why sexual offences should not be proved and tried in just the same way as any others.

2. PREVIOUS CONSISTENT STATEMENTS ADMITTED AS PART OF THE RES GESTAE

The term 'res gestae' is a blanket phrase when applied to the admissibility of statements, and may roughly be said to denote relevance through

---

5 See further, below, ch XVIII.
6 See for example, *Sparks v R* [1964] AC 964 at 979.
7 See *R v Kooyman* (1979) 22 SASR 376 at 380, 381.
8 Cmnd 4991, para 232.
9 In *Commonwealth v Cleary* (1898) 172 Mass 175 Justice Holmes described it as 'a perverted survival', see also Wigmore para 1140.
10 Canadian Criminal Code, s 275. See Dawson 'The Abrogation of Recent Complaint: Where Do We Stand Now' (1984) 27 Crim LQ 57.
11 See, for example, Evidence (Amendment) Ordinance (No 2) 1985, s 76C(1) (ACT); Crimes Act, s 405B (NSW); Acts Amendment (Sexual Assaults) Act 1985, s 15 enacting new s 36BD (WA); Evidence Amendment Act 1985, s 3 (New Zealand).
12 See *R v Newsome* (1980) 71 Cr App Rep 325.
13 See, below, p 290.

contemporaneity—part of the story.[14] The different types of statement that may be admitted under this head are considered later. At this stage it is necessary to say only that the credibility of a witness's testimony may be confirmed by the narration by himself or someone else of a statement to the same effect as his evidence if it can be said to form part of the transaction to which his evidence relates. In *Milne v Leisler*,[15] for instance, the question was whether the plaintiff contracted to sell goods on the footing that A, to whom the goods were delivered, was the agent of B, or on the basis that A was acting on his own behalf. On the first assumption, the defendant was liable in conversion, but not on the second. After the plaintiff had sworn that A purported to contract as agent for B, he was allowed to put in evidence letters written by him to his firm's representative referring to the sale and asking for inquiries to be made concerning the solvency of B. Normally, letters by a party to his agent are excluded as irrelevant, or too remotely relevant, because of the facility with which a man can manufacture evidence for himself, but, in this instance, the letters were received, not as direct proof of the sale to B, but on account of their strong tendency to confirm the plaintiff's testimony. The crucial facts were that the letters could be regarded as part of the events to which the plaintiff was deposing. If a witness says, that, in consequence of the naming of a referee, he made certain inquiries in order to determine whether a particular person should be a party to a contract of sale to which he also deposes, the letters containing those inquiries are better evidence than his testimony.

In *Spittle v Spittle*,[16] on the other hand, a wife who had been negotiating a settlement of outstanding financial questions with her husband was not allowed to call her daughter to depose to the fact that, very soon after she received a cheque from her husband, she told her daughter that she had taken it on account. The statement could not, in any sense of the word, be said to have formed part of the settlement.

If the facts of *Milne v Leisler* were to recur, the letter would be admissible with the leave of the court under the Civil Evidence Act 1968, as direct evidence of the fact to which it referred, and not merely as evidence of consistency although, in the particular circumstances, this would be largely if not entirely a distinction without a difference because the plaintiff deposed to most if not all of the facts in question, but it seems that he would still be able to insist on the reception of the letter as evidence of consistency without the necessity of obtaining the leave of the court, for the Act of 1968 is solely concerned with the reception of statements as evidence of the facts stated. If the facts of *Spittle v Spittle* were to recur, the wife would, with the leave of the court, be able to prove what she said to her daughter and to call her daughter to do likewise under the Civil Evidence Act 1968. The wife's remarks would be admitted as evidence that the cheque was taken on account although, as the greater includes the lesser, the remarks would also constitute evidence of consistency.

In *R v Fowkes*[17] a man commonly known as 'the butcher' was charged with murder. The deceased's son gave evidence that he and a police officer were sitting in a room with his father when a face appeared at the window

14 See note by F P in *Homes v Newman* [1931] 2 Ch 112 at 120.
15 (1862) 7 H & N 786.
16 [1965] 3 All ER 451, [1965] 1 WLR 1156.
17 Stephen *Digest of the Law of Evidence* (12th edn) 8.

through which the fatal shot was then fired. At the trial he said that he thought the face was that of 'the butcher'. He was allowed to swear how he had shouted 'There's Butcher' when the face appeared, and the police officer, who had not seen the face, was allowed to depose to the shouting of the name Butcher. Sir James Stephen commented on this case as follows:

> It is ... obvious that the fact that he said at the time 'There's Butcher' was far more likely to impress the jury than the fact that he was at the trial uncertain whether the person he saw was the butcher, though he was disposed to think so.

This meagrely reported decision is unaffected by any intervening legislation. Although there is really no authority on the point, it is certainly arguable that previous statements of witnesses constituting part of the res gestae are admissible as hearsay statements, and not merely as evidence of consistency.[18] If this is so, the conditions of admissibility are, in this very limited class of case, less restrictive in criminal than in civil proceedings. On facts such as those of *R v Fowkes*, evidence of what the son said at the time of the shooting would be admissible under the Civil Evidence Act 1968 but only on compliance with specified conditions or with the leave of the court.[19] It is further arguable that the importance of this exception may have grown as a result of the relaxation of the condition for the admissibility of res gestae statements following the decision of the Judicial Committee of the Privy Council in *Ratten v R*.[20]

3. PREVIOUS CONSISTENT STATEMENTS ADMITTED TO REBUT AFTERTHOUGHT

When giving judgment in *R v Coll*,[21] Holmes J said:

> It is I think clear that the evidence of a witness cannot be corroborated by proving statements to the same effect previously made by him; nor will the fact that his testimony is impeached in cross-examination render such evidence admissible. Even if the impeachment takes the form of showing a contradiction or inconsistency between the evidence given at the trial and something said by the witness on a former occasion it does not follow that the way is open for proof of other statements made by him for the purpose of sustaining his credit. There must be something either in the nature of the inconsistent statement, or in the use made of it by the cross-examiner to enable such evidence to be given.

The fact that the whole of the witness's testimony is attacked will not bring the exception into play.[1] Nor is it enough that an inconsistent statement has been used to discredit the witness.[2] It has been said that the nature of the cross-examination must be such that it can be interpreted as containing the direct question 'when did you first invent this story?'[3]

18 See R N Gooderson in [1957] CLJ 55 at 78.
19 The distinction would probably have been preserved by cl 37 of the draft Bill attached to the 11th Report of the Criminal Law Revision Committee.
20 [1972] AC 378, [1971] 3 All ER 801.
21 (1889) 25 LR Ir 522 at 541.
 1 *Fox v General Medical Council* [1960] 3 All ER 225, [1960] 1 WLR 1017.
 2 *R v Beattie* (1989) 89 Cr App Rep 302 explicitly, endorsing these remarks in *Coll*; cp dicta in *Ahmed v Brumfitt* (1967) 112 Sol Jo 32. In Canada the rule appears to be less strict, see *R v Simpson* (1988) 46 DLR (4th) 466 at 482.
 3 *Flanagan v Fahy* [1918] 2 IR 361.

If it is alleged that a prisoner's story is a recent concoction, a previous statement concerning the nature of his defence becomes admissible,[4] so too does a statement made by an accused's wife to a solicitor before she had seen her husband after his arrest if it is suggested in cross-examination that her evidence was the result of collusion with him;[5] and an allegation that a policeman is fabricating his testimony allows his notebook to be put in evidence.[6] Generally speaking the previous statement will be put to the witness in re-examination, but circumstances are conceivable in which he would be asked about it in-chief. This might be done when the cross-examination of a previous witness had contained a suggestion of fabrication by himself and the succeeding witness, or at a criminal trial when something of the sort had been suggested at the proceedings before the magistrates.

The question whether a situation has arisen in which a previous statement may be proved under this head is, both in civil and criminal cases, largely a matter for the judge's decision. It is difficult to improve on the following observations of a former Chief Justice of Australia:

> In as much as the rule forms a definite exception to the general principle excluding statements made out of Court and admits a possibly self-serving statement made by the witness, great care is called for in applying it. The judge at the trial must determine for himself, upon the conduct of the trial before him, whether a case for applying the rule of evidence has arisen—and must exercise care in assuring himself not only that the account given by the witness in his testimony is attacked on the ground of recent invention or reconstruction or that a foundation for such an attack has been laid—but also that the contents of the statement are in fact to the like effect as his account given in his evidence and that having regard to the time and circumstances in which it was made it rationally tends to answer the attack.[7]

Section 3(1)(b) of the Civil Evidence Act 1968 provides that:

> Where in any civil proceedings ... a previous statement made by a person called as [a witness] is proved for the purpose of rebutting a suggestion that his evidence has been fabricated, that statement shall by virtue of this section[8] be admissible as evidence of any fact stated therein of which direct oral evidence would be admissible.[9]

At common law, and therefore in criminal cases, the statement is simply

---

4 *R v Roberts* [1942] 1 All ER 187 at 191 per Humphreys J.
5 *R v Oyesiku* (1971) 56 Cr App Rep 240. See also *R v Okai* [1987] Crim LR 259.
6 *R v Benjamin* (1913) 8 Cr App Rep 146.
7 Dixon CJ in *Nominal Defendant v Clements* (1961) 104 CLR 476 at 479. This statement was cited in the Court of Appeal (Criminal Division) in *R v Oyesiku*, above. Other important Australian authorities are *Woodward v Shea* [1952] VLR 313; *Francombe v Holloway* [1957] VLR 139; *Lavelle v R* [1957] Tas SR 162; *Transport and General Insurance Co Ltd v Edmundson* (1961) 106 CLR 23; *Wojcic v Incorporated Nominal Defendant* [1967] VR 263 leaving open, at 282, the question whether, if a party's testimony is contradicted in cross-examination by an admission, it is permissible for him to prove an earlier statement under the recent invention rule (this point was not mentioned on appeal in [1969] VR 323); *Damon v Snyder* [1970] VR 81. (Cross-examination on answers to interrogatories inconsistent with testimony held not to be within the recent invention rule.)
8 These words, which occur quite frequently in the Act, are necessitated by the fact that, in consequence of the Act, hearsay statements are only admissible in civil cases by virtue of a statutory provision or agreement.
9 There is a similar provision in cl 33 of the draft Bill annexed to the 11th Report of the Criminal Law Revision Committee.

admissible as circumstantial evidence negativing the suggestion of after-thought or fabrication; but, in view of the requirement of close correspond-ence between the statement and the witness's testimony, the distinction is unimportant, if not non-existent.

4. OTHER EXCEPTIONS

Although the existence of other common law exceptions to the general prohibition of proof of a witness's prior consistent statements was recognised before 1968, it was not until the publication of an important article in that year by Gooderson[10] that anything like a thorough account was given of them. A brief reference must be made to three further exceptions mentioned in that article, statements by the accused when arrested, statements by the accused when incriminating articles are recovered from his possession, and statements by witnesses when identifying the accused out of court.[11] Finally a new category seems to have emerged resembling, but not identical to, some of those discussed above.

(i) Statements on arrest

Perhaps this exception would be better described as 'statements made by the accused to the police when taxed with incriminating facts', for such statements are admissible whether or not there is an arrest. If they are partly or wholly adverse to the accused they are admissible for or against him as confessions, provided that they satisfy the conditions established by the Police and Criminal Evidence Act 1984.[12] If they[13] are partly inculpatory and partly exculpatory, then both parts are admissible as evidence of their truth.[14] This is allowed partly because it would be unfair to admit the inculpatory part, but not a qualification or explanation in the exculpatory part; and partly because any direction discriminating between them would be hard for the judge to formulate and for the jury to understand. If no part of them is adverse to the accused they have been held to be admissible because:

> A statement made voluntarily by an accused person to the police is evidence in the trial because of its vital relevance as showing the reaction of the accused when first taxed with incriminating facts.[15]

If an exculpatory statement has no such relevance, perhaps because made only after careful consideration and upon legal advice, it need not be admitted.[16] If admitted, it is still, unlike a confession, not evidence of the

---

10 (1968) CLJ 64.
11 A further exception is the previous statement contained in a writing used to refresh memory made evidence in the case by cross-examination on other parts of the document (p 279 above).
12 S 76.
13 This point applies to all 'mixed statements' whether made on arrest, or at any other time before trial.
14 *R v Sharp* [1988] 1 All ER 65, [1988] 1 WLR 7; *R v Duncan* (1981) 73 Cr App Rep 359.
15 *R v Storey* (1968) 52 Cr App Rep 334 at 337.
16 *R v Newsome* (1980) 71 Cr App Rep 325, explaining *R v Pearce* (1979) 69 Cr App Rep 365. See also *R v Steel* (1981) 73 Cr App Rep 173 at 185, where the statement was made, not to the police, but to the accused's solicitor. See also *R v Squire* [1990] Crim LR 341.

facts stated in it, and the judge need neither take it into account in deciding whether or not there is a case to answer,[17] nor draw it to the jury's attention, if the accused fails to testify at his trial.[18] It is not clear that the slight relevance of such a statement either on grounds of consistency of story or as showing reaction is worth the risk of attempting to explain so illogical and anomalous a rule to the jury. It would have been much better to have swept the rule aside as part of a general reform of the hearsay rule in criminal cases, as recommended by the Criminal Law Revision Committee.[19]

(ii) Statements made on recovery of incriminating articles

We saw in ch 1 that, if someone is found in possession of recently stolen goods, there is a presumption of fact that he was either the thief or a guilty handler of them. What he says by way of explanation is therefore admissible on principles similar to those discussed in the last paragraph and, if he is subsequently charged, it may be valuable proof of consistency if he tells the same story in court.[20]

(iii) Previous identification of the accused

To quote Ferguson J, a judge of the Supreme Court of New South Wales, '... evidence has been admitted in criminal trials from time immemorial of the identification of the accused (by witnesses) out of court'.[1] There can be no doubt that identification at the time of or soon after the offence will often strengthen the value of the witness's identification of the accused in court, and nothing more need be said in order to justify the reception of statements forming part of his act of identification.[2]

There is no suggestion in the cases that any of the three last mentioned exceptions to the rule prohibiting proof of prior consistent statements applies to civil proceedings, and, in view of the general admissibility of such statements under the Civil Evidence Act 1968, as evidence of any fact of which direct oral evidence by the maker would be admissible, it is unlikely that there ever will be any authority dealing with the common law in these situations. The following would be a test case: A is suing B for negligence in a running down action; an hour after the accident, a police officer tells B that A has said that B was driving with gross negligence, giving details. B at once retorts that it was all A's fault, giving details in his turn. Assuming that B were to give evidence, his statement would be admissible as proof of consistency at his trial for reckless driving. B's statement would also be admissible with the leave of the court in the running down action under the Civil Evidence Act 1968. But would it be admissible as of right at common law on the ground that it is sufficient to tender it as evidence of consistency and not as evidence of a fact of which B could give oral evidence and has

17 *R v Storey* above.
18 *R v Barbery* (1975) 62 Cr App Rep 248.
19 Cmnd 4991, para 232, draft Bill cl 33. See also Elliott and Wakefield 'Exculpatory Statements by Accused Persons' [1979] Crim LR 428.
20 Among the English authorities cited by Gooderson are *R v Abraham* (1848) 3 Cox CC 430; *R v Exall* (1866) 4 F & F 922; *R v Muller* (1865) 4 F & F 383 n, and 388–389 n (a murder case); *R v Manzano* (1860) 2 F & F 64–65 n. See also *R v Graham* (1972) 7 CCC (2d) 93.
1 *R v Fannon* (1922) 22 SR NSW 427 at 430.
2 For the position where the maker of the statement gives no evidence of identification or gives hesitant evidence, see pp 290 above and 722 below.

already done so? If such a distinction as the above, one well warranted by judicial statements, is tenable, the answer is 'yes'; but is the distinction tenable? Surely a time comes when the distinction between admitting a witness's statement as evidence of a fact of which he can and does give oral evidence and as evidence of consistency ceases to exist.

(iv) Previous statements alleged to have been concocted

It has been held[3] that where it is alleged in cross-examination that a document, amounting to a previous consistent statement and used by the witness to refresh his memory, has been concocted, then, if the form of the document might be taken by the jury to indicate that the allegation is false,[4] it is admissible in evidence at the instance of the party calling the witness. This differs from the rule relating to cross-examination on parts of the document not used to refresh memory as discussed above, in that here the cross-examination need not extend to any such part. It differs from the rule relating to rebutting afterthought by reference to a previous consistent statement, since here it is the previous consistent statement itself which is alleged to have been concocted. When such a document has been admitted it is not evidence of the truth of its contents, except to the extent that they relate to its own authenticity.

5. STATEMENTS VALIDATED BY SCIENTIFIC MEANS

Wigmore once said that 'if ever there is devised a psychological test for the valuation of witnesses, the law will run to meet it.[5] Three possibilities which have been considered involve the use of lie-detectors, truth drugs and hypnosis. None has been received with any enthusiasm. Evidence of the use of a lie-detector has been rejected by the Supreme Court of Canada, whether the relevant subject testifies,[6] or chooses not to do so.[7] In the latter case the accused had been given a truth-drug, and the evidence of the psychiatrist who administered it was admitted at the trial. The admissibility of that evidence was not in issue before the Supreme Court, and in any event did not consist of statements of fact relevant to the issues made under the influence of the drug. That situation did however arise in New Zealand in *R v McKay*.[8] The evidence was rejected because it infringed the rules excluding previous consistent statements and hearsay, because it would distort the process of trial, and because it was unreliable.[9] In Scotland facilities for taking such a statement have been refused, once again because it would involve distortion of the trial process.[10] The evidence of statements made during, and indeed after, a hypnotic trance which had been induced,

---

3 *R v Sekhon* (1987) 85 Cr App Rep 19.
4 This is vital, cp *R v Fenlon* (1980) 71 Cr App Rep 307; *R v Dillon* (1983) 85 Cr App Rep 29n.
5 Para 924a.
6 *R v Beland and Phillips* (1987) 43 DLR (4th) 641.
7 *Phillion v R* [1978] 1 SCR 18, not accepting the contrary decision in *R v Wong* [1977] 1 WWR 1, but following the majority view in the United States, stemming from *Frye v United States* 293 F 1013 (1923).
8 [1967] NZLR 139.
9 See Mathieson 'The Truth Drug: Trial by Psychiatrist' [1967] Crim LR 645.
10 *Meehan (petitioner)* 1970 JC 11.

apparently inadvertently, by a police interrogator, was rejected by the Supreme Court of Canada in *Horvath v R*, largely on grounds of unreliability.[11] Despite arguments in favour of the admission of such statements,[12] it is submitted that the unproven reliability of these techniques, together with the danger of the jury's attributing more weight to such unfamiliar scientific evidence than it deserves, would justify the English courts in following the example of their counterparts in the rest of the common law world in excluding such statements.

D. UNFAVOURABLE AND HOSTILE WITNESSES

A party calling a witness to prove certain facts may be disappointed by his failure to do so, and his difficulties may be increased by the witness's manifest antipathy to his cause. This lies at the root of the distinction between unfavourable and hostile witnesses. An unfavourable witness is one called by a party to prove a particular fact in issue or relevant to the issue who fails to prove such fact, or proves an opposite fact. A hostile witness is one who is not desirous of telling the truth at the instance of the party calling him.[13] It will be convenient to state the common law with regard to unfavourable and hostile witnesses separately, and then to mention the relevant statutory provisions—s 3 of the Criminal Procedure Act 1865, and the Civil Evidence Act 1968; but something must first be said of the prohibition against a party impeaching his own witness.

1. THE PROHIBITION AGAINST IMPEACHING A PARTY'S OWN WITNESS[14]

A party against whom a witness is called may impeach him in various ways. He may cross-examine him by means of leading questions, ask him about his previous inconsistent statements and prove them if they are denied—a matter which is now covered by statute; he may cross-examine him with regard to his discreditable conduct in the past with a view to showing bad character, or he may ask the witness about his previous convictions or the existence of bias, and prove these two matters by other evidence if they are denied. Finally a party may call evidence to show that the opponent's witness is not to be believed on oath. The prohibition against a party impeaching his own witness means that there is a general rule preventing a litigant from taking any of the above steps with regard to witnesses called by him. It is for the judge to determine whether and to what extent a witness is unfavourable to the party calling him, and no such determination should be made before

11 [1979] 2 SCR 376. See also *R v Geering* (1984) 39 SASR 111, and cp *Van Vliet v Griffiths* (1978) 19 SASR 195.
12 See for example, Haward and Ashworth 'Some Problems of Evidence Obtained by Hypnosis' [1980] Crim LR 469, and Harnon 'Evidence Obtained by Polygraph: An Israeli Perspective' [1982] Crim LR 340. For an excellent exposition of the problems see Elliott 'Lie-Detector Evidence: Lessons from the American Experience' in Campbell and Waller (eds) *Well and Truly Tried* (1982).
13 Stephen *Digest of the Law of Evidence* (12th edn) art 147.
14 III *Wigmore* para 896 f. See also Bryant (1982) 32 Univ of Tor LJ 412, (1983) 33 Univ of Tor LJ 108.

the witness has been sworn and given a chance to come up to his proof.[15] Such procedure renders a voir dire generally unnecessary on this issue.

Various reasons have been given for the rule. It is said that a party ought not to have the means of discrediting his witness, or that he guarantees the trustworthiness of the evidence he adduces, or that it would be unfair to subject the witness to two cross-examinations. Whatever its basis may be, the rule seems to work well enough in ordinary circumstances as applied to unfavourable witnesses, but it would be ludicrous to apply it to a hostile witness in its full rigour.[16]

2. UNFAVOURABLE WITNESSES

At common law a party was allowed to contradict his own witness by calling other evidence[17] if he was unfavourable, but this did not amount to a modification of the prohibition against discrediting his witness because it did not involve resort to any of the methods mentioned at the beginning of the last section. In *Ewer v Ambrose*[18] someone whom the defendant called to prove a partnership proved the contrary, and it was held that the defendant could rely on the testimony of other witnesses in support of the existence of the partnership. In the words of Holroyd J :

> If a witness proves a case against the party calling him, the latter may show the truth by other witnesses. But it is undoubtedly true, that if a party calls a witness to prove a fact, he cannot, when he finds the witness proves the contrary, give general evidence to show that the witness was not to be believed on his oath, but he may show by other evidence that he is mistaken as to the fact which he is called to prove.

This last kind of evidence would necessarily concern the issue more directly than evidence with regard to the witness's credibility, and, in order to appreciate the enormity of the injustice which might be occasioned by rejecting it, a case may be supposed in which a party has four witnesses to support his version of the facts. If he happened to begin by calling a witness who disproved his case, he would be deprived of the testimony of the other three. If he called these before the one who disproved his case, it would have been a question for the jury upon the evidence whether they gave credit to the three or the one. The order in which the witnesses happen to be called ought not to make any difference.[19] Of course, there is a sense in which a

---

15 *R v Darby* [1989] Crim LR 817. Still less should previous statements inconsistent with an anticipated hostile line of response to examination-in-chief be put to the witness at this stage.

16 The rule is abrogated by r 607 of the United States Federal Rules (following the Model Code and Uniform Rules), but the Criminal Law Revision Committee was in favour of its retention (11th Report, para 162).

17 If the original evidence takes the form of an interrogatory the conflicting testimony may even come from the very same witness, see *Mundy v Bridge Motors Pty Ltd* (1987) 45 SASR 125.

18 (1825) 3 B & C 746. If the prosecution calls a witness to identify the accused and he fails to do so, he is not contradicted by evidence that he did identify the accused given by a police officer who saw him do so at a parade (*R v Osborne and Vertue* [1973] QB 678, [1973] 1 All ER 649), although the officer's evidence gives rise to hearsay problems as not yet fully considered in the English cases.

19 This is the basis of the judgment of Littledale J in *Ewer v Ambrose*. See also *Bradley v Ricardo* (1831) 8 Bing 57.

man is being discredited if someone asks the court to believe what another man says in preference to his testimony concerning a fact in issue or relevant to the issue, but, although the question is one of degree, the discrediting is a great deal more obvious if one of the methods mentioned at the beginning of the last section is adopted. When this is done, the whole of his testimony is impugned, but this is not necessarily the case when he is contradicted with regard to a particular fact. If a party contradicts part of the testimony of an unfavourable witness, he is not precluded from relying on the rest of that testimony.

3. HOSTILE WITNESSES[20]

The judge may allow the examination-in-chief of a hostile witness to be conducted in the manner of a cross-examination to the extent to which he considers it necessary for the purpose of doing justice.[1] If the witness is not compellable, the possibility of being cross-examined as a hostile witness should be explained before the witness is sworn.[2] The witness may be asked leading questions, challenged with regard to his means of knowledge of the facts to which he is deposing or tested on such matters as the accuracy of his memory and perception; but the party by whom he is called cannot ask about his previous bad conduct and convictions, nor can he adduce evidence of the witness's doubtful veracity. This is the result of the common law, but it used not to be clear whether a statement inconsistent with his present testimony could be proved against a hostile witness—a matter that became increasingly important with the growth of the practice among attorneys of taking a proof of the evidence which a person was prepared to give.[3] As Erle CJ observed:[4]

> There are treacherous witnesses who will hold out that they can prove facts on one side in a cause and then, for a bribe or for some other motive, make statements in support of the opposite interest. In such cases the law undoubtedly ought to permit the party calling the witness to question him as to the former statement, and ascertain, if possible, what induces him to change it.

In *R v Fraser and Warren*,[5] Lord Goddard CJ said that if, in a criminal case, counsel for the prosecution has a statement contradicting a Crown witness who says, at the trial, that he is unable to identify the accused, he should at once show the statement to the judge and ask for leave to cross-examine the witness, but it is doubtful whether the mere existence of an inconsistency between a witness's previous statement and his testimony at the trial will necessarily lead the judge to allow the witness to be treated as hostile. In a civil case, the mere fact that the witness is the other litigant does not mean that he may be treated as hostile.[6] Although the matter has been much more fully discussed in the Commonwealth than in this country, there seems to be

---

20 See Newark 'The Hostile Witness and the Adversary System' [1986] Crim LR 441.
1 *Bastin v Carew* (1824) Ry & M 127.
2 *R v Pitt* [1983] QB 25, [1983] 3 All ER 63.
3 See, for example, the difference of opinion in *Wright v Beckett* (1834) 1 Mood & R 414.
4 *Melhuish v Collier* (1850) 15 QB 878 at 890.
5 (1956) 40 Cr App Rep 160. See also *R v Pitt* [1983] QB 25, [1982] 3 All ER 63; *R v Mann* (1972) 56 Cr App Rep 750.
6 *Price v Manning* (1889) 42 Ch D 372.

no doubt that, in deciding whether to allow the witness to be treated as hostile, the judge may have regard to the witness's demeanour, the terms of any inconsistent statement and the circumstances in which it was made.[7] As the matter is dependent on judicial discretion, the judge's decision will seldom be reversed by an appellate tribunal.[8] There can, however, be little doubt that an English court would not react with comparable disfavour to that shown by the High Court of Australia[9] to the idea of calling a witness known to be hostile for the sole purposes of cross-examining by reference to a previous inconsistent statement.

Although there does not appear to be a fully reported case on the point,[10] it is believed that judges take different views on the question whether a party who has obtained leave to treat his witness as hostile has a right to re-examine him. If the hostility is made manifest only at the stage of re-examination, then cross-examination is naturally permitted.[11]

4. STATUTORY PROVISIONS

(i) Criminal Procedure Act 1865, s 3

Section 22 of the Common Law Procedure Act 1854 was passed in order to settle the law in civil cases with regard to proof of inconsistent statements by a party's own witness. As was pointed out five years later in *Greenough v Eccles*,[12] the terms of the section were confusing so far as unfavourable witnesses were concerned, but they were re-enacted in s 3 of the Criminal Procedure Act 1865.

This governs a party's right to impeach a hostile witness in civil and criminal cases alike at the present day.[13] It reads as follows:

> A party producing a witness shall not be allowed to impeach his credit by general evidence of bad character, but he may, in case the witness shall, in the opinion of the judge, prove adverse, contradict him by other evidence, or, by leave of the judge, prove that he has made at other times a statement inconsistent with his present testimony; but before such last-mentioned proof can be given the circumstances of the supposed statement, sufficient to designate the particular occasion, must be mentioned to the witness, and he must be asked whether or not he has made such statement.

The prohibition on general evidence of bad character applies to hostile and unfavourable witnesses alike. This part of the section is declaratory of the common law and means that the witness cannot be asked about his bad

---

7 *The People v Hannigan* [1941] IR 252; *R v Hunter* [1956] VLR 31 (citing *R v Harris* (1927) 20 Cr App Rep 144 at 146 and doubting whether *Coles v Coles and Brown* (1866) LR 1 P & D 70 supports the view that demeanour alone can be considered); *R v Hayden and Slattery* [1959] VLR 102; *McLellan v Bowyer* (1962) 106 CLR 94; *Wawanesa Mutual Insurance Co v Hanes* (1961) 28 DLR (2d) 386.
8 *Rice v Howard* (1886) 16 QBD 681. In a sufficiently strong case a new trial could be ordered by an appellate tribunal (see the review of the authorities by the High Court of Australia in *McLellan v Bowyer* above).
9 See *Blewitt v R* (1988) 80 ALR 353.
10 See *R v Wong* [1986] Crim LR 683.
11 As in *R v Powell* [1985] Crim LR 592; *R v Norton and Driver* [1987] Crim LR 687.
12 (1859) 5 CBNS 786.
13 See *R v Booth* (1981) 74 Cr App Rep 123 (leave required before accused could put inconsistent statement to his own hostile witness).

conduct on former occasions or his previous convictions, in order that he may be discredited, while the party calling him cannot adduce evidence of his mendacious disposition. In *Greenough v Eccles* it was decided that 'adverse' means hostile, so the concluding portions of the section are unambiguous so far as the proof of such a witness's previous statements is concerned. The section gives rise to two remaining questions—its effect on the old law concerning unfavourable and hostile witnesses and the evidential value of the inconsistent statements that are proved or admitted under the Act.

(a) Unfavourable witnesses. The words 'he may, in case the witness shall, in the opinion of the judge, prove adverse, contradict him by other evidence' suggest that a party cannot do this when his witness is merely unfavourable and not, in the opinion of the judge, hostile. If this is so, the section has altered the common law as illustrated by cases such as *Ewer v Ambrose*.[14] It appears to be universally agreed that this is not the effect of the section, and, as long ago as 1859, Cockburn CJ said of the identical provision in the Common Law Procedure Act 1854:

> There has been a great blunder in the drawing of it, and on the part of those who adopted it . . . Perhaps the better course is to consider the second part of the section as altogether superfluous and useless.[15]

The alternative, and probably the sounder method, of ignoring the implications of the section is that adopted by Williams and Willes JJ:[16]

> We think the preferable construction is, that in case the witness shall, in the opinion of the judge, prove 'hostile', the party producing him may not only contradict him by other witnesses, as he might heretofore have done, and may still do, if the witness is unfavourable, but may also, by leave of the judge, prove that he has made inconsistent statements.

Whatever means may be adopted in order to reach it, the conclusion is that an unfavourable witness can be contradicted with regard to facts in issue or relevant to the issue, he cannot be cross-examined or discredited in any other way.

(b) Hostile witnesses. Section 3 of the 1865 Act has not affected the common law according to which the judge has a discretion to allow a hostile witness to be examined by means of leading questions or with reference to a previous statement[17] for this does not amount to impeachment of credit 'by general evidence of bad character'. In *R v Thompson*[18] the accused was convicted of incest with his daughter who was called as a witness by the prosecution. After answering some formal questions she said that she did not wish to give evidence. The judge allowed her to be treated as hostile with the result that she was examined on a statement she had made to the police and by means of leading questions. The Court of Appeal held that the judge had acted properly and affirmed the conviction. The witness did not deny making the

---

14 (1825) 3 B & C 746, p 296 above.
15 *Greenough v Eccles* (1859) 5 CBNS 786 at 806.
16 The quotation is from 28 LJCP 160 at 163.
17 *Clarke v Saffery* (1824) Ry & M 126; *Bastin v Carew* (1824) Ry & M 127.
18 (1976) 64 Cr App Rep 96.

statement to the police but, even if she had done so, it is doubtful whether s 3 would have applied to the case for the girl's statement was not 'inconsistent with her present testimony'. If the section does not apply in such circumstances, it is questionable whether the statement can be proved.[19]

(c) Evidential value of previous inconsistent statements. A question naturally arises concerning the use that may be made of inconsistent statements when they are admitted by, or proved against, the witness. Are they evidence of the facts stated, or do they merely constitute a ground for disbelieving the witness's testimony? As s 3 of the Act of 1865 only deals with procedure, the answer depends on the common law which still governs criminal cases on this point. Although judicial expression of the first view has not been wanting,[20] the English judges' view of the common law is that statements of witnesses who are not parties put in evidence under s 3 of the Criminal Procedure Act 1865 (and the same is true of those proved or admitted under s 4 and s 5, set out in the next section of this chapter), cannot be treated as proof of the facts stated.[1] When the witness is a party, his previous statement may be admissible as evidence of the facts stated because it is an admission.[2]

An illustration of the common law is provided by *R v White.* Several witnesses called by the prosecution had previously made statements to the police indicating that the accused had participated in a riot. At the trial these witnesses gave evidence in which they said that the accused did not participate in the riot. The previous statements were admitted, and the judge told the jury that they could choose between the witnesses' evidence at the trial and their statements to the police. The jury must have acted on the latter for they returned a verdict of guilty; but the conviction was quashed because:

> quite obviously it is one thing to say that, in view of an earlier statement, the witness is not to be trusted: it is another thing to say that his present testimony is to be disbelieved and his earlier statement, which he now repudiates, is to be substituted for it.[3]

The Court of Criminal Appeal has said:

> when a witness is shown to have made previous statements inconsistent with the evidence given by that witness at the trial the jury should not merely be directed that the evidence given at the trial should be regarded as unreliable; they should

---

19 The submission that it could not be proved is made in Archbold (42nd edn) para 4-305, and see *R v Booth* above. A different view is taken in Canada, see *McInroy and Rouse v R* [1979] 1 SCR 588.

20 See the judgment of Pollock CB in *A-G v Hitchcock* (1847) 16 LJ Ex 259, where he spoke of the jury being at liberty to believe either the one account or the other. The same view was taken by Estey J in the Supreme Court of Canada in *McInroy and Rouse v R* above.

1 *R v Dibble* (1908) 1 Cr App Rep 155; *R v White* (1922) 17 Cr App Rep 60; *R v Birch* (1924) 93 LJKB 385; *R v Harris* (1927) 20 Cr App 144; *R v Golder, Jones and Porritt* [1960] 3 All ER 457, [1960] 1 WLR 1169; *R v Oliva* [1965] 3 All ER 116, [1965] 1 WLR 1028; *R v Moore* (1957) 25 CR (Can) 159.

2 The witness is not likely to be a party in the case of statements admitted under s 3, but might be in the case of those admitted under s 4 and s 5. A non-party witness may of course render his previous statement evidence of the facts stated by admitting its truth in cross-examination (*Birkett v A J Little Ltd* [1962] NSWR 492).

3 Per Lord Hewart CJ (1922) 17 Cr App Rep 60 at 64.

also be directed that the previous statements whether sworn or unsworn do not constitute evidence upon which they can act.[4]

In that case the jury had been warned that the testimony was unreliable, so the apparent suggestion that a direction to disregard the testimony is mandatory, was obiter.[5] It has not always been acted upon in England,[6] and despite similar remarks in earlier,[7] and blanket endorsement in later,[8] cases, any such necessity has been convincingly criticised by courts of high authority elsewhere in the Commonwealth,[9] and even in England.[10] Circumstances are quite conceivable in which so completely satisfactory an explanation is given that it would be perverse to require the jury to regard the testimony as unreliable. It should perhaps be added that if the prior inconsistent statement should be unequivocally accepted as accurate by the witness when put to him, it is then, in effect, incorporated into his testimony, and as such capable of being accepted as evidence of the truth of its contents.[11]

(ii) Civil Evidence Act 1968

Section 3(1)(a) of the Civil Evidence Act 1968 provides that:

> Where in any civil proceedings—(a) a previous inconsistent or contradictory statement made by a person called as a witness in those proceedings is proved by virtue of section 3 of the Criminal Procedure Act 1865, that statement shall, by virtue of this subsection be admissible as evidence of any fact stated therein of which direct oral evidence by him would be admissible.

There is thus a complete conflict between the statutory civil and common criminal law governing the evidential effect of the previous inconsistent statements of a hostile witness.

If facts such as those of *R v White*[12] were to recur, the appeal would probably still have to be allowed if the judge suggested to the jury that they might choose to act on either of the two statements of the witness, his testimony or the statement which he made to the police. On the other hand, if the claim were a civil claim for damages caused by the riot, such a direction could well be held to have been proper. As there is similar conflict with respect to the evidential effect of an inconsistent statement proved or admitted to have been made by any witness under cross-examination, it is worthwhile considering the merits of the conflict. Before doing so, however, it must be emphasised that the practical effect is likely to be negligible in the majority of cases, for the only safe course to adopt will be to ignore both the testimony and the inconsistent statement. The type of situation in which it is

---

4 *R v Golder, Jones and Porritt* [1960] 3 All ER 457 at 459. See also *R v Oliva* [1965] 3 All ER 116, [1965] 1 WLR 1028; *R v Pearson* [1964] Qd R 471; *R v Schmahl* [1965] VR 745.
5 See *Driscoll v R* (1977) 137 CLR 517 at 537.
6 See *R v Williams* (1913) 8 Cr App Rep 133.
7 *R v Harris* (1927) 20 Cr App Rep 144 at 147, 148.
8 Eg *R v Oliva* [1965] 3 All ER 116, [1965] 1 WLR 1028.
9 In Australia in *Driscoll*, above; in Canada in *Deacon v R* [1947] 3 DLR 772; in New Zealand in *R v Morgan* [1981] 2 NZLR 164.
10 *R v Pestano* [1981] Crim LR 397.
11 *R v Carrington* [1969] NZLR 790. Though its weight would normally be impaired by the initially inconsistent testimony.
12 See p 300 above.

arguable that the tribunal of fact should be able to act on the statement rather than the testimony is that in which there is reason to suppose that the witness quarrelled with the party in whose favour the statement operates after it was made or was 'got at' by the opposite party.

It is sometimes said that the approach of the common law under which the previous inconsistent statement merely neutralises the maker's testimony is the logical one, because rejection of the testimony does not entail acceptance of the statement; but this is simply another instance of the pseudo-logic occasionally indulged in by lawyers. Everything depends upon the contents of the statement and testimony respectively. Of course the rejection of W's evidence that he was in Rome on 1 May because he had previously said that he was in Carthage throughout that day does not entail acceptance of this latter fact; but acceptance of W's previous statement that he was not in Rome on 1 May does entail rejection of his testimony that he was there during that day. Statement and testimony usually cancel each other out because there is no particular reason why one should be preferred to the other. The testimony is on oath, but, in the absence of a convincing explanation of the inconsistency, it is the testimony of someone who has, or may have, lied on the same point on a previous occasion.

The common law approach, and hence that of the present criminal law, may, however, be justified by practical considerations. The earlier statement may have been put into the mouth of its maker by an over-enthusiastic police officer or solicitor, it will generally not have been made on oath, and the maker will generally not have been subject to cross-examination when it was made.[13] The solemnity of the occasion may lend support to the truth of the testimony and it will only be in rare cases that acceptable evidence tending to show that the statement rather than the testimony was true will be available.

(iii) Proposals of the Criminal Law Revision Committee

Nonetheless, cl 33 of the draft Bill attached to the 11th Report of the Criminal Law Revision Committee contained a provision identical to s 3(1)(a) of the Civil Evidence Act 1968. The report also recommended the adoption of a modernised version of s 3 of the Criminal Procedure Act 1865, together with the retention of the prohibition on a party's impeaching his own witness by evidence of bad character; the new clause would have made it plain that both unfavourable and hostile witnesses could be contradicted by other evidence without the leave of the court because it did not refer to the point.[14] It now seems most unlikely that this draft clause will be enacted.[15]

---

13 These objections do not apply to a deposition.
14 The clause (cl 11) read as follows: 'In any [criminal] proceedings the party calling a witness shall in no circumstances be allowed to impeach his credibility as a witness by evidence tending to establish that he is a person of bad disposition or reputation; but, subject to that restriction, where in any [criminal] proceedings a party calls a witness who—(a) gives evidence adverse to that party; or (b) gives evidence which is inconsistent with a statement made by the witness on a previous occasion, that party may, with the leave of the court, cross-examine him as if he were a witness called by another party.'
15 No such clause appeared in any version of the Police and Criminal Evidence Act 1984 or the Criminal Justice Act 1988 though in certain of the latter circumstances s 26 could perhaps be invoked.

SECTION 3. CROSS-EXAMINATION AND RE-EXAMINATION

The object of cross-examination is two-fold, first, to elicit information concerning the facts in issue or relevant to the issue that is favourable to the party on whose behalf the cross-examination is conducted, and secondly to cast doubt upon the accuracy of the evidence-in-chief given against such party. So far as cross-examination to the issue is concerned, the ordinary rules with regard to the admissibility of evidence apply so that the prosecution cannot cross-examine the accused on the contents of an inadmissible confession,[16] and, in criminal cases, the rule against hearsay applies with as much force to the answers given by a witness in cross-examination as it does to those given by him in-chief. Thus, in *R v Thomson*,[17] it was held that a doctor charged with aborting a woman since deceased had been rightly refused permission to ask a prosecution witness in cross-examination whether the deceased had not told her that she intended to operate on herself and later that she had in fact done so. If the accused had called a witness to prove these statements, they would have been inadmissible hearsay and they would not have lost that character by being elicited in cross-examination. There are decisions to the same effect in civil cases,[18] but it seems that, in civil proceedings, the court would now have a discretion to admit statements of deceased persons elicited from a witness under cross-examination as evidence of any fact of which the deceased could have given direct oral evidence.[19]

Any matter upon which it is proposed to contradict the evidence-in-chief given by the witness must normally be put to him so that he may have an opportunity of explaining the contradiction,[1] and failure to do this may be held to imply acceptance of the evidence-in-chief, but is not an inflexible rule and it has been held to be unsuitable to proceedings before lay justices.[2] In criminal proceedings material proposed to be put to the accused in cross-examination should normally have been led by the prosecution as part of its case-in-chief.[3] Leading questions may be employed in cross-examination,[4] but, whether this is directed to the issue or the credit of the witness, the judge has a discretion under which he may disallow questions which he considers to be improper or oppressive, and

---

16 *R v Treacey* [1944] 2 All ER 229, 30 Cr App Rep 93; endorsed in *Wong Kam-ming v R* [1980] AC 247 at 259, [1979] 1 All ER 939 at 945; see also *R v Brophy* [1982] AC 476, [1981] 2 All ER 705, where it is apparently regarded as too obvious to need separate explanation. See also *R v Neville* [1985] 2 Qd R 398 where cross-examination was forbidden on a previous inconsistent statement which had formed the foundation of a charge of which the witness had been acquitted.

17 [1912] 3 KB 19.

18 *Beare v Garrod* (1915) 85 LJKB 717; *Sharp v Loddington Ironstone Co Ltd* (1924) 132 LT 229.

19 Civil Evidence Act 1968, s 2, s 8; RSC Ord 38, r 29; it is assumed that a statement is 'given in evidence' within the meaning of this rule if the statement is elicited in cross-examination.

1 *Browne v Dunn* (1893) 6 R 67; *R v Fenlon and Neal* (1980) 71 Cr App Rep 307. See also *Allied Pastoral Holdings Pty Ltd v Comr of Taxation* [1983] 1 NSWLR 1; *Machado v Berlet* (1986) 32 DLR (4th) 634 applying the rule to a video recording of the plaintiff.

2 *O'Connell v Adams* [1973] Crim LR 313.

3 *R v Dartey* (1987) 84 Cr App Rep 352.

4 *Parkin v Moon* (1836) 7 C & P 408.

this would include leading questions of the second kind mentioned above (p 269).[5]

All witnesses are liable to be cross-examined except one who is called for the sole purpose of producing a document and one who is not examined-in-chief because he had been called by mistake.[6] A witness who does not come within these excepted categories is liable to be cross-examined, not merely by the opponent of the party calling him, but also by all other parties.[7] All parties have the right to cross-examine witnesses not called by them, whether or not the witness is himself a party, whether or not the witness has given evidence against the party seeking to cross-examine him, and even though the witness is a co-accused.[8] Of course it would be wrong to allow a party to endeavour to discredit a witness who had not given evidence against him, but, so far as cross-examination to the issue is concerned, it is difficult to disagree with the following statement of a South African judge: 'An accused ought, if a fair trial is what is aimed at, to be at liberty to cross-examine a co-accused or any witness not called by him who may not have inculpated him in any way in order to establish facts which might tend to support an alibi.'[9] The absence of a right to discredit in such a situation led the other member of the court to prefer to speak of the accused having a right to put questions to rather than cross-examine his co-accused.

The matters that call for further treatment at this stage are the previous contradictory statements of witnesses under cross-examination (a subject which may conveniently be followed by some general remarks concerning cross-examination on documents), and the outline of the rule that a witness's answers to questions that are collateral to the issue must be treated as final. More detail upon these matters, and in relation to impugning the credit of a witness is postponed until the next chapter. A final brief part mentions re-examination.

---

5 See the statement of the Bar Council set out in Phipson *Law of Evidence* (13th edn) 807, 808. In New Zealand the use of hypothetical questions has been regulated, see *Practice Note* [1985] 1 NZLR 386.

6 *Wood v Mackinson* (1840) 2 Mood & R 273. The position of a witness called by the judge is not altogether clear. In *R v Tregear* [1967] 2 QB 574 at 580, the judge said that counsel for the prosecution and defence should both have an opportunity of examining and cross-examining the witness he was calling. It has been held in South Australia that there is no absolute right to cross-examine a witness on a voir dire; *R v Henderson and Panagaris* (1984) 14 ACR 274. It is not necessarily vital that cross-examination cannot be completed, if the witness breaks down for example, so long as an appropriate warning is given, *R v Wyatt* [1990] Crim LR 343.

7 *Allen v Allen* [1894] P 248 at 254; *Dryden v Surrey County Council and Stewart* [1936] 2 All ER 535 at 537–8 (adversity of interest enough); *Re Baden's Deed Trusts, Baden v Smith* [1967] 3 All ER 159; unless his having been called by a formal opponent has merely pre-empted his being called by the party seeking to cross-examine, *Governors of Peabody Donation Fund v Sir Lindsay Parkinson* [1983] CLY 1660 (not reported on this point in subsequent proceedings).

8 *R v Fenlon and Neal* (1980) 71 Cr App Rep 307; *R v Hilton* [1972] 1 QB 421, [1971] 3 All ER 541; *Murdoch v Taylor* [1965] AC 574, especially per Lord Morris at 584. *R v Hadwen* [1902] 1 KB 882; *State v Langa* 1963 (4) SA 941; *Nyense v R* [1962] R & N 271; but see *Gemmel and McFadyen v MacNiven* 1928 JC 5.

9 Harcourt J in *State v Langa* 1963 (4) SA 941 at 945. On the whole subject see an article by I G Carvell [1965] Crim LR 419.

A. PREVIOUS INCONSISTENT[10] STATEMENTS[11]

The proof of previous statements[12] of a witness under cross-examination that are inconsistent with his evidence-in-chief is governed by ss 4 and 5 of the Criminal Procedure Act 1865,[13] but their evidential effect is dependent on the common law and the Civil Evidence Act 1968.

1. CRIMINAL PROCEDURE ACT 1865, S 4

Under s 4 of the Criminal Procedure Act 1865:

> If a witness, upon cross-examination as to a former statement made by him relative to the subject-matter of the indictment or proceeding, and consistent with his present testimony, does not distinctly admit that he has made such statement, proof may be given that he did in fact make it; but before such proof can be given, the circumstances of the supposed statement, sufficient to designate the particular occasion, must be mentioned to the witness, and he must be asked whether or not he has made such statement.

This is, almost, if not entirely, declaratory of the common law.[14] If a statement is admitted or proved under the section, it merely impugns the testimony of the witness under cross-examination (unless he happens to be a party when the statement may amount to an admission); it does not constitute evidence of the facts stated at common law.[15] Under s 3(1)(a) of the Civil Evidence Act 1968 the statement is, however, also admissible in civil proceedings as evidence of any fact of which the maker could have given oral evidence.[16]

2. CRIMINAL PROCEDURE ACT 1865, S 5

Section 5 of the Act of 1865 applies to cases in which the previous statement is in writing. Between 1820 and 1854, they had been complicated by the rule

10 There is no English authority on what constitutes an inconsistency for this purpose (see *Carbury v Measures* (1904) 4 SR NSW 569 and V *Wigmore* para 1040). There is a Victorian authority for the sound view that, if the statement is both consistent and inconsistent, the whole must go in (*R v Titijewski* [1970] VR 371 citing *R v Riley* (1866) 4 F & F 964).

11 See generally Bryant 'The Adversary's Witness: Cross-examination and Proof of Prior Inconsistent Statements' (1984) 62 Crim BR 43.

12 The statement may be proved in the form of an audio-visual tape, see *R v Andrews* [1987] 1 Qd R 21.

13 These sections apply to civil as well as criminal cases (s 1), and they re-enact ss 23 and 24 of the Common Law Procedure Act 1854.

14 See the judgment of Parke B in *Crowley v Page* (1837) 7 C & P 789. The only doubtful point seems to have concerned the position when the witness did not clearly deny or admit the statement. See *R v Hart* (1957) 42 Cr App Rep 47 at 50. This case confirms that the section is in no way confined to previous statements on oath.

15 See *R v Askew* [1981] Crim LR 398.

16 For a discussion of this conflict between civil and criminal proceedings, see p 301 above. There was a provision corresponding to s 4 of the Act of 1865 in cl 12 of the Bill annexed to the 11th Report of the Criminal Law Revision Committee, and under cl 33 the previous statement could have constituted evidence of the facts stated, but no such provision was included in the Police and Criminal Evidence Act 1984 or in the Criminal Justice Act 1988, though similar provisions have been enacted in some Commonwealth jurisdictions, see eg Evidence Act 1977–81, s 101 (Queensland).

laid down by the judges when advising the House of Lords in relation to the divorce proceedings brought against Queen Caroline.[17] Wigmore referred to it as a rule which: 'for unsoundness of principle, impropriety of policy, and practical inconvenience in trials, committed the most notable mistake that can be found among the rulings upon the present subject'.[18] It was that, if a witness was to be cross-examined with regard to a previous statement made by him in writing, he must be shown the document before any questions were asked with regard to it. If he admitted that it was his statement, it could be read as the evidence of the cross-examining party, who was not obliged to inquire whether there was any explanation of the inconsistency. If the witness did not admit that the statement was his, it could be proved by another witness and read as part of the case of the cross-examining party. This procedure was attended by at least three disadvantages.

First, it was unfair to the cross-examiner because it deprived him of the invaluable weapon of surprise. In certain situations, the most effective procedure is to ask the witness whether he has ever said the contrary of what he now says on oath and to show him the previous statement only if he answers the question in the negative.

Secondly, the procedure under consideration was unfair to the cross-examiner by obliging him to read the statement as part of his evidence. This might have affected the order of the counsel's speeches, because even if the cross-examiner called no other witnesses, he had adduced evidence within the meaning of the common law rules concerning the order of speeches.[19] Those rules then applied at a criminal trial and the adduction of evidence by the accused gave the prosecution the last word. Moreover, there are certain situations in which the cross-examiner will not desire to put the witness's statement in evidence at all. In *R v Ford*,[20] for instance, counsel for the defence wanted to show a police officer called by the Crown his deposition in order to induce him to vary his answer to a question concerning a statement made by the prisoner. On the authority of *The Queen's Case* it was held that the correct course was to read the deposition to the witness. This would have had the disadvantage of showing the jury that the witness had, on many matters, told the same story as he told in court, and the reading of the deposition might have been more favourable to the Crown in some respects than the casting of doubt on one point of the witness's evidence would have been helpful to the accused. What counsel for the defence wants to do in such a case is to be able to ask the witness to read the deposition to himself, and then to inquire whether he adheres to the statement made in his evidence-in-chief. If the witness says 'no', counsel for the defence has achieved his object; if the witness says 'yes', then only should it be necessary for counsel for the defence to decide whether to use the deposition to contradict the witness; if he does so, the deposition then becomes evidence in the case.

Finally, the ruling in *The Queen's Case* could operate harshly from the point of view of the witness, because the cross-examiner was not obliged to

17 *The Queen's Case* (1820) 2 Brod & Bing 286.
18 IV *Wigmore* 497.
19 See the judges' directions in 7 C & P 676.
20 (1851) 5 Cox CC 184.

give him an opportunity of explaining the inconsistency between his former statement and present testimony.

Section 5 of the Criminal Procedure Act 1865 reads as follows:

> A witness may be cross-examined as to previous statements made by him in writing or reduced into writing relative to the subject-matter of the indictment or proceeding, without such writing being shown to him; but if it is intended to contradict such witness by the writing, his attention must, before such contradictory proof can be given, be called to those parts of the writing which are to be used for the purpose of so contradicting him; provided always, that it shall be competent for the judge, at any time during the trial, to require the production of the writing for his inspection, and he may thereupon make such use of it for the purposes of the trial as he may think fit.

This appears to overcome all the disadvantages of the ruling in *The Queen's Case* to which reference has been made. The witness can be asked whether he made a statement and be cross-examined on the general nature of its contents without being shown the document.[1] The cross-examiner is not obliged to put it in evidence, even if he shows it to the witness, but he must do so if he wishes to use the document as a contradictory statement[2] and the witness must be given an opportunity of explaining the contradiction.[3] The document is never evidence of the facts stated in it by virtue of s 5 because the proviso with regard to the judge making such use of it as he may think fit does not extend to his directing the jury to choose between it and the testimony of the witness.[4]

A cross-examiner cannot make the contents of a document evidence in a case simply by requiring the person under cross-examination to read it aloud. Thus, in *R v Gillespie and Simpson*,[5] the manageress and cashier of a store were charged with theft and false accounting, the case against them being that they had accounted for sums less than those shown to have been received by documents prepared by salesgirls. Some of the girls gave evidence, but documents prepared by others were handed to the accused in cross-examination with a request, notwithstanding their dissent from what was said in the documents, to read them aloud. This was duly done and the judge referred to the documents in his summing-up. The procedure was held to have been improper by the Court of Appeal who quashed the convictions:

> As it seems to this court, if a document is produced to a witness and the witness is asked; 'Do you see what that document purports to record?' the witness may say 'I see it, I accept it as true' in which case the contents of the document become evidence: or he may say: 'I see what is there written, I do not accept it as true', whereupon that which is purported to be recorded in the document is not evidence

1 Wrottesley *The Examination of Witnesses* (2nd edn) 61 f. Cross-examining counsel must have the document with him even if he does not intend to contradict the witness with it. (*R v Yousry* (1914) 11 Cr App Rep 13; *R v Anderson* (1929) 21 Cr App Rep 178).

2 *R v Riley* (1866) 4 F & F 964; *R v Wright* (1866) 4 F & F 967.

3 Even if this means re-calling a witness before the Court of Appeal if the statement has been made after the trial, *R v Conway* (1979) 70 Cr App Rep 4.

4 *R v Birch* (1924) 18 Cr App Rep 26. Clause 13 of the Bill attached to the 11th Report of the Criminal Law Revision Committee contained a provision similar to s 5 of the Act of 1865; a statement admissible under that section is admissible as evidence of a fact stated in it under s 3(1)(a) of the Civil Evidence Act 1968. It would have been admissible as evidence of the facts stated in a criminal case if cl 33 of the draft Bill had been adopted.

5 (1967) 51 Cr App Rep 172, applied in *R v Cooper* (1985) 82 Cr App Rep 74.

against that person who has rejected the contents; it becomes what one might call non-evidence, the document itself being nothing but hearsay.[6]

B. CROSS-EXAMINATION ON DOCUMENTS GENERALLY[7]

But there are situations in which a document may become evidence of the facts stated in it by virtue of the common law rules concerning cross-examination. If, at the trial, a party calls for and inspects a document held by his adversary, he is bound to put it in evidence if required to do so, provided the document was not being used to refresh the memory of one of the adversary's witnesses. If the document was being used for this purpose, neither the inspection, nor cross-examination on such parts of the document as were used to refresh memory, makes it evidence in the case, though cross-examination on other parts will have this effect.

In *Stroud v Stroud*,[8] a divorce case in which a doctor was giving evidence on behalf of the wife, the husband's counsel called for and inspected medical reports from other doctors which were in the hands of the doctor who was testifying although he was not referring to them for any purpose. Wrangham J held that the reports were thus made evidence in the case at the option of the wife. Unfortunately Wrangham J did not say, any more than do any of the older authorities on cross-examination on documents, whether or not they were used to refresh memory,[9] or for what purpose the reports could have been made evidence in the case. They might have contained matter consistent with the doctor's testimony or inconsistent with the evidence of one of the husband's witnesses or their contents might have been received as hearsay statements in support of the wife's case.

In Australia, it has been held that a document called for in cross-examination may become evidence of the facts stated in it at the option of the party thus obliged to produce it, although the rule against hearsay would have prevented him from relying on the document for this purpose in the first instance. Thus, in *Walker v Walker*[10] a wife was applying for a maintenance order against her husband. She made a statement in-chief with regard to his income, and was cross-examined concerning her means of knowledge of this matter. She mentioned a letter received by her father from an accountant who had been making enquiries. Counsel for the husband called for the letter, and it was held that he had rightly been obliged to put it in evidence at the request of the wife's counsel. A majority of the High Court was also of the opinion that the trial judge had been correct in treating the letter as some evidence of the husband's means.

The Criminal Law Revision Committee recommended the reversal of the

6 Winn LJ.
7 For a helpful set of notes see H H Glass (ed) *Evidence Seminars* p 136.
8 [1963] 3 All ER 539, [1963] 1 WLR 1080. The headnote to *Senat v Senat* [1965] P 172, [1965] 2 All ER 505 suggests that that case conflicts with *Stroud v Stroud*, but this is doubtful because the diaries with which *Senat's* case were concerned were used to refresh memory.
9 *Wharam v Routledge* (1805) 5 Esp 235; *Wilson v Bowie* (1823) 1 C & P 8; *Calvert v Flower* (1836) 7 C & P 386; *Palmer v Maclear and M'Grath* (1858) 1 Sw & Tr 149.
10 (1937) 57 CLR 630. The rule was not applied to criminal proceedings in *R v Weatherstone* (1968) 12 FLR 14, and has been recommended for abolition by the Australian Law Reform Commission, Interim Report No 26 (1985) para 617. For a consideration of the limits of the decision in *Walker v Walker*, see *O'Brien v Clegg* [1951] SRQ 1.

effect of *Stroud v Stroud* by a provision that, where a party calls for and inspects a document in the possession of an opposing party or of a witness called by such party, his doing so shall not of itself entitle the opposing party to make the document evidence in the proceedings.[11] So far as civil cases are concerned, this result has been partially achieved by the Civil Evidence Act 1968. Section 1 provides that in any civil proceedings a statement other than one made by a person while giving oral evidence in those proceedings shall be admissible as evidence of a fact stated only to the extent permitted by the Act, or any other statutory provision, or by agreement. The documents put in evidence in *Stroud v Stroud* and *Walker v Walker* were admitted by virtue of the common law, but they would not be wholly inadmissible under the Act of 1968 because the court would have a discretion to admit them as evidence of any fact of which the maker could have given direct oral evidence.[12] A similar effect may sometimes be achieved on criminal cases by the operation of s 23 of the Criminal Justice Act 1988.

C. FINALITY OF ANSWERS TO COLLATERAL QUESTIONS

1. THE GENERAL RULE

There is a sound general rule, based on the desirability of avoiding a multiplicity of issues, that the answers given by a witness to questions put to him in cross-examination concerning collateral facts must be treated as final. They may or may not be accepted by the jury, but the cross-examiner must take them for better or worse and cannot contradict them by other evidence.[13]

As relevance is a matter of degree, it is impossible to devise an exhaustive means of determining when a question is collateral for the purpose of the rule under consideration; Pollock CB said in the leading case of *A-G v Hitchcock*:[14]

> The test whether a matter is collateral or not is this: if the answer of a witness is a matter which you would be allowed on your own part to prove in evidence—if it have such a connection with the issues, that you would be allowed to give it in evidence—then it is a matter on which you may contradict him.

The defendant was charged with using a cistern for making malt without complying with various statutory requirements. One Spooner gave evidence of the use of the cistern and was asked in cross-examination on behalf of the defendant whether he had not told Cook that the excise officers had offered him twenty pounds to say that the cistern had been used. Spooner denied that he had ever made such a statement, and it was held that the defendant could not ask Cook to narrate the alleged conversation. If Cook had been able to prove that Spooner had actually received a bribe from the excise

11 11th Report, para 223, draft Bill cl 29.
12 Civil Evidence Act 1968, s 8; RSC Ord 38, r 29.
13 Nor should he suggest to the witness that he can, *S v Damalis* 1984 (2) SA 105.
14 (1847) 1 Exch 91 at 99. Pollock CB was really saying no more than that a witness may be contradicted on matters relevant to the issue (see per Ogilvy-Thompson JA in *S v Sinkankanka* [1963] 2 SA 531 at 539). See also *Palmer v Trower* (1852) 8 Exch 247.

officers, his testimony would have been admissible because it would have tended to show bias under an exception to the rule prohibiting contradictory evidence on collateral issues.[15]

The effect of the judgments in *Hitchcock*'s case is aptly stated in the following passage from an American author:

> Independent evidence may be given to prove a self-contradictory statement by a primary witness only if (a) the statement contradicts testimony by the primary witness about a matter directly in issue in the litigation, or (b) the statement contradicts testimony by the primary witness as to 'those matters which affect the motives, temper and character of the witness, ... with reference to his feelings toward one party or the other'.[16]

The Australian case of *Piddington v Bennett and Wood Pty Ltd*[17] prompts speculation on the merits of the finality rule. One of the plaintiff's witnesses in a running-down action was asked in cross-examination how he accounted for his presence at the scene of the accident, and he said that he had been to the bank on behalf of the named person. A new trial was ordered on the ground that the judge had wrongly allowed the bank manager to give evidence to the effect that no business was done on that day on behalf of the man named by the witness. Similar speculations are prompted by the Irish case of *R v Burke*[18] in which a witness was giving evidence through an interpreter. He was cross-examined about his knowledge of English, and it was held that evidence could not be given to contradict his statement that he was ignorant of the language.

No doubt the questions of how a witness came to be where he was and whether an interpreter was really necessary were collateral, but the first could have been a step towards challenging the witness's presence at the accident,[19] and the second casts doubt on the honesty of the whole of his testimony. The indubitable value of the finality rule should not blind us to the undesirability of a closed list of exceptions to it.

2. EXCEPTIONS TO THE GENERAL RULE

The nature of the cross-examination will sometimes entitle the party calling the witness to call another one to testify to matters which could not have been deposed to in the absence of the cross-examination. For example, if the plaintiff in a running-down case is cross-examined in such a way as to suggest that he has suppressed information about a later accident in which he sustained injuries, his solicitor may be called to prove the prompt disclosure of those injuries. The point is directly relevant to the amount of damages

---

15 For a clear, recent re-statement by the Supreme Court of Canada of the effect of this rule prohibiting rebuttal of other types of attack on credibility, see *Krause v R* (1986) 33 DLR (4th) 267.

16 Maguire *Evidence, Common Sense and Common Law* 67. The sub-quotation is from the judgment of Pollock CB.

17 (1940) 63 CLR 533.

18 (1858) 8 Cox CC 44.

19 This has been held to go to the issue in Nova Scotia (*Tzagarakis v Stevens* (1968) 69 DLR (2d) 466, a decision which seems to follow from *Toohey v Metropolitan Police Comr* [1965] AC 595, [1965] 1 All ER 506).

claimed,[20] but cases of this sort do not constitute a real exception to the rule that a witness's answers to collateral questions or questions concerning credit only are final.

There are three well-recognised exceptions—the fact that a witness has been convicted of a crime, the fact that he is biased in favour of the party calling him and the fact that he has previously made a statement inconsistent with his present testimony. Nothing more need be said about the third exception, and both of the other two will be discussed in the following chapter.

D. RE-EXAMINATION

The subject of re-examination can be disposed of briefly. Leading questions may not be put, any more than they may be put in-chief; previous consistent statements can only be put to the witness if rendered admissible by the terms of the cross-examination, or, with the leave of the Court, under the Civil Evidence Act 1968, s 2, or to refresh memory.[1] The most important rule is that the re-examination must be confined to matters arising out of the cross-examination, and new matter may only be introduced with the leave of the judge. Thus, in *Prince v Samo*,[2] an action for malicious arrest arising out of the non-payment of a loan alleged by the plaintiff to be a gift, the plaintiff had given evidence at the trial of one of the defendant's witnesses for perjury. The plaintiff's attorney was present at the trial, and he was called as a witness on behalf of his client in the present proceedings. The attorney could not be asked in-chief about statements made by the plaintiff at the earlier trial on account of the rule against hearsay, and the prohibition on evidence of a witness's prior consistent statements; but he was asked in cross-examination whether the plaintiff had not said, in the course of his evidence in the previous proceedings, that he had repeatedly been insolvent. It was held that he could not be asked in re-examination about other portions of the plaintiff's earlier evidence which had no connection with the statement concerning his insolvency. The rule is sound in principle because it prevents the reception of inadmissible evidence in re-examination, under the guise of dealing with points emerging from the cross-examination, and any hardship that the rule may occasion can be mitigated by the judge.

The terms of the cross-examination may, however, let significant and prejudicial evidence in through the re-examination although such evidence would not be admissible in-chief. Perhaps the most striking example is provided by a case in which it was held that a suggestion to a child witness in cross-examination that her testimony was activated by hatred for the accused, would permit re-examination to show that such hatred was derived from the witness's belief that the accused had attempted to murder someone.[3]

---

20 *Drakos v Smith* [1958] VLR 536; the solicitor's evidence was also admissible on the ground that it rebutted the cross-examiner's allegation of recent invention. Had the defendant been in a position to rebut the plaintiff's denials of his failure to disclose the later accident, no doubt he would have been allowed to call a witness to do so.
1 *R v Harman* [1985] Crim LR 326.
2 (1838) 7 Ad & El 627.
3 *R v Phair* [1986] 1 Qd R 136. See also *R v Nation* [1954] SASR 189; *Wojcic v Incorporated Nominal Defendant* [1969] VR 323; *R v Singleton* [1986] 2 Qd R 535.

CHAPTER VIII

Character and credibility

This chapter, and the two which follow, deal with the important and complicated topic of how far evidence may be adduced bearing upon the record and disposition of a person when either directly or indirectly relevant to matters before the court. Like much of the law of evidence the topic is made more difficult by confusion of terminology, by the disparity of contexts to which the terminology is applied, by the vicissitudes of history, and by the impact of piecemeal statutory change. The topic is at its most important when it is concerned with the character of the accused person in a criminal case. Special rules have been developed at common law to deal with the extent to which the prosecution can lead in chief evidence showing the accused in a discreditable light, in England generally described as similar fact evidence. Cross-examination of the accused about such matters is governed by the Criminal Evidence Act 1898. Those two topics will be dealt with in the chapters which follow. This chapter will deal with the rules which govern the use of evidence relating to the character of witnesses, and other cases where character is for some reason or another relevant. In relation to non-party witnesses such questions go to the credibility of the witness, in the other cases they may go more directly to the issues before the court. It is convenient to divide the chapter into three principal sections dealing with the character of a party's own witness, the character of an opponent's witness, and other cases where character is in issue. It is always necessary to consider the distinctions between evidence of good character and of bad; evidence of disposition, of reputation, of record, and of discreditable conduct; evidence going to the issue and evidence going only to credit; and whether the evidence is to be led in chief, to be the subject of cross-examination, or to be adduced in rebuttal.

SECTION 1. CHARACTER OF PARTY'S OWN WITNESS

Evidence explicitly commending the good character of the party's own witness is rarely led, even though as going to the credibility of the witness, a matter which is automatically in issue, it might logically be thought material and relevant. Thus in *R v Turner* Lawton LJ said: 'in general evidence can be called to impugn the credibility of witnesses but not led in chief to bolster it up.'[1] It is nevertheless common for a party to present his witnesses with as respectable an appearance as possible,[2] and introductory questions are commonly asked about the employment and marital status of the witness so

---

1 [1975] QB 834 at 842, [1975] 1 All ER 70 at 75; see also Lord Ellenborough CJ in *Bamfield v Massey* (1808) 1 Camp 460 at 460, 461. See further, above, p 294 on the use of scientific means to accomplish this.
2 See Cmnd 4991, para 135.

as to enhance such an impression.[3] If the impression conveyed in this way is totally false, it may be sufficiently serious to provide grounds for a successful appeal,[4] or even, if it emerges after an appeal, for the conviction of a lower court to be quashed by certiorari.[5] The court accepts that in general a party tenders a witness as capable of being believed. If a party, and especially the prosecution in a criminal case, tenders a witness whose character may be impugned, for example by proof of previous convictions, the court expects the prosecution to be candid and to reveal such convictions to the accused's advisers,[6] and to the court.[7] In such cases the party asks the court to accept the testimony of the witness despite his bad character.

In general a party is neither inclined, nor permitted, to impeach the credibility of his own witness,[8] not even when the witness is the opposing party.[9] This rule is enshrined by the Criminal Procedure Act 1865 to the extent that it prohibits a party from impeaching his own witness 'by general evidence of bad character',[10] and was defended by the Criminal Law Revision Committee,[11] largely on the basis that a party should not be in a position to intimidate a witness into testifying, perhaps falsely, in his favour. This argument fails to address the situation where a party might discover only after a witness has testified adversely just why he should have chosen to do so.[12] For this reason the rule has been condemned as unconstitutional in the United States, at least as concerns the accused in a criminal trial,[13] and has been widely abrogated by statute.[14] It clearly cannot be applied to a hostile witness in its full rigour. Apart from the statutory provision for inconsistent statements dealt with in the previous chapter, the rules relating to the impeachment of hostile witnesses are still governed by the common law in other respects. It seems clear that the witness cannot be impeached by evidence of convictions or discreditable acts unconnected with his testimony, so far as those matters are not governed by the statutory prohibition against general evidence of bad character, which must be understood in its common

---

3 Such introductory questioning of the accused in a criminal case should be very carefully confined so as to avoid any suggestion that it amounts to giving evidence of good character under the Criminal Evidence Act 1898, s 1 (f) (ii); see *R v Coulman* (1927) 20 Cr App Rep 106 (regular employment); *R v Baldwin* (1925) 18 Cr App Rep 175 (marital status). See further, ch X below.

4 *Meek v Fleming* [1961] 2 QB 366, [1961] 3 All ER 148, where the court was deliberately left with the impression that a police witness, sued for assault, had retained the rank of chief inspector, when he had in fact been demoted to sergeant for being concerned with the presentation of false evidence to a court.

5 *R v Knightsbridge Crown Court, ex p Goonatilleke* [1986] QB 1, [1985] 2 All ER 498.

6 *Practice Direction* [1966] 2 All ER 929, [1966] 1 WLR 1184, though the prosecution is under no obligation to go beyond the revelation of previous convictions in disclosing matter which might impugn the credibility of one of its witnesses, *R v Collister, R v Warhurst* (1955) 39 Cr App Rep 100.

7 But not necessarily to the jury, as this remains a matter ultimately within the discretion of prosecution counsel, *R v Carey and Williams* (1968) 52 Cr App Rep 305.

8 As noted above at p 296. See also III *Wigmore* A para 896.

9 See *Skender v Barker* (1987) 44 DLR (4th) 106 at 125.

10 S 3, above p 298.

11 Cmnd 4991, paras 162–4. These arguments were rejected by the Australian Law Reform Commission, Research Paper No 8 'Manner of Giving Evidence' ch 9.

12 See Lord Denman CJ in *Dunn v Aslett* (1838) 2 Mood & R 122.

13 *Chambers v Mississippi* 410 US 285 at 294 (1973), though this view has been rejected in Canada, see *R v Williams* (1985) 44 CR (3d) 351.

14 See, for example, r 607 of Federal Rules (following the Model Code and Uniform Rules).

law sense of reputation.[15] Nor may he be cross-examined about his general veracity. It is however equally clear that he can be cross-examined about his means of knowledge, and general capacity. It is slightly less certain whether or not he can be cross-examined about possible bias against the party calling him, but the better view is that he may be so cross-examined.[16]

SECTION 2. CHARACTER OF OPPONENT'S WITNESS

An opponent's witness may be discredited in a wider variety of ways than one's own. In addition to demonstrating lack of knowledge or capacity and inconsistent statements, it is possible to raise his previous convictions, discreditable conduct, bias, corruption or lack of veracity. There are however two general restrictions. The first is that the matter must be relevant, at least to the witness's credibility,[17] though this sometimes seems rather notional. If it is relevant only to credit, the general rule is that evidence may not be adduced to rebut the witness's denial. Thus in *R v Cargill*[18] where the accused was charged with a sexual offence against a child he was not permitted to adduce evidence to rebut her denial of being a prostitute, despite the fact that she had, in error, been allowed to assert in chief that she was a virgin. Since she was a child, consent was not in issue, and her prostitution, even if it could be proved, was relevant only to credit. The second general restriction is that the judge has the duty to prevent questioning of an unduly offensive, vexatious or embarrassing character,[19] and to prevent the process of the court from being abused to torture witnesses by oppressive cross-examination.[20] It is now convenient to consider the different ways of attacking the character of an opponent's witness. Convictions, which are the subject of an explicit statutory rule, will be considered first. They can be regarded as affecting credit only on the basis that they show the witness in a generally unfavourable light. Since the same light is shed by equally discreditable conduct which does not happen to have become the subject of a conviction, it is necessary to consider also evidence of that character. Traditionally, bias in the sense of underlying and undue sympathy or hostility felt by the witness towards a party has been regarded as relevant to credit, and has been distinguished from corruption, in the sense of more specific interference with testimony, typically by way of bribery. Finally there is a special technique of the common law permitting an attack upon the general veracity of a witness. For convenience of exposition these will be considered separately, but similar principles underpin them all.

---

15 *R v Rowton* (1865) Le & Ca 520, discussed further below at p 332.
16 Though there are dicta to the contrary in *Fenton v Hughes* (1802) 7 Ves 287 at 290, and in *R v Ball* (1839) 8 C & P 745 at 746, the point seems settled by *R v Chapman* (1838) 8 C & P 558 at 559, *Dunn v Aslett* (1838) 2 Mood & R 122 at 123, and *Melhuish v Collier* (1850) 15 QB 878 at 890.
17 In *Wentworth v Rogers (No 10)* (1987) 8 NSWLR 398 a line of questioning which, if anything, showed the witness to disapprove of perjury was disallowed (the general effect would have been unattractive and prejudicial).
18 (1913) 8 Cr App Rep 224.
19 *Vassiliades v Vassiliades* (1941) 18 Cyprus LR 10 at 22 per Lord Wright; *Wong Kam-ming v R* [1980] AC 247 at 260, [1979] 1 All ER 939 at 946 per Lord Edmund-Davies. See also *Fanjoy v R* (1985) 21 DLR (4th) 321.
20 *Re Mundell* (1883) 48 LT 776 at 778.

A. CONVICTIONS

It was relatively rare for witnesses who had convictions to be regarded as competent to give evidence at common law.[1] The question became important only after the passage of the Evidence Act 1843. It was considered by the Common Law Commissioners who recommended in 1853 that cross-examination be confined to 'offences which imply turpitude and want of probity, and more especially absence of veracity—as for instance, perjury, forgery, obtaining money or goods under false pretences and the like.'[2] For some reason this limitation was not included in the ensuing statutory provision which now reads:

> A witness may be questioned as to whether he has been convicted of any ... misdemeanour and upon being so questioned, if he either denies or does not admit the fact, or refuses to answer, it shall be lawful for the cross-examining party to prove such conviction.[3]

Whatever the reason for enacting the statute in this form it was generally taken to authorise cross-examination about any previous conviction.[4] The Criminal Law Revision Committee recommended the requirement of an explicit link between the conviction and the credibility of the witness, leaving the interpretation of such provision to the courts without further guidance. It is to be regretted that no such provision has yet been included in any subsequent legislation.[5] It should be noted that although convictions which are 'spent' under the provisions of the Rehabilitation of Offenders Act 1974 are technically admissible in criminal proceedings,[6] the court, as a matter of practice, requires leave to be sought before permitting cross-examination on such convictions.[7] Cross-examination is subject to the discretion of the judge to disallow such questioning, a discretion recommended to be exercised as benevolently to the accused as possible.[8]

The statute itself provides for proof of the conviction if the witness should deny it,[9] thus constituting an explicit statutory exception to the general rule that denial of a collateral matter cannot be rebutted.[10]

1 In *Bugg v Day* (1949) 79 CLR 442 at 467, Sir Owen Dixon took the view that at common law questions had to be restricted to convictions for offences involving the veracity of the witness.
2 Second Report of Her Majesty's Commissioners for Inquiry into the Process, Practice and Pleading in the Superior Courts of Law (1853) at 21.
3 Criminal Procedure Act 1865, s 6. For historical background see Ladd 'Impeachment of One's Own Witness—New Developments' (1936) 4 U Chi LR 69.
4 In *Clifford v Clifford* [1961] 3 All ER 231 at 232, [1961] 1 WLR 1274 at 1276, per Cairns J, 'It has never, I think, been doubted that a conviction for any offence could be put to a witness by way of cross-examination as to credit, even though the offence was not one of dishonesty'. But see *R v Sweet-Escott* (1971) 55 Cr App Rep 316 at 320.
5 Cmnd 4991, paras 159–61, draft Bill cl 10(1).
6 S 7(2)(a), and 25 year old convictions have been permitted to be put to an accused person aged under 50, *R v Bailey* [1989] Crim LR 723.
7 *Practice Note* [1975] 2 All ER 1072, [1975] 1 WLR 1065. Non-compliance with the direction is however not necessarily fatal to a conviction, *R v Smallman* [1982] Crim LR 175.
8 *R v Nye* (1982) 75 Cr App Rep 247. See also *D v Yates* (1986) Times, 3 December.
9 The marginal note to the section suggests that it was principally designed to facilitate such proof.
10 Under the old law a false denial could always provide the basis for a charge of perjury, *R v Baker* [1895] 1 QB 797. See now *R v Sweet-Escott* (1971) 55 Cr App Rep 316. See also *R v Livingstone* [1987] 1 Qd R 38.

B. DISCREDITABLE ACTS

The traditional rule was laid down by Lawrence J in *Harris v Tippett*:

> I will permit questions to be put to a witness as to any improper conduct of which
> he may have been guilty for the purpose of trying his credit; but, when the
> questions are irrelevant to the issue on the record, you cannot call witnesses to
> contradict the answers he gives.[11]

If the question imputes a crime with which the witness has not been charged
he may claim the benefit of the privilege against self-incrimination so as to
refuse to answer.[12] Subject to that, and to the judge's discretion to disallow
improper questions, cross-examination about discreditable acts was widely
permitted. The width and tone of such cross-examination caused some
disquiet which was not wholly stilled by a new rule of court made in 1883.[13]
Principles governing the discretion to disallow cross-examination to credit
were propounded by Stephen, incorporated into the Indian Evidence Act,
and endorsed by Sankey LJ in *Hobbs v Tinling & Co Ltd*[14] to the effect that
(i) questions are proper only when answers would seriously impair the
credibility of the witness; (ii) questions are improper if they relate to matters
so remote in time or of such a character that if true they could not seriously
impair the credibility of the witness; and (iii) questions are improper if there
is a substantial disproportion between the importance of the imputation
against the witness's character and the importance of his evidence to the
issue to be decided.[15]

If a question is allowed, then as stated above, the rule used to be that the
witness's denial could not be rebutted on a purely collateral matter, but here
as elsewhere there are now signs of a more liberal approach to rebuttal,
certainly in criminal cases. A recent example is *R v Busby*[16] where it was
suggested that a police witness for the prosecution had fabricated an oral
confession and threatened a potential witness for the defence so as to prevent
him from testifying. Both allegations were denied by the police officer, and
the defence proposed to call the man who had been threatened to rebut the
denial of a threat. The judge refused to permit rebuttal applying the
traditional collateral matter rule, but the Court of Appeal quashed the
conviction on the basis that the defence should have been allowed to rebut
the denial because it went to a fact in issue. This seems quite contrary to the
decision in *Harris v Tippett*,[17] and to most tests for the distinction between

---

11 (1811) 2 Camp 637 at 638.
12 In the early nineteenth century he could invoke an analogous privilege in respect of
   questions the answers to which would disgrace him.
13 Ord 36 r 38, not carried over into the new rules in 1965.
14 [1929] 2 KB 1 at 51.
15 These principles still allow considerable latitude to a cross-examiner, see *R v Longman and
   Richardson* [1969] 1 QB 299, [1968] 2 All ER 761, where it was put to a witness not only
   that she was generally unreliable but that she was a drunkard, suffered from hallucinations,
   entertained groundless fears, was a prostitute and a deliberate perjurer, and in the words
   of the court her whole history and background were brought out.
16 (1981) 75 Cr App Rep 79. See also *R v Mendy* (1976) 64 Cr App Rep 4, where a witness's
   denial that he had received an improper communication to assist his testimony for the
   accused was permitted to be rebutted.
17 (1811) 2 Camp 637.

credit and issue,[18] in effect, substituting substantial relevance as a test for allowing rebuttal, and coming close to assimilating it with the third part of the test quoted above from *Hobbs v Tinling* for deciding whether to allow the original question to be put. It should be noted that in this case the argument seems simply to have been that a man who would tamper with potential witnesses in the way alleged was a man whose testimony was likely to be unreliable, and one who ought not to be believed when there was a conflict with the testimony of the accused who alleged that the witness's evidence of an oral confession was a fabrication. It was not suggested that there was any special animus against the accused, or that the witness's testimony had been secured by corruption.[19] A similar approach is also apparent in the Divisional Court's agreement[20] that 'a matter going to the credit of a witness in a criminal case cannot be said to be collateral to the vital issue; . . . especially where . . . the witness in question provides the only evidence upon that issue.'

C. BIAS

Bias was more important under the old law when incompetence on account of interest was widespread. If a wife was totally incompetent to testify for a spouse, it was not unnatural for a court to allow a witness to be asked whether she was the mistress of the party for whom she was testifying, and even for her denial to be rebutted.[1] In the modern law it is quite clear that many witnesses, such as parties and their close relatives, are likely to be biased, and there is no special need to bring this out. In some cases it may not be obvious, and it is then perhaps desirable to make the true position clear by permitting rebuttal of a denial.[2] It seems similarly reasonable in a case where some special factor is present in addition to foreseeable bias, such as the information passed to the accused's husband while he was waiting outside the court before giving his evidence in his wife's favour in *R v Mendy*,[3] to allow it to be brought out, once again by rebuttal of a denial. The English courts have not had reason to consider the question whether an admission of bias for one reason lets in evidence of bias for another reason; the Supreme Court of Victoria has held that it does not.[4]

---

18 Various formulations were advanced in *A-G v Hitchcock* (1847) 1 Exch 91 at 99. For further discussion see *R v Funderburk* [1990] 1 WLR 587.
19 It has been suggested that the issue in *Busby* is better characterised as one of bias, see Wolchover 'Attacking Confessions with Past Police Embarrassments' [1988] Crim LR 572, but if so, it is bias in an extended sense overlapping this category.
20 In *R v Knightsbridge Crown Court, ex p Goonatilleke* [1986] QB 1 at 11. For further examples of liberality see also *R v Marsh* (1985) 83 Cr App Rep 165; *R v Barton* (1986) 85 Cr App Rep 5 at 13.
1 See *Thomas v David* (1836) 7 C & P 350. In *R v Richardson and Longman* [1969] 1 QB 299, [1968] 2 All ER 761, a witness was even permitted to be called to rebut the testimony of a mistress that she was afraid of her paramour.
2 As in *R v Phillips* (1936) 26 Cr App Rep 17, where relations between the accused and his wife and children had become poisoned.
3 *R v Mendy* (1976) 64 Cr App Rep 4.
4 *Bakopoulos v General Motors Holdens Ltd* [1973] VR 190.

D. CORRUPTION

Corruption requires separate treatment, if only because the bias cases have been expressly distinguished on the ground of constituting a separate area.[5] The scope for an allegation of corruption is limited because if the corruption were attempted by a party to the proceedings, it could in any event be proved as a form of admission by conduct.[6] The whole area was reviewed in *A-G v Hitchcock*[7] where a witness for the prosecution in an excise case was cross-examined as to whether he had said that he had been offered a bribe to testify, impliedly falsely, for the prosecution. The prosecution argued that his denial of so saying could not be rebutted because it was a collateral matter, and more collateral than his denial of the actual receipt of a bribe would have been, which, they argued, could not have been rebutted either. The defence argued that the matter was not completely extrinsic. The court held that the denial could not be rebutted because the question was collateral in the sense that even if it could be shown that the witness had said that he had been offered a bribe it would constitute no disparagement of him. This however would seem to make the question not merely collateral, but wholly irrelevant. His denial of having said he had been offered a bribe might indeed disparage him if false, but it was already well-established by 1847 that it was impermissible to make an irrelevant allegation, merely in the hope of securing a false denial which could be rebutted so as to discredit the witness.[8] It seems hard to contend that saying that a bribe has been offered in any way reveals that one has been accepted. In such a situation the man who has accepted a bribe will either keep quiet if he is speaking to a stranger, or say that he has accepted it if speaking to a close friend. The only man who is likely to say that that he has been offered a bribe is one who implies that he has rejected it. It seems that if the issue relates to the solicitation of a bribe by the witness,[9] or his acceptance of it,[10] rebuttal is permitted. In *A-G v Hitchcock* the court had been careful not to accede to the full width of the argument advanced by the prosecution, though it is hard to fit the case of an actual bribe into the formulations of the various tests for the distinction between collateral and crucial issues propounded by the different judges. It may however be the case that here too the only test is the importance of the allegation in the context of the case. This certainly seems to have been the view of Lord Hewart CJ in *R v Phillips*,[11] where the question was whether the denial of the child victims of alleged incest by their father that they had been schooled by their mother could be rebutted.[12]

E. LACK OF VERACITY

From the very beginning of the modern law of evidence it has been possible to call a witness to swear that the opponent's witness cannot be believed

---

5 In *A-G v Hitchock* (1847) 1 Exch 91 at 100.
6 *Moriarty v London, Chatham and Dover Rly Co* (1870) LR 5 QB 314.
7 See above.
8 *Spenceley v De Willott* (1806) 7 East 108.
9 *Jackson v Thomason* (1861) 8 Jur NS 134.
10 *R v Denley* [1970] Crim LR 583.
11 (1936) 26 Cr App Rep 17.
12 The rebuttal was to have been by two women to whom they had admitted that this was so, but it is not clear why this would not have been inadmissible as hearsay.

upon his oath.[13] It was established that the impugning witness must speak from his personal knowledge,[14] but that he could not refer to particular events to justify his belief.[15] The general form of the question went from the general to the more particular, by asking first 'Have you the means of knowing what the general character of the witness is?', and then 'From such knowledge of his general character would you believe him on oath?'[16] It was not necessary that the witness need have personal knowledge of false testimony by the witness,[17] and even if he did, he would not be allowed to refer to it under the ban on collateral matters.[18] The rule was reconsidered in *R v Brown and Hedley*[19] in the light of the decision in *R v Rowton*[20] that a witness could not express his personal opinion of the accused's character in rebuttal of a character witness called by the accused. The reasoning of the court was not wholly satisfactory, but the outcome was to endorse the existing practice, and to condense the questioning to elicit a simple asseveration that the impugning witness would not believe the opponent's witness on his oath.[1] It became very rare in practice for this cumbersome, anomalous and unconvincing exercise to be conducted.[2] Its continued availability was however endorsed by a unanimous House of Lords in *Toohey v Metropolitan Police Comr.*[3] In *R v Richardson and Longman*[4] strenuous efforts were made to impugn the credibility of a key witness for the prosecution. The defence called a witness in the hope that he would testify that this witness could not be believed on her oath if she were frightened, and her own evidence was that she was frightened of the accused. The trial judge allowed the witness to be asked if he were aware of her reputation for veracity, and whether he would believe her on oath. After a caution from the trial judge the witness replied that in certain particulars she could be believed, whereupon the judge intervened to prevent any qualification of that statement, though the witness had got so far as to indicate that he wished to make some qualification. Nor, despite counsel's persistence, would the trial judge allow the witness to be asked to give an opinion of her credibility on oath on the basis of his personal knowledge of her. It was held that the further question should have been permitted, and that a witness is allowed to express his opinion of the veracity of another on the basis both of the general reputation for veracity, *and* of his personal knowledge, of the impugned witness. No final view was expressed about the intervention to prevent qualification, though the court seemed to incline to the view that qualification is impermissible if it is adduced only as a means of introducing

---

13 Wigmore traces the rule back to 1664.
14 *Trial of O'Connor* (1798) 26 How St Tr 1192, 27 How St Tr 32.
15 *R v Rudge* (1805) Peake Add Cas 232, a decision of Lawrence J who also presided in *Harris v Tippett* (1811) 2 Camp 637.
16 See *Mawson v Hartsink* (1802) 4 Esp 102.
17 *R v Bispham* (1830) 4 C & P 392.
18 *R v Hemp* (1833) 5 C & P 468.
19 (1867) 10 Cox CC 453 (a better report than (1867) 1 CCR 70).
20 (1865) Le & Ca 520.
 1 See also *R v Watson* (1817) 2 Stark 116 at 152 for this form of question.
 2 None of the Lords of Appeal, nor any of the counsel, in *Toohey*, below, could recall its ever having happened, and leading counsel for the prosecution was Mr J H Buzzard, first Treasury counsel, editor of Archbold's *Criminal Pleading, Evidence and Practice*, a lawyer of quite unrivalled experience of criminal trials.
 3 [1965] AC 595, [1965] 1 All ER 506.
 4 [1969] 1 QB 299, [1968] 2 All ER 761.

in chief particular reasons for the qualification, though cross-examination about such reasons is permissible.

This longstanding rule is to be distinguished from the situation in which the witness's lack of veracity is imputed to some specific medical or mental condition.[5] This issue was raised in *R v Gunewardene*[6] where the accused, a doctor charged with abortion, wished to call a medical witness to testify that a prosecution witness was suffering from a disease which made him incapable of telling the truth. The Court of Criminal Appeal upheld the trial judge's refusal to allow this on the basis that it infringed the rule relating to the rebuttal of a denial of a collateral matter,[7] and might lead to great inconvenience. This decision was overruled by the House of Lords in *Toohey v Metropolitan Police Comr*[8] where the accused was charged with assault. He wished to call medical evidence that the victim who had testified for the prosecution was suffering from hysteria. The trial judge refused to permit such evidence, and was upheld by the Court of Criminal Appeal, on the strength of *R v Gunewardene*. In the House of Lords counsel did not seek to support that decision, and it was overruled, the rule being held to be that:

> Medical evidence is admissible to show that a witness suffers from some disease or defect or abnormality of mind that affects the reliability of his evidence. Such evidence is not confined to a general opinion of the unreliability of the witness, but may give all the matters necessary to show not only the foundation of and the reasons for the diagnosis but also the extent to which the credibility of the witness is affected.[9]

It seems clearly right that such evidence should be before the jury, and the possibility in these circumstances of prolonging the trial unduly is remote. There is some danger of attempts to influence the jury's assessment of the credibility of a witness by calling medical evidence to prove matters within the jury's normal competence, such as the propensity of some witnesses, who could perfectly well tell the truth, to tell lies.[10] Such cases are best dealt with on the basis of the relevance of the evidence, and the proper function of expert witnesses.[11] The rule in *Toohey* applies just as much to evidence adduced by the prosecution as by the defence, and to evidence adduced in chief as much as in rebuttal.[12] It is however possible that a court will be more inclined to receive expert testimony as to the effect of a marginal mental condition upon a witness's veracity when it is offered to rebut testimony that the witness should not be believed on oath,[13] than where it is offered in advance of any attack.[14]

5 See Pattenden 'Conflicting Approaches to Psychiatric Evidence on Criminal Trials: England, Canada and Australia' [1986] Crim LR 92; *Murphy v R* (1989) 86 ALR 35.
6 [1951] 2 KB 600, [1951] 2 All ER 290.
7 In so doing it appeared not to have been apprised of dicta to the contrary in *A-G v Hitchcock* (1847) 1 Exch 91 at 95, and *R v Hill* (1851) 20 LJMC 222 at 225.
8 [1965] AC 595, [1965] 1 All ER 506.
9 At 609, 512.
10 See *R v Ashcroft* [1954] Qd R 81 at 85; *R v MacKenney* (1980) 72 Cr App Rep 78.
11 See below ch XIII. The attempt in *R v MacKenney* to limit the decision in *Toohey* to total incapacity to tell the truth appears to be inconsistent with the last sentence of Lord Pearce's speech quoted above.
12 *R v Eades* [1972] Crim LR 99.
13 As in *R v Taylor* (1986) 31 CCC (3d) 1 (allegation of sexual abuse by borderline schizophrenic).
14 As in *R v B* [1987] 1 NZLR 362 (allegation of sexual abuse by slightly retarded twelve year old).

Although not strictly relevant to impugning the testimony of an opponent's witness by medical evidence, it is convenient to consider here the question of how far a statement tendered by the prosecution can be discredited by medical evidence of the condition of the maker at the time that the statement was made. It has been argued above[15] that the court has, at least, a discretion to reject a confession made by an accused person suffering at that time from mental instability. Under s 76 of the Police and Criminal Evidence Act 1984 a confession may be excluded if it were obtained in consequence of anything done which was likely in the circumstances existing at the time to render a confession unreliable. It might well be argued that to question a mentally disturbed person was so likely.[16] In such cases it would seem right that the defence should be able to adduce medical evidence of the accused's condition at such a time.[17] Such evidence has been admitted in Commonwealth jurisdictions.[18] To the extent that *Toohey* is relied upon to justify these decisions it is somewhat questionable whether it goes so far.[19] In these cases the accused himself often testifies inconsistently with his confession, and it would appear that the expert evidence could be regarded as simply bolstering the testimony of the accused in the way criticised by the Court of Appeal in *R v Turner*.[20]

Sometimes lack of veracity may be approached by reference to previous cases in which a witness's evidence on a related matter has been disbelieved. Thus if the witness has himself been subsequently convicted of perjury in respect of a similar charge upon which he testified, a conviction may be quashed.[1] Similarly, if a witness has given evidence in former proceedings either against the same accused on another matter, where the evidence was similar[2] or part of the same statement,[3] or against other accused in respect of the very same subject matter,[4] and a verdict of acquittal[5] is entered in circumstances indicating that the witness's evidence must have been disbelieved by the jury; then evidence of such an acquittal becomes admissible to impugn the veracity of the witness.[6]

15 See above, p 191.
16 As recognised by the prescription of a mandatory direction to the jury of the need for caution in convicting upon such a basis, Police and Criminal Evidence Act 1984, s 77.
17 Expert medical evidence of the accused's condition at the time of confessing adduced to impugn its reliability was admitted in *R v Kilner* [1976] Crim LR 740; *R v Davis* [1979] Crim LR 167; and *R v Powell* [1980] Crim LR 39.
18 See *Sinclair v R* (1947) 73 CLR 316; *Jackson v R* (1962) 108 CLR 591; *Phillion v R* [1978] 1 SCR 18 (though this aspect of the case was not the subject of the appeal); *Murphy v R* (1989) 86 ALR 35.
19 See *R v McKay* [1967] NZLR 139 at 153.
20 [1975] QB 834 at 842, [1975] 1 All ER 70 at 75. See also *R v Moore* [1982] 1 NZLR 242.
1 *R v Savin* (1972) unreported but referred to in *R v Cooke* (1986) 84 Cr App Rep 286 at 290.
2 *R v Doosti* (1985) 82 Cr App Rep 181.
3 *R v Hay* (1983) 77 Cr App Rep 70.
4 *R v Cooke*, above.
5 The Supreme Court of Canada has held it improper to put to an expert witness the confession of guilt by a former co-accused in respect of the very same matter upon which the witness proposed to testify in a manner inconsistent with such a result, *R v Howard* (1989) 69 CR (3d) 193.
6 Though it is not permissible to use merely disparaging remarks about the witness's evidence made by judges in other cases, see *Humphries v R* (1987) 75 ALR 31.

SECTION 3. CHARACTER OF PARTY

There are a number of rather miscellaneous situations to be considered in this section. Strictly not all of the subjects are parties, for example, prosecutions for rape are normally undertaken by the police, and not by the complainant, whose character may be put in issue. The first part of this section deals with the admissibility of evidence of character in relation to such cases, loosely categorised, as the character of the prosecutor. The second part is concerned with the rules of common law governing the character of the accused in those cases where it is not adduced in chief by the prosecution, for example where the character of the accused is put in issue by a character witness called on his behalf. The third part deals with the admissibility of character evidence in civil cases, excluding those where it is led in chief under the so-called similar facts rule. The final part deals with the extent to which the law permits rehabilitation of character so impugned.

A. PROSECUTOR

By far the greatest accumulation of authority has accreted around the question of the admissibility of evidence and questioning as to the character of the complainant on an allegation of rape or allied crimes. There are a number of reasons for this. One is that rape is rare in being a crime where the state of mind of the complainant is important; in evidential terms, her disposition may be relevant to the question of whether or not she consented. It is also a defence to rape that the accused believed the complainant to be consenting, so her reputation for unchastity may become relevant. It has also been remarked that sexual intercourse, whether or not consensual, most often takes place in private, and leaves few visible traces of having occurred. Evidence is often effectively limited to that of the parties, and much is likely to depend upon the balance of credibility between them. This has important effects for the law of evidence since it is capable of reducing the difference between questions going to credit and questions going to the issue to vanishing point.[7] If the only issue is consent and the only witness is the complainant, the conclusion that the complainant is not worthy of credit must be decisive of the issue. The difficulties caused by these factors are also present in relation to much of the evidence used to resolve them. If it is sought to prove consent by evidence that the complainant is sexually promiscuous, it is likely to be just as difficult for the defence to rebut her denials of such promiscuity as it is for the prosecution to prove that she did not consent on the occasion in issue. If it is alleged that she has made a previous false allegation of rape it is unclear how its falsity could be satisfactorily established. In other words the collateral issues in such cases are likely to prove particularly time-consuming, difficult to resolve and confusing to the jury.

It is also likely to be more than usually unfair to confront the complainant with isolated examples of her extrinsic sexual behaviour at the trial without warning, since sexual activity tends to occur frequently, and it really would be tantamount to forcing her to defend her whole life in a way clearly less true than in the case of, say, allegations of crime. It has already been noted

7 See *R v Viola* [1982] 3 All ER 73 at 77, [1982] 1 WLR 1138 at 1143.

that the law has, in other respects, been influenced by the supposition that the testimony of complainants of sexual crimes may be tainted by considerations not obvious to juries. It should now be noted that juries in sexual cases may be influenced by considerations not intended by the law.[8] It must finally be remembered that the common law has developed during a period of rapidly changing sexual manners. Is it then at all surprising that the law should be confused and confusing, and latterly the subject of investigation and legislative reform?

ι ne position broadly established at common law at the beginning of the nineteenth century was that the complainant could be cross-examined about her promiscuity in general,[9] but not about particular acts of intercourse with named men.[10] This position crystallised into rules prohibiting rebuttal of her denials by adducing evidence of particular acts of sexual intercourse,[11] subject to three exceptions. According to these her denials could be rebutted by evidence of her prostitution,[12] of other acts of intercourse with the accused,[13] or of other sexual acts constituting part of the surrounding circumstances.[14] It seems that such rebuttal was usually justified on the basis that it went to consent, though this argument was not available in *R v Barker*, where it was regarded as going to credibility.[15] The concept of prostitution was itself somewhat vague, and became interpreted in such a wide manner that it defeated one of the professed objects of the general ban on rebuttal of denials, namely, that it exposed the complainant to cross-examination upon the whole of her sexual life without notice.[16] It was also possible to adduce extrinsic evidence, cross-examine and rebut if denied on all the surrounding circumstances of the incident in question, including the sexual behaviour of the complainant.[17]

This state of the law was widely regarded as unsatisfactory, and became the subject of investigation and reform in many parts of the common law world.[18] In England the Advisory Group on the Law of Rape reported that the present law was widely criticised, and itself expressed the view that:

8 See Kalven and Zeisel *The American Jury* (1966) 249–54.
9 *R v Clarke* (1817) 2 Stark 241.
10 *R v Hodgson* (1812) Russ & Ry 211.
11 *R v Holmes* (1871) 12 Cox CC 137.
12 *R v Barker* (1829) 3 C & P 589.
13 *R v Martin* (1834) 6 C & P 562; *R v Riley* (1887) 16 Cox CC 191.
14 *R v Turner* [1944] KB 463, [1944] 1 All ER 599.
15 (1829) 3 C & P 589. It should be noted that in *Thomas v David* (1836) 7 C & P 350, *R v Cargill* (1913) 8 Cr App Rep 224, and *R v Richardson and Longman* [1969] 1 QB 299, [1968] 2 All ER 761, it was accepted that an allegation of prostitution impugned the credit of a witness.
16 See *R v Krausz* (1973) 57 Cr App Rep 466 at 474, 'Evidence which proves that a woman is in the habit of submitting her body to different men without discrimination, whether for pay or not, would seem to be admissible.'
17 However much it might show the complainant to be 'a filthy, nasty woman, utterly filthy' per Charles J in *R v Turner* [1944] KB 463, [1944] 1 All ER 599.
18 There is specific legislation in Scotland, in Canada, in many of the Australian jurisdictions and in New Zealand. In the United States 'rape shield' statutes are in force in almost all of the states, and Federal law appears in r 412 of the Federal Rules. The truly bewildering variety of approaches is analysed and summarised in the Australian Law Reform Commission's Research Paper No 11 'Character and Conduct'.

In contemporary society sexual relationships outside marriage, both steady and of a more casual character, are fairly widespread, and it seems now to be agreed that a woman's sexual experiences with partners of her own choice, are neither indicative of untruthfulness nor of a general willingness to consent.[19]

Notwithstanding this general view the committee was not prepared to bar all cross-examination, or evidence in rebuttal, as to the complainant's sexual history. It was generally prepared to countenance it when the evidence was relevant to an issue in the case, and seems to have taken the view that it would always be so relevant if it related to other acts involving the accused himself, or when the acts involving other men bore a striking resemblance to that with which the accused was charged. These precepts were embodied in a complicated clause in a Bill presented to Parliament implementing the committee's recommendations.[20] It was regarded as much too complicated by some of the Law Lords,[1] and a less elaborate provision was adopted as s 2 of the Sexual Offences (Amendment) Act 1976:[2]

2(1) If at a trial any person is charged with a rape offence to which he pleads not guilty, then, except with the leave of the judge, no evidence and no question in cross-examination shall be adduced or asked at the trial, by or on behalf of any defendant at the trial, about any sexual experience of a complainant with a person other than that defendant.

2(2) The judge shall not give leave in pursuance of the preceding sub-section for any evidence or question except on an application made to him in the absence of the jury by or on behalf of a defendant; and on such an application the judge shall give leave if and only if he is satisfied that it would be unfair to that defendant to refuse to allow the evidence to be adduced or the question to be asked.

The section goes on to provide that it does not authorise the asking of any questions which could not otherwise be asked.[3] This is a very limited provision. It applies only to 'rape offences',[4] and more importantly it makes no attempt to regulate evidence relating to the complainant's sexual activities with the accused himself, nor does it apply at all to evidence of anything other than 'sexual experience'. Acceptance of the common law in relation to activities with the accused himself was recommended by the advisory group, apparently on the basis that it was relevant to consent. The rationale for this wholesale exemption is quite unclear. It seems to suggest that once a woman has consented to have intercourse with a man she will never again refuse. This is hardly a self-evident proposition, and it looks very odd beside the established rule that a husband can rape his wife after they have formally separated,[5] and even odder beside the recommendation of the Criminal Law Revision Committee that no special defence should be available to husbands,

19 Cmnd 6352, para 131.
20 The group's report did not itself contain a draft Bill.
1 See 376 HL Official Report (5th series) cols 1518–20.
2 For criticism of this general scheme see Temkin 'Evidence in Sexual Assault Cases' (1984) 47 MLR 625; *Rape and the Legal Process* (1987) chs 3, 5.
3 S 2(4).
4 Defined in s 7(2) to exclude indecent assault and forcible buggery of a woman, though the common law appears to have applied to the former, see *R v Holmes* (1871) LR 1 CCR 334 at 336. Though the tendency will be to interpret common law rules in adjacent areas sympathetically, see *R v Funderburk* [1990] 1 WLR 587.
5 *R v Clarke* [1949] 2 All ER 448, 33 Cr App Rep 216; *R v Miller* [1954] 2 QB 282, [1954] 2 All ER 529; *R v O'Brien* [1974] 3 All ER 663.

wherever the parties have ceased to cohabit.[6] It is hard to see why special rules should apply to this situation, different from those that apply in relation to third parties.[7] In both, the critical consideration should be the precise contribution which admission of the evidence will make to the just resolution of the issues between the parties in the circumstances of the case. The advisory group was concerned to exclude evidence of a vague and general character, but the Act appears not to affect such evidence which is still left to the operation of the rules of common law. The advisory group took the view that evidence of sexual behaviour with third parties should be admitted only where it was relevant to an issue in the case, normally consent, and admitted then only when it showed a striking similarity to the acts alleged by the accused. The Act seeks to accomplish this result by its reference to the new and undefined term 'sexual experience', and by imposing the overriding condition that the judge shall allow the question or evidence only where it would be unfair to the defendant to refuse. While it is clear that acts of intercourse with other men constitute 'sexual experience', it is surprising to find that conversations about such acts also constitute 'sexual experience' even in the absence of any suggestion that the conversations had any basis in fact.[8] How much further it might go, or how specifically it should be related to particular incidents with particular men is a matter for speculation. It would presumably not include having undergone sexual education at school,[9] or having associated with prostitutes.[10] It is less clear that evidence of solicitation as a prostitute does not amount to being about 'sexual experience'. The whole basis both of the common law and of the advisory group's recommendations on this matter is obscure. Both the judges[11] and the group[12] recognise that prostitutes can be raped. It is much less clear why an allegation of prostitution is regarded as being relevant to consent. Prostitutes customarily demand payment in advance for their services. It is rare for the accused to allege such payment in cases where he seeks to raise the complainant's prostitution in evidence. In the absence of such payment it seems less, rather than more, likely that the complainant will have consented. Here too a better rule would be to allow the question to be raised when it is shown by the special circumstances to be relevant. Thus in a case like *R v Krausz*[13] where the allegation was that the complainant habitually, and unusually, demanded payment only after the consummation of the act, there is a real issue as to consent to which the disputed evidence is relevant. It is easy to understand why the advisory group approved of the common

6 15th Report on Sexual Offences (Cmnd 9213) para 2.85. A substantial minority would not even have excluded cohabiting spouses.
7 Such a change has now been recommended by the Criminal Law Revision Committee, 15th Report on Sexual Offences (Cmnd 9213) para 2.90.
8 *R v Hinds and Butler* [1979] Crim LR 111. In *R v Viola* [1982] 3 All ER 73, [1982] 1 WLR 1138, no regard was paid to these words at all and the court appears to have accepted that evidence of the complainant's having made unaccepted, and less than explicit, sexual advances to particular men, and having a naked man in her flat, amounted to evidence of her sexual experience. Compare *Beck v R* [1984] WAR 127 (evidence that woman had previously cut man's pubic hair not within statute unless followed by sexual intercouse).
9 See *R v Byczko (No 1)* (1977) 16 SASR 506.
10 One of the allegations in *R v Barker* (1829) 3 C & P 589.
11 See Byles J in *R v Holmes* (1871) LR 1 CCR 334 at 337.
12 Para 136.
13 (1973) 57 Cr App Rep 466. See also *R v Starkey* (1987) 26 ACR 113 (previous acts of consensual sexual activity involving bondage to show that tying up not necessarily determinative of lack of consent).

law's allowing rebuttal in those circumstances; it is incomprehensible in the light of their general approach why they approved of the decision in *R v Clay*,[14] where the only evidence was of isolated acts of prostitution some twenty years before the incident in question. It is hard to avoid the conclusion that trials for rape are, in fact, conducted upon the basis of a contest more about the character of the complainant than anything else.[15] The prosecution frequently seeks to assert the prior virginity of the complainant in support of its contention that she would never say yes, and the defence seeks to assert her prior sexual experience in support of its contention that she would never say no. Such contentions are so patently irrational that it would surely be better to go further in guiding the courts towards concentration upon the issues to which the character of the complainant, in its widest sense, is truly relevant.[16] The Act does not purport to offer more by way of guidance than that the evidence or questioning should be allowed if refusal would be unfair to the defendant. In most cases where leave is sought the defence appears to suggest that the evidence or questioning is relevant to consent,[17] and it certainly seems to have been the intention both of the advisory group[18] and of Parliament[19] that it should go to an issue in the case. Although this was emphasised in *R v Viola*[20] to be the general effect, it is understandable that in *R v Cox*,[1] where the complainant could be shown to have made an admittedly false complaint of rape in very similar circumstances in the past, it was held to have been unfair to the accused not have allowed the complainant to be questioned about the incident. It is, if anything, even more surprising to find that despite the statutory wording which appears to exclude it as a consideration, in *R v Hinds and Butler*,[2] the judge took the probable effect of the questioning of the complainant into account in determining whether to give leave. In *R v Viola*[3] the Court of Appeal has, it is submitted quite correctly, stressed the importance of determining the relevancy of the evidence or questioning, that it should normally relate to an issue, and perhaps most important of all that it should be related to the way in which the trial is being run. It is made quite clear that s 2(2) invests the trial judge with a duty to be exercised in the light of his judgment, and not with a discretion, and that the Court of Appeal may properly substitute its own judgment for his. It should be emphasised that the difference between a

14 (1851) 5 Cox CC 146.
15 See *R v Gun* (1977) 17 SASR 379; Kalven and Zeisel *The American Jury* (1966) pp 249–54; Adler 'Rape—The Intention of Parliament and the Practice of the Courts' (1982) 45 Mod LR 664; *Rape on Trial* (1987) ch 6.
16 But see Elliott 'Rape Complainants' Sexual Experience with Third Parties' [1984] Crim LR 4.
17 Eighty per cent of Adler's example.
18 Paras 134–8.
19 See 376 HL Official Report (5th series) col 1518 and 911 HC Official Report (5th series) col 1989.
20 [1982] 3 All ER 73 at 77, [1982] 1 WLR 1138 at 1143.
 1 (1986) 84 Cr App Rep 132, where it was felt that the force of the point would be lost without reference to the sexual intercourse which had then taken place.
 2 [1979] Crim LR 111, though despite the fact that the complainant was only 14 years old and had already made an attempt to commit suicide, leave was granted.
 3 [1982] 3 All ER 73, [1982] 1 WLR 1138. In *Viola* the issue was consent, see also *R v Fenlon and Neal* (1980) 71 Cr App Rep 307, where the court was prepared to allow questions only to account for the presence of semen at the relevant time, and *Gregory v R, Sharwood v R* (1983) 57 ALJR 629, where the evidence refuted the complainant's denial of other sexual acts at the same time and place.

defence of lack of consent and of belief in lack of consent is far from decisive. In the latter case the issue relates to belief at the time of the act that the victim is consenting then, not to belief at some earlier time that she is likely to consent.[4] In either case the evidence of previous sexual experience must relate strictly and strongly to proof of the relevant issue, and a simple allegation of belief in consent conveys no general warrant for such cross-examination.[5]

There are a number of other situations in which the character of the prosecutor or victim of a crime may be regarded as relevant. Thus in *Toohey v Metropolitan Police Comr*[6] the defence hinged completely on the personality of the alleged victim, namely, that he was subject to hysteria and quite capable of misunderstanding, exaggerating and over-reacting to the most solicitous of treatment. The House of Lords had no doubt that such evidence was admissible irrespective of whether the victim had testified or not. Similarly, if self-defence is pleaded in defence of a charge of murder the accused may show that the deceased was of violent disposition,[7] or where there are special features of the defence dependent upon facets of the victim's character, for example, that the killing occurred in the course of resisting a violent homosexual advance, then those relevant aspects may be proved also.[8] In all such cases it is however essential that the evidence shall be relevant,[9] and relevant at the stage of the proceedings at which it is raised.[10]

A further possible situation is one in which the accused asserts that a third party committed the crime with which he is charged, and wishes to adduce evidence of that person's character in support of such assertion. Most of the English case-law is concerned with allegations made with respect to a co-accused, and will be considered in the next section. It is sufficient to note here that the rules are no less generous when the alleged criminal is a third party, and that in civil cases they are most generous of all.[11]

B. ACCUSED

The most common situations involving evidence of the character of the accused are those in which it is adduced in chief by the prosecution, and in which the accused is cross-examined about it. These are dealt with in the two following chapters. This section is concerned with those cases where the accused adduces evidence of his own good character, and the extent to which that opens the way to cross-examination, or rebutting evidence, and cases where the accused seeks to adduce evidence, or cross-examine, as to the bad character of his co-accused.

4 *R v Barton* (1987) 85 Cr App Rep 5.
5 *R v Brown* (1988) Crim LR 828.
6 [1965] AC 595, [1965] 1 All ER 506.
7 But not, it seems, in Scotland, see *Brady v HM Advocate* 1986 SCCR 191.
8 As in *R v Biggin* [1920] 1 KB 213.
9 See *R v Harmer* (1985) 28 ACR 35.
10 In *R v Wells Street Stipendiary Magistrate, ex p Deakin* [1980] AC 477, sub nom *Gleaves v Deakin* [1979] 2 All ER 497, it was held that the reputation of the prosecutor for criminal libel was not relevant at the stage of the committal proceedings, but could be raised at the trial.
11 *Hurst v Evans* [1917] 1 KB 352 at 355.

1. GOOD CHARACTER

The accused has been permitted to adduce evidence of his own good character from very early times.[12] Questions arise as to the interconnected issues of the precise purpose for admitting such evidence, the type of evidence to be permitted, and the effect of such evidence when admitted. Evidence of the good character of the accused could be admitted because it goes to the issue of guilt or innocence, because it supports the credibility of the accused, or simply so as to predispose the jury in the accused's favour. Since such evidence was admitted long before the accused became a competent witness it is clear that, in origin at least, it was not admitted to support his credibility as a witness. In the leading case of *R v Rowton*[13] only Baron Martin was at all inclined to accept that it was admitted simply so as to predispose the jury in favour of the accused. So far as relevance to an issue is concerned the process of reasoning was explained in *R v Stannard*:

> the object of laying it before the jury is to induce them to believe, from the improbability that a person of good character should have conducted himself as alleged, that there is some mistake or misrepresentation in the evidence of the prosecution, and it is strictly evidence in the case.[14]

Attempts are sometimes made to distinguish between relevance to innocence simpliciter, and relevance via disbelief of the prosecution's witness.[15] This seems both confusing and pointless though the judgments in *R v Rowton* show some difference of emphasis. Thus Cockburn CJ said:

> It has been put that evidence in favour of the character of a person on his trial raises a collateral issue. I can hardly think that it is a collateral issue in the proper sense of the term. It becomes one of the points on which the jury are to found their verdict.[16]

While Willes J said:

> it is a mistake to suppose because only the prisoner can raise the question of character, that therefore it is evidence on a collateral issue. It is not. It is evidence which is admissible, because it makes it less probable that that which the prosecution has averred . . . should be true. It is evidence strictly relevant to the issue.[17]

Both of these purposes, excluding only simple prejudice in favour of the accused, re-appear in recent cases. The accused may now testify, and in *R v Bellis* Lord Widgery CJ said that 'possession of a good character is primarily a matter which goes to credibility.'[18] In cases where the accused does not exercise his option to testify he is still entitled to have evidence of his good

---

12 See *R v Turner* (1664) 6 State Tr 565 at 613; *R v Harris* (1680) 7 State Tr 926 at 929.
13 (1865) 34 LJMC 57 at 65.
14 (1837) 7 C & P 673 at 674.
15 See *R v Trimboli* (1979) 21 SASR 577.
16 (1865) 34 LJMC 57 at 60.
17 (1865) 34 LJMC 57 at 66.
18 [1966] 1 All ER 552n at 552, [1966] 1 WLR 234 at 236; see also *R v Falconer-Atlee* (1973) 58 Cr App Rep 348; *R v Callum* [1975] RTR 415.

character considered as relevant to the issue,[19] a view which has recently been re-emphasised.[20] It has even been held proper in one such case to direct the jury that good character enhances the credibility of an out-of-court assertion.[21] If the accused does testify, he is presumably entitled to have his good character considered on both grounds. Despite an apparent suggestion to the contrary in *R v Levy*,[1] it is submitted that this remains the case whether or not there is an issue between two co-accused. As between them, one is entitled to elicit, or adduce, explicit evidence of bad character against the other, constrained only by considerations of relevancy,[2] and can cross-examine explicitly to the other's bad character free from discretionary control,[3] it seems very odd to hold that he cannot adduce evidence of his own good character for fear of damaging his co-accused by implicit comparison. Indeed in *Bracewell* this very situation was accepted by the Court of Appeal to have occurred at the trial without the slightest hint of criticism of such a procedure.[4]

When the only possible purpose was relevance to the issue it made good sense to restrict the evidence of character to those aspects relevant to the nature of the charge. Thus when the accused was charged with treason it was held that evidence of his good character should not be general, but limited to his character for loyalty and as being peaceable.[5] The rule seems however to have been disregarded both before 1898,[6] and after.[7] It was accepted by all of the judges in *R v Rowton* that such evidence could not consist of particular examples of good acts, since it did not follow that the accused never acted otherwise.[8] It was impossible to maintain such a rule consistently in practice once it was accepted that answers to questions in cross-examination could constitute evidence of good character, since such questions invariably condescend to particularity.[9] Nevertheless the rule still retains sufficient vitality in this respect to have prevented a man accused of

---

19 *R v Bryant, R v Oxley* [1979] QB 108, [1978] 2 All ER 689. In Australia it now seems clear that the accused is entitled to a direction which does not explicitly exclude either ground, see *R v Murphy* (1985) 63 ALR 53 at 64; *R v Palazoff* (1986) 23 ACR 86, esp at 96.
20 *R v Cohen* (1990) Times, 15 March. See also *R v Berrada* (1989) Times, 20 February; *R v Marr* [1989] Crim LR 743.
21 *R v Chapman* [1989] Crim LR 60, though this seems to raise a number of potential problems, for example if there are a number of conflicting extra-judicial statements.
1 [1987] Crim LR 48.
2 See *R v Miller* [1952] 2 All ER 667, 36 Cr App Rep 169; *Lowery v R* [1974] AC 85, [1973] 3 All ER 662; *R v Bracewell* (1978) 68 Cr App Rep 44.
3 *Murdoch v Taylor* [1965] AC 574, [1965] 1 All ER 406.
4 This case which seems not to have been brought to the attention of the Court in *Levy* is actually stronger in that the evidence was much more narrowly focussed on the trait in question.
5 *R v Turner* (1817) 32 State Tr 957 at 1007.
6 See *R v Burt* (1851) 5 Cox CC 284 (evidence of general good character on a charge of receiving); for judicial recognition of widespread abuse in the older law, see *R v Jones* (1809) 31 State Tr 251 at 310.
7 See *R v Savory* (1942) 29 Cr App Rep 1 (good character as railway porter on a charge of indecent assault); for judicial recognition of widespread abuse in the newer law, see *R v Butterwasser* [1948] 1 KB 4 at 6, [1947] 2 All ER 415 at 416.
8 (1865) 34 LJMC 57 at 67; though in *R v Williamson* (1807) 3 C & P 635, Lord Ellenborough CJ permitted a male mid-wife charged with manslaughter to adduce evidence of his kind and skilful attention to other women.
9 See *R v West* (1890) 112 CCCt Cas 724 for a particularly harsh example in which the negative answer given by a police witness when asked by counsel for the defence whether anything was known against the accused was held to amount to evidence of good character sufficient to permit rebuttal.

homosexual offences from adducing evidence of particular heterosexual acts as evidence of his proclivities.[10]

The matter for decision in *R v Rowton*, as will be seen below, related to the type of evidence which could be adduced in rebuttal of good character, but by parity of reasoning the majority held that a witness to the good character of the accused could speak only to the accused's reputation, and not to his personal opinion of the accused's disposition. The court confessed its unfamiliarity with any practice in this area and even admitted the rule to be anomalous and illogical. It is also arguable that it confused general evidence of character, with which it was concerned, with evidence of general character, with which the principal authorities cited to it were concerned. Nevertheless the limitation, in this context at least, of evidence of character to signify reputation has not, so far, been overruled. No detailed analysis of such reputation evidence has been attempted in England, but it was suggested by *Wigmore*[11] that it should extend to reputation in any relevant field,[12] and need not be confined to reputation in the local community. Given the tendency to apply the rule to issue, as well as credibility, this seems good sense.[13] Though if it is taken to imply a narrowing of possible sources of information then there must be an increased danger of conflict with the rule against hearsay.[14] Nor has much attention been devoted here to the question of how much need be done to constitute evidence of good character.[15] As noted above it was in one case held to apply where a question was asked in cross-examination of a prosecution witness about the absence of convictions.[16] This has stimulated distinctions in South Australia between negative good character,[17] good character, and positive good character.[18] This seems needlessly elaborate.

The final question here relates to the effect of the evidence when adduced. It was long considered that its effect was for the jury to take it into account only when otherwise left in doubt. It was then claimed in *R v Bliss Hill*[19] that this reduced its effect to nil, since if the jury was in doubt the accused was in any event entitled to be acquitted. This is unconvincing because there must be a point at which the jury requires only the slightest extra evidence to feel the reasonable doubt sufficient to acquit the accused, and that surely must have been the situation contemplated.[20] Even so, it is certainly more

---

10 *R v Redgrave* (1981) 74 Cr App Rep 10.
11 Para 245 et seq, a view accepted in many American jurisdictions, see also Federal Rules of Evidence, r 803(21).
12 For example among business associates.
13 It has been adopted in Canada, see *R v Levasseur* (1987) 35 CCC (3d) 136.
14 The borderline could not have been very far away in *Levasseur* where the witness testified on the basis of his own limited knowledge and that of fifteen business acquaintances with whom he had discussed the accused's reputation in business matters.
15 See further below p 401.
16 See also *R v Lopatta* (1983) 35 SASR 101 where a question was asked of a prosecution witness as to whether the accused was a good person.
17 Absence of convictions, suggested distinction in *R v Mandica* (1980) 24 SASR 394 at 406.
18 Doing good works in the community, canvassed by the trial judge as reported in *R v Palazoff* (1986) 43 SASR 99 at 111.
19 (1918) 13 Cr App Rep 125. Re-affirmed in *R v Brittle* (1965) 109 Sol Jo 1028. See also *R v Falconer-Atlee* (1973) 58 Cr App Rep 348 at 358; *R v Lawrence* [1984] 3 NSWLR 674.
20 This may account for the persistence of the older form of direction, see *R v Islam* (1969) 113 Sol Jo 185.

straightforward to let the evidence go to the jury with whatever cautionary direction the trial judge feels appropriate.[1]

2. REBUTTAL

It was settled in *R v Butterwasser* that the bad character of the accused can be brought out at common law only when the accused has put his character in issue. It is not enough for him to attack the character of the witnesses for the prosecution:

> I do not see on what principle it can be said, that if a man does not go into the box and put his character in issue, he can have evidence against him of previous bad character when all that he has done is to attack the witnesses for the prosecution. The reason is that by attacking the witnesses for the prosecution and suggesting that they are unreliable, he is not putting his character in issue; he is putting their character in issue.[2]

The problem then is to determine when the accused does put his character into issue at common law. The most obvious way is to call witnesses to testify as to his good character, indeed if character means reputation, it is not clear that the accused could testify to his own good character. It seems that if the witness testifies to the accused's good character without premeditation, for example, in response to a question in cross-examination, not requiring an answer relating to the accused's character, such character will not normally be put in issue. In *R v Gadbury*[3] the question was asked by the accused's counsel, but was not intended to elicit evidence of good character even though the answer to the matter in issue could incidentally be construed as showing the accused's good character; while in *R v Redd*[4] a witness who had been called by an unrepresented defendant to do no more than prove a document, blurted out his encomium of the accused without external stimulation. On the other hand it has been held that rebuttal cannot be shut out or restricted by confining the evidence of the accused's good character to a particular period,[5] or trait.[6] The character of the accused may exceptionally be put in issue by operation of law, as in the case of a child presumed to be *doli incapax*.[7]

It is possible to rebut evidence of the accused's good character either by eliciting evidence of his bad character in cross-examination, or by leading extrinsic evidence of it. Despite some uncertainty[8] and confusion[9] in the

---

1 The judge is under no absolute duty to direct the jury's attention to the accused's good character, *R v Aberg* [1948] 2 KB 173 at 175; *R v Smith* [1971] Crim LR 531; *R v Callum* [1975] RTR 415 at 420; see also *Simic v R* (1980) 144 CLR 320 at 333. Nor is he bound to direct them to disregard it simply because the accused has been shown in cross-examination to have previous convictions, *R v Manwaring* [1983] 2 NSWLR 82.
2 [1948] 1 KB 4, [1947] 2 All ER 415.
3 (1838) 8 C & P 676.
4 [1923] 1 KB 104.
5 *R v Shrimpton* (1851) 2 Den 319.
6 *R v Winfield* (1939) 27 Cr App Rep 139.
7 *R v B, R v A* [1979] 3 All ER 460, [1979] 1 WLR 1185, though this seems a very harsh rule when the accused disclaims any reliance upon the presumption.
8 It was doubted in *R v Wood and Parker* (1841) 5 Jur 225.
9 Although accepted as a general rule in *R v Redd* [1923] 1 KB 104, both the authorities which were relied upon (*R v Gadbury* (1838) 8 C & P 676 and *R v Shrimpton* (1851) 2 Den 319) depended upon particular statutory provisions.

earlier law, it now seems settled that a witness may be asked about the accused's previous convictions.[10] It is equally possible to ask about the accused's previous bad acts, notwithstanding the *Rowton* rule as to the inadmissibility of evidence of good acts for the accused in chief.[11] This seems to have been put beyond doubt by the decision of the Court of Appeal in *R v Bracewell*[12] where such cross-examination was justified by the accused's having put his good character in issue, when it would not be countenanced on the basis of simple relevance to facts in issue. There have been suggestions that the witness can be cross-examined as to rumours about the accused,[13] but this seems to have been an unfortunate attempt to restrict cross-examination to reputation, and to be inconsistent with subsequent authority.[14] No final decision was reached in *R v Waldman*[15] as to whether the witness could be cross-examined about a previous acquittal. The court seemed prepared to accept that the same principles apply at common law as apply under the Criminal Evidence Act 1898. In *Maxwell v D P P*[16] the House of Lords had held that an acquittal could not be used in cross-examination to the extent that it was relied upon to suggest that the accused had really been guilty despite his acquittal. It could however be put if relevant as a genuine acquittal, as for example by providing a reason for the accused to act carefully so as to avoid the danger of a further false accusation. It has already been noted that extrinsic evidence may be led to rebut a denial on a material issue. Thus since the accused's good character is relevant to issue as well as to credibility it would seem that a denial by a character witness of the accused's previous convictions or of his bad acts could be rebutted by leading evidence. This seems to be the case. Adduction of the accused's previous convictions was upheld in *R v B, R v A*,[17] and in *R v Bracewell*[18] the court was prepared to allow evidence of specific bad acts. The prosecution may also adduce evidence to rebut evidence of his good character given by a witness on his behalf. In *R v Rowton*[19] only Baron Martin had any doubt that in such a case the prosecution had such a right, the problem which caused most difficulty related to the nature of that evidence. The accused, who was charged with an offence of indecency, called witnesses to testify that he was a moral and well-conducted man, and the prosecution called a witness in rebuttal to swear that while he knew nothing of the opinion of the neighbourhood, the opinion of the witness and of his brothers who had attended the accused's school, was that he was a man 'capable of the grossest indecency and the most flagrant immorality'. It was not suggested that these three brothers constituted a community within which

---

10 *R v Waldman* (1934) 24 Cr App Rep 204, a strong case because the undoubted admissiblity of a previous conviction was held to outweigh the dubious admissibility of a previous acquittal; *R v Winfield* (1939) 27 Cr App Rep 139; *R v B, R v A* [1979] 3 All ER 460, [1979] 1 WLR 1185.

11 *R v Hodgkiss* (1836) 7 C & P 298; *R v Rogan and Elliott* (1846) 1 Cox CC 291.

12 (1978) 68 Cr App Rep 44.

13 *R v Wood and Parker* (1841) 5 Jur 225.

14 *R v Savory* (1942) 29 Cr App Rep 1, where the prosecution was not permitted to cross-examine the character witness about complaints made of the accused in the relevant respect which had not become the subject of formal proceedings against him.

15 (1934) 24 Cr App Rep 204.

16 [1935] AC 309.

17 [1979] 3 All ER 460, [1979] 1 WLR 1185.

18 (1978) 68 Cr App Rep 44.

19 (1865) Le & Ca 520; 34 LJMC 57.

the accused's reputation was bad. The dispute centred around the question of whether it was permissible for the witness to express his personal opinion of the accused's disposition, or whether he was limited to reporting the reputation of the accused. The dissentient minority argued that the whole purpose of the evidence was to determine whether or not the accused had a disposition to acts of indecency upon which he had acted. It was more direct to derive it from the witness's personal knowledge of that disposition than to try to infer it from the general consensus of opinion in the neighbourhood which constituted the accused's reputation. The majority argued rather narrowly that precedent supported the view that as neither particular acts nor personal opinions could be given in support of the accused's good character, so it would be wrong to allow its refutation by different means. This defence is somewhat ironic since the authorities were by no means so opposed either to evidence of particular acts[20] or of personal opinion[1] as the court supposed, but arguments of general principle were available. If the evidence is restricted to that of reputation the trial can be insulated from the confusion, surprise and prejudice likely to be engendered by collateral attack in the form of counter-examples of particular discreditable acts. The fatal flaw in such argument however is in the nature of the evidence being defended. Evidence of reputation, general or specific, is thoroughly unconvincing. It necessarily rests upon hearsay, gossip and rumour, and permits a witness without perjury to state something which he believes to be unjustified, and which he knows will be used as the foundation for an inference which he believes to be false. It is uncomfortable to have to rely upon a rule defended by the Supreme Court of the United States only on the ground that 'to pull one misshapen stone out of the grotesque structure is more likely simply to upset its present balance between adverse interests than to establish a rational edifice'.[2] It is hardly surprising to find that the rule was roundly condemned by commentators,[3] ignored in practice,[4] and rejected as a model for the construction of the now much more important provisions of the Criminal Evidence Act 1898.[5]

3. CO-ACCUSED

Another area largely governed by common law rules is that dealing with evidence of the bad character of a co-accused. It is not wholly governed by the common law since cross-examination of a co-accused is subject to the provisions of the Criminal Evidence Act 1898, and will be dealt with in ch X. This part is concerned with the question of how far other witnesses can be cross-examined about the co-accused's character, and how far evidence of the bad character of a co-accused can be led either to rebut any denial, or simply to inculpate the co-accused.

20 See for example *R v Williamson* (1807) 3 C & P 635.
 1 See for example *R v Turner* (1817) 32 State Tr 957.
 2 *Michelson v United States* 335 US 469 at 486 (1948).
 3 See Stephen *History of Criminal Law* (1882) vol 1 p 450, 'The decision [in *Rowton*] settled the law, but in practice it is impossible to act upon it, and it may be doubted whether it is desirable to try to do so.'
 4 See for example *R v West* (1890) 112 CCC Sess Pap 724, where the rebuttal consisted in part of evidence of the accused's known association with criminals.
 5 See *R v Dunkley* [1927] 1 KB 323 at 329.

The case of *R v Miller*[6] provides a convenient starting point. The co-accused were charged with offences in connection with the evasion of customs duties. The defence of one of them was that he had not been concerned, and that the offences were all committed by another of the co-accused. In pursuance of that defence he asked a witness for the prosecution whether or not it was true that the offences stopped when that co-accused was sent to prison, and re-started only after he was released. Devlin J held that such a question was perfectly proper, and that if necessary it could be justified by calling evidence in support. In his judgment a co-accused was bound only by considerations of relevance, though such relevance would require careful consideration, and the decision:

> does not open the field to any question of this kind by counsel for an accused person against the character of another accused. In the ordinary way the character of the accused is no more relevant at the hands of the defence that it is at the hands of the prosecution.[7]

The authority of that decision has been accepted by the Privy Council[8] and by the Court of Appeal.[9] In both the question arose out of a similarly 'cut throat' defence. In *Lowery* the two co-accused were alone present when a young girl was viciously murdered. The crime must have been committed by one or the other, or by both acting in concert. Each accused adduced evidence of the unlikelihood of his having committed the murder. In the case of Lowery such evidence took the form of evidence of his reputation, his aversion to the sadism involved in the murder, and his generally favourable prospects and happy family circumstances motivating him towards good behaviour. King, Lowery's co-accused, sought to adduce expert psychiatric testimony indicating that of the two, Lowery had the personality more disposed towards the commission of acts of the type in question. Each supplemented his evidence with direct testimony of the other's dominant role at the time of the incident. The expert evidence called by King was admitted at the trial over Lowery's protests, and the decision was upheld both by an appellate court in Victoria, and by the Privy Council. The Privy Council took pains to deny that the psychiatric evidence was related either to crime or to criminal tendencies,[10] or even amounted to evidence of the character of the two men.[11] It is hard to square this approach to the nature of character evidence with the Privy Council's earlier statement that an accused person puts his character in issue when he asks the jury 'to take the view that he is not one who would be disposed to have committed or would be likely to have committed the crime in question.'[12] It is also instructive to note that the Privy Council endorsed the view of the court below that the evidence could not have been led by the prosecution. It may be best to regard *Lowery* as a case very much influenced by its special facts,[13] and the way in which the case was run. The psychiatric evidence might well have been regarded as inappropriate for use by the prosecution, either because its

---

6 [1952] 2 All ER 667, 36 Cr App Rep 169. See also *R v Gibb and Mckenzie* [1983] 2 VR 155.
7 At 669, 172.
8 *Lowery v R* [1974] AC 85, [1973] 3 All ER 662.
9 *R v Neale* (1977) 65 Cr App Rep 304, where *Miller* is referred to as 'famous'.
10 At 101, 671.
11 At 102, 672.
12 At 102, 671.
13 It was so treated in *R v Turner* [1975] QB 834 at 842, [1975] 1 All ER 70 at 75.

prejudicial effect, which may have been vast, would then have exceeded its true probative value, which may have been small, or because it was simply irrelevant to the contention of the prosecution that the two men were acting in concert.

In *R v Bracewell*,[14] just as in *Lowery*, two men were charged with a brutal murder, this time of a very old man in the course of a burglary. Here too each claimed that the killing was done by the other when alone with the victim. Bracewell wished to cross-examine his co-accused's mistress, his own sister, who was a witness for the prosecution, about violent, and uncontrolled, attacks which his co-accused had made upon her. The Court of Appeal upheld the trial court's refusal to permit such cross-examination at that stage on the basis that it was insufficiently relevant, and because it was, unlike the evidence in *Miller* and *Lowery*, factually controversial and so capable of raising a confusing collateral issue. However Lockwood, the co-accused, had himself tried to cast the blame upon Bracewell by contrasting his own professional coolness as an experienced burglar with Bracewell's panicky inexperience. The Court of Appeal took the view that this put his character in issue, and that Bracewell could, for that reason alone, cross-examine him about his uncontrollable episodes of violence towards his mistress, and if they were denied, adduce evidence of them. It is immaterial that the co-accused are acting not as part of a joint enterprise, but individually, if their acts so overlap as to engender a defence drawing a comparison between them.[15]

The importance of the nature of the defence in determining the relevance of the evidence was further stressed in *R v Neale*.[16] In that case Neale's defence to charges of arson and manslaughter arising out of a fire in an institution was that he was not present at the relevant time. He wished to adduce evidence that his co-accused, Burr, had on two previous and on two subsequent occasions set fires while acting alone. It was held that the only question to be considered was whether or not the evidence was relevant to his defence. It was decided that it was not, because even if accepted it could not logically found an inference that on this occasion Burr was acting alone, rather than in concert with Neale. The logic of that argument would seem to be equally applicable whether Neale's argument were that he was not present at all, or that although present he did not participate.

It is possible to derive from these cases a reasonably coherent pattern of admissibility.

At one end of the scale there will be cases, though none of these are among them, where the evidence of the accused's evil disposition will be so strong, and so relevant to the case of both the prosecution and co-accused, that it will be admissible at the instance of either. It is possible to imagine a situation in which a girl and two men are alone together taking drugs. The girl complains of having been given a highly unusual incapacitating drug, and of then being raped by both men. One co-accused may have a long history of having used this drug to secure sexual intercourse, but put forward the defence that the whole episode is a drug-induced fantasy on the part of the girl and his co-accused. His co-accused may defend himself on the basis that the drug was also used to incapacitate him, and that his participation was imagined by the girl who was the victim only of his co-accused. In these

14 (1978) 68 Cr App Rep 44.
15 *R v Douglass* [1989] Crim LR 569.
16 (1977) 65 Cr App Rep 304.

circumstances it is submitted that both prosecution and the second co-accused could cross-examine, and lead evidence, of the first co-accused's previous use of this highly unusual drug.

The next position on the spectrum of relevance is occupied by the situation, of which *Miller*, and perhaps *Lowery*,[17] provide examples, where the bad character of the co-accused is necessarily brought out by evidence which is clearly relevant to the defence of the co-accused, though not at all to the case for the prosecution. There too the co-accused is entitled to cross-examine a witness,[18] and lead evidence, without waiting for character to be put in issue, and without the need to balance probative effect against possible prejudice, as required in the case where such evidence is to be led by the prosecution, and without any danger of the exercise of judicial discretion to prevent him.

The next gradation, illustrated by *Bracewell*, is that in which the evidence is not sufficiently relevant to the issues either for the prosecution, or for the co-accused. It seems to be the case that the accused may however introduce general evidence of his good character, even though it would not meet the standard of relevance required for evidence of his bad character tendered initially by either prosecution or co-accused. It seems reasonable that when good character has been claimed by such evidence that a co-accused should be permitted to attempt to rebut it by evidence coming up to the same standard of relevance. It is less clear whether it would become relevant in rebuttal if the co-accused contented himself with an attack on the character of his co-accused in that respect, probably it would not by analogy with the decision in *R v Butterwasser*,[19] though cross-examination of the co-accused would be allowed under the Criminal Evidence Act 1898, s 1(f), if he were to testify. The final position on the spectrum is illustrated by the facts of *Neale*.[20] Here the evidence is insufficiently relevant either at the instance of prosecution or of co-accused, and so in the absence either of good character being claimed by the co-accused, or of any attack being made upon the character of the other, there is no ground for its admission.

C. PARTIES TO CIVIL PROCEEDINGS

Evidence of character may be relevant in civil proceedings in a number of different ways. Quite apart from its possible relevance as 'similar fact' evidence it may itself be an issue, as in defamation cases, or it may be used to impugn the credibility of a party witness. It seems that the general good character of a party may not be adduced, unlike that of the accused in criminal proceedings. This was clearly stated by Eyre CB in *A-G v Bowman*,[1] a suit for a penalty, and elaborated by Baron Martin in *A-G v Radloff*:

---

17 It is uncertain how crucial it was that the co-accused had put his character in issue. In Canada it appears not to be necessary, *R v Kendall and McKay* (1987) 35 CCC (3d) 105.

18 The Criminal Evidence Act 1898, s 1(f), might sometimes prevent cross-examination of the co-accused himself.

19 [1948] 1 KB 4, [1947] 2 All ER 415, where the attack was on witnesses for the prosecution. The problem is more theoretical than real because there will normally in this situation, even in the case of an attack, be an implicit comparison suggesting that the attacker's character is better than that of the co-accused, so putting his own in issue.

20 See also *R v Priestley and Mason* (1985) 19 ACR 388.

1 (1971) 2 Bos & P 532 (n).

In criminal cases evidence of the good character of the accused is most properly and with good reason admissible in evidence, because there is a fair and just presumption that a person of good character would not commit a crime; but in civil cases such evidence is with equal good reason not admitted, because no presumption would fairly arise, in the very great proportion of cases, from the good character of the defendant, that he did not commit the breach of contract or of civil duty alleged against him.[2]

As one would expect exactly the same rule applies to evidence of good character of the plaintiff.[3]

A plaintiff's character may be directly in issue on the question of liability in an action for defamation when justification is pleaded, and the question whether specific acts, rumours or reputation can be received will depend upon the pleadings in the particular case.[4] The plaintiff's character is also relevant to the amount of damages recoverable by him in proceedings for defamation. In *Scott v Sampson*[5] it was decided that the evidence which might be adduced in mitigation of damages for defamation must be confined to the plaintiff's reputation, and might not consist of rumours or testimony concerning specific acts. This case was subsequently approved by the House of Lords.[6] It is clear that the evidence of reputation must relate to the segment of the plaintiff's life to which the defamation relates, and some of their Lordships pointed to the difficulty of drawing up a sharp distinction between evidence of specific acts and evidence of reputation. Although evidence of specific acts is not admissible to show that they were performed, it may be admissible to show that the plaintiff has the reputation of being a man who is in the habit of performing such acts.[7] Such matters as rumours and specific acts may be put to the plaintiff in cross-examination as to credit, his answers are final in accordance with the general rule, and the judge must endeavour to separate the issue of credibility from that concerning the quantum of damages when he sums up to the jury.[8]

In an action for defamation, the plaintiff's previous convictions for offences relevant to the alleged defamation may be proved in mitigation of damages[9] as well as in cross-examination to credit:

They are the raw material upon which bad reputation is built up. They have taken place in open court. They are matters of public knowledge. They are acted on by people generally as the best guide to his reputation and standing.[10]

---

2 (1854) 10 Exch 84 at 97.
3 *Cornwell v Richardson* (1825) 1 Ry & M 305. See also *Deep v Wood* (1983) 143 DLR (3d) 246.
4 *Maisel v Financial Times Ltd* (1915) 84 LJKB 2145.
5 (1882) 8 QBD 491.
6 *Plato Films Ltd v Speidel* [1961] AC 1090, [1961] 1 All ER 876. In that case there was a plea of justification and the decision turned on the propriety of the particulars in the defendant's defence. When justification is not pleaded, particulars of matters to be relied upon in mitigation of damages must be furnished, otherwise the defendant may not give evidence of them without the leave of the judge (RSC Ord 82, r 7). The plaintiff may be cross-examined on such matters, although no particulars have been furnished, but the cross-examination goes to credit, not to the diminution of damages.
7 *Waters v Sunday Pictorial Newspaper Ltd* [1961] 2 All ER 758, [1961] 1 WLR 967.
8 *Hobbs v Tinling & Co Ltd* [1929] 2 KB 1.
9 Similarly the character of a complainant of sexual harassment may be relevant to the detriment suffered, see *Snowball v Gardner Merchant Ltd* [1987] ICR 719.
10 *Goody v Odhams Press Ltd* [1967] 1 QB 333 at 340, [1966] 3 All ER 369 at 372.

They are also in defamation cases conclusive evidence of the accused having committed the offence of which he has been convicted.[11]

The exclusionary rules of the law of evidence play a very limited role in modern civil law, and it is certain that there are very many more examples of evidence of the character of a party being adduced without the slightest advertence to this branch of law.

SECTION 4. REHABILITATION

As noted above[12] it is generally impermissible to support the credibility of a witness in advance of an attack, even when one is reasonably anticipated.[13] The witness may of course deny any allegation made against him, and if the allegation is made in cross-examination not of him but of a subsequent witness, the impugned witness may even be recalled for re-examination in order to have an opportunity to make such a denial.[14] If a witness were impeached by calling evidence as to his lack of veracity, it was always open to a party to call a witness in rebuttal to affirm his veracity.[15] There seems to have been some confusion as to the permissibility of adducing evidence to rebut a specific allegation of misconduct falling short of the commission of a crime, when such an allegation was permitted.[16] It can certainly be argued that the same need to conduct a trial expeditiously which dictates the general rule that denials should not be rebutted by extrinsic evidence should be applied to evidence in support of them. On the other hand some have felt that a simple denial in response to cross-examination may be too unconvincing a response, at least when the allegation can be answered conclusively.[17] It is even less clear whether when a witness has been cross-examined about particular facts, testimony of general character can be led to rehabilitate the witness. This was denied in *Bamfield v Massey*, but permitted in *R v Clarke*[18] where not only was evidence of good general conduct after serving a term of imprisonment permitted to rehabilitate the witness against the effect of the conviction, but particular good acts were also allowed. Similarly in more modern times such general rehabilitation was permitted in *A-G v O'Sullivan*,[19] but disallowed in *R v Wood*,[20] though in the latter it might well have been thought that the whole question was irrelevant to any issue before the court.

---

11 Civil Evidence Act 1968, s 13. Acquittals are however no evidence of innocence.
12 See above, p 312.
13 *Bamfield v Massey* (1808) 1 Camp 460.
14 *R v Noel* (1834) 6 C & P 336.
15 *R v Murphy* (1753) 19 State Tr 693 at 723, 724.
16 Compare *Bamfield v Massey* above; *Dodd v Norris* (1814) 3 Camp 519; *Bate v Hill* (1823) 1 C & P 100; *Provis v Reed* (1829) 5 Bing 435; and *Doe d Reed v Harris* (1836) 7 C & P 330.
17 See for example IV *Wigmore* para 1104.
18 (1817) 2 Stark 241. But see *R v Redgrave* (1981) 74 Cr App Rep 10, where the accused was not allowed to prove particular heterosexual acts to rehabilitate his character as a man of normal sexual inclinations.
19 [1930] IR 552.
20 [1951] 2 All ER 112n, 35 Cr App Rep 61.

CHAPTER IX

Similar fact evidence[1]

This chapter complements the discussion of character and credibility in ch VIII, and together with it lays the foundations for the discussion of cross-examination of the accused in ch X. These three chapters cover topics which lie at the very heart of the law of evidence as it applies in criminal cases. The subject matter of this chapter is the exclusionary rule which in Commonwealth jurisdictions is commonly known as the 'similar facts' rule, terminology which is less common in the United States, and is certainly misleading.[2] It is indeed doubly misleading because it describes the exclusionary rule in a phrase more apt to describe one of the principal exceptions to it,[3] and because it suggests a unifying factor between the situations in this area which they do not necessarily possess.[4] The terminology is nevertheless too deeply engrained to be abandoned. If it cannot be abandoned, it must be explained. It is used here to connote that part of the law of evidence concerned with the rule which prevents a party, usually the prosecutor, from leading evidence showing the discreditable disposition[5] of the other, usually the accused, as derived from his discreditable acts, record, possessions, or reputation. The chapter is not concerned with evidence of these matters when they are themselves in issue, as they would be if justification were pleaded in an action for libel based upon allegations that the plaintiff had taken things which did not belong to him, been convicted of theft, been found in possession of housebreaking implements, and had the reputation of being dishonest.

As noted above this subject is at its most important in criminal proceedings. The reason is simply that such evidence is believed to be very influential in its effect upon a jury.[6] It is likely both to help prove the guilt of the accused, and to prejudice the jury against him. The prosecution justifiably seeks its inclusion for the former purpose, and the defence equally justifiably seeks it exclusion for the latter reason. The dilemma created by these competing aims generates the problems discussed in the first section of this chapter which deals with the rules at common law excluding 'similar fact' evidence when tendered in chief by the prosecution in a criminal case. The remaining,

---

1 See monographs, from a Canadian perspective by Piragoff *Similar Fact Evidence* (1981), and from an Australian, by Forbes *Similar Facts* (1987).
2 See *R v Green* (1988) 40 CCC (3d) 333 at 353.
3 This seems to be the best explanation of the terminological distinction made in *R v Lewis* (1982) 76 Cr App Rep 33 at 35.
4 See Elliott 'The Young Person's Guide to Similar Fact Evidence—1' [1983] Crim LR 284 at 288.
5 Throughout this chapter the term 'disposition' is used to denote a propensity to act, think or feel in a particular way.
6 This commonly held belief is largely confirmed by the results of empirical investigation, see 'Juries and the Rules of Evidence' [1973] Crim LR 208, McCabe and Purves *The Jury at Work* (1972) Table 4.

and much less important, sections deal with those few statutory rules which affect the position in criminal cases, and the position in civil proceedings.

SECTION 1. EXCLUSION AT COMMON LAW IN CRIMINAL PROCEEDINGS

This aspect of the law of evidence was said by the Criminal Law Revision Committee to constitute 'far the most difficult of all the topics which we have discussed'.[7] It is also one of the most keenly litigated, and has been described by Lord Hailsham as a 'pitted battlefield'.[8] Its legendary difficulty is largely a reflection of the dilemma created by the clash of probative force and prejudicial effect which is at its most strident in this area. Significant confusion of terminology, long historical development and the absence of statutory intervention by throwing more weight upon the precise formulation of appellate opinions than they can reasonably bear have, no doubt, all contributed to the problem. They are less significant than the basic dilemma which is fundamentally insoluble, and inescapable. The first part of this section will set out the two most significant landmarks in the development of the exclusionary rule. Its scope, constituent elements and application will then be examined in turn. An attempt to cut the Gordian knot by invocation of judicial discretion will be considered, and the final part will examine some suggestions for reform of the rule. A preliminary formulation of the rule is that evidence of the character or of the misconduct of the accused on other occasions (including his possession of discreditable material), tendered to show his bad disposition, is inadmissible unless it is so highly probative of the issues in the case as to outweigh the prejudice it may cause.[9]

A. DEVELOPMENT OF THE RULE[10]

An exclusionary rule seems to have been established by the beginning of the nineteenth century, and is stated in recognisably modern terms in *R v Cole*: 'in a prosecution for an infamous crime, an admission by the prisoner that he had committed such an offence at another time and with another person, and that he had a tendency to such practices, ought not to be admitted'.[11] The application of the rule was uncertain throughout the nineteenth century.[12] It was first considered by a final appellate court in *Makin v A-G for New South Wales*.[13] This was an important case not only because of the eminence of the court which decided it, but also because on its facts it

---

7 Cmnd 4991, para 70.
8 *D P P v Boardman* [1975] AC 421 at 445, [1974] 3 All ER 887 at 898.
9 This formulation has twice been explicitly approved by the Supreme Court of Canada, *R v Robertson* (1987) 39 DLR (4th) 321 at 338; *R v D (LE)* (1989) 50 CCC (3d) 142 at 161.
10 The history of the rule is traced by Stone 'The Rule of Exclusion of Similar Fact Evidence (England)' (1933) 46 Harv LR 954.
11 As reported in Phillips *Evidence* (1814) at 69. The original judge's note is appended to the judgment in *R v Sims* as reported in [1946] KB 531 at 544.
12 Compare the reasoning in the poisoning cases of *R v Geering* (1849) 18 LJMC 215, *R v Winslow* (1860) 8 Cox CC 397, and *R v Hall* (1887) 5 NZLR 93, for example. Nor did these varieties exhaust the possibilities, in the infamous case of Neill Cream the evidence of other poisonings was admitted by Hawkins J 'as corroboration', Shore *Trial of Neill Cream* (1923) at 154.
13 [1894] AC 57.

represented a construction of the rule admitting similar fact evidence more readily than in any previous example. Makin and his wife were tried for the murder of a baby which it was alleged they had taken in for informal adoption upon the payment of a small payment by the infant's mother. As asserted by the Supreme Court of New South Wales,[14] and accepted by the Privy Council,[15] there was ample evidence that the accused were guilty as charged. The mother was able to give evidence of the transaction handing the child over, of deceit and evasion by the accused when she tried to see it again, including an attempt to pass off a different child as hers, and of the identity of clothing found on the child's dead body. There was evidence of damaging admissions made by the accused both by word and action. The premium was plainly inadequate to support the child for very long. There was evidence that the accused received the baby in good health one day in one set of premises, removed surreptitiously to another two days later without the child, and that a corpse found wearing the baby's clothes was found secretly buried on the premises from which the accused had so departed. Such circumstantial evidence would surely have been sufficient for a verdict of guilty, even on so serious a charge. The prosecution was not content however and wished to adduce evidence of a number of other mothers who had placed babies with the accused on the payment of similarly inadequate premiums. The accused had flatly denied having received any of these children. The prosecution also tendered evidence of thirteen bodies of babies having been found on three different sets of premises occupied at different times by the accused. It was argued that this evidence tended to rebut any possible defence of accidental death, and showed a systematic course of conduct by the accused, vulgarly known as 'baby farming'. The defence attempted to counter this argument by asserting that the evidence of the other bodies was admissible only to show the mens rea of the accused once it had been shown that it was a result of their acts that the baby had met its death, but that there was no clear evidence of that. The evidence was in fact admitted to rebut the accused's presumed[16] defence that they had not engaged in a systematic practice of 'baby farming'. This was shown by the direct evidence of the five mothers who testified to having handed over their babies, and by the finding of so many dead bodies of babies in so many different premises occupied by the accused which rendered quite incredible any suggestion that there was no connection between the bodies found on the premises, and the acts of the accused while they lived there. The majority of the Supreme Court denied that it was necessary to show even a prima facie connection between the acts of the accused and the deaths of any of the babies before evidence of the latter became admissible, though the denial was obiter since the court, as noted above, held that there was plenty of evidence of such a connection in the case before them. In more analytical and less descriptive terms the evidence tending to show other discreditable acts, and through them the disposition of the accused to commit the discreditable act in issue, was admissible to corroborate circumstantial evidence both of the commission of the actus reus of the crime and of the

---

14 (1893) 14 LR NSW 1 at 19.
15 At 64.
16 Derived from statements made to the police during interrogation, and at an inquest into the deaths of the children. At the trial the accused seem merely to have put the prosecution to their proof.

mens rea required for it. It should be noted that at no stage did the accused raise a defence of accidental death, they simply disclaimed all connection with either mother or baby, and all knowledge of any of the bodies. It was against this background that the Privy Council delivered the passage characterised so appreciatively by the House of Lords in *D P P v Boardman*:[17]

> It is undoubtedly not competent for the prosecution to adduce evidence tending to show that the accused had been guilty of criminal acts other than those covered by the indictment, for the purpose of leading to the conclusion that the accused is a person likely from his criminal conduct or character to have committed the offence for which he is being tried. On the other hand, the mere fact that the evidence adduced tends to show the commission of other crimes does not render it inadmissible if it be relevant to an issue before the jury, and it may be so relevant if it bears upon the question whether the acts alleged to constitute the crime charged in the indictment were designed or accidental, or to rebut a defence which would otherwise be open to the accused.[18]

It is also significant that this passage was both preceded and succeeded by a warning that its application might prove extremely difficult. The source of such difficulties was identified by Lord Hailsham as residing in the fact that while the rule depends heavily on questions of weight and degree best left to a jury, the function of the rule, because it combines considerations of relevance and prejudice, properly falls to be decided in advance,[19] by the judge. There was for a long time a tendency to construe Lord Herschell's words as if they were part of a criminal statute, and in particular to treat the examples given in the second sentence as if they constituted a closed list of rigid categories. These words are more naturally read as stressing the importance of, and illustrating by examples, the relevance of the evidence to the issues in the case.[20]

It was certainly in such a sense that they were read in *D P P v Boardman*, the most authoritative modern restatement of this principle.[1] In that case the accused, a middle-aged headmaster, was charged with one count of buggery, and two of incitement to buggery with pupils at this school. Each count

---

17 [1975] AC 421, [1974] 3 All ER 887, 'always been accepted as expressing cardinal principles' (Lord Morris at 438, 892); 'can [not] be better stated' (Lord Hailsham at 435, 905); 'stated with crystal clarity' (Lord Salmon at 461, 912). And as a result still frequently cited, see eg *A-G of Hong Kong v Siu Yuk-shing* [1989] 1 WLR 236; *R v Lunt* (1986) 85 Cr App Rep 241; *R v Shore* (1988) 89 Cr App Rep 32. For criticism of such survival see Carter 'Similar Fact Evidence since *Boardman*' (1985) 48 MLR 29; Mirfield 'Similar Facts—Makin Out' (1987) 46 CLJ 83. Zuckerman 'Similar Fact Evidence—The Unobservable Rule' (1987) 103 LQR 187 regards *Boardman* as representing little, if any, advance on *Makin.*
18 [1894] AC 57 at 65.
19 The various stages at which such questions arise were helpfully dissected in *R v Scarrott* [1978] QB 1016, [1978] 1 All ER 672.
20 That this represented the view of the profession in England even before the decision in *Makin* is shown by the terms of a letter, appended to the relevant volume of the Law Reports, (1893) 14 LR (NSW) 1, written to Windeyer J by Hawkins J, an English judge with very extensive experience of presiding over criminal trials, and who when asked to comment on the judgment of the Supreme Court of New South Wales wrote, 'Relevancy to the issue is . . . all that is required to make evidence (not otherwise objectionable) admissible.'
 1 [1975] AC 421, [1974] 3 All ER 887, see also commentary in Hoffman 'Similar Facts After *Boardman*' (1975) 91 LQR 193; Cross 'Fourth Time Lucky—Similar Fact Evidence in the House of Lords' [1975] Crim LR 62; and Tapper 'Similar Facts: Peculiarity and Credibility' (1975) 38 MLR 206.

related to a different youth, and in his evidence each youth recounted other incidents involving himself which, if true, amounted to criminal offences. No application was made for separate trials, nor does any objection seem to have been taken to the admission of evidence of the other incidents involving a particular youth on the count relating to that youth. The count of buggery and evidence on one of the counts of incitement related to an incident in which the accused had sought to play the passive role. Because neither the second incitement itself, nor the other incident related by that victim, possessed that peculiarity, the trial judge instructed the jury that the evidence on that count neither corroborated, nor was itself corroborated by, evidence on the other counts.[2] The trial judge held that all of the evidence on the remaining counts was mutually corroborative, though it should be noted that a number of the incidents adduced in relation to the count of buggery did not explicitly suggest a passive role on the part of the accused. It was argued that the evidence on one count should have been held irrelevant to the determination of the other.[3] Their Lordships all held the evidence to have been rightly considered relevant and admissible to guilt on the other count. The speeches are inconsistent in some aspects of their reasoning, but unanimous in requiring the 'similar fact' evidence to be more than barely relevant to guilt.[4] This decision has been accepted elsewhere by the highest courts in the Commonwealth,[5] and must constitute the starting point for further examination of the modern law.

B. SCOPE OF THE RULE

The first point to note is that the rule excludes only evidence that is otherwise relevant. It is an exclusionary exception to the general and fundamental principle that all relevant evidence is prima facie admissible. It has been perceptively noted that many of the difficulties experienced by the courts in their attempts to apply Lord Herschell's remarks in *Makin* might have been eliminated if his two famous sentences had been delivered in the converse order, making it clear that the second was not so much an exception to the first, as the first to the second.[6] The operation of this limitation upon the scope of the rule is not always easy to recognise. In the first place the baneful tendency to use 'relevant' and 'admissible' interchangeably clouds the issue. A second problem is that the rule demands exclusion when prejudicial effect exceeds probative force. Relevance, as will be seen, is merely one element constituting probative force, and if the evidence is to be excluded in any event there is no point in the court's agonising over the distinction between excluding the evidence because it is insufficiently relevant, and excluding it

---

2 Evidence must be both admissible and credible before it can amount to corroboration *D P P v Kilbourne* [1973] AC 729, [1973] 1 All ER 440.

3 The verdict on the second incitement count had been quashed by the Court of Appeal.

4 It should be 'of close or striking similarity' (Lord Morris at 441, 895); 'striking similarity' (Lord Wilberforce at 444, 897); 'striking resemblance' (Lord Hailsham at 455, 907); 'exhibit very striking peculiarities' (Lord Cross at 460, 911); and 'be uniquely or strikingly similar' (Lord Salmon at 462, 913). The phrase 'striking similarity' is derived from *R v Sims* [1946] KB 531 at 540, [1946] 1 All ER 697 at 701.

5 See *Sutton v R* (1984) 152 CLR 528 (Australia); *R v Hsi En Fong* [1985] 1 NZLR 222 (New Zealand); *R v Robertson* (1987) 39 DLR (4th) 321 (Canada).

6 Schiff *Evidence in the Litigation Process* (3rd edn, 1988) p 821; McNamara 'Dissimilar Judgments on Similar Facts: Part II' (1984) 57 ALJ 143.

because its prejudicial effect exceeds its probative force, all elements considered. This difficulty is illustrated by two cases of high authority.

In *Noor Mohamed v R*[7] the accused was charged with the murder of his mistress. She had undoubtedly died as a result of cyanide poisoning, and the accused, who was a goldsmith and who was on bad terms with her, had access to cyanide. There was however no evidence that the accused had administered poison to her. The prosecution wished to adduce evidence of the death of the accused's former wife, with whom he had also been on bad terms, as a result of cyanide poisoning. The accused had never been charged with causing her death, but there was some evidence that he might have tricked her into taking the cyanide. The court reasoned that even assuming it to be established that he had tricked her, it still did not follow that, in the absence of the slightest evidence of such a trick in the instant case, he had tricked his mistress. This sounds like the language of irrelevance, but the court was so adamant in rejecting dicta in *R v Sims*[8] that similar fact evidence was prima facie admissible so long only as it was logically probative, that it may be that the Privy Council thought the evidence was of too much prejudice rather than of too little relevance.

Much the same analysis may be made of a case decided soon afterwards in the House of Lords. In *Harris v D P P*[9] the accused, a policeman, was charged on eight counts of breaking into shops in a market he was patrolling, and of stealing part of the cash on the premises. The evidence on the first seven was exiguous, amounting to little more than that all the thefts were committed by a similar technique, that all had occurred when the accused was on duty and could have been in the area, and that none had occurred when he was not on duty. The evidence on the eighth count implicated the accused more directly since a trap had been set, and the accused had been identified in the area, had been seen to disappear briefly before going to the assistance of the policemen whom he knew and who had set the trap, and marked money was found in a place which he could have reached in the time he was absent. He was acquitted by the jury on the first seven counts, but found guilty on the eighth. The House of Lords quashed his conviction on the ground that the jury should have been warned that 'the evidence called in support of the earlier counts did not in itself provide confirmation of the last charge.'[10] Once again this suggests that it was irrelevant, but it is probably more accurate to attribute the failure of probative force to lack of cogency rather than to irrelevance.[11] Perhaps the clearest example of lack of relevance is a case where the accused has been acquitted on a charge involving the conduct relied upon as constituting the similar fact evidence. In *G (an infant) v Coltart*[12] the accused was charged on two counts of stealing, to both of which the defence was that there was no intention permanently to deprive. There was good evidence of such an intention on the first count, but as the principal witness was abroad, no evidence was offered and the accused acquitted. It

---

7 [1949] AC 182, [1949] 1 All ER 365, one of very few cases of murder reported this century in which the similar fact evidence has been excluded.

8 [1946] KB 531, [1946] 1 All ER 697.

9 [1952] AC 694, [1952] 1 All ER 1044. See also *Sweitzer v R* (1982) 137 DLR (3d) 702.

10 At 711, 1050.

11 In *R v Miller* [1952] 2 All ER 667, 36 Cr App Rep 169, it was regarded as relevant that the commission of crimes did not occur when one of the accused was in prison, though the cases are not exactly comparable.

12 [1967] 1 QB 432, [1967] 1 All ER 271. See also *R v Holloway* [1980] 1 NZLR 315.

was held that the prosecution was not able to rely upon an alleged intent to deprive in the first case since it was negated by the acquittal. This may perhaps be regarded as irrelevance of rather technical a character. In *R v Rodley*[13] it was straightforward. The accused was charged with housebreaking with intent to commit rape. His conviction was quashed because of the admission of evidence of his subsequently entering a nearby house by climbing down a chimney and having consensual intercourse with the occupant. However bizarre, such evidence was simply irrelevant, and excluded as such without any need to rely upon the rule excluding evidence of similar facts.[14]

The second condition which must be satisfied before the rule may be invoked is that the evidence should be relevant by way of an argument relying at some stage upon an inference drawn from the disposition of the accused. The distinction is drawn most clearly by Lord Hailsham in *Boardman*:

> what is not to be admitted is a chain of reasoning and not necessarily a state of facts. If the inadmissible chain of reasoning be the *only* purpose for which the evidence is adduced as a matter of law, the evidence itself is not admissible. If there is some other relevant, probative purpose than the forbidden type of reasoning, the evidence is admitted, but should be made subject to a warning from the judge that the jury must eschew the forbidden reasoning.[15]

This is a most important requirement, and understood correctly, helps make the similar facts rule much more comprehensible. It is worth examining some of the ways in which evidence of the relevant discreditable conduct of the accused may be relevant otherwise than by way of an argument involving a step relying upon his disposition so suggested. In these cases the evidence, if sufficiently relevant according to ordinary standards of relevance, is admissible without reference to the similar facts rule, though the evidence may, in appropriate cases, be excluded by the exercise of the judge's discretion if he believes that to admit it will be unduly prejudicial to the accused.

In some cases the revelation that the accused has committed a crime is inherent in the background to the facts of the case, and no one even considers making an objection. Thus in *R v Neale*[16] the accused was a resident in an institution for ex-Borstal boys where the crime had been committed, so it could be inferred that he had at some time in the past committed a crime. Similarly in *R v Straffen*[17] the accused's presence in the area at the relevant time could be fixed only by reference to the time at which he had escaped

---

13 [1913] 3 KB 468.
14 This also seems to be the best explanation of *R v Tricoglus* (1976) 65 Cr App Rep 16 (accused charged with rape committed after victim picked up by 'kerb crawler' in city centre, evidence of 'kerb crawling' by accused in city centre on other occasions held inadmissible). *R v Neale* (1977) 65 Cr App Rep 304, discussed in ch VIII is another example. See also *R v Horry* [1949] NZLR 791 (accused charged with indecent assault of woman tricked into meeting him, evidence of similar tricks upon other women not accompanied by any indecency held to be irrelevant).
15 [1975] AC 421 at 453, [1974] 3 All ER 887 at 907, emphasis in original. It will however be argued that the consequences of drawing the distinction are over-stated in this passage, and that such a chain of reasoning is acceptable in a few exceptional cases.
16 (1977) 65 Cr App Rep 304.
17 [1952] 2 QB 911, [1952] 2 All ER 657.

from Broadmoor.[18] So too in *R v Malik*[19] where the accused was charged with stirring up racial hatred by reference to his experience in prison it was inevitable that the jury should become aware that he had been convicted of other crimes. Sometimes the commission of an extrinsic crime is part and parcel of the crime with which the accused is charged. A good example of this is furnished by the old case of *R v Salisbury*[20] where the accused was a letter carrier, and the substance of the crime charged against him was the taking of notes from one letter to replace notes taken by him from another. Clearly evidence of both takings had to be given. In *R v Ellis*[1] the accused was charged with embezzling six marked coins from a till in the shop where he was employed. It was not possible to monitor the exact extent of his depredations from the till without alerting him, and the prosecution was allowed to prove the total deficiency from the till, which corresponded to the total in the accused's possession at the end of the day, although he was charged only in respect of the marked coins. In *R v Cobden*[2] the matter was a stage further removed as three men were charged with breaking into a railway booking office and stealing property from it. None of that property was found in the possession of one of the three accused, but it was held permissible to prove similar break-ins in other booking offices on the same night, since the third accused might have received his share of the night's takings exclusively from those. Bramwell B opined that 'the events of that night relating to these burglaries are so intermixed that it is impossible to separate them.' Sometimes the other crime relates to the means for committing the principal crime with which the accused is charged, for example the theft of a car.[3]

In all of these cases the fact that the impermissible line of reasoning is not involved can be tested by supposing the extrinsic matter to be in no way discreditable to the accused and so not indicative of an evil disposition, and then seeing if that would make any difference. It can easily be seen that it would make no difference to the reasoning in cases like *Neale*, *Straffen* and *Malik* that the relevant institution had been, say a boarding school, rather that some sort of penal institution. Similarly in cases like *Salisbury*, *Ellis* or *Cobden* it would be immaterial that the accused had interchanged or mixed something to which he was perfectly entitled with the stolen property, nor would it have made the slightest difference in cases like *Mortimer* and *Thomas* that the car in question had been innocently lent to the accused. It follows that the forbidden line of reasoning has no necessary place in such cases, and that the evidence is, in principle, admissible. This is not to say however that

---

18   One of the most spectacular examples of this genre where the similar fact point was argued is provided by *R v Sims and Anderson* [1967] Qd R 432, where the accused who had escaped from prison were charged with breaking into a nearby house and stealing clothes, and sought, rightly without success, to suppress evidence that their discarded prison clothing had been found on the premises.

19   [1968] 1 All ER 582n, [1968] 1 WLR 353.

20   (1831) 5 C & P 155. See also a case referred to in *R v Whiley* (1804) 2 Leach 983 at 985 (shirt stolen from one house found in another burgled on the same night).

1   (1826) 6 B & C 145.

2   (1862) 3 F & F 833.

3   As in *R v Mortimer* (1936) 25 Cr App Rep 150 (theft of cars used to run down female cyclists). In *R v Thomas* (1949) 33 Cr App Rep 74, Lord Goddard CJ deplored the joinder of charges for such ancillary offences, in that case offences under the Road Traffic Act in relation to the taking and reckless driving of a car in which a rape, which constituted the principal charge, was alleged to have been committed.

the judge should not be alert to warn the jury against the forbidden line of reasoning as suggested by Lord Hailsham,[4] and to prevent attention being drawn to associated, but logically unconnected, criminality, by severing the indictment as suggested by Lord Goddard.[5]

Two cases involving young children may be considered in this context. A particularly difficult situation arose in *R v Chambers*[6] where the accused was charged with the rape of his ten year old grand-daughter. No similar fact evidence was adduced in chief, but when the witness admitted under cross-examination that the act had occasioned her no pain, it was held that she could be asked in re-examination whether the accused had done the same thing before on other occasions. Once again it was strictly immaterial that what occurred was discreditable to the accused. Any occurrence, however innocent and however unconnected with the accused, which might have had the same result would have been equally relevant. It is however clear that this explanation was extremely prejudicial, and in the modern law every sinew would be strained to prevent such a question being asked, whether by some form of bowdlerisation, or exclusion at the discretion of the judge. Another case best considered in this connection is *R v Mackie*[7] where the accused was convicted of the manslaughter of a child. The prosecution tendered evidence of previous assaults upon the child by the accused in order to explain the child's fear of the accused, which was relevant to explain the circumstances of his death. It was held that the evidence was admissible to show the disposition of the child, not that of the accused. It is arguable that it was immaterial how the child came to have that disposition, and that it could just as easily have been caused by previous assaults by another.[8] It is submitted that it was because the case was not strictly covered by the similar facts rule that the evidence was held to be admissible, even though its prejudicial effect was conceded by the Court of Appeal to exceed by far its probative force.[9]

It is possible to categorise these various cases as being those in which the evidence from which the inference of the accused's disposition is drawn is so closely entwined and involved with the evidence directly relating to the facts in issue that it would amount to distortion to attempt to edit them out. Such an approach is potentially dangerous because the notion of involvement is rather vague, and could easily be used to smuggle in otherwise inadmissible similar fact evidence by an extended view of what is to count as a single event. English courts have so far insisted on very close involvement, and in

4 See also *R v Ducsharm* [1956] 1 DLR 732.
5 See also Lord Cross, with whom Lord Wilberforce expressly agreed on this point, in *Boardman* at 459, 911. The problem becomes more and more acute as the evidence nears the point of admissibility because of its high probative force, see generally Weinberg 'Multiple Counts and Similar Fact Evidence' in Campbell and Waller (eds) *Well and Truly Tried* (1982).
6 (1848) 3 Cox CC 92.
7 (1973) 57 Cr App Rep 453.
8 There are some parallels with *Toohey v Metropolitan Police Comr* [1965] AC 595, [1965] 1 All ER 506.
9 Identification from police photographs is another situation in which the accused's discreditable past is incidentally revealed to the jury, and where admissibility is not governed by the similar facts rules, but the discretion to exclude on the balance between probative force and prejudicial effect comes into play, see *Alexander v R* (1981) 34 ALR 289; *R v Aziz* [1982] 2 NSWLR 322.

R v Devins[10] were reluctant to accept that where a theft took place in connection with an affray that it could be assumed that there was sufficiently close involvement for a confession of commission of the theft to be admitted on the charge of affray.

Similar reasoning has also been applied in the rather different situation where the whole history of the relationship between the victim and accused is opened up. Although in *R v Berry*[11] the Court of Appeal attempted to limit such an approach in a case where prior acts of violence were tendered to prove the nature of the relationship by excluding the evidence, this view was subsequently repudiated[12] on the basis that prior events might be proved as part of an ongoing relationship when that was relevant. It is accepted that in such a case the evidence is not automatically inadmissible provided it is sufficiently probative. It is submitted though that it still falls within the ambit of the exclusionary rule, and that the question of its inadmissibility is to be determined by the application of the ordinary process of balancing probative force against prejudicial effect. It would be wrong to regard it as falling outside the rule on the same basis as those cases where the evidence showing evil disposition is merely incidental, as in the prison location or intermingling type of case. In them argument from disposition plays no part in the argument; here it plays a prominent part, and so the ordinary rule assessing the balance of probative force and prejudicial effect should be applied.[13]

Two other possible situations which have been mooted as falling outside the range of cases where the similar fact evidence is relevant because it shows the accused's bad disposition are those where it is relied upon to corroborate a witness, and those where it is used to rebut a suggestion of coincidence. Both have some plausibility, but it is submitted that both are better regarded as falling within the scope of the rule.

The argument in the case of corroboration depends upon a line of reasoning illustrated by the facts of *R v Chitson*.[14] The accused was charged with having had unlawful carnal knowledge of a servant girl under the age of fifteen living in his household. She testified[15] that he had told her of having done the same thing to a girl in another part of the country of whom she could have known in no other way. It was held that he could be cross-examined about his relationship with that girl, and letters that he had written to her were put to him. The relevance of this evidence was to corroborate the complainant's testimony:

> Although the latter questions did no doubt tend to prove that he was of bad character, still they also in our opinion tended to show that he was guilty of the offence with which he was charged, for if he had made that statement to the

---

10 [1985] LS Gaz 3082. The doctrine has been further developed in Australia, see (1946) *O'Leary v R* (1946) 73 CLR 566; though strictness of interpretation varies, cp *Bell v R* (1985) 63 ALR 433 and *R v Hocking* [1988] 1 Qd R 582. It was extensively elaborated by McHugh J in *Harriman v R* (1989) 63 ALJR 694.

11 (1986) 83 Cr App Rep 7.

12 In *R v Williams* (1986) 84 Cr App Rep 299 by reference to *R v Ball* [1911] AC 47.

13 Contrary to dicta in *Williams* citing the 6th edition of this work.

14 [1909] 2 KB 945.

15 Since she alleged that he told her this after the commission of the crime, its initial relevance to the issues is obscure.

prosecutrix at the time alleged by her, that fact would strongly corroborate her evidence that the prisoner was the person who had had connection with her.[16]

The reasoning in *Chitson* was criticised by the majority of the House of Lords in *Jones v D P P*,[17] on the ground that cross-examination of the accused about such matters was not properly justified under the provisions of the Criminal Evidence Act 1898, s 1.[18] The decision was however vindicated on the basis that the questioning showed nothing not revealed by the evidence in chief. The vindication reveals a flaw in this line of reasoning. For the evidence to have been admitted in chief it must have been regarded as probative of the accused's guilt. Similarly for evidence to corroborate a witness's testimony it must not merely support it, but also implicate the accused in a material particular. It could have done those things in *Chitson* only by showing the accused's bad disposition, and if tendered to do that, came within the scope of the rule excluding similar fact evidence as formulated earlier.[19] Nevertheless it is accepted that the use of similar fact evidence to corroborate testimony constitutes a very significant, and sometimes overlooked, differentiating factor in determining exactly how the rule is to be applied.[20]

The other situation sometimes asserted as one in which the similar fact evidence does not operate by way of showing the accused's bad disposition is when it is tendered to rebut a suggestion of coincidence. This argument is elegantly deployed by Hoffman in relation to the facts of *Makin*.[1] He asserts that the evidence of finding all of the bodies operated on a statistical basis. It was inherently improbable that all thirteen of the children should have died by accident. The only plausible explanation was that Makin had killed them. Makin's disposition plays no part in this argument, it is only *after* the argument has been made, and *because* it succeeds, that Makin's bad disposition is established. This is an interesting approach. It should perhaps be noted that in fact the prosecution case was that Makin was engaged in a system of taking in children at inadequate premiums and killing them. It was integral to this case that Makin took in a large number of children, that his disposition was murderous, and that this supported their case that he murdered the child in respect of which he was charged. It may also be noted that the defence never raised any question of accident at the trial. Nevertheless the case could have been run differently, and the argument should be considered on its merits. It is conceded that the statistical argument does not rely upon Makin's disposition. It is however submitted that the best that the statistical argument can establish is that Makin must have murdered most of the children. If there had been only one death the possibility of accident was not rebutted. It was only when there were so many that it became incredible all could be accidental. This is not however enough for the prosecution. They must establish not that most of the deaths were deliberately caused, but that one

---

16 [1909] 2 KB 945 at 947.
17 [1962] AC 635 at 665, [1962] 1 All ER 569 at 576.
18 See further ch X below.
19 The report contains no indication that the admissibility of the evidence in chief in *Chitson* was ever questioned.
20 See part D below.
 1 Hoffman 'Similar Facts after *Boardman*' (1975) 91 LQR 193 at 198.

in particular was deliberate.[2] It has however already been established that one death might be accidental. It is only because of the association of this one with all of the others that any inference can be drawn that it too was deliberate. In other words the last and essential link in the chain of reasoning still depends upon the accused's disposition.[3] For that reason it is rightly within the scope of the similar fact rule.[4]

The third condition which evidence must satisfy in addition to being relevant, and relevant by way of an argument from the accused's disposition, before the similar fact rule can be applied to it, is that the evidence must be discreditable to the accused in some way. It is noticeable that in the famous passage quoted above from *Makin* Lord Herschell refers only to 'criminal acts' and 'criminal conduct or character'. It is quite clear that discredit extends further than evidence of the commission of crimes. In some cases the evidence in question suggests no more than immorality,[5] in others it is of some, in itself non-criminal, aspect of the criminal act. One of the clearest examples of the first sort is provided by *R v Ball*.[6] In that case a brother and sister were charged with incest contrary to the Punishment of Incest Act 1908. In order to show that sexual intercourse had occurred between them at a time after the passage of the Act when they were sharing a bed the prosecution wished to prove that the brother had fathered his sister's child, conceived before incest became a crime under the Act. In that case the act while not criminal when committed subsequently became criminal; in *R v Shellaker*[7] the act, although criminal at the time of commission, had ceased to be subject to criminal proceedings at the time it was adduced in evidence owing to lapse of time; in both the evidence was nevertheless held admissible. The question was also mooted in *R v Barrington*.[8] In that case the prosecution sought to bolster the evidence of three young complainants of various acts of indecency by the accused with evidence from three other girls. The evidence of those girls indicated that the accused had gone through much the same preliminary technique of recruiting them ostensibly for baby-sitting, by the same false pretences, and had attempted to induce them into a compliant attitude and compromising situation by the use of similar inducements, including the provision of pornographic magazines and photographs. It was not however alleged that any acts of indecency or criminal conduct had occurred. The court admitted the evidence notwithstanding. *Ball* was not cited to the court, which was wrongly informed that there were no reported cases in which similar fact evidence had been admitted even though no

---

2 As Lord Herschell himself once said in a civil case in this context 'Cases of this description are not determined upon probabilities, but upon evidence of what happened upon the particular occasion', *Kennedy v Dodson* [1895] 1 Ch 334 at 338.

3 But see Ligertwood *Australian Evidence* (1988) at p 68 for a contrary view arguing that, if a disposition at all, this is not the *prior* disposition with which the rule is concerned.

4 As it should be, since even if Hoffman's argument were accepted, it would be highly unlikely to correspond to the reasoning of the jury.

5 As in *R v Butler* (1986) 84 Cr App Rep 12 where it consisted of the details of consensual heterosexual acts, and of the places where they occurred. But see *R v Von Einem* (1985) 38 SASR 207 at 211 where it was suggested, it is submitted wrongly, that allegations of homosexuality fell outside the rule to the extent that it had been legalised in South Australia.

6 [1911] AC 47, 6 Cr App Rep 31.

7 [1914] 1 KB 414, 9 Cr App Rep 240.

8 [1981] 1 All ER 1132, [1981] 1 WLR 419. See also *R v Seaman* (1978) 67 Cr App Rep 234, where the evidence was also of acts probably preliminary to commission of a crime, though not there of an inherently discreditable character.

crime had occurred. Instead, the court relied upon cases where the non-criminal circumstances of other crimes had been stressed. It should also be noted that in a number of cases the accused's propensity had been proved by the possession of articles of an indecent character even though such possession was in itself no offence and there was no suggestion that they had ever been used in connection with the commission of the offence.[9] In the case of other articles it has been held that evidence of possession of implements only of the sort actually used for the housebreaking in question are admissible.[10] In these cases the possession of certain articles may not be unequivocally discreditible in itself, though they may be capable of being used for discreditible purposes. It seems that if there is a suggestion that otherwise innocent articles, such as walkie-talkie radios and imitation police uniforms, may be used for criminal purposes it is not necessary that any such occasion on which they have been so used need be identified, provided that there is some issue to which their possession is sufficiently relevant.[11]

As has already been noted, and as will be seen later, the similar fact rule depends upon the relevance of the evidence under consideration to the issues in the case. This usually requires detailed comparison of the facts in issue and the evidence showing the accused in a discreditable light. It is thus necessary to examine that other conduct in some detail. Many of the details, often the most important, are not essential features of the criminality or discreditability of the other conduct, but incidental to it. It was suggested in *R v Novac*[12] that evidence of surrounding circumstances, not in themselves criminal, could not be adduced if they were not sufficiently proximate to the commission of the crime charged. In that case the evidence related to the place at which young boys were solicited for indecent purposes. The suggestion has however been rejected in subsequent cases.[13] This seems to reflect no more than a difference between the opinion of the different courts as to the relevance of the evidence in question. It is highly unlikely that the Court of Appeal was in *Novac* seeking to cast any doubt upon one of the most famous of all similar fact cases, *R v Smith*,[14] where a number of undoubtedly innocent features of the conduct in question were stressed, such as the celebration of marriage with a lady,[15] taking out insurance on her life, exhibiting solicitude about her health, and purchasing a bath for her use. These features were rightly admitted, and emphasised, since they were

---

9 See *Thompson v R* [1918] AC 221, 13 Cr App Rep 61 (photographs); *R v Twiss* [1918] 2 KB 853 (photographs). But see *R v Gillingham* [1939] 4 All ER 122, 27 Cr App Rep 143, where the court seemed to require at least possible use in a crime of the sort in question, but took a broad view of the possible uses of indecent photographs (heterosexual photographs to stimulate homosexual activity); and *R v Wright* (1989) Times, 27 April where the court was unwilling to accept such evidence where the defence was one of concoction.

10 *R v Manning* (1923) 17 Cr App Rep 85; *R v Taylor* (1923) 17 Cr App Rep 109. See also *Guay v R* [1979] 1 SCR 18 (indecent book used in commission of crime).

11 *R v Reading* [1966] 1 All ER 521n, [1966] 1 WLR 836.

12 (1977) 65 Cr App Rep 107 at 112.

13 *R v Scarrott* [1978] QB 1016 at 1025, [1978] 1 All ER 672 at 679; *R v Barrington* [1981] 1 All ER 1132 at 1141, [1981] 1 WLR 419 at 430.

14 (1915) 11 Cr App Rep 229. See also *Lanford v General Medical Council* [1990] AC 13, [1989] 2 All ER 921.

15 In fact the marriage was bigamous, but clearly the proof of it still falls into the class of case where the evidence of the discreditable nature is relevant otherwise than as showing the accused's disposition.

vitally relevant to establish the circumstantial basis for the inference that all of these ladies had been murdered by the accused.

It can now be seen that evidence revealing the accused's discreditable disposition is excluded under the similar facts rule only when such disposition is an essential step in the argument.[16] If the evidence of disposition is irrelevant, it is excluded for that reason. If it is relevant, but upon a line of argument unconnected with the accused's discreditable disposition, it is, in principle, admissible, but remains subject to exclusion by way of judicial discretion if its prejudicial effect is regarded as sufficiently outweighing its probative value.

C. ELEMENTS OF THE RULE[17]

The rule comprises two elements conveniently set out by Lord Wilberforce in *Boardman*:

> Whether in the field of sexual conduct or otherwise, there is no general or automatic answer to be given to the question whether evidence of facts similar to those the subject of a particular charge ought to be admitted. In each case it is necessary to estimate (i) whether, and if so how strongly, the evidence as to other facts tends to support, ie to make more credible, the evidence given as to the fact in question; (ii) whether such evidence, if given, is likely to be prejudicial to the accused. Both these elements involve questions of degree.[18]

The two elements to which reference is made have been called above 'probative force' and 'prejudicial effect'. Both are composite notions, and will be considered in turn.

1. PROBATIVE FORCE

The probative force of similar fact evidence depends upon three principal factors: (a) the cogency of the evidence showing the accused's bad disposition; (b) the extent to which proof of such disposition supports the inference sought to be drawn from it; and (c) the degree of relevance of that inference to some fact in issue in the proceedings. These three variable factors interact with each other, and to some extent strength in one can compensate for weakness in another.[19] The skeleton of this analysis is sketched out here, many of the examples are discussed in more detail in the next part of this section.

16 The importance of distinguishing between the admissibility of evidence of discreditable matters which does and does not proceed by way of an argument relying upon disposition has received statutory recognition in Police and Criminal Evidence Act 1984, s 74(3).
17 For a helpful discussion see Williams 'The Problem of Similar Fact Evidence' (1979) 5 Dal LJ 281.
18 [1975] AC 421 at 442, [1974] 3 All ER 887 at 896.
19 Thus in *R v Wilmot* (1988) 89 Cr App Rep 341 the number of incidents outweighed minor dissimilarities, and it should be noted that an initial ruling of inadmissibility was reversed when evidence of further similar incidents became available.

(i) Cogency of evidence showing bad disposition

There is a wide range of possibilities, from the accused's plea of guilty[20] or his confession of extrinsic discreditable conduct[1] or disposition,[2] or his conviction for the conduct after a trial,[3] to such weak possibilities as charges for which the evidence is scanty,[4] or even, of which he has already been acquitted.[5] In some cases the probative force consists solely of an inference sought to be drawn from equivocal conduct,[6] from statements made by the accused,[7] from the possession of articles,[8] or even of letters written by a third party.[9] In some cases the evidence was too weak to be accepted. It is interesting that in some cases less cogently established evidence is tendered when stronger is available. This tends to occur where the accused has previously been convicted of similar offences, so the evidence is clearly cogent, but is charged with a large number of incidents of the same character in different counts in the current indictment, all of which are denied. This is not at all uncommon in cases of homosexuality.[10] It appears to reflect a sentiment not very different from that inspiring the plea of autrefois convict, namely a desire not to make the accused suffer twice for the same act.

A further dimension of the cogency of evidence of bad disposition relates to the danger of collaboration between the witnesses to the evidence extrinsic to the charge and those to the conduct in respect of which the accused is being tried. This sometimes seems to be regarded as a matter of weight, and thus as having little bearing on admissibility,[11] but there is high authority to the contrary.[12] It assumes particular importance where the principal justification for the admission of the evidence of bad disposition lies in the corroboration it affords a primary witness.[13] One of the facts which renders the whole area so confusing is that it is impossible to insulate questions of weight from those of relevance and admissibility, compelling the judge to decide in advance, and as a matter of law, what is essentially a jury question. It must however be conceded that if it is determined in favour of admissibility, the role of the jury is not excluded since it then has an opportunity to decide for itself whether the evidence is worthy of reliance.[14]

20 Eg *R v Benson* [1985] 2 Qd R 117.
1 Eg *R v Straffen* [1952] 2 QB 911, [1952] 2 All ER 657.
2 Eg *R v King* [1967] 2 QB 338, [1967] 1 All ER 379.
3 Eg *R v Harrison-Owen* [1951] 2 All ER 726, 35 Cr App Rep 108. But see *R v Shepherd* (1980) 71 Cr App Rep 120, suggesting that the fact of conviction will rarely be relevant, and this case is expressly excluded from the generally curative effect of s 74 of the Police and Criminal Evidence Act 1984. The same difficulty exists in Australia, see *Tedge v R (No 2)* [1979] WAR 89.
4 Eg *Harris v D P P* [1952] AC 694, [1952] 1 All ER 1044, where the evidence was so scanty that the accused was acquitted on the relevant counts.
5 Eg *R v Ollis* [1900] 2 QB 758, 19 Cox CC 554.
6 Eg *R v Hall* [1952] 1 KB 302, [1952] 1 All ER 66, the first two counts.
7 Eg *R v Horwood* [1970] 1 QB 133, [1969] 3 All ER 1156.
8 Eg *R v Mustafa* (1976) 65 Cr App Rep 26.
9 *R v Cole* (1941) 28 Cr App Rep 43.
10 *Boardman* and *Kilborne* both fall into this category.
11 Eg *R v Johannsen* (1977) 65 Cr App Rep 101 at 105.
12 *D P P v Boardman* [1975] AC 421 at 459, [1974] 3 All ER 887 at 910 and *R v Scarrott* [1978] QB 1016 at 1028, [1978] 1 All ER 672 at 682. See further below p 365.
13 As in *Boardman*.
14 Such a dual function is not unknown elsewhere in the law of evidence, for example, in relation to the weight to be attached to confessions unsuccessfully alleged to have been obtained in circumstances rendering them inadmissible.

(ii) Strength of the inference from evidence of bad disposition

It is obvious that the cogency of the evidence counts for nothing unless it tends to prove what it is tendered to prove, and unless that matter is itself relevant to a fact in issue. The former of these two questions has to be resolved in the light of the other evidence in the case and the form of reasoning to be adopted. The greatest difficulty is experienced in cases where it is necessary to show by the extrinsic evidence, because of the absence of direct oral testimony of the matter, both that a criminal act occurred, and that, if it did, it was the accused who committed it.[15] In some cases identity may be conceded, indeed be undeniable, but the commission of a criminal act hotly disputed.[16] *Straffen* fell into the converse category where the commission of the crime by someone was undeniable, but dispute centred upon the identity of the accused as the criminal in the absence of direct testimony of identification. It is in such cases that the courts require the very strongest evidence of similarity, indeed peculiarity, of technique because the evidence must by itself be so compelling as to be the equivalent of a signature, or the discovery of the accused's fingerprints in each separate connection.[17] It is suggested that the connection must be so compelling that the accused would be entitled to be acquitted if he could prove his innocence of a further crime involving exactly the same characteristics. In other cases where there is direct evidence of the commission of the crime, and it is merely sought to corroborate such evidence, as in *Boardman,* a lower standard of peculiarity may be tolerated, and in cases where there is still more compelling further evidence, such as keeping an appointment to meet at a pre-arranged place at a pre-arranged time, even less similarity is required, as in *Thompson* where evidence of no more than homosexual disposition sufficed. Similarly if the issue is solely as to the intent, motive or knowledge of the accused, the commission of the act and the identity of the actor being conceded,[18] this requirement sinks lower still, as stated most clearly in a recent Canadian case:

> The degree of similarity required will depend upon the issues in the particular case, the purpose for which the evidence is sought to be introduced and the other evidence . . . That test [striking similarity] has been applied when the Crown seeks to prove identity, but the test is less stringent where the evidence is adduced to show knowledge, intent or state of mind or . . . to refute the defence of accident.[19]

15 Though usually as a matter of tactical necessity only one of these issues will be fought seriously. *Makin v AG for New South Wales* [1894] AC 57, *R v Smith* (1915) 11 Cr App Rep 229, and *Noor Mohamed v R* [1949] AC 182 all fall into this category in theory, but in none of them was it seriously argued that if the victim was deliberately killed, it was done by someone other than the accused, so effectively putting such cases into the following category.

16 As in *R v Ball* [1911] AC 47, 6 Cr App Rep 31.

17 See *R v Carroll* (1985) 19 ACR 410 where it was held inadmissible to identify the accused, who lied about an alibi, as the man who had abducted a female infant, dressed her in adult underwear, sexually assaulted her, bitten her on the thigh, damaged her right eye, and strangled her, by evidence that he had been subsequently divorced having on a number of occasions apparently bitten the thigh of his own female infant and once damaged her eye, though she had not been strangled, and it could not be proved whether or not she had been sexually assaulted or dressed in adult underwear.

18 As in *R v Ollis* [1900] 2 QB 758, 19 Cox CC 554, the first two counts in *R v Hall* [1952] 1 KB 302, [1952] 1 All ER 66, or *R v Rance and Herron* (1975) 62 Cr App Rep 118.

19 *R v Carpenter (No 2)* (1982) 142 DLR (3d) 237. See also *Sutton v R* (1984) 51 ALR 435 at 451 per Brennan J.

(iii) Degree of relevance to facts in issue

This is the second of the two questions mentioned at the beginning of the last section. Even if, say, the act of the accused can be established by reference to evidence of bad disposition, its establishment is no more than prejudicial if the act of the accused, so established, is not in dispute. In a sense a plea of not guilty puts every element of the crime into issue, as Lord Goddard said in *Sims*:

> the accused should not be able, by confining himself at the trial on one issue, to exclude evidence that should be admissible and fatal if he ran two defences; for that would make the astuteness of the accused or his advisors prevail over the interests of justice.[20]

However the stringency of such a view has now been recognised, and in the light of adverse comments in *Noor Mohamed* Lord Goddard himself expressed the more traditional and generous view in *R v Hall*:

> in criminal cases . . . the prisoner does not plead in writing; he pleads orally and a plea of not guilty is a plea of the general issue, and when the general issue is pleaded all defences are open to a prisoner, but it would not, on that account, be right at once in all cases to assume that a prisoner is going to set up a defence which is theoretically open to him.[1]

The question is clearly complicated by the paucity of pre-trial proceedings in criminal cases, and by the frequent desire of the defence to show its hand at as late a stage as possible. It is nevertheless clear that the line of defence taken[2] by the accused may either contract or expand the ambit of relevance of evidence of bad disposition. Thus a charge of rape might be defended on the grounds of alibi, impotence or consent of the victim. If the alibi line is chosen the prosecution could adduce evidence of any relevant conduct of the accused, including criminal conduct, which took place in circumstances inconsistent with his alibi. If the impotence line is taken the prosecution could adduce evidence of any acts of sexual intercourse, including criminal acts, to rebut the defence.[3] But other acts of criminality which might be proved on the first hypothesis would not now be relevant because of the different line taken by the accused. If the defence were consent of the victim, then neither evidence of general criminality, nor of intercourse with others would be admissible.[4] Sometimes when the nature of the defence lets in a new range of extrinsic material it becomes relevant in a much wider way than would otherwise have been the case. Thus in *R v Mitchell*[5] the accused

---

20 [1946] KB 531 at 539, [1946] 1 All ER 697 at 701.
 1 [1952] 1 KB 302 at 307, [1952] 1 All ER 66 at 68.
 2 It may occasionally occur that the accused initially develops a line of defence perhaps on the voir dire, making similar fact evidence admissible, but subsequently resiles from it. It has been held in South Australia that in such a case it would be wrong to quash a conviction simply because the evidence had been admitted at a time when it seemed likely to be relevant, see *R v Wright* (1986) 19 ACR 17.
 3 See for example *R v Solomons* 1959 (2) SA 352, where the accused's denial of possession of a knife let in evidence of other stabbings, and *R v Ward* [1963] Qd R 56, where the accused's denial of knowing how to drive let in evidence of driving offences.
 4 See *R v Rodley* [1913] 3 KB 468. See also *R v Clermont* (1986) 32 DLR (4th) 306.
 5 (1952) 36 Cr App Rep 79. This is a better example than the more usual *R v Chitson* [1909] 2 KB 945 because, as noted above, it is not there completely clear why the prosecution witness was permitted to testify to a conversation which ocurred a day after the events in question. See also *R v Hasler, ex p A-G* [1987] 1 Qd R 239.

denied not only the commission of the acts in question, but also the conversation leading up to them. For this reason the prosecution was able to corroborate the evidence of its principal witness with evidence of further discreditable conduct of the accused which could have come to the knowledge of the victim only by way of such a conversation. It then became a matter of little consequence how different the details of the two incidents were.

It is sometimes possible by unwavering concentration upon the matters actually put in issue by the nature of the defence to protect the accused by insisting upon a similarly restricted scope of the evidence admitted to rebut them. Thus in *U S v Cook*[6] where the accused argued that he would not have committed the instant offence because he would not have wanted to run the risk of violating his parole, it was held to be prejudicial to give the highly unpleasant details of another breach of parole, for the purpose simply of showing that this consideration did not balk very large with him. It should have been enough simply to restrict the evidence to an unspecific allegation of a deliberate breach of parole.

This raises the closely related question of cumulative testimony. In the United States the same Federal Rule[7] which bestows a discretion to exclude unduly prejudicial evidence also bestows one to exclude needlessly cumulative evidence. Suppose the accused raises alibi as a defence, and that the prosecution has plenty of convincing evidence to rebut it quite apart from evidence of his commission of a crime which also tends to rebut it. Should the prosecution be allowed to adduce evidence of the crime in addition to its other evidence to rebut the alibi? The answer is not straightforward. On the one hand if there is plenty of other evidence the issue might plausibly be regarded as being as little in real contention as one in respect of which the accused has made an explicit concession, and thus the evidence of the extrinsic crime might seem simply prejudicial. On the other hand the issue *is* still open, and there is no predicting what view the jury might take of any particular piece or pieces of evidence. Nor is it manifestly just that the weaker the case for the prosecution the worse off the accused should become so far as the admission of evidence of discreditable extrinsic matters is concerned. It is submitted that the least unsatisfactory procedure depends upon the delicate art of balancing proof and prejudice.[8]

2. PREJUDICIAL EFFECT

It is clear from the discussion above that evidence of discreditable extrinsic conduct or disposition can be relevant in a large number of different ways, for example by showing a system of discreditable conduct and so tending to prove criminal intent; by showing a particular modus operandi and so tending to identify the accused as the criminal; by showing something discreditable about the accused which only the accused could have communicated to the witness and which was communicated as part of the technique of committing the crime and so tending to corroborate the witness; or by showing some unusual and discreditable attribute of the accused and

---

6 538 F 2d 1000 (1976).

7 Rule 403.

8 In the analogous context of cross-examination to the accused's record discussed below at p 408 it will be seen that cumulation is one of the considerations recommended to be taken into account, *R v Britzman* [1983] 1 All ER 369 at 374.

so tending to corroborate identification of the accused by a witness. There is nothing inherently prejudicial in these processes of reasoning. If the accused's system were in no way discreditable, say a particular and highly unusual system of arranging a client's affairs so as to reduce tax before a change in the law made it illegal, if after the change such an arrangement were found to have been made, there could be no objection to proving that system as tending to show the unlikelihood of a coincidence, and thus that the accused was involved in the, now illegal, arrangement. If the accused could be shown to be in the habit of wearing outlandish clothes, such as an Indian head-dress, in perfectly innocent pursuits, there could be no objection to proving such an unusual habit as tending to show that the accused was the criminal who was also so attired. If the accused could be shown to be in the relevant location at the relevant time his alibi would equally be disproved whether his activities there and then were innocent or discreditable. If the accused told the victim something perfectly innocent, say the number of his bank account, as part of his technique of committing a fraud, the witness's knowledge of that number would corroborate his testimony just as much as if his knowledge related to some discreditable act of the accused. If the accused has some innocent attribute, say being a bird-watcher, and the criminal also has this attribute, then the fact that the person identified as the criminal by the witness also happens to be a bird-watcher strengthens the inference that the identification is accurate, just as much as if it related to some discreditable characteristic.

It is thus apparent that it is not the line of reasoning as such which prejudices the accused, nor even the fact that as a result of its application he is more likely to be convicted. It is rather the tendency of the evidence indicating a bad disposition to persuade the jury to convict the accused for reasons other than its logical force which constitutes the justification for excluding such evidence.[9] Its admission is undesirable at two levels. The first relates to the trial process itself, and constitutes what is usually understood by prejudice in this context. Beyond it there lie further ranges of institutional perils which will accrue whenever prejudice of the former type occurs.

(i) Trial level[10]

In the absence of any satisfactory psychological studies of the reasoning processes of actual juries, or even of a sufficient corpus of reliable scientific evidence derived from carefully controlled experiments, it is not possible to do more than speculate upon the lines of argument which may occur.[11]

---

9 See *R v Wilmot* (1988) 89 Cr App Rep 341 at 348 where 'proper' and 'improper' prejudice are distinguished. See also *R v Da Silva* [1990] 1 All ER 29 where, it is submitted the Court went too far in reducing this concept. As Street CJ said in *R v Stalder* [1981] 2 NSWLR 9 at 20, 'It is not *mere* prejudice, no matter how inevitable or grave that may be, which is the touchstone; it is *undue* or *disproportionate* prejudice having regard to the probative significance of the evidence upon an issue falling for determination by the jury' (emphasis in original). See also *Sutton v R* (1984) 51 ALR 435 at 450, 451, per Brennan J.

10 See *R v D (LE)* 50 CCC (3d) 142 where the Supreme Court of Canada held that the direction to the jury had not sufficiently guarded them against these very dangers.

11 For some North American evidence see Doob and Kirshenbaum 'Some Empirical Evidence on the Effect of s 12 of the Canada Evidence Act Upon An Accused' (1972) 15 Crim LQ 88; Note 'Other Crimes Evidence at Trial: Of Balancing and Other Matters' (1961) 70 Yale LJ 763, quoting Broeder's reflections on the evidence obtained from the Chicago jury study.

Common sense suggests a number of possibilities. The first, and the most obvious, is that the jury might simply take the view that the evidence shows the accused to be bad, that crimes are more often committed by the bad than by the good, and hence the evidence tends to show the accused likely to be guilty. It has already been suggested that there is statistical support for this reasoning process, and it is strengthened the greater the similarities and peculiarities of the evidence are, and the stronger the probative force in the ways outlined above.[12] In short, the principal danger is that the jury may concentrate too much upon the moral infirmities of the accused, and too little upon other factors in the case leading to the opposite conclusion. It may be swayed more by revulsion for the accused than persuasion by the rest of the evidence. It is for very similar reasons that the court is required to be sparing in the admission of gruesome photographs or particularly revolting details of the crime committed so as not to permit the accused to be made a scapegoat for the jury's abhorrence of the crime which has been committed, and for its determination that the wrong not go unpunished.

A different danger is that the jury, after hearing the evidence of the accused's discreditable extrinsic conduct or disposition may not try sufficiently conscientiously to determine whether or not the accused really is guilty of the crime with which he is charged. In the former case the danger is that the jury may too readily infer from the evidence that the accused is guilty, here the danger is that the jury may simply infer from the evidence that the accused is the sort of man who ought to be punished whether he has been proved guilty of the crime with which he has been charged, or not. They may feel that once it has been proved that the accused has committed crimes in the past, or that he has a disposition which makes it likely that he will commit crimes in the future, then he ought to be punished for what he has already done or be prevented from doing what he might go on to do, and that for these reasons he should be convicted and sentenced. If the evidence consists of crimes for which the accused has already been convicted he may suffer from a tendency for the jury not to give him the same benefit of any doubt which might have been given to one with no previous convictions. A jury may well wish to be much more sure before inflicting upon a man for the first time all the opprobrium which attaches to those found guilty of crimes. If such opprobrium already attaches to him the jury may not regard a mistake as quite so serious a matter.

A slight variant on this line of reasoning is that the jury may feel that the accused has probably committed many other crimes beyond those for which he has previously been convicted, but in some cases has gone undetected, in others has not been charged because of insufficient evidence, and in others has been acquitted upon a technicality of some sort. It might then seem eminently fair to convict him on the current charge, guilty or innocent. A similar line of reasoning may be applied in the class of case where the evidence in dispute relates to a large number of incidents in respect of which the accused has not so far been convicted, including some where the incidents

---

12 It has been argued that this statistical evidence may not be so strong as it seems at first sight unless the statistics are related only to cases in which the accused has chosen to stand trial, the plausible thesis being that many of those with previous convictions who are in fact guilty, plead guilty; while many of those with previous convictions who are in fact innocent, plead not guilty; see Lempert and Salzburg *A Modern Approach to Evidence* (2nd edn, 1982) p 217.

are charged in other counts in the indictment,[13] and others where the evidence does not constitute a separate count in the indictment, but is merely used to support it.[14] In these cases the remarks made by Lord Hewart CJ in *R v Bailey* are most pertinent:

> the risk, the danger, the logical fallacy is indeed quite manifest to those who are accustomed to thinking about such matters. It is so easy to derive from a series of unsatisfactory allegations, if there are enough of them, an accusation which at least appears satisfactory. It is so easy to collect from a mass of ingredients, not one of which is sufficient, a totality which will appear to contain what is missing. That of course is only another way of saying that when a person is dealing with a considerable mass of facts, in particular if those facts are of such a nature as to invite reprobation, nothing is easier than confusion of mind; and, therefore, if such charges are to be brought in a mass, it becomes essential that the method upon which guilt is to be ascertained should be stated with a punctilious exactness.[15]

A rather different danger operating at this level is that the jury may become genuinely confused, and concentrate so much upon resolving the question of whether the accused really did commit the extrinsic discreditable acts urged against him, that once having done so, the verdict upon them is simply substituted for that upon the issue which the jury is really trying. Even where there is no danger of simple substitution of one bad act for another, the intrusion of an issue of extrinsic discreditable conduct may deflect attention from the real issue of intrinsic discreditable conduct. This possibility was canvassed in *R v Mackie*:

> the jury might have considered that the evidence admitted was evidence of excessive chastisement on the part of the appellant which made it unnecessary for them to consider whether the conduct on April 4 was itself so excessive or unreasonable as to be unlawful, and they might have been misled into thinking that they need not trouble whether it was lawful or unlawful in the light of what has been proved about the appellant's earlier conduct; in either case he was morally responsible for the boy's death.[16]

(ii) Secondary prejudice

If prejudice of this sort is tolerated at the trial, and if evidence of bad disposition is admitted whenever it is barely relevant to the issues of the accused's guilt, an undesirable ripple effect is likely to occur. It may be expected that prosecutors will rely upon such evidence more and more, and in the absence of any explicit restriction will sometimes seek to use it even to establish a prima facie case. At an earlier stage the police may be inclined to base their enquiries still more strongly upon the personalities and propensities of criminals known to be living in their areas. This danger is likely to be at its most acute in relation to identification evidence, since eye witnesses are very likely to be shown photographs of those with criminal records in an

---

13 As in *Scarrott.*
14 As in *Makin.*
15 [1924] 2 KB 300 at 305, 18 Cr App Rep 42 at 44. It should be noted that in this case the prejudice appears to have been so profound as to have induced the jury to convict upon one count upon which prosecuting counsel conceded that there was not even a case to answer, see [1924] 2 KB 300 at 303, 18 Cr App Rep 42 at 42.
16 (1973) 57 Cr App Rep 453 at 464.

attempt to detect the criminal. It is well known how unreliable such identification can be,[17] and how much danger it already creates. If criminal records are themselves to be more readily adduced in evidence these dangers will be seriously enlarged. Not only will the police be more likely to rely upon such matters to find people to charge, they will also be in a much stronger position to exert pressure to plead guilty or to confess by persuading the accused that a man with such a record stands little chance of acquittal in a contested case. Some people will have records so damning and will be so vulnerable to successful prosecution as to become easily manipulated by the police. No doubt most prosecutors and most policemen are both honourable, and energetic and are unlikely to change their current practices, but it is not unduly cynical to suppose that there could be some who might be tempted into an easier and more certain path to secure convictions to clear up crimes, especially when convinced of the accused's guilt.

Greater admissibility of evidence of extrinsic discreditable conduct or disposition would also lead to the complication and prolongation of the process of trial. Some such conduct might have occurred long before the trial, and the means of proving it might be most unsatisfactory. Since the accused can be expected to deny the truth of such allegations as vigorously as possible, the chances of a scrupulous jury remaining unconvinced beyond reasonable doubt might be unduly high, and the administration of justice easily be brought into disrepute by the spectacle of continual re-litigation of past events, perhaps with differing results, or in relation to conduct for which the perpetrator was never charged at the time. The proliferation of such issues will inevitably slow litigation down still more. It will complicate trials by requiring very careful direction of juries on the weight and point of previous judicial findings, and will lead to special difficulty where indictments contain multiple counts and involve several co-accused. All this will generate more and more appeals.

The matter can also be viewed from the perspective of rehabilitation. The modern tendency is to encourage rehabilitation of offenders so far as possible by making it possible to live down a criminal past, and not have it brought up against one over and over again.[18] If having a criminal record becomes a passport to police scrutiny, harassment and unjustified reconviction, all of these aims will be frustrated. Indeed to the extent that such a system did lead to unjustified conviction, it would rapidly poison the atmosphere in prisons still further, and generate still greater contempt for the forces of law. It should also be noted that the effects would be cumulative. More convictions would mean longer records, and so increase the chances of reconviction still further.

D. APPLICATION OF THE RULE

In *Makin v A-G for New South Wales* Lord Herschell introduced his celebrated passage by saying: 'the principles which must govern the decision of the case are clear, though the application of them is by no means free from difficulty'.[19] He concluded it by saying: 'The statement of these general

17 See below p 715.
18 Rehabilitation of Offenders Act 1974; see s 7(2)(a), which exempts references in evidence in criminal proceedings.
19 [1894] AC 57 at 65.

principles is easy, but it is obvious that it may often be very difficult to draw the line and to decide whether a particular piece of evidence is on the one side or the other.'[20]

These passages were re-echoed and approved in *D P P v Boardman*.[1] One of the problems relates to the nature of the rule, which was recognised in *Boardman* to depend upon questions of degree and weight, but ones which have to be decided by the judge rather than by the jury. The various stages at which the rule may have to be considered were summarised by Scarman LJ in *R v Scarrott*.[2] He distinguished the pre-arraignment stage from the trial stage. At the former he took the view that the judge could exercise his discretion to sever the indictment if he felt that the evidence relevant to one count would not, because of this rule, be admissible on the others.[3] At the trial stage the question of admissibility ought to be decided in the absence of the jury at the outset of the trial.[4] The judge is not however rendered functus officio by the judgments he makes at so early a stage without having had the opportunity to take into account the way the trial develops. He may still permit evidence which would have been relevant to a severed count to be tendered if he becomes convinced, contrary to his provisional view, of its admissibility. He may also instruct the jury to disregard evidence which he now believes himself wrong to have allowed,[5] or in a really serious case, where such a course is likely to be ineffective to prevent prejudice, he may discharge the jury and order a fresh trial.

These considerations make the application of the rule a difficult one for the judge to perform.[6] It was perhaps for such a reason that in the years between *Makin* and *Boardman* a tendency grew up to consider the application of the rule in terms of rigid categories which dictated either admission or exclusion. An early example is provided by the judgment of Bray J in *R v Bond*: 'A careful examination of the cases where evidence of this kind has been admitted shows that they may be grouped under three heads . . .'[7] This practice was roundly condemned in *Boardman* because 'where what is important is the application of principle, the use of labels or definitive

20 At 65.
1 [1975] AC 421, [1974] 3 All ER 887; see Lord Morris at 438, 892, and Lord Hailsham at 450, 903.
2 [1978] QB 1016, [1978] 1 All ER 672.
3 In England this matter is governed by Indictment Rules 1971, r 9 as interpreted by the House of Lords in *Ludlow v Metropolitan Police Comr* [1971] AC 29, [1970] 1 All ER 567, and dicta of Lords Cross and Wilberforce in *Boardman* which apparently suggest a more generally liberal approach are to be construed as applying only where there is serious danger of prejudice on account of the unpleasant nature of the evidence, see *R v McGlinchey* [1983] Crim LR 808; *R v Wells* [1989] Crim LR 67; but cp *R v Wilmot* (1988) 89 Cr App Rep 341; *Lanford v General Medical Council* [1989] 3 WLR 665 at 673. In Australia a more liberal approach has prevailed, especially in sexual cases where prejudice is so rife, and no special factor, as required by *Ludlow*, need be shown, see *De Jesus v R* (1986) 68 ALR 1; *R v Cranston* [1988] 1 Qd R 159. See also Weinberg 'Multiple Counts and Similar Fact Evidence' in (eds) Campbell and Waller *Well and Truly Tried* (1982).
4 See Lord Cross in *Boardman* at 459, 910.
5 As occurred in *R v Flack* [1969] 2 All ER 784, [1969] 1 WLR 937.
6 It should be noted that the rule applies to criminal proceedings at all levels including summary proceedings, see, for example, *R v Rochford Justices, ex p Buck* (1978) 68 Cr App Rep 114.
7 [1906] 2 KB 389 at 414, 21 Cox CC 252. *R v Flack* [1969] 2 All ER 784, [1969] 1 WLR 937, illustrates the persistence of the tendency up to the period of *Boardman*. There is even some evidence of its continued survival, see *R v Lewis* (1982) 76 Cr App Rep 33.

descriptions cannot be either comprehensive or restrictive'.[8] Some of the labels so applied in the past such as 'innocent association', and 'system', were explicitly condemned.[9] All of their Lordships seem to have agreed that the matters to be considered involved the interpretation of principle by the application of logic and commonsense which 'are not susceptible of exact codification when applied to the actual facts of life in its infinite variety'.[10] Such a view opens rather than closes the door to exemplification of, and to the provision of guidelines for, the application of the rules, so long as such examples and guides are not regarded as automatic shackles or escape hatches.

As decided in *Boardman*, and as formulated here, the application of the rule depends upon the precise balance between probative force and prejudicial effect. Probative force itself depends upon relevance and cogency. Relevance is heavily influenced by the line of defence adopted by the accused, and cogency by the other evidence in the case. These two practical considerations, rather than time-worn cliches of presentation, govern the form of exemplification here. Issues are considered simply in terms of the elements which arise in any criminal case, such as the occurrence of an actus reus, its commission by the accused, and his intention, motive and state of knowledge in so committing it.

They are affected, not only by the formal definition of the crime, but also by the defences actually advanced by the accused, or reasonably open to him. These constitute the primary vehicle for the exemplification which follows, but within them there operate considerations of cogency, and predominantly the question of whether or not there is direct testimony of the commission of the crime. If there is, the similar fact evidence operates to corroborate it; if there is not, the similar fact evidence operates simply as circumstantial evidence of guilt.

1. COMMISSION OF CRIME

In many cases the commission of a crime cannot be denied, and the only question to be decided is the identity of the criminal.[11] In others although it would be possible to deny that any crime were committed, the line of defence operates to convert the case into one of identity or participation.[12] This leaves cases where the evidence is sufficiently equivocal for the commission of any crime at all to remain open to doubt. The most common cases are those of 'victimless' offences, the commission of which may leave no physical trace, and of murder where there may either remain insufficient evidence of the cause of death to exclude the possibility of a natural cause,[13] or where it may be possible for the accused to allege accident,[14] or suicide.[15] In the case

---

8 Lord Morris at 439, 893.
9 By Lord Wilberforce at 443, 896.
10 Lord Hailsham at 452, 904.
11 Many cases of murder and robbery fall into this category, *R v Straffen* [1952] 2 QB 911, [1952] 2 All ER 657, and *R v Robinson* [1952] 2 All ER 334; sub nom *Practice Note* [1953] 1 WLR 872, are typical examples.
12 *Thompson v R* [1918] AC 221, 13 Cr App Rep 61, and *R v Neale* (1977) 65 Cr App Rep 304, are clear examples.
13 As in *Makin*.
14 As in *R v Smith* (1915) 11 Cr App Rep 229.
15 As in *Noor Mohamed v R* [1949] AC 182, [1949] 1 All ER 365.

of many sexual offences there is direct testimony from the victim for the similar fact evidence to corroborate. In murder and in the case of 'victimless' offences it is less likely that there will be such direct testimony. It is useful to consider the two situations separately.

At one time it was thought that evidence of the accused's bad disposition could not be relied upon to establish the existence of an actus reus. This view was firmly rejected in *Makin* where the evidence of finding the other bodies was admitted solely to show that the Makins had developed a system of taking babies in at low sums, insufficient to support them, and then murdering them, thus helping to prove it more likely that the child in respect of which they were charged had been murdered by them than that it had died from natural causes. So too in *Smith* the evidence of the other deaths tended to rebut a possible defence of accident. It was inherently implausible that so many accidents would happen. The main authority on the 'victimless' crime situation is *R v Ball*.[16] A brother and sister were accused of incest. There was evidence that they had been living in the same household, sleeping in the same bed, and passing themselves off as man and wife. In addition there was evidence that the sister had borne her brother's child, conceived before incest became a criminal offence. The House of Lords received the evidence of the conception of the child to show the disposition of the accused to have sexual relations with each other, and hence that such relations took place when they were sharing a bed. The case is particularly significant in this context as the Court of Criminal Appeal had refused to uphold the trial judge's admission of the similar fact evidence just because it was being used to show the commission of the actus reus which it held an impermissible purpose.

In all of these cases where the evidence is used to show the commission of a criminal act in the absence of direct testimony to that effect, the evidence of disposition needs to be particularly strong. In the traditional terminology these often tend to be the cases where 'system' is alleged. *Makin* and *Smith* might well have been decided differently if there had been no more than one other example, just as happened in *Noor Mohamed*. The disposition was however made out in the one case because there were so many other examples, plus a good deal of circumstantial evidence; and in the other because the situations were so remarkably similar to each other in all of their details.[17] In *Ball* much depended upon the circumstantial evidence, and the way in which Scrutton J, the trial judge, wisely widened the period within which the commission of the crime was alleged.

Where there is direct testimony of the commission of the crime, usually from the victim in sexual cases, the evidence need not be so strong. These are the cases sometimes categorised as ones of 'innocent association'. The accused admits an opportunity for the commission of the crime, but denies that advantage was taken of it. The more compromising and contrived the opportunity the more readily the evidence will be admitted. Thus in *R v*

---

16 [1911] AC 47, 6 Cr App Rep 31. A leading Australian example is *Martin v Osborne* (1936) 55 CLR 367 (evidence of regular trips to establish operation of unlicensed bus service).

17 It is interesting to note that suspicion was cast upon Smith by a letter written to the police by the husband of the landlady of the premises in which the second victim had been murdered categorised as commenting upon the 'striking similarity' between that death and the third, a report of the inquest upon which he had read in his newspaper, see Watson 'Trial of Joseph Smith' *Notable British Trials* (1922) at 28.

King[18] the accused not only made the acquaintance of the victims, who were total strangers to him, in a public lavatory frequented by homosexuals, but then invited the boys back to his flat where he shared a bed with one of them. Here the supporting evidence was so strong that evidence of a general disposition to homosexuality was of sufficient probative force to be admitted. Where the supporting evidence is not so strong, as in *R v Horwood*,[19] where the initial meeting was less questionable, and where no such close contact as sharing a bed was admitted, evidence of the accused's homosexuality was excluded. A similar situation arises when the accused denies commission of a sexual crime on the basis that the victim consented. Here too, if the probative force of the evidence exceeds its prejudicial effect, which may well be great, it may be admitted.[20]

There have been a number of reported cases[1] since *Boardman* in which the commission of a criminal act has been in issue, but in all of them there has been some direct testimony of the commission of the act in question. They provide no clear guidance to the amount of probative force required. In some the evidence relied upon as being strikingly similar has been regarded as relating to no more than the stock-in-trade of the perpetrator of the crime in question. In some there has been stress upon the corroborative factor. Where a number of different witnesses, without any suggestion of collaboration, all testify that the same thing has happened, it is significant, particularly where the detail is either unusual,[2] or tallies in some very minute particulars over a large number of cases.[3] As Lord Cross indicated in *Boardman* the essence of the argument is the unlikelihood of a coincidence of testimony, and that unlikelihood increases the more peculiar the circumstances and the greater the number of instances. It does however then become absolutely vital that the testimony should be truly independent, and free from any danger of collaboration, or any other cause common to the witnesses. Indeed in *Boardman* Lord Wilberforce emphasised that this:[4]

> may be a real possibility; something much more than mere similarity and absence of proved conspiracy is needed if this evidence is to be allowed. This is well illustrated by *Kilbourne*'s case where the judge excluded 'intra group' evidence because of the possibility *as it appeared to him*, of collaboration between boys who knew each other well. This is . . . the right course rather than to admit the evidence unless a case of collaboration or concoction is made out.

18 [1967] 2 QB 338, [1967] 1 All ER 379, the case was treated as if the evidence had been led in chief rather than elicited in cross-examination with the result that the Criminal Evidence Act 1898, s 1(f), which should have governed it, was ignored.
19 [1970] 1 QB 133, [1969] 3 All ER 1156.
20 *R v Wilmot* (1988) 89 Cr App Rep 341.
 1 They include *R v Novac* (1976) 65 Cr App Rep 107; *R v Johannsen* (1977) 65 Cr App Rep 101; *R v Scarrott* [1978] QB 1016, [1978] 1 All ER 672; *R v Inder* (1977) 67 Cr App Rep 143; *R v Clarke* (1977) 67 Cr App Rep 398; *R v Downes* [1981] Crim LR 174; *R v Barrington* [1981] 1 All ER 1132, [1981] 1 WLR 419; *R v Lewis* (1982) 76 Cr App Rep 33 (as to one incident); *R v Lunt* (1987) 85 Cr App Rep 241.
 2 This was an important factor in *Boardman* (two separate suggestions that the middle-aged party played the passive role in homosexual conduct with youths), and in *Barrington* (two separate reports of the impersonation of the same minor celebrity).
 3 *R v Sims* [1946] KB 531, [1946] 1 All ER 697, is a very good example where four victims all alleged that they had been induced to sit with the accused in order to play cards, and the court stressed that 'whereas the jury might think one man might be telling an untruth, three or four are hardly likely to tell the same untruth unless they were conspiring together'.
 4 [1975] AC 421 at 444, [1974] 3 All ER 887 at 897.

Although Lord Cross agreed on this point, the other members of the House were more equivocal, and in *R v Scarrott*[5] the Court of Appeal was content to leave the matter to the discretion of the judge. The court was prepared to accede to the trial judge's view that the question could be ventilated in summing-up, and decided by the jury. It is submitted that the question is so important[6] that the procedure suggested by Lords Cross and Wilberforce should be adopted in all cases where there are grounds for suspecting concoction. The admissibility of similar fact evidence of this type is likely to be just as damaging to the accused as that of a disputed confession, and it is appropriate to pursue an analogous course. So if the defence alleges some such concoction and adduces some credible evidence of it, the prosecution should be required to satisfy the judge on a voir dire that there is no real possibility that such concoction has occurred. Such an approach was endorsed by the High Court of Australia in *Hoch v R*.[7] If the prosecution succeed on the voir dire the evidence should be admitted, but the defence remain free to attack its cogency, in much the same way as it remains free to attack the cogency of a confession admitted after a contested voir dire.

If the evidence emanates from one witness, it will also be less cogent for similar reasons, however many incidents are recounted and however similar their details, since it is little more difficult to concoct accounts of many incidents than to concoct an account of one.[8]

2. COMMISSION BY ACCUSED

Quite often the commission of an act constituting the crime cannot be denied. This applies to many cases of murder, rape, robbery, burglary and theft. In this situation the accused must usually seek to deny that he is the criminal. Here too the cases may be divided according to whether there is, or is not, direct testimony of the accused's commission of the crime. A very straightforward example of a situation in which there was no such direct testimony is provided by *R v Straffen*.[9] The accused had been immured in Broadmoor after being found unfit to plead to two charges of having killed two small girls without having molested them sexually, and then having left their bodies unconcealed where they could readily be discovered. He escaped, and soon afterwards while he was still in the vicinity of the hospital, a small girl was killed not having been molested sexually, and her body was left unconcealed in a place where it could readily be discovered. Straffen admitted having seen the girl, but denied he had killed her. The evidence was held to have been rightly admitted for the purpose of showing that Straffen was the murderer. It should be noted that it was agreed on all sides that the similarities between all of the crimes were very strong, and that the accused's involvement in the earlier crimes was established as a virtual certainty. The court argued that the evidence was admitted because it

5 [1978] QB 1016 at 1027, [1978] 1 All ER 672 at 680. See also *R v Narain (No 2)* [1988] 1 NZLR 593 at 595.
6 By diminishing the cogency and probative force of the evidence, see *Hoch v R* (1988) 81 ALR 225.
7 Above, and the analogy with confessions explicitly drawn by Dawson and Brennan JJ.
8 This consideration may have influenced the Court in *R v Tetlow* (1986) 27 ACR 198 to reject evidence of a course of previous injections of the same drug by the same accused upon the same victim over a continuing period culminating in the occasion charged.
9 [1952] 2 QB 911, [1952] 2 All ER 657.

showed the identity of the murderer. This is somewhat specious. In all criminal cases it is necessary to show that the man charged is the man who committed the relevant crime, and *Thompson* which the court relied upon differed in that there was there, as argued below, evidence of *identification* to be corroborated. It is the existence of cases like *Straffen*, where as Lord Cross put it in *Boardman* 'the evidence of the other murders . . . was simply evidence to show that Straffen was a man likely to commit a murder of that particular kind', that prevents unqualified acceptance of Lord Hailsham's view quoted above that the 'inadmissible chain of reasoning' inevitably leads to exclusion. If the chain is strong enough, and relevant enough to a live issue, evidence of bad disposition alone may, exceptionally, be admitted. It is however vital in this situation to be sure that the evidence is strong enough. It must identify the accused in the same sort of way as the discovery of his fingerprints at the scene of the crime. In *R v Mansfield*[10] the strength of the evidence could have been no more than barely sufficient. The accused was charged with offences arising out of three fires which occurred on his employer's premises. There was evidence that he was present at the seat of the fire on all three occasions, there was some weak evidence of suspicious behaviour by him, and there was similarly weak evidence that all of the fires had been started by the use of a similar, though in itself by no means peculiar, technique. It should be noted that here the accused's involvement in the other fires was denied, and the technique was not particularly unusual. So in those respects the evidence was much less strong than that in *Straffen*. The factor which must have tilted the balance was that the fires occurred in three different locations, and once it was accepted that an employee had started all three, it became clear that only two employees had been in all three locations, and there was no suggestion whatever that the other had been involved. *Mansfield* is a good illustration of the need to consider the similar fact evidence in the context of all of the other evidence in the case, which there strengthened its probative force considerably.[11]

It is more common for that other evidence of the accused's involvement to be the direct testimony of a victim. That was the situation in one of the pre-*Boardman* cases to reach the House of Lords. In *Thompson v R*[12] the accused was charged with offences of gross indecency involving two boys. According to their account he committed the offences with them in a public lavatory, and made an appointment to meet them there again. A trap was set. Thompson arrived at the arranged time and place. He spoke to the boys, gave them money, and then the trap was sprung. He was found to be carrying powder puffs,[13] and to have indecent photographs of boys in his lodgings. His defence was that he was not the man who had committed the offences, and that the boys had mis-identified him. The evidence of his disposition to homosexuality as shown by his possessions was admitted to corroborate the evidence of identification: 'That the boys should pick out as

---

10 [1978] 1 All ER 134, [1977] 1 WLR 1102.
11 See also *R v Mills* [1986] 1 Qd R 77 where there were only two possible assailants, and there was evidence of previous injury inflicted upon the same child by the accused on earlier occasions.
12 [1918] AC 221, [1918–19] All ER Rep 521.
13 Assumed by the court to indicate a disposition to homosexual practices.

the guilty person someone who, unknown to them, possessed these objects, confirms their accuracy.'[14]

It should be noted that in this sort of case, just because the similar fact evidence is not the sole means of identifying the accused it need not be quite so uniquely denominative of him. In *Thompson* the evidence showed the accused to have a disposition to homosexuality, or perhaps to paedophilia, but it went no further, and without the element of direct supporting testimony would certainly be decided differently today.[15] The importance of this factor was stressed in a number of other cases. One of the more influential was *R v Robinson* where the accused was charged in respect of two separate robberies. He was identified practising for one, and committing the other. The importance of these acts of identification was stressed: 'if Robinson is not a guilty man, he is a singularly unfortunate man. He is identified by different people, or said to be identified by entirely different people, in respect of two entirely different raids.'[16]

The strength of the inference depends, as in all such cases, upon the cogency of the evidence. Two important factors here are the certainty of the implication of the accused in both events, and the independence of the witnesses who testify to it.[17] Thus in *R v Tricoglus*,[18] although two of the acts were sufficiently similar and peculiar, the direct testimony of the accused's involvement in them was unsatisfactory. An example of a case in this category where the evidence was probably sufficiently strong only because it confirmed direct identification of the accused, is provided by *R v Mustafa*. The accused was charged with four offences involving the use of a stolen credit card to buy large quantities of frozen meat from specialist freezer stores. Apart from the identification testimony, there was evidence of finding a stolen credit card, of a different brand, and a paper containing attempts to forge its signature in the accused's dwelling. Despite the fact that it was a different card, a different signature, and that the attempted forgeries were not of consistently high quality, the evidence was admitted because: 'in the particular circumstances . . . the Access card evidence does bear a similarity to the Barclaycard frauds sufficiently striking to make it admissible in *corroboration of identification*.'[19]

3. VOLUNTARY ACT OF ACCUSED

The prosecution must always establish that the commission of the actus reus was voluntary. In the absence of some special line of defence this can usually

14 Lord Sumner at 233, 527. See also Viscount Finlay at 226, 523 'to show the probability of the truth of the boys' story as to identity', and Lord Atkinson at 224, 522 'to prove . . . that the boys were not making any mistake whatever in their identification of him'.
15 Although at the time some of their Lordships seemed to have regarded these traits as very much more unusal and peculiar than would be generally thought today, in *Boardman* Lord Cross said that the expression of such views in *Thompson* 'sounds nowadays like a voice from another world'. Evidence of things found in the accused's possession, used to support direct testimony, is often very weak, see also *Morris v R* (1983) 1 DLR (4th) 385.
16 Direction of trial judge, quoted only in (1953) 37 Cr App Rep 95 at 106.
17 This makes it very difficult to understand the reasoning in *Perkins v Jeffery* [1915] 2 KB 702, 25 Cox CC 59 where, on a charge of indecent exposure, the court was more ready to accept evidence by the complainant of previous exposure to her, than evidence by other female witnesses of exposure to them.
18 (1976) 65 Cr App Rep 16.
19 (1976) 65 Cr App Rep 16 at 31 (emphasis supplied).

be inferred from the nature of the act in question. Sometimes physical contact, capable of amounting to an indecent assault is claimed to have occurred involuntarily, and similar fact evidence can be adduced to show other cases of similar contact.[20] Occasionally, and usually in the last straits of desperation, the accused does not deny the commission of the relevant act, but denies all recollection of having done it. In some such cases similar fact evidence has been admitted to rebut this defence. This was the accused's line of defence in *R v Mortimer*[1] when charged with the murder of a female cyclist by driving a car at her. The court admitted evidence of his having driven at three other women cyclists at around the same time. This case seems to have been overlooked in *R v Harrison-Owen*[2] where the accused who had been found in a house at night after taking keys from a car outside, and who first gave a false explanation for being there and then attempted to run away, raised as a defence that he had no recollection of having entered the house. The trial judge took the initiative in having his long record of previous convictions for housebreaking and burglary put in. In the Court of Appeal Lord Goddard CJ took the view that this was to confuse accident and intent, apparently confining accident to the situation, like that in *Makin* or *Smith*, in which any actus reus was denied, and held that the evidence should have been excluded.[3] In the nature of things there can be no direct testimony from any other witness of the accused's mental processes, so no possibility of corroboration arises here.

4. INTENTION OF THE ACCUSED

Sometimes the criminality of an act depends upon the purpose for doing it. An early example of this sort of case is provided by *R v Bond* where the accused, a doctor, was charged in respect of the abortion of a girl whom he had impregnated. His defence was that the girl had spontaneously miscarried when he was engaged in a routine procedure, not designed to accomplish such a result. The prosecution was permitted to call another girl whom he had also impregnated, to testify to an unsuccessful attempt to abort her, to which she had been induced to submit by his claim that had 'put dozens of other girls right'. Although there was some division of opinion among the judges, the reasoning was succinctly expressed by Lawrence J:

> That the same accident should repeatedly occur to the same person is unusual, especially so when it confers a benefit on him. The degree of improbability will depend upon the number of times it is shown to have occurred and the similarity of the circumstances on each occasion.[4]

A steady trickle of similar cases has subsequently approved the admissibility

---

20   As in *R v Huijser* [1988] 1 NZLR 577.
 1   (1936) 25 Cr App Rep 150, although the court said that the evidence showed his intent, his defence was simply that his mind went blank and he did not know what he had done.
 2   [1951] 2 All ER 726, 35 Cr App Rep 108.
 3   It is interesting that both in this case, and in *R v Coombes* (1960) 45 Cr App Rep 36 where a similar point arose, the similar fact evidence comprised previous convictions, the facts of which were not elaborated.
 4   [1906] 2 KB 389 at 420, 21 Cox CC 252 at 273.

of similar fact evidence for this purpose.[5] It is less common to permit the prosecution to use similar fact evidence to rebut a defence of self-defence, though it equally relates to the motivation of an admitted voluntary act. It has been said that such evidence will only rarely be admissible, and a high requirement of similarity insisted upon.[6]

It is sometimes appropriate to show the state of knowledge of the accused as a step on the way to showing his intent. This line of reasoning is well illustrated by one of the oldest cases, *R v Francis*,[7] which involved a charge of attempting to obtain money from a pawnbroker by the false pretence that a diamond ring was genuine. Blackburn J admitted the evidence at first instance, and his decision was upheld by the Court for Crown Cases Reserved,[8] on the basis that the evidence of other attempts to pass false articles as genuine, including the same ring, showed that the accused was not mistaken about the falsity of the ring. In these cases it may not be necessary to show quite the same high degree of similarity as is required in cases where the establishment of an actus reus is in question. In *R v Ollis*[9] it was immaterial that the accused had been acquitted in respect of the conduct which was relied upon to establish knowledge of the state of his bank account.[10] Such a consideration may have motivated the court in *R v Rance and Herron*[11] to re-phrase the test so as to require 'positive probative value'. In that case the accused director of a building company was charged with making a corrupt payment to a local councillor in respect of securing a contract from the local authority. His defence was that he signed both the false authorisation and the cheque without knowing the true state of affairs. The prosecution was allowed to adduce evidence of two other transactions in which the accused had signed false papers for a similar purpose, though in one of them he had handed the money over in a parcel. It should perhaps be noted that there was direct testimony that he really did know the true state of affairs, and the similar fact evidence simply corroborated that testimony. Because it was immaterial to establishing such knowledge that the situations exhibiting it should be identical the use of the new form of words is unexceptionable. It is however important that it should not be allowed to weaken the rigour of the exclusionary rule when the evidence is relied upon for a different purpose, and where the probative force of the evidence is quite different.

---

5 For example, *Perkins v Jeffery* [1915] 2 KB 702, 25 Cox CC 59 (to show that exposure was with indecent intent); *R v Hall* [1952] 1 KB 302, [1952] 1 All ER 66 (on first two counts to show that handling of victim was with indecent intent); *R v Williams* (1986) 84 Cr App Rep 299 (to show that threats were intended to be taken seriously). See also *Thompson v R* (1989) 86 ALR 1 (to show that deaths apparently caused by a car accident were really murder by shooting); *R v Seaman* (1978) 67 Cr App Rep 234 (to show that removal of goods from self-service shop without paying was deliberate); *R v Lewis* (1982) 76 Cr App Rep 33 (on three counts to show that handling of victims was with indecent intent). In *R v Rodley* [1913] 3 KB 468 there was no suggestion that it was inappropriate to show the intent with which the breaking had been accomplished by similar fact evidence, the evidence was simply insufficiently probative of that intent.
6 *R v Beggs* [1989] Crim LR 898.
7 (1874) 43 LJMC 97.
8 This case was apparently overlooked when it was asserted in *Makin* that only one case had previously been decided in the Court for Crown Cases Reserved.
9 [1900] 2 QB 758, 19 Cox CC 554.
10 Though on the facts it is extremely difficult to disagree with the dissenting opinion of Bruce J, with whom Ridley J concurred.
11 (1975) 62 Cr App Rep 118.

E. ROLE OF DISCRETION[12]

As noted above, the rule excluding evidence of the accused's bad disposition extends back at least to the early years of the nineteenth century. There appears to be no English case in which any judicial discretion to exclude such evidence was mentioned before the beginning of the twentieth century.[13] Its appearance seems to derive from the judge's general control over the proceedings before him, and was for many years expressed in terms of judicial persuasion of counsel not to press for the admission of similar fact evidence even though strictly admissible.[14] Its development so soon after the decision in *Makin,* and the analogy of the cognate discretion in relation to cross-examination under the Criminal Evidence Act 1898, s 1(f), suggest that it was used to soften the rigidity with which the words of Lord Herschell so rapidly came to be interpreted. Under pressure from counsel the discretion metamorphosed from being one of persuasion to becoming one of exclusion.[15] This function was recognised by the Privy Council in *Noor Mohamed v R.*[16] Although no pronouncement on this aspect of the judge's discretion could form part of the ratio decidendi of the House of Lords in *R v Sang* it was recognised to exist, and to have an exclusionary function. Lord Scarman may even have intended to allude to the change in function in his remark that 'the discretion now extends further than was contemplated by Lord Halsbury LC and Lord Moulton in *R v Christie,* or even by Lord Simon in *Harris's* case'.[17]

In the same way as there existed two different versions of the function of any such discretion there also existed two different formulations of the circumstances in which it could be exercised. In *Noor Mohamed,* the first really authoritative asseveration of its exclusionary function, Lord Du Parq considered that it should be applied only to cases 'in which it would be unjust to admit evidence of a character gravely prejudicial to the accused even though there may be some tenuous ground for holding it technically admissible'.[18] This approach stresses the trifling probative value of the evidence to be excluded. The alternative formulation stresses the disproportion between probative force and prejudicial effect. In *R v Sang* Lord Fraser adverted to the discrepancy, and supported the latter formulation:

> The judge in these circumstances has a discretion to exclude the evidence not only if its probative weight is 'trifling' (see *Noor Mohamed v R*), but whenever its prejudicial effect would be 'out of proportion to [its] true evidential value': see *Harris v D P P,* Viscount Simon quoting Lord Moulton in *R v Christie.* I read the

---

12 See above ch IV section 2 part B. For fuller discussion, to which the editor is much indebted, see Pattenden *Judicial Discretion and Criminal Litigation* (1990) 235–243.

13 Such a discretion was referred to, but not exercised, by Darling J in *R v Ollis* [1900] 2 QB 758 at 780, 19 Cox CC 554 at 566. The earliest reported case in which the discretion seems to have been exercised is *R v Miller* (1901) 65 JP 313.

14 It was put in this way by Lords Moulton and Reading in *R v Christie* [1914] AC 545 at 559, 564, [1914–15] All ER Rep 63 at 69, 71. Although *Christie* was not itself a similar fact case, this view seems to have been anticipated in *R v Shellaker* [1914] 1 KB 414 at 418, 9 Cr App Rep 240 at 244. It was repeated in the House of Lords in this form by Viscount Simon in *Harris v D P P* [1952] AC 694 at 707, [1952] 1 All ER 1044 at 1048.

15 It was so treated by Humphreys J in *R v Cole* (1941) 28 Cr App Rep 43 at 51.

16 [1949] AC 182 at 192, [1949] 1 All ER 365 at 370.

17 [1980] AC 402 at 452, [1979] 2 All ER 1222 at 1243.

18 At 192, 370.

latter expression as meaning that the discretion can be exercised where the prejudicial value of the evidence would greatly exceed its probative value.[19]

It is interesting that only one member of the House of Lords in *Sang* had been party to the decision in *Boardman*, which, for perfectly good reasons, was not cited. It will be apparent from Lord Fraser's formulation of the discretion quoted above that there is a problem in reconciling it with Lord Wilberforce's formulation of the exclusionary rule in *Boardman* quoted earlier.[20] If the exclusionary rule is designed to balance probative force and prejudicial effect it is hard to see how there will ever be any evidence to which the discretion can, as formulated by Lord Fraser, ever apply.

It is submitted that *Boardman* is good authority for the proposition that the balancing of probative force and prejudicial effect is required by the exclusionary rule. Thus Lord Cross said:

> the reason for this general rule is not that the law regards such evidence as inherently irrelevant, but because it is believed that if it were generally admitted jurors would in many cases think that it was more relevant than it was—so that ... its prejudicial effect would outweigh its probative value ... In the end—although the admissibility of such evidence is a question of law not of discretion—the question ... must be one of degree.[1]

The problem arises because most of their Lordships also recognise the continued existence of a discretion to exclude, formulated in virtually identical terms. Thus Lord Salmon said that the trial judge: 'still, of course, has a discretion to exclude [relevant and admissible similar fact evidence] on the ground that its probative value is minimal and altogether outweighed by its likely prejudicial effect.'[2] A third view expressed by Lord Morris seems to have been that the two processes should take place simultaneously: 'at whatever stage a judge gives a ruling he must exercise his judgment and his discretion having in mind both the requirements of fairness and also the requirements of justice'.[3]

It has nowadays become increasingly realised that the notion of 'discretion' may be used in a number of different senses.[4] It may be used either in a 'strong' sense to recognise that its possessor has a choice of alternatives free of binding criteria, or in a weak sense to recognise that its possessor is bound by criteria, but criteria formulated in such a way that he has to exercise his personal judgment in determining whether or not they have been satisfied. In another context within the law of evidence it has been decided that the judge's task is of the latter type, and that the terminology of discretion is best

---

19 At 446, 1238.
20 Part C.
1 This was clearly the line taken by Lord Wilberforce, and Lord Hailsham also said, at 451, 904, 'the evidence is to be excluded under the first rule in *Makin* because its prejudicial effect may be more powerful than its probative effect.'
2 At 463, 913. Lord Hailsham also said at 453, 906 'The judge also has a discretion, not as a matter of law, but of good practice, to exclude evidence, whose prejudicial effect, though the evidence be technically admissible on the decided cases, may be so great in the particular circumstances as to outweigh its probative value to the extent that a verdict of guilty might be considered unsafe or unsatisfactory.'
3 At 439, 893.
4 For a theoretical examination of the use of the concept see Dworkin 'Model of Rules I' in *Taking Rights Seriously* (1977) at 27, 31.

eschewed to avoid possible confusion.[5] In this context the difference is between taking the view that the judge can properly decide that the prejudicial effect of evidence outweighs its probative value, and still admit it; and taking the view that once the judge has decided that the prejudicial effect outweighs its probative value he is bound to exclude it.[6] It is submitted that the latter is clearly the better view. It also accords better with the authorities both before and after *Boardman*. Thus in *R v Doughty* Lord Parker CJ had said:

> Where the evidence of indecency is tenuous to a degree and where, even if held to be indecent, it is a different form of indecency, then the court can only exercise its discretion in one way, by excluding that evidence, the reason being that its prejudicial value is quite overwhelming. The court feels . . . that . . . this discretion could properly be exercised in only one way, by excluding the evidence.[7]

It has been noted above that the House of Lords has rejected the notion that a proposition permitting exercise only in one way can properly be regarded as a discretion.[8] It seems therefore that as stated by Lord Cross in the passage quoted above from *Boardman*, and as stated by Lord Scarman in *Sang*, 'The law, not the judge's discretion, determines what is admissible evidence'.[9] Although perhaps less plangent, the same approach can be seen to inform the practical guidance for trial judges offered by the Court of Appeal in *R v Scarrott*.[10] The phraseology of that advice has clearly been chosen with great care, and it is significant to note the shift of emphasis between the description of the judge's role at the pre-arraignment stage where the judge has a real discretion,[11] and that of his role at the trial stage. In describing the former, Scarman LJ said:

> It is important to appreciate that *at this stage*, the pre-arraignment stage, the ultimate decision of the judge is *an exercise of judicial discretion* . . . *at this stage* the judge is taking no final decision as to the admissibility of evidence.

But in describing the latter, he said: 'it will *then* be for the judge to rule, in accordance with *the laws of evidence*, whether the evidence is admissible or not.'[12] It is significant that there is no further use of the word 'discretion' once the trial stage has been reached.[13] This is quite consistent with the view expressed by Devlin J in the influential case of *R v Miller*, though there in the

5 *R v Viola* [1982] 3 All ER 73 at 77, [1982] 1 WLR 1138 at 1142, in the not wholly dissimilar context of making a judgment about the fairness of cross-examination of a complainant in a case of rape about her sexual experience.
6 The argument becomes even stronger if the proposition is framed in the terms quoted above from Lord Salmon in *Boardman* and from Lord Fraser in *Sang*.
7 [1965] 1 All ER 560 at 562, [1965] 1 WLR 331 at 334. In *R v Novac* (1976) 65 Cr App Rep 107 at 111, Bridge LJ also suggests the discretion as being capable of exercise only one way.
8 See above ch IV section 2 part B noting the treatment of similar view advanced in *R v Flynn* [1963] 1 QB 729, [1961] 3 All ER 58, by the House of Lords in *Selvey v D P P* [1970] AC 304 at 331, [1968] 2 All ER 497 at 510.
9 At 454, 1245.
10 [1978] QB 1016, [1978] 1 All ER 672.
11 Partly because the decision has to be made upon an inadequate basis, and can be revised in the light of later developments.
12 At 1028, 681, emphasis supplied.
13 The Court of Appeal also avoided use of the word in its decision on this point in *R v Barrington* [1981] 1 All ER 1132, [1981] 1 WLR 419.

context of cross-examination, that: 'if the court is of the opinion that the prejudicial effect outweighs its relevance, then it has the power, and, indeed, the *duty* to exclude the question.'[14] It has also been held that the court has a duty to consider the question, and an appeal allowed where the trial judge failed to do so.[15]

It is worth considering the results of the contrary view that a discretion exists in the usual sense. As noted above such a view would justify a judge's decision to admit evidence even though he found that its prejudicial effect exceeded, or perhaps even greatly exceeded, its probative value. This may be regarded as fanciful, though even that tells significantly against any such view. It is not so fanciful to suppose that an appellate court might, despite disagreeing with the trial judge's assessment, nevertheless feel obliged to uphold his decision if he had taken the right considerations into account. Indeed this very situation occurred in *R v Mackie* where the Court of Appeal said: 'we agree that the prejudicial effect of the evidence admitted was enormous and far outweighed its value in proving that the child was frightened of the appellant', but then went on to decide that: 'the judge was entitled to exercise his discretion as he did and to admit this evidence'.[16] It is much easier to avoid such injustice elsewhere if exclusion is recognised to be by application of a rule, subject to the ordinary processes of appellate review.

Another possible consequence of regarding the discretion in the usual way relates to the effect of such a view upon the operation of the basic exclusionary rule. The only possible way of reconciling such a discretion with the rule, is to divorce the question of prejudicial effect from that of probative force. The rule then excludes only those cases where there is insufficient probative force, and the discretion excludes even those where it is sufficient, if that force is greatly outweighed by its prejudicial effect. It can then be argued that the existence of a discretion cast in such terms shows that some evidence of, to use Lord Salmon's formulation quoted above, 'minimal probative value', passes the test. It may next be possible to attempt to utilise the change of terminology in *R v Rance and Herron*[17] to 'positive probative value' to suggest that similar fact evidence is always, prima facie, admissible so long as it is barely relevant, and subsequent exclusion wholly reliant upon the operation of the trial judge's discretion, itself minimally subject to appellate control. Such an argument would seem very far-fetched had it not been adopted by the Full Court of the Supreme Court of Victoria in *R v Chee*.[18] It has however been subsequently disavowed both in Victoria,[19] and still more authoritatively by the High Court of Australia.[20]

It may thus be accepted that the similar facts rule operates, as Lord Wilberforce explained in *Boardman*, to exclude evidence the prejudicial effect

14 [1952] 2 All ER 667 at 669, 36 Cr App Rep 169 at 171, emphasis supplied.
15 *Cottle v R* [1977] AC 323 at 328. Although the term 'discretion' was employed, it seems clear that it was used in the loose sense to mean 'judgment'. No question of applying both rule and discretion arose, principally because no question of the admissibility of the evidence relating to one count on another was considered at all.
16 (1973) 57 Cr App Rep 453 at 464, 465.
17 (1975) 62 Cr App Rep 118.
18 [1980] VR 303. Criticised in Tapper 'Proof and Prejudice' in Campbell and Waller (eds) *Well and Truly Tried* (1982). Traces of a similar argument can be discerned in *R v Downes* [1981] Crim LR 174.
19 *R v Vaitos* (1982) 4 A Crim R 238 at 297.
20 *Perry v R* (1982) 44 ALR 449 at 453, 454, and a further attempt to resurrect it was quelled in no uncertain terms by the High Court of Australia in *Sutton v R* (1984) 51 ALR 435.

of which exceeds its probative force. Does this leave any role for the operation of an exclusionary discretion? Many commentators have argued that it does not.[1] This view appears not to be shared by very many judges.[2] In a sense this is unimportant. It does not matter very much that a discretion should be regarded as existing despite having been rendered redundant by the re-formulation of the exclusionary rule, so long at least as reasoning like that in *Chee* can be avoided. It remains to be considered whether a more useful role can be ascribed to such a discretion in this context. Two possibilities suggest themselves. The first is that there may still, as will be seen in the next section, be a role for such a discretion when the evidence showing the accused's bad disposition has been admitted under a statutory rule. The second is consequential upon the restriction of the common law rule as formulated here to the exclusion of evidence showing the accused's bad disposition *when that disposition constitutes an essential step in the process of reasoning*. This formulation then leaves simple relevance to govern admissibility when disposition forms no part of the chain of reasoning. It will nevertheless often be desirable to exclude such evidence to avoid the possibility of causing prejudice. If the accused's presence at the scene of a theft with which he is charged is supported by evidence of, say, his promiscuous homosexuality with others in the area at the time, it might well be thought right to exclude the evidence. Such an interpretation of the use of the discretion is also quite consistent with the decision of the Court of Appeal in *R v Mackie*[3] where the evidence was not admitted to show the accused's propensity, and where it was made quite clear that a discretion, and not a rule, was being applied, since the Court of Appeal refused to intervene once it was satisfied that the trial judge had taken the correct considerations into account, even though it disagreed with his judgment of them. Another case illustrating the usefulness of the discretion in this context is *R v Fitzpatrick*.[4] The accused was charged with two offences of indecency which occurred very soon after each other, perhaps within a three minute period. The Court of Criminal Appeal took the view that the only possible basis for the admission of evidence of the one on the other was that they occurred during one continuous period of sexual excitement. Such an argument may be regarded as falling outside the scope of the similar fact rule as defined here, but the court held that the trial judge should at least have considered the possible application of the discretion to exclude on the basis of the preponderance of possible prejudicial effect over probative value.

This view accordingly preserves a useful role for the discretion, and helps to explain the judicial re-affirmation of its continued existence. Its role has nevertheless diminished since *Boardman* swept away the rigid categorisation of admission and exclusion, and it may be expected to become progressively less prominent as the implications of the decision in *Boardman* become ever more apparent.

1 See for example, Cowen and Carter *Essays on the Law of Evidence* (1956) at 155; Hoffman 'Similar Facts after *Boardman*' (1975) 91 LQR 193 at 204; Eggleston *Evidence, Proof and Probability* (1978) at 82; Pattenden *Judicial Discretion and Criminal Litigation* (1990) at 240.
2 But see *Perry v R* (1982) 44 ALR 449 at 469 per Wilson J; and *Sutton v R* (1984) 51 ALR 435 at 439 per Gibbs CJ, and at 464 per Dawson J.
3 (1973) 57 Cr App Rep 453.
4 [1962] 3 All ER 840, [1963] 1 WLR 7.

F. REFORM OF THE RULE

As noted earlier in this chapter the English rule is a product of the common law, and has in its most recent manifestation in *Boardman* been adopted and approved throughout the Commonwealth. Apart from one small area[5] and one small jurisdiction[6] there has been little statutory intervention. In the United States the matter is largely governed by statute, in the case of the Federal jurisdiction by rr 403 and 404 of the Federal Rules. They broadly correspond to the English common law rule,[7] and have made no significant improvement in dealing with the problem.[8] It is thus necessary to consider the various suggestions made by law reform bodies.

The only one to suggest any really radical change was the English Criminal Law Revision Committee in its 11th Report.[9]

A number of possibilities were considered. Three were discussed in some detail. Under the first of these[10] evidence of the commission by the accused of any other offence falling into the same class as that with which he was currently charged would be admitted. The committee was prepared to draft broad classes of offence, though they recognised that there would be difficult overlaps, for example rape often involves both sex and violence. This was rejected on the basis that it would be too prejudicial to the accused, might undermine the confidence of the public and might discourage criminals from reforming. It is not at all clear how it would have worked because it was explicitly recognised that it would not be necessary that the evidence in respect of the other offences be similar to that in the instant case. It is unclear whether the proposal was intended as an addition to, or as a substitution for, the existing law. This would mean that the other offence could always be proved if it fell into the appropriate class, irrespective of the very greatest difference in circumstances, a serious danger in view of the enormous width of the classification proposed, and irrespective of the defence raised by the accused. Conversely it could never be proved if it fell into a different class, or indeed in no class at all because no offence was committed,[11] however relevant it might be in view of the particular circumstances, or of the defence raised by the accused.

The second radical proposal was that the accused's convictions should be read out at the beginning of the trial.[12] Here it was made clear that the proposal would have been complementary to any other rules permitting relevant similar fact evidence to be adduced. This proposal was probably intended to have more effect on the rules about cross-examination than on the similar fact rules. It was rejected on the basis that it would be even more inclined than the previous proposal to cause prejudice, injustice and despair.

---

5 Proof of mens rea on handling charges under Theft Act 1968, s 27(3).
6 Evidence Ordinance (Singapore), also applicable in Christmas and Cocos (Keeling) Islands.
7 Though it must be remembered that they are wider in scope in governing also cross-examination of the accused, in the absence of any enactment corresponding to Criminal Evidence Act 1898, s 1(f), and civil cases, which are still often heard by juries.
8 For short summaries from a British perspective see Australia Law Commission Research Paper 11 'Character and Conduct' 71–9, and Tapper 'Proof and Prejudice' in Campbell and Waller (eds) *Well and Truly Tried* (1982) 188–196.
9 Cmnd 4991.
10 See para 89.
11 In a case like *Barrington* for example.
12 Para 90.

The proposal which recommended itself to the committee was more complicated.[13] In part it represented a codification of the existing law as understood by the committee.[14] It was felt desirable to establish a form of words which could provide a fresh starting point, free from the necessity to conform to existing decisions.[15] The major innovation was to extend the admissibility of similar fact evidence in cases where the accused admitted the conduct in respect of which he was charged. It has been shown above that in practice similar fact evidence is under the existing rules more readily admitted in such situations. If such admissibility is to be taken still further it runs the risk of distorting the process of the trial. The problem is that it then gives the accused every incentive to deny his involvement in the crime. The committee anticipated this objection, but felt that it was unlikely to cause substantial difficulty since it would usually be difficult to combine the accused's real defence, of say absence of intent, with a denial of commission of the relevant acts. While this may be true it is certainly arguable that the gain is not worth the price of the dilemma into which an accused who really had no criminal intent will be placed if he has a long record of previous convictions. The committee also found the relevant provisions difficult to draft,[16] and found their form subjected to some criticism.[17] One of the situations which they most wished to change by this proposal was, they thought, exemplified in *R v Slender*,[18] where the prosecution was prevented from adducing evidence that the accused had previously obtained money by the false pretence that he needed it to get to Cheltenham, upon the current charge that he had obtained money by the false pretence that he needed it to spend the night in Cheltenham. It is submitted that the evidence ought to have been regarded as admissible under the existing rules, and that the proposed change would be quite uncertain of achieving a better result since there could be endless debate about precisely what the accused would have to admit before he could be regarded as admitting the conduct in respect of which he was charged. This proposal excited considerable opposition, not least from legally qualified members of the House of Lords.[19] It has found no place in the Police and Criminal Evidence Act 1984. As an ancillary part of its recommendations on this matter the committee provided for the admission in evidence of the accused's convictions in certain circumstances. It was noted in ch II above that this part of the committee's draft clause has been incorporated into the new Act. This tends to confirm the view that the committee's general recommendations are now most unlikely to be enacted.[20]

In other Commonwealth countries where the law has been under review no similarly radical proposals have been made. In Canada dispute has arisen about the desirability even of enacting a general statement of the existing

13 Paras 91–101, draft Bill cl 3.
14 Professor Cross, a member of the committee, felt that it would have been better for the committee to have adopted an approach closer to that taken here, see Cross 'Clause 3 of the Draft Criminal Evidence Bill, Research and Codification' [1973] Crim LR 400.
15 Para 100.
16 See Cross [1973] Crim LR 400.
17 See Tapper 36 MLR 56.
18 [1938] 2 All ER 387, 26 Cr App Rep 155; though there is room for doubt about the true facts in that case.
19 338 H L Official Report (5th series) cols 1546–678.
20 As anticipated by Professor Cross, see [1973] Crim LR 400.

position,[1] while in Australia the Law Reform Commission has contented itself with the provision of guidelines to assist in striking the balance between probative force and prejudicial effect which it regards as the most accurate representation of the current state of the law.[2]

SECTION 2. STATUTORY PROVISIONS

Two statutes abrogate the rule discussed in this section in the particular circumstances to which they apply, namely s 1(2) of the Official Secrets Act 1911, and s 27(3) of the Theft Act 1968.

Section 1(1) of the Official Secrets Act 1911 (as amended by the Official Secrets Act 1920), punishes various forms of spying if the accused's purpose was prejudicial to the State. Section 1(2) provides that it shall not be necessary to show that the accused person was guilty of any particular act tending to show a purpose prejudicial to the safety or interests of the State and, notwithstanding that no such act is proved against him, he may be convicted if, from the circumstances of the case, or his conduct, or his known character as proved, it appears that his purpose was a purpose prejudicial to the safety or interests of the State. The wording of this subsection shows that evidence of the accused's misconduct may be given although it is relevant only because it shows that he is the kind of man whose purpose in doing certain acts might be of the type proscribed by the statute.

Section 27(3) of the Theft Act 1968, reads as follows:

> Where a person is being proceeded against for handling stolen goods (but not for any offence other than handling stolen goods), then at any stage of the proceedings, if evidence has been given of his having or arranging to have in his possession the goods the subject of the charge, or of his undertaking or assisting in, or arranging to undertake or assist in, their retention, removal, disposal or realisation, the following evidence shall be admissible for the purpose of proving that he knew or believed the goods to be stolen goods:
>
> (a) evidence that he has had in his possession, or has undertaken or assisted in the retention, removal, disposal or realisation of, stolen goods from any theft taking place not earlier than twelve months before the offence charged; and
> (b) (provided that seven day's notice in writing has been given to him of the intention to prove the conviction) evidence that he has within the five years preceding the date of the offence charged been convicted of theft or handling stolen goods.

The subsection re-enacts with some significant differences,[3] s 43(1) of the Larceny Act 1916, which, in its turn, re-enacted s 19 of the Prevention of Crimes Act 1871. Section 19 abrogated the effect of the decision in *R v Oddy*.[4] In that case, the third count of the indictment charged the accused with knowingly receiving stolen cloth which was found in his possession shortly after the theft, and the trial judge admitted evidence of the fact that other

---

1 The Canadian Law Reform Commission recommended such legislation in its 1975 Report, the Joint Task Force was unanimous in rejecting this recommendation in 1980, but the Uniform Law Conference in 1981 did decide to enact legislation.
2 Research Paper No 11 'Character and Conduct' (1982) proposal 6.
3 On which see the 8th Report of the Criminal Law Revision Committee (Cmnd 2977, 1966), paras 157–9.
4 (1851) 2 Den 264. If the facts were to recur the decision would still be the same because there were also counts for theft.

cloth which had been stolen three months previously was also found in the accused's house. The Court for Crown Cases Reserved held that he ought not to have done so, as the evidence merely went to show that the accused was in the habit of receiving stolen cloth. It would have been different if there had been some further connecting link between the two items of evidence. For example, if the cloth had been stolen by the same person the fact of the discovery of both pieces in the accused's house would have been relevant as suggesting the existence of some arrangement for its disposal between the thief and the receiver.[5] Proof of guilty knowledge is, however, a notoriously difficult matter, in a receiving case, and the statutory provisions may be regarded as supplementary to the case-law concerning the provisional presumption arising from the accused's possession of the property mentioned in the indictment shortly after the theft.[6]

This provision has proved so unpopular with English judges as to be given a highly restricted interpretation.[7] In particular there has been anxiety that it be restricted to proof of guilty knowledge,[8] and, despite the apparently mandatory language, the court has invested itself with, and applied, discretion to exclude evidence should there be any danger of this restriction being undermined.[9] Similar motives have led to the application of a strictly literal construction being placed upon the ambit of the evidence admitted under the provision. Thus in the case of s 27(3)(a) it has been determined that no surrounding detail of the previous possession can be adduced beyond the barest description of the relevant goods.[10] Similarly in relation to s 27(3)(b) no more than the formal details of the relevant conviction may be adduced, and in this case not extending even to a description of the relevant goods.[11] It has been argued[12] that this effort has been counter-productive since the elimination of detail makes it very difficult for the jury to evaluate the true significance of the evidence, and gives rise to the possibility of exacerbating the very prejudice which it is designed to eliminate. The prosecution is in no way hampered since it can adduce any detail which is sufficiently relevant under the ordinary similar facts rules which the provision supplements, while the accused has no ready means to avoid the prejudice since it would hardly help his cause to draw attention to the variety and versatility of his previous criminal conduct.

SECTION 3. CIVIL CASES

Although some early civil cases[13] rejected similar fact evidence as *res inter alios acta*, it was soon accepted that the rule of exclusion was certainly no

---

5 *R v Dunn* (1826) 1 Mood CC 146; *R v Mansfield* (1841) Car & M 140; *R v Powell* (1909) 3 Cr App Rep 1. Admissibility at common law has been unaffected by the statutes.
6 See p 32, above.
7 It is no more popular in its local form in Australia, see *R v Cresswell* (1987) 8 NSWLR 56 where faint ambiguity in the drafting of the starting point for time beginning to run was resolved in favour of inadmissibility.
8 *R v Wilkins* (1975) 60 Cr App Rep 300; *R v Bradley* (1979) 70 Cr App Rep 200.
9 *R v Herron* [1966] 2 All ER 26; see above p 182.
10 *R v Wood* (1987) 85 Cr App Rep 287, preferring *R v Bradley* (1979) 70 Cr App Rep 200 to *R v Smith* [1918] 2 KB 415.
11 *R v Fowler* (1987) 86 Cr App Rep 219; cp *R v Brosnan* [1951] NZLR 1030 at 1039.
12 By Smith in his note in the Criminal Law Review to the case of *R v Bradley* [1980] Crim LR 173, and Munday 'Handling the Evidential Exception' [1988] Crim LR 345.
13 *Spencely v De Willott* (1806) 7 East 108 (usurious contracts); *Holcombe v Hewson* (1810) 2 Camp 391 (bad beer).

stricter than that in criminal cases.[14] The real question was whether there was a special rule of exclusion at all, or whether it were not rather a question of simple relevance in each case. In some cases the nature of the issue determined the question in favour of admissibility, as Stephen J remarked in *Brown v Eastern and Midlands Rly Co*: 'when the question is whether a particular act is a public nuisance, it is difficult to see how it can be proved to be so except by shewing cases in which it has interfered with a public right'.[15] Similarly evidence of previous complaints about accidents was admitted to show that the proprietors of a dock knew of its dangerous condition,[16] and previous outbreaks of skin complaints among the defendant barber's customers to show his negligent practice.[17]

The enactment of enforceable rights against discrimination has extended the admissibility of similar fact evidence in civil proceedings. Thus in *West Midlands Passenger Executive v Singh*[18] the Court of Appeal accepted that statistical evidence of consistent employment practice in relation to particular ethnic groups was both necessary and relevant to prove discrimination, and an order for discovery was upheld. In other cases where a claim does not depend upon showing consistent practice, but where previous malpractice might be sought to be used in cross-examination such discovery may be regarded as oppressive.[19] It should be noted however that in the criminal sphere there is no requirement that systematic conduct need be alleged as part of the definition of the offence in order for similar fact evidence to be admitted.[20] The general tendency has indeed been for further relaxation. In more recent times there has been further relaxation of the exclusionary rules in civil cases, and Lord Reid doubted whether the same considerations which justified the rule in criminal cases applied in the civil law.[1] The most authoritative recent statement of the position was made by Lord Denning MR in *Mood Music Publishing Co Ltd v de Wolfe*. The plaintiffs in an action for infringement of copyright wished to tender evidence of previous infringements of copyright by the defendant. The trial judge decided the question of admissibility on considerations of ordinary relevance without reference to any special exclusionary rule. In this he was upheld by the Court of Appeal, on the basis that no more than such relevance was required in civil cases by contrast with criminal cases:

> The criminal courts have been very careful not to admit such evidence unless its probative value is so strong that it should be received in the interests of justice; and its admission will not operate unfairly to the accused. In civil cases the courts will admit evidence of similar facts if it is logically probative, that is if it is logically relevant in determining the matter which is in issue; provided that it is not

---

14 *Blake v Albion Life Assurance Society* (1878) 4 CPD 94 (fraudulent trading). See also *Thorpe v Greater Manchester Chief Constable* [1989] NLJR 467 (certificate of the results of disciplinary proceedings involving acts of similar misconduct by the relevant policemen).
15 (1889) 22 QBD 391 at 393, 58 LJQB 212 at 214.
16 *Moore v Ransome's Dock* (1898) 14 TLR 539. See also *McKenna v Greco* (1981) 125 DLR (3d) 268 (previous violence in defendant's hotel to show knowledge of likelihood of violence).
17 *Hales v Kerr* [1908] 2 KB 601, 77 LJKB 870.
18 [1988] 2 All ER 873.
19 See *Thorpe v Greater Manchester Chief Constable* [1989] 2 All ER 827. See also *Kennedy v Dodson* [1895] 1 Ch 334.
20 See especially *R v Bond* [1906] 2 KB 389.
 1 *Cummings (McWilliams) v Sir William Arrol & Co* [1962] 1 All ER 623 at 630, [1962] 1 WLR 295 at 305.

oppressive or unfair to the other side; and also that the other side has fair notice of it and is able to deal with it.[2]

This passage may be interpreted as applying in civil cases a similar sort of balancing approach to the rules for admissibility of similar fact evidence as applies in criminal cases. The factor favouring admissibility is the probative force of the evidence. Lord Denning's remarks seem to suggest that simple relevance is sufficient, but some cases seem to take a strict view of the circumstances in which other discreditable conduct is relevant, denying such categorisation to other acts of similar police misconduct,[3] fraudulent overcharging for similar services on other occasions,[4] other cases of cattle suffering disease after consuming the defendant's feed,[5] and other fraudulent misrepresentations made to different tenants in respect of the same building development.[6] However, in other cases fraudulent representations to the purchasers of shares,[7] and forgeries of the signatures of some other members of the same family, have been regarded as sufficiently relevant.[8] As in criminal cases the estimation of probative force is a complex one depending upon the precise circumstances of the case and the issues being contested. The factors to be weighed against such probative effect are however different on account of the peculiar position of the accused in criminal cases. There is very high authority accounting for the existence of an exclusionary discretion in criminal cases solely by reference to the accused's vulnerability to prejudice.[9] It has accordingly been held in Australia that in civil cases there is no comparable exclusionary discretion in respect of similar fact evidence on the basis of an excess of prejudice over probative force.[10] It is significant that Lord Denning refers not to prejudice, but to oppression and unfairness. This approach has been elaborated by Warner J in *Berger v Raymond & Sun Ltd*[11] where a question of forgery by a defendant of some share transfers was in issue. Evidence of other transfers alleged to have been forged by the defendant was adduced. Warner J took the view that *Mood Music* had equated the test for the admissibility of similar fact evidence in criminal and civil cases,[12] but that the discretion to exclude operated upon a different basis. He adverted to such factors as the burden imposed upon the defendant in adducing evidence, the lengthening of the trial, and the undesirability of re-litigating issues disposed of in previous proceedings. Given the weight of authority opposed to the existence of an exclusionary discretion in civil proceedings it seems that Warner J was employing the term to indicate

---

2 [1976] Ch 119 at 127, [1976] 1 All ER 763 at 766.
3 *Thorpe v Greater Manchester Chief Constable*, above.
4 *British Coal Corpn v Dennis Rye Ltd* (1988) Times, 7 March.
5 *Laubscher v National Foods Ltd* 1986 (1) SA 553.
6 *HW Thompson Investments Pty Ltd v Allen Property Services Ltd* (1984) 77 FLR 254 refusing to follow earlier decisions admitting such evidence; *Peet & Co Ltd v Rocci* [1985] WAR 164.
7 *MacDonald v Canada Kelp Co Ltd* (1973) 39 DLR (3d) 617.
8 *Berger v Raymond & Son Ltd* [1984] 1 WLR 625.
9 *R v Christie* [1914] AC 545 at 559, 564, [1914–15] All ER Rep 63 at 69, 71; *Ibrahim v R* [1914] AC 599 at 609, [1914–15] All ER Rep 874 at 878. See further p 180 above.
10 *Manenti v Melbourne Tramways* [1954] VLR 115 at 118, approved by the full court in *David Syme & Co Ltd v Mather* [1977] VR 516 at 531. See also Forbes 'Extent of the Judicial Discretion to Reject Prejudicial Evidence in Civil Cases' (1988) 62 ALJ 211.
11 [1984] 1 WLR 625.
12 Relying also upon the decision of the Court of Appeal in *Sattin v National Union Bank* (1978) 122 Sol Jo 367 (evidence of previous loss of jewellery by bank admissible to prove negligence in respect of the instant loss).

factors relevant to the exercise of the rule as to admissibility which were incapable of precise determination, and hence ultimately depended upon the assessment of the judge.[13] Indeed the affirmation by Warner J of the essential similarity of the approach in both criminal and civil cases lends weight to the view that exclusion is by rule, albeit one involving the assessment of imprecise elements, and not by discretion.

13 His remarks seem to have been so interpreted by Carter J in *Taylor v Harvey* [1986] 2 Qd R 137.

CHAPTER X

Criminal Evidence Act 1898

Section 2 of this chapter is mainly a gloss on the last one, for s 1(f) of the Criminal Evidence Act 1898 defines the extent to which the accused may be cross-examined on the subject of his disposition and character; some points of a more general nature are discussed in section 1.

SECTION 1. THE GENERAL EFFECT OF THE ACT

We have already seen how s 1 of the Act made the accused and his spouse competent witnesses for the defence in all criminal cases,[1] and the limited extent to which the accused's spouse is compellable as a witness on his behalf, or competent or compellable as a witness for the prosecution or a co-accused has likewise been considered.[2] Two matters will be considered, first, the position of an accused who does not give evidence, and second, the position of one who does.

Section 1(a) of the Act provides that the person charged can be called as a witness only on his own application. It is doubtful whether many people in 1898 would have favoured a provision under which the accused would have become a compellable witness in the sense that he would be liable to imprisonment for contempt if he refused to answer questions, and it is difficult to believe that their numbers have greatly increased in the meantime. Nevertheless, in any system under which the accused is neither incompetent to give evidence on his own behalf nor compellable to answer questions put to him by the prosecution or the judge, adverse inferences are liable to be drawn from his failure to go into the witness box. This danger would not exist if the tribunal of fact were unaware of the accused's right to give evidence if he chooses to do so, but from the coming into force of the Act of 1898 onwards, magistrates have not been in this state of ignorance, and it is improbable that every member of any jury is in such a state to-day. The Act of 1898 can thus be said to have confronted the accused with the choice of opting not to give evidence with the consequential risk that adverse inferences will be drawn, or going into the witness box and thus exposing himself to cross-examination which might cause him to incriminate himself. Reflections of this nature even led some lawyers to regard the Act as a retrograde step. After it had been in force for as long as 16 years Mr Ernest Williams wrote:

---

1 Ch V.
2 Ch V. See Police and Criminal Evidence Act 1984, s 80.

No sooner have we elaborated precautions for insuring the voluntary character of confessions than we strike a blow at the underlying principle, and substitute the moral compulsion of the witness box for the physical compulsion of the rack.[3]

No present day lawyer would seriously advocate the repeal without replacement of the 1898 Act, but it certainly raises problems concerning an accused who chooses not to testify.

The problem raised by the Act with regard to an accused who does choose to testify concerns the position of an accused with a criminal record. Is he to be liable to cross-examination to credit on his previous convictions and bad character like any other witness, or is he to be protected against such cross-examination and, if so, to what extent?

It should be noted that despite reference in s 1 of the Criminal Evidence Act 1898 to a 'person charged with an offence' it seems that it applies not so much to an 'offence', as to an indictment,[4] so that an accused charged on an indictment containing more than one count cannot elect to testify upon some counts, but not upon others. Once he has elected to testify as to one, he is exposed to cross-examination as to all, unprotected as to the others by the privilege against self incrimination.[5]

A. THE ACCUSED WHO DOES NOT GIVE EVIDENCE

If common sense were to be given free rein it would be proper, once an accused is a competent witness, to draw inferences from his failure to testify in certain circumstances. One obvious example would be a murder case in which the accused was proved to have been in the deceased's company shortly before his death; another would be a case of theft or handling in which the accused was found in possession of the stolen goods, and there are many others. But one of the objects of the law of evidence is to prevent common sense from having a free rein because there are cases in which to permit it might lead to an unjust result. The accused might refrain from testifying, not because he was guilty, but because he feared cross-examination on his record, wished to protect a friend or was afraid that he might be obliged to disclose some compromising information about his actions, such as the fact that he had spent the night with his mistress. One answer to the first point is to prohibit the cross-examination of the accused on his record unless he is sufficiently misguided to say that he has a good character, but we shall see that this is not to everybody's taste. So far as the other points are concerned, there are those who would rest content with Bentham's observation that 'probabilities and not improbabilities constitute the true ground of legislative practice;'[6] but it would be idle to deny that these points are taken very seriously by a large number of people.

1. POSSIBLE COURSES

In the case of a trial by jury, three courses were open to the framers of the legislation of 1898. The first would have been to prohibit any comment by

3 (1914) 30 LQR 297.
4 In which several counts may validly be joined.
5 *R v Phillips* (1987) 86 Cr App Rep 18.
6 *Works* (Bowring edn) v 7, p 27.

the judge or prosecution on the accused's failure to testify; the second would have been simply to prohibit comment by the prosecution; and the third would have been to make an express provision that the judge could, if he thought fit, draw the jury's attention to such inferences as might properly be drawn from the accused's failure to testify. The first course was ultimately adopted by the legislature of New South Wales,[7] and a provision permitting comment either by the judge or the prosecution was held to be an infringement of the fifth amendment of the United States Constitution in *Griffin v California*[8] by rendering it costly for the accused to exercise his privilege not to be a witness against himself. The second course is that adopted by the Act. The third course was recommended in the 11th Report of the Criminal Law Revision Committee.[9]

It is by no means clear that the first course would have been particularly advantageous to the accused. In the words of the dissenting judgment in *Griffin*'s case:

> How can it be said that the inferences drawn by a jury will be more detrimental to a defendant under the limiting and carefully controlling language of the instruction here involved than would result if the jury were left to roam at large with only its untutored instinct to guide it, to draw from the defendant's silence broad inferences of guilt.[10]

The answer of the majority was: 'What the jury may infer, given no help from the court, is one thing. What it may infer when the court solemnises the silence of the accused into evidence against him is quite another.'[11]

2. JUDICIAL COMMENT[12]

Section 1(b) of the 1898 Act provided that the failure of any person charged with an offence to give evidence shall not be made the subject of any comment by the prosecution.[13] So far as counsel is concerned the ban is absolute, and prohibits all comment by the prosecution, favourable or unfavourable.[14] The Act had not been in force for very long before the courts decided, on the principle *expressio unius est exclusio alterius*, that there

---

7 Crimes Act 1900, s 407(2), though this has not by any means insulated the courts from consideration of alleged comment, see for a very strong example *R v Greciun-King* (1981) 4 A Crim R 88. The judge is released from restriction if any such comment is made by a co-accused.

8 380 US 606 (1965). But see *US v Robinson* 108 S CtR 864 (1988) permitting prosecutional comment in response to an explicit claim that the accused had not been given an opportunity to answer the charge against him.

9 Para 110f.

10 380 US 621.

11 380 US 614.

12 For comment on the accused's silence before trial, see p 34 above; for comment on the accused's failure to call a witness see *R v Gallagher* [1974] 3 All ER 118, [1974] 1 WLR 1204 and *R v Staines* (1974) 60 Cr App Rep 160; for comment on failure to testify or to put in cross-examination at preliminary proceedings a defence advanced for the first time at the trial see *R v Maiden and Petty* (1988) 35 ACR 346.

13 Police and Criminal Evidence Act 1984, s 80(8), extends the prohibition to comment upon the failure to testify of the accused's spouse; for comment on failure to call a spouse see *R v Naudeer* [1984] 3 All ER 1036.

14 *R v Everelt*; *R v Riley* (1989) Times, 29 December, disapproving any suggestion to the contrary in *R v Brown and Routh* [1983] Crim LR 38.

was no ban on comment by the judge.[15] For some time it appears to have been thought that the decision when, and how, to comment were within the unfettered discretion of the judge,[16] but it is now clear that the discretion is subject to appellate control.[17] The reported decisions most certainly do not suggest any tendency on the part of English judges to 'solemnise the silence of the accused into evidence against him.'

In *R v Mutch*,[18] the Court of Appeal concluded that, in almost every case, the comment should take the form described by Lord Parker CJ in *R v Bathhurst*.[19] Lord Parker had said that the jury should be told, if the judge were minded to make any comment at all, that:

> the accused is not bound to give evidence, that he can sit back and see if the prosecution have proved their case, and that, while the jury have been deprived of the opportunity of hearing his story tested in cross-examination, the one thing they must not do is assume that he is guilty because he has not gone into the witness box.

Bathhurst's case was one in which diminished responsibility was pleaded in answer to a murder charge, and the conviction was quashed because the judge had gone too far in commenting on the accused's failure to testify. It was recognised that the number of diminished responsibility cases in which any comment should be made must be small, but it was also pointed out that, when comment is proper, it must take a different form in a case in which the burden of proof is borne by the accused.[20]

The conviction was also quashed in *R v Mutch*, a case of robbery in which the defence was a simple denial, because the trial judge had suggested that the jury might draw unfavourable inferences from the fact that the accused had not been called to suggest an innocent explanation of facts proved by the prosecution. The Court of Appeal recognised that there were such cases in which a direction might be proper, but these were cases in which the undisputed or clearly established facts involved the accused to such an extent as to call for an innocent explanation if there were one.[1]

In *R v Sparrow*,[2] the Court of Appeal recognised that the interests of justice called for a strong comment. Someone charged as a joint principal in a murder case did not give evidence in support of his plea that he was guilty of manslaughter only because he had agreed with his co-accused that the latter's gun should be used only to frighten, not to shoot at, anyone attempting to apprehend them and did not go into the witness box to support it. Even so, the Court, while applying the proviso to s 2(1) of the Criminal Appeal Act 1968, had no doubt that the trial judge had erred in suggesting

15 *R v Rhodes* [1899] 1 QB 77; on the same principle it has been held that comment on behalf of a co-accused is permissible (*R v Wickham, R v Ferrara* and *R v Bean* (1971) 55 Cr App Rep 199); and for a very full discussion of the English antecedents of the American rule in the latter context see *De Luna v US* 308 F 2d 140 (1962).
16 *R v Voisin* [1918] 1 KB 531 at 536.
17 *Waugh v R* [1950] AC 203.
18 [1973] 1 All ER 178.
19 [1968] 2 QB 99, [1968] 1 All ER 1175.
20 'He [the accused] is not bound to go into the witness box, no-one can force him to go into the witness box, but the burden is upon him, and if he does not, he runs the risk of not being able to prove his case.'
1 *R v Corrie and Watson* (1904) 68 JP 294; *R v Bernard* (1908) 1 Cr App Rep 218.
2 [1973] 2 All ER 129, [1973] 1 WLR 488.

that it was essential for the accused to go into the witness box in order that such a plea should succeed.[3]

All that can be said on the authorities is that the questions whether the judge should make any comment, and how far he should go in commenting, depend on the particular facts, and that it is essential for the judge to make two things plain to the jury, first, that the accused has a right not to testify,[4] second, that they must not assume that he is guilty because he does not do so. *R v Sparrow* also decides that the mere fact that the judicial comment on this failure occurs several times in the course of the summing up does not render it improper.

3. THE RECOMMENDATION OF THE CRIMINAL LAW REVISION COMMITTEE

Whilst there are no doubt many people who consider that the present English law represents the best solution to the problem of ensuring that justice is done to an accused who chooses not to give evidence, it has two defects. The first is the comparatively minor one that it is too vague on the subject to the extent to which the judge can go when he is minded to comment; the second, and far more serious defect is that the law generates the myth that there is a distinction between conferring on a judge the power to comment on the failure of an accused to testify and permitting him to point out to a jury what inferences could, in all the circumstances, be properly drawn from that fact, while leaving it to them to decide whether such inferences should be drawn. Even the superficially mild reminder that the jury has been deprived of the opportunity of hearing the accused's story tested in cross-examination is an invitation to infer that he has so little confidence in his story that he is not prepared to be cross-examined upon it, unaccompanied by the observation that there may be other reasons for not wishing to be cross-examined. The provision in cl 5(3) of the draft Bill attached to the 11th Report of the Criminal Law Revision Committee that the court[5] or jury, in determining whether the accused is guilty of the offence charged, may draw such inferences from his failure to testify as appear proper at least had the merit of remedying the two defects which have been mentioned.

Two objections, which may only amount to one, were raised against the proposal. They are that it would violate the accused's 'right to silence', and relieve the prosecution of the burden of proving the accused's guilt. The right to silence is a right not to be obliged to answer, or to be pressurised into answering, questions, and it was said that the proposal of the Criminal Law Revision Committee would have increased the pressure on the accused to assume the obligation of answering questions by going into the witness box. It was also said that the burden of proving his innocence would have been shifted to the accused if the court or jury were empowered to draw inferences from his failure to testify. These objections seem to be more appropriate to

---

3 It seems however that even counsel is entitled to draw attention to the fact that the prosecution evidence has been allowed to go uncontradicted, and to suggest possible explanations which might have been advanced, *R v Brown and Routh* [1983] Crim LR 38.

4 *R v Davison* [1972] 3 All ER 1121, [1972] 1 WLR 1540.

5 Ie a magistrates' court trying a case summarily. This has been recognised to represent the law in New Zealand, see *Trompert v Police* [1985] 1 NZLR 357.

the granting by the Act of 1898 to the accused of the option to testify than to the proposal of the Criminal Law Revision Committee. Inferences are bound to be drawn from the accused's failure to give evidence, and to that extent the Act of 1898 lightened the prosecution's burden of proof. The real choice seems to be between the prohibition of comment by the judge as well as the prosecution and a provision of a kind proposed by the Criminal Law Revision Committee. A provision, such as that which exists in some Commonwealth jurisdictions, including Queensland, that comment may come from the prosecution as well as the judge, would merely tend to perpetuate the myth that there is a rational distinction between commenting on, and pointing to inferences that can be properly drawn from, the accused's failure to testify. Under the committee's proposal, just as much as under the present law, it would have been necessary for the judge to have insisted that a direct inference of guilt must never be drawn from this failure; it simply detracts from the weight of any special defence that the accused may raise and, in some, but by no means all, circumstances, adds to the weight of the prosecution's case.[6] In Singapore the accused may formally be called upon to testify, and warned that his failure to do so may entitle adverse inferences to be drawn.[7] The Privy Council, in construing this provision, has expressed the view that such inferences have always been available in England, and that the comments of the judge might properly direct the jury as to the extent of such permissible adverse inference without any necessary impairment of the principles of natural justice, or of the obligation upon the prosecution to prove its case beyond reasonable doubt.[8]

Clause 5(3) of the Criminal Law Revision Committee's draft Bill also provided that the accused's failure to give evidence may, on the basis of proper inferences, have been treated as corroboration of evidence given on behalf of the prosecution. We have seen that, under the present law, the accused's failure to give evidence cannot be treated as corroboration,[9] but, if the failure is something which can detract from the weight of a defence or add to the weight of the prosecution's case, it is difficult to see why it should not corroborate. If, on facts such as those of *R v Sparrow*,[10] evidence that Sparrow had been heard to agree to the use of a gun by his co-accused had been given by an accomplice, it is as difficult to see why he should not be corroborated by the accused's failure to testify as it is to see how, under the present law, the judge could sum up to the jury without sinking into gibberish. The accused's absence from the witness box would call for strong comment as something which the jury should bear in mind when considering the weight of his defence, but the judge would have to go on to say that, notwithstanding what he had said by way of comment, they must not treat the fact on which comment was made as corroborative of the accomplice's evidence.

---

6 Clause 56 of the Draft Canadian Code reads: 'The accused in a criminal proceeding cannot be compelled to be a witness but the judge, prosecutor and defence counsel may comment on his failure to testify and the trier of fact may draw all reasonable inferences therefrom.'
7 Criminal Procedure Code, s 188(2).
8 *Haw Tua Tau v Public Prosecutor* [1982] AC 136 at 154.
9 See p 250 above.
10 See p 386 above.

B. THE ACCUSED WHO DOES GIVE EVIDENCE

In the words of Lord Sankey:

> When Parliament by the Act of 1898 effected a change in the general law and made the prisoner in every case a competent witness, it was in evident difficulty and it pursued the familiar English system of compromise.[11]

If the ordinary rules governing the examination and cross-examination of witnesses were to be applied to the accused without restriction or modification, he would have been unduly favoured in one respect and unduly prejudiced in another. He would have been unduly favoured because he could have claimed the privilege against self-incrimination on the ground that his answer to a question might show that he had committed the crime under investigation. This danger was met by proviso (e) to s 1 of the Act under which he may be asked any question in cross-examination notwithstanding that it would tend to incriminate him as to the offence charged, and it has been held that the proviso applies when one prisoner confines his evidence to statements exculpating his co-accused.[12]

It was thought that the accused would have been unduly prejudiced if he had anything in the nature of a criminal record because he would have been exposed to cross-examination concerning his past misdeeds as a matter affecting his credibility. This danger was met by s 1(f) which is itself a compromise because cross-examination as to credit is neither wholly prohibited nor invariably permitted. Its principal effect is to provide the accused with a shield which is only thrown away if he gives evidence of his good character or casts imputations on the prosecutor or the witnesses for the prosecution. When the shield is thrown away, the accused is liable to be cross-examined on his criminal record and past misdeeds.

Although the accused who gives evidence is technically in the same position as any other witness, subject to the important exceptions made by s 1(e) and s 1(f) of the Act of 1898, it would be unrealistic to regard their positions as substantially similar from the practical point of view. We have already seen that it is difficult, in practice, to discriminate between the use to be made of the answers given by the accused in cross-examination to credit and cross-examination to the issue. The sanctions of the law of perjury may operate quite differently in the case of the accused from the way in which they apply to an ordinary witness. The latter is confronted with the choice of telling the truth or taking the risk of a prosecution for perjury. This risk is bound to appear in a somewhat different light if the choice is to take it or run the risk of conviction for the more serious offence charged.[13] Considerations of this nature have led the judges to be a great deal more solicitous about the propriety of the cross-examination of the accused than that of any other witness. No doubt they have a discretion to disallow questions in each case, but it is most often stressed in relation to the

---

11 *Maxwell v D P P* [1935] AC 309 at 317.

12 *R v Rowland* [1910] 1 KB 458. S 1(e) is not expressly confined to cases in which the accused is giving evidence 'on his own behalf', and the court would not read these words into the proviso. Whether this provision was really necessary is open to doubt; no such provision appeared in earlier legislation making the accused a competent witness, and no difficulty appears to have been experienced, see Criminal Law Amendment Act 1885.

13 See 19 MLR 704.

questioning of the prisoner under the Act of 1898.[14] Counsel for the prosecution is repeatedly admonished not to drive the accused into throwing his shield away.[15] Even if this was not, in any sense, the purpose of the cross-examination, it may be held to have been improper because the crucial question is its effect upon the minds of the jury, not the purpose with which it was administered.[16] A further safeguard is provided by the requirement that Crown counsel should obtain the approval of the judge before embarking on cross-examination under s 1(f).[17]

Section 1(f) has, however, led to numerous difficulties so far as its construction is concerned, and it is now necessary to consider them.

SECTION 2. THE INTERPRETATION OF S 1(f)[18]

Section 1 (f) reads as follows:

> A person charged and called as a witness in pursuance of this Act shall not be asked, and if asked shall not be required to answer, any question tending to show that he has committed or been convicted of or been charged with any offence other than that wherewith he is then charged, or is of bad character, unless—
>> (i) the proof that he has committed or been convicted of such other offence is admissible evidence to show that he is guilty of the offence wherewith he is then charged; or
>> (ii) he has personally or by his advocate asked questions of the witnesses for the prosecution with a view to establish his own good character, or has given evidence of his good character, or the nature or conduct of the defence is such as to involve imputations on the character of the prosecutor or the witnesses for the prosecution; or
>> (iii) he has given evidence against any other person charged in the same proceedings.[19]

It will be observed that the section begins with a prohibition on four types of question—those tending to show previous charges, those tending to show previous offences, those tending to show previous convictions and those tending to show bad character. Reference is then made to the situations in which such questions are permitted. So far as sub-paras (f)(ii) and (iii) are concerned, the situations must be brought into existence by the accused himself; he must either put his character in issue, or cast imputations on the witnesses for the prosecution or give evidence against someone charged in the same proceedings. No action on the part of the accused is necessary to render questions admissible under s 1(f)(i), but the omission from this part

---

14 See especially *R v Baldwin* (1925) 18 Cr App Rep 175.
15 *R v Eidinow* (1932) 23 Cr App Rep 145.
16 *R v Ellis* [1910] 2 KB 746; *R v Sugarman* (1935) 25 Cr App Rep 109.
17 *R v McLean* (1926) 19 Cr App Rep 104. Appeals have been allowed on account of improper questioning by the judge (*R v Ratcliffe* (1919) 14 Cr App Rep 95) and counsel for a co-accused (*R v Roberts* [1936] 1 All ER 23) as well as counsel for the prosecution. Under s 399 of the Crimes Act (Victoria), the judge's leave to cross-examine under the equivalent of s 1(f)(ii) must be obtained in the absence of the jury.
18 Section 1(f) must be read subject to s 16(2) of the Children and Young Persons Act 1963. Someone aged 21 or more cannot be asked about convictions before he was 14. The proviso must also be read subject to the practice direction of 30 June 1975, made in consequence of the Rehabilitation of Offenders Act 1974, see ch VIII, section 2, part A above.
19 The words 'in the same proceedings' were substituted for 'with the same offence' by the Criminal Evidence Act 1979.

of the proviso of any reference to the fact that the accused has been charged with another offence or is of bad character renders it difficult to reconcile some of the decisions with the strict words of the statute.

It will be convenient to begin by considering the construction of the prohibition and then to discuss the situations in which cross-examination is permitted under s 1(f).

A. THE PROHIBITION

Although the prohibition is absolute in its terms, it does not prevent questions concerning his record being put to the accused in-chief on the comparatively rare occasions when he wishes to testify on that subject. Such words as 'shall not be asked' and 'shall not be required to answer' are considered to be inapplicable to evidence which is tendered voluntarily in-chief.[20]

Problems have been raised with regard to the relation between the prohibition and proviso (e), the meaning of the words 'tending to show', the meaning of the word 'charged' and the relation of the prohibition to the permissions conferred by the rest of s 1(f). These problems were considered by the House of Lords in the leading cases of *Jones v D P P*,[1] *Stirland v D P P*[2] and *Maxwell v D P P*.[3]

1. THE RELATION OF PROVISO (e) TO PROVISO (f)[4]

According to proviso (e) the accused may be asked any question in cross-examination notwithstanding that it would tend to criminate him as to the offence charged. Its relation to proviso (f) was not discussed before *Jones's* case, but the two main views on the subject expressed in *Jones's* case were discernible in the earlier authorities. They may be described as the 'literal' and 'broad' views respectively. According to the literal view, proviso (e) permits questions tending directly to criminate the accused as to the offence charged, while proviso (f) prohibits, subject to exceptions which must be construed literally, questions tending to incriminate the accused indirectly as well as those which simply go to his credit as a witness. This view is supported by *R v Cokar*[5] where cross-examination about a previous charge was held to have infringed the statute although it related to an issue concerning liability, as distinct from credibility. At his trial for breaking and entering with intent to steal, Cokar's defence was that he had entered the house in question for the sake of warmth and in order to have a sleep. In the course of his cross-examination, he denied that he knew it was no offence to enter a house in order to go to sleep, and the trial judge allowed counsel for the prosecution to put questions concerning a previous charge of breaking and entering which had resulted in an acquittal. It was probable that the accused had learned, in connection with that charge that it is not an offence

20 *Jones v D P P* [1962] AC 635 at 663, [1962] 1 All ER 569 at 575 per Lord Reid.
1 [1962] AC 635, [1962] 1 All ER 569.
2 [1944] AC 315, [1944] 2 All ER 13.
3 [1935] AC 309.
4 See McNamara 'Cross-Examination of an Accused as to Collateral Crimes Relevant to Guilt' (1983) 9 Adel LR 290.
5 [1960] 2 QB 207, [1960] 2 All ER 175. The literal view is also supported by the tenor of Lord Sankey's speech in *Maxwell's* case.

to enter a house in order to go to sleep. He was convicted, and his conviction was quashed by the Court of Criminal Appeal on the ground that the question concerning the previous charge had been wrongly admitted. Section 1(f)(ii) and (iii) did not apply to the case because Cokar had neither put his character in issue, nor cast imputations nor given evidence against a co-accused, while questions concerning charges resulting in anything other than a conviction were held to be outside the purview of s 1(f)(i) from which the word 'charged' is omitted.[6]

According to the broad view, proviso (e) permits questions which tend to criminate the accused as to the offence charged directly or indirectly, and, in cases to which none of the exceptions apply, the prohibition in proviso (f) relates solely to cross-examination to credit. This view is supported by *R v Chitson*[7] and *R v Kurasch*.[8] Chitson was charged with unlawful intercourse with a girl of fourteen. In the course of her evidence in-chief, the prosecutrix stated that he had told her that he had done the same thing to another girl. There was no evidence whether this other girl was beneath or above the age of sixteen at the material time, but it was held by the Court of Criminal Appeal that the prisoner had been properly examined with regard to his relations with her because, although the questions did no doubt tend to show that he was of bad character, they also tended to incriminate him as to the offence charged; if he had had intercourse with the other girl, that fact would confirm the prosecutrix's statement with regard to what he told her. If the other girl had been under sixteen at the material time, the case would have come within s 1(f)(i) because evidence that Chitson had committed another offence would have been admissible in-chief[9] but, if the other girl was over sixteen at the material time, no offence would have been committed against her; nevertheless despite the omission of the words 'bad character' from s (1)(f)(i) the cross-examination was held to be permissible because it was relevant to an issue in the case. In *R v Kurasch*, the appellant was charged with a conspiracy to defraud by means of a mock auction. His defence was that he was merely the servant of the proprietress of the auction room, and a question suggesting that she was his mistress was held by the Court of Criminal Appeal to have been properly put to him in cross-examination simply because it was relevant to the issue. The accused had done nothing to throw his shield away under s 1(f)(ii) or (iii), and, as the question merely tended to show immorality as opposed to the commission or conviction of another offence, the case fell outside the literal words of s 1(f)(i).

2. THE MEANING OF 'TENDING TO SHOW'—JONES V DIRECTOR OF PUBLIC PROSECUTIONS

In *Jones v D P P*[10] a majority of the House of Lords sanctioned a construction of s 1(f) which does much to reduce the practical effect of the difference

6 This reasoning leads to the perverse result that the cross-examination would have been permissible if the accused had acquired his knowledge in the course of a case in which he had been convicted rather than acquitted.
7 [1909] 2 KB 945. See also *R v Kennaway* [1917] 1 KB 25.
8 [1915] 2 KB 749.
9 Even then a sufficient foundation for the cross-examination should have been laid by the evidence in-chief; cf the treatment of *R v Kennedy* by the majority of the House of Lords in *Jones v D P P*.
10 [1962] AC 635, [1962] 1 All ER 569. The text represents part of an article by Sir Rupert Cross in 78 LQR 407.

between the two views concerning the relationship of provisos (e) and (f). Jones was charged with the murder of a Girl Guide. His evidence was an uncorroborated alibi that he had been with a prostitute, and he deposed to the details of a conversation he had had with his wife on his return home. It was necessary for him to explain why, before setting up his alibi, he had endeavoured to establish another one which would have been corroborated. He did so by stating, in the course of his evidence in-chief, that he had previously been in trouble with the result that he was afraid that the police would not pay much attention to an uncorroborated alibi. The alibi which Jones ultimately set up bore a striking resemblance to that which he had set up at an earlier trial resulting in his conviction for the rape of another Girl Guide. He was cross-examined with regard to the resemblances between the two alibis and between the conversations with his wife to which he deposed at each trial. Although the terms of the cross-examination did not actually show that he had committed another offence, it was common ground among the members of the House of Lords who heard the appeal that the questions suggested that he was a person of bad character who had previously been suspected of, if not charged with, a serious crime. Jones was convicted, and the propriety of the cross-examination was challenged in the Court of Criminal Appeal. That court held that proviso (f) had not been infringed because the words 'tending to show' mean 'make known to the jury', and the jury had already been made aware of the fact that the accused had previously been in trouble by means of his evidence in-chief.[11] Jones appealed to the House of Lords, and the House was unanimously in favour of dismissing the appeal. Lords Simonds, Reid and Morris did so for the reason given by the Court of Criminal Appeal, but Lords Denning and Devlin expressly disagreed with it. They were in favour of dismissing the appeal on the broader ground that the cross-examination was relevant to the issue of the prisoner's liability because it tended to disprove his alibi; a considerable strain was put on the credulity of the jury when they were asked to believe that identical alibis were true, and that identical conversations took place between Jones and his wife. Lords Simonds, Reid and Morris were of course also of the opinion that the cross-examination was relevant for this reason, but, in their view, that did not of itself suffice to render the questions admissible under the statute. Had Jones not alluded in-chief to his previous trouble, the majority would have allowed the appeal.[12]

The view that 'tending to show' means 'make known' or 'reveal' to the jury for the first time goes a long way towards reducing the practical effect of the difference between the literal and broad views concerning the relation between provisos (e) and (f) of the Criminal Evidence Act 1898, if it applies to cases in which the evidence tending to show bad character has been given by the prosecution.

There is now further authority on the interpretation of these words. In *R v Anderson*[13] the accused was charged, together with a number of others, with various terrorist offences, having been found in possession of apparently incriminating articles such as a gun, false documents, and a large amount of

---

11 *R v Jones* [1962] AC 635, [1961] 3 All ER 668.
12 Unless they would have been prepared to apply what is now the proviso to s 2(1) of the Criminal Appeal Act 1968, and dismiss the appeal on the ground that there had been no miscarriage of justice.
13 [1988] QB 678, [1988] 2 All ER 549 (51 MLR 785).

cash. Her explanation, advanced for the first time at her trial, was that she had come from Northern Ireland to escort escaped prisoners on their route to the continent of Europe, and that most of the materials found in her possession were there for that purpose. The prosecution were permitted to ask her in cross-examination whether she was a 'wanted' person in Northern Ireland, their aim being to show that, as such, she would be most unlikely to have been chosen to play the role she professed. They had not adduced the evidence in-chief, because at that time they had had no inkling of the line of defence which made such evidence relevant. The defence argued that s 1(f) prohibited such cross-examination.[14] The trial judge allowed the cross-examination, and the appeal was dismissed upon the basis that the nature of the accused's defence had itself revealed the commission of crimes,[15] and that no further prejudice would be occasioned to her by the cross-examination. This was regarded as equivalent to the situation in *Jones* as not tending to show any of the prohibited matters, in the sense of revealing them to the jury for the first time.

It should however be noted that in *Anderson*, in critical distinction from *Jones*, not even the most imperceptive juror could have supposed the accused to be 'wanted' at the relevant time in respect of crimes which had then been undiscovered, or even uncommitted. The decision thus seems to erode the natural meaning of the words of the prohibition still further. Lord Lane CJ consoled himself with the reflection that little damage had been done since the prosecution, having been taken by surprise by the defence, would have been successful in an application to re-open its case so as to call in-chief evidence of the matters in fact put to the accused in cross-examination, and that the course adopted in *Anderson* had done no more than short-circuit the process. It is submitted that this ignores the grave disadvantage to the accused[16] of having such material sprung upon her in cross-examination, without prior argument in the absence of the jury, without the production of a suitable prosecution witness,[17] and by means of leading questions. It was to prevent just such a situation that s 1(f) was enacted in the first place.

In fact it seems that the same result could have been better achieved in *Anderson*, without undue distortion of the wording of the section, by the simple application of s 1(f)(i)'s permission of questions relating to the commission of a crime as showing the accused's guilt.[18]

It has been held elsewhere that nothing further is shown when details of the relevant offences have already been adduced by the accused in attempting to have confessional material excluded at a voir dire,[19] or where they have already been brought before the jury in relation to other charges,[20] or by a special form of pleading.[1] Neither of these situations seems very satisfactory

14 And that it was not permitted by s 1(e) either.
15 Such as illegal possession of firearms, forgery and conspiracy. It should also be noted that here the prosecution justified its cross-examination by 'revelations' of matters different from those charged, not shown to be true, and which the prosecution itself necessarily maintained to be false. I am grateful to Mr David Kell for pointing this out to me.
16 Which had been recognised in *Jones*.
17 Who would then be available for cross-examination by the defence.
18 By rebutting a defence raised by the accused. The court adverted to this justification but while expressing its inclination to accept it, for some reason preferred the justification criticised above.
19 *R v Vuckov and Romeo* (1986) 40 SASR 498.
20 Although the evidence of them had been held insufficient even to raise a case to answer.
 1 *Dodds v HM Advocate* 1987 SCCR 678.

either. In the former it is submitted that the accused should no more be inhibited in the conduct of his defence by fear of the use of such material than of that of confessional material.[2] In the latter the party prejudiced was in no way himself responsible for the prior revelation to the jury.

It cannot be denied that the majority view in *Jones* does diminish the protection apparently bestowed by the natural meaning of the words of the prohibition in s 1(f). Nor, however, can it reasonably be denied that such a reading bestows an anomalous and unjustifiable degree of protection. In particular there seems no reason why the accused should not be exposed to cross-examination on any evidence admitted in chief, whether it consists of evidence of convictions for or commission of crimes,[3] or whether it consists of evidence of charges or of bad character.[4] It would be better for evidence admitted in chief, and for that available for use in cross-examination to cohere.[5] If similar fact evidence has been admitted in chief, then the accused, if he choose to testify, should be exposed to cross-examination about such matters. If such evidence has not been so adduced, though admissible, then the prosecution should be permitted to re-open its case to adduce it in chief, subject to satisfying the requirements for so re-opening its case. This would give the accused the choice of whether to expose himself to further cross-examination by testifying in denial of such further evidence. If the evidence is inadmissible in chief as similar fact evidence, or if the prosecution is unable to satisfy the conditions for re-opening its case, then the accused should not be exposed to cross-examination in relation to such evidence.

3. THE MEANING OF 'CHARGED'—STIRLAND V DIRECTOR OF PUBLIC PROSECUTIONS

In *Stirland v D P P*[6] the House of Lords decided that the word 'charged' as used in s 1(f) means 'charged in court'. Accordingly, when a prisoner accused of forgery put his character in issue and said that he had never been charged before, it was reasonable to suppose that he was using the word in this sense, and the trial judge should have disallowed questions concerning the suspicions that had been entertained against the accused by one of his employers. Lord Simon LC concluded his speech with six propositions to some of which it will be necessary to refer later. The first summarises the effect of s 1(f). According to the second, the accused may be cross-examined as to any of the evidence he has given in-chief, including statements concerning his good record, with a view to testing his veracity or accuracy or to showing that he is not to be believed on oath.[7] The accused had been questioned before leaving his previous employment and was presumably well aware of the suspicions. Accordingly, he could presumably have been cross-examined on the subject if he had said in-chief that he had never previously been suspected of an offence. Lord Simon's fifth proposition was that it is no disproof of good character that a man has been suspected or

---

2 See above p 168.
3 As permitted by s 1(f)(i) when relevant to guilt.
4 Apparently, on the natural interpretation of s 1(f)(i), incapable of being so used.
5 As has been achieved by amendment of the relevant provisions in other jurisdictions.
6 [1944] AC 315, [1944] 2 All ER 13. See also *R v Wadey* (1935) 25 Cr App Rep 104; and *R v Nicoloudis* (1954) 38 Cr App Rep 118.
7 See p 397 below.

accused of a previous crime. Such questions as 'Were you suspected' or 'Were you accused' are inadmissible because they are irrelevant to the issue of character and can only be asked if the accused has sworn expressly to the contrary. When he does this, he may be said to have adopted a particular method of putting his character in issue. According to the sixth proposition, the fact that a question put to the accused is irrelevant is no reason for quashing his conviction, though it should have been disallowed by the judge. If the question is not only irrelevant but is unfair to the accused as being likely to distract the jury from considering the real issues and so lead to a miscarriage of justice, it should be disallowed, and if not disallowed, is a ground on which an appeal against conviction may be based. As there had been no miscarriage of justice, *Stirland*'s appeal was in fact dismissed.

In *R v Smith*[8] on a charge of assault the accused was asked in-chief whether she had ever been convicted of such an offence, and gave a negative response. She was then cross-examined about a pending[9] charge for such an offence. The court held this to be improper, apparently on the ground of unfairness,[10] and because the question went to the issue rather than to credibility.

4. THE RELATION OF THE PROHIBITION TO THE PERMISSION CONFERRED BY THE REST OF S 1(f)— MAXWELL V DIRECTOR OF PUBLIC PROSECUTIONS

When the accused has thrown away the shield provided by the first part of s 1(f), it would be wrong to suppose that he can always be asked questions tending to show that he has committed, been convicted of or charged with other offences or is of bad character, because such questions must be relevant either to his liability[11] or else to his credit.[12] Accordingly, it was decided by the House of Lords in *Maxwell v D P P*[13] that, although a doctor charged with manslaughter by means of an illegal operation gave evidence of his good character, he ought not to have been asked whether a similar charge of which he was acquitted had been made against him in the past. In the instant case, it was impossible to say that the fact that the accused had been acquitted on a previous charge was relevant, or that it tended to destroy his credibility as a witness, and the appeal was allowed. Lord Sankey LC recognised the possibility of circumstances in which the fact of a charge resulting in an acquittal might be elicited. Among the instances he mentioned was that of a man charged with an offence against the person who might be asked whether he had uttered threats against his victim because he was angry with him for having brought an unfounded charge. A further instance is suggested by the later case of *R v Waldman*[14] in which the Court of Criminal Appeal upheld a

---

8 [1989] Crim LR 900.
9 The Act leaves it unclear whether 'charge' in s 1(f) is limited to adjudicated charges.
10 The short report makes no reference to s 1(e).
11 Although relevance is required, it is not necessary to show the same preponderance of probative force over prejudicial effect as must be shown to justify admission in chief, see *R v Bracewell* (1978) 68 Cr App Rep 44; the same is true in Canada, *R v Farrant* (1983) 147 DLR (3d) 511.
12 In *R v Cooper* (1985) 18 ACR 1 a new trial had to be ordered for this reason, despite the manifest guilt of the accused.
13 [1935] AC 309.
14 (1934) 24 Cr App Rep 204. *Maxwell*'s case was in fact decided earlier in 1934 although it was not reported in the Appeal Cases.

conviction for receiving stolen goods although the accused, who had put his character in issue, had been asked about a previous acquittal on an earlier charge of receiving. The court appears to have considered that *Maxwell's* case could be distinguished because the question was addressed to a character witness as well as to Waldman, and because the question was linked with one concerning a possibility that a previous acquittal of receiving might be relevant to the accused's guilty knowledge on a subsequent occasion because the previous investigation ought to have stimulated the most careful inquiries in the later transaction, and thus militated against the credibility of statements to the effect that the accused acquired goods cheaply without asking questions about their origin.

It should be emphasised that both *Maxwell v D P P* and *R v Waldman* were concerned with situations in which the shield had been thrown away. When this is not the case, it is extremely doubtful whether the accused could be asked about a previous charge resulting in an acquittal owing to the restricted phraseology of s 1(f)(i).[15]

B. THE INTERPRETATION OF S 1(f)(i)[16]

Section 1(f)(i) allows the accused to be questioned about other offences when proof that he has committed or been convicted of them is admissible to show that he is guilty of the offence charged. The subsection makes no reference to questions about charges or about bad character. There is surprisingly little direct authority on its interpretation.[17] The effect of the reasoning of the majority of the House of Lords in *Jones* is to make it clear that when evidence of a previous offence has been adduced in chief, cross-examination of the accused about such offence is permitted, at least to the extent that it reveals no more of the prohibited matters.[18] In that situation the prohibition is inoperative, so there is no need to rely upon this subsection. This reduces its practical effect considerably, and may help to explain the dearth of authority. It does not however deprive it of all effect because the subsection requires the justifying evidence to be 'admissible', not 'to have been admitted', thus leaving open the possibility of cases where no revelation of the otherwise prohibited matter has been made. It was nevertheless said in *Jones* that where cross-examination about such matter is intended, some foundation should normally be laid for it by adducing evidence of the otherwise prohibited matter in chief.[19] The Court of Criminal Appeal regarded such a course as desirable because unless it were taken, if:

---

15 Such cross-examination appears to have been permitted in Tasmania, see *R v Unsworth* [1986] Tas R 173 at 174.

16 See Cross 'The Criminal Evidence Act 1898, s 1(f)(i)' (1960) 76 LQR 537; Tapper 'The Meaning of Section 1(f)(i) of the Criminal Evidence Act 1898' in Tapper (ed) *Crime, Proof and Punishment* (1981).

17 Although Wigmore regarded it as the most important part of the section, I *Wigmore* p 662.

18 This was how the majority in *Jones* justified the decisions in *R v Chitson* [1909] 2 KB 945, 79 LJKB 10 and *R v Kennaway* [1917] 1 KB 25, 12 Cr App Rep 147.

19 [1962] AC 635, [1962] 1 All ER 569 at 668, 578 (Lord Denning), at 685, 589 (Lord Morris).

the accused desired to dispute or explain the alleged similarity of circumstances or pattern of the two offences he would thereby be deprived of any opportunity to cross-examine prosecution witnesses and be exposed to the gravely prejudicial effect of suggestive questions to which his negative answer might be of no avail.[20]

This still leaves a residual class of case where the prosecution has a good reason for choosing not to adduce the prohibited matter in chief, perhaps from a desire not to prejudice the accused unnecessarily, or to spare a possible witness,[1] or because the relevance of such evidence becomes apparent only after an unanticipated defence has been raised.

The last of these possibilities was the one which had occurred in *R v Cokar*.[2] It will be recalled that the prosecution were not there permitted to cross-examine the accused about a previous charge of which he had been acquitted in order to show that it was the source of his knowledge of the efficacy of a particular line of defence to a charge of burglary. The reason for this was apparently the omission from s 1(f)(i) of any reference to charges or to bad character. This confirms that natural reading of the subsection as an exception to the prohibition in the enacting part, and not as a condition for lifting the prohibition in its entirety.[3] It also illustrates the absurdity of the result so achieved. It is surely much less likely that a defence will be raised a second time after it has failed,[4] than after it has succeeded,[5] yet it is only in the former case that the subsection permits cross-examination. The subsection is so badly drafted[6] that the High Court of Australia has refused to adopt a literal construction of it,[7] while some Australian jurisdictions have amended earlier legislation incorporating the original English form.[8]

The provision refers to proof of commissions and of convictions. It will generally be the circumstances of the commission of the crime that are relevant to prove guilt.[9] The reference to convictions may have been included to cater for cross-examination in those cases where proof of a conviction is expressly permitted by statute.[10] As noted by Lord Devlin in *Jones*[11] the inclusion in s 1(f)(i) of 'such' appears to confine its ambit to specified criminality. As he further noted, this reading has nothing whatever

20 [1962] AC 635 at 646, [1961] 3 All ER 668 at 675.
1 As in *Jones*.
2 [1960] 2 QB 207, [1960] 2 All ER 175, above p 390.
3 The appearance of 'such' in s 1(f)(i) can be justified only upon this basis, though the consequence is that its effect is quite different from that of s 1(f)(ii) and s 1(f)(iii) which must be construed as defining conditions for a total relaxation of the prohibition in the enacting part.
4 As in *Jones*.
5 As in *Cokar*. See also *R v Cohen* [1938] 3 All ER 380, 26 Cr App Rep 190, where cross-examination showing bad character was held impermissible in accordance with this construction, but where the court appeared to believe cross-examination about previous convictions still more impermissible. Such a view accords much better with common sense than with the drafting of the subsection.
6 See *R v Anderson* [1988] QB 678 at 686, [1988] 2 All ER 549 at 554. A private member's amendment to the original draft of the prohibition in s 1(f) was accepted during the passage of this sub-section, see 60 Official Report (4th series) col 712 (30 June 1898), and no consequential amendment to s 1(f)(i) appears to have been proposed.
7 *Attwood v R* (1960) 102 CLR 353.
8 For example see Evidence Act 1977 (Qld), s 15: Crimes Act 1900 (as amended) (NSW), s 413A: Evidence Act Amendment Act 1983, s 2(a) (S Aust).
9 See Lord Morris in *Jones* at 687, 590. See also *R v Shepherd* (1980) 71 Cr App Rep 120.
10 See Ch IX section 2 above.
11 At 700, 598.

to recommend it as a matter of policy. If it is relevant to the issue to show that the accused was in prison on a particular occasion in the past, but unnecessary, and perhaps prejudicial to show what his precise offence was on that occasion, it is hard to see why the prosecution should be forced to be specific.[12]

The purpose of cross-examination of the accused under this subsection is expressed as being 'to show that he is guilty of the offence wherewith he is then charged'. This seems to exclude any suggestion that it could be used simply to discredit the accused, either generally or with regard to some particular part of his testimony. In *Jones* Lord Reid refused to accept a wide reading of 'to show that he is guilty' as including anything tending to convince the jury that he is guilty, however indirect the route.[13] It has, however, been submitted[14] that the suggestion advanced, and not rejected, in *R v Anderson*[15] that it comprehend rebuttal of a defence actually advanced should be accepted. The majority in *Jones* was also explicit in rejecting any general application of the second proposition advanced by Viscount Simon in *Stirland v D P P*[16] permitting cross-examination of the accused as to any statement made by him in chief with a view to 'testing his veracity'. The application of that proposition was confined to cases in which, as in *Stirland*, the accused came within one of the other parts of s 1(f).[17]

C. THE INTERPRETATION OF S 1(f)(ii)

It will be convenient to divide the discussion of s 1(f)(ii) into two main parts—cases in which the accused puts his character in issue, and those in which the nature or conduct of the defence involves imputations on the character of the prosecutor or one of his witnesses.

1. CHARACTER IN ISSUE

In order that the first part of the second exception to the prohibition may be brought into play, the court must be satisfied that the accused: 'has personally or by his advocate asked questions of the witnesses for the prosecution with a view to establish his own good character, or has given evidence of his good character'. This clearly excludes cases where the reference to good character is elicited from defence witnesses only as a result of cross-examination by the prosecution.[18] The latter phrase is apt to cover a case in which the prisoner calls a witness to character but does not cross-examine on the subject or allude to it in his own evidence in-chief. It is not sufficient that counsel raises the accused's good character in his opening if nothing falling explicitly

---

12 Cf *R v Miller* [1952] 2 All ER 667, 36 Cr App Rep 169.
13 At 663, 575.
14 Above p 393.
15 [1988] QB 678 at 688, [1988] 2 All ER 549 at 556.
16 [1944] AC 315, [1944] 2 All ER 13.
17 Nor may such evidence be admitted to support the credibility of prosecution witnesses unless it is brought under one of the other exceptions, *R v Weekes* [1983] Crim LR 801. For a most helpful discussion, and for some unreported authority allowing cross-examination to credit under s 1(f)(i), see Pattenden 'The Purpose of Cross-Examination under Section 1(f) of the Criminal Evidence Act 1898' [1982] Crim LR 707.
18 See *R v Stronach* [1988] Crim LR 48.

under this provision should be elicited or adduced.[19] The exception is not brought into play when a defence witness volunteers a statement concerning the character of the accused which he had not been asked to make;[20] nor is the exception brought into play by the accused's reference to one of his many previous convictions as a ground for fearing the police because it would be wrong to infer that he meant that the occasion of the conviction was the only occasion on which he had previously been in trouble.[1] It may be noted that the exception makes no reference to the consequence of eliciting the accused's good character by cross-examination of a co-accused, or a witness called by him. It is uncertain how far the accused puts his own character in issue by suggesting a favourable contrast with the bad character of others who might have committed the crime. If those others are called as witnesses for the prosecution the matter is governed by the second limb of s 1(f)(ii). If they are not so called it seems to depend upon exactly how pointedly the contrast is made. Thus in *R v Lee*[2] where the accused was charged with theft from a house in which he was lodging it was held not sufficient that he had pointed out that others with criminal records had access to the house. In *R v Bracewell*[3] by contrast it was regarded as sufficient that one of two men accused of murder in the course of a burglary had contrasted his own cool professionalism with the panic-prone inexperience of his companion. A general examination by the accused in the course of his evidence into the circumstances surrounding the alleged crime with a view to establishing innocence does not expose him to cross-examination under s 1(f)(ii). Thus, in *R v Ellis*,[4] a dealer was charged with obtaining cheques from a customer by false pretences concerning the cost price of antiques and he answered questions about his conduct towards the alleged victim with a view to negativing any intent to defraud. The Court of Criminal Appeal held that he ought not to have been asked questions under s 1(f)(ii) as the evidence had not been given with a view to establishing good character. No doubt it had that tendency, but an assertion of innocence might equally well be said to be tantamount to giving evidence of character. The position is the same if the accused calls witnesses to his business transactions which are in question.[5]

Generally speaking the accused's own evidence of his character takes the form of allusions to his innocent or praiseworthy past, and the decisions certainly do not indicate any great reluctance on the part of the courts to hold that he has put his character in issue by such a reference. A man's allegations concerning his regular attendance at mass,[6] his assertion that he had been earning an honest living for a considerable time,[7] and his affirmative answer to the question whether he is a married man with a

---

19 *R v Ellis* [1910] 2 KB 746. It is also unclear how far the mere repetition in court of words claiming a good character uttered upon arrest (*R v Solomon* (1909) 2 Cr App Rep 80); or a claim made in a letter probably intended to read only in mitigation of sentence (*R v Parker* (1924) 18 Cr App Rep 14) will suffice. See also *Malindi v R* [1967] 1 AC 439, [1966] 3 All ER 285.

20 *R v Redd* [1923] 1 KB 104.

1 *R v Thompson* [1966] 1 All ER 505, [1966] 1 WLR 405 following dicta of Oliver J in *R v Wattam* (1952) 36 Cr App Rep 72 at 78.

2 [1976] 1 All ER 570, [1976] 1 WLR 71.

3 (1978) 68 Cr App Rep 44.

4 [1910] 2 KB 746.

5 *R v Stronach* [1988] Crim LR 48.

6 *R v Ferguson* (1909) 2 Cr App Rep 250.

7 *R v Baker* (1912) 7 Cr App Rep 252.

family in regular work[8] have been treated as instances in which the shield provided by s 1(f) would be thrown away. There seems to be some doubt whether a reference to honourable discharge from the army would have this effect,[9] and similar uncertainty prevails with regard to the statement by a man charged with traffic offences that he disapproved of speeding.[10] In *R v Samuel*,[11] the Court of Criminal Appeal did not experience much difficulty in arriving at the conclusion that someone who was charged with larceny by finding put his character in issue when he gave evidence with regard to previous occasions on which he had returned lost property to its owner.

It is necessary to consider the meaning of 'character' as used in s 1(f) in general and the first part of s 1(f)(ii) in particular, the purpose of cross-examination under the exception, the question of the divisibility of the accused's character, and the availability of judicial discretion to disallow cross-examination otherwise allowed by this part.

(i) The meaning of character

We have seen that, in ordinary language, 'character' may mean either the reputation or the disposition of the person about whom the inquiry is being made, and that, at common law, a character witness might only be asked about the reputation of the accused.[12] The word is used no less than four times in proviso (f) and, in *R v Dunkley*,[13] a case concerned with imputations against a witness for the prosecution, Lord Hewart CJ said:

> It is not difficult to suppose that a formidable argument might have been raised on the phrasing of this statute, that the character which is spoken of is the character which is so well known in the vocabulary of the criminal law—namely, the general reputation of the person referred to; in other words that 'character' in that context and in every part of it, in the last part no less than in the first, in the third part no less than in the second, bears the meaning which the term 'character' was held to bear, for example, in the case of *R v Rowton*.[14]

Lord Hewart concluded that it was much too late in the day to consider such an argument because it could not prevail without the revision, and, to a great extent, the overthrow of a very long series of decisions. When speaking of the first part of s 1(f)(ii) in *Stirland v D P P*,[15] Lord Simon LC said:

> There is perhaps some vagueness in the use of the term 'good character' in this connection. Does it refer to the good reputation which a man may bear in his own circle, or does it refer to the man's real disposition as distinct from what his friends and neighbours may think of him?

Lord Simon was inclined to think that both conceptions were combined in s 1(f).

In *Jones v D P P*,[16] Lord Denning took Lord Hewart's view that it is too

---

8 *R v Coulman* (1927) 20 Cr App Rep 106 per Swift J in the course of the argument.
9 *R v Parker* (1924) 18 Cr App Rep 14.
10 *R v Beecham* [1921] 3 KB 464.
11 (1956) 40 Cr App Rep 8.
12 See p 332 above.
13 [1927] 1 KB 323 at 329. See also *Malindi v R* [1967] 1 AC 439, [1966] 3 All ER 285.
14 (1865) Le & Ca 520.
15 [1944] AC 315 at 324, [1944] 2 All ER 13 at 17.
16 [1962] AC 635 at 671, [1962] 1 All ER 569 at 580.

late to argue that 'character' as used in the Act of 1898 means 'reputation' and nothing else, but Lord Devlin expressed the opinion that this was the meaning intended by the draftsman of the statute.[17] He also thought that the point was still open at the level of the House of Lords. The effect of such a construction would be revolutionary and difficult to apply. When the accused testifies to his own good character, he must almost inevitably speak of his own good past acts[18] and it would certainly upset past decisions if it were to be held that a man who swore that he had led a good clean life and gone to mass every Sunday had not 'given evidence of his own good character'. If, throughout the entirety of s 1(f) 'character' were to mean 'reputation', it would be difficult to construe that part of s 1(f)(ii) under which the accused loses his shield if the nature or conduct of his defence involves imputations on the 'character of the prosecutor or the witnesses for the prosecution'. It would then become possible to argue that someone who swore that a policeman had extracted a confession from him by violence was not casting imputations on the character of a witness for the prosecution.

It was just such an argument that was rejected by the House of Lords in *Selvey v D P P*,[19] a case turning on the construction of the second part of s 1(f)(ii), in which someone accused of buggery alleged that the prosecutor had offered to go on the bed with him for a pound, told him that he had already gone on the bed for that sum with another man, and, because his offer was rejected, dumped indecent photographs in the accused's room out of pique. It may therefore now be taken to be settled law that 'character' when used in the Act of 1898 means both disposition and reputation.

(ii) The purpose of cross-examination under the first half of s 1(f)(ii)[20]

There are three possible purposes for such cross-examination. It could be used simply to rebut the good character claimed by the accused; it could be used to discredit the accused so that his testimony should not be believed; or it could be used to go directly to the issue and to show that the accused is guilty as charged.

The first of these interpretations was rejected in *R v Richardson* and *R v Longman* where Edmund Davies LJ both summarised the argument, and gave the answer of the Court of Appeal:

> it is contended . . . that evidence of bad character can do no more than rebut or cancel out the evidence of good character and the jury must be instructed not to be influenced by the evidence of bad character in general assessment of the accused's credibility. We do not think that this is the general practice, and we have the gravest doubts whether a jury could be expected to understand such a direction, which verges on the metaphysical . . . In our view, evidence of character, when properly admitted, goes to the credibility of the witness concerned, whether

17 [1962] AC 635 at 699, [1962] 1 All ER 569 at 604.
18 See per Lord Denning in *Plato Films v Speidel* [1961] AC 1090 at 1143: 'The plaintiff cannot speak as to his own character and reputation because he does not know what other people think of him, or at any rate he cannot give evidence as to what they think of him.' Lord Devlin considers that the word 'character' means 'reputation' throughout the law of evidence (see *Dingle v Associated Newspapers* [1961] 2 QB 162 at 195 and 198; see also Fridman in (1962) 1 Sol Q 211).
19 [1970] AC 304, [1968] 2 All ER 497.
20 See Pattenden 'The Purpose of Cross-Examination Under Section 1(f) of the Criminal Evidence Act 1898' [1982] Crim LR 707.

the evidence discloses good character or bad character. If the accused calls evidence of good character and is shown by cross-examination to have a bad character, the jury may give this fact such weight as they think fit when assessing the *general* credibility of the accused. They cannot be expected to execute the metaphysical feat of treating the evidence as relevant to credibility on one issue, but irrelevant on another, and they are not required to do so.[1]

This passage shows that such evidence goes to the credibility of the accused. In some cases it is incapable of doing more. Thus in *R v Wood*[2] the evidence was of conviction for a *subsequent* offence, and was accepted as showing the bad character of the accused, not at the time of the commission of the offence with which he was charged, but at the time of his trial for it. Similarly in *R v Winfield*[3] the evidence was of convictions for offences totally dissimilar to those with which the accused was charged. In most cases however the evidence is also capable of showing the accused's guilt of the offence charged. It has already been seen that rebuttal of the accused's good character before 1898 must necessarily have gone to show his guilt.[4] It is also well-established that after 1898 possession of a good character is not *only* relevant to credibility, but also goes directly to the issue of guilt or innocence.[5] It might thus be supposed that refutation of it by cross-examination to bad character would also go to the same issue, and it is possible so to construe some remarks of Lord Sankey in *Maxwell v D P P*:

> if the prisoner by himself or his witness seeks to give evidence of his own good character, for the purpose of showing that it is unlikely that he committed the offence charged, he raises by way of defence an issue as to his good character so that he may fairly be cross-examined on that issue just as any witness called by him as to his good character may be cross-examined to show the contrary.[6]

There appear to be no reported cases in which cross-examination under this part of s 1(f)(ii) has been accepted as unequivocally going to the issue of guilt or innocence. The nearest approach to such acceptance is exhibited by the judgment of Lord Goddard CJ in *R v Samuel*[7] where it was explained that in the case of the accused the distinction between cross-examination to credit and issue is rather illusory, but even then it was accepted that technically the cross-examination ought to be regarded as going to credit. The view that cross-examination under this part cannot go directly to the issue of guilt or innocence is supported by another part of Lord Sankey's speech in *Maxwell* where he said:

> the question whether a man has been convicted, charged or acquitted, even if it goes to credibility, ought not to be admitted if there is any risk of the jury being misled into thinking that it goes not to credibility but to the probability of his having committed the offence with which he is charged.[8]

1 [1969] 1 QB 299 at 311, [1968] 2 All ER 761 at 767, emphasis in original.
2 [1920] 2 KB 179, 14 Cr App Rep 149.
3 [1939] 4 All ER 164, 27 Cr App Rep 139.
4 See above ch VIII, section 3, part B(1).
5 *R v Bellis* [1966] 1 All ER 552 n, [1966] 1 WLR 234; *R v Bryant, R v Oxley* [1979] QB 108 at 119, [1978] 2 All ER 689 at 696.
6 [1935] AC 309 at 319, 24 Cr App Rep 152 at 171.
7 (1956) 40 Cr App Rep 8 at 12.
8 [1935] AC 309 at 321, 24 Cr App Rep 152 at 173. See also *R v Smith* [1989] Crim LR 900.

This view has also been taken by the High Court of Australia,[9] is in accordance with the best recent view of the purpose of cross-examination under the second limb of s 1(f)(ii),[10] and accords with the general principle that the prosecution should not be allowed to reveal the bad character of the accused to the jury unless they can demonstrate that its probative force is likely to exceed its prejudicial effect, and that this should normally be done by seeking to lead such evidence in chief, rather than to elicit it in cross-examination without first having laid a foundation.

(iii) The divisibility of the character of the accused

When the prisoner urges that he ought to be believed when he swears that he was innocent of a sexual crime because he has a good character for sexual morality, it certainly does tend to refute his contention to show that he was convicted of an indecent assault; but it is open to question whether a conviction for theft has the same effect. This raises the issue of the propriety of a dictum in *R v Winfield* on the assumption that the accused was cross-examined about his character. According to this dictum: 'there is no such thing known to our procedure as putting half a prisoner's character in issue and leaving out the other half'.[11] It will be recollected that Winfield was convicted of indecent assault upon a woman and that he called a witness to speak of his good behaviour with ladies. He had previously been convicted of larceny, and it is not clear whether this conviction was put to his character witness, in which case the matter fell to be determined by the common law principles that have already been discussed, or whether the cross-examination concerning the conviction was of Winfield himself under s 1(f)(ii) of the Act of 1898. In either event, the Court of Criminal Appeal appears to have approved of the cross-examination, although their observations on the subject were obiter dicta because the conviction was quashed on account of the inadequacy of the direction to the jury on the subject of corroboration. So far as the cross-examination of the prisoner was concerned, it ought not to have been used by the jury as a direct means of establishing his guilt, because it was relevant only on the very doubtful footing that a thief is more likely to commit an indecent assault than an honest man. Its relevance to the credibility of the prisoner's testimony is not much greater, although there is a little more force in the argument that a convicted thief is more likely to lie than others.

Viewed as a matter affecting credibility, however, Winfield's cross-examination can be justified on the footing that having put his character in issue, he forfeited his right to be treated, as regards cross-examination, otherwise than as an ordinary witness, and an ordinary witness may be cross-examined about a conviction for any offence. The law on this subject may not be beyond reproach, but it is the outcome of the view that cross-examination about a conviction for any offence is permissible under s 6 of

9 *Donnini v R* (1972) 128 CLR 114 at 123; *Matusevich v R* (1977) 137 CLR 633 at 659; see also *R v Beech* (1978) 20 SASR 410 at 420; *R v Maiden and Petty* (1988) 35 ACR 346.
10 See *R v Watts* [1983] 3 All ER 101, 77 Cr App Rep 126, and below p 410.
11 (1939) 27 Cr App Rep 139. *Winfield's* case is discussed from the point of view of the Criminal Evidence Act 1898, by R N Gooderson in 11 CLJ 386. The case is considered above, p 331, from the point of view of the cross-examination of a character witness at common law.

the Criminal Procedure Act 1865,[12] and has nothing to do with the Criminal Evidence Act 1898. Lord Simon's third proposition in *Stirland's* case[13] was:

> An accused who 'puts his character in issue' must be regarded as putting the whole of his past record in issue. He cannot assert his good conduct in certain respects without exposing himself to inquiry about the rest of his record so far as this tends to disprove a claim to good character.

R v Winfield was cited, and it remains to be seen whether this will be held tantamount to House of Lords' approval of the course that was adopted in that case.

(iv) Discretion to disallow questioning

Most of the learning about the judicial discretion to prevent cross-examination under s 1(f)(ii) relates to the second limb as will be seen below. It should be noted here that in *R v Thompson*[14] the Court of Criminal Appeal recognised the existence of a discretion to disallow cross-examination under the first limb. The application of the discretion should be considered when a particular piece of evidence, capable of being construed as a claim to a better character than is wholly justified, is adduced to explain a special feature of the prosecution case. It should also be noted that in *Thompson* the trial judge had to overcome some reluctance in the prosecutor to conduct such cross-examination.

2. IMPUTATIONS ON THE CHARACTER OF THE PROSECUTOR OR THE WITNESSES FOR THE PROSECUTION[15]

Turning to the second part of s 1(f)(ii)—cases in which 'the nature or conduct of the defence is such as to involve imputations on the character of the prosecutor or the witnesses for the prosecution', there are several decisions favourable to the accused in which the statutory words have been given their natural meaning. Thus, an attack upon the conduct of a magistrate or police officer not called as a witness for the Crown,[16] and a suggestion by someone accused of murder that the deceased had made indecent approaches to him,[17] have been held to fall outside the proviso so that they did not warrant cross-examination under it; but a strictly literal construction of s 1(f)(ii) would be unfavourable to the accused because it would mean that, in many cases, a plea of not guilty coupled

---

12 See p 315 above. See also *R v Morris* (1959) 43 Cr App Rep 206 (cross-examination on conviction for dishonesty permitted by imputation of immorality against prosecution witnesses on charge of incest).

13 [1944] AC 315 at 324, [1944] 2 All ER 13 at 18.

14 [1966] 1 All ER 505, [1966] 1 WLR 405.

15 See articles in (1961) Crim LR 142 and 213, and 29 MLR 492. See also Munday 'Reflections on the Criminal Evidence Act 1898' (1985) CLJ 62.

16 *R v Westfall* (1912) 7 Cr App Rep 176.

17 *R v Biggin* [1920] 1 KB 213. Cases are conceivable in which the prosecutor would not be called as a witness, and imputations on his character would nonetheless expose the accused to cross-examination under the Act.

with an assertion of innocence in the witness box would render the accused liable to cross-examination on his criminal record, on account of the tacit suggestion that the prosecutor or one of his witnesses had been guilty of perjury. The avoidance of such a conclusion has led to an uneasy conflict of authority palliated by an extensive exercise of the court's discretion. The authorities will be briefly reviewed before the rationale of the later part of s 1(f)(ii) and the purpose of the cross-examination which it permits are considered.

(i) Imputations

It is not possible to lay down any clear definition of what amounts to an imputation since so much necessarily depends upon the detailed facts of particular cases. Some general guidance may be furnished by the following examples. A mere denial of guilt, even one couched in emphatic language, is not necessarily an imputation upon the prosecutor.[18] Nor is an allegation of relatively venial misconduct, such as drunkeness or swearing.[19] It is not however necessary that the allegation be of the commission of a criminal offence, immorality may be sufficient.[20] It may be enough that the allegation is elicited only as a result of cross-examination by the prosecution,[1] or that it goes beyond a limited admission of bad character by the prosecution witness in question,[2] or that it raises no issue extrinsic to the evidence which has been given by the witness in question.[3] It is immaterial whether the matter alleged is accepted to be true, as it normally will be when previous convictions are alleged; or is denied, as it usually will be when improper conduct is alleged. The most common situation is one in which the accused challenges the circumstances surrounding a purported confession put in evidence by a police witness for the prosecution. The problem is here most acute. The accused with a long criminal record has a double dilemma. He is likely to be at risk if he chooses to challenge the confession without himself giving evidence.[4] If he does choose to testify, he is then confronted with a choice between failing to contest an alleged confession which might well prove fatal to any chance of an acquittal,[5] and contesting it, with the result of letting in evidence of his previous

18 *Selvey v DPP* [1970] AC 304, [1968] 2 All ER 497, Viscount Dilhorne's fourth proposition.
19 *R v McLean* [1978] Crim LR 430, the court was quite explicit that the decision had nothing to do with discretion.
20 *R v Jenkins* (1945) 31 Cr App Rep 1 (woman's heterosexual immorality); *R v Bishop* [1975] QB 274, [1974] 2 All ER 1206, (man's homosexual immorality).
 1 *R v Rappolt* (1911) 6 Cr App Rep 156. But see *R v Jones* (1909) 3 Cr App Rep 67; *R v Stratton* (1909) 3 Cr App Rep 255; *R v Eidinow* (1932) 23 Cr App Rep 145.
 2 *R v Cohen* (1914) 10 Cr App Rep 91. But see *R v Watson* (1913) 8 Cr App Rep 249.
 3 *R v Marshall* (1899) 63 JP 36.
 4 Such a practice attracts strong judicial disapproval, see *R v O'Neill, R v Ackers* (1950) 34 Cr App Rep 108 at 111; *R v Callaghan* (1979) 69 Cr App Rep 88 at 91.
 5 Research conducted on behalf of the Royal Commission on Criminal Procedure by Baldwin and McConville revealed that, overall, fewer than 5 per cent of those alleged to have made a written confession, and fewer than 10 per cent of those alleged to have made an oral confession, were acquitted after a trial in the Crown Court 'Confessions in Crown Court Trials' (1980) Research Study No 5, Table 3.2; similar results were found by Vennard in relation to summary trials, 'Contested Trials in Magistrates' Courts' (1980) Research Study No 6, Table 3.1.

record, which is likely to prove equally fatal.[6] It is clear that any allegation of gross misconduct by a police witness in securing a confession,[7] or of concocting one,[8] will amount to an imputation. Attempts have been made to alleviate the harshness of this result by suggesting that this conclusion can be avoided if there is no more than a conflict of testimony between the accused and a single police witness about the making of a confession,[9] or if the suggestion is not made explicitly, but merely left as a matter of inference.[10] The most recent decisions reject both lines of argument.[11] The simple truth of the matter is that, in the absence of any plausible explanation by way of mistake or misunderstanding,[12] it is an imputation upon the character of a witness for the prosecution to allege that he has either coerced or concocted the confession to which he has testified.

(ii) Reading words into s 1(f)(ii)

It is often said that s 1(f) is to be construed literally. If so, it should be noted that the second limb of 1(f)(ii) requires that the questions be 'such as to' involve imputations, and by contrast with the formulation of the first limb not necessarily 'with a view to' doing so. This suggests that an unintended imputation should be enough to forfeit protection. Such a view was not accepted before the development of discretion as a form of longstop protection.[13] It now seems that this limb is to be read literally, and that discretion should be used to mitigate its effects.[14] It may also be noted that this limb mentions both the nature and the conduct of the defence, though it is rare for any explanation of the difference between them to be advanced.[15] Closely akin to the questions of what does or does not amount to an 'imputation' is the question whether it can be said that the accused is only exposed to cross-examination concerning his record when the nature or conduct of the defence is such as to involve 'unnecessary' or 'unjustifiable' imputations upon the character of the prosecutor or the witnesses for the prosecution. If the answer is in the negative, the prisoner who alleges that it was not he, but a Crown witness, who committed the crime charged, that the prosecutrix who asserts his guilt of rape was a consenting party to acts of immorality or that the man he assaulted was

---

6 See 'Juries and the Rules of Evidence' [1973] Crim LR 208; McCabe and Purves *The Jury at Work* (1972) Table 4; Doob and Kirshenbaum 'Some Empirical Evidence on the Effect of s 12 of the Canada Evidence Act Upon an Accused' (1972) 15 Crim LQ 88. Doubts were, however, expressed by the Supreme Court of Canada about the conclusiveness of these studies in *Corbett v R* (1988) 41 CCC (3d) 385 at 401.

7 *R v Cook* [1959] 2 QB 340, [1959] 2 All ER 97.

8 *R v Clark* [1955] 2 QB 469, [1955] 3 All ER 29.

9 Wolchover 'Cross-Examination of the Accused on his Record when a Confession is Denied or Retracted' [1981] Crim LR 312, attempting to reconcile the decisions in *R v Tanner* (1977) 66 Cr App Rep 56 and *R v Nelson* (1978) 68 Cr App Rep 12.

10 Cohen 'Challenging Police Evidence of Interviews and the Second Limb of Section 1(f)(ii)—Another View' [1981] Crim LR 523. In *Tanner* the judge intervened to make the suggestion explicit, as he did in his ruling in *R v Britzman, R v Hall* [1983] 1 All ER 369, [1983] 1 WLR 350.

11 *Britzman* above; *R v Owen* (1985) 83 Cr App Rep 100 at 104.

12 Though a court is likely to construe these concepts fairly broadly in order to prevent every conflict of evidence from entitling the prosecution to cross-examine so as to reveal the accused's record, see *R v St Louis and Fitzroy Case* (1984) 79 Cr App Rep 53.

13 *R v Preston* [1909] 1 KB 568, 2 Cr App Rep 24.

14 *R v Watts* [1983] 3 All ER 101, 77 Cr App Rep 126.

15 Some attempt was made in *O'Hara v HM Advocate* 1948 JC 90.

the aggressor will be unable to develop his defence without throwing his shield away. After an early tendency to answer the question in the affirmative,[16] an emphatic negative was the reply of a full Court of Criminal Appeal in *R v Hudson*,[17] a prosecution for larceny to which the defence was that the crime had been committed by a Crown witness. Soon after *Hudson*'s case, however, it came to be recognised that the court has a discretion to prohibit cross-examination under s 1(f)(ii) although it is permissible as a matter of law.[18]

In *R v Turner*[19] the Court of Criminal Appeal decided, on the strength of the preponderance of earlier authority, that allegations by someone accused of rape that the prosecutrix had not merely consented to intercourse but had also been guilty of gross indecency as a preliminary, did not, as a matter of law, deprive him of his shield, the case being one in which: 'some limitation must be placed on the words of the section since to decide otherwise would be to do grave injustice never intended by Parliament.' With this exception, the difficulties mentioned in the last paragraph have been met, in so far as they have been met at all,[20] by the exercise of the court's discretion.

The facts of *Selvey v D P P*[1] are given above, p 401. The case is primarily of importance because the authorities on the second half of s 1(f)(ii) were reviewed by the House of Lords. According to Lord Dilhorne they establish the following propositions:[2]

(a) The words of the statute must be given their ordinary natural meaning;
(b) the section permits cross-examination of the accused as to character both when imputations on the character of the prosecutor and his witnesses are cast to show their unreliability as witnesses independently of the evidence given by them and also when the casting of imputations is necessary to enable the accused to establish his defence;
(c) in rape cases the accused can allege consent without placing himself in peril of cross-examination;
(d) if what is said amounts in reality to no more than a denial of the charge, expressed, it may be, in emphatic language, it should not be regarded as coming within the section.

The rape cases may either be treated as sui generis[3] or else explained on the ground that the defence of consent is nothing more than a denial by the accused that the prosecution has established one of the essential ingredients of the charge,[4] there is certainly no disposition on the part of the courts to extend the scope of these decisions.

16 *R v Bridgwater* [1905] 1 KB 131; *R v Preston* [1909] 1 KB 568.
17 [1912] 2 KB 464. Decisions to the same effect are *R v Cohen* (1914) 10 Cr App Rep 91; *R v Jenkins* (1945) 31 Cr App Rep 1; *R v Sargvon* (1967) 51 Cr App Rep 394; and *R v Bishop* (above). See also *Kerwood v R* (1944) 69 CLR 561; *Dawson v R* (1961) 106 CLR 1.
18 *R v Watson* (1913) 8 Cr App Rep 249; *R v Cook* [1959] 2 QB 340, [1959] 2 All ER 97.
19 [1944] KB 463, [1944] 1 All ER 599.
20 See *R v Brown* (1960) 44 Cr App Rep 181, for a case of self-defence in which they were hardly met.
1 [1970] AC 304.
2 At 339. See *R v Nelson* (1978) 68 Cr App Rep 12, applying propositions 2 and 4 (b and d).
3 *R v Cook* [1959] 2 QB 340 at 347.
4 *R v Turner* [1944] KB 463 at 469.

(iii) The discretion of the court and the duty to warn

In *Selvey*'s case the House of Lords confirmed, after full argument, the existence of a judicial discretion to prohibit cross-examination in spite of the fact that it is permitted as a matter of law by the terms of s 1(f)(ii);[5] but the House denied the existence of a general rule that the discretion should be exercised in favour of the accused when the proper development of his defence necessitates the casting of imputations on the prosecutor or his witnesses.[6] In *R v Britzman, R v Hall*[7] the Court of Appeal suggested guidelines for the application of this discretion. These were that it should be exercised in favour of the defence if the imputation amounted to no more than a denial of a single act or short series of acts relating to a single incident or interview, though not where the denial was of everything occurring over an extended period; that allowance should be made for the strain imposed by cross-examination of the accused, and too much weight should not be placed upon the phraseology of particular answers; and that the discretion should normally be exercised in favour of the defence when the evidence against him was overwhelming. It cannot be pretended that such guidelines offer very substantial protection. The fact that the existence of the discretion was not recognised in the early days of the Criminal Evidence Act is a matter to be borne in mind when the early decisions are under consideration; it is possible that some of them should now be treated as cases in which there was an imputation although the judge would have been justified in prohibiting cross-examination in the exercise of his discretion, had he known that he possessed such a thing. Even now, in cases in which the judge does not apply his mind to the question of discretion, the Court of Appeal may exercise its own discretion.[8] It may also uphold the judge's decision to allow cross-examination on a different ground from that upon which he relied.[9]

In *R v Cook*,[10] the Court of Criminal Appeal stressed the importance of giving some sort of warning to the defence that it was going too far. It was said that it has always been the practice for prosecuting counsel to indicate in advance that he is going to claim his rights, or for the judge to give the defence a caution. This is especially needful when the prisoner is unrepresented,[11] but can be regarded as giving the accused the best of both worlds when he is represented by counsel.[12]

---

5 In New Zealand where the discretion is formally open ended it is construed as if it were appended to the English statute, see *R v Potter* [1984] 2 NZLR 374; *R v Kalo* [1985] 1 NZLR 219. A similar discretion is applied in Canada where the statute is of much broader scope, see *Corbett v R* (1988) 41 CCC (3d) 385.
6 As had been suggested in *R v Flynn* [1963] 1 QB 729, [1961] 3 All ER 58.
7 [1983] 1 All ER 369 at 374, [1983] 1 WLR 350 at 355.
8 *R v Watts* [1983] 3 All ER 101, 77 Cr App Rep 126, where the purpose for conducting the cross-examination could not be achieved.
9 *R v Clark* [1955] 2 QB 469 at 473.
10 Above.
11 For the appropriate procedure at a summary trial see *R v Weston-Super-Mare JJ, ex p Townsend* [1968] 3 All ER 225n.
12 See *R v Brown* (1960) 44 Cr App Rep 181; *R v McGee and Cassidy* (1979) 70 Cr App Rep 247.

(iv) The rationale of the second half of s 1(f)(ii)

The rationale of this part of s 1(f)(ii) was stated in the following passage in a judgment of Channell J:

> If the defence is so conducted, or the nature of the defence is such, as to involve the proposition that the jury ought not to believe the prosecutor or one of the witnesses for the prosecution upon the ground that his conduct—not his evidence in the case, but his conduct outside the evidence given by him—makes him an unreliable witness, then the jury ought also to know the character of the prisoner who either gives that evidence or makes that charge, and it then becomes admissible to cross-examine the prisoner about his antecedents and character with the view of showing that he has such a bad character that the jury ought not to rely upon his evidence.[13]

In other words, it is a case of tit for tat.[14]

(v) Purpose of the cross-examination allowed by the second half of s 1(f)(ii)[15]

Such a rationale means that cross-examination under this limb of s 1(f)(ii) is directed to the credibility of the accused. There is room for difference of opinion as to whether it merely goes to the credibility of his imputation upon the prosecutor,[16] or more generally to the credibility of the whole of his testimony.[17] In some cases the sequence of events determines that the cross-examination is capable of going only to credibility.[18] More often it is logically capable of going also to the issue of guilt or innocence. The practice of the courts seems to indicate that it is often so used.[19] There are however weighty dicta, and decisions, prohibiting the use of such cross-examination to show the accused's guilt directly.[20] It is always difficult to distinguish intelligibly between questions going to the credibility of the accused's testimony and questions going to his guilt. The zenith of such difficulty is achieved in a situation where the subject matter of the previous convictions is not particularly suggestive of general dishonesty, but is highly suggestive of the accused's guilt of the offences with which he is now charged. If such previous convictions are not to be used as evidence going to guilt, then the more that emerges about the underlying facts the greater the likelihood of prejudice. The question of how far it is permissible

---

13 *R v Preston* [1909] 1 KB 568 at 575. See also per Singleton J in *R v Jenkins* (1945) 31 Cr App Rep 1 at 14–15: 'It is only fair that the jury should have material to enable them to determine whether to believe the accused or the prosecution'.

14 This policy has been held in Canada not to infringe the Canadian Charter of Rights and Freedoms, *Corbett v R* (1988) 41 CCC (3d) 385.

15 See Pattenden 'The Purpose of Cross-Examination Under Section 1(f) of the Criminal Evidence Act 1898' [1982] Crim LR 707.

16 As suggested by the formulation in *R v Cook* [1959] 2 QB 340 at 348, [1959] 2 All ER 97 at 101.

17 As suggested by the formulation in *Preston* quoted in the text.

18 As in *R v Coltress* (1978) 68 Cr App Rep 193.

19 Thus in *Selvey* itself the trial judge permitted only convictions on similar subject matter to be put to the accused.

20 Among the weightiest are the dicta in *Maxwell* quoted above at p 402, decisions turning on this point include *R v Vickers* [1972] Crim LR 101, and *R v Watts* (1983) 77 Cr App Rep 126. See also *R v Bransden* (1981) 27 SASR 474 at 480.

to reveal such facts has created some confusion.[1] It seemed at one time that the use of convictions for similar offences, carrying no special connotation of dishonesty might be eliminated.[2] As noted above,[3] the latest authority has swung back towards the practice adopted by the trial judge in *Selvey*. In a series of cases the Court of Appeal resiled from its views in *Watts*. Thus cross-examination as to convictions for drug offences,[4] for sexual offences,[5] and for theft from a person[6] have all been approved in the course of reverting to the guidance offered by *Selvey*. No real attempt has been made in any of these decisions to explain how it is possible both to affirm, as they all do, the proposition that the cross-examination relates to the worthiness of belief of the accused in his attack on the prosecution witnesses, with their explicit endorsement of the use of convictions for offences bearing a close resemblance to those charged against the accused, even though not necessarily involving an element of dishonesty.

The guidance offered by this line of authority appears to combine both a rationale of negating the effect of the accused's attack, and one of more generally impugning the credit of the accused. It is odd that an attempt was made to suppress potentially prejudicial detail only in *Owen*, which was the only one of the cases where the conviction did necessarily savour to some extent of dishonesty.

This part of s 1(f)(ii) is liable to place counsel for the defence in an embarrassing position. Assuming that the prosecution has, as it should,[7] informed him of his client's record, and of the known records of witnesses for the prosecution,[8] he cannot cross-examine the witnesses without exposing the accused to retaliation in kind. On the other hand failure to attack the witnesses' credibility may lead the jury to treat unreliable evidence as though it were trustworthy. It is still more unfair if other defence witnesses have had records which the prosecution may attack with impunity. This difficulty could be countered by a practice under which counsel for the Crown informs the court of such matters as the previous convictions of his witnesses, but there is no general rule to that effect.[9]

It is to be hoped that further consideration will be given to this area of the law. It is submitted that the accused should be exposed to cross-examination as to his record, and especially as to the details of his conduct in the past, only if such evidence would be admissible in chief. The difference between the criterion being its having been admitted, as

1 In *R v Shepherd* (1980) 71 Cr App Rep 120, the use of the convictions alone was condemned, for fear that the jury might use the underlying facts for an improper purpose; in *R v Duncalf* [1979] 2 All ER 1116, [1979] 1 WLR 918, the use of underlying facts was encouraged; while in *R v France* [1979] Crim LR 48, the use of the underlying facts was condemned but the use of the fact of conviction approved.

2 In *R v Watts* [1983] 3 All ER 101, 77 Cr App Rep 126 Lord Lane LCJ described the direction to regard cross-examination as to such offences as affecting only credibility as requiring the jury to perform 'feats of intellectual acrobatics'.

3 At p 183.

4 *R v Burke* (1985) 82 Cr App Rep 156.

5 *R v Powell* [1986] 1 All ER 193, [1985] 1 WLR 1364.

6 *R v Owen* (1985) 83 Cr App Rep 100.

7 *Practice Direction* [1966] 2 All ER 929, [1966] 1 WLR 1184.

8 See *R v Collister, R v Warhurst* (1955) 39 Cr App Rep 100; *R v Parks* (1961) 3 All ER 633, [1961] 1 WLR 1484; *R v Matthews* (1975) 60 Cr App Rep 292. See also *R v Kelly* [1987] IR 596.

9 *R v Carey, R v Williams* (1968) 52 Cr App Rep 305.

suggested above[10] in relation to the discussion of s 1(f)(i), and its being merely admissible as suggested here, may be justified upon the basis that here it is the accused who brings the conditions into effect by himself conducting the defence in such a way as to suggest his own good character, or to cast imputations upon the character of the witnesses for the prosecution. If this course were to be adopted it should be made clear that such cross-examination would go both to issue and to credit, so far as these can be distinguished in the case of the accused. It would further help to avoid anomaly if, as also suggested above,[11] the archaic rule that a conviction for any offence at however remote a date on a charge of any crime be regarded as relevant to credit, were to be abolished.

D. THE INTERPRETATION OF S 1(f)(iii)

The rationale underlying s 1(f)(iii) according to which the accused may be cross-examined about his past misconduct if he has 'given evidence against any other person charged in the same proceedings' is, presumably, that he is in the same position as a witness for the prosecution so far as the co-accused is concerned, and nothing must be done to impair the right of a person charged to discredit his accusers. Accordingly it has been held that the court has no discretion to refuse leave for a co-accused to cross-examine under s 1(f)(iii) if it considers that the subsection applies to the case,[12] although it would have such a discretion if the application under the subsection were made by the prosecution.[13] It should also be remembered that the judge has a separate discretion to order separate trials which may be used to prevent prejudice which might otherwise be caused by the absence of a discretion to prevent cross-examination by a co-accused under s 1(f)(iii).[14] The construction, scope and purpose of cross-examination under this proviso will now be considered.

1. CONSTRUCTION

(i) 'Given evidence against'

Much more weight has been cast upon the construction of these words in the proviso as a result of the decision that there is no discretion to disallow cross-examination under it by a co-accused. In *Varley* the Court of Appeal attempted to clarify matters. The accused, and one Dibble, were accused

10 At p 396.
11 At p 315.
12 *Murdoch v Taylor* [1965] AC 574, [1965] 1 All ER 406, but note Lord Pearce's dissent on this point and see *Sandlon v H M Advocate* 1983 JC 22. Earlier authorities include *R v Ellis* [1961] 2 All ER 928, [1961] 1 WLR 1064; *R v Stannard* [1965] 2 QB 1, [1964] 1 All ER 34. See Carvell 'The Criminal Evidence Act 1898 s 1(f)(iii)' [1965] Crim LR 419. In Tasmania there may be a discretion, *Hill v R* [1953] Tas SR 54; though later cases in other Australian jurisdictions recognise no discretion, see for example, *R v Ransom* (1979) 22 SASR 283 at 285. For cross-examination by co-accused generally see p 333 above.
13 See *Matusevich v R* (1977) 137 CLR 633.
14 *R v Varley* [1982] 2 All ER 519, 75 Cr App Rep 242. It is unlikely to be sufficient to justify the exercise of such discretion merely that 'cut throat' defences are being run. See also *R v Hoggins* [1967] 3 All ER 334, [1967] 1 WLR 1223; *R v Ditroia and Tucci* [1981] VR 247.

of participating in a robbery. Dibble's defence was that although he did participate, he was acting under the coercion of Varley. Varley's defence was that he had not been involved at all. He argued that such a defence ought not to be construed as amounting to giving evidence 'against' Dibble. The Court of Appeal reviewed a number of decisions,[15] and distilled from them the following propositions:

> (1) If it is established that a person jointly charged has given evidence against the co-defendant that defendant has the right to cross-examine the other as to previous convictions and the trial judge has no discretion to refuse an application. (2) Such evidence may be given either in chief or during cross-examination. (3) It has to be objectively decided whether the evidence either supports the prosecution case in a material respect or undermines the defence of the co-accused. A hostile intent is irrelevant. (4) If consideration has to be given to the undermining of the other's defence care must be taken to see that the evidence clearly undermines the defence. Inconvenience to or inconsistency with the other's defence is not of itself sufficient. (5) Mere denial of participation in a joint venture is not of itself sufficient to rank as evidence against the co-defendant. For the proviso to apply, such denial must lead to the conclusion that if the witness did not participate then it must have been the other who did. (6) Where the one defendant asserts or in due course would assert one view of the joint venture which is directly contradicted by the other such contradiction may be evidence against the co-defendant.[16]

It should be noted that a co-defendant retains an interest capable of being undermined so long as he persists in his plea of not guilty, however much his case may have been damaged by the time the question arises.[17] It may also be noted that the second of these propositions is not easily reconciled with the literal wording of the proviso, and in particular with the absence from (iii) of the reference to 'asking questions' which is present in proviso (ii). It also seems that the application of these principles will do little to avert the result regretted by Lord Reid in *Murdoch v Taylor* that:

> an accused person with previous convictions, whose story contradicts in any material respect the story of the co-accused who has not yet been convicted, will find it almost impossible to defend himself, and if he elects not to give evidence his plight will be as bad.[18]

(ii) 'Any other person charged in the same proceedings'

The Act of 1898 originally referred to cases in which evidence was given against any other person 'charged with the same offence'. These words were unduly restrictive because there are many joint trials in which the accused cannot by any stretch of the imagination be said to be charged with the same offence. The phraseology was criticised in the House of Lords when they held, in *Metropolitan Police Comr v Hills*,[19] that two

15 *Murdoch v Taylor* [1965] AC 574, [1965] 1 All ER 406; *R v Stannard* [1965] 2 QB 1, [1964] 1 All ER 34; *R v Davis* [1975] 1 All ER 233, [1975] 1 WLR 345; *R v Bruce* [1975] 3 All ER 277, [1975] 1 WLR 1252; *R v Hatton* (1976) 64 Cr App Rep 88.
16 At 522, 246.
17 *R v Mir, Ahmed and Dalil* [1989] Crim LR 894.
18 [1965] AC 574 at 582, [1965] 1 All ER 406 at 408.
19 [1980] AC 26, [1978] 2 All ER 1105. The authorities are discussed and the solution which has been adopted is suggested in an article by Mirfield in [1978] Crim LR 725.

motorists who had collided with the result that a pedestrian was killed were not charged with the same offence when tried together on successive counts of the same indictment for causing death by dangerous driving. The Criminal Evidence Act 1979 substituted the words 'charged in the same proceedings' for 'charged with the same offence'. The new wording is wide enough to cover all the old cases in which cross-examination was held to have been impermissible and there is no obvious reason why it should cause difficulty.

2. SCOPE

In *R v Lovett*[20] Lovett was charged with stealing a television set and G, his co-accused, was charged with handling it. Lovett cast serious imputations on a witness for the prosecution and gave evidence against G. G's counsel immediately cross-examined him on his previous convictions; he was convicted and G was acquitted. On Lovett's appeal the Court of Appeal held that cross-examination under s 1(f)(iii) as it then was worded was improper because the two accused were not charged with the same offence but, as counsel for the prosecution had intended to seek leave to cross-examine under s 1(f)(ii), the Court of Appeal exercised the discretion which the judge would have had and dismissed the appeal. On the authority of *R v Seigley*,[1] the court expressed the view that the prosecution may, subject to the discretion of the judge to prohibit such a course, cross-examine under s 1(f)(iii). As the law then stood the prosecution could not have been allowed to cross-examine under that proviso in *R v Lovett*, and it is only in very exceptional circumstances that an application for leave to do so would be likely to succeed. A possible instance would be a case in which two persons charged in the same proceedings each gave evidence against the other, but, because they both had criminal records, neither cross-examined the other under s 1(f)(iii). There is, however, something to be said for the conclusion of the High Court of Australia that the Crown has no power to cross-examine under an identically worded proviso.[2]

The High Court of Australia held in the same case, contrary to what was said in *R v Lovett*, that the accused has no right, where imputations have been cast by a co-accused on a witness for the prosecution, to cross-examine under s 1(f)(ii). Such a right is difficult to justify on principle, although it is not excluded by the wording of the statute. It might occasionally have been useful before the wording of s 1(f)(iii) was changed. For example the Court of Appeal recognised that G might have sought leave to cross-examine Lovett under s 1(f)(ii), but it is not easy to think of situations in which it would now be called for.

There appears to be no authority on the extent to which one co-accused may invoke s 1(f)(i) in order to cross-examine another about the commission of crimes or previous convictions. A literal construction presents no impediment to such a course, and it might be useful in cases

20 [1973] 1 All ER 744, [1973] 1 WLR 241.
1 (1911) 6 Cr App Rep 106.
2 *Matusevich v R* (1977) 137 CLR 633. The decision turned in part on the absence of a statutory requirement of an application for leave to cross-examine such as is required in the equivalent to s 1(f)(ii) in s 399 of the Crimes Act of Victoria.

where the cross-examination was intended to go to more than the co-accused's credit. It should be noted though that in such a case the wording of the first proviso would exclude cross-examination about charges or bad character falling short of the commission of crimes, and that it would have to show the co-accused's guilt of the crime with which *he* was charged.

3. PURPOSE OF CROSS-EXAMINATION UNDER S 1(f)(iii)[3]

There seems little doubt that the only purpose of such cross-examination is to attack the credibility of the accused. It was so stated in *Murdoch v Taylor*.[4] In many cases credibility and issue are so intertwined that a court is likely, even without reference to s 1(f)(i), to permit cross-examination so long as some issue of credibility can be discerned.[5] Nor is it necessarily fatal to a conviction that the trial judge fails to explain this limited purpose to the jury, again no doubt because of the difficulty of distinguishing between the various purposes in the case of a defendant.[6]

E. PROPOSALS FOR REFORM

In the course of its comprehensive re-examination of the whole of the law of evidence in criminal cases the Criminal Law Revision Committee formulated a number of far-reaching reforms of this part of the law.[7] Some of the suggestions attracted criticism,[8] only one of them has been so far enacted in England,[9] and none are included in the Police and Criminal Evidence Act 1984. It may thus be supposed that they are unlikely to be enacted in their original form without some further investigation into the whole structure of a criminal trial, and it is no longer profitable to consider them in detail.[10]

Very many different approaches have been proposed to the solution of the problem of cross-examination of the accused who gives evidence. There are two basic traditions, that current in North America and that obtaining elsewhere in the common law world. The North American tradition has tended to favour treatment of the accused as an ordinary, but not compellable, witness.[11] As such he is free to choose whether or not to testify, but if he chooses to do so, he enjoys no special protection. There is

---

3 See Pattenden 'The Purpose of Cross-Examination Under Section 1(f) of the Criminal Evidence Act 1898' [1982] Crim LR 707.
4 [1965] AC 574 at 584 (Lord Morris), at 593 (Lord Donovan), [1965] 1 All ER 406 at 409 and at 416.
5 *R v Reid* [1989] Crim LR 719.
6 *R v Hoggins* [1967] 3 All ER 334, [1967] 1 WLR 1223.
7 Cmnd 4991 paras 114–136, draft Bill cll 6, 7 and 15.
8 See Tapper (1973) 36 MLR 167.
9 Though some have been included in the Criminal Procedure Code of Singapore, see *Haw Tua Tau v Public Prosecutor* [1982] AC 136, [1981] 3 All ER 14; *Jaykumal v Public Prosecutor* [1982] AC 156; and in the New South Wales Crimes Act 1900, see s 413A(4).
10 For such discussion see the 5th edition of this work (1979).
11 Although in Canada the Uniform Law Conference has now proposed a measure within the alternative tradition, see Report of Canadian Task Force, App 3; and in the United States the Commonwealth of Pennsylvania has operated within that tradition since 1911, see Tapper 'The Meaning of s 1(f)(i) of Criminal Evidence Act 1898' in Tapper (ed) *Crime, Proof and Punishment* (1981) pp 307–10.

little room for doubt that this inhibits many accused persons with criminal records from testifying.[12] Within this tradition, where the same rules have to apply to the accused as apply to other witnesses, the only means of amelioration would seem to be either to make the accused a compellable witness, or to reform the techniques for the cross-examination of all witnesses to such an extent that the accused would be no longer so inhibited. It should be noted that no more than the fact of a conviction can be put, that the judge has a discretion to disallow even this,[13] and that the Canadian courts are endowed with a discretion to disallow any other oppressive cross-examination of the accused.[14]

In the tradition deriving from the Criminal Evidence Act 1898 the accused is treated differently from other witnesses, and accorded special protection in cross-examination. Here the difficulty lies in deciding upon the precise nature and detail of that protection. There is widespread dissatisfaction with the current state of the law in virtually every jurisdiction within the tradition, and it is hardly surprising to discover that there is no unanimity in proposals for reform.[15] Here too the principal difficulty is to reconcile the desirability of having as much evidence before the jury as will enable them to come to a more accurate judgment of the worth of the accused's testimony with the prejudice such evidence may cause and the danger of inhibiting the accused from testifying at all. It is suggested that the basic aim of this branch of the law of evidence should be to get as much evidence relating directly to the commission of the crime before the jury as is possible. This will not be achieved if the accused chooses not to testify. It is worth re-examining the whole question of cross-examination so as to discredit a witness, in the light of the principle that evidence should be more probative than prejudicial. Such a re-examination might well remove some of the more objectionable lines of cross-examination, and help persuade the accused to testify.

---

12 Report of Canadian Task Force p 411. This was explicitly accepted by the Criminal Law Revision Committee, Cmnd 4991 para. 127(ii).

13 *Corbett v R* (1988) 41 CCC (3d) 385.

14 See *Fanjoy v R* (1985) 21 DLR (4th) 321; *Brown and Murphy v R* (1985) 21 DLR (4th) 761.

15 The Criminal Law Revision Committee rehearses very sharp disagreements on many points. The various suggestions are well analysed by the Australian Law Reform Commission in its Research Paper No 11 'Character and Conduct' ch 8. In addition to those mentioned above, that paper considers positions in the United States Federal Rules, and different variations in particular states; proposals in the Canadian Law Reform Commission's Evidence Code; proposals in the Ontario Law Reform Commission's Report on Evidence and draft Code; and proposals in the New South Wales Working Party Report on the Course of the Trial.

CHAPTER XI

Privilege

A witness is said to be privileged when he may validly claim not to answer a question or to supply information which would be relevant to the determination of an issue in judicial proceedings. Because the effect of such rules is to deprive the tribunal of relevant evidence powerful arguments are required to justify their existence, and the tendency of the modern law of evidence has been to reduce both their number and their scope.[1] Only three heads of privilege are sufficiently important to require discussion here, the privilege against self-incrimination, legal professional privilege and a privilege for statements made without prejudice as part of an attempt to settle a dispute. A few preliminary observations are also necessary.

In the first place, as the privilege is that of a particular person or class, matters covered by it may always be proved by the evidence of other witnesses. Parke B once said:

Where an attorney entrusted confidentially with a document communicates the contents, or suffers another to take a copy, surely the secondary evidence so obtained may be produced. Suppose the instrument were even stolen, and a correct copy taken, would it not be reasonable to admit it?[2]

It was on the authority of Parke B's remark that the Court of Appeal allowed copies of proofs of witnesses with notes on the evidence in a former action brought by the plaintiff's predecessor in title to be put in by the defendant in *Calcraft v Guest*,[3] the originals having been handed over by the defendant's solicitor to the plaintiff to whom they belonged. Such secondary evidence cannot however be used if it consists of, or is derived from, a document brought into court by an opponent, or his legal representative, and then improperly obtained.[4] The Law Reform Committee felt that such a rule should apply generally in cases where secondary evidence had been obtained by the commission of a crime or tort, but refrained from making any recommendation pending the 11th Report of

---

1 Recommendations to this effect in the 16th Report of the Law Reform Committee (Cmnd 3472, 1967) and in the 11th Report of the Criminal Law Revision Committee (Cmnd 4991, 1972) have been largely implemented in Civil Evidence Act 1968, s 16, and Police and Criminal Evidence Act 1984, s 80 (9). Any statute conferring a new privilege is liable to be construed strictly, *Pallin v Department of Social Welfare* [1983] NZLR 666, *R v House* [1983] NZLR 252.

2 *Lloyd v Mostyn* (1842) 10 M & W 478 at 481–2 in the course of argument.

3 [1898] 1 QB 759. Quaere whether this decision has not overruled *R v Leverson* (1868) 11 Cox CC 152.

4 *ITC Film Distributors v Video Exchange Ltd* [1982] Ch 431, [1982] 2 All ER 241. If there has been no impropriety in obtaining such a document, it may apparently be used, see *R v Tompkins* (1977) 67 Cr App Rep 181; for a more restrictive view in New Zealand see *R v Uljee* [1982] 1 NZLR 561.

the Criminal Law Revision Committee.[5] No recommendation was made upon this matter, nor was it dealt with in the Police and Criminal Evidence Act 1984. The matter is thus left to the general common law rules relating to the admissibility of illegally obtained evidence, where as will be explained more fully in the next chapter the rules in England generally favour admissibility more than those in some other common law jurisdictions, and very much more than the rules in the United States.[6]

Secondly, the personal nature of the privilege means that a party will not necessarily be entitled to succeed on an appeal, or obtain an order for a new trial when the claim to privilege of his own, or his opponent's witness has been wrongly rejected or accepted in the court below. There is express authority for this view in a case in which the witness had unsuccessfully invoked the privilege against self-incrimination,[7] and practically all the decisions of appellate courts in which the judge's ruling on a question of privilege has been varied or reversed relate to issues in which the person claiming the privilege was a party to, and not merely a witness in, the proceedings. Many of them are concerned with the discovery of documents, or the propriety of interrogatories for, as often as not, the issue of privilege is raised in interlocutory proceedings before the actual trial of a civil action.

Thirdly, according to English law, no adverse inference should be made from the fact that the privilege is claimed.[8]

The last general observation concerns the effect of upholding a claim to privilege. This involves withholding important information from the court at the expense of what may be abstract justice to one of the parties. It follows that there should be good cause, plainly shown, for the existence of any privilege,[9] and it remains for us to consider whether this is so in the case of all the privileges discussed in this chapter. The crucial question is whether there is some interest protected by the privilege which is at least as significant as the proper administration of justice. It is, of course, important not to exclude the possibility that the law is defective on account of its failure to recognise certain legitimate claims to privilege, and not merely because of its protection of interests which do not merit such solicitude. The influence of public opinion must never be ignored. The proper administration of justice mentioned above includes the notion of

---

5 Cmnd 3472 para 32. The committee assumed that secondary evidence of a privileged document could be given however it had been obtained; see also Lord Simon's view in *Waugh v British Railways Board* [1980] AC 521 at 536, [1979] 2 All ER 1169 at 1177.

6 The Report of the Law Reform Committee refers to r 26 of the Uniform Rules which confers very wide protection on the privilege holder; there is no equivalent in the new, and now current, Federal Rules under which privilege is governed by the common law.

7 *R v Kinglake* (1870) 22 LT 335. In *Doe d Egremont v Date* (1842) 3 QB 609, a decision on title deeds, a distinction was suggested between cases in which the witness's claim to privilege was successful in which event a party could contend that he had been deprived of a possible means of proving a fact, and those in which it failed, in which event the aggrieved party cannot complain because the privilege might have been waived, but the distinction does not seem to have been taken in other cases.

8 *Wentworth v Lloyd* (1864) 10 HL Cas 589 at 590–592. The contrast with r 233 of the Model Code is striking: 'if a privilege to refuse to disclose, or a privilege to prevent another from disclosing, matter is claimed and allowed, the judge and counsel may comment thereon, and the trier of fact may draw all reasonable inferences therefrom'; but this rule was not adopted by the Uniform Law Commissioners (see Uniform Rules, r 39).

9 VIII *Wigmore* p 67.

the rejection of relevant evidence because its reception would be unduly offensive to contemporary public opinion. It follows that that which was the subject of privilege in one generation should not necessarily be privileged in the next and vice versa.

SECTION 1. THE PRIVILEGE AGAINST SELF-INCRIMINATION[10]

A. STATEMENT, HISTORY AND RATIONALE OF THE RULE

1. STATEMENT OF THE RULE

The rule is that no one is bound to answer any question if the answer thereto would, in the opinion of the judge, have a tendency to expose the deponent to any criminal charge, penalty or [in a criminal case] forfeiture which the judge regards as reasonably likely to be preferred or sued for.[11]

The privilege extends to the production of documents and things, and, subject to the unimportant modification in square brackets, it applies to civil and criminal cases alike. In the United States it appears that the privilege does not permit samples of 'body fluids or substances' to be withheld.[12] We have seen that, at any rate as far as blood tests are concerned, the provision of samples of this nature may not be ordered at common law, although this is the outcome of the protection of personal liberty rather than the privilege against self-incrimination.[13] A witness cannot claim to be privileged from answering questions on the ground that the answers will expose him to civil liability either at the suit of the Crown or of any other person.[14] Nor will exposure to other unpleasant consequences be enough, such as rendering the witness liable to bankruptcy,[15] or to professional disciplinary, proceedings.[16] It has further been

10 VIII *Wigmore* (McNaughton revision), paras 2250–51 contains a classic statement of the history and rationale of the rule. See also Edmund Morgan 'The Privilege against Self-Incrimination' (1949) 34 Minn LR 1, and Levy *Origins of the Fifth Amendment* (1968). For a modern Australian perspective, see McNicol *A Non-curial Privilege Against Self-Incrimination* Contemporary Legal Issues Series No 2 (1984).

11 Per Goddard LJ in *Blunt v Park Lane Hotel Ltd* [1942] 2 KB 253 at 257, [1942] 2 All ER 187 at 189.

12 See also in Australia *Controlled Consultants Pty Ltd v Comr for Corporate Affairs* (1985) 57 ALR 751 at 755, 756; and in the United States Uniform Rules 25(c); *Schmerber v California* (1966) 384 US 757, the Uniform Rules and the decision in *Schmerber's* case confine the privilege, even in the case of an accused, to evidence of a testimonial or communicative nature, but this is, of course, subject to the rights accorded to an accused by the constitutional proviso against unreasonable searches.

13 See p 39 above. Such samples may however be ordered under the conditions set out in the Police and Criminal Evidence Act 1984, ss 61–65.

14 Witnesses Act 1806.

15 *Re XY, ex p Haes* [1902] 1 KB 98.

16 See *Re Fang and College of Physicians and Surgeons of Alberta* (1985) 25 DLR (4th) 632; *Re Johnstone and Law Society of British Columbia* (1987) 40 DLR (4th) 550; *Re Prousky and the Law Society of Upper Canada* (1987) 41 DLR (4th) 565, though in Canada the position has been much affected by the Canadian Charter of Rights and Freedoms which these decisions construe. In the United States the privilege has been held not to extend to protect a foreign bank account from compulsory disclosure, *Doe v US* 108 S Ct 2341 (1988), nor to prevent the accused from being shown to be 'a sexually dangerous person', *Allen v Illinois* 106 S Ct 2988 (1986).

suggested that the privilege may need to be curtailed so far as it is deployed to defeat a motion for civil contempt in the very same proceedings.[17]

It will be convenient to say something about the history and rationale of the rule before mentioning some miscellaneous points and considering various statutory provisions.

2. HISTORY OF THE RULE

Three types of answers are contemplated as the possible subject-matter of a claim to privilege in the above statement—those which expose the deponent to the risk of a criminal charge, those which put him in danger of a penalty, and those which might lead to a forfeiture. It used to be customary to include within the rule answers which would tend to show that the deponent had committed adultery. Each of these matters has a different history, the result of which is that the so-called privilege against self-incrimination covers a wider ground than the liability to criminal punishment.

(i) Liability to a criminal charge

We have seen that the privilege against self-incrimination in the narrow sense of the word originated in the unpopularity of the procedure in the Star Chamber under which those who were charged with an offence were interrogated on oath.[18] This contributed to the rule that the accused could not testify in a criminal case, and the idea that no one could be obliged to jeopardise his life or liberty by answering questions on oath came to be applied to all witnesses in all proceedings in the course of the seventeenth century. The rule extends beyond answers that would directly criminate the witness to those which might be used as a step towards obtaining evidence against him. In *R v Slaney*,[19] for instance, a witness who was giving evidence at a prosecution for a criminal libel contained in an advertisement in a newspaper was asked whether he knew who wrote to the proprietors with the advertisement, and, after he had answered in the affirmative, Lord Tenterden CJ upheld his objection to stating the name of the writer of the letter:

> You cannot only not compel a witness to answer that which will criminate him, but that which tends to criminate him: and the reason is this, that the party would go from one question to another, and though no question might be asked, the answer of which would directly criminate the witness, yet they would get enough from him whereon to found a charge against him.

At one time it was thought that it would be sufficient to establish the claim to privilege if the witness swore that his answer would tend to criminate him, but we shall see that it is now clear that the court must examine the matter a little more closely.

17 *Crest Homes plc v Marks* [1987] AC 829 at 859, [1987] 2 All ER 1074 at 1082.
18 See p 204 above.
19 (1832) 5 C & P 213. See also *Short v Mercier* (1851) 3 Mac & G 205 at 217 per Lord Truro.

(ii) Liability to a penalty

The rule that a witness cannot be obliged to answer a question if the answer would expose him to the risk of a penalty seems to have originated in the doctrine that equity would not assist a common informer by making an order for discovery in his favour. This rule survived the Judicature Acts.[20] Proceedings for penalties, as opposed to compensation,[1] were virtually obsolete, but the Law Reform Committee considered that the privilege should continue so long as penalties are recoverable in some civil proceedings.[2] The category of penalties in respect of which the privilege may be claimed has been augmented by accession to the European Economic Communities, since penalties imposed for breach of the terms of the EEC Treaty, and of Council Regulations, have been held to qualify.[3]

(iii) Liability to forfeiture

The inclusion of answers tending to establish liability to a forfeiture within this privilege is attributable to the rule that equity would not grant discovery or order interrogatories in aid of a forfeiture of property which also survived the Judicature Acts. When declining to grant discovery in an action for the forfeiture of a lease in *Earl of Mexborough v Whitwood U D C*,[4] Lord Esher referred to the equitable rule against assisting common informers or aiding a forfeiture of property, saying:

> The rule by which a witness is protected from being called on to answer questions which may tend to criminate himself is often referred to in connection with this subject, but it has really nothing to do with the two rules to which I have referred.

The Law Reform Committee could see no reason for the continued existence of this branch of the privilege against self-incrimination now that the courts possess wide powers of relief against forfeiture, and it was accordingly abolished, so far as civil cases are concerned, by s 16(1)(a) of the Civil Evidence Act 1968.[5]

(iv) Liability to a finding of adultery

There can be little doubt that answers which might be used to establish the witness's adultery were once thought to be included in the common law privilege against self-incrimination, but this view was rendered obsolete by the decision of the Court of Appeal in *Blunt v Park Lane Hotel Ltd*.[6] That was an action for slander based on an allegation that the

---

20 *Hunnings v Williamson* (1883) 10 QBD 459; *Martin v Treacher* (1886) 16 QBD 507.
1 *Adams v Batley* (1887) 18 QBD 625.
2 16th Report, para 13.
3 *Rio Tinto Zinc Corpn v Westinghouse Electric Corpn* [1978] AC 547, [1978] 1 All ER 434. It is also of importance in other common law jurisdictions where regulations are enforced by the imposition of penalties, often by a commission or tribunal, see *Pyneboard Pty Ltd v Trade Practices Commission* (1983) 45 ALR 609.
4 [1897] 2 QB 111 at 115; *Seddon v Commercial Salt Co Ltd* [1925] Ch 187.
5 There was a corresponding provision in cl 16(1)(a) of the draft Bill annexed to the 11th Report of the Criminal Law Revision Committee.
6 [1942] 2 KB 253, [1942] 2 All ER 187. See also *Evans v Evans and Blyth* [1904] P 378, and *Elliot v Albert* [1934] 1 KB 650.

plaintiff had been guilty of adultery. She objected to answering interrogatories which the defendants wished to administer in support of their plea of justification, but the court held that formal ecclesiastical censure of laymen for adultery was obsolete, and described the plaintiff's plea that her answers might expose her to the risk of not being allowed to partake of the sacrament as 'fanciful'. Goddard LJ stated the rule in the terms quoted at the beginning of this section, and it will be seen that he adopted the words of Bowen LJ in *Redfern v Redfern* except that he made no allusion to the possibility of ecclesiastical censure.

3. RATIONALE OF THE MAIN BRANCH OF THE RULE

Turning to the question of the rationale of the main head of the privilege, the idea that a man should be compelled to give answers exposing himself to the risk of criminal punishment is probably still repellent to public opinion, although it is no longer based on the unpopularity of the Star Chamber. There is the additional consideration that people must be encouraged to testify freely, and they might not be prepared to come forward as witnesses in the absence of some kind of privilege against incrimination. Although reliance on the privilege will sometimes obstruct the course of justice in the case in which it is claimed, and may militate against the discovery of crimes which ought to be traced in the public interest, there is probably sufficient justification for protecting a witness from exposing himself to the peril of criminal proceedings. When it is invoked as a justification of the accused's right not to testify and the suspect's right not to answer the questions of investigating officials, additional bases of the privilege which are frequently mentioned are the need to keep the officials up to scratch and the desirability of requiring them, as representatives of the state, to shoulder the entire burden of establishing the accused's guilt.

Considerations of this character have in some jurisdictions led to the extension of the doctrine of protection against self-incrimination beyond the confines of an evidential privilege into the status of a constitutional right. Thus in Canada the Supreme Court has remarked:

> Recent case law has taken the traditional doctrine of privilege and placed it on a new plane. Privilege is no longer regarded merely as a rule of evidence which acts as a shield to prevent privileged materials from being tendered in evidence in a courtroom. The courts, unwilling to restrict the concept, have extended its application well beyond those limits.[7]

Such an extension carries implications for the sort of proceedings in which the privilege can be claimed, the range of matters in respect of which it can be claimed, and particularly whether it can be claimed for evidence other than voluntary communications, how far the protection extends to material non-incriminating in itself but from which incriminating material can be derived, and how to construe statutes purporting to abrogate the privilege. In Australia, where a similar view is developing, such questions

7 *Solosky v R* (1979) 105 DLR (3d) 745 at 757 (the generality of these remarks occurred within the context of a claim for solicitor and client privilege).

are in the process of being worked out.[8] It is submitted that such an approach conflates a number of quite separate rules having different rationales, different histories and different incidents, with the consequent dangers of confusion and anomaly explained in the dissenting opinions of Brennan J in the High Court of Australia.[9]

B. MISCELLANEOUS POINTS

There are three further points to be considered so far as the common law on this subject is concerned—the question whether the privilege extends to answers which would criminate the witness's spouse, the question whether the privilege extends to answers which would criminate the witness under foreign law and the part played by the judge in determining the criminating tendencies of a question to which the witness objects.

1. INCRIMINATION OF SPOUSE

In civil cases s 14(1)(b) of the Civil Evidence Act 1968 has extended the privilege to questions tending to criminate a spouse. The Criminal Law Revision Committee recommended a similar rule for witnesses in criminal proceedings, excepting only the accused and his spouse,[10] though no such rule has as yet been enacted. It was unwilling to recommend such a general rule in respect of the accused or the spouse of the accused, nor has any such rule been included in the Police and Criminal Evidence Act 1984. Despite some old dicta to the contrary it seems that the privilege did not extend so far at common law.[11] Thus in *R v Pitt*[12] it was held that a spouse should be advised that if she chose to testify for the prosecution she would be treated like any other witness. In such circumstances she can be treated as hostile. All of this would be quite futile if she could nevertheless claim a privilege against incriminating her spouse. It need hardly be added that there is no privilege against incriminating strangers.[13]

---

8 *Sorby v Commonwealth* (1983) 46 ALR 237 is the leading case, and its implications are explored in *Trade Practices Commission v TNT Management Pty Ltd* (1984) 53 ALR 214; *Scanlon v Swan ex p Swan* [1984] 1 Qd R 21; *Re Packer v Deputy Commissioner of Taxation* (1984) 53 ALR 589; *Controlled Consultants Pty Ltd v Comr for Corporate Affairs* (1985) 57 ALR 751; and *Police Service Board v Morris* (1985) 58 ALR 1. See McNicol *A Non-Curial Privilege Against Self-incrimination* Contemporary Legal Issues Series No 2 (1984). See also in *New Zealand, Apple and Pear Marketing Board v Master and Sons Ltd* [1986] 1 NZLR 191.

9 Notably in *Pyneboard Pty Ltd v Trade Practices Commission* (1983) 45 ALR 609 at 623; and *Sorby* above at 261; Brennan J holds a similar view in relation to the closely related topic of legal professional privilege, see *Baker v Campbell* (1983) 49 ALR 385 at 418.

10 Cmnd 4991 para 169.

11 Dicta of Bayley J in *R v All Saints, Worcester* (1817) 6 M & S 194 at 201; compare Lord Diplock in *Rio Tinto Zinc Corpn v Westinghouse Electric Corpn* [1978] AC 547 at 637, [1978] 1 All ER 434 at 465, 'At common law ... the privilege against self-incrimination was restricted to the person claiming it and not anyone else.'

12 [1983] QB 25, [1982] 3 All ER 63.

13 *R v Minihane* (1921) 16 Cr App Rep 38. See also *Concrete Construction Pty Ltd v Plumbers and Gasfitters Employees' Union of Australia* (1987) 71 ALR 501.

2. INCRIMINATION UNDER FOREIGN LAW

In the *King of the Two Sicilies v Willcox*,[14] it appears to have been decided that the privilege does not extend to answers that might incriminate the witness under foreign law because the judge ought to be able to determine the question whether disclosure would entail penal consequences as a matter of law. In the *United States of America v McRae*,[15] on the other hand, it was decided that, where the provisions of the foreign law were admitted on the pleadings, there could be no order for discovery if the production of documents might have penal consequences thereunder. In the circumstances it is impossible to state the common law on this matter with any certitude. Section 14(1)(a) of the Civil Evidence Act 1968, expressly confines the privilege to 'criminal offences under the law of any part of the United Kingdom and penalties provided for by such law'.[16] Even then the court retains a discretion, at least in respect of discovery, and its exercise of such discretion may be influenced by the prospect of incrimination under foreign law.[17]

3. THE ROLE OF THE JUDGE

The privilege applies to answering, it does not facilitate the prevention of the relevant question being asked.[18] The judge will often warn a witness that he is not obliged to answer criminating questions, but there is no rule of law to this effect, and the fact that the witness was ignorant of his rights does not prevent the court from utilising his evidence in the case in which it was given, or in subsequent criminal proceedings brought against him.[19] The practice to be followed when someone objects to answering a question because he might be incriminated if he were to do so was laid down in *R v Boyes*.[20] The witness's mere statement that his answer might have this effect is not sufficient, although it is on oath and even if there is no doubt concerning his bona fides. The court must see, from the circumstances of the case and the nature of the evidence which the witness is called to give that there is reasonable ground to apprehend danger to him from his

---

14 (1851) 1 Sim NS 301. To the same effect are dicta in *Re Atherton* [1912] 2 KB 251 at 255.
15 (1868) 3 Ch App 79.
16 There was a corresponding provision in cl 15(1)(a) of the draft Bill attached to the 11th Report of the Criminal Law Revision Committee, but no such clause appeared in the Police and Criminal Evidence Act 1984. It is not without interest that the United States Supreme Court appears to have approved the application of the privilege to incrimination under foreign law generally in *Murphy v Waterfront Commission of New York Harbour* 378 US 52 (1964), although the actual case was concerned with incrimination under State Law. The position in Canada is similar to that in England, *Spencer v R* (1985) 21 DLR (4th) 756; while in Australia it seems uncertain, see *Comr of Australian Federal Police v Cox* (1989) 87 ALR 163 at 167.
17 *Arab Monetary Fund v Hashim* [1989] 3 All ER 466, [1989] 1 WLR 565.
18 *Allhusen v Labouchere* (1878) 3 QBD 654 at 660. Contrast the introductory words of the Criminal Evidence Act 1898, s 1(f).
19 *R v Coote* (1873) LR 4 PC 599. Cf *S v Lwane* 1966 (2) SA 433. For the stage in the proceedings at which the objection should be taken, see *Spokes v Grosvenor Hotel Co* [1897] 2 QB 124; *A J Bekhor v Bilton* [1981] QB 923, [1981] 2 All ER 565. It seems that a warning is not mandatory in relation to incrimination under foreign law, *R v Bateman and Cooper* [1989] Crim LR 590.
20 (1861) 1 B & S 311; *Re Reynolds, ex p Reynolds* (1882) 20 Ch D 294.

answer.[1] There must be no nice balancing of odds,[2] the judge must come to the conclusion that such danger is real and appreciable with reference to the ordinary operation of law in the ordinary course of things, not a danger of an imaginary and insubstantial character, having reference to some extraordinary and barely possible contingency so improbable that no reasonable man would suffer it to influence his conduct.

In *Boyes*'s case, a witness who had been handed a pardon under the Great Seal was obliged to answer a question with reference to its subject matter although he might still have been impeached for the offence according to strict legal theory because a pardon cannot be pleaded in answer to an impeachment. If a witness has already made himself liable to a criminal prosecution by an admission, his refusal to answer may be held not to be bona fide.[3] If the offence was of a trifling nature, or committed many years ago, a court might be inclined to regard the danger as too insubstantial to allow the plea to succeed. It will also be responsive to diminution of particular dangers in the light of changes of practice, and alert to the risk of defendants seeking to avoid civil liability by exaggerating dangers of prosecution.[4] If the danger is real, the court will not be deterred by commercial inconvenience from upholding the privilege. Thus in *Rank Film Distributors Ltd v Video Information Centre*, where the defendant raised the privilege to defeat the application of an Anton Piller order summarily requiring him to furnish certain information about his infringement of copyright in certain video films, the danger of a criminal charge of conspiracy to defraud was very real. The House of Lords upheld the claim for privilege even though it accepted that the result of so doing would be the practical destruction of the usefulness of Anton Piller orders.[5]

As noted above, the common law rule was that the privilege against self-incrimination applied only to the crimination of the claimant. In England there seems to be no doubt that the privilege can be claimed by any entity having legal personality,[6] but this is not the case in North America,[7] and has come under some attack in Australia.[8] In *Rio Tinto Zinc*

---

1 *Triplex Safety Glass Co v Lancergaye Safety Glass (1934) Ltd* [1939] 2 KB 395, [1939] 2 All ER 613, approved in *Rio Tinto Zinc Corpn v Westinghouse Electric Corpn* [1978] AC 547, [1978] 1 All ER 434.

2 *Re Westinghouse Electric Corpn Uranium Contract Litigation N D L Dock 235* [1977] 3 All ER 703 at 726.

3 *Brebner v Perry* [1961] SASR 177, where various English authorities are mentioned.

4 *Rank Film Distributors Ltd v Video Information Centre* [1982] AC 380 at 441, [1981] 2 All ER 76 at 80.

5 See Lord Fraser at 445, 83. It was thought necessary to enact s 72 of Supreme Court Act 1981 to restore the position, though in New Zealand a similar result has been achieved at common law, see *Thorn EMI Ltd v Kitching and Busby* [1984] FSR 342. For a similarly stringent approach in the context of *Mareva* injunctions, see *Sociedad N de C Angola UEE v Lundqvist* (1990) Times, 15 February.

6 *Triplex Safety Glass Co Ltd v Lancegaye Safety Glass (1934) Ltd* [1939] 2 KB 395, [1939] 2 All ER 613; *Rio Tinto Zinc Corpn v Westinghouse Electric Corpn* [1978] AC 547, [1978] 1 All ER 434.

7 *US v White* 322 US 694 (1944); *Braswell v US* 108 S Ct 2284 (1988); *R v Judge of General Sessions of the Peace for the County of York, ex p Corning Glassworks of Canada Ltd* (1970) 16 DLR (3d) 609; *R v N M Paterson & Sons Ltd* [1980] 2 SCR 679; *R v Amway Corpn* (1989) 56 DLR (4th) 309.

8 Especially by Justice Murphy in a number of cases including *Rochfort v Trade Practices Commission* (1982) 43 ALR 659; *Pyneboard Pty Ltd v Trade Practices Commission* (1983) 45 ALR 609; *Sorby v Commonwealth* (1983) 46 ALR 237; *Controlled Consultants Ltd v Comr for Corporate Affairs* (1985) 57 ALR 751.

Corpn v Westinghouse Electric Corpn the question of the extent to which an individual director could claim the privilege in relation to material which might incriminate his company was raised. It was not necessary for their Lordships to express a final view on this question, which they felt required further consideration, since if some such privilege were not recognised that of the company might be rendered nugatory.[9]

Anything that a person was wrongly compelled to say after he had claimed his privilege was treated as having been said involuntarily, with the result that it was inadmissible in subsequent proceedings brought against him,[10] but the provisions and, to some extent, the construction of statutes have prevented this result from being reached in a number of cases.

C. STATUTORY PROVISIONS

It is not unknown for some modern statutes to make explicit endorsement of the operation of this privilege.[11] It is, however, more common to find some degree of statutory abridgement of the privilege. Such statutory intervention is often necessary to facilitate effective extra-curial investigations. This scenario is well-illustrated by recent developments in the field of the law relating to intellectual property. In order to secure the elimination of 'piracy' in respect of copyright in such things as recordings and computer programs, the courts developed a special summary procedure, the Anton Piller order, requiring a defendant to provide materials and to answer enquiries. Given the operation of criminal sanctions in the area, compliance with such orders could lead to self-incrimination and, as noted above, in *Rank Film Distributors Ltd v Video Information Centre*[12] the House of Lords upheld the privilege at common law. Almost immediately legislation was enacted as s 72(1) of the Supreme Court Act 1981 to abrogate the privilege, but in compensation also provided instead that:

(3) ... no statement or admission made by a person—
 (a) in answering a question put to him in any proceeding to which subsection (1) applies; or
 (b) in complying with any order made in such proceedings,
shall, in proceedings for any related offence or for the recovery of any related penalty, be admissible in evidence against that person or (unless they married after making of the statement or admission) against the spouse of that person.
(4) Nothing in subsection (3) shall render any statement or admission made by a person as there mentioned inadmissible in evidence against that person in proceedings for perjury or contempt of court.

9 *In Rochfort v Trade Practices Comrs* the privilege was refused to the executive secretary of an unincorporated association in respect of documents which might incriminate the association. Cf *Upjohn & Co v US* 449 US 383 (1981) for the position in the United States.
10 *R v Garbett* (1847) 1 Den 236; it is not clear that this result can be reconciled with the new test provided by s 76(2) of the Police and Criminal Evidence Act 1984. Obiter dicta to the same effect in *R v Coote* (1873) LR 4 PC 599, have however been used in New Zealand to assist the court to resist a claim to the privilege on an Anton Piller application because it made the chance of criminal proceedings being brought more remote, *Thorn EMI Video Ltd v Kitching and Busby* [1984] FSR 342.
11 See, for example, the Consumer Protection Act 1987, s 47(2).
12 [1982] AC 380, [1981] 2 All ER 76.

This technique of abrogating the privilege in return for abstention from use of the material so obtained has been extensively employed for many years, particularly under the old bankruptcy legislation. It can lead to difficulty in establishing the range of proceedings in respect of which the material so obtained cannot be used.[13] It should be noted also that here the abrogation of the privilege is wider than its restoration in such proceedings.[14]

Other statutes have a more draconian effect. They do not simply abolish the privilege for the purpose of a particular examination and then restore it to a limited extent. Their effect is that the privilege is abolished for all purposes in the cases to which they apply. The net result is that, if information has been lawfully obtained pursuant to statutory provisions and there is no restriction on the use which can be made of the information, the person giving it cannot object to its being used in evidence against him either on the ground that such use would infringe his privilege against self-incrimination or because the information would not have been given voluntarily.[15]

To a large extent this is the result of the decision of the majority of the Court for Crown Cases Reserved in *R v Scott*.[16] It turned on the construction of s 117 of the Bankruptcy Law Consolidation Act 1849 under which it was lawful for the official receiver to examine the debtor 'touching all matters relating to his trade dealings or estates'. A subsequent section provided for the punishment of false answers as perjury, but there was no provision explicitly permitting subsequent use of the answers in any legal proceedings. Under some pressure the debtor answered questions of the relevant kind, and it was held that his answers were admissible against him at his subsequent trial for mutilating his books. The court declined to apply a proviso that the answers could not be used in subsequent criminal proceedings against the debtor. Among the grounds for this conclusion was that:[17]

> When the legislature compels parties to give evidence accusing themselves, and means to protect them from the consequences of giving such evidence, the course of legislation has been to do so by express enactment.

The existence of statutes providing that information obtained in a particular inquiry may be used in evidence against the person questioned could be invoked in favour of a converse argument that the absence of such words implies the continued availability of the privilege against self-incrimination.[18] It must be admitted, however, that most statutory provisions favour the conclusion of the majority in *R v Scott*.

---

13 S 72(5) of the Supreme Court Act 1981 contains a definition of a 'related offence' and a 'related penalty' in terms which the House of Lords found it difficult to construe in *Crest Homes plc v Marks* [1987] AC 829, [1987] 2 All ER 1074; see also *Universal City Studios v Hubbard* [1984] Ch 225, [1984] 1 All ER 661.

14 The abrogation extends to materials discovered while the restoration is limited to admissions and statements.

15 *R v Scott* (1856) Dears & B 47; *R v Coote* (1873) LR 4 PC 599; *Customs and Excise Comrs v Harz* [1967] 1 AC 760, [1967] 1 All ER 177; *George v Coombe* [1978] Crim LR 47.

16 Above. Cf *R v Sloggett* (1856) Dears CC 656 where the point was left open.

17 Lord Campbell at 60.

18 *R v Savundra Nayagan and Walker* (1968) 52 Cr App Rep 637 at 644; but see *R v Harris* [1970] 3 All ER 746, [1970] 1 WLR 1252.

The number and effect[19] of these abrogations of the privilege should give pause for thought on the part of anyone who regards the privilege as a fundamental principle of English law. These statutes relate not only to the investigation of serious offences such as infringements of s 1 of the Official Secrets Act 1911,[20] but also to such matters as taxation, gambling and road traffic.[1]

Section 1(e) of the Criminal Evidence Act 1898 provides that the accused may be asked any question in cross-examination notwithstanding that it would tend to incriminate him as to the offence charged. This was thought an essential corollary to the main provision of the Act enabling the accused to give evidence on his own behalf. His position with regard to questions tending to show that he had committed other offences is governed by special provisions in s 1(f) already considered in ch X above.

It seems now to have been accepted[2] that the Canadian Charter of Rights and Freedoms has colonised the privilege against self-incrimination in that jurisdiction by enacting in s 11(c) that a person accused of crime may not be compelled to testify, and in s 13 that a witness may not have incriminating evidence used against[3] him in subsequent proceedings.[4] Contrary to some early indication[5] it seems unlikely that the ambit of the privilege will be extended by reference to s 7 of the Charter, since so expanded a concept is not regarded as a 'principle of fundamental justice' in Canada.[6] In civil proceedings a witness can rely only upon the protection offered by the Charter against use of his testimony in any subsequent proceedings.[7]

Where the privilege has been abrogated it may nevertheless be just, and within the discretion of the court, to stay contemporaneous civil proceedings, so that the criminal proceedings can be completed without such encroachment upon the accused's position.[8]

---

19 In the United States since the decision of the Supreme Court in *Counselman v Hitchcock* 142 US 547 (1892) it has become more common for abrogation of the privilege to lead to complete immunity from prosecution for the relevant offence rather than merely to the inadmissibility in it of evidence so obtained.

20 See s 6 of the Act of 1920 under which it is an offence to withhold information from a duly authorised officer of police.

1 On the whole subject see Heydon 'Statutory Restrictions on the privilege against Self-incrimination' (1971) 87 LQR 214.

2 *Thomson Newspapers v Director of Investigation and Research* (1986) 34 DLR (4th) 413 at 418 (leave was given to appeal to the Supreme Court of Canada, but at the time of writing no further report was available).

3 This has been held not to prevent use to impugn credit, *R v B (WD)* (1987) 45 DLR (4th) 429.

4 The exegesis of this concept has proved problematical, see eg *R v Dubois* [1985] 2 SCR 350; *R v Mannion* [1986] 2 SCR 272.

5 *R L Crain v Couture and Restrictive Trade Practices Commission* (1983) 6 DLR (4th) 478.

6 *Thomson Newspapers* above, see also *R v McKinlay Transport* (1987) 48 DLR (4th) 765. This reflects long experience of s 5 of the Canada Evidence Act which merely provided use immunity.

7 *Caisse Populaire Laurier d'Ottawa Ltee v Guertin (No 2)* (1983) 150 DLR (3d) 541; *Saccomanno v Swanson* (1987) 34 DLR (4th) 462.

8 *Jefferson Ltd v Bhetcha* [1979] 2 All ER 1108, [1979] 1 WLR 898. See for a similar approach in Australia, *Kirk v Comr of Australian Federal Police* (1988) 81 ALR 321; and in Canada, *Saccamanno v Swanson*, above.

N 2. LEGAL PROFESSIONAL PRIVILEGE[9]

~1ATEMENT AND RATIONALE OF THE RULE[10]

In civil and criminal cases, confidential[11] communications passing between a client and his legal adviser need not be given in evidence by the client and, without the client's consent, may not be given in evidence by the legal adviser in a judicial proceeding if made either:

(1) to enable the client to obtain, or the adviser to give, legal advice; or

(2) with reference to litigation that is actually taking place or was in the contemplation of the client.

Communications passing between the legal adviser or client and third parties need not be given in evidence by the legal adviser if they come within (2) above.

It is pointed out in para 17 of the 16th Report of the Law Reform Committee that the privilege covers three kinds of communication:

(a) communication between the client or his agents and the client's professional legal advisers;

(b) communications between the client's professional legal advisers and third parties, if made for the purpose of pending or contemplated litigation;

(c) communications between the client or his agent and third parties, if made for the purpose of obtaining information to be submitted to the client's professional legal advisers for the purpose of obtaining advice upon pending or contemplated litigation.[12]

In the following discussion, communications under heads (b) and (c) may be taken together, and the term 'legal adviser' simply includes a solicitor and a barrister. Counsel's opinion taken by a solicitor is privileged under all three heads of the rule either because counsel counts as the client's legal adviser, or else because he is the alter ego of the solicitor.[13] The privilege extends to communications to salaried legal advisers in that capacity.[14]

Communications from police forces seeking the legal advice of the Director

---

9 Lord Wilberforce has criticised this label as inaccurate because the privilege is that of the client, *Waugh v British Railways Board* [1980] AC 521 at 531, [1979] 2 All ER 1169 at 1172; see also *AM & S Europe v EC Commission* [1983] QB 878 at 894, 910, [1983] 1 All ER 705 at 718, 730. The expression has however achieved statutory endorsement, see e g Companies Act 1985, s 452; Merchant Shipping Act 1979, s 28(3); Health and Safety at Work etc Act 1974, s 20(8); the rubric to s 33 of the Administration of Justice Act 1985 (assimilating licensed conveyancers); and s 47(1) of the Consumer Protection Act 1987. In some other statutes one of the two adjectives is omitted, see e g Finance Act 1975, Sch 4, para 5(3) ('professional privilege'), and Police and Criminal Evidence Act 1984, ss 10 and 11 ('legal privilege').

10 The rule stated below applies to communications with a foreign legal adviser and to cases in which the litigation contemplated is foreign *(Re Duncan, Garfield v Fay* [1986] P 306, [1968] 2 All ER 395). It also extends to proceedings under the rules of the European Economic Community, see *AM & S Europe v EC Commission* [1983] QB 878, [1983] 1 All ER 705.

11 *Gardner v Irvin* (1879) 4 Ex D 49 at 53.

12 See also the definition in Police and Criminal Evidence Act 1984, s 10, p 437 below.

13 *Bristol Corpn v Cox* (1884) 26 Ch D 678. See also *Koowarta v Bjelke-Petersen* (1988) 92 FLR 104, where claims for public policy immunity in respect of cabinet documents failed, but a claim in respect of counsel's opinion succeeded.

14 *Alfred Crompton Amusement Machines Ltd v Comrs of Customs and Excise (No 2)* [1972] 2 QB 102 at 129, [1972] 2 All ER 353 at 376 (this point was neither raised nor questioned in the subsequent proceedings in the House of Lords).

of Public Prosecutions have, in England,[15] been treated on the basis of public policy immunity,[16] but upon considerations of policy very similar to those applicable here. The privilege has been extended by statute to patent,[17] and to trademark,[18] agents in respect of civil proceedings, and to licensed conveyancers.[19] It has also been held to extend to employees' representatives at industrial tribunals for the purposes of the litigation in hand.[20] It is not otherwise enough that someone without formal legal professional qualification is performing the functions of a legal adviser, such as a legal aid officer in a prison.[1]

1. COMMUNICATIONS BETWEEN CLIENT AND LEGAL ADVISER

The first head of legal professional privilege was the last to gain full recognition by the courts for it was not until *Greenough v Gaskell* was decided in 1833[2] that it was clear that the privilege attaches to communications between client and legal adviser, even though no litigation was contemplated by the client. In that case Lord Brougham said:[3]

> If the privilege was confined to communications connected with suits begun, or intended or expected or apprehended, no-one could safely adopt such precautions as might eventually render any proceedings successful, or all proceedings superfluous.

Although the privilege under consideration applies to communications made with the object of retaining a solicitor's services even if they are not in fact retained, the relationship of solicitor and client must at least be contemplated and the communications must be fairly referable to that relationship: 'The mere fact that the person speaking is a solicitor and the person to whom he speaks is his client affords no protection.'[4] It has been

---

15 For the position in Australia see *A-G (NT) v Kearney* (1985) 158 CLR 500; *Waterford v Commonwealth of Australia* (1987) 71 ALR 673.
16 *Evans v Chief Constable of Surrey* [1988] QB 588, [1989] 2 All ER 594, see further below p 468.
17 Copyright, Designs and Patents Act 1988, s 280, enlarging the privilege previously bestowed by Patents Act 1977 to include non-litigious communications. For the situation in Australia see *Sepa Waste Water Treatment Pty Ltd v JMT Welding Pty Ltd* (1986) 6 NSWLR 41.
18 Copyright, Designs and Patents Act 1988, s 284, reversing the position at common law, see *Dormeuil Freres SA v Dormiere Menswear Ltd* [1983] RPC 131.
19 Administration of Justice Act 1985, s 33.
20 *M and Grazebrook Ltd v Wallens* [1973] 2 All ER 868, [1973] ICR 256.
 1 *R v Umoh* (1986) 84 Cr App Rep 138, although in some circumstances immunity may be available on grounds of public policy, or the evidence may be excluded in criminal proceedings by way of discretion under s 78 of the Police and Criminal Evidence Act 1984 if the fairness of the proceedings might be jeopardised by its admission.
 2 1 My & K 98; some would say not until the judgment of Lord Selbourne in *Mintet v Morgan* (1873) 8 Ch App 361.
 3 At 103.
 4 *Minter v Priest* [1930] AC 558 at 568 per Lord Buckmaster; *Wilson v Rastall* (1792) 4 Term Rep 753; *Greenlaw v King* (1838) 1 Beav 137; *Thomas v Rawlings* (1859) 27 Beav 140; *Smith v Daniell* (1875) LR 18 Eq 649. The mere fact that a solicitor advising trustees is himself a trustee does not exclude the privilege *(O'Rourke v Darbishire* [1920] AC 581). For the position where a solicitor acts for two parties see *Baugh v Cradocke* (1832) 1 Mood & R 182; *Perry v Smith* (1842) 9 M & W 681; *Warde v Warde* (1851) 3 Mac & G 365; *Harris v Harris* [1931] P 10.

held to cover information communicated by the solicitor to the client for the purpose of tendering advice, despite the information emanating from a third party, being passed on as received, and there being no litigation in prospect.[5] It does not, however, include communications to a client from his opponent's solicitor, since such a communication is hardly likely to convey legal advice,[6] though if such a communication contemplates settlement of a dispute it may be within the protection conferred by the privilege to be described in the next section of this chapter. The ambit of communications passing between solicitor and client covered by this privilege is not to be construed too narrowly, and extends to all communications relating to the normal legal business of a solicitor, thus extending to routine communications between them in relation, for example, to a conveyancing transaction.[7]

Privilege may however be claimed by one not strictly a client of the legal adviser, if he has an interest in common with such a client, for example as a joint tenant or as one of several victims of a common calamity.[8] Such privilege cannot be claimed against such other party,[9] and only in respect of communications made while the common interest exists, not after it has ended.[10]

The privilege extends to communications by the client's agent[11] to the clerk or other subordinate of the adviser and vice versa; but there is an important distinction between the head of legal professional privilege under consideration and that which will be discussed shortly arising from the fact that, when litigation is not contemplated, communications between the adviser and third parties to enable him to obtain information before giving his opinion are not always privileged. This was decided in the leading case of *Wheeler v Le Marchant*,[12] where the defendant was obliged to produce reports made to his solicitor by a surveyor with regard to property that became the subject of litigation, the litigation not having been contemplated when the reports were made. Cotton LJ observed that documents such as those with which the case was concerned had hitherto only been protected when made in contemplation of some litigation, and he did not consider that all communications between a solicitor and a third person in the course of advising clients ought to be protected.

---

5 *Re Getty (Sarah C) Trust* [1985] QB 956, [1985] 2 All ER 809.
6 *Hadley v Baddock* [1987] WAR 98.
7 *Balabel v Air India* [1988] Ch 317, [1988] 2 All ER 246; but see *R v Inner London Crown Court, ex p Baines & Baines* [1988] QB 579, [1987] 3 All ER 1025 which appears not to have been cited in *Balabel*.
8 *Buttes Gas and Oil Co v Hammer (No 3)* [1981] QB 223, [1980] 3 All ER 475 (unaffected on this point by subsequent proceedings).
9 *Cia Barca de Panama SA v George Wimpey & Co* [1980] 1 Lloyd's Rep 598 at 614.
10 *Talbot v Marshfield* (1865) 2 Drew & Sm 549.
11 See *Mudgway v New Zealand Insurance Co Ltd* [1988] 2 NZLR 283 where the agent was not an employee but a third party acting as *agent*, and so distinguished from a true third party.
12 (1881) 17 Ch D 675.

2. COMMUNICATIONS WITH THIRD PARTIES FOR THE PURPOSE OF PENDING OR CONTEMPLATED LITIGATION[13]

In order that communications between the client or his legal adviser and third parties should be privileged, there must be a definite prospect of litigation in contemplation by the client, and not a mere vague anticipation of it;[14] but it is not necessary that a cause of action should have arisen;[15] nor is it essential that the third party should anticipate litigation.[16] The communication must have been made, or the document brought into existence, for the purpose of enabling the legal adviser to advise or act with regard to the litigation. In the ordinary case this requirement gives rise to no particular difficulty. Communications with and proofs of witnesses are clearly privileged,[17] and a mere request for information, unaccompanied by any suggestion that it was required for legal advice, is equally clearly not privileged, however probable the litigation may have been at the time the request was made.[18] There were, however, a number of difficult borderline cases in which the communication was made for more than one purpose, and it was difficult to say much more with regard to the decisions in these cases than that they showed that the utilisation of the communication in litigation must have been one of its main purposes, even though the client may have intended to settle the claim without litigation if he could.[19]

Examples of material which had been held not to be privileged are reports to the directors of a railway company made simply for the purpose of conveying information even if litigation is contemplated,[20] information supplied by a member of a trade union to officials of the union to enable them to decide whether to refer his claim for wrongful dismissal to the union's solicitor for legal action,[1] and the report of a private inquiry into an accident aimed primarily at preventing the recurrence of such an event.[2] Examples falling on the other side of the line were reports of an accident made to the director of a company to be placed before the company's solicitors,[3] and correspondence by the Transport Commission with its

---

13 The privilege extends to communications passing between the members of a business organisation or government department and its salaried permanent legal advisers *(Alfred Crompton Amusement Machines Ltd v Customs and Excise Comrs (No 2)* [1972] 2 QB 102, [1972] 2 All ER 353, the point was not argued before the House of Lords), and there can be little doubt that this would be true of confidential communications in order to obtain legal advice simpliciter.
14 Bray on *Discovery*, cited by Lord Denning MR in *Alfred Crompton Amusement Machines Ltd v Customs and Excise Comrs (No 2)* above at 377.
15 *Bristol Corpn v Cox* (1884) 26 Ch D 678.
16 *Di Pietrantonio v Austin Hospital (Heidelberg)* [1958] VR 325.
17 *Curling v Perring* (1835) 2 My & K 380.
18 *Anderson v Bank of British Columbia* (1876) 2 Ch D 644.
19 *Ogden v London Electric Rly Co* (1933) 149 LT 476.
20 *Wooley v North London Rly Co* (1869) LR 4 CP 602.
1 *Jones v Great Central Rly Co* [1910] AC 4.
2 *Longthorn v British Transport Commission* [1959] 2 All ER 32, [1959] 1 WLR 530; *Warner v Women's Hospital* [1954] VLR 410.
3 *Southwark Water Co v Quick* (1878) 3 QBD 315; *Ankin v London and North Eastern Rly Co* [1930] 1 KB 527.

servants concerning the cause of an accident intended to be placed before the Commission's solicitors.[4]

In *Alfred Crompton Amusement Machines Ltd v Customs and Excise Comrs (No 2)*[5] the company notified the commissioners in 1967 that they were dissatisfied with the agreed formula under which they had been paying purchase tax. The prescribed procedure in the event of disagreement was that the commissioners should state their opinion concerning the basis on which purchase tax was payable and, if this was not accepted, the taxpayer could proceed to arbitration. The commissioners expressed their opinion in 1968 and the parties proceeded to arbitration. Both the Court of Appeal and House of Lords took the view that the commissioners had reasonably anticipated arbitration since the receipt of the company's notification of dissatisfaction with the agreement in 1967. The commissioners claimed legal professional privilege in respect of (1) communications with their salaried legal advisers in order to obtain advice, (2) communications with their legal advisers in order to obtain evidence for the anticipated arbitration, (3) internal communications with their officers and agents concerning the proper assessment of the purchase tax payable by the company, and (4) documents received in confidence from third parties concerning the market value of machines sold by the company. There was no argument in the House of Lords with regard to the first set of communications, so the decision of the Court of Appeal that they were privileged stands; the House held that privilege attached to the second set, even if it were assumed that litigation had to be anticipated to found it; but the majority held that the third and fourth sets were not subject to legal professional privilege because they came into existence for one single purpose—to assist the commissioners to form an opinion about the basis on which purchase tax should be paid by the company, and not for the dual purpose of enabling an opinion to be formed and resisting the company's contentions in the arbitration. It was held that the third and fourth sets of communications ought not to be disclosed in the public interest, a matter which is considered in the next chapter.

Having regard to the decision under heads (3) and (4) everything said in the House about dual or multiple purpose communications was obiter, but the majority favoured a restrictive view with regard to the recognition of privilege in such cases. Two major vehicles existed for the expression of such a view. The privilege could be restricted to communications made solely for the purpose of seeking legal advice, or to those made for the dominant purpose of seeking such advice. The former position was adopted by the majority of the High Court of Australia in *Grant v Downs*.[6] In that case the plaintiff was suing for negligence in respect of an accident which took place in a hospital. A series of reports about the nature of the circumstances was submitted to the Department of Public Health, partly to help improve procedures in such hospitals and partly in order to inform the defendant's legal advisers. The majority of the High Court examined the nature of the claim to legal professional privilege by large corporate bodies in the light of

---

4 *Seabrook v British Transport Commission* [1959] 2 All ER 15, [1959] 1 WLR 509; *Britten v Pilcher & Sons* [1969] 1 All ER 491.
5 [1974] AC 405, [1973] 2 All ER 1169. See also *Silver Hill Duckling Ltd v Minister of Agriculture* [1987] IR 289.
6 (1976) 135 CLR 674 (Stephen, Mason and Murphy JJ).

all the authorities, including the leading English cases. It exhibited a rather sceptical approach to the very existence of the privilege, while conceding it to be 'so firmly entrenched in the law that it is not to be exorcised by judicial decision.' It nevertheless determined to limit its availability very drastically in the case of communications of this type by requiring them to be made solely for the purpose of submission to legal advisers or for use in legal proceedings. Barwick CJ was unwilling to be quite so restrictive, and was prepared to allow the privilege not only when this was the sole purpose, but also when it was merely the dominant one.[7] In England the House of Lords has rejected the approach of the majority in *Grant v Downs* in favour of that proposed by Barwick CJ. In *Waugh v British Railways Board*[8] the situation was virtually identical to that in the Australian case, except that the accident happened on the railway. The House of Lords was unanimous in approving of the 'dominant' purpose test, and overruling previous decisions of the lower courts to the extent of any inconsistency with it. Their Lordships felt that a 'sole purpose' test would go too far in denying privilege for communications whose overwhelming purpose was for litigation, but for which some other minor purpose could be discovered. Lord Russell who initially favoured the more restrictive approach, was eventually persuaded that it would mean that it would be virtually impossible ever to raise a claim for privilege on this basis. None of their Lordships anticipated any difficulty in applying a test of dominance, which is familiar in other branches of the law.[9]

The rationale of legal professional privilege is inseparable from the adversary system of litigation which would become unworkable if no document could ever be kept from an opponent. But as the privilege applies to some communications in the absence of the prospect of any litigation at all, this must be supplemented by what Lord Wilberforce regarded as the more powerful reason of encouraging the client to confide fully and candidly in his legal adviser.[10]

A problem arises on account of the fact that this second head of privilege requires litigation to have been contemplated in order to protect communications from third parties. It arises particularly in relation to original documents which are not subject to the privilege because themselves not made in contemplation of litigation, but which are then copied for the purpose of litigation. Some authorities have been cast in broad terms, such as those used by James LJ in *Anderson v Bank of British Columbia*:[11]

---

7 Jacobs J adopted a third formulation in requiring this purpose to account for the existence of material
8 [1980] AC 521, [1971] 2 All ER 1169.
9 It has subsequently been applied to documents made in the course of an inquiry into the conduct of the police under s 49 of Police Act 1964 following a complaint and threat of legal action, *Neilson v Laugharne* [1981] QB 736, [1981] 1 All ER 829 (compare *Konia v Morley* [1976] 1 NZLR 455 where the same result was reached even on the basis of the older test), and to reports on the cause of a suspicious fire commissioned by the solicitors to the insurers of the relevant premises, *Re Highgrade Traders Ltd* [1984] BCLC 151. *Waugh* has been approved in Canada, see *Levin v Boyce* [1985] 19 DLR (4th) 128 citing cases from various Canadian jurisdictions; for New Zealand see *Guardian Royal Exchange Assurance of New Zealand Ltd v Stuart* [1985] 1 NZLR 596; and for South Africa see *A Sweidan and King (Pty) Ltd v Zim Israel Navigation Co Ltd* (1986) (1) SA 515.
10 *Waugh v British Railways Board* [1980] AC 521 at 531, [1979] 2 All ER 1169 at 1172.
11 (1876) 2 Ch D 644 at 676.

as you have no right to see your adversary's brief, you have no right to see that which comes into existence merely as the materials for the brief.

In cases where copies of documents held by third parties have been made specifically for the litigation in respect of which disclosure is sought the privilege has been upheld.[12] If, however, the originals would have been unprivileged in the hands of the opponent, then merely copying them for the purposes of the litigation should not shield them from discovery.[13] This is, however, qualified in the case of documents procured by the advisers themselves for the purposes of the litigation, since where such a collection of documents has been so prepared its principles of selection, editing, organisation and classification might themselves indicate the substance of the party's case.[14] It now seems that, at least in the case of individual documents not originally procured by the advisers, that privilege is not available for copies of unprivileged documents, whether the original is in the hands of the client,[15] or third party,[16] and even though the copy has been made for the purpose of securing legal advice in the litigation.

3. GENERAL

(i) A rule of evidence

In England the rule has been regarded as a rule of evidence, and applied only to prevent compulsory disclosure either by way of pre-trial discovery, or in the actual course of judicial[17] or quasi-judicial proceedings.[18] In many other parts of the Commonwealth the extension of the rule to proceedings not falling within so strict a category, or in respect of earlier and more peripheral activities relevant to such proceedings has been the subject of intense judicial debate. A movement seems to be developing to elevate the privilege into something more nearly resembling a basic constitutional principle, expressed in the rhetoric of rights.[19] In Australasia after some uncertainty,[20] and despite some dissent,[1] current opinion favours such an

---

12 *The Palermo* (1883) 9 PD 6; *Watson v Cammell Laird & Co (Shipbuilders and Engineers) Ltd* [1959] 2 All ER 757, [1959] 1 WLR 702. See also *Hodgkinson v Simms* (1988) 55 DLR (4th) 577 where the court applied the principle to a single document.
13 *Chadwick v Bowman* (1886) 16 QBD 561.
14 *Lyell v Kennedy (No 3)* (1884) 27 Ch D 1.
15 *R v Board of Inland Revenue, ex p Goldberg* [1988] 3 All ER 248, [1988] 3 WLR 522 where the privilege was, in fact, allowed, but the case was held in *Dubai Bank Ltd v Galadari* [1989] 3 All ER 769 at 775, [1989] 3 WLR 1044 at 1052 to have been wrongly decided.
16 *Dubai Bank* above.
17 Even then the privilege will not operate to prevent disclosure of communications relating to legal advice on *other* unrelated proceedings, for example when the personal liability to tax of a solicitor is in question, *R v I R C, ex p Taylor (No 2)* [1989] 3 All ER 353.
18 See Diplock LJ in *Parry-Jones v Law Society* [1969] 1 Ch 1 at 9, [1968] 1 All ER 177 at 180. It does not protect the identity of the client (or presumably of the lawyer) *Bursill v Tanner* (1885) 16 QBD 1. But in *AM & S Europe v EC Commission* [1983] QB 878 at 895, 896, [1983] 1 All ER 705 at 719, 720, Adv-Gen Warner seemed to suggest that there was no reason not to apply the Commonwealth approach, as exhibited in the *West-Walker* and *Shell Canada* cases (below), to the construction of English statutes.
19 See *Sorby v Commonwealth* (1983) 46 ALR 237 at 262 per Brennan J.
20 See *Crowley v Murphy* (1981) 34 ALR 496; *O'Reily v Comrs of the State Bank of Victoria* (1982) 57 ALJR 130; *Baker v Campbell* (1983) 49 ALR 385; and in New Zealand, *IRC v West-Walker* [1954] NZLR 191; *Rosenberg v Jaine* [1983] NZLR 1.
1 Most notably from Brennan J.

extension of the doctrine beyond the strict field of the law of evidence. It is arguable, given the rather jaundiced view held in Australia of this privilege, that its extension to the procedures of Commissions of Inquiry and administrative bodies will make little inroad into the basic principle of the availability of relevant evidence. Its apparent capacity to apply in derogation of valid search warrants, by the application of very strict principles of construction to the relevant empowering legislation, may lead to greater encroachment.[2] In Canada a similar step appears to have been taken, and some of the Canadian cases appear to have been influential in Australia. In one case[3] a search warrant was quashed because it was directed to the seizure of documents subject to privilege, and in another the principle underlying the privilege was applied to regulate the opening of mail passing between a solicitor and his client, who was in prison.[4] It now seems well-established there also that the legal effects of the relationship between solicitor and client extend beyond the protection from disclosure in legal proceedings of relevant communications which pass between them.[5] So far however the doctrine appears not to have been extended so far as to protect communications which implicate third parties.[6] The position is nevertheless far from being fully worked out, and further development seems inevitable.

(ii) The privilege as that of the client

Legal professional privilege in both of its aspects is that of the client.[7] It enures for the benefit of his successors in title with regard, for instance, to documents handed over by him,[8] and the Court of Appeal accordingly held that the original of the proofs and notes on evidence with which the case of *Calcraft v Guest*[9] were concerned were privileged from production. The fact that they had been brought into existence for the purposes of a particular action which had been concluded was treated as immaterial. Lindley MR stated this conclusion in terms of a general rule—'once privileged, always privileged'; but it is important to remember that this simply means that, once a particular client's privilege has attached to a document, it remains for his benefit and that of his successors in title. It is not necessary that subject

---

2 See especially *Baker v Campbell* and *Rosenberg v Jaine*, above; *Arno v Forsyth* (1986) 65 ALR 125; *Federal Comr of Taxation v Citibank Ltd* (1989) 85 ALR 588.
3 *Re Borden and Elliot v R* (1975) 70 DLR (3d) 579, it is unlikely that the same result could have been achieved in England at common law, see *R v King* [1983] 1 All ER 929 at 932, [1983] 1 WLR 411 at 415, rejecting dicta in *Frank Truman Export Ltd v Metropolitan Police Comr* [1977] QB 952 at 962, [1977] 3 All ER 431 at 440.
4 *Solosky v R* [1980] 1 SCR 821, without however going so far as to sever all evidentiary connection, with the result that the claim was disallowed.
5 *Descoteaux v Mierzwinski* (1982) 141 DLR (3d) 590 (here too the discussion was strictly obiter and did not govern the actual result); *Re Ontario Securities Commission and Greymac Credit Corpn* (1983) 146 DLR (3d) 73; *Re Director of Investigation and Research and Shell Canada Ltd* (1975) 55 DLR (3d) 713. See also Kasting 'Recent Developments in Lawyer and Client Privilege' (1978) 24 McGill LJ 115; Chasse 'The Solicitor–Client Privilege and Search Warrants' (1977) 36 CRNS 349.
6 *Re Gowling and Henderson v R* (1982) 136 DLR (3d) 292, where some doubt was expressed upon the general policy of expansion of the privilege at the expense of the public interest in the detection and successful prosecution of criminal activities.
7 *Wilson v Rastall* (1792) 4 Term Rep 753.
8 *Minet v Morgan* (1873) 8 Ch App 361; followed in *Crescent Farm (Sidcup) Sports Ltd v Sterling Offices Ltd* [1972] Ch 553, [1971] 3 All ER 1192.
9 [1898] 1 QB 759, above.

matter or parties be identical.[10] A time may come when the party denying the continued existence of the privilege can prove that the party relying on it no longer has any interest to protect, as where a solicitor takes a statement from a witness who has been party to the proceedings, and the prosecution wish to use the communication against the witness.[11] In *Schneider v Leigh*[12] the plaintiff had claimed damages for personal injuries against a company, whose solicitor obtained the usual medical report—a document in relation to which the company enjoyed the ordinary litigant's privilege. The report was made by the defendant and the plaintiff contended that it libelled him. It was held that the defendant could claim no privilege with regard to his report. This case illustrates what Lord Atkin once described as the 'double nature' which problems relating to professional privilege may assume. First, there is the question whether the document or statement need be put in evidence—a general question of adjectival law; and, secondly, there is the question whether the occasion on which the statement (ex hypothesi before the court) was published is an occasion of absolute or qualified privilege—a question with which the substantive law of defamation is concerned.[13] On facts such as those of *Schneider v Leigh*, a plea of qualified privilege might ultimately succeed although the pleas of professional privilege failed.[13] It seems that the result would be different if the claim against the witness were in respect of the very same subject matter in the original litigation.[14]

If a lawyer swears that a question cannot be answered without disclosing communications made to him professionally by his client his oath is conclusive unless it appears from the nature of the question that the privilege cannot be applicable.[15]

There is little case-law on this subject due no doubt to the fact that the issue of legal professional privilege is most frequently raised in connection with pre-trial discovery of documents which the judge has power to inspect.[16]

At common law the rule was clear that legal professional privilege did not attach to documents or things which had come into existence before the relationship of solicitor and client had become established, even though submitted to a legal adviser for his advice,[17] or sent by him to a third party in connection with litigation.[18] The privilege was regarded as that of the client, and if the document or thing were not protected in the hands of the client it could not attract protection merely by being submitted to a legal adviser. The rule is now stated by the Police and Criminal Evidence Act

---

10 *The Aegis Blaze* [1986] 1 Lloyd's Rep 203.
11 *R v Ataou* [1988] 2 All ER 321, [1988] 2 WLR 1147. See also *R v Craig* [1975] 1 NZLR 597.
12 [1955] 2 QB 195, [1955] 2 All ER 173.
13 *Minter v Priest* [1930] AC 558 at 579.
14 *Lee v South West Thames Regional Health Authority* [1985] 2 All ER 385, [1985] 1 WLR 845.
15 *Morgan v Shaw* (1819) 4 Madd 54.
16 A power which the majority of the High Court of Australia in *Grant v Downs* (1976) 135 CLR 674 felt should be exercised more readily.
17 *R v Peterborough Justices, ex p Hicks* [1978] 1 All ER 225, [1977] 1 WLR 1371 (forged power of attorney deposited for legal advice in relation to impending prosecution).
18 *R v King* [1983] 1 All ER 929, [1983] 1 WLR 411 (document sent by defence to handwriting expert to use for comparison with prosecution documents in connection with impending prosecution). This case disapproved comments in *Frank Truman Export Ltd v Metropolitan Police Comr* [1977] QB 952, [1977] 3 All ER 431, and endorsed the criticism of them made in the 5th edn (1979) of this work.

1984. It expressly repeals previous legislation so far as it authorised searches for items subject to legal privilege,[19] and goes on to provide that:

(1) Subject to subsection (2) below, in this Act 'items subject to legal privilege' means—

(a) communications between a professional legal adviser and his client or any person representing his client made in connection with the giving of legal advice to the client;

(b) communications between a professional legal adviser and his client or any person representing his client or between such an adviser or his client or any such representative and any other person made in connection with or in contemplation of legal proceedings and for the purposes of such proceedings; and

(c) items enclosed with or referred to in such communications and made—
  (i) in connection with the giving of legal advice; or
  (ii) in connection with or in contemplation of legal proceedings and for the purposes of such proceedings; when they are in the possession of a person who is entitled to possession of them.

(2) Items held with the intention of furthering a criminal purpose are not items subject to legal privilege.[20]

The first of these subsections has been authoritatively stated[1] to re-state the common law. It should be noted that in s 10(1)(c) it seems that 'made' refers to items enclosed or referred to, and not to the communication itself. The second subsection is discussed more fully below.[2] Other confidential material passing between solicitor and client, although not protected by this privilege,[3] is nevertheless subject to a special procedure to secure access under the Police and Criminal Evidence Act 1984.[4]

(iii) Communications between the parties and their representatives

It looks like a truism to say that privilege cannot be claimed for communications passing between one party and another or his agent, but the cases show that problems can arise under this head. In *Grant v South Western and County Properties Ltd*[5] the plaintiff caused a tape-recording to be made of a conversation between himself and one of the defendants and it was held that he could not claim privilege from discovery of the recording. So far as the defendant was concerned there was no intention that it should be placed before the plaintiff's solicitor; so far as the plaintiff himself was concerned, what he said to the defendant could not be privileged. From the point of view of the privilege the recording was the equivalent of a letter and copy letter exchanged between the parties.

In *Baker v London and South Western Rly Co*,[6] a case in which executors were claiming damages for personal injuries to the deceased, the defendants

---

19 S 9(2).
20 S 10.
1 By Lord Goff in *R v Central Criminal Court, ex p Francis & Francis* [1989] AC 346 at 392, [1988] 3 All ER 775 at 797.
2 In section 2 part B.
3 Police and Criminal Evidence Act 1984, s 14(2).
4 See *R v Central Criminal Court, ex p Francis & Francis* above, *R v Inner London Crown Court, ex p Baines & Baines* [1988] QB 579, [1987] 3 All ER 1025.
5 [1975] Ch 185 at 199.
6 (1867) LR 3 QB 91.

d that their medical officer had visited him and negotiated a settlement. s held that the officer's report was not privileged from production on discovery. The decision seems to have been correct on its particular facts because, subject to the without prejudice rule, there is no reason why privilege should attach to discussions aimed at achieving a settlement. The judgment contains a suggestion that privilege could never attach to an agent's report of what took place at an interview with the opposite party, but there is subsequent authority for the proposition that statements taken from the victim on behalf of a potential defendant for the purpose of laying them before his solicitor are privileged in accident cases.

In *Feuerheerd v London Omnibus Co*[7] the plaintiff mistakenly believed that she was making a statement to her solicitor about the accident in which she had sustained her injuries, when she was in fact being interrogated by the company's claims manager. It was held that the defendants could claim privilege for the statement as a documentary record made for the purpose of laying it before their solicitors. The Court of Appeal laid stress on the fact that the manager acted in good faith. Had he not done so the claim to privilege would presumably have failed on the ground that the defendants could not take advantage of their agent's wrong.[8] There was no discussion of the effect of the plaintiff's mistake as to the person to whom she was speaking. Subject to this point there is no obvious reason why the victim's statement should be differentiated in this context from those of other witnesses taken on behalf of a potential defendant shortly after the occurrence of an accident. A cynic is entitled to ask why, if the victim does not take the precaution of getting a copy of his statement at the time it was made, he should have a right to its production on discovery in order to trim his evidence accordingly.[9]

B. EXCEPTIONS TO THE RULE

Legal professional privilege may always be waived by the client.[10] It may also be waived by his counsel's conduct of his case in court, even though acting under a mistake, and against the client's interests and wishes.[11] Waiver may be implied from the use of a privileged document in court, for

---

7 [1918] 2 KB 565.

8 Although it might have been argued that, if a person may steal a document and put it in evidence, there is no reason why evidence should not be given of what occurred at any interview obtained by deception.

9 See the judgment of Thesiger J in *Britten v F H Pilcher and Sons Ltd* [1969] 1 All ER 491. See also per Cotton LJ in *Kennedy v Lyell* (1883) 23 Ch D 387 at 404. In Australia see *Aydin v Australian Iron and Steel Pty Ltd* [1984] 3 NSWLR 684; *Hadley v Baddock* [1987] WAR 98.

10 Or, if deceased, by his personal representative, *Chant v Brown* (1849) 7 Hare 79, *Doe d Marriott v Hertford* (1849) 19 LJQB 526; or, if bankrupt, by his trustee in bankruptcy, *Re Konigsberg (a bankrupt)* [1989] 3 All ER 289. For a different view in Canada in relation to a receiver see *Re Ontario Securities Commission and Greymac Credit Corpn* (1983) 146 DLR (3d) 73.

11 *Great Atlantic Insurance Co v Home Insurance Co* [1981] 2 All ER 485 at 494, [1981] 1 WLR 529 at 539. The same may apply to any waiver made under the ostensible authority of the client's legal adviser, see *Causton v Mann Egerton (Johnsons) Ltd* [1974] 1 All ER 453, [1974] 1 WLR 162, but see *Frank Truman Export Ltd v Metropolitan Police Comr* [1977] QB 952 at 957, [1977] 3 All ER 431 at 436. See also *R v CKC* (1987) 62 CR (3d) 131 where privilege was held not to have been waived in Canada when a report was disclosed by counsel as part of an unauthorised plea bargain.

example by its use for the purposes of cross-examination.[12] An agreement to waive the privilege attaching to a medical report will not, however, be implied from the acceptance of the opposite party's unconditional production of his medical report.[13] Nor, where a communication passing between potential joint-defendants is privileged on account of anticipation of proceedings by one of them, may such privilege be waived, without authority by the other.[14] The fact that a conversation between a client and his solicitor takes place in the presence of a third party does not necessarily amount to a waiver,[15] although it will no doubt usually be held to have this effect.

The extent of pre-trial waiver may be determined by the party making it,[16] except that it is always necessary to reveal enough of the transaction so as not to mislead. The same applies to waiver by the conduct of litigation.[17] This means that the whole of a document must normally be revealed unless its different parts deal with totally different subject matter.[18] It does not mean that waiver so made extends to all otherwise privileged documents dealing with any matter merely mentioned in such a document.[19] It may also be possible to waive protection in respect of one head of privilege, for example between client and legal adviser, without waiving it in respect of another, for example documents brought into existence for the purpose of subsequently ensuing litigation.[20] It should also be noted that waiver applies only for the purposes of the proceedings, or part of the proceedings,[1] in which the privilege was waived. Thus documents handed over to the police by the plaintiff in a civil suit, for the purpose of prosecuting the defendant

---

12 *Nea Karteria Maritime Co v Atlantic and Great Lakes S Co (No 2)* [1981] Com LR 138. See also *Buttes Gas and Oil Co v Hammer (No 3)* [1981] QB 223 at 268, [1980] 3 All ER 475 at 502 (unaffected on this point by subsequent proceedings). Mention of a privileged document in an affidavit will not necessarily amount to waiver, *Tate & Lyle International Ltd v Government Trading Corpn* [1984] LS Gaz R 3341.

13 *Causton v Mann Egerton (Johnsons) Ltd*, above. For special rules relating to the discovery of privileged medical reports see RSC Ord 38, rr 36–38.

14 *Lee v South West Thames Regional Health Authority* [1985] 2 All ER 385, [1985] 1 WLR 845. Still less does such communication itself imply waiver, see *Vancouver Hockey Club Ltd v National Hockey League* (1987) 44 DLR (4th) 139.

15 *R v Braham and Mason* [1976] VR 547.

16 *Lyell v Kennedy (No 3)* (1884) 27 Ch D 1 at 24.

17 *Nea Karteria Maritime Co v Atlantic and Great Lakes SS Co (No 2)* [1981] Com LR 138. In *Pozzi v Eli Lilley* (1986) Times, 3 December it was said to be immaterial in this respect whether part of a document was disclosed on discovery or used in open court.

18 *Great Atlantic Insurance Co v Home Insurance Co* [1981] 2 All ER 485 at 490, [1981] 1 WLR 529 at 538. This has been held in Australia to go too far in relation to privilege at the stage of discovery (as opposed to trial), *Curlex Manufacturing Pty Ltd v Carlingford Australia General Insurance Ltd* [1987] 2 Qd R 335, after consideration of a number of older English cases; and in New Zealand has been restricted to applying to parts of a single document, *Mudgway v New Zealand Insurance Co* [1988] 2 NZLR 283.

19 *General Accident Fire and Life Assurance Corpn Ltd v Tanter* [1984] 1 All ER 35, [1984] 1 WLR 100. See also *A-G for The Northern Territory v Maurice* (1986) 69 ALR 31 where the High Court of Australia insisted that the test was whether use of part only of the material, or even oblique reference to it, would be unfair or misleading.

20 *George Doland Ltd v Blackburn, Robson, Coates & Co* [1972] 3 All ER 959, [1972] 1 WLR 1338, but see *General Accident Fire and Life Assurance Corpn Ltd v Tanter*, above.

1 *Goldman v Hesper* [1988] 3 All ER 97, [1988] 1 WLR 1238 where legal professional privilege attaching to documents put forward on taxation of costs under Ord 62, r 29(7) was waived, to the extent that disclosure was voluntary, for that purpose only. See also *R v Harper-Taylor and Bakker* [1988] NLJR 80.

in that suit, remained privileged in the civil suit.[2] The same applies to civil proceedings, even to the extent of different actions between the same parties.[3]

In addition to the possibility of waiver there are four exceptions to the rule which must be considered in turn—communications made in order to facilitate the perpetration of a crime or fraud, facts discovered in the course of the relationship, information tending to establish the innocence of an accused and statutory provisions.

1. COMMUNICATIONS TO FACILITATE CRIME OR FRAUD

In the leading case of *R v Cox and Railton*,[4] the Court for Crown Cases Reserved decided that, if a client applies to a lawyer for advice intended to guide him in the commission of a crime or fraud, the legal adviser being ignorant of the purpose for which his advice is wanted, the communication between the two is not privileged. Accordingly a solicitor was compelled to disclose what passed between the prisoners and himself when they consulted him with reference to drawing up a bill of sale that was alleged to be fraudulent. As Stephen J pointed out when delivering the judgment to the court, if the law were otherwise, a man intending to commit treason or murder might safely take legal advice for the purpose of enabling himself to do so with impunity, and the solicitor to whom the application was made would not be at liberty to give information against his client in order to frustrate his criminal purpose.[5] If the lawyer participates in the criminal purpose he ceases to act as a lawyer. Stephen J concluded that the court must judge whether the evidence is admissible on the special facts of each particular case, and every precaution should be taken against compelling unnecessary disclosures. The doctrine of *R v Cox and Railton* has been applied to civil cases[6] in which fraud was alleged and it has since been stressed that there should be prima facie evidence that it was the client's intention to obtain advice in furtherance of his criminal or fraudulent purpose before the court will consider whether the situation comes within the exception to the rule relating to professional privilege.[7] The judge retains a discretion to exclude evidence if he believes that the public interest in supporting a party in the preparation of his case outweighs that of disclosure, and this is particularly likely to be exercised against disclosure at an interlocutory stage, especially when the fraud amounts to an allegation that the legal proceedings have themselves been brought fraudulently. It has been remarked[8] that if this were not so a party need only allege fraud in bringing any proceedings to secure sight of the whole of his opponent's brief. The same consideration applies to an allegation of fraud in securing legal aid in respect of launching proceedings.[9] Still less is the privilege likely to be lost in

2 *British Coal Corpn v Dennis Rye Ltd (No 2)* [1988] 3 All ER 816, [1988] 1 WLR 1113.
3 *Dinham v British Steel Corpn* [1986] CLY 115.
4 (1884) 14 QBD 153.
5 Cf *R v Smith* (1915) 11 Cr App Rep 229.
6 *Williams v Quebrada Railway, Land and Copper Co* [1895] 2 Ch 751; *Gamlen Chemical Co (UK) Ltd v Rochem Ltd (No 2)* (1979) 124 Sol Jo 276.
7 *O'Rourke v Darbishire* [1920] AC 581; *Bullivant v A-G for Victoria* [1901] AC 196.
8 By Hoffman J in *Chandler v Church* [1987] NLJ Rep 451.
9 *R v Snaresbrook Crown Court, ex p DPP* [1988] QB 532, [1988] 1 All ER 315.

respect of communications with their legal advisers by innocent assignees of goods obtained by the fraud of third parties.[10]

In *R v Central Criminal Court, ex p Francis & Francis*[11] the majority of the House of Lords took the view that s 10(2) of the Police and Criminal Evidence Act 1984 had left this rule unaffected, and in particular that its reference to the intention with which documents were held was capable of referring to the intention, not of the adviser but of the client, with the result that documents held innocently by a solicitor remain outside the protection of the privilege if the client's intention is fraudulent. It seems that the restriction to 'furthering a criminal purpose' is probably no more restrictive than the position at common law in its reliance upon the concept of 'fraud', which in this context had been held not to extend to every act or scheme which was unlawful such, for example, as an inducement of breach of contract;[12] or an unsolicited letter to a client advising him that certain conduct could lead to his being prosecuted;[13] or a conveyance without consideration designed to defeat creditors.[14] It seems that in order to determine whether documents fall within this exception the judge himself is entitled to inspect them.[15]

2. FACTS DISCOVERED IN THE COURSE OF THE RELATIONSHIP

The privilege only applies to communications; a solicitor can be obliged to disclose the identity of his client[16] and the privilege does not prevent the disclosure of facts observed by either party in the course of their relationship as client and legal adviser. In *Brown v Foster*,[17] for instance, it was held that a barrister who saw a book produced at the trial of his client could testify without the client's consent, in subsequent proceedings, on the question whether it contained a particular entry when he previously saw it at the preliminary examination. Similarly, in *Dwyer v Collins*,[18] it was held that the plaintiff's attorney must say whether he had a particular document in court with him although he could not be obliged to produce it. In *Conlon v Conlons Ltd*[19] the defence to a claim for damages for personal injury alleged that the plaintiff had agreed to accept a sum in full settlement. In his reply, the plaintiff denied that his solicitor had been authorised to settle the claim and it was held that he could be obliged to answer an interrogatory as to whether he had authorised his solicitor to negotiate a settlement. If settlements made before the issue of a writ are to be binding the client's instruction to his solicitor in this regard ought to be held to be outside the rule relating to legal professional privilege, for a solicitor has no implied authority to conclude negotiations at that stage, although he may bind his client by doing so later.

If a third party is consulted by a legal adviser for the purposes of litigation,

10 *Banque Keyser Ullmann SA v Skandia (UK) Insurance Co Ltd* [1986] 1 Lloyd's Rep 336.
11 [1989] AC 346, [1988] 3 All ER 775.
12 *Crescent Farm (Sidcup) Sports Ltd v Sterling Offices Ltd* [1972] Ch 553, [1971] 3 All ER 1192.
13 *Butler v Board of Trade* [1971] Ch 680, [1970] 3 All ER 593.
14 See *Re Konigsberg (a bankrupt)* [1989] 3 All ER 289, [1989] 1 WLR 1257.
15 *R v Governor of Pentonville Prison, ex p Osman* [1989] 3 All ER 701.
16 *Bursill v Tanner* (1885) 16 QBD 1.
17 (1857) 1 H & N 736; *Re Cathcart, ex p Campbell* (1870) 5 Ch App 703.
18 (1852) 7 Exch 639.
19 [1952] 2 All ER 462.

perhaps as a potential witness, a question may arise as to the extent to which privilege can be claimed in respect of communications to him.[20] Since there is no property in a witness,[1] the third party is compellable. He is then free to testify, subject only to the ordinary operation of legal professional privilege, which will not protect documents submitted to him for expert advice, not otherwise protected.[2]

3. INFORMATION TENDING TO ESTABLISH INNOCENCE

In *R v Barton*[3] the accused, a legal executive, was charged with fraudulent conversion of the assets of an estate. He served a solicitor, who was in fact a Crown witness, with a subpoena incorporating a notice to produce documents relating to the estate which he claimed would tend to establish his innocence. Although it was not clear whether the documents had been brought into existence in connection with advice tendered by the solicitor to his client or for the purpose of litigation contemplated by the client, there seems to have been no doubt that they were privileged. Nevertheless Caulfield J ordered the solicitor to produce them and made the following observations when doing so:

> If there are documents in the possession or control of a solicitor which, on production, help to further the defence of an accused man, then in my judgment no privilege attaches. I cannot conceive that our law would permit a solicitor or other person to screen from a jury information which, if disclosed to the jury, would perhaps enable a man either to establish his innocence or to resist an allegation made by the Crown.

We shall refer again in the next chapter to the doctrine that rules under which evidence may be inadmissible in the public interest must yield in situations in which it is reasonable to suppose that reception of the evidence might have the effects mentioned by Caulfield J. The merits of the doctrine are obvious,[4] but its precise implications and limitations, if any, have not been worked out. It seems, however, to apply to statements sought to be used only to discredit a witness, and if the witness testifies for the prosecution it has been held that the burden of proving that no privilege attaches is borne by the accused.[5]

Although there is no reason to doubt that privilege may be successfully pleaded on behalf of the client of a solicitor called by the prosecution in a criminal case,[6] we shall see that the client's right to confidentiality as against

20 It has been held that legal professional privilege will not itself provide a basis for restraining disclosure of such communications by the supplier, *W v Egdell* [1990] 1 All ER 835, [1990] 2 WLR 471.

1 *Harmony Shipping Co SA v Davis* [1979] 3 All ER 177, [1979] 1 WLR 1380.

2 *R v King* [1983] 1 All ER 929, [1983] 1 WLR 411. See also *R v Ward* (1980) 3 ACR 171.

3 [1972] 2 All ER 1192, [1973] 1 WLR 115.

4 In Australia it has, however, been rejected, at least in application to statements made by potential prosecution witnesses, *Cain v Glass* (1985) 3 NSWLR 39.

5 *R v Ataou* [1988] 2 All ER 321, [1988] 2 WLR 1147, criticised by Allan in (1988) 138 NLJ 668. In *R v Dunbar and Logan* (1982) 138 DLR (3d) 221, the court considered the situation of the two accused with conflicting interests in relation to the confidence being retained. In South Africa the accused may be required to go further in establishing a claim to defeat the privilege, *S v Safatsa* 1988 (1) SA 868.

6 As it was in *R v Ataou*, above.

third parties in respect of the contents of a letter written to him by his solicitor may have to yield to the Crown's right to prove them in a public prosecution.[7]

4. STATUTE

There are few if any statutes abrogating legal professional privilege by express reference and the subject has not attracted much case-law so far as implied abrogation is concerned. In this respect there is a striking contrast with the privilege against self-incrimination.

Jones v G D Searle & Co Ltd[8] shows that s 33 of the Limitation Act 1980 is a clear instance of a statutory exception to the rule of legal professional privilege for the plaintiff was required to answer an interrogatory inquiring whether the legal advice he had received was favourable or unfavourable. The subsection empowers the court to give leave to bring an action out of time having regard to a number of factors affecting the delay, including the nature of the advice received.

It has however become increasingly common to preserve the privilege by express provision,[9] and in criminal cases the Police and Criminal Evidence Act 1984 has not only insulated material covered by the privilege from the issue of search warrants, but has also invalidated all previous legislation to the extent of any inconsistency.[10]

C. LEGAL PROFESSIONAL PRIVILEGE AND THIRD PARTIES[11]

A legal adviser owes a twofold duty to his client with regard to confidential communications. In the first place he must claim privilege for them in legal proceedings and second he must not disclose their contents to anyone without the client's consent. The problem with which we are concerned arises when those contents have become known to a third party who wishes to prove them in litigation against the client. The disclosure may have been due to the adviser's wilful or negligent breach of duty, to accident, or to the wrongful act of a third party. The information sought to be proved in the litigation may be the outcome of oral communication or the previous reading of a document, but more often than not it will be contained in a copy of a privileged document. We have seen that in *Calcraft v Guest*[12] the Court of Appeal allowed copies of proofs of witnesses with notes on the evidence in a former action brought by the plaintiff's predecessor in title to be put in by the defendant. In this case the originals had accidentally fallen into the defendant's hands, but the principle of the decision applies to all methods of obtaining. It overlaps with the rule which has already been mentioned in section 2 of ch IV and to which further reference is made in ch XII section

---

7 *Butler v Board of Trade* [1971] Ch 680, [1970] 3 All ER 593.
8 [1978] 3 All ER 654, [1979] 1 WLR 101.
9 See for example Data Protection Act 1984, s 31(2); Banking Act 1987, ss 39(13), 41(11) and 42(6) (there limited to documents).
10 S 9(2).
11 J D Heydon 'Legal Profession Privilege and Third Parties' 37 MLR 601.
12 [1898] 1 QB 759.

3, that illegally and improperly obtained evidence is admissible provided that it is relevant. A recent example of the operation of this principle is provided by *Re Briamore Manufacturing*[13] where inadvertent disclosure of privileged documents was made. The party to whom such disclosure was permitted made notes and copies of some, but the mistake had been discovered before receipt of a request for copies of all, which was refused. It was held to be futile to maintain such refusal since as a result of *Calcraft v Guest*[14] the party to whom such disclosure had been mistakenly made could use all of his secondary evidence at the trial,[15] and it was clearly preferable to have the trial conducted on the basis of the best evidence, namely the original documents.

One exception to the principle of *Calcraft v Guest* occurs when a document subject to legal professional privilege is brought into court by one party, is improperly obtained by his opponent, and is then sought to be put into evidence by the wrongdoer. In *ITC Film Distributors v Video Exchange Ltd*[16] Warner J restrained the use of documents obtained in such a way on the basis that the interests of the proper administration of justice required him to do so. This restriction does not however apply when the party seeking to use the document has obtained it without impropriety. Thus in *R v Tompkins*[17] a note which the accused had written to his counsel was found on the floor of the courtroom during an adjournment and handed to prosecuting counsel who was thus enabled to secure devastating effect in cross-examination.

By far the most common occurrence is that in which there is no impropriety[18] but under the pressure of litigation[19] a privileged document is disclosed in error. If *Calcraft v Guest* stood alone there would be little question but that privilege would be lost, and secondary evidence of the privileged material admissible. But it does not stand alone. In *Lord Ashburton v Pape*[20] the defendant, a bankrupt, obtained possession of correspondence passing between Lord Ashburton and his solicitor, taking copies before he returned it. Lord Ashburton sought an injunction against any use being made of those copies on the general ground that equity will act to restrain a breach of confidence. It was unclear exactly how these two rules related to each other.[1] The matter has now been clarified by the decision of the Court

13 [1986] 3 All ER 132, [1986] 1 WLR 1429.
14 Above, which was conceded to apply.
15 It is not futile if the secondary evidence is incomplete, and the fact that an application is made strongly suggests that the party making it has not got all that he wishes, see *Hooker Corpn Ltd v Darling Harbour Authority* (1987) 9 NSWLR 538.
16 [1982] Ch 431, [1982] 2 All ER 241. No such rule appears to exist in Canada, see *R v Dunbar and Logan* (1982) 138 DLR (3d) 221.
17 (1977) 67 Cr App Rep 181. See also *Re Girouard and the Queen* (1982) 138 DLR (3d) 730; but in New Zealand it has been held that a policeman could not testify to a conversation between a solicitor and his client which he had, without any impropriety, overheard, *R v Uljee* [1982] 1 NZLR 561, a decision preferred to *Tompkins* in obiter dicta by Nourse LJ in *Goddard v Nationwide Building Society* [1987] QB 670 at 686, [1986] 3 All ER 264 at 272.
18 Though in *English and American Insurance Co Ltd v Herbert Smith & Co* [1988] FSR 232 the Vice-Chancellor intimated that to peruse plainly confidential material, known at the time to be privileged was not entirely innocent, even though received in error.
19 Especially where discovery is expedited, in *Transamerica Computer Co Ltd v IBM Corpn* 573 F 2d 646 (1978) no fewer than 1,138 privileged documents were inadvertently disclosed when 17 million pages had had to be vetted in 3 months.
20 [1913] 2 Ch 469.
1 See Tapper 'Privilege and Confidence' (1972) 35 MLR 83; Heydon 'Legal Professional Privilege and Third Parties' (1974) 37 MLR 601.

of Appeal in *Goddard v Nationwide Building Society Ltd*[2] that the matter is governed by the principle of *Ashburton v Pape* so long as any relief is practicable, that is until the documents have been used, or otherwise relied upon, in the relevant litigation. It is not necessary to commence separate proceedings; an application can be made at any time. This relief is however limited to documents which are both confidential *and* subject to legal professional privilege. *Ashburton v Pape* cannot be used to prevent use of unprivileged, but nevertheless confidential material. It in no way depends upon the impropriety of the other party, or of anyone at any stage. Although all equitable remedies are to some extent discretionary it seems that in these circumstances it will be rare for the discretion to be exercised in favour of disclosure.[3] Nor does it matter that the inadvertence leading to the disclosure is that of a party in conducting the very litigation in which the document is to be used,[4] though in such cases considerations of implied waiver may also arise.[5]

The resultant law can be criticised on two grounds: (1) the contrast between *Calcraft v Guest* and *Lord Ashburton v Pape* makes the client's success in getting evidence excluded depend on the date at which he found out that he was the victim of a wrongdoer;[6] (2) the distinction between public prosecutions and other legal proceedings is unjustified. If they can be answered, the answer to the first criticism seems to be that trials at which it was claimed that the contents of a confidential document ought not to be put in evidence, although no previous injunction had been obtained, would be unduly protracted by the collateral inquiry into the circumstances in which the document was obtained; while the answer to the second criticism may be that, in criminal proceedings, the accused receives as much protection as he should receive from the law of privilege in the strict sense and it would be going too far to afford him the protection afforded by the law of confidentiality.

D. THE CLAIMS OF OTHER RELATIONSHIPS

The distinction between professional privilege and the protection of confidentiality lies at the root of the present law concerning the disclosure by doctors and priests of statements made by a patient or penitent. There is no doubt that the voluntary disclosure of such matters would be restrained by injunction. There is equally no doubt that such statements are not privileged from compulsory disclosure in court by the person to whom they are made. For this reason it may be doubted whether an injunction would ever extend to compulsory disclosure in court, but this has not been the

---

2 Above.
3 At least in the absence of some such factor as inordinate delay.
4 *Guinness Peat Properties v Fitzroy Robinson Partnership* [1987] 2 All ER 716, [1987] 1 WLR 1027. In this case some stress is placed upon the fact that the mistake should be an obvious one, but it is not clear that this should be regarded as essential.
5 See above p 438.
6 The time of application was regarded as important in *ITC Film Distributors v Video Exchange Ltd* [1982] Ch 431, [1982] 2 All ER 241, but doubts were expressed in *Universal City Studios Inc v Hubbard* [1984] 1 All ER 661 at 665, [1984] 2 WLR 492 at 496, and in *Goddard* May LJ expressed a wish for intervention by the House of Lords to resolve the still unsatisfactory position.

subject of case-law to date.[7] The problem with which we are now concerned is whether the equivalent to legal professional privilege which covers confidential communications between client and legal adviser in the course of obtaining advice should be extended to other relationships. Does the fact that legal advice inevitably takes the form of a statement like 'If you do so and so it could lead to litigation', coupled with the fact that full and free disclosure is essential to the obtaining of good advice about litigation, justify the peculiar treatment by English law of the lawyer-client relationship?

It is hardly surprising that privilege should, at different times, have been claimed for confidential communication between friends,[8] documents in the possession of an accountant relating to his client's affairs[9] and even for information supplied to a pursuivant of the Royal College of Heralds.[10] All these claims have been unsuccessful.

It is only necessary to add a few remarks on the subject of the non-recognition by the law of privilege of the relationship between priest and penitent, and physician and patient. There are, however, two points that should be stressed before this is done. In the first place, although law rather than discretion may be in control 'if it comes to the forensic crunch', the court has a discretion to disallow questions unless they are relevant and necessary, or such as to serve a useful purpose in relation to the proceedings in hand,[11] secondly it is a mistake to suppose that the choice lies between a privilege of complete secrecy on the one hand, and on the other hand, compulsory disclosure without restriction. It is possible, and sometimes desirable, that the claimant to the privilege should decline to produce documents or give evidence until he is ordered to so so by the court. Such a course is contemplated by statute and approved by the cases. Thus, s 7 of the Bankers' Books Evidence Act 1879, assumes that an application will be made to the court for an order for inspection of a banker's books, and in *R v St Lawrence's Hospital*[12] Lord Goddard CJ approved the refusal of medical officers to disclose their communications with the visitors to a hospital under the Mental Deficiency Acts without the order of the court. When such an order is made, it can be on such terms as, for example, that no use will be made of the information disclosed outside the particular proceedings before

7 An injunction may however be granted to prevent such disclosure to a foreign court, *XAG v A bank* [1983] 2 All ER 464, [1983] 2 Lloyd's Rep 535.

8 *Duchess of Kingston's Case* (1776) 20 State Trials 355.

9 *Chantrey Martin & Co v Martin* [1953] 2 QB 286, [1953] 2 All ER 691. There would be no obligation to disclose if the documents were the client's property but that is not the result of the law of privilege.

10 *Slade v Tucker* (1880) 14 Ch D 824. See also *Jones v Great Central Rly Co* [1910] AC 4 (trade union official). So far as bankers are concerned, their contractual duty is not to disclose the state of their customer's account without his consent except under order of the court or pursuant to a public duty (*Tournier v National Provincial and Union Bank of England* [1924] 1 KB 461). See also *R v Daye* [1908] 2 KB 333. In the case of a company's bankers support is to be found in s 452 of the Companies Act 1985.

11 *A-G v Mulholland* [1963] 2 QB 477 at 489 and 492 per Lord Denning MR and Donovan LJ respectively.

12 *R v St Lawrence's Hospital, Caterham Statutory Visitors, ex p Prichard* [1953] 2 All ER 766 at 772. A statute may affect the terms upon which an order for discovery may be made (see *McIvor v Southern Health and Social Services Board* [1978] 2 All ER 625). See also *Church of Scientology of California v Department of Health and Social Security* [1979] 3 All ER 97.

the court.[13] Non-compliance with the order would constitute a contempt of court,[14] but it must be admitted that there are circumstances in which disclosure, even on the most stringent terms as to dissemination of the information, is abhorrent to the witness. He may not consider himself to be adequately protected by the discretion of the court simply because there are cases in which the question is both relevant and, from the point of view of the party putting it, necessary.

1. PRIEST AND PENITENT

The most obvious case for the creation of a new privilege is that of the Roman Catholic priest called upon to testify with regard to that which took place in the confessional.[15] There is very little judicial authority on the subject, but such as there is, like the opinion of all the text-writers, is against the existence of any privilege according to English law. The only legal arguments that could be advanced in support of the priest's refusal to testify concerning statements in the confessional would be first, that the privilege must have existed at the time of the Reformation, and it has not been displaced by any statute or authoritative decision since that date; secondly, that disclosure would incriminate the priest by the canon law; and thirdly that the privilege is implicitly recognised by the decision in *R v Hay*.[16] Sir James Fitzjames Stephen appears to have answered the first point conclusively when he said:

I think the modern law of evidence is not so old as the Reformation, but has grown up by the practice of the Courts, and by decisions in the course of the last two centuries. It came into existence at a time when exceptions in favour of auricular confessions to Roman Catholic priests were not likely to be made. The general rule is that every person must testify to what he knows. An exception to the general rule has been established in regard to legal advisers, but there is nothing to show that it extends to clergymen, and it is usually so stated as not to include them.[17]

So far as the argument based on the possibility of self-incrimination is concerned, we have seen that it is doubtful whether at common law the

13 See the order in *Chantrey Martin & Co v Martin* (above). In wardship and custody proceedings there may be disclosure to the court leaving it to the discretion of the judge to decide whether there should be any disclosure to the parties; see for example *Official Solicitor v K* [1965] AC 201, [1963] 3 All ER 191; *Re M* [1973] QB 108, [1972] 3 All ER 321. The number of such cases may be increasing, see *Science Research Council v Nasse* [1980] AC 1028, [1979] 3 All ER 673 (anti-discrimination legislation); and *Campbell v Tameside Metropolitan Borough Council* [1982] QB 1065, [1982] 2 All ER 791 (psychologists' reports on children).

14 Even in the absence of a special order it amounts to contempt to use a document obtained by discovery for any purpose ulterior to the purposes of the litigation in which it was obtained, *Harman v Secretary of State for the Home Office* [1983] 1 AC 280, [1962] 1 All ER 532.

15 The usual claim is that the privilege is that of the penitent, but it is sometimes said that it should belong to the priest alone as distinct from being exercisable by him on behalf of an absent person.

16 (1860) 2 F & F 4.

17 *Digest of the Law of Evidence* (12th edn) 220, where all the authorities are collected apart from the dictum in *Wheeler v Le Marchant* (1881) 17 Ch D 675 at 681, which is also against the existence of the privilege.

privilege protects answers that would criminate the witness by any foreign system of law,[18] and it is still more doubtful whether it would be held to extend to answers prohibited by the canon law.

In *R v Hay*,[19] the prisoner was charged with larceny of a watch. A Roman Catholic priest had handed it to the police, and the priest was asked in court from whom he had received the watch. He was compelled to answer this question. The judgment stressed the point that he was being asked about a fact as distinct from a communication,[20] and it is perhaps just arguable that the case impliedly recognised a privilege in the case of communications, but it can hardly displace the bulk of authority which, though inconclusive, is undoubtedly against the existence of the privilege. Were the problem to arise in an acute form in practice, most judges would probably sympathise with Best CJ when he said 'I, for one, will never compel a clergyman to disclose communications made to him by a prisoner; but if he chooses to disclose them I shall receive them in evidence'.[1]

A privilege is conferred on penitential communications by statute in various parts of the Commonwealth,[2] as well as by the American Model Code and Uniform Rules,[3] but both the Law Reform Committee and the Criminal Law Revision Committee were opposed to any change in the English law.[4]

There may be circumstances in which a clergyman can invoke some recognised privilege or exemption, as when he assists in without-prejudice negotiations between estranged spouses—a matter that is discussed in section 3, or when he is a prison chaplain and the Home Secretary prohibits him from testifying with regard to statements made to him by prisoners—a head of public policy that has, as yet, not been considered by the court; but the mere fact that a clergyman is a marriage guidance counsellor and can only give evidence derived from meetings between the litigating spouses does not confer any privilege on him as distinct from the privilege enjoyed by the parties to without-prejudice negotiations.[5]

2. PHYSICIAN AND PATIENT[6]

There is more judicial authority on the subject of communications between doctors and their patients than there is on statements made to clergymen. It

---

18 The matter is discussed by Nokes 'Professional Privilege' (1950) 66 LQR 88.

19 (1860) 2 F & F 4. The privilege is recognised in Eire as that of the priest (*Cook v Carroll* [1945] IR 515; see the discussion in (1959) 12 Northern Ireland Legal Quarterly 160).

20 Cf *Brown v Foster* p 441 above.

 1 *Broad v Pitt* (1828) 3 C & P 518 (obiter). A clergyman was obliged to disclose an admission of adultery made in conversation by a friend in *Normanshaw v Normanshaw and Measham* (1893) 69 LT 468.

 2 In Canada the situation has been affected by s 2 of the Canadian Charter of Rights and Freedoms, but at most it permits privilege only on a case by case basis, and was rejected in respect of a confession to a Lutheran pastor in *R v Fosty* (1989) 68 CR (3d) 382. But see dicta in *Re Church of Scientology and R* (1987) 31 CCC (3d) 449.

 3 For an American case applying the privilege see *Mullen v US* 263 F2d 275 (1958).

 4 16th Report of the Law Reform Committee, paras 46–7; 11th Report of the Criminal Law Revision Committee, paras 272–5.

 5 *Pais v Pais* [1971] P 119, [1970] 3 All ER 491.

 6 When the claim to privilege is made it is always treated as that of the patient.

is uniformly against the existence of any privilege,[7] although Buller J once said it was much to be regretted that legal professional privilege had not been extended to medical persons.[8] The problem is much more likely to arise in practice than that which relates to statements made to clergymen, for these are only likely to be relevant to litigation when they constitute admissions, and in many cases, no one will know whether they were made, whereas questions concerning medical treatment are both more likely to arise in a law suit, and more likely to be the subject of such knowledge as could warrant the calling of a doctor as a witness.

Rule 221 of the American Law Institute's Code of Evidence accords the privilege in civil actions and prosecutions for misdemeanour in the case of confidential communications reasonably necessary for the treatment in hand, r 27 of the Uniform Rules is to the same effect. This matter is also dealt with by statute in various parts of the Commonwealth, but both the Law Reform Committee and the Criminal Law Revision Committee were against any change in the English law.[9]

In the legislation which has been enacted to date it has been found necessary to provide for exceptions. Not only is there a tendency to confine medical privilege to civil proceedings, a restriction which some would advocate in the case of the priest and penitent, it has also been found desirable to impose special limitations in civil cases. Examples are actions for medical negligence brought by a patient against his doctor, cases in which the patient's sanity is in issue and claims by the patient in respect of personal injuries the nature, duration, extent or effect of which is in issue.

A doctor, like a clergyman, may be able to rely on some other head of privilege or exemption, such as that which relates to negotiations between estranged spouses or the possible protection from disclosure on the ground of public interest of communications with the Minister relating to the National Health Service.[10]

3. CONCLUSIONS

In a much quoted paragraph[11] Wigmore mentioned four preconditions of a privilege of the lawyer-client type.[12] They are that:

(1) the communications must originate in a confidence that they will not be disclosed;

(2) the element of confidentiality must be essential to the full and satisfactory maintenance of the relationship between the parties;

---

7 *Duchess of Kingston's Case* (1776) 20 State Trials 355; *R v Gibbons* (1823) 1 C & P 97; *Wheeler v Le Merchant* (1881) 17 Ch D 675 at 681; *Garner v Garner* (1920) 36 TLR 196; *Hunter v Mann* [1974] QB 767, [1974] 2 All ER 414; *R v Smith* [1979] 3 All ER 605, [1979] 1 WLR 1445; *Campbell v Tameside Metropolitan Borough Council* [1982] QB 1065, [1982] 2 All ER 791.
8 *Wilson v Rastall* (1792) 4 Term Rep 753 at 760. See also per Lord Edmund Davies in *D v National Society for the Prevention of Cruelty to Children* [1978] AC 171 at 245. He long thought that the law should be altered.
9 16th Report of the Law Reform Committee, paras 48–52; 11th Report of the Criminal Law Revision Committee, para 276.
10 66 LQR 92.
11 Para 2285.
12 In *Slavotych v Baker* [1976] 1 SCR 254 at 260 Spence J expressed approval of this approach, but his remarks were obiter, and subsequently criticised by McLachlin (now a Justice of the Supreme Court of Canada) in 'Confidential Communications and the Law of Privilege' (1977) 11 UBCLR 266.

(3) the relationship must be one that in the opinion of the community ought to be sedulously fostered;

(4) the injury that would inure to the relationship by the disclosure of the communication must be greater than the benefit gained through the correct disposal of the litigation.

Wigmore had no doubt about the compliance of the lawyer-client privilege with these conditions. He was unsympathetic to medical privilege and suggested that, in its case, preconditions 2 and 4 are not fulfilled, while he thought that there might be some uncertainty with regard to precondition 3 in the case of the priest-penitent privilege, with which he was sympathetic. Some people would no doubt disagree with him on both points. It is difficult to assess the merits of the present English law until it is known whether, 'when it comes to the forensic crunch', the judge has a discretion to exclude even relevant and necessary questions in civil proceedings. The House of Lords was equally divided on this point in *D v National Society for the Prevention of Cruelty to Children.*[13]

E. IDENTITY OF INFORMANT

As will be seen in the following chapter, it has been recognised as being contrary to public policy to require the names of informants to the police, or to some other bodies conducting similar functions, to be revealed in civil proceedings. An allied privilege has occasionally been claimed by journalists.[14] The privilege differs from the professional privileges considered above in that the claim is not normally made in respect of the content of the communication, which has usually been revealed already;[15] and in the absence of any clear recognition that the privilege belongs to the informant and not to the journalist himself. Such a privilege is recognised in some other jurisdictions,[16] but at least in an absolute form, was rejected here.

The question was considered by the House of Lords in *British Steel Corpn v Granada Television Ltd.*[17] A confidential document belonging to the plaintiffs came into the hands of the defendants, and was knowingly used as part of a television programme. The plaintiffs secured an order for the return of the documents, but the defendants mutilated them so as to try to conceal any indication of the identity of their supplier. The plaintiffs then sought an order for the revelation of his identity. It transpired that an undertaking to respect the anonymity of the source had been given. The majority of their Lordships was quite clear that journalists had no privilege akin either to that of lawyer and client, or in respect of the non-disclosure of their sources of information akin to that of the police. It was said that such a privilege would:

---

13 [1978] AC 171, [1976] 2 All ER 993. See above p 193.

14 *A-G v Clough* [1963] 1 QB 773, [1963] 1 All ER 420; *A-G v Mulholland* [1963] 2 QB 477, [1963] 1 All ER 767. See also *McGuiness v A-G of Victoria* (1940) 63 CLR 73; *Wran v Australian Broadcasting Commission* [1984] 3 NSWLR 241.

15 In *Moysa v Alberta (Labour Relations Board)* (1989) 60 DLR (4th) 1 the unsuccessful claim related to information conveyed *by* the journalist to a known party.

16 It is recognised in many United States jurisdictions; for an extensive discussion see *Branzburg v Hayes* 408 US 665 (1972).

17 [1981] AC 1096, [1981] 1 All ER 417.

place journalists (how defined?) in a favoured and unique position as compared with priest-confessors, doctors, bankers, and other recipients of confidential information and would assimilate them to the police in relation to informers.[18]

This decision caused some disquiet in the media of communication, and a new statutory privilege was created in an attempt to assuage it:

> No court may require a person to disclose, nor is any person guilty of contempt of court for refusing to disclose, the source of information contained in a publication for which he is responsible, unless it be established to the satisfaction of the court that disclosure is necessary in the interests of justice or national security or for the prevention of disorder or crime.[19]

It was not clear that this section would have a very radical effect upon the law as established in *Granada*. It was recognised there that even though there was no absolute immunity, the judge still had some discretion in relation to questioning about the source.[20] The vague formula in the statute appeared to impose little more constraint upon, or to offer very much more guidance for, the action of the court. It was however clearer that the burden of satisfying the court that the conditions existed was upon the party desirous of disclosure, and that within the relevant area disclosure was governed by the statutory rule, and not by discretion.[1]

The judge nevertheless retains discretion after the Act to refuse to order disclosure in an extreme case even when the conditions for disclosure have been satisfied.[2] There has now been a certain amount of interpretation of this provision. In particular the concept of disclosure being *necessary* has been clarified. In *Secretary of State for Defence v Guardian Newspapers Ltd*[3] Lord Diplock pointed out that this requirement was mandatory, and it has been further explained that administrative convenience is insufficient.[4] It seems that where an end, such as the assessment of damages, can be achieved without disclosure, but by other means, such as a firm jury direction, the availability of such means removes any *necessity* for disclosure.[5] In the case of prosecution of crime it has been held that the reference is to crime in general, and not to a specific crime, so there is no need to demonstrate that some particular crime will be prevented by disclosure,[6] nor that disclosure would necessarily prevent the commission of further crime,[7] if it would have that tendency. In the case of the interest of the administration of justice, the concept is to be construed narrowly, typically referring to proceedings in a

18 Lord Wilberforce at 1171, 457. See also Viscount Dilhorne at 1181, 465; Lord Fraser at 1196, 476; Lord Russell concurred.
19 Contempt of Court Act 1981, s 10. Much the same result seems to have been reached in Canada as a matter of the construction of s 2 of the Canadian Charter of Rights and Freedoms, see *The Citizen v Coates* (1986) 29 DLR (4th) 523.
20 See ch IV, section 2(b)(iii) above.
1 *Secretary of State for Defence v Guardian Newspapers Ltd* [1985] AC 339, [1984] 3 All ER 601.
2 *Re Insider Dealing Inquiry* [1988] AC 660 at 703, [1988] 1 All ER 203 at 208.
3 Above at 350, 607.
4 In the *Insider Dealing* case, above, at 704, 208, the meaning was said by Lord Griffiths to lie between being 'indispensable' and 'useful or convenient', and capable of being paraphrased as 'really needed'.
5 *Maxwell v Pressdram Ltd* [1987] 1 All ER 656, [1987] 1 WLR 298.
6 *Insider Dealing*, above, at 705, 209.
7 See also *X v Y* [1988] 2 All ER 648.

court of law,[8] including interlocutory proceedings,[9] or proceedings to identify a tortfeasor,[10] though there must be evidence of some intention to initiate such proceedings.[11] Neither the privilege in respect of police informants,[12] nor that of lawyer and client,[13] can be claimed to the prejudice of the defence in criminal case. There is no such expressed limitation here, and as noted above the accused would bear the burden of establishing grounds for disclosure.

SECTION 3. STATEMENTS MADE WITHOUT PREJUDICE

As part of an attempt to settle a dispute, the parties frequently make statements 'without prejudice'. When this is done, the contents of the statement cannot be put in evidence without the consent of both parties, the case being one of joint privilege. The statements often relate to the offer of a compromise, and, were it not for the privilege, they would constitute significant items of evidence on the ground that they were admissions. Obviously it is in the public interest that disputes should be settled and litigation reduced to a minimum, so the policy of the law is in favour of enlarging the cloak under which negotiations may be conducted without prejudice. This policy is carried out by means of a rigorous insistence on the absence of any magic in the form of words used by the parties, everything being made to depend upon their intention and the objective circumstances of the case, but difficulty occasionally arises as to the scope and effect of the privilege. A specialised application of the same general principles relates to without-prejudice negotiations between estranged spouses—a matter which has come to the fore of recent years.

A. SCOPE AND EFFECT

This privilege has been authoritatively stated to be 'founded on the public policy of encouraging litigants to settle their differences rather than litigate them to a finish'.[14] The detail represents no more than a number of illustrations of this guiding principle. It follows that literal use of the phrase 'without prejudice' is no more than indicative that evidence[15] prefaced by it may be intended to lead to the settlement of a dispute, and so be protected.[16] It is certainly immaterial that a different formulation is adopted, or the words used elsewhere than at the beginning of a document.[17] It is unnecessary to use the words, or any equivalent, if it is clear from the surrounding

---

8 *Guardian Newspapers Ltd*, above, at 350, 607.

9 *Guardian Newspapers Ltd*, above.

10 *X Ltd v Morgan-Grampian (Publishers) Ltd* [1990] 2 All ER 1, [1990] 2 WLR 1000.

11 *Handmade Films (Productions) Ltd v Express Newspapers Plc* [1986] FSR 463.

12 See below ch XII, section 1, part A(3).

13 See above section 2, part B(3).

14 By Lord Griffiths in *Rush & Tompkins Ltd v Greater London Council* [1989] AC 1280 at 1299 [1988] 3 All ER 737 at 739.

15 The rule applies to oral as well as to documentary statements.

16 *South Shropshire District Council v Amos* [1987] 1 All ER 340 at 344, [1986] 1 WLR 1271 at 1277.

17 *Cory v Bretton* (1830) 4 C & P 462.

circumstances that the evidence is part of a continuing negotiation,[18] or obtained pursuant to one.[19] Conversely, use of the phrase is inefficacious if the statement is not made as part of a genuine attempt to negotiate a settlement. Thus evidence of letters written by a debtor to his creditors declaring his inability to pay was admissible in bankruptcy proceedings as an act of bankruptcy, despite having been headed 'without prejudice'.[20] Even when genuinely made in the context of a negotiation it seems that a statement can be put in evidence for some purpose not directly linked to the meaning of the statement, such as to identify the handwriting of a party.[1] It is less certain whether an English court would require some element of equivocation in an admission so headed and made in the general context of a negotiation.[2] Another difficult situation arises in relation to a simple statement of a legal claim so headed. If the document contains no other hint of any intention to negotiate it will be insufficient,[3] but the court will be astute to detect such an intention, and it is certainly not the case that a letter first intimating a dispute can never be made without prejudice.[4]

If the privilege can be established it is sometimes uncertain exactly what it prohibits. It seems clear that it can prevent use, not only by parties to the relevant negotiation, but also by third parties.[5] A party to negotiations to settle a dispute might well be inhibited from making damaging admissions if he knew that they could be used by a different adversary. Similarly, solicitors for the parties may claim privilege for statements made in letters written on their clients' behalf in proceedings in which they are sued personally;[6] but the statement in respect of which privilege is claimed must have some bearing on negotiations for a settlement.[7]

For some purposes reference can be made to without prejudice statements. Thus if the negotiations succeed, and constitute a binding contract, this may be proved by the use of without prejudice material.[8] It has also been said that it is permissible to refer to such statements, and the dates upon which they were made, in order to establish laches.[9] On the other hand no such reference can be made upon an application to secure costs.[10] These decisions may be reconciled upon the basis that in the former it was not necessary to do more than establish the context within which the letters were written,

---

18 *Paddock v Forrester* (1842) 3 Man & G 903, where the heading of the first of a series of letters invested later ones with the privilege, and *Oliver v Nautilus S S Co* [1903] 2 KB 639, where so labelling a later document invested an earlier one with the privilege.

19 *Rabin v Mendoza & Co* [1954] 1 All ER 247, [1954] 1 WLR 271.

20 *Re Daintrey, ex p Holt* [1893] 2 QB 116. Similarly an illegal threat as in *Kurtz & Co v Spence & Sons* (1887) 58 LT 438, or a libel is not protected simply because headed 'without prejudice'.

1 *Waldridge v Kennison* (1794) 1 Esp 143.

2 So held in Australia in *Davies v Nyland* (1974) 10 SASR 76 at 91, adopting the view of Wigmore; but see *Thomson v Austen* (1823) 1 LJ OS KB 99.

3 *Buckinghamshire County Council v Moran* [1989] 2 All ER 225, [1989] 3 WLR 152.

4 *South Shropshire District Council v Amos*, above.

5 *Rush & Tompkins v Greater London Council*, above. In Canada see *I Waxman and Sons Ltd v Texaco Canada Ltd* (1968) 67 DLR (2d) 295.

6 *La Roche v Armstrong* [1922] 1 KB 485.

7 *Field v Comrs of Railways for New South Wales* (1957) 99 CLR 285, where the authorities are reviewed.

8 *Tomlin v Standard Telephones & Cables Ltd* [1969] 3 All ER 201, [1969] 1 WLR 1378.

9 By Lindley LJ in *Walker v Wilsher* (1889) 23 QBD 335 at 338. See also *McFadden v Snow* (1951) 69 WN NSW 8 where it was decided in Australia that such a statement could be referred to in order to rebut an inference of an admission by otherwise apparent silence.

10 *Simaan General Contracting Co v Pilkington Glass Ltd* [1987] 1 All ER 345, [1987] 1 WLR 516.

whereas in the latter reliance had to be placed upon the contents of the documents as admissions. Similar considerations have caused difficulty in relation to disputes about the taxation of costs. The general rule is that negotiations made without prejudice cannot be taken into account when considering questions of costs.[11] This principle has, however, been eroded to the extent that the court will permit a sort of hybrid 'without prejudice' statement to be made, which reserves the right to refer to it, but only on questions of costs.[12] The reason for this is simply that such an erosion is more likely to promote speedy settlement.[13]

B. WITHOUT-PREJUDICE NEGOTIATIONS BETWEEN ESTRANGED SPOUSES

If a solicitor is consulted by both husband and wife, professional privilege may attach to statements made to him by either of them so that he may not disclose them in subsequent matrimonial proceedings without the consent of the makers.[14] The ordinary law concerning without-prejudice statements applies to negotiations between the parties personally, or between their solicitors, which take place with a view to compromising a matrimonial cause; but some recent cases have been concerned with statements made to a mediator and the question arises as to whether he can decline to give evidence concerning them without the consent of the parties. The answer is in the affirmative, and although this would probably be the case with all negotiations carried on through a mediator, the promotion of marital harmony is an additional reason in favour of the promotion of the fullest possible privilege when the dispute is between husband and wife. A reconciliation between estranged spouses is not the same thing as the compromise of a disputed claim.

In *McTaggart v McTaggart*[15] a probation officer was obliged to give evidence concerning that which had passed at an interview between the parties at which he had been present. The spouses each gave evidence about this interview, and the Court of Appeal accordingly held that such privilege as attached to their statements to the probation officer had been waived, but the court had no doubt that the statements were privileged although the privilege was that of the parties. In *Mole v Mole*[16] it was decided that the privilege existed when only one of the parties had enlisted the services of a probation officer, so that he could not give evidence about a letter written to him by the other party without that person's consent. It was emphasised that a similar privilege would apply when one or other of the parties approached a doctor, clergyman or marriage guidance counsellor with regard to his or her matrimonial differences, and there was said to be a tacit understanding that negotiations were to be without prejudice in such cases. In *Henley v*

---

11 *Walker v Wilsher* above, applied to arbitrations in *Stotesbury v Turner* [1943] KB 370.
12 *Calderbank v Calderbank* [1976] Fam 93, [1975] 3 All ER 333; *Cutts v Head* [1984] Ch 290, [1984] 1 All ER 597, now given statutory effect by RSC Ord 22, r 14.
13 It seems that such a reservation might not be effective in relation to a money claim, where payment into court under RSC Ord 16, r 10 remains the more appropriate procedure.
14 *Harris v Harris* [1931] P 10.
15 [1949] P 94, [1948] 2 All ER 754.
16 [1951] P 21, [1950] 2 All ER 328; see also *Pais v Pais* [1971] P 119, [1970] 2 All ER 491.

Henley[17] the initiative in endeavouring to effect a reconciliation was taken by a clergyman, a friend of the parties, and it was held that the privilege attached to statements made to him.

In *Bostock v Bostock*[18] it was held that a solicitor could be obliged to give evidence about an interview which took place between the parties to divorce proceedings at his office, although one of the parties objected to his doing so. The ground of the decision was that the interview was not expressly stated to be without prejudice, but, even if this is good law so far as without prejudice negotiations with regard to an ordinary dispute are concerned, it is most unlikely that the case will be followed in the divorce court.[19]

In *Theodoropoulas v Theodoropoulas*,[20] it was held that, where spouses were endeavouring to effect a reconciliation in the presence of a third person, neither one of the parties, nor the third person, could give evidence of the terms of the conversation without the consent of the other party. In Canada *Sinclair v Roy*[1] takes the matter at least two steps further in applying the rule to prevent parties interviewed separately in the process of mediation from calling the mediator, even to give objective evidence, such as the fact that statements were made, quite irrespective of their truth.[2]

It is often suggested that the privilege should be that of the mediator, at any rate when he is a marriage guidance officer, but the Law Reform Committee was against the creation of a statutory privilege for court welfare officers and marriage guidance counsellors.[3] No privilege attaches in affiliation proceedings to a statement made by the respondent to a case worker acting for an adoption society.[4] It has been held in Alberta that no privilege attaches to a statement made by the respondent in affiliation proceedings to a welfare officer who was making inquiries on behalf of the applicant. The matrimonial cases were distinguished on the score of public policy, the welfare officer not being a conciliator.[5]

---

17 [1955] P 202, [1955] 1 All ER 590.
18 [1950] P 154, [1950] 1 All ER 25.
19 *Pool v Pool* [1951] P 470, [1951] 2 All ER 563 is against *Bostock v Bostock* and the latter case was doubted by the Court of Appeal in *Mole v Mole*. It was distinguished in *G v R* [1981] 2 NZLR 91.
20 [1964] P 311, [1963] 2 All ER 722.
1 (1985) 20 DLR (4th) 748.
2 There in order to rebut a claim of recent fabrication.
3 16th Report, paras 39–40.
4 *R v Nottingham JJ, ex p Bostock* [1970] 2 All ER 641, [1970] 1 WLR 1117.
5 *Re Child Welfare Act, Brysh v Davidson* (1963) 42 DLR (2d) 673. See also *Constable v Constable* [1964] SASR 68 (husband's admission of adultery to children's welfare officer not privileged because officer was not conciliator), but see *G v R* above, where a new head of privilege was recognised in this situation.

CHAPTER XII

Public policy

Relevant evidence must be excluded on the ground of public policy when it concerns certain matters of public interest considered to be more important than the full disclosure of facts to the court and when it relates to miscellaneous matters connected with litigation. These subjects are discussed in the first two sections of this chapter. Evidence which has been illegally obtained—considered in section 3—is not usually discussed under the head of public policy. There is nothing in the nature of a general exclusionary rule but, if such a rule were ever to be developed, the basis might well be the desirability of discouraging a resort to illegality by the police.[1] The public interest in the conviction of guilty criminals would have to be weighed against the public interest in the preservation of basic civil liberties.

This topic is made more difficult by the very wide variety of situations to which it can be considered to apply. An important distinction is between its application at the stage of discovery, and its application during the course of the trial. In the former context it is sometimes difficult to differentiate between rules which apply generally to discovery, and those which are peculiar to a claim for immunity on the basis of public interest. It is also necessary to distinguish between those considerations which relate to a claim for inspection by the court, and those which relate to actual production. As will be seen, a wide spectrum of public interests may be urged in favour of immunity, some of them apparent upon the face of the documents in question, and others apparent only to those possessing intimate acquaintance with the operation of the public service, and with the psychology of those who work in it, or supply information to it. A final complicating factor is that while in many cases a party may share the public interest concerned, and be instrumental in ensuring that it is brought to the attention of the court, this will not necessarily be so. The court must itself always be alert to the possibility of such an interest being involved. Such a possibility may be very hard to detect in cases where the claim does depend upon knowledge of esoteric, and perhaps secret, aspects of the conduct of affairs of state.

Before considering some of the major varieties of claim, it is worth mentioning the impact of the factors set out above upon the terminology of this branch of the law, upon the question of waiver and upon the admissibility of secondary evidence of excluded matter.

At one time this branch of the law of evidence was subsumed under the rubric of 'Crown Privilege'. The reasons for abandoning such a categorisation were stated by Lord Simon as long ago as 1942:

---

1 Just such a justification for just such a rule has been propounded by the High Court of Australia, see *R v Ireland* (1970) 126 CLR 321 at 355; *Bunning v Cross* (1978) 141 CLR 54 at 74.

The withholding of documents on the ground that their publication would be contrary to the public interest is not properly to be regarded as a branch of the law of privilege connected with discovery. 'Crown privilege' is for this reason not a happy expression. Privilege, in relation to discovery, is for the protection of the litigant and could be waived by him, but the rule that the interest of the state must not be put in jeopardy by producing documents which would injure it is a principle to be observed in administering justice, quite unconnected with the interests or claims of the particular parties in litigation, and, indeed, is a rule on which the judge should, if necessary, insist even though no objection is taken at all.[2]

In *Rogers* Lord Simon expressed the view that the term privilege was properly applicable only to a claim which could be waived. This view has recently been reasserted by Lord Fraser in *Air Canada v Secretary of State for Trade (No 2)*: 'Public interest immunity is not a privilege which may be waived by the Crown or by any party.'[3] At first sight this view might seem inconsistent with some dicta of Lord Cross in *Alfred Crompton Amusement Machines Ltd v Customs and Excise Comrs (No 2)*[4] to the effect that where the claim is made in order to protect the interests of third parties in the confidentiality of information supplied to public authorities the privilege can be waived. There is no real inconsistency however. Before waiver can take place there must be some claim based upon public interest to be waived. It is material to the determination of that question whether or not the suppliers of information are willing for it to be revealed. It may well in many cases be hard to demonstrate a public interest in keeping information secret on behalf of those quite willing for it to be revealed, if that is the only basis for the claim.[5] In such a case the correct analysis is not that a valid public interest claim is waived, but that no public interest is ever established.[6]

In similar fashion where the archive of an international organisation was accorded inviolability on the same basis as that of a diplomatic mission, the House of Lords held that no objection could be taken to the use in litigation of documents which had been voluntarily communicated to third parties.[7] The act of communication prevented such documents from any longer attracting immunity, and the situation should be distinguished from deliberate waiver for the purposes of litigation. In these circumstances it is sometimes said where consent has been given to the release of the relevant information, and a fortiori where it has in fact been released, that the claim for immunity is not waived, but rather evaporates.[8]

Nor is the question of the admissibility of secondary evidence free from confusion. The general rule in this case was stated many years ago by Bayley J: 'If the document cannot, on principles of public policy be read in evidence, the effect will be the same as if it was not in evidence, and you may not prove

---

2 *Duncan v Camell Laird & Co Ltd* [1942] AC 624 at 641. See also *Rogers v Secretary of State for the Home Department* [1973] AC 388, [1972] 2 All ER 1057.

3 [1983] 2 AC 394 at 436, [1983] 1 All ER 910 at 917; *Carey v The Queen in right of Canada* (1986) 35 DLR (4th) 161 at 173; *Fletcher Timber Ltd v A-G* [1984] 1 NZLR 290 at 291.

4 [1974] AC 405 at 434, [1973] 2 All ER 1169 at 1185. See also *Peach v Metropolitan Police Comr* [1986] QB 1064 at 1071, [1986] 2 All ER 129 at 131 (applying the same view to statements made to the police in the course of an internal inquiry).

5 Indeed it might sometimes even be regarded as contrary to the public interest that information should be withheld when its suppliers wished it to be revealed.

6 Such an analysis is suggested by Brightman LJ in *Hehir v Metropolitan Police Comr* [1982] 2 All ER 335 at 341, [1982] 1 WLR 715 at 723.

7 *Shearson Lehman Bros Inc v Maclaine Watson Co Ltd (No 2)* [1988] 1 All ER 116.

8 *Multi-Guarantee Co Ltd v Cavalier Insurance Co* (1986) Times, 24 June.

the contents of the instrument.'[9] It is important to understand that this prohibition is limited to secondary evidence of the *documents*, and does not necessarily extend to secondary evidence of the matters dealt with in the documents. Indeed it is often a reason for upholding public interest immunity that the information contained in the relevant documents adds nothing to information in the hands of the parties which they may adduce in evidence without constraint.[10] This is not however to deny where the claim is based upon the vital importance of the contents of some documents, a national defence secret for example, that any oral evidence of the matter in question might be prohibited.

It may thus be appreciated that while there are clear analogies between claims for private privilege which were considered in the previous chapter and those under consideration here, there are nevertheless important points of distinction emphasised by the use of the currently fashionable terminology of 'public interest immunity'.

Far and away the most important ground of exclusion on account of public interest is that of state interest discussed in the early part of section 1. Before referring to matters of detail, it would be well to emphasise the devastating effect which the exclusion of evidence at the instance of the head of a government department can have on the substantive rights of litigants. It may render it totally impossible for them to rely on matters which would otherwise have constituted an unanswerable cause of action or a complete defence. An example is provided by *Hennessy v Wright*.[11] That was a libel action brought against the proprietor of a newspaper in respect of a statement imputing that the plaintiff, the governor of a colony, had sent home garbled reports to the Colonial Secretary, and the defendant was, in effect, prevented from setting up the defence of justification. The Colonial Secretary would not produce the originals of the reports, the court would not order discovery of copies that were in the possession of the plaintiff, and, even if witnesses who could depose to the contents of the reports had been available, their evidence would have been inadmissible. The words used by Field J when dismissing the application for discovery are memorable:

> First, the publication of a state document may involve danger to the nation. If the confidential communications made by servants of the Crown to each other, by superiors to inferiors, or by inferiors to superiors, in the discharge of their duty to the Crown were liable to be made public in a court of justice at the instance of any suitor who thought proper to say '*fiat justitia ruat caelum*', an order for discovery might involve the country in war. Secondly, the publication of a state document may be injurious to servants of the Crown as individuals. There would be an end of all freedom in their official communications, if they knew that any suitor could legally insist that any official communication, of no matter how secret a character, should be produced openly in a court of justice.

9 *Cooke v Maxwell* (1817) 2 Stark 183 at 186. See also Lynskey J in *Moss v Chesham UDC* (17 January 1945, unreported) cited in Simon 'Evidence Excluded by Considerations of State Interest' (1955) CLJ 62, 'if it is contrary to public interest to produce the original documents, it must be equally contrary to public interest to produce copies which the maker of the document has kept for his own information.'

10 *See Air Canada v Secretary of State for Trade (No 2)* [1983] 2 AC 394 at 442, [1983] 1 All ER 910 at 920, where Lord Wilberforce emphasised this point by describing the available documents as 'primary' evidence of the contentions advanced, and those for which immunity was claimed as 'secondary'.

11 (1888) 21 QBD 509.

There is no great enthusiasm for the second justification of the exclusionary rule but *Hennessy v Wright* might well be followed today.

SECTION 1. MATTERS OF PUBLIC INTEREST

This category of evidence is now recognised to be wider than it once was, and to be capable of modification by the courts, as Lord Hailsham remarked in *D v National Society for Prevention of Cruelty to Children*: 'The categories of public interest are not closed and must alter from time to time whether by restriction or extension as social conditions and social legislation develop.'[12] That remark was made in the context of an extension of public interest outside the confines of central government. It was also based upon a claim for the preservation of the anonymity of a supplier of information. That consideration raises the question of the basis for making such a claim. On occasion it is raised because the public interest demands that a particular piece of information not be revealed, and sometimes because it demands that a particular source of information remain inviolate. Such demands are not, of course, mutually exclusive. The basis of the claim may also affect the procedure for determining it, and in particular the desirability of the court's inspecting the relevant document in order to assist its decision. It is best to examine first the considerations and procedure which govern the clearest cases, those where vital interests of state are affected, and then to go on to consider how far the principles that apply there extend to other less vital interests of state, to reports of parliamentary proceedings, to the police, to local government and to matters of a confidential nature. It is finally necessary to consider how far the rules extend to criminal cases.

A. VITAL INTERESTS OF STATE[13]

The importance of particular pieces of information or classes of source to the interests of the state must obviously vary, not only from subject to subject but also from time to time. There can be no clearly defined line between cases where such vital interests are at stake and those where they are not. It is now recognised that many factors enter into any such estimation, and such recognition has contributed to the current practice of assessing the relative importance of the policies suggesting suppression, and those favouring disclosure. Some particular pieces of information are of so important a nature at some times that it is hard to see how any contravening policy in favour of the administration of justice could outweigh them. Thus in *Asiatic Petroleum Co Ltd v Anglo-Persian Oil Co Ltd*,[14] the defendants, acting under the direction of the Board of Admiralty, refused to produce a letter to their agent on the ground that it contained information concerning the government's plans with regard to one of the Middle Eastern campaigns of the First World War. The information had, of course, been given to the

12 [1978] AC 171 at 230, [1977] 1 All ER 589 at 605.
13 See Street 'State Secrets—A Comparative Study' (1951) 14 MLR 121; Simon 'Evidence Excluded by Considerations of State Interest' (1955) 13 CLJ 62; Zuckerman 'Privilege and Public Interest' in *Crime, Proof and Punishment* (ed Tapper) (1981).
14 [1916] 1 KB 822.

defendants by the Board of Admiralty under the seal of the strictest security, but as Swinfen-Eady LJ observed :[15]

> The foundation of the rule is that the information cannot be disclosed without injury to the public interests, and not that the documents are confidential or official, which alone is no reason for their non-production: the general public interest is paramount to the interests of the suitor.

The defendant's objection was upheld, and a similar principle was successfully invoked in *Duncan v Camell Laird & Co Ltd*,[16] where the defendants to a claim for damages for negligence in relation to the construction of a submarine were directed by the Board of Admiralty to object to the production of numerous documents in their possession in their capacity as government contractors. The structure of our submarines is clearly a matter that affects our national security, and ought to be kept secret while the country is at war, as in that case.[17]

In both cases the interest of the state would have been threatened by disclosure of the particular information contained in the relevant documents. In others the claim may be based upon the character of the source of information, or the class to which it belongs. Here too there may be classes of such vital interest to the state that documents belonging to them should not be produced. As Lord Salmon said in *Rogers v Secretary of State for the Home Department*:[18]

> There are also classes of documents and information which for years have been recognised by the law as entitled in the public interest to be immune from disclosure. In such cases the affidavit or certificate of a Minister is hardly necessary. I refer to such documents as Cabinet minutes, minutes of discussions between heads of government departments and despatches from ambassadors abroad.

The reasons in such a case are however a little less direct, and were stated by Lord Reid in *Conway v Rimmer*:[19]

> I do not doubt that there are certain classes of documents which ought not to be revealed whatever their content may be. Virtually everyone agrees that cabinet minutes and the like ought not to be disclosed until such time as they are only of historical interest; but I do not think that many people would give as the reason that premature disclosure would prevent candour in the cabinet. To my mind the most important reason is that such disclosure would create or fan ill-informed or captious public or political criticism. The business of government is difficult enough as it is, and no government could contemplate with equanimity the inner workings of the government machine being exposed to the gaze of those ready to criticise without adequate knowledge of the background and perhaps with some axe to grind.

15 At 830.
16 [1942] AC 624, [1942] 1 All ER 587.
17 It should be noted that the public interest in the security even of such pieces of information is ephemeral and could hardly prevail once the campaign had been fought, or the design of the submarine become common knowledge. Class claims are likely to be less time-sensitive.
18 [1973] AC 388 at 412, [1972] 2 All ER 1057 at 1071. Confidential communications passing between the British government and the governments of other states have been protected on this basis, *Buttes Gas and Oil Co v Hammer (No 3)* [1981] QB 223, [1980] 3 All ER 475 (unaffected on this point by subsequent proceedings).
19 [1968] AC 910 at 952, [1968] 1 All ER 874 at 888.

Nevertheless despite cabinet papers being regarded as the archetype of such a class, and despite a tendency to re-attach rather more weight to considerations of candour in such a case,[20] the courts still regard the matter as one requiring a balance to be struck, and are not prepared to countenance automatic immunity even for cabinet papers,[1] nor in either Australia[2] or Canada[3] for documents held by the state's intelligence services. It should be noted that while the only basis for immunity from disclosure in our courts is the public interest of the United Kingdom, and the interests of a foreign state are thus not, in principle, alone sufficient,[4] two possible qualifications might be made. The first is that now that this country is a member of the European Community similar considerations apply to confer immunity in respect of the interests of organs of the Community, including the European Commission.[5] The second is that a government may regard its own interests as being affected, and so certify, by the disregard of its own courts for the public interests of a foreign state.[6] This is particularly likely where the foreign state is a confidential source of vital information which is likely to dry up if revealed.[7] It should also be noted that the discretionary power of the court extends to refusing to issue letters of request in relation to evidence seeking to impugn the motives of a foreign legislature.[8] In striking a balance the court will take into account factors such as the seriousness of the claim for which disclosure is sought,[9] whether or not the government is itself a party or alleged to have acted unconscionably,[10] the relevance of the

---

20 See Lord Wilberforce in *Burmah Oil Co Ltd v Bank of England* [1980] AC 1090 at 1112, [1979] 3 All ER 700 at 707.
 1 *Air Canada v Secretary of State for Trade (No 2)* [1983] 2 AC 394 at 432, [1983] 1 All ER 910 at 915. Similar views have prevailed in Australia in *Sankey v Whitlam* (1978) 142 CLR 1; in New Zealand in *Environmental Defence Society Inc v South Pacific Aluminium Ltd. (No 2)* [1981] 1 NZLR 153; in Canada in *Carey v The Queen in right of Canada* (1986) 35 DLR (4th) 161; and in the United States in *Nixon v US* 418 US 683 (1974). In Canada the same approach has been utilised in relation to the oral evidence of a cabinet minister, *Smallwood v Sparling* (1982) 141 DLR (3d) 395, but see *Re Mulroney and Coates* (1986) 27 DLR (4th) 118. Some aspects of the question there have been affected by the statutory provisions of s 36 of the Canada Evidence Act, see *Gold v The Queen in right of Canada* (1986) 25 DLR (4th) 285.
 2 *Alister v R* (1983) 50 ALR 41.
 3 *Re Henrie and Security Intelligence Review Committee* (1988) 53 DLR (4th) 568.
 4 *Buttes Gas and Oil Co v Hammer (No 3)*, above.
 5 *Hasselblad (GB) Ltd v Orbinson* [1985] QB 475, [1985] 1 All ER 173. But see *Silver Hill Duckling Ltd v Steele* [1987] IR 289 where meetings of the Standing Veterinary Committee of the European Community were held not to attract immunity, though it is not clear whether this was because the body was insufficiently august, or that inspection of the relevant documents revealed no basis for any claim.
 6 This was considered at some length, though ultimately rejected on its application to the particular facts, in *A-G (UK) v Heineman Publishers Australia Pty Ltd* (1988) 78 ALR 449, largely on the basis that the courts no longer accept as binding any such certification, and that it is more in the public interest that they abstain from deciding upon the merits of any claim based, even at one remove, upon the public policy of a foreign state.
 7 As in *Nestle Australia Ltd v Federal Comr of Taxation* (1986) 67 ALR 128 at 136.
 8 *Settebello Ltd v Banco Totta & Acores* [1985] 2 All ER 1025, [1985] 1 WLR 1050. The court left open the question whether or not such evidence would have been admissible at all in English proceedings.
 9 Thus in *Henrie*, above, the fact that it related to security clearance so as to permit promotion within the government service was thought insufficiently compelling.
10 See *Burmah Oil*, above, at 1128, 720. See also *Sankey v Whitlam*, above at 540; *Carey*, above, at 188. In these circumstances there is a danger that justice will not be done because the interest of the government has been assimilated to that of the state, and a certainty that it will not have been seen to be done.

particular evidence to the dispute,[11] taking into account other possible sources of evidence,[12] and on the other side, the nature of the state's interest,[13] and the length of time which has elapsed since the relevant discussion took place.[14] In one Canadian case the fact that the government had set up the relevant Royal Commission before which the evidence was sought to be tendered was regarded as favouring admissibility.[15]

The appropriate procedure for determining the question was set out most clearly by Bingham J in *Air Canada* at first instance. Although his judgment was reversed on one point, his general approach was endorsed both by the House of Lords and by the Court of Appeal, where he was described as an acknowledged authority upon the subject.[16]

It should first be noted that the question is usually vented at the preliminary stage of discovery.[17] If the government is itself a party, or otherwise closely involved,[18] the question will normally be raised by a certificate made either in the ordinary case by a Minister,[19] or in a case where the documents relate to the papers of a previous administration, by a Permanent Under-Secretary.[20] The certificate should set out the precise grounds upon which immunity is claimed, and may also claim immunity in respect of oral evidence of the documents. If the government is not a party, nor closely involved, it is open for one of the parties to seek a certificate from the government.[1] The question may in any event always be raised by a party, or by a witness, and should be taken by the Court on its own initiative whenever it appears to arise.[2] There is, however, the difficulty that in cases where the danger to the public interest arises in respect of a class of documents, the courts may not be equipped to recognise it in the absence of some formal intimation from the government.[3] It was left open in *Sankey v Whitlam*[4] whether a deliberate decision by the government not to certify damage to the public interest should be regarded as conclusive.

Once apprised of the question the court must first determine whether the claim for immunity is on its face a valid one. In most cases this will involve perusal of the certificate to ascertain that the class into which the document falls either is, or is closely analogous to, one which has been recognised

11 See *Hospitals Consolidated Fund of Australia v Hunt* (1983) 76 FLR 408.
12 An important consideration in *Air Canada*, above.
13 Preferring disclosure of discussion even at the highest level if the subject was of commercial rather than security matters, see *Hospitals Fund of Australia*, above.
14 *A-G v Jonathan Cape Ltd* [1976] QB 752 at 770, [1975] 3 All ER 484 at 496. See also *Sankey v Whitlam*, above, at 528.
15 *Re The Queen and the Royal Commission into the Donald Marshall Junior Prosecution* (1988) 51 DLR (4th) 705.
16 By Lord Denning at [1983] 2 AC 394 at 412, [1983] 1 All ER 161 at 182.
17 Similar principles apply to interrogatories, Ord 26, r 4. See also *Whitlam v ACP Ltd* (1985) 73 FLR 414 at 417.
18 Perhaps because a public corporation is a party.
19 Who may however be a junior Minister, *Continental Reinsurance Corpn (UK) Ltd v Pine Top Insurance Ltd* [1986] 1 Lloyd's Rep 8 at 12.
20 As in *Air Canada*.
 1 In *Buttes Gas and Oil Co v Hammer (No 3)* [1981] QB 223, [1980] 3 All ER 475, such an application was made, but was unsuccessful.
 2 *Rogers v Home Secretary* [1973] AC 388 at 400, [1972] 2 All ER 1057 at 1065. It is permissible for the question to be raised on appeal without notice as it was in the *Buttes Gas* case. The failure of a party to challenge the certificate is no admission of the truth of its contents, *Sethia v Stern* Independent, 30 October 1987.
 3 See Lord Salmon in *Rogers* at 412, 1070; Lord Fraser in *Air Canada* at 436, 917.
 4 Above at 549.

before; that there is no reason to suppose that the documents do not fall within that class; and that proper consideration has been given to the matter by an appropriate person.

The court must next determine whether the party seeking production can show that there is a public interest in such production. It was at that point that the higher courts differed from Bingham J in *Air Canada*. The public interest involved is that of the administration of justice, and it was held that this implied that the party seeking production must show that the document sought was not only relevant to the dispute between the parties, but also that it would assist his own case. In that case the documents in question related to fixing landing fees at Heathrow Airport. The plaintiffs contended that the Secretary of State had acted upon criteria different from those specified by the relevant statutory provision, and sought discovery of relevant documents which included some cabinet papers, and documents relating to meetings held between the Secretary of State and his advisers, and between the advisers. The plaintiff was not in a position to demonstrate that these documents would support his case, and even if they did, it was felt that they could add nothing to other evidence of the matters in question which was already available to the plaintiffs. This point, one of the law of discovery rather than that of evidence, decided the appeal.

If it could have been demonstrated that the public interest in the administration of justice would have been likely to have been promoted by disclosure, the judge's task would have been to compare the public interest in such disclosure with that set out in the certificate, or discerned by the court, in favour of suppression. Only if the court were in doubt about the balance, or provisionally in favour of disclosure would it seek to inspect the documents in question.[5] In the latter case it would normally always inspect to confirm its provisional view before ordering disclosure, and in the case of a lower court would postpone disclosure pending any appeal.[6] It is important to distinguish the separate questions of whether the document should be inspected by the court, and that of whether it should be disclosed to the other party. These questions arise at different stages of the reasoning process, and must not be run together.[7]

Although it may at one time have seemed otherwise, the court's power to inspect applies equally to claims based on the contents of particular documents and to those based upon their provenance, in the latter case even to those where the class of documents is of the most vital state interest, such as cabinet papers.[8] This has become clearer now that it is recognised that the power to inspect is not limited to cases where the court is in doubt as to whether the documents really fall within the public interest claimed in the certificate, but also extends to cases where the doubt is whether or not that claim overbalances the countervening public interest in the administration

5 Inspection by the court is sometimes allowed by a party despite his claim for immunity, see Lord Wilberforce in *Burmah Oil* at 1116, 711 citing *Tito v Waddell* [1975] 3 All ER 997, [1975] 1 WLR 1303 and *Barty-King v Ministry of Defence* [1979] 2 All ER 80, [1978] STC 218.
6 In *Burmah Oil* Lord Keith said at 1136, 727 that a judge should not even undertake inspection without allowing time for an appeal, but he invoked Lord Reid in *Conway v Rimmer* as authority for this, and it seems clear that Lord Reid was referring only to production. In *Air Canada* Bingham J accordingly proposed the procedure stated in the text on this question, and was said by Lord Fraser to have adopted the proper practice.
7 *Continental Reinsurance Corpn (UK) Ltd v Pine Top Insurance Ltd* [1986] 1 Lloyd's Rep 8.
8 See e g Lord Fraser in *Air Canada* at 432, 915.

of justice. A further advantage of inspection is that it may enable the court to secure partial disclosure of documents. In some cases it may be possible, without distortion, to sever the parts most relevant to the litigation from those disclosure of which would be overly inimical to vital interests of state.[9] It is also possible in some cases for the courts to restrict disclosure to the legal advisers of the parties,[10] to order proceedings to be held in camera,[11] and to impose orders restricting the reporting of proceedings.[12] It is always the case that documents disclosed upon discovery should be used only for the purposes of the litigation in question, and not for any ulterior purpose,[13] even after being put in evidence in open court.[14]

B. OTHER INTERESTS OF STATE

It has already been noted that the line separating vital interests of state from those to be considered here is imprecise. It can hardly be denied however that some claims made on behalf of central government are of much less pressing importance than those discussed above.

Many such claims were allowed in the climate prevailing before the decision of the House of Lords in *Conway v Rimmer*.[15] Thus the Inland Revenue successfully objected to the production of a company's balance sheets at the hearing of a misfeasance summons against one of its directors;[16] the Minister of Transport successfully objected to the production of a report on a railway accident made to him under various statutory provisions at the hearing of an action for negligence against a railway company;[17] the Home Office successfully objected to the production of reports made by doctors and police officers concerning the mental condition of a prisoner awaiting trial and his assault on the plaintiff, a fellow prisoner, who was claiming damages from the Home Office;[18] and the Secretary of State for War successfully objected to the production in a divorce case of documents concerning attempts to reconcile the parties, of the Soldiers', Sailors' and Airmen's

9 See eg Lord Keith in *Burmah Oil* at 1135, 726.
10 *Church of Scientology of California v Department of Health and Social Security* [1979] 3 All ER 97, [1979] 1 WLR 723, though it seems that the court should not discriminate between counsel and solicitors, *WEA Records Ltd v Visions Channel 4 Ltd* [1983] 2 All ER 589, [1983] 1 WLR 721.
11 In the very case which enunciated the general obligation for courts to sit in public it was recognised that they could sit in camera if the administration of justice so required, *Scott v Scott* [1913] AC 417. This inherent power has been supplemented in certain cases by explicit statutory provision, for example, Official Secrets Act 1920, s 8(4).
12 Contempt of Court Act 1981, s 11, stilling doubts vented in *A-G v Leveller Magazine Ltd* [1979] AC 440, [1979] 1 All ER 745.
13 *Riddick v Thames Board Mills Ltd* [1977] QB 881, [1977] 3 All ER 677.
14 *Home Office v Harman* [1983] 1 AC 280, [1982] 1 All ER 532. This case is particularly significant since the material revealed had been the subject of a claim to public interest immunity, and the documents had been ordered to be produced only after inspection by the judge, *Williams v Home Office* [1981] 1 All ER 1151.
15 [1968] AC 910, [1968] 1 All ER 874.
16 *Re Joseph Hargreaves Ltd* [1900] 1 Ch 347. The balance sheets were in the hands of the Inland Revenue authorities for the purposes of tax assessment and the objection to production was founded on the desirability of secrecy. See also *Hughes v Vargas* (1893) 9 TLR 551, and contrast *Honeychurch v Honeychurch* [1943] SASR 31 where a number of English authorities are discussed.
17 *Ankin v London and North-Eastern Rly Co* [1930] 1 KB 527.
18 *Ellis v Home Office* [1953] 2 QB 135, [1953] 2 All ER 149.

Families Association.[19] The strength of the public interest justifying the suppression of such documents is highly questionable, and in one case the Lord Chamberlain was even successful in withholding from a slander suit communications made to him regarding the suitability of the female plaintiff for invitations to court functions.[20]

It is, now, much less likely that such claims will succeed. In most cases the claim will be based upon the argument that the public service will be impaired if the documents are revealed, and that in its turn will almost invariably be based upon the need to protect the class of documents to which those in question belong. In 1973 the House of Lords twice considered the situation where ordinary business documents came into the possession of Commissioners of Customs and Excise. In *Norwich Pharmacal Co v Customs and Excise Comrs*[1] the plaintiffs sought disclosure of import documents which would reveal the names of unlicensed importers of a patented drug, of which they were sole licensees in this country. This information came into the possession of the respondents in the course of their statutory duties, and they regarded themselves as bound not to disclose it to anyone else.[2] The House of Lords rejected this argument on the basis that it could not be regarded either as inimical to the interests of the persons concerned, or to the proper administration of the customs service, that the names of wrongdoers[3] should be revealed. The other parallel case was *Alfred Crompton Amusement Machines Ltd v Customs and Excise Comrs*[4] in which the documents in question were business documents, such as invoices, submitted by third parties to the commissioners in order to try to ascertain the true value of the plaintiff's machines for the purposes of calculating the correct amount of purchase tax payable in respect of them. Here, where the third parties were not wrongdoers, the House felt that the balance of interests fell fairly evenly, and was inclined to hold in such circumstances in favour of the claim for public interest. Although a party claiming immunity has a very heavy burden to make out that claim,[5] once the balancing stage has been reached the scales must tip decisively in favour of disclosure before it will be ordered.[6]

As noted above the argument for suppression in these lower level cases almost invariably rests upon the need to preserve the confidentiality of a class of documents. In *Conway v Rimmer* Lord Reid justified such 'class' claims upon the need to promote candour in communication, and to protect the public service from captious and ill-informed criticism. The former

---

19 *Broome v Broome* [1955] P 190, [1955] 1 All ER 201; distinguished in *Whitehall v Whitehall* 1957 SLT 96. See also *Anthony v Anthony* (1919) 35 TLR 559, and compare *Gain v Gain* [1962] 1 All ER 63, [1961] 1 WLR 1469, especially on the question of the admissibility of oral evidence of the contents of the relevant documents.
20 *West v West* (1911) 27 TLR 189 and 476.
1 [1974] AC 133, [1973] 2 All ER 943.
2 They were however unable to point to any explicit statutory restriction, and it seems that even if they had been able to do so, the Court would not have regarded it as preventing disclosure under proper authority in legal proceedings in the absence of an explicit provision to that effect, see *Rowell v Pratt* [1938] AC 101, [1937] 3 All ER 660. The effect of various statutory restrictions upon the disclosure of information is analysed in Eagles 'Public Interest Immunity and Statutory Privilege' (1983) 42 CLJ 118. See also *Townsley v Allan* [1985] Tas R 123.
3 Only re-importers could have been innocent.
4 [1974] AC 405, [1973] 2 All ER 1169.
5 See the formulation of Lord Edmund-Davies in *Burmah Oil Co Ltd v Bank of England* [1980] AC 1090 at 1125, [1979] 3 All ER 700 at 717.
6 *Burmah Oil* at 1127, 719.

justification, which was not much favoured even by Lord Reid, has subsequently been treated with scepticism. In *Burmah Oil* Lord Wilberforce thought this had been overdone,[7] but he felt that the latter argument had remained intact. There are however signs that it too is now being questioned. Thus in *Air Canada* Bingham J noted that while those criticised can always claim such criticism to be captious 'the extent to which it is ill- informed is naturally affected by the extent to which the relevant documents are available'.[8] The problem for the party seeking disclosure is that because of the requirements of the English[9] law of discovery as reiterated in *Air Canada* he must show that the documents are very likely to assist his case before he has had any opportunity to see them. While it is perfectly reasonable to prevent anything in the nature of 'fishing', it should not be forgotten that the party must in any event have shown on the pleadings a valid cause of action and some material to support it. In such circumstances it would not seem unreasonable, at least in this category of case, to put the burden of showing that the documents are not 'very likely to assist the plaintiff's case' upon the party resisting disclosure. He will know from the pleadings what the case is, and he has access to the documents enabling him to be able to assess their relevance to it. Then only if he is unable to satisfy the court that the documents are not likely to assist will the court inspect. There is some danger that the result of *Air Canada* will otherwise be to claw back by the principles of discovery what *Conway v Rimmer* had achieved in liberalising the law of evidence.

No distinction is drawn between cases in which the Crown or a government department is a party to the proceedings, and those in which the parties are private citizens or corporations. The former class of case has, however, increased since the Crown Proceedings Act 1947, came into force, and although an order for discovery may be made against the Crown under s 28 of that statute, it is expressly made subject to this doctrine of public policy.

C. REPORTS OF PROCEEDINGS IN PARLIAMENT

Questions have arisen as to the immunity from use in evidence of reports of proceedings in Parliament. It has been settled since 1688 that proceedings in Parliament ought not to be questioned in any court.[10] In *Church of Scientology v Johnson-Smith*[11] this was interpreted broadly to exclude the use of such reports in evidence in any proceedings,[12] except so far as they established matters of historical fact,[13] such as the presence in the chamber of a

---

7 At 1112, 707, but see Lord Keith at 1133, 724.
8 See also Lord Keith in *Burmah Oil* at 1134, 725.
9 It is significant that in jurisdictions where the roles of discovery are different there has been much less inclination to refuse inspection upon any such basis, even in the case of higher state documents, see in New Zealand *Fletcher Timber Ltd v A-G* [1984] 1 NZLR 290 at 293; and in Canada *Carey v the Queen in right of Canada* (1986) 35 DLR (4th) 161 at 194.
10 Bill of Rights 1688, art 9.
11 [1972] 1 QB 522, [1972] 1 All ER 378. Different views have been expressed in Australia as to the width of the immunity, compare *R v Murphy* (1986) 64 ALR 498 where a narrow view was taken with *R v Jackson* (1987) 8 NSWLR 116 where the approach was much broader.
12 Including proceedings for judicial review, *R v Secretary of State for Trade, ex p Anderson Strathclyde plc* [1983] 2 All ER 233.
13 No leave of the House of Lords has ever been required to use such reports, nor of the House of Commons since its resolution of 31 October 1980.

particular person on a particular day. It seems to be the case that the judge has the duty, as in other public policy situations, to intervene on his own initiative if the point is not taken by the parties.[14]

D. POLICE MATTERS[15]

Information may come into the hands of the police either in the course of an internal inquiry, or from outside the police force in the ordinary course of the business of the police. *Conway v Rimmer*,[16] the genesis of much of the modern law on the whole topic of public interest immunity, itself fell into the former category. In that case the appellant had been a probationary police constable. He was accused by a fellow probationer of stealing a cheap torch, and was ultimately prosecuted by the respondent, a superintendent in that police force. The prosecution was unsuccessful, but the appellant was dismissed from the police force. He brought an action for malicious prosecution and sought disclosure of probationary reports upon him, made both before and after the allegations of theft, and of a report to the Director of Public Prosecutions about the circumstances of the alleged theft. The Home Secretary claimed Crown privilege for these reports upon the basis that their disclosure would be injurious to the public interest. The House of Lords was unwilling to be bound by such a claim in respect of ostensibly routine documents such as the probation reports, or even in the case of the report to the Director of Public Prosecutions after the occasion of the prosecution had passed. It was clearly regarded as relevant that the documents were of crucial importance to the outcome of the case.[17]

More often the issue is raised in relation to information which comes to the police from external sources. The facts of *Rogers v Secretary of State for the Home Department*[18] provide a neat transition to that situation. An applicant to the Gaming Board for a gaming licence was unsuccessful. Subsequently he came into possession of a copy of a letter written to the board by a police officer in relation to his application which, he alleged, contained defamatory statements about him. He sought to prosecute the officer for criminal libel, and served witness summonses upon the secretary of the Gaming Board and the relevant chief constable to give evidence, and to produce relevant documents including the original letter. The summonses were set aside by the Divisional Court. The House of Lords upheld this decision, not on the basis that the letter was a policy document, but because its production might jeopardise the working of the public service. The House was impressed by the fact that the police in responding to inquiries from the Gaming Board, and the board itself, depended upon the provision of information from members of the public, and that such sources might be threatened if protection from disclosure could not be guaranteed. Exactly the same line of reasoning was applied back to statements made for the purpose of a police

---

14 *R v Murphy*, above, at 519.
15 It was explicitly denied in Australia in *R v Robertson, ex p McAuley* (1983) 71 FLR 429 at 438 that police documents are sufficiently homogenous to constitute a class of documents to which immunity can attach.
16 [1968] AC 910, [1968] 1 All ER 874. See also *Konia v Morley* [1976] 1 NZLR 455.
17 They were requested by both parties.
18 [1973] AC 388, [1972] 2 All ER 1057.

disciplinary inquiry in *Neilson v Laugharne*.[19] The Court of Appeal decided
that the test in every such case was whether disclosure would inhibit the
performance of the statutory function in question, and there they held that
disclosure of statements made for the purpose of such an inquiry in a
subsequent civil action would have just such an effect.

This view may, however, lead to difficulty after a complaint has failed
whether the complainant persists and brings a civil action nevertheless,[20] or
the policeman sues for defamation.[1] In the former case the claim for
immunity so as to bar cross-examination on an inconsistent statement by the
plaintiff succeeded, though the decision was subsequently doubted,[2] and
seems to have been disregarded in practice so far as use in cross-examination
is concerned.[3] In the latter case the problem was evaded by drawing a
somewhat implausible distinction between a statement in support of a
complaint, which cannot be used; and the complaint itself, which can. It has
been further held where the complaint amounted to an allegation of a serious
crime committed by the police that statements made in connection with it
are not subject to immunity.[4] Despite such difficulty the basic rule has been
reaffirmed by the Court of Appeal,[5] subject only to the consideration that
the class is merely prima facie one for immunity, and that in exceptional
circumstances a judge may find that the public interest is better served by
disclosure than by suppression.[6]

Where application is made for statements in the hands of the police, or
reports made by them to prosecuting authorities the general difficulty with
public policy immunity is compounded by a further analogy with legal
professional privilege, by the law of discovery, and by the general effect of
the position of the accused in criminal proceedings.[7] It seems that if the
application is not so general as to be disallowed on the basis that it amounts
to 'fishing', then documents should be identified with some particularity, and
reasons for disclosure or suppression elaborated in detail.[8] In such a case the
party seeking disclosure must first satisfy the normal rules for discovery.
This may be particularly difficult in a case where there is an onus of proof
upon the resisting party, for example in an action for wrongful arrest.[9] Even
if this hurdle can be cleared it seems that the analogy with legal professional
privilege may make it difficult to overcome immunity on ordinary balancing
principles.

These arguments rely in part upon analogy with a much older line of
authority, concerned with the preservation from disclosure in civil cases of

19 [1981] QB 736, [1981] 1 All ER 829.
20 As in *Hehir v Metropolitan Police Comr* [1982] 2 All ER 335, [1982] 1 WLR 715.
1 As in *Conerney v Jacklin* [1985] Crim LR 234.
2 By Lord Denning MR in *Campbell v Tameside Metropolitan Borough Council* [1982] QB 1065
at 1072, [1982] 2 All ER 791 at 795.
3 See letter in (1986) 136 NLJ 14.
4 *Peach v Metropolitan Police Comr* [1986] QB 1064, [1986] 2 All ER 129.
5 In other jurisdictions such complaints are subject to no general rule of immunity but dealt
with in every case by the operation of the normal balancing principles, see *Ninness v Graham*
(1986) 70 ACTR 1; *R v Delong* (1989) 69 CR (3d) 147.
6 *Makanjuola v Metropolitan Police Comr* [1989] NLJR 468. This is a particularly strong case
because the complainant sought disclosure of her own statement, but was still refused.
7 See section G below. There may also, in some jurisdictions, be further complications on
account of local privacy provisions, see e g *Davidson v Solicitor-General of Canada* (1987) 41
DLR (4th) 533.
8 *R v Robertson, ex p McAuley* (1983) 71 FLR 429.
9 As in *Evans v Chief Constable of Surrey* [1989] 2 All ER 594.

the identities of those providing information for public prosecutions.[10] This line which extends back at least to the eighteenth century was endorsed in the leading case of *Marks v Beyfus*.[11] In an action for an alleged conspiracy to prosecute maliciously, the plaintiff called the Director of Public Prosecutions and wished to ask the name of the person who gave the information leading to the prosecution for which the Director had been responsible. The Court of Appeal held that the prosecution was a public one, that, in such a case, the information sought by the plaintiff ought to be withheld, and that the trial judge had rightly disallowed the question.[12] The ban on the disclosure of the name of the informant appears to have been confined to 'public prosecutions', but there is no modern authority on the implication of this term. It has also been suggested that a distinction be drawn between those who provide information upon a regular, and often paid, basis, who would be popularly known as 'informers' and to whom the rule should apply, and those ordinary citizens who just happen quite by chance to possess some relevant information which they pass on to the police in the spirit of public duty, who would not be so regarded, and to whom the rule should not apply.[13] Such a distinction might however prove very difficult to apply with any consistency.

Rogers reaffirms that the court should take the point if it has not been taken by the parties,[14] and by implication that it may not be waived.[15] Its facts also provide the clearest possible example of the inadmissibility of secondary evidence since the plaintiff was prevented from using his copy of the relevant original. In Canada the Supreme Court has characterised this situation as amounting to an absolute prohibition on the disclosure of the informant's identity, even to a Commission inquiring into illegal disclosure of confidential information to the police.[16] The same court has also held that the prohibition must extend outside judicial proceedings, and that it precludes any notion of balancing.[17]

If, as most formulations of the rule suggest, and as will be discussed more fully below in part G, the immunity does not apply when disclosure of the information is required by the defence to establish innocence in a criminal

10 The strength of this analogy was strongly questioned by the Supreme Court of Canada in *Bisaillon v Keable* (1983) 2 DLR (4th) 193, where a number of differences between the rules relating to the ordinary public interest immunity and the special rules relating to informers are emphasised.

11 (1890) 25 QBD 494. The rule was discussed in *R v Hardy* (1794) 24 State Tr 199 at 808. The rule is similar in Scotland, see *Friel v Chief Constable of Strathclyde* 1981 SC 1.

12 The objection may be taken by the judge on his own initiative, *A-G v Briant* (1846) 15 M & W 169.

13 *Tipene v Apperley* [1978] 1 NZLR 761 (in this case the contest related mainly to the release to a potential plaintiff of the substance of the information).

14 At 400, 1060.

15 See also Oliver LJ in *Neilson v Laugharne* at 753, 839. Though it appears that in practice the police do disclose the names of witnesses of road accidents to solicitors for the plaintiff in subsequent civil litigation. Statements by witnesses to the police are nevertheless regarded as the proper subject matter for public interest immunity. See 237 H L Official Report (5th series) cols 1191–3. It is arguable that no public interest is involved when the informants either consent, or might reasonably be supposed to consent, to the disclosure of their identity, see Brightman LJ in *Hehir v Metropolitan Police Comr* [1982] 2 All ER 335 at 341, [1982] 1 WLR 715 at 723, and above p 457. It seems reasonable to presume that this is the case when the statement is made in anticipation of becoming a witness in open court, *Tipene v Apperley*, above.

16 *Solicitor-General of Canada v Royal Commission of Inquiry into the Confidentiality of Health Records in Ontario* [1981] 2 SCR 494.

17 Note 16 (above) and *Bisaillon v Keable* (1983) 2 DLR (4th) 193.

trial, the justification advanced in *Rogers* in terms of the drying up of sources
of information is open to question. As Lord Reid himself said in *Conway v
Rimmer* it is a:

> curious result that 'freedom and candour of communication' is supposed not to be
> inhibited by knowledge of the writer that his report may be disclosed in a criminal
> case, but would still be supposed to be inhibited if he thought that his report might
> be disclosed in a civil case.[18]

E. LOCAL GOVERNMENT MATTERS

Immunity is granted, and only granted, in the public interest. If no public
interest is asserted, but only an interest of a local authority it will not be
accepted as alone constituting a valid ground for immunity.[19] It often
happens however that a matter of national concern raising a clear public
interest is entrusted to a local authority. In such a case it is not conclusive
against the recognition of immunity from disclosure that the claim is made
by the local authority, even though it may be unsupported by an affidavit
from a Minister. Still less is it conclusive in favour of immunity that the
question arises in wardship proceedings.[20] Thus in *D v National Society for the
Prevention of Cruelty to Children* the House of Lords recognised, obiter, such a
claim in relation to information given to the local authority to enable it to
discharge its statutory duties in relation to the care of children.[1] It is however
likely to be rare that a claim for public interest immunity, raised only by a
local authority, and supported by affidavits not from Ministers, but local
professional advisers, will prevail against the public interest in the
administration of justice, especially in a case where the documents are of the
utmost significance to the outcome of the litigation for which they are
required.[2] In this area, as in others involving public policy immunity, the
principles laid down in *Air Canada* regarding balancing for both inspection
and disclosure are appropriate.[3]

F. CONFIDENTIAL MATTERS

It was stated quite clearly by Lord Cross in *Alfred Crompton Amusement Machines
Ltd v Customs and Excise Comrs (No 2)* that : '"Confidentiality" is not a separate
head of privilege, but it may be a very material consideration to bear in
mind when privilege is claimed on the ground of public interest.'[4] This
proposition has impeccable historical credentials,[5] and has subsequently

18 At 942, 882. See also Oliver LJ in *Neilson v Laugharne* at 752, 837 in his discussion of the
'confidentiality' argument.
19 *Blackpool Corpn v Locker* [1948] 1 KB 349, [1948] 1 All ER 85, as interpreted by Lord
Edmund-Davies in *D v National Society for the Prevention of Cruelty to Children* [1978] AC 171
at 245, [1977] 1 All ER 589 at 618.
20 *Re M (A Minor)* (1990) Times, 4 January, disapproving *Re S* [1987] Fam 199.
 1 *Re D (infants)* [1970] 1 All ER 1088, [1970] 1 WLR 599, is similar, but *Campbell v Tameside
Metropolitan Borough Council* [1982] QB 1065 at 1077, [1982] 2 All ER 791 at 798, shows its
strictly confined ambit. See also *Gaskin v Liverpool City Council* [1980] 1 WLR 1549; *Re S and
W (minors)* (1982) 12 Fam Law 151.
 2 See e g *Campbell v Tameside MBC*, above.
 3 *Re M*, above.
 4 [1974] AC 405 at 433, [1973] 2 All ER 1169 at 1184.
 5 See VIII *Wigmore* para 2286.

been re-affirmed by the House of Lords.[6] It is necessary to re-state it on account of the modern approach to public interest immunity exhibited in the quotation from Lord Hailsham's speech in *D v National Society for the Prevention of Cruelty to Children* with which this section of the chapter began. The judgments in the Court of Appeal in that case exhibit the conflicting views current at the time. There was on the one hand Lord Denning's view that breach of confidence was a sufficient basis for making a claim for immunity from disclosure on the basis of public interest, and would prevail unless over-balanced by the public interest in the administration of justice. On the other there was the view of the majority that the categories of public interest immunity were strictly limited to the sorts of claim on behalf of central government which had been recognised in the past. The House of Lords attempted to steer a middle course between these views. The case arose out of the visit without any prior warning of an inspector of the NSPCC to the home of the mother of a young child. It transpired that the visit was to investigate an allegation that the child had been ill-treated. There was no evidence of such ill-treatment, and no subsequent proceedings were set in train. The mother was most upset by the incident, and eventually brought an action for negligence against the NSPCC in respect of its conduct in the matter, pursuant to which she sought discovery of all relevant documents in its possession, some of which would be very likely to reveal the identity of the society's informant. The society sought an order that no such documents should be discovered. This application was dismissed by the master, upheld by the judge, and dismissed by the majority of the Court of Appeal, but only over the dissent of Lord Denning. It may be noted that there could be no reasonable doubt that such documents existed, and that they would assist the plaintiff's case. It is also the case that the plaintiff was interested only in the identity of the informant, and that the society relied upon no certificate or affidavit from any official in support of its claim that it would be contrary to the public interest to make such a revelation to the plaintiff. Nor was the issue capable of being disposed of simply as a matter for the discretion of the judge at the stage of discovery. The case was accepted, and discussed, by the House of Lords on the basis that it affected the law of evidence,[7] in the sense that the decision involved also the range of questions which could be put at the trial of the action. The unanimous view of the House was that it could not be regarded as fatal that no arm of central government was involved, so long as the defendant's claim were capable of subsumption under a head of public policy, at least analogous to one previously recognised. In the particular case it was felt that there was a clear analogy to the public policy of preserving from disclosure in a civil case the identity of informants to the police.

Such an approach opens up the field of public interest immunity just because the closeness of the necessary analogy is left for subsequent development. The facts of the case demonstrate that the analogy may be

---

6 Eg *D v National Society for the Prevention of Cruelty to Children* [1978] AC 171 at 238, [1977] 1 All ER 589 at 612; *Science Research Council v Nassé* [1980] AC 1028 at 1080, [1979] 3 All ER 673 at 691.

7 See Lord Diplock at 219, 595, Lord Hailsham at 221, 600, and Lord Simon at 241, 615.

close enough even though no organ of central government is involved, and notwithstanding the absence of official certification of any public interest.[8]

The House regarded the role of confidence as being essentially confirmatory, in the sense that it is unlikely that the argument for refusing disclosure of any statement made otherwise than in confidence would ever be supported by a public policy so strong as to override the public interest in the proper administration of justice.

The ambit of this extension of public interest immunity was soon afterwards explored in two discrimination cases, eventually heard together by the House of Lords.[9] In both cases discrimination was alleged in relation to employment; in both the claimant sought disclosure of confidential reports upon the successful applicants; and in both disclosure was ordered at a lower level, but denied by the Court of Appeal. One of the respondents rested its case upon a claim for public interest immunity. This was rejected by the whole House. Most of their Lordships were concerned to point out that there was no such analogy to a recognised form of public interest immunity as there had been in *D v National Society for the Prevention of Cruelty to Children*. It was pointed out that the interest of the employers, even though one was a public body, was of a private and not a public nature. Nor was Parliament's expression of public policy in setting up the relevant commissions compatible with a public interest immunity which would effectively prevent them from discharging their statutory functions.

Despite some dicta in *D v National Society for the Prevention of Cruelty to Children* tending to elide the distinction between private privilege and public interest immunity in some respects, the House clearly reaffirmed its acceptance of the doctrine that any immunity based upon public interest cannot be waived by the parties, and must be taken up by the court even if not explicitly claimed by one of them.[10] On the other hand a court may be more prepared to protect the confidentiality of documents secured by compulsory process, such as discovery, than those divulged voluntarily, for example, in an arbitration.[11]

G. CRIMINAL PROCEEDINGS[12]

It seems clear that rules both of privilege and of public policy immunity apply differently in criminal proceedings.[13] It has already been noted that

---

8 This may however be relevant to the burden of proof which Lord Edmund-Davies at 246, 619 here regarded as being borne by the party resisting disclosure, apparently at the standard of the balance of probabilities, by contrast to his view in *Burmah Oil* at 1127, 719 and repeated in *Air Canada* at 442, 922 that the burden in those cases, where there was such a certificate, was borne by the party seeking disclosure, and at an apparently high standard ('the scales must come down decisively').

9 *Science Research Council v Nassé, Leyland Cars (BL Cars Ltd) v Vyas* [1980] AC 1028, [1979] 3 All ER 673.

10 See Lord Wilberforce at 1067, 681; Lord Edmund-Davies at 1074, 686; Lord Fraser at 1082, 693.

11 *Shearson Lehman Hutton Inc v Maclaine Watson Co Ltd* [1989] 1 All ER 1056, [1988] 1 WLR 946.

12 See Wharam 'Crown Privilege in Criminal Cases: The Background' [1971] Crim LR 675.

13 Said in *R v Brown and Daley* (1987) 87 Cr App Rep 52 at 57 'always to have been accepted'. But see *R v Robertson* (1983) 21 NTR 11. It has also been recognised by statute, see Iron and Steel Act 1982, s 33(1). Some statutory provisions of a like character, such as the Interception of Communications Act 1985, s 9 which prohibits any evidence or cross-examination on certain sensitive matters, apply indifferently to both civil and criminal proceedings alike.

a claim to legal professional privilege may be overridden when the evidence may enable the accused to resist an allegation made by the Crown or to establish his innocence.[14] In relation to public policy immunity it was stated by the Lord Chancellor that:[15]

> if medical documents, or indeed other documents, are relevant to the defence in criminal proceedings, Crown privilege should not be claimed.

It was made clear that the rule was far-reaching and applied even to prosecutions for minor offences. It should however be noted that the reference is to the practice of claiming Crown privilege, and not to its non-existence as a matter of law. Indeed such existence is rather presumed by the form of the statement, and may well be necessary since it can hardly be supposed that there are no means of preventing disclosure of the most vital national secrets just because they are relevant to the defence of one accused of some most trivial offence.

One of the more sensitive aspects of public policy immunity in this connection is that relating to police matters, and especially to evidence tending to reveal the identity of informers.[16] Here too the general rule is relaxed in favour of the defence, as Lord Simon of Glaisdale recognised in *Rogers v Home Secretary*:[17]

> Sources of police information are a judicially recognised class of evidence excluded on the grounds of public policy *unless their production is required to establish innocence in a criminal trial.*

The earliest cases[18] involved vital state interests and were resolved in favour of the application of the privilege. In less important situations the cases diverged,[19] and in the leading case of *Marks v Beyfus*[20] it was regarded as a matter for discretion[1] by the judge at the trial. It is for the defence to show[2] that disclosure is necessary for the proper presentation of the defence

---

14 P 442, above, *R v Barton* [1972] 2 All ER 1192, [1973] 1 WLR 115. The rules apply in the ordinary way to evidence required by the prosecution, see *R v King* [1983] 1 All ER 929 at 931, [1983] 1 WLR 411 at 414.

15 197 HL Official Report (5th series) col 745 quoted by Lord Reid in *Conway v Rimmer* [1968] AC 910 at 942, [1968] 1 All ER 874 at 881.

16 See Eagles 'Evidentiary Protection for Informers' [1982] 6 Crim LJ 175 for a full and helpful summary of this topic.

17 [1973] AC 388 at 407, [1972] 2 All ER 1057 at 1067 (emphasis supplied) citing *R v Hardy* (1794) 24 State Tr 199, *Hennessy v Wright* (1888) 21 QBD 509, and *Marks v Beyfus* (1890) 25 QBD 494. See also *Roviaro v US* 353 US 53 (1957) for a similar approach in the United States.

18 *R v Hardy*, above, *R v Watson* (1817) 32 State Tr 1, *R v Cobbett* (1831) 2 State Tr NS 789, and *R v O'Connor* (1846) 4 State Tr NS 935.

19 In *A-G v Briant* (1846) 15 LJ Ex 265, disclosure was not compelled, while in *R v Richardson* (1863) 3 F & F 693, and *Webb v Catchlove* (1886) 3 TLR 159, the contrary view prevailed. See also *Thomson v Neilson* 1900 8 SLT 147.

20 At 498. The position seems not to be materially different in Ireland where a number of cases have allowed privilege not to disclose the names of informers in criminal cases, see eg *A-G v Simpson* [1959] IR 105, discussed in O'Connor 'The Privilege of Non-Disclosure and Informers' (1980) 15 IJ (NS) 111.

1 In *R v Hallett* [1986] Crim LR 462 it was emphasised that it was not truly a matter of discretion since once the judge found the relevant condition to be established he was bound to allow the evidence to be given or questions to be asked.

2 *R v Hennessey* (1978) 68 Cr App Rep 419 at 426.

case.[3] The judge should take into account the nature of the information to be revealed and its importance to the accused's defence.[4] For example if the defence is that the accused was inveigled into a compromising situation by a particular third person, the fact that the third person was an informer with a motive for so behaving ought not to be suppressed.[5] The court is not however prepared to countenance 'fishing' expeditions, and has refused to lift the immunity when the accused did not know the identity of certain persons who might have been informers and in a position to 'plant' incriminating material.[6] A more controversial step has been the extension of immunity to protect the identity, not of informers, but of those who make premises available to the police as observation posts. In *R v Rankine* it was said that:[7]

> the reasons which give rise to the rule that an informer is not to be identified apply with equal force to the identification of the owner or occupier of premises used for surveillance *and to the identification of the premises themselves.* The cases are indistinguishable, and the same rule must apply to each.

It is vital to note that the words emphasised above do not constitute a separate basis for protection, but are subordinate to the consideration of protecting the identity of the owner or occupier. If taken as an independent basis the reasoning could easily be extended to the protection of methods of surveillance. Such a further extension was attempted in *R v Brown and Daley*[8] where the police refused to describe cars used for surveillance purposes. As the court pointed out such an extension would distort the reason for the rule, and destroy the analogy with the case of informers. The critical difference is that in the case of an informer the prosecution must elect either to take the direct benefit of the informer's information by calling him to testify, in which case his identity is revealed and he is available for cross-examination, or to secure only indirect benefit from his information by using it to lead them to evidence which they can then adduce without revealing his identity. If the extension to the identity of observation posts were to be accepted the prosecution would be able to secure the direct benefit of evidence observed from the post while at the same time insulating that evidence from any effective cross-examination by suppressing any indication of its location. Since this information will normally be necessary for such cross-examination it is to be expected that the occasions for applying the analogy to informers, and suppressing the information, will be rare. In particular it will be necessary for the prosecution to satisfy the court that there was a particular need for the observation post, and for anonymity, before any such suppression is even considered.[9] On the other hand in neither the case of an informer nor of

---

3 This formulation of the test seems to have been adopted in *R v Williams* [1988] Crim LR 113.

4 In a number of jurisdictions a distinction is made between relaxation of the immunity where it helps the defence directly, but reluctance to do so when it might merely show that a warrant was unlawfully obtained, see *Hilton v Wells* (1985) 59 ALR 281; *R v Hunter* (1987) 57 CR (3d) 1; *McCray v Illinois* 386 US 300 (1967).

5 *R v Williams*, above; *R v Agar* [1989] NLJ 1116.

6 *R v Hardy* [1988] Crim LR 687.

7 [1986] QB 861 at 867, [1986] 2 All ER 566 at 570, emphasis supplied.

8 (1987) 87 Cr App Rep 52.

9 *R v Johnson* [1989] 1 All ER 121, [1988] 1 WLR 1377.

an owner of an observation point should the defence be permitted to exploit the exception as a substitute for discovery.[10] Nor should an order ever be made *ex parte*.[11]

If a Crown witness's evidence is contradictory of a statement made by him, the prosecution should show the statement to counsel for the defence so that he can cross-examine upon it, and orders to hand over such a statement have been made.[12]

SECTION 2. MISCELLANEOUS MATTERS CONNECTED WITH PREVIOUS LITIGATION

The judges of the superior courts cannot be compelled to give evidence concerning cases tried by them, and more or less closely analogous rules exist concerning the evidence of arbitrators, jurors or barristers.

A. EVIDENCE OF JUDGES OF THE SUPERIOR COURTS

In *R v Gazard*[13] it was held that a chairman of quarter sessions ought not to be compelled to go before the grand jury in order to depose what a witness had said in a previous case tried by him. Patteson J said: 'It would be dangerous to allow such an examination as the judges of England might be called upon to state what occurred before them in court.' It has since been held that the judges of inferior courts can be compelled to do this,[14] but the remarks of Patteson J suggest that a privilege based upon the dignity of their office is conferred on the judges of the superior courts, although it is impossible to say exactly how far the privilege extends because there are very few authorities on the subject as the judges do not appear to object to giving evidence, at least from the well of the court, concerning that which occurred in cases tried by them when they can assist subsequent litigation by so doing. In *Buccleuch (Duke) v Metropolitan Board of Works*[15] Cleasby B said:

> With respect to those who fill the office of judge it has been felt that there are grave objections to their conduct being made the subject of cross-examination and comment (to which hardly any limit could be put) in relation to proceedings

10 *R v Robertson* (1983) 21 NTR 11.
11 *R v Guildhall Justices, ex p DPP* (1983) 78 Cr App Rep 269.
12 *R v Clarke* (1930) 22 Cr App Rep 58; *R v Hall* (1958) 43 Cr App Rep 29. If the witness is not called, there is no obligation to hand over his statement (*R v Bryant* (1946) 31 Cr App Rep 146), but the witness must be made available to the defence if it is known that he can give material evidence; it should be noted that rigid adherence to this practice can lead to injustice, see *R v Lawson* (1989) 90 Cr App Rep 107 at 115. See also *Baksh v R* [1958] AC 167, the conflicting views of Lord Denning MR and Diplock LJ in *Dallison v Caffery* [1965] 1 QB 348, at 369 and 375, [1964] 2 All ER 610 at 618 and 622, and the guidelines for the disclosure of information to the defence at trials on indictment in *Practice Note* [1982] 1 All ER 734. Power to make rules on the subject for summary proceedings was conferred by s 48 of the Criminal Law Act 1977.
13 (1838) 8 C & P 595.
14 *R v Harvey* (1858) 8 Cox CC 99.
15 (1872) LR 5 HL 418 at 433. A subpoena may be issued against a magistrate's clerk to bring and produce notes of proceedings before the magistrates (*McKinley v McKinley* [1960] 1 All ER 476, [1960] 1 WLR 120).

before them; and, as everything which they can properly prove can be proved by others, the courts of law discountenance and I think I may say prevent them being examined.

B. EVIDENCE OF ARBITRATORS

So far as arbitrators are concerned, it is settled that they can be compelled to give evidence with regard to occurrences at the arbitration, and to state what matters were included in the submission, but they must not be asked questions about the reasons for their award.[16] Such a limitation may be justified on the ground that the evidence would be irrelevant as the reasons for an award could only be material at the hearing of an application to have it set aside, but there is also the point that the award must be treated as final in the absence of any proceedings of this nature.

C. EVIDENCE OF JURORS

There is a settled rule that jurors may not give evidence of discussions that took place in the jury box or jury room concerning the cases in which they were acting. Even if they are all prepared to swear that they intended to return a verdict for a greater sum of damages than that which appeared on the record, no alteration can be made.[17] Hard as it is, the point made in the judgment that it is better for the plaintiff to suffer an inconvenience than that his application should be allowed is probably a sound one. If the statement of all the jurors concerning their intentions would justify a variation of the verdict, what would happen if some, or a majority of them, made such a statement? The exclusionary rule is confined to evidence of discussions concerning their verdict that took place between the jurors.[18] Accordingly in *Ellis v Deheer*,[19] a new trial was ordered on the ground that some jurymen had not been present in court when their verdict was announced, and it is probable that the fact that one of the jurors did not understand English would be a good ground for setting aside their verdict. As Lord Atkin observed, finality is a good thing, but justice is better.[20]

---

16 *Buccleuch's* case (above), applied to a member of a medical board under the National Insurance (Industrial Injuries) Act 1946, in *Ward v Shell Mex and BP Ltd* [1951] 2 All ER 904.

17 *Jackson v Williamson* (1788) 2 Term Rep 281. See also *Nesbitt v Parrett* (1902) 18 TLR 510; and *R v Thompson* [1962] 1 All ER 65.

18 In *R v Hood* [1968] 2 All ER 56, 52 Cr App Rep 265, the Court of Appeal admitted an affidavit sworn by a juror relating to his knowledge of the accused's previous convictions, but ostensibly only on the basis that it dealt exclusively with extrinsic matters and did not relate to discussions between jurors or to the reasons for verdict, though it is hard to understand how such a limitation applied in the circumstances there present.

19 [1922] 2 KB 113.

20 *Ras Behari Lal v The King-Emperor* (1933) 102 LJPC 144, disapproving in the Privy Council the decision of the Court of Criminal Appeal in *R v Thomas* [1933] 2 KB 489. For evidence of statements by jurors to third parties see *R v Syme* (1914) 10 Cr App Rep 284; *R v Armstrong* [1922] 2 KB 555; *R v Box* [1964] 1 QB 430, [1963] 3 All ER 240.

D. EVIDENCE OF ADVOCATES

There are obvious reasons why an advocate should not give evidence in a case in which he is acting, and it is not customary to compel him to testify in later litigation concerning such matters as the terms of a compromise of a previous suit, but the whole question is more dependent on professional etiquette than anything in the nature of an exclusionary rule of evidence,[1] and nothing more need be said about it in a work of this nature.

SECTION 3. ILLEGALLY OBTAINED EVIDENCE[2]

Cast into its simplest terms, the problem with which this section is concerned is whether there is a rule under which relevant evidence must be excluded because it was obtained illegally, for example, by a crime, tort, breach of contract or an infringement of official regulations such as those which bind the police when carrying out investigations. So far as the present English law is concerned, the short answer is that confessions may not be admitted if they were obtained by oppression, or made in consequence of anything said or done likely in the circumstances to render them unreliable;[3] but, subject to this important qualification, there is no such rule as that which has been suggested. The cases which lead to this conclusion are few, and there has been no full examination of the principles at stake by an English court. Yet these principles are of the highest significance. On the one hand, there is the general rule that all relevant evidence is admissible, and the fact that it was obtained illegally is immaterial so far as the case before the court is concerned; in particular, the method by which incriminating evidence was obtained may be thought not to justify the release of a guilty man, although it may warrant punitive or remedial proceedings against those responsible for the illegality. On the other hand, there is the argument that the slightest encouragement of illegal methods of obtaining evidence, and in particular, the barest toleration of improper police practice is a worse evil than the escape of an occasional criminal. To quote from an important judgment in a Scottish case:[4]

> The law must strive to reconcile two highly important interests which are liable to come into conflict—(a) the interest of the citizen to be protected from illegal or irregular invasions of his liberties by the authorities, and (b) the interest of the state to secure that evidence bearing upon the commission of a crime and necessary to enable justice to be done shall not be withheld from courts of law on any mere formal or technical ground. Neither of these objects can be insisted upon to the uttermost. The protection for the citizen is primarily protection for the innocent citizen against unwarranted, wrongful and perhaps high-handed interference, and the common sanction is an action for damages. The protection

1 See *R v Jacquith and Emode* [1989] Crim LR 508 where the Court of Appeal suggested reconsideration of such etiquette after a barrister had testified in a case in which he was acting.
2 Cowen and Carter *Essays on the Law of Evidence* essays 2 and 3; Gottlieb 'Confirmation by Subsequent Facts' (1956) 72 LQR 209; Glanville Williams 'Evidence Obtained by Illegal Means' [1955] Crim LR 339, and Heydon [1973] Crim LR 603 and 690.
3 Police and Criminal Evidence Act 1984, s 76.
4 Lord Cooper in *Lawrie v Muir* 1950 JC 19 at 26.

is not intended as a protection for the guilty citizen against the efforts of the public prosecutor to vindicate the law. On the other hand the interest of the state cannot be magnified to the point of causing all the safeguards for the protection of the citizen to vanish, and of offering a positive inducement to the authorities to proceed by irregular methods.

We shall see that the most recent Scots decisions have gone far towards providing for a compromise between the two conflicting interests by according a large measure of discretion to the trial judge. The conflicting interests have produced conflicting views in the United States. The impropriety of acquitting A, who is guilty, on account of the illegal conduct of B, was forcefully put by Cardozo J when he said:

A room is searched against the law, and the body of a murdered man is found. If the place of discovery may not be proved, the other circumstances may be insufficient to connect the defendant with the crime. The privacy of the home has been infringed, and the murderer goes free.[5]

The contrary view was forcefully put by Holmes J when he said:

We must consider the two objects of desire both of which we cannot have and make up our minds which to choose. It is desirable that crimes should be detected, and to that end too all available evidence should be used. It is desirable that the government should not itself foster and pay for other crimes, when they are the means by which the evidence is to be obtained. If it pays its officers for having got evidence by crime I do not see why it may not as well pay them for getting it in the same way, and I can attach no importance to protestations of disapproval if it knowingly accepts and pays and announces that in future it will pay for the fruits. We have to choose, and for my part I think it a less evil that some criminals should escape than that the government should play an ignoble part.[6]

The American authorities are mainly concerned with the provisions of the Constitution of the United States, and anything in the nature of a detailed discussion is beyond the scope of this book; but it is relevant to point out that the American courts have hitherto adhered fairly rigidly to the doctrine of the exclusion of the 'fruits of the poisoned tree', and, by way of contrast with the English courts, have stressed the disciplining of the police as the motivation of the exclusionary rule. To quote from the majority judgment in the leading case of *Mapp v Ohio*:[7] '... the purpose of the exclusionary rule is to deter—to compel respect for the constitutional guarantees [against illegal searches] in the only effective available way— by removing the incentive to disregard it.' The cost to the public due to acquittals caused by the exclusion of reliable real evidence is, however, a

5 *The People v Defoe* 242 NY 413 (1926).
6 *Olmstead v United States* 277 US 438 (1928).
7 367 US 656 (1961); the judgment was quoting from that in *Elkins v US* 364 US 206 (1960) at 217. The underlying psychology is highly questionable. The 'bent' police officer thinks that no point will be taken on his illegal methods of obtaining evidence or that, if it is, he will be able to lie himself out of trouble.

matter of some judicial concern in the United States, and has now led to a change of approach.[8]

The English cases that will now be briefly considered concern either the admissibility of facts discovered in consequence of inadmissible confessions, or else the admissibility of evidence procured in consequence of some unlawful act such as illegal search. The distinction is necessitated by the rule prohibiting the reception of involuntary confessions.

A. FACTS DISCOVERED IN CONSEQUENCE OF INADMISSIBLE CONFESSIONS

The English law on this topic now has been put upon a statutory basis by s 76 of the Police and Criminal Evidence Act 1984 which provides:

(4) The fact that a confession is wholly or partly excluded in pursuance of this section shall not affect the admissibility in evidence—
(a) of any facts discovered as a result of the confession; or
(b) where the confession is relevant as showing that the accused speaks, writes or expresses himself in a particular way, of so much of the confession as is necessary to show that he does so.

(5) Evidence that a fact to which this subsection applies was discovered as a result of a statement made by an accused person shall not be admissible unless evidence of how it was discovered is given by him or on his behalf.

(6) Subsection (5) above applies—
(a) to any fact discovered as a result of a confession which is wholly excluded in pursuance of this section; and
(b) to any fact discovered as a result of a confession which is partly so excluded, if the fact is discovered as a result of the excluded part of the confession.

These provisions are intended to clarify what had become a particularly unsatisfactory and unsettled area of the common law. Subsection (4) follows the recommendations of the 11th Report of the Criminal Law Revision Committee,[9] and is consistent with the reasoning of the Royal Commission on Criminal Procedure.[10] Subsection (5) however adopts the minority view of the Criminal Law Revision Committee.[11]

The effect of sub-s (4) is intended to preserve the position established in the old case of *R v Warickshall*[12] where a woman who was charged as an accessory after the fact to theft and as a receiver of stolen goods was improperly induced to make a confession in the course of which she said that the property in question was in her lodgings where it was in fact found. The court held that the exclusion of a confession 'forced from the

8 See *United States v Leon* 104 S Ct 3405 (1984) (no exclusion if constable acts in good faith upon basis of apparently valid warrant); *Segura v United States* 104 S Ct 3380 (1984) (no exclusion where link between illegality and discovery so attenuated as to dissipate any taint); *Immigration and Naturalisation Service v Lopez-Mendoza* 104 S Ct 3479 (1984) (no application to deportation proceedings). For an accessible, concise and recent statement of the position in the United States, see Stuntz 'The American Exclusionary Rule and Defendants' Changing Rights' [1989] Crim LR 117.
9 Cmnd 4991, para 68, draft Bill cl 2(5)(a) and (c).
10 Cmnd 8092, para 4.123f.
11 Para 69. The Royal Commission did not descend to this level of detail.
12 (1783) 1 Leach 263, re-affirmed in *R v Berriman* (1854) 6 Cox CC 388.

mind by the flattery of hope, or by the pressure of fear' was not based on any breach of public faith that might be involved in its reception, but was due to the fact that the confession comes in so questionable a shape, when it is to be considered as evidence of guilt, that no credit ought to be given to it. But:

> this principle respecting confessions has no application whatever as to the admission or rejection of facts, whether the knowledge of them be obtained in consequence of an extorted confession or whether it arises from any other source; for a fact, if it exist at all, must exist invariably in the same manner whether the confession from which it derives be in other respects true or false. Facts thus obtained, however must be fully and satisfactorily proved without calling in the aid of any part of the confession from which they may have been derived.[13]

It was immaterial that the 'fact' which was discovered was a document.[14] The Criminal Law Revision Committee also took the view that other forms of evidence derived indirectly from an inadmissible confession should be permitted. A confession may be of evidential value because it shows that its maker writes, speaks or expresses himself in a particular way and thus helps to identify him as the culprit. For example, in *R v Voisin*[15] the accused was convicted of the murder of a woman, part of whose body was found in a parcel in which there was also a piece of paper with the words 'blady belgiam'. The accused had been asked by a police officer if he had any objection to writing down the two words 'bloody Belgian' and had said 'Not at all' and had written down 'Bladie Belgiam'. The accused appealed unsuccessfully against his conviction on the ground, among others, that this writing ought to have been rejected as he had not been cautioned before being asked to write the words down. There was no question of an inadmissible confession, but it seemed to the Criminal Law Revision Committee that, if the words had been written in an inadmissible confession, it would be right that they should be admissible for the purpose of showing that the accused writes, speaks or expresses himself in a particular way; and sub-s (4) so enacts.

It can be argued that in exactly the same way it ought to be possible to rely upon an otherwise inadmissible confession to show that it was the accused who provided the information leading to the discovery of the relevant facts, or to show his knowledge of some independently verifiable circumstance.[16] The latter possibility seems to have aroused little, if any, judicial discussion, was specifically rejected by the Criminal Law Revision Committee, and is not provided for in the new Act. The former situation has aroused more concern. In some cases where the location of the facts found in consequence of the otherwise inadmissible confession was less

---

13 At 264.
14 *R v Leathem* (1861) 8 Cox CC 498. The extremely unsatisfactory case of *R v Barker* [1941] 2 KB 381, [1941] 3 All ER 33 which appeared to assimilate false accounts with a confession of false accounting, and which was overturned on its facts by Finance Act 1942, s 34 (see now Taxes Management Act 1970, s 105), appears to be inconsistent with s 76(4)(a) as a matter of law, and can be supported now only upon the basis of the judge's discretion, see Lord Diplock in *R v Sang* [1980] AC 402 at 435, [1979] 2 All ER 1222 at 1229.
15 [1918] 1 KB 531, [1918-19] All ER Rep 491.
16 See Andrews 'Involuntary Confessions and Illegally Obtained Evidence in Criminal Cases' [1963] Crim LR 15, 77.

indicative of the accused's guilt than in *Warickshall*, the court permitted the prosecution to testify that it was the accused whose statement revealed the location of the goods.[17] This practice was endorsed by a majority of the Criminal Law Revision Committee, and a provision included in its draft Bill.[18] No such provision has however been made in the Police and Criminal Evidence Act 1984, presumably upon the ground that to admit such evidence would tend to subvert the exclusion of the confession itself.[19]

B. THE ADMISSIBILITY OF EVIDENCE PROCURED IN CONSEQUENCE OF ILLEGAL SEARCHES AND OTHER UNLAWFUL ACTS[20]

The English authorities on the admissibility of evidence procured in consequence of an illegal search are uniformly in favour of its reception although there are not many of them. In *Jones v Owen*[1] a constable searched the appellant illegally and found a quantity of young salmon in his pocket. This evidence was held to be admissible on a charge of unlawful fishing, Mellor J expressing the view that:

> It would be a dangerous obstacle to the administration of justice if we were to hold, because evidence was obtained by illegal means, it could not be used against a party charged with an offence.

In *Elias v Pasmore*[2] Horridge J concluded that the interests of the state must excuse a seizure of documents which would otherwise be unlawful if it appears that such documents were evidence of a crime committed by anyone. The case was not directly concerned with the admissibility of illegally obtained evidence, but it is frequently cited in this context and was mentioned by Lord Goddard CJ when giving the advice of the Judicial Committee of the Privy Council in *Kuruma, Son of Kaniu v R*,[3] an appeal from Kenya whose law on this subject may be taken to have been the same as that of England. The accused had been convicted of being in unlawful possession of ammunition which had been discovered in conse-

---

17 *R v Grant* (1801) and *R v Hodge* (1794) cited in East 2 Pleas of the Crown 658. Practice was far from consistent, for different approaches see *R v Griffin* (1809) Russ & Ry 151; *R v Gould* (1840) 9 C & P 364; *R v Garbett* (1847) 2 Car & Kir 474 at 490; *R v Berriman* (1854) 6 Cox CC 388.

18 Para 69, cl 2(5)(b).

19 It seems clear that in Scotland, no part of an inadmissible confession can be received however much of it is confirmed (*Chalmers v HM Advocate* 1954 JC 66). In Canada the position has since 1982 been determined by the relevant provisions of the Canadian Charter of Rights and Freedoms, and especially by s 24(2) under which evidence obtained in breach of the provisions of the Charter which would be likely to bring the administration of justice into disrepute must be excluded. The Supreme Court of Canada has interpreted this provision in such a way as to permit the use of real evidence obtained despite breach, but not any part of the confession or conduct of the accused leading up to such obtention, *R v Black* (1989) 50 CCC (3d) 1. Subsequently discovered facts are admissible under the Indian Evidence Act 1872, s 27.

20 For a comparative survey of the position in the Commonwealth and in the United States, see Polyviou *Search and Seizure* (1982) ch 7.

1 (1870) 34 JP 759.

2 [1934] 2 KB 164. This case must be read with *Ghani v Jones* [1970] 1 QB 693, [1969] 3 All ER 1700.

3 [1955] AC 197, [1955] 1 All ER 236.

quence of a search of his person by a police officer below the rank of those who were permitted to make such searches. Although they referred the case to the Colonial Secretary on other grounds, the board were of opinion that the evidence had been rightly admitted. Their view was that, if evidence is relevant, it matters not how it was obtained. Their Lordships made it plain that they were not qualifying the law with regard to the admissibility of confessions in any way whatsoever.

The English authorities on the admissibility of evidence obtained by some unlawful act other than an illegal search are even scantier, but they generally bear out the view, so laconically expressed by Crompton J in *R v Leatham*,[4] when he said: 'It matters not how you get it if you steal it even, it would be admissible in evidence.' This dictum was cited in *Kuruma*'s case, and it will be recollected that *Calcraft v Guest*,[5] the leading authority on the admissibility of secondary evidence of privileged documents was decided on a similar principle. In *ITC Film Distributor v Video Exchange Ltd*[6] however where the material in question was found to have been obtained by means of a contempt of court it was held that it should not be admitted.[7]

A further much litigated area of possible illegality is that relating to the detection of alcohol in the body of someone suspected of committing a road traffic offence. Such detection will normally involve a breath, blood or urine test, and may thus necessitate an arrest in order to accomplish it. It now seems that even if the test is conducted only after, and in consequence of, an illegal arrest, the evidence is nevertheless admissible in subsequent proceedings for driving with excess alcohol in the body.[8] Similarly in *R v Apicella*,[9] where an intimate sample was taken from a suspect without his consent,[10] the court was clear that the sample, being relevant to help identify the suspect as the criminal, was technically admissible.

It may therefore be concluded that, under English law, illegally obtained evidence is admissible as a matter of law, provided that it involves neither a reference to an inadmissible confession of guilt, nor the commission of an act of contempt of court. There was however an accumulating body of authority suggesting that as a matter of discretion the trial judge could exclude evidence from a criminal trial if the strict rules of admissibility would operate unfairly against the accused, and illustrated by the example

4 (1861) 8 Cox CC 498 at 501. See the same judge in *Phelps v Prew* (1854) 3 E & B 430 at 441. See also *Stockfleth v De Tastet* (1814) 4 Camp 10. To the same effect is *Lord Ashburton v Pape* [1913] 2 Ch 469 at 473.
5 [1898] 1 QB 759, and see p 443 above.
6 [1982] Ch 431, [1982] 2 All ER 241.
7 It seems that the same will apply where although the document may have been obtained perfectly lawfully, for example on discovery, its use in different proceedings would amount to contempt, per Waller LJ in *Riddick v Thames Board Mills Ltd* [1977] QB 881 at 911, [1977] 3 All ER 677 at 702.
8 *Fox v Chief Constable of Gwent* [1986] AC 281, [1985] 3 All ER 392. This situation is to be distinguished from that where an offence of refusing a test is charged, since the conditions may there require that the arrest be lawful, *Morris v Beardmore* [1981] AC 446, [1980] 2 All ER 753.
9 (1985) 82 Cr App Rep 295.
10 Though this was not realised by the person taking the sample because the suspect was in custody and had been previously informed by a prison officer that he must submit.

of a document obtained by a trick.[11] The House of Lords subsequently
decided[12] in *R v Sang*[13] that any such discretion was much more
circumscribed than such dicta suggested, and applied only in respect of
evidence obtained from the accused[14] after the commission of an offence.
The reference to trickery was taken to refer to situations where the accused
was so induced to deliver up a document, or a piece of real evidence
contrary to the principle underlying the privilege against self-incrimination, and thought also to underlie the exclusion of involuntary confessions.[15]

This position has now been affected by the passage of s 78 of the Police
and Criminal Evidence Act 1984 which provides that:

> In any proceedings the court may refuse to allow evidence on which the
> prosecution proposes to rely to be given if it appears to the court that, having
> regard to all the circumstances, including the circumstances in which the
> evidence was obtained, the admission of the evidence would have such an
> adverse effect on the fairness of the proceedings that the court ought not to
> admit it.

This provision is cast in terms of such vagueness and generality as to
furnish little guidance to the court. It is clearly capable of generating a
more rigorous attitude to the exclusion of illegally obtained evidence[16]
than applied either before the decision in *Sang*, or as there enunciated. It
is also capable of letting in still more illegally obtained evidence. First
indications are that little has so far changed. In *Fox v Chief Constable of
Gwent*[17] the House of Lords regarded it as justifying the refusal of the
magistrates to exercise their discretion to exclude the evidence that the
police had acted 'in good faith, and that the specimen itself had been
obtained without inducement, threat . . ., trick or other impropriety'. The
discretion conferred by s 78 was however regarded as being properly
applicable in another breath test case, *Matto v Wolverhampton Crown Court*,[18]
where the police officers acted in knowing derogation of their powers in
requiring a specimen from a suspect on his own private land. *Matto* held[19]

11 Formulated in those terms by Lord Goddard CJ in *Kuruma, Son of Kaniu v R* [1955] AC
197 at 204, [1955] 1 All ER 236 at 239. Further dicta are to be found in *R v Payne*
[1963] 1 All ER 848, [1963] 1 WLR 637; *Callis v Gunn* [1964] 1 QB 495 at 501, [1963]
3 All ER 677 at 680; *King v R* [1969] 1 AC 304 at 319, [1968] 2 All ER 610 at 617;
and *Jeffery v Black* [1978] QB 490 at 498, [1978] 1 All ER 555 at 559.
12 Although technically obiter outside the area of entrapment it is clear that it will be
highly persuasive, see Lord Roskill in *Morris v Beardmore* [1981] AC 446 at 469, [1980]
2 All ER 753 at 767. Discretion to exclude evidence obtained by illegal means was
denied in *R v Adams* [1980] QB 575, [1980] 1 All ER 473, and *Cameron v Charles Simpson
Motors* [1980] CLY 2630, on the basis of *Sang*.
13 [1980] AC 402, [1979] 2 All ER 1222.
14 It is unclear how far it applies to evidence obtained from the accused's premises, see
p 187 above.
15 It is not clear how this doctrine could be reconciled with the decision in *R v Derrington*
(1826) 2 C & P 418, where a letter obtained from the prisoner by the turnkey under a
false promise that he would post it was admitted in evidence for the prosecution. Cf *R
v Pamenter* (1872) 12 Cox CC 177.
16 Though in some areas, as a result of statutory intervention, it may be difficult to prove
that illegality has taken place, see the bar on adducing evidence and conducting cross-
examination imposed by s 9 of the Interception of Communications Act 1985.
17 Above at 290, 395. S 78 had been enacted, but not brought into force, at the relevant
time.
18 [1987] RTR 337.
19 At 346.

that the new statutory discretion was certainly no less extensive than that which existed at common law. In at least one lower court case it also appears to have been decided that simple breach of the relevant provision of a Code of Practice in not informing a suspect of the grounds for his arrest or the purpose of searching him gave sufficient justification for exercising the discretion under s 78 to exclude the substances so found from evidence. It is uncertain whether this heralds a new approach. English courts could choose to model their practice upon that of another Commonwealth jurisdiction.

In Scotland the discretion is inclusionary. Illegally obtained evidence is excluded in the absence of an excuse for its reception.[20] There are even signs that the discretion may exist under Scots law in civil cases, while there has been no parallel development in English procedure. In the Scots divorce case of *Rattray v Rattray*,[1] it was held that a letter from the wife of the co-defendant must be received although it had been stolen from the post office by the husband who had suffered criminal punishment on account of his conduct. Lord Young dissented because he thought that the court was bound to take notice of the statute law enacting that the pursuer's conduct was a crime, and to reject as evidence anything obtained by a violation of the law. This case was followed in *Maccoll v Maccoll*,[2] but the judge said that, had he been a member of the court in *Rattray v Rattray* he would have dissented with Lord Young and on the same grounds.

In Canada, as noted above, the whole position is now governed by the Charter of Rights and Freedoms. This has adopted a position intermediate between the English[3] rule that evidence is in principle admissible however it has been obtained subject only to an exclusionary discretion, and the American rule that illegally obtained evidence must, in principle, be excluded. The Canadian compromise is to exclude evidence obtained in breach of the Charter, but only if its admission is likely to bring the administration of justice into disrepute. It is obvious that such a position requires detailed elaboration, and the Supreme Court of Canada has already been deluged with appeals to this end. The leading case at present is probably *R v Collins*,[4] and it seems broadly to regard the administration of justice as brought into disrepute more by evidence secured by conscripting the accused against himself[5] than by other forms of illegality. The test also recognises that the administration of justice may sometimes

---

20 *Lawrie v Muir* 1950 JC 19; *McGovern v H M Advocate* 1950 JC 33. In *H M Advocate v Turnbull* 1951 JC 96 the evidence was excluded by the judge. For a case in which the Scots courts would have been prepared to receive illegally obtained evidence because of the danger that the accused would destroy the evidence against him, see *Hay v H M Advocate* 1968 JC 40.

1 1897 25 R (Ct of Sess) 315.

2 1946 SLT 312.

3 It also represented the previous position in Canada, see *R v Wray* (1970) 11 DLR (3d) 673.

4 [1987] 1 SCR 265, where Lamer J set out the principles according to which s 24(2) of the Charter is to be construed. See also an influential article by Morisette 'The Exclusion of Evidence under the Canadian Charter of Rights and Freedoms: What to Do and What Not to Do' (1984) 29 McGill LJ 521; Paccioco *Charter Principles and Proof in Criminal Cases* (1987); though the pace of development is so swift that both of these sources are already somewhat dated.

5 A concept extended to include the illegal obtention of constituent parts of the human body, see *R v Therens* (1985) 18 DLR (4th) 655 (breath); *R v Dyment* (1988) 55 DLR (4th) 503 (blood).

also be brought into disrepute by the exclusion of reliable evidence, and that the good faith of the police,[6] or even the obnoxious reaction of the suspect,[7] may cure any technical illegality from this point of view.[8]

By contrast, in Australia, the position is determined by the common law and the following statement of Barwick CJ is applied:

> On the one hand there is the public need to bring to conviction those who commit criminal offences. On the other hand there is the public interest in the protection of the individual from unlawful and unfair treatment. Convictions obtained with the aid of unlawful and unfair acts may be obtained at too high a price. Hence the judicial discretion.[9]

The notions of public policy and fairness are combined in this statement. The former is predominant in the following remark made by Kingsmill Moore J in the Supreme Court of Eire: 'I am disposed to lay emphasis not so much on alleged unfairness to the accused as on the public interest that the law should be observed in the investigation of crime.'[10] Stress is also laid on this aspect of the matter in the most recent opinions in the High Court of Australia.[11]

C. EVIDENCE THAT IS NOT OBTAINED ILLEGALLY

The ratio decidendi of some of the cases is not that relevant evidence is admissible although it was obtained illegally, but that such evidence is admissible because it was not obtained illegally. In *R v Palfrey, R v Sadler*[12] it was held that a blood sample was admissible evidence against someone charged with driving while unfit through drink contrary to what is now s 4 of the Road Traffic Act 1988, in spite of the fact that it had been taken after the warning required by s 7(7) for the purpose of driving with excessive blood alcohol contrary to s 5. The warning states that failure to supply a sample may result in imprisonment, fine or disqualification from driving. The prosecution relied on what is now s 6(1) according to which a sample may be evidence for the prosecution on a charge under s 4 if taken with the accused's consent. There was no evidence of want of consent apart from the circumstances in which the sample was obtained. The Court of Appeal seems to have regarded these as irrelevant with the result that the sample was lawfully taken. In *Callis v Gunn*[13] it was held that, although no one can be obliged to allow his finger-prints to be taken in the absence of a court order, the police were not acting illegally in requesting a suspect to allow his prints to be taken, even though they did not administer any caution.

6 Or other infringer of Charter principles, see *R v Lerke* (1986) 25 DLR (4th) 103.
7 See *Tremblay v R* (1987) 45 DLR (4th) 445.
8 *Sieben v R* (1987) 38 DLR (4th) 427.
9 *R v Ireland* (1970) 126 CLR 321 at 335.
10 *People (A-G) v O'Brien* [1965] IR 142 at 160.
11 *Bunning v Cross* (1978) 141 CLR 54; *Cleland v R* (1983) 57 ALJR 15.
12 [1970] 2 All ER 12, [1970] 1 WLR 416 not followed in *Elliot v Burns* [1973] NI 81.
13 [1964] 1 QB 495, [1963] 3 All ER 677; *R v Beet* (1977) 66 Cr App Rep 188 (results of urine test admissible on drugs charge though taken without caution).

In *R v Maqsud Ali, R v Ashiq Hussain*,[14] Pakistanis suspected of murder went voluntarily with police officers to a room in the Bradford town hall in which, unknown to them, there was a microphone connected with a tape-recorder in another room. They were left alone in the room and proceeded to have a conversation in which incriminating remarks were made. The Court of Criminal Appeal held that the trial judge had rightly admitted the tape-recording of the incriminating conversation in evidence: 'The criminal does not act according to the Queensbury rules. The method of the informer and of the eavesdropper is commonly used in the detection of crime. The only difference here was that a mechanical device was the eavesdropper.'[15]

In *R v Murphy*,[16] the Courts-Martial Appeal Court held that the accused had been rightly convicted by a court martial of disclosing information useful to an enemy when the disclosure had been made to police officers posing as members of a subversive organisation. Lord MacDermott CJ said:

Detection by deception is a form of police procedure to be directed and used sparingly and with circumspection: but as a method it is as old as the constable in plain clothes and, regrettable though the fact may be, the day has not yet come when it would be safe to say that law and order could always be enforced and the public safety protected without occasional resort to it.[17]

D. CONCLUSION

In conclusion it is respectfully submitted that the remarks of Cardozo J and Holmes J which were cited at the outset of this discussion are both tendentious. So far as those of Cardozo J are concerned, if a room is searched and a dead body is found in it, it would certainly be a terrible thing if the guilty occupant were allowed to go free on a charge of murder because the search was technically illegal, but there must be some limit to this doctrine. What if admission were gained to the room in consequence of a violent assault, or what if the whereabouts of the corpse were ascertained by means of prolonged torture of the accused? On the other hand, in spite of the contrary opinion of Holmes J, the government does not foster and pay for other crimes whenever illegally obtained evidence is admitted. It is a mistake to suppose that the choice lies between admitting the evidence and leaving the aggrieved party to pursue such civil or criminal remedies against the wrongdoer as may be available, or rejecting the evidence as a warning to officialdom that convictions cannot be obtained by illegal action. Such an approach assumes that the conduct of the police is exclusively influenced by the number of convictions obtained.

14 [1966] 1 QB 688, [1965] 2 All ER 464. For evidence of tape-recording generally, see p 48 above. The jury were warned to be careful about the translation. For other cases in which eavesdropping was held not to render the evidence inadmissible, see *R v Stewart* [1970] 1 All ER 689n, [1970] 1 WLR 907 and *R v Keeton* (1970) 54 Cr App Rep 267.

15 At 469 per Marshall J.

16 [1965] NI 138.

17 At 147–8. For English cases on agents provocateurs see *R v Mullins* (1848) 3 Cox CC 526; *R v Bickley* (1909) 2 Cr App Rep 53; *Brannan v Peek* [1948] 1 KB 68, [1947] 2 All ER 572; *Sneddon v Stevenson* [1967] 2 All ER 1277, [1967] 1 WLR 1051; *R v Mealey, R v Sheridan* (1974) 60 Cr App Rep 59; *R v McEvilly* (1973) 60 Cr App Rep 150; *R v Sang* [1980] AC 402, [1979] 2 All ER 1222.

It leaves out of account the all-important sanctions provided by the opinion of those who pursue the same occupation as the person by whom the evidence was illegally obtained. Is it to be supposed that when the Lord Chief Justice said, 'The sooner the Bristol police study, learn and abide by the Judges' Rules, the better',[18] the conduct of the police of Bristol was unaffected because his Lordship admitted a confession obtained in consequence of a breach of those rules? What was deplorable was the total absence of criticism of the behaviour in cases such as *Jeffrey v Black*[19] where there was no element of emergency and the suspected offence was comparatively venial. Since the enactment of the Police and Criminal Evidence Act 1984 and the implementation of the Codes of Practice under s 66 a more healthily critical attitude has become apparent. In spite of the great weight of opinion to the contrary, too much importance may be attached to the rejection of illegally obtained evidence as an incentive to good behaviour on the part of the police. Bad behaviour, it is felt, is prompted by the hope that it will not be brought to the notice of the court,[20] not by the belief that evidence discovered in consequence of it will be received in any event.

18 *R v Mills and Lemon* [1947] KB 297 at 299, [1946] 2 All ER 776 at 777.
19 [1978] QB 490, [1978] 1 All ER 555.
20 By precipitating a plea of guilty it may often achieve its purpose behind the scenes.

CHAPTER XIII

Opinion[1]

The rule excluding evidence of opinion has come to be of far greater importance in the law of the United States than it is in that of this country. As long ago as 1898, Thayer said, 'the quantity of decisions on the subject is most unreasonably swollen'[2] and he was speaking of the position in America. In 1940, Wigmore felt able to assert that, so far as the United States was concerned, the rule 'had done more than any other rule of procedure to reduce our litigation towards a state of legalised gambling'.[3] In England, the reported decisions on the subject are comparatively few, and it is difficult to believe that the exclusionary rule gives rise to much trouble in practice. An explanation of this difference is offered in the following passage from an important book review:[4]

> At the outset of the nineteenth century, the English writers, with the English love of conciseness, had laid down the general proposition that 'a witness must state facts not opinions'. In this country, the bench and bar were not misled by this statement, Starkie, for instance, showed its limitations in practice (3rd edn, 1842, p 173): 'It has been said that a witness must not be examined in-chief as to his belief or persuasion, but only as to his knowledge of the fact . . . But, with respect to persuasion or belief as founded on facts within the actual knowledge of the witness, the position is not true.' In other words, we have never felt any hesitation, on this side of the Atlantic, in admitting statements by witnesses which are a compendious mode of summarising a sequence of inference, based upon perceived facts.

Although the bulk of transatlantic case law on the subject may be due to an over-rigid adherence to the proposition that witnesses must state facts, not opinions, the English practitioner's gain has, to some extent, been the English writer's loss, for the mass of material has obliged lawyers and judges in the United States to subject the rule to deeper scrutiny than it has received in this country, and much reliance is placed on their work in this chapter.

---

1 See generally Law Reform Commission of Australia Research Paper No 13 'Opinion Evidence'.
2 *Preliminary Treatise on Evidence at the Common Law* 525.
3 VII *Wigmore* p 27.
4 P A Landon reviewing King and Pillinger's *Opinion Evidence in Illinois* in 60 LQR 201.

SECTION 1. STATEMENT AND ILLUSTRATIONS OF THE EXCLUSIONARY RULE[5]

A. STATEMENT OF THE RULE

A witness may not give his opinion on matters which the court considers call for the special skill or knowledge of an expert unless he is an expert in such matters, and he may not give his opinion on other matters if the facts upon which it is based can be stated without reference to it in a manner equally conducive to the ascertainment of the truth.[6]

In the law of evidence 'opinion' means any inference from observed facts, and the law on the subject derives from the general rule that witnesses must speak only to that which was directly observed by them. The treatment of evidence of opinion by English law is based on the assumption that it is possible to draw a sharp distinction between inferences and the facts on which they are based.[7] The drawing of inferences is said to be the function of the judge or jury, while it is the business of a witness to state facts. But the law recognises that, so far as matters calling for special knowledge or skill are concerned, judges and jurors are not necessarily properly equipped to draw the right inferences from facts stated by witnesses. A witness is therefore allowed to state his opinion with regard to such matters provided he is expert in them.

Although the distinction between fact and inference is clear enough up to a point, there are borderline cases. The statement that a car was being driven on the left side of the road is plainly one of fact, while the assertion that a particular piece of driving was negligent is equally a matter of inference from observed facts. Statements concerning speed, temperature, or the identity of persons, things and handwriting are, however, indissolubly composed of fact and inference. The law makes allowances for these borderline cases by permitting witnesses to state their opinion with regard to matters not calling for special knowledge whenever it would be virtually impossible for them to separate their inferences from the facts on which those inferences are based.

There are thus two broad spheres of evidence of opinion. The first concerns matters calling for specialised skill or knowledge. In this sphere the only questions are whether the subject of inquiry does raise issues calling for expertise and whether the witness is a qualified expert. The rule of evidence is exclusionary only in the sense that the testimony of non-experts is excluded on matters calling for a specialist. In the other sphere of evidence of opinion, such evidence will be excluded if the subject is one with regard to which fact and inference can conveniently be kept separate.

In so far as is possible for them to do so, the courts set themselves against receiving evidence from any witness as to the very matter which the judge or jury has to decide. This is because litigants are entitled to have their disputes settled by a judge, with or without a jury, and not by the statement of witnesses. If witnesses are too readily allowed to give their opinion

---

5 In the following pages much use has been made of material in VII *Wigmore* ch 67; Maguire *Evidence, Common Sense and Common Law* 24–31, and Cowen and Carter *Essays on the Law of Evidence* essay 5.

6 See *Sherrard v Jacob* [1965] NI 151 at 157–8 per Lord MacDermott.

7 For an alternative view based upon the disputability of an assertion, see Cox J in *R v Perry (No 4)* (1982) 28 SASR 119 at 123.

concerning an ultimate issue, there is a serious danger that the jury will be unduly influenced:

> If a cardinal of the Roman Catholic church is testifying before a jury mainly composed of Catholics, and states that, in his opinion, the defendant was driving negligently, it can hardly be supposed that the verdict would be other than for the plaintiff.[8]

This is an extreme case, but the reception of evidence of opinion on this kind of question is always liable to prevent a jury from troubling to make up its own mind. Even when they are receiving expert evidence, it has generally been the practice of the judges to prevent a witness from stating his opinion on an ultimate issue, such as the reasonableness of a covenant in restraint of trade,[9] the validity of a patent, or the construction of a document: 'The admission of the opinion of eminent experts upon the issues leads to the balance of opinions and tends to shift responsibility from the bench or the jury to the witness box.'[10] The exclusion of opinion evidence on the ultimate issue can easily become something of a fetish, and we shall see that the law has been explicitly relaxed for civil proceedings by s 3 of the Civil Evidence Act 1972.[11]

B. ILLUSTRATION OF THE EXCLUSIONARY EFFECT OF THE RULE

1. NON-EXPERT OPINION ON MATTERS CALLING FOR EXPERTISE

In so far as it is exclusionary, two classes of case are contemplated in the formulation of the rule at the beginning of this section, and it is hardly surprising that there should be but few reported decisions falling within the first class. A litigant would normally have to be in desperate straits before he thought of calling a witness who was not an expert on the matter in question to give his opinions on a subject involving special skill or knowledge.[12] This may have been the position of counsel for the defence in *R v Loake*[13] when he applied to the Court of Criminal Appeal for leave to call fresh evidence in support of the accused's plea of insanity. Among the witnesses he wished to call were a friend of the accused who saw him three days before the crime was committed and formed the opinion that he was insane, together with a magistrate who had come to a similar conclusion after visiting the prisoner in his cell. The court disposed of the application so far as these witnesses were

---

8 60 LQR 202.

9 *Haynes v Doman* [1899] 2 Ch 13.

10 *Joseph Crosfield & Sons Ltd v Technichemical Laboratories Ltd* (1913) 29 TLR 378 at 379.

11 But no similar statutory relaxation has been made for criminal proceedings, contrary to the recommendation of the Criminal Law Revision Committee, see Cmnd 4991 para 270, and draft Bill cl 43.

12 Though it may be hard to separate such cases from those where a witness tendered as an expert is held to have inappropriate or insufficient expertise, see *Seyfert v Burnaby Hospital Society* (1986) 27 DLR (4th) 96 (emergency physician inappropriate to testify to qualities required of emergency physician); *Gaudiuso v Walker* (1989) 56 DLR (4th) 355 (doctor competent to testify to medical examination but not to theory of scientific tests used).

13 (1911) 7 Cr App Rep 71.

concerned by saying that the friend's evidence was clearly inadmissible, and the magistrate was not an expert. Non-experts may be asked to state whether they consider a person with whom they are well acquainted to be sane, but this has been said to be no more than a 'compendious mode of ascertaining the result of the actual observation of the witness, from acts done, as to the habits and demeanour' of such person.[14] There was no suggestion that either of the proposed witnesses in *Loake*'s case were at all intimately acquainted with the accused.

2. CASES NOT CALLING FOR EXPERTISE

An expert's opinion is admissible to furnish the court with scientific information which is likely to be outside the experience and knowledge of a judge or jury. If on the proven facts a judge or jury can form their own conclusions without help, then the opinion of an expert is unnecessary. In such a case if it is given dressed up in scientific jargon it may make judgment more difficult. The fact that an expert witness has impressive scientific qualifications does not by that fact alone make his opinion on matters of human nature and behaviour within the limits of normality any more helpful than that of the jurors themselves; but there is a danger that they may think it does.[15]

These words provide us with as clear an explanation as can be asked for of the basis of the second limb of the exclusionary rule. Evidence of opinion on matters not calling for expertise is generally excluded because, like the evidence of non-experts on matters calling for expertise, it does not help the court. At best it is superfluous, and it could be a cause of confusion.

In *R v Chard*[16] the Court of Appeal held that the judge had rightly excluded medical evidence concerning the intention at the material time of someone charged with murder where there was no question of his being insane or suffering from diminished responsibility. A judge and jury are as competent as a psychiatrist to form an opinion about the past intention of a normal man. On similar grounds it has been held that expert evidence is inadmissible to explain the ordinary meaning of words such as 'obscene or indecent'[17] or 'calculated to deprave or corrupt',[18] or perhaps on 'severe impairment',[19] when used in a modern general Act of Parliament. Expert opinion may never be received on a question of domestic law.[20]

R v Turner, the case from which the passage quoted above is taken, is more controversial on account of the problem of reconciling it with the decision

---

14 Per Parke B in *Wright v Doe d Tatham* (1838) 4 Bing NC 489 at 543–4. Cf *R v Davies* [1962] 3 All ER 97, [1962] 1 WLR 1111.
15 Per Lawton LJ in *R v Turner* [1975] QB 834 at 841, cited with approval by Lord Wilberforce in *Director of Public Prosecutions v Jordan* [1977] AC 699 at 718. For a Canadian case involving the same principle see *R v Cusmack* (1955) 20 CR 365. For a nineteenth-century English case see *Ramadge v Ryan* (1832) 9 Bing 333; cf *Greville v Chapman* (1844) 5 QB 731.
16 (1971) 56 Cr App Rep 268.
17 *R v Stamford* [1972] 2 QB 391, [1972] 2 All ER 427.
18 *R v Anderson* [1972] 1 QB 304, [1971] 3 All ER 1152. For possible exception see *Director of Public Prosecutions v A B and C Chewing Gum Ltd* [1968] 1 QB 159, [1967] 2 All ER 504 pp 501, 502.
19 *R v Hall* (1987) 86 Cr App Rep 159.
20 See *R v Century 21 Ramos Realty Inc* (1987) 37 DLR (4th) 649.

of the Privy Council in *Lowery v R*.[1] The accused unsuccessfully pleaded
provocation in answer to a charge of murder of his girlfriend whom he
alleged that he had killed in a fit of rage caused by her sudden confession of
infidelity. He appealed on the ground that the judge had wrongly refused to
allow him to call a psychiatrist. This witness would have sworn that the
accused was not mentally ill; that he had a deep relationship with the girl
which was likely to cause an explosive outburst of rage at her confession;
and that his subsequent behaviour showed profound regret at what he had
done. The Court of Appeal held that no evidence was called for with regard
to the first of these matters which was undisputed, and that jurors do not
need a psychiatrist to tell them how ordinary folk who are not suffering from
mental illness are likely to react to the stresses and strains of life. This would
appear to provide a basis for reconciling their decisions with *Lowery v R* in
which case, it will be recollected, Lowery and King were charged with
murder which must have been committed by either or both of them and the
Privy Council held that the judge has acted properly in allowing King to
call a psychiatrist to swear that he was less likely to have committed the
crime than Lowery. Juries do not need to be told that normal men are liable
to lose control of themselves when their women admit to infidelity, but they
require all the expert assistance they can get to help them determine which
of two accused has the more aggressive personality. Another way of
reconciling the cases would be to treat the fact that Lowery had put his
character in issue as crucial to the decision of the Privy Council, the
psychiatric evidence then being admissible to impugn the credibility of his
testimony. Unfortunately we are left without any guidance on the subject
from the Court of Appeal who contented themselves with saying that *Lowery*'s
case was decided on its special facts.[2]

In England there is little inclination to extend the category of those in
respect of whom expert psychiatric testimony may be received. Thus in *R v
Masih*[3] such evidence was held inadmissible[4] in relation to a borderline
mental defective.[5] Some slight flexibility in this formulation has however
been exploited to admit such evidence outside these strict limits in the case
of the young.[6]

In some Australian cases stress has been placed upon the difference
between expert psychiatric evidence in relation to testimony for the purpose
of testing its credibility, and in relation to out of court statements for the

---

1 [1974] AC 85, [1973] 3 All ER 662 (p 334 above). See Pattenden 'Conflicting Approaches
   to Psychiatric Evidence in Criminal Trials: England, Canada and Australia' [1986] Crim
   LR 92.
2 It would probably be a mistake to regard *R v Turner* as closing the door to the admissibility
   of psychiatric evidence on behalf of the accused in all cases of provocation, especially
   having regard to changes in the substantive law on the subject effected by *D P P v Camplin*
   [1978] AC 705, [1978] 2 All ER 168.
3 [1986] Crim LR 395. See also in Canada *Roy v R* (1988) 62 CR 3d 127, and in New
   Zealand *R v B* [1987] 1 NZLR 362.
4 Explicitly rejecting the more liberal Australian view taken in *Schultz v R* [1982] WAR 171,
   subsequently affirmed by the majority of the High Court of Australia in *Murphy v R* (1989)
   86 ALR 35.
5 The general rule was stated to be that an intelligence quotient of less than 70 was required
   to justify the admissibility of expert psychiatric evidence of credibility.
6 See Beaumont 'Psychiatric Evidence: Over-Rationalising the Abnormal' [1988] Crim LR
   290, though in Australia no comparable exception has been made for alcoholics, *R v Haidley
   and Alford* [1984] VR 229.

same purpose, or as going to an issue in the case.[7] In a somewhat similar fashion a distinction has also been made between the rejection of expert evidence as to the sincerity of views expressed by individual members of the public in response to a survey, and its acceptance as the expert's opinion of the public's view, even though derived from perusal of the results of the survey.[8]

SECTION 2. EXPERT OPINION[9]

The courts have been accustomed to act on the opinion of experts from early times. As long ago as 1553 Saunders J said:

> If matters arise in our law which concern other sciences or faculties we commonly apply for the aid of that science or faculty which it concerns. This is a commendable thing in our law. For thereby it appears that we do not dismiss all other sciences but our own, but we approve of them and encourage them as things worthy of commendation.[10]

The learned judge's assertion was amply borne out by copious citations, but the early expert was often a member of the jury, and there was no question of his opinion being disregarded by that body. Expert witnesses began to play their modern role in the eighteenth century. In *Folkes v Chadd*[11] Mr Smeaton, the famous engineer, was allowed to testify concerning his opinion whether an embankment had caused the silting of a harbour.

> Mr Smeaton understands the construction of harbours, the causes of their destruction, and how remedied. In matters of science no other witnesses can be called . . . Handwriting is proved every day by opinion; and for false evidence on such questions a man may be indicted for perjury.[12]

In *Beckwith v Sydebotham*,[13] Lord Ellenborough allowed shipwrights to testify concerning the seaworthiness of a ship. He said that, where there was a matter of skill or science to be decided, the jury might be assisted by the opinion of those peculiarly acquainted with it in their professions or pursuits. As the truth of the facts stated in them was not certainly known, their opinion might not go for much, but still it was admissible evidence. In cross-examination, they might be asked what they would think of the state of facts contended for by the other side. His Lordship was referring to a difficulty that is encountered in the reception of all kinds of expert evidence. In the vast majority of cases, the witnesses will not have perceived the occurrences with which the case is concerned. In *Beckwith v Sydebotham* for instance, the shipwrights had not examined the ship whose seaworthiness was in issue, therefore their opinion had to be based on assumed facts. It is for the court to

7 *R v Barry* [1984] 1 Qd R 74.
8 *Ritz Hotel Ltd v Charles of the Ritz Ltd* (1988) 15 NSWLR 158 at 175. In England such evidence has been held not to be expert, nor even opinion, *Reckitt & Colman Products Ltd v Borden Inc (No 2)* [1987] FSR 407.
9 See Hammelmann 'Expert Evidence' (1974) 10 MLR 32, and Learned Hand 'Historical and Practical Considerations Regarding Expert Testimony' (1901) 15 Harv LR 40.
10 *Buckley v Rice-Thomas* (1554) 1 Plowd 118 at 124.
11 (1782) 3 Doug KB 157.
12 Per Lord Mansfield.
13 (1807) 1 Camp 116.

determine which party's version of the occurrences in issue is to be accepted. Accordingly, every effort must be made not to call upon the expert to give an opinion on the veracity of the ordinary witness in the case, or the validity of any inference concerning the existence of a disputed fact. This can only be done by framing a series of hypothetical questions[14]—a procedure which, however necessary it may be, certainly complicates the issues in a particular case.

The facts upon which an expert's opinion is based must be proved by admissible evidence, and he should be asked in-chief what those facts are.[15] If he observed them, he may testify to their existence, but, when the facts in question are dependent on ordinary human powers of perception, the expert may be contradicted by a lay witness, as when a police officer and a doctor give different accounts of the behaviour of someone accused of drunken driving when he was being questioned at a police station.[16] A doctor may not state what a patient told him about past symptoms as evidence of the existence of those symptoms because that would infringe the rule against hearsay, but he may give evidence of what the patient told him in order to explain the grounds on which he came to a conclusion with regard to the patient's condition.[17] In these cases an opinion based solely upon uncorroborated statements by the patient is not automatically admissible, but is likely to be of very little weight, and the jury should be instructed appropriately.[18] A valuer may express his opinion concerning the appropriate rent for particular premises even though he has not got first hand knowledge of comparable rents, but he may not give evidence about comparable rents of which he has not got personal knowledge.[19]

The functions of expert witnesses were succinctly stated by Lord President Cooper in *Davie v Edinburgh Magistrates*[20] when he said:

> Their duty is to furnish the judge with the necessary scientific criteria for testing the accuracy of their conclusions, so as to enable the judge or jury to form their own independent judgment by the application of these criteria to the facts proved in evidence.

The Court of Session repudiated the suggestion that the judge or jury is bound to adopt the views of an expert, even if they should be uncontradicted, because: 'The parties have invoked the decision of a judicial tribunal and

---

14 Although in Canada it has been denied, it is submitted wrongly, that any matter which it is not proposed to adduce in evidence can be used as the basis for such an hypothetical question, *R v Howard* (1989) 69 CR (3d) 193 at 201.
15 *R v Turner* [1975] QB 834 at 840. See also *R v Abbey* (1982) 138 DLR (3d) 202.
16 *Sutton v Prenter* [1963] Qd R 401. On the dual role of an expert witness see per Cooke J in *Seyfang v G D Searle* [1973] QB 148 at 151. If an expert offers an opinion as a layman, and not as an expert, this must be brought to the attention of the jury, *R v Cook* [1982] Crim LR 670.
17 A statement explicitly approved in *R v Bradshaw* (1985) 82 Cr App Rep 79 at 83. *Ramsay v Watson* (1961) 108 CLR 642; *Leis v Gardner* [1965] Qd R 181; *Leonard v British Colombia Hydro and Power Authority* (1965) 49 DLR (2d) 422.
18 *R v Bradshaw* above, ibid. See also *Lortie v R* (1986) 54 CR (3d) 228.
19 *English Exporters (London) Ltd v Eldonwall Ltd* [1973] Ch 415, [1973] 1 All ER 726. See also *City of St John v Irving Oil Co Ltd* [1966] SCR 581.
20 [1953] SC 34 at 40.

not an oracular pronouncement by an expert'.[1] This case reaffirmed the view that an expert might adopt statements made in scientific works as part of his testimony, and portions of such works might be put to him in cross-examination. To this extent they may be used as evidence in the case, but the judge is entitled to form an opinion on the basis of other parts of the book.[2]

The testimony of an expert is likely to carry more weight, and more readily relate to an ultimate issue than that of an ordinary witness. It is thus understandable that higher standards of accuracy and objectivity should be required, especially when the expert is testifying for the prosecution in a serious criminal case.[3] For similar reasons it has been provided[4] that advance notice must be given of the intention to adduce expert evidence in criminal proceedings, and an opportunity provided to examine the factual basis for any such evidence of opinion.[5] Such evidence of opinion may however be given in the form of a written report in derogation of the hearsay rule, whether or not[6] its maker attends to give oral evidence.[7]

No useful purpose would be served by an endeavour to enumerate the matters which have been treated by the courts as requiring a sufficient degree of specialised knowledge to render expert evidence admissible.[8] They include medical and scientific questions, the meaning of technical terms, questions of commercial practice or market value, the provisions of a foreign system of law and the identity of a person's handwriting—a subject which is discussed in ch XIX. Sometimes a field may not have developed sufficiently for the court to recognise it as one of appropriate expertise, as stated in a leading American case:[9]

> Just when a scientific principle or discovery crosses the line between the experimental and the demonstrable stages is difficult to define . . . while the courts will go a long way in admitting expert testimony deduced from a well-recognised scientific principle or discovery, the thing from which the deduction is made must be sufficiently established to have gained general acceptance in the particular field in which it belongs.

On this basis expert evidence has been rejected in Australia on some aspects of the behaviour of bush fires,[10] identification by reference to bite marks,[11]

1 [1953] SC 34 at 40. Though if there is nothing in the case to contradict unanimous expert evidence in favour of the accused the trier of fact is not entitled to reject it, *R v Bailey* (1977) 66 Cr App Rep 31. See also *R v Hall* (1988) 36 ACR 362; *Towne Cinema Theatres Ltd v R* (1985) 18 DLR (4th) 1 (community standard of obscenity).
2 *Collier v Simpson* (1831) 5 C & P 73.
3 See *Preece v H M Advocate* [1981] Crim LR 783.
4 Police and Criminal Evidence Act 1984, s 81; Crown Court (Advance Notice of Expert Evidence) Rules 1987 (SI 1987 No 70 (L.2)). No comparable provisions apply in the magistrates' courts.
5 If no such notice or opportunity is given or afforded the evidence can be adduced only by leave of the court.
6 Then only by leave of the court.
7 Criminal Justice Act 1988, s 30.
8 See *Re Pinion, Westminster Bank Ltd v Pinion* [1965] Ch 85 at 98, [1964] 1 All ER 890 at 891. See also *Scottish Shire Line Ltd v London and Provincial Marine and General Insurance Co Ltd* [1912] 3 KB 51 at 70 and *Carter v Boehm* (1766) 3 Burr 1905.
9 *Frye v United States* 293 F 1013 (1923) at 1014, a decision which has spawned considerable discussion in many overseas jurisdictions.
10 *Casley-Smith v F S Evans & Sons Pty Ltd* (1988) 49 SASR 314.
11 *Lewis v R* (1987) 88 FLR 104; *R v Carroll* (1985) 19 ACR 410.

and doubted in the case of reconstruction of a road accident.[12] Even if the field of expertise is sufficiently well-established, the guidance it provides must also be sufficiently relevant to a matter in issue.[13] If the court comes to the conclusion that the subject of investigation does not require a sufficient degree of specialised knowledge to call for the testimony of an expert, evidence of opinion will be excluded, unless the case is one in which non-expert opinion is admissible.[14] Thus in *R v Mackenney*[15] a psychologist was not permitted to give evidence of his opinion of the likelihood of a witness telling lies. He was not medically qualified, and even if he had been, the only evidence he could have given related not to the incapacity of the witness to tell the truth,[16] but to his disinclination to do so, which the jury was able, and indeed bound, to decide for itself.

It is for the judge to determine[17] whether the witness had undergone such a course of special study or experience as will render him expert in a particular subject, and it is not necessary for the expertise to have been acquired professionally. In *R v Silverlock*,[18] for example, the Court for Crown Cases Reserved considered that a solicitor might be treated as an expert in handwriting even if he had acquired his knowledge as an amateur. Most of the reported cases on the subject of a witness's skill are concerned with evidence of foreign law discussed in ch XX. Specialisation is a matter of degree. It is not necessary for a doctor to have specialised in studies concerned with the rate at which the blood destroys alcohol before he can give evidence on such a subject based on analysts' tables,[19] a stenographer who has familiarised herself with the contents of a tape recording may be treated as a temporary expert,[20] and a police officer's experience in investigating traffic accidents may make him an expert for the purpose of reconstructing a particular motor accident[1] or for testifying to the normal dosage of a drug addict.[2] But experience in driving does not make a bombardier an expert on the subject of the capabilities of someone charged with dangerous driving.[3] Addiction to a drug may give sufficient experience to permit credence to be given to the addict's identification of a substance as that drug.[4]

12 *R v Faulkner* [1987] 2 Qd R 263.
13 *R v Tilley* [1985] VR 505 accepted stylistic analysis as a sufficiently well-developed field but denied that it was appropriate to apply it to the material available. See also *R v Watson* [1987] 1 Qd R 440 at 465.
14 *United States Shipping Board v The St Albans* [1931] AC 632; *Clarke v Ryan* (1960) 103 CLR 486. See also *Transport Publishing Co Pty Ltd v Literature Board of Review* (1957) 99 CLR 111; *Weal v Bottom* (1966) 40 ALJR 436.
15 (1981) 76 Cr App Rep 271. See also *R v Smith* [1987] VR 907 (where evidence of a psychologist was rejected on the question of the reliability of eye-witness identification).
16 Which is permissible, *Toohey v Metropolitan Police Comr* [1965] AC 595, [1965] 1 All ER 506; see also *Re J (a minor)* (1984) Times, 23 January.
17 See *R v Bonython* (1984) 38 SASR 45 for a particularly clear exposition of the issues to be considered by the judge in determining the admissibility of expert opinion.
18 [1894] 2 QB 766; *R v Bunnis* (1964) 50 WWR 422. Cf *Clark v Ryan* (above).
19 *R v Somers* [1963] 3 All ER 808, [1963] 1 WLR 1306; *R v Richards* [1974] 3 All ER 696, [1975] 1 WLR 131.
20 *Hopes and Lavery v H M Advocate* 1960 JC 104.
 1 *R v Oakley* [1979] RTR 417; *R v Murphy* [1980] QB 434, [1980] 2 All ER 325.
 2 *White v H M Advocate* 1986 SCCR 224. In Australia police evidence as to the sort of pipes used by drug addicts has been regarded as evidence of fact and not opinion at all, *R v Barker* (1988) 34 ACR 141.
 3 *R v Davies* [1962] 3 All ER 97, [1962] 1 WLR 1111. See also *Seyfert v Barnaby Hospital Society* (1986) 27 DLR (4th) 96; *Gaudiuso v Walker* (1989) 56 DLR (4th) 355, above p 490.
 4 *R v Chatwood* [1980] 1 All ER 467, [1980] 1 WLR 874.

Although the expert witness has not escaped criticism,[5] he is probably the best means, compatible with the adversary system, of furnishing the judge and jury with information on matters calling for expertise. In their 17th Report the Law Reform Committee considered, but did not recommend, an extension to civil proceedings generally of the Admiralty practice under which the judge sits with assessors, or the adoption of a regular practice of appointing experts by the court,[6] but the report contains a number of recommendations designed to reduce controversy on matters of expertise and increase the usefulness of expert testimony. These recommendations are embodied in RSC Ord 38, rr 35–44 made in accordance with the provisions of s 2 of the Civil Evidence Act 1972. The broad effect of these rules is that parties to civil litigation will be prevented from calling experts unless they have applied to the court for leave to do so, and the court may order disclosure of the experts' reports to the opposite party.[7] The range of controversy will thus be defined and, as s 1 of the Act of 1972 enables hearsay evidence of opinion to be given, it is possible to dispense with the actual calling of the expert in uncontroversial cases.[8] It is possible also to restrict the number of expert witnesses,[9] though it is not possible to eliminate them completely, nor even, in advance of trial, to rule on the admissibility of any particular branch of expertise.[10] It may sometimes be advantageous for, and there is nothing to prevent,[11] a party calling his opponent's expert.

SECTION 3. NON-EXPERT OPINION

When, in the words of an American judge,[12] 'the facts from which a witness received an impression were too evanescent in their nature to be recollected, or too complicated to be separately and distinctly narrated', a witness may state his opinion or impression. He is better equipped than the jury to form it, and it is impossible for him to convey an adequate idea of the premises on which he acted to the jury:

5 See the observations of Lord Campbell at the hearing of the *Tracy Peerage Claim* (1843) 10 Cl & Fin 154 at 177, of Jessel MR in *Plimpton v Spiller* (1877) 6 Ch D 412, and of Lord Tomlin in *British Celanese Ltd v Courtaulds Ltd* (1935) 152 LT 537 at 543.
6 See John Basten 'The Court Expert in Civil Trials' (1977) 40 MLR 184.
7 Such disclosure should encompass the substance of the relevant opinion, note *Ollett v Bristol Aerojet Ltd* [1979] 3 All ER 544, [1979] 1 WLR 1197; it applies to expert medical opinion in all categories of case, see RSC (Amendment) 1987 (SI 1987 No 1423) so extending the ambit of the provision; and it applies as much to expert party witnesses as to any others, *Shell Pensions Trust Ltd v Pell Frishmann and Partners* [1986] 2 All ER 911.
8 Although the decision turned on the Foreign Tribunals Evidence Act 1856, *Seyfang v G D Searle & Co* [1973] QB 148, [1973] 1 All ER 290 emphasises the differences between an expert witness who has no particular connection with the facts in issue and an ordinary witness. The courts are loth to compel him to testify or to break confidences. But see *Harmony Shipping Co S A v Saudi Europe Line Ltd* [1979] 3 All ER 177, [1979] 1 WLR 1380 (handwriting expert originally instructed by plaintiff compellable for defendant), and *R v King* [1983] 1 All ER 929, 77 Cr App Rep 1 (enabling the prosecution to call in a criminal case an expert first consulted by the defence, and requiring him to produce samples of handwriting submitted to him).
9 Order 38, r 4. For discussion of a similar rule in South Australia see, *McCutcheon v Grimmond* (1986) 40 SASR 404.
10 *Sullivan v West Yorkshire Passenger Transport Executive* [1985] 2 All ER 134.
11 *Burton v Chemical Vessel Services Ltd* [1984] CLY 1525.
12 Gibson J cited in VII *Wigmore* p 12.

Unless opinions, estimates and inferences which men in their daily lives reach without conscious ratiocination as a result of what they perceived with their physical senses were treated in the law of evidence as if they were mere statements of fact, witnesses would find themselves unable to communicate to the judge an accurate impression of the events they were seeking to describe.[13]

There is nothing in the nature of a closed list of cases in which non-expert opinion evidence is admissible. Typical instances are provided by questions concerning age,[14] speed,[15] weather, handwriting and identity in general. Proof of handwriting is discussed in ch XIX, but a word may be said here about the question of identification.

When a witness says, 'that is the man I saw the other day', pointing to someone in court, or 'that is the man whose wedding I attended', pointing to a figure in a photograph,[16] or, 'that is a copy of a picture of which I have seen the original',[17] there is clearly a sense in which it is true to say that he is expressing an opinion. He is not simply narrating what he has perceived in the past; but the perception on which his statements are founded cannot be conveyed to the jury in the same way that the premises for or against an inference of negligence can be narrated. In *Fryer v Gathercole*[18] in order to prove the publication of a libellous pamphlet to friends of a female witness she was allowed to swear that she received a pamphlet from the defendant, lent it to friends in succession and put her name on it when it was ultimately returned to her. She said that she believed the pamphlet returned by the last borrower to be identical with that received from the defendant, but she could not swear to this fact because it was possible that another pamphlet had been substituted for the original. Pollock CB disposed of an objection to the effect that her evidence was mere opinion by saying: 'There are many cases of identification where the law would be rendered ridiculous if positive certainty were required from witnesses', and Parke B said in the course of the argument; 'In the identification of person you compare in your mind the man you have seen with the man you see at the trial. The same rule belongs to every species of identification.' Every fact on which the identification is based cannot be satisfactorily given in evidence.

In some cases a non-expert witness has been allowed to give evidence of opinion on a subject on which expert testimony would have been admissible. Acquaintances of a person whose sanity is in issue may be asked whether they consider him sane, but this is not so much a demand for an opinion as a 'compendious mode of ascertaining the result of the actual observations of the witness'. Did the witness observe any action by the accused characteristically associated with persons of dubious sanity? Similarly, in *R v Davies*,[19] the Courts Martial Appeal Court held that on a charge of drunken driving, a non-medical witness might state that he formed the impression that the

---

13 17th Report of the Law Reform Committee, para 3.
14 *R v Cox* [1898] 1 QB 179.
15 Road Traffic Regulation Act 1984, s 89.
16 *R v Tolson* (1864) 4 F & F 103.
17 *Lucas v Williams & Sons* [1892] 2 QB 113.
18 (1849) 13 Jur 542.
19 [1962] 3 All ER 97, [1962] 1 WLR 1111. See also *Sherrard v Jacob* [1965] NI 151; *R v German* [1947] 4 DLR 68; *Burrows v Hanlin* [1930] SASR 54; *R v McKimmie* [1957] VLR 93; *R v Spooner* [1957] VLR 540; *R v Kelly* [1958] VLR 412; *A-G (Rudley) v James Kenny* (1960) 94 ILTR 185 (77 LQR 166); *Blackie v Police* [1966] NZLR 910; *Graat v R* (1982) 144 DLR (3d) 267.

accused had been drinking but it was said that he must state the facts on which that impression was based, and it was also held that the witness ought not to have been allowed to add that he believed the accused to be unfit to drive, although an expert could have testified to this effect. In an interesting decision in South Africa[20] it has been held that lay eyewitness evidence of a collision between motor vehicles was to be preferred to expert evidence reconstructing the collision from physical traces alone,[1] unless it were completely incredible.

In *R v Beckett*,[2] the accused was charged with maliciously damaging a plate glass window worth more than five pounds. The fact that the window was worth more than five pounds was an essential ingredient of the offence, and it was held to have been proved by the statement of an assistant superintendent of the post office who swore that the window was worth more than five pounds. In cross-examination it became clear that his evidence was largely based on hearsay, but the Court of Criminal Appeal upheld the conviction on the footing that the case was proved by the witness's statement of his personal opinion as to the value of the window. The basis of the admissibility of this evidence was not considered by the court, and the decision is perhaps open to question on the ground that it raises insoluble problems of degree. Is it confined to non-expert opinion concerning the value of commonplace objects? If so, what are commonplace objects? Does it apply where the witness opines that the value of an article exceeds a specified sum by a considerable amount? If so, what is a considerable amount? But *R v Beckett* was cited in a South Australian case in which it was said that the court may always act on non-expert opinion as to value when no specialised knowledge is required.[3]

SECTION 4. ULTIMATE ISSUES

A considerable body of authority has asserted that evidence of opinion may not be proffered on an ultimate issue. This rule was supposed to apply both to expert[4] and to lay[5] opinion. In the early case of *R v Wright* some of the judges were said to doubt:

> whether the witness could be asked his opinion on the very point which the jury were to decide, viz. Whether, from the other testimony given in the case, the act as to which the prisoner was charged was, in his opinion, an act of insanity.[6]

A more recent, and more stringent, formulation was made by Neville J in *Joseph Crosfield & Sons (Ltd) v Techno-Chemical Laboratories (Ltd)*: 'It is not competent in any action for witnesses to express their opinions upon any of the issues, whether of law or fact, which the court or a jury has to determine.'[7]

20 *Motor Vehicle Assurance Fund v Kenny* 1984 (4) SA 432.
1 As noted above p 495 this is a subject sometimes thought only marginally of a sufficient status to be appropriate for the admission of expert testimony.
2 (1913) 8 Cr App Rep 204.
3 *Wise v Musolino* [1936] SASR 447. In some cases judicial notice may be taken that the value of an object exceeds the specified sum or evidence of its purchase price might suffice.
4 See, for example, *North Cheshire and Manchester Brewery Co v Manchester Brewery Co* [1899] AC 83 at 85.
5 See, for example, *R v Davies* [1962] 3 All ER 97, [1962] 1 WLR 1111.
6 (1821) Russ & Ry 456 at 458.
7 (1913) 29 TLR 378 at 379.

So far as the rule is justified upon the basis that it prevents usurpation of the function of the trier of fact, it was condemned by Wigmore as 'a mere bit of empty rhetoric',[8] the point being that the trier of fact is always free to reject the guidance offered by the opinion. The justification appeared to confuse the admissibility of evidence with its having conclusive weight. Yet it can hardly be denied that in those circumstances when opinion is admitted it is likely to carry more weight than other evidence. It is perhaps more appropriate to criticise the uncertainty both of the formulation of the rule and of the policy underlying it. The law, and especially the criminal law, is rarely precise in the demarcation of issues, and tends to eschew the formal characterisation of any of them as ultimate. It may be for this reason that some recent overseas authority has formulated the rule in different terms as excluding opinion only on the application of an essentially legal standard, such as that of negligence or incapacity to marry:

> When a standard, or a measure, or a capacity has been fixed by law, no witness whether expert or non-expert, nor however qualified, is permitted to express an opinion as to whether the person or the conduct, in question, measures up to that standard; on that question the court must instruct the jury as to the law, and the jury draw its own conclusion from the evidence.[9]

Despite its support by some textbooks,[10] commentators[11] and law reformers,[12] it is suggested that this approach offers no more certain guidance than its predecessor. It seems to assume a clear distinction between those issues which involve the application of legal standards and those which do not, but in truth all legal rules are cast in ordinary English words and carry legal consequences. It merely happens that under the pressure of the need to subsume new and unforeseen circumstances under such rules those words gradually depart further and further from their ordinary non-legal meaning. At some indeterminate point they may be regarded as having a specific legal meaning as opposed to their ordinary non-legal meaning.

It is submitted that the better and simpler solution, largely implemented by English case-law, and in civil cases recognised in explicit statutory provision, is to abandon any pretence of applying any such rule, and merely to accept opinion whenever it is helpful to the court to do so, irrespective of the status or nature of the issue to which it relates.[13] As most admissible lay opinion is admitted as a convenient summary of the conclusion drawn from a myriad of imperfectly describable details, and most expert opinion admitted to instruct the court in the application of unfamiliar terms and concepts, and as there have been said to be important differences between them in this respect,[14] it is best to treat them separately.

8 Evidence (Chadbourn rev) para 1920.
9 *Grismore v Consolidated Products Co* 5 NW 2d 646 at 663 (1942), approved in *R v Tonkin and Montgomery* [1975] Qd R 1 at 42. See also *R v Palmer* [1981] 1 NSWLR 209.
10 See, for example, Phipson *Evidence* (13th edn) 27–47.
11 See, for example, Calvert 'Proof of Guilt in Drunken Driving Cases' (1966) 17 NILQ 496.
12 See, for example, Australian Law Reform Commission 'Opinion Evidence' Research Paper No 13, para 20.
13 This is the approach of the United States Federal Rule 704, and see *Graat v R* (1982) 144 DLR (3d) 267.
14 *R v Davies* [1962] 3 All ER 97, [1962] 1 WLR 1111.

A. EXPERT WITNESSES

The common law rule that an expert witness may not be asked the question which the court has to decide is supported by civil cases.[15] The rule is based on the undesirability of allowing the expert to become involved in the decision making process, but it is not difficult to think of cases in which an expert's opinion on the ultimate issue might be of considerable assistance to the court. An instance given by the Law Reform Committee in their 17th report[16] is a case raising the question whether a professional man acted with the requisite degree of competence. The rule was frequently circumvented by what amounted to nothing more than a play upon words. For example, in one of the early medical negligence cases, it was held that a doctor who had been in court throughout the proceedings might not be asked whether he thought that the defendant was guilty of any want of skill, although he could be asked whether anything he had heard suggested improper conduct on the part of the defendant.[17] The Law Reform Committee did not think that they were proposing much, if any, change in the practical administration of the law when recommending the enactment of what is now s 3(1) of the Civil Evidence Act 1972: '. . . where a person is called as a witness in any civil proceedings, his opinion on any relevant matter[18] on which he is qualified to give expert evidence shall be admissible in evidence.' The greater use of the jury might be thought to justify the retention of the common law rule in criminal proceedings,[19] but there are signs that it is being eroded in this sphere without the aid of legislation.[20]

In *R v Mason*[1] the defence to a charge of murder was that the deceased had committed suicide, and a doctor who had heard the evidence was asked whether it was his opinion that the fatal wound had been inflicted by someone other than the deceased. The Court of Criminal Appeal held that his answer was admissible as an opinion based upon an assumed state of facts and, in *R v Holmes*,[2] the same court decided that a doctor called in support of the accused's plea of insanity might be asked in cross-examination whether the prisoner's conduct after the crime indicated that he knew the nature of his act and that it was wrong, although these are of course the very points which determine the applicability of the M'Naghten rules. A doctor who has examined a motorist charged with drunken driving is regularly asked whether, in his opinion, the accused was so drunk as not to have proper control of his car.

In *DPP v AB and C Chewing Gum Ltd*,[3] it was held that a child psychiatrist's

---

15 See, for example, *Sills v Brown* (1840) 9 C & P 601; *Rich v Pierpont* (1862) 3 F & F 35; *North Cheshire Brewery v Manchester Brewery Co* [1899] AC 83 at 85; *Haynes v Doman* [1899] 2 Ch 13 at 24; *British Celanese Ltd v Courtaulds Ltd* (1935) 152 LT 537 at 543.
16 Para 63.
17 *Rich v Pierpont* (1862) 3 F & F 35.
18 Under s 3(3) this includes an issue in the proceedings in question.
19 It may also justify control of the form of the question, for example, requiring the witness to quantify his degree of certainty in such terms as 'beyond reasonable doubt', see *Hendry v H M Advocate* 1987 SCCR 396.
20 Clause 43 of the Bill annexed to the 11th Report of the Criminal Law Revision Committee contained provisions identical with those of s 3(1) of the Civil Evidence Act 1972, but they did not appear in the Police and Criminal Evidence Act 1984.
1 (1911) 7 Cr App Rep 67.
2 [1953] 2 All ER 324, [1953] 1 WLR 686; *Bleta v R* [1964] SCR 561.
3 [1968] 1 QB 159, [1967] 2 All ER 504.

evidence about the effect which 'battle cards' sold with packets of bubble gum would have on children of various ages from five upwards ought to have been admitted on the issue, in a prosecution under the Obscene Publications Act 1959, whether the cards were likely to deprave and corrupt the children. In the ordinary case jurors and magistrates are as capable as anyone else of judging the likely effects of a publication[4] but, where children are concerned, 'any jury and any Justices need all the help they can get.' Lord Parker CJ pointed out that the psychiatrist was not, strictly speaking, being asked the very question which the court had to decide, but he said of the prohibition on questions on the ultimate issue:

> I cannot help feeling that with the advance of science more and more inroads have been made into the old common law principles. Those who practise in the criminal courts see every day cases of experts being called on the question of diminished responsibility, although technically the final question 'Do you think he was suffering from diminished responsibility?' is strictly inadmissible, it is allowed time and time again without any objection.[5]

The exception to the rule that evidence is inadmissible on the meaning of ordinary words used in general acts of Parliament recognised in the *A B and C Chewing Gum* case was questioned by Lord Dilhorne in *Director of Public Prosecutions v Jordan*[6] but the House of Lords was concerned with a different point in that case.

The question was whether the statutory provision in s 4 of the Obscene Publications Act 1959 for the reception of expert evidence on an ultimate issue, the availability of the defence of 'public good', covered evidence that an article, indubitably obscene within the meaning of s 1, had therapeutic effects on sexually abnormal people. It was held that this was not within the expression 'or other objects of public concern' following on the words 'in the interests of science, literature, art of learning'.[7]

No particular concern for the ultimate issue was shown in the case, and it is an interesting fact that it was not mentioned in the opinion in *Lowery v R*,[8] although it loomed large in the deliberations of the Supreme Court of Canada in *Lupien v R*[9] in which evidence which came very near to infringing the rule was held to be admissible by a bare majority.

B. NON-EXPERT WITNESSES

The existence of a particular issue may necessitate the reception of evidence which is not that of an expert and yet is nothing short of a witness's opinion concerning an ultimate issue in the case. In *Mansell v Clements*[10] the question

---

4 *R v Calder and Boyars Ltd* [1969] 1 QB 151, [1968] 3 All ER 644; *R v Anderson* [1972] 1 QB 304, [1971] 3 All ER 1152. See also *Ingram v Macari* 1983 JC 1.
5 [1968] 1 QB 159 at 164, [1967] 2 All ER 504 at 506. See also *R v Palmer* [1981] 1 NSWLR 209 at 214, SC.
6 [1977] AC 699 at 722.
7 See also *Re A-G's Reference (No 3 of 1977)* [1978] 3 All ER 1166, [1978] 1 WLR 1123 (expert evidence inadmissible to show article of value in sex education); and cf *R v Skirving, R v Grossman* [1985] QB 819, [1985] 2 All ER 705 (expert evidence admissible to prove effects of cocaine).
8 [1974] AC 85, [1973] 3 All ER 662 (see p 334 above).
9 (1970) 9 DLR (3d) 1.
10 (1874) LR 9 CP 139.

on a claim for commission was whether a third party bought a house from the defendant through the intervention of the plaintiff, an estate agent. The judge put the following question to the purchaser: 'Would you, if you had not gone to the plaintiff's office and got the card, have purchased the house?' The answer was 'I think not.' On appeal it was held that a verdict in favour of the plaintiff could have been justified without reference to the question and answer, but the judge was a member of the appellate court and he maintained his view concerning the propriety of the question.

Subject to the exceptional type of situation which has just been mentioned, it would seem that, if non-expert opinion is in reality evidence of fact given ex necessitate in the form of evidence of opinion, there should be no question of its inadmissibility because it deals with ultimate issues.[11] This is borne out by the form of s 3(2) of the Civil Evidence Act 1972, which suggests that no change in the law was intended:

> It is hereby declared that where a person is called as a witness in any civil proceedings, a statement of opinion by him on a relevant matter[12] on which he is not qualified to give expert advice, if made as a way of conveying relevant facts personally perceived by him, is admissible as evidence of what he perceived.

So far as criminal cases are concerned, the decisions on drunken driving indicate a difference of approach between the English and Northern Irish courts on the one hand, and the courts of Eire and Canada on the other.

In all these cases there are two questions although they may be phrased in different ways: (a) had the accused taken drink?, and (b) was he unfit to drive through drink? Factual evidence may be available with regard to the first, but we approach the realm of opinion evidence when someone who did not see the accused take drink deposes to his impression that the accused had done so. The second question can be answered only by opinion evidence.

We have seen that, in *R v Davies*,[13] the Court of Criminal Appeal allowed a non-expert who had not seen the accused take drink to answer the first question in terms of his impression, but not the second; there is no doubt that an expert, a doctor who had examined the accused, for example, would have been allowed to give his opinion with regard to both questions. The Court of Criminal Appeal allowed the non-expert to give his opinion on the first question because it was a compendious mode of stating the facts on which the opinion was based, the fact that the accused had a lurching gait and slurred speech etc. The objection to the witness answering the second question was stated to be that it involved the very point the court had to decide. In Eire, a non-expert has been allowed to give his opinion on both questions, on the first because the question whether a man was under the influence of drink is, like questions concerning identity, a question which cannot be adequately answered by enumerating observed facts, the second because it did not differ in this respect from the first.[14] In the Divisional Court of Northern Ireland, Lord MacDermott would have followed the Irish practice, but the majority preferred the English.[15] According to Lord MacDermott:

11 For example evidence of handwriting, see further, below p 690.
12 'In this section "relevant matter" includes an issue in the proceedings in question' (s 3(3)).
13 [1962] 3 All ER 97, [1962] 1 WLR 1111. For a full citation of authorities, see n 19 on p 498 above.
14 *A-G (Rudely) v James Kenny* (1960) 94 ILTR 185.
15 *Sherrard v Jacob* [1965] NI 151.

As in the case of the inference that a person is under the influence of drink, the inference that the same person was incapable of having proper control may depend on the whole picture, on the conjoint effect of numerous facts and circumstances which lead to a sound conclusion but cannot be faithfully or completely reproduced in evidence.[16]

The majority view was based on the courts' unwillingness to allow any witness to depose to ultimate issues, and it treated the first question as a compendious method of ascertaining observed facts.

SECTION 5. REASONS FOR THE EXCLUSION OF CERTAIN KINDS OF EVIDENCE OF OPINION

There have been two main and two subsidiary reasons for the exclusion of those kinds of evidence of opinion that fall within the rule stated at the beginning of this chapter. The two main reasons are founded on the principle that evidence of opinion is excluded when its reception would not assist, and might even mislead, the court. In the first place it is said that opinion evidence is irrelevant,[17] and this is largely true of non-expert opinion on a subject requiring expertise as well as opinion evidence concerning matters which do not call for expertise, although some writers prefer to say that the evidence is insufficiently relevant to be admissible.[18] Secondly, it is said that the reception of opinion evidence would usurp the functions of the jury. To the extent that this suggests that the witness might undesirably indicate what factual evidence he accepted or rejected, the danger can be avoided by stressing the hypothetical basis for any opinion; to the extent that it suggests an opinion might be unduly influential, it has been discussed in the previous section.

The two subsidiary reasons for the rejection of certain kinds of evidence of opinion are the fact that a witness who merely speaks to his opinion cannot be prosecuted for perjury, and the danger that the reception of such evidence might indirectly evade other exclusionary rules. The first reason is of some antiquity,[19] but, although Lord Mansfield had it in mind when he said, in *Folkes v Chadd*,[20] that Mr Smeaton could have been prosecuted if he had wilfully given false testimony, no great stress is placed upon it at the present day. As a matter of substantive law, the precise extent of the proposition is debatable. There is more force in the second reason, but it has not been stressed by the judges. The exclusionary rules most likely to be indirectly infringed by the reception of opinion evidence are those according to which irrelevant matter and hearsay are inadmissible. A witness can always be cross-examined on the grounds for his opinion, and, if these appear to be irrelevant the evidence can be ignored. The relationship of the opinion rule to the rule against hearsay calls for separate consideration.

16 At 163. See also *Graat v R* (1982) 144 DLR (3d) 267.
17 Goddard LJ in *Hollington v Hewthorn & Co Ltd* [1943] KB 587 at 595, [1943] 2 All ER 35 at 40.
18 Cowen and Carter *Essays on the Law of Evidence* 169.
19 *Adams v Canon* (1621) 1 Dyer 53b.
20 See p 493 above.

SECTION 6. THE RULE AGAINST HEARSAY AND EVIDENCE OF OPINION

The rule with regard to evidence of opinion originated in the same doctrine as that to which the rule against hearsay can be traced—every witness must be able to say that he had seen or heard that to which he deposes. He must have been 'oyant' and 'voyant',[1] but the two rules are now quite distinct although the same item of evidence may occasionally call for a consideration of both of them. For example, A is prepared to swear that he heard B, who witnessed a collision between two cars driven by C and D, say, some time after the event, that it was due to the negligence of D. A's evidence would clearly infringe the rule against hearsay if tendered to prove D's negligence on his prosecution for careless driving, because an assertion other than one made by a person while giving oral evidence would be tendered as evidence of the truth of that which was asserted. The evidence would also be inadmissible because B's assertion was an assertion of opinion of a kind that could not have been received if proffered by B himself from the witness box. If A had been at hand at the time of the collision, and he had heard B make some exclamation concerning the negligent manner in which D was driving, it is possible that he would be allowed to relate the assertion as evidence of D's negligence, although B was not called as a witness.[2] This is because there may be an exception to the rule against hearsay covering exclamations concerning an event made contemporaneously with its occurrence. So far as the opinion rule is concerned, B's opinion was spontaneous, or impulsive, as it was not the result of deliberation on his part; accordingly A's evidence as to what B said would probably be admissible.

The leading case on evidence calling for consideration of both the hearsay and the opinion rules is *Wright v Doe d Tatham*[3] which was elaborately argued on three occasions between 1830 and 1838. The sanity of a deceased testator named Marsden was in issue, and those who contended that he was sane when he executed his will tendered three letters written to him by acquaintances at the time. The writers of these letters had since died, and it was contended that the documents ought to be received (a) because they concerned business matters and showed that their authors regarded the addressee as sane, and (b) because Marsden displayed his sanity in the manner in which he acted on the letters. They were rejected in the Court of King's Bench, the judges in Exchequer Chamber were evenly divided and a majority of the judges advised the House of Lords that the letters were inadmissible. The judgment of the King's Bench was accordingly affirmed. The second ground upon which it was contended that the letters should be received was of no particular moment as it raised a question of fact. Evidence of the conduct of the testator is always admissible in such a case provided it is relevant, but the majority view was that there was no sufficient proof that Marsden had acted on the letters so as to indicate a rational appreciation of their contents. The first ground upon which it was contended that the evidence was admissible raised problems in connection with the rule against hearsay and the reception of opinion which have never since been fully

---

1 Thayer *Preliminary Treatise on Evidence at the Common Law* 523–4.
2 See per Pollock CB in *Milne v Leisler* (1862) 7 H & N 786 at 796.
3 (1838) 4 Bing NC 489. An analogous case is *Backhouse v Jones* (1839) 9 LJCP 99 where the statements were oral.

examined in England.[4] The letters indicated that the writers treated Marsden as sane, therefore they were equivalent to an assertion of that fact, therefore they infringed the rule against hearsay, and the majority of the judgments proceeded on this footing. If the writers of the letters had been called as witnesses they could have been asked for their views concerning the testator's sanity. However, it does not follow that a layman's opinion on such an issue is admissible because the question is, as we have seen, merely 'a compendious mode of ascertaining the result of the actual observation of the witness, from acts done, as to the habits and demeanour of the deceased'. Accordingly it is arguable that the letters had to be rejected both because their reception would have infringed the rule against hearsay and also because they were mere statements of opinion on a matter with regard to which an ordinary witness's opinion, unsupported by details concerning his observations, would have been inadmissible. This seems to have been the view of the majority of the judges, although it was only Parke B who gave much consideration to this aspect of the case.

As noted above, an opinion is generally admissible only if it is based upon facts which have been, or are to be, proved by admissible evidence.[5] It follows that it may not be based upon hearsay, unless it can be admitted notwithstanding the rule excluding hearsay. It may be useful to summarise these situations.[6] In some cases the opinion may be based upon statements which fall within an exception to the hearsay rule. In civil cases the matter is now governed entirely by statute as will be explained in ch XV below. Thus if an expert rely for his opinion upon facts related to him by a third party who had observed them, this would provide a sufficient foundation for the admissibility of his opinion. Spontaneous statements made in the circumstances examined more fully in ch XVIII below may also provide such a foundation. A more usual situation is one in which the opinion is based upon expertise in part derived from hearsay material, which may indeed be incorporated into the expert's evidence, notwithstanding that he has no personal knowledge of its factual basis, and which may either be in the form of general works of reference,[7] particular studies,[8] or information gleaned from others in the course of professional life.[9] In *R v Zundel*,[10] it was necessary to prove the basic facts of The Holocaust. The court took the view that while judicial notice[11] might be taken of such a notorious matter based upon historical treatises, it was better[12] to prove it by calling expert witnesses

4 For a very thorough examination in Canada, see *R v Zundel* (1985) 35 DLR (4th) 338 at 384.
5 Above p 493.
6 See further, Pattenden 'Expert Opinion Evidence Based on Hearsay' [1982] Crim LR 85.
7 *Rowley v London and North Western Rly Co* (1873) LR 8 Exch 221 (mortality tables). See also *Borowski v Quayle* [1966] VR 382 (standard pharmaceutical guide).
8 *H v Schering Chemicals Ltd* [1983] 1 All ER 849 at 853, [1983] 1 WLR 143 at 148 (research studies into drug). See also *R v Abadom* [1983] 1 All ER 364, 76 Cr App Rep 48 (statistics of refractive index of samples of glass).
9 *English Exporters (London) Ltd v Eldonwall Ltd* [1973] Ch 415 at 420, [1973] 1 All ER 726 at 730 (general knowledge of property values derived from reports of transactions conducted by others). See also *Wilson v H M Advocate* 1988 SCCR 384 (briefings of police, as to methods of importing drugs).
10 (1987) 35 DLR (4th) 338.
11 See further above p 65.
12 Because an expert witness could be cross-examined, and because of the undesirability of establishing by judicial notice a major part of the prosecution case.

who could themselves rely upon historical treatises,[13] and also contemporaneous documents of the sort relied upon by historians in preparing such treatises. An opinion will not be admissible if it is based upon more specific hearsay not falling under any such exception,[14] though the dividing line between generic and specific hearsay may occasionally prove difficult to draw with any precision. If the opinion is not solely based upon inadmissible hearsay, then the statements may be proved not as evidence of their truth, but as an additional basis for the opinion.[15]

13 Such use of treatises constitues an acknowledged exception to the hearsay rule.
14 See *Eldonwall* and *Borowski* above, in each of which some bases for the opinion were excluded for this reason; *Mobil Oil Corpn v Registrar of Trademarks* (1983) 51 ALR 735 (excludes opinion survey evidence in trademark case).
15 *R v Abbey* (1982) 138 DLR (3d) 202.

CHAPTER XIV

The rule against hearsay[1]

The rule against hearsay is one of the oldest, most complex and most confusing of the exclusionary rules of evidence. Lord Reid has said that it was 'difficult to make any general statement about the law of hearsay which is entirely accurate.'[2] One of the reasons is that its definition, and the ambit of exceptions to it are both unclear. Because its exercise often tells against the reception of apparently satisfactory evidence, and because objections to it have been said to be based on the far from unattractive fallacy that 'whatever is morally convincing, and whatever reasonable beings would form their judgments and act upon, may be submitted to the jury',[3] there has been an understandable tendency for courts to decline to exclude such evidence. In many cases this is done because it never occurs to anyone that the evidence could be construed as hearsay. Even in those cases where the problem is recognised, it is nevertheless often left quite unclear whether the evidence is admitted because it does not fall within the scope of the exclusionary rule at all, or whether although within the scope of the rule it falls within, or constitutes, an exception to it. The rule and its exceptions will occupy this and the four following chapters. This chapter will be concerned with the nature of the rule, and the following chapters with its application in different types of proceedings, and with a particular class of exceptions.

A preliminary formulation of the rule has already been advanced,[4] and reference made to the distinction between hearsay and original evidence. This chapter will consider these matters further, and in particular the nature and development of the rule, its application to different types of proceedings, and the nature of attempts at reform.

SECTION 1. DEVELOPMENT AND RATIONALE OF THE RULE

This section opens with a short statement of the hearsay rule, goes on to trace the outline of its history and then explains why such an exclusionary rule was thought to be necessary.

---

1 Two useful monographs are Tregarthen *The Law of Hearsay Evidence* (1915) and Baker *The Hearsay Rule* (1950). The number of extremely valuable American studies of the topic include Morgan *Some Problems of Proof Under the Anglo-American System of Litigation* (1956) p 106, Tribe 'Triangulating Hearsay' (1974) 87 Harvard LR 957, and Park 'McCormick on Evidence and the Concept of Hearsay' (1981) 65 Minn LR 423. Many of the topics considered in this chapter were discussed in Cross 'The Periphery of the Rule Against Hearsay' (1969) 7 Melb ULR; more recent British discussion may be found in Guest 'The Scope of the Hearsay Rule' (1985) 101 LQR 385; and Ashworth and Pattenden 'Reliability, Hearsay and the English Criminal Trial' (1986) 102 LQR 292.
2 *Myers v D P P* [1965] AC 1001 at 1019, [1964] 2 All ER 881 at 884.
3 By Coleridge J in *Wright v Tatham* (1838) 5 Cl & Fin 670 at 690.
4 Above, p 42.

A. STATEMENT

The rule applies to all kinds of assertion, whether made orally, in writing or by conduct.[5] It is sometimes uncertain how far it extends to assertions implied by words or deeds.

According to the rule against hearsay as formulated in ch I, an assertion other than one made by a person while giving oral evidence in the proceedings is inadmissible as evidence of any fact asserted. This formulation conflates two common law rules, the rule that the previous assertions of the witness who is testifying are inadmissible as evidence of the facts stated (sometimes spoken of as the 'rule against narrative', or the 'rule against self-corroboration'), and the rule that assertions by persons other than the witness who is testifying are inadmissible as evidence of the facts asserted (the rule against hearsay in the strict sense).

At common law there is only one clear exception to the first rule, an informal admission proved by the party who made it. There are many common law exceptions to the rule against hearsay in the strict sense. If A proves that B, the defendant in a running-down action, admitted to him that he was not keeping a proper look-out, A's evidence of what was said is admissible against B under an exception to the rule against hearsay in the strict sense; but if B admits in the course of his evidence that he told A that he was not keeping a proper look-out, reliance may be placed by the plaintiff on the previous assertion of the defendant as evidence of the facts asserted.[6]

In ch VII we saw that, at common law, the previous consistent assertions of witnesses are usually inadmissible as evidence of consistency though inconsistent assertions might be proved, not as evidence of the facts asserted, but in order to cast doubt on the witness's testimony. We also saw that previous consistent assertions might be proved by way of exception to the general exclusionary rule in the case of complaints of sexual offences, assertions forming part of the res gestae, assertions rebutting a suggestion that the witness's testimony was a recent invention and sundry assertions of the accused. In these cases the witness's previous assertions are not, strictly speaking, received as evidence of the facts asserted, and they are therefore not received under exceptions to the rule against hearsay.

The law of evidence distinguishes between a witness's assertions of fact and opinion. This should be reflected in a complete formulation of the rule against hearsay. A full version of that adopted in this book should therefore read: any assertion other than one made by a person while giving oral evidence in the proceedings is inadmissible as evidence of any fact or opinion asserted.

This chapter is primarily concerned with the rule against hearsay in the strict sense. It has never been fully formulated judicially, but most authorities concur in the view that:

Evidence of a statement made to a witness by a person who is not himself called as a witness may or may not be hearsay. It is hearsay and inadmissible when the object of the evidence is to establish the truth of what is contained in the statement.

5 *Chandrasekera (alias Alisandiri) v R* [1937] AC 220, [1936] 3 All ER 865 (signs made by woman dying as a result of her throat being cut).
6 The exception of the admission has been described as the only 'clear' one because of the possibility that previous statements of witnesses received as part of the res gestae are received as evidence of the facts stated.

It is not hearsay and is admissible when it is proposed to establish by evidence, not the truth of the statement, but the fact that it was made.[7]

This crucial distinction was overlooked by the trial judge in the case from which the above extract from the advice of the Judicial Committee of the Privy Council is taken. The appellant was charged with being in possession of firearms without a lawful excuse and his defence was that he was acting under duress in consequence of threats uttered by Malayan terrorists. The judge would not allow the accused to state what had been said by the terrorists and the Judicial Committee advised that the conviction should be quashed because the reported assertions were tendered as original evidence and ought to have been received as such.[8]

The rule against hearsay applies just as much to evidence elicited in cross-examination as to evidence in-chief. A deceased workman's statements to his widow on returning home after an accident have been held inadmissible at common law as evidence of its cause on a number of occasions.[9] If a widow narrates in cross-examination what her deceased husband told her about the cause of his injuries or illness, her assertion is no more admissible as evidence of that fact than it would have been if made in-chief.[10]

B. HISTORY

No aspect of the hearsay rule seems free from doubt and controversy, least of all its history. Legal historians are divided between those who ascribe the development of the rule predominantly to distrust of the capacity of the jury to evaluate it, and those who ascribe it predominantly to the unfairness of depriving a party of the opportunity to cross-examine the witness.[11] It does however seem to be agreed that the rule developed at the same time as the modern form of trial. At an earlier period the functions of jurors and witnesses had overlapped; jurors were expected to rely upon their own knowledge, and in some forms of trial the production of witnesses was conclusive. It was not before the end of the seventeenth century that the general rule crystallised into one where jurors were expected to rely only upon the evidence presented to them in court, and witness to testify only to what they had themselves seen and heard. If such witnesses were to be allowed to testify to the assertions of others the former rule would become emasculated, and the whole developing procedure of trial undermined. Thus in his justification of the rule Chief Baron Gilbert said:

> though a person testify what he hath heard upon oath, yet the person who spoke it was not upon oath; and if a man had been in court and said the same thing and had not sworn it, he had not been believed in a court of justice.[12]

7 *Subramaniam v Public Prosecutor* [1956] 1 WLR 965 at 969; that approach, and the one adopted in this work, was explicitly approved by the Supreme Court of Canada in *R v Abbey* (1982) 138 DLR (3d) 202.
8 For a similar oversight by a trial judge, see *R v Willis* [1960] 1 All ER 331, [1960] 1 WLR 55; and for one by magistrates, see *Woodhouse v Hall* (1980) 72 Cr App Rep 39.
9 *Gilbey v Great Western Rly Co* (1910) 102 LT 202; see also *Amys v Barton* [1912] 1 KB 40.
10 *Beare v Garrod* (1915) 113 LT 673; see p 303 above. In *R v Summers* (1986) 22 ACR 47 an appeal was allowed on account of cross-examination permitted to elicit such hearsay.
11 Holdsworth, Thayer and Wigmore favoured the former view, and Morgan the latter.
12 *The Law of Evidence* (2nd edn, 1760) p 152.

It should not be forgotten that many elements inevitably contribute to a rule so central and extensive as the hearsay rule. Many rules of independent origin are related to it by way of amplification, such as the rules relating to the previous assertions of witnesses; and some by way of exception, such as that allowing the use of the dying declarations of victims to identify their assailants.[13] It was inter-connected, especially during the period of its development with the rules insisting upon the sanction of the oath and upon the disqualification of particular categories of witness. It is ultimately futile to seek a single coherent explanation for the development of the rule, or to relate its modern form to any such explanation. Even Morgan is forced to concede the influence of distrust of the jury, the explanation he otherwise rejects, in justifying resistance to reform.[14]

It certainly seems that by the beginning of the nineteenth century the rule excluding hearsay had become well-established, and the emphasis shifted to definition of its range and the establishment of exceptions. The former question lay at the heart of perhaps the most influential authority on the development of the rule, *Wright v Doe d Tatham*.[15] The issue arose from a disputed will in which the testator had left substantial property to his steward. Those entitled on intestacy claimed that the deceased had been mentally incompetent. The issue roused passions to a considerably degree,[16] and led to a series of lawsuits and appeals throughout the 1830s, culminating when the House of Lords took the opinions of the judges. Part of the evidence against the deceased's competence consisted of evidence of taunts asserting insanity and his lack of spirited reaction to them. Part of the evidence in favour of his competence consisted of letters written to him, apparently upon the basis that he was sane. The issue was complicated by the fact that the assertion implied from these circumstances was one of opinion, and by dispute as to the inferences to be drawn from the evidence as to the deceased's reactions to the taunts or letters. In the end the evidence of the taunts was accepted[17] to help to show the testator not to have sufficient capacity, and the letters rejected to help to show capacity. The numerous opinions are mainly significant for the indications they give of the reasons felt at that time to justify the rule, and hence exceptions to it, including a famous discursus by Baron Parke on the application of the rule to conduct. It seems likely that the spectacular character of this litigation, and its result, both focused attention upon the rule and inhibited the development of new exceptions to it. Although some judges continued to argue for the development of exceptions upon 'the reasons and principles which have induced the tribunals of this country to admit exceptions in other cases',[18] the more common attitude was that of Lord Blackburn who refused to admit hearsay because 'unless it is to be brought within some one of the exceptions, it would

---

13 Shown by Thayer to antedate the rule by some centuries.
14 *Some Problems of Proof Under the Anglo-American System of Litigation* (1956) p 117.
15 (1837) 7 Ad & El 313, (1838) 5 Cl & Fin. Other stages in the drama are reported in 2 Russ & Myl 1 (1830), 1 Ad & El 3 (1833), and (1837) 7 Ad & El 359.
16 The first trial was removed to York because feelings ran too high in Lancashire to empanel an unprejudiced jury, though three later trials took place in Lancashire including one in which a verdict was entered for the defendant. Many of the leading lawyers of the day, including some who were judges in later stages of the proceedings, acted in the earlier as advocates, judges or, in one case, as a witness.
17 No serious attempt was made to exclude this evidence, its admission was however suggested by the devisee to justify the admission of the letters.
18 *Sugden v Lord St Leonards* (1876) 1 PD 154 at 241.

fall within the general rule that hearsay evidence is not admissible'.[19] As Thayer pertinently remarked the real difference was between those who regarded the exclusion of hearsay as a principal rule subject to inclusionary exceptions, and those who regarded the admission of relevant evidence as the principal rule subject to exclusionary exceptions. The matter was however effectively closed by the declaration of Lord Reid in *Myers v DPP* that:

> If we are to extend the law it must be by the development and application of fundamental principles. We cannot introduce arbitrary conditions or limitations; that must be left to legislation: and if we do in effect change the law, we ought in my opinion only to do that in cases where our decision will produce some finality or certainty. If we disregard technicalities in this case and seek to apply principle and common sense, there are a number of parts of the existing law of hearsay susceptible of similar treatment, . . . The only satisfactory solution is by legislation following on a wide survey of the whole field . . . A policy of make do and mend is no longer adequate.[20]

It should be noted that so to restrict the creation by the judges of new exceptions to the hearsay rule can have the effect of distorting the law's response in this area. If a useful and cogent piece of evidence should technically be regarded as hearsay, and if the most natural means of securing its admissibility, namely by the creation of a specific judicially crafted exception, is denied, then there is a danger that other less desirable expedients may be adopted. One possibility is to adopt an interpretation of substantive or more basic procedural law so as to admit the evidence despite the hearsay rule; another is so to manipulate the definition of hearsay that it is regarded as falling outside the proscription of the rule altogether. For example if a statute requiring reasonable suspicion is interpreted subjectively it may well justify the admissibility of hearsay as providing grounds for suspicions, although it would not suffice for proof.[1] An example of a more basic procedural rule[2] would be the suggestion that at common law where objection has deliberately not been taken by an opponent to the admission of hearsay then the judge is justified in leaving it to the jury. In England although it has been denied that hearsay may be so admissible either in criminal or in civil proceedings,[3] it seems occasionally[4] to have been accepted upon such a basis in civil proceedings even before the passage of the Civil Evidence Act 1968. The alternative technique is to define hearsay in such a manner that the relevant assertion falls outside the rule so stated. Both

---

19 *Sturla v Frecchia* (1880) 5 App Cas 623 at 647.
20 [1965] AC 1001 at 1021, [1964] 2 All ER 881 at 885. The comment was made in full knowledge of the recommendations of the Law Reform Committee for wholesale reform of the rule, and probably in the expectation of their adoption by the Criminal Law Revision Committee, see further section 3 below.
1 See *Shaaban Bin Hussein v Chong Fook Kam* [1970] AC 942, [1969] 3 All ER 1626. If reasonable suspicion is interpreted objectively then hearsay may not be admissible, see *Tucs v Manley* (1985) 62 ALR 460.
2 More discussed in Australia than here, see *Cross on Evidence* (3rd Australian edn, 1986) pp 94–98; *R v McGookin and Robinson* (1986) 20 ACR 438.
3 *R v Gibson* (1887) 18 QBD 537 at 542. See also Harrison 'Hearsay Admitted Without Objection' (1955) 7 Res Judiocatae 58.
4 *Re Allied Produce Co Ltd* [1967] 3 All ER 399, [1967] 1 WLR 1469. It should however be noted that the hearsay rule has never applied in winding up proceedings in quite the same way as it applies elsewhere.

approaches seem to have been involved in *WW v Kennedy*[5] where a previous statement, the making, but not the truth of which, was acknowledged by the witness, was held admissible. A more straightforward and successful attempt at manipulation of the definition is to be seen in cases holding that such evidence as a photofit identification,[6] or a statement of intention[7] made by a third party[8] fall outside the definition of hearsay.

C. RATIONALE

As noted above, the development of the hearsay rule coincided with the stabilisation of a recognisably modern form of trial. Whether the exclusion of hearsay was based upon distrust of the abilities of the jury to evaluate it, or upon faith in the power of cross-examination, or both, it remains to be seen what frailties required such elaborate precautions.[9] Their examination may reveal a basis both for the principles of defining and applying the rule in borderline situations, and for developing exceptions to it.

It is helpful to start by contrasting the reasoning process involved in the acceptance of direct testimony with that involved in the acceptance of hearsay. If a witness testifies to a relevant event which he has himself observed, say 'that x existed', the jury is invited to accept that the witness did perceive x, that he has remembered correctly what he perceived,[10] that there is no ambiguity in his relation of x to the court, and that he is sincere in his testimony. Rules of competence may disqualify such direct testimony in extreme cases, and sincerity may be promoted by the sanction of the oath and the prospect of prosecution for perjury, but the principal guaranties for these factors are provided by the witness's availability for cross-examination to probe into them. At the end of the day the jury must be satisfied both that the witness believes that x existed, and that his belief is justified.

It is obvious that any danger in accepting these conclusions is multiplied when hearsay is tendered. In such cases the jury must be satisfied that the witness believes he heard a third party say 'x exists'; that the witness's belief was justified; that the third party believed that x existed; and that the third party's belief was justified. It must do this in the absence of any safeguard from the ordinary conditions of testimony in relation to the third party; in the absence of any opportunity to probe the third party by cross-examination; and despite the diminution of the value of these safeguards in relation to the testifying witness on account of the severance of any direct link between his testimony and the proposition which the jury is invited to support as a result of it. A direct witness, who asserts that x existed can be cross-examined much more fruitfully about his perception and memory of x

5 1988 SCLR 236.
6 *R v Cook* [1987] QB 417, [1987] 1 All ER 1049.
7 *Walton v R* (1989) 84 ALR 59.
8 Any relevant statement by a party opponent would be admissible as an admission excepted from the general exclusion on hearsay.
9 Such frailties have led to convictions being regarded as obtained contrary to basic principles of justice even in jurisdictions with a totally different tradition and form of trial when dependent upon evidence from anonymous informants, *Kostovski v Netherlands* European Court of Human Rights (1989) Times, 22 November.
10 The results of considerable scientific investigation into these factors are presented and evaluated in the Australian Law Reform Commission's Research Paper No 3 'Hearsay Evidence' (1981) ch 2.

of which he claims experience, than the hearsay witness, who merely testifies that he heard a third party say 'x exists', can be cross-examined about what he claims he heard.

It is largely because of the increased dangers of impaired perception, bad memory, ambiguity and insincerity, coupled with the decreased effectiveness of conventional safeguards, that hearsay is regarded as so particularly vulnerable as to require a special exclusionary rule. Because dangers of ambiguity and insincerity relate to the existence of belief while those of impaired perception and bad memory relate to its reflection of reality, some commentators explicitly utilise the difference between them in their definition of hearsay.[11] Because cross-examination is often supposed to be more effective in relation to perception and memory, the diminution of such dangers in particular circumstances is often used to help to justify special exceptions.[12]

In defining hearsay implicit reference is made to the existence of these dangers in applying the exclusionary rule only to situations in which the out-of-court assertion is tendered for the truth of that which it asserts. If it is tendered merely as original evidence of the fact of its having been asserted, or of the belief of its auditor in the truth of the matter asserted, no question arises as to the sincerity, memory or perception of utterance of the third party, and in many cases there is little possibility of ambiguity. All four dangers are much more likely to be present if the assertion is tendered to prove the truth of the matter asserted. Definitions of the type advanced here have been categorised as assertion-based definitions because of their concentration upon the role played by the assertion.[13] Other definitions which stress the absence from the courtroom of the original source of the information have been categorised as declarant-based definitions. The principal reason for adopting the former approach is to cater for the assimilation of the exclusion both of the out-of-court assertions of third parties, and of those of the witness who is testifying.

It must also be remembered that if the hearsay rule is to be effective it must exclude circumstantial as well as direct inference. As Thayer put it:

> the hearsay rule operates in two ways: (a) it forbids using the credit of an absent declarant as the basis of an inference, and (b) it forbids using in the same way the mere evidentiary fact of the statement as having been made under such and such circumstances.[14]

There would be little point in excluding testimony that a named third party said 'x exists' for the purpose of showing directly that x existed, if the same testimony were nevertheless to be accepted as evidence that the third party *said* that x existed, perhaps coupled with testimony as to the third party's general high reputation for credibility, and then to permit the jury to draw from these circumstances what conclusion it pleased.

It is the exclusion of testimony inviting this sort of circumstantial inference which will be found to cause some difficulty in borderline cases, and which compels a restrictive approach to the basic definition of hearsay. Even on the basis of such an approach hearsay often goes unrecognised, if the

11 Lempert and Salzburg *A Modern Approach to Evidence* (2nd edn, 1982) pp 357, 358.
12 See eg United States Federal Rules of Evidence, r 803 (24) and r 804(b)(6).
13 Park 'McCormick on Evidence and the Concept of Hearsay' (1981) 65 Minn LR 423.
14 Thayer *Legal Essays* (1907) p 270.

definition were more widely drawn hardly any piece of testimony would be completely free of its tentacles.

SECTION 2. APPLICATION OF THE RULE

Before embarking upon a survey of different circumstances to which the hearsay rule is relevant it is salutary to remember Lord Reid's remark at the beginning of this chapter. It has to be recognised that the vagueness of the definition of the rule and of its exceptions, the absence of a clear and consistent rationale for applying it or refusing to do so, the failure to recognise the potential application of the rule in a number of situations, and the blurred distinction between direct and circumstantial use of such evidence, have together created a morass of authority and example, quite devoid of clear and consistent holding. Thoroughfares through this swamp do not occur naturally; they must first be constructed. Nor has the situation been much assisted by voluminous academic survey.[15] A surfeit of markers has been placed, but they point in different directions.

In this section it is proposed to distinguish three major modes of assertion, by writing, by speech, and by conduct. Each will be considered in turn, and an attempt made to explain the difficulties to be found in relation to it, at common law. There will inevitably be some overlapping between the sub-divisions when similar considerations apply to each. It makes little d˙ˉerence for example whether a bet is written on a slip, made over the telephone, or conveyed by tic-tac. Implied assertions are not treated as a separate category, but will be considered according to whether they are implied from writing, speech or conduct. Other points which will occur in a number of parts include the question of the use of the assertion for purposes other than the truth of what it asserts, for example as a lie or as original evidence, the question of whether the writing, speech or conduct can be classified as an assertion, and the question of negative hearsay.

A. WRITING

The rule as stated above applies to previous assertions both of witnesses and of third parties. The former situation rarely causes much difficulty, and the operation of the rule is well-illustrated by the situation which arose in *R v Harman*.[16] In that case, after giving evidence, witnesses were quite properly cross-examined by reference to subsequent statements which they had made.[17] The party calling these witnesses then attempted to rehabilitate them in re-examination by putting to them different statements which they had made and invited the witness to agree that these were likely to be more reliable. While such statements may quite properly be used to refresh

15 In addition to the contributions noted at p 508 above, see for example McCormick 'The Borderland of Hearsay' (1930) 39 Yale LJ 489, Morgan 'Hearsay and Non-Hearsay' (1935) 48 Harv LR 1138, Falknor 'Silence as Hearsay' (1940) 89 U Pa LR 192, Ladd 'The Hearsay We Admit' (1952) 5 Okla LR 269, Maguire 'The Hearsay System: Around and Through the Thicket' (1961) 14 Vand LR 741, Finman 'Implied Assertions as Hearsay' (1962) 14 Stan LR 682, Weinberg 'Implied Assertions and the Scope of the Hearsay Rule' (1973) 9 Melb ULR 268.
16 [1985] Crim LR 326.
17 See ch VII p 311 above.

memory when the appropriate conditions have been met,[18] or to rebut
suggestions of previous inconsistency,[19] they cannot, at common law, be used
as evidence of the truth of the matters asserted without breach of the hearsay
rule.

Myers v D P P[20] is the leading recent case on the operation of the rule in
relation to the written assertions of third parties. The accused was charged
with frauds involving passing off stolen cars as models re-built from wrecks.
In order to avoid detection the stolen cars had to have their own identifying
numbers removed, and the identifying numbers of the wrecked cars
substituted for them. Unfortunately for this enterprise the number cast into
the cylinder block could not be changed. The prosecution case thus rested
upon the discrepancy in the relevant cars between the numbers which could
be changed, which corresponded to those of a wrecked car, and the one
which could not be changed and accordingly corresponded to that of a stolen
car. In order to establish the relevant combinations of numbers the
prosecution called as a witness the custodian of the manufacturer's records.
These consisted of microfilmed copies of record cards which passed along the
production line with the vehicle, and onto which the relevant numbers were
entered. After having been filmed the original records were destroyed. It
was not denied that the records were inherently reliable, nor that no oral
testimony would have been credible, even if those who wrote the numbers
on the cards could have been identified and found. It was however held by
the House of Lords that these records amounted to hearsay, and came within
no recognised exception to the rule.[1] This result occasioned some disquiet,
and was reversed by special legislation providing for the admissibility of
business records in criminal proceedings to be discussed in detail in ch XVII
below.

This case may be contrasted with one decided in the Court of Criminal
Appeal shortly before *Myers*, and which had some influence on the
dissentients, and on the court below. *R v Rice*[2] was also a car fraud case. It
was relevant to establish that Rice flew from London to Manchester on a
particular day. The prosecution proposed to do so by putting in evidence a
used ticket for the relevant flight bearing Rice's name. It was perhaps
unfortunate from the point of view of the prosecution that the ticket was for
two seats, and it was also part of the case that the second seat had not been
occupied by the man whose name appeared on it. Nevertheless the Recorder,
and the Court of Criminal Appeal, agreed in holding that the ticket, having
been produced from the repository of tickets used on that particular flight,
could be admitted as circumstantial evidence from which the jury could
draw what inference it chose. The Recorder was quite explicit in rejecting
any suggestion that this breached the hearsay rule. This result can be
supported only by taking an extremely strict view of what amounts to an

---

18 See ch VII p 271 above.
19 See ch VII p 290 above.
20 [1965] AC 1001 [1964] 2 All ER 881, followed in *R v Sealby* [1965] 1 All ER 701; *R v Van
    Vreden* (1973) 57 Cr App Rep 818; *R v Patel* [1981] 3 All ER 94, (1981) 73 Cr App Rep
    117; distinguished in *R v Wood* (1982) 76 Cr App Rep 23. The evidence rejected in *Myers*
    would now be admissible under the Criminal Justice Act 1988, ss 24, 27.
1 Two of their Lordships dissented, principally on the ground that a new exception should
   be recognised, but also argued faintly that the records could perhaps be admitted as
   circumstantial evidence to confirm other evidence in the case, the ground which had
   succeeded in the Court of Criminal Appeal, *R v Myers* [1964] 1 All ER 877.
2 [1963] 1 QB 857, [1963] 1 All ER 832.

assertion. If an assertion is defined in this context as words primarily intended to assert a state of fact, it is possible to contend that the names of the passengers inscribed on an airline ticket are not primarily intended to assert anything. The whole ticket is primarily intended to be used as a valid warrant for travelling on an aeroplane. As such it may be permissible to treat it as a piece of real evidence, and to allow it to be proved as one of the circumstances of the case from which the jury is entitled to make common-sense inferences. It is indeed difficult, on the facts of *Rice*, even to identify the maker of an assertion, or what precisely the assertion was. It is far from inconceivable that the clerk writing the ticket simply asked whose name should be inserted. It would have been different if the prosecution had sought to tender a list of passengers compiled by the airline as a result of the scrutiny of the used tickets. Then the document would have been intended to assert the identities of the passengers, and the author of the assertion would have been the official who compiled the list. That quite different situation was the one which occurred in *Myers*, which may explain why the majority there made so little attempt to discredit the decision in *Rice*, even though it had been the cornerstone of the argument which had succeeded in the Court of Criminal Appeal.

It is readily conceded that the line between that which is primarily intended to assert, and that which is not, will often be difficult to draw, and that opinions might legitimately differ as to where in relation to it the fact of *Rice* ought to be placed.[3] In many cases intention may properly be inferred from the external and objective manifestations normally taken to signify intention.[4] It is nevertheless contended that concentration upon the presence of an intention to assert provides the most defensible watershed between hearsay and non-hearsay both as a matter of logical coherence and of practical common-sense.[5]

The principal authority opposed to such a line of reasoning is the old and unsatisfactory case of *Wright v Doe d Tatham*.[6] It may be recalled that the issue concerned the mental competence of a testator. Those who asserted his competence wished to tender in evidence a number of letters, some of them written to him years earlier. None of these letters, naturally enough, explicitly asserted the competence of the testator. Had they done so, there could be no question but that they would have been hearsay, just as much as similar letters written to third parties. It was thus argued that to admit the letters in their own right, irrespective of any act done in consequence of receiving them by the testator, as circumstantial evidence of his competence, would undermine the foundations of the hearsay rule. It was felt that the same objections which could have been made to letters explicitly stating the authors' opinions of the testator's sanity applied also to letters from which such opinions could be implied. It may be accepted that the letters in question

---

3 The reasoning in *Rice* was doubted in *R v Lydon* (1987) 85 Cr App Rep 221 at 224. In Australia it was rejected by Gibbs J in *Re Gardener* (1968) 13 FLR 345 (another air ticket case), and by Cox J in *R v Romeo* (1982) 30 SASR 243 at 264 where an invoice was rejected as evidence implicating the person named on it. In all of these cases the remarks were strictly obiter dicta.

4 See Guest 'Hearsay Revisited' (1988) Current Legal Problems, see also Seligman 'An Exception to the Hearsay Rule' (1912) 26 Harv LR 146 at 148, 149.

5 For a different view see Wellborn 'The Definition of Hearsay in the Federal Rules of Evidence' (1982) 61 Tex LR 49.

6 (1837) 7 Ad & El 313; 5 Cl & Fin 650 (1838).

were particularly inadequate for the purpose of proving the testator's sanity, but it is submitted that this was mainly because the circumstance of their having been written could not justify the inference which it was sought to draw from it. It was just not sufficiently relevant to that question that some time before the will had been made, a few laymen had written occasional letters addressed to the testator, which on one of several possible explanations were consistent with a belief in his sanity.[7] Explained in that way the decision need not be regarded as an irremovable obstacle to a more rational approach to the treatment of hearsay.

In *Rice* then the document was, while in *Wright v Tatham* it was not, a fact from which an inference relevant to the issue could reasonably be drawn. In other cases the document may itself be a fact in issue. Thus in *Stobart v Dryden* the plaintiff proved the due execution of a deed upon which he was suing by calling testimony to verify the handwriting of the deceased attesting witness. That witness's out-of-court confession of having altered the deed was held to be hearsay, and inadmissible.[8] One unsuccessful argument for its admissibility was that, as the plaintiff used the declaration of the subscribing witness, evidenced by his signature, to prove the execution, the defendant might use any declaration of the same witness to disprove it. The answer given by Baron Parke was:

> that evidence of the handwriting in the attestation is not used as a declaration by the witness, but to show the fact that he put his hand in that place and manner, in which in the ordinary course of business he would have done, if he had actually seen the deed executed. A statement of the attesting witness by parol, or written on any other document than that offered to be proved, would be inadmissible. The proof of actual attestation of the witness is, therefore, not the proof of a declaration but of a fact.[9]

It is obvious that many legal documents have an operative effect, and hence cannot be regarded as asserting any state of fact. Thus contracts and wills generally fall outside the scope of the hearsay rule. In the case of related documents it is sometimes more difficult to draw the line. The difficulty is well illustrated by *Re Wright, Hegan v Bloor*. A testatrix who executed a power of appointment in 1917 wrote a letter to the appointee in 1911 saying that she regarded herself as bound by a bargain made with his father concerning the exercise of the power. In deciding that the appointment was a fraud upon the power, P O Lawrence J said:

> in principle the court ought to set aside the appointment if it is satisfied that the appointor made the appointment *under the belief that he was bound by the corrupt bargain*, or even without any evidence as to his belief, if the appointor *states* that he had made such a bargain and that he intends to carry it out, and then makes an appointment in accordance with it.[10]

On the first hypothesis the letter was received under what is probably best regarded as an exception to the hearsay rule as evidence of the testatrix's state of mind in 1911—a state which might be presumed to have continued

---

7   There was certainly no shortage of more relevant evidence including that of dozens of witnesses who gave oral evidence on both sides, and many uncontested letters upon which the testator could be shown to have acted.
8   It could not be received under the Civil Evidence Act 1968.
9   (1836) 1 M & W 615 at 624.
10 [1920] 1 Ch 108 at 119 (italics supplied).

until 1917; but the letter constituted original evidence upon the second hypothesis.

First hand oral testimony is available only for events which have taken place in relatively modern times. For older events it is useful to have recourse to circumstantial inferences drawn from non-assertive documents. In *Malcolmson v O'Dea* an assembly book of 1679 containing fishing leases granted by a predecessor in title of the plaintiff was held to be admissible evidence of the lessor's enjoyment of the fishing rights when the leases were granted. Willes J said:

> The proof of ancient possession is always attended with difficulty. Time has removed the witnesses who could speak to acts of ownership of their own personal knowledge, and resort must necessarily be had to written evidence. In some cases written statements of title are admitted even when they amount to mere assertions as in the case of a right affected the public generally;[11] but the entry now under consideration is admissible according to a rule equally applicable to a fishery in a private pond as to one in a public navigable river. The rule is that ancient documents coming out of proper custody and purporting on the face of them to show exercise of ownership, such as a lease or a licence, may be given in evidence without proof of possession or payment of rent under them as being in themselves acts of ownership and proofs of possession.[12]

In some other cases the temptation to rely upon the written assertion of a third party may occur not so much because of the lapse of time, but because the assertion may not seem quite so much like an assertion at all. In this category it is useful to consider such writings as labels upon objects and stamps upon documents.

The former circumstance arose in two cases heard by the Privy Council soon after the decision in *Myers*. In one[13] it was held that the words 'produce of Morocco' inscribed on bags of coriander seed were hearsay, and inadmissible as original evidence of the country of origin; in the other[14] it was held that labels upon, and even words indelibly stamped into,[15] various implements were also inadmissible hearsay to prove what they asserted, namely the country of origin. They had been placed upon the goods to make that assertion, and for no other purpose. They were thus rightly regarded as hearsay.

It is hard to reconcile these decisions with that in *Miller v Howe*[16] where the question was whether a particular breath testing device which had been used had been the one approved by the Home Secretary, an 'Alcotest 80'. In that case it was indicated that a label to that effect on the device would have been sufficient evidence of its identity, and even that the presence of such a label on the box containing the device was sufficient. This decision is itself inconsistent with the reasoning in *R v Cook*[17] where it seems to have been

11 They are then admissible under an exception to the rule against hearsay discussed in the next chapter.
12 (1863) 10 HL Cas 593 at 614. See also *Bristow v Cormican* (1878) 3 App Cas 641; *Neill v Duke of Devonshire* (1882) 8 App Cas 135.
13 *Patel v Comptroller of Customs* [1966] AC 356, [1965] 3 All ER 593. See also *Holmden v Bitar* (1987) 47 SASR 509 (labels on tins of paté).
14 *Comptroller of Customs v Western Electric Co Ltd* [1966] AC 367, [1965] 3 All ER 599.
15 In *Myers* itself no question was raised about the admissibility of evidence of the number acutally cast into the engine block.
16 [1969] 3 All ER 451, [1969] 1 WLR 1510.
17 (1980) 71 Cr App Rep 205.

assumed that a date stamp upon a document was hearsay.[18] It is submitted that, in principle, such a writing can be admitted consistently with the hearsay rule only when it is an identifying part of an object the identity of which is in issue, and not when it simply asserts a characteristic of the object.[19] Such a test discriminates between the number on the block in *Myers* and the letters on the handle in *Western Electric*. It seems to have been in the mind of the court in *Miller v Howe*, though it is very dubious whether that case can be brought within it, and still less the postmark cases.[20]

In these cases it seems that the writing, when properly admissible at all, is relevant not as an assertion of a state of facts, but as itself a fact, which affords circumstantial evidence upon the basis of which the jury may draw an inference as it may from any other relevant circumstance of the case. This reasoning was explicitly applied by the Court of Appeal in *R v Lydon*[1] in holding that the words 'Sean rules', found on a piece of paper near a gun discarded after the commission of a robbery, were relevant not to prove the truth of what they asserted, but because they were more likely to have been written by someone called Sean than not, and afforded some circumstantial support to the identification of the accused, whose name was Sean, as the robber.[2] There are however also cases where the writing does assert a state of fact, which is capable of being either true or false, but where the jury is invited to draw an inference, not from its truth to the fact which is asserted, but from its falsity to the asserter's state of mind. Thus in *R v Steel*[3] the accused who was charged with murder wished to tender evidence of a false alibi given to the police by another man who had been questioned about the killing. The question of its being hearsay was raised, and the court expressed its tentative view that it was, but was able to dispose of the case on the ground that it was in any event irrelevant because there might be any number of reasons for giving a false alibi. This seems correct. The only point of tendering a third party's statement as false can be to help to prove either the converse of that asserted, or a consciousness of guilt in the third party. It is unnecessary for the former purpose since ex hypothesi it must be possible to show by other evidence that the fact asserted is false, and the mere falsity of a proposition cannot as a matter of logic establish an inconsistent positive, as Scrutton LJ pointed out in *Hobbs v Tinling*:

---

18 Though it was, in fact, admitted under the business records exception. There is however some old and unreasoned English authority for the use of a postmark as admissible evidence of the place of posting at common law, *Perkin's* case (1826) 1 Lew CC 99. See also *R v Kelly* (1975) 12 SASR 389 and *R v Leroy* (1984) 55 ALR 338.

19 A similar distinction between matters going to the content and to the identity of a document was made in some older English cases, such as *Bucher v Jarratt* (1802) 3 Bos & P 143 at 146, and *Boyle v Wiseman* (1855) 11 Exch 360 at 367. See also more recent Australian cases, such as *Comr of Railways (NSW) v Young* (1962) 106 CLR 535 and *Ritz Hotel Ltd v Charles of the Ritz Ltd (No 21)* (1988) 14 NSWLR 128.

20 A more disturbing application of the same problem occurred in *R v Fizzell* (1987) 31 ACR 213 where the court rejected a forensic scientist's evidence of analysis which she had performed because she had relied upon the sample having been correctly taken and labelled by an absent assistant prior to her analysis.

1 (1987) 85 Cr App Rep 221 at 224.

2 Much the same reasoning was adopted by the High Court of Australia in *R v Chin* (1985) 16 ACR 147 where the fact that two suspects had both supplied the same five digit Malaysian business telephone number on their visa application was held admissible to help prove their prior acquaintance before coming to Australia.

3 Reported on this point only in (1981) 73 Cr App Rep 173. See also *R v Blastland* [1986] AC 41, [1985] 2 All ER 1095.

If by cross-examination as to credit your prove that a man's oath cannot be relied on, and he has sworn that he did not go to Rome on May 1st, you do not, therefore, prove that he did go to Rome on May 1st; there is simply no evidence on the subject.[4]

Nor on a similar basis is it likely to be sufficiently relevant for the latter purpose, for as *Steel* shows there may be any number of reasons for lying besides consciousness of guilt. This reasoning will dispose of almost all practical difficulty in such circumstances. The view that such a statement is hearsay is more dubious. It is not adduced as evidence of its truth, and it is hard to see how the lack of any opportunity to cross-examine weakens any inference to be drawn from it, since the roles of cross-examiner and examiner-in-chief are effectively reversed. In any rare case where it is sufficiently relevant, there is no special danger in allowing the statement to be recounted, shown to be false, and the jury left to draw what inference it chooses.

A similar question of an assertion implied by the production of a document is involved when it is sought to proceed by way of negative inference. In *R v Patel*[5] it was held to be hearsay when an immigration official recounted his unsuccessful scrutiny of Home Office records of valid registrations to show that a third party was an illegal immigrant. It would have made no difference if the records had themselves been produced. In order for the inference to be established it was necessary to call evidence of the method of compilation and custody; without it no inference as to the non-existence of the conditions necessary for such a record to exist could be drawn. Just such a course was taken in *R v Shone*[6] where the prosecution was permitted to prove, by calling the relevant record-keepers, that certain car parts had been stolen from a supplier, by showing that the records relating to those parts had not been inscribed as they would have been if they had been supplied in the course of the business. In that case it seems that between them the witnesses were able to prove the course of record-keeping from their own personal knowledge. It seems much more dubious when they have to rely upon information supplied by others, for example when the records are widely distributed, but it may occasionally be possible to surmount such difficulties by presenting such evidence as that of an expert whose expertise is in part derived from hearsay.[7] It might be better to address the special problems of negative hearsay by specific statutory provision.[8]

B. ORAL ASSERTIONS

The main difference between written and oral assertions is that in the former case there is some tangible evidence of the form of the third party's assertion, at least in those cases where the objection is not to hearsay upon hearsay. In the case of an oral assertion, the trier of fact must always rely upon the witness's version of the out-of-court assertion. In considering the various examples which follow, the main difference is that in the case of oral

4 [1929] 2 KB 1 at 21.
5 [1981] 3 All ER 94, 73 Cr App Rep 117.
6 (1983) 76 Cr App Rep 72.
7 This seems to be the only plausible explanation of the decision in *R v Muir* (1983) 79 Cr App Rep 153.
8 Like s 7 of the Civil Evidence (Scotland) Act 1988. See also US Federal Rules of Evidence, ss 803(7), (10); Evidence Act 1898, s 14 CH (New South Wales).

assertions there is often some difficulty in distinguishing clearly between arguments that such assertions are admissible because they fall outside the definition of hearsay, and that they are admissible as falling within an exception to the hearsay rule, especially that for contemporaneous utterances to explain a fact in issue or the asserter's state of mind or body.

The ordinary operation of the rule in relation to oral assertions is illustrated by cases such as *R v Gibson*[9] where a conviction for unlawful wounding was quashed because the prosecutor had been allowed to narrate a statement which he heard an unidentified woman make immediately after a stone had been thrown at him. The statement was 'The man who threw the stone went in there', and the maker of the statement pointed to the prisoner's house.

Sometimes the rule operates to the prejudice of the accused in a criminal case. In *Sparks v R*[10] an appeal from Bermuda, the accused, a white man, was charged with an indecent assault on a girl between three and four years old. About an hour and a half after the event, the child told her mother that a coloured boy did it. The child did not give evidence and the Judicial Committee held that the trial judge had rightly rejected the evidence of what the child had said to her mother, although the accused's appeal against conviction was allowed upon other grounds. No point was made with regard to the fact that the child would have been incompetent to testify if she had been called, and it appears that the decision would have been the same, if the victim had not testified, whatever her age.

In *R v Turner*[11] the Court of Appeal affirmed a striking illustration of the effect of the hearsay rule when holding that the judge had correctly refused to receive evidence that a third party, not called as a witness, had admitted to having committed the offence charged. The admission had in fact been withdrawn, but the decision would have been the same if the person who had made the admission had died, or become unavailable as a witness for some other reason, without withdrawing it.[12]

Further illustration of the breadth of the hearsay rule is provided by some old English cases in which it was held that a witness cannot give admissible evidence of the place or date of his own birth.[13] In more modern times, the fact that a witness cannot testify to his age without infringing the rule against hearsay has been stressed by the South African and Australasian courts.[14]

It should also be noted that the rule cannot be evaded by avoiding direct reference to the assertion. Thus in *R v Saunders*[15] a conviction for conspiracy to defraud was quashed on account of the reception of a police witness's answers to the following questions: 'Did you make inquiries as to whether any trade had been done by the prisoners?' and 'Did you, as a result of such inquiries, find that any had been done?' The answer to the first was in the

9 (1887) 18 QBD 537. It is possible that the statement might now be received as part of the res gestae, see ch XVIII below.
10 [1964] AC 964, [1964] 1 All ER 727. The statement was rejected as part of the res gestae because not sufficiently proximate in time.
11 (1975) 61 Cr App Rep 67 at 87.
12 See also *Re Van Beelen* (1974) 9 SASR 163; *Demeter v R* [1978] 1 SCR 538; *R v O'Brien* [1978] 1 SCR 591.
13 *R v Erith (Inhabitants)* (1807) 8 East 539; *R v Risworth (Inhabitants)* (1842) 2 QB 476; *R v Day* (1841) 9 C & P 722; *R v Rogers* (1914) 111 LT 1115.
14 *R v Corris* [1931] TPD 471; *R v Young* [1923] SASR 35; *Carlton and United Breweries v Cassin* [1956] VLR 186; *Smith v Police* [1969] NZLR 856.
15 [1899] 1 QB 490; *Buckley v I R C* [1962] NZLR 29; cf *R v Wilkins* (1849) 4 Cox CC 92.

affirmative, and the second met with a negative response. Although the matter is not discussed in the report, the rule against hearsay was infringed because the court was asked to act on assertions made to the witness by third persons with regard to the prisoners' business, and these third parties should have been called as witnesses.[16]

Cases of this sort serve as a reminder of the impropriety of the devices mentioned by Devlin LJ to make that which is in reality hearsay look as if it were nothing of the sort. The first:

consists in not asking what was said in a conversation or written in a document but in asking what the conversation or document was about; it is apparently thought that what would be hearsay if fully expressed is permissible if decently veiled. The other device is to ask by means of 'yes' or 'no' questions what was done (just answer yes or no. Did you go to see counsel? Do not tell us what he said but as a result of it did you do something? What did you do?). This device is commonly defended on the ground that counsel is asking only about what was done and not about what was said. But in truth what was done is relevant only because from it there can be inferred something about what was said.[17]

In all of these cases the objection was that the oral assertion was in one way or another adduced as evidence of the truth of the proposition asserted. In other cases the fact that it was made may in itself be in some sense in issue irrespective of its truth or falsity. The decision most commonly cited for the importance of this distinction is *Subramaniam v Public Prosecutor*.[18] In that case the defence to a charge of the unauthorised possession of ammunition was that the accused had been acting under duress. He sought to testify to threats offered to him by terrorists, but it was held at the trial that such evidence was hearsay. The Privy Council pointed out however that since it was the belief of the accused that was relevant, it was sufficient to prove merely that the threats were made.[19] Other cases where the utterance is used not for its truth, but to explain the state of mind, knowledge or emotion of the auditor include those where it is material to know the testator's belief as to the content of a will he is executing,[20] whether someone alleging fraud was misled,[1] the nature of a husband's belief concerning the destination of his wife on leaving him,[2] or the belief of the police in the existence of grounds for securing a warrant.[3] In these situations direct evidence of the utterances

---

16 It is especially dangerous hearsay because the inference is negative in character, and would require particularly convincing support in terms of evidence of the exhaustiveness of the relevant enquiries and the reliability of responses to them.

17 *Glinski v McIver* [1962] AC 726 at 780, [1962] 1 All ER 696 at 723.

18 [1956] 1 WLR 965.

19 The reasoning is equally acceptable when the absence of an oral utterance is in issue, see *R v Chapman* [1962] 2 QB 436, [1969] 2 All ER 321 (absence of complaint by doctor to proposal to administer breath test to his patient), though an alternative analysis categorising silence as a form of conduct is also possible.

20 *Doe d Small v Allen* (1799) 8 Term Rep 147 (statement to testator that second will duplicate of first admissible on issue of validity of second).

1 *Gray v New Augarita Porcupine Mines Ltd* [1952] 3 DLR 1 (statement by one company director to another admissible as suggesting that it was of such a nature that it could not mislead).

2 *Hoare v Allen* (1801) 3 Esp 276 (wife's statement to husband that she was going to her uncle admissible to rebut suggestion that husband had connived at her leaving him in order to go to defendant). This is another case where the utterer of the assertion was an incompetent witness.

3 See 1981 Report of the Royal Commission on Criminal Procedure (Cmnd 8092) para 3.66; *Minnesota v Purdy* 153 NW 2d 254 (1967).

of third parties capable of inducing such beliefs is not hearsay, and is admissible because it is not tendered as proof of the fact it asserts.

Similar reasoning has also been applied in the slightly different situation where the making of a statement has been used as evidence not of the state of mind of the person hearing it, but that of the person making it. Here again so long as the assertion is not being used as evidence of the truth of any matter asserted, it is admissible. Thus in *Woodhouse v Hall*[4] where it was necessary for the prosecution to prove that premises were being used for immoral purposes, a policeman was allowed to give evidence of an oral offer of immoral services to him on the premises. Here too it is sufficient that the utterance fall short of itself establishing a fact in issue, if its making is relevant to the issue. Thus in *R v Edmunds*[5] a demand for money made by the complainant was permitted to be proved in a trial for rape. It is also possible to have recourse to the statement of an absent third party made at the time of performing an otherwise equivocal action to explain the nature of the action. Thus in *Walters v Lewis*[6] the defendant was allowed to call a witness to say that he had heard the defendant's wife say 'this money is to pay for the sheep' when handing it over to a servant. The purpose of the evidence was simply to explain the nature of the wife's act.[7] The borderline of hearsay is however very close at this point, and it may be thought that *Lister v Smith*[8] crossed it in making no distinction between evidence of the statement of a testator, at the time of making a formally valid codicil and at other times, that he did not intend it to take effect.[9] The difference between the two situations is that when the words are uttered at the time of the act they explain, they can be regarded as part of that act which is independently relevant, but when they are uttered separately they can have no purpose other than to make an assertion about the quality of the earlier act. Such circumstantial relevance also appears to offer the best explanation of a number of Australasian cases involving betting.[10] The usual pattern in such cases is that the police seek to justify a charge of using premises for unlawful betting by tendering evidence of the receipt of telephone calls from third parties apparently making bets. In some cases the admission of this evidence is justified upon the basis that they are statements accompanying a relevant act. This is quite implausible since the words uttered constitute the relevant act of telephoning rather than accompany it. In these cases the fact that such

---

4 (1980) 72 Cr App Rep 39 the reasoning of which was applied by the Court of Appeal in *R v Wilson* (28 October 1983 unreported) (LEXIS).

5 (1833) 6 C & P 164.

6 (1836) 7 C & P 344.

7 It was regarded as irrelevant that the absent third party was an incompetent witness. See also *R v Lord Gordon* (1781) 21 St Tr 485 (words uttered during riot); *Hayslep v Gymer* (1834) 1 Ad & El 162 (words accompanying delivery of money).

8 (1863) 3 Sw & Tr 282.

9 It is hard to reconcile the reasoning with that in *Stobart v Dryden* (1836) 1 M & W 615 or *Re Wright, Hegan v Bloor* [1920] 1 Ch 108, though the evidence would now be admissible under the Civil Evidence Act 1968.

10 *Davidson v Quirke* [1923] NZLR 552; *Lenthall v Mitchell* [1933] SASR 231; *Marsson v O'Sullivan* [1951] SASR 224; *McGregor v Stokes* [1952] VLR 347; *Marshall v Watt* [1953] Tas SR 1; *Gorman v Newton* [1958] SR Qd 169; *Mathewson v Police* [1969] NZLR 218; *Police v Machirus* [1977] 1 NZLR 288; *Fingleton v Lowen* (1979) 20 SASR 312. Most American cases have admitted the evidence on similar grounds, see for example *State v Tolisano* 70 A 2d 118 (1949); but it is now sometimes accepted that this result is achieved only on account of the restrictive definition of hearsay in the Federal Rules, see *US v Zenni* 492 F Supp 464 (1950).

calls are made is itself a relevant piece of circumstantial evidence from which the jury may draw an inference as to the beliefs held by the callers, and the reasons for such beliefs. The calls do not themselves assert anything. They are neither true nor false. It is submitted that the ban on circumstantial inference is restricted to circumstantial inference from explicit assertions. A defensible line can be drawn between evidence of a call explicitly asserting premises to be used for betting, which is hearsay and admissible neither directly as evidence of the nature of the premises, nor circumstantially as evidence of the belief of such callers;[11] and evidence of the receipt of calls ostensibly placing bets which is admissible directly to show that such calls were made, and circumstantially to show the beliefs of their makers. A similar line of reasoning was adopted by the Privy Council in *Ratten v R.* In that case the accused was charged with the murder of his wife. The disputed evidence was that of a telephone operator testifying to receiving a call from the deceased, asking for the police in a distressed voice. Here too Lord Wilberforce expressed the view that the evidence of the call having been made was not hearsay:

> The mere fact that evidence of a witness includes evidence as to words spoken by another person who is not called is no objection to its admissibility. Words spoken are facts just as much as any other action by a human being. If the speaking of words is a relevant fact, a witness may give evidence that they were spoken. A question of hearsay only arises when the words are relied on 'testimonially', ie as establishing some fact narrated by the words.[12]

It is submitted that the operator's evidence was admissible directly to show that the call had been made in a distressed voice, and that the jury was rightly instructed that it could use it circumstantially to justify the inference that the maker had been in a state of fear at the time of making it. It would have been quite different if the call had asserted that the accused was threatening the deceased with his gun. In that case it would have been hearsay of the fact it asserted, and to preserve the force of that rule it could not be used circumstantially to justify an inference of the fact asserted. Telephone calls create special difficulties because of the necessity to pass information over the line between physically separated parties to identify each to the other.[13] It has been suggested that a special exception should be made to the hearsay rule to admit statements made in such a way identifying the speaking party.[14] In the absence of any such exception a direct assertion of identity will attract the operation of the hearsay rule.[15] It seems to have been hardly necessary, nor even consistent with *Ratten*, for it to have been held in *R v Harry*[16] that an inquiry by drug seekers, over the telephone situated in a given flat where drugs had been found, for a co-defendant, was

11 See *R v Ryan* (1984) 55 ALR 408 where an explicit assertion of the identity of the caller was rejected as evidence of his identity.
12 [1972] AC 378 at 387, [1971] 3 All ER 801 at 805.
13 In *Coles v R* (1984) 9 ACR 419 the court appears to have been prepared to assume that where telephone calls were made to a given number that the subscriber could be taken to be the person answering it, at least in the absence of any convincing evidence to the contrary. But in *R v Chedzey* (1987) 30 ACR 451 where a scientific device for tracing calls was used, the court was not prepared to accept that the number so traced was in truth the origination of the call.
14 Deane J in *Walton v R* (1989) 84 ALR 59 at 77.
15 See *R v Ryan* (1984) 55 ALR 408.
16 (1988) 86 Cr App Rep 105.

inadmissible hearsay when tendered to show the belief of the callers that the co-accused, so named, was the only supplier there.

It is difficult to explain the reception of the evidence in *Lloyd v Powell Duffryn Steam Coal Co Ltd*.[17] A claim was made upon the behalf of the posthumous child of a miner killed in an accident. He had not been married to the child's mother, and in order to establish the necessary condition of dependency the plaintiff sought to rely upon assertions by the deceased that he was the father of the child and intended to marry the mother. In the Court of Appeal[18] the evidence had been rejected upon the ground that such statements did not fall within the exception to the hearsay rule in favour of the assertions of deceased persons against interest. In the House of Lords the defendant was represented by different counsel, and the plaintiff succeeded on altogether different arguments. Although the speeches are not wholly consistent it seems that some of their Lordships regarded the statements as not amounting to hearsay. This may be interpreted as suggesting that they were regarded as providing circumstantial evidence from which the state of mind of the deceased could be inferred:

> The significance consists in the improbability that any man would make these statements, true or false, unless he believed himself to be the father of the child ...[19]
>
> The testimony of the witness is to the act, ie to the deceased speaking these words, and it is the speaking of the words which is the matter that is put in evidence and which possesses evidential value. The evidence is, therefore, not in any respect open to the objection that it is secondary or hearsay evidence.[20]

Some of their Lordships laid stress upon the fact that the hearsay rule is less vigorously applied to issues of status, and given both the well-known exceptions in favour of declarations as to contemporaneous state of mind and body, and the absence of any danger of perception or memory, it is possible to understand the rather generous view which was taken.

A different sort of complication arises when it is sought to prove a fact by the combination of the testimony of two different witnesses. In general if witness A testifies that witness B told him that he perceived a crime committed by X that evidence is hearsay of the commission of the crime by X. On the other hand this normally causes no problem as B's evidence that X committed the crime, being based upon his own perception, is not hearsay, but admissible direct evidence. The problem arises when B is unable to give such direct evidence to the court. This difficulty has arisen in two main situations, when B can no longer testify either because he has forgotten or for some other reason; and when the court cannot understand B's testimony without interpretation.

The former situation is exemplified by a number of cases in which a car number is observed by one person and recorded at his behest by another. By the time of trial the person who observed the number can no longer remember what it was, and the person who recorded it cannot testify to having observed it. In *R v McLean*[1] both persons were available to testify, but the Court of Criminal Appeal felt obliged to reject the evidence of the

---

17 [1914] AC 733.
18 Sub nom *Ward v Pitt & Co* [1913] 2 KB 130.
19 Lord Atkinson at 741.
20 Lord Moulton at 752.
 1 (1967) 52 Cr App Rep 80.

recorder as hearsay, and of the observer as to having dictated it correctly as irrelevant. It should be noted that if the observer had written down the number himself, or perhaps even if he had seen it being written by the recorder and checked its accuracy at the time, he could use it to refresh his memory in court, and so give direct oral evidence of the number.[2]

In all of these cases the issue hinged upon the identification of a car, but the principle is no different if it relates to the identification of a human being. Here authority appears to point in the opposite direction. In *R v Burke and Kelly*[3] the victim of a crime identified the accused as the criminal shortly afterwards, but by the time of the trial was unable to repeat the feat. Baron Lefroy then permitted the prosecution to call a police witness to swear to such identification. A similar situation occurred in *R v Osbourne and Virtue*[4] where the police officer in charge of an identification parade was permitted to testify to the identification of the accused by a witness who gave evidence at the trial, but could not then remember that she had identified the accused. No hearsay point was taken, and the car number cases were not cited.[5] The presence of the two witnesses in court may be regarded as mitigating the danger of relying upon the evidence since both are available for cross-examination, but the usefulness of such cross-examination is greatly reduced when the only witness to have made the relevant observation is able to remember nothing about it, save that it was reported accurately. It is indeed hard to see upon what basis such a saving can be affirmed, given the premise. Nevertheless the High Court of Australia, after hearing full argument on the point, has held evidence of an out-of-court identification not to be hearsay.[6]

The other situation in which similar problems arise is that in which the observer cannot express himself in a language which the court can understand. Here too it can be argued that no witness can be allowed to testify what another asserted in order to prove the truth of that assertion, and that it can make no difference that the witness is an interpreter, and that the other is present, if he cannot testify directly. In *R v Attard*[7] when the interrogation of a Maltese took place out of court, the police officer who took notes of the answers furnished by an interpreter was not permitted to give

---

2 This course was suggested in *Jones v Metcalfe* [1967] 3 All ER 205, [1967] 1 WLR 1286, and applied in *R v Kelsey* (1982) 74 Cr App Rep 213. See also *Grew v Cubitt* [1951] 2 TLR 305. In *R v Townsend* [1987] Crim LR 411 the witness had run out of ink, but it was possible to treat the paper afterwards so as to reproduce the number which would have been inscribed, and the witness was permitted to refresh memory by reference to the treated version. Similar evidence has been admitted in other jurisdictions, see *S v Tuge* 1966 (4) SA 565; *Bradpiece v South British Insurance Co Ltd* 1966 (2) SA 629; *Guy and Finger v R* [1978] WAR 125.

3 (1847) 2 Cox CC 295.

4 [1973] QB 678, [1973] 1 All ER 649; this is also allowed in Scotland, see *Smith v HM Advocate* 1986 SCCR 135 where the evidence is permitted even though it contradicts that of the witness at the trial.

5 The point appears to have been first taken by Libling 'Evidence of Past Identification' [1977] Crim LR 268; see further below p 722.

6 *Alexander v R* (1981) 145 CLR 395. Gibbs CJ accepted this only in the case where the identifying witness was prepared to swear to the correctness of his previous identification. It has been held to apply even more strongly to identification of a voice out of court, *R v Smith* [1984] 1 NSWLR 462. The majority view appears to prevail in New Zealand, see *R v Howard* [1987] 1 NZLR 347; in Canada now see *R v Swanston* (1982) 33 BCLR 391. In the United States evidence of prior identification is deemed not to be hearsay, Federal Rules of Evidence, r 801 (d) (1) (C).

7 (1958) 43 Cr App Rep 90.

evidence of those answers. In that case the interpreter was not called to give evidence. The wholly beneficial consequence was that the Home Office issued a circular suggesting that interpreters make notes of their interpretation, and be prepared to give evidence. It is submitted that adoption of such a procedure is much more likely to be conducive to the tender of satisfactory evidence, than to rely upon the unassisted oral testimony of the questioner and interpreter, effectively untestable by cross-examination. It may sometimes be the case that the interpreter is unable to take a note, perhaps because he cannot write.[8] In such a case however a note could be taken by the questioner, and agreed by the interpreter, which would be sufficient to allow it to be used to refresh the memory of either party. An alternative and still better way of resolving the problem is to take a sound recording of the interrogation which can then be used in a convenient way by both parties and by the court.[9]

The problem of implied assertions can also arise in relation to speech. It is submitted that the best solution is that advanced above in relation to writing namely, that the rule should apply to exclude only that speech which is primarily intended to assert the proposition of fact which it is adduced to prove. In some cases a relevant assertion can be implied from an irrelevant explicit assertion. Thus if A is heard to say 'I saw X drown his wife', and it transpires that X's wife survived, the implied assertion that A saw X perform acts which would have led to his wife drowning, is clearly hearsay of X's action even though it makes no explicit assertion of them.

There will still be cases where the borderline between speech primarily intended to be assertive, and that which is not will be very difficult to draw. It is submitted that the borderline may properly be drawn somewhere between a hypothetical variation upon the facts of *R v Gibson*[10] whereby the witness deposes not that he was told that the man ran into a particular house, but that he heard a witness say 'Hello Gibson' to him. It can be argued that such a remark is not primarily intended to assert the identity of Gibson, but to greet him personally. Upon this analysis the greeting can be retailed to the court as evidence of the speaker's belief in Gibson's presence, and inferentially of his presence. On the other hand the remark of the bystander in *Teper v R*[11] may be thought to fall on the other side of the line. In that case the appellant had been convicted of the arson of his own shop. The only evidence to contradict his alibi was that of a policeman who swore that, in approaching the shop some twenty-five minutes after the conflagration began he heard a woman in the crowd of spectators exclaim to a passing motorist who bore some resemblance to the accused, 'Your place burning and you going away from the fire.' The only function of this utterance is to assert the presence of the owner of the shop and remark upon the peculiarity of his conduct. As such it was, it is submitted rightly, regarded as hearsay, and held to be inadmissible evidence of the presence of the accused at the scene, so long as it fell within no recognised exception to the hearsay rule.

No question of hearsay is involved if a statement is adduced as demonstrably

---

8 This occurred in *Gaio v R* (1960) 104 CLR 419, where the High Court of Australia admitted the evidence though different judges justified its admission in different ways. See also *R v Mutchke* [1946] AD 874; and for a summary of the position in the United States, see 12 ALR 4th 1017.

9 The procedure adopted in *R v Maqsud Ali* [1966] 1 QB 688, [1965] 2 All ER 464.

10 (1887) 18 QBD 537; see above p 522.

11 [1952] AC 480, [1952] 2 All ER 447. The statement was rejected as part of the res gestae.

false. Thus in *A-G v Good* where a wife's untrue statement that her husband was away from home was received on the issue whether he intended to defraud his creditors, Garrow B said:

> The doubt on the present occasion has originated in calling that hearsay evidence which has no approximation to it. The answer is received as a distinct fact in itself, to be compared and combined with other facts; . . . Suppose an unreasonable time had intervened between the demand of entrance and the opening of the door . . . is not that a circumstance to be inquired into with a view to the fact under investigation . . .[12]

Another situation in which a false statement may be adduced for the circumstantial inference to be drawn from it is, for example, one where the witness swears that he heard a person whose sanity is in issue claiming to be Napoleon, or one where in order to help fix the time of a person's death a witness swears that he heard the deceased asserting, at a relevant time, his innocence of possession of goods subsequently found to have been in his pocket.

C. CONDUCT

If, as submitted above, the hearsay rule bites only upon express assertions it is obvious that examples of conduct as hearsay are going to be rare. The High Court of Australia has remarked that 'acts (other than certain acts of communication) cannot of themselves constitute hearsay and, strictly speaking, lie outside the rule'.[13] The clearest case of an act of communication is one in which the acts constitute a form of sign language. *Chandrasekera v R*[14] is a convenient example. The accused was charged with the murder of a woman by cutting her throat. Before her death she had in the presence of witnesses, and in response to the question of who had attacked her, made signs indicative of driving oxen, and had pointed at a policeman and made signs of slapping her face. These signs were immediately interpreted as referring to the accused who drove oxen, and had been in trouble for slapping a policeman's face. Similarly it could make no difference whether a witness at an identification parade said to someone on the parade 'you are the man who attacked me', or in response to a direction to tap her attacker on the shoulder was seen to tap the accused's shoulder.[15] A slightly less direct form of communication occurs when people agree to play a part in the reconstruction of events in which they were involved. It is increasingly common for such reconstructions to be used by the police in the investigation of crime, and by medical and social workers in the treatment and diagnosis of the sexual abuse of young children. It is becoming common for such

---

12 (1825) M'Cle & Yo 286 at 290. See also *Mawaz Khan v R and Amanat Khan* [1967] 1 AC 454, where it was alleged that a false alibi had been concocted by two co-accused, and Lord Hodson said of the statement at 462 'they can without any breach of the hearsay rule be used, not for the purpose of establishing the truth of the assertions contained therein, but for the purpose of asking the jury to hold the assertions false and to draw inferences from their falsity.'

13 *Ahern v R* (1988) 80 ALR 161 at 163, though in fact the Court adopted a laxer view on the facts before it. See also *R v McKinnon* (1989) 70 CR (3d) 10.

14 [1937] AC 220, [1936] 3 All ER 865.

15 As in *R v Osbourne, R v Virtue* [1973] QB 678, [1973] 1 All ER 649. See also *US v Ross* 321 F2d 61 at 69 (1963) (name on list pointed out as that of accused).

reconstructions to be recorded on videotape, often with a sound commentary. It is accordingly necessary to consider the evidentiary status of such taped reconstructions. It seems that it accordance with the views expressed above such reconstructions will, in principle, be regarded as forms of assertion, and hence as hearsay. The Privy Council made this clear in *Li Shu-ling v R*:[16]

> If the three performers who made the film had described their act in out-of-court statements those statements would be hearsay and not admissible. A demonstration given on film is open to the same objection.

In most criminal cases the principal performer is the accused, and the film, may, provided that the appropriate safeguards for the admission of confessional assertions[17] have been satisfied, be admitted[18] under the appropriate exception to the hearsay rule.[19] In the child sexual abuse cases however the child, who is sometimes encouraged to play with dolls representing the relevant human beings, is rarely a party and such films cannot easily be brought within any exception to the hearsay rule.[20] Strong judicial misgivings[1] of the dangers inherent in the procedures involved in the making of such films indicate the need for caution in any proposal for wholesale abandonment of the hearsay rule.

In a number of recent cases questions have arisen as to the admissibility of 'photofit' pictures compiled by witnesses. These seem in principle no different from the cases mentioned above, and hence to amount to hearsay, and to be inadmissible in the absence of a recognised exception to the hearsay rule. Despite Lord Morris's explicit rejection in *Sparks v R*[2] of the notion that the hearsay rule operates differently in relation to questions of identification, such a view now seems to have prevailed in relation to 'photofit' identification. In *R v Cook*[3] the Court of Appeal held the construction of a photofit picture, or of a drawing made to the specification of a witness,[4] not to fall within the hearsay rule. It was reasoned that such situations were analogous to the taking of a contemporaneous photograph.[5] In so holding the court appears to have assumed equivalent objectivity in the combination of human beings composing 'photofit' or drawing, and camera. It is submitted that such an assessment is extremely optimistic, and that the chances of error and misdescription are very much greater in the former situations, and so great

---

16 [1988] AC 270 at 278, [1988] 3 All ER 138 at 141.

17 Including discretionary safeguards which may be particularly appropriate given that accused persons are unlikely to be accomplished actors, may be susceptible to leads offered, perhaps inadvertently, by other actors in the reconstruction, and given that a film is invariably more dramatic than any form of reconstruction in words alone rendering it extremely difficult to affect the jury's impression once the film has been shown to them.

18 Such tapes were admitted in Australia in *R v Lowery and King* [1972] VR 554 and in *Collins v R* (1980) 31 ALR 257, in Canada in *R v Tookey and Stevenson* (1981) 58 CCC (2d) 421, and in the *United States People v Dabb* 32 Cal 2d 491 (1948).

19 See further below ch XVIII, section 1.

20 See now Children Act 1989, s 96(3) and regulations made thereunder, Children (Admissibility of Hearsay Evidence) Order 1990 (SI 1990 No 143).

1 See, for example, *Re E (A Minor)* (1990) Times, 2 April.

2 [1964] AC 964 at 981, [1964] 1 All ER 727 at 735.

3 [1987] QB 417, [1987] 1 All ER 1049. See also *R v Constantinou* [1989] Crim LR 571, and discussion below at p 719.

4 See *R v Percy Smith* [1976] Crim LR 511.

5 Such photographs are certainly admissible as real evidence and, as such, lie outside the hearsay rule, see further, above, p 47.

as to justify the application of the hearsay rule in the ordinary way to such out-of-court descriptions and actions.

In this area the greatest, though almost entirely theoretical, difficulty is caused by the possibility of implying assertions from conduct. It might never have arisen but for some remarks of Baron Parke in *Wright v Doe d Tatham* where he said:[6]

> the supposed conduct of the family or relations of a testator, taking the same precautions in his absence as if he were a lunatic; his election, in his absence, to some high and responsible office; the conduct of a physician who permitted a will to be executed by a sick testator; the conduct of a deceased captain on a question of sea-worthiness, who, after examining every part of the vessel, embarked in it with his family; all these, when deliberately considered, are, with reference to the matter in issue in each case, mere instances of hearsay evidence, mere statements, not on oath, but implied in or vouched by the actual conduct of persons by whose acts the litigant parties are not to be bound.

While it is clear that an out-of-court explicit assertion of sea-worthiness by the captain would be hearsay, and inadmissible, it does not necessarily follow that evidence of his conduct apparently evincing a belief in such a state of affairs must also be so categorised and so treated. The fact of acting upon his belief must reduce the danger of insincerity. Nor is it clear where such an analysis of conduct as hearsay would end. Every human action can be presented as an implied assertion of the actor's belief in the satisfaction of the conditions under which he would be prepared to perform it.[7] Any such analysis would inevitably lead to confusion since much hearsay so extensively defined would go unrecognised, and injustice would occur on account of the anomalies which would flood into the problem of the admissibility of evidence.[8] Further support for this approach is provided by the reasoning preferred by the Privy Council in *Ratten v R*[9] so far as the implication was based upon the conduct of the caller.

It is submitted that it is better to accept the dictates of commonsense, and to restrict the definition of implied hearsay to that implied by conduct itself intended to be assertive.

Baron Parke's view was not necessary for his decision in *Wright v Doe d Tatham*. It remains to be seen whether there is any authority to support it.

6 (1837) 7 Ad & El 313 at 387.
7 It is rarely suggested in England that involuntary conduct can be categorised as hearsay, see *R v Turner* [1975] QB 834 at 840, [1975] 1 All ER 70 at 73, ('the facts on which the psychiatrist based his opinion were hearsay save for those which he observed for himself during his examination of the appellant such as his appearance of depression and his becoming emotional when discussing the deceased girl and his own family'); in the United States there is some divergence of opinion, compare *Bagwell & Stewart Inc v Bennett* 107 SE2d 824 (1959) (not hearsay to prove vomiting when odour emitted by factory inhaled), with *Norriss v Detroit United Railway* 151 NW 747 (1915) (evidence of doctor that patient flinched when pressure applied to ankle held to be hearsay). Absence of involuntary reaction has even on occasion been accepted, see *Anthony v Public Transit Co* 130 A 895 (1925) (to show loss of sensation in limb).
8 A salutary warning is provided by *Iowa v Menilla* 158 NW 645 (1916) in which evidence of the flight of a third party was held to be inadmissible hearsay of the third party's guilt of the offence with which the accused stood charged, but evidence of his having attempted to conceal a revolver was held admissible evidence of his guilt.
9 [1972] AC 378, [1971] 3 All ER 801, above p 525. Their Lordships went on to consider the admissibility of the evidence as *res gestae*, but not because they thought it strictly necessary to do so, see below p 661.

One possible class of situation is that in which the actor's conduct evinces some consciousness of guilt, for example driving away after an accident or fleeing the scene of a crime. In *Holloway v McFeeters*[10] the judges in the majority appeared to take the view that evidence that a driver must have been aware of having hit a pedestrian, but had driven away without reporting the matter was hearsay, though all of them favoured the admission of the evidence for one reason or another. Dixon J was however prepared to permit the evidence to be received as a circumstance of the death, and to permit inferences to be drawn from it, even though on his view of the issues no exception to the hearsay rule was available. Flight from the scene of a crime is traditionally regarded as hearsay in the United States, though once again invariably admitted either as a confession if it is the accused's flight, or under an extension of the declaration against interest exception if it is that of a third party.[11] The problem is likely to remain more theoretical than practical in this country so long as the court sticks to the robust view expressed in *R v Steel*[12] that there are so many various possible motives for human conduct that its mere occurrence will very rarely warrant the implied assertion of just one of them. It should also be noted that in the many cases where a party attempts to bribe witnesses from the other side,[13] tells demonstrable lies in or out of court,[14] or remains silent in the face of an accusation which demands an answer[15] the court does not regard it as necessary to labour over the exercise of first classifying the evidence as hearsay and then justifying its admission by invocation of an exception to the exclusionary rule.

Other situations raising the issue of conduct as implied hearsay involve the treatment of things or persons. In *Manchester Brewery v Coombs* the defendant wished to prove that beer supplied by the plaintiff had been of poor quality. He proposed to call witnesses to testify to complaints which had been received from customers. Farwell J was disposed to permit such testimony for the interesting reason that in his view:[16]

> Counsel can certainly ask as to facts—Did the customer order beer? Did he finish it? What did he do with it? If the matter is left there with the answer that he tasted and left it or threw it away, the judge cannot avoid drawing an inference . . .

This is the exact converse of the reasoning in *Wright v Tatham*. There it was argued that since an explicit assertion would clearly be hearsay, conduct justifying the same inference must also be excluded on the same basis; here it is argued that since conduct is clearly admissible, there is no point in excluding assertions to the same effect.[17] A rather similar view seems to have

---

10 (1956) 94 CLR 470.
11 See *Chambers v Mississippi* 410 US 295 (1973) where the Supreme Court held the exclusion of defence evidence of the flight of a third party on a hearsay basis to be unconstitutional.
12 [1981] 2 All ER 422, [1981] 1 WLR 690.
13 *Moriarty v London, Chatham and Dover Railway Co* (1870) LR 5 QB 314.
14 *R v Lucas* [1981] QB 720, [1981] 2 All ER 1008.
15 *Bessela v Stern* (1877) 2 CPD 265.
16 (1900) 82 LT 347.
17 Where such conduct is not also available, reported statements of reasons given by customers, not themselves called to give evidence, are excluded as hearsay, see *Tilk v Parsons* (1825) 2 C & P 201, unless the reasons are relevant to an issue irrespective of their truth or falsity, for example to show that rejection of goods was on account of rumours spread by the defendant, *International Tobacco Ltd SA v United Tobacco Co (South) Ltd* 1953 (3) SA 343.

inspired the opinion expressed by Morris LJ in *Re Jenion, Jenion v Wynne* that:[18]

> Evidence of a bare and isolated declaration not linked with evidence of conduct and action gives no guidance to the truth if no heed be paid to the declaration itself.

That case was concerned with the admissibility of statements tending to show the illegitimacy of certain children. Statements to that effect by the deceased mother were admitted under the pedigree exception to the hearsay rule, but the Court of Appeal was also prepared to admit statements made by the putative father as original evidence. This may be somewhat dubious, but it is clear from the quoted passage that Morris LJ, whatever might have been his doubts on that score, was not prepared to take the same view of conduct towards the children on the part of the putative father.

There seems then to be no clear authority in favour of treating conduct not primarily intended to be assertive as hearsay in English law,[19] and a number of more modern contra-indications to outweigh the dicta of Baron Parke.

SECTION 3. REFORM OF THE RULE[20]

Although Wigmore regarded the hearsay rule as the 'most characteristic rule of the Anglo-American law of Evidence—a rule which may be esteemed, next to jury trial, the greatest contribution of that eminently practical legal system to the world's methods of procedure',[1] not all views have been quite so complimentary, with for example both Lord Reid[2] and Lord Diplock[3] judicially categorising it as absurd.

It was seen in section 1 above that the hearsay rule developed alongside that of the newer form of trial by jury, and was concerned to prevent its being undermined by the introduction of evidence which could not easily be tested by cross-examination in open court. Both of these justifications are now much weaker than once they were. The overwhelming majority of trials are now conducted without a jury, and a more literate and technologically advanced society provides and depends upon more reliable methods of keeping track of what has happened than can possibly be provided by the unassisted recollection of witnesses, even though exposed to cross-examination by an opponent.

It remains true however that in some circumstances such records are not available, and the hearsay rule can then be relied upon to prevent the deliberate dilution of proof by straining out the testimony of those with direct personal knowledge of relevant events, and by seeking to substitute

---

18 [1952] Ch 454 at 484, [1952] 1 All ER 1228 at 1245.
19 Some American authority does recognise conduct as hearsay, see, for example, *Thompson v Manhattan Railway Co* 42 NY Sup 896 (App Div, 1896) (treatment by doctor hearsay when tendered to show nature of injury), though in many such cases there is some suggestion that the conduct was regarded as hearsay only because it was itself induced by the assertions of a fourth party, and thus the objection may really have been to hearsay upon hearsay.
20 Different approaches to reform of the rule are extensively discussed in Law Reform Commission of Australia Research Paper No 9 *Hearsay Law Reform—Which Approach* (1982).
1 5 Wigmore *Evidence* 1364.
2 In *Myers v D P P* [1965] AC 1001 at 1019, [1964] 2 All ER 881 at 884.
3 In *Jones v Metcalfe* [1967] 3 All ER 205 at 208, [1967] 1 WLR 1286 at 1291.

for it the bland reportage of those who know only what they have been told by others. The business of reform thus seeks to prevent the rule from causing unnecessary difficulty, while at the same time preserving its efficiency. For many years the task was left to the judges to proceed by way of elaboration of the rule and the development of exceptions in the course of deciding cases, the traditional method of the common law. This has the advantage of proceeding step by step, and of permitting the isolation, or even retraction, of a step in the wrong direction. It is particularly well-suited to the detection of situations in which the rule is peculiarly prone to cause difficulty, and of those in which the absence of cross-examination is unlikely to create serious risks. It is less adept in securing such situations from deliberate manipulation, and in providing a secure foundation of certainty for the adoption of new techniques of record-keeping. To achieve these ends, it may be thought that legislative intervention provides a more appropriate means of change.

Some pressure for change has been felt for many years, and in many different jurisdictions. The fruits of that pressure will be explored in the following chapters, this section will no more than outline the operation of the principal engines to apply it, namely common law and statute.

A. COMMON LAW

As noted in section 1, the hearsay rule is a generic term which came to be applied to a number of cognate rules excluding evidence of much the same character for much the same reasons. It began to crystallise in judicial decisions principally during the later eighteenth and earlier nineteenth centuries. It may be said that the sharpening analysis of the range of the rule, and the elaboration of exceptions to it, particularly towards the end of that period, constitute the contribution of the common law to the reform of the rule. The recognition of exceptions probably illustrates the nature of that contribution most clearly. It has been suggested that the aim of reforming the rule is to prevent its rigid application causing unnecessary hardship, while at the same time preserving its efficiency. This suggests that hearsay should be admitted where it is especially difficult to secure other evidence, provided that there is some guarantee of its reliability. It will be seen that in the development of exceptions to the rule sometimes one of these factors predominates, and sometimes the other.

The most obvious difficulty is created in cases where the evidence occurred so long ago that no one who can speak from their own personal knowledge is left alive. This led to the creation of a number of exceptions where the statement was made by a deceased person. The weakness of reform by common law is indicated by the fact that analogous situations, such as those where the witness could not be found, was overseas, had gone mad, or could not reasonably be expected to remember the matter were rarely provided for. One of the strengths of this procedure is however also indicated by the fact that the death of its maker was never a sufficient condition for the admissibility of a statement. Some further necessity, or a special warrant of reliability was invariably required. Thus an exception was created for statements of family pedigree.

It may also be necessary to rely upon hearsay when there is only one person who can have any direct knowledge of the relevant matter, such as his own bodily sensations, emotions and intentions. Another group of exceptions has been created to cope with the difficulty posed by this situation. Sometimes the very nature of the matter to be proved excludes the possibility of a witness having direct personal knowledge free from the taint of hearsay. Thus a witness may indeed have direct personal knowledge of a person's reputation, but that knowledge can come only from hearsay since it is fundamental to the nature of a reputation that it may be undeserved. If a man's reputation as an adulterer is in issue, no amount of evidence of his having committed or not having committed adultery can prove it, but only evidence of the assertions of others, and that is relevant quite irrespective of the personal knowledge of those making such assertions.

Occasionally the problem relates to the form in which the evidence is presented. Very often evidence of what is technically and strictly hearsay, such as the time of day derived from seeing a public clock, or the name of a town derived from reading a sign, is accepted without any adversion to a problem. The most common case where trouble can be caused arises in connection with the basis for an expert opinion. It is sometimes impossible for such an opinion to be tendered without placing implicit reliance upon the assertions of others, ranging from those to be found in established works of reference, through independent studies to isolated pieces of casual information. As noted in ch XIII above, some such hearsay is accepted just because expert opinion cannot be entirely pruned of it.

The second factor is reliability. It may in very exceptional cases be sufficient to justify the creation of an exception, that for the admission of statements in certain public records may provide an example, though even there necessity is often also present. More frequently it has, by itself, been insufficient to justify the creation of an exception, as illustrated by *Myers v D P P* where it was conceded that the records were perfectly reliable. It may however help to hew out from the broader face of necessity those categories of case where an exception can be allowed. Thus in the case of deceased persons it has been felt that if the statement was against the interest of its maker, made in the course of duty, or made in the belief of imminent death, then there was a sufficient guarantee of truthfulness to justify the reception of the evidence. Yet here too the deficiencies of the common law as a vehicle for reform have become apparent. It seems no more than an accident of the history of the development of the rule that a proprietary interest, but not a penal interest, could guarantee the truth of the statement of a deceased person, or that a deceased person under the belief of imminent demise would tell the truth about the identity of his assailant, but about nothing else.

In those cases reliability was furnished otherwise than by the availability of the declarant for cross-examination. Such availability may itself constitute a sufficient guarantee of reliability in some circumstances of necessity, for example when a witness who has given evidence in earlier proceedings dies, or is too ill to testify. Here the law is careful to ensure that the guarantee shall be sufficient, and so insists that the proceedings relate to the same matter, and that the opportunity to cross-examine was available to the same party. It may be noted that in this case the common law took account of illness as well as death, perhaps because the opportunity to cross-examine was thought a particularly substantial safeguard. Once again the infirmity of the common law method is indicated by the exemption from this relaxation of cases where the witness cannot be produced to testify for some other reason, such as not being able to be found.

The passage from *Myers* which was quoted earlier[4] has in England marked the end of any further likelihood of reform of the hearsay rule by way of the development of common law exceptions. In other jurisdictions the courts are less restricted. Thus in the area of business records, both the High Court of Australia before *Myers*,[5] and the Supreme Court of Canada after that decision,[6] have felt able to develop the common law. So also in the United States when it was sought to establish the cause of a defect in a building, the court felt able to refer, by witting exception to the hearsay rule, to a contemporary newspaper account of the fire in the building some fifty years earlier, and to justify its reference on the simple ground that the evidence was admissible because it was 'necessary and trustworthy, relevant and material'.[7]

B. LEGISLATION

In *Myers* Lord Reid recommended reform of the rule 'by legislation following on a wide survey of the whole field'. He seems to have taken the view that the rule was too diverse, yet too interconnected in its parts, for the fortuitous litigation of an arbitrary collection of cases, to reshape it in a coherent manner. In view of his recommendation of a wide survey of the whole field, it might have been regarded as ironic that the legislature's immediate response was to pass legislation, specifically limited to the admission of business records in criminal cases. It should not be overlooked that similar specific legislation had been used to plug gaps in the rule for many years, for example, the Bankers' Books Evidence Act 1879. The existence of such pockets of legislation provided a further reason to abandon the common law as a vehicle for reform. The ordinary principles of statutory interpretation proceed upon the presumption that a statute intends to affect only that to which it expressly refers, particularly when derogating from the common law. Given such a principle, and given the existence of statutes on a number of isolated subjects, it becomes very difficult to invoke common law exceptions in related areas. For example, if there is a specific exception for bankers' books, it becomes difficult to create a common law exception for, say, other financial records relied upon in the conduct of business.

The result has been that in most Commonwealth jurisidictions Lord Reid's advice has been accepted, general surveys have been conducted, and in many cases their results enshrined in legislative enactment. In England the situation has been complicated by the fact that the survey recommended by Lord Reid was divided between the Law Reform Committee, and the Criminal Law Revision Committee. This complication was further aggravated by the adoption of different styles of approach by the two bodies. The Law Reform Committee issued its reports on evidence topic by topic as it completed its work, and in particular its recommendations on hearsay in 1966.[8] The Criminal Law Revision Committee published its single composite report on evidence, including hearsay, in 1972.[9] The Law Reform Committee

---

4 See above p 512.
5 *Potts v Miller* (1940) 64 CLR 282.
6 *Ares v Venner* [1970] SCR 608.
7 *Dallas County v Commercial Union Assurance Co Ltd* 286 F 2d 388 (1961) at 397.
8 *Hearsay Evidence in Civil Proceedings* (Cmnd 2964).
9 *Evidence (General)* (Cmnd 4991).

included recommendations, but no draft legislation. The Criminal Law Revision Committee included both. The Law Reform Committee's recommendations were largely accepted and very soon embodied in legislation.[10] The proposals of the Criminal Law Revision Committee were considered as a whole, met with an unfavourable overall reception, and some of its hearsay proposals have only recently been enacted, and then in a rather different form and context.[11]

These delays and differences of approach have not only postponed the attainment of a complete and comprehensive statutory code of hearsay evidence, but have overlaid the old crazy paving of the common law with a number of statutory patches of different ages and extents. The overall result has been to divide the law relating to the admissibility of hearsay by reference to four different distinctions, between common law and statute, between higher and lower courts, between civil and criminal proceedings, and between oral and documentary evidence. The broad outline is indicated in the Table.[12]

	HIGHER		LOWER	
	Civil	*Criminal*	*Civil*	*Criminal*
Oral	S	CL	CL	CL
	1968, s 2			
Documentary	S	S	S	S
	1968, s 4	1988, ss 23, 24	1938, s 1	1988, ss 23, 24

It is necessary to offer some explanation of this state of affairs. The first attempt at general, as opposed to specific, reform of the hearsay rule was made by the Evidence Act 1938.[13] The statute was confined to civil cases, though at all levels, and applied only to documentary hearsay, which was made admissible provided that it satisfied a number of conditions, the most important of which was that the maker of the statement should have had personal knowledge of the matters contained in it, and either be called to give evidence, or fall within one of a number of excepted categories, such as being dead or beyond the seas. The statute also indicated various factors affecting the weight of evidence admitted under it. Its limited scope, and the nature of some of the conditions limited the effectiveness of the Act. It was first supplemented by the Criminal Evidence Act 1965, designed specifically to deal with the admissibility of business records in criminal cases in response to the decision in *Myers*. A more thorough survey was undertaken by the Law Reform Committee which recommended replacement of the 1938 Act by a more comprehensive statute applying to oral as well as documentary hearsay, and by sweeping in common law exceptions and admission by

10 Civil Evidence Act 1968, Part I.
11 Police and Criminal Evidence Act 1984, Part VII, itself subsequently largely replaced by Part II of the Criminal Justice Act 1988.
12 This Table mentions only the major provisions. S indicates that hearsay is admitted by the statute of the date mentioned beneath, viz Evidence Act 1938, Civil Evidence Act 1968 or Criminal Justice Act 1988, while CL indicates that the admissibility of hearsay is principally governed by the common law.
13 Lord Maugham was responsible for piloting the Act through Parliament, and he discussed the subject in an article in 17 Can BR 469. There are now corresponding statutes in many parts of the Commonwealth.

agreement, thus providing a completely statutory foundation for the admission of hearsay in civil proceedings. This was accomplished by Part I of the Civil Evidence Act 1968 which also made specific provision for evidence from computers. The Act departed from the scheme recommended by the committee in providing for application to civil proceedings in magistrates' courts,[14] but as no commencement order has so far been made to apply the 1968 Act to such courts, the 1938 Act continues to apply to such proceedings in them, by default.[15] Nor was there any relief by way of inclusionary discretion, even in cases involving the custody of children.[16] This statutory reform of the rule in the higher civil courts was brought to a conclusion by the enactment of the Civil Evidence Act 1972, extending the new regime to statements of opinion.[17]

Meanwhile the Criminal Law Revision Committee reported on evidence in 1972, and recommended a far-reaching scheme of reform for criminal cases designed:

(i) to admit all hearsay evidence likely to be valuable to the greatest extent possible without undue complication or delay to the proceedings;
(ii) to ensure that evidence should continue to be given for the most part orally by allowing hearsay evidence only if the maker of the statement cannot be called or it is desirable to supplement his oral evidence.
(iii) to include necessary safeguards against the danger of manufactured hearsay evidence;
(iv) to follow the scheme of the Civil Evidence Act 1968 as far as the differences between civil and criminal proceedings allow.[18]

It is unnecessary to explore the details of this scheme any further since the Committee's recommendations for the reform of the law of evidence attracted heavy criticism, principally on account of recommendations in relation to different areas of the law, and were not enacted in the form proposed.

Instead the Police and Criminal Evidence Act 1984 made more limited provision for the admission of documentary hearsay in all criminal proceedings, and altered the rules for the admissibility of confessions. It included a provision different[19] from that in the 1968 Act to admit statements in documents produced by computers, but did not admit oral hearsay, apart from the special rules about confessions. It repealed the Criminal Evidence Act 1965. Even before the enactment of the Police and Criminal Evidence Act 1984 the area was subjected to further investigation at the hands of a departmental Committee chaired by Lord Roskill into the conduct of criminal proceedings arising from fraud. A complete chapter of the Committee's report[20] was devoted to the rules of evidence. The Committee

---

14 The Law Reform Committee preferred to wait until the Criminal Law Revision Committee reported with its proposals, so that a unified system could be operated in magistrates' courts, most of the work of which is criminal rather than civil, see Cmnd 2964 paras 48–52.
15 See *R v Wood Green Crown Court, ex p P* [1982] 4 FLR 206.
16 *Bradford City Metropolitan Council v K* [1990] 2 WLR 532 now mitigated by the passage of the Children Act 1989, s 96(3).
17 Implementing the 17th Report of the Law Reform Committee *Evidence of Opinon and Expert Evidence* (Cond 4489).
18 Cmnd 4991 para 238.
19 S 69, discussed further below at p 634. In the original drafts of the Bill the clause was to be similar to s 5 of the Civil Evidence Act 1968, but was amended in committee.
20 Fraud Trials Committee Report (1986) ch 5.

recommended an extension of the admission of hearsay in fraud cases, and recognised that it might be necessary to extend the ambit of its recommendations to all criminal proceedings. As a result Part II of the Criminal Justice Act 1988 was enacted,[1] extending the admissibility of documentary hearsay in criminal proceedings.

In Scotland the Scottish Law Commission recommended[2] the radical step of abolishing the hearsay rule completely in civil proceedings, irrespective of its form or remoteness. This recommendation was accepted, and has been enacted in s 2 of the Civil Evidence (Scotland) Act 1988. It will be interesting to observe its operation, and it has been recommended[3] that an investigation be mounted into whether or not such a system would be appropriate in England and Wales.

Many other jurisidictions have considered, or are considering reform of the hearsay rule by legislative means.[4] None of them is satisfied with the unreformed operation of the rule; none of them agree on how it should be reformed. It is proposed to examine the operation of the rule in England and Wales in the following chapters, considering separately its operation in civil and criminal proceedings.

---

1 An earlier and more radical bill had lapsed when Parliament was dissolved in 1987.
2 SLC No 100 (1986) para 3.37, recommendation 8.
3 Civil Justice Review Cm 394 (1988), para 270, recommendation 26.
4 The different schemes for reform are conveniently set out, documented and criticised in Research Paper No 3 *Hearsay Evidence Proposal* (1981) of the Australian Law Reform Commission.

CHAPTER XV

Hearsay statements in civil proceedings

SECTION 1. THE CIVIL EVIDENCE ACT 1968, PART I

At a risk of some repetition and an overlap with the later sections of this chapter it is proposed to give a brief general account of the main objects and effects of Part I of the Civil Evidence Act 1968. Some special cases on problems of construction are considered in sections 2–4 of this chapter. The purpose of the following outline is simply to facilitate comprehension of these sections.

A hearsay statement is defined in ch I as an assertion other than one made by a person while giving oral evidence in the proceedings tendered as evidence of the facts asserted. Part I of the 1968 Act governs the admissibility of such statements in civil proceedings. This is made clear by s 1 which is designed to abolish the common law on the subject. It reads as follows:

> (1) In any civil proceedings a statement other than one made by a person while giving oral evidence in those proceedings shall be admissible as evidence of any fact [or matter of opinion] stated [or dealt with] therein to the extent that it is so admissible by virtue of any provision of this part of this Act or by virtue of any other statutory provision or by agreement of the parties, but not otherwise.
>
> (2) In this section 'statutory provision' means any provision contained in, or in an instrument made under, this or any other Act, including any Act passed after this Act.

A number of other statutes, and instruments made under them provide for the admissibility of hearsay statements in civil proceedings[1] but none of them is of general application. The words in square brackets have been inserted in s 1 of the 1968 Act set out above because s 1(1) of the Civil Evidence Act 1972 provides that Part I of the earlier Act shall apply in relation to statements of opinion as it applies in relation to statements of fact; 'subject to the necessary modifications and in particular to the modification that any reference to a fact stated in a statement shall be construed as a reference to a matter dealt with therein'. Occasional references to s 1 of the 1972 Act (the only section dealing with hearsay statements) are made later in this chapter, but it can be ignored for the time being.

It should be noted that the Act refers in terms to its application in any civil proceedings, a term further defined in s 18 to include:

> in addition to civil proceedings in any of the ordinary courts of law—
> (a) civil proceedings before any other tribunal, being proceedings in relation to which the strict rules of evidence apply; and
> (b) an arbitration or reference, whether under an enactment or not,

---

1 Some examples are mentioned in section 1 of the next chapter.

but does not include civil proceedings in relation to which the strict rules of evidence do not apply.

The Act has never been commenced for civil proceedings in magistrates' courts, so they remain governed by the Evidence Act 1938 and the common law.[2] Neither does it apply to wardship proceedings in the High Court,[3] nor to some sorts of interlocutory proceedings,[4] since the strict rules of evidence do not apply to them. Despite widespread acquiescence in the admission of hearsay in other proceedings relating to children, hearsay reports were excluded[5] in such proceedings when the point was taken, both in the High Court[6] and in the magistrates' court.[7] Such consequences highlighted anomalies between different levels of court, different types of proceeding, and different uses of the same evidence. The result was deplored,[8] and further piecemeal reform has been made by s 96 of the Children Act 1989 which empowers the Lord Chancellor to make orders[9] admitting hearsay in civil proceedings in connection with the upbringing, maintenance or welfare of a child, thus creating a further set of anomalies. This is all part of the price paid for the retention of some elements of the hearsay rule in England.[10]

The principal objects of Part I of the Civil Evidence Act 1968 (comprising ss 1–10) are: to ensure that all first-hand hearsay statements are admissible, provided certain conditions are fulfilled; to allow second-hand hearsay statements to be received if contained in a record; to prevent the party against whom the statement is tendered from being taken by surprise by its adduction at the trial; and to give the court a wide inclusionary discretion but, except when the maker of the statement is called as a witness, no exclusionary discretion.[11]

By a 'first-hand' hearsay statement is meant a statement made by A and proved either by his direct oral evidence, or by the production of the document in which he made it, or by the direct oral evidence of a witness who heard him make it. If a witness swears that A told him that B had said something, or if a document asserts that the author was told something by others, or that he is repeating what he read in another document, the hearsay statement proved by the witness or narrated in court by the author of the document is 'second-hand'. In theory this process can be prolonged indefinitely so that there could be third, fourth or fifth-hand hearsay. The

2 *R v Wood Green Crown Court, ex p* (1982) 4 FLR 206. That position was dealt with in ch XX of the third edition (1967) of this book. The only important subsequent decision is *Dass v Masih* [1968] 2 All ER 226 in which the Court of Appeal said (obiter) that statements of opinion are admissible under s 1 of the Evidence Act 1938.

3 *Official Solicitor v K* [1965] AC 201, [1963] 3 All ER 191.

4 RSC Ord 41, r 5(2), see *Savings and Investment Bank Ltd v Gasco Investments (Netherlands) BV (No 2)* [1988] Ch 422, [1988] 1 All ER 975.

5 At least to prove the truth of any assertions made by them see *Re C (A Minor) (Contempt)* [1986] 1 FLR 578.

6 *K v K* [1989] 3 All ER 740, [1989] 3 WLR 933.

7 *Bradford City Metropolitan Council v K* [1990] 2 WLR 532.

8 See Spencer 'Children's Evidence: a Catastrophic Decision?' (1989) 139 NLJ 1309.

9 This power was immediately exercised by making the Children (Admissibility of Hearsay Evidence) Order 1990 (SI 1990 No 143). The complexity referred to is compounded by the application of part of the Order to the High Courts and county courts, of part to the juvenile court, and by the exclusion from its ambit of magistrates' courts.

10 In Scotland the rule has been totally abolished in civil proceedings by the Civil Evidence (Scotland) Act 1988, s 2.

11 There is also an exclusionary discretion in the case of statements made in former proceedings, but that is a matter of detail to be dealt with later.

term 'second-hand hearsay statement' may, however, be taken to include all hearsay statements that are not first-hand.

The first of the above objectss of the 1968 Act is achieved by s 2 which provides that the oral or written out-of-court statements of any person, whether called as witness in the proceedings or not, shall, 'subject to this section and to rules of court', be admissible in-chief as evidence of any fact stated therein of which direct oral evidence by him would be admissible. The words in inverted commas point to the existence of conditions of admissibility.[12] Two of them are to be found in the section itself. The first is in s 2(3), designed to ensure that only first-hand hearsay statements shall be admissible under the section. It provides that the statement must either be 'made in a document' or else proved by the direct oral evidence of the maker or someone who heard or otherwise perceived it being made. The second is in s 2(2) according to which, when the maker of the statement is called as a witness, it is admissible only with the leave of the court. This is a wise provision, for the pointless proliferation of the previous statements of witnesses is to be deplored although they may, exceptionally, be of considerable probative value.

Rules of court have been made under wide powers conferred by s 8. One of these provides for a further condition of admissibility of statements under s 2 and, at the same time, carries out the object of avoidance of surprise. The party desiring to tender a statement in evidence under s 2 must give notice of that fact to all other parties. The notice must contain details of the statement and, where appropriate, indicate which of the reasons for not calling the maker mentioned in s 8 is applicable to the case. These are that the maker is dead, beyond the seas, unfit to attend, cannot be identified or found, or cannot reasonably be expected to have any recollection of matters relevant to the accuracy of the statement. If the recipient of the notice does nothing, the statement must be admitted (subject to the requirement of leave under s 2(2) if the maker is called, a matter as to which the party serving the notice would have an option if the maker were available). He may, however, serve a counter-notice requiring the maker of the statement to be called unless one of the specified reasons for not doing so was mentioned in the notice. In this latter event the recipient of the notice may contest the existence of the reason, and the issue may be decided before the trial. If a counter-notice requiring the maker of the statement to be called is served, the party serving the original notice must call him.

The rules confer on the court a discretion to admit the statement under s 2 although no notice was served, a counter-notice requiring the maker to be called has not been obeyed, and in spite of the absence of any of the specified reasons for not calling him. A strong case for the exercise of the discretion will of course have to be made out. Possible instances would be those in which an intended witness dies or becomes ill at or shortly before the trial, or is detained in another court. The proceedings might of course be adjourned, but the judge might take the view that an adjournment was unnecessary.

To summarise the law with regard to the admissibility of first-hand hearsay statements in civil proceedings, such a statement is admissible:

---

12 Any factual basis for the satisfaction of such conditions must itself be established by admissible evidence, or be the subject of a recognised presumption, *R v Nicholls* (1976) 63 Cr App Rep 187. See also *Fiefia v Department of Labour* [1983] NZLR 704.

(1) with the leave of the court when the maker is called as a witness; (2) as of right when notice of desire to tender it in evidence has been served and either one of the reasons specified in s 8 for not calling the maker of the statement as a witness exists, or else no counter-notice has been served, and he is not called; (3) at the discretion of the court in any other case. The student should now be able to see that, rather than creating a huge exception to it, the Civil Evidence Act 1968 may be said to have abolished the rule against hearsay as hitherto known to civil cases. An accurate statement of the rule in relation to proceedings to which the Act applies would have to be in terms of a general ban on second-hand hearsay statements subject to important exceptions.

Such statements are admissible under ss 4 and 5 of the Act when contained in records. Under the first of these sections the record must have been compiled by someone acting under a duty to keep it, such as that which exists in many businesses, trades and professions. The record must have been compiled from information supplied by someone with personal knowledge of the facts stated. A statement is nonetheless a statement for being contained in a record. Accordingly, when the information is supplied directly to the compiler, a statement contained in a record may be admissible under both s 2 and s 4. This overlap is largely immaterial because the conditions of admissibility of first-hand hearsay statements under s 2 and statements contained in a record compiled from information directly supplied are to all intents and purposes identical.[13] If what was said by the supplier of the information is proved by the production of the record (and not by his evidence, production of a document of which he was the author or the direct oral evidence of the compiler who heard him) the statement contained in the record is technically a second-hand hearsay statement, but the big difference between s 2 and s 4 is that the latter provides for the transmission of information to the compiler through intermediaries, each of whom must have acted under a duty. This permits the reception of statements which could not possibly be proved under s 2. The original supplier of the information need not have acted under a duty. If he is called as a witness, the record can only be proved with the leave of the court. Statements admissible under s 4 are governed by substantially the same provisions as those governing statements admissible under s 2 with regard to the service of notice and counter-notice, the permissible reasons for not calling the supplier of the information and the discretion of the court.

Second-hand hearsay statements are also admissible under the highly specialised s 5 dealing with computerised records, a matter of growing importance in relation to which it may well prove to be desirable to amend some of the existing elaborate provisions.

Various common law rules are preserved by s 9. First and second-hand hearsay statements may be admissible under them, but, for the purpose of civil proceedings, these rules are converted into statutory provisions under which certain statements are admissible as evidence of the facts stated by virtue of s 9. The conditions of admissibility are the common law ones and there are no requirements with regard to the service of notices or counter-notices.

Although the Act is quite unequivocal in requiring admissible hearsay to

---

13 The only difference of any significance between the various provisions concerns computer records (because of different linkages between the provisions), see further below, p 558.

comply with its provisions, including those of s 9 incorporating some hitherto common law rules, this requirement sometimes seems to have been overlooked, and hearsay admitted by reference to the pre-existing law.[14] It should be noted that the enactment of some, previously common law, exceptions in s 9 may operate in tandem with s 2(1) to admit some statements under the latter which are not first hand. The requirement in s 2(1) is that the maker of the statement admitted under it should have been himself competent to give evidence of the relevant matter. Section 9 preserves, inter alia, the old common law exception for admissions. Thus a witness who himself heard an admission could give oral evidence of it, and that evidence would help prove the fact admitted. Thus under the Act an admission recorded in a document made by a third party may be admitted under the combination of the two sections, because the author of the document recording it could, had he been called, have given oral evidence of the admission.[15]

Perhaps the most common course for the admission of hearsay in civil proceedings is by agreement of the parties. In many cases they agree because they appreciate that to insist upon strict compliance with the conditions imposed by the Act would needlessly add to the costs and cause delay. In many cases agreement may be presumed from the absence of objection. If however the admission of hearsay evidence is objected to, it cannot be said to have been admitted by consent, even if the objection was raised for some quite different reason.[16]

SECTION 2. STATEMENTS ADMISSIBLE UNDER THE CIVIL EVIDENCE ACT 1968, SS 2 AND 3

Section 2(1) of the Civil Evidence Act 1968 reads:

> In any civil proceedings a statement made, whether orally or in a document or otherwise, by any person, whether called as a witness in those proceedings or not, shall, subject to this section and to rules of court, be admissible as evidence of any fact [or matter] stated [or dealt with] therein of which direct oral evidence by him would be admissible.[17]

The rest of s 2 and the rules of court call for a distinction between the cases falling within the two rules conflated in the formulation of the rule against hearsay adopted in this book and s 1(1) of the Civil Evidence Act 1968,[18] the

14 *Knight v David* [1971] 3 All ER 1066, [1971] 1 WLR 1671 (admissibility of tithe map, but where the court may have applied s 9 without explicit reference); *Re Armvent* [1975] 3 All ER 441, [1975] 1 WLR 1679, and *Re St Piran* [1981] 3 All ER 270, [1981] 1 WLR 1300 (admissibility of inspectors' reports on company winding-up petitions, perhaps explicable by reference to the statutory basis of winding-up procedure and the very limited purpose for which they are admitted); *Savings and Investment Bank Ltd v Gasco Investments (Netherlands) BV* [1984] 1 All ER 296.
15 *The Ymnos* [1981] 1 Lloyd's Rep 550.
16 *K v K* [1989] 3 All ER 740, [1989] 3 WLR 933.
17 The words in square brackets are added in consequence of s 1(1) of the Civil Evidence Act 1972.
18 The subsection is set out on p 540 above. 'We have chosen as our first topic "the hearsay rule", in which we include not only the strict hearsay rule ("what the soldier said is not evidence") but also what is sometimes mis-called the rule against narrative ("what the witness himself said outside the witness box is not evidence")' (13th Report of the Law Reform Committee, para 5).

case in which the maker of the statement is called as a witness and that in which he is not called.

A. THE PREVIOUS STATEMENTS OF WITNESSES

1. STATEMENTS ADMISSIBLE UNDER S 2

The previous statement of a witness, consistent or inconsistent with his testimony, is admissible under s 2 of the Act on two conditions, first, that the party calling the witness should have notified all other parties within the prescribed time before the trial[19] of his desire to give the statement in evidence, and second, that the trial judge should give leave for the statement to be given in evidence.

(i) Notice

One of the objects of the notice procedure for which provision is made by Ord 38, rr 21–26 is to prevent surprise; another is to provide an incentive for parties upon whom a notice is served to agree to the reception of a hearsay statement without the necessity of calling the maker. It is unlikely that a party who has a witness available to prove a crucially important fact would not want to call him, but that party must nonetheless serve all other parties with notice of his desire to give a statement of that witness in evidence, if such be his desire, and the object of the requirement is to prevent him from taking his adversaries by surprise. Parties to litigation are seldom in complete accord on the question what is or is not an important fact; provision is therefore made by Ord 38, r 26 for the service of a counter-notice requiring the person named in the original notice as the maker of the statement to be called as a witness. If that person is available as a witness, and he is not called, after receipt of a counter-notice by the party who served the original notice, the statement will, subject to the discretion of the court to rule otherwise, be inadmissible in evidence. An incentive not to serve a counter-notice without good cause is provided by Ord 38, r 32 under which, if it appears to the court that it was unreasonable to require the maker of the statement to be called, the costs of the preparation of the counter-notice may be disallowed and the party serving it may also be required to pay costs occasions by it.

(ii) Leave

Section 2(2) of the Civil Evidence Act 1968, reads in part as follows:

> Where in any civil proceedings a party desiring to give a statement in evidence by virtue of this section has called or intends to call as a witness in the proceedings the person by whom the statement was made, the statement—
> (a) shall not be given in evidence by virtue of this section on behalf of that party without the leave of the court; and
> (b) without prejudice to paragraph (a) above, shall not be given in evidence by virtue of this section on behalf of that party before the conclusion of the examination-in-chief of the person by whom it was made . . .

19 See Ord 38, r 21.

To a large extent this subsection embodies the reaction of the Law Reform Committee to what was thought to be a lax practice which prevailed, under the Evidence Act 1938. A party could call a witness, ask him to verify his proof of evidence and put it in as of right, thus avoiding any examination-in-chief:

> Examination-in-chief by question and answer without leading questions on matters in dispute plays an important part in our system of eliciting the truth under the adversary system. As every judge and advocate knows, witnesses often fail to 'come up to their proofs' in examination-in-chief—and this is one of the commonest ways in which truth will out.[20]

There are three exceptions to the prohibition of the reception of the witness's previous statement before the conclusion of his examination-in-chief. In the first place, the court may allow the statement to be proved by an earlier witness, and might do so, for instance, where a party to a running-down action intended to call someone who had made a statement soon after the accident to a police officer who gives his evidence first and wishes to be released. Secondly, the court may allow a witness to narrate his previous statement in the course of his examination-in-chief on the ground that to prevent him from doing so would adversely affect the intelligibility of his evidence. For instance the most natural way for a witness to give his evidence may involve his stating what he said to his wife on a particular occasion, and perhaps also what she said to him; interruptions inspired by the rule against hearsay have, it is believed, been too frequent in the past. These exceptions are contained in s 2(2) of the 1968 Act. The third is the result of Ord 38, r 43, relating to reports of experts. When an expert is called as a witness in accordance with the procedure outlined on p 497, his report may be given in evidence at the beginning of his examination-in-chief or at any other time directed by the court. Such a provision is desirable because the examination-in-chief of an expert as to opinion is quite different from the examination-in-chief of the ordinary witness as to fact; it may often take the form of a request to enlarge upon the report.

(iii) Discretion

Under Ord 38, r 29(1), the court has a discretion to admit a statement, if it thinks it just to do so, although no notice of desire to give the statement in evidence has been served. In *Morris v Stratford-on-Avon U D C*[21] the plaintiff had been struck, five years before the trial, by a lorry driven by an employee of the defendants who gave evidence for them. His evidence was inconsistent and confused, and although no notice concerning a previous statement had been served on the plaintiff, the judge allowed the defendants to adduce a proof of evidence which a driver had given to a representative of their insurers some nine months after the accident. The judge's decision was upheld by the Court of Appeal. The court did not think it mattered whether the case was regarded as one in which there was one discretion or two, the discretion under Ord 38, r 29, to waive the failure to give notice, and the discretion to grant leave to give the statement in evidence under s 2(2). The defendants had no particular reason to suppose that their driver would give

20 13th Report of the Law Reform Committee, para 32.
21 [1973] 3 All ER 263, [1973] 1 WLR 1059.

confused evidence, and the Court of Appeal took the view that it would perhaps be unfortunate if the Civil Evidence Act were to be so interpreted that a party's advisers would feel it necessary to advise that notice should be served if ever there were the remotest possibility that leave to give the statement in evidence would have to be sought. At the same time, the court recognised that failure to give the prescribed notice was a serious matter, that notice should always be given when it was thought an application for leave to give a statement in evidence would be made at the trial, and that justice to the opposite party might sometimes require an adjournment if the prescribed notice were not served.[1]

2. STATEMENTS ADMISSIBLE UNDER S 3

There are no requirements concerning the service of a notice or the necessity of obtaining the leave of the court before the previous statement of a witness becomes admissible under s 3 of the Civil Evidence Act 1968. It is necessary only to set the section out and to indicate in footnotes the pages in this book at which the statements mentioned in the section have been discussed and the precise extent to which it changes the law.

Section 3 reads as follows:

(1) Where in any civil proceedings—
(a) a previous inconsistent or contradictory statement made by a person called as a witness in those proceedings is proved by virtue of section 3, 4 and 5 of the Criminal Procedure Act 1865;[2] or
(b) a previous statement made by a person called as aforesaid is proved for the purpose of rebutting a suggestion that his evidence has been fabricated,[3] that statement shall by virtue of this subsection be admissible as evidence of any fact [or matter] stated [or dealt with] therein of which direct oral evidence by him would be admissible.[4]

(2) Nothing in this Act shall affect any of the rules of law relating to the circumstances in which, where a person called as a witness in any civil proceedings is cross-examined on a document used by him to refresh his memory, that document may be made evidence in those proceedings; and where a document or any part of a document is received in evidence in any such proceedings by virtue of any such rule of law, any statement made in that document or part by the person using the document to refresh his memory shall by virtue of this subsection be admissible as evidence of any fact [or matter] stated [or dealt with] therein, of which direct oral evidence by him would be admissible.[5]

---

1 Such an adjournment was granted in *Minnesota Mining and Manufacturing Co v Johnson and Johnson Co* [1977] FSR 210.
2 For s 3 (hostile witnesses) see p 299 above; for ss 4–5, see pp 305–307 above; the law is changed because previous inconsistent statements are made admissible as evidence of the facts stated, although it does not follow that they will often be acted on as such.
3 See p 288 above. The law is changed because at common law the previous statement is admissible only to rebut fabrication, not as evidence of the facts stated; but it is doubtful whether the change is more than nominal.
4 Words in square brackets due to Civil Evidence Act 1972, s 1(1).
5 See pp 277–278 above. It is open to question whether the provision for the reception of the statement as evidence of the facts stated alters the common law.

B.   THE PREVIOUS STATEMENTS OF NON-WITNESSES

The oral or written statement of someone who is not called as a witness is admissible as of right as evidence of any fact or opinion stated of which he could have given direct oral evidence[6] under s 2(1) of the Civil Evidence Act 1968, if (i) the statement is proved in accordance with the terms of s 2(3); (ii) one of the reasons for not calling the maker as a witness mentioned in s 8 of the Act and Ord 38, r 25, exists; and (iii) the appropriate notice has been served on all other parties to the proceedings by the party wishing to give the statement in evidence. The court has a discretion to admit the statement although the second and third of the above requirements have not been met if it thinks it just to do so, and the Act contains guidelines about the weight to be attached to the statement if admitted, as well as rules concerning the admissibility of evidence impugning the credibility of the maker. These requirements, guide-lines and rules may be described as the 'main provisions'; after they have been considered, some special cases will be mentioned.

1.   THE MAIN PROVISIONS

(i)   Proof in accordance with s 2(3)

Section 2(3) of the Civil Evidence Act 1968, reads in part as follows:

> Where in any civil proceedings a statement which was made otherwise than in a document is admissible by virtue of this section no evidence other than direct oral evidence by the person who made the statement or any person who heard or otherwise perceived it being made, shall be admissible for the purpose of proving it . . . .

The object of this provision is to ensure that only first hand hearsay statements are admissible under s 2(1). B may prove what he heard A say, but C may not prove what B told him A said. A's written statement that he saw X hit Y is clearly admissible as evidence of that fact, and B's written statement that A had told him that he saw X hit Y is equally clearly inadmissible as evidence of the assault. The term 'document' is very broadly defined by s 10(1) as including in addition to a document in writing, a map, plan, photograph, disc, tape, film or microfilm. 'Statement' includes 'any representation of fact [or expression of opinion][7] whether made by words or otherwise.' We shall see that this could give rise to problems concerning the admissibility of implied assertions under s 2, but, for the time being, it is only necessary to refer to a few problems which could be raised in exceptional circumstances, by the concept of a 'statement made in a document.'

The obvious instance of such a statement has already been given. A's written assertion that he saw X hit Y; but what if A were to dictate the words 'I saw X hit Y' to B? It is to be assumed that, if B duly wrote the statement down and A checked the writing, any court would hold, on the ordinary principles of agency, that A had made a statement in a document. Doubt begins to creep in if it is assumed that A dictated the statement to B

---

6   *Re Koscot Interplanetary (UK) Ltd, Re Koscot AG* [1972] 3 All ER 829 (so excluding hearsay upon hearsay).

7   Some such words are necessary to allow for the Civil Evidence Act 1972, s 1(1).

but did not check what B wrote.[8] To cope with this possibility, the Criminal Law Revision Committee recommended the following sub-clause:

> Where a person makes an oral statement to or in the hearing of another person who, acting at the instance of the maker of the statement reduces it (or the substance of it) into writing at the time or reasonably soon afterwards, thereby producing a corresponding statement in a document, the statement in the document shall be treated . . . as having been made in the document by the maker of the oral statement not only where he has, but also where he has not, signified his acceptance of it as his.[9]

The courts may well reach the same conclusion on the construction of s 2(3) of the 1968 Act without the aid of any such sub-clause.

If B were to eavesdrop on a conversation in which A told C that he saw X hit Y, A's statement could be proved by B; but, if B were to write the statement down, it is hard to believe that any court would hold that A's statement was made in a document. Doubt again begins to creep in if one assumes that A's statement to C was recorded on a concealed tape recorder of which A was unaware.

The combined effect of the common law rule, discussed in ch XIX, that secondary evidence (including oral evidence) may be given of the contents of a document which cannot be found after due search for the original and the provisions of s 2 of the 1968 Act could be to render second, third or even fourth hand hearsay admissible, but the facts would have to be sufficiently exceptional to render the point of no more than theoretical interest. Suppose A writes a letter to B stating that he saw X hit Y, and the letter cannot be found after due search, its contents could be proved under s 2(3) by a letter written by B to C in which B narrated the substance of what A had written to him, and this process might, in theory, be continued. However remote the letter ultimately placed before the court was from that written by A to B, it is A's statement made in that lost letter which is the statement 'made in a document' and received as evidence that X hit Y. Section 6(1) provides for the proof of statements contained in documents by the production of the original or a copy of the document, authenticated in such a manner as the court may approve; but, in the case put, it is assumed that there is no copy of A's letter to B, the only evidence of its contents being the statements in the successive letters from B to C, C to D etc.

(ii) Reasons for not calling the maker

The following are the reasons, mentioned in s 8 of the Act and incorporated in Ord 38, r 25, for not calling the maker of the statement as a witness: that he is dead, beyond the seas,[10] or unfit[11] by reason of his bodily or mental condition to attend as a witness,[12] or that, despite the exercise of reasonable

---

8 See *R v Calabria* (1982) 7 ACR 207 (statement dictated to secretary by solicitor while questioning witness who subsequently died, held witness was supplier of information).

9 Clause 31(6) of the draft Bill, see paras 254–5 of the 11th Report. The draft Bill contained provisions as to hearsay substantially similar to those of the Civil Evidence Act 1968. No such provision appears in the Criminal Justice Act 1988.

10 Guernsey is beyond the seas, *Rover International Ltd v Cannon Films Sales Ltd (No 2)* [1987] 3 All ER 986, [1987] 1 WLR 1597.

11 This expression is not apt to render admissible the assertions of a child too young to testify, *K v K* [1989] 3 All ER 740, [1989] 3 WLR 933, but now see Children Act 1989, s 96.

12 These facts may be proved by medical certificate s 8(5).

diligence, it has not been possible to identify or find him, or that he cannot reasonably be expected to have any recollection of matters relevant to the accuracy of the statement. These conditions are disjunctive. It has thus been held necessary to show only that the maker was 'beyond the seas', and unnecessary to go on to show in such a case that he cannot with reasonable diligence be found.[13]

(iii) Notice

The notice to be served by the party desiring to give the statement in evidence must, where he contends that there is one, specify which of the reasons upon which he relies for not calling the maker. The party upon whom the notice is served may then serve a counter-notice only if he contends that the maker of the statement can, or should, be called. In that event, the court may, on the application of any party, decide these questions before the trial.[14]

(iv) Discretion

Under Ord 38, r 29, the court has a broad inclusionary[15] discretion to admit a statement although no notice of desire to tender it in evidence was served, although a counter-notice requiring the maker to be called has not been complied with, and although none of the reasons for not calling the maker exists. In *Ford v Lewis*[16] the plaintiff, a girl of five at the time, was struck by a van driven by the defendant who was in a mental hospital at the time of the trial. Although no notice had been served in respect of either statement, the trial judge admitted a statement made by the defendant at some time during the period of nearly ten years which elapsed between the accident and the trial, and hospital notes[17] suggesting that the plaintiff's father, who had been with her at the time of the accident, was drunk. The reason given by the defendant's counsel for not serving the notices was that he was afraid that the plaintiff's witnesses might 'trim' their evidence to meet the defendant's statement. A new trial was ordered on the plaintiff's appeal against judgment for the defendant because it could not be right to exercise the discretion conferred by Ord 38, r 29, in favour of someone who had deliberately flouted the rules.

(v) Weight and credibility

Section 6(3) enjoins the court, when estimating the weight to be attached to a statement to have regard to the questions whether it was made contemporaneously with the events to which it refers, and whether the maker had any incentive to conceal or misrepresent facts.

---

13 *Piermay Shipping Co SA v Chester* [1978] 1 All ER 1233, [1978] 1 WLR 411, approving *Rasool v West Midland Passenger Transport Executive* [1974] 3 All ER 638. Both the vagueness of the expression 'beyond the seas' and the disjunction of the conditions have been remedied in the drafting of the comparable provision for criminal cases in the Criminal Justice Act 1988, s 23(2).
14 Ord 38, r 27. The word 'should' is required on account of the fifth reason.
15 S 8(3)(a) explicitly denies any general *exclusionary* discretion.
16 [1971] 2 All ER 983, [1971] 1 WLR 623.
17 Admissible under s 4 of the 1968 Act.

Section 7 provides that, when the maker of the statement is not called as a witness, any evidence which would, had he been called, have been admissible for the purpose of destroying his credibility, may be adduced; but evidence may not be given on matters as to which the maker's denials in cross-examination to credit would have been final. This simply means that evidence may be given of bias, previous convictions, bad reputation for veracity, mental or physical condition tending to show unreliability and, subject to notice by the person tendering the statement,[18] inconsistent statements.[19]

(vi) No counter-notice

There is a further situation in which the statement of a non-witness is admissible under s 2, namely, that in which the party desiring to give in evidence a statement of an available witness has served the appropriate notice on all other parties and has not been served with a counter-notice requiring the maker of the statement to be called. The party serving the notice has an option whether to call the maker of the statement as a witness, and if he opts against calling him, the court has no discretion to exclude the statement, although, if the maker is called, the statement will be admissible only with the leave of the court in accordance with the provisions of s 2(2) set out on p 545.

2. SPECIAL CASES

(i) Statements in former proceedings

The proviso to s 2(3) of the Civil Evidence Act 1968, reads:

> Provided that if the statement in question was made by a person while giving oral evidence in some other legal proceedings (whether civil or criminal), it may be proved in any manner authorised by the court.

Accordingly Ord 38, r 28, enables any party, upon whom notice of intention to give in evidence a statement made in former proceedings has been served, to apply to the court for directions as to whether, and, if so, upon what conditions, the party desiring to give the statement in evidence will be permitted to do so, and as to the manner in which the statement and any other evidence given in the former proceedings should be proved.

Special provision had to be made for such a case because the party desiring to give the statement in evidence might otherwise simply prove a portion of the testimony of a witness in former proceedings, leaving out unfavourable passages; or the witness may have been disbelieved or contradicted by other evidence. All these matters may be dealt with on the application for directions.

Two further points may be mentioned. In the first place, this is the one instance in which the court has a discretion to exclude the statement of someone not called as a witness under s 2, even though notice of desire to give it in evidence has been duly served; the statement of a witness who had been thoroughly discredited in the former proceedings would be a case in

18 Ord 38, r 31.
199 For details see p 305 above.

point. Secondly, if, as will usually happen, the court directs that the statement, and possibly much other evidence given in the former proceedings, be proved by a transcript of those proceedings, second-hand hearsay will be received at the trial for the testimony of the witnesses in the former proceedings will be proved by the hearsay statement of the shorthand writer, assuming of course that he is not called as a witness.

(ii) Co-defendants or co-plaintiffs

A party's informal admissions are admissible evidence against him at common law, and the common law on this subject is preserved by s 9 of the Act. Admissions are therefore fully discussed below; but, to quote para 30 of the 13th Report of the Law Reform Committee:

> One of the most striking effects of the rule against hearsay in its present form is that the out-of-court statement by one of two co-defendants is inadmissible evidence against the other, even though the statement seriously inculpates the maker and is, for that reason, very probably true. The commonest example is the divorce case in which the respondent's admission of adultery with the co-respondent is no evidence against the co-respondent.

Not the least of the merits of the Civil Evidence Act 1968, is that it puts an end to this absurdity. If A and B are co-defendants, and A has made a statement implicating B, the plaintiff may (whether or not the statement also implicates A) serve notice on A and B of his desire to give the statement in evidence; B can then serve a counter-notice requiring the plaintiff to call A as a witness. It is, however, undesirable that a party should be obliged to call one of his opponents as his witness. In the case which has just been put, this problem might have been solved by means of the general discretion of the court under Ord 38, r 29(1), to admit the statement even though A was not called by the plaintiff; but Ord 38, r 29(2), expressly states that the court may exercise its discretion if a refusal to do so might oblige the party desiring to give the statement in evidence to call an opposite party. If, in the example which has just been given, A were to give evidence, the plaintiff could put his statement to him in cross-examination, but if, as would be most likely, the court were prepared to exercise its discretion, the statement could form part of the plaintiff's case against B. If it also implicated A, it would be admissible against him by virtue of s 9, he therefore could not serve a counter-notice requiring the plaintiff to call him.[20]

Everything said above applies to cases in which one of two plaintiffs has made a statement implicating the other.

(iii) Statements by servants or agents of a party

A further absurd result of the common law avoided by the Act of 1968 was that, if the servant or agent of a party had made a statement adverse to that party's case, it often happened that the statement could not be proved against that party, even if made with regard to a transaction in relation to which the maker was vicariously liable. For example, if a lorry driver were to admit that he had not been keeping a proper look out when, in the course of

---

20 Civil Evidence Act 1968, s 9(5). The notice and counter-notice procedure does not apply to admissions.

his employment, he ran A down, A could not rely on the statement as evidence against the driver's employer; he can do so now thanks to s 2 of the 1968 Act, but B can serve him with a counter-notice requiring him to call the driver. To quote again from the 13th Report of the Law Reform Committee:

> Although not 'hostile' in the technical sense, such a witness might be unfavourably disposed towards the party who was forced to examine him in-chief and favourably disposed towards his cross-examiner.[1]

This is another matter which could have been dealt with under the general discretion conferred upon the court by Ord 38, r 29(1), but Ord 38, r 29(2), expressly states that the court may exercise its power to allow a statement to be given in evidence under s 2 although the maker is not called, when its refusal to do so might oblige the party desiring to give the statement in evidence to call the servant or agent of the opposite party. In the example given above, there would of course be no objection to B calling his driver if minded to do so.

(iv) Probate actions

It sometimes happens that a party to a probate action wishes to prove statements made by the deceased as evidence of the facts stated. Indeed, he may wish to prove the deceased's account of the contents of his lost will. There would be no point in serving the opposite party with notice of desire to give the statements of the deceased in evidence because the opposite party would be unable to contest the death of the deceased. Accordingly Ord 38, r 21(3), provides that no notice need be served in such a case.

The above reference to the deceased's account of the contents of his lost will provokes a general question with regard to the construction of s 2(1) of the Civil Evidence Act 1968. It renders a statement admissible 'as evidence of any fact [or matter][2] of which direct oral evidence by [the maker] would be admissible'. It is clear that the reference to direct oral evidence by the maker is to the direct oral evidence he could have given in the proceedings had he been called, and, at any rate for the pedant, this raises problems in relation to cases in which the death of the maker of the statement is a pre-requisite of the action in which the statement is tendered in evidence. The concept of the deceased giving direct oral evidence in an action for probate of his own will is not an easy one, and there is the same difficulty with regard to a will construction summons or a claim under the Fatal Accidents Acts in respect of the death of the maker of the statement. It is to be hoped that the courts will avoid the apparent impasse by holding that the 1968 Act requires them to imagine a probate action, will construction summons or claim under the Fatal Accidents Acts at the hearing of which the deceased miraculously appears to give evidence.

(v) Undefended divorces

The object of the notice of desire to give a statement in evidence under s 2 is to enable the opposite party to consider whether he wishes the maker of the

---

1 Para 31.
2 Civil Evidence Act 1972, s 1(1).

statement to be called as a witness if available, to consider the validity of any reason given for not calling the maker and generally to make inquiries concerning the circumstances in which the statement was made. There is therefore no point in serving such a notice in undefended proceedings and the Matrimonial Causes Rules accordingly provide that the notice need not be served in undefended divorce cases.

(vi) Implied assertions

It has been noted that 'statement' for the purposes of the Civil Evidence Act 1968, includes 'any representation of fact [or expression of opinion],[3] whether made in words or otherwise'. Does this include implied assertions?[4] It is submitted that it does not, and that 'representation' connotes an intention to assert the existence of a fact, or the entertainment of an opinion. If so, the Act is in conformity with the general approach to the nature of hearsay advanced above. It certainly seems that the Criminal Law Revision Committee held such a view since it recommended specific amendment of the definition in s 10 just so that it should encompass such implied assertions.[5] This seems unnecessary. If the very same definition of statement applies both to define the evidence excluded by the Act, and to the exceptions to that exclusion, it follows that matters falling outside the definition are quite outside the scope of the Act, and unaffected by it. They are then governed by the common law. It has been argued above that at common law the concept of hearsay applied only to exclude express assertions primarily intended to assert a proposition of fact, or the circumstantial use of the making of such assertions to prove the existence of the fact so asserted.[6] The compilation of documents, making of greetings, and doing of acts not primarily intended to assert anything, could accordingly be put in evidence as a circumstance available for the derivation of any inference which could be drawn from them as a matter of ordinary logic and common-sense.

SECTION 3. STATEMENTS CONTAINED IN RECORDS ADMISSIBLE UNDER THE CIVIL EVIDENCE ACT 1968, SS 4 AND 5

Only documents which are, or are part of, a 'record' can be admitted under s 4(1). This vital condition for admissibility is left undefined by the Act, but has been considered in a number of cases. In *Re Koscot Interplanetary (UK) Ltd*[7] Megarry J expressed the view that it was not apt to cover the anonymous schedule of legal proceedings undertaken in the United States adduced before him. Further consideration was given to the question in *H v Schering Chemicals*[8] where Bingham J was prepared to take into account cases construing the word 'record' in the context of the Evidence Act 1938,[9] and

3 Civil Evidence Act 1972, s 1(1).
4 See p 531 above.
5 Cmnd 4991, draft Bill cl 41(3).
6 See p 516 above. The same reasoning applies to expressions of opinion.
7 [1972] 3 All ER 829.
8 [1983] 1 All ER 849, [1983] 1 WLR 143.
9 *Thrasyvoulos Ioannou v Papa Christoforos Demetrious* [1952] AC 84, [1952] 1 All ER 179 (surveyor's report not a 'continuous record' for purpose of Act identical in wording to Evidence Act 1938, s 1(1)(i)(b)).

the Criminal Evidence Act 1965.[10] He held that all of the cases were consistent with the view that the sort of record in question must be one which a historian would regard as original or primary, either giving effect to a transaction, or containing a contemporaneous register of information supplied by those with personal knowledge. He accordingly ruled that the research reports, articles and letters in medical journals before him did not qualify. This approach was approved by Peter Gibson J in *Savings and Investment Bank Ltd v Gasco Investments (Netherlands) BV*,[11] applied to a report on a company by Board of Trade inspectors, and garnished with the further requirement that it should not amount to a selection of material submitted together with comments and conclusions. It has further been held that selective notes of an interview with a potential witness made by a solicitor did not qualify as a 'record' when it was not intended that they should be used otherwise than as an aide-memoire.[12]

The difficulty created by this approach is that if such a report is not a record, it is very difficult to see how its contents ever can be proved, short of repeating the very same process according to which it was originally compiled, which is clearly impractical. It ought to be possible to put such a report in evidence, subject to its being proved by its authors. This result could be achieved by treating the report as a record, and requiring the normal notice procedures to be followed. The liberalising aim of the Evidence Act 1938 was frustrated by restrictive interpretation, and led to dissatisfaction eventually culminating in the passage of the 1968 Act. The approach now adopted by judges at first instance seems to be in some danger of duplicating that entire saga, though fortunately it is still not too late for the Court of Appeal to reaffirm the intention of the legislature by adopting a broader approach to the meaning of 'record' in s 4. It is ironical that unless this is done civil proceedings will be governed by a more restrictive rule than criminal, where the limitation to 'records' has now been removed.[13]

A. RECORDS ADMISSIBLE UNDER S 4

1. STATEMENTS ADMISSIBLE BOTH AS STATEMENTS UNDER S 2 AND AS STATEMENTS IN RECORDS UNDER S 4

Section 4(1) of the Civil Evidence Act 1968 reads:

> Without prejudice to s 5 of this Act [dealing with computerised records], in any civil proceedings a statement contained in a document shall, subject to this section and to rules of court, be admissible as evidence of any fact stated therein of which direct oral evidence would be admissible, if the document is, or forms part of, a record compiled by a person acting under a duty from information which was

10 *R v Tirado* (1974) 59 Cr App Rep 80 (file of letters not a 'record'); and *R v Jones and Sullivan* [1978] 2 All ER 718, [1978] 1 WLR 195 (bills of lading and cargo manifests part of 'record').
11 [1984] 1 All ER 296; itself approved in *R v Governor of Pentonville Prison, ex p Osman* [1989] 3 All ER 701. Compare the more liberal approach in *Campofina Bank v ANZ Banking Group* [1982] 1 NSWLR 409.
12 *Re D (A Minor) (Wardship: Evidence)* [1986] 2 FLR 189.
13 See Criminal Justice Act 1988, s 24, replacing Police and Criminal Evidence Act 1984, s 68; and remarks in *R v Cunningham* [1989] Crim LR 435.

supplied by a person (whether acting under a duty or not) who had, or may reasonably be supposed to have had, personal knowledge of the matters dealt with in that information and which, if not supplied by that person to the compiler of the record directly, was supplied by him to the compiler of the record indirectly through one or more intermediaries each acting under a duty.

The main purpose of this subsection is to provide for the reception of hearsay statements which are not first hand, i e they are neither made in a document, nor proved by the direct oral evidence of the maker, nor proved by a witness who heard or otherwise perceived them being made. Many first hand hearsay statements are, however, admissible both as a statement under s 2 and as a statement contained in a record under s 4.

The overlap between s 2 and s 4 is of little practical importance[14] because (agreement or acquiescence by failure to serve a counter-notice requiring an available witness to be called apart) the person who originally supplied the information from which a record admissible under s 4 is compiled must either be called as a witness, or be unavailable for the reasons specified in Ord 38, r 25, i e because he is dead, beyond the seas, unfit, untraceable, or someone who cannot reasonably be expected to have any recollection of the matters dealt with in the information. These are the same reasons as those governing the admissibility of statements under s 2 when the maker is not called. There are similar rules governing the notice which must be served on opposite parties by someone who wants to give in evidence a record admissible by virtue of s 4, and the counter-notice which may be served.[15] These rules correspond with those governing the admissibility of statements under s 2, and everything said with regard to the admissibility of first hand hearsay (as a statement) applies to its admissibility (as a record) under s 4. The supplier of the information is to all intents and purposes in the same position as the maker of a statement admissible under s 2. If he is called as a witness, the record cannot be given in evidence without the leave of the court, and generally not before the conclusion of his examination-in-chief.[16] It seems, however, that where there is a choice between s 2 and s 4, it is better to tender the statement under the latter, thus bringing the record directly before the court instead of treating it as a document which must be produced to the court as one used to refresh memory.

It has been said that a transcript of a witness's evidence in former proceedings is admissible both as a statement under s 2 and as a record under s 4;[17] it has even been suggested that a transcript of the judge's summing up in a criminal case is admissible in subsequent civil proceedings as a record under s 4,[18] although it is perhaps open to question whether the judge 'supplies' information to the shorthand writer even if, contrary to the view taken with regard to the Evidence Act 1938,[19] the witness supplies information to the shorthand writer.

14 There is a slight difference in the linkage to s 5 relating to computer records, see further, below, p 558.
15 RSC Ord 38, r 21, r 23 and r 26.
16 Civil Evidence Act 1968, s 4(2).
17 *Taylor v Taylor* [1970] 2 All ER 609; but see *Re D (A Minor) (Wardship: Evidence)* [1986] 2 FLR 189 for a different view of notes of evidence taken by a solicitor.
18 *Taylor v Taylor*, above.
19 *Barkway v South Wales Transport Co Ltd* [1949] 1 KB 54, [1948] 2 All ER 460.

2. STATEMENTS CONTAINED IN RECORDS ADMISSIBLE UNDER S 4 ALONE

As an example of a recorded statement admissible under s 4 alone we may take the case of a lorry driver who informs a fellow servant that he delivered a load at X; the fellow servant makes a note of this fact and passes the note on to another servant who destroys it after entering the delivery in a book. This process can be continued for any length without affecting the admissibility of the ultimate record, provided the compiler and all the intermediaries were acting under a duty.

It is important to bear in mind that the original supplier of the information need not act under a duty. Hospital records are only one of many sets of records compiled from inquiries in relation to which the original source of information, the patient, can hardly be said to have been acting under a duty to supply it.

The existence of a duty to pass the information on and to compile the record reduces the chance of erroneous repetition which is the great weakness of hearsay upon hearsay. Section 4(3) reads:

> Any reference in this section to a person acting under a duty includes a reference to a person acting in the course of any trade, business, profession or other occupation in which he is engaged or employed or for the purpose of any paid or unpaid office held by him.

It is not clear how far this provision is from being exhaustive. If, after an accident, A, a police officer acting under a duty, records a statement by B, who did not see the accident, that C told him that one of the drivers was driving without lights, and it proves to be impossible to trace C, is the record admissible? The answer turns upon the question whether B could be said to have been acting under a duty to pass the information on to A. Is a mere social duty, or the moral duty of citizens to help the police, sufficient?

Although the original supplier of the information need not have been acting under a duty, he must have had a personal knowledge of the matters dealt with in the information, or have been someone who may reasonably be supposed to have had such knowledge. This is something which will often have to be inferred from the nature of the record and all the circumstances of the case.[20] In *Knight v David*,[1] for example, the plaintiff in an action concerning title to land tendered in evidence a map and apportionment survey made under the Tithe Act 1836 . It was held that these documents were admissible under s 4[2] because a living person could have testified to the fact that the machinery prescribed by the Tithe Act had been used and that a certain person was entered as proprietor. The fact that the commissioners had acted on information supplied by people with personal knowledge of the matters upon which they gave information was inferred.

The personal knowledge requirement does not apply to a record containing a statement of opinion of which the original supplier of the information could have given direct oral evidence as an expert.[3] Experts do

---

20 Civil Evidence Act 1968, s 6(2). But see *Fiefia v Department of Labour* [1983] NZLR 704.

1 [1971] 3 All ER 1066, [1971] 1 WLR 1671.

2 Although the judge preferred to rest his decision on the common law, preserved by s 9, a section to which no express reference was made.

3 Civil Evidence Act 1972, s 1(2).

not always have to have personal knowledge of that to which they depose; their information is, for example, frequently derived from books.

Everything said above in section 1 with regard to the credibility of the maker of the statement when he is not called as a witness applies to the original supplier of the information from which a record admissible under s 4 is compiled, but evidence on this subject is not likely to be forthcoming in the case of a record of any antiquity.

B. STATEMENTS CONTAINED IN RECORDS ADMISSIBLE UNDER S 5: COMPUTERISED RECORDS[4]

The Law Reform Committee regarded the difficulty of dealing with modern systems of record-keeping as one of the defects of the older law.[5] It believed that its recommendations for what are now ss 2 and 4 of the Civil Evidence Act 1968 would remedy them.[6] This aim was further enhanced by the adoption of a wide definition of a document to include:

> any disc, tape, sound track or other device in which sounds or other data (not being visual images) are embodied so as to be capable (with or without the aid of some other equipment) of being reproduced therefrom.[7]

It is likely that such provision would have coped with computers perfectly well.[8] It was however thought necessary to make special provision for computers in s 5:

> (1) In any civil proceedings a statement contained in a document produced by a computer shall, subject to the rules of court, be admissible as evidence of any fact stated therein of which direct oral evidence would be admissible, if it is shown that the conditions mentioned in sub-section (2) below are satisfied in relation to the statement and computer in question.

The conditions referred to are of great complexity, but in summary require the computer to have been used regularly for processing information of the type concerned, that it should have been working properly during that period and that the information constituting the basis for the document tendered in evidence should be of the sort ordinarily supplied. Still more complex and Byzantine provisions regulate the situation when two or more computers are used in combination to produce the document.[9] A computer is very broadly defined as 'any device for storing and processing information'.[10]

A singular defect of these provisions is that unlike s 2 or s 4 they make no

---

4 See generally Tapper *Computer Law* (4th edn, 1990) chs 9, 10; *Encyclopedia of Information Technology Law* (1990) ch 11; for American Law see Bender *Computer Law* Vol 3.
5 Cmnd 2964 para 16(a).
6 Cmnd 2964 para 19.
7 Civil Evidence Act 1968, s 10(1)(c).
8 The Criminal Evidence Act 1965 has generally worked well in its application to computers, and no special difficulty has been experienced in other jurisdictions which rely on general business record statutes, or on the common law. See *R v Weatherall* (1981) 27 SASR 238, where the common law was applied to admit a computerised record which failed to satisfy the requirements of the local specialised computer provisions.
9 S 5(3).
10 S 5(6).

requirement whatever that any person at any stage of the process shall have had personal knowledge of the accuracy of the information from which the tendered document is derived. It thus becomes vital to understand the relationship of s 5 to the other principal inclusionary sections. The most common overlap will be between s 4 and s 5 as many computer records will be compiled in the course of duty. Since the conditions for the operation of s 4 and s 5 are different, there are two cases to consider. The first is that in which one of the conditions for s 4 is not satisfied, say that the supplier neither has, nor can reasonably be supposed to have had, personal knowledge of the matters dealt with, but where all the conditions for s 5 are satisfied. The second is that in which one of the conditions for s 5 is not satisfied, say that the document in question was not derived from information supplied to the computer in the ordinary course of its activities, but where all the conditions for s 4 are satisfied.[11] The former situation is provided for by expressing s 4 to be without prejudice to s 5. This must mean that a computerised record which fails to fulfil the requirements of s 4, but does satisfy those of s 5, is nonetheless admissible. On the other hand s 5 is *not* expressed to be without prejudice to s 4, so it would appear that in the latter situation a computerised record which fails to fulfil the requirements of s 5, but does satisfy those of s 4, remains inadmissible.[12] In other words the requirements of the computerised record section prevail over those of the documentary record section whenever a computerised record is concerned. As a matter of drafting this is quite satisfactory; approval for the result must however be withheld on account of the manifest inferiority of the particular conditions imposed by s 5. It is however worth noting that s 2, unlike s 4, is not expressed to be without prejudice to s 5, so it seems that documents which fail to satisfy the requirements of s 2 remain inadmissible notwithstanding their satisfaction of the requirements of s 5.[13]

Section 5(4) provides for the certification by the appropriate person of compliance with the conditions set out in s 5(2) as evidence of the matters stated, and Ord 38 r 24 requires the notice of desire to give in evidence a statement under s 5 to contain particulars of the persons who occupied a responsible position in relation to the management of the computer and the supply of information to it. The party upon whom such notice is served may, by counter-notice, require these persons to be called as witnesses with the result that he will have an opportunity of cross-examining them.

Although these provisions were extended within the United Kingdom,[14] and have been copied outside,[15] they have attracted some criticism,[16] mainly

11 *R v Wood* (1982) 76 Cr App Rep 23 furnishes a good example of a perfectly reliable computer record which although admissible in criminal proceedings under the Criminal Evidence Act 1965 would be excluded from civil proceedings because of the stringency of this provision in s 5.

12 It should be noted that s 5, but not s 4, is expressly excluded from the relaxation of the ban on hearsay evidence of opinion enacted by the Civil Evidence Act 1972, s 1.

13 S 2 is not expressly excluded from the relaxation of the ban on hearsay evidence of opinion enacted by the Civil Evidence Act 1972, s 1.

14 See Finance Act 1972, s 34(5); Armed Forces Act 1981, s 9.

15 Eg Victoria Evidence Act 1958, s 55B; Queensland Evidence Act 1977, s 95.

16 See comments on the operation of s 5 submitted to the Australian Law Commission by the London Common Law Bar Association, reproduced by the Australian Law Reform Commission in its Paper No 3 p 83; comments made by an unnamed London commercial silk quoted in *Didcott Legislation Regarding the Admissibility of Computer Generated Evidence* (1980) para 20; and comments by the Scottish Law Commission SLC 100 (1986) para 3.66.

on account of their needless complexity and their omission to cater for the single most common cause for the inaccuracy of computer output, namely inaccurate input.

Most recently in the United Kingdom,[17] and in some other jurisdictions, the remedy has been to draft improved,[18] or differently based,[19] legislation specifically orientated to computers. In others, it is submitted more satisfactorily, computer output has been subsumed under legislation relating to business records generally.[20] The best solution may well be that originally envisaged by the Law Reform Committee, namely to provide a liberal regime within which no distinction is made either between manual and computer records, or between business and private documents.

SECTION 4. STATEMENTS ADMISSIBLE UNDER THE CIVIL EVIDENCE ACT 1968, S 9

Section 9 in effect preserves some common law exceptions to the hearsay rule, but it formally converts them into statutory provisions by providing that statements admissible under them shall be admissible by virtue of s 9. This course was necessitated partly by the fact that second-hand hearsay is admissible under these exceptions in cases falling outside s 4 and s 5, and partly by the inappropriateness of the notice procedure to such cases. The effect of s 9(5) is that statements admissible under the section may be proved at the trial although no preliminary notices have been served. Section 9(2) specifies four common law rules under which evidence is admissible by virtue of s 9(1); s 9(4) specifies three common law rules under which a statement tending to establish reputation or family tradition is received, and, where such evidence cannot, by service of the appropriate notice, be rendered admissible by virtue of s 2 or s 4, it is made admissible by virtue of s 9(3)(a).

A. STATEMENTS ADMISSIBLE BY VIRTUE OF S 9(1)

The following are the rules under which statements are admissible by virtue of s 9(1):

Any rule of law—
(a) whereby in any civil proceedings an admission adverse to a party to the proceedings, whether made by that party or by another person, may be given in evidence against that party for the purpose of proving any fact stated in the admission;
(b) whereby in any civil proceedings published works dealing with matters of a public nature (for example, histories, scientific works, dictionaries and maps) are admissible as evidence of facts of a public nature stated therein;

---

17 Police and Criminal Evidence Act 1984, s 69, so far limited to criminal proceedings, see further ch XVII below.
18 Eg Evidence Act 1929, ss 45a–51 (South Australia).
19 Eg Computer Evidence Act 1983 (South Africa).
20 Notably in the United States, but the same solution has been adopted in a number of Australian jurisdictions including the Commonwealth, see eg Evidence Act 1905, Part IIIA (added in 1978, amended 1985) (Commonwealth); Evidence Act 1898, Part IIC (added in 1976) (New South Wales); and Evidence Act 1910, Part III, Division IIB (added 1981) (Tasmania).

(c) whereby in any civil proceedings public documents (for example, public registers, and returns made under public authority with respect to matters of public interest) are admissible as evidence of facts stated therein;

(d) whereby in any civil proceedings records (for example, the records of certain courts, treaties, Crown grants, pardons and commissions) are admissible as evidence of facts stated therein.[1]

Admissions are included because they may involve proof of second-hand hearsay[2] as when someone not called as a witness admits, on the strength of what the mother told him, that a child was his, and the statement could not be proved under s 2 because of s 2(3), or under s 4, because it is not contained in a record. The maker of an admission hardly has claims to be protected from surprise by service of a notice of desire to tender it in evidence and the adoption of such a course could result in service of a counter-notice obliging his opponent to call him. The case-law on admissions, applicable alike to civil and criminal proceedings, is extensive. It is summarised in the next chapter.

There is no need to deal at length with the second of the above rules, also applicable to civil and criminal proceedings alike. It is not difficult to think of historical facts which could be proved in a contemporary court of law only by recourse to the works mentioned and Lord Halsbury was merely stating the dictates of common sense when he said: 'Where it is important to ascertain ancient facts of a public nature, the law does permit historical works to be referred to.'[3] It was by analogy with those dictates that the report of the engineer responsible for the construction of the Thames tunnel, made in 1844, was admitted in 1904 as evidence of the nature of the soil above it in *East London Rly Co v Thames Conservators*,[4] but it is regrettably true that a higher degree of technicality has been allowed to creep into this branch of the law. In the case of old maps, for instance, great stress is laid on the existence of a public duty on the part of those who prepared them[5] and, in *Fowke v Berington*,[6] Habbington's *Survey of Worcestershire* was excluded on the issue whether a church was the old parish church. The book was tendered as evidence on the condition of the church when Habbington saw it in the seventeenth century and, because there was no reference to public repute, the court treated this fact as one which was not of a public nature. The exclusion of evidence of such obvious relevance has been the subject of judicial regret,[7] but the conversion of the common law rule into a statutory provision cannot of itself effect any change in this regard.[8]

Statements in public documents constitute a vast heterogeneous mass of exceptions to the hearsay rule applicable in civil and criminal cases. They are dealt with in the next chapter.

The fourth rule, also applicable in civil and criminal cases, does not call for comment.

1 S 9(2).
2 Conversely a statement admitted under s 4 or s 2 may itself record an admission made by a third party, see, above, p 544.
3 *Read v Bishop of Lincoln* [1892] AC 644 at 653.
4 (1904) 90 LT 347. The report had become part of the technical expertise of the relevant witness.
5 Contrast *A-G v Horner (No 2)* [1913] 2 Ch 140 with *A-G v Antrobus* [1905] 2 Ch 188 where, however, the duty was statutory.
6 [1914] 2 Ch 308.
7 *A-G v Horner (No 2)*, above.
8 Civil Evidence Act 1968, s 9(6).

B. EVIDENCE OF REPUTATION ADMISSIBLE BY VIRTUE OF S 9(3)(a)

Section 9(3)(a) provides that, in any civil proceedings, a statement which tends to establish reputation or family tradition with respect to any matter and which, if the Act had not been passed, would have been admissible in evidence by virtue of the common law rules mentioned in s 9(4) shall be admissible by virtue of s 9(3)(a), in so far as it is not capable of being rendered admissible under s 2 or s 4.

The following are the rules mentioned in s 9(4):

Any rule of law—
(a) whereby in any civil proceedings evidence of a person's reputation is admissible for the purpose of establishing his good or bad character;
(b) whereby in any civil proceedings involving a question of pedigree, or in which the existence of a marriage is in issue, evidence of reputation or family tradition is admissible for the purpose of proving or disproving pedigree or the existence of the marriage as the case may be;
(c) whereby in any civil proceedings evidence of reputation or family tradition is admissible for the purpose of proving or disproving the existence of any public or general right or of identifying any person or thing.

Taylor contended that evidence of reputation had nothing to do with the hearsay rule—the immediate object of inquiry being 'the concurrence of many voices which raises a presumption that the fact in which they concur is true.'[9] Hearsay statements are nonetheless hearsay statements because there are many of them, but it is important to distinguish, as Taylor does, between the establishment of reputation and the use made of it when established. Reputation is established by a witness's evidence concerning the sayings and doings of a plurality of people. Accordingly it has been said that a witness may not narrate a single person's statement of either the fact reputed or reputation unless it is the pedigree declaration of a member of the family with regard to a genealogical issue.[10] There is therefore no question of an infringement of the rule against hearsay so far as the establishment of reputation is concerned, but that rule is infringed whenever reputation is tendered as evidence of the facts reputed. If a witness deposes to a tradition concerning the existence of a public right prevailing in the community, or the neighbourhood's treatment of a couple as man and wife, he is recounting the express or implied assertions of a number of other people in order to establish the truth of that which was asserted.

The above distinction is taken in s 9(3)(b) of the Civil Evidence Act 1968. The subsection provides that a statement which tends to establish reputation or family tradition under the rules mentioned in s 9(4) shall be admissible as evidence of the matters reputed or handed down, whether tendered under s 2 or s 4, or by virtue of s 9(3)(a); but, if the subsection had stopped there, it would have been difficult to tender reputation as evidence of the matters reputed under s 2 or s 4. As reputation is a multiplicity of statements, how could the notice procedure be applied? How could it be made clear whether the statements were first or second-hand hearsay? To meet such difficulties s 9(3)(b) provides that, for the purposes of Part I of the Act, reputation shall

9 *Law of Evidence* (12th edn) 367.
10 *Shedden v A-G* (1860) 30 LJPM & A 217.

be treated as a fact and not as a statement or multiplicity of statements dealing with the matter reputed.

The result is that there will be many cases in which statements proving reputation can be given in evidence under s 2 or s 4 as tending to establish the facts reputed. For example, if A deceased told B that, according to the tradition prevailing in the locality of X, Y land was common land, or that, according to the tradition prevailing in the A family, his grandmother was illegitimate, these statements of fact could be proved by B as evidence that Y was common land, or that A's grandmother was illegitimate, under s 2 of the 1968 Act. Very often, however, evidence of this nature will be in the form of a statement by A deceased to B that sundry deceased elders of X had told him that Y was common land, and s 9(3) was enacted to meet such cases.

Nothing need be said about evidence of character, but reference must be made to the matters of pedigree and public or general rights mentioned in s 9(4) because, at common law, they are the subject of technical requirements some of which will very probably be held to have survived the Act.

1. PEDIGREE

At common law there is an exception to the hearsay rule under which the oral or written declarations of deceased persons, or declarations to be inferred from family conduct, are, subject to the conditions of admissibility mentioned below, admissible as evidence of pedigree. The evidence often takes the form of direct assertions of fact, as in the old leading case of *Goodright d Stevens v Moss*[11] where the question was whether a child was the legitimate offspring of its parents (since deceased), and Lord Mansfield admitted the parents' declarations, proved by the persons to whom they were made, to the effect that the child was born before their marriage. Such declarations would now, like any other first-hand hearsay statement, be admissible under s 2 of the 1968 Act. Lord Mansfield said that tradition is sufficient in point of pedigree, and referred to the treatment of a child as illegitimate (a matter which is best regarded as original evidence), an entry in a family Bible, an inscription on a tombstone and a pedigree hung up in the family mansion. Without undue strain of language, the inscription on the tombstone could be proved under s 2 of the Act as a statement made in a document by someone who cannot be identified or found. Whether the entry in the family Bible or the hanging pedigree would be admissible under s 2 would depend on the form of statement to be given in evidence, but, and this is particularly true of the hanging pedigree, they might well have to be tendered as evidence of family tradition under s 9 because second or third-hand hearsay would be involved. Lord Eldon said that the tradition must prevail among persons having such a connection with the person to whom it relates that it is natural and likely, from their domestic habits and connections, that they are speaking the truth and could not be mistaken;[12] but this is a matter of weight rather than admissibility, although it is clear that, in order to be admissible, the tradition must be family tradition, and not, for example, that prevailing among the neighbours.

11 (1777) 2 Cowp 591; *Murray v Milner* (1879) 12 Ch D 845; *Re Turner, Glenister v Harding* (1885) 29 ChD 985.
12 *Whitelocke v Baker* (1807) 13 Ves 510 at 514.

The common law conditions of admissibility of pedigree statements or, to employ the more usual word 'declarations', are:

(i)   that the declarant should have been dead;
(ii)   that the declarations should relate to a question of pedigree, ie have a genealogical purpose;[13]
(iii) that the declarant should have been a blood relation, or the spouse of a blood relation, of the person whose pedigree is in issue;[14] and
(iv)   that the declaration should have been made before the dispute in which it is tendered had arisen.[15]

All these conditions are now irrelevant so far as declarations of fact, as distinct from reputation, are concerned, provided they can be rendered admissible under s 2. For example, the issue being A's legitimacy, A's mother writes to B from America to say that she has heard of the dispute and may as well state the truth, viz that she never married A's deceased father; the mother's statement is admissible under s 2 as one made in a document by a person who is overseas. If the issue is whether the defendant to an action for breach of contract is an infant, an affidavit sworn by his deceased father in relation to another case is admissible, although the question is not one of pedigree.[16] If the issue is which of the twins C and D is the elder, the statement of a deceased nurse that she was present at the birth and marked C's foot as that of the first born may be proved under s 2 by the person to whom it was made.[17]

It is therefore only in a very restricted sense that s 9 can be said to have preserved this common law exception to the hearsay rule. A statement tending to establish family reputation or tradition which would, but for the Act, have been admissible for the purpose of proving pedigree is admissible by virtue of s 9 only if the common law conditions of admissibility are satisfied. Accordingly, if A's deceased father told him that his deceased father had often said that, according to family tradition, his grandfather had only one child, A may prove these statements under s 9, although they would be inadmissible as hearsay upon hearsay under s 2; but if A's father had made these statements to B a stranger, B could not prove them under s 9, and they would still be inadmissible under s 2. On the other hand, if C would prove that D, a deceased retainer of the X family, had told him that, according to the family tradition X's grandfather was illegitimate, it seems that, although the statement would be inadmissible by virtue of s 9, because inadmissible at common law as it was not the statement of a blood relation, the statement may be proved under s 2, since s 9(3)(b) permits reputation to be treated as a question of fact if given in evidence under Part I.

13 *Haines v Guthrie* (1884) 13 QBD 818; cf *Hood v Beauchamp* (1836) 8 Sim 26 and *Shields v Boucher* (1847) 1 DeG & Sm 40.
14 *Johnson v Lawson* (1824) 2 Bing 86; *Shrewsbury Peerage Case* (1858) 7 HL Cas 1 at 23; *Berkeley Peerage Case* (1811) 4 Camp 401; on problems of legitimacy and legitimation see *Hitchens v Eardley* (1871) LR 2 P & D 248; *Re Jenion, Jenion v Wynne* [1952] Ch 454, [1952] 1 All ER 1228; *Re Perton Pearson v A-G* (1885) 53 L T 707; *Re Davy* [1935] P 1, followed in *Battle v A-G* [1949] P 358. See also *Monkton v A-G* (1831) 2 Russ & M 147 and *B v A-G* [1965] P 278, [1965] 1 All ER 62.
15 *Berkeley Peerage Case*, above.
16 Cf *Haines v Guthrie*, above.
17 Cf *Johnson v Lawson*, above.

2. PUBLIC OR GENERAL RIGHTS[18]

At common law an oral or written declaration by a deceased person concerning the reputed existence of a public or general right is admissible as evidence of the existence of such right provided the declaration was made before the dispute in which it is tendered had arisen, and, in the case of a statement concerning the reputed existence of a general right, provided the declarant had competent knowledge.

A public right is one affecting the entire population, such as a claim to tolls on a public highway,[19] a right of ferry,[20] or the right to treat part of a river bank as a public landing place.[1] Declarations by deceased persons tending to prove or disprove the existence of such rights are admissible at common law, and evidence of this nature is received on cognate questions such as the boundaries between counties and parishes,[2] and the question of whether a road is public or private.[3]

A general right is one that affects a class of persons such as the inhabitants of a particular district, the tenants of a manor, or the owners of certain plots of land. Examples are rights of common,[4] the rights of corporations[5] and a custom of mining in a particular district.[6] The distinction from public rights is not precise and important, if important at all, only because it has been said that no evidence of competent knowledge of the subject-matter of the reputed right on the part of the declarant is necessary when the right is public because: 'in a matter in which all are concerned, reputation from anyone appears to be receivable; but of course it would be almost worthless unless it came from persons who were shown to have some means of knowledge as by living in the neighbourhood, or frequently using the road in dispute'. If, however, the alleged right is a general one, such as a mining right under certain land; 'hearsay from any person wholly unconnected with the place in which the mines are found, would not only be of no value, but probably altogether inadmissible'.[7]

A far more crucial distinction is that between public or general rights on the one hand and private rights on the other hand, for the latter cannot be proved by evidence of reputation.[8] But here again the distinction is none too precise, all that can be said is that a public or general right must be enjoyed by the claimant as a member of the public or as a member of some clearly defined class. Evidence of a reputation is admissible when private and public

---

18 Except where admissibility under the Civil Evidence Act is being considered, what is said under this head could apply in criminal proceedings.
19 *Brett v Beales* (1830) 10 B & C 508.
20 *Pim v Curell* (1840) 6 M & W 234.
1 *Drinkwater v Porter* (1835) 7 C & P 181.
2 *Brisco v Lomax* (1838) 8 Ad & El 198; *Evans v Rees* (1839) 10 Ad & El 151.
3 *R v Bliss* (1837) 2 Nev & PKB 464.
4 *Evans v Merthyr Tydfil U D C* [1899] 1 Ch 241.
5 *Davies v Morgan* (1831) 1 Cr & J 587.
6 *Crease v Barrett* (1835) 1 Cr M & R 919.
7 *Crease v Barrett*, above; see also *Rogers v Wood* (1831) 2 B & Ad 245. Even in the case of a general right, the declarant need not be proved to have been resident in the neighbourhood (*Duke of Newcastle v Broxtowe Hundred* (1832) 4 B & Ad 273).
8 *R v Antrobus*(1835) 2 Ad & El 788; *Talbot v Lewis* (1834) 1 Cr M & R 495; *Lord Dunraven v Llewellyn* (1850) 15 QB 791 (see *Evans v Merthyr Tydfil U D C* [1899] 1 Ch 241 for the limits of this decision); *White v Taylor* [1969] 1 Ch 150, [1967] 3 All ER 349.

rights coincide, as when the boundaries between two estates are coterminous with those between two hamlets.[9]

The common law conditions of admissibility of hearsay statements concerning reputed public or general rights are:

   (i)   the death of the declarant;

   (ii) that the declaration should have been made before the dispute in which it is tendered;[10] and

   (iii) that the declaration should concern the reputed existence of the right as opposed to a particular fact from which the existence of the right may be inferred.[11]

This last requirement marks a great distinction between the admissibility of pedigree declarations and the admissibility of declarations concerning public or general rights. In the case of each the declarant must be dead, and the statement must have been made before the dispute arose; but, whereas proof of reputation is merely one way of establishing pedigree by hearsay at common law, it is the only way of doing so in the case of public or general rights.

All the above conditions must be fulfilled if evidence of the reputed existence of such rights is to be admissible by virtue of s 9 of the Civil Evidence Act 1968; but is this true of a statement which can, by virtue of s 9(3)(b) be treated as a statement of fact and thereby rendered admissible by virtue of s 2? For example, if A, formerly the oldest inhabitant of a village, were to write from America, after a dispute had arisen concerning rights of common, stating that, according to the tradition which had prevailed in the village community, those rights were enjoyed only by the occupiers of certain lands, could A's statement be received under s 2 as one made in a document by someone who is overseas? It is submitted that the answer is in the affirmative because the exclusion of statements made after a dispute has arisen is a common law restriction on the reception of hearsay under a particular exception to the hearsay rule and it has suffered the same fate as other restrictions on the admissibility of hearsay evidence at common law. Evidence of reputation is second-hand hearsay and this would be inadmissible under s 2 were it not for s 9(3)(b), but that subsection authorises the treatment of reputation as a matter of fact for the purposes of all of Part I of the 1968 Act.

A further, and possibly more difficult, question relates to the effect of the Act on the third common law condition of admissibility, that the declaration should concern the reputed existence of the right as opposed to a particular fact from which it might be inferred. In the past this has produced decisions of breathtaking absurdity. For example, in *Mercer v Denne*[12] the issue was whether the fishermen of Walmer had a customary right of immemorial

9 *Thomas v Jenkins* (1837) 6 Ad & El 525.

10 *Berkeley Peerage Case* (1811) 4 Camp 401; the fact that the declaration was made to provide against future controversy does not affect its admissibility, nor does the existence of a general motive to misrepresent (*Moseley v Davies* (1822) 11 Price 162) but see the judgment of Joyce J in *Brocklebank v Thompson* [1903] 2 Ch 344 where, however, the remarks about interested persons were obiter.

11 *R v Lordsmere (Inhabitants)* (1866) 16 Cox CC 65 (conviction for non-repair as evidence road public).

12 [1905] 2 Ch 538; see also *R v Bliss* (1837) 7 Ad & El 550; *R v Berger* [1894] 1 QB 823; and *A-G v Horner (No 2)* [1913] 2 Ch 140.

antiquity to dry their nets on part of the foreshore. In support of the contention that the custom could not have existed throughout the relevant period, a survey, depositions and old maps were produced. They showed that the sea had run over the portion of foreshore in respect of which the customary right was claimed, but they were rejected because they amounted to statements of particular facts and had nothing to do with the reputed existence of the custom. Is the condition of admissibility under consideration simply a common law restriction on the reception of hearsay under an exception to the general rule excluding such evidence, or is it an independent rule, which can equally well be described as one of evidence or substantive law, which has survived the partial abolition of the hearsay rule in civil cases? Perhaps it would be rash to predict the courts' answer to this question, but it is to be hoped that *Mercer v Denne* and the congeries of similar decisions have not survived the Civil Evidence Act 1968. The survey, depositions and old maps appear to have been documents in which statements were made by persons who could, if living, have given direct oral evidence with regard to the condition of the foreshore.

Whatever view may ultimately be taken by the courts on the matters mentioned above, some of the absurd results of past decisions will be avoided for the future, so far as rights of way are concerned, on account of the provisions of the Highways Act 1959, s 35.[13] The section provides that any map, plan or history of locality is admissible to show whether a way has or has not been dedicated as a highway, or the date when such dedication took place. Such weight is to be given to the above documents as the court considers justified by the circumstances, including the antiquity of the document, the status of the person by whom it was made, its purpose, and the custody in which it was kept or from which it was produced.

SECTION 5. CRITICISMS AND COMPARISONS

Since admissions and statements in public documents, discussed in the next chapter, are admissible in civil proceedings by virtue of s 9 of the Civil Evidence Act 1968, it is arguable that anything in the nature of a general appraisal of that Act should be deferred until they have been discussed; but, although it may well prove to be a permanent measure, s 9 is so obviously meant to be a temporary provision, pending the codification of the law of evidence, that this seems to be the best place for a brief assessment of the merits of the 1968 Act.[14]

It would be hard to maintain that the Act provides a perfect solution to the hearsay problem, but it is submitted that the solution it does provide is among the best that has so far come into force. After some criticisms have been considered, an attempt will be made to justify the above submission by reference to the United States Federal Rules. It must be confessed, however, that it would be unwise to set too much store by a solution to the hearsay problem which applies only to civil cases; the great merit of the American solution is that it also applies to criminal proceedings.

13 Re-enacting the Rights of Way Act 1932. See also National Parks and Access to the Countryside Act 1949.
14 Review was recommended in the Civil Justice Review (1988) para 270, and was referred to the Law Commission in 1989.

A. CRITICISMS

Reference has already been made to what are little more than points of drafting on which it would be possible to improve. These include the desirability of some clarification of the concept of a statement 'made in a document',[15] the difficulty of applying s 2 literally to cases, such as probate actions, will construction summonses and claims under the Fatal Accidents Acts, in which the death of the testator or victim of the tort whose statement a party might wish to tender as evidence of a fact of which 'direct oral evidence by [the maker] would be admissible', is a condition precedent to the bringing of the action,[16] and the desirability of tightening the definition of the conditions justifying the absence of the maker.[17] A few more substantial criticisms have been made. It was suggested[18] that the absence of any definition of 'record' was leading to an over-restrictive application of s 4. The scheme of the Act is generally orientated towards making more go to weight than to admissibility, and there are those who would wish to go further in allowing in second-hand hearsay.[19] Substantial criticism was also addressed to the computer provision. It is doubtful if any special provision is necessary at all, but if it is to be retained it would be sensible to introduce some check on the reliability of the information fed into the machine, and preferably, in the course of doing so, to simplify the conditions for admissibility. It might also be desirable to restrict the width of the definition of a computer.

A criticism which has not yet been mentioned concerns the somewhat elaborate notice procedure. The point is frequently made that parties are not always so advanced in their preparations for trial as to be able to give notice within the prescribed time (usually 21 days before the hearing). It certainly does seem somewhat superfluous to require notice of desire to give a statement in evidence in cases in which the maker is to be called as a witness, the leave of the court for the reception of the statement being required in any event; but this point can be met by a generous exercise of the court's discretion such as that which occurred in *Morris v Stratford-upon-Avon U D C.*[20] When the maker of the statement is not to be called as a witness, the argument in favour of an obligation to give notice of desire to give the statement in evidence, if it is to be admissible as of right, is far stronger.

B. THE FEDERAL RULES

There are five possible solutions to the hearsay problem.[1] The first is to assume that, generally speaking, all is well with the present law, leaving it to the courts to make such modifications as the occasion demands; but, as we have seen, such a solution could be adopted in England only if it were

15 See p 548 above.
16 See p 553 above.
17 See p 550 above.
18 See p 554 above.
19 See p 543 above.
20 See p 547 above.
 1 They are rehearsed in this form by the New Zealand Law Commission in an options paper 'Hearsay Evidence', Preliminary Paper No 10 (1989).

assumed that no modifications will be called for, because the House of Lords has, by a majority, set itself against the creation of further common law exceptions to the hearsay rule.[2] The second is to rationalise the existing exceptions by legislation, and to create new ones by the same means. This course has been adopted in the United States. It has much to commend it, notably continuity with the common law; but it does tend to produce a most unwieldy list of exceptions. There are no less than 31 in the Uniform Rules, and, though the arrangement is more logical and has more regard to practical convenience, we shall see that there are nearly as many in the Federal Rules. The third possible solution is that adopted by the Civil Evidence Act 1968, the partial abolition of the rule by permitting, subject to safeguards, first-hand hearsay statements to be proved in all cases in which the maker is unavailable, by permitting, subject to the discretion of the court, the proof of all such statements when the maker is called, and by allowing for the reception of a fairly wide class of second-hand hearsay statements. A fourth possible solution mooted by the Law Reform Commission of Australia is to admit hearsay at the discretion of the judge. Such an approach could either exclude hearsay in principle, subject to a broad inclusionary discretion, in which case it might resemble the second and third solutions; or admit all relevant hearsay in principle, subject to a broad exclusionary discretion, in which case it would resemble the fifth solution. The fifth solution is that of total abolition: hearsay, however remote, would, in theory, be admissible without restriction. This solution which seems to work perfectly well in civil law jurisdictions and in informal tribunals within England and Wales[3] has now been adopted for all civil proceedings in Scotland.[4] This course was recommended by the Scottish Law Commission,[5] and the legislation goes still further in making such hearsay, however remote, admissible without imposing any notice procedure. It is to be hoped that if this measure proves to be successful it may be emulated in England and Wales.

After giving a definition of hearsay like that adopted in this book,[6] r 801 of the Federal Rules provides that certain statements are not to be treated as hearsay. These are the previous inconsistent statements of witnesses: 'given under oath subject to the penalty of perjury at a trial, hearing, or other proceeding, or in a deposition,'[7] previous consistent statements rebutting fabrication or proving identification soon after the perception of the person identified, and a party's admissions. A general ban on the reception of hearsay is then followed by two groups of exceptions. The first group comprises situations in which hearsay statements are admissible although the maker is available. It includes statements made for the purpose of medical diagnosis or treatment, and the number of situations in this group is no less than 23. Hearsay statements included in the second group are

---

2 *Myers v D P P* [1965] AC 1001, [1964] 1 All ER 877.
3 See above p 14.
4 Civil Evidence (Scotland) Act 1988, s 2.
5 In its Report 'Evidence' SLC No 100 (1986).
6 '"Hearsay" is a statement, other than one made by the declarant while testifying at the trial or hearing, offered in evidence to prove the truth of the matter asserted.' This approach has been criticised by some American commentators, see eg Wellborn 'The Definition of Hearsay in the Federal Rules of Evidence' (1982) 61 Tex LR 49.
7 An enlargement of the common law of little practical value, cf Civil Evidence Act 1968, s 3.

admissible only if the maker is unavailable. There are four of them, of which the one of the greatest general interest is formulated as follows:

> A statement which was at the time of its making so far contrary to the declarant's pecuniary or proprietary interest, or so far tended to subject him to civil or criminal liability, or to render invalid a claim by him against another, that a reasonable man in his position would not have made the statement unless he believed it to be true. A statement tending to expose the declarant to criminal liability and offered to exculpate the accused is not admissible unless corroborating circumstances clearly indicate the trustworthiness of the statement.[8]

Each group of exceptions concludes with 'a statement not specifically covered by any of the foregoing exceptions but having comparable circumstantial guarantees of trustworthiness,' an interesting provision leaving the development of the law to the courts.

It does scant justice to the carefully thought out set of rules to point to two situations where, it is submitted, the statements ought to be admissible, and yet they are not admissible; but such situations are almost bound to arise whenever the hearsay problem is dealt with by a general prohibition followed by a number of specific exceptions, instead of being followed by a general permission with qualifications. The situations in question are first, that which arose in *Morris v Stratford-upon-Avon U D C*[9] in which a witness unexpectedly gave confused and inconsistent evidence, and second, the case in which the maker of the statement has not perceived the event described in it recently. Someone age 20 tells his friend that he vividly remembers how, on his 16th birthday, his father hit his mother. It is absurd not to allow the friend to prove this statement as evidence of the assault if the maker is not available.

Finally, it should be stressed that the Federal Rules are in some respects much laxer than the Civil Evidence Act with regard to the admissibility of hearsay. Statements made for the purpose of medical diagnosis by someone who is available as a witness ought never to be admissible as of right unless he is called. It is just the kind of case where 'truth will out' in cross-examination if it has not already come out in the examination-in-chief.

---

8 Federal Rules 1975, r 804(3).
9 See p 547 above; or the witness may have become senile since he made the statement as in *Harvey v Smith-Wood* [1964] 2 QB 171, [1963] 2 All ER 127, a decision on the Evidence Act 1938.

CHAPTER XVI

Hearsay statements in civil and criminal cases

This chapter is concerned with statements in public documents and admissions. They are the two most important common law exceptions to the hearsay rule, although the treatment of the first involves a reference to a number of statutory provisions. In each instance the exception is now applicable to civil cases by virtue of s 9(1) of the Civil Evidence Act 1968. The common law relating to statements in public documents still applies in criminal proceedings,[1] but the Police and Criminal Evidence Act 1984, s 76, has changed the conditions under which admissions are admissible in criminal proceedings.[2]

Two other common law rules under which hearsay statements are admissible in civil and criminal proceedings, in the former by virtue of s 9(1), were mentioned in section 4 of the last chapter. They are the rule whereby published works, dealing with matters of a public nature, are admissible as evidence of facts of a public nature stated therein, and the rule whereby records (for example, the records of certain courts, treaties, Crown grants and commissions) are admissible as evidence of the facts stated therein. Nothing more need be said with regard to the first, and, for the purposes of a work of this nature, the second may be treated as part of the more general rule under which statements in public documents are admissible.

Pedigree declarations and statements concerning public rights were also dealt with in the last chapter. Although the common law rules on these subjects apply to civil and criminal proceedings alike, it was thought to be more convenient to deal with them in a chapter concerned with hearsay statements in civil cases, firstly because, so far as the latter are concerned, the common law has to some extent been affected by the Civil Evidence Act, and secondly because the number of occasions on which resort is likely to be had to them in a criminal case is minimal.

---

1 As supplemented by the provisions of Part II of the Criminal Justice Act 1988.
2 Although in criminal proceedings admissions are now governed entirely by statute, it will be seen that they have in the past contributed greatly to the development of the common law, and may yet do so.

SECTION 1. STATEMENTS IN PUBLIC DOCUMENTS

A. STATEMENT AND ILLUSTRATIONS OF THE EXCEPTION TO THE HEARSAY RULE

1. STATEMENT OF THE EXCEPTION

In civil and criminal cases, statements in public documents are generally admissible evidence of the truth of their contents.[3] In criminal cases they are admissible by virtue of the common law and a heterogeneous mass of statutes, including the Criminal Justice Act 1988 to the extent that the conditions imposed by ss 23 and 24 are satisfied. In civil cases, if they were admissible at common law, they are now admissible by virtue of s 9(1) of the Civil Evidence Act 1968; in some cases in which they were not admissible at common law they may be admissible, subject to compliance with the notice procedure, under s 2 or s 4 of that Act. If admissible in a civil case under some other statute, as many documents are, there is no question of their being rendered admissible under s 2 or s 4 of the 1968 Act for RSC Ord 38, r 21(2) states that the notice procedure shall not apply 'in relation to any statement which is admissible as evidence of the fact stated therein by virtue not only of the said ss 2, 4 and 5 [of the Civil Evidence Act 1968] but by virtue also of any other statutory provision'. All that is required is that the conditions of admissibility laid down in the other statute should be complied with; usually there are none and the document is admissible in evidence on production of the original (or where permitted a copy) to the court.

The most succinct formulation of this exception to the hearsay rule is that of Phillimore J in *Wilton & Co v Phillips*.[4] 'A public document coming from the proper place or a certified copy of it is sufficient proof of every particular stated in it.' In *Re Stollery, Weir v Treasury Solicitor*,[5] Scrutton LJ expressed the opinion that this was simply a restatement of the law laid down in the leading cases of *Irish Society v Bishop of Derry*[6] and *Sturla v Freccia*.[7] Some limit must, however, be placed upon the generality of Phillimore J's statement, in view of the explanation of *Bird v Keep*[8] adopted in *Re Stollery, Weir v Treasury Solicitor*. In *Bird v Keep* it was held that a death certificate was inadmissible evidence of the cause of death mentioned therein on information supplied by a coroner.[9] This conclusion was technically obiter dictum because the Court of Appeal considered that the cause of death was sufficiently proved by other evidence, but it was justified in *Re Stollery* on the ground that, as the registrar of births, deaths and marriages is bound by statute to record the verdict of a coroner's jury, and as that verdict was inadmissible evidence of the facts on which it was based, it would be absurd to treat the registrar's certificate as any proof of this particular fact. Such a certificate does, however, constitute evidence of the date, as well as the fact of the birth,

---

3 In the United States the matter is governed by the Federal Rules of Evidence, r 803 (8)(c) which has been held to encompass opinion as well as fact, if based upon factual findings, *Beech Aircraft Corporation v Rainey* 109 S Ct R 439 (1988).
4 (1903) 19 TLR 390.
5 [1926] Ch 284 at 318.
6 (1846) 12 Cl & Fin 641.
7 (1880) 5 App Cas 623.
8 [1918] 2 KB 692.
9 *Bird v Keep* was followed in *Chapman v Amos* (1959) 18 DLR (2d) 140.

marriage or death recorded,[10] and, as was decided by the Court of Appeal in *Re Stollery*, a birth certificate may constitute a link in the evidence relating to the marriage of the parents of the child whose birth is recorded. A birth certificate is likewise evidence of the paternity of the person named therein as the father.[11]

2. ILLUSTRATIONS OF THE EXCEPTIONS

(i) Registers

The admissibility of certificates of birth, marriage and death is now governed by statute; but, so far as the registers themselves are concerned, Lord Blackburn pointed out that:

> In many cases, entries in the parish register of births, marriages and deaths, and other entries of that kind, before there were any statutes relating to them, were admissible, for they were 'public' then, because the common law of England making it an express duty to keep the register, made it a public document in that sense kept by a public officer for the purposes of a register, and that made it admissible.[12]

In *Lyell v Kennedy*[13] Lord Selborne said:

> Foreign registers of baptisms and marriages or certified extracts from them are receivable in evidence in the courts of this country as to those matters which are properly and regularly recorded on them when it sufficiently appears (in the words of Mr Hubbock's learned work on evidence) that they 'have been kept under the sanction of public authority and are recognised by the tribunals of the country' (i e of the country where they are kept) 'as authentic records'.

To this day, therefore, the contents of certain foreign registers are treated as proof of the facts stated by virtue of the common law. On the principle discussed by Lord Blackburn, an entry in a vestry book has been received as evidence of the election of a parish officer,[14] a statement in the log book of one of the King's ships was evidence at common law of the time of sailing,[15] and entries in coastguards' books have facilitated proof of the state of the weather.[16] For similar reasons, entries in books kept by universities may be received to prove the granting of degrees,[17] and the public books of a corporation might be received at common law as evidence of matters of

10 *Wilton & Co v Phillips* (above); *Re Goodrich's Estate, Payne v Bennett* [1904] P 138; *Brierley v Brierley and Williams* [1918] P 257. Now that hearsay statements of opinion are admissible under the Civil Evidence Act 1968 (Civil Evidence Act 1972, s 1), a doctor's statement of the cause of death would be admissible under s 4.
11 *Jackson v Jackson and Pavan* [1960] 3 All ER 621. See also *Carlton and United Breweries Ltd v Cassin* [1956] VLR 186 (statement of age on marriage certificate evidence of that fact).
12 *Sturla v Freccia* (1880) 5 App Cas 623 at 644. In *R v Halpin* [1975] QB 907 it was suggested that it would have been more accurate if Lord Blackburn had spoken of registers of baptisms, marriages and burials because the parish officer would not have had personal knowledge of births and deaths and was under no duty to enquire into their occurrence.
13 (1889) 14 App Cas 437 at 448–9.
14 *R v Martin* (1809) 2 Camp 100.
15 *D'Israeli v Jowett* (1795) 1 Esp 427.
16 *The Catherina Maria* (1866) LR 1 A & E 53.
17 *Collins v Carnegie* (1834) 1 Ad & El 695.

public interest stated in them,[18] although this subject is now mainly governed by statute.

(ii) Returns

We have already seen that inquisitions, assessments, surveys, reports and returns are admissible as proof of the truth of their contents when made under public authority and in relation to matters of public interest or concern.[19] The leading authority is *Irish Society v Bishop of Derry*[20] in which case the bishop's return to a writ from the exchequer stating the vacancies and advowsons in his diocese was received as evidence of these matters because it consisted of statements made by a public officer in discharge of a public duty. On similar principles, inquisitions and surveys of manors belonging to the Crown or the duchies of Cornwall and Lancaster have been admitted to show the manorial customs and boundaries specified therein.[1] Land tax assessments and poor rate books have likewise been received as evidence of the ownership and occupation of land to which they related.[2] In *A-G v Antrobus*,[3] tithe maps were received as evidence of the non-existence of certain rights of way when they were prepared because they were prepared after a public inquiry. Perhaps it is not going too far to regard a public statute as the outcome of a parliamentary inquiry. However that may be, recitals in such statutes are evidence of the facts stated,[4] as are the contents of parliamentary journals and governmental gazettes so far they relate to acts of state.[5]

(iii) Certificates

Registers and returns are made pursuant to a public duty for the public benefit in circumstances in which there is usually some public check on their accuracy, and it was no doubt the absence of one or more of these guarantees of reliability that accounted for the reluctance of the common law to admit the mere certificate of a fact as evidence of that fact's existence.[6] The stock exception was the notary's certificate when treated as evidence of the due protest of a bill of exchange,[7] and there may have been others,[8] but the reception of certificates as evidence of the facts stated has been authorised by numerous statutes.

---

18 *Shrewsbury (Warden etc of Mercers etc) v Hart* (1823) 1 C & P 113.
19 See p 109, above.
20 (1846) 12 Cl & Fin 641; *Tanenbaun v Helpvic Ltd* (1960) 22 DLR (2d) 333 following *Gyfford v Woodgate* (1809) 11 East 297.
1 *Duke of Beaufort v Smith* (1849) 4 Exch 450.
2 *Doe d Strode v Seaton* (1834) 2 Ad & El 171; *Smith v Andrews* [1891] 2 Ch 678 (poor rate books).
3 [1905] 2 Ch 188.
4 *R v Sutton* (1816) 4 M & S 532.
5 *R v Holt* (1793) 5 Term Rep 436, followed in *Walt Disney Productions Ltd v H John Edwards Publishing Co (Pty) Ltd* (1955) 55 SR (NSW) 162. The *London Gazette* is made evidence of a variety of matters by statute.
6 *Omichund v Barker* (1745) Willes 538 at 549–50.
7 *Brain v Preece* (1843) 11 M & W 773 at 775.
8 When, in *Krajina v Tass Agency* [1949] 2 All ER 274, the court accepted the certificate of the Soviet ambassador that Tass was a department of the Soviet state, was it receiving hearsay evidence or taking judicial notice?

3. RATIONALE OF THE EXCEPTION

(i) Necessity

The object of many of these statutes is to obviate the necessity of calling an official to produce a register or return for which he is responsible, and it is sometimes said to be a principal justification for this exception to the hearsay rule that an enormous amount of public time would be wasted if it did not exist. It seems, however, that there is some confusion of thought in regarding this as a principal justification for the exception. No one would wish to deny the merits of any rule of law designed to prevent the waste of public time involved in calling a public official for the sole purpose of producing a document, but the waste of time which may have been caused by the necessity of adopting this procedure in the past was due to the rule requiring the production of an original document when reliance is to be placed on its contents, rather than the rule against hearsay. In nine cases out of ten this latter rule would be infringed when the original register or return was produced to prove its contents, because it is only when the official has personally observed some matter to which his report relates that the reception of hearsay evidence can be avoided. There is, of course, a necessity for the reception of such evidence in many of the cases in which public documents have been received to prove the truth of their contents; but this arises from the impossibility of procuring better evidence, and it is quite unconnected with the question of saving time.

(ii) Reliability

In *Irish Society v Derry*, the bishop was an interested party in the sense that some of the advowsons belonged to him, but, in the opinion of Parke B, this did not affect the reliability of the return to the extent of rendering it inadmissible. He said:

> In public documents, made for the information of the Crown, or all the King's subjects who may require the information they contain, the entry by a public officer is presumed to be true when it is made, and it is for that reason receivable in all cases, whether the officer or his successor may be concerned in such cases or not.

Parke B might have added 'and whether the entry consists of hearsay upon hearsay or not', for second or third-hand hearsay is undoubtedly received under this particular exception. It is evidence of belief on the part of the person making the entry.

Public duties are usually carried out, and failure to do so is often likely to be detected. The presumption mentioned by Parke B is probably justified by the facts.

B. CONDITIONS OF ADMISSIBILITY—THE NATURE OF A PUBLIC DOCUMENT

It is clear from the above illustrations that there are several different kinds of public document. Different conditions of admissibility may apply to the different kinds of document when the somewhat heterogeneous exception to the hearsay rule now under consideration is invoked. As most of these conditions are common to most of the documents, it will be convenient to consider them under the head of the definition of a public document before referring to the different categories of public documents.

1. THE DEFINITION OF A PUBLIC DOCUMENT

In *Sturla v Freccia*,[9] the report of a committee appointed by the Genoese government on the fitness of a candidate for the post of consul which contained a statement of his age was rejected as evidence of that fact. The grounds on which the House of Lords held that the evidence should be rejected were that the report was not made under a strict duty to inquire into all the circumstances it recorded, it was not concerned with a public matter, it was not intended to be retained, and it was not meant for public inspection. A word must be said about each of these matters which may be treated as the usual pre-requisites of a document's admissibility as a public document although the last appears in the forefront of Lord Blackburn's description which has been quoted on a number of subsequent occasions. He said he understood:

> a public document to mean a document that is made for the purpose of the public making use of it, and being able to refer to it. It is meant to be where there is a judicial or quasi-judicial duty to inquire, as might be said to be the case with the bishops acting under the writs issued by the Crown.[10]

(i) Public duty to inquire and record

In the case of returns, special stress is laid upon the duty to inquire, while the duty to record is more to the fore in the case of registers and certificates. It has, however, been said that, even in the latter case, the admissibility of a register depends on the public duty of the person compiling it to make an entry after satisfying himself of the truth of the statement.[11] The duty must be imposed on a public official in that capacity. Surveys made under private authority have been held to be admissible, although they were kept in a public office,[12] and baptismal registers kept by nonconformists or Quakers were inadmissible as evidence of the facts stated at common law.[13] Even if a duty to report to a public authority is imposed upon an official by statute, his report will not constitute proof of the truth of its contents if made solely in

---

9 (1880) 5 App Cas 623.
10 At 643–4.
11 Per Erle J in *Doe d France v Andrews* (1850) 15 QB 756. A gratuitous annotation to an official record is thus inadmissible, *Re Simpson* [1984] 1 NZLR 738 (annotation on death certificate that the deceased's issue had been adopted).
12 *Daniel v Wilkin* (1852) 7 Exch 429. The surveys might well be admissible under s 4 of the Civil Evidence Act 1968.
13 *Re Woodward, Kenway v Kidd* [1913] 1 Ch 392. In so far as they are not admissible by virtue of some other statute they would now be admissible under the Civil Evidence Act 1968 (*Re H's Estate* [1949] VLR 197).

order to provide a check upon himself.[14] Nor is it enough to make a report in anticipation of an official request.[15]

(ii) Public matter

It was recognised in *Sturla v Freccia* that a matter may be public although it is not the concern of the entire community. Accordingly, the court rolls of a manor have been received as evidence of a custom,[16] but entries in a corporation's books were sometimes rejected at common law because they did not concern a public matter.[17] It is, however, doubtful whether this is something with regard to which any high degree of precision can be achieved.

In *R v Halpin*[18] it was held that a company's file of statutory returns kept in the register of companies was admissible evidence that the appellant was a director at the material time because, under modern conditions, it is sufficient if one person (the officer making the return) has a duty to satisfy himself as to the facts stated and another (the registration officer) has a duty to record those facts.

(iii) Retention

If a document is brought into existence for a temporary purpose it cannot be received under this head. Thus, in *Heyne v Fischel & Co*,[19] it was held that records compiled by the post office showing the times at which telegrams were received were inadmissible as there was no intention that they should be retained for public inspection, and Crown surveys were rejected on account of their temporary purpose in *Mercer v Denne*.[20]

(iv) Public inspection

The possibility that the public may refer to the document undoubtedly enhances the credibility of its contents; but the decision in *Lilley v Pettit*[1] which turned on this requirement may be thought to justify Professor Baker's comment that:

> Accessibility of the public to documents should never have been raised from the status of an additional reason for admitting official records to that of a condition of admissibility.[2]

Lilley v Pettit was a case in which a woman was prosecuted for making a false

14 *Merrick v Wakley* (1838) 8 Ad & El 170.
15 *Newbold v R* [1983] 2 AC 705, though such a report would now be admissible in England under s 24 of the Criminal Justice Act 1988.
16 *Heath v Deane* [1905] 2 Ch 86.
17 *Hill v Manchester and Salford Waterworks Co* (1833) 5 B & Ad 866.
18 [1975] QB 907, [1975] 2 All ER 1124.
19 (1913) 30 TLR 190.
20 [1905] 2 Ch 538; see also *White v Taylor* [1969] 1 Ch 150, [1967] 3 All ER 349. There is no requirement of permanence for the admissibility of statements contained in records under s 4 of the Civil Evidence Act 1968.
1 [1946] KB 401, [1946] 1 All ER 593. Cf *Andrews v Cordiner* [1947] KB 655, [1947] 1 All ER 777 an affiliation case in which regimental records were admitted under the Evidence Act 1938, as they would be under the Act of 1968.
2 Baker *The Hearsay Rule* 137.

statement with regard to the paternity of her child in entering it as that of her husband. The prosecution tendered in evidence the regimental records of the army unit in which her husband had been serving abroad at all material times, but the Divisional Court held them to be inadmissible because they were not kept for the use and information of the public who had not got access to them. Accordingly the prosecution failed. The result is no doubt surprising, but the principle on which it was reached was already deeply embedded in our law,[3] and has since been adopted by the Privy Council.[4]

2. THE DIFFERENT CATEGORIES OF PUBLIC DOCUMENTS

The distinction between registers, returns and certificates taken in the foregoing illustrations of the exception is that of Wigmore.[5] Apart from its convenience from the point of view of exposition, it may have practical significance because the general conditions of admissibility which have just been enumerated undoubtedly undergo some modification when applied to different species of public document. In the case of registers, it may be fatal to the reception of the entry to prove that it was not made promptly[6] or in accordance with the prevailing practice relating to the keeping of the register.[7] Any excess of jurisdiction would be fatal to some types of return.[8] There would, however, be no point in endeavouring to lay down hard-and-fast rules, inferred from the cases, concerning the further conditions of admissibility which may have to be satisfied in the case of certain public documents, for each decision is highly dependent on its specific facts.

SECTION 2. ADMISSIONS

A party's statements adverse to his case are received as evidence of the truth of their contents in civil and criminal proceedings. Difficulties may sometimes be occasioned by the fact that the person making the statements is not technically a party. The guardian of an infant is not a party to care proceedings brought under the Children and Young Persons Act 1969, but, although he was not called as a witness, his admissions concerning the treatment of the child were received in *Re Humberside County Council v D P R (An Infant)*[9] on the ground that the hearsay rule does not apply to such proceedings. In *R v Phillips*[10] the Court of Criminal Appeal might be thought to have considered that the accused's daughters' statements (the making of which they denied in court) that they had been 'schooled' by their mother would, if they had been proved under the Criminal Procedure Act 1865, s 4, have constituted evidence of that fact. Though the relevance of that fact was

3 See, for example, *A-G v Horner (No 2)* (p 2, above)
4 *Thrasyvoulos Ioannou v Papa Christoforos Demetrious* [1952] AC 84, [1952] 1 All ER 179; see also *R v Kaipianen* (1954) 17 CR 388.
5 V *Wigmore* para 631 f.
6 *Doe d Warren v Bray* (1828) 8 B & C 813.
7 *Fox v Bearblock* (1881) 17 Ch D 429; *Doe d Davies v Gatacre* (1838) 8 C & P 578.
8 *Evans v Taylor* (1838) 7 Ad & El 617.
9 [1977] 3 All ER 964, [1977] 1 WLR 1251. This position now has statutory authorisation, see Children (Admissibility of Hearsay Evidence) Order 1990 (SI 1990 No 143).
10 (1936) 26 Cr App Rep 17.

indisputable, the daughters were not parties to the proceedings. However, the court may have meant to do no more than say that the accused should have been allowed to call the witnesses to prove the girls' out-of-court statements in order to neutralise their testimony.[11]

When they are made by the accused in a criminal case, admissions are received upon special conditions set out in the Police and Criminal Evidence Act 1984, s 76, described as 'confessions', and defined to include: 'any statement wholly or partly adverse to the person who made it, whether made to a person in authority or not and whether made in words or otherwise'.[12] When disserving statements are made by a party to civil litigation, they are said to be admissions and must be distinguished from the formal admissions which may be made for the purpose of particular proceedings and were mentioned in ch II. Formal admissions bind the party by whom they were made, but the informal admissions we are about to consider may always be contradicted or explained away by their maker,[13] when it is for the tribunal of fact to determine the weight to be attached to them. They may constitute the sole, though sufficient, evidence in support of a civil judgment,[14] or even a conviction of crime.[15]

This section is confined to admissions. As we have seen, they are admissible in civil cases by virtue of s 9(1) of the Civil Evidence Act 1968. In that context, an admission 'includes any representation of fact whether made in words or otherwise',[16] so long as it is adverse to the party against whom it is tendered and made by him or someone in privity with him. Conduct which was not intended to amount to a representation may constitute circumstantial evidence against the agent because it warrants an inference of consciousness of guilt or the weakness of a party's case, as when he suborns witnesses,[17] or remains silent when a denial of things said against him could reasonably have been expected.[18]

When considering the following account of the common law, the reader should bear in mind the possibility that, although a statement does not qualify for reception as a common law admission by virtue of s 9(1), it may yet be possible to give it in evidence in civil proceedings under s 2 or s 4 of the 1968 Act. This would of course entail notice of desire to do so, with the possibility of a counter-notice which might require the opposite party to be called as a witness, but there will always be the further possibility of the court's exercising its discretion either to admit the statement although no notice has been served, or to dispense with compliance with the counter-notice. From the point of view of the party wishing to give it in evidence under the Act, the advantage of a statement's coming within the category of

---

11 See *R v Turner* (1975) 61 Cr App Rep 67 at 87.
12 S 82(1).
13 See for example, *Smith v Smith* [1957] 2 All ER 397, [1957] 1 WLR 802.
14 *M'Kewen v Cotching* (1857) 27 LJ Ex 41.
15 *R v Sullivan* (1887) 16 Cox CC 347, an Irish case in which the English authorities are reviewed; *McKay v R* (1936) 54 CLR 1.
16 Civil Evidence Act 1968, s 9(2).
17 *Moriarty v London Chatham and Dover Rly Co* (1870) LR 5 QB 314; *R v Watt* (1905) 20 Cox CC 852.
18 *Bessela v Stern* (1877) 2 CPD 265; cf *Weidemann v Walpole* [1891] 2 QB 534; and, for an example in a criminal case, see *R v Edwards* [1983] Crim LR 539; but it is not enough that the accused fails to deny an element in the charge against him when it has not been proved by the prosecution, *Chappell v D P P* (1988) 89 Cr App Rep 82.

admissions is that it can be given in evidence as of right without the necessity of going through the notice procedure.

Admissions by words may be made in any form and any circumstances. In *R v Simons*,[19] for instance, it was proposed, on a charge of arson, to call a witness to prove what the prisoner said to his wife on leaving the magistrate's room after committal, and Alderson B allowed the witness to be called because 'What a person is overheard saying to his wife, or even saying to himself, is evidence.'

An oral admission may be proved although it concerns the contents of a document which is not produced in circumstances in which secondary evidence would be inadmissible. In *Slatterie v Pooley*,[20] the plaintiff sued on a covenant indemnifying him against debts set out in the schedule to a deed which was inadmissible for want of a proper stamp. An oral admission by the defendant that a certain debt was included in the schedule was received because, according to Parke B:

> The reason why such parol statements are admissible, without notice to produce, or accounting for the absence of the written instrument, is that they are not open to the same objection which belongs to parol evidence from other sources, where the written evidence might have been produced; but such evidence is excluded from the presumption of its untruth, arising from the very nature of the case, where better evidence is withheld; whereas what a party himself admits to be true, may reasonably be presumed to be so.

The decision has been criticised because it flouts the best evidence rule and ignores the danger of inaccuracy attendant on the repetition of an admission,[1] but the foregoing quotation seems to provide an adequate answer to the first point, and ample allowance was made by Parke B for the second when he added 'the weight and value of such testimony is quite another question'.

The fact that an admission was made under threats or in consequence of other pressures may greatly affect its weight, but does not appear to render it inadmissible. Thus in *Morleys of Brixton v Minott*[2] an admission by an employee was admitted in an unfair dismissal case without regard to any question of inducement or breach of the Judges' Rules. It should be borne in mind, however, that the rules of evidence may be waived by the parties to civil cases, and this may mean that an admission made pursuant to an agreement not to use it in evidence would be inadmissible.

A. CONDITIONS OF ADMISSIBILITY

An admission being any statement, express or implied, oral or written, which is adverse to a party's case, the only conditions of admissibility, when the statement emanates from the party himself concern the capacity in which he is acting and the reception of the entirety of the statement; there is also

---

19 (1834) 6 C & P 540; cf *Rumping v D P P* [1962] 3 All ER 256; *R v Maqsud Ali* [1966] 1 QB 688, [1965] 2 All ER 464 (tape-recording of private conversation in foreign language). An infant's admissions are evidence against him (*Alderman v Alderman and Dunn* [1958] 1 All ER 391).

20 (1840) 6 M & W 664.

1 *Lawless v Queale* (1845) 8 ILR 382; Taylor *Law of Evidence* (12th edn) vol 1, 286.

2 [1982] ICR 444. See also *Jogender Singh, Bains v Yorkshire Insurance Co Ltd* (1936) 38 DLR (2d) 417 (confession of arson in action on insurance policy).

the question whether he must have had personal knowledge of the facts stated. When these matters have been considered, it will be necessary to say something about cases in which the statement does not directly emanate from the party himself. These cases give rise to problems relating to documents found in the possession of the parties, vicarious admissions and statements made in the presence of the parties.

1. CAPACITY OF THE PARTY

If someone sues or is sued in a personal capacity, admissions made by him when acting in a representative capacity, as when he was litigating as guardian of an infant,[3] may be proved against him; but, when he is litigating in a representative capacity, admissions that would affect him in his personal capacity may not be proved against him. Thus, in *Legge v Edmonds*,[4] a mother had made statements which could have been received as evidence of her adultery if she had been sued personally, and it was held that they were inadmissible in proceedings brought against her as administratrix of her late husband's estate in which proceedings the legitimacy of her child was in issue. The common law rule was justified by the broader principle that persons other than the maker of an admission ought not to be bound by it. Granted that this is a valid principle, it would clearly be improper to allow those represented by the maker of an admission to be affected by it, at any rate when it did not concern a matter in which his and their interest was identical; but the justification was no different from the justification of the hearsay rule on the ground that the statement could not be contradicted or questioned by the other party when it was made, and it could now be rendered admissible in civil proceedings under s 2 of the 1968 Act.

2. RECEPTION OF ENTIRE STATEMENT

When a statement contains items favourable to a party's case in addition to the admission, the party relying on the latter cannot prevent the other items from being proved. Accordingly, the debit side of an account may be tendered as an admission against one party, but this will mean that the credit side may be treated as evidence against his adversary.[5] The self-serving nature of the parts of a statement that are favourable to the maker of an admission will no doubt affect their weight but there seems to be no reason why they should not be treated as evidence of the truth of that which they assert.[6]

3. THE QUESTION OF PERSONAL KNOWLEDGE

An admission is of evidential value only to the extent that its maker has personal knowledge of the matters it contains. In *Comptroller of Customs v Western Electric Co* the Judicial Committee held that an admission that goods

3 *Beasley v McGrath* (1804) 2 Sch & Lef 31; *Stanton v Percival* (1855) 5 HL Cas 257.
4 (1855) 25 LJ Ch 125 at 141.
5 *Harrison v Turner* (1847) 10 QB 482.
6 *Smith v Blandy* (1825) Ry & M 257 at 259.

were manufactured in the United States which was based solely on markings to that effect on the goods was of no more value than the markings themselves, which were inadmissible hearsay, 'If a man admits something of which he knows nothing it is of no real evidential value.'[7] On the other hand, it is immaterial that the admission relates to a matter of opinion if the opinion is formed upon a sufficient basis of personal experience.[8] The point is well illustrated in handling cases. The prosecution must prove both that the goods in question were in fact stolen, and also that the accused so believed. If the accused's knowledge is, or may reasonably be supposed to be, derived from his own personal knowledge it is admissible on both issues, but if it is derived solely from what he has been told by another, while it is still relevant to prove his belief, it is valueless to prove that the goods were in fact stolen.[9]

It is probably better to regard such admissions as valueless rather than inadmissible.[10] A witness has been allowed to narrate a party's statement of his own age as evidence of that fact,[11] although it is not a matter of which the party could be said to have personal knowledge. Even a party's assertion that he believes what his agent told him to be true may constitute evidence against him.[12] There must, however, be some evidence of belief in, or acceptance of, the fact admitted.[13] In such a case it can be argued that the accused in adopting the statement waives any objection.[14]

Similar reasoning may be applied to cases where the accused makes admissions in terms of conclusions of law which it is for the trier of fact to determine.[15]

B. DOCUMENTS IN THE POSSESSION OR CONTROL OF A PARTY

The fact that documents were found in the possession of a party may be proved for a variety of purposes. So far as the present inquiry is concerned, the only question is the extent to which they may be received as evidence against the party of the truth of their contents. On principle, a strong case should be necessary for the reception of the document for such a purpose, and this may account for the paucity of authority on the subject. Such as there is certainly warrants Professor Baker's conclusion that it is difficult to prove an admission against a party by his mere possession of the documents of a third person.[16] If it is clear that a party had access to and control over the contents of a document, they may be proved against him as evidence of their truth. In *Alderson v Clay*,[17] for instance, the books of a society of which

---

7 [1966] AC 367 at 371, [1965] 3 All ER 599 at 601.

8 *Bird v Adams* [1972] Crim LR 174; *R v Chatwood* [1980] 1 All ER 467, [1980] 1 WLR 874. See also *R v Brady* (1980) 2 ACR 42; *R v Dillon* [1983] Qd R 627; *Reardon v Baker* (1987) 25 ACR 203 (in all, admissions by drug addict of the nature of a substance in issue).

9 *R v Hulbert* (1979) 69 Cr App Rep 243; *R v Korniak* (1983) 76 Cr App Rep 145.

10 For a different view, see Scott 'Controlling the Reception in Evidence of Unreliable Admissions' [1981] Crim LR 285.

11 *R v Turner* [1910] 1 KB 346 at 362; see also *R v Jones* (1933) 24 Cr App Rep 55.

12 *Lustre Hosiery Ltd v York* (1936) 54 CLR 134.

13 *Bulley v Bulley* (1874) 9 Ch App 739.

14 *Strev v R* (1989) 70 CR (3d) 10.

15 *Rhone Poulenc Agrochimie SA v UIM Chemical Services Pty Ltd* (1985) 75 ALR 601.

16 *Baker The Hearsay Rule* 43. But see *R v Madden* [1986] Crim LR 804.

17 (1816) 1 Stark 405.

the defendant was a member were received as evidence that purchase of goods was duly authorised with the result that he was liable to the vendor. Perhaps it is on the ground that he exercises some control over their contents that affidavits by a third person used by a party to legal proceedings may be tendered as evidence against him in subsequent proceedings,[18] but this may be treated as a vicarious admission.

C. VICARIOUS ADMISSIONS[19]

Admissions by those in privity with a party to litigation may be given in evidence against him. The phrase 'in privity' as used here is not a technical term. It includes predecessors in title, referees, all manner of agents and sundry other miscellaneous cases. The statements received under these heads were generally against the interest of the declarants when they were made, and no doubt they would have been covered by another of the common law exceptions to the hearsay rule relating to declarations against interest discussed in the next chapter had this not come to be restricted in two important respects—the requirement that the maker of the statement must be dead when it is tendered, and the rule that the statement must have been against his pecuniary or proprietary interest when made. This topic will diminish in importance now that hearsay statements in documents are more widely admissible in criminal proceedings,[20] but what is said here remains relevant where there are no business documents or the admission is oral. It must be frankly recognised that there is no single rational basis for the reception of vicarious admissions as the subject is one in relation to which it is difficult to distinguish rules of substantive law from rules of evidence.

It will be convenient to begin by mentioning two important cases in which there is no privity between the maker of the statement and the party against whom it is tendered, so that it cannot be received as a vicarious admission. After this has been done, the standard examples of such admissions will be mentioned.

1. CASES IN WHICH THERE IS NO PRIVITY

(i) Co-defendants, etc

The out-of-court admission of a co-defendant, co-plaintiff or co-accused is not admissible evidence against his fellow party to the litigation by virtue of the mere fact that they are joint parties or said to be jointly involved in a particular transaction. This rule operates not only to bar use of such an admission as evidence in-chief, but also to prevent use being made of the admission in cross-examination of the third party.[1] This principle applies in all cases, but is most vividly illustrated by its application to divorce

---

18 *Brickell v Hulse* (1837) 7 Ad & El 454; *Richards v Morgan* (1863) 4 B & S 641. *Saunders v Saunders* [1965] P 499 (retention of letter from third party evidence of retainer's state of mind, but not of truth of contents).
19 Hanbury *Principles of Agency* ch 10; Fridman *The Law of Agency* ch 20; Morgan 'The Rationale of Vicarious Admissions' 42 HLR 461.
20 As a result of Part II of the Criminal Justice Act 1988, see further ch XVII below.
1 *R v Windass* (1988) 89 Cr App Rep 258.

proceedings where the result is that in a divorce case there might be a finding that A committed adultery with B on account of A's extra-judicial admission, although there is no finding that B committed adultery with A because the admission comes within the rule against hearsay and outside any exception to it so far as B is concerned.[2] Wigmore characterised the conclusion as 'perfectly logical ... [but] also perfectly and absurdly artificial'.[3] A's statement could now be rendered admissible against B under s 2 of the Civil Evidence Act 1968, by the service of the appropriate notice by the petitioner.[4] An equally odd conclusion could be reached at a trial for incest. In criminal cases the matter is complicated by the provisions of s 74 of the Police and Criminal Evidence Act 1984[5] which allow proof of the conviction[6] of one co-defendant to be used against another. Nevertheless so strong is judicial repugnance to the unfairness of permitting the admission of one co-defendant to be used against another[7] that the court has applied its discretion under s 78 of the Police and Criminal Evidence Act 1984 to prevent a plea of guilty by one party to an act of gross indecency with the other to be admitted at the trial of the other in respect of the very same act.[8]

(ii) Party and witness in former proceedings

We have seen that affidavits of third persons used by a party in former proceedings may be received as evidence against him in subsequent litigation. The authorities on this subject were said to be in an uncertain and unsatisfactory condition by Atkin LJ in *British Thomson-Houston Co Ltd v British Insulated and Helsby Cables Ltd.*[9] In that case the majority of the Court of Appeal decided that a transcript of the oral testimony of a witness, called by the plaintiffs in former proceedings, could not be tendered in evidence against them in the litigation before the court merely because the testimony was that of a witness upon whose evidence reliance had previously been placed by the plaintiffs. Atkin LJ conceded that, in different circumstances, the transcript might have been admissible as evidence of the plaintiff's knowledge of a particular fact, or, had this been the case, on the footing that the witness was the plaintiff's agent in the transaction to which he deposed.[10] The decision in the *British Thompson-Houston* case may in due course be applied to affidavits, but, until this is done, the authorities on the latter subject necessitate the treatment of a third person's affidavit used by a party in previous proceedings as a species of admission so far as subsequent litigation is concerned. The point is somewhat academic since, in both cases, resort will now normally be had to the provisions of the Civil Evidence Act 1968, concerning the admissibility of statements made in former proceed-

---

2   *Morton v Morton, Daly and McNaught* [1937] P 151, [1937] 2 All ER 470; *Rutherford v Richardson* [1923] AC 1.
3   IV *Wigmore* 117.
4   See SI 1980 No 977.
5   See further above p 105.
6   Including a plea of guilty.
7   Warnings not to use a plea of guilty in this way are customary, see *R v Moore* (1956) 40 Cr App Rep 50. See also *Simpson v R* (1988) 62 CR (3d) 137.
8   *R v Mattison* [1989] NLJR 1417.
9   [1924] 2 Ch 160 at 168.
10 At 170.

ings,[11] although the point might become less academic if the court were minded to exercise its exclusionary discretion in the case of the affidavit.

In the unlikely event of the question arising in a criminal case, it is difficult to believe that someone else's affidavit used by the accused in former proceedings (civil or criminal) would be held to be evidence against him of the facts stated in it.

2. PREDECESSORS IN TITLE

The statement of a predecessor in title of a party to the litigation in which it is tendered is admissible evidence against him provided it relates to the title and was made when the maker had the interest qualified by the statement.[12] This rule appears to be the outcome of the substantive law under which no better title is acquired than that which was enjoyed by the predecessor. The limitations on the rule should be noted. The successor is not, as such, bound by his predecessor's admissions which do not concern the title, nor is he affected by a statement of a predecessor who had parted with his interest in the property when it was made.

3. REFEREES

Statements made by someone to whom a party has referred others for information may be proved against him as admissions concerning the subject-matter of the reference. In *Williams v Innes*,[13] the defendants were executors of a deceased's estate. They referred the plaintiff to one Ross for information concerning the assets, and it was held that that which Ross said could be proved against the defendants for:

> If a man refers another upon any particular business to a third person, he is bound by what this third person says or does concerning it, as much as if that had been said or done by himself.

Similarly, if a defendant claims to retain goods on behalf of a named person, that person's statements become admissible evidence for the plaintiff in conversion.[14]

4. AGENTS

(i) Agents' admissions in general

Statements made by an agent within the scope of his authority to third persons during the continuance of the agency may be received as admissions against his principal in litigation to which the latter is a party. So far as the reception of admissions is concerned, the scope of authority is a strictly limited conception. It is sometimes said that the agent must be authorised to

11 See p 552, above.
12 *Woolway v Rowe* (1834) 1 Ad & El 114; *Falcon v Famous Players Film Co Ltd* [1926] 2 KB 474.
13 (1808) 1 Camp 364; *Daniel v Pitt* (1806) 1 Camp 366 at 369; *R v Mallory* (1884) 13 QBD 33. See also *Kroon v J L Clark Cotton Co Pty Ltd* 1983 (2) SA 197.
14 *Harrison v Vallance* (1822) 1 Bing 45.

make the admission, but that is a confusing statement for admissions are often received although no one was expressly or impliedly authorised to make them. A better way of putting the matter is to say that the admission must have been made by the agent as part of a conversation or other communication which he was authorised to have with a third party. The authority to have such conversations or make such communications is frequently not co-terminous with an authority to act on behalf of the principal[15]—a point which has an important bearing on the limited extent to which a servant's admissions concerning acts done by him in the course of his employment may as such be proved against his master.

In *Kirkstall Brewery Co v Furness Rly Co*[16] the plaintiff claimed damages for the loss of a parcel, and it was held that a statement made by the defendants' stationmaster to a policeman suggesting that the goods had been stolen by a servant of the defendants could be proved against them. In *Great Western Rly Co v Willis*,[17] on the other hand, the plaintiff claimed damages for the defendants' failure to deliver cattle promptly, and it was held that a statement made by a night inspector to the plaintiff suggesting that the beasts had been forgotten was inadmissible as evidence against the defendants. The conversation with which the last-mentioned case was concerned took place a week after delivery was due, but it seems that the real distinction between the two cases lies in the different circumstances in which the statements were made, as well, perhaps, as the larger scope of the stationmaster's authority. He was authorised to put the police in motion, and this necessarily included authority to draw attention to suspects, even if they should happen to be the company's servants, but the night inspector had no authority to answer inquiries of the kind that the plaintiff was making.

The statement of the agent which is tendered as an admission must, on the preponderance of authority, have been made to a third person, not to the principal.[18] Thus, in *Re Devala Provident Gold Mining Co Ltd*,[19] a shareholder claimed to have his name removed from the company's register on the ground of misrepresentation in the prospectus, and it was held that a report made by the chairman to a meeting of the company could not be received against the company as an admission of the falsity of the prospectus. Fry J said that though the chairman was the agent of the company, the statement was not made in a transaction between the company and a third party, and, in his view, 'When an agent is making a confidential report to his principal, the report is not admissible evidence in favour of a third party.' The fact that the applicant was a shareholder in the company was held to make no difference.

It is necessary to prove the existence of the agency before the admissions

---

15 See *Scott v Fernhill Stud Poultry Farm Pty Ltd* [1963] VR 12 holding a company not bound by a director's admissions.
16 (1874) LR 9 QB 468; *Fraser Henleins Pty Ltd v Cody* (1944) 70 CLR 100; *Lewis v Crafter* [1942] SASR 30.
17 (1865) 18 CBNS 748. Assuming that the statement was one of fact or, what is most unlikely, opinion, of which the maker could have given direct oral evidence, it could now be received under s 2 of the Civil Evidence Act 1968.
18 See *Industrial Distributors (Central Scotland) Ltd v Quinn* 1984 SCCR 5.
19 (1883) 22 Ch D 593; *The Solway* (1885) 10 PD 137 is to the contrary, but it was criticised as being against previous English authority in *Swan v Miller, Son and Torrance Ltd* [1919] 1 IR 151 at 176 and 185. It should be noted, however, that agents' reports could be rendered admissible under s 2 of the Civil Evidence Act 1968. See also *Warner v Women's Hospital* [1954] VLR 410.

of the agent can be received against the principal.[20] It may sometimes be possible to imply the existence of the agency from the surrounding circumstances.[1] It is not sufficient, at common law,[2] to rely upon the agent's own statements of that fact, because they are hearsay.[3] The agent could, of course, give evidence of the making of any operative statement without infringing the rule.

The statement tendered as an admission must have been made by the agent during the continuance of his agency. In *Peto v Hague*,[4] an action for penalties for selling coal in short measure, the defendant's manager was said to have made certain statements to a witness, and they were held to be admissible because they related to a sale which was about to take place; but Lord Ellenborough said: 'What he might have said respecting a former sale made by the defendant, or on another occasion, would not be evidence to affect his master.' Relatively few agents have authority to speak about past transactions, and, once an agent's employment as such has ceased altogether, he can have no authority to do so.

It seems that the same rules concerning the requirement of personal knowledge apply in the case of admissions by agents as in that of admissions by parties, but this is subject to the proviso that an agent, such as a solicitor, who is instructed to pass on information, need not accept it in any way, and yet his statement may be evidence against his principal.[5] It seems to be the case if an agent for a principal gathers information from employees, and makes an admission based on such information that the principal will be bound unless there is some overt qualification or disclaimer.[6]

It is now proposed to indicate very briefly how the foregoing principles are applied in the case of the specific agencies of employment and partnership.

(ii) Master and servant

A direct result of the requirement that the making of the admission must be within the scope of the agent's authority if it is to be received against the principal, is that a servant's admission is usually inadmissible in cases in which it is sought to make his master vicariously liable in tort. So far as this branch of the law of evidence is concerned, servants are treated as agents, and, so far as the course of employment is concerned, authority to do acts is

---

20 *G(A) v G(T)* [1970] 2 QB 643, [1970] 3 All ER 546; *R v Evans* [1981] Crim LR 699. See also *Maxwell v I R C* [1959] NZLR 708.

1 *R v Turner* (1975) 61 Cr App Rep 67 (acting as barrister representing a party); compare *Wagstaff v Wilson* (1832) 4 B & Ad 339 (acting as party's attorney insufficient), and *R v Evans* (above) (acting as clerk to party's solicitor insufficient). See also *Smart v Popper and Casswell* (1987) 26 ACR 140 (solicitor representing client who was present in court).

2 In appropriate circumstances it is now possible to invoke the Civil Evidence Act 1968, see *G(A) v G(T)* (above) where the only reason for not doing so was that the proceedings took place in the magistrates court.

3 *R v Evans* (above). *Edwards v Brookes (Milk) Ltd* [1963] 3 All ER 62, [1963] 1 WLR 795 cannot be supported to the extent of any inconsistency after *Myers v D P P* [1965] AC 1001, [1964] 2 All ER 881.

4 (1804) 5 Esp 134; *The Prinses Juliana, Esbjerj (Owners) v Prinses Juliana (Owners)* [1936] P 139, [1936] 1 All ER 685. Such statements could be rendered admissible under the Civil Evidence Act 1968.

5 See p 582, above. *The Actaeon* (1853) 1 Ecc & Ad 176.

6 *Welsbach Incandescent Gas Lighting Co v New Sunlight Incandescent Co* [1900] 2 Ch 1. See also *Claiborne Industries Ltd v National Bank of Canada* (1989) 59 DLR (4th) 533.

far wider than authority to speak about them. In *Burr v Ware R D C*[7] the Court of Appeal would not allow an interrogatory against the defendants about admissions of negligence made by one of their drivers at an inquest. The proceedings arose out of a fatal accident alleged to have been caused by the driver's negligence, but the interrogatory was disallowed because, though the driving was in the course of employment, the admissions would not be evidence against the employer. Such an admission may be brought before the court by the simple device of making the driver a defendant but, in theory at least, the admission will only be evidence against him. Wigmore said 'this rule as now universally administered makes a laughing stock of court methods';[8] it is just as well that the servant's statement can now be rendered admissible against his master under s 2 of the Civil Evidence Act 1968.[9]

(iii) Partners

An admission made by a partner concerning partnership affairs in the ordinary course of business is evidence against the firm. This common law principle is now embodied in s 15 of the Partnership Act 1890. Admissions by one of several people jointly interested in any contract or property are evidence against the others provided they were made during the existence of the interest.[10]

5. MISCELLANEOUS CASES

The list of miscellaneous agencies could be indefinitely prolonged, but, in the main, it will be found that the question of the reception of vicarious admissions depends on the substantive law. This is certainly the case so far as admissions by one of several trustees or executors are concerned, and the same is true of the solicitor's authority to bind his client.

(i) Admissions by a deceased

Another such case, though strictly not one of agency, is *Marks v Portsmouth Corpn*,[11] in which it was held that the defendant to an action under the Fatal Accidents Acts could rely on an admission by the deceased. The admission suggested contributory negligence which was then a complete defence to proceedings under the Acts. Such a statement would, however, be equally admissible today as affecting damages. In *Marks*'s case, there was no claim under the Law Reform (Miscellaneous Provisions) Act 1934, but a relevant

---

7 [1939] 2 All ER 688; 55 LQR 490; *Johnson v Lindsay* (1889) 53 JP 599; *Price Yards Ltd v Tiveron Transport Co Ltd and Barbe* (1958) 11 DLR (2d) 669. A ship owner is bound by the captain's informal admissions, but not those of the crew, though these may be received as part of the res gestae. A statement in the engineer's log-book had been received against the ship owner (*The Earl of Dumfries* (1885) 10 PD 31). In *Bruff v Great Northern Rly Co* (1858) 1 F & F 344, it was held that a secretary's admission could not be admitted as proof of the receipt of a letter by a company. *Burr v Ware R D C* was not followed in *Botes v Van Deventer* [1966] 3 SA 182.

8 IV *Wigmore* para 1078, n 2.

9 See p 553, above.

10 *Jaggers v Binnings* (1815) 1 Stark 64.

11 (1937) 157 LT 261.

admission by the deceased would surely be received in such an action which is brought in his right. In fact there is less room for argument about the admissibility of the deceased's statement in such a case than in that of the action under the Fatal Accidents Acts because the decision in *Marks v Portsmouth Corpn* is difficult to reconcile with the principle that those Acts confer an entirely new action on the dependants.[12]

(ii) Conspirators

The admissions of one conspirator are receivable against the other if they relate to an act done in furtherance of the conspiracy, but not otherwise.[13] For example, in *R v Blake and Tye*,[14] the accused were charged with a conspiracy to pass goods through the customs without paying duty. Tye had made entries incriminating Blake as well as himself in two books. In one case the entry was a necessary part of the fraud, in the other case it was solely for the purposes of record and for Tye's convenience. It was held that the first entry was admissible against Blake as something tending to the advancement of the common object, but the second merely constituted evidence against Tye because it was not concerned with the disposal of the plunder.

In determining whether there is such a common purpose as to render the acts and extra-judicial statements done or made by one party in furtherance of the common purpose evidence against the others, the judge may have regard to these matters, although their admissibility is in issue, as well as to other evidence.[15] This doctrine is obviously liable to produce circularity in argument:

> Since what A says in B's absence cannot be evidence against B of the truth of what was said unless A was B's agent to say those things, how can one prove that A was B's agent to say them by showing what A said?[16]

The answer is that the agency may be proved partly by what A said in the absence of B, and partly by other evidence of common purpose. It makes no difference which is adduced first, but A's statements will have to be excluded if it transpires that there is no other evidence of common purpose; it is another instance of conditional admissibility.[17]

In England this view of the law has been accepted without cavil, or much elaboration.[18] In other jurisdictions questions have arisen both as to the

---

12 *Seward v The Vera Cruz* (1884) 10 App Cas 59 at 70. It was for this reason that *Marks v Portsmouth Corpn* was questioned and not followed in *Evans v Hartigan* [1941] SR (NSW) 179. Those who have doubts about *Marks*'s case could take steps to render the statement admissible under s 2 of the Civil Evidence Act 1968 (see also the doubt raised, unnecessarily it is hoped, on p 553, above).

13 Though it should be noted that in many cases out-of-court assertions and actions of conspirators may be admissible as circumstantial evidence of a conspiracy quite independently of reliance upon any admission, express or even implied, and so arguably outside the operation of the hearsay rule.

14 (1844) 6 QB 126; see also *R v Hardy* (1794) 24 State Tr 1065; *R v Hunt* (1820) 3 B & Ald 566; *R v Whitaker* [1914] 3 KB 1283.

15 *Ahern v R* (1988) 80 ALR 161.

16 *R v Mayet* 1957 (1) SA 492 at 494.

17 *Tripodi v R* (1961) 104 CLR 1; *Ahern*, above, at 171.

18 *R v Donat* (1985) 82 Cr App Rep 173 at 179; *R v Governor of Pentonville Prison, ex p Osman* [1989] 3 All ER 701; *R v Windass* (1988) 89 Cr App Rep 258. It has however influenced attitudes against the use of convictions for conspiracy under s 74 of the Police and Criminal Evidence Act 1984, see, above, p 105.

standard which the extrinsic evidence of conspiracy should reach, and whether the question once having been decided by the judge so as to admit the evidence should be subject to reconsideration by the jury. Since there is little difference here between the preliminary question and the final issue, namely whether the accused was party to the conspiracy, it would be futile to require the preliminary issue to be decided upon proof beyond reasonable doubt. The better view is that the judge should decide[19] the preliminary issue on a prima facie basis.[20] It is submitted that since the evidence has been admitted upon such a basis it is unnecessarily confusing for the jury to be given an opportunity to reject it upon the application of a different standard of proof from that which they will have to be instructed to apply to the ultimate question of guilt or innocence of participation in the conspiracy.[1]

The rule under consideration is not confined to charges of conspiracy as it is based on implied agency, and would apply, for example, to charges of aiding and abetting, even though the secondary party was not charged; but it is in relation to conspiracy trials that the rule may operate most oppressively. If there is a series of counts charging separate offences and a concluding count alleging conspiracy, evidence may be admissible against all the accused on the last count, although it would not be admissible against more than one of them on any of the separate counts.[2] The evidence often takes the form of directions given and acts done by the other parties which can take a much broader form when there is a conspiracy charge than when the charge relates to one specific transaction.

(iii) Husband and wife

Further enumeration of the examples of vicarious admissions would be out of place, but it may be added that the admissions of one spouse are not, as such, received against the other, although an agency may be held to exist on the particular facts,[3] or one spouse may have rendered the other's statement admissible evidence against himself or herself by inviting a third party to treat the other as a referee.[4]

---

19 In the United States the Federal Rules of Evidence permit hearsay, including the hearsay of the alleged co-conspirators, to be used in the determination of that preliminary question, Federal Rules of Evidence, rr 104(a), 1101(d)(1); *Bourjaily v US* 107 S Ct 2775 (1987).
20 Used for some other issues of fact upon which the admission of evidence depends, see *R v Robson and Harris* [1972] 2 All ER 699, [1972] 1 WLR 651. In *Ahern* (1988) 80 ALR 161 the High Court of Australia preferred the term 'reasonable evidence' to 'prima facie case' but thought there to be no real distinction of meaning. But see *R v Buckton* [1985] 2 NZLR 257 suggesting that the standard of the balance of probabilities be adopted at this stage; this is also the position in the United States, *Bourjaily v US*, above.
1   This seems the predominant view in other common law jurisdictions, see *Ahern*, above (Australia); *Buckton* above (New Zealand); and *Bourjaily*, above (United States). But Canada adopts a different view, *R v Carter* [1982] 1 SCR 938; *R v Barrow* (1987) 45 DLR (4th) 487.
2   *R v Griffiths* [1966] 1 QB 589, [1965] 2 All ER 448.
3   *Clifford v Burton* (1823) 1 Bing 199; see also *G(A) v G(T)* [1970] 2 QB 643, [1970] 3 All ER 546 (parent and child).
4   *R v Mallory* (1884) 13 QBD 33.

D. STATEMENTS IN THE PRESENCE OF A PARTY

Statements made in the presence of a party are admissible as an introduction[5] to his or her reaction to them which may or may not prove to be relevant. The question whether an adverse inference should be drawn from that reaction has to be determined by the jury where there is one. The principle of conditional admissibility is applied with the result that such statements can be proved although it may become necessary to disregard them. This is the consequence of the decision of the House of Lords in *R v Christie*[6] in 1914. It will be convenient to consider the authorities down to that date, the results of *R v Christie* and some practical difficulties which still make themselves felt from time to time.

1. THE CASES BEFORE 1914

Two tendencies were discernible in the cases decided before 1914. In the first place some of the older authorities seemed to favour a purely mechanistic approach by admitting the statement once it was proved to have been made in the presence or hearing of a party without pausing to consider the purpose for which it was received.[7] The second and more rational solution required the judge to decide whether there was evidence, in the shape of words or conduct on the part of the party in whose presence the statement was made, which would justify the jury in inferring that its truth was admitted. On this second view, the judge's decision constituted a preliminary finding of fact affecting the admissibility of evidence, and it had to be made before the statement could be narrated to the jury. Thus, in *R v Norton*,[8] a conviction for an offence against a young girl was quashed because there was, in the opinion of the Court of Criminal Appeal, no evidence that the accused had admitted the truth of the girl's allegation that he was the culprit made in response to a question put by him in the presence of witnesses. The court observed that, at trials on indictment, there would generally be no difficulty in deciding whether there was evidence, fit to be submitted to the jury, that the accused admitted the whole or part of a statement. His answer appears on the depositions, and the chance that the evidence with regard to it may be different at the trial is small enough to be disregarded. Pickford J added that there did not seem to be any practical difficulty where evidence of the answer did not appear in this way, for:

---

5 It is thus the accused's reaction to the statement which constitutes the evidence so it is not necessary to call the maker of the statement if its terms can be proved by a third party, see *Glass v Tudhope* 1986 SCCR 49; and the statement cannot amount to corroboration of its acceptance, *Annan v Bain* 1986 SCCR 60.

6 [1914] AC 545. *R v Christie* was anticipated by *R v Grills* (1910) 11 CLR 400. For conditional admissibility see p 59, above. *Christie's* case is also important on evidence of identification, p 724 below; self-corroboration, p 281, above; complaints, p 282, above; and res gestae. The boy's statement was not admissible under the latter head because of the interval of time intervening between the assault and the remarks, but this type of reasoning may require reconsideration after *Ratten v R* [1972] AC 378, [1971] 3 All ER 801. For an example of the application of the principle in a civil case, see *Chantler v Bromley* (1921) 14 BWCC 14.

7 *Neile v Jakle* (1849) 2 Car & Kir 709; *R v Cox* (1858) 1 F & F 90. See also the argument of counsel in *R v Smith* (1897) 18 Cox CC 470.

8 [1910] 2 KB 496.

The fact of a statement having been made in the prisoner's presence may be given in evidence, but not the contents, and the question asked what the prisoner said or did on such a statement being made. If his answer, given either by word or conduct, be such as to be evidence from which an acknowledgment may be inferred, then the contents of the statement may be given and the question of admission or not in fact left to the jury; if it be not evidence from which such an acknowledgment may be inferred, then the contents of the statement should be excluded.[9]

2. R V CHRISTIE

In *R v Christie* the House of Lords held that the requirement that the judge should, in the first instance, determine whether there was evidence from which an admission of a statement made in a party's presence could be inferred, was not a rule of law, although it constituted a salutary rule of practice, which ought to be followed in most criminal cases. Christie had been convicted of an indecent assault on a small boy who gave his evidence unsworn, describing the assault, and identifying the accused as his assailant, but saying nothing about having identified him soon after the event. The boy's mother and a constable then gave evidence that, shortly after the offence was alleged to have been committed, the boy went up to Christie saying, 'That is the man', and described the assault, to which the reply was. 'I am innocent'. On the authority of *R v Norton*, the Court of Criminal Appeal quashed the conviction, because the evidence of the mother and constable had been wrongly admitted as Christie had denied the truth of the boy's statement. The House of Lords dismissed the Crown's appeal because the trial judge had misdirected the jury on the question of corroboration, but laid down that there is no fixed rule of law that statements made in the presence of a party cannot be received in evidence until a foundation has been laid for their admission by proof of facts from which, in the opinion of the presiding judge, a jury might reasonably draw the inference that the accused had so accepted the statements as to make them in whole or in part his own. In the words of Lord Atkinson:

> The rule of law undoubtedly is that a statement made in the presence of an accused person even upon an occasion which should be expected reasonably to call for some explanation or denial from him, is not evidence against him of the facts stated save so far as he accepts the statement so as to make it in effect his own. If he accepts the statement in part only, then to that extent alone does it become his statement. He may accept the statement by word or conduct, action or demeanour, and it is the function of the jury which tries the case to determine whether his words, action, conduct or demeanour at the time when the statement was made amounts to an acceptance of it in whole or in part. It by no means follows, I think, that a mere denial by the accused of the facts mentioned in the statement necessarily renders the statement inadmissible, because he may deny his statement in such a manner and under such circumstances as may lead a jury to disbelieve him, and constitute evidence from which an acknowledgment can be inferred by them.[10]

The fact that the allegations made in the statement were denied by the

9 At 500.
10 At 554.

accused cannot be conclusive in all cases, for his denial of a violent assault might be distinctly relevant, if he pleaded self-defence at his trial.[11]

3. PRACTICAL DIFFICULTIES

(i) Charges, interrogations and the direction to the jury

Although they do not do so in as many words, the speeches in *R v Christie* indorse the principle of common sense stated by Cave J in *R v Mitchell*[12] that, when people are speaking on even terms, and a charge is made, the fact that the person charged does nothing to repel it is some evidence to show that he admits its truth. The Judicial Committee of the Privy Council acted on this principle in *Parkes v R*[13] when affirming the accused's conviction of the murder of a young woman. Her mother came out of the room in which she had found her bleeding from stab wounds and asked him why he had done it. He said nothing and, when the woman's mother took hold of him, he threatened her with a knife. The jury were directed that there was evidence from which they could infer his acceptance of the truth of the accusation. The earlier decision of the Judicial Committee in *Hall v R*[14] was distinguished. In that case a conviction of unlawful possession of ganja had been quashed because the accused's silence, when informed by a police officer that one of the occupants of a house in which a quantity of the drug was found had said that it was his, had been treated as something which could amount to an acknowledgment of the truth of the allegation. He had not been cautioned when the officer addressed him but Lord Diplock said that: 'the caution merely serves to remind the accused of a right which he already possesses at common law.' The distinction between *Parkes v R* and *Hall v R* lay in the fact that, in the former case, the allegation was not made by a person endeavouring to find out who had committed the crime and the parties were on even terms, but, in *R v Chandler*,[15] the Court of Appeal questioned the consistency of everything said by Lord Diplock in *Hall*'s case with the speeches in *R v Christie*.

Chandler was convicted of a conspiracy to defraud. He had been interviewed by the police at a police station in the presence of his solicitor. He was cautioned at the interview. Both before and after caution he answered some questions, but declined to answer others. In accordance with previous authority applying to cases in which the accused has answered some police questions but refused to answer others[16] evidence was admitted of his reaction to the unanswered questions as well as of his answers to the others. The conviction was quashed because the judge had told the jury to consider whether the refusal to answer some of the questions had been due to Chandler's insistence on his common law right of silence, or to his knowledge that the answers might incriminate him, but the court said that the parties were on even terms and that the jury should have been directed to consider whether by words, conduct, action or demeanour, the accused had accepted the implications of some of the questions he did not answer. No doubt the

11 Per Lord Moulton at 560.
12 (1892) 17 Cox CC 503 at 508; see p 252, above. See also *Bessela v Stern* (1877) 2 CPD 265.
13 [1976] 3 All ER 380, [1976] 1 WLR 1251.
14 [1971] 1 All ER 322.
15 [1976] 3 All ER 105, [1976] 1 WLR 585.
16 *R v Mann* (1972) 56 Cr App Rep 750.

decisions can be reconciled on their facts, but the question which of the two directions is appropriate, a direction to draw no inference from the accused's silence when charged by the police, or one in conformity with Lord Atkinson's remarks in *R v Christie*, is liable to raise difficult problems. It may also be complicated by interaction with the general rules governing the proper direction in a case where stolen goods have been found on the accused's premises.[17]

The decision in *R v Christie* that, as a matter of law, the correct procedure is for the prosecution to adduce evidence of the making and contents of the statement in the first instance, leaving the judge to tell the jury to disregard it if there is nothing in the nature of an acknowledgment by the accused or it is not relevant for some other reason, has necessitated frequent insistence by the Court of Appeal on the importance of emphasising the point that statements made in the presence of the accused are relevant only as an introduction to his reactions to them.[18] It is hard to believe that the jurors can always rid themselves of the impression made by the statement when told to disregard it. The solution of allowing proof of nothing more than the fact that a statement was made suggested by Pickford J in *R v Norton* is not very satisfactory, but, in some circumstances at least, a trial within a trial may be desirable before anything is heard of the statement.[19]

(ii) Co-accused's statement

Difficulties used to arise when two people were under arrest for the same crime and one of them was informed of a statement implicating him which had been made by the other. The maker of the statement could not be called as a witness for the prosecution if tried together with the person implicated by it; but, to quote Lord Goddard CJ when speaking of a state of affairs which existed when *R v Christie* was decided:

> There used to be a practice by which the police would give evidence before the jury to the following effect: 'I saw the prisoner. I told him that John Smith had been arrested and had said "Yes, I was there and he (the prisoner) was with me".' Then the prisoner made a statement and said, perhaps, that he was not there at all, but that was a means of getting before the jury the statement of John Smith.[20]

This practice is, in effect, condemned by para 17.4 of the Code of Practice for Police Questioning made under the Police and Criminal Evidence Act 1984, s 66 which provides that, if a police officer wishes to draw the attention of someone charged with an offence to a statement by someone else charged with the same offence, he should hand him a copy without saying or doing anything to invite a reply. If someone who has thus received a copy of his co-accused's statement desires to make a reply, the usual caution should be administered, after which it would be perfectly proper to receive what he said in evidence. If the reply made by a prisoner to whom his co-accused's statement has been improperly read is intelligible without reference to the statement, it may be received in evidence against him as a confession,

---

17 *R v Raviraj* (1986) 85 Cr App Rep 93, see further, above, p 33.
18 *R v Curnock* (1914) 111 LT 816; *R v Altschuler* (1915) 11 Cr App Rep 243; *R v Pilley* (1922) 16 Cr App Rep 138; *R v Adams* (1923) 17 Cr App Rep 77.
19 For trials within a trial in Commonwealth cases in this context see *R v Thomas* [1970] VR 674; and *R v Thompson* (1974) 16 CCC (2d) 374.
20 *R v Mills and Lemon* [1947] KB 297 at 299, [1946] 2 All ER 776 at 777.

otherwise it may be excluded.[1] Even if made technically admissible by the accused's reaction, such a statement may well be regarded as unduly prejudicial, and excluded in the exercise of the judge's discretion.[2]

(iii) Nature of the reply

Another practical difficulty which may be occasioned by the procedure of proving the contents of a statement made in the presence of an accused person without reference, in the first instance, to his reply, may be caused by the nature of the latter. In *Turner v Underwood*,[3] for instance, the accused was charged with infringement of a byelaw by indecent behaviour in a railway train. When the complaint was narrated to him by a railway police sergeant, the accused said, 'I have done time for this before'. This was not a case in which previous convictions could have been proved in-chief, but it was held that there is no rule of law that what a prisoner says in relation to the charge is not evidence against him, even if it relates to his past record. Accordingly it was decided that evidence of the narration of the complaint and the accused's reply was properly received as the reply amounted to an admission of a deliberate act of indecency; but Lord Goddard CJ added that:

> It is the practice as a rule in cases which are tried before juries that where the court knows there is something said by a man in his statement which admits a previous conviction, or shows other matter reflecting on his character, the court sees that that is not read out to the jury.[4]

(iv) The danger of the mechanical approach

When qualified by discretionary practices and the Codes of Practice, the law concerning the admissibility of statements made in the presence of a party may work well enough; but there is always a danger of a reversion to the old mechanical practice of allowing such statements to go to the jury without a reference to the evidential purpose served by them on the facts of the particular case. In *R v Black*,[5] for instance, the Court of Criminal Appeal held that the absence of comment from the accused, who was charged with poisoning his wife, on her statements to him concerning her symptoms after taking medicine which he had procured was evidence from which the jury might draw inferences. It is not suggested that this view was incorrect, but one could have wished for a more detailed consideration of the kind of inference that could be drawn—the probative value of the evidence. As long as due regard is had to this in every case, it cannot be said that there is anything seriously amiss with the law laid down in *R v Christie*. The logic of that decision is hard to escape, but it has to be applied with caution.

In the day to day administration of justice, the question whether the

1 See *R v Mills and Lemon* (above); *R v Gardner and Hancox* (1915) 11 Cr App Rep 265, decided under a similar provision in the old Judges' Rules.
2 Such discretion may be exercised under either s 78 or s 82(3) of the Police and Criminal Evidence Act 1984, or in the case of an admission in a document prepared for the purpose of criminal proceedings or investigations under that conferred by s 26 of the Criminal Justice Act 1988. See *R v Taylor* [1978] Crim LR 92 for the position under the old law; and *R v Martin* (1984) 14 ACR 73 for that in Australia.
3 [1948] 2 KB 284, [1948] 1 All ER 859.
4 At 286, 860, respectively.
5 (1922) 16 Cr App Rep 118.

prisoner was present when a statement was made is undoubtedly a convenient test of admissibility, but it is open to question whether the bald assertion that all statements made in the presence of the accused are admissible can be accepted, even if it is recognised that the admissibility may only be conditional. To take the facts of a Queensland case,[6] if a man is arrested on a charge of drunken driving and his friends shout advice to him to refuse medical examination and insist on the presence of his own doctor in order to procure as much delay as possible so that he may have time to sober up, the evidence should surely be rejected from the outset in the absence of something showing that the accused accepted his friends' views that it was necessary for him to do as suggested.

---

6 *Mahoney v Fielding* [1959] Qd R 479, following *Barnett v McGregor* [1959] SR Qd 296. See also *R v Bailey* [1956] SASR 153; *Thatcher v Charles* (1961) 104 CLR 57; *R v Lindsay* [1963] Qd R 386; *Woon v R* (1964) 109 CLR 529; and *R v Spring* [1958] NZLR 468.

CHAPTER XVII

Hearsay in criminal proceedings

The Police and Criminal Evidence Act 1984 and the Criminal Justice Act 1988 have transformed this subject from one primarily determined by common law rules to one dominated by statute. These Acts, unlike the Civil Evidence Act 1968, do not in terms supplant the whole of the common law, but have taken over so much of the ground, that the old rules of the common law now govern only a very small part of the field, although since the legislation employs a number of concepts developed by the common law, so it will for some time have an influence upon the interpretation of the new law. The arrangement of this chapter will reflect these changes. The first two sections will examine what are now mainly statutory areas, first that covering confessions and closely related topics, and then one encompassing some different types of documentary hearsay. The third and last section will consider the remaining fragments of the common law. It should be noted that some topics strictly speaking within the scope of the title of this chapter are considered elsewhere. In particular some discussion of criminal cases in their bearing on the admissibility of public documents and admissions were considered in the previous chapter, and statements accompanying and explaining relevant acts, spontaneous statements relating to an event in issue, statements concerning the maker's contemporaneous state of mind or emotions, and statements of contemporaneous physical sensation are discussed in the next chapter dealing with res gestae, even when within the context of criminal proceedings.

SECTION 1. CONFESSIONS[1]

Some areas of law relevant to this topic have already been mentioned in previous chapters,[2] and this section will concentrate upon the substance of the law embodied in s 76 of the Police and Criminal Evidence Act 1984. Before examining that provision in detail, it is still helpful to consider the development and rationale of the old law relating to confessions, and some of the various proposals made for its reform.

---

1 This enormous topic has in the past been the subject of a number of monographs, among them Joy *On Confessions* (1842), still an important historical source. For a stimulating and perceptive modern view see Mirfield *Confessions* (1985).
2 The standard of proof of the conditions for admissibility was considered in ch I, respective roles of judge and jury and the application of discretion to exclude were considered in ch IV, the privilege against self-incrimination in ch XI, the admissibility of evidence discovered by illegal means in ch XII and the nature of admissions in ch XVI.

A. DEVELOPMENT

The Police and Criminal Evidence Act 1984 defines a confession to include:
'any statement wholly or partly adverse to the person who made it, whether
made to a person in authority or not and whether made in words or
otherwise'.[3] It is thus clear that when made otherwise than by a witness
testifying in court it amounts to hearsay as defined in this work. At common
law, however, confessions were subsumed under the general exception in
favour of admissions for the reason given by Parke B quoted in the previous
chapter.[4] Some confessions, made to persons in authority and categorised as
'involuntary', were nevertheless excluded from that relaxation. In the early
years of the development of the law of evidence, hearsay in general and
confessions in particular were admitted without serious question.[5] Although
Lord Sumner in *Ibrahim v R*[6] asserts that the exclusion goes back to Hale, this
must be understood as a reference to later editions of his book. In the original
editions the reference is to confession only in the sense of a plea. It is however
interesting to note that in that context, some early statutes do refer to such
pleas being acceptable, only where the party 'shall willingly without
violence' confess.[7] The origin of the true exclusionary rule is to be found in
the mid-eighteenth century, and achieved its first clear and authoritative
formulation in the case of *R v Warickshall*:

> a confession forced from the mind by the flattery of hope, or by the torture of fear,
> comes in so questionable a shape when it is to be considered as the evidence of
> guilt, that no credit ought to be given to it; and therefore it is rejected.[8]

It is interesting to note that the court went out of its way to assert that the
rationale of the rule was based entirely on considerations of credit, having
first denied quite explicitly that it depended upon any 'regard to public
faith'. In origin the rule has little or no connection with the privilege against
self-incrimination either.[9] That doctrine had developed a century or so
earlier, in reaction to the oaths required by the Courts of High Commission
and Star Chamber. The line between judicial proceedings in which that
doctrine came to flourish, and extra-curial investigations was however
blurred by the investigatory functions of magistrates, which were not clearly,
or finally, distinguished until after the establishment of a regular police
force, and the passage of the Indictable Offences Act 1848.[10]

Between the end of the eighteenth century and the middle of the
nineteenth the rules excluding confession were elaborated in a series of
judgments at first instance. The conditions of that period were described by
Lord Hailsham as:

---

3 S 82(1).
4 See p 580.
5 See 3 Wigmore *Evidence* para 818, upon which the editor has relied extensively in this
   section.
6 [1914] AC 599 at 610.
7 1 Edw VI Cl 2 s 22 (1547), and 5 and 6 Edw VI c 11 s 8 (1554).
8 (1783) 1 Leach 263 at 263, 264.
9 See Wigmore 'Nemo tenetur seipsum prodere' (1891) 5 HLR 71, and Morgan 'The
   Privilege Against Self-Incrimination' (1949) 34 Minn LR 1.
10 The form of caution established by that legislation had an impact upon the attitudes of the
    judiciary to confessions secured by the police, see *R v Baldry* (1852) 2 Den 430.

a time when the savage code of the eighteenth century was in full force. At that time almost every serious crime was punished by death or transportation. The law enforcement officers formed no disciplined police force and were not subject to effective control by the Central Government Watch Committee or an inspectorate. There was no legal aid. There was no system of appeal. To crown it all the accused was unable to give evidence on his own behalf and was therefore largely at the mercy of any evidence, either perjured or oppressively obtained, that might be brought against him. The judiciary were therefore compelled to devise artificial rules designed to protect him against dangers now avoided by other and more rational means.[11]

By mid-century, not without some grave judicial misgivings, it was accepted that, in the words of Baron Parke:

> By the law of England, in order to render a confession admissible in evidence, it must be perfectly voluntary; and there is no doubt that any inducement in the nature of a promise or of a threat held out by a person in authority vitiates a confession.[12]

Thereafter the formulation of the rule remained relatively constant,[13] but became more and more rigid as a developing case-law filled out the interstices of the definition by the determination of particular disputes. In England this prevented the rule from extending beyond inducements in the shape of threats or promises,[14] though these were often construed with some ingenious generosity. This meant that in order to accommodate the exclusion of confessions obtained by the use of reprehensible police methods, not on any view involving the use of either promises or threats, it was necessary to develop rules of practice.[15] Since the evolution of such a rule of practice could hardly be left to the vagaries of dozens of unco-ordinated decisions, the scene was set for the promulgation of the English Judges' Rules attempting to encapsulate a set of rules of fair police practices, though without the sanction of automatic enforcement. It also meant that in order to provide for automatic exclusion in the most egregious cases of malpractice, it was ultimately necessary to amplify the formulation of the exclusionary rule to include a reference to oppression.[16] Conversely the consequence of construing individual decisions on particular facts as rules of law was that some forms of words, which many felt could hardly have induced the most timorous of suspects to confess falsely, became automatic warrants for

11 *D P P v Ping Lin* [1976] AC 574 at 600, [1975] 3 All ER 175 at 182. See also the remarks of Lord Diplock in *R v Sang* [1980] AC 402 at 436, [1979] 2 All ER 1222 at 1230.
12 *R v Baldry* (1852) 2 Den 430 at 444.
13 The leading authorities are *R v Thompson* [1893] 2 QB 12 and *Ibrahim v R* [1914] AC 599.
14 In Australia the courts were more prepared to take a wider and less blinkered view of the impediments to voluntariness, see *Cornelius v R* (1936) 55 CLR 235 where Dixon J made an explicit contrast with the position in England. See also *Wan v US* 266 US 1 (1924), for a similar statement of the American position by Justice Brandeis.
15 It seems that they had developed by 1905, see *R v Knight and Thayre* (1905) 20 Cox CC 711 per Channell J.
16 It was first introduced by Lord Parker CJ in his judgment in *Callis v Gunn* [1964] 1 QB 495 at 501, [1963] 3 All ER 677 at 680, and shortly afterwards incorporated as part of principle (e) of the introduction to the new Judges' Rules of 1964. It may seem difficult to accommodate confessions obtained by actual torture within the classical formulation of the rule, unless one implies a promise to desist if a confession should be made, as in *R v Gardner* (1932) 51 NZLR 1648, but see *D P P v Ping Lin* [1976] AC 574 at 606, [1975] 3 All ER 175 at 188 per Lord Salmon.

exclusion.[17] This concentration on particular facts was aggravated by the practice for a time of allowing both judge and jury an opportunity to decide upon the voluntary character of a confession, the judge deciding merely whether or not a particular form of words was capable of amounting to an inducement.[18] In recent years the old rule has been clarified, and in some respects its working improved. Thus in *Customs and Excise Comrs v Harz and Power*[19] the House of Lords rejected the view that the inducement or threat need relate to the prosecution, a view which never made any sense in relation to a threat of physical violence. On the other hand the requirement that the inducement must come from, or at least be attributable to,[20] a person in authority was retained.[1]

The basic roots of the technicality in which the modern law had become enmeshed were addressed in *D P P v Ping Lin*.[2] The accused was charged with conspiracy to supply drugs. When interviewed by the police he sought a deal which was refused, but he nevertheless confessed to being a supplier of drugs in a small way. Later in the interview, in response to further suggestions and after refusing to bargain, the police officer remarked that he was sure that if the accused assisted the police, as the accused proposed, the judge would take such assistance into account when determining sentence, whereafter the accused made further admissions. The question certified by the Court of Appeal in effect raised the whole issue of the interpretation of the voluntariness test, and its application to the case. The House of Lords was at pains to stress the simplicity of the test, and the need to apply it as a question of fact, unencumbered by reference to authorities turning on particular circumstances or forms of expression.[3] It was denied, in particular, that any impropriety need be proved on the part of the person in authority inducing the confession,[4] or that a subjective intent to induce the confession need be shown.[5] The effect was to emphasise that the question of the exclusionary test was one of fact, especially one of causation, to be construed on a common-sense basis and necessarily determined without reference to authority, just because everything depended upon the particular circumstances in which the particular suspect was placed. In this way the judge could approach the question just as it would be approached by a jury, whose function in this situation he was unusually, but unavoidably, assuming.

17 Here too some jurisdictions avoided such consequences by robust intervention, thus the colony of Victoria as early as 1857 enacted a provision providing that only inducements 'really calculated' to cause untrue admissions were to lead to exclusion, now Evidence Act 1958, s 149.
18 This view was engendered by dicta in *R v Bass* [1953] 1 QB 680 at 684, criticised by Dixon CJ in *Basto v R* (1954) 91 CLR 628 at 640, rejected in *Chan Wei Keung v R* [1967] 2 AC 160, [1967] 1 All ER 948, and that rejection finally accepted in *R v Burgess* [1968] 2 QB 112, [1968] 2 All ER 54n. See p 170 above.
19 [1967] 1 AC 760, [1967] 1 All ER 177.
20 *R v Cleary* (1963) 48 Cr App Rep 116; *R v Moore* (1972) 56 Cr App Rep 373.
1 *Deokinanan v R* [1969] 1 AC 20, [1968] 2 All ER 346. But see the cogent criticism of this requirement in Mirfield 'Confessions—The Person in Authority Requirement' [1981] Crim LR 92.
2 [1976] AC 574, [1975] 3 All ER 175.
3 Lord Morris at 594, 177; Lord Hailsham at 600, 182; Lord Kilbrandon at 604, 186; and Lord Salmon at 606, 187–8.
4 Lord Morris at 594, 178; Lord Hailsham at 602, 184, disapproving a suggestion to the contrary in *R v Isequilla* [1975] 1 All ER 77 at 82, [1975] 1 WLR 716 at 721–22, though the result of that case was approved on other grounds.
5 Lord Hailsham at 601, 184.

B. RATIONALE

The House of Lords declined to speculate in *Ping Lin*[6] upon exactly what basis the exclusion of involuntary confessions was to be justified. A number have been suggested, both in relation to the rules excluding involuntary confessions, and to the exercise of exclusionary discretions which apply to confessional statements, and to other evidence obtained by illegal means itself sometimes regarded as being governed by analogous policies. The general ground for accepting admissions, that what a party says against his own interests may be presumed to be true, has not always been accepted in relation to confessions. Thus Wigmore cites the same eminent English judge asserting first in 1798 that 'confession is a species of evidence which, though not inadmissible, is regarded with great distrust',[7] and in 1820 that 'confession generally ranks high, or I should say, highest in the scale of evidence'.[8] This discrepancy is plausibly enough explained on the basis that *when satisfactorily established* to have proceeded from a genuine motive and to have been accurately recorded, a confession may well be worthy of the highest esteem, but just because this is the case, such high regard will also be sought by the less scrupulous for statements which merely purport to satisfy these conditions. In contested criminal cases, given that the accused is present in court, has not pleaded guilty and has retracted his confession, there must always be a possibility that the statement falls into the latter category.[9] The requirement that a confession be 'voluntary' may be regarded as demanding satisfaction of quite different rationales. As noted above, *Warickshall* stressed the need for the confession to be credit-worthy, and to that end distinguishes sharply between the making of an oral statement which may or may not be false, and the finding of objects which it assumes to be automatically cogent, though it must be conceded that it is rare for evidence of the latter sort to prove very much without the assistance of testimony, or other circumstantial evidence. In *Baldry* the court was anxious to point out that involuntary confessions are not presumed to be false,[10] but that it is nevertheless dangerous from the point of view of the administration of justice to admit them. *Ibrahim* referred to the rule as one of policy, but abstained from elaborating the nature of that policy. The modern cases, at the same time as clarifying the operation of the rule, have suggested a more diffused basis for it in policy. Thus one further strand intertwined with reliability in the modern approach, and to be discerned both in Lord Reid's speech in *Harz and Power*[11] and in Lord Diplock's in *Sang*,[12] is that of the basis for the privilege against self-incrimination, a vindication of the right of the

---

6 [1976] AC 574 at 595 (Lord Morris), at 607 (Lord Salmon), [1975] 3 All ER 175 at 178 and 188.
7 Sir William Scott in *Williams v Williams* (1798) 1 Hag Con 299 at 304.
8 *Mortimer v Mortimer* (1820) 2 Hag Con 310 at 315.
9 See per Cave J in *R v Thompson* [1893] 2 QB 12 at 18.
10 In *Burns v R* (1975) 132 CLR 258 at 262, the High Court of Australia was equally insistent that voluntary confessions were not to be presumed to be true.
11 [1967] 1 AC 760 at 820, [1967] 1 All ER 177 at 184.
12 [1980] AC 402 at 436, [1979] 2 All ER 1222 at 1230. The passage is somewhat difficult to interpret since after mentioning the principle *nemo debet prodere se ipsum* in relation to the justification for modern confession law, Lord Diplock relates it to the *discretion* to exclude, going on to describe that as a sanction upon the improper conduct of the prosecution, contrasting it with the power only to secure a fair trial, and denying the existence of any comparable sanctioning power in relation to obtaining any other evidence.

individual not to be subjected to official pressure to condemn himself.[13] Two other members of the House, so far from contrasting the basis of this privilege with that of ensuring a fair trial, seem to equate them.[14] Lord Salmon makes no reference to the basis for self-incrimination, but refers only to the preservation by the judge of a fair trial by excluding involuntary confessions.[15] This rationale, concerned so closely with the rights of the accused at his trial, seems to exemplify what has been called the 'protective principle'.[16] It is clearly intended to be distinguished from what the Criminal Law Revision Committee referred to as the 'disciplinary principle', the thrust of which is more to deter improper police practices than to protect the rights of the accused. Yet this principle itself has found expression in recent decisions, for example in *Wong Kam-ming v R* Lord Hailsham said:

> any civilised system of criminal jurisprudence must accord to the judiciary some means of excluding confessions or admissions obtained by improper methods. This is not only because of the potential unreliability of such statements, but also, and perhaps mainly, because in a civilised society it is vital that persons in custody or charged with offences should not be subjected to ill treatment or improper pressure in order to extract confessions.[17]

The generality and instrumentality of these words suggest that Lord Hailsham's principal concern was with the control of police behaviour.[18] Indeed the rationale is sometimes put on a still higher plane, and, quite irrespective of the deterrent force of a decision upon police practice, related to the court's expression of abhorrence for the methods used. Thus in *King v R* Lord Hodson expressed the view of the Privy Council by saying:

> This is not, in their opinion, a case in which evidence has been obtained by conduct of which the Crown ought not to take advantage. If they had thought otherwise they would have excluded the evidence even though tendered for the suppression of crime.[19]

This view has received even stronger support in Australia where the High Court has explicitly rejected a fair play rationale in favour of such a view: 'It is not fair play that is called in question in such cases but rather society's right to insist that those who enforce the law themselves respect it.'[20] It should be noted that in both of these cases the issue related to the discretion to exclude real evidence secured after a breach of proper procedure, and in *Bunning v Cross* was said 'not to entrench upon the quite special rules which apply to the case of confession evidence'. Yet it can hardly be argued today that a weaker justification is required to restrain the application of pressure to human beings to force them to confess, than is required to prevent intrusion into private property. The further step of explicit extension to disputed confessions was taken by the High Court of Australia in *Cleland v*

---

13 See also *R v Keenan* [1989] 3 All ER 598 at 603 where the modern law under s 76 of the Police and Criminal Evidence Act 1984 is ascribed to such a rationale.

14 See Lord Fraser at 449–50, 1241, and Lord Scarman at 455, 1246.

15 Lord Salmon at 445, 1237.

16 See Ashworth 'Excluding Evidence as Protecting Rights' [1977] Crim LR 723.

17 [1980] AC 247 at 261, [1979] 1 All ER 939 at 946.

18 For a still more explicit reference to this rationale see *R v Trump* (1979) 70 Cr App Rep 300 at 303.

19 [1969] 1 AC 304 at 319, [1968] 2 All ER 610 at 617.

20 *Bunning v Cross* (1978) 19 ALR 641 at 659.

R,[1] in accordance with the position that the discretion to exclude had always been wider in Australia, than in England,[2] but not so different in the result from the position in Scotland.[3] It should be noted that under modern English law discretionary exclusion under s 78 of the Police and Criminal Evidence Act 1984 extends to means of obtaining evidence having an adverse effect upon the fairness of the proceedings, a provision which has been explicitly held to extend to confessions.[4] In Canada this area, like so much of the law of evidence, has been affected by the advent of the Canadian Charter of Rights and Freedoms. Under art 24(2) of the Charter any evidence in breach of the rights guaranteed by the Charter must be excluded 'if it is established that, having regard to all the circumstances, the admission of it in the proceedings would bring the administration of justice into disrepute'. This will, in many cases, operate in relation to confessions by way of breach of the right to counsel guaranteed under the Charter.[5]

The explicit rejection of such rationales is as significant as the espousel of such a variety has been, as an indication of the uncertainty of the law in this area. In *R v Warickshall* the court was clear that:

It is a mistaken notion that the evidence of confessions and facts which have been obtained from prisoners by promises or threats, is to be rejected from a regard to public faith: no such rule ever prevailed.[6]

In stark contrast when, in *Wong Kam-ming v R*, counsel for the respondent began his argument by expressing the reliability principle he was sharply upbraided by Lord Diplock with the assertion that such an argument was contrary to authority.[7] Nor do the views in *R v Sang* support a general disciplinary policy in this area, for as expressed by Lord Diplock:

It is no part of a judge's function to exercise powers over the police or prosecution as respects the way in which evidence to be used at the trial is obtained by them. If it was obtained illegally there will be a remedy in civil law; if it was obtained legally but in breach of the rules of conduct of the police, this is a matter for the appropriate disciplinary authority to deal with. What the judge at the trial is concerned with is not how the evidence sought to be adduced by the prosecution has been obtained, but with how it is used by the prosecution at the trial.[8]

It should be noted that by excluding confessions from this reasoning Lord Diplock was countenancing just that split between the rationales in respect of police methods in obtaining confessions and in obtaining other evidence which was rejected by the High Court of Australia in *Cleland v R*[9] Lord Diplock's view distinguishes sharply, and perfectly understandably, between police practice in inducing speech and in searching premises. It is less clear

---

1 (1982) 43 ALR 619.
2 Justified by Murphy J at 631 on the basis of the lower standard of proof for the voluntariness of a confession in Australia.
3 *Cleland v R* per Gibbs CJ at 624.
4 *R v Mason* [1987] 3 All ER 481 at 484.
5 *R v Manninen* [1987] 1 SCR 1233. A vast jurisprudence has already developed around the Charter in general, and this article in particular, see Paccioco *Charter Principles and Proof in Criminal Cases* (1987).
6 (1783) 1 Leach 263.
7 [1980] AC 247 at 251.
8 [1980] AC 402 at 436, [1979] 2 All ER 1222 at 1230. See also *R v Delaney* (1989) 88 Cr App Rep 338 at 341.
9 (1982) 43 ALR 619.

how Lords Fraser and Scarman, who extend discretionary exclusion to some searches, can subscribe to the same rationale. It is hard to see why it is so much worse for the police to search the accused's premises improperly than so to search those of anyone else. If anything, the former seems marginally less iniquitous.

It can thus be seen that the cases exhibit no unanimity of approach, and it was partly for this reason that in *D P P v Ping Lin* the House of Lords took the view that any general reform must be left to the legislature.[10]

C. PROPOSALS FOR REFORM

There has been no shortage of such proposals in common law jurisdictions. In England two of the most interesting and influential have been those made by the Criminal Law Revision Committee in its 11th Report,[11] and those made by the Royal Commission on Criminal Procedure.[12] It should be noted that these two reports considered the admissibility of confessions in two different contexts, the former within that of the whole range of rules of evidence which apply in criminal cases, and the latter within that of the whole process of police investigation into crime. As will become apparent, these different contexts coloured, to some extent, the recommendations which were made.

1. CRIMINAL LAW REVISION COMMITTEE

The principal defect in the existing law in the eyes of the Criminal Law Revision Committee was clearly that the existing law had become over-technical, and that confessions were being excluded upon the basis of 'inducements' which, although falling within the ambit of previous precedent, were highly unlikely to have had any real effect upon the suspect. It was thus inclined to introduce a new test based upon the likelihood, in the prevailing circumstances, of the confession's being reliable. It stressed however that the court should not assess the reliability of the confession actually made, but should instead consider a hypothetical confession made in the circumstances of the actual case. It envisaged that in the very same situation a confession of the commission of a serious crime might thus be sustained while that of a more minor one could be vitiated.[13] It is perhaps dubious whether such a refined distinction would make much impression upon the minds of those required to administer it, and whether in fact the issue of the reliability of a hypothetical confession could be kept quite so separate from that of the reliability of the confession actually made. The committee, by contrast, decided to retain its view of the then current law, and to retain the concept of inadmissibility on account of oppression,[14] in this case irrespective of any consideration of hypothetical reliability, presumably on the basis that the concept of oppression at common law was

10 [1976] AC 574, [1975] 3 All ER 175, at 595, 179 (Lord Morris), at 600, 182, (Lord Hailsham) at 607, 188 (Lord Salmon).
11 Cmnd 4991 (1972) pp 34–47, draft Bill cl 2, pp 212–214.
12 Cmnd 8092 (1981) ch 4.
13 Para 65.
14 Simply substituting the terminology of 'oppressive treatment', para 60, draft Bill cl 2(2)(a).

decisive of such a question against admissibility. It also envisaged the retention of a discretion in the court to exclude in cases of serious impropriety falling short of oppression and not threatening reliability.[15]

The committee decided to endorse the views expressed in *Customs and Excise Comrs v Harz and Power*[16] that no distinction should be drawn between full confessions and admissions of some elements of the offence charged only,[17] and also that there should be no need for a relevant inducement to relate to the crime charged. It then took the further logical step of extending its provisions to inducements offered by persons generally, and of not limiting them to those offered by persons in authority, thus recommending the overthrow of the decision in *Deokinanan v R*.[18]

It adhered to its view of the common law in deciding that the inadmissibility of involuntary confessions applied only to evidence adduced by the prosecution.[19] Because it felt it to be controversial, it also reaffirmed the view that the burden of proof borne by the prosecution should be proof beyond reasonable doubt,[20] and that although normally the issue would be raised by the accused, nevertheless the judge could in appropriate circumstances raise the issue of his own volition.[1]

It should be remembered that these recommendations were made in the context of a plan for widespread reform of the hearsay rule. It was thus quite unnecessary to make any special provision for the admissibility of the confession of one person upon the trial of another. For the same reason there was no need for the committee to address its mind to the question of wholly exculpatory statements. In fact the committee treated confessions and most other forms of hearsay quite separately. It did however incorporate into its proposals about confessions, explicit provision for the admissibility of evidence discovered as a result of inadmissible confessions, and of the fact that it was discovered as a result of a statement made by the accused.[2]

An even more dramatic and still more controversial aspect of the committee's report bearing upon these proposals, was its recommendation that the accused's 'right of silence' should be curtailed to the extent that adverse inferences, or even corroboration of other evidence, could be drawn from his failure to mention during interrogation facts subsequently relied upon by him at his trial.[3] This naturally entailed drastic revision of the Judges' Rules and of the whole environment of the interrogation of suspects. It was indeed largely the radicalism of these suggestions, rather than any more technical points of the law of evidence which brought about the hostile reception to the Report, and prevented its implementation in the form recommended.

15 Paras 61 and 278, cl 45(8).
16 [1967] 1 AC 760, [1967] 1 All ER 177.
17 In the same vein the committee recommended that its provisions should apply to the exculpatory parts of partially inculpatory statements.
18 [1969] 1 AC 20, [1968] 2 All ER 346. Para 58, cl 2(2) by necessary implication.
19 Para 53.
20 Cl 2(2), and see Annex 2 p 213.
 1 Para 54, cl 2(3).
 2 Paras 68 and 69, sub-cll 2(5)(a) and 2(5)(b).
 3 Paras 28–34, cl 1.

2. ROYAL COMMISSION

The Royal Commission investigated and reported in the aftermath of the reaction to the Criminal Law Revision Committee's report. It is important to note also that it was a differently constituted body, set up under different powers, adopted a different method and had different, though to some extent overlapping, terms of reference. The Criminal Law Revision Committee was overwhelmingly composed of trained lawyers, many of them with long practical experience, whereas on the Royal Commission lawyers constituted a tiny minority. The Royal Commission, partly on account of its different status and partly perhaps in the light of reaction to the proposals of the Criminal Law Revision Committee, set about its task in a very different way. In particular it conducted extensive research studies, and engaged in a much more widespread exercise of consultation and the solicitation of evidence. It did not incorporate its proposals into a draft Bill. It should also be re-emphasised that its main focus of concern was upon pre-trial criminal procedure, and recommendations about the law of evidence were incidental to that focus.

The research studies produced interesting information and statistics about a number of matters. Among other things they tended to dispel some of the concerns which had exercised the Criminal Law Revision Committee. It was found, for example, that contrary to the view expressed by the Criminal Law Revision Committee,[4] it is not the case that very much time is taken up in court on issues relating to the admissibility of statements made, or alleged to have been made, by accused persons.[5] It was also discovered that the furore about the judicial treatment of exercise by the suspect of his right to silence, which had sunk the committee's proposals, appeared to be based upon the false premise that suspects did actually choose to remain silent, when in fact this was true of only a tiny proportion of those questioned.[6] At a less fundamental level, it was also discovered by reference to experience elsewhere that at least two of the objections to tape-recording which had bothered the committee,[7] namely the ease of tampering with tapes and the danger of feigning improprieties, were not supported by the evidence of that experience.[8]

The commission differed from the committee on the issue of the right to silence, preferring to retain the essence of the present situation in which judicial comment on the exercise of that right is strictly limited. This was justified on the basis that any other course would be unfair in placing too much pressure upon suspects, and that it would be contrary to the basic philosophy of an accusatorial system. These reasons are unconvincing. The commission's own research had revealed just how much psychological pressure to speak already exists and how rarely it is resisted, so it is dubious whether this marginal addition would make very much difference. Nor is it clear exactly why the basis of the accusatorial system which the committee tended to see in terms of the burden of proof borne by the prosecution, would be undermined by an inference drawn from the accused's silence, when it is

---

4 Para 54.
5 Paras 4.7 and 4.8, and evidence cited therein.
6 Paras 4.43–4.46, and evidence cited therein.
7 Para 52.
8 Paras 4.23 and 4.24.

not generally considered to be so undermined by the use at trial of other forms of explicit or implicit acknowledgement of guilt occurring in the course of pre-trial investigation. Nevertheless the commission was content to endorse the existing position, which its research had shown not to amount to such a substantial clog upon the process of prosecution as had previously been supposed. It was less content with the 'voluntariness' and 'oppression' rules. It felt that they were far too vague to give any realistic guidance to police officers in the course of an investigation. It also felt that too great a gap had opened up between the legal notion of 'involuntary', enshrined in the doctrine of threats and promises from persons in authority, and the psychological notion, arguably borne out by the high incidence of statements made by those interrogated, which its own research had revealed. Notwithstanding its professed scepticism about the disadvantages and difficulties of ex post facto judicial assessment of the propriety of police behaviour during an interrogation,[9] the commission recommended that in the case of police behaviour involving 'violence, threats of violence, torture or inhuman or degrading treatment' any evidence found to have been obtained by such methods should be excluded automatically by the trial judge.[10] In the case of less heinous behaviour the commission recommended the automatic admissibility of evidence so obtained, subject only to the impact of defence submissions and cross-examination, if any, and to a compulsory judicial warning about the risks of the unreliability of evidence obtained in breach of a new and expanded code of police procedure for the treatment of suspects and the conduct of investigations.[11]

It can hardly be denied that the commission's treatment of the law of evidence is, even conceding its limited focus, vestigial in the extreme. No clear distinction is made between exclusion by rule and exclusion by discretion, nor between a confessional statement, evidence discovered in consequence of such a statement, or those parts of the statement confirmed by the evidence, nor between the protection of the right to silence by bestowing upon the suspect a more realistic opportunity to decide whether or not to speak, or by restricting the judge's right to comment upon such an exercise. It does not address itself at all to the admissibility of exculpatory statements, to the admissibility of confessions otherwise than at the instance of the prosecution, or the question of how far confessions of one suspect can be evidence against another. It is thus hardly a blueprint for a comprehensive code of evidence in this area.[12]

D. POLICE AND CRIMINAL EVIDENCE ACT 1984[13]

This legislation now governs the admissibility of confessions, and requires consideration in detail. Questions arise as to its extent, the conditions which it imposes for admissibility, and its effect.

9 See Para 4.72.
10 Para 4.132.
11 Para 4.133.
12 In that respect it falls far short of the Australian Law Reform Commission's Research Paper No 15 'Admissions' (1983) or that of the New Zealand Evidence Law Reform Committee's Report on Confessions (1987).
13 For early appraisal of the operation of this legislation see Birch 'The Pace Hots Up: Confessions and Confusions Under the 1984 Act' [1989] Crim LR 95.

1. EXTENT

Section 76 of the Police and Criminal Evidence Act 1984 establishes its extent by providing:

(1) In any proceedings a confession made by an accused person may be given in evidence against him in so far as it is relevant to any matter in issue in the proceedings and is not excluded by the court in pursuance of this section.

This is supplemented by s 82 which states that:

(1) 'confession' includes any statement wholly or partly adverse to the person who made it, whether made to a person in authority or not, and whether made in words or otherwise.

Two sets of issues arise as to the extent of these provisions, the first relating to substantial, and the second to procedural, delimitation. These will be considered in turn.

(i) Substantial delimitation

In the first category it is necessary to elucidate the notion of a 'statement', whether it extends to matters of opinion as well as those of fact, the precise extent of the phrase 'made in words or otherwise', and the vexed notion of how far, if at all, purely exculpatory statements are caught by the words 'wholly or partly adverse'.

There is, in this part of the Act, no further definition of 'statement', by contrast to the preceding part where it is defined in accordance with the definition in the Civil Evidence Act 1968.[14] That definition, as amended, now includes an expression of opinion, so it is reasonable to construe 'confession' here as excluding any expression of opinion.

It will be noticed that to amount to a confession any statement must be, at least in part, adverse to its maker. A question may arise as to the position with regard to a statement wholly exculpatory in intention and apparent effect when made, but which by the time of trial, has become damaging to the accused either because it can be shown to be false, or because it is inconsistent with the defence raised at the trial. In *Piché v R*[15] the Supreme Court of Canada held, by a majority, that such an exculpatory statement must also satisfy the voluntariness test, adopting the reasoning of Chief Justice Warren in *Miranda v Arizona*:[16]

no distinction may be drawn between inculpatory statements and statements alleged to be merely 'exculpatory'. If a statement made were in fact exculpatory it would, of course never be used by the prosecution. In fact, statements merely intended to be exculpatory by the defendant are often used to impeach his testimony at trial or to demonstrate untruths in the statement given under interrogation and thus to prove guilt by implication. These statements are incriminating in any meaningful sense of the word.

It was also sought to buttress the argument by reference to the choice of the

14 S 72(1).
15 (1970) 11 DLR (3d) 709.
16 384 US 436 at 477 (1966).

wider term 'statement' in *Ibrahim v R*,[17] and the stress put upon its repetition in principle (e) of the introduction to the Judges' Rules by Lord Reid in *Customs and Excise Comrs v Harz and Power*.[18] It is however quite clear that *Ibrahim* was in fact concerned with incriminating statements, and there is no reason to suppose in any case that the choice of words had any deep significance, while Lord Reid was concerned only to equate admissions with full confessions. In principle it seems that an exculpatory statement of this sort is not used as evidence of its truth,[19] indeed it is used only because it is false, and does no more than demonstrate an inconsistency to discredit its maker. As such it does not fall foul of the hearsay rule, and ought to be admitted. The equation of admissions falling short of confessions with exculpatory statements is extremely misleading. It is perfectly conceivable, as Lord Reid remarked, that a man may under pressure falsely tell all, or part, of what the person inflicting the pressure wants to hear, namely an admission. It is quite implausible to suppose that he will falsely tell him what he does not want to hear, namely a denial. An argument to the contrary might be raised upon the decision in *R v Treacy*[20] where it was said that an inadmissible confession could not be used as a previous inconsistent statement for the purpose of discrediting its maker. The difference is however that in such a case the prosecution does not reject the truth of the statement it is tendering, indeed by tendering it on the voir dire it has affirmed its truth in the very same proceedings, and by tendering it at the trial it is seeking a verdict in accordance with the truth of what it asserts. It is submitted that the Act does not for these reasons extend to wholly exculpatory statements, but instead applies only to statements made as being, at least in part, adverse. This is in full accord with the robust view of the Court of Appeal that 'a denial does not become an admission because it is inconsistent with another denial'.[1] The Court of Appeal has further asserted that it would be odd to consider an unequivocal denial to be regarded, even for these purposes, as a confession.[2]

This raises the further vexed question of implied admissions, and whether they are covered by the Act. If the accused who has made a false denial fails to testify, the most likely relevance of the false denial is to show consciousness of guilt. Such consciousness may also be shown by such things as making false,[3] or evasive,[4] statements, remaining silent when speech could have been expected,[5] refusing to supply a sample of real evidence,[6] putting in a false notice of alibi,[7] attempting to suborn witnesses,[8] calling witnesses to give

---

17 [1914] AC 599.
18 [1967] 1 AC 760 at 819, [1967] 1 All ER 177 at 182.
19 *Mawaz Khan v R* [1967] 1 AC 454, but see Elliott and Wakeham 'Exculpatory Statements by Accused Persons' [1979] Crim LR 428; Mirfield *Confessions* pp 82–88.
20 [1944] 2 All ER 229.
 1 *R v Pearce* (1979) 69 Cr App Rep 365 at 370.
 2 *R v Sat-Bhambra* (1988) 88 Cr App Rep 55 at 61. See also *R v Doyle* [1987] 2 Qd R 732 at 746; *R v Coats* [1932] NZLR 401.
 3 *R v Knight* [1966] 1 All ER 647, [1966] 1 WLR 230; and see *R v Lucas* [1981] QB 720, [1981] 2 All ER 1008.
 4 *Woon v R* (1964) 109 CLR 529.
 5 *R v Chandler* [1976] 3 All ER 105, [1976] 1 WLR 585; and a fortiori assaulting an accuser, *Parkes v R* [1976] 3 All ER 380, [1976] 1 WLR 1251.
 6 *R v Smith* (1985) 81 Cr App Rep 286.
 7 *R v Rossborough* (1985) 81 Cr App Rep 139.
 8 *Moriarty v London Chatham and Dover Rly Co* (1870) LR 5 QB 314.

testimony known to be false,[9] or fleeing.[10] It is submitted that unless the conduct can be regarded as indicating acceptance of an assertion made by another, consciousness of guilt derived from such statements or conduct can amount only to circumstantial evidence, and consistent with the view expressed in ch XIV cannot amount to hearsay. In such a case it is admissible if relevant, irrespective of its motivation, save in so far as that may so reduce the weight of such evidence as to suggest that it ought to trigger the exercise of the judge's discretion to exclude because the prejudicial effect is likely to exceed probative value, a particularly likely situation here when the conduct or statement may have many other plausible explanations besides consciousness of guilt.[11] If an accused person is subjected to improper pressure to confess, his running away may clearly stem from a desire to avoid the pressure, rather than from a consciousness of guilt. This is a matter of simple common-sense, and there is no need to achieve the exclusion of any adverse inference from such conduct by so tortuous a chain of reasoning as first categorising it as hearsay and in principle inadmissible, then as falling within an inclusionary exception for admissions implied from conduct, and finally excluding it as coming within the exception to that exception for involuntary admissions. It might be argued that this view deprives the second part of the expression 'in words or otherwise' of any meaning, on the basis that even an allegation accepted by conduct, remains a statement in words irrespective of its mode of adoption. Such an argument seems to place insufficient emphasis upon the mode of adoption by the accused which is what turns it into an admission, and which is hypothesised to be made otherwise than in words. It should also be noticed that the concluding words are undeniably apt to cover evidence of admissions deduced from the conduct of the accused in the course of a re-enactment of the crime, arranged by the police.[12]

(ii) Procedural delimitation

These matters comprehend such issues as the extent to which the section applies to use of confessional material by the defence, and especially by a co-accused, how far it applies to statements made in other curial proceedings, to what extent it applies to magistrates, and the stage at which particular exclusionary rules apply.

The wording of the Act seems to distinguish between its general extent which is to all confessions made by an accused person, and the special restrictive conditions which apply only to those put in evidence by the prosecution. The result appears to be that the accused may himself adduce the confessions of a co-accused without regard to the restrictive conditions laid down, but, since such a confession would fall within the terms of sub-s 76(1), can secure the advantage of the effects given by the Act. This seems to have been the position at common law,[13] and is in complete accord with

9 *R v Perera* [1982] VR 901.
10 *R v Gay* [1976] VR 577.
11 This is consistent with the approach adopted in *Lucas*, and in *R v Dowley* [1983] Crim LR 168, an appeal was allowed because the dangers had not been clearly enough spelled out.
12 *Li Shu-ling v R* [1989] AC 270, [1988] 3 All ER 138. Also accepted elsewhere see *Collins v R* (1980) 31 ALR 257; *R v Tookey and Stevenson* (1981) 58 CCC (2d) 421; *People v Dabb* 32 Cal 2d 491 (1948).
13 But see in Australia *Wade v Gilroy* (1986) 83 FLR 15.

the view that the principal evidential constraint upon the accused in his own defence is relevance. As between co-accused there will rarely be scope for the exercise of any exclusionary discretion. In particular, one co-accused may always cross-examine his co-accused upon the basis of a confession, even if it is, and has been held to be, inadmissible for the prosecution.[14] If, on the other hand, the confessional statement is not one made by an accused person, then admissibility is governed either by the common law in the case of an oral statement, or by the provisions of Pt II of the Criminal Justice Act 1988 in the case of a statement in a document. An oral statement by a third party will normally be excluded[15] by the ordinary operation of the hearsay rule.[16] Such a confessional documentary statement may however be admitted under Pt II of the Criminal Justice Act 1988 if the conditions there prescribed can be satisfied.[17] It should however be noted that nothing in Pt II affects the operation of s 76 of the Police and Criminal Evidence Act 1984 in the case of statements made by the defendant.[18] Such a confession is admissible only upon the satisfaction of the conditions prescribed by s 76.

The next point to be made on the extent of the section relates to the question of the admissibility of confessions made in other proceedings, or at earlier stages of the same proceedings.[19] There is nothing in the wording of s 76 to suggest that it does not apply to statements made in the course of judicial proceedings just as much as to those not so made. It would follow that the common law rules admitting statements made in other proceedings,[20] pleas of guilty to associated offences,[1] and pleas of guilty which have been withdrawn,[2] will remain applicable since it is inherently unlikely that the conditions for exclusion will be capable of being established in such situations.[3]

The admissibility of statements on the voir dire has been more controversial. As noted earlier[4] the position at common law seems to have been changed in some respects by the section. It is best to consider the matter in two stages, first to consider to what extent admissions can be extracted on the voir dire, and then to what extent they can be adduced at the trial. Section 76 makes no explicit reference to the propriety of asking about the

14 *R v Rowson* [1986] QB 174, [1985] 2 All ER 539; *Lui Mei-lin v R* [1989] AC 288, [1989] 1 All ER 359.
15 Unless it falls within a recognised exception, see section 3 below.
16 *Sussex Peerage Case* (1844) 11 Cl & Fin 85. The same rule applies in Australia, see *Re Van Beelen* (1974) 9 SASR 163; but not in Canada, *R v O'Brien* (1977) 76 DLR (3d) 513, or the United States, Federal Rule 804(3)(b) requiring corroboration, and see *Chambers v Mississippi* 410 US 295 (1973).
17 See further section 2 below.
18 Criminal Justice Act 1988, ss 23(4), 24(3). Cp *R v England* [1978] Tas SR 79.
19 The editor has relied heavily in this section upon Pattenden 'Informal Judicial Admissions of Criminal Activity: A Comparative Study of England, Canada and the United States' (1983) 32 ICLQ 812.
20 *R v McGregor* [1968] 1 QB 371, [1967] 2 All ER 267.
1 *R v Bastin* [1971] Crim LR 529.
2 *R v Rimmer* [1972] 1 All ER 604.
3 In *R v Scott* (1856) Dears & B 47 at 58, Lord Campbell CJ said 'Such an objection [involuntariness] cannot apply to a lawful examination in the course of a judicial proceeding'. In *McGregor* also the vigour of Lord Parker CJ's repudiation of the notion of the inadmissibility of a statement on oath in judicial proceedings points in the same direction. But see *Seymour v A-G for Commonwealth* (1984) 53 ALR 513; *Clyne v R* (1985) 81 FLR 197.
4 At pp 168–171.

truth or falsity of a confession on the voir dire,[5] so the matter is left to the common law. This is in a somewhat uncertain state. In the case of such an issue being initiated by the prosecution there was conflict between a decision of the Court of Criminal Appeal that such questioning was permissible,[6] and one of the majority of the Privy Council, that it was not.[7] In the case of the issue's being initiated by the defence the House of Lords seems to have held that such questioning was proper.[8] This would probably have remained an academic issue at common law in view of the further finding that no reference could be made to such an admission at the trial. On ordinary principles of statutory interpretation however this happy result seems to have been overturned by the new statutory provisions. Section 76 applies to confessions in unrestricted terms, and makes them admissible at the instance of the prosecution in all cases, unless the conditions of sub-s (2) cannot be disproved. But as noted above, there is, in the case of an admission on the voir dire every reason to suppose that such conditions will be held to be disproved.[9] It would seem to follow that judicial confessions made at whatever stage are thus admissible. This effect appears to resurrect the conflict between *Hammond* and the majority view in *Wong Kam-ming*. In the first draft of the Bill, as noted above, such a conflict was to have been resolved by a specific provision in favour of *Hammond* and the minority in *Wong Kam-ming*, but that provision was withdrawn, and the Act is now silent on the propriety of questions as to the truth or falsity of a confession on the voir dire.[10] On balance it seems, notwithstanding the strict doctrine of precedent, more likely in the circumstances that the views of the majority of the Law Lords in *Wong Kam-ming* will prevail, especially as no disapproval of that decision was expressed by the House of Lords in *Brophy*.[11] It does seem however that the general intention of *Wong Kam-ming* and *Brophy* to protect the accused from damaging use at the trial of proceedings on the voir dire has been frustrated by the drafting of the new statutory provisions so as to exclude confessions, only upon the satisfaction of conditions which judicial proceedings will rarely, if ever, satisfy in the United Kingdom.

'Proceedings' are defined by s 82(1) to mean criminal proceedings, though no indication is given of whether that expression is meant to comprehend all stages of such proceedings at which evidence might be tendered.[12] It is clear that they comprehend proceedings before magistrates, and s 76(2) in its

---

5 The Bill, as introduced, included a subsection specifically permitting such questioning, but it was withdrawn.

6 *R v Hammond* [1941] 3 All ER 318, 28 Cr App Rep 84.

7 *Wong Kam-ming v R* [1980] AC 247, [1979] 1 All ER 939.

8 *R v Brophy* [1982] AC 476, [1981] 2 All ER 705. It is left unclear to what extent the questioning there did relate to an extra-judicial confession, and to what extent its adduction by the defence would permit cross-examination by the prosecution. In any event the situation there was atypical in that it was the defence which was alleging the confession to be true.

9 Above 169. The same result was reached by the Supreme Court of Canada in *Boulet v R* (1978) 75 DLR (3d) 223 at 236, and in none of *Hammond, Wong Kam-ming* nor *Brophy* was the question so much as raised. The regressive effect of voir dires into voir dires is surely to be avoided if at all possible.

10 Commentators are not so much silent as divided, compare Murphy 'Truth on the Voir Dire' [1979] Crim LR 364 with Arvay 'Voir Dire Evidence: A Commentary on *Wong Kam-ming* and its application to Canada' (1981) 23 Cr LQ 173.

11 It seems still permissible to ask the question in Australia, see *Frijaf v R* [1982] WAR 128; but not in South Africa *S v De Vries* 1989 (1) SA 228.

12 Compare Criminal Evidence Act 1898, s 1.

mandatory terms seems to have imposed an obligation upon magistrates to consider the admissibility of a confession as a separate preliminary matter in summary proceedings,[13] and perhaps also in committal proceedings.[14] A different view was however taken in respect of an application to consider discretionary exclusion under s 78 as a preliminary matter.[15] The reasoning was based upon a supposed difference between the obligation under s 76(2) to take a decision on admissibility in advance of the evidence being tendered, and the decision under s 78 which could be taken at any time. It is doubtful however whether this view can survive the interpretation of ss 76 and 78 of the Police and Criminal Evidence Act 1984 in *R v Sat-Bhambra*[16] as referring only to the future, so that once the evidence has been adduced their direct effect has been spent. The effect of any such view is however slight, since the judge may still discharge the jury, or direct it to disregard the confession, under his general discretionary powers, preserved by s 82(3) of the Police and Criminal Evidence Act 1984.

2. CONDITIONS

Confessions are made admissible under the conditions set out in s 76:

> (2) If, in any proceedings where the prosecution proposes to give in evidence a confession made by an accused person, it is represented to the court that the confession was or may have been obtained—
> (a) by oppression of the person who made it; or
> (b) in consequence of anything said or done which was likely, in the circumstances existing at the time, to render unreliable any confession which might be made by him in consequence thereof,
> the court shall not allow the confession to be given in evidence against him except in so far as the prosecution proves to the court beyond reasonable doubt that the confession (notwithstanding that it may be true) was not obtained as aforesaid.
> (8) . . . 'oppression' includes torture, inhuman or degrading treatment, and the use of threat or violence (whether or not amounting to torture).

It is convenient to discuss these conditions under four headings, oppression, unreliability, causation and burden of proof.

(i) Oppression

The adjectival form of this word seems to have entered English law in this context in Lord Parker CJ's judgment in *Callis v Gunn* where he said with reference to statements by accused persons to the police that it was:[17]

---

13 *R v Liverpool Juvenile Court, ex p R* [1988] QB 1, [1987] 2 All ER 668.
14 *R v Oxford City Justices, ex p Berry* [1988] QB 507, [1987] 1 All ER 1244. Though in most cases refusal to consider the admissibility of a confession will not be sufficient to justify judicial review of the decision to commit, such remedies being discretionary.
15 *Vel v Owen* [1987] Crim LR 496, see also *Carlisle v DPP* (1987) Lexis Transcript 9 November.
16 (1988) 88 Cr App Rep 55, intimating that the 1984 legislation had altered the procedure determined by *R v Watson* [1980] 2 All ER 293, [1980] 1 WLR 991.
17 [1964] 1 QB 495 at 501, [1963] 3 All ER 677 at 680.

a fundamental principle of law that no answer to a question and no statement is admissible unless it is shown by the prosecution not to have been obtained in an oppressive manner and to have been voluntary in the sense that it has not been obtained by threats or inducements.

It then appeared in its substantive form as a condition negating the categorisation of a confession as 'voluntary' in principle (e) in the introduction to the new Judges' Rules of January 1964.[18] In *R v Prager*,[19] a case in which the confession of a sergeant in the Royal Air Force on charges of espionage made after a prolonged, but interrupted, interrogation was held not to have resulted from oppression, the Court of Appeal adopted a statement made by Sachs J in *R v Priestley*:[20]

> Whether or not there is oppression in an individual case depends upon many elements... They include such things as the length of time of any individual period of questioning, whether the accused person had been given proper refreshment or not, and the characteristics of the person who makes the statement. What may be oppressive as regards a child, an invalid or an old man or somebody inexperienced in the ways of this world may turn out not to be oppressive when one finds that the accused person is of a tough character and an experienced man of the world.

The court also relied upon the following quotation from an address given by Lord MacDermott to the Bentham club in 1968:

> Questioning which by its nature, duration or other attendant circumstances (including the fact of custody) excites hopes (such as the hope of release) or fears, or so affects the mind of the suspect that his will crumbles and he speaks when otherwise he would have remained silent.

These terms, perhaps because delivered extra-judicially, seem remarkably far-reaching, a very large number of remarks and actions might affect a man's mind so as to induce him to speak when otherwise he would have remained silent. Although approved by the Criminal Law Revision Committee,[1] this test was criticised by the Royal Commission as imprecise and unsatisfactory.[2] The terminology of oppression nevertheless received the endorsement of the legislature as indicated above, though it provided only an inclusive definition repeating the substantive form of the old Judges' Rules.[3] Its construction was considered by the Court of Appeal in *R v Fulling*.[4] In that case a woman accused of fraud at first refused to make a statement to the police. At one point during an interview she alleged that she was told by her interrogator that her lover had been engaged in a sexual affair with another woman, who was incarcerated in the next cell. She claimed that this

---

18 Themselves accepted as an accurate statement of English law as it then stood by the House of Lords in *Customs and Excise Comrs v Harz and Power* [1967] 1 AC 760, [1967] 1 All ER 177.
19 [1972] 1 All ER 1114, [1972] 1 WLR 260.
20 See the note in (1967) 51 Cr App Rep 1 in which Sachs J expressly disavowed any intention of making a categorical definition.
1 Cmnd 4771, para 60.
2 Cmnd 8092, paras 4.71 and 4.72.
3 Although the Criminal Law Revision Committee had proposed to use the phrase 'oppressive treatment'.
4 [1987] QB 426, [1987] 2 All ER 65, see commentary in [1987] All ER Annual Review 120.

upset her, and that in her anxiety to get away from the police station she then confessed. She contended that the confession should be excluded under s 76(2)(a) as having been obtained by oppression. The trial court rejected this view, and was upheld by the Court of Appeal on the basis that the Police and Criminal Evidence Act 1984 was a codifying Act, and to be construed without necessary reference to the old law. This was explained upon the basis that the newly extended grounds of exclusion on the basis of unreliability were sufficient to cover many of the situations previously within the wider old ambit of 'oppression'. It is perhaps the more surprising that no reference was made to the partial definition in s 76(8). Instead the court applied a dictionary definition:[5]

> Exercise of authority or power in a burdensome, harsh or wrongful manner; unjust or cruel treatment of subjects, inferiors, etc; the imposition of unreasonable or unjust burdens.

and drew attention to one of the quotations, 'There is not a word in our language which expresses more detestable wickedness than *oppression*.'[6] The conclusion drawn from this reasoning was that it would be rare to establish oppression without some impropriety on the part of the interrogator. In this respect it should be noted that the first phrase of the partial definition in s 76(8) appears also in Article 3 of the European Convention on Human Rights, to which the United Kingdom is a party, and was discussed in a case arising out of the treatment of detainees in Northern Ireland.[7] It thus seems likely that s 76(8) will be interpreted so as to conform with the accepted construction of that Convention. The term 'violence' does not appear in the Convention, nor is it a term of art in English law. It seems possible that it will, because of its connection with the notion of torture in s 76(8), be construed as connoting a substantial application of force. It must certainly indicate more than a mere battery as the legislature would presumably have used a term of art if to do so would have implemented its intention, and the requirement of so small a degree of force would be prone to cause disputes in far too many perfectly reasonable and acceptable situations.

It is somewhat uncertain how far the effect of the conduct on the particular individual is to be taken into account under this head.[8] In the case of a mentally disturbed suspect it seems that the fact that questioning might disturb him is irrelevant to the operation of the exclusionary conditions of s 76(2)(a), unless the asking of such questions was a deliberate attempt to exploit the suspect's mental condition.[9] It is clear from the context that more than mere incarceration or interrogation in a police station is required to constitute oppression. The difficulty is to know exactly how much more. Under the old law in *R v Hudson*[10] where a retired local government officer of 57, who had led a quiet life, was arrested at his home at 6.30 a.m. on a Sunday morning by a posse of seven police, on a charge not subsequently preferred against him, subjected to a total of 700 questions on and off for 25 hours out of 50 spent in custody during a hot summer, and then charged

5 *Oxford English Dictionary* third definition.
6 Original emphasis.
7 *Republic of Ireland v United Kingdom* (1978) 2 EHRR 25.
8 It seems to have been decisive in *R v Gardner* [1986] CLY 1499, but that was decided before *Fulling*, and may have been over-influenced by the old law.
9 *R v Miller* [1986] 3 All ER 119, [1986] 1 WLR 1191.
10 (1980) 72 Cr App Rep 163.

only a year after release with the, non-arrestable, offence of corruption, the court excluded a written statement upon this basis, remarking that 'the very serious factor of unlawfulness' made the inference 'almost irresistible'. This may be contrasted with *R v Hughes*[11] where conditions were uncomfortably cold rather than hot, and where there were also breaches of the proper practice governing interrogation, though they were not so serious. In that case the court thought it right that no point was raised on oppression, and instead considered the case on the basis of the discretion conferred by s 78 of the Police and Criminal Evidence Act 1984.[12] Much may depend upon the notion of 'wrongful' in the dictionary definition adopted in *Fulling*. It seems that it is capable of applying to breaches of the Code of Practice for the interrogation of offenders, provided that they are sufficiently numerous and serious. In *R v Davison*,[13] as in *Hudson*, they were further aggravated by failure to charge for the offence with which the interrogation was principally concerned, and the ground of oppression was held not to have been disproved.

(ii) Unreliability

Although, as noted above,[14] the danger of unreliability has always been regarded as one of the factors underpinning the development of the exclusionary rule for confessions in English law, it had never previously played a part in the formulation of the test for admissibility which had been traditionally cast in terms of 'voluntariness'.[15] The introduction of this notion into the English test for exclusion was recommended by the Criminal Law Revision Committee in its 11th Report.[16] It was not however endorsed by the Royal Commission as a test for admissibility, but was simply to be regarded as an important matter going to the weight of those confessions obtained otherwise than by 'oppressive treatment'.[17] The new legislation adopts the principle proposed by the Criminal Law Revision Committee, doing no more than broaden the nature of the conduct affecting reliability from 'threat or inducement'[18] to 'anything said or done'. Neither version limits such conduct to that performed by persons in authority. The Criminal Law Revision Committee stressed that the test was not to be based upon the actual, but the potential, unreliability of a confession made in the relevant circumstances, which took into account such matters as the seriousness of the offence. It will be noted that s 76(2) refers explicitly to the 'circumstances existing at the time'. This seems to reflect the concern of the Criminal Law Revision Committee that the judge should try to recreate in his mind the conditions as they seemed to the accused at the moment of interrogation, though the Royal Commission was sceptical of the feasibility of such an

11 [1988] Crim LR 519.
12 Such overlapping of 'oppression' and discretionary exclusion existed even under the old common law discretion before the passage of s 78, see *R v Platt* [1981] Crim LR 622, and *R v Gowan* [1982] Crim LR 821.
13 [1988] Crim LR 442.
14 At p 601.
15 The state of Victoria has however had a test formulated in such terms since 1857, and New Zealand since 1895.
16 Cmnd 4991, para 65.
17 This term is here used to connote the gamut of conduct regarded by the Royal Commission as justifying automatic exclusion.
18 Draft bill, cl 2(2)(b).

exercise.[19] There seems no reason to suppose that the English provisions will not be interpreted in a manner similar to those already in force in New Zealand and Victoria where despite minor differences of phraseology the Court have interpreted their respective provisions as referring to potential rather than to actual unreliability, and as requiring consideration of all the circumstances.[20]

In an apparent effort to encourage such an interpretation s 76 makes explicit reference to the possibility of the confession's being true despite its potential unreliability, and this view is further strengthened by the absence from the section as enacted of any authorisation to ask about the truth or falsity of a confession. There can be little doubt that the reason for such concern is some unease about the danger of the preliminary test for admissibility before the judge becoming one of whether or not a given confession is reliable,[1] and, given such a test, that the jury may then infer that any confession proved before them has already been considered by the judge to be reliable. It is certainly possible, given the unsophistication of some criminal proceedings, that the subtle difference between the tests to be imposed by judge and jury will be overlooked, and in such cases the problem of keeping each to its separate role will be as obscure and unsatisfactory as it was in the aftermath of the decision in *R v Bass*.[2]

It should also be noted that in Victoria and New Zealand the courts regard an unreliability test as in no way antithetical to the continued existence of a wide discretion to exclude on the ground of unfairness.[3] The Police and Criminal Evidence Act 1984, s 82(3) explicitly retains the existing discretion in England, but it was less generously interpreted than in Australia.[4] Two interlocking factors seem to have influenced subsequent development in England, first the much more ready application of the new statutory discretion to exclude evidence on the ground of 'unfairness', which has been explicitly extended to apply to confessions,[5] and second the extremely detailed guidance for the behaviour of the police provided by the Codes of Conduct given statutory force by Pt VI of the Police and Criminal Evidence Act 1984. The general tendency has been to take the Code as a rough guide to the likelihood of reliability, so that failure to comply is some

---

19 Cmnd 8092, para 4.72, although uttered in the context of oppression it is just as applicable here.
20 *Cornelius v R* (1936) 55 CLR 235; *R v Coats* [1932] NZLR 401, suggesting that the change in terminology in New Zealand in 1905 to 'in fact likely' from 'really calculated' was specifically designed to prevent an interpretation forcing admissibility upon the court whenever it believed the confession true.
 1 In *R v Tyrer* (1990) 90 Cr App Rep 446 the Court of Appeal considered the trial judge to have come close to confusing these matters by taking into account other evidence given at the trial proper which indicated that the confession was probably true.
 2 [1953] 1 QB 680, [1953] 1 All ER 1064.
 3 *R v Gardner* (1932) 51 NZLR 1648; *R v Lee* (1950) 82 CLR 133; *Cleland v R* (1983) 43 ALR 619; *R v Larson and Lee* [1984] VR 559. In those jurisdictions however reliability operates positively to admit involuntary confessions which would otherwise be excluded, and in such cases the discretion seems not to have been applied, indeed in the ACT where there is a similar provision legislation has been enacted to provide such a power, see ACT Evidence Ordinance 1971, s 68(3); and similar legislation has been recommended for New Zealand.
 4 See above p 191.
 5 *R v Mason* [1987] 3 All ER 481 at 484, [1988] 1 WLR 139 at 144.

indication of potential unreliability,[6] and compliance some indication of potential reliability.

Although in *R v Fulling*[7] it was stated that impropriety by the police is not a necessary condition to the establishment of potential unreliability under s 76(2)(b), the operation of this head is conditioned upon 'anything said or done'[8] which is likely in the circumstances to induce unreliability. It should be noted that the test is objective in the sense that it is immaterial that the police are unaware of the factors inducing the potential unreliability,[9] or that they acted in perfect good faith.[10] If the mental condition of the suspect is such that any statement he makes is likely to be unreliable, it might be thought that even the most innocuous remark might satisfy this requirement. Such a view was rejected by the Court of Appeal in *R v Goldenberg*,[11] in respect of the interviewing of a drug addict who might have been desperate for release in order to satisfy his addiction, where it was emphasised that the stimulus must be external[12] to the suspect,[13] and likely to have an effect upon him.[14] On the other hand it seems that in the case of such a suspect very little pressure may take the case over the line, and into the area of potential unreliability.[15] As noted above breaches of the Codes of Practice may influence a court in deciding that oppression has not been disproved. It will, if anything, be easier to contend that unreliability under this head has been disproved.[16]

(iii) Causation

Under the previous law one way of avoiding the artificial construction of particular forms of words as automatically amounting to an inducement was to require a convincing demonstration that they had in fact caused the accused to confess. Thus in *Ping Lin* Lord Hailsham remarked that:[17]

> It is the chain of causation which has to be excluded by the prosecution and not the hypostatisation of any part of it.

Given the difficulties to which the notion of causation has led in other areas

6 But by no means conclusive, see *R v Delaney* (1989) 88 Cr App Rep 338, or exclusive see *DPP v Blake* (1989) 89 Cr App Rep 179.
7 [1987] QB 426 at 432, [1987] 2 All ER 65 at 70.
8 It is immaterial that the crux of the stimulus is constituted by an omission, such as the provision of a period of rest, *R v Trussler* [1988] Crim LR 446.
9 *R v Everett* [1988] Crim LR 826.
10 *DPP v Blake* (1989) 89 Cr App Rep 179.
11 (1989) 88 Cr App Rep 285.
12 It need not however emanate from the police, but can come from a third party, *R v Harvey* [1988] Crim LR 241.
13 This was thought to stem from the requirement of a causal link between stimulus and reaction, but it is not clear why self-stimulus cannot be causally linked to reaction, for example, by taking hallucinogenic drugs.
14 See also *R v Maguire* (1989) 90 Cr App Rep 115 where statements made by a child questioned innocuously by a police officer, but in the absence of a responsible adult, were not rejected.
15 See *R v Delaney* (1989) 88 Cr App Rep 338, where while interviewing an educationally subnormal and emotional youth accused of a horrific assault on a small child the police officers underplayed the seriousness of the matter, and emphasised the suspect's need for psychiatric help.
16 See eg *R v Doolan* [1988] Crim LR 747.
17 [1976] AC 574 at 602, [1975] 3 All ER 175 at 184.

of the law,[18] it might have been feared that such concentration might prejudice the simplicity of the test for admissibility aimed at in *Ping Lin*, but such fears were allayed by the decision of the Court of Appeal in *R v Rennie*.[19] In that case the accused claimed that he had confessed because he was under stress, had been threatened by the police and wanted to prevent the rest of his family being charged with complicity in the frauds of which he was suspected. His evidence to this effect had received some support from one of the police witnesses who had testified that he believed that the accused had confessed in order to prevent the involvement of his family. Nevertheless the Court of Appeal while recognising that in most cases there are mixed motives for confessing, and that some of them may be inspired by something said or done by the interrogator, felt that it would be wrong to apply 'any refined analysis of the concept of causation'. The judge should instead apply the spirit of the test in much the same way as it would be applied by a jury. In a mixed motive case this would appear to require a determination of the dominant motive. Exactly the same approach is appropriate to the conditions imposed by s 76(2).[20] It should perhaps be noticed that there is a slight difference in the drafting of the two conditions in that the first relating to oppression is introduced by the word 'by', whereas the second which relates to unreliability is introduced by the phrase 'in consequence of'. If anything should turn on that difference, it would presumably be to require less in the way of the demonstration of a causal link in the case of oppression, which may perhaps more readily be inferred, and where the law will be more anxious to mark its disapproval.

It is important to note that in order to qualify for exclusion a causal link must always be established between something said or done by the interlocutor and the person making the confession.[1] It may often be necessary to determine whether an admission is made as a result of whatever has been said or done, or rather in recognition of the implausibility of previous statements, perhaps revealed by what has been said or done.[2] A spontaneous confession seems admissible, however unreliable it may be in the light of the accused's mental or emotional state. It may, however, in such circumstances, be excluded by the judge at his discretion,[3] and even if it be admitted, the weight to be attached to the confession of a person in such a state would obviously be small.

It had become well-established in the old law that a confession which, considered in isolation, appeared to satisfy the conditions for being voluntary, might nevertheless be excluded if preceded by an earlier involuntary confession. It would be so excluded if either the factors tainting the earlier confession continued to apply, or if the fact of having made such a confession could itself be regarded as precipitating its successor.[4] There is nothing in the new Act to displace so sensible an approach.[5]

18 See Hart and Honoré *Causation in the Law* (2nd edn 1985).
19 [1982] 1 All ER 385, [1982] 1 WLR 64.
20 And has been so applied, see *R v Phillips* (1987) 86 Cr App Rep 18.
 1 *R v Goldenberg* (1989) 88 Cr App Rep 285 at 290.
 2 As in *R v Tyrer* (1990) 90 Cr App Rep 446.
 3 See p 191 above.
 4 *R v Smith* [1959] 2 QB 35, [1959] 2 All ER 193. See also *Hobbins v R* (1982) 135 DLR (3d) 244, and *HM Advocate v Docherty* 1981 JC 6.
 5 See *R v Waters* [1989] Crim LR 62.

(iv) Burden of proof

At common law it was for the prosecution to prove beyond reasonable doubt that a confession was voluntary.[6] Section 76(2) explicitly retains both incidence and standard. It also provides that the matter is to be tested whenever 'it is represented to the court' that one of the conditions has been satisfied. It has been held that merely to cross-examine so as to suggest the satisfaction of the invalidating conditions of s 76 is not sufficient.[7] This might have appeared to suggest that the court could no longer[8] take the point of its own motion, but any such argument has been pre-empted by explicit provision allowing such a course.[9] In most cases, of course, the defence will itself raise the point, usually with the prosecution informally and before the trial, so that a disputed confession will not be opened before its admissibility has been tested. Breach of the provisions of the Codes of Practice requiring the documentation of action by the police may operate to prevent the prosecution from being able to negate the exclusionary conditions of s 76.[10]

3. EFFECT

The principal intended effect of the legislation is to exclude confessions as evidence of the truth of their contents, but this effect is qualified by further provisions also set out in s 76 as follows:

(4) The fact that a confession is wholly or partly excluded in pursuance of this section shall not affect the admissibility in evidence—
(a) of any facts discovered as result of the confession; or
(b) where the confession is relevant as showing that the accused speaks, writes or expresses himself in a particular way, of so much of the confession as is necessary to show that he does so.
(5) Evidence that a fact to which this subsection applies was discovered as a result of a statement made by an accused person shall not be admissible unless evidence of how it was discovered is given by him or on his behalf.

These sections raised three matters which require to be mentioned, the admissibility of subsequently discovered facts, the circumstantial use which can be made of confessions, and the extent to which any part of an excluded confession may be given when it is confirmed by finding real evidence which it mentions. All three of these matters have already been considered.[11]

---

6 See *DPP v Ping Lin* [1976] AC 574 at 597 at 599, [1975] 3 All ER 175 at 178 and 180. The standard of proof had however been considered doubtful by the Criminal Law Revision Committee (Cmnd 4991, Annex 2 p 213), and see p 605 above.
7 *R v Liverpool Juvenile Court, ex p R* [1988] QB 1, [1987] 2 All ER 668.
8 See the guidance provided in *Ajodha v The State* [1982] AC 204 at 222, [1981] 2 All ER 193 at 202.
9 S 76(3), in accordance with the Criminal Law Revision Committee's recommendation and draft bill, Cmnd 4991, para 54, cl 2(3).
10 *R v Delaney* (1989) 88 Cr App Rep 338 at 342.
11 See ch XI, section 3, above.

E. QUESTIONING SUSPECTS[12]

This topic has come under intense scrutiny since the report of the Criminal Law Revision Committee, notably by the Royal Commission on Criminal Procedure, and has been put on a new footing by the Police and Criminal Evidence Act 1984 and the Codes of Practice issued thereunder.[13] Their application and interpretation have generated a considerable amount of modern case law.[14]

During the nineteenth century the police gradually assumed the major responsibility for the detection, apprehension, and questioning of those suspected of the commission of crimes. They were also expected to collect evidence for, and to initiate, most prosecutions in England and Wales. Statutory authorisation for many of these functions was often absent, and its absence sometimes created problems, especially in relation to questioning, given the strict limitations on compulsory questioning by judicial tribunals,[15] and given the combination of stringency and uncertainty surrounding the exclusion of incriminating statements made to persons in authority. After being highlighted by a number of inconsistent decisions, and failing any direct legislative intervention, the matter was regulated by the judges who issued a set of rules to guide the police in 1912. These rules were supplemented from time to time by Home Office circulars, and in 1964 replaced by a further set of Judges' Rules.[16] The general scheme was that admissibility continued to be governed by the general law relating to confessions, but it was still possible for the trial judge to exclude evidence obtained as a result of a breach of the Judges' Rules at his discretion.[17] The Royal Commission on Criminal Procedure was sceptical of many aspects of this procedure. In its view it left the police without adequate guidance, both in the definition of the circumstances triggering different remedies,[18] and in the uncertainty of application ex post facto in the different atmosphere of the courtroom.[19] Its principal recommendation therefore was the adoption of a very restricted test for inadmissibility, the publication of a much more comprehensive code of practice to govern questioning, determined by the need to ensure conditions conducive to reliability, and a greater readiness to direct the jury that breach of the Code might endanger reliability. The Police and Criminal Evidence Act 1984, as noted above, has in s 76 adopted a less stringent test for inadmissibility, but has in s 66 prescribed the publication of Codes of Police Practice in relation to search and seizure, and to detention, treatment, questioning and identification. The Royal Commission recommended that breach of any such code should not in itself automatically lead to exclusion of evidence obtained thereby, unless it involved violence, threats of violence,

---

12 For much valuable background to the current position see Gooderson 'The Interrogation of Suspects' (1970) 48 Can BR 270.
13 At the time of writing the formulation of these Codes was under review by the Home Office.
14 Described in *R v Keenan* [1989] 3 All ER 598 at 601 as a 'flood'.
15 See Indictable Offences Act 1848 and Criminal Evidence Act 1898.
16 Issued as a *Practice Note* by the Court of Criminal Appeal [1964] 1 All ER 237, [1964] 1 WLR 152, and supplemented by Administrative Directions in Home Office Circular No 31/1964.
17 See above p 191.
18 Cmnd 8092, para 4.70.
19 Ibid, paras 4.72 and 4.131.

torture or inhuman or degrading treatment.[20] In any other case it recommended neither automatic, nor even discretionary, exclusion, but simply made breach a factor relevant to weight. Two principal areas of dispute concern the interpretation and application of the Codes of Practice, and the significance to be attached to the accused's silence in the face of police questioning.

1. CODES OF PRACTICE

The Codes of Practice cover ground similar to that previously governed by what the Royal Commission described as 'jigsaw pieces of two centuries of police and legal history'. They are designed to regulate such matters as the rights of a suspect to communication with third parties, rights to legal advice and to medical treatment; and to provide guidance to the police on such things as the conduct of searches, the administration of a caution, the provision of interpreters, and in all cases the compilation of adequate documentation of what occurs. Particular attention is paid to the treatment of juveniles, the mentally ill and the mentally handicapped. Indeed in the case of the last of those categories a special statutory warning is required of the need for caution before convicting such an accused upon the basis of his confession, if made otherwise than in the presence of an independent person.[1] As the Codes of Practice prohibit the taking of a statement from such a person in the absence of an independent person, unless the stringent conditions for urgent interviews are satisfied,[2] s 77 is either taking a sledgehammer to crack a nut, or else contemplates the tendering of statements obtained in breach of the Codes.[3] If the latter, it must also contemplate judicial abstinence from the exercise of any exclusionary discretion. It will be recalled that the Royal Commission was unhappy about reliance upon such an exclusionary discretion in relation to breach of the Code in general, and the early drafts of the Bill contained no explicit reference to any such discretion, though *R v Sang* provided common law authority for its existence in relation to 'admissions and confessions and generally with regard to evidence obtained from the accused after the commission of the offence'.[4] At a late stage in its passage new and explicit provision was made in the Police and Criminal Evidence Act 1984 for such a discretion:[5]

> (1) In any proceedings the court may refuse to allow evidence on which the prosecution proposes to rely to be given if it appears to the court that, having regard to all the circumstances in which the evidence was obtained, the admission of the evidence would have such an adverse effect upon the fairness of the proceedings that the court ought not to admit it.
>
> (2) Nothing in this section shall prejudice any rule of law requiring a court to exclude evidence.

20 Ibid, para 4.132.
1 Police and Criminal Evidence Act 1984, s 77.
2 Code of Practice for the Detention, Treatment and Questioning of Persons by Police Officers, para 13 and Annex C.
3 In *R v Lamont* [1989] 2 All ER 187 the Court of Appeal insisted upon such a warning being given in an appropriate case, and because it had not, was able to abstain from deciding whether the evidence should have been excluded altogether. See also *R v Moss* (1990) Times, 17 March.
4 [1980] AC 402 at 437, [1979] 2 All ER 1222 at 1231.
5 S 78.

It should be noted that sub-s (2) is designed to preserve the exclusionary rule set out in s 76. This is necessary because this section, unlike the clause it replaced, is of general application, and applies across the whole range of the law of evidence in criminal proceedings.[6] Nor does this new discretion derogate from the common law discretion discussed in *Sang*, since s 82(3) provides that:

> Nothing in this Part of this Act shall prejudice any power of a court to exclude evidence (whether by preventing questions from being put or otherwise) at its discretion.

Section 78 was expressed in such vague terms that it was hard to anticipate in advance how it would be applied.[7] There was indeed some warrant for regarding s 76 as constituting an exclusive new codification of the rules relating to confessions, but as noted above any such view was rejected at an early stage in *R v Mason*.[8] Although, as also noted, the Codes of Practice have been accepted as providing some indication of the satisfaction of the conditions of admissibility under s 76, their implementation has mainly been by way of triggering the exercise of the discretion to exclude conferred by s 78. It seems by its specific reference to the matter to contemplate that the fairness of proceedings may be affected by the way in which evidence was obtained. Remarkably little attention seems to have been paid to any distinction which might be drawn between the fairness of the treatment of the accused and the effect of such treatment upon the fairness of the proceedings.[9] The effect of such failure is to blur any substantial distinction between the conditions for inadmissibility by rule under s 76 and by discretion under s 78. In many, if not most, cases discretionary exclusion is held in reserve in case a claim under s 76 should fail.[10] The principal differences between the two sections are that exclusion under s 76 is by rule, and that under s 78 by discretion. In the case of s 76 the burden of disproof of the relevant conditions is always on the prosecution, whereas under s 78 the incidence of burden of persuading the court to exercise its discretion is equivocal.[11] Procedurally s 78 presents serious difficulties to the judge who has to exercise his discretion before all the evidence and relevant information is before him, and in particular in ignorance of the line of defence to the main charge, and how the accused will react, so far as himself testifying is concerned, whichever way the discretion is exercised.[12] This presents further problems on appeal when the court has to put itself in the position of the trial judge, and ignore any such matters even though they have by then been revealed.[13]

---

6 'Proceedings' are defined as criminal proceedings by s 82(1).
7 See remarks to this effect in *R v Keenan* [1989] 3 All ER 598 at 603.
8 [1987] 3 All ER 481 at 484, [1988] 1 WLR 139 at 144.
9 See Birch 'The Pace Hots Up: Confessions and Confusions Under the 1984 Act' [1989] Crim LR 95.
10 See, for example, *R v Delaney* (1989) 88 Cr App Rep 338 at 340.
11 In *R v Keenan* [1989] 3 All ER 598 at 605 it appears to be suggested that it varies according to the circumstances, though in *Vel v Owen* [1987] Crim LR 496 it was said not to be borne by the prosecution. In Australia it is borne by the accused, see *MacPherson v R* (1981) 147 CLR 512 at 519, 520; *Cleland v R* (1982) 151 CLR 1 at 19, 20 where Deane J applied the same principle to the *Bunning v Cross* discretion.
12 These difficulties are explained at some length in *R v Keenan* [1989] 3 All ER 598, [1989] 3 WLR 1193.
13 *R v Parris* (1988) 89 Cr App Rep 68.

The relationship between breaches of the Codes and the operation of s 78 have come before the Court of Appeal in two main contexts; first, where the trial judge has found no breach of the Codes, and has not otherwise excluded the evidence under his discretion, and second, those where the trial judge has found breach of the Codes, but has excercised his discretion against excluding the evidence. The Court of Appeal is in principle more likely to intervene in the former situation in which the judge may not have addressed his mind to the exercise of the discretion at all,[14] or only upon a hypothetical basis.[15]

Although it has authoritatively, and it is submitted logically, been stated in connection with s 78 that breach of the Codes of Practice does not automatically trigger the application of the exclusionary discretion,[16] there are sometimes signs of such a tendency. In one case real evidence was excluded under the discretion because it could not be proved that the accused had been told why he was being searched.[17] It is very hard to see how this could have caused unfairness to the subsequent proceedings. The basic problem is that the Codes of Practice cover a multitude of topics, occurring at different stages in the investigation and prosecution of crime, and it is far from obvious that all can be brought within the precise terms of section 78. Conversely there may well be other matters which are not dealt with under the Codes which should trigger such an exclusionary discretion.[18]

Two linked, and particularly contentious matters, have concerned the implementation by the Codes of the right conferred by s 58 of the Police and Criminal Evidence Act 1984 for a person arrested and in police custody to consult a solicitor, and the duty upon the police to comply with the detailed requirements of Code C in the case of 'interviews'. In *R v Walsh*[19] the Court of Appeal seems to have taken the view that s 58 and the Codes provided a prima facie standard of fairness, though it also pointed out that s 78 seems by the use of the phrase '*such* an adverse effect' to contemplate *some* situations of venial unfairness insufficient to justify the exclusion of evidence thereby obtained because the effect is not adverse enough. Any breach should be 'significant and substantial', and while bad faith might exalt into that category behaviour which might otherwise fall short, the converse did not follow. If there were significant and substantial unfairness, then it would be sufficient to justify discretionary exclusion whether or not there were bad faith. The right of access to a solicitor is so fundamental a part of the scheme of the Police and Criminal Evidence Act 1984 that a court is highly likely to exercise its discretion to exclude a confession obtained after wrongful refusal of such access, and to construe the grounds[20] for proper refusal of such access

---

14 In *R v Parris* (1988) 89 Cr App Rep 68 the trial judge appears to have been under the impression that he was obliged to consider s 78 *only* if satisfied that a breach of the Code had been shown.

15 See *R v Samuel* [1988] QB 615, [1988] 2 All ER 135.

16 *R v Parris* (1988) 89 Cr App Rep 68 at 72.

17 *R v Fennelley* [1989] Crim LR 142, see also *R v Woodall* [1989] Crim LR 288.

18 As in *R v Woodall* [1989] Crim LR 288 where there appears neither to have been a breach of the Code nor any unfairness in obtaining the admission, but its use was nevertheless regarded as making subsequent proceedings unfair since it had been volunteered 'off the record', and no subsequent reference had been made to it until the first day of the trial.

19 [1989] Crim LR 822.

20 As set out in Police and Criminal Evidence Act 1984, s 58(8), Code C para 6.3 and Annex B.

narrowly.[1] In *R v Alladice*[2] however the court was able to disregard a breach of these provisions on the basis that the suspect asserted, at the trial within a trial on the voir dire, not that in the absence of legal advice he had spoken instead of remaining silent, but that he had not confessed at all. It will be rare for that to be regarded as sufficient since the accused might still be prejudiced in the subsequent proceedings because he is then unable to corroborate his account of what has taken place.[3]

If these provisions conferring a right to legal advice are to be effective it becomes increasingly important to regulate any other contact between the police and the suspect. To this end the Codes set out elaborate rules to govern 'interviews' between police and suspects, both at a police station and outside. It seems that any questioning of a suspect designed to obtain admissions of guilt will constitute an 'interview', however informal and unpremeditated the situation.[4] On the other hand questioning someone encountered at the scene of a crime with a view to dispelling suspicion does not necessarily amount to an 'interview'.[5] It may be anticipated that so fine a distinction in a sensitive area will require further clarification by the Court of Appeal. This scheme of regulation is intended to inhibit both manufacture by the police of 'admissions', and false allegations by suspects of such police conduct. The requirements of documentation are a vital part of the scheme.[6] It is just as true in relation to s 78 as it was in relation to s 76 that failure to complete such documentation deprives the court of the basis for exercising its discretion and, despite any difference in burden of proof, failure to provide it is likely to be fatal, especially when adopted as deliberate policy.[7]

The Code of Practice is also concerned to prevent statements being taken from juveniles, the mentally ill, the mentally handicapped, those incapacitated by drink or drugs, non-English speakers or the deaf, except upon the satisfaction of appropriate conditions, just because they may be unreliable.[8] Accordingly breach of the Code in relation to such matters has led to discretionary exclusion under s 78.[9] The discretion conferred by s 78 also provides a means whereby statements spontaneously blurted out by those so disadvantaged may be excluded.[10]

---

1 *R v Samuel* [1988] QB 615, [1988] 2 All ER 135. But see *R v Dunford* [1990] NLJ Rep 517.
2 (1988) 87 Cr App Rep 380.
3 *R v Parris* (1988) 89 Cr App Rep 68.
4 *R v Absolam* (1989) 88 Cr App Rep 332; *R v Keenan* [1989] 3 All ER 598, [1989] 3 WLR 1193.
5 *R v Maguire* (1989) 90 Cr App Rep 115.
6 They are usually vital whether interviews take place within or outside police stations, though opinions have differed as to whether the rules relating to the review of any alleged admissions apply in the same way to both, compare *R v Kingsley Brown* [1989] Crim LR 500 with *R v Parchment* [1989] Crim LR 290 and *R v Brezeanu* [1989] Crim LR 650.
7 *R v Canale* [1990] Crim LR 329 . But see *R v Matthews* [1990] Crim LR 190 where a different exercise of the discretion was not overturned, perhaps because of the strength of the rest of the evidence.
8 See Cmnd 8092, para 4.133.
9 *R v Fogah* [1989] Crim LR 141 (juvenile, and no appropriate adult), *Timothy v DPP* [1989] Crim LR 893 (drunkenness, though a note of a request for a specimen of breath was not excluded); but see *R v Clarke* [1989] Crim LR 892 (deaf, but discretion not exercised because the condition was not known to the police).
10 Compare *R v S and J* (1983) 32 SASR 174.

2. SILENCE

There has been much discussion of the question as to whether a suspect should retain a right to remain silent in the face of police questioning,[11] without fear of adverse inference or comment at any subsequent trial. In its Eleventh Report the Criminal Law Revision Committee recommended that such adverse inferences could be drawn, and that the form of caution should be amended to reflect the new position.[12] This matter was re-examined in detail by the Royal Commission. It found that very few suspects did remain silent in the face of police questioning,[13] and felt that the proposals of the Criminal Law Revision Committee were in principle incompatible with English criminal procedure. They therefore recommended retention of the current situation including the conventional caution.[14] That situation has been arrived at only gradually, and is far from clear or stable. Already in Northern Ireland provisions[15] have been introduced changing the caution and permitting reference to failure to mention facts during interrogation which are later relied upon at the trial. Similar recommendations have been made by a Home Office Working Party for application in the United Kingdom.[16]

From time to time appellate courts have, with varying results, heard appeals upon the ground that the trial judge went too far when commenting in his summing up on the accused's silence when charged.[17] The upshot of most of these decisions seems to be that, although the accused's silence may be treated as something which has a bearing on the weight of his evidence, it is not something which can support an inference that the story told by him in court is untrue, still less can it amount to corroboration of the evidence given against him:[18]

> It is one thing to make an observation with regard to the force of an alibi, and to say that it is unfortunate that the defence was not set up at an earlier date so as to afford the opportunity of its being tested; it is another thing to employ that non-disclosure as evidence against the accused person and as corroborating the evidence of an accomplice.

Since those words were spoken s 11 of the Criminal Justice Act 1967 has made special provision with regard to notice of alibis in the case of trials on

---

11 *Rice v Connolly* [1966] 2 QB 414, [1966] 2 All ER 649.
12 Cmnd 4991, paras 28–52, draft bill, cl 1.
13 Cmnd 8092, paras 4.43–4.46 summarising the results of no fewer than three separate studies made under the auspices of the Royal Commission.
14 They recommended a minor change in the form of the caution to make it clear that statements made before the caution was issued might nevertheless be reported to the court. This recommendation has not been adopted, see Code of Practice para 11.5.
15 Criminal Evidence (Northern Ireland) Order 1988. For comment see Jackson 'Recent Developments in Criminal Evidence' (1989) 40 NILQ 105.
16 *Report on Right to Silence* Home Office 13 July 1989, trenchantly criticised by Zuckerman 'Trial by Unfair Means—The Report of the Working Party on the Right of Silence' [1989] Crim LR 855.
17 The principal authorities include *R v Tate* [1908] 2 KB 680; *R v Feigenbaum* [1919] 1 KB 431; *R v Littleboy* [1934] 2 KB 408; *R v Hoare* [1966] 2 All ER 846, [1966] 1 WLR 762; *R v Sullivan* (1966) 51 Cr App Rep 102; *Hall v R* [1971] 1 All ER 322; *R v Gilbert* (1977) 66 Cr App Rep 237; *R v Raviraj* (1987) 85 Cr App Rep 93.
18 Lord Hewart CJ in *R v Littleboy*, above, at 413.

indictment,[19] and it has been held that the judge should not comment on the accused's failure to mention an alibi when arrested.[20]

Although said to be very fine,[1] the distinction made in the quotation above has been applied to other defences[2] but the dominant view persists that the judge should generally make no comment on the accused's pre-trial silence when charged or questioned by someone in authority.[3] Severe misgivings have been expressed about such apparent abnegation of the normal role of the judge in directing the jury, especially in view of the strengthened right to consult a lawyer conferred by the Police and Criminal Evidence Act 1984, and the Lord Chief Justice has been stung to remark:[4]

> Despite the fact that the explanation or defence could, if true, have been disclosed at the outset and despite the advantage which the defendant has gained by these tactics, no comment may be made to the jury to that effect. The jury may in some cases put two and two together, but it seems to us that the effect of section 58 [of the Police and Criminal Evidence Act 1984] is such that the balance of fairness between prosecution and defence cannot be maintained unless proper comment is permitted on the defendant's silence in such circumstances. It is high time that such comment should be permitted together with the necessary alteration to the words of the caution.

It should however be noted that in certain situations the stringency of the prohibition has been mitigated. For example if the accused and the person questioning him can be said to be on equal terms, a summing-up on the lines of Lord Atkinson's speech in *R v Christie*[5] may be appropriate.[6] It is arguable that the presence of a solicitor does equalise the terms, and this may provide a partial explanation of the decision in *R v Smith*[7] where the Court of Appeal allowed comment on the accused's refusal during such an interview to permit a sample of his hair to be taken for comparison with hair found on an incriminating object. It may also be incumbent upon the court to make some comment in connection with a different rule, such as the presumption of knowledge arising from possession of recently stolen property.[8] Nor is it improper for the judge to emphasise both the nature of possible adverse inferences and the prohibition upon drawing them.[9] It is to be hoped that the current review will eliminate the need for such unsatisfactory distinctions and disingenuous directions.

---

19 See p 26 above.
20 *R v Lewis* (1973) 57 Cr App Rep 860.
1 Lord Salmon in *R v Sullivan*, above, at 105; apparently on the basis that it was too favourable to the accused.
2 See *R v Ryan* (1964) 50 Cr App Rep 144 at 148.
3 *R v Gilbert*, above, and further p 35 above; see also *R v Coombs* [1983] NZLR 748.
4 *R v Alladice* (1988) 87 Cr App Rep 380 at 385. See also *R v McNamara* (1988) 87 Cr App Rep 246 at 253.
5 [1914] AC 545.
6 *R v Chandler* [1976] 3 All ER 105, [1976] 1 WLR 585.
7 (1985) 81 Cr App Rep 286.
8 *R v Aves* (1950) 34 Cr App Rep 159; *R v Raviraj*, above.
9 *R v McNamara*, above.

SECTION 2. STATUTORY PROVISIONS APPLICABLE IN CRIMINAL PROCEEDINGS

In *Myers v DPP*[10] Lord Reid recommended wholesale statutory revision of the law of hearsay. Such wholesale reform has yet to take place in relation to the admissibility of hearsay in criminal cases. At the time *Myers* was decided the whole question was under review by the Criminal Law Revision Committee, and it made sweeping recommendations for change in the Eleventh Report,[11] largely adopting the pattern established for civil proceedings by the Civil Evidence Act 1968.[12] Those recommendations were not accepted, and instead a series of piecemeal measures has been adopted, especially in the field of business records, relating both to general documentary evidence and to the more specialised field of computer output. It is convenient to deal with these matters separately, before dealing with s 9 of the Criminal Justice Act 1967, which, however important it may be in practice, requires less attention here.

A. DOCUMENTARY EVIDENCE[13]

The first response to the decision in *Myers* was to legislate on a stop-gap basis in the Criminal Evidence Act 1965 so as to admit business records of a broadly defined character upon the satisfaction of certain conditions, principally that the record be documentary in character, that the supplier of the information contained in it have, or be reasonably expected to have, personal knowledge of the truth of that information, and that there be some acceptable reason for not calling such supplier.[14] This legislation was repealed and replaced by s 68[15] of the Police and Criminal Evidence Act 1984. Even before s 68 had been brought into force it was subjected to further examination by the Roskill Committee into the conduct of trials for fraud, a vital aspect of which was considered to be the admissibility of documentary evidence.[16] The Committee accordingly recommended further relaxation of the hearsay rule though subject to retaining a measure of judicial control of the admissibility of documents without prejudicing preparation for the trial. Its solution was to permit documents to be admitted as evidence of the truth of their contents at the discretion of the judge, such inclusionary discretion to be exercised at a special hearing in advance of the trial.[17] Although an initial bill went some way towards the adoption of these proposals the final version subsequently enacted as Pt II of the Criminal Justice Act 1988 is more limited. It deals separately with first-hand

---

10 [1965] AC 1001 at 1022, [1964] 2 All ER 881 at 886. See further, above p 516.
11 Cmnd 4991 (1972) paras 224–265, and draft bill, cls 30–41.
12 Though with some differences mainly reflecting the greater fear of manufactured evidence in criminal proceedings.
13 See Birch 'The Criminal Justice Act 1988 (2) Documentary Evidence' [1989] Crim LR 15.
14 Including his being unidentifiable, or there being no prospect of his having any recollection of the information required.
15 Supplemented by s 69 dealing with computer output, further explained in part B below, and by Sch 3 expanding and expounding a number of points in detail.
16 Para 5.32.
17 Para 5.36, but subject to special rules relating to the admissibility of proofs of evidence so as not to prejudice the basic orality of a criminal trial, para 5.37.

documentary hearsay, with business documents and with documents prepared for the purposes of criminal proceedings or investigations, as well as incorporating some general provisions. Each of these topics requires separate consideration.

1. FIRST-HAND HEARSAY

This is governed by s 23 of the Criminal Justice Act 1988 which provides that:

(1) Subject—
    (a) to subsection (4) below;
    (b) to paragraph 1A of Schedule 2 to the Criminal Appeal Act 1968 (evidence given orally at original trial to be given orally at retrial); and
    (c) to section 69 of the Police and Criminal Evidence Act 1984 (evidence from computer records), a statement made by a person in a document shall be admissible in criminal proceedings as evidence of any fact of which direct oral evidence by him would be admissible if—
        (i) the requirements of one of the paragraphs of subsection (2) below are satisfied; or
        (ii) the requirements of subsection (3) below are satisfied.

(2) The requirements mentioned in subsection 1(i) above are—
    (a) that the person who made the statement is dead or by reason of his bodily or mental condition unfit to attend as a witness;
    (b) that—
        (i) the person who made the statement is outside the United Kingdom; and
        (ii) it is not reasonably practicable to secure his attendance; or
    (c) that all reasonable steps have been taken to find the person who made the statement, but that he cannot be found.

(3) The requirements mentioned in subsection 1(ii) above are—
    (a) that the statement was made to a police officer or some other person charged with the duty of investigating offences or charging offenders; and
    (b) that the person who made it does not give oral evidence through fear or because he is kept out of the way.

(4) Subsection (1) above does not render admissible a confession made by an accused person that would not be admissible under section 76 of the Police and Criminal Evidence Act 1984.

In some respects these conditions carry over improvements upon the drafting of the comparable provisions applicable in civil proceedings, for example in referring to the maker as being 'outside the United Kingdom'[18] and in making the relevant conditions in sub-s 2(b) cumulative.[19] It is to be expected that like the comparable provision in the Police and Criminal Evidence Act 1984 this condition will be construed against the background of the whole history of the litigation and not judged simply on the basis of the situation at the moment when the issue arises.[20] It should be noted that the existence of the factual substratum of such conditions must be proved by evidence, and

18 Rather than 'beyond the seas', cp *Rover International Ltd v Cannon Film Sales Ltd (No 2)* [1987] 3 All ER 986, [1987] 1 WLR 1597.
19 Cp *Piermay Shipping Co SA v Chester* [1978] 1 All ER 1233, [1978] 1 WLR 411.
20 *R v Bray* [1988] Crim LR 829.

cannot be left to be presumed, even if it means that a voir dire has to be held.[1]

This provision corresponds to s 2 of the Civil Evidence Act 1968, and as such does go beyond the previous provision in criminal proceedings which was limited to business records or those made pursuant to a duty. The shoulder note refers to 'First-hand' hearsay, and as in the 1968 Act this restriction is principally accomplished by insistence that direct oral evidence by the maker of the relevant statement should have been admissible. Since witnesses cannot generally adduce hearsay such terminology normally restricts the operation of this provision to first-hand hearsay. This is however subject to a qualification in that where an exception to the hearsay rule operates then a witness can testify to hearsay, and if such evidence is recorded in a document it is submitted that it will be admissible in criminal proceedings.[2]

The Act is confined to statements made in documents,[3] tendered as evidence of fact,[4] and effectively to cases where the maker is unavailable to give oral evidence, though in relation to this provision unavailability is more strictly confined than in relation to the business documents admitted under s 24. For this reason sub-s 4 is likely to have a very limited effect.[5]

Subsection 3 appears to have been designed to overcome the defects in the existing law[6] exposed by *R v O'Loughlin and McLaughlin*,[7] whereby the pressure was required to have been exerted by or on behalf of the accused. The section makes no explicit requirement that the fear need relate to the maker himself. It should be noted that any statement admitted under this provision will also require the leave of the court under s 26, and that it may still be excluded at the discretion of the court[8] either pursuant to the new discretion conferred by s 25, or that conferred by s 78 of the Police and Criminal Evidence Act 1984, or any exclusionary discretion operating at common law, such as where its prejudicial effect exceeds the probative force of the evidence.

2. BUSINESS DOCUMENTS

The Act repeals s 68 of the Police and Criminal Evidence Act 1984, and in its place provides in s 24 as follows:

1 *R v Nicholls* (1976) 63 Cr App Rep 187; *Bermudez v Chief Constable of Avon and Somerset* [1988] Crim LR 452.
2 As it is in civil proceedings, see *The Ymnos* [1981] 1 Lloyd's Rep 550.
3 Unlike s 2 of the Civil Evidence Act 1968, though 'document' is given an extended meaning by Sch 2, para 5 incorporating the definition contained in s 10 of the Civil Evidence Act 1968, see, above, p 558.
4 Evidence of opinion has been admitted under some earlier legislation despite similar apparent restriction, see *Dass v Masih* [1968] 2 All ER 226 under the Evidence Act 1938 and *Wallhead v Ruston & Hornsby Ltd* (1973) 14 KIR 285 under the Civil Evidence Act 1968. Explicit provision is made in Part III of the Criminal Justice Act 1988 for the admission of expert reports in derogation of the hearsay rule, see s 30.
5 The conditions under which confessions are admitted are generally incompatible with these conditions, except perhaps in a rare case involving more than one accused.
6 In Criminal Justice Act 1925, s 13(3).
7 [1988] 3 All ER 431, 85 Cr App Rep 157.
8 Explicitly preserved by s 28(1)(b).

(1) Subject—
  (a) to subsections (3) and (4) below;
  (b) to paragraph 1A of Schedule 2 to the Criminal Appeal Act 1968; and
  (c) to section 69 of the Police and Criminal Evidence Act 1984, a statement in a document shall be admissible in criminal proceedings as evidence of any fact of which direct oral evidence would be admissible, if the following conditions are satisfied—
      (i) the document was created or received by a person in the course of a trade, business, profession or other occupation, or as the holder of a paid or unpaid office; and
      (ii) the information contained in the document was supplied by a person (whether or not the maker of the statement) who had or may reasonably be supposed to have had, personal knowledge of the matters dealt with.
(2) Subsection (1) above applies whether the information contained in the document was supplied directly or indirectly but, if it was supplied indirectly, only if each person through whom it was supplied received it—
  (a) in the course of a trade, business, profession or other occupation; or
  (b) as the holder of a paid or unpaid office.
(3) Subsection (1) above does not render admissible a confession made by an accused person that would not be admissible under s 76 of the Police and Criminal Evidence Act 1984.
(4) A statement prepared otherwise than in accordance with section 29 below or an order under paragraph 6 of Schedule 13 to this Act or under section 30 or 31 below for the purposes—
  (a) of pending or contemplated criminal proceedings; or
  (b) of a criminal investigation, shall not be admissible by virtue of subsection (1) above unless—
      (i) the requirements of one of the paragraphs of subsection (2) of section 23 above are satisfied; or
      (ii) the requirements of subsection (3) of that section are satisfied; or
      (iii) the person who made the statement cannot reasonably be expected (having regard to the time which has elapsed since he made the statement and to all the circumstances) to have any recollection of the matters dealt with in the statement.

This provision reverts to the categorisation of admissibility in this area by reference to business[9] rather than duty.[10] However, given the expansive definition, and the incorporation of s 23 to deal with first-hand hearsay, this is unlikely to cause any difficulty.[11] A much more significant change is from the terminology of 'record' to that of 'statement in a document'. It seems that this will free the law from the unduly restrictive interpretation attached to the notion of a record.[12] It also squares with the view advanced above that the hearsay rule applies only to intended, and not to implied, assertions. A further indication of liberalisation is that it is necessary now only that the document be *received* in the course of business, not that it be supplied or made in the course of business. It remains necessary that the supplier of the information have personal knowledge. It is not however clear that the rigid distinction between the maker of the statement

9 As in the Criminal Evidence Act 1965.
10 As in s 68 of the Police and Criminal Evidence Act 1984.
11 All subsequent reference in this part to 'business' is intended to refer to the extended meaning.
12 In cases such as *R v Tirado* (1974) 59 Cr App Rep 80; *R v Jones and Sullivan* [1978] 2 All ER 718, [1978] 1 WLR 195; *R v Cunningham* [1989] Crim LR 435; *R v Governor of Pentonville Prison, ex p Osman* [1989] 3 All ER 701, see further above p 555.

contained in the document[13] and the supplier of the information contained in it has always been applied satisfactorily. For example it is far from clear why the condition in subsection 24(4)(b)(iii) relating to the absence of recollection of the matters dealt with in the statement should be applied to the maker of the statement rather than to the supplier of the information which it contains.

Although the statement should have been admissible in the mouth of some witness at some stage, and must have been supplied by someone with personal knowledge, there is no restriction upon the length of the chain of supply so long as every subsequent reception takes place in the course of business. It should be noted that intermediate reception need not be in documentary form.

In contrast to the position in some other jurisdictions[14] no explicit provision is made in relation to statements of negative purport. It might be thought that this would cause difficulty in the light of the condition requiring personal knowledge, since the negative cannot be within anyone's personal knowledge. Such an argument was advanced in at least two cases under the old law. In *R v Patel*[15] the court did not need to decide the question, but seemed to think that the proper custodian of the records could testify to their mode of creation, leaving the jury to infer from the absence of the inclusion of a particular person's name as a legal immigrant that he had immigrated illegally. In *R v Shone*[16] the argument was rejected, and a custodian was allowed to testify that certain stock records did not contain an indication of the stock's having been used legitimately, from which the jury was permitted to infer that the stock had left the relevant premises as the result of an illegal act. If the suggestion is that such a use does not infringe the hearsay rule, but rather represents no more than a circumstantial use of the record, the argument seems to be inconsistent with the decision in *Myers v D P P*[17] since it should make no difference whether the inference is superficially positive or negative. In *Myers* itself, although the records were tendered to prove the positive association of a series of numbers, it was equally essential to the argument that no record contained the association of numbers actually found on the cars alleged to have been stolen. *Shone* seems to be one more example of failure to appreciate that the hearsay rule is undermined by circumstantial inference.[18]

Here again evidence admitted under the provisions of s 24 may be excluded at the discretion of the court under the provisions of s 25, those of s 78 of the Police and Criminal Evidence Act 1984 or at common law.

3. DOCUMENTS PREPARED FOR CRIMINAL PROCEEDINGS OR INVESTIGATIONS

In order to deal with the problem of manufacture and to preserve the general orality of the criminal trial special conditions are imposed by s 26

13 Presumably the maker of the document.
14 Such as New South Wales by the new Part IIC of the Evidence Act 1898, s 14CH, and the United States by Federal Rules of Evidence, r 803(7).
15 (1981) 73 Cr App Rep 117.
16 (1983) 76 Cr App Rep 72.
17 [1965] AC 1001, [1964] 1 All ER 877.
18 The dangers of such an approach are graphically illustrated by *R v Muir* [1984] Crim LR 101.

of the Criminal Justice Act 1988 for documents, otherwise admissible under the provisions of ss 23 or 24 which appear to the court to have been prepared for the purposes of criminal proceedings or investigations.[19] It is necessary to secure the leave of the court to give such material in evidence, and such leave may be obtained only if the court regards such admission as in the interests of justice, having regard to the contents of the statement and to the risk of unfairness to the accused if the statement cannot be controverted and its maker does not attend to give oral evidence. It seems likely that this explicit reference in the body of the Act to such statements will overcome the difficulty felt under the old law in considering proofs of evidence or depositions to qualify as documentary records,[20] and this view appears to be confirmed by the first cases to be decided under the new provisions.[1]

4. GENERAL PROVISIONS

The Act makes a number of useful improvements of a general nature. In particular it provides for the admission of copies of any document, whether admitted under the provisions of the Act or otherwise, at any remove from the original, and subject only to authentication in any manner approved by the court.[2] It also paves the way for rules to be made so as to provide for evidence to be furnished to the court in any form[3] notwithstanding the existence of evidence in original form from which the evidence tendered has been derived.[4] The whole aim is to improve the comprehensibility to the jury of the material tendered in evidence. It is to be hoped that any such rules will be astute to prevent the diversion of any dispute from the ascertainment of the facts themselves to the techniques of their presentation. It can hardly be denied that the simplification achieved by graphic, statistical or summary presentation can sometimes be achieved only at the cost of distortion induced by the selective choice of scale, starting point or categorisation.

In relation to evidence admissible under ss 23 and 24 of the Act provision is made for a special exclusionary discretion in the interests of justice by s 25. The guidelines for the exercise of this discretion are set out in subsection (2) as follows:

> Without prejudice to the generality of subsection (1) above, it shall be the duty of the court to have regard—
> (a) to the nature and source of the document containing the statement and to whether or not, having regard to its nature and source and to any other circumstances that appear to the court to be relevant, it is likely that the document is authentic;
> (b) to the extent to which the statement appears to supply evidence which would not otherwise be available;

19 Expert reports admissible under s 30 are expressly excluded from the range of this provision.
20 See *R v Martin* [1988] 3 All ER 440, [1988] 1 WLR 655; *R v Cunningham* [1989] Crim LR 435.
1 See *R v Cole* [1990] 2 All ER 108.
2 S 27.
3 For example, by the use of charts, statistical analysis or summaries.
4 S 31.

(c) to the relevance of the evidence that it appears to supply to any issue which is likely to have to be determined in the proceedings; and
(d) to any risk, having regard in particular to whether it is likely to be possible to controvert the statement if the person making it does not attend to give oral evidence in the proceedings, that its admission or exclusion will result in unfairness to the accused or, if there is more than one, to any of them.

It may be noted that these guidelines may on occasion clash with each other. Thus the more the evidence is necessary under (b) and relevant under (c) the more risk there is likely to be under (d). It is somewhat unclear how these guidelines are to be reconciled with the different considerations under s 26 when a document admissible under s 23 or s 24 has been prepared for the purpose of criminal proceedings. Since s 26 requires leave to be obtained it would appear that it will be for the prosecution to satisfy the court of the absence of risk to the accused under s 26, rather than to leave it to the accused to persuade the court to exclude the document on such a basis under s 25, though s 25 is not formally subordinated to s 26.

Some detailed considerations relating to the weight to be attached to evidence admissible under these provisions are provided by Sch 2.[5] It makes admissible evidence which could have been used to discredit a witness testifying to the information contained in a document whether in such a case it could have been adduced in chief or used only to cross-examine, and permits the use of inconsistent statements by such a witness to show contradiction.[6] Although it hardly seems necessary, explicit provision is made forbidding the use of a statement admitted under the Act from being used to corroborate the evidence of its supplier when such corroboration is required.[7] It is significant that para 3 which explicitly deals with the estimation of weight is now cast in much more general terms than under the old law by permitting reference to any circumstances from which any inference can reasonably be drawn to its accuracy or otherwise. This seems to allow reference to matters bolstering as well as to those diminishing weight. A final matter relates to the universal importation of definitions from the Civil Evidence Act 1968 to the extent of the overlapping of terminology, and to the definition of 'confession' from the Police and Criminal Evidence Act 1984.

Since, unlike the Civil Evidence Act 1968, these provisions contemplate the use of documentary hearsay, only where the supplier of the information is unavailable to give evidence, there is no need for any notice procedure. This has made it possible for the provisions to apply to the lower courts as much as to the higher.

B. COMPUTER RECORDS[8]

It was thought necessary to make special provisions for the admission of computer records in evidence in criminal proceedings just as in civil.

---

5 Which replaces Part I of Sch 3 to the Police and Criminal Evidence Act 1984 in a more simplied form.
6 Though in such a case it would not apparently be admissible to show the truth of its contents.
7 Sch 2, para 2. It seems unnecessary because it does not come from an independent source, and so could not corroborate at common law in any case. See p 247 above.
8 See further Tapper *Computer Law* (4th edn, 1990) chs 9 and 10.

Criticism of those provisions has however been heeded, and s 69 of the Police and Criminal Evidence Act can be seen to be very different in form:

(1) In any proceedings, a statement in a document produced by a computer shall not be admissible as evidence of any fact stated therein unless it is shown—
   (a) that there are no reasonable grounds for believing that the statement is inaccurate because of improper use of the computer.
   (b) that at all material times the computer was operating properly, or if not, that any respect in which it was not operating properly or was out of operation was not such as to affect the production of the document or the accuracy of its contents; and
   (c) that any relevant conditions specified in rules of court under subsection (2) below are satisfied.

Although it seemed at one time as though such special provision might be omitted from the Criminal Justice Act 1988 the principal enabling provisions[9] of that legislation have explicitly been made subject to s 69 of the Police and Criminal Evidence Act 1984. It will be immediately apparent that this is a much clearer and more straightforward provision than s 5 of the Civil Evidence Act 1968.[10] It is supported by further supplementary provisions in Part II of Sch 3 to the Police and Criminal Evidence Act 1984, and provision is made for rules of court to be drafted. The Schedule is however more concerned with questions of procedure and weight than with amplifying the conditions for admissibility.

The most significant difference is in the relationship between this section and the enabling provisions of the Criminal Justice Act 1988. One of the weakest features of the regime for civil cases is the precedence accorded to the computer provision, despite its lack of any requirement of personal knowledge.[11] There is no such requirement here either, but the structure is quite different. Because s 69 is negative in form, and because ss 23 and 24 of the Criminal Justice Act 1988 are made subject to s 69 of the Police and Criminal Evidence Act 1984, the result is that any hearsay statement produced by a computer must satisfy the requirements of both sections.[12] Thus since ss 23 and 24 both require personal knowledge, it follows that no such statement produced by a computer can be admitted unless the supplier of its information has personal knowledge of its truth. In effect, records produced by computers have to clear two hurdles rather than one. It is certainly arguable that the second, focused particularly on computers, is unnecessary, and that the safeguards incorporated in ss 23 and 24[13] are quite sufficient to cope with records produced by computers just as much as those produced by any other means. It should be noted that in the Police and Criminal Evidence Act 1984 no attempt was made to define a computer. This seemed, and still seems, sensible since there can be no reason for giving the word anything other than its ordinary English

---

9 Ss 23 and 24.
10 See Ch XV, section 3, part B, above.
11 See pp 558–9 above.
12 The structure was exactly the same before the repeal of s 68 of the Police and Criminal Evidence Act 1984, see *R v Minors and Harper* [1989] 2 All ER 208, 89 Cr App Rep 102.
13 And their accompanying provisions.

meaning. Unfortunately Sch 2[14] of the Criminal Justice Act 1988 incorporates the unsatisfactory definition of a computer contained in the Civil Evidence Act 1968.[15] It is to be hoped that this will not cause any undue problems. The increasing use of computerised word-processing systems for the production of documents, and the widespread diffusion of personal computer systems does however mean that more and more documents are going to become subject to s 69, and many of them will not bear on their face any indication of having been produced by a computer. It is suggested that this phenomenon also points in the direction of abandoning special provision for documents produced by computers, and towards that of subjecting them to exactly the same regime as any other documents.[16]

Since the effect of these provisions is to require personal knowledge on the part of the supplier of the information, it is necessary to consider the case law relating to records produced by computer under the similar requirement of the Criminal Evidence Act 1965, since there is no reason to take a different approach. The one difficulty under the existing law occurred in *R v Pettigrew*[17] where in the special case of a dual purpose computer which was both recording information and performing an automated task, it was held that no personal knowledge had been proved. In fact it seems that had proof of the commission of the automated task been tendered in the same way as proof of the operation of other scientific devices any problem could have been avoided.[18] Subsequent cases had no trouble with this requirement in relation to use of the computer solely as a calculator,[19] or as recording information.[20] The terminology of s 69 suggests all statements in documents produced by computers, such as those in *Pettigrew* or *Wood*, should satisfy the conditions imposed by s 69,[1] but this should not prove unduly onerous, being little more than is already required by the application to computers of the rules applying to other scientific devices. To the extent that the statement represents real hearsay, for example in a case like *Ewing*, then the provisions of ss 23 or 24 will also, and rightly, have to be satisfied. In many cases of records produced by computers, advantage will have to be taken of the provisions of s 24(4) permitting the use of the record when the maker of the information cannot reasonably be expected to remember the information. It may also be necessary to have recourse to the presumption that a computer was operating properly when its output shows no internal sign of malfunction, and it has been retained as a record by a business or professional person.[2]

It is also worth noting that special provision is made in the Code of Practice for the Searching of Premises and the Seizure of Property issued

14 Para 5. It seems extremely doubtful whether this result in relation to the definition of a computer was intended.
15 See, above, p 558.
16 As is achieved in other jurisdictions such as New South Wales and the United States by the use of general business record provisions to cater for computer output.
17 (1980) 71 Cr App Rep 39.
18 *R v Spiby* (1990), Times 16 March, see also pp 31, 48 above.
19 *R v Wood* (1983) 76 Cr App Rep 23; *Castle v Cross* [1985] 1 All ER 87. See also *R v McHardie and Danielson* [1983] 2 NSWLR 733.
20 *R v Ewing* [1983] 2 All ER 645.
1 Though a different view seems to have been taken in *Sophocleous v Ringer* [1988] RTR 52 and in *R v Spiby*, above.
2 See *R v Governor of Pentonville Prison, ex p Osman* [1989] 3 All ER 701 at 727; *R v Spiby*, above.

under the Police and Criminal Evidence Act 1984 for requiring relevant information held in a computer to be supplied in a visible and legible form.[3]

C. CRIMINAL JUSTICE ACT 1967, S 9

Provided the conditions specified in s 9 of the Criminal Justice Act 1967, are fulfilled, agreed statements of facts may be admitted in evidence at any criminal trial to the same extent and with the same effect as oral evidence.[4] The principal conditions are that the statement should be signed and contain a declaration of the maker's knowledge that it was made subject to penalties in the event of its being used in evidence if the maker knew it to be false or did not care whether it was true, that a copy should have been served on the opposite party, and that no notice of objection should have been received from that party within seven days. It is also possible for the parties to agree to the reception of such a statement at or before the trial, although the provisions with regard to service of a copy of the statement and non-receipt within seven days of notice of objection have not been fulfilled.

If a defendant wishes to challenge such evidence he should serve notice under s 9(2)(d), and if he challenges it at the trial without doing so, the court may order an adjournment, and may charge him with the costs.[5] It is important to preserve the orality of criminal proceedings, and maintenance of the rule in *Browne v Dunn*[6] that the defence case should be put to the witnesses for the prosecution in cross-examination wherever possible.

SECTION 3. STATEMENTS OF DECEASED PERSONS ADMISSIBLE AT COMMON LAW

Statements as to pedigree and statements concerning public or general rights were discussed in ch XV.[7] Having regard to the restricted nature of the issues on which they are admissible, the number of criminal cases to which the law governing the reception of such statements is relevant at the present day is small. In practice, the number of criminal cases to which the law governing the admissibility of declarations against interest and in the course of duty is relevant may not be much larger, but these declarations are admissible on every possible issue, although the conditions of their admissibility have a circumscribing effect. The conditions were evolved in civil cases and in a milieu which has little relevance to the principles on which hearsay should be admissible in contemporary criminal proceedings; but, in spite of the rather unrealistic nature of the process, there seems to be no alternative to giving an account of these two common law exceptions to the hearsay rule commensurate in detail with the rest of

3 Para 6.5.
4 *Ellis v Jones* [1973] 2 All ER 893.
5 *Lister v Quaife* (1982) 75 Cr App Rep 313, although if this is not done and the trial proceeds in the absence of the prosecution witnesses, the trier of fact is not bound to accept the truth of their statements.
6 (1893) 6 R 67; see p 303 above.
7 See pp 563 and 565 above.

this book. The law governing the admissibility of dying declarations in homicide cases is no less antediluvian than that governing the admissibility of declarations against interest and in the course of duty. As a minimal step in law reform, the statements of all deceased persons on every relevant matter should be made admissible in all criminal cases.

A. DECLARATIONS AGAINST INTEREST

1. STATEMENT AND ILLUSTRATIONS OF THE EXCEPTION

(i) Statement

In criminal cases the oral or written declaration by a deceased person of a fact which he knew to be against his pecuniary or proprietary interest when the declaration was made, is admissible as evidence of that fact and of all collateral matters mentioned in the declaration provided the declarant had personal knowledge of such fact and matters. Although practically all the authorities mentioned under this head and head B are civil, they govern criminal cases. Practically all the statements received or rejected under these common law exceptions to the hearsay rule would be admissible in civil proceedings under the Civil Evidence Act 1968.

(ii) Illustrations

(a) Statements against pecuniary interest. The simplest instance of a declaration against pecuniary interest would be a bare acknowledgement of indebtedness. The acknowledgement must be 'bare' in the sense that it is unilateral, for, if it is contained in a statement concerning an executory contract concluded by the declarant, the statement is not regarded as one that was against his interest when it was made. Thus, in *R v Inhabitants of Worth*,[8] an entry in a deceased farmer's book relating to a contract of service was held inadmissible as evidence of the hiring because the agreement was for the mutual benefit of the parties and the employer would have been liable only for salary if the services were duly rendered. A declaration by a deceased workman to the effect that he had promised to marry the mother of the child on whose behalf workmen's compensation was claimed was held to be inadmissible as evidence of the promise by the Court of Appeal in *Ward v H S Pitt & Co* which was reported together with *Lloyd v Powell Duffryn Steam Coal Co.*[9]

A statement acknowledging the receipt of money on behalf of a third person is plainly admissible under this head.[10] In the old leading case of *Higham v Ridgway*,[11] an entry made by a deceased male midwife stating that he had delivered a woman of a child on a certain day and referring to the payment of his charges was received as evidence of the date of the child's birth. In the words of Lord Ellenborough CJ: 'If this entry had been produced when the party was making a claim for his attendance, it

---

8 (1843) 4 QB 132; cf *Bagot's Executor and Trustee Co Ltd v Fudge* [1949] SASR 297; *Conley v Conley* (1968) 70 DLR (2d) 352.
9 [1913] 2 KB 130.
10 *Short v Lee* (1821) 2 Jac & W 464 at 478; *Middleton v Melton* (1829) 10 B & C 317.
11 (1808) 10 East 109.

would have been evidence against him that his claim was satisfied.' Lord Ellenborough added that: 'It is idle to say that the word "paid" only shall be admissible in evidence, without the context, which explains to what it refers.' He was, of course, speaking of the admissibility of the collateral statement concerning the date of the child's birth, and it will be necessary to refer to this aspect of the case later. On the preponderance of authority, if payment of a statute-barred debt is acknowledged, the receipt does not amount to a declaration against pecuniary interest because the payment revives the debtor's liability, and even if the entirety of a statute-barred debt were discharged, the receipt could hardly be said to be against the creditor's interest because it does not provide evidence of a release from an antecedent legal liability.[12]

(b) Statements against proprietary interest. So far as declarations against proprietary interest are concerned, possession is prima facie evidence of ownership. A statement by the possessor to the effect that he is not the owner will therefore amount to a declaration against interest. The remarks of a tenant naming the person from whom he rented certain houses may accordingly be received as evidence of the fact that the reversion was vested in that person,[13] of the amount of the rent[14] and of the fact that it was paid,[15] provided, of course, that these last two matters were mentioned in the statement. It has even been held that, where a man was found to be felling timber, his declaration that someone else was the proprietor of the estate was admissible evidence as to who was the owner[16]—a conclusion which prompted Tregarthen to remark that:

> Surely the law never appeared decked with a more luxuriant pair of ears than when it enunciated this judgment. The same train of reasoning would admit the bawdry of a tramp under a hedge on the presumption that he was lord of the manor.[17]

(c) No derogation from superior title. The principle underlying the cases mentioned in the last paragraph is subject to the qualification that a tenant may not derogate from his landlord's title. This qualification was the basis of the decision in *Papendick v Bridgwater*[18] where the plaintiff claimed a right of common appurtenant to a farm, and the statement of a deceased tenant of the farm negativating the existence of such a right was rejected as evidence for the defendant. Wigmore criticised this decision on the ground that it confuses the rules of evidence concerning the admissibility of declarations against interest with the substantive law that a tenant

12 *Newbold v Smith* (1885) 29 Ch D 882; *Briggs v Wilson* (1854) 5 De G M & G 12; cf *Bradley v James* (1853) 13 CB 822. The conflict was left unresolved by the Court of Appeal in *Coward v Motor Insurers' Bureau* [1963] 1 QB 259, [1962] 1 All ER 531. Perhaps it is arguable that, after this case, a release from a moral obligation to pay money is against interest. The receipt for a payment within the limitation period would be against interest on the principle of *Higham v Ridgway*.
13 *Peacable d Uncle v Watson* (1811) 4 Taunt 16.
14 *R v Birmingham Overseers* (1861) 1 B & S 763.
15 *R v Exeter Guardians* (1869) LR 4 QB 341.
16 *Doe d Stansbury v Arkwright* (1833) 5 C & P 575.
17 Tregarthen *The Law of Hearsay Evidence* 105.
18 (1855) 5 E & B 166; *Crease v Barrett* (1835) 1 Cr M & R 919; *Scholes v Chadwick* (1843) 2 Mood & R 507.

cannot dispute his landlord's title;[19] but this is surely a case in which the substantive law is rightly reinforced by a qualification of the logical implications of a rule of evidence. There is much to be said for Coleridge J's observations that nothing would lead to greater inconvenience than that the landlord should be ousted of his rights by loose declarations of his tenants. *Papendick v Bridgwater* was distinguished in *Blandy-Jenkins v Dunraven (Earl)*[20] where the fact that the tenant of a predecessor in title of the defendant paid money under a compromise of an action of trespass brought by one of the plaintiff's predecessors in title was received as a declaration against interest. The bringing of the action showed that the plaintiff's predecessor performed acts of ownership and the compromise was not tendered as a denial of the title of the landlord of the other party.

(iii) Rationale of the exception

In *Ward v H S Pitt & Co*,[1] Hamilton LJ recognised, as many others had done before,[2] that it is on the guarantee of truth, based on a man's conscious statement of a fact (even if it be to his own hindrance), that the whole theory of admissibility depends. He added that this seems sordid and unconvincing because: 'Men lie for so many reasons and some for no reason at all and some tell the truth without thinking or even in spite of thinking about their pockets'; but he concluded that it is too late to question the piece of eighteenth-century philosophy on which the exception is based, and it is difficult to dissent from either the observations on the rationale or the conclusions with regard to it.

2. CONDITIONS OF ADMISSIBILITY

(i) Death of declarant

Stephen v Gwenap[3] conclusively established that the death of the declarant is a prerequisite of admissibility under this head. The defendant to an action on a loan wished to prove that he had made some payments on account to an agent for the plaintiff, and he proposed to produce the books of the agent who had absconded, but he was not allowed to do so because there was no evidence that the agent was dead.

(ii) Statement must be against the pecuniary or proprietary interest of the declarant when it was made

There are three matters to be considered in connection with the requirement that the statement must have been against the interest of the declarant when it was made—the nature of the interest, the necessity of the statements being presently, not merely contingently, against interest, and the question whether it is sufficient that the statement should have

19 V *Wigmore* 279.
20 [1899] 2 Ch 121.
 1 [1913] 2 KB 130 at 138.
 2 See Baker *The Hearsay Rule* 66–7 for examples.
 3 (1831) 1 Mood & R 120. At common law, the declarant's death must be proved like other preliminary facts upon which the admissibility of evidence depends unless death can be presumed (*Doe d Earl of Ashburnham v Michael* (1851) 17 QB 276).

been prima facie contrary to the interest of the declarant although it might have been to his advantage in certain circumstances.

(a) The nature of the interest. The House of Lords is generally thought to have decided in the *Sussex Peerage Case*[4] that a declaration by a deceased person is not admissible as evidence of its truth on the ground that it exposed him to a criminal, as opposed to a pecuniary or proprietary, liability. It was held that a declaration by a deceased clergyman concerning a marriage at which he had officiated was inadmissible as evidence of the marriage although the celebrant was liable to criminal punishment under the Royal Marriages Act 1772. Lord Brougham said:

> The rule as understood now is that the only declarations of deceased persons receivable in evidence are those made against the proprietary or pecuniary interest of the maker,

but Professor Baker has pointed out that Lord Campbell was also of opinion that, even if declarations exposing the declarant to criminal liability were admissible, the statement with which the House was concerned would still have been inadmissible as there was no evidence that the clergyman was aware of the dangers to which he was exposing himself by his statement. The marriage was celebrated abroad and he might have believed that the statutory prohibition did not extend to it. Professor Baker asks whether it is not possible that, in a more definite case, where it was obvious that the declarant must have known what the consequences of his statement would be, the statement might be received. It is doubtful whether this course could be adopted by any court lower than the House of Lords but few would disagree with Professor Baker's conclusion that there is a crying need for reform if the law is too firmly established to allow for an affirmative answer to this question.[5]

Lord Brougham expressed himself with characteristic force when he said:[6]

> to say, if a man should confess a felony for which he would be liable to prosecution, that therefore, the instant the grave closes over him, all that was said by him is to be taken as evidence in every action and prosecution against another person, is one of the most monstrous and untenable propositions that can be advanced.

He evidently regarded as one instance of the monstrosity the fact that, if A made an extrajudicial statement incriminating himself and B, the statement would, on the argument he was seeking to refute, be admissible against B in criminal proceedings brought after A's death. But this could be the consequence of a declaration against pecuniary interest, as when A acknowledges his liability to repay money which he says was embezzled by B and himself, and dies before B is brought to trial.

The *Sussex Peerage Case* was followed by the United States Supreme Court in *Donnelly v US*,[7] but there is much force in the following observations made by Holmes J in a famous dissent:

4 (1844) 11 Cl & Fin 85.
5 Baker *The Hearsay Rule* 70.
6 (1844) 11 Cl & Fin 85 at 112.
7 228 US 243 (1913). Cf *Chambers v Mississippi* 410 US 295 (1973).

The confession of Joe Dick, since deceased, that he committed the murder for which the plaintiff in error was tried, coupled with circumstances pointing to its truth, would have a very strong tendency to make anyone outside of a court of justice believe that Donnelly did not commit the crime . . . [t]he exception to the hearsay rule in the case of declarations against interest is well known; no other statement is so much against interest as a confession of murder; it is far more calculated to convince than dying declarations, which would be let in to hang a man; . . .

It is said that, if declarations by deceased persons against penal interest were to be admissible, there would be a spate of criminal cases in which the accused adduced perjured evidence by witnesses of confessions of the crime charged allegedly made by people since deceased, but this is a somewhat unconvincing manifestation of the proverbial dread of encouraging the manufacture of evidence. Nevertheless, due attention would have to be paid to the circumstances in which the alleged confession was made before it could be allowed to have an exculpatory effect. Holmes J's statement was avowedly based on the assumption that there was no ground for connecting Donnelly with Dick, and we have seen that, although a statement against penal interest by someone who is not available as a witness is admissible under r 804(3) of the US Federal Rules, there must be corroborating circumstances if it is offered to exculpate the accused.[8]

The effect of recent decisions of the Supreme Court of Canada is that declarations of deceased persons against penal interest are admissible to exculpate the accused, although they were held to be inadmissible on the particular facts.[9]

In *Re Perton, Pearson v A-G,*[10] Chitty J was prepared to receive a deceased's statement that he was illegitimate as evidence of that fact on the ground that the statement was against interest, and, although the judge mentioned the social stigma attaching to illegitimacy, he appears to have based his conclusion on the fact that the statement might have affected the proprietary rights of the deceased in an adverse manner.

There is no conclusive authority on the extent to which an acknowledgment of a tortious liability will suffice. On principle, there seems to be no reason why such an acknowledgment as that A has assaulted B should not amount to a statement against A's pecuniary interest, but, in some cases, the form of the declaration may give rise to difficulty. 'I was negligent' might be excluded as a statement of opinion when a statement of fact is essential.[11] It has, however, been held in Canada,[12] that a statement by an injured passenger (since deceased) that a motorist had driven well on the occasion of an accident was admissible as tending to exempt the motorist from liability to the passenger.

In *Coward v Motor Insurers' Bureau,*[13] the Court of Appeal held that the

---

8 See p 570 above.
9 *Demeter v R* (1977) 75 DLR (3d) 251; *R v O'Brien* (1977) 76 DLR (3d) 513; *Lucier v R* (1982) 132 DLR (3d) 244. Cf *Re Van Beelen's* case (1974) 9 SASR 163 (confession by someone unavailable as a witness on account of his mental state inadmissible).
10 (1885) 53 LT 707. This is a difficult case because of the vague terms of the judgment. The judge did not consider the requirement that the statement should be against the declarant's present interest when made.
11 The first condition mentioned by Hamilton LJ in *Ward v Pitt* [1913] 2 KB 130 at 137 could be cited in support of this view.
12 *Watt v Miller* [1950] 3 DLR 709; but see *R v Schwarz* [1923] SASR 347.
13 [1963] 1 QB 259, [1962] 1 All ER 531.

acknowledgment of a moral obligation to pay money was against the pecuniary interest of its maker. Oral declarations by the deceased suggesting the evidence of an arrangement to pay for lifts to work were held to be admissible although they did not amount to the acknowledgment of a legal debt; but it has been contended with some force that the decision represents an extension of the old law.[14]

It is possible that a statement in answer to inquiries which might lead to liability as co-respondent in divorce proceedings is against interest in this context.[15]

(b) Statement must be presently against interest. Granted that the interest must be pecuniary or proprietary:

> The rule is that an admission which is against the interest of the person who makes it, at the time when he makes it, is admissible; not that an admission which may or may not turn out at some subsequent time to have been against his interest is admissible.[16]

Accordingly it was decided in the case from which this remark is taken that the acknowledgment of a debt by a bankrupt in his statement of affairs could not be regarded as against interest merely because he might subsequently have assets out of which the debt could be paid. In *Massey v Allen*,[17] the entry by a stockbroker in his day-book that he had purchased certain shares on behalf of a client was held not to amount to a declaration against interest although it would have affected the stockbroker adversely if the shares had increased in value. The requirement that the declaration must have been against interest when made is, in fact, the basis of the rule that any reference to a contract by one party while it is still executory so far as the other is concerned is insufficient to bring the exception under consideration into play; but the principle applies in many other situations. Thus, in *Smith v Blakey*,[18] it was the duty of the plaintiffs' confidential clerk (since deceased) to keep them advised of all business transacted at their branch office in Liverpool. He wrote them a letter stating that he had received three cases of shoes from the defendant, giving details of the terms on which they were received, and it was held that the letter was inadmissible as evidence of these terms because the possibility that the clerk would have been liable if the cases had been lost was too remote to render the letter a statement against his pecuniary or proprietary interest.

The goods were received at the plaintiffs' office, so the decision does not conflict with those in which an entry charging the entrant with the receipt of money on behalf of a third person has been proved under this head.

(c) Statement must simply be prima facie against interest when made. In *Smith v Blakey*, Blackburn J said:

14 Nokes in 25 MLR 458.
15 *B v A-G* [1965] P 278, [1965] 1 All ER 62.
16 Brett MR in *Re Tollemache, ex p Edwards* (1884) 14 QBD 415–416.
17 (1879) 13 Ch D 558.
18 (1867) LR 2 QB 326.

No doubt when entries are against the pecuniary interest of the person making them, and *never could be made available for the person himself,* there is such a probability of their truth that such statements have been admitted after the death of the person making them, as evidence against third persons, and not merely of the precise fact which is against interest, but of all matters involved in or knit up with the statement.

The words in italics have been approved in dicta in other cases,[19] but they are unduly rigorous, for there can be very few declarations which never could be made available for the declarant, and there are several decisions which can only be supported on the footing that it is sufficient if 'the entry prima facie and in its natural meaning, standing alone, was against interest'.[20] In *Re Adams, Benton v Powell,*[1] the question was whether a woman's will was in existence at the time of her death, and a statement by her husband (since deceased) that he had destroyed the original after his wife's death and referring to its terms was received in evidence because he was in possession of real property and hence, presumptively its owner. This property formed part of his wife's estate, and the will gave him a life interest in it. Accordingly, when all the facts were investigated, the husband's reference to the will was not one that never could be made available for him as, without it, he would have had no rights in relation to the property, but, on principles which have already been illustrated, the statement that he had been given a life interest was, prima facie and standing alone, against his interest. It is therefore submitted that this is all that is required under the present law.[2]

(iii) Declarant must have known statement to be against his interest

In *Tucker v Oldbury Urban Council,*[3] a claim for workmen's compensation was made on behalf of the dependents of a deceased workman, and the Court of Appeal held that statements made by him to the effect that the injury to his thumb which caused his death was due to a whitlow were inadmissible as declarations against interest:

> Such declarations are admitted on the ground that declarations made by persons against their own interest are extremely unlikely to be false. It followed therefore that to support the admissibility it must be shown that the statement was to the knowledge of the deceased contrary to his interest.[4]

This was said to be an essential pre-requisite of admissibility in *Ward v H S Pitt & Co,*[5] and, on principle, its soundness is beyond dispute; but there are several cases in which it is difficult to believe that the condition was fulfilled.[6] It is doubtful whether many laymen know that possession is prima facie evidence of ownership, so it is hard to believe that those who are in possession

19 *Ward v H S Pitt & Co* [1913] 2 KB 130 at 137.
20 The test propounded by Jessel MR in *Taylor v Witham* (1876) 3 Ch D 605 at 607.
 1 [1922] P 240; see also *Sly v Sly* (1877) 2 PD 91.
 2 This was the view of Greer J in *Republica de Guatemala v Nunez* (1926) 42 TLR 625 at 628, and of Hodgson J in *Roberts v Burns Philp Trustee Co* (1985) 5 NSWLR 72 at 78.
 3 [1912] 2 KB 317. The statement was also excluded as an admission binding on the claimant because she was suing in her own right and not that of the deceased.
 4 Fletcher-Moulton LJ at 321.
 5 [1913] 2 KB 130 at 137.
 6 *R v Exeter Guardians* (above); *Taylor v Witham* (above).

and credit themselves with a qualified title know that they are making declarations against their interest. This point was put most forcefully by an American writer when he said:

> By applying a rule of thumb test as to when a statement is against pecuniary or proprietary interest, and devising ingenious theories of interest, courts have admitted statements which the declarants could not conceivably have believed against their interest . . . To support an English case we are required to believe that the life tenant of enclosed land was aware of a presumption that open pieces of waste land by the side of the highway belonged to the owner of the adjoining enclosed land between which and the highway the pieces lie; and this in spite of the fact that the life tenant came into possession of his estate two years after the waste land itself had been enclosed and was in the possession of another.[7]

In short, the technicality of this branch of the law prevents the application of sound principle in all but the simplest cases. The requirement as to the declarant's knowledge that the statement was against his interest may be advanced as a ground for rejecting evidence in a novel case, but it would be idle to pretend that the requirement has been considered frequently in the past.

(iv) Personal knowledge of facts stated

The authorities conflict on the question whether the declarant must have had personal knowledge of the facts stated in order that his declaration should be admissible evidence of their existence, and the opinion of text writers is also divided.[8] In *Crease v Barrett*,[9] a deceased clerk's entry of the payments made in respect of the workings of a particular mine for which he took responsibility of a lessee of the mineral rights was admitted in order to show that payments were made to the lessee in respect of that mine; for the clerk in fact had no knowledge that the ore for which he received payment had been raised from the mine in question. This is a decision to the effect that personal knowledge of the facts stated is unnecessary, but the preponderance of authority favours the opposite conclusion. *Crease v Barrett* involved the reception of hearsay upon hearsay under this head, for the clerk was told that the ore in respect of which payment was entered by him had been raised from the mine in question, and hearsay upon hearsay was also received in *Re Perton, Pearson v A-G*,[10] where the deceased's declaration of his own illegitimacy was admitted, for no one can have personal knowledge of his illegitimacy; but, in *Roe d Lord Trimlestown v Kemmis*,[11] the *Sussex Peerage Case*[12] and *Sturla v Freccia*,[13] the need for personal knowledge was stressed in

---

7 Jefferson in 58 HLR 15 at 18–19. This entire article repays careful study by those who are still seriously concerned with this exception to the hearsay rule. The English case is *Grey v Redman* (1875) 1 QBD 161.

8 See Baker *The Hearsay Rule* 73–5.

9 (1835) 1 Cr M & R 919; *Percival v Nanson* (1851) 7 Exch 1 is to the same effect, but it is not so clear that there was, in fact, absence of personal knowledge on the part of the declarant.

10 (1885) 53 LT 707 (above).

11 (1843) 9 Cl & Fin 749 at 780.

12 (1844) 11 Cl & Fin 85 at 112.

13 (1880) 5 App Cas 623 at 632–3. 'Declarations made against interest involve as a necessary element that the subject matter of the declaration must have been within the direct personal knowledge of the person making the declaration' (Lord Selborne).

the House of Lords, and, in *Lloyd v Powell Duffryn Steam Coal Co*,[14] in the Court of Appeal where this requirement formed part of the ratio decidendi as the deceased's statement that he was the father of the claimant did not satisfy the condition that: 'the fact stated is one of which he has peculiar knowledge or direct personal knowledge to the exclusion of hearsay'. It is therefore submitted that this condition is part of the present law, although it must be stressed that there is quite a strong body of opinion to the contrary.

3. COLLATERAL MATTERS

More often than not, a statement against interest is tendered to prove some fact other than that which it was against the declarant's interest to state. In *Higham v Ridgway*,[15] for instance, the receipt was not tendered in order to prove that the midwife's charges were paid, but so as to establish the date on which the child was delivered. The doctrine of this case has frequently been followed, although Parke B appears to have thought that the authorities had gone too far.[16] In *Taylor v Witham*,[17] a receipt for payment on account of twenty pounds against a debt for two thousand pounds mentioned in the same entry enabled the debt to be proved, and the only question so far as the present law is concerned is whether any rule governing the extent of this doctrine can be stated. When an account containing receipts and disbursements is produced, the question seems to be whether the statements on the one side and the other are so blended together that the one cannot be read without the other,[18] but it is impossible to go beyond this as everything depends on the facts of the particular case. This is shown by the use of necessarily vague expressions to the effect that a declaration against interest renders admissible 'all that formed an essential part of it', or 'closely connected and related matters', and no useful purpose would be served by an attempt to give further illustrations of their meaning.

B. DECLARATIONS IN THE COURSE OF DUTY[19]

1. STATEMENT AND ILLUSTRATIONS OF THE EXCEPTION

(i) Statement

In criminal cases the oral or written statement of a deceased person made in pursuance of a duty to record or report his acts is admissible evidence of the truth of such contents of the statement as it was his duty to record or report, provided the record or report was made roughly contemporaneously with

---

14 [1913] 2 KB 130. For the facts, and the grounds on which the House of Lords allowed an appeal, see p 526 above.

15 (1808) 10 East 109.

16 *Davies v Humphreys* (1840) 6 M & W 153 at 166.

17 (1876) 3 Ch D 605. Some of the other cases in which the principle of *Higham v Ridgway* has been applied are *Webster v Webster* (1858) 1 F & F 401; *In the Goods of Thomas* (1871) 41 LJP & M 32; *Sly v Sly* (above); *Hudson v Swiftsure (Owners), The Swiftsure* (1900) 82 LT 389; *Re Adams, Benton v Powell* (above); *Homes v Newman* [1931] 2 Ch 112.

18 *Doe d Kinglake v Beviss* (1849) 7 CB 456.

19 Many of the situations considered below will now be covered by the provisions of Part II of the Criminal Justice Act 1988, though the common law remains available as an alternative channel for admissibility in criminal, as it is *not* in civil, proceedings.

the doing of the act, and provided the declarant had no motive to mirepresent the facts.

(ii) Illustrations

In *Price v Earl of Torrington*,[20] an action for the price of beer sold and delivered, entries which a deceased drayman employed by the plaintiff had made, or caused to be made, in the plaintiff's books were received as evidence of the delivery of beer. In *Pritt v Fairclough*,[1] a copy of a letter made by a deceased clerk in pursuance of his duty to his employer was received as evidence of the contents of the original. In *Mellor v Walmesley*,[2] entries made by a deceased surveyor in his field book were received as evidence of the high-water mark on the seashore. The surveyor had been employed by the local authority to make a survey in connection with a proposed drainage scheme and the grounds on which the field book was admitted were stated by Romer LJ to be that: 'it was his duty to make measurements. He could not make a plan without taking measurements and he could not discharge his duty without making these entries'.

(iii) Rationale of the exception

The grounds of the exception appear to be that, in many cases, it would be impossible to obtain other evidence of a servant's acts after his death, and, in most cases, the likelihood of detention if errors were made together with the sanction of dismissal if the duty were unfulfilled afford some guarantee of the trustworthiness of the statement.

2. CONDITIONS OF ADMISSIBILITY

The conditions of admissibility are that the declarant should be dead, he must have been under a duty to do an act and record or report it, the act must have been performed, the statement must have been made roughly contemporaneously with it and the declarant must have had no motive to misrepresent the facts.

(i) Death of declarant

Nothing need be said with regard to the first of these requirements.

(ii) Duty to act and record or report

So far as the second is concerned, a specific duty must have been owed by the declarant to another person and it must have related to the acts of the declarant.

(a) Specific duty to another. In *Smith v Blakey*[3] the plaintiffs' confidential clerk

---

20 (1703) 1 Salk 285.
1 (1812) 3 Camp 305.
2 [1905] 2 Ch 164.
3 (1867) LR 2 QB 326 (p 643 above); *R v O'Neally* [1952] VLR 499.

was under a general duty to report what took place at their Liverpool office, but he owed no particular duty with regard to the receipt of the shoes and the report of the transaction to his principals. In the words of Blackburn J: 'The duty must be to do the very thing to which the entry relates and then to make a report or record of it.' In *Mercer v Denne*,[4] a report alluding to damage by the sea to the walls of Walmer castle was excluded because there was no evidence concerning the instructions which had been given to the surveyor who made it in 1816.

In *R v Inhabitants of Worth*[5] and *Massey v Allen*,[6] attempts were made to prove the employer's entry of a contract of hiring, and the broker's entry of a purchase of shares as declarations in the course of duty; but the attempts failed because, in each case, the duty, such as it was, was purely self-serving. An entry by a deceased doctor concerning his patient's disease was excluded on similar grounds in *Mills v Mills*,[7] although it was recognised that the case would have been different if the doctor had been under a statutory duty to make the entry, and, had he practised in partnership, he might have owed a duty to his partner to make notes of all his cases. A similar strict view of the law was taken in *Simon v Simon, Hogarth, Preston and Shaw*,[8] where a deceased doctor's report concerning the physical condition of the intervener in a divorce case was held to be inadmissible. Though in the possession of the intervener's solicitors, the report had not been made for the purposes of the divorce proceedings, and Bucknill J said that he could not see that the doctor had any duty to record the result of his examination. In *Rawlins v Rickhards*,[9] a deceased solicitor's entry of an attendance at which a deed was executed was received as evidence of execution. The decision is, however, out of accord with those that have previously been mentioned in this paragraph, and its validity has since been doubted.[10]

Entries by a solicitor's clerk may, of course, be received under the exception to the hearsay rule which is now being considered on account of the duty owed to his employer, and, in some cases, the duty to record may have been owed by the solicitor to his client. This is probably the best way of accounting for the decision in *Doe d Patteshall v Turford*[11] where one of the partners in a firm of solicitors served a notice to quit, and his indorsement of service was received as evidence of that fact after his death.

(b) Duty must relate to acts of declarant. When speaking of the reception of declarations in the course of duty, Sir Robert Phillimore said:

---

4 [1905] 2 Ch 538, CA.
5 (1843) 4 QB 132 (p 638 above).
6 (1879) 13 ChD 558 (p 643 above).
7 (1920) 36 TLR 772. See also *Dawson v Dawson and Heppenstall* (1905) 22 TLR 52, excluding a statement by a deceased doctor to a patient concerning the nature of her illness. Cf *Palter Cap Co v Great West Life Assurance Co* [1936] 2 DLR 304, where a consultant owed a duty to a general practitioner.
8 [1936] P 17.
9 (1860) 28 Beav 370.
10 *Hope v Hope* [1893] WN 20; *Eckroyd v Coulthard* (1897) 32 L Jo 161.
11 (1832) 3 B & Ad 890. The explanation was given in *R v Worth (Inhabitants)* (1843) 4 QB 132 at 139.

Entries in a document made by a deceased person can only be admitted where it is clearly shown that the entries relate to an act or acts done by the deceased person and not by third parties.[12]

Accordingly, one of the reasons why he rejected entries made in a ship's logbook by a deceased mate was the fact that it concerned the navigation of another ship. In *Brain v Preece*,[13] it was the duty of workmen to give an account of coal delivered by them to a foreman (since deceased), and the foreman, in his turn, caused entries to be made concerning the deliveries. These entries were held to be inadmissible as the foreman had not got personal knowledge, and the recording process was one step less direct than that employed in *Price v Torrington*. Similarly in one of the very rare modern cases[14] decided under this exception it was held that the exception is confined to statements of fact and does not extend to expressions of opinion.[15] A scientific officer was commissioned to investigate a suspicious fire. He made notes of his observations and stated his opinion, but died before proceedings commenced. It was held that the notes of his observation were admissible under this head, but not the expression of his opinion. The proper course was to commission a further opinion to be made upon the basis of the original observations. Any other view would be incompatible with the requirement of contemporaneity.

(iii) Act must have been performed

In *Rowlands v De Vecchi*,[16] an office book containing a record of letters to be posted and kept by a clerk who had since died was rejected as evidence that a particular letter copied in the book had been posted. It seems, therefore, that the exception only covers records of acts done by the deceased, not records of acts to be done by him.

(iv) Contemporaneity

It is impossible to lay down a precise rule with regard to the requisite degree of contemporaneity between the doing of the act and the production of the report. In *Price v Torrington*, the entry was made in the evening of acts performed in the daytime and it was received, but, in *The Henry Coxon*,[17] entries concerning a collision at sea made in a ship's logbook two days after the event were rejected. All that can be said with certainty is that:

> The measure of contemporaneousness is not that period of time within which it is consistent with his duty to his employer that the party making the entry might wait to make his record.[18]

In the case from which this remark is taken, a report prepared a month after a survey was made was rejected although the surveyor had been prevented

12 *The Henry Coxon* (1878) 3 PD 156.
13 (1843) 11 M & W 773.
14 *R v McGuire* (1985) 81 Cr App Rep 323.
15 For a discussion of different senses of opinion in this context see *Apsassin v The Queen in right of Canada* (1987) 37 DLR (4th) 257.
16 (1882) Cab & El 10; cf *R v Buckley* (1873) 13 Cox CC 293.
17 (1878) 3 PD 156.
18 *Re Djambi (Sumatra) Rubber Estates Ltd* (1912) 107 LT 631, at 634 per Hamilton LJ.

from preparing it by illness. It seems, therefore, that the standard of contemporaneity under this head is strict, and this is doubtless due to the fact that the probative value of the record is increased by its promptness.

(v) Absence of motive to misrepresent

A further ground for the rejection of the entries in *The Henry Coxon* was that the mate had every reason to misrepresent the part played in the collision by his ship. Although the authority is somewhat scanty, it may therefore be assumed that the absence of a motive to misrepresent is one of the conditions precedent to the reception of declarations in the course of duty to prove the truth of that which they assert.

3. CONTRAST WITH DECLARATIONS AGAINST INTEREST

The most important respect in which the law relating to declarations in the course of duty as an exception to the hearsay rule differs from that governing declarations against interest is that the former, unlike the latter, can never be received as evidence of collateral facts. This was decided in *Chambers v Bernasconi*,[19] where the certificate of an officer whose duty it was to record the day and hour of an arrest was rejected as evidence of the place at which it occurred although this was stated in the certificate and the officer had died before the trial. Further respects in which the rules governing the two exceptions differ are the absence of any requirement as to contemporaneity and motive to misrepresent as conditions precedent to the reception of declarations against interest.[20] If, contrary to the submission that has already been made, personal knowledge of the declarant should be held to be unnecessary when a statement against his interest is received as evidence of its truth, yet another difference between the two exceptions to the hearsay rule that have so far been considered in this section of this chapter will have been brought to light.

Blackburn J once accounted for the exclusion of collateral matter in the case of declarations in the course of duty by reference to the need for contemporaneity which went, in his view, to the essence of admissibility.[1] It seems that he would also have been prepared to justify the distinction on the ground that collateral facts are, so to speak, outside the purview of the duty to record; but there is probably no rational basis for any of the distinctions mentioned in the last paragraph.

---

19 (1834) 1 Cr M & R 347. This could now be proved under the Police and Criminal Evidence Act 1984.
20 The judgment of Jessel MR in *Taylor v Witham* (1876) 3 ChD 605 at 607, suggests that a motive to misrepresent goes to weight rather than admissibility in the case of declarations against interest, and no case seems to require strict contemporaneity before such statements can be received.
1 *Smith v Blakey* (1867) LR 2 QB 326 at 333.

C. DYING DECLARATIONS

1. STATEMENT AND ILLUSTRATIONS OF THE EXCEPTION

(i) Statement

The oral or written declaration of a deceased person is admissible evidence of the cause of his death at a trial for his murder or manslaughter provided he was under a settled hopeless expectation of death when the statement was made and provided he would have been a competent witness if called to give evidence at that time.[2]

(ii) Illustrations

In *R v Woodcock*,[3] a man was charged with the murder of his wife, and her statement concerning the cause of her injuries given on oath to a magistrate was received in evidence against the accused for although the deceased said nothing of her impending death, the court was satisfied that she must have known she was on the point of dying. Eyre CB said:

> The principle on which this species of evidence is admitted is, that they are declarations made in extremity, when the party is at the point of death, and when every hope of this world is gone; when every motive to falsehood is silenced, and the mind is induced by the most powerful considerations to speak the truth; a situation so solemn and so awful is considered by law as creating an obligation equal to that which is imposed by a positive oath administered in a court of justice.

In *R v Mosley*,[4] the deceased did not die until eleven days after he made a statement implicating the accused, but he constantly said he was sure he would not get better in spite of encouragement from his surgeon who did not regard the case as hopeless. The judges were unanimously of opinion that the declarations had been properly received in evidence. In *R v Errington*,[5] on the other hand, similar declarations were excluded because the deceased did no more than say that he regarded himself as in great danger. In *R v Scaife*,[6] the deceased's statement that the accused would not have struck him in the absence of provocation was received as evidence favourable to the accused.

(iii) Rationale of the exception

The passage from the judgment of Eyre CB in *R v Woodcock* is the classic statement of the rationale of this exception to the hearsay rule. The theory is that no one would wish to die with a lie on his lips. The exception has been held to have no application in a community such as the indigenous people of Papua New Guinea where the next life is believed to be spent in comfort on

2 There is no requirement that such a statement need be corroborated, *Nembhard v R* [1982] 1 All ER 183, [1981] 1 WLR 1515.
3 (1789) 1 Leach 500.
4 (1825) 1 Mood CC 97.
5 (1838) 2 Lew CC 148.
6 (1836) 2 Lew CC 150.

a neighbouring island and there is no sanction against lying when at the point of death.[7]

2. CONDITIONS OF ADMISSIBILITY

The conditions on which dying declarations are admitted in evidence are the death of the declarant, that the trial should be for his murder or manslaughter, that his statement should relate to the cause of his death, that he should have been under a settled hopeless expectation of death and that he could have been a competent witness.

(i) Death of declarant

Nothing need be said with regard to the first of these conditions.

(ii) Trial for murder or manslaughter

The second is the outcome of restrictions placed at the beginning of the nineteenth century on what bade fair to become a general principle under which dying declarations might be received.[8] In *R v Mead*[9] the accused was charged with perjury. He obtained an order for a new trial and shot the deceased before it took place. A dying declaration made by the deceased concerning the transaction out of which the prosecution for perjury arose was rejected, Abbot CJ saying that dying declarations are only admissible where the death of the deceased is the subject of the charge, and the circumstances of the death are the subject of the declaration. This case really settled the law, but, as late as 1860, an unsuccessful attempt was made to obtain the reception of a woman's dying declaration on a charge against the accused of procuring her abortion.[10]

(iii) Statement must relate to cause of declarant's death

The words of Abbott CJ indicate that the declaration is admissible only in so far as it relates to the cause of the deceased's death, and this is borne out by observations in *R v Murton*.[11] *R v Baker*[12] is to the contrary, for a statement made by a cook shortly before her death from poison believed to have come from a cake, to the effect that she had put nothing wrong in the cake was admitted on the trial of another servant for murdering the master of the house who had also eaten some of the cake. It is doubtful whether the case has much bearing on the law relating to dying declarations, for Coltman J took refuge in the language of res gestae by treating the two deaths as part of the same transaction. Perhaps the cook's remark is best regarded as a

---

7 *R v Madobi* (1963) 6 FLR 1.
8 See *Wright d Clymer v Littler* (1761) 3 Burr 1244.
9 (1824) 2 B & C 605.
10 *R v Hind* (1860) 8 Cox CC 300. There is no authority on causing death by dangerous driving or abetting suicide.
11 (1862) 3 F & F 492 at 494; *R v Buck* [1941] 1 DLR 302. Questions of remoteness of causation and the admissibility of deceased's statements of opinion could arise but have not been discussed in the English cases.
12 (1837) 2 Mood & R 53.

statement accompanying and concerning a relevant event—the death of the master of the house.

(iv) Declarant's settled hopeless expectation of death

In the *Sussex Peerage Case*[13] Lord Denman said:

> With regard to declarations made by persons in extremis, supposing all necessary matters concurred, such as actual danger, death following, and a full apprehension at the time of the danger of death, such declarations can be received.

This suggests that the danger of death and the apprehension of it are to be treated separately, but the cases are all concerned with the second, and, in the absence of any authority, there is no point in speculating on the course that would be adopted with regard to a statement made by someone who believed himself to be dying when this was not the case although death in fact followed shortly after the making of the statement.

A number of judgments insist on the necessity of proving the apprehension of a speedy end on the part of the declarant. The words 'settled hopeless expectation' come from the judgment of Willes J in *R v Peel*.[14] They were approved by the Court of Criminal Appeal in *R v Perry*,[15] where the suggestion that there must be a settled hopeless expectation of *immediate* death was criticised.[16] We have already seen that, in *R v Mosley* the death did not occur until eleven days after the statement. In one case, the interval was as much as three weeks.[17] It is immaterial that the deceased should have entertained hopes of recovery after the statement was made, so long as he or she had abandoned all hope of life when it was made.[18] The absolute necessity of compliance with this latter requirement was vividly illustrated by *R v Jenkins*.[19] This was a murder case in which the deceased made a statement implicating the accused. The statement was written down by a magistrate's clerk who included the words that it was made 'with no hope of my recovery', and read it over to the deceased. Before signing the statement she caused it to be amended so as to read 'with no present hope of my recovery', and it was held that the statement could not be received in evidence on account of the suggestion that the deceased entertained a faint hope of recovery. The express declaration of the deceased is treated as the best proof of settled hopeless expectation of death. But other considerations may also be taken into account, such as his having talked about the devolution of his property, the fact that he took leave of his family and the fact that he made arrangements about his funeral.[20] The courts have, however, been extremely reluctant to infer knowledge on the part of the deceased of his or her impending death from the surrounding circumstances. In *R v Morgan*,[1] for instance, the deceased's head was all but cut off, but

13 (1844) 11 Cl & Fin 85 at 112.
14 (1860) 2 F & F 21.
15 [1909] 2 KB 697.
16 The suggestion came from the judgment of Lush J in *R v Osman* (1881) 15 Cox CC 1. It was queried by Charles J in *R v Gloster* (1888) 16 Cox CC 471.
17 *R v Bernadotti* (1869) 11 Cox CC 316.
18 *R v Hubbard* (1881) 14 Cox CC 565; *R v Austin* (1912) 8 Cr App Rep 27.
19 (1869) LR 1 CCR 187.
20 *R v Spilsbury* (1835) 7 C & P 187 at 190.
1 (1875) 14 Cox CC 337; *R v Cleary* (1862) 2 F & F 850; *R v Bedingfield* (1879) 14 Cox CC 341; *R v Rogers* [1950] SASR 102.

Denman J held that he could not admit the dying declaration for this reason alone and the prosecution proceeded without it.

(v) Competence of declarant

In *R v Pike*,[2] the statement of a child of four made shortly before his death was rejected at the trial of the accused for the child's murder. According to Parke B: 'It is quite impossible that she, however precocious her mind, could have had that idea of a future state which is necessary to make such a declaration admissible.' This suggests that Parke B would have excluded the dying declaration of an atheist, although it is doubtful whether the court would embark on the necessary inquiries. Now that the old restrictions on the competency of witnesses have been abolished, it is difficult to think of cases other than those of young children in which a dying declaration would have to be excluded on account of the incompetency of the declarant. No doubt the principle of *R v Pike* would apply to the statement of a lunatic. It will be recollected that, in *R v Woodcock*, the deceased was the accused's wife, but, in cases of violence, the accused's spouse is a competent witness for the prosecution, and it is hard to imagine a case of murder or manslaughter which would not come within this category.[3]

(vi) Hearsay upon hearsay

No doubt if A, an adult under a settled hopeless expectation of death who has since died of gun-shot wounds, were to tell B that X had caused those wounds, and B were to pass that information on to C, C would not be allowed to prove B's statement as evidence that X killed A; but what if A and B had both been shot and mortally wounded by the same person? If, just before he died, A were to tell B that he had seen that X was their assailant, and B in his turn, just before he died, were to say to C; 'A told me that he saw that it was X who did it', could B's hearsay statement concerning the cause of his death be proved by C? It is hardly surprising that there is no authority, but the example is sometimes cited by those who contend that, if and when the common law of hearsay in criminal cases next comes to be reformed, it should be borne in mind that second-hand hearsay may be very relevant. A's statement to B as to the cause of his death comes within a exception to the hearsay rule as does B's statement to C as to the cause of his death; for this reason the latter would be admissible under r 805 of the Federal Rules.[4]

---

2 (1829) 3 C & P 598. In *R v Perkins* (1840) 9 C & P 395 the declaration of a child of ten was received, he having been questioned about his belief whether he would be punished for lying. In *R v Austin* (above) the point was raised in argument that the deceased would, if she had lived, have been an accomplice of the accused. Nothing was said in the judgment about the need for a direction concerning the desirability of corroboration, but presumably such a direction would now be given. In *R v Drummond* (1784) 1 Leach 337 the dying declaration of a convict was excluded, but the case is no longer authoritative, so far as its particular facts are concerned, after the abolition of the incompetency of convicted witnesses.

3 If a doctor were prosecuted for manslaughter in consequence of an illegal operation performed by him on his wife with her consent would her dying declaration be admissible against him? The fifth condition of admissibility may be stated too widely in the text although it is so stated by other writers on the law of evidence.

4 'Hearsay included within hearsay is not excluded under the hearsay rule if each part of the combined statements conforms with an exception to the hearsay rule provided in these Rules.'

SECTION 4. MISCELLANEOUS COMMON LAW EXCEPTIONS TO THE HEARSAY RULE

After dealing with testimony in former proceedings, it is proposed to say a little about evidence of age because it seems to involve exceptions to the hearsay rule at certain points.

A. TESTIMONY IN FORMER PROCEEDINGS[5]

A number of statutes provides for the reception of depositions and statements of fact at subsequent stages of a criminal trial,[6] and it has been held at common law that the trial court may read a deposition taken at a coroner's inquisition when the deponent committed suicide after the inquest.[7] The statutes providing for the reception at the trial proper of depositions taken at committal proceedings when the deponent has died or is ill are to a large extent enactments of the common law.[8]

In *R v Hall*[9] the jury had disagreed at the first trial. At his second trial the accused wished to put in evidence of the deposition and a transcript of the evidence of a Crown witness who had died between the two trials. He wished to do this because the witness had been unsatisfactory in some respects. The trial judge admitted the deposition, but rejected the transcript and the Court of Appeal allowed the accused's appeal because, although he had a discretion to exclude it, the judge should have admitted the transcript. The decision turned on the common law and it seems that the conditions of admissibility of testimony in former proceedings are that the evidence should have been for or against the same accused, in relation to substantially the same facts, by a witness unable to attend the trial through death or illness[10] but not, it seems, absence from the jurisdiction.[11]

It is sometimes said that evidence of this nature, whether it was originally given at an earlier stage of the same trial or in separate proceedings, is not received under an exception to the hearsay rule. This is because it was given on oath and was subject to cross-examination. It is true that the evidence has been said to be of 'as high a nature, and as direct and immediate as viva voce testimony,'[12] but the court is deprived of the opportunity of first-hand experience of the witness's demeanour, and much of the force of cross-examination is lost if it does not take place before the tribunal which has to accept or reject the evidence. At any rate, there is no doubt that the reception

---

5 See also pp 551 and 632 above. Statutes permitting the use of such testimony have been held to be consistent with the Canadian Charter of Rights and Freedoms. *Potvin v R* (1989) 68 CR (3d) 193.
6 Eg Criminal Justice Act 1925, s 13; Criminal Law Amendment Act 1867, s 6; Magistrates' Courts Act 1980, s 105; Children and Young Persons Act 1933, s 43; Children and Young Persons Act 1963, s 27; Criminal Appeal Act 1968, s 8(4) and Sch 2; Criminal Justice Act 1988, s 26.
7 *R v Cowle* (1907) 71 JP 152.
8 *R v Beeston* (1854) Dears CC 405 at 411 and 414.
9 [1973] QB 496, [1973] 1 All ER 1. See also *R v McGregor* [1968] 1 QB 371, [1967] 2 All ER 267.
10 Finally confirmed by the Court of Appeal in *R v Thompson* [1982] QB 647 at 659, [1982] 1 All ER 907 at 914.
11 *R v Scaife* (1851) 17 QB 238 at 243.
12 *Wright v Doe d Tatham* (1834) 1 Ad & El 3 at 22.

of the evidence infringes the hearsay rule as formulated in this book; it must therefore be accounted for on the basis that it constitutes a common law exception to that rule which has to a large extent been taken over by statute.

B. EVIDENCE OF AGE

As we saw in ch XIV, one of the stock illustrations of the breadth of the hearsay rule is provided by cases in which it has been held that a witness cannot give admissible evidence of the date of his birth, and the same decision has been reached with regard to the witness's place of birth. Generally speaking, these cases give rise to no problem because age can be proved under a variety of well recognised exceptions to the hearsay rule (notably that relating to statements in public documents), by appearance, or by the recollection of past events by the person whose age is in question. It seems, however, that hearsay is allowed to creep in; where no recognised exception to the rule under which it is prohibited applies, on account of the different methods of proving the identity of a person named in a birth certificate that have been permitted by the courts in civil and criminal cases. Let us assume that A's age is to be proved by production of a certificate referring to the birth of someone named A. Clearly it will be necessary for the court to be satisfied that the A mentioned in the certificate is the same person as the A whose age is to be proved, and the courts have admitted hearsay evidence on this point without stating that they are doing so.

In *R v Weaver*,[13] it was that of a child's grandmother who, though present at its birth, was not present at the registration; in *Wilton & Co v Phillips*[14] the evidence was that of a brother of the person whose age was in issue, and he does not appear to have been present either at the birth or registration; in *Re Bulley's Settlement*,[15] there was only an affidavit sworn by the claimant to a fund stating that he had reached his majority, and in *R v Bellis*,[16] the clerk to a board of guardians simply deposed to the result of inquiries which he had previously made about the age of the prosecutrix. In each of these cases the court acted on statements which must necessarily have been based on information supplied to the makers by third parties. It is submitted that this kind of evidence of age should be expressly treated as received under an exception to the hearsay rule.

---

13 (1873) LR 2 CCR 85.
14 (1903) 19 TLR 390.
15 [1886] WN 80.
16 (1911) 6 Cr App Rep 283.

CHAPTER XVIII

The doctrine of res gestae[1]

Unlike most of the principles of the law of evidence, the doctrine of the res gestae is inclusionary. Under it evidence may be received although it infringes the rule against hearsay, the opinion rule or the rule which generally prohibits evidence of bad disposition on the part of one of the parties, and there may be other exclusionary rules which are mitigated by the operation of the doctrine. Its inclusionary effect accounts for the fact that it is discussed after all the exclusionary rules other than those relating to documentary evidence have been considered.

We have seen that the assertion that an item of evidence forms part of the res gestae roughly means that it is relevant on account of its contemporaneity with the matters under investigation.[2] It is part of the story. An endeavour is now to be made to ascertain the extent to which the categories of admissibility under this head can be precisely stated. It will be convenient to begin by considering four exceptions to the hearsay rule (still partly applicable to criminal cases) which are associated with the doctrine of res gestae.

SECTION 1. FOUR EXCEPTIONS TO THE HEARSAY RULE ASSOCIATED WITH THE DOCTRINE OF RES GESTAE IN CRIMINAL CASES

These are statements accompanying and explaining a relevant act, spontaneous statements relating to an event in issue, a person's statements concerning his contemporaneous state of mind or emotion, and a person's statements concerning his contemporaneous physical sensation. A fair amount of reference to civil cases is inevitable, but it is important to bear in mind that, if statements are to be received as evidence of the facts stated in civil proceedings, steps must now be taken to render them admissible under the Civil Evidence Act 1968. When this is done, the only question, so far as admissibility is concerned, will be the relevancy of the statement; would it have been admissible if contained in the direct oral evidence of the maker? Such special conditions of admissibility as the common law may attach to the statements (a matter on which there is uncertainty on several points) have ceased to apply in civil cases owing to the abolition of all common law exceptions to the hearsay rule.

At one time it was customary for distinguished writers, and even the most

1 Useful articles on this difficult subject are Morgan 'A Suggested Classification of Utterances Admissible as Res Gestae' (1922) 31 Yale LJ 229; Stone 'Res Gestae Reagitatae' (1939) 55 LQR 66; Nokes 'Res Gestae as Hearsay' (1954) 70 LQR 370; and Gooderson 'Res Gestae in Criminal Cases' (1956) CLJ 199; (1957) CLJ 55.
2 See p 27, above.

eminent judges,[3] to assert, apparently without qualification, that statements received as part of the res gestae are never received under an exception to the hearsay rule; but the facts of the numerous cases cited by the writers are such as to render the contention quite untenable,[4] and, so far from the assertion being repeated by eminent judges, Lord Reid once urged, in the course of the argument, that the question of res gestae could arise only if a statement were received as a hearsay statement.[5] His Lordship was of course concerned with the facts of the particular appeal; statements received as original evidence have, in the past, been said to constitute part of the res gestae on a number of occasions. The phrase, which the law of evidence could well do without, is used in a variety of senses with the result that evidence said to be received as part of the res gestae is sometimes hearsay and sometimes original.

A. STATEMENTS ACCOMPANYING AND EXPLAINING RELEVANT ACTS

1. STATEMENT AND ILLUSTRATIONS OF THE EXCEPTION

More than a hundred years ago, Parke B spoke of 'proof of the quality and intention of acts by declarations accompanying them' as an exception to the rule against hearsay that has been recognised from very early times on the ground of necessity or convenience.[6] The existence of this exception has not always been recognised by legal writers, but it is vouched for by numerous decisions. The rule was stated by Grove J to be that:

> Though you cannot give in evidence a declaration per se, yet when there is an act accompanied by a statement which is so mixed up with it as to become part of the res gestae, evidence of such a statement may be given.[7]

This does not indicate the purpose for which the evidence may be tendered, but there is a number of cases in which a statement was plainly received in order to establish the truth of its contents. This exception to the hearsay rule may be justified on the score of necessity because 'the proper person to explain and justify a voluntary act is the man who acted',[8] as well as on the ground that the fact that the statement was made contemporaneously with the act enhances the probability that it was true.

It has repeatedly been held that, if a bankrupt goes or remains abroad, his

3 Per Lord Atkinson in *R v Christie* [1914] AC 545 at 553.
4 It is sufficient to refer to *R v Foster* (1834) 6 C & P 325, a case of manslaughter by reckless driving in which the deceased's statement made shortly after the collision was admitted 'as the best possible testimony that, under the circumstances, can be adduced to show what it was that knocked the deceased down.'
5 *Ratten v R* [1972] AC 378 at 381.
6 *Wright v Doe d Tatham* (1837) 7 Ad & El 313 at 384.
7 *Howe v Malkin* (1878) 40 LT 196.
8 Per Lord Normand in *O'Hara v Central S M T Co* [1941] SC 363 at 376.

intention in doing so can be proved by his declarations which may be oral or written.[9] In the words of Lord Denman:

> The principle of admission is, that the declarations are pars rei gestae, and therefore it has been contended that they must be contemporaneous with it; but this has been decided not to be necessary, and on good grounds, for the nature and strength of the connection with the act are the material things to be looked to; and although concurrence of time cannot but be always material evidence to show the connection, yet it is by no means essential ... The substantive act proved *aliunde* is the departure from home, that is equivocal: the declaration made during the continuance of the act shows the intention with which it was done.[10]

In *Skinner & Co v Shew & Co*[11] the question was whether a third party had been induced to break off contractual negotiations with the plaintiff by the defendant's threat of legal proceedings, and the court allowed the whole of a letter from the third party to the plaintiff to be read, because it both constituted the act of repudiation and contained the third party's reasons for discontinuing the negotiations. The statement of the latter, which was not that of a witness who was testifying, was thus admitted as evidence that it was the defendant's threat which caused the breakdown of the negotiations; but it is important to note the limited purpose for which declarations accompanying an act may be proved at common law. They are evidence of the actor's intention in acting, or his reasons for doing so, but they are not admissible to prove the existence of any fact mentioned in the statement of those reasons. For instance, in *Skinner & Co v Shew & Co*, the letter from the third party to the plaintiff was not received as evidence of the fact that the defendant had made the threats mentioned—a matter which was adequately proved by a letter from the defendant to the third party.

It is generally considered that this point was overlooked in *R v Edwards*[12] where, on a charge of murder, evidence that the deceased, the accused's wife, deposited an axe and a carving knife with a neighbour, saying that she felt safer with them out of the way, was received, apparently in order to prove previous threats by the accused.

2. CONDITIONS OF ADMISSIBILITY

It seems that there are also three conditions with which the statements must comply before they can be received under this head—they must relate to the act, they must be roughly contemporaneous with it and they must be made by the actor. Before these conditions are considered, it should be stressed that the act which the statements accompany must itself be in issue or relevant to the issue. The point was pithily put by Coltman J, when he said he was not aware:

9 *Rawson v Haigh* (1824) 2 Bing 99; *Bateman v Bailey* (1794) 5 Term Rep 512; *Robson v Kemp* (1802) 4 Esp 233; *Rouch v Great Western Rly Co* (1841) 1 QB 51. These cases should be distinguished from *Ridley v Gyde* (1832) 9 Bing 349, and *Smith v Cramer* (1835) 1 Bing NC 585, where the debtor's statements were received as original evidence.

10 *Rouch v Great Western Rly Co* (1841) 1 QB 51 at 62.

11 [1894] 2 Ch 581; *Re Workmen's Compensation Acts, Cullen v Clarke* [1963] IR 368.

12 (1872) 12 Cox CC 230.

of any case where the act done is in its nature irrelevant to the issue and where the declaration is *per se* inadmissible in which it has been held that the union of the two has rendered them admissible.[13]

The statement is, so to speak, parasitic on the act with regard to its admissibility. Unless the act can be shown to be of at least some possible relevance without reference to the statement the latter may not be proved as evidence of the truth of its contents.

(i) Statement must relate to the act it accompanies

In *R v Bliss*[14] the question was whether a road was public or private, and it was sought to prove a statement by a deceased owner of adjacent land who, when planting a tree, said that he was doing so on the boundary of his estate. This evidence was rejected because the declaration had no connection with the act done, and the doing of the act could not make such a declaration evidence.

(ii) Contemporaneity

The *raison d'être* of this exception to the hearsay rule is that the statement throws light on the nature of a relevant act because of its proximity to it. In the absence of such proximity, the statement would lack connection with the act and become a mere hearsay assertion about it. This distinction was taken by Lord Denman in *Peacock v Harris*[15] when he said: '[A] contemporaneous declaration may be admissible as part of a transaction, but an act done cannot be varied or qualified by insulated declarations made at a later time.' Contemporaneity is a matter of degree, and no useful purpose would be served by an elaborate citation of authority.

(iii) Statement must be by the actor

In *Howe v Malkin*,[16] it was sought to prove a statement concerning the boundaries of property made by the plaintiff's father contemporaneously with the performance of some work on the land by builders, and the evidence was rejected as it did not come within the exception to the hearsay rule now under consideration because the declaration was by one person, and the accompanying act was that of another. Phipson once said that the admissibility of statements accompanying acts is by no means so strictly confined because it is everyday practice in criminal cases to receive the declarations of the victim as well as the assailant, while in cases of conspiracy, riot and the like, declarations of all concerned in the common object, although not defendants, are admissible.[17] It seems, however, that, so far as the first of these points is concerned, the declarations of the victim are received under the next exception to the hearsay rule to be discussed, while, so far as the second point is concerned, the declarations of rioters are usually

13 *Wright v Doe d Tatham* (1837) 7 Ad & El 313 at 361. Though it now seems that an evidentiary issue such as an act of identification may suffice, *R v McCay* [1990] Crim LR 338.
14 (1837) 7 Ad & El 550.
15 (1836) 5 Ad & El 449.
16 (1878) 40 LT 196.
17 Phipson *Law on Evidence* (11th edn) 83.

received as original evidence,[18] or as assertions of their states of mind, and those of conspirators as admissions by agents.[19]

B. SPONTANEOUS STATEMENTS RELATING TO AN EVENT IN ISSUE MADE BY PARTICIPANTS OR OBSERVERS

1. STATEMENT AND ILLUSTRATIONS OF THE EXCEPTION

As stated above[20] hearsay statements may be admitted in civil proceedings only if they comply with the conditions laid down by the Civil Evidence Act 1968, and neither explicitly,[1] nor implicitly,[2] is any provision made for the admission of res gestae statements under that legislation.

The exception does however remain in force in relation to criminal proceedings, and has recently been clarified by the Privy Council,[3] and re-affirmed by the House of Lords.[4] Much of the difficulty of this exception had been created by the very strict view of the ambit of the exception taken in *R v Bedingfield*.[5] It is no longer necessary to consider that decision in detail since its authority was drastically weakened by *Ratten*, and it was finally and formally overruled by *Andrews*. Those decisions provide the appropriate starting point for any discussion of the modern law.

Ratten was convicted in Victoria of murdering his wife by shooting her. His defence was that the gun had discharged accidentally while he was cleaning it. There was evidence that his wife was alive and well at about 1.12 p.m., and the accused said that, after he had telephoned for an ambulance following the shooting, the police telephoned him at about 1.20. The prosecution adduced the evidence of a telephone operator who swore that, at about 1.15 a woman had telephoned from the accused's number asking in an hysterical tone for the police, and that after losing contact with the caller she had called the police, who in their turn called the accused's number. The Judicial Committee held that the telephone operator's evidence had been rightly received. Their ratio decidendi was that the evidence was not hearsay because the telephone call was being used to contradict the accused's statement that the only outgoing call from his number at the relevant time was that for the ambulance, by which time his wife was undoubtedly dead. Furthermore, the operator's evidence that the caller was a woman, speaking in an hysterical voice and expressing a wish to be connected to the police, was something from which the jury could, if they were so minded, infer that Mrs Ratten was in a state of anxiety or fear owing to an existing or impending emergency.

18 *R v Lord Gordon* (1781) 21 State Tr 485.
19 See p 589 above.
20 Ch XVI, and p 657.
1 S 9 which incorporates many of the old common law exceptions does not incorporate res gestae statements.
2 The general conditions for admissibility under ss 2, 4 and 5 bear little resemblance to the conditions for the admission of res gestae statements at common law.
3 In *Ratten v R* [1972] AC 378, [1971] 3 All ER 801.
4 In *R v Andrews* [1987] AC 281, [1987] 1 All ER 513.
5 (1879) 14 Cox CC 341.

On this view the jury was not asked to assume that any assertion of fact made by the caller was true, but the Judicial Committee also dealt with the case on the assumption that the words used by the caller involved an assertion of the truth of some fact stated, for example that she was being attacked by the accused. This raised the question of the proper criteria for the reception of hearsay statements under this head of the res gestae doctrine. Lord Wilberforce said :[6]

[T]he test should be not the uncertain one whether the making of the statement was in some sense part of the event or transaction.[7]. . . As regards statements made after the event it must be for the judge, by preliminary ruling, to satisfy himself that the statement was so clearly made in circumstances of spontaneity or involvement in the event that the possibility of concoction[8] can be disregarded. Conversely, if he considers that the statement was made by way of narrative of a detached prior event so that the speaker was so disengaged from it as to be able to construct or adapt his account, he should exclude it. And the same must in principle be true of statements made before the event.

This spontaneity test was applied in a number of subsequent cases by the Court of Appeal. In *R v Nye*; *R v Loan*[9] Loan was charged with an assault on the victim, immediately after a car which the prosecution contended had been driven by Nye and in which Loan was a passenger, had run into the back of the victim's car. The police were summoned and arrived after a short interval during which the victim had been sitting in his car recovering from the effects of the assault. He then identified Loan, and not Nye, as his assailant. The court held that the identification was spontaneous as he had not been in a condition to concoct a story while recovering from the blows which he had received. After suggesting a gloss to Lord Wilberforce's test according to which the judge must be satisfied of the absence not merely of concoction, but also of error, the court held that the case was one in which it was safe to assume that the victim had not made a mistake. The test was further applied in *R v Turnbull*[10] to prove a victim's identification of his assailant very soon after an assault from which he subsequently died; in *R v Boyle*[11] a statement made by an old lady from whom the accused had removed a clock was admitted to show that the accused had removed it without her consent; in *R v O'Shea*[12] the statements of an elderly man who had jumped from a window were admitted to show his reason for doing so; and finally at the trial in *R v Andrews* an identifying statement was received in facts almost identical to those in *Turnbull*.

In *R v Andrews* it was argued that *Bedingfield* had survived *Ratten*, and so provided an opportunity for the House of Lords to restate the law, which it did in five numbered propositions :[13]

---

6 At 389.
7 This test seems none the less to have been applied by the High Court of Australia in *Vocisano v Vocisano* (1974) 130 CLR 267, 3 ALR 97, but see *Walton v R* (1989) 84 ALR 59 where Mason CJ suggests at 68 that those remarks were obiter dicta and that the rule in Australia is the same as that in England.
8 Distortion or error (see below).
9 (1977) 66 Cr App Rep 252.
10 (1985) 80 Cr App Rep 104.
11 (6 March 1986, unreported), though in *R v Andrews* Lord Ackner doubted whether the evidence had been hearsay at all in that case.
12 (24 July 1986, unreported).
13 At 300, 520.

(1) The primary question which the judge must ask himself is: can the possibility of concoction or distortion be disregarded? (2) To answer that question the judge must first consider the circumstances in which the particular statement was made, in order to satisfy himself that the event was so unusual or startling or dramatic as to dominate the thoughts of the victim, so that his utterance was an instinctive reaction to that event, thus giving no real opportunity for reasoned reflection. In such a situation the judge would be entitled to conclude that the involvement or the pressure of the event would exclude the possibility of concoction or distortion, providing that the statement was made in conditions of approximate but not exact contemporaneity. (3) In order for a statement to be sufficiently 'spontaneous' it must be so closely associated with the event which has excited the statement that it can fairly be stated that the mind of the declarant was still dominated by the event. Thus the judge must be satisfied that the event which provided the trigger mechanism for the statement was still operative. The fact that the statement was made in answer to a question is but one factor to consider under this heading. (4) Quite apart from the time factor, there may be special features of the case, which relate to the possibility of concoction or distortion . . . The judge must be satisfied that the circumstances were such that, having regard to . . . [such] special feature[s]. . ., there was no possibility of any concoction or distortion to the advantage of the maker or the disadvantage of the accused. (5) As to the possibility of error in the facts narrated in the statement, if only the ordinary fallibility of human recollection is relied upon, this goes to the weight attached to and not to the admissibility of the statement and is therefore a matter for the jury. However, here again there may be special features that may give rise to the possibility of error . . . In such circumstances the trial judge must consider whether he can exclude the possibilities of error.

It should be noted that the House of Lords appears to have accepted the gloss made in *Nye and Loan* with regard to error, though only where it arises from some special feature. A further gloss added by *Andrews* itself equates the danger of distortion with that of concoction, and again requires that the inference arise from some special feature of the case, presumably based upon evidence admitted, or at least to be admitted. More generic weaknesses go only to weight.

It seems immaterial that the statement is elicited by questioning, so long as the principle of 'spontaneity' can be held to have been satisfied. Perhaps the analogy of the instigation of complaints in sexual cases may be thought apposite.[14] Spontaneity will partly be a function of the intrinsic excitement of the event, partly of the declarant's degree of involvement in it, and partly of the separation in time between the event and the declaration.[15] In one case,[16] where the event was no more than a collision causing damage to a coach driven by the declarant, his identification of the accused as the other driver some twenty minutes later was not regarded as sufficiently spontaneous. If these conditions are taken into account by the trial judge an appellate court is unlikely to interfere with his decision. It must be stressed however that where the declarant is available as a witness he should normally be called, and not only is the statement likely to be excluded if there is any suspicion of an attempt deliberately to shield a witness from cross-

---

14 See above p 284.
15 In Canada proneness of the class of witness to concoct has been taken into account in relation to the acceptability of a given temporal separation between event and declaration, *R v Khan* (1988) 44 CCC (3d) 197 at 210.
16 *Tobi v Nicholas* (1987) 86 Cr App Rep 323. See also *Re Plumbers and Gasfitters* (1987) 72 ALR 415 at 434.

examination, but even when a witness is not present owing to the incompetence of the prosecution the same attitude is likely to be adopted.[17]

2. CONDITIONS OF ADMISSIBILITY

Two further questions, not mentioned by the House of Lords in *Andrews* might nevertheless, in the light of remarks in some of the cases, be regarded as further conditions for admissibility. Must the statement concern the event in issue 'directly'? Must there be other evidence of the event than the statement itself in order to render the latter admissible?

(i) Directness

The first question is prompted by Lord Normand's treatment of *R v Gibson*[18] in *Teper v R.*[19] Teper was charged with arson, and the Judicial Committee held that the trial judge should have rejected a police officer's evidence of the remark of an unidentified bystander made to a passing motorist, said by the officer to resemble the accused, expressing surprise at the fact that he was going away from the vicinity of his burning shop, such evidence having been tendered in rebuttal of the defence of alibi. There was every reason why the statement should have been excluded. It was of dubious contemporaneity, having been made some twenty-five minutes after the fire began, and there was no evidence that it was made by someone who witnessed the earlier stages of the conflagration. Furthermore, it did not relate to the commission of the alleged crime at all; but Lord Normand said:

> For identification purposes in a criminal trial the event with which the words sought to be proved must be so connected as to form part of the res gestae, is the commission of the crime itself, the throwing of the stone, the striking of the blow, the setting fire to the building or whatever the criminal act may be.

The allusion to the throwing of the stone is a reference to *R v Gibson*, a case of unlawful wounding in which it was conceded on appeal that the prosecutor's evidence that he heard a woman, who was not called as a witness, say, immediately after he had been struck by a stone, 'The man who threw the stone went in there' ought to have been rejected, although the accused was found in the house to which the woman had pointed. Lord Normand agreed that these words were closely connected in time and place with the assault:

> But they were not directly connected with that event itself. They were not words spontaneously forced on the woman by the sight of the assault, but were prompted by the sight of a man quitting the scene of the assault and they were spoken with the purpose of helping to bring him to justice.

This reasoning is as pedantic as that by which it is sometimes sought to support *R v Bedingfield*[20] namely, that there were two transactions in that

17 Ibid.
18 (1887) 18 QBD 537.
19 [1952] AC 480 at 487. Reference may also be made to Lord Normand's judgment in *O'Hara v Central S M T Co* 1941 SC 363.
20 (1879) 14 Cox CC 341.

case, the assault, and the quest for assistance; the requirement that the statement should have directly concerned the event may be valid when the question is whether the statement can be treated as the equivalent of an act of identification, but it would still seem unduly technical to say that the remark with which *Gibson's* case was concerned did not 'directly' concern the throwing of the stone.[1] In many cases strict restriction to the act of commission of the relevant crime is inappropriate in the light of the reasoning in *Ratten*. The event exciting the statement, and guaranteeing the absence of concoction, may easily be something other than the commission of the crime, say the sight of a pickpocket being chased. This is doubly frustrating where, as in *Teper*, not only was the event, the recognition of the accused incognito at the site of his burning shop, just as exciting whenever it occurred, but his presence there at either time was equally fatal to his alibi.

It is difficult, if not impossible, to apply the requirement that the statement should 'directly' concern the event to cases in which it was made shortly before the occurrence of the event. Nevertheless the requirement was included in cl 37 of the draft Bill attached to the 11th Report of the Criminal Law Revision Committee which read as follows:

> In any [criminal] proceedings a statement made by a person otherwise than in a document shall be admissible as evidence of any fact stated therein if—
>   (a) it directly concerns an event in issue in those proceedings which took place in the presence, sight or hearing of that person, and
>   (b) it was made by him as an immediate reaction to that event . . .[2]

(ii) Other evidence

As Lord Wilberforce pointed out in *Ratten v R*,[3] if it were not the case that there must be other evidence than that contained in the statement of the maker's association with the event, the statement would be lifting itself into the area of admissibility, but he did not regard this as something which prohibited any reference to the statement on the question of admissibility. In *Ratten's* case the other evidence may be said to have consisted of the accused's admission that the deceased met her death at his hands albeit, on his account of the facts, accidentally. In the South African case of *R v Taylor*,[4] where, on a charge of culpable homicide, witnesses near to the room in which the deceased was killed heard her exclaim 'John, don't hit me any more or you will kill me', a serious question of admissibility might have arisen had they not also heard the sounds of a scuffle.

3. RATIONALE AND UTILITY

As developed in the United States, the justification of this exception to the hearsay rule is the probability of the truth of the statement which is said to

---

1 *Gibson's* case will require reconsideration in the light of Lord Wilberforce's approval ([1972] AC 378 at 391) of *People v De Simone* (1919) 121 NE 761.
2 This clause was not included in the Police and Criminal Evidence Act 1984 or the Criminal Justice Act 1988.
3 [1972] AC 378 at 391.
4 (1961) 3 SA 614. For other South African cases in which the statements seem to have been treated as original evidence, see *R v Le Roux* (1897) 14 SC 424; *R v De Lew* [1927] NPD 276, and *R v Nichols* [1931] NPD 550.

be guaranteed to some extent by the fact that the event to which it is related was an exciting one.[5] The theory may be said to be that there are certain occurrences which will shake the truth out of the most consummate liar. After *Ratten* and *Andrews*, a similar justification may come to be recognised in this country; but the psychology underlying the assumption has been questioned,[6] and it is open to question whether special provision should be made in a code of evidence for the reception of hearsay statements of the kind we have been considering. Were those responsible for the Civil Evidence Act 1968, right in not including a special clause relating to such statements? Were the members of the Criminal Law Revision Committee right to include such a clause? So far as the first question is concerned, the statements in all the cases we have been considering could have been rendered admissible in civil proceedings by virtue of the Civil Evidence Act 1968; but a statement by a young child cannot be made admissible under the 1968 Act and it can be argued that a special res gestae clause is desirable to cater for such a case. For example, in civil proceedings on facts such as those of *Sparks v R*,[7] in which the child's hearsay statement would be inadmissible even if it could be brought within the res gestae principle at common law. It is, however, very doubtful whether it is necessary to have a special clause to cater for this remote contingency.

There is rather more justification for such a clause in the case of criminal proceedings because, in addition to the incompetency of young children, there are the facts that the accused's spouse is compellable for the prosecution only in those cases specified in the Police and Criminal Evidence Act 1984, s 80(3), and the co-accused is not a compellable witness for the accused, nor even competent for the prosecution. Nonetheless, it may well be thought unnecessary to complicate an evidence code with special clauses to cover comparatively remote contingencies.[8]

C. STATEMENTS CONCERNING THE MAKER'S CONTEMPORANEOUS STATE OF MIND OR EMOTION

1. STATEMENT AND ILLUSTRATIONS OF THE EXCEPTION

A person's declaration of his contemporaneous state of mind or emotion are admissible as evidence of the existence of such state of mind or emotion.

In *Thomas v Connell*[9] it was held on appeal that a bankrupt's statement that he knew he was insolvent was admissible to prove his knowledge of that fact at the time when he made a payment to the defendant. The statement was of course no evidence of the insolvency, and this point was emphasised by Parke B when he said:

---

5 VI *Wigmore* ch 59.
6 Hutchins and Slesinger 'Some Observations on the Law of Evidence' (1928) 28 Col LR 432, discussed in Australian Law Reform Commission Research Paper No 3 p 37.
7 [1964] AC 964, [1964] 1 All ER 727. The statement was made about an hour and a half after the assault. Were the facts to recur in criminal proceedings, it is just possible that the statement could be held admissible as part of the res gestae in view of the new approach in *Ratten v R* [1972] AC 378, [1971] 3 All ER 801.
8 But see 11th Report of the Criminal Law Revision Committee, para 261.
9 (1838) 4 M & W 267.

If a fact be proved aliunde, it is clear that a particular person's knowledge of that fact may be proved by his declaration. . . and under the impression that such evidence was admissible after proof of the fact to which it related, I postponed the reception of such declaration in a cause of *Craven v Halliley* tried by me at York until after the fact was proved.

A person's declarations may likewise be proved in order to show his belief that defamatory statements referred to a particular individual,[10] his political opinions,[11] his affection for his spouse,[12] his dislike of his child,[13] and his fear of some burglars which prevented him from reporting their conduct to the police.[14]

2. THE REQUIREMENT OF CONTEMPORANEITY

The only condition precedent to the admissibility of statements under this head is that they should relate to the maker's contemporaneous state of mind or emotion. The cases show that, as in the situations which have been previously discussed, contemporaneity is a question of degree. In *R v Vincent, Frost and Edwards*[15] the question was whether a public meeting caused alarm, and a policeman was allowed to swear that a number of bystanders had told him that the assembly frightened them. Although the report is silent on the point, the complaints must in some sense have referred to the past feelings of the complainants. In *R v Kay*,[16] on the other hand, where the question was whether a woman was aware, at the time of her marriage, that she had been falsely described in the banns, her mother's evidence that the woman said, after the marriage, that she knew of the false description before it took place, was held to be inadmissible.

3. LIMITED PURPOSE FOR WHICH DECLARATIONS OF CONTEMPORANEOUS STATE OF MIND OR EMOTION MAY BE RECEIVED

The reason for this exception to the hearsay rule is usually regarded as being that a person's statements are the best, and sometimes the only, means of demonstrating his state of mind. To that extent even direct statements of state of mind, comprehending such states as knowledge, memory, belief, opinion, intention and emotion, may be accepted notwithstanding any technical objection to such a means of proof as hearsay.[17] It is however one thing to accept breach of the hearsay rule so far as demonstration of the existence of the given state of mind is concerned, and quite another to determine its relevance to the issues in dispute.

10 *Du Bost v Beresford* (1810) 2 Camp 511; *Cook v Ward* (1830) 4 Moo & P 99; *Jozwiak v Sadek* [1954] 1 All ER 3.
11 *R v Tooke* (1794) 25 St Tr 344 at 390.
12 *Trelawney v Coleman* (1817) 1 B & Ald 90; *Willis v Bernard* (1832) 8 Bing 376.
13 *R v Hagan* (1873) 12 Cox CC 357.
14 *R v Gandfield* (1846) 2 Cox CC 43.
15 (1840) 9 C & P 275.
16 (1887) 16 Cox CC 292.
17 In some situations the line between hearsay and original evidence is very fine in this area.

It has already been noted[18] that in *Thomas v Connell*[19] the bankrupt's statement of his knowledge of his insolvency could not be used as a basis for inferring the fact of such insolvency. It had to be proved by other means. The converse was held in *R v Gunnell*[20] where it was decided that a statement that a fact exists is not admissible as evidence of the knowledge of the recipient of such a statement that the fact exists. In that case the issue was whether the fact of Gunnell's fraud was known before his examination in bankruptcy. If it had not previously been disclosed he could take advantage of a special statutory defence. The prosecution called on Marshall to testify that another, Andrews, had told him of Gunnell's fraud before the date of the examination, and that hence it had not been disclosed, in the sense of made known for the first time, during the bankruptcy proceedings themselves. It can be seen that the inference that it had been disclosed rested upon double hearsay, what Gunnell told Andrews, and what Andrews told the witness. It is not however clear why the exception to the hearsay rule cannot be applied twice. Each speaker is declaring or demonstrating his own state of mind, namely his 'knowledge' of Gunnell's fraud. It may be true that information acquired at third-hand is generally less cogent than information acquired at second-hand, but it is not clear that it is different in kind. The real question should have been whether on the construction of the statute it had become so remote as to be accounted rumour rather than knowledge.

Such questions are particularly acute in relation to the states of mind of knowledge, memory and belief. The court must be specially sensitive to avoid infringement of the hearsay rule, and scrupulous to inhibit inference of the underlying fact, known, remembered or believed. In some cases, such as *Thomas v Connell*, the issue directly involves the relevant state of mind. It is more tricky if it is merely argued that the state of mind is relevant to facts is issue. The problem is well illustrated by the case of *R v Blastland*.[1] The accused was charged with the murder of a young boy with whom he admitted having homosexual relations early on the evening of the boy's murder, though he denied otherwise harming him in any way. He claimed that a third man had been lurking near by, and so implied that another had the opportunity to commit the crime. His description of the man agreed with that of a local homosexual who was interviewed by the police, and in relation to whom statements were taken from others. Those statements were made available to the defence, and the accused wished to adduce evidence that the third man had made statements indicating his knowledge of the killing before it had become public. The House of Lords held evidence of such knowledge inadmissible, adopting a very narrow view of its relevancy. It was suggested that because there were a number of innocent explanations of the acquisition of that knowledge it would be no more than speculative to infer that it had been acquired in the course of the commission of the crime, and it thus had insufficient relevance to any issue in the case. The court was further struck by the anomaly that would be created by the rule that a direct

---

18 Above p 667.
19 (1838) 4 M & W 267.
20 (1867) 16 Cox CC 154.
 1 [1986] AC 41, [1985] 2 All ER 1095. See also *R v Roberts* (1984) 80 Cr App Rep 89, a case very similar on its facts.

'confession' of guilt by the third party would be inadmissible,[2] if such a statement were to be admitted. It would be tantamount to allowing evidence to prove indirectly that which could not be proved directly. This is the classic argument against allowing circumstantial undermining of the hearsay rule. It could be met in either of two ways. First, by distinguishing between the circumstantial and testimonial aspects of confessions, treating the former, in this instance exhibitions of knowledge, as more akin to real evidence discovered pursuant to the testimonial narrative.[3] Alternatively the exception for statements against interest by deceased persons could be expanded to include statements by living persons against penal interest.[4] The anomaly aside, it becomes a matter of determining whether evidence of the third party's knowledge of the commission of the crime at the particular time is sufficiently relevant to the accused's defence to justify its admission. It is certainly arguable, especially in the case of someone accused of so heinous a crime, that little harm would have been done by admitting the evidence, allowing its cogency to be attacked by reference to the alternative innocent explanations, and leaving its ultimate weight to be determined by the jury.

4. DECLARATIONS OF INTENTION

Declarations of intention need special consideration because proof of intention is required in very many different legal contexts, and is generally regarded as being particularly difficult to establish without reference to its declaration by the person in question. This view was very clearly expressed by Mellish LJ in *Sugden v Lord St Leonards*:[5]

> wherever it is material to prove the state of a person's mind, or what was passing in it, and what were his intentions, there you may prove what he said, because that is the only means by which you can find out what his intentions are.

The concluding words are greatly exaggerated since intention very often is proved in the absence of any express declaration of it by the relevant party. It is a curious phenomenon that declarations of intention are more prone to be used to establish the performance of the act intended, than are declarations of knowledge, memory or belief, perhaps because the clash with the hearsay rule is less overt. The phenomenon is surprising because it can hardly be doubted that the inference to the commission of the act from a statement of intention to perform it is more precarious than the inference of commission from a statement of memory of having performed it. Given equal sincerity in either case, it is more likely that something will occur to frustrate a sincere intention to act than that memory of having acted will be mistaken. Of course in either case there will be considerable variation in reliability depending upon the distance in time between the statement and the act, and in relation to different degrees of detail of the act intended or remembered.

---

2 As hearsay not falling within any exception to the rule at common law. It is noteworthy that just such 'confessions' had been made at various stages by the third man, although subsequently retracted.

3 As suggested by Andrews 'Involuntary Confessions and Illegally Obtained Evidence in Criminal Cases' [1963] Crim LR 15, 77.

4 In the United States this result will in many cases be achieved by r 804(b)(3) of the Federal Rules of Evidence, see above pp 570, 642.

5 (1876) 1 PD 154 at 251.

Since there is usually little question but that the existence of intention can be proved by way of express declaration, whether by exception to the hearsay rule or as original evidence, the focus of attention must again concentrate on the relevancy of the utterance. In the case of declarations of intention questions may be raised in relation to the persistence of any such intention, and its eligibility to prove the commission of the act intended. These will be considered separately.

(i) Prospectant or retrospectant continuance of intention

In *Robson v Kemp*[6] Lord Ellenborough said: 'If the declarations of the bankrupt had been made before his act (a fraudulent assignment) they may show with what intention it was done', and in *Re Fletcher, Reading v Fletcher*,[7] Cozens-Hardy MR said 'It is common practice, particularly in criminal cases, to prove intention at a particular time by words and acts at a subsequent date'. A's declaration of intention on 1 January is received as testimonial evidence of that fact under an exception to the rule against hearsay, and the existence of the intention is then treated as an item of circumstantial evidence to prove the continuance of the intention up to 1 February, or its antecedent existence on 1 December. Obviously a point will be reached at which A's intention on 1 January is so remote as to be irrelevant to the question of his intention at another time, and, equally clearly, it is impossible to lay down rigid rules to determine when that point will be reached.

The danger that evidence will be concocted is something that must be borne in mind when the admissibility of the parties' declarations of intention is considered for it is on account of this danger that self-serving statements of the parties are generally rejected at common law. Illustrations of the rejection of such statements have already been given in ch VII when the general prohibition on the proof of a witness's prior consistent statements was discussed. A party's self-serving statements are, generally speaking, equally inadmissible at common law when he is not called as a witness. This is well illustrated by the exclusion of the accused's self-serving declarations of intention in criminal cases decided before he was allowed to give evidence on his own behalf.[8]

In *R v Petcherini*[9] it was held that a priest charged with blasphemously burning the scriptures could not call witnesses to prove statements made by him in sermons before the occasion in respect of which he was prosecuted. He contended that he had said that only immoral books should be destroyed and Crampton J said:

> Declarations made two or three days, or even a week, previous to the transaction in question cannot be evidence, otherwise it would be easy for a man to lay grounds for escaping the consequences of his wrongful acts by making such declarations.

---

6 (1802) 4 Esp 233.
7 [1917] 1 Ch 339 at 342.
8 It remains the case in relation to wholly exculpatory statements, whether of fact or of intent.
9 (1855) 7 Cox CC 79. See also the statement of Eyre CJ in *R v Hardy* (1794) 24 State Tr 199 at 1093 (quoted at p 2 above).

(ii) **Previous declarations of intention as evidence of the performance of a subsequent act**[10]

It remains to be considered whether a declaration of intention to perform an act is admissible to prove that the act was performed. It should first be noted that where the declaration is by a party in civil proceedings it may be proved as an admission by his opponent, and in criminal cases it seems that the prosecution can prove statements of intent by the accused on a similar basis, for example on a charge of murder that the accused threatened to kill the deceased.[11]

In civil proceedings the problem has mainly been discussed in relation to wills. The leading case is *Sugden v Lord St Leonards*[12] where the testator was known to have taken great care in drafting his will, but after his death all that remained in the box thought to contain it were a number of codicils and holograph notes apparently made at the time of drafting it. His daughter, who had acted as housekeeper, was however able to remember its terms, and her version of the will was accorded probate. On appeal the question arose of what use could be made of the pre-testamentary[13] declarations of the testator, principally deduced from his holograph notes. It was held by the majority[14] of the five judge court that such pre-testamentary declarations were admissible as proof of the contents of the will. This decision found little favour with the House of Lords, and was said in *Woodward v Goulstone* to have reached 'the very verge of the law, and was not to be extended'. Some support for it can be found in earlier decisions[15] relating to disputes about the terms of executed wills, and in the light of the criticisms of the House of Lords[16] its effects may extend no further.

In criminal cases the English authorities are in some disarray. Evidence of a declaration to visit the accused, who was subsequently accused of murdering the declarant, was excluded in two Old Bailey cases, once[17] by Lord Cockburn CJ on the basis 'that it was only a statement of intention which might or might not have been carried out.' On the other hand in *R v Buckley*[18] a declaration by a policeman that he was going to observe the suspected

---

10 See Hutchins and Slesinger 'State of Mind to Prove an Act' (1929) 38 Yale LJ 283.
11 *R v Ball* [1911] AC 47 at 68; *R v Williams* (1986) 84 Cr App Rep 299. See also *Plomp v R* (1964) 110 CLR 234; *R v Andrews* [1987] 1 Qd R 21.
12 (1876) 1 PD 154.
13 He had in addition made post-testamentary declarations of the contents of the will, and these were also held admissible evidence of its contents. The pronouncements of the court as to both categories were however regarded as unnecessary for its decision, and thus strictly, no more than obiter dicta, see Lord Cockburn CJ at 224, Jessel MR at 243, and Mellish LJ at 250.
14 Lord Cockburn CJ, with whom Baggalley JA and James LJ agreed; Jessel MR thought that even then they were admissible only as circumstantial evidence; and Mellish LJ was prepared to admit them only to corroborate other evidence.
15 See *Doe d Shallcross v Palmer* (1851) 16 QB 747; *Johnson v Lyford* (1868) LR 1 P & D 546.
16 (1886) 11 App Cas 469 at 485. Though there are a few cases where such evidence seems to have been admitted without argument on this point, see *Marshall v Wild Rose (Owners)* [1910] AC 486 (declaration that deceased workman was going on deck to get some air); *Tracey v Kelly* (1930) WC & Ins Rep 214 (declaration that leaving room to relieve nature). See also *Dobson v Morris* (1985) 4 NSWLR 681 (declaration of destination of journey) where the question was considered.
17 *R v Wainwright* (1875) 13 Cox CC 171, see also *R v Pook*, ibid 172.
18 (1873) 13 Cox CC 293.

criminal activities of the man accused of his murder was admitted by Lush J on assize.[19] In that case no question of hearsay was however raised.

The issue has since been considered only sporadically. In *R v Thomson*,[20] an appeal against conviction for abortion on a woman who had died before trial, it was held that her statement of intention to perform the operation herself had been rightly excluded as evidence for the defence together with her later assertions that she had procured her own miscarriage. The reception of such later assertions as testimonial evidence of their truth would have been an obvious infringement of the hearsay rule, and it may have been felt, much as was argued in *Blastland*,[1] that it would be anomalous to allow in the declarations of intention to prove indirectly what more direct assertions were not allowed to prove.[2]

There is no more modern English case in which the issue has been squarely addressed.[3] It has however been recently considered by the High Court of Australia in *Walton v R*.[4] The accused was charged with the murder of his wife, after having lured her into meeting him in the local town centre. After receiving a telephone call in which she declared that the caller was her husband, she said that she intended to meet him in the town centre. The High Court admitted evidence of such declarations, despite any hearsay element, as original evidence of her intentions from which the jury could draw appropriate inferences, though they could not use them as direct testimonial evidence, of her having met her husband at the appointed place. In so admitting the declarations of intention the High Court appears to have accepted a famous line of American authority stemming from *Mutual Life Insurance Co v Hillmon*.[5] In that case insurance had been taken out on Hillmon's life, and a claim was made in respect of a man killed in the wilds of Colorado. The defendants claimed that the body was not that of Hillmon, but that of one Walters, who had written letters declaring his intention of accompanying Hillmon on the relevant trip. At the trial[6] the judge excluded these letters as hearsay, but the Supreme Court of the United States held[7] that they were admissible as relevant original evidence of Walters' intentions. Despite subsequent criticism of this decision by the Supreme Court,[8] and by other

---

19 After consulting his colleague Mellor J.
20 [1912] 3 KB 19.
 1 Above p 668.
 2 Considerations of just such an anomaly led the majority in *Sugden v Lord St Leonards* to apply the same rules as to both pre- and post-testamentary declarations.
 3 In *R v Moghal* (1977) 65 Cr App Rep 56 dicta suggested that a declaration of intent to kill by the principal offender, as conceded by the prosecution despite her previous acquittal, would have been admissible at the trial of an alleged accomplice, though these dicta were doubted by the House of Lords in *Blastland* at 60, 1104.
 4 (1989) 84 ALR 59, see Odgers '*Walton v The Queen*—Hearsay Revolution' (1989) 13 Crim LJ 201. See also *R v Hendrie* (1985) 37 SASR 581 where the victim's declaration of intention to have repairs done to her bedroom by the accused was admitted to explain the absence of a struggle in any other part of the house, her raped and murdered body having been found in the bedroom.
 5 145 US 284 (1892).
 6 In fact the third trial, the jury having disagreed at the first two, and there were a further three, the last of which also found in favour of the plaintiff only to be reversed by the Supreme Court. The issue was finally settled in the widow's favour by the insurance companies.
 7 For an account of the genesis of this decision see Maguire 'The Hillmon Case—Thirty Three Years After' (1925) 38 Harv LR 109.
 8 By Cardozo J in *Shepard v US* 290 US 96 (1933).

eminent American judges,[9] it has been extended to allow such declarations of intention to implicate second parties, and to permit proof of declarations as to past facts in interpretation of such declarations.[10] It is however generally recognised in the United States that the admission of declarations for such purposes can be permitted only by way of exception to the hearsay rule.[11] Such extensions were also involved in the reasoning accepted in *Walton*, though without the invocation of any special exception. It is submitted that in England it would be necessary to subsume any such evidence under an exception, presumably this one. In view of the criticism of any such extension by the House of Lords in *Woodward v Goulstone*[12] and in *Blastland*, and of the reluctance to create wholly new exceptions exhibited in *Myers v DPP*[13] it seems unlikely that the same development would be likely to take place here, especially to the disadvantage of the accused in a criminal prosecution.

5. THE PUBLIC'S STATE OF MIND[14]

A New Zealand judge has invoked the decision in *R v Vincent, Frost and Edwards*[15] in aid of the solution of a problem in relation to the law of hearsay evidence which is more likely to arise in civil than in criminal cases. The problem concerns the admissibility of market research surveys. For example, the plaintiff in a passing off action alleges that members of the public believe that the goods sold under a particular description by the defendant are identical with his. Extensive inquiries by means of questionnaires are made on his behalf. How can the results of these inquiries be placed before the court by admissible evidence? One answer given by Mahon J[16] was that the person responsible for the questionnaires should simply state the purport of the answers received as hearsay statements of the beliefs of those who gave them just as the policeman deposed to what the bystanders had told him about the fears excited in them by the public meeting in *R v Vincent, Frost and Edwards*. The alternative answer was that no hearsay problem was raised because the person responsible for the questionnaires was simply giving evidence of the fact that a particular opinion was held by a number of members of the public. English courts initially admitted evidence of the kind with which Mahon J was concerned without consideration of the theoretical problems involved.[17] In *Lego System A/S v Lego M Lemelstrich*[18] the theoretical problem was addressed, and the view expressed by Mahon J that such evidence was not hearsay accepted.[19] The argument is mainly directed to reception of the expert evidence of those who have conducted a professionally

9 By Traynor J in *People v Alcalde* 148 P 2d 627 (Cal, 1944) at 633.
10 *US v Annunziato* 293 F 2d 373 (2nd Cir, 1961).
11 See Federal Rules of Evidence, r 803(3).
12 Above p 671.
13 [1965] AC 1001, [1964] 1 All ER 877, see also above p 516.
14 See Farmer 'The Admissibility of Survey Evidence in Intellectual Property Cases' (1984) 7 UNSWLR 57; Sorensen and Sorensen 'The Admissibility and Use of Opinion Research Evidence' (1953) 28 NYULR 1213.
15 (1840) 9 C & P 275 (see p 667, above).
16 *Customglass Boats Ltd v Salthouse Bros Ltd* [1976] 1 NZLR 36.
17 *Bailey & Co Ltd v Clarke Son and Morland* [1938] AC 557; *General Electric Co v General Electric Co Ltd* [1972] 2 All ER 507, [1972] 1 WLR 729.
18 [1983] FSR 155.
19 Most recent Australian authority seems to have accepted a similar approach, see *Shoshana Pty v 10th Cantanae Pty* (1987) 79 ALR 279.

designed survey. It may be that in this way it is possible to counter the otherwise cogent objection that such evidence quite blatantly relies upon the sincerity and reliability of the expression of opinion by the person interviewed as genuinely representing that opinion. This sort of evidence highlights the theoretical danger of accepting the express assertion of an absent party as accurately representing what is asserted, a danger at least as great when what is asserted is a statement of opinion as it is when it is a statement of memory. It would however be inconvenient to have to call respondents for cross-examination in sufficient numbers for the evidence to be cogent, and it may well be the case that the relevant science is now sufficiently advanced for cross-examination of the expert as to survey design to be sufficient to guard against the dangers of insincerity.[20] It is submitted that while such evidence may usefully be admitted there is still need for further theoretical consideration. It is certainly arguable that by regarding such evidence as hearsay, and thus in civil proceedings subject to the procedural requirements of Order 38, it will be easier to ensure adequate survey design, than simply by taking the glib view that no hearsay problem is involved at all.

D. STATEMENTS OF CONTEMPORANEOUS PHYSICAL SENSATION

1. STATEMENT AND ILLUSTRATIONS OF THE EXCEPTION

A person's statements concerning his contemporaneous physical sensation are admissible evidence of that fact. In *Gilbey v Great Western Rail Co*[1] Cozens-Hardy MR entertained no doubt that:

> Statements made by a workman to this wife of his sensations at the time, about the pains in his side or head, or what not—whether the statements were made by groans, or by actions, or were verbal statements—would be admissible to prove these sensations.

The Master of the Rolls also held that the workman's assertion of the cause of his condition was inadmissible at common law, and his view of the law on both points is supported by a long line of authority.[2] For example, as long ago as 1846 it was said:

> If a man says to his surgeon 'I have a pain in the head', or 'in such a part of my body', that is evidence, but if he says to the surgeon. 'I have a wound', and was to add 'I met John Thomas who had a sword and ran me through the body with it', that would be no evidence against John Thomas.[3]

The long line of authority on the admissibility of statements of contempora-

---

20 But see *Reckitt & Colman Products Ltd v Borden Inc (No 2)* [1987] FSR 407 where scepticism was expressed as to the expert status of some such evidence. See further p 493, above.

1 (1910) 102 LT 202.

2 *Aveson v Lord Kinnaird* (1805) 6 East 188; *R v Johnson* (1847) 2 Car & Kir 354; *R v Conde* (1867) 10 Cox CC 547; *R v Gloster* (1888) 16 Cox CC 471.

3 *R v Nicholas* (1846) 2 Car & Kir 246 at 248 per Pollock CB.

neous physical sensation can hardly be said to have been shaken by the judgment of the Court of Criminal Appeal in *R v Black*,[4] but the court's hesitancy to admit evidence under this head is, at first sight, a little surprising. The accused had been convicted of murdering his wife by arsenical poisoning, and statements made by the deceased concerning her bodily symptoms after taking medicine procured by the accused were proved at the trial by the persons to whom they were made. When dismissing the appeal Avory J said:

> If it had appeared that these were statements made behind the back of the appellant, it would have required grave consideration whether they could have been admitted, but the court is satisfied that they were made in his presence in such circumstances as to require some comment or answer from him, and that the absence of any such comment was evidence from which the jury might draw an inference.

We saw in ch XVI that statements made in the presence of a party can be proved as something that may render his conduct in the face of them relevant, although the judge must tell the jury to ignore them if there is no evidence of such conduct. In view of the words used by Avory J it can only be assumed that the requisite evidence was present in *R v Black*.

2. THE REQUIREMENT OF CONTEMPORANEITY

It seems that the difficulty experienced by the Court of Criminal Appeal in deciding on the admissibility of the deceased's statements concerning her symptoms was that the statements related to past symptoms. In the course of the argument, Salter J said:

> Surely 'contemporaneous' cannot be confined to feelings experienced at the actual moment when the patient is speaking. It must include such a statement as 'Yesterday I had a pain after meals'.

This is a matter upon which it is impossible to lay down anything in the nature of a rigid rule. At a trial for murder by means of an illegal operation in *R v Gloster*,[5] Charles J insisted that questions to a witness with regard to the deceased's statements about her symptoms must be confined to her contemporaneous symptoms, and added that nothing in the nature of a narrative is admissible as to who caused them or how they were caused. In *Aveson v Kinnaird*,[6] usually regarded as among the earliest cases in which a deceased person's statements of bodily symptoms were received as evidence of their existence, utterances by a woman whose life had recently been insured by her husband made to a friend who found her in bed during the day, were received, not merely to prove the existence of the symptoms but also, it seems, to establish their previous existence when the deceased had been examined by a doctor some ten days earlier. In some cases the evidence may relate to presently lost memory of past fact, and in such a case, if later

---

4 (1922) 16 Cr App Rep 118.
5 (1888) 16 Cox CC 471.
6 (1805) 6 East 188. In *Tickle v Tickle* [1968] 2 All ER 154, [1968] 1 WLR 937, what the doctor said to the patient was held admissible as original evidence relevant to the latter's belief concerning his health. See also *Ramsay v Watson* (1961) 108 CLR 642.

loss of memory is itself memory, it will be immaterial that it relates, as indeed it must, to past fact.[7]

It has been held in Australia to be immaterial that the person who experienced and declared the symptoms at the time does not testify although available to do so.[8] There is plainly force in Wigmore's view that in such a case the contemporary statements of the witness as to his symptoms are likely to be more reliable than his later recollection of them in the witness box. The Civil Evidence Act 1968 provides a means of solving this problem in civil proceedings, but it may still raise a difficulty in criminal cases.

SECTION 2. STATEMENTS FORMING PART OF THE RES GESTAE RECEIVED AS ORIGINAL EVIDENCE

Statements received as original evidence are frequently said to form part of the res gestae. The making of such statements may be in issue or relevant to the issue. When the question is whether operative words were used, they are often said to be part of the res gestae, and this is also the case with regard to reported statements received as a matter affecting the credibility or weight of other evidence. It must be borne in mind that statements which can, in appropriate cases, be received under the four exceptions to the hearsay rule which have just been discussed may, in other cases, constitute original evidence.[9] A statement accompanying a relevant act may owe its significance to its falsity rather than its truth,[10] a statement made contemporaneously with a relevant event may have a significance which is quite unconnected with its truth or falsity, as when the fact that someone who was assaulted screamed, 'You're throttling me', is admitted to explain why people rushed to his assistance; a statement of affection may owe its significance to the circumstances in which it was made, as when terms of endearment used by a co-respondent to the respondent are proved in a divorce case (the sincerity of the utterance being beside the point), and statements of contemporaneous physical sensation may have probative value as something said in the presence of a party explicitly or implicitly, and accepted by him.[11] In every case the vital question is neither the nature of the statement, nor the circumstances in which it was made, nor the best manner of describing it, but the purpose for which it is tendered in evidence.

SECTION 3. EVIDENCE OF OPINION RECEIVED AS PART OF THE RES GESTAE

It seems that in certain cases evidence which would infringe both the rule against hearsay and the opinion rule may be received as part of the res gestae although it would be excluded if it consisted of statements made at a time which was at all remote from the events to which they relate. The typical

---

7 See *R v Wogandt* (1988) 33 ACR 31.
8 *R v Perry (No 2)* (1981) 28 SASR 95; *Batista v Citra Constructions Pty Ltd* (1986) 5 NSWLR 351.
9 See per Lord Blackburn in the *Dysart Peerage Case* (1881) 6 App Cas 489 at 502; *Re Jenion* [1952] Ch 454, so far as the declaration of the putative father was concerned.
10 *A-G v Good* (1825) M'Cle & Yo 286; *Ridley v Gyde* (1832) 9 Bing 349.
11 *R v Black* (above).

example is provided by the reception of a bystander's statements alleging negligence on the part of one of the drivers involved in a motor accident,[12] for we have seen that a witness may not state his deliberate opinion on the matter. Although there is no authority on the point, it is possible that, if the bystander was called as a witness, he could narrate his own statements made contemporaneously with the occurrences to which he was deposing. It is also possible that, on a trial for murder by poisoning, the deceased's statement immediately after he had eaten an apple to the effect that it had poisoned him would be received although some such statement as, 'I believe something in the apple I ate two days ago to be the cause of my present suffering', would be excluded.[13]

SECTION 4. FACTS RECEIVED AS PART OF THE RES GESTAE

We have seen that facts are sometimes allowed to be proved on the footing that they form part of the res gestae. In this context too the phrase seems merely to denote relevance on account of contemporaneity.[14] We saw, however, in ch IX, that it had a further implication in that evidence of facts forming part of the same transaction as that under inquiry may be received notwithstanding the general rule that evidence must be excluded if it does no more than show that someone is disposed to commit crimes or civil wrongs in general, or even crimes or civil wrongs of the kind into which the court is inquiring.[15] Contemporaneity, continuity or the fact that a number of incidents are closely connected with each other gives the evidence an added relevance which renders it admissible in spite of its prejudicial tendencies. It is however important that such evidence should have substantial relevance quite independent of any argument from the accused's disposition, and that mere contemporaneity should not be used as a device for evading the rigour of the general conditions for the admissibility of evidence of disposition.[16]

SECTION 5. RES GESTAE AND OTHER EXCLUSIONARY RULES

We have already seen that the doctrine of res gestae renders admissible the prior consistent statements of witnesses in spite of the common law prohibition on the proof of such statements in order to confirm present testimony. To gain sufficient weight to be admissible as part of the res gestae under this head, the statement must have formed part of the transaction to which the witness is deposing as in *Milne v Leisler*;[17] alternatively it must

---

12 As contemplated by Pollock CB in *Milne v Leisler* (1862) 7 H & N 786.
13 Cf *Chapdelaine v R* [1935] SCR 53.
14 *R v Moore* (p 27, above); cf *R v Hill* (1908) 1 Cr App Rep 158 where, however, the basis on which the evidence was held to be admissible is obscure.
15 See p 288, above.
16 In England this principle seems to be adopted, see *R v Rodley* [1913] 3 KB 468; *R v Fitzpatrick* [1962] 3 All ER 840, [1963] 1 WLR 7. It was perhaps unduly stretched in Australia in *O'Leary v R* (1946) 73 CLR 566; see also *Harriman v R* (1989) 88 ALR 161, and increasingly scant regard seems to be paid to it in the United States, see e g *ex p State of Alabama* (*In re Davenport v Alabama*) 426 So 2d 472 (1982).
17 (1862) 7 H & N 786; (p 289, above).

have accompanied the act or event about which the witness is speaking.[18] The doctrine of res gestae may sometimes serve to qualify the rule that a witness's prior inconsistent statements are not evidence of the facts stated unless the witness happens to be a party, in which case his previous statement may constitute an admission. Suppose, for example, that, at the trial of Fowkes, the son had said that he had never identified the culprit as the Butcher. The son's statements on the occasion under investigation might have been proved by the policeman as affirmative evidence that it was the Butcher who fired the shot, and not merely as something casting doubt on the son's testimony.[19]

Although there is no English authority on the subject, it is possible that an otherwise inadmissible confession would be rendered admissible by the res gestae doctrine. Suppose, for example, that a policeman were to chase a suspect from the scene of a murder and that, when he caught up with him, the policeman were to say 'If you don't tell me who killed the deceased I will kill you'. If the suspect were to reply 'I did', this spontaneous admission might be received, although it would plainly be inadmissible if made long after the event at a police station in response to such a threat as that which has been suggested.[20]

---

18 *R v Fowkes*, cited in Stephen *Digest of the Law of Evidence* (12th edn) art 3.
19 The example is taken from R N Gooderson (1957) CLJ 70.
20 This example is also taken from R N Gooderson in (1957) CLJ 67.

CHAPTER XIX

Documentary evidence[1]

Darling J once said that a document is 'any written thing capable of being evidence' and he added that it is immaterial on what the writing may be inscribed.[2] This was sufficient to dispose of the issue with which he was concerned, the question whether a writing inside a sealed envelope was a document for the purposes of a subpoena duces tecum, but it is clear that the word may have a broader meaning in many contexts. These are not confined to cases, such as the Civil Evidence Act 1968 and the Police and Criminal Evidence Act 1984, in which there is an enlarging statutory definition. For the purposes of the Rules of the Supreme Court concerning discovery the word has been held to include a tape-recording[3] and a facsimile transmission,[4] and, on the authority of the former, a majority of the Court of Appeal held that a film is a document for the purpose of the County Court Rules governing the same subject.[5] It seems however that films, tapes and video recordings are not to be regarded as documents for the purposes of excluding authenticated copies as evidence of their contents, even though the original may be in existence.[6] So too, it has been held,[7] and enacted,[8] that photocopies of documents may be admitted without accounting for the absence of the original provided that they are authenticated to the satisfaction of the court.

If a litigant wishes to rely upon the provisions of a document, he must render the court conversant with its terms. To this end it is generally incumbent upon him to produce the original, but he is dispensed from doing so in the circumstances mentioned in section 1. In many cases the court will require to be satisfied that the document was duly executed before admitting it in evidence, and this is discussed in section 2. Finally, difficult problems may arise with regard to the extent to which extrinsic evidence is admissible when it relates to the terms of a transaction embodied in a document, or the meaning of the words used in a written instrument. The principal rules are mentioned in section 3.

---

1 For a useful modern monograph on Australian law see Brown *Documentary Evidence in Australia* (1988).
2 *R v Daye* [1908] 2 KB 333 at 340.
3 *Grant v South Western and County Properties* [1975] Ch 185, [1974] 2 All ER 465.
4 *Hastie and Jenkerson v McMahon* (1990) 134 Sol Jo 725.
5 *Senior v Holdsworth, ex p Independent Television* [1976] QB 23, [1975] 2 All ER 1009. For a fuller citation of authorities see Phipson *Law of Evidence* (13th Edn) para 36.01.
6 *Kajala v Noble* (1982) 75 Cr App Rep 149.
7 *R v Wayte* (1982) 76 Cr App Rep 110 at 116.
8 Police and Criminal Evidence Act 1984, s 71. See also Administration of Justice Act 1982, s 66; Criminal Justice Act 1988, s 27.

SECTION 1. PROOF OF THE CONTENTS OF A DOCUMENT

A. THE GENERAL RULE

1. STATEMENT AND ILLUSTRATIONS OF THE GENERAL RULE

(i) Statement

A party relying on the words used in a document for any purpose other than that of identifying it must, as a general rule, adduce primary evidence of its contents. This is often spoken of as the most important survival of the best evidence rule, although it antedates that rule by several centuries. So vestigial has the best evidence rule become that its operation is effectively limited to cases where a party has possession of an original document, and wilfully refuses to produce it.[9] The typical example of primary evidence in this context is the original document, but there are others which will be mentioned after the rule has been illustrated. It is subject to important exceptions of which the most notable relates to public documents, the contents of which may be proved by the production of a copy.

(ii) Illustrations[10]

The simplest illustration is provided by a case in which a party wishes to put his correspondence with his adversary in evidence. He will normally have the originals of letters received from his adversary, but he will be unable to prove the contents of his replies by the production of copies unless the case has been brought within one of the exceptions to the general rule by service of a notice to produce.[11] Other obvious illustrations are afforded by cases in which a party wishes to rely upon the terms of any document of which he merely has a copy or a more or less perfect recollection, but the rule may be brought into play in circumstances in which the possibility of its application is considerably less obvious. In *Macdonnell v Evans*,[12] a witness for the plaintiff was asked in cross-examination whether a letter of his which was produced was written in reply to a letter charging him with forgery. The last-mentioned letter was not produced, and the question was disallowed because it assumed that there was a document in existence which should have been proved by production of the original. Similarly, in *Augustien v Challis*,[13] the plaintiff alleged that the defendant, a sheriff, had negligently caused a fieri facias to be withdrawn. The defendant sought to justify his conduct on the ground that rent was due to the debtor's landlord whose claim had priority to that of the plaintiff. The defendant called the landlord who testified to the fact that rent was due to him, but admitted that it was payable under a lease. This document was not produced and the landlord's evidence was thus

---

9 See *R v Governor of Pentonville Prison, ex p Osman* [1989] 3 All ER 701 at 728.
10 The same rule applies in Scotland; for a recent application see *Inverclyde District Council v Carwell* [1987] SCLR 145.
11 In civil cases this will be deemed to have taken place by virtue of the exchange of lists of documents (Ord 27, r 4(3)) and the requirement of proof by the original may be waived by agreeing a bundle of correspondence.
12 (1852) 11 CB 930, *Potts v Miller* (1940) 64 CLR 282; *Lakeman v Finlay* [1959] SR (NSW) 5.
13 (1847) 1 Exch 279, see also *Twyman v Knowles* (1853) 13 CB 222.

rendered inadmissible because: 'The moment it appears that there is a lease, you cannot speak about its contents without producing it.'[14] The lease had to be consulted in order to determine the amount of rent, if any, due to the landlord.

It is important to remember that the rule has its limitations. In the first place, it applies only to cases in which direct reliance is placed on the words used in a document. In *R v Holy Trinity, Kington-upon-Hull (Inhabitants)*[15] it was held that the fact that a pauper was a tenant in a particular parish could be proved without reference to the original lease, as could the value of the premises. Relationships such as those of landlord and tenant, or partnership,[16] may be created by a document, but they can be proved by other evidence, such as the payment of rent or a witness's assertion that someone is his partner.

In the second place, the rule does not prevent reference being made to the terms of a document for the purpose of identifying it. A distinction must be drawn between referring to the contents of a document as marks of identification and as a means of communicating ideas:

> For the purpose of identifying anything, whether it be a writing or anything else, proof may be given to show what it is; and therefore, in an action of trover for a promissory note, the contents of the promissory note may be stated verbally by a witness; the reason is, that the evidence is not of the contents as evidence, but for the purpose of identification.[17]

Finally, and a fortiori, if the bare fact of the existence of a document is in issue, it may be proved without recourse to the original, but the rule applies the moment reliance is placed upon the contents. In *R v Elworthy*,[18] for instance, a solicitor was charged with perjury in having wilfully denied on oath that a draft of a statutory declaration had been prepared. No notice to produce the draft was given, but the Court for Crown Cases Reserved considered that this would not have excluded parol evidence of the existence of the draft and its possession by the accused. But the prosecution went further, and gave evidence of alterations in the draft in order to show that the accused's denial was wilful and, for this reason, the conviction was quashed. It was not a case in which it could be said that the indictment gave notice to the prisoner that he would be required to produce a particular document as, for instance, on a prosecution for forgery.

2. TYPES OF PRIMARY EVIDENCE OF THE CONTENTS OF A DOCUMENT

(i) The original

The primary evidence par excellence of the contents of a document is the original. Generally speaking there can be no great difficulty in determining

14 Per Parke B at 280.
15 (1827) 7 B & C 611.
16 *Alderson v Clay* (1816) 1 Stark 405.
17 *Boyle v Wiseman* (1855) 11 Exch 360 at 367 per Martin B citing *Whitehead v Scott* (1830) 1 Mood & R 2. See also *Railways Commissioner for New South Wales v Young* (1962) 35 ALJR 416.
18 (1867) LR 1 CCR 103. See also *Maks v Maks* (1986) 6 NSWLR 34 where the court was prepared to accept evidence of the existence of a document relied upon for the purposes of denying costs, but not for those of affording the relief sought.

which of several documents is the original; but it is sometimes necessary to have regard to the purpose of which or the party against whom the contents are tendered in evidence. In the case of a telegram, if the contents are tendered in evidence against the sender, the original is the message handed in at the post office,[19] so far as the receiver is concerned, there are many cases in which the original will be the written message received by him. A counterpart lease, executed only by the lessee, is the original so far as he and those claiming under him are concerned,[20] although the other part is the original as against the lessor. If duplicates of a deed are executed by all the parties to it, each duplicate is an original,[21] and, when this is so, each of them must be accounted for before secondary evidence of the contents of the deed becomes admissible.[1] An unsigned carbon copy of a letter, or one produced by means of a duplicating machine,[2] is not the original when the contents of the signed top copy are in issue. Similarly, if the question concerns the contents of a town planning notice served on a third person, the notice so served is the only original,[3] but there are cases where, as between the parties to the proceedings, the copy of a bill or invoice may, in effect, be treated as a duplicate original because it is unnecessary for the person producing it to account for the original.[4] There are also cases in which any number of printed copies of a document may be treated as originals where, for example, the question concerns the contents of a placard and not the terms of the author's manuscript.[5]

(ii) Copy of document requiring enrolment

There are certain private documents which must be filed in a court or other public office and, when they are thus filed, the copy issued by the court or other office may be treated as the original. Once again, everything turns on the purpose for which the contents are tendered in evidence. The probate is, for instance, conclusive evidence of the words of the will in respect of which the grant was made and, for this purpose, it constitutes primary evidence, but, on questions of construction, the court may examine the original. Thus, in *Re Battie-Wrightson*,[6] the probate of the will of a testatrix who had an account at seven banks stated that she bequeathed the balance of her account 'at the said bank' to a named person. There was no indication which bank account was intended, but the original will contained an erasure referring to a specific bank in the clause preceding the bequest which the court was thus enabled to construe. The probate had not superseded the document executed by the testatrix for all purposes.

---

19 *R v Regan* (1887) 16 Cox CC 203.
20 *Roe d West v Davis* (1806) 7 East 363.
21 *Forbes v Samuel* [1913] 3 KB 706.
 1 *Alivon v Furnival* (1834) 1 Cr M & R 277.
 2 *Nodin v Murray* (1812) 3 Camp 228; cf *Durston v Mercuri* [1969] VR 507 (signed carbon may in some circumstances be the original).
 3 *Andrews v Wirral Rural Council* [1916] 1 KB 863.
 4 *Philipson v Chase* (1809) 2 Camp 110 as explained in *Andrews v Wirral Rural Council* (above); *Colling v Treweek* (1827) 6 B & C 394; *Buckley v Macken* [1961] NZLR 46.
 5 *R v Watson* (1817) 2 Stark 116.
 6 *Re Battie-Wrightson, Cecil v Battie-Wrightson* [1920] 2 Ch 330.

(iii) Admission of a party

We have already seen that it was decided in *Slatterie v Pooley*,[7] that the informal admission by one party to litigation constitutes primary evidence against him of the contents of a document. His opponent is thus dispensed from the necessity of producing the original or showing that the case comes within one of the exceptions to the rule requiring this to be done. The mere fact that the contents of a deed are recited in a later deed produced by one of the parties does not dispense with the necesssity of producing the original of the earlier document if his opponent wishes to rely on other parts of it.[8]

3. TYPES OF SECONDARY EVIDENCE OF THE CONTENTS OF A DOCUMENT[9]

Reference may be made to the different kinds of secondary evidence that can be given of the contents of a document before the circumstances in which such evidence is admissible by way of exception to the general rule are considered. Secondary evidence may take the form of all manner of different types of copy, including those proved by testimony to have been checked against the original which are known as 'examined copies',[10] those bearing a certificate of their accuracy called 'certified copies', 'office copies', examined in the court office in which they are filed, and 'government printer's copies' which are employed to prove the contents of certain other kinds of public documents such as statutes, treaties and royal proclamations. Other public documents are proved by examined or certified copies, and these kinds of secondary evidence, as well as that of less formal copies, are also employed in the case of private documents. These may also be proved by the oral evidence of persons able to recollect their contents.

According to the old rules there were no degrees of secondary evidence,[11] so oral evidence of the contents of a document could be adduced without accounting for the absence of any copies that may have been in existence, and there were no preferences between different kinds of copy. This was because the best evidence rule prohibited only the adduction of evidence which, by its very nature, disclosed the existence of a better means of proof. The production of the copy of a deed shows that the original is, or was, in existence, and this is also the case when a witness deposes to the contents of a writing which is not before the court; but a copy does not show that others were made, and oral evidence of the contents of the document does not suggest the existence of any but the original. The proposition that there were no degrees of secondary evidence was, however, of merely general application. In the case of many public documents, oral evidence of their contents would be received only if copies were unavailable, and the contents of a will that had been admitted to probate could never be proved by oral testimony so long as the original or probate was in existence. It remains to

---

7 (1840) 6 M & W 664 (see p 580, above); *Price v Woodhouse* (1849) 3 Exch 616.
8 *Gillett v Abbott* (1838) 7 Ad & El 783.
9 See generally Australian Law Reform Commission Research Paper No 4 'Secondary Evidence of Documents' (1981).
10 As to photographs of the locus in quo see *Hindson v Ashby* [1896] 2 Ch 1 at 21.
11 *Doe d Gilbert v Ross* (1840) 7 M & W 102.

be seen how far such exceptions will survive the demise of the best evidence rule.[12]

There is authority for the view that the copy of a copy is inadmissible,[13] but there is also authority on the other side,[14] and there seems to be no reason why the copy of a copy should not be received in evidence provided the witness producing it, or some other witness, makes it clear that the copy produced is a true copy of the first copy and that that copy was, in its turn a true copy of the original. In *R v Collins*[15] it was necessary for the prosecution to prove that the accused knew that his bank account was inoperative. The prosecution called an assistant bank manager who produced a copy of the unsigned carbon copy of a letter sent by his colleague to the accused informing him that his account was closed. The accused had been called upon to produce this letter and, as he had not done so, secondary evidence was admissible. But the Court of Criminal Appeal held that the letter had not been properly proved by the bank manager because he did not swear that the copy produced was a true copy of the carbon or that the carbon was a true copy of the original apart from the signature. Had the bank manager testified to these matters, it seems that the court would have considered the letter to have been properly proved by his evidence.[16]

B. EXCEPTIONS TO THE GENERAL RULE

Mention must be made of six exceptions to the general rule—cases in which the contents of a document may be proved by secondary evidence. These occur when the original is in the possession or control of the opponent of the party wishing to rely on the document and the opponent fails to produce it after receipt of a notice requiring him to do so; when the document is in the possession of a stranger who lawfully refuses to produce it after service of a subpoena duces tecum; when the original cannot be found after due search; when, though it is known to be in existence, the production of the original is, for practical purposes, impossible; when the production of the original would be highly inconvenient owing to the public nature of the document, or because it is an entry in a banker's book. This list of exceptions is not exhaustive, but it covers the important instances in which secondary evidence of the contents of a document may be adduced.

1. OPPONENT'S FAILURE TO PRODUCE DOCUMENT AFTER NOTICE

(i) Nature and purpose of notice to produce

A notice to produce informs the party upon whom it is served that he is required to produce the documents specified therein at the trial to which the

12 *Garton v Hunter* [1969] 2 QB 37, [1969] 1 All ER 451.
13 *Everingham v Roundell* (1838) 2 Mood & R 138.
14 *Lafone v Griffin* (1909) 25 TLR 308.
15 (1960) 44 Cr App Rep 170; see the helpful case note by Hudson 24 MLR 178. The appellant's landlady testified to having communicated the contents of the letter to him when he was in hospital, and the court accordingly applied what is now the proviso to s 2 of the Criminal Appeal Act 1968.
16 A photocopy of a copy was accepted in *R v Wayte* (1982) 76 Cr App Rep 110.

notice relates. The notice does not compel production of the documents in question, but the fact that it has been served provides a foundation for the reception of secondary evidence. If a party wishes to compel his opponent to produce documents, the proper course is for him to serve the opponent with a subpoena duces tecum and this will be adopted when the party is not in a position to adduce satisfactory secondary evidence, or when an issue turns on the form of the original as when handwriting is material.[17] Notice to produce is not served in order to give the opponent notice that the documents mentioned in it will be used by the other party, and thus to enable the opponent to prepare counter-evidence, but so as to exclude the objection that all reasonable steps have not been taken to procure the original document. Accordingly, when the original is in court, notice to produce may be served during the trial.[18] The party serving the notice must put the documents it mentions in evidence if required to do so by the opponent upon whom the notice was served. The notice cannot be employed as a means of gaining inspection of documents without using them if they turn out to be unfavourable.[19] The party served with a notice to produce cannot rely upon the original of a document it mentions if secondary evidence of the contents of the document has been given in consequence of non-compliance with the notice.[20]

In civil cases, the parties exchange lists of documents after the close of the pleadings, and, under RSC Ord 27, r 4(3):

> a party to a cause or matter by whom a list of documents is served on any other party ... shall be deemed to have been served by that other party with a notice requiring him to produce at the trial of the cause or matter such of the documents specified in the list as are in his possession, custody or power.

(ii) When service of notice is excused

In certain circumstances, service of notice to produce is excused, and a party may adduce secondary evidence of the contents of a document if the original is not produced by his opponent. The most important case in which this is so is when the document in question is itself a notice,[1] whether it be a notice to produce, notice of dishonour of a bill of exchange or notice by the prosecution of intention to rely on the accused's previous convictions. Another case in which there is no need to serve notice to produce is when the nature of proceedings is such as to inform a party that he is required to produce the originals of certain documents at the trial. Obvious instances are provided

---

17 The accused should not be served with a subpoena duces tecum in a criminal case. The service of a notice to produce is unobjectionable because the accused need not comply with it. If he does not do so, he cannot be ordered to produce the original on account of the privilege against self-incrimination (*Trust Houses Ltd v Postlethwaite* (1944) 109 JP 12); but the privilege does not apply to answers to questions when the accused is giving evidence and he may then perhaps be ordered to produce documents in his control (*R v Adams* [1965] VR 563).
18 *Dwyer v Collins* (1852) 7 Exch 639.
19 *Wharam v Routledge* (1805) 5 Esp 235. Quaere whether this will apply to cases coming within Ord 27, r 4(3).
20 *Doe d Thompson v Hodgson* (1840) 12 Ad & El 135.
1 *R v Turner* [1910] 1 KB 346; *Practice Note* in [1950] 1 All ER 37n; cf *Andrews v Wirral Rural Council* [1916] 1 KB 863 showing that a subpoena is necessary in order to obtain production of a notice served on a stranger to the litigation.

by prosecutions for the the the theft or a document[2] or driving a motor vehicle without being adequately insured.[3] Service of notice to produce is also excused when possession of a document is admitted[4] or admitted to have been lost[5] by the opponent.

2. STRANGER'S LAWFUL REFUSAL TO PRODUCE DOCUMENT

When the original of a document is in the possession of a stranger to the litigation, the proper course for the party desiring to prove the contents of the document is to serve him with a subpoena duces tecum. The stranger may, however, be able to establish a claim to privilege in respect of the document when secondary evidence of its contents becomes admissible.[6]

The governing principle is the same as that which covers the next exceptions to the general rule that are mentioned—it is impossible to compel production of the document, and it will apply in cases in which the person in possession of the original is beyond the jurisdiction of the court, or makes a lawful claim to diplomatic immunity,[7] but the principle does not apply when a stranger served with a subpoena duces tecum wrongfully refuses to produce the document,[8] for in such a case he may be made liable for any damage caused by his disobedience to the subpoena, and he may even be imprisoned for non-compliance with its terms.

3. LOST DOCUMENT

When the original of a document cannot be found after due search, its contents may be proved by secondary evidence. The requirement as to due search will be satisfied in different ways according to the differing circumstances of each case.[9] A party may adduce secondary evidence of the contents of a document if his opponent admits to having lost it or if a stranger served with a subpoena duces tecum does likewise. The contents of a lost will may be proved by secondary evidence to the same extent as those of any other lost document.[10]

4. PRODUCTION OF ORIGINAL IMPOSSIBLE

The production of the original of a document may be physically impossible in which case secondary evidence of its contents is admissible. It has been

---

2 *R v Aickles* (1784) 1 Leach 294.
3 *Machin v Ash* (1950) 49 LGR 87; *Bracegirdle v Apter* (1951) 49 LGR 790. In these cases secondary evidence was received of the accused's certificate of insurance.
4 *Dwyer v Collins* (1852) 7 Exch 639.
5 *R v Haworth* (1830) 4 C & P 254.
6 *Mills v Oddy* (1834) 6 C & P 728. Secondary evidence is also admissible if the opponent obtained possession from someone served with a subpoena duces tecum (*Leeds v Cook* (1803) 4 Esp 256).
7 *R v Nowaz* [1976] 3 All ER 5, [1976] 1 WLR 830 showing that there is no difference in this context between civil and criminal cases.
8 *R v Inhabitants of Llanfaethly* (1853) 2 E & B 940.
9 *Brewster v Sewell* (1820) 3 B & Ald 296.
10 *Sugden v Lord St Leonards* (1876) 1 PD 154.

said that inscriptions on tombstones and walls are proved by copies every day.[11] Secondary evidence is likewise admissible when the production of the original is legally prohibited by, for example, a foreign court with custody of it,[12] or a law requiring it to remain affixed to the walls of a particular place such as a factory.[13]

5. PUBLIC DOCUMENTS

In *Mortimer v M'Callan*,[14] it was held to be unnecessary to cause the originals of the books of the Bank of England to be produced. Alderson B said that if they were not removable on the ground of public inconvenience, that was upon the same footing in point of principle as in the case of that which is not removable by the physical nature of the thing itself.[15] At common law, the contents of numerous public documents[16] could be proved by copies of various kinds on account of the inconvenience that would have been occasioned by production of the originals. The mode of proving public documents is now governed by a host of statutes[17] and, in a work of this nature, it is possible only to mention a few that are of more or less general application.

Private Acts of Parliament are, where necessary, proved by the production of a Queen's Printer's or Stationery Office copy.[18] Royal proclamations may be proved by production of a Queen's Printer's copy or of the gazette containing them, or of a copy certified to be correct by the appropriate official.[19] Orders in Council and statutory instruments are proved in the same way.[20] Journals of either House of Parliament are proved by production of a Queen's Printer's copy.[1]

---

11 Per Alderson B in *Mortimer v M'Callan* (1840) 6 M & W 58. Some kinds of inscriptions, e g those on banners, may be treated as equivalent to public speeches rather than writings, in which case the banners do not have to be produced (*R v Hunt* (1820) 3 B & Ald 566; for criticisms of the vague judgments in this case see 65 LQR 65).
12 *Alivon v Furnival* (1834) 1 Cr M & R 277.
13 *Owner v Bee Hive Spinning Co Ltd* [1914] 1 KB 105.
14 (1840) 6 M & W 58.
15 See also per Pollock CB in *Sayer v Glossop* (1848) 2 Exch 409 at 441: 'If in point of law you cannot compel a party who has the custody of a document to produce it, there is the same reason for admitting other evidence of its contents as if its production were physically impossible.'
16 See p 576, above, for a definition of a public document.
17 See *Wills on Evidence* (3rd edn) App A.
18 Evidence Act 1845, s 3; Documentary Evidence Act 1882, equating Stationery Office copies with those of the Queen's Printer or Government Printer referred to in other statutes. Under s 3 of the Interpretation Act 1978, every Act is a Public Act to be judicially noticed as such, unless the contrary is expressly provided by the Act; it applies to Acts coming into force after 1890 and re-enacts an earlier provision applying to Acts passed since 1850. Generally speaking, therefore, it is unnecessary to produce any particular copy of a modern statute.
19 Evidence Act 1845, s 3; Documentary Evidence Act 1868, s 2.
20 *R v Clarke* [1969] 2 QB 91, [1969] 1 All ER 924. Cases sometimes have to be adjourned so as to give a party an opportunity of producing a Stationery Office copy. The courts vary in their attitude towards insistence on the proper proof of statutory instruments and Orders in Council, sometimes describing it as the imprescriptible right of a litigant to have it properly proved and, on other occasions, describing the insistence on proper proof as a technical triviality (see *Duffin v Markham* (1918) 88 LJKB 581; and *Tyrrell v Cole* (1918) 120 LT 156). Cf *Snell v Unity Finance Ltd* [1964] 2 QB 203, [1963] 3 All ER 50, suggesting judicial notice may be taken of all statutory instruments.
1 Evidence Act 1845, s 3.

Byelaws are proved under s 238 of the Local Government Act 1972, by the production of a printed copy indorsed with a certificate purporting to be be signed by the proper officer containing details concerning the making and confirming of the byelaw and certifying that the document is a true copy.

Proclamations, treaties and other acts of state of any foreign state or British colony may be proved either by examined copy or by a copy authenticated with the seal of the foreign state or British colony.[2]

Records of the Supreme Court may be proved by production of any document sealed or stamped with the seal or stamp of the court.[3]

Records preserved in the Public Record Office are proved by copies certified by the Keeper of the Public Records,[4] and entries in registers which may be held on computer, kept in the Patent Office, are proved by copies certified by the Comptroller,[5] like those relating to companies which may also be held on computer[6] and may be proved by copies signed or sealed by the Registrar.[7]

Finally, two more general provisions may be noted: the effect of s 1 of the Evidence Act 1845 is that when a statute permits a document to be proved by certified or sealed copy, it is unnecessary to prove certification or sealing, the mere production of the certified or sealed copy sufficing; under s 14 of the Evidence Act 1851, whenever any book or other document is of such a public nature as to be admissible in evidence on production from proper custody and no statute exists which renders its contents provable by means of a copy, it may be proved by certified or examined copy. The upshot of these two provisions, together with those of numerous special statutes, is that a very large number of copy documents may be put in evidence on mere production to the court, without there being any question of accounting for the original or proving the accuracy of the copy.

6. BANKERS' BOOKS

At common law, bankers' books, other than those of the Bank of England, are private documents; but the inconvenience which would have been occasioned by the necessity of producing the originals as and when required for the purposes of any litigation has been avoided by the Bankers' Books Evidence Act 1879. Provided that the book is one of the ordinary ones of the bank, the entry was made in the ordinary course of business, the book is in the custody of the bank, and the copy has been examined against the original (all of which matters can be proved by the affidavit or the testimony of an officer of the bank),[8] a copy of an entry in a banker's book shall, in all legal proceedings, be received as prima facie evidence of such entry, and of the

---

2 Evidence Act 1851, s 7. Despite some technical difficulty it appears that s 7 applies to the Republic of Ireland, as it applies elsewhere, see *R v McGlinchy* [1985] 9 NIJB 62.
3 Supreme Court Act 1981, s 132.
4 Public Records Act 1958, s 9.
5 Patents Act 1977, s 32, as substituted by the Patents, Designs and Marks Act 1986, Sch 1.
6 Companies Act 1985, s 723.
7 Ibid, s 709(1).
8 Ss 4–5.

matters, transactions and accounts therein recorded.[9] The application of these provisions has been very sensibly extended to modern forms of book-keeping such as microfilmed and computerised records.[10] This reform does not, however, extend beyond the form of the records to their substance, and it seems that copies of letters sent by the bank,[11] or of cheques and paying-in slips,[12] would still not be covered by the provisions. Under s 7 any party to a legal proceeding can apply, if necessary ex parte, for an order that he be at liberty to inspect and take copies of any entries in a banker's books for the purpose of such proceedings. This section, like the rest of the Act, applies to both civil and criminal proceedings.[13] In civil proceedings it is well-established that the provision is to be applied according to the ordinary rules of discovery,[14] and in particular that it cannot be used to compel the revelation of incriminating matters.[15] There is no discovery in criminal proceedings, and for many years the application of the Act in such proceedings was left untested. In *Williams v Summerfield*[16] it was however held that to apply the same ban on self-incrimination would frustrate the operation of the Act to criminal proceedings, and that an application could be granted upon conditions analogous to those applying to search warrants. The order is such a serious invasion of privacy that it should not be made without the most careful consideration, and the court granting it should satisfy itself that there is other evidence to support the charge,[17] and that the order is limited to entries strictly relevant, especially temporally, to the charge.[18] It is generally desirable that notice be given to anyone affected by an order,[19] though it should be noted that the account need not be that of a party to the proceedings, and may even be that of a person incompetent to testify.[20] These safeguards may in some circumstances lead courts to approve of action under these provisions in preference to those under less fastidious statutory provisions.[1]

---

9 S 3. The section creates an exception to the hearsay rule as to the transactions to which the entry relates (*Harding v Williams* (1880) 14 Ch D 197, questioned in argument in *Arnott v Hayes* (1887) 56 LJCh 844 at 847, but see *Myers v Director of Public Prosecutions* [1965] AC 1001 at 1028 and 1033). See also *Elsey v Taxation Commissioner of Commonwealth of Australia* (1969) 121 CLR 99.

10 A new definition clause, s 9, substituted by Banking Act 1979 Sch 6, has applied since 1982, although *Barker v Wilson* [1980] 2 All ER 81, [1980] 1 WLR 884, had already indicated the capacity of judicial interpretation to achieve the same result. See also *ANZ Banking Group Ltd v Griffiths* (1988) 49 SASR 385; *R v Saffron* (1988) 36 ACR 262 at 290.

11 *R v Dadson* (1983) 77 Cr App Rep 91.

12 *Williams v Williams* [1988] QB 161, [1987] 3 All ER 257.

13 Which in Scotland include a criminal petition, *Carmichael v Sexton* 1985 SCCR 333.

14 *Re Bankers' Books Evidence Act 1879, R v Bono* (1913) 29 TLR 635.

15 *Waterhouse v Barker* [1924] 2 KB 759.

16 [1972] 2 QB 512, [1972] 2 All ER 1334.

17 *Re v Nottingham City Justices, ex p Lynn* (1984) 79 Cr App Rep 238. The court will be wary of a situation in which the charge is laid simultaneously with the application for the order so as formally to satisfy the requirements of the section.

18 In *R v Marlborough St Stipendiary Magistrate, ex p Simpson* (1980) 70 Cr App Rep 291, orders were quashed, largely on this basis. A party cannot necessarily prevent an order being made by proclaiming an intention to plead guilty, *Owen v Sambrook* [1981] Crim LR 329.

19 *R v Grossman* (1981) 73 Cr App Rep 302.

20 *R v Andover Justices, ex p Rhodes* [1980] Crim LR 644, where this was, in fact, regarded as a further reason for making the order.

1 See *R v Epsom Justices, ex p Bell* [1988] NLJR 165.

SECTION 2. PROOF OF THE EXECUTION OF PRIVATE DOCUMENTS

The statutes which enable the contents of public documents to be proved by means of copies also dispense with the necessity of proving that the documents have been properly executed. In the case of a public document, therefore, the mere production of the appropriate copy will suffice to put it in evidence, but something more than production is required in the case of a private document. The court will require to be satisfied by evidence that it was duly executed, unless it is more than twenty years old and comes from the proper custody, in which event there is a presumption of formal validity. The due execution of a private document is proved by showing that it was signed by the person by whom it purports to have been signed and, when attestation is necessary, that it was attested. Accordingly, proof of handwriting and attestation will be discussed before various presumptions applicable to documents are considered.[2] The section concludes with a brief reference to the Stamp Acts.

A. PROOF OF HANDWRITING

There are three types of evidence of handwriting which call for discussions— testimonial evidence, opinion and comparison.

1. TESTIMONIAL EVIDENCE

The testimonial evidence may take one of the following forms: the testimony of the person whose handwriting is to be proved; his admissible hearsay statement; the testimony of someone who saw the document executed (whether he be an attesting witness or a bystander); and an admissible hearsay statement of someone other than the person whose handwriting is in question. Nothing need be said with regard to any of these forms of testimonial evidence except that it is usually unnecessary, in the first instance, for a witness to the signature to do more than swear that he saw someone sign in a particular name. The name will, in itself, be sufficient evidence of the identity of the signatory with the person whose handwriting is to be proved,[3] unless there are circumstances calling for investigation, or unless, perhaps, the name is a very common one.[4]

---

2 In civil cases, the due execution of a document is frequently the subject of a formal admission for the purposes of a particular trial and such an admission is deemed to have taken place under and subject to the provisions of Ord 27, rr 1 and 2. Proof of due execution is dispensed with when the document is in the possession of the opponent who refuses to produce it on notice (*Cooke v Tanswell* (1818) 8 Taunt 450; *Poole v Warren* (1838) 8 Ad & El 582). This is also the case when the opponent produces the document but claims an interest under it (*Pearce v Hooper* (1810) 3 Taunt 60). The due execution of a document might be formally admitted in a criminal case under s 10 of the Criminal Justice Act 1967.

3 *Roden v Ryde* (1843) 4 QB 626.

4 *Jones v Jones* (1841) 9 M & W 75.

2. OPINION

Witnesses who have not seen the document in question written or signed may depose to their opinion that the writing is that of a particular person. Such opinon may be based upon the witness's acquaintance with the handwriting of the person in question through having seen him write on former occasions. It makes no difference whether these occasions were many or few, and whether the signature was merely that of the signatory's surname without the addition of the Christian names appearing on the document before the court,[5] although these matters will affect the weight of the evidence.

It is unnecessary that the witness who thus deposes to his opinion should have seen the person whose writing is in question write at all, for it will be sufficient if he has received documents purporting to be written or signed by him,[6] and the capacity in which he has done so is immaterial, although this may affect the weight of the evidence:

> The clerk who constantly read the letters, the broker who was ever consulted upon them, is as competent to judge whether another signature is that of the writer of the letters, as the merchant to whom they were addressed. The servant who has habitually carried letters addressed by me to others has an opportunity of obtaining knowledge of my writing though he never saw me write or received a letter from me.[7]

There must, however, have been a sufficient opportunity for the witness to acquire such knowledge of the handwriting in question as to make it worthwhile receiving his evidence.[8]

3. COMPARISON

There is a general sense in which it is true to say that:

> All evidence of handwriting, except where the witness sees the document written, is in its nature comparison. It is the belief which a witness entertains on comparing the writing in question with an example in his mind derived from some previous knowledge.[9]

but, under s 8 of the Criminal Procedure Act 1865, handwriting may also be proved by comparison in a more specific sense of the word. A document which is proved[10] to have been signed or written by the person whose handwriting is in issue is first produced, and this is compared with the writing which is being considered by the court. On the basis of such a

---

5 *Lewis v Sapio* (1827) Mood & M 39.
6 *Harrington v Fry* (1824) 1 C & P 289.
7 *Doe d Mudd v Suckermore* (1837) 5 Ad & El 703 at 750 per Lord Denman CJ.
8 *R v O'Brien* (1911) 7 Cr App Rep 29; *Pitre v R* [1933] 1 DLR 417 (sight of two letters and two postcards insufficient).
9 *Doe d Mudd v Suckermore* (1837) 5 Ad & El 703 at 739 per Patteson J.
10 The section applies to civil and criminal cases and in both instances the standard of proof is the one normally appropriate to those proceedings, *R v Ewing* [1983] QB 1039, [1983] 2 All ER 645. See also *R v Sim* [1987] 1 NZLR 356.

comparison, an expert in these matters may give evidence.[11] The rigour of the old law restricting a witness to testifying to points of comparison rather than to the identity of two pieces of handwriting has probably not survived s 3 of the Civil Evidence Act 1972.[12]

Although the evidence may be thought to be of less weight, an opinion with regard to the handwriting of the two documents may be given by a witness who is not an expert, or the document may be submitted to the court in order that the handwriting on each of them may be compared. The document which is thus submitted to the jury for comparison with the one in dispute need not be relevant to the issues in the case in any other way,[13] and, if he gives evidence, the person whose handwriting is under consideration may be asked to write in court so that his writing may be compared with that on the document in question.[14]

Conclusions based on comparison of handwriting by those who are not experts must obviously be treated with considerable caution, and there are several instances in which the Court of Criminal Appeal has quashed a conviction after examining two specimens of handwriting which had been submitted to the jury at the trial.[15] It is wrong for a judge to invite the jury to make a comparison without the guidance of an expert although, where they have to be allowed to consider exhibits, he cannot do more than warn them of the risks of comparison.[16] In Australia, where the rule seems more lax, the question has been raised of possible prejudice to the accused as a result of counsel asking the accused to provide a specimen by writing in court during cross-examination.[17] It has been held that a policeman who induced a prisoner to write while under arrest in order that his handwriting might be compared with that on a threatening letter which he was alleged to have written, was a biased witness and that his evidence of opinion based on a comparison ought not to have been submitted to the jury,[18] and, in *R v Harvey*,[19] it was said that the jury ought not to act on a comparison of the handwriting in books found in the possession of the prisoner with that on a document alleged to have been forged by him. These decisions may have turned on their special facts, for it appears to have been ruled in a later case that evidence by a policeman that he had seen the accused write for his own purposes pending trial was admissible.[20]

In spite of the variety of the methods by which handwriting may be

---

11 *R v Silverlock* (1894) 2 QB 766. It may be necessary to establish the basis of such expertise on a voir dire, though questions of methodology go to weight rather than to admissibilty, *R v Bonython* (1984) 15 ACR 364.

12 See also *R v Mazzone* (1985) 43 SASR 330 at 339.

13 *Birch v Ridgway* (1858) 1 F & F 270; *Adami v R* (1959) 108 CLR 605. It may even be an otherwise inadmissible confession, see *S v Duna* 1984 (2) SA 591.

14 *Cobbett v Kilminster* (1865) 4 F & F 490.

15 *R v Smith* (1909) 2 Cr App Rep 86; *R v Rickard* (1918) 13 Cr App Rep 40.

16 *R v O'Sullivan* [1969] 2 All ER 237; [1969] 1 WLR 497; *R v Tilley* [1961] 3 All ER 406, [1961] 1 WLR 1309; *R v Smith* (1968) 52 Cr App Rep 648. See also *Daley v R* [1979] Tas SR 75.

17 *R v McCarthy and Martin* (1984) 14 ACR 73.

18 *R v Crouch* (1850) 4 Cox CC 163. Perhaps this case is best regarded as turning on an analogy with those in which the answers to questions improperly put by policemen to prisoners in custody were rejected.

19 (1869) 11 Cox CC 546.

20 *R v McCartney and Hansen* (1928) 20 Cr App Rep 179. For further cases turning on the proof of handwriting see *Lucas v Williams & Sons* [1892] 2 QB 113 and *R v Hope* (1955) 39 Cr App Rep 33. See also *R v Day* [1940] 1 All ER 402.

proved, there might be great difficulty in employing them to authenticate handwriting of any antiquity, and that is why the presumption of due execution to which reference will be made shortly is of the utmost utility.

B. PROOF OF ATTESTATION

For historical reasons to be mentioned at the end of the discussion, it is convenient to deal separately with proof of the attestation of wills and other documents required by law to be attested.

1. WILLS

If it becomes necessary to prove the due execution of a will, it is essential to call one of the attesting witness if any are available. Before other evidence is admissible, it must be shown that all the attesting witnesses are dead, insane, beyond the jurisdiction or that none of them can be traced. This requirement holds good even if the execution can be proved by those who saw it though they were not attesting witnesses, but the witness is treated as if he had been called by the court so he may be cross-examined by the party seeking to prove execution,[1] professional privilege cannot be claimed in respect of his previous statements to solicitors concerning execution,[2] and any other evidence may be given if he denies execution or refuses to testify.[3]

If none of the attesting witnesses can be called for the reasons indicated in the previous paragraph, steps must be taken to prove the handwriting of at least one of them. This constitutes secondary evidence of attestation.

If evidence of handwriting is unobtainable, evidence of those who saw the will executed, or any other evidence from which an inference of due execution can be drawn becomes admissible, but it seems that every effort must first be made to prove the handwriting of one of the attesting witnesses.[4] If a will is proved to have been in existence after the testator's death, a copy may be admitted to probate on proof that the original was signed by the testator and bore the signature of two attesting witnesses, although the person giving this evidence is unable to recollect their names.[5] It should perhaps be added that, when probate is sought in common form, the rigorous requirements as to proof of due execution to which reference has just been made do not apply.

2. OTHER DOCUMENTS REQUIRED BY LAW TO BE ATTESTED

In the case of the comparatively few documents, other than wills, to the validity of which attestation is essential, it may be proved by the testimony

1 *Oakes v Uzzell* [1932] P 19; *Re Webster, Webster v Webster* [1974] 3 All ER 822, [1974] 1 WLR 1641 (general cross-examination by both parties permissible).
2 *Re Fuld's Estate (No 2), Hartley v Fuld* [1965] P 405, [1965] 2 All ER 657.
3 *Bowman v Hodgson* (1867) LR 1 P & D 362; *Re Ovens's Goods* (1892) 29 LR Ir 451, *Re Vere-Wardale, Vere-Wardale v Johnson* [1949] P 395, [1949] 2 All ER 250.
4 *Clarke v Clarke* (1879) 5 LR Ir 47.
5 *Re Phibb's Estate* [1917] P 93; *Re Webb, Smith v Johnson* [1964] 2 All ER 91, [1964] 1 WLR 509.

of one of the subscribing witnesses, but it is unnecessary to call any of them if the person wishing to prove due execution does not desire to do so. He may content himself with proving the handwriting of an attesting witness, and, if he is unable to do this, he may have recourse to other evidence.

3. HISTORY OF THE PRESENT LAW

The rule that one of the subscribing witnesses of an attested document must be called unless they were all unavailable used to apply to all attested documents, whether attestation was required by law or not. Lord Ellenborough said that the rule was 'as fixed, formal and universal as any that can be stated in a court of justice'.[6] It probably originated in the ancient requirement that the witness to a deed should, where possible, be summoned to sit with the jury in the days when that body was composed of witnesses rather than triers of fact. In more modern times, the rule was justified on the ground that the parties to a document must be taken to have agreed that the document should not be given in evidence unless the attesting witness was called when possible,[7] but, by virtue of s 7 of the Criminal Procedure Act 1865 (which applies to civil and criminal cases), instruments to the validity of which attestation is not necessary may be proved as if there had been no attesting witnesses thereto, and s 3 of the Evidence Act 1938 provides that in any proceedings, civil or criminal, an instrument to the validity of which attestation is requisite may, instead of being proved by an attesting witness, be proved in the manner in which it might be proved if no attesting witness were alive. The only exception is the case of testamentary documents to which the section is expressly stated to be inapplicable. Section 7 of the Criminal Procedure Act 1865, and s 3 of the Evidence Act 1938, are the authorities for the foregoing treatment of the proof of attestation.

C. PRESUMPTIONS RELATING TO DOCUMENTS

Attestation, like handwriting, would not be easily proved in the case of a document of any antiquity, but practical difficulties are, in the main, obviated by the presumption of due execution that attaches to a document proved or purporting to be not less than twenty years old, provided it is produced from proper custody. 'Proper custody' is that which was reasonable and natural under the circumstances of the particular case. Expired leases may be expected to be in the custody of either lessor or lessee and those claiming under them, a family Bible may properly be in the custody of any member of the family. Proper custody in this context does not mean the most appropriate custody possible. Papers relating to a bishopric have been held to come from proper custody when found among the family papers of a deceased bishop and not, as they should have been, in the possession of the bishop for the time being,[8] but, in the absence of further explanation, the parish clerk's house is not a place of proper custody for the parish registers.[9]

---

6 *R v Harringworth (Inhabitants)* (1815) 4 M & S 350. See Stephen *Digest of the Law of Evidence* (12th edn) n XIII.
7 *Whyman v Garth* (1853) 8 Exch 803 per Pollock CB.
8 *Meath (Bishop) v Marquess of Winchester* (1836) 3 Bing NC 183.
9 *Doe d Lord Arundel v Fowler* (1850) 14 QB 700.

The other basic fact of the presumption—the age of the document—is prescribed by s 4 of the Evidence Act 1938, for criminal and civil cases. At common law the period was thirty years.

Several other useful presumptions relating to documents may be mentioned. A document is presumed to have been executed on the date it bears;[10] alterations in a deed are presumed to have been made before execution, otherwise the entire deed might be avoided, but alterations in a will are presumed to have been made after execution because they would not invalidate the entire testament.[11] It is sometimes said that there is a presumption that a deed, even when less than twenty years old, was duly sealed, but this is not a presumption which is at all clearly established by the authorities.[12]

D. THE STAMP ACT 1891

In civil proceedings, stamp objections are taken by the court and cannot be waived by the parties.[13] If the original of a document is lost, or not produced after notice, it is presumed to have been duly stamped. If a document is shown to have been unstamped at a particular time, the ordinary provisional presumption of continuance applies, and there is evidence on which the court may find that the document was never properly stamped, but there is at least one case where language is used which suggests that the court must find that a lost document was duly stamped when the question is left doubtful by the evidence.[14]

SECTION 3. THE ADMISSIBILITY OF EXTRINSIC EVIDENCE AFFECTING THE CONTENTS OF A DOCUMENT

Having dealt with what may be called the 'exclusiveness' of a document as evidence of its terms, it is now necessary to consider its conclusiveness. The general effect of the rule considered in section 1 was that the contents of a document may be proved only on production of the original. The major problems with which this section is concerned are first, whether, once a transaction has been embodied in a document, evidence may be given of terms other than those it mentions, and, second, the extent to which evidence may be given of the meaning of the terms used in the document. In each instance, the problem is one of the admissibility of 'extrinsic evidence', an expression which means any evidence other than the document the contents of which are under consideration. It is often said to be 'parol evidence', but no doubt this is because it usually takes the form of oral testimony, but it may consist of other documents.

10 *Aderson v Weston* (1840) 6 Bing NC 296.
11 *Doe d Tatum v Catomore* (1851) 16 QB 745.
12 *Re Sandilands* (1871) LR 6 CP 411; *National Provincial Bank of England v Jackson* (1886) 33 Ch D 1 at 11 and 14; *Re Balkis Consolidated Co Ltd* (1888) 58 LT 300.
13 *Bowker v Williamson* (1889) 5 TLR 382. Unstamped documents may be proved in criminal proceedings.
14 *Closmadeuc v Garrel* (1856) 18 CB 36.

A. THE CONCLUSIVENESS OF A DOCUMENT AS EVIDENCE OF THE TERMS OF THE TRANSACTION IT EMBODIES

1. STATEMENT AND ILLUSTRATIONS OF THE RULE

(i) Statement

Extrinsic evidence is generally inadmissible when it would, if accepted, have the effect of adding to, varying or contradicting the terms of a judicial record, a transaction required by law to be in writing, or a document constituting a valid and effective contract or other transaction.[15] Most judicial statements of the rule are concerned with its application to contracts, and one of the best known is that of Lord Morris who regarded it as indisputable that:

> Parol testimony cannot be received to contradict, vary, add to or subtract from the terms of a written contract or the terms in which the parties have deliberately agreed to record any part of their contract.[16]

Another well-known statement is that of Lord Denman when he said:

> If there be a contract which has been reduced into writing, verbal evidence is not allowed to be given of what passed between the parties, either before the written instrument was made, or during the time that it was in a state of preparation, so as to add to or subtract from, or in any manner to vary or qualify the written contract.[17]

Statements of this nature are best regarded as statements of the effect of the substantive law of merger which is now based on the presumed intention of the parties.[18] If the court is satisfied that they effectively agreed to be bound by a written instrument, they are bound by its terms though unacquainted with them,[19] and though one of the parties believes that something said in the course of the negotiations is still binding. In such circumstances, it would be pointless to admit extrinsic evidence with regard to those negotiations because it is irrelevant.[20] It is for the same reason that evidence that one of the parties to a written agreement did not intend to be contractually bound is inadmissible.[1] Evidence of antecedent negotiations is relevant and admissible if they retain their contractual effect or legal significance after the writing has been brought into existence. Such evidence is always admissible if tendered to establish the existence of a contract

---

15 The position is similar in Scotland, *Smith v Mackintosh* [1989] SCLR 83.

16 *Bank of Australasia v Palmer* [1897] AC 540 at 545.

17 *Goss v Lord Nugent* (1833) 5 B & Ad 58.

18 The law of merger originated in deeds and the rules of pleading, but it had come to apply to written contracts as part of the substantive law by the eighteenth century; compare Bacon's Maxims (reg 25) with Viner's Abridgement (contract g 18); contrast *Countess of Rutland's Case* (1604) 5 Co Rep 25 B with *Meres v Ansell* (1771) 3 Wils 275. See also Salmond 'The Superiority of Written Evidence' (1890) 6 LQR 75 and Wigmore 'A Brief History of the Parol Evidence Rule' (1904) 4 Columbia Law Review 33–7. For further developments, see Wedderburn in [1959] CLJ 58.

19 *Parker v South Eastern Rly Co* (1877) 2 CPD 416 at 421.

20 *Lambert v Lewis* [1982] AC 225 at 263, [1980] 1 All ER 978 at 1002 (unaffected on this point by the subsequent decision in the House of Lords).

 1 *Smith v Mansi* [1962] 3 All ER 857, [1963] 1 WLR 26.

collateral to the writing, or the conclusion of a contract which is partly oral and partly in writing. Evidence of antecedent negotiations is likewise admissible when it is relevant owing to such provisions of the substantive law as the requirement of what is now s 14(3) of the Sale of Goods Act 1979, that the buyer should make known to the seller that he relies on his skill and judgment.[2]

(ii) Illustrations

(a) Judicial records. Once it has been drawn up, the order of a court is conclusive evidence of that which was directed by the judge. Steps may be taken to have clerical errors corrected, and there may be an appeal, but, in any other proceedings, extrinsic evidence of the terms of the decision would be irrelevant.

(b) Transactions required by law to be in writing. Even when a transaction is required by law to be in writing, extrinsic evidence is admissible in aid of the interpretation of the document, but that does not constitute an infringement of the rule under consideration. Additional or different terms may not be proved by extrinsic evidence. In *Re Huxtable*,[3] a testator bequeathed four thousand pounds to C 'for charitable purposes agreed between us'. It was held that, though evidence was admissible to show what purposes had been agreed, it was not permissible to adduce evidence tending to show that only the income of the bequest was to be devoted to these purposes. That would have contradicted the will, whereas proof of the agreed purposes did not have this effect. In *Re Rees*,[4] a testator left part of his estate 'to my trustees absolutely, they well knowing my wishes concerning the same'. The Court of Appeal affirmed the judge's decision, reached without resort to extrinsic evidence, that, as a matter of construction, the estate was given on trust, and accordingly evidence showing that, in the events which had happened, the testator intended his trustees to take it beneficially was inadmissible because it would contradict the terms of the will as construed by the court.

(c) Written contracts. In *Angell v Duke*,[5] the defendant agreed in writing to let a house to the plaintiff together with the furniture therein. The plaintiff tendered evidence that, before the execution of the writing, the defendant had orally agreed to send in additional furniture, but it was held that such evidence was inadmissible because, having once executed the writing, without making the terms of the alleged parol agreement part of it, the plaintiff could not afterwards set up that agreement. It would have contradicted the restriction of the written document to furniture already in the house. In *Newman v Gatti*[6] an actress signed an agreement to understudy a named principal who left the employment of the defendant during the

---

2 *Gillespie Bros & Co v Cheney Eggar & Co* [1896] 2 QB 59; *Manchester Liners Ltd v Real Ltd* [1922] 2 AC 74 at 85; *The Preload Company of Canada Ltd v The City of Regina* (1958) 13 DLR (2d) 305.
3 *Re Huxtable, Huxtable v Crawford* [1902] 2 Ch 793.
4 *Re Rees, Williams v Hopkins* [1950] Ch 204, [1949] 2 All ER 1003.
5 (1875) 32 LT 320, but see [1959] CLJ 65–6, *Kaplan v Andrews* [1955] 4 DLR 553.
6 (1907) 24 TLR 18; see also *Grimston v Cunningham* [1894] 1 QB 125 and *Aetna Factors Corporation Ltd v Breau* (1957) 10 DLR (2d) 100.

currency of the agreement. It was held that the actress could not give evidence of an oral undertaking that she should have the right to take the place of the principal because there was no evidence that this was to be a term of the contract. The Court of Appeal recognised that in some cases a collateral verbal contract for which the consideration was the entering into the principal contract might be proved, or it could happen that, after the written contract had been drawn up, the parties realised that it did not deal with a situation which might arise, and agreed to provide for that event, but the mere fact that a promise made during the negotiations preceding a written agreement is believed to be binding by the promisee when he signs the document does not prevent the doctrine of merger from operating.

The distinction between an addition, a variation and a contradiction has not been discussed by the courts. With the possible exception of *Angell v Duke* the cases mentioned in the last paragraph were treated primarily as ones in which an effort was made to give extrinsic evidence of additional terms. A case which was treated as one of attempted variation is *Re Sutro (L) & Co and Heilbut, Symons & Co*.[7] A written contract having provided for the sale of rubber to be shipped to New York, evidence of a practice under which the goods were dispatched by rail for part of the journey was held to be inadmissible. The admissibility of evidence of a variation of a written contract which has once been concluded is plainly dependent on the substantive law. If, having regard to the rules of consideration, the variation is effective, and if, having regard to statutory provisions such as s 2 of the Law of Property (Miscellaneous Provisions) Act 1989, it is enforceable, evidence of its terms will be received. When these conditions do not apply, such evidence will be irrelevant.

> After the agreement had been reduced into writing, it is competent to the parties, at any time before breach of it, by a new contract not in writing, either altogether to waive, dissolve, or annul the former agreement, or in any manner to add to, or subtract from, or vary or qualify the terms of it, and thus to make a new contract, which is to be proved, partly by the written agreement, and partly by the subsequent verbal terms engrafted upon what will thus be left of the written agreement.[8]

These words were spoken in a case in which the plaintiff had agreed in writing to sell a number of lots of land to the defendant and tendered evidence of a subsequent oral agreement discharging him from the duty of making a good title to one of the lots. The evidence was held to be inadmissible on account of the Statute of Frauds 1677,[9] but the court was clearly of opinion that evidence of the subsequent contractual variation or discharge of a written agreement is admissible in the ordinary case.[10]

Decisions which primarily turned on the question whether extrinsic evidence could be received of terms contradicting those of a written agreement are *Henderson v Arthur*[11] and *Evans v Roe*.[12] In the first case, a lease having been executed under which rent was payable in advance, the lessee

---

7 [1917] 2 KB 348.
8 *Goss v Lord Nugent* (1833) 5 B & Ad 58 per Lord Denman CJ.
9 See now s 2 of the Law of Property (Miscellaneous Provisions) Act 1989.
10 A parol discharge as distinct from a variation was held effective in a case coming within s 4 of the Sale of Goods Act 1893 (now repealed), in *Morris v Baron & Co* [1918] AC 1.
11 [1907] 1 KB 10; see also *Goldfoot v Welch* [1914] 1 Ch 213.
12 (1872) LR 7 CP 138.

was not allowed to give evidence of a prior undertaking by the lessor to accept rent in arrears. In the second case, evidence of a contemporaneous oral agreement that a written contract of service from week to week was to last for a year was rejected. To the same effect are cases in which, when a person has signed an agreement as 'owner'[13] or 'proprietor',[14] evidence that he was acting as agent for an undisclosed principal has been held to be inadmissible, as contradicting the unambiguous statement in the agreement.[15]

2. EXCEPTIONS TO AND CASES FALLING OUTSIDE THE RULE

The case of a subsequent variation or discharge of a written agreement to which reference has already been made may be treated as an exception to the rule under consideration. Transactions required by law to be in writing may be discharged or varied by a parol contract, subject, in the case of a variation, to the requirements of the relevant statutes such as s 3 of the Law of Property (Miscellaneous Provisions) Act 1989.[16] Evidence tending to establish such a contract may be regarded as evidence varying or contradicting the terms of the original document. The same can be said of evidence varying or discharging a contract embodied in a document when writing is not a necessary condition of its validity or enforceability. The cases about to be considered can be regarded as exceptions to the rule or as falling outside it according to taste.

(i) Public registers

Oral evidence has been received and accepted although it had the effect of establishing different tonnage of a ship than that mentioned on the register of ships[17] and a different proprietorship of a taxicab than that shown on the register of hackney carriages.[18] No reasons were given for the first of these decisions. In the second case, the judgments of the Court of Appeal were exlusively concerned with the construction of the relevant statutes. The upshot seems to be that, subject to the terms of the statute under which it is kept, the contents of a public register are not conclusive.[19] Extrinsic evidence affecting their truth is therefore admissible.

---

13 *Humble v Hunter* (1848) 12 QB 310.
14 *Formby Bros v Formby* (1910) 102 LT 116. This case, and *Humble v Hunter*, were said to be no longer law by Scott LJ in *Epps v Rothnie* [1945] KB 562 at 565, [1946] 1 All ER 146 at 147 (sed quaere). The cases are discussed below. *Humble v Hunter* was held to be good law in *Murphy v Rae* [1967] NZLR 103.
15 See the converse case of *Universal Steam Navigation Co v J McKelvie & Co* [1923] AC 492 and contrast *Automobile Renault Canada Ltd v Maritime Import Autos Ltd and Kyley* (1962) 31 DLR (2d) 592.
16 *Morris v Baron & Co*, above.
17 *The Recepta* (1889) 14 PD 131.
18 *Kemp v Elisha* [1918] 1 KB 228.
19 See e g British Nationality Act 1981 s 45, which makes certificates merely prima facie evidence of the matters entered on the registers, but conclusive of other matters not so entered; see also *R v Secretary of State for the Environment, ex p Simms* (1989) Times, 27 November construing ss 53 and 56 of the Wildlife and Countryside Act 1981 to the effect that while a 'definitive' map was conclusive of its contents in independent proceedings such status does not preclude the admission of inconsistent evidence in proceedings designed to correct the map itself.

(ii) Cases concerning the validity or effectiveness of a written contract or other document

Extrinsic evidence is admissible to show that a written contract or any other document is void for mistake,[20] or illegality,[1] or for non-compliance with the provisions of a statute,[2] or voidable on account of a fraudulent or innocent misrepresentation.[3] It is also permissible to prove by extrinsic evidence that a deed or written contract, unconditional on its face, was delivered as an escrow or signed subject to a condition precedent to its effectiveness as in *Pym v Campbell*,[4] where the defendants agreed in writing to buy an invention from the plaintiff, subject to the oral stipulation that the transaction was conditional on the approval of the invention by the defendant's engineer. Extrinsic evidence was received concerning this stipulation and the fact that the invention had not been approved. Such evidence is also admissible to negative the implication of a warranty[5] or to raise an equitable defence.[6] The rule under consideration can hardly be said to be infringed in any of the cases mentioned in this paragraph because it applies only to valid and effective transactions.

(iii) Consideration

The absence of consideration invalidates a simple contract in writing, and this may always be proved by extrinsic evidence. The fact that a bill of exchange contains the words 'for value received' does not render evidence that it was an accommodation bill inadmissible in cases where the fact is relevant. When a deed contains no reference to consideration, or mentions a nominal consideration, extrinsic evidence concerning a real consideration has been held to be admissible. Thus, in *Turner v Forwood*,[7] the plaintiff entered into an agreement under seal with a company and a director in which he assigned a debt due to him from the company for a thousand and fifteen pounds to the director in consideration of ten shillings, and it was held that oral evidence might be given of an antecedent agreement by the director to pay in full for the debt. The principle underlying such decisions appears to be that, as no consideration need, in general, be expressed in a deed in order that it should be effective, the parties may often be taken to have intended that their arrangements should be carried out, partly by a contract under seal, and partly by parol. As a matter of conveyancing

20 *Henkel v Royal Exchange Assurance Co* (1749) 1 Ves Sen 317; *Wake v Harrop* (1861) 7 Jur NS 710; *Cowen v Truffitt Bros Ltd* [1899] 2 Ch 309; *Roe v Naylor* (1918) 87 LJKB 958 at 968 (non est factum); *Craddock Bros v Hunt* [1923] 2 Ch 136; *U.S.A. v Motor Trucks Ltd* [1924] AC 196.

1 *Collins v Blantern* (1767) 2 Wils 341.

2 *Campbell Discount Co Ltd v Gall* [1961] 1 QB 431, [1961] 2 All ER 104.

3 *Dobell v Stevens* (1825) 3 B & C 623.

4 (1856) 6 E & B 370; *Wallis v Littell* (1861) 11 CBNS 369; *Lindley v Lacey* (1864) 17 CBNS 578; *Davis v Jones* (1856) 17 CB 625; *Pattle v Hornibrook* [1897] 1 Ch 25, distinguished in *Smith v Mansi* [1962] 3 All ER 857, [1963] 1 WLR 26. See also *Frontier Finance Ltd v Hynes and Niagara Sewing Machine Co* (1956) 10 DLR (2d) 206. In *Re Tait* [1957] VLR 405, instructions for a will were admitted to show that a revocation clause was conditioned on the insertion of other clauses inadvertently omitted.

5 *Burges v Wickham* (1863) 3 B & S 669.

6 *Martin v Pyecroft* (1852) 2 DeGM & G 785, followed in *Scott v Bradley* [1971] Ch 850, [1971] 1 All ER 583, *Wake v Harrop* (1861) 1 H & C 202.

7 [1951] 1 All ER 746; *Clifford v Turrell* (1845) 1 Y & C Ch Cas 138 (affirmed 14 LJ Ch 390); *Frith v Frith* [1906] AC 254.

practice, it became usual to insert a nominal consideration in many deeds in order to avoid the implication of a use, so it was reasonable to infer that, so far as the intention of the parties was concerned, these cases were the same as those in which no consideration was inserted in a deed. There is no authority dealing with the admissibility of extrinsic evidence to vary a real consideration stated in a deed. In *Turner v Forwood*, Lord Goddard CJ was not prepared to say that the principle applied by him was confined to cases in which a nominal consideration was expressed in a deed, but, if the principle is extended, the question as to what undertakings are to be treated as part of the consideration would give rise to difficulty.

(iv) The real nature of the transaction

When it is relevant, having regard to the principles of common law and equity involved, extrinsic evidence may be given of the real nature of any transaction, whether it is recorded in a document in pursuance of legal requirements or at the instance of the parties. Thus evidence has been received to show that an apparent sale was really a mortgage,[8] and a secret trust could never be established without recourse to extrinsic means of proof.

(v) Capacity of parties[9]

We have seen that, if someone signs a document as 'owner' or 'proprietor', extrinsic evidence of agency is inadmissible. This may be on the principle that only one person can comply with such descriptions, so the evidence would inevitably contradict the document. Extrinsic evidence of agency has been received in the case of such other forms of signatures as 'charterer'[10] 'tenant'[11] and 'landlord'.[12] It is possible, however, that the true basis of the decisions exluding the extrinsic evidence was that it was a term of the contracts with which the court was dealing that the signatory should have been owner or proprietor. They were treated with reserve by Lord Shaw and said to be no longer law by Scott LJ.[13] Extrinsic evidence has been received of the fact that the successive indorsers of a bill of exchange were co-sureties,[14] and, in *Young v Schuler*,[15] where it was not clear whether the defendant had signed a guarantee as agent for a company or with the intention of making himself personally liable, evidence was received of his contemporaneous declaration to the latter effect. It might have been treated as an admission, but it seems to have been received on the principle, to be discussed later, under which declarations of intention are admissible in cases of equivocation.

---

8 *Re Duke of Marlborough, Davis v Whitehead* [1894] 2 Ch 133.
9 For the admissibility of extrinsic evidence to show who was purchaser and who vendor, see *Newell v Radford* (1867)LR 3 CP 52.
10 *Fred Drughorn Ltd v Rederiaktiebolaget Transatlantic* [1919] AC 203.
11 *Danziger v Thompson* [1944] KB 654, [1944] 2 All ER 151.
12 *Epps v Rothnie* [1945] KB 562, [1946] 1 All ER 146.
13 In *Drughorn's* case and *Epps v Rothnie* respectively; but see *Murphy v Rae* [1967] NZLR 103.
14 *Macdonald v Whitfield* (1883) 8 App Cas 733. See also *Rolfe, Lubell & Co v Keith* [1979] 1 All ER 860.
15 (1883) 11 QBD 651.

(vi) Collateral undertakings, contracts partly oral and partly in writing or subject to usage

We have seen that the Court of Appeal recognised in *Newman v Gatti*,[16] that a collateral oral contract might be proved when it was concluded in consideration of the execution of a written contract. In *De Lassalle v Guildford*,[17] for instance, the plaintiff made it plain to his landlord, the defendant, that he would not execute a lease unless the defendant gave a warranty concerning the healthy condition of the drains. Such warranty was given orally, and the lease was duly executed. The lease did not refer to the state of the drains, but it was held that this fact did not prevent the adduction of oral evidence concerning the warranty.

A court may likewise come to the conclusion that the parties intended their contract to be partly oral and partly in writing, in which case the oral parts may be proved by parol testimony. In *Harris v Rickett*,[18] the defendant was allowed to prove that a written agreement for a loan was accompanied by an oral stipulation that a bill of sale would be given. The plaintiff contended that the effect of this evidence was to add to or vary the writing but Pollock CB said that: 'the rule relied on by the plaintiff only applies when the parties to an agreement reduce it to writing and agree or intend that writing should be their agreement.' A further example of the use of extrinsic evidence is provided by cases in which one party has been allowed to establish a trade usage provided it is not inconsistent with the writing.[19]

> In all contracts, as to the subject-matter of which known usages prevail, parties are found to proceed with the tacit assumption of these usages, they commonly reduce into writing the special particulars of their agreement but omit to specify these known usages, which are included, however, as of course, by mutual understanding, evidence therefore of such incidents is receivable. The contract in truth is partly express and in writing, partly implied or understood and unwritten.[20]

(vii) Memoranda

In some cases, after an oral contract has been concluded, a memorandum relating to the whole or part of the transaction is prepared by one of the parties and handed to the other. The document may then be treated as a mere memorandum, and, as it has no contractual effect, additional matter may be proved. Whether the writing is to be treated thus, or whether it will be held to be, not a memorandum, but a contractual document, depends on the intention of the parties, which must, in the absence of direct evidence, be ascertained by means of the inferences which a reasonable man would draw from the terms of the document and the surrounding circumstances. In *Aleen*

---

16 (1907) 24 TLR 18; see also *Bristol Tramways etc Carriage Co v Fiat Motors* [1910] 2 KB 831 at 838; and *Heilbut, Symons & Co v Buckleton* [1913] AC 30 at 47.

17 [1901] 2 KB 215; *Morgan v Griffith* (1871) LR 6 Exch 70; *Erskine v Adeane* (1873) 8 Ch App 756; *City and Westminster Properties (1934) Ltd v Mudd* [1959] Ch 129, [1958] 3 All ER 733. A possible distinction between this last case and *Angell v Duke* is that in *Angell v Duke* the lessee did not insist on the provision of further furniture being part of the consideration for his executing the lease. Cf *Couchman v Hill* [1947] KB 554, [1947] 1 All ER 103.

18 (1959) 4 H & N 1.

19 The distinction between usages which add to and contradict a document is difficult. Contrast *Brown v Byrne* (1854) 3 E & B 703 with *Krall v Burnett* (1887) 25 WR 305.

20 Per Coleridge J in *Brown v Byrne* (1854) 3 E & B 703.

v Pink,[1] the plaintiff bought a horse from the defendant who handed him a receipt for the purchase price, and it was held that this did not preclude the plaintiff from proving an oral warranty of the fitness of the animal. Lord Abinger CB concluded that the paper appeared to have been meant merely as a memorandum of the transaction, or an informal receipt for the money, not as containing the terms of the contract itself. This case may be contrasted with *Hutton v Watling*[2] in which a document providing for the sale of a business by the defendant to the plaintiff and containing an option to purchase the land on which the business was carried on was treated as contractual by the Court of Appeal with the result that the defendant's evidence, in an action for specific performance of the option, that no option was given, was held to be inadmissible. The court treated the matter as one of construction, adding that:

> The true construction of a document means no more than that the court puts upon it the true meaning, being the meaning which the other party, to whom the document was handed or who is relying upon it, would put upon it as an ordinary intelligent person construing the words in a proper way in the light of the relevant circumstances.[3]

The cases on collateral contracts, contracts partly oral and partly in writing, contracts subject to usage and memoranda raise the question whether, at least in its application to contracts, what is often called the parol evidence rule is anything more than an empty tautology.[4] If the law is simply that extrinsic evidence is inadmissible when the parties intended that a document should contain their entire contract, extrinsic evidence is naturally inadmissible because it is irrelevant. Cases like *Hutton v Watling* show that the rule is not a tautology because the parties are bound by the terms of a document if a reasonable man would have considered the document to be a contractual one. This is so even if one of them thought that the contract contained additional terms not mentioned in the document or that a clearly expressed term to which he had agreed bore a special meaning.[5]

(viii) Proceedings between strangers

There is little doubt that, in proceedings between strangers to transactions required by law to be in writing, the circumstances in which extrinsic evidence is admissible are the same as those in which such evidence is admissible in proceedings between the parties to the document, but there is some authority for the view that extrinsic evidence is always admissible when the document merely embodies a transaction to the validity of which

---

1 (1838) 4 M & W 140; as between the parties a bill of lading is a memorandum, *Ardennes SS (Cargo Owner) v Ardennes S S (Owners)* [1951] 1 KB 55, [1950] 2 All ER 517, cf *Leduc v Ward* (1888) 20 QBD 475, turning on the point that the bill is conclusive evidence of the terms of the shipment as between shipowner and indorsee under the Bills of Lading Act 1855. Another case in which a post-contractual document was treated as a memorandum is *Bank of Australasia v Palmer* [1897] AC 540.
2 [1948] Ch 398, [1948] 1 All ER 803; *Stuart v Dundon* [1963] SASR 134.
3 Per Lord Greene MR at 403, 805 respectively.
4 See the discussion of this point by G H Treitel in *The Law of Contract* (6th edn) 156.
5 See the speech of Lord Denning in *London County Council v Henry Boot & Sons Ltd* [1959] 3 All ER 636 at 641. The parties may be bound by terms to which they have agreed although they both think the terms have a different meaning from that ultimately placed on them by the court.

the writing is not essential even if it has the effect of varying, adding to, or contradicting the terms of the writing. In *R v Inhabitants of Cheadle*[6] the parish was allowed to call a pauper whose settlement was in issue to swear that a deed of conveyance to which he was party was, contrary to its express terms, unsupported by consideration. In *R v Adamson*,[7] the accused was charged with obtaining money by false pretences as a premium payable under a deed of partnership executed by the prosecutor. It was held that the prosecutor could give evidence of a different consideration for the payment of the premium than that stated in the deed. Stephen treated these cases as authorities for a general exception to the rule prohibiting extrinsic evidence adding to, varying or contradicting the terms of a document,[8] but this rule certainly applies in some cases in which one of the parties to the proceedings was not a party to the writing. In *Mercantile Bank of Sydney v Taylor*,[9] for instance, the bank was not allowed to adduce evidence of an oral agreement between themselves and one of sereral sureties, of whom the defendant was another, that the guaranteed debt should not be included in a release from liability given by them. The evidence received in *R v Inhabitants of Cheadle* would now be admissible in proceedings between parties to the deed[10] and *R v Adamson* may simply indicate that the rule does not apply in criminal proceedings. The authorities are too scanty to be a convenient subject for any generalisation.[11]

The Law Commission, although at first inclined to recommend abolition of the rule, ultimately came to the conclusion that it had become too ineffective to cause serious difficulty, and that more disruption would probably be caused by formal abolition than by leaving it alone.[12]

B. EXTRINSIC EVIDENCE IN AID OF INTERPRETATION[13]

It has been said that:

> The admission of extrinsic circumstances to govern the construction of a written instrument is in all cases an exception to the general rule of law which excludes everything dehors the instrument.[14]

But statements of this nature must be read with caution, for it would be impossible to interpret most documents if some extrinsic matter were not allowed to be proved. If a testator bequeaths 'my piano to my son John',

---

6 (1832) 3 B & Ad 833. Contrast the operation of the rule that a document is exclusive evidence of its terms as illustrated by *Augustien v Challis* (1847) 1 Exch 279.

7 (1843) 2 Mood CC 286.

8 *Digest of the Law of Evidence* (12th Edn) art 99.

9 [1893] AC 317.

10 See *Frith v Frith* [1906] AC 254.

11 It has been held in South Africa that the rule does not apply between strangers (*Davies v Brooklands Car Sales* 1956 (1) SA 745).

12 Law Commission No 154 (Cmnd 9700) (1986) Part III. The term 'parol evidence rule' as used in this paper is confined to the rule so far discussed in this section. The paper is not concerned with the rules discussed in section 1 and in the remainder of this section.

13 Now that s 21 of the Administration of Justice Act 1982 has implemented the recommendations of the 19th Report of the Law Reform Committee on the Interpretation of Wills (Cmnd 5301), it has been possible to eliminate much of the discussion of the old case law to be found in some previous editions of this work.

14 Per Sir T Plumer MR in *Colpoys v Colpoys* (1822) Jac 451.

evidence must perforce be received to show that there were in existence at his death a chattel and a person corresponding to these descriptions. In the words of James LJ: 'You must always, of course, have evidence who are the persons mentioned, and you must also have evidence of what are the things bequeathed'.[15] The main problem in relation to the construction of a will was the extent to which it was permissible to go beyond these matters in cases of disputed interpretation, and a similar problem arises with regard to the construction of other documents[16]—if there is a doubt concerning the persons or things to which the document refers, is it permissible to consider the surrounding circumstances and the extrinsic declarations of the parties in order to resolve the doubt, or must the document be held void for uncertainty? In some cases there may be no alternative to the adoption of the latter course. If a testator leaves his estate to 'Lady   ', or to 'One or other of my daughters Joan and Jane', even if it is proved that he was acquainted with women of title, or the father of daughters named Joan and Jane respectively, no further evidence might be forthcoming, in which case there would hardly be a rational alternative to holding that he died intestate. There is, however, an infinite variety of degrees of doubt concerning the certainty with which a document may be interpreted. At the one extreme there are the cases of complete uncertainty to which reference has just been made, at the other there is the case of virtually complete certainty as where a man leaves everything to 'my only son John', and it is proved that he had but one son and that son's name is John.

The extent to which a document may be treated as conclusive as to the meaning of its terms is thus a question of degree. It can hardly ever be completely so, because some extrinsic evidence must be received but the nature of such evidence, and the purposes for which it may be used in a case in which the meaning of a document is disputed, depends on the standard of interpretation by which the litigation must be decided.

1. STANDARDS OF INTERPRETATION

Wigmore[17] spoke of four possible standards—the popular, the local, the common and the individual. The popular standard refers to the ordinary meaning of words; the local standard refers to possible variations of the popular within a particular community, trade or religious sect; the common standard covers the sense in which the words were understood by both parties to a contract, while the individual standard is that of one party to a transaction and is, in general, relevant only in cases of will construction. Subject to the need to resort to extrinsic evidence in order to ascertain the persons and things covered by the words used, the application of the popular standard is a matter of exegesis aided by judicial notice rather than evidence. Judicial notice may be taken of some local or trade usages, but these are matters which usually have to be proved. The application of the common and individual standards calls, in the absence of anything in the nature of a formal admission, for extrinsic evidence which can be either circumstantial

---

15 *Sherratt v Mountford* (1873) 8 Ch App 928 at 929.
16 The rules apply similarly to documents whether or not required to be evidenced or made in writing, and whether or not referring to future liabilities, *Perrylease Ltd v Imecor AG* [1987] 2 All ER 373, [1988] 1 WLR 463.
17 Paras 2458 and 2460.

or testimonial. Assuming that no exclusionary rules apply, the fact that the parties to a contract have a common objective may warrant an inference concerning the meaning they attached to certain clauses, just as the speech habits of a testator may justify a particular construction of the words used by him. The meaning of the contracting parties and the testator could also, subject to exclusionary rules, be proved in the one case by their direct oral evidence and, in either case, by their out of court statements.

According to Wigmore, the application of each of the above standards should be, and to a large extent is, provisional. This means that extrinsic evidence in aid of interpretation may take a variety of forms and be adduced for a number of different purposes varying with the facts of the particular case, but Wigmore did not deny the existence of restrictions on its admissibility. Such restrictions may, as a matter of law, rule out one or more of the standards which have just been mentioned.

In the first place, there was a general rule (subject to very limited exceptions) excluding the statements of intention of the testator or contracting parties as evidence of the sense in which words were used by them in the will or written contract under consideration. In the case of wills, that general rule has been abrogated by s 21 of the Administration of Justice Act 1982 for wills taking effect after 1 January 1983.

Secondly, the individual standard must always be inapplicable when the court is concerned with the construction, as opposed to the existence, avoidance or rectification of a contract:

> The words used may, and often do, represent a formula which means different things to each side, yet be accepted because that is the only way to get agreement and in the hope that disputes will not arise. The only course there can be is to try to ascertain the natural meaning.[18]

But the most important of all the restrictions on the application of any standard of interpretation but the popular is the survival or, assuming it has not survived, the influence, of what may be called the 'plain meaning' rule. According to this rule, if the words of a document apply exactly to a particular person or thing in their ordinary natural sense, extrinsic evidence cannot be received to displace it. In other words, if the document contains names or descriptive phrases which are wholly appropriate when the popular standard of interpretation is applied, resort cannot be had, in the case of a contract, to the common standard, and, in the case of a will, to the individual standard:

> Suppose . . . a testator left a legacy to his son *John*, and suppose he had a son *John* who had been living away from him, and there was another person named *John* living with him who was not his son, but whom he called his son, in such a case would any evidence be admitted that his son *John* was not the person intended to be benefited? How can the fact of a testator being in the habit of calling a person his son who is not his son be evidence of surrounding circumstances? It is really evidence of the intention of the testator. . . [19]

---

18 Per Lord Wilberforce in *Prenn v Simmonds* [1971] 3 All ER 237 at 241.
19 Per Kay LJ in *Re Fish, Ingham v Rayner* [1894] 2 Ch 83 at 86. The Administration of Justice Act 1982, s 21, would now allow such evidence to be adduced.

2. INTERPRETATION OF WILLS

Most of the discussion of the admissibility of extrinsic evidence in aid of interpretation has been derived from learning devoted to the rules governing the interpretation of wills. A number of principles, representing the common law of his day, was drawn up by Wigram in 1831. Wills created special problems because of the expectations and disappointments so often generated by death. The resolution of disputes so created is rendered particularly difficult because of the unavailability as a witness of the testator, who would have been the one to know most about the matters in issue. It was, of course, for such reasons that the law insisted upon strict formal requirements for the making, and proof, of a will. Much of the rigidity of the rules excluding extrinsic evidence in aid of the interpretation of wills was explained by the quite understandable desire to prevent the formal rules from being undermined. All extrinsic evidence was looked upon with suspicion, but none with more than the testator's direct statement of his intentions. It would hardly have made sense to insist upon strict formal rules for making wills, and then to allow any vague expression to be interpreted in the light of informal statements of the testator.

On the other hand a succession of cases exemplified the unsatisfactory nature of a system of rigid exclusionary rules, which often defeated the intentions of the testator completely. Thus in *Doe d Chichester v Oxenden*[20] the will referred to 'my estate of Ashton', and was construed so as to apply strictly to the testator's actual estate at Ashton, despite clear evidence that he was in the habit of including other nearby estates in his references to 'the Ashton estate'. The rigidity of these principles was further exemplified by a decision of the House of Lords in this century. In *Higgins v Dawson*[1] the question was whether pecuniary legacies were payable out of the entire residuary estate of a testator or only out of such estate after two sums due to the deceased on mortgages had been deducted. The testator had bequeathed 'all the residue and remainder' of these sums to named persons after 'payment of my debts, funeral and testamentary expenses'. In favour of the contention that the sums due on mortgage should be liable to bear their portion of the legacies, it was sought to adduce evidence that, when he made his will, the testator's estate, apart from these sums, was insufficient to meet the legacies so that he must have intended to charge them on the mortgage debts. It was held that the evidence was inadmissible because the language used by the testator clearly meant that the residue of the sums due on mortgage was to be calculated without deducting anything in respect of the legacies. In both of these cases the words bore on their face a plain, and apparently unambiguous, meaning.

Similar difficulties are created by incomplete description or misdescription. Thus in one case[2] land was devised to John Hiscocks the eldest son of John Hiscocks. John Hiscocks had two sons: Simon, the eldest, and John, his second son, who was however his eldest son by a second marriage. It was held that this fact, and a number of other circumstances pointing to an

---

20 (1816) 3 Taunt 147.
 1 [1902] AC 1. A less rigid line was taken in *NSPCC v Scottish NSPCC* [1915] AC 207. *Higgins v Dawson* was distinguished by the New Zealand Court of Appeal in *Re Bell, Bell v Bell* [1964] NZLR 912 on the strength of *Re Knight, Re Wynn, Midland Bank Executor and Trustee Co Ltd v Parker* [1957] Ch 441, [1957] 2 All ER 252.
 2 *Doe d Hiscocks v Hiscocks* (1839) 5 M & W 363.

intention that the second son should benefit, were admissible in evidence; but it was also held that the testator's declarations of intention were inadmissible.[3]

The old law distinguished such a situation from an equivocation where the description in the will clearly intends unique denotation, but is capable of applying to more than one instance. Here even the old law went a step further, and allowed use of the testator's informal declarations of intent to help resolve the ambiguity. In *Doe d Gord v Needs*[4] land was devised to 'George Gord, the son of Gord', and extrinsic evidence showed that there were two persons answering that description. Evidence was admitted of the testator's declarations of intention indicating which of the two he meant to benefit. In the words of Parke B:

> There is no blank before the name of Gord the father, which might have occasioned a doubt whether the devisor had finally fixed on any certain person in his mind. The devisor has clearly selected a particular individual as his devisee ... The evidence of the declarations of the testator has not the effect of varying the instrument in any way whatever; it only enables the court to reject one of the subjects, or objects, to which the description in the will applies; and to determine which of the two the devisor understood to be signified in the description in the will.

These rules were overlaid by further strata of learning devoted to such questions as whether the misdescription or equivocation was required to be patent, as in *Doe d Gord v Needs*, or could be discerned only after the reception of extrinsic evidence, as in *Doe d Chichester v Oxenden*. Then there were anomalies stemming from the reception of extrinsic evidence to show special meanings of particular terms, as in *Smith v Wilson*,[5] or even of particular names, as in *Re Ofner, Samuel v Ofner*[6] where the testator's declaration of intention to benefit a particular person was admitted merely to show his habit of misdescribing that person, and so indirectly to construe the use of the same misdescription in the will.

In addition there was some variation between the rules relating to the interpretation of wills and of other documents, such as contracts where extrinsic evidence was admissible, not only to resolve an ambiguity or uncertainty but also to raise one, as where the terms of a conversation were admitted to show that 'your wool' mentioned in the defendant's agent's written offer to buy included a quantity of wool produced by the plaintiff from other farms.[7]

For these reasons the whole question of the interpretation of wills was referred to the Law Reform Committee, which reported in 1973.[8] The whole Committee favoured an extension of the use of extrinsic evidence to resolve ambiguities, misdescription, partial description and equivocation. It was divided on how far to permit the use of direct evidence of the testator's dispositive intentions. The majority took the view that to allow it in all cases would go further than the rules applying to other documents, and would

3 See also *Charter v Charter* (1874) LR 7 HL 364.
4 (1836) 2 M & W 129.
5 (1832) 3 B & Ad 728 ('a thousand rabbits' held to mean 'twelve hundred rabbits').
6 [1909] 1 Ch 60.
7 *Macdonald v Longbottom* (1860) 1 E & E 987 at 989 per Byles J.
8 19th Report (Cmnd 5301).

lead to uncertainty, expense and delay.[9] This view was accepted, and s 21 of the Administration of Justice Act 1982 embodies it:

> (1) This section applies to a will—
>   (a) in so far as any part of it is meaningless;
>   (b) in so far as the language used in any part of it is ambiguous on the face of it;
>   (c) in so far as evidence, other than evidence of the testator's intention, shows that the language used in any part of it is ambiguous in the light of surrounding circumstances.
>
> (2) In so far as this section applies to a will extrinsic evidence of the testator's intention, may be admitted to assist in its interpretation.

This section should be read in conjunction with s 20 which extends the application of the equitable doctrine of rectification to wills, and thus allows words to be added to the probate, not, as before, merely to be omitted.

It is not intended that the section will enable a court to make a testator's will for him. Thus it will not allow complete blanks to be filled in, nor, it is submitted, will it allow vestigial coding to be expanded.[10] The use, and limitations, of the new law were demonstrated in *Re Williams, Wiles v Madgin*[11] where a letter written by a testatrix to her solicitor explaining her intentions was admitted to help construe her will, but was unable to remedy the deficiency, which there was the omission of words of gift. The instructions indicated an order of preference of potential beneficiaries, but was of too vague and preparatory a nature to be regarded as more than instructions for a draft. It was held however that the letter could be used only to attempt to resolve the ambiguity, justifying its admission, and not for any other purpose. The admissibility of this letter under the new provisions may be compared with the inadmissibility of counsel's opinion to help construe a settlement drawn up in consequence of it.[12]

The new section clearly retains the possibility of reference to the testator's direct statement of intention in cases of patent equivocation like *Doe d Gord v Needs*,[13] or to resolve the problem of misdescription or incomplete description, thus adding to the evidence admissible if facts like those of *Doe d Hiscocks v Hiscocks*[14] or *Charter v Charter*[15] were to recur. It would be of still more assistance in cases like *Doe d Chichester v Oxenden*[16] or *Higgins v Dawson*[17] where anything but direct evidence of the testator's intention would be admissible to demonstrate the ambiguity, and then, even including such direct evidence of intention, to resolve it.

It seems likely, and is to be hoped, that these provisions will achieve the

---

9 Para 54.
10 As in *Clayton v Lord Nugent* (1844) 13 M & W 200 where the letters K, L and M were used and a key made after the will was rejected.
11 [1985] 1 All ER 964.
12 *Rabin v Gerson Berger Association Ltd* [1985] 1 All ER 1041, [1985] 1 WLR 595.
13 (1836) 2 M & W 129.
14 (1839) 5 M & W 363.
15 (1874) LR 7 HL 364.
16 (1816) 3 Taunt 147.
17 [1902] AC 1.

aim of the Law Reform Committee to make this branch of the law simpler and more logical. It has been seen that more satisfactory results would apparently have been achieved in the difficult problems thrown up by the old cases, and with the entry into force of these new provisions it seems that a complicated and confusing chapter of the law of evidence can now be closed.

CHAPTER XX

Proof of frequently recurring matters

There is a sense in which this chapter is redundant, for almost every point made in it can be found elsewhere in this book. The collection under one head of the different ways in which evidence may be given of certain matters which frequently have to be proved in litigation may, however, be of some use to the student, if not to the practitioner. The proof of handwriting and certain kinds of document, both private and public was considered in the last chapter as well as the important provisions of the Bankers' Books Evidence Act 1879. It is now proposed to consider the proof of foreign law, identification, birth, death, age, marriage and legitimacy, judgments, convictions and other orders of the court and various other miscellaneous matters. Reference will from time to time be made to judicial notice and presumptions, although it is not customary to describe them as means of proof. The possibility of a fact being admitted formally or informally should be borne in mind when the following paragraphs are being read.

SECTION 1. FOREIGN LAW[1]

We saw in ch IV that, so far as the English courts are concerned, foreign law is a question of fact which since 1920 has to be decided by the judge.[2] We also saw in ch IV that, in this context, 'foreign law' comprises the law of Scotland, the law of the British dominions and colonies and, to some extent, the laws of Eire and Northern Ireland as well as the law of a foreign country in the strict sense of the term.

The general rule is that foreign law must be proved by an expert witness who will, in a disputed or complicated case, give his evidence on oath in the ordinary way. In simple routine cases it is not uncommon for the evidence to be by affidavit, or resort might be had to the Civil Evidence Act 1968.[3] The effect of the general rule is that foreign law cannot usually be the subject of judicial notice,[4] or, at common law, inferred from previous English decisions on the same subject.[5] Before s 4(2), (5) of the Civil Evidence Act 1972 came into force it had to be proved afresh by an expert in each case. There are, however, certain cases in which foreign law is the subject of judicial notice or something taken to have been established by a previous English decision, and there are also some special statutory provisions

1 For a much fuller discussion and citation of authority see Dicey and Morris *Conflict of Laws* (11th edn) ch 9.
2 The same is true in Scotland, see *Armour v Thyssen Edelstahlwerke AG* [1989] SCLR 26.
3 *Markes v Markes* (1955) 106 LJ 75 (a decision on the Evidence Act 1938); *Kirsh v Kirsh* [1958] SASR 258.
4 *Brenan and Galen's Case* (1847) 10 QB 492 at 498.
5 *M'Cormick v Garnett* (1854) 23 LJCh 777.

governing the proof of foreign law. These matters will be considered before reference is made to the question of the qualification of the expert when testifying in cases to which the general rule applies.

The burden of proof rests on the party asserting that foreign law differs from English law. This is frequently expressed, rather infelicitously, by saying that there is a presumption that foreign and English law are the same.

A. JUDICIAL NOTICE AND PREVIOUS DECISIONS

We saw in ch II that judicial notice may be taken of notorious facts, and, in some exceptional cases, the English courts have treated certain items of foreign law as matters of notoriety. The most famous instance is provided by *Saxby v Fulton*[6] in which judicial notice was taken of the fact that roulette is legal in Monte Carlo. Judicial notice might also be taken of the common law of Northern Ireland,[7] or of European Community Law,[8] and the House of Lords will take judicial notice of Scots law.[9] Under the Maintenance Orders Act 1950, s 22(2), judicial notice must be taken of the law with regard to maintenance orders in every part of the United Kingdom. It also seems to be settled that once a statute passed in a British possession is properly before an English court, that court may construe the statute with the result that a body of case law on the subject may be created.[10] The principal statute is the Evidence (Colonial Statutes) Act 1907, which is confined to British possessions, and it is not clear how far the English courts will construe foreign legislation without the guidance of an expert witness. There are cases in which the English courts appear to have done this, and their decisions are then, presumably, binding on other courts within the limits of the doctrine of precedent.[11]

Section 4(2) of the Civil Evidence Act 1972 permits the reception as evidence of foreign law of any previous determination by an English court of the point in question, provided it is reported in citable form,[12] and provided notice of intention to rely upon it has been given to the other parties to the proceedings.[13] The foreign law is to be taken to be in accordance with the determination unless the contrary is proved. It makes no difference whether the point was determined in civil or criminal

---

6 [1909] 2 KB 208; see also *Re Turner, Heyding v Hinchliff* [1906] WN 27.
7 *Re Nesbitt* (1844) 14 LJMC 30 at 33. See Nokes 'Irish Law in English Courts' [1960] ICLQ 564.
8 European Communities Act 1972, s 3.
9 This is on account of the House's appellate jurisdiction in civil cases. It is doubtful whether the House of Lords would take judicial notice of Scots criminal law, should the question ever arise. The House would take judicial notice of the law of Northern Ireland.
10 *Re Sebba, Lloyds Banks, Ltd v Hutson* [1959] Ch 166, [1958] 3 All ER 393, following *Re Goetze, National Provincial Bank Ltd v Mond* [1953] Ch 96, [1953] 1 All ER 76. See also 22 MLR 317; 24 MLR 312. In *Mahadervan v Mahadervan* [1964] P 233 at 240, [1962] 3 All ER 1108 at 1113 it was said that an English court can construe a written foreign law once it is in evidence. Most of the decisions on this matter relate to countries to which the Evidence (Colonial Statutes) Act 1907 applies, although, in several instances, no reference is actually made to the Statute. See also *Shariff v Azad* [1967] 1 QB 605, [1966] 3 All ER 785.
11 In *Re Cohn* [1945] Ch 5, the English court appears to have construed a provision in the German Civil Code with expert evidence, and presumably its decision on the point constitutes a precedent.
12 Ie in a report which could, if the question had been one of English law, have been cited as authority in any court in England or Wales.
13 See RSC Ord 38, r (7).

proceedings, but foreign law may only be proved in this way in civil proceedings.[14]

B. OTHER STATUTORY PROVISIONS

Under the Evidence (Colonial Statutes) Act 1907,[15] copies of Acts, Ordinances and Statutes passed by or under the authority of the legislature of any British possession shall be received in evidence by all courts of justice in the United Kingdom if purporting to be printed by the Government Printer[16] without any proof given that the copies were so printed. The term 'British possession' means any part of Her Majesty's dominions exclusive of the United Kingdom.[17] It is clear that this statute enables an English court to receive a statute or subordinate legislation of a British possession in evidence on the mere production of a Government Printer's copy, but the Act of 1907 would not be much use if this were all that it has achieved, and it has been held in a number of cases that the English courts may construe the statute, acting on its provisions as so construed without anything in the nature of expert evidence.[18]

There has long been provision for ascertaining foreign law by special reference to a foreign court. Within the Commonwealth this can be accomplished by the use of the British Law Ascertainment Act 1859.[19] Although the law to which it refers is strictly not 'foreign', of perhaps greater importance is the provision in art 177 of the Treaty of Rome that any subordinate court of a member country of the European Community may, if it considers it necessary to give judgment, refer any question of the interpretation of Community law to the European Court for its opinion, and that any final court must do so. In *Bulmer (HP) Ltd v Bollinger SA*[20] the Court of Appeal set out guidelines to assist in determining when such reference was to be considered necessary, and for determining whether to exercise discretion to do so where it exists.

Although the Evidence (Foreign, Dominion and Colonial Documents) Act 1933 does not, strictly speaking, relate to the proof of foreign law, it contains useful provisions which should never be forgotten in cases involving a foreign element. Put very briefly, its effect is that Orders in Council may be made with regard to the proof, by authenticated copy, of extracts from public registers in the foreign country or dominion to which the order applies. The certificate is not merely evidence of the contents of the register, but also evidence of the facts stated. The statute is therefore of great utility in connection with the proof of births, deaths and marriages occurring abroad. In the case of a marriage, it will generally dispense with the necessity

14 There was a corresponding provision in the draft Bill attached to the 11th Report of the Criminal Law Revision Committee, but it was omitted from the Police and Criminal Evidence Act 1984 and from the Criminal Justice Act 1988.

15 See also the Colonial Laws Validity Act 1865, s 6.

16 Ie the Government Printer of the possession.

17 Quaere whether this statute still applies to all Commonwealth countries.

18 See the numerous cases cited in *Jasiewicz v Jasiewicz* [1962] 3 All ER 1017, [1962] 1 WLR 1426.

19 The comparable provision in relation to non-British law, the Foreign Law Ascertainment Act 1861, was never invoked, and consequently repealed in 1973.

20 [1974] Ch 401, [1974] 2 All ER 1226. See also *Customs and Excise Comrs v ApS Samex (Hanil Synthetic Fiber Industrial Co)* [1983] 1 All ER 1042.

of calling an expert in the relevant foreign law in order to swear that the certificate would be accepted as evidence of the marriage in question in the courts of the foreign country. A number of Orders in Council have been made under the Act.

C. EXPERT WITNESS

When a case falls within the general rule requiring proof of foreign law by an expert, the witness must be properly qualified. There has never been any doubt that a judge or regular practitioner in the jurisdiction whose law is in question is properly qualified,[1] but this was once thought to be both a sufficient and necessary condition. In *Bristow v Sequeville*[2] a jurisconsult, adviser to the Prussian consulate in London who had studied law in Leipzig and knew that the Code Napoleon was in force in Saxony was not allowed to give evidence concerning the Code. A number of cases departed from this rigid attitude over the years, and it seems that Civil Evidence Act 1972, s 4(1) did no more than enact the common law in declaring that a person suitably qualified on account of knowledge or experience is competent to give evidence of foreign law irrespective of whether he has acted or is qualified to act as a legal practitioner in the country in question.[3]

This leaves open the question of what constitutes a suitable qualification. It seems that practical experience will suffice, even though gained as business man,[4] banker,[5] diplomat,[6] or Governor-General,[7] rather than as legal practitioner. A teacher of the law of the jurisdiction in question may be sufficiently qualified,[8] though it is doubtful whether a student would be. Conversely the evidence of a legal practitioner may be rejected if he cannot be shown to have practical experience.[9] There may indeed be room for argument as to what counts as practical experience.[10] A more lenient view used to be taken of the qualifications regarded as suitable, when there were particularly few witnesses,[11] though modern communications and relaxation of the hearsay rule should reduce the need for such leniency today.

The decision whether the proposed witness is properly qualified is made by the judge as a condition precedent to the admission of the evidence. In coming to a conclusion on a question of foreign law, the English courts may

1 *Baron De Bode's Case* (1845) 8 QB 208.
2 (1850) 5 Exch 275.
3 It is to be hoped that this is the case since the recommendation of the Criminal Law Revision Committee in Cmnd 4991 draft Bill cl 44 that a similar provision be enacted for criminal proceedings has not been implemented in the Police and Criminal Evidence Act 1984 nor in the Criminal Justice Act 1988.
4 *Vander Donckt v Thellusson* (1849) 8 CB 812.
5 *Ajami v Customs Controller* [1954] 1 WLR 1405.
6 *Re Dost Aly Khan's Goods* (1880) 6 PD 6.
7 *Cooper-King v Cooper-King* [1900] P 65.
8 *Brailey v Rhodesia Consolidated Ltd* [1910] 2 Ch 95 (Reader in Roman-Dutch Law at Council for Legal Education); contrast *Bristow v Sequeville* (above) (a former student).
9 *Cartwright v Cartwright and Anderson* (1878) 26 WR 684 (English barrister as to law of Canada when he had appeared in the Privy Council on Canadian appeals, but not in the relevant area of law).
10 In *R v Brady* (1980) 57 FLR 198 the witness carried on a tax consultancy practice involving schemes operating under the law of Liechtenstein which he had studied only at second hand, and was held entitled to give evidence on the general basis of the law, but not of its detailed application.
11 See *Direct Winters Transport v Duplate Canada Ltd* (1962) 32 DLR 2d 278.

consider foreign statutes and decisions referred to by the expert witness, and, in the event of a conflict of expert testimony, the English judge must resolve it.[12]

SECTION 2. EVIDENCE OF IDENTITY

Evidence of identity is required in a wide variety of situations. Most often it relates to the identity of persons, but sometimes relates to the identity of objects. In a sense all litigation involves questions of the identity of persons, since the relevant order must relate to the same person as was implicated in the events upon the proof of which the order was made. The most common situation however occurs in criminal cases where it can be established that a crime has been committed, and witnesses are prepared to testify that they observed the accused in circumstances making it likely that he committed it. Sometimes the presence of the accused in a relevant place is controverted, but sometimes his presence may be admitted, and the question arises as to whether it was the accused or others of those also present who acted in a particular way.[13] Identification can, of course, be equally central in civil cases, for example, whether a particular claimant to an estate is the rightful heir.[14]

Evidence of identity is at its most vulnerable when it purports to be based upon the identification by a human being of the features of another human being, whether those features are identified by sight, hearing, smell or, just conceivably,[15] touch, based upon an evanescent contact in the past. Sometimes the past occasion has been captured in more permanent form, for example, on a video or tape recording, in which case the jury may make their own identification, perhaps assisted by identification testimony from witnesses who have greater familiarity with the accused.[16] Identification may also be accomplished by the use of circumstances rather than testimonial evidence, or by presumption. This section will consider identification by direct, circumstantial and presumptive evidence separately, but the first is by far the most important.

A. DIRECT EVIDENCE

This part will first consider the reasons why direct evidence of identity poses particular problems, then the reactions of courts and law reformers to their perception of such problems. It will then go on to consider the modern law, mentioning in turn the different forms of identification, the question of the procedure for considering them, and finally the proper direction to be given to the jury.

---

12 *Re Duke of Wellington* [1947] Ch 506, [1947] 2 All ER 854.
13 This has been regarded as not requiring the same consideration of caution as identification in the normal sense, *R v Oakwell* [1978] 1 All ER 1223.
14 As in the famous nineteenth century case of the Tichborne claimant, a dispute which could probably by modern methods of genetic testing nowadays be settled with complete certainty.
15 Taste does seem inconceivable.
16 *Kajala v Noble* (1982) 75 Cr App Rep 149; *R v Fowden and White* [1982] Crim LR 588; *R v Grimer* [1982] Crim LR 674. But not if the witnesses have no more previous knowledge of the accused than the jury itself, see *R v Leaney* (1989) 50 CCC (3d) 289.

1. SPECIAL PROBLEMS[17]

It was stated by the Criminal Law Revision Committee in its Eleventh Report that:[18]

> We regard mistaken identification as by far the greatest cause of actual or possible wrong convictions. Several cases have occurred in recent years when a person has been charged or convicted on what has later been shown beyond doubt to have been mistaken identification.

This is far from being a new concern. It was because of the mistaken identification[19] of Adolph Beck that a Committee of Inquiry was set up, and, following receipt of its report,[20] that the Court of Criminal Appeal was established. Similarly it was concern over miscarriages of justice in two cases on the basis of mis-identification that caused the government to set up a departmental committee under the chairmanship of Lord Devlin to review all aspects of the law and procedure relating to identification in criminal cases.[1]

The reasons for such difficulty are apparent. A very substantial psychological literature[2] has demonstrated that the processes involved are riddled with weaknesses, from initial perception to eventual recall. Articulation is particularly difficult, and suggestibility, both in the sense of accepting externally inspired suggestions and in applying internal preconceptions, is high. These defects are compounded by the inability of conventional cross-examination to reveal their weaknesses. Identification is a largely internal and isolated process so, unlike other evidence, it resists probing based upon its coherence with the rest of the surrounding evidence. It is also usually sincerely believed in by the witness, and the witness's view is more likely to be reinforced than to be weakened by the passage of time and by challenge. The courts are generally reluctant to allow challenge to evidence based upon abstract or theoretical studies divorced from the facts of the instant case, and in this context have refused to admit evidence designed to show the general weakness of evidence of identification.[3] The cumulative effect of these factors is to reduce the probative value of the evidence while at the same time increasing its prejudicial effect, given that in this context prejudice connotes adducing evidence which the jury is likely to credit more than is warranted.

Problems are compounded when the variation between different situations is taken into account. For example if the person identified is well-known to the identifier, sometimes distinguished as recognition as opposed to identification,[4] this might be regarded in many cases as decreasing the risk of mis-identification, except that there is a known tendency for an identifier

---

17 See Jackson 'The Insufficiency of Identification Based on Personal Impression' [1986] Crim LR 203.
18 Cmnd 4991 (1972) para 196.
19 By no fewer than fifteen different women.
20 Cmnd 2315 (1905).
 1 HC Paper 338 (1976).
 2 Some of it is conveniently summarised in the Interim Report of the Australian Law Reform Commission No 26 Vol 1 paras 419–421 (1985).
 3 See *R v Smith* [1987] VR 907; cp Holdenson 'The Admission of Expert Evidence of Opinion as to the Potential Unreliability of Identification Evidence' (1988) 16 Melb ULR 521.
 4 See, for example, *R v Ryan* [1990] Crim LR 50. See also *People v Stafford* [1983] IR 165.

to assimilate a perception to someone who is already known. The procedure for initial identification may also be suggestive, for example in using photographs, or may reinforce an initially uncertain perception, for example, by reference to an elicited description, or image. Quite apart from anything else physical conditions will vary greatly from one situation to another, and perceptive abilities from one person to another. Even in the case of a given individual it is unlikely to be obvious, or known, how distorted perceptive faculties may become as a result of the stress or trauma of perhaps being the victim of, or even an eyewitness to, a particularly distressing event like the commission of a brutal crime.

2. LEGAL REACTION

These problems have become better understood in modern times, especially as a result of the development of psychological research into perception and recall. This increased awareness was first translated into intervention at a high judicial level in *People v Casey (No 2)*[5] where the Supreme Court of Ireland took the view that a warning of the dangers of acting upon evidence of identification should always be given to the jury, and in the instant case ordered a re-trial because no such warning had been given. It should be noted that in that case the purported identification was by a number of strangers to the accused, some of them victims or children or both, and in poor light and otherwise difficult conditions.

This approach was however rejected by the House of Lords in *Arthurs v A-G for Northern Ireland*,[6] significantly enough a case in which the accused was well-known to the identifying police witness. It was there held that there is no inflexible rule that a warning should always be given, still less a requirement that there should be corroborating material. The House of Lords appeared to leave open the question of whether a warning should be mandatory in a case where the accused was previously unknown to the identifying witness,[7] but in a subsequent case of that nature[8] the Court of Criminal Appeal rejected any such view, and the House of Lords refused leave to appeal.[9]

Although such an approach stressed the need for a proper direction to the jury in general terms on the strength of the prosecution case many still felt this insufficient. Some groups felt the need for a corroboration requirement[10] and, in at least one case,[11] the still more stringent requirement that such corroboration should not itself consist of further identification evidence of the same character as that requiring corroboration. The Criminal Law Revision Committee in its Eleventh Report recommended a mandatory caution, but not any special form of words.[12] This recommendation was to apply whether or not the accused was previously known to the witness, and

5 [1963] IR 33.
6 (1970) 55 Cr App Rep 161.
7 A position indorsed by Hailsham LC in *DPP v Kilbourne* [1973] AC 729 at 740.
8 *R v Long* (1973) 57 Cr App Rep 871.
9 See also dicta of Gibbs J to the same effect in the High Court of Australia in *Kelleher v R* (1974) 131 CLR 534 at 551.
10 Submissions to this effect were received by the Devlin Committee from the Law Society, the British Legal Association and the National Council for Civil Liberties.
11 The submission of *Justice* to the Devlin Committee.
12 Cmnd 4991 (1972) para 199 and draft bill, cl 21.

irrespective of the number of acts of identification. The Devlin Committee went further, impelled to some extent by the fact that in one of the cases which inspired its investigation[13] such a general direction had been given, but without being effective to prevent a demonstrably wrong conviction. The Devlin Committee was thus inspired to recommend something more radical. It resisted the suggestion of a corroboration requirement, partly because there frequently is corroboration in the evidence of other identifying witnesses, partly because corroboration had become enmeshed with technicality and partly because of the burden that it would impose in clear and simple cases.[14] Its recommendation was that the trial judge should in every case give a very strong direction to the jury that evidence of identification alone is not sufficient to satisfy the high burden of proof in criminal cases, and explain to them exactly why this is so. It recommended further that the jury be directed that only in a limited range of exceptional circumstances would a conviction depending upon identification evidence be justified.[15] Like the Criminal Law Revision Committee the Devlin Committee took the view that in the then state of the law it was necessary for any such change to be introduced by statute.

This view was however overtaken by the highly influential decision of the Court of Appeal in *R v Turnbull*.[16] Since the Court of Appeal took the view that the direction of juries was a matter of practice, it felt competent to prescribe the proper direction. It took its cue from the recommendations of the Devlin Committee, and in particular stressed the need for some explanation of the need for special caution in accepting evidence of identification. It went on to require the judge to direct the jury in some detail about the quality of the evidence of identification. It was in this stress upon quality that the court departed from the Devlin recommendations. It was not to countenance an automatic direction to acquit upon the basis of identification evidence alone, even in the absence of exceptional features in the Devlin sense, provided that the quality was good. It was indeed felt that the concept of exceptional features was undesirable, and for the very reason which commended it to the Devlin Committee, namely that it would be likely to generate a considerable corpus of precedent. The Devlin Committee welcomed this as being indicative rather than definitive, but the Court of Appeal clearly feared the growth of excessive technicality, it is submitted, rightly.

These guidelines seem to have precluded statutory intervention. The Royal Commission in Criminal Procedure did however recommend that identification procedures be made the subject of statutory regulation.[17] Section 66(b) of the Police and Criminal Evidence Act 1984 accordingly required the issue of a Code of Practice for the identification of suspects by police officers. It should be noted that despite its title this code deals in detail with identification by lay witnesses under the supervision of the police. This

---

13 That of *Dougherty*, see Devlin Report ch 2.
14 Paras 4.36–4.42.
15 For discussion of the Devlin Committee's Report see Glanville Williams 'Evidence of Identification' [1976] Crim LR 407, and for a bibliography see Khan 'Judicial Warnings in Identification Cases'(1978) 122 Sol Jo 377.
16 [1977] QB 224, [1976] 3 All ER 549, indorsed by the Privy Council in *Reid v R* [1989] 3 WLR 771.
17 Cmnd 8092 (1981) para 3. 138.

Code regulates procedures in most of the common situations to be mentioned in the next section.

3. DIFFERENT PROCEDURES FOR IDENTIFICATION

The most common situation is identification by a witness, but exceptionally identification may be accomplished by the jury directly.

(i) Identification by witnesses

There are many different procedures for identification by witnesses, depending upon the particular circumstances of a given case. Sometimes the witness is able to describe the criminal in sufficient detail for a suspect to be identified, and sometimes such description is taken beyond words and expressed by a drawing or amalgamation of pre-recorded features in a so-called 'photofit'. A different technique is to show the witness a series of photographs in the hope that the witness will be able to recognise one of them as being that of the criminal. Once a suspect has been initially identified by one of these methods, opportunity is often presented for confirmation of his identification by the relevant witness. Such confirmation is normally, and preferably, attempted by means of an identification parade, but may also take the form of a group identification where a number of people are presented to the witness otherwise than on a formal parade, or by individual confrontation with the witness, the least satisfactory form of such confrontation being one which takes place in court during the trial itself, frequently referred to as 'dock identification'. It will be helpful to say a little more about the evidential repercussions of each of these approaches.

(a) Description. The Devlin Committee pointed out[18] that psychological research indicated that descriptions given by witnesses were likely to be a good deal more unreliable than acts of identification. It nevertheless recommended that statutory provision be made for the police to secure a description from an identifying witness, and for the imposition of a duty to supply such description to the defence. In the case of a witness actually called by the prosecution to identify the accused it recommended that such a description should itself become admissible in evidence.[19] In *R v Turnbull*[20] the Court of Appeal recommended that any descriptions materially differing from the appearance of the accused should automatically be supplied to the defence, any other supplied upon request, and that the trial judge should specifically direct the jury as to any material discrepancy between such a description and the actual appearance of the accused.

(b) Drawings or photofit compilations.[1] These techniques are designed to overcome the difficulty frequently experienced in trying to describe a criminal. Instead an artist attempts to draw to the witness's description, or,

18 Para 5.8.
19 Para 5.15.
20 At 228, 552.
1 For a comprehensive collation of United States authority see the annotation at 42 ALR 3d 1217.

given that adequately competent artists are in short supply, someone assembles drawings or photographs of parts of a face, in the hope that by trial and error a representation will be obtained more satisfying to the witness, and more readily applied by investigators. In *R v Smith*,[2] one of the first English cases[3] to consider the point, it was argued that a sketch produced at the witness's behest was hearsay, just as much as would have been a dictated verbal description. This argument was rejected on the basis that the artist performed a purely passive function, acting no more independently than a pen in the witness's hand. Different results were achieved in 1982: one court rejected a 'photofit' as equivalent to a previous consistent statement by the identifying witness, though conceding possible use to refresh memory,[4] while another admitted it, though in that case the witness who had composed it had subsequently failed to identify the accused at a parade.[5] The matter was finally resolved in *R v Cook*[6] where the Court of Appeal held that such a photofit picture infringed neither the hearsay rule nor that against previous consistent statements, and was hence admissible, just like a photograph. It seems that here again the court must have taken the view that the composer of the photofit picture was acting purely passively. This may seem implausible, but, if accepted, disposes of the hearsay rule. It is far from clear that the rule against previous consistent statements can be surmounted. It seems that the victim was prepared to identify the accused at the trial, though she had during the investigation experienced some difficulty in doing so. The court's view was simply that a photofit representation is sui generis, and not being a statement at all, cannot amount to a previous consistent statement. At this point it really does seem to raise similar problems to those in *R v Smith*. If the analogy of a photograph is taken, it would be tantamount to saying that a photograph identified out of court by the witness as being that of the criminal would be admissible whether or not the witness testified. If the witness did not testify it is submitted that the photograph would be inadmissible because it could not be linked to the criminal except by hearsay. Similarly here the photofit can be linked to the criminal only by the initial statement of the witness that it resembled her attacker. If she testifies, it is that assertion, and not the photofit itself, which amounts to the previous consistent statement. She is in effect testifying that the accused looks like the man in the dock, and that she said so earlier as demonstrated by the photofit which is now produced. This regrettable line of reasoning has now been taken a stage further in *R v Constantinou*[7] by holding that even where such a photofit constitutes the only evidence of identification it is unnecessary to give the normal '*Turnbull*' warning, though one would think that in these circumstances it was more, rather than less, necessary.

(c) Photographs. The problems of using photographs to assist the identification of offenders were thoroughly analysed by the High Court of Australia

2 [1976] Crim LR 511.
3 Though a drawing was admitted as early as 1817, see *R v Watson* (1817) 32 State Tr 1 at 125 (1817).
4 *R v O'Brien* [1982] Crim LR 746.
5 *R v Okorodu* [1982] Crim LR 747.
6 [1987] QB 417, [1987] 1 All ER 1049. Apparently accepted by Brooking J in *R v Hentschel* [1988] VR 362.
7 [1989] Crim LR 571.

in *Alexander v R*.[8] A distinction was made between their use as an aid to detection by the police, and their use as evidence of identification in court, recognising that their use for the former purpose might infect their use for the second. It was pointed out that identification from photographs suffers from these defects; first, because it happens in the absence of the accused there is no opportunity to see whether or not it has been conducted fairly, without prompting; second, because the act of picking out a photograph as resembling the criminal can subtly crystallise into firm recognition of the subject of the photograph as the criminal at a subsequent stage; and, third, because any revelation of initial identification by reference to photographs in the possession of the police may suggest the possession of a criminal record.[9] These defects work to some extent in a cumulative fashion, since it is difficult for the defence to expose the frailties of the procedure employed without at the same time drawing attention to the provenance of the photographs, and by inference to the accused's record.

The cases suggest that these dangers can be minimised consistent with efficient detection procedures by showing photographs only in batches,[10] and only before apprehension of the suspect.[11] Even then such a procedure must be recognised to weaken the strength of subsequent identification despite a properly conducted parade.[12] It seems however that failure to comply with such practices will not itself automatically lead to the inadmissibility of such evidence.[13] Nor does it seem that a judge is necessarily bound to warn the jury of the danger of inferring a criminal record from the use of photographs,[14] or of the weakening of other identification evidence because of initial photographic identification, though such matters might well affect the general fairness of the direction to the jury on the question of identification. It should also be noted that the Code of Practice made under s 66 of the Police and Criminal Evidence Act 1984 is quite explicit in providing that photographs must not be shown to identifying witnesses if the suspect is available for a parade or group identification.[15]

Although there have been strong statements as to the inadmissibility of identifying photographs adduced in evidence, especially when they indicate possession of a criminal record,[16] it seems that such photographs are not in all circumstances inadmissible.[17] It is however likely that a judge would normally exercise his discretion to exclude unduly prejudicial evidence in many such cases, even as a matter of common law,[18] and quite apart from any breach of the Code of Practice, at least in relation to photographs clearly indicating the accused's possession of a criminal record.[19] On the other hand,

8 (1981) 34 ALR 289.
9 See *R v Varley* (1914) 10 Cr App Rep 125.
10 See *R v Ormsby* [1985] 1 NZLR 311.
11 See *R v Goss* (1923) 17 Cr App Rep 196; *R v Haslam* (1925) 19 Cr App Rep 59.
12 *R v Dwyer and Ferguson* [1925] 2 KB 799.
13 *R v Seiga* (1961) 45 Cr App Rep 220, and as decided in *Alexander* itself.
14 *R v Lawrenson* [1961] Crim LR 398; *R v Seiga* above.
15 Code D para 2.6.
16 *R v Wainwright* (1925) 19 Cr App Rep 52 at 54.
17 *R v Maynard* (1979) 69 Cr App Rep 309.
18 In Australia it seems that the *Bunning v Cross* discretion may also apply, see Gibbs CJ and Stephen and Murphy JJ in *Alexander v R* (1981) 34 ALR 289; *R v Burchielli* [1981] VR 611; *R v Shannon* (1987) 29 ACR 434.
19 *R v Governor of Pentonville Prison, ex p Voets* [1986] 2 All ER 630, [1986] 1 WLR 470. See also *R v Coleman* (1987) 87 FLR 175.

if the photographs, even though coming from police custody, do not indicate their provenance, and have relevance, for example, as explaining the failure of the identifying witness to pick out the accused on account of a recent change of appearance, then they may well be both admissible, and admitted.[20]

(d) Identification parades. A properly conducted identification parade is generally accepted as being the least unsatisfactory method of identifying a suspect. The parade is conducted impartially, the accused is able to see what takes place, and choice is made from a number of persons of similar general appearance. The Code of Practice in England sets out elaborate regulations governing the conduct of a parade.[1] These give the suspect some control. He can insist that a parade take place, provided only that it is practicable to hold one.[2] He can refuse to participate, though he will then be at risk of identification by confrontation with the identifying witness. They also permit him to object to the constitution of the parade. It seems that if the police have assembled enough persons of similar general appearance the suspect may not insist upon the inclusion of persons of his own choice.[3] If the police are, however, unable to assemble enough such persons then the defence should be allowed a reasonable time to find sufficient to make up the number.[4]

The prescribed procedure requires the witness to identify the suspect clearly during the course of the parade. Difficulty can occur if this is not done, or if the witness is subsequently unable or unwilling to identify the accused. As noted above, one of the advantages of a parade is that the suspect has an opportunity to monitor the fairness of the procedure. This is reduced to the extent that evidence may be admitted of events occurring out of his presence, especially when they are relied upon to contradict what did apparently occur. Thus in *R v Creamer*[5] the accused objected to evidence that a witness, having apparently failed to identify him at the parade, subsequently told the investigating officer that she had done so, but had been frightened to speak. The Court of Appeal accepted that this diminished the value of the evidence, but felt that to exclude the evidence would encourage intimidation. The problem of witnesses failing to make a clear identification at a parade is illustrated by the facts of *R v Osbourne and Virtue*.[6] Two ladies attended an identification parade, and allegedly identified the accused in the normal way. At the trial however one of them said that she could not remember identifying anyone, and the other said that the man she identified was not the accused. The officer supervising the parade was then called, and testified that they had, in fact, both identified the accused. His evidence was objected to, not on hearsay grounds, but as contradicting the evidence of the ladies. This was unfortunate since the evidence does raise very difficult hearsay

---

20 *R v Byrne and Trump* [1987] Crim LR 689.
1 Annex A to Code D.
2 Code D para 2.1; see *R v Conway* (1990) Times, 30 January.
3 *R v Thorne* [1981] Crim LR 702.
4 *R v Britton and Richards* [1989] Crim LR 144.
5 (1984) 80 Cr App Rep 248.
6 [1973] QB 678, [1973] 1 All ER 649.

problems.[7] Although in *Sparks v R*[8] Lord Morris had declared that 'There is no rule which permits the giving of hearsay evidence merely because it relates to identity', it is hard to resist the view that there is such a rule, at least in relation to acts of identification at an identity parade, as indicated by the admission of the evidence in *Osbourne*'s case.[9] It can hardly be argued that there is any difference between touching a man on the shoulder, and saying 'He is the man who did it'. If a third party testified to the latter it would appear to be a clear assertion, and in cases where the principal identifier does not testify, not capable of being regarded simply as supporting the credibility of a witness, but instead used as evidence of the truth of what it asserts. This is recognised more frankly in the United States.[10]

The Code of Practice provides for the possibility that a witness may require more than the opportunity to inspect a static and silent line of human beings. In particular it provides for them to be required to adopt a particular posture, to move or speak. It does however require the witness first to attempt to identify the criminal by appearance alone, since the parade has been assembled on that basis. Identification by voice is particularly contentious[11] since the human ear is generally less discriminating than the eye, and the variation between the aural abilities of people differ greatly.

(e) Group or street identification. This involves the witness seeing the suspect among a group of other people, but not on a formal parade. Sometimes the accused is assembled with others, and sometimes the witness observes a succession of individuals in a particular situation over a period of time. Under the Code of Practice group identification is suggested in cases where the suspect refuses or fails to participate in a parade,[12] or if the supervising officer thinks it advisable so as to avoid intimidation. The Code provides that so far as possible the conditions applying to the composition of parades shall be applied to group identification.[13] The Code is less specific about the conduct of a street identification, but evidence derived from it will clearly be strengthened the closer its conditions approximate to those of a parade or group identification. In some circumstances a video recording may be taken

7 See Libling 'Evidence of Past Identification' [1977] Crim LR 268 and Weinberg 'The Admissibility of Out-of-Court Identification Evidence in Criminal Cases' (1980) 12 Melb ULR 543.

8 [1964] AC 964 at 981, [1964] 1 All ER 727 at 735.

9 In *R v McCay* [1990] 1 WLR 645 the admission of such evidence was said to have statutory authorisation as a result of s 66 of the Police and Criminal Evidence Act 1984 and the terms of the Code of Practice governing identification, and especially Annex A para 7. Such evidence is now widely admitted both as to visual and aural identification, see above p 527, and has been said to constitute a special exception, see *R v Cook* [1987] QB 417 at 425, [1987] 1 All ER 1049 at 1051, 1052. In *R v Collings* [1976] 2 NZLR 104 at 114 the Court of Appeal drew a distinction between statements part of the act of identification which were admissible, and those not part of it which were rejected as inadmissible hearsay.

10 A specific provision in the Federal Rules of Evidence, r 801(d)(1)(C) redefined hearsay to exclude such statements. See also IV Wigmore *Evidence* para 1130.

11 Different approaches have been taken by different states in Australia, compare *R v Hentschel* [1988] VR 362 with *R v Smith* (1986) 7 NSWLR 444.

12 In Australia it has been held to be wrong to trick the accused into participating in a group identification, *R v Shannon* (1987) 29 ACR 434.

13 This appears to have been overlooked in *R v Ladlow* [1989] Crim LR 219 where the judge seems to have thought it permissible to include more than two suspects in a group, but not in a parade.

of a group or street identification, but it seems wrong to use it as evidence of identification made on such an occasion, and worse to use it after committal proceedings to try to improve the quality of the evidence of the identifying witness.[14]

(f) Confrontation.[15] A confrontation between the witness and the suspect will be arranged only as a last resort if parade or group identification is impracticable.[16] The reason for this is that a confrontation in which the witness is asked 'Is this the man?', is somewhat analogous to a leading question. Provision is made in the code for confrontation through a one-way screen if necessary, though in such cases only if the suspect is represented at the confrontation, or a video recording is made of it.

(g) Dock identification. The least satisfactory method of all is to ask the witness to identify the man in the dock as the criminal. It has all the disadvantages of a confrontation, and compounds them by being still more suggestive.[17] For these reasons the Devlin Committee recommended that dock identification should become a purely formal matter, allowed only where identification had been made by a parade unless the judge takes the view that to hold a parade would be impractical or unnecessary.[18] Where a witness does identify the accused in his evidence at the trial it seems that evidence of a prior identification by him can be led.[19] A majority of their Lordships seem to have regarded such evidence as bolstering that of the witness, 'What was done and said out of court goes to show that the witness was able to identify at the time and to negative anything in the nature of an afterthought'.[20] It would be more consistent with principle to wait for some such attack to take place before permitting rebuttal in this way.

(ii) Identification by jury

If a crime has been recorded on film, video or sound recording, or by a still photograph, it may be possible for the jury to make their own identification of the criminal with the man on trial before them, for example in *Kajala v Noble*[1] where the incident had been captured on a television camera as part of a news broadcast. In such cases it is permissible for a witness to depose to the identity of the person depicted on the film, if for some reason or another

---

14 *R v Smith and Doe* (1986) 85 Cr App Rep 197. It is interesting that no reference was made to *R v Cook* above where Watkins LJ also delivered the judgment of the court.
15 A confrontation is sometimes engineered otherwise than by the police, see *R v O'Leary* (1988) 87 Cr App Rep 387.
16 *R v Ladlow* above indicates the court's distaste for this method of identification since the correct conduct of parades would have required some 231 parades over a bank holiday, and the conditions for a group identification could not strictly have been fulfilled, but still the convictions were quashed because confrontation had been preferred to either of these options.
17 *Davies and Cody v R* (1937) 57 CLR 170.
18 The alternative of permitting the accused to stand elsewhere in the court before the attempt at identification was rejected as likely to be ineffective (such a technique had been adopted in one of the cases which had led to the Committee's being set up).
19 *R v Christie* [1914] AC 545.
20 Lord Haldane LC at 551.
 1 (1982) 75 Cr App Rep 149. See also in Australia *R v Palmer* (1980) ACR 458; *R v Goodall* [1982] VR 33; *R v Smith* (1983) 33 SASR 558.

it is desirable to supplement it.[2] Discrimination of sound is much more difficult, and it will be rare for a court to leave a sound recording to the jury to compare with the voice of the accused.[3] If however the sound recording has been analysed by an expert, then it may be right for the recordings used by the expert to be submitted to the jury so as to assist their evaluation of his testimony.[4]

4. PROCEDURE

Two procedural questions may arise in relation to evidence of direct identification, first whether the evidence should be allowed to go to the jury at all, and second, if it is, the question of the proper direction to be given to the jury. The first involves the issue of whether a voir dire should be used in such cases, and the second of what, if any, warning should be given.

(i) Voir dire

Under the old law it was determined that a voir dire should never be held in relation to evidence of identity.[5] This followed from the analysis undertaken by the Court of Appeal in *R v Turnbull*[6] which had determined that such evidence was either of such poor quality that the case should be withdrawn from the jury in the absence of any support, but if of better quality, or if supported, then the only question was one of weight rather than of admissibility, and there was no need for a voir dire. It was suggested in *R v Beveridge*[7] that the passage of s 78 of the Police and Criminal Evidence Act 1984 had transformed this situation in its enactment of a statutory discretion to exclude evidence likely to operate unfairly. Such a view was received coolly by the court, and apparently rejected by it in the subsequent case of *R v Flemming*[8] on the basis that identification evidence still differed from evidence of a confession admitted under s 76 where a voir dire was appropriate, since s 76 imposes a persuasive burden of proof upon the prosecution in relation to admissibility, while s 78 does not. Given the unpopularity of holding a voir dire, this view seems likely to prevail in England.[9]

(ii) Direction to the jury

As noted above the framework for such a direction was provided by *R v Turnbull*. A judge should always warn the jury of the special need for caution in relying on evidence of identification, and instruct them of the reason for

2 *R v Fowden and White* [1982] Crim LR 588; *R v Grimer* [1982] Crim LR 674. See also *Bowie v Tudhope* 1986 SCCR 205.
3 See *R v Smith* (1986) 7 NSWLR 444; *R v Brownlowe* (1986) 7 NSWLR 461.
4 *R v Bentum* (1989) 153 JP 538.
5 *R v Walshe* (1982) 74 Cr App Rep 85, though it seems that voir dires were, in fact, sometimes held, see, for example, *R v Maynard* (1979) 69 Cr App Rep 309.
6 [1977] QB 224, [1976] All ER 549.
7 [1987] 85 Cr App Rep 255.
8 [1987] Crim LR 690, rejecting the contrary practice adopted in *R v Leckie and Ensley* [1983] Crim LR 543.
9 But perhaps not so rigidly in Australia, see *R v Hallam and Karger* (1985) 42 SASR 126, cp *R v Rowley* (1986) 23 ACR 371.

giving such a warning. He should then direct the jury to examine closely the circumstances in relation to each act of identification. He should also remind the jury of any specific weaknesses in the evidence. If, in his view, the quality of the evidence of identity is good he can leave it to the jury even in the absence of supporting evidence, subject always to the warning of the need for caution having been given. If, in the judge's view, the quality of the evidence is poor he should withdraw the case from the jury unless there is some other evidence to support its correctness. The judge should identify what evidence can be relied upon as providing such support, and which cannot. In particular he should explain that the accused's absence from the witness box can prove nothing, though it may leave prosecution evidence uncontradicted,[10] and that a false alibi may be put forward for reasons unconnected with consciousness of guilt.[11] The guidance could perhaps be criticised for not more clearly indicating just how poor the evidence needed to be before a case should be withdrawn from the jury by the judge, and when a warning was sufficient.[12] It also failed to indicate whether further visual identification evidence could be relied upon as support. The answer to this was supplied in *R v Weeder*[13] where it was held that only high quality identification evidence could provide support.

These guidelines have been accepted in many Commonwealth jurisdictions,[14] but not in all.[15] Two situations which do not seem to require the full *Turnbull* treatment are first those where the real question is not whether or not someone was present on a particular occasion, but whether they were performing a particular act,[16] and second those where the issue is not one of personal identification, but rather circumstantial identification. This is well illustrated in *R v Bartels*[17] where the witnesses saw the accused running close to their apartment shortly after they had seen a crime committed some way off. They could not have made out the features of the criminal at the distance, and they did not have the man continuously in their sight. However no one else appeared to be in the vicinity, and the obvious way for the criminal to run was in their direction. The accused admitted that he was the man they saw, but denied that he had committed the crime, and suggested that the real criminal must have run off in a different direction.

It has been stressed that when the jury is cautioned it is wrong either to weaken the caution by putting counter-arguments,[18] or by the judge failing to make it clear that he is himself endorsing, and not merely recapitulating, cautionary arguments put by the defence.[19]

---

10 The judge should be slow to emphasise this, especially where the rest of the evidence is weak, *R v Allan* (1990) Times, 2 January.
11 This was further emphasised in *R v Keane* (1977) 65 Cr App Rep 247.
12 It was so criticised by Wilson J in the Supreme Court of Canada in *Mezzo v R* (1986) 30 DLR (4th) 161.
13 (1980) 71 Cr App Rep 228.
14 For example in Canada, *Mezzo v R*, above, in most Australian jurisdictions, and in New Zealand, *Auckland City Council v Brailey* [1988] 1 NZLR 103.
15 For example New South Wales, see *R v De-Cressac* (1985) 1 NSWLR 381.
16 As in *R v Oakwell* [1978] 1 All ER 1223 (which of a crowd was the assailant); *R v Curry and Keeble* [1983] Crim LR 737 (a similar situation); *Auckland City Council v Brailey* [1988] 1 NZLR 103 (which of two people in a car was driving it).
17 (1986) 44 SASR 260.
18 *R v Keane* (1977) 65 Cr App Rep 247.
19 *R v Browne, Moorehouse and Blewitt* (1987) 30 ACR 278.

In England it has been said[20] that 'It would be wrong to interpret or apply *Turnbull* inflexibly'. It purports, after all, to offer no more than guidelines, and so flexible has this interpretation become that there are examples both of appeals being allowed despite an impeccable *Turnbull* direction,[21] and disallowed despite a quite inadequate *Turnbull* direction.[1]

It should be noted that the judge's discretion to exclude evidence pursuant to s 78 of the Police and Criminal Evidence Act 1984 may be applied in respect of evidence of identification,[2] and occasionally the judge will feel inclined to exercise his discretion only after initially permitting the evidence to be adduced. In such a case he should do no less than direct the jury to disregard the evidence altogether.

It seems that in the case of voice identification it is necessary also to warn the jury that if the witness identifying the voice was not previously familiar with it, it must possess very unusual and distinctive characteristics before such identification can be relied upon.[3]

B. CIRCUMSTANTIAL EVIDENCE OF IDENTITY

When there is no doubt that an act has been done, and the question is whether it was the act of a particular person, all relevant evidence is normally admissible in order to prove or disprove that fact. Obvious instances are afforded by cases in which the criminal has left traces behind him. The fact that the crime was probably committed by a left-handed man and that the accused was left-handed, or any other physical or mental peculiarity exhibited by the criminal may be shown to have been exhibited by the accused. This is, however, a branch of the law in which it is often necessary to have regard to the general prohibition on evidence which merely goes to show criminal tendencies, or a disposition to commit particular crimes on the part of the accused. From the point of view of relevancy, these should often be admissible because they go to show that the accused was a member of a comparatively small class of which the criminal was also a member, but the prejudicial nature of the evidence will render it inadmissible unless the tendency or disposition is of particular relevance to a matter in issue in the proceedings.

There is, of course, a variety of other factors which will go to prove membership of a restricted class. On a charge of bigamy, it is necessary for the prosecution to prove that the accused duly went through a ceremony of marriage with the first spouse. Since 1914, the latter has been a competent witness for the prosecution, and the necessary identification can often be accomplished by his or her direct evidence. But, where this is not forthcoming and where there is no other direct proof of the first marriage, such as that of a witness who was present at its celebration, it may be established by circumstantial evidence of which a material item would be the identity of the accused's name with that of the person named in a marriage certificate

---

20 By Scarman LJ in *R v Keane*, above, at 248.
21 *R v Pope* (1986) 85 Cr App Rep 201 (where the court seemed remarkably unaware of black vernacular usage).
1 *R v Clifton* [1986] Crim LR 399.
2 See *R v Quinn* (1990) Times, 31 March.
3 *R v E J Smith* [1984] 1 NSWLR 462, approved by the Court of Appeal at (1986) 7 NSWLR 444.

produced by the prosecutor. Standing by itself it would probably be insufficient in any case, but a conviction for bigamy has been upheld by the Court of Criminal Appeal on such evidence coupled with the fact that the accused cohabited with a woman of the same name as the other person mentioned in the marriage certificate and referred to her as his wife.[4]

Personal identity may be established by many other factors than that of name, obvious instances are provided by occupation, education, and mental or physical idiosyncrasies. In the *Lovat Peerage Case*,[5] it was held that the fact that an ancestor was reputed to have been guilty of manslaughter coupled with the fact that a similar tradition prevailed with regard to the lineage of one of the claimants was some evidence that the latter was the descendant of the former. The sole question with regard to the admissibility of circumstantial evidence of this nature is whether a particular characteristic is sufficiently rare, or a class sufficiently small, to make it worthwhile for the court to hear evidence tending to show possession of that characteristic or membership of that class.[6]

The most cogent circumstantial evidence of identity is likely to be evidence of fingerprints, or of DNA traces in relevant tissue.[7] In practice such evidence is likely to be conclusive.

C. PRESUMPTIVE EVIDENCE OF IDENTITY

Although it is highly exceptional for presumptions to operate against the accused in criminal cases at common law, such a presumption was made in Scotland in *Rollo v Wilson*[8] where the accused sought acquittal on the basis that the prosecution had failed to prove that he was the person summoned to appear in court, despite his having so appeared in answer to the summons. If such an extraordinary claim were to be made in England there seems no reason to believe that it would not be resolved in a similar manner.

---

4 *R v Birtles* (1911) 6 Cr App Rep 177.
5 (1885) 10 App Cas 763.
6 'Where a certain circumstance, feature or mark may commonly be found associated with a large number of objects, the presence of that feature or mark in two supposed objects is little indication of their identity, because, on the general principle of relevancy, the other conceivable hypotheses are so numerous, ie the objects that possess that mark are numerous and therefore two of them possessing it may well be different. But where the objects possessing the mark are only one or a few, and the mark is found in two supposed instances, the chances of their being different are nil, or are comparatively small . . . Suppose there existed a parent named John Smith whose heirs are sought, and there is also a claimant whose parent's name was John Smith. The name John Smith is associated with so many persons that the chances of two supposed persons of that name being different are too numerous to allow us to consider the common mark as having appreciable probative value. But the chances may be diminished by adding other common circumstances going to form the common mark. Add, for instance, another name-circumstance,—as that the name of each supposed person was John Barebones Bonaparte Smith, here the chances of there being two persons of that name in any district however large are instantly reduced to the minimum' (II *Wigmore* p 386)
7 See further, above p 40.
8 (1988) SCCR 312.

SECTION 3. BIRTH, AGE, DEATH, MARRIAGE AND LEGITIMACY

A. BIRTH

There are four methods of proving birth. Far and away the most usual at the present day is the production of a certified copy of an entry in the register of births which may be received as evidence of the facts stated under the exception to the rule against hearsay relating to statements in public documents.[9] The court will require some evidence identifying the person whose birth is in question with the person referred to in the birth certificate. This might take the form of a direct statement by the person in question if he were testifying to the date or place of birth, though the evidence is at best hearsay and at worst pure guesswork. It could also be provided by someone who was present at the birth, or by the informant to the Registrar; but, more often than not, the evidence of identity will be supplied by an affidavit in which the deponent, usually a member of the family of the person whose birth is in question, will depose to his or her belief that the person is or was the same person as the one referred to in the exhibited birth certificate. The testimony of someone present at the birth to that fact, its place or date is a second and separate method of proving these matters. They may also be proved, in civil proceedings, by statements admissible by virtue of the Civil Evidence Act 1968, and, in criminal proceedings, under exceptions to the hearsay rule relating to the declarations of deceased persons,[10] or perhaps under the provisions of Part II of the Criminal Justice Act 1988.

B. AGE

There are four ways in which a person's age can be proved; two of them depend on direct evidence and two on the exceptions to the hearsay rule relating respectively to statements in public documents and declarations of deceased persons.

1. DIRECT EVIDENCE

A person's age may be proved by direct evidence (a) by the testimony of those present at his birth and (b) by inferences from his appearance which are permitted in special cases by certain statutes.[11] In the nature of things, it is not often that resort can be made to the first of these methods, and, in many instances, its use would, to some extent, involve reliance on hearsay. For example, A's grandmother was present at his birth, and she sees a child whom she believes to be A once a quarter for the next ten years, after which she testifies to A's age in court. It cannot be said that she knows that A is the

---

9 Births and Deaths Registration Act 1953, s 34. See ch XVI, section 1. As to certified extracts from foreign registers, see the Evidence (Foreign Dominion and Colonial Documents) Act 1933 and as to births on board ship the Merchant Shipping (Returns of Births and Deaths) Regulations 1972, made under s 75 of the Merchant Shipping Act 1970.
10 Ch XVII, section 2.
11 Children and Young Persons Act 1933, s 99; Criminal Justice Act 1948, s 80(3); Magistrates' Courts Act 1980, s 150(4); Sexual Offences Act 1956, s 28(5).

child at whose birth she was present exclusively by means of her own observation. Even the mother's evidence of the child's age might well be based on hearsay evidence of identity at the earliest stages of the child's life. The court is authorised to act on inspection with regard to questions of age by several statutes, but quite apart from these provisions the general effect of which is to make the result of the inspection prima facie proof of age, such result would presumably be evidence of age in every case.[12] It would be a kind of real evidence, though, in many instances, it would not be sufficient for the court to act on it without more.

2. HEARSAY

Probably the most usual way of proving age is the production of a birth certificate as evidence of the date of the birth specified therein under the exception to the hearsay rule relating to statements in public documents.[13] Evidence of the identity of the person whose age is in question with the person named in the certificate will be required.

In criminal cases age may be proved by declarations by deceased persons against interest or in the course of duty, and, when a genealogical issue is involved, by the pedigree declaration of a deceased relation. In these cases too, it may be necessary to find some evidence identifying the person referred to in the statement with the person whose age is in issue.

C. DEATH

There are six heads under which a person's death may be proved. It is not necessary to refer to any of them in detail. The first and most usual way to prove death is to rely on a death certificate coupled with some evidence identifying the person named therein with the person whose death is in question.[14] Secondly, in a criminal case, reliance may be placed on the declaration of a deceased person made against interest or in the course of duty or, when a genealogical question is in issue, the pedigree declaration of a deceased relation. Evidence of identity may also be necessary in these cases. Thirdly, death may be proved by statements admissible under the Civil Evidence Act 1968 or the Criminal Justice Act 1988. Even where the presumption is inapplicable, the court may feel warranted in inferring death from a protracted period of absence the length of which will vary according to the facts of each case. The fifth and sixth methods of proving death are to rely either on the evidence of someone who was present at its occurrence, or else on the evidence of someone who, though not present at its occurrence, was able to identify the corpse as that of the person whose death is in issue.

---

12 *Wallworth v Balmer* [1965] 3 All ER 721, [1966] 1 WLR 16.
13 See the Births and Deaths Registration Act 1953, s 34 and, as to foreign registers, the Evidence (Foreign, Dominion and Colonial Documents) Act 1933. See also Merchant Shipping (Returns of Births and Deaths) Regulations 1979.
14 Section 34 of the Births and Deaths Registration Act 1953; Merchant Shipping (Returns of Births and Deaths) Regulations 1979.

D. MARRIAGE

When a marriage is in issue, the first thing that has to be proved is the celebration of a marriage ceremony. In certain cases, this may be presumed from proof of cohabitation and repute. Subject to this further possibility, the person seeking to prove a marriage ceremony may rely on the same methods as those discussed in connection with the proof of birth. Evidence may be adduced from someone who was present at the wedding[15] and this is the method of proof almost invariably adopted in matrimonial cases.[16] Declarations that a couple were married may be received, in criminal cases, under exceptions to the hearsay rule relating to the statements of deceased persons as being against interest, or in the course of duty, or as to pedigree in cases involving a genealogical issue; and in civil cases, under the Civil Evidence Act 1968 or in criminal cases, under the Criminal Justice Act 1988. The third and most usual method consists in the production of a marriage certificate coupled with evidence identifying the persons mentioned in the certificate with those whose marriage is to be proved. When he or she is available, such evidence will generally be supplied by one of the parties to the marriage. Whenever a certificate is available, the courts require it to be produced in addition to receiving the evidence of the parties as to the ceremony.

The second thing to be proved by someone who is seeking to establish a marriage is that the ceremony constituted a formally valid marriage. Generally speaking, it will have to be shown that a form recognised by the law of the place of celebration was adopted, but there are exceptions in the case of marriages celebrated abroad.[17] If the ceremony took place in England or Wales, the certificate is evidence of the marriage to which it relates,[18] but, in other cases, it will be necessary to produce expert evidence by a witness or by affidavit of formal validity according to the local law. This could be a costly requirement, and there are accordingly eight exceptions the last two of which will no doubt supersede the others. These exceptions relate first to marriages celebrated in Scotland and Northern Ireland, certificates of which are recognised by the English courts as evidence of the facts stated under various statutory provisions.[19] Secondly, if the marriage took place in a British possession under a statute proved by virtue of the provisions of the Evidence (Colonial Statutes) Act 1907, it is not the practice of the courts to require expert evidence of the validity of the marriage according to the local law, although such evidence may be required if there is any doubt whether the statute in question in still in force.[20] Thirdly, if the marriage took place in a country to which the Evidence (Foreign, Dominion and Colonial Documents) Act 1933, has been applied by Order in Council, a certificate produced under that Act is evidence of the marriage to which it refers, and the English courts will require no further evidence of the formal validity of

---

15 This includes a party to the marriage.
16 Statements may be received under the Civil Evidence Act 1968.
17 For details see Dicey and Morris *Conflict of Laws* (11th edn) p 613f.
18 Marriage Act 1949, s 65.
19 Registration of Births, Deaths and Marriages (Scotland) Act 1854; *Drew v Drew* [1912] P 175 (Scotland); Evidence Act 1851; *Whitton v Whitton* [1900] P 178 (Eire before 1921, and Northern Ireland).
20 The authorities are comprehensively reviewed in *Jasiewicz v Jasiewicz* [1962] 3 All ER 1017, [1962] 1 WLR 1426.

the marriage, although they will of course require the usual evidence of identity. A further exception to the requirement of proof of formal validity according to the local law is provided by the Foreign Marriage Act 1892. All that is required is evidence that a marriage celebrated under that statute complied with its requirements. The fifth and sixth exceptions relate to marriages celebrated abroad according to the rites of the Church of England and it is unnecessary to go into details in a work of this nature.[1]

In spite of the numerous exceptions to the requirement of proof of formal validity under the local law, the general rule remained and it was often necessary to procure the attendance of an expert witness, or to obtain leave to read an affidavit by him to the effect that the certificate of the marriage would be recognised in the courts of the country in question. It was, for instance, held to be necessary in the case of an Irish marriage,[2] even in an undefended divorce, as neither the Evidence (Colonial Statutes) Act, nor the Evidence (Foreign, Dominion and Colonial Documents) Act, applied to Eire.

It is because of such possibilities that the seventh and eighth exceptions to the requirement of proof by testimony or affidavit of the legal validity of a foreign marriage are of great importance. Under r 40(1) of the Matrimonial Causes Rules 1977, the celebration and validity of a marriage, which took place outside England and Wales may be proved, in any matrimonial proceedings in which the existence and validity of the marriage is not disputed, by the evidence of one of the parties and the production of the foreign marriage certificate or a certified copy of an entry in a foreign register of marriages. In other cases in which the existence and validity of the marriage is not disputed, reliance may be placed on the evidence of one of the parties and the production of such a certificate or certified copy as a statement or record admissible by virtue of the Civil Evidence Act 1968 or the Criminal Justice Act 1988. Before this Act came into force, it was becoming increasingly common for the courts to accept a foreign marriage certificate as evidence of the validity of the marriage under the Evidence Act 1938,[3] and it could be given in evidence, even without the evidence of one of the parties under the Act of 1968, as prima facie evidence both of the celebration of the marriage and of its validity according to the relevant foreign law.

E. LEGITIMACY

In order to establish a child's legitimacy, reliance may be placed on the presumption of legitimacy. For this purpose it is simply necessary to prove that the child was born or conceived during its mother's marriage to her husband, after which it is incumbent on those denying legitimacy to prove illegitimacy. Legitimacy may also be proved, in criminal cases, under

---

1 Marriages celebrated according to the rites of the Church of England in the Channel Islands are recognised on production of a certificate with evidence of identification because they are in the diocese of Winchester (*Pritchard v Pritchard* (1920) 37 TLR 104). According to *Ward v Dey* (1846) 1 Rob Eccl 759, marriages celebrated according to the rites of the Church of England in any British possession may be recognised on production of a certificate with evidence of identity, but it is not clear how far this doctrine extends today.
2 *Todd v Todd* [1961] 2 All ER 881.
3 *Henaff v Henaff* [1966] 1 WLR 598.

exceptions to the rule against hearsay, notably that relating to pedigree declarations by deceased persons perhaps under the Criminal Justice Act 1988; and, in civil cases, by statements admissible under the Civil Evidence Act 1968. It might also be proved by a statement in a public document, for the statements as to paternity in birth certificates are evidence of their truth. Finally, reliance might be placed on a declaration of legitimacy which is a judgment in rem and therefore binding on the whole world.

SECTION 4. JUDGMENTS AND CONVICTIONS

If the proof of judgments and convictions were not exhaustively covered by statutory provisions, it would be necessary to produce the actual record of the court and to call evidence identifying the relevant parties with the person mentioned in the record. The different statutory provisions may be summarised under the heads of civil and criminal cases.

A. CIVIL CASES

A judgment of the House of Lords may be proved by production of the journal of the House. Judgments of the Court of Appeal and High Court may be proved by production of an office copy made in the central office or district registry.[4] Judgments of the County Court may be proved by a certified copy of the entry in the registrar's book.[5] Judgments of the magistrates in civil matters are also proved by the production of a certified extract from the court book.[6] There are special statutory provisions relating to proceedings in bankruptcy.[7] Foreign or colonial judgments may be proved by production of an examined copy[8] or a copy sealed with the seal of the court under the provisions of s 7 of the Evidence Act 1851. In all the above cases, production of the relevant document will usually be sufficient to establish its authenticity because the court will take judicial notice of the seal or certificate attached to the document, but oral evidence may be required to identify the parties to the judgment with the person whose rights the court is considering, or those through whom such persons claim. Evidence of this nature is, however, often rendered unnecessary by some kind of formal admission.[9]

B. CRIMINAL CASES

Proof of convictions in criminal cases has been revolutionised by the passage of the Police and Criminal Evidence Act 1984, s 73, which must be rendered in full:

4 RSC Ord 38, r 10; Supreme Court Act 1981, s 132.
5 County Courts Act 1984, s 12(2).
6 Magistrates' Courts Rules 1981, rr 66 and 68.
7 Bankruptcy Act 1914, ss 137(2), 139 and 148(2).
8 An examined copy is one examined against the original. As evidence of the examination is usually necessary, proof by examined copy is rare. Some cases are governed by separate statutory provision eg Child Abduction and Custody Act 1985, s 22.
9 Which is equally admissible in a criminal court, *R v Stokes* [1988] Crim LR 110.

(1) Where in any proceedings the fact that a person has in the United Kingdom been convicted or acquitted of an offence otherwise than by a Service court is admissible in evidence, it may be proved by producing a certificate of conviction or, as the case may be, of acquittal relating to that offence, and proving that the person named in the certificate of conviction or, as the case may be, of acquittal relating to that offence, and proving that the person named in the certificate as having been convicted or acquitted of the offence is the person whose conviction or acquittal of the offence is to be proved.

(2) For the purposes of this section a certificate of conviction or of acquittal—

(a) shall, as regards a conviction or acquittal on indictment consist of a certificate, signed by the clerk of the court where the conviction or acquittal took place, giving the substance and effect (omitting the formal parts) of the indictment and of the conviction or acquittal; and

(b) shall, as regards a conviction or acquittal on a summary trial, consist of a copy of the conviction or of the dismissal of the information, signed by the clerk of the court where the conviction or acquittal took place or by the clerk of the court, if any, to which a memorandum of the conviction or acquittal was sent; and a document purporting to be a duly signed certificate of conviction or acquittal under this section shall be taken to be such a certificate unless the contrary is proved.

(3) References in this section to the clerk of a court include references to his deputy and to any other person having the custody of the court record.

(4) The method of proving a conviction or acquittal authorised by this section shall be in addition to and not to the exclusion of any other authorised manner of proving a conviction or acquittal.

This provision was recommended by the Criminal Law Revision Committee, and is adopted almost verbatim from the Bill annexed to its Eleventh Report.[10] Although stated to be in addition to other methods of proving convictions or acquittals, it has permitted the repeal or modification of a number of now obsolete provisions in relation to criminal proceedings.[11] It is unclear why s 14 of Perjury Act 1911 has been retained since it seems to add little to these provisions. There does however seem to have been a quite deliberate decision to retain as additional methods written statements admitted under Magistrates' Courts Act 1980, s 102 or Criminal Justice Act 1967, s 9, admissions under Criminal Justice Act 1967 s 10, and proof by means of finger-prints under Criminal Justice Act 1948, s 39. The former provisions have been mentioned earlier, the last requires evidence of the previous conviction and that the finger-prints of the person convicted are the same as those of the person against whom it is sought to prove the conviction. This evidence may take the form of three certificates. First there is the certificate of conviction signed by or on behalf of the Commissioner of Metropolitan Police exhibiting copies of finger-prints and stating that they are the finger-prints of the person who was convicted. Second there is a certificate signed by or on behalf of the prison or remand centre where the person against whom it is sought to prove the conviction was detained in connection with any criminal proceedings; this certificate states that the exhibited finger-prints were taken from the person in question while he was detained. Last there is another certificate signed by or on behalf of the

10 Cmnd 4991, Annex 1 cl 26.
11 Evidence Act 1851, s 13; Criminal Procedure Act 1865, s 6; and Prevention of Crimes Act 1871, s 18.

Commissioner of the Metropolitan Police stating that the finger-prints exhibited to the two previous certificates are identical.

Under s 31 of the Road Traffic Offenders Act 1988, the endorsement of a licence is prima facie evidence of a conviction. This provision is in addition to the other statutory provisions dealing with the proof of previous convictions which have just been mentioned; but its object is to enable justices to determine sentence and it does not supersede the other methods of proving convictions at the trial.[12]

SECTION 5. MISCELLANEOUS

It would obviously be possible to protract a chapter of this sort indefinitely, but proof of most other frequently recurring points are dependent on special statutory provisions such as those of the Companies Act 1985, and the Insolvency Act 1985. It will be convenient to conclude with the proof of custom and ownership, two matters which are dependent on widely differing branches of the common law of evidence.

A. CUSTOM AND USAGE

There are four ways in which the existence of a custom or usage may be proved. They constitute direct, circumstantial and hearsay evidence. The first method consists of the testimony of a witness who deposes from his personal knowledge to the actual existence of the custom or usage. He states that he is well aware of the fact that lessees in a given locality have been in the habit of removing 'way-going' crops, that is crops sown by the tenant before the termination of his lease,[13] or of any other custom or usage. The evidence may be based on the observation of many instances, and it may sometimes be based on reputation or hearsay. A second method of proving custom which also comes into the category of direct evidence is for a witness to testify to particular instances of its exercise. He refers to cases in which he or someone observed by him exercised the custom, but he does not generalise on the subject. The third way of proving a custom or usage depends on circumstantial evidence. It consists of evidence of a comparable custom in other localities similar to the one in question. Finally, what is probably the most typical way of proving a custom is to rely on the declaration of a deceased person concerning public or general rights,[14] admissible, in criminal proceedings, under a common law exception to the hearsay rule and, in civil cases, under the Civil Evidence Act 1968.

B. OWNERSHIP

There are also four main ways in which ownership of real or personal property may be proved. The first consists of production of the documents

---

12 *Stone v Bastick* [1967] 1 QB 74, [1965] 3 All ER 713, also requiring a certificate of disqualification to refer only to the offence in respect of which the disqualification was imposed.

13 Cf *Wigglesworth v Dallison* (1779) 1 Doug KB 201.

14 See p 565 above.

of title which must, of course, be duly authenticated in the sense that their due execution must be proved unless they are produced from proper custody in circumstances giving rise to the presumption in favour of due execution in the case of documents more than twenty years old. Possession is prima facie evidence of ownership, and a second way in which ownership may be proved is by proof of possession of the property in question. In the case of real estate, proof of connected property in circumstances rendering it probable that the owner of such connected property would, in addition, be the owner of the property in question may rank as a third means of proving ownership. Finally ownership may be proved by admissible hearsay statements.

Index